ORGANIZATIONAL BEHAVIOR

Sixth Edition

Western Michigan University
MGMT 2500

Robert Kreitner
Arizona State University—Tempe

Angelo Kinicki
Arizona State University—Tempe

McGraw-Hill Custom Publishing

Boston Burr Ridge, IL Dubuque, IA Madison, WI New York San Francisco St. Louis
Bangkok Bogotá Caracas Lisbon London Madrid
Mexico City Milan New Delhi Seoul Singapore Sydney Taipei Toronto

Organizational Behavior, Sixth Edition
Western Michigan University, MGMT 2500

1 2 3 4 5 6 7 8 9 0 PLK PLK 0 9 8 7 6 5

ISBN 0-07-325903-9

Editor: Tamara Immell
Production Editor: Carrie Braun
Printer/Binder: Plastikoil of Pennsylvania

About the Authors

ROBERT KREITNER, PHD (pictured right) is an Emeritus Professor of Management at Arizona State University and a member of the ASU College of Business Faculty Hall of Fame. Prior to joining ASU in 1975, Bob taught at Western Illinois University. He also taught organizational behavior at the American Graduate School of International Management (Thunderbird). Bob is a popular speaker who has addressed a diverse array of audiences worldwide on management topics. Bob has authored articles for respected journals such as *Organizational Dynamics, Business Horizons,* and *Journal of Business Ethics.* He also is the co-author (with Fred Luthans) of the award-winning book *Organizational Behavior Modification and Beyond: An Operant and Social Learning Approach,* and the author of *Management,* 9th edition, a best-selling introductory management text.

Among his consulting and executive development clients have been American Express, SABRE Computer Services, Honeywell, Motorola, Amdahl, the Hopi Indian Tribe, State Farm Insurance, Goodyear Aerospace, Doubletree Hotels, Bank One–Arizona, Nazarene School of Large Church Management, US Steel, and Allied-Signal. In 1981–82 he served as Chairman of the Academy of Management's Management Education and Development Division. Bob grew up in western New York State. After a four-year enlistment in the US Coast Guard, including service on the icebreaker EASTWIND in Antarctica, Bob attended the University of Nebraska–Omaha on a football scholarship. Bob also holds an MBA from the University of Nebraska–Omaha and a PhD from the University of Nebraska–Lincoln. While working on his PhD in Business at Nebraska, he spent six months teaching management courses for the University in Micronesia. In 1996, Bob taught two courses in Albania's first-ever MBA program (funded by the US Agency for International Development and administered by the University of Nebraska–Lincoln). He taught a summer leadership program in Switzerland from 1995 to 1998. Bob and his wife, Margaret, live in Phoenix with three cats and a pet starling. They enjoy travel, hiking, woodcarving, and fishing.

ANGELO KINICKI is a Professor and Dean's Council of 100 Distinguished Scholar at Arizona State University. He joined the faculty in 1982, the year he received his doctorate in business administration from Kent State University. His specialty is Organizational Behavior.

Angelo is recognized for both his research and teaching. He has published over 75 articles in a variety of leading academic and professional journals, and has coauthored three textbooks. Angelo's success as a researcher also resulted in his selection to serve on the editorial review boards for the *Academy of Management Journal, Journal of Vocational Behavior,* and the *Journal of Management.* He received the All Time Best Reviewer Award from the *Academy of Management Journal* for the period of 1996–1999. Angelo's outstanding teaching performance resulted in his selection as the Graduate Teacher of the Year and the Undergraduate Teacher of the Year in the College of Business at Arizona State University. He also was acknowledged as the Instructor of the Year for Executive Education from the Center for Executive Development at Arizona State University.

One of Angelo's strengths is his ability to teach students at all levels within a university. He uses an interactive environment to enhance undergraduates' understanding about management and organizational behavior. He focuses MBAs on applying management concepts to solve complex problems; PhD students learn the art and science of conducting scholarly research.

Angelo also is a busy consultant and speaker with companies around the world. His clients are many of the *Fortune* 500 companies as well as a variety of entrepreneurial firms. Much of his consulting work focuses on creating organizational change aimed at increasing organizational effectiveness and profitability. One of Angelo's most important and enjoyable pursuits is the practical application of his knowledge about management and organizational behavior.

Angelo and his wife Joyce have enjoyed living in the beautiful Arizona desert for 21 years, but are natives of Cleveland, Ohio. They enjoy traveling, golfing, and hiking.

With love to Margaret, my forever hiking buddy on
life's winding trail.

—B.K.

To Joyce and Nala: Joyce, I would not be who I am without you. I
treasure your continued love, friendship, support, positive energy,
and excellent cooking. Nala's unconditional love is a source of
energy that always lifts my spirits.

—A.K.

Preface

Things move very fast in today's Internet-linked global economy. Competition is intense. Speed, cost, and quality are no longer the trade-offs they once were (meaning improvement in one came at the expense of one or both of the others). Today's customers want immediate access to high-quality products and services at a reasonable price. Thus, managers are challenged to simultaneously speed up the product creation and delivery cycle, cut costs, and improve quality. (And to do so in an ethical manner.) Regardless of the size and purpose of the organization and the technology involved, people are the common denominator when facing this immense challenge. Success or failure hinges on the ability to attract, develop, retain, and motivate a diverse array of appropriately-skilled people. The human factor drives everything. To know more about workplace behavior is to gain a valuable competitive edge. The purpose of this textbook is to help present and future managers better understand and manage people at work.

Although this Sixth Edition of *Organizational Behavior* is aimed at undergraduate business students in similarly named courses, previous editions have proven highly versatile. *Organizational Behavior* has been used effectively in MBA programs, executive education and management development programs, and industrial and organizational psychology programs around the world. (Note: A special European edition is available.) This textbook is the culmination of our combined half-century of teaching experience and research into organizational behavior and management in the United States, Pacific Rim, and Europe. Thanks to detailed feedback from students, professors, and practicing managers, this Sixth Edition is more refined and better organized. Many new changes have been made in this edition, reflecting new research evidence, new management techniques, and the fruits of our own learning process.

Organizational Behavior, Sixth Edition, is a product of the *total quality management* (TQM) process described in Chapter 1. Specifically, it is *user driven* (as a result of carefully listening to our readers), developed through close *teamwork* between the authors and the publisher, and the product of *continuous improvement.* Our TQM approach has helped us achieve a difficult combination of balances. Among them are balances between theory and practice, solid content and interesting coverage, and instructive detail and readability. Students and instructors say they want an up-to-date, relevant, and interesting textbook that actively involves the reader in the learning process. Our efforts toward this end are evidenced by many new topics and real-life examples, a stimulating art program, timely new cases and boxed inserts, end-of-chapter experiential exercises for both individuals and teams, and more than two dozen exercises integrated into the text. We realize that reading a comprehensive textbook is hard work, but we also firmly believe the process should be interesting (and sometimes fun).

GUIDED TOUR

Structural Improvements in the Sixth Edition

Part One in this Sixth Edition provides a foundation of understanding as well as a cultural context for the study of organizational behavior. In Parts Two through Four, the material flows from micro (individuals) to macro (groups and organizations) topics. Once again, we have tried to achieve a workable balance between micro and macro topics. As a guide for users of the previous edition, the following structural changes need to be noted:

- This Sixth Edition is one chapter shorter than the fifth edition. There are now four major parts, down from five.

- Ethics coverage has been improved, expanded, and featured in a separate Learning Module following Chapter 1. Like a normal chapter, Learning Module A includes a real-life opening vignette, an International OB box, an OB Exercise, and a Group Exercise. New in this edition are Ethical Dilemmas at the end of each chapter to give students the opportunity to wrestle with today's tough ethical issues.

- Self-management now is covered in Chapter 5 in conjunction with self-concept.

- Chapter 6 is a new chapter covering personal values, attitudes, abilities, and job satisfaction. It expands our treatment of key individual differences in Chapter 5.

- Chapter 8, one of the two motivation chapters, now features a major new section on intrinsic motivation and rewards.

- As requested by reviewers, Chapter 10 on improving performance with feedback and rewards now includes a major section on positive reinforcement.

- Learning organizations are now covered in Chapter 18 and stress is covered in Chapter 19.

- The Learning Module on Research Methods in OB has been moved to the end of the text.

Brief Contents

New and Expanded Coverage

Our readers and reviewers kindly tell us how much they appreciate our efforts to keep this textbook up-to-date and relevant. Toward that end, you will find the following new topics featured in the Sixth Edition: Human capital and social capital (Chapter 1), Learning Module A: Expanded coverage of ethics, Nine cultural dimensions and leadership lessons from the GLOBE project (Chapter 4), Work-versus-family life conflict and balance (Chapter 6), Major new section on intrinsic motivation (Chapter 8), Improving decisions through knowledge management (Chapter 11), and Cialdini's six principles of influence and persuasion (Chapter 16). In addition, this edition includes significantly improved coverage of the following topics:

Chapter 1
Human and social capital, Internet/E-business revolution

Chapter 2
Workforce demographics for 2000–2010

Chapter 3
Socialization tactics, development networks underlying mentoring

Chapter 4
How culture overrides national boundaries, cultural paradoxes, nine cultural dimensions and leadership lessons from the GLOBE project, tips for landing a foreign assignment

Chapter 5
Branden's six pillars of self-esteem, the proactive personality, four characteristics of emotional intelligence, emotional contagion, emotional labor

Chapter 6
Work-versus-family life balance and conflicts, cognitive and behavioral components of attitudes, Ajzen's theory of planned behavior, organizational commitment, job involvement, withdrawal cognitions, costs of employee turnover, job satisfaction/job performance research update

Chapter 7
Golem effect (how leader's low expectations hurt performance)

Chapter 8
Alderfer's ERG theory of needs, major new section on intrinsic motivation/rewards, sense of meaningfulness/choice/competence/progress

Chapter 9
Equity and interactional justice

Chapter 10
Modern incentive pay plans

Chapter 11
Assumptions of rational decision making, improving decisions through knowledge management, tacit versus explicit knowledge, advantages and disadvantages of group-aided decision making

Chapter 12
Social skills for building social capital, social exchanges in the workplace, behavioral categories of sexual harassment

Chapter 13
Knowledge/skills/abilities (KSAs) for team players, how to manage virtual teams, empowering self-managed teams

Chapter 14
Conflict metaphors and meaning

Chapter 15
New list of male and female communication differences

Chapter 16
Cialdini's six principles of influence and persuasion, keeping organizational politics within bounds

Chapter 17
Contrasting 360-degree ratings of leadership for women and men, leadership traits identified by famous leaders, updated path-goal theory of leadership

Chapter 18
New model of environmental uncertainty

Chapter 19
Commitment to change, resilience to change, primary and secondary appraisal of stress.

AACSB Coverage

In keeping with the curriculum recommendations from AACSB International (The Association to Advance Collegiate Schools of Business; www.aacsb.edu) for greater attention to managing in a global economy, managing cultural diversity, improving product/service quality, and making ethical decisions, we feature this coverage:

- A full chapter on international organizational behavior and cross-cultural management (Chapter 4). Comprehensive new coverage from the landmark GLOBE project. To ensure integrated coverage of international topics, 21 all-new boxed features titled "International Organizational Behavior" can be found in this Sixth Edition.

- Chapter 2 offers comprehensive and up-to-date coverage of managing diversity.

- Principles of total quality management (TQM) and the legacy of W Edwards Deming are discussed in Chapter 1 to establish a quality-improvement context for the entire textbook. Also, many quality-related examples have been integrated into the textual presentation.

- As outlined next, this Sixth Edition includes comprehensive coverage of ethics-related concepts, cases, and issues.

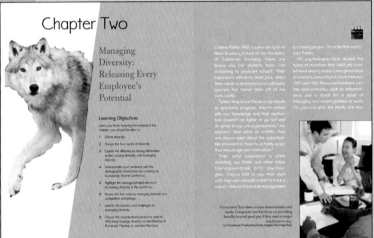

Learning Module A

Ethics and Organizational Behavior

Renee Hinton says it was hard enough when she was laid off last August from Global Crossing Ltd. after 14 years with the company and its predecessor. But when the former fiber-optic darling declared bankruptcy...[in 2002], it dragged the systems manager into bankruptcy, too.

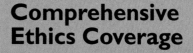

Like thousands of other laid-off employees, Ms. Hinton was required to take her severance package in spread-out payments rather than a lump sum. With the company's bankruptcy filing, those payments stopped. Medical benefits also were terminated. Many of the workers' 401(k) retirement plans, loaded with Global Crossing shares, became nearly worthless as the stock price plunged.

But for many Global Crossing executives, the outcome has been quite different... . Global Crossing's new chief executive, John Legere, received a $3.5 million signing bonus when he took the job in October [2001]—even though he was already employed as CEO of Asia Global Crossing, a separately traded affiliate... . At about the same time, Asia Global Crossing and Global Crossing forgave a $10 million loan to Mr. Legere, and Global Crossing eased the terms of an $8 million loan to Thomas Casey, Global's departing chief executive, according to filings the company made with the government.

The company also moved up its last pay date by a week so that executives and others still employed at Global could get paid before the company declared bankruptcy... . Severance payments to the already laid-off workers weren't paid.

Furthermore, in recent months Global Crossing made 11th-hour lump-sum pension payouts totaling $15 million to high-ranking executives, most of them no longer with the company.[1]

Was Global Crossing acting ethically? Explain your rationale.

The opening vignette highlights the relationship between decision making and ethical behavior. It also underscores the fact that top management's ethical or unethical behavior can significantly affect the lives of employees such as Renee Hinton. Ethics and ethical behavior are receiving greater attention today. This interest is partly due to reported cases of questionable or potentially unethical behavior involving companies like Global Crossing, Enron, Tyco, and Arthur Andersen and the associated costs of unethical behavior.

For instance, US industries lose about $400 billion a year from unethical and criminal behavior. Another nationwide survey revealed that 20% of the respondents were asked to do something that violated their ethical standards; 41% complied.[2] Unethical behavior is a relevant issue for all employees. It occurs from the bottom to the top of an organization. For example, a recent survey of 1,000 senior-level executives revealed that as many as one-third lied on their resumes.[3] Maybe this result should not be surprising because there are more benefits to lying, such as a higher salary and stock

33

Ethical Dilemma

Sexy but Sexless Relationships?

Situation

You're the ground crew manager in Chicago for a major commercial airline company. During lunchtime in your office, you run across a curious article while browsing *Fast Company* magazine's Web archives. You begin to read:

"You're intensely together on a project, things are going well, and the adrenaline gets pumping," says David R Eyler. "The chemistry feels right, but you don't want to mess up your personal or professional relationships by having an affair. You recognize that you've got something good here, and you set limits on your behavior."

Can you have a sexy but sexless relationship? Researchers are embracing a new notion that sexual attraction between co-workers may not be bad. It may, in fact, be beneficial.

Eyler and Andrea P Baridon, authors of three books on men and women in the workplace and senior staff members of the National Center for Higher Education in Washington, propose an unconventional alternative to an illicit affair. Instead of giving in to sexual attraction, you manage it. They call the relationship *More than Friends, Less than Lovers*—the title of a book they published in 1991.[97]

The article goes on to say researchers have found men and women using "sexual synergy" to achieve goals in the workplace. Five tips are offered for keeping these close, but not too close, relationships within bounds.

What is your reaction? (Explain the ethical reasoning for your choice.)

1. Hmmm. A little harmless flirting might boost productivity and be good for morale.

2. This is a surefire invitation to sexual harassment abuses and charges. What a stupid idea! (*Tip:* Refer back to Table 12–5, Behavioral Categories of Sexual Harassment.)

3. I should discuss this with our human resource department to check our stance on workplace romances and their relationship to our sexual harassment policy.

4. I could pass a copy of this article around to see if we have a problem with sexual harassment.

5. Invent other options. Discuss.

For an interpretation of this situation, visit our Web site, **www.mhhe.com/kreitner.**

Comprehensive Ethics Coverage

Ethics is covered early and completely in Learning Module A (following Chapter 1) to set a proper moral tone for managing people at work. Ethical issues are raised throughout the text. New to this Sixth Edition are 19 Ethical Dilemmas (one following each chapter). They raise hard-hitting ethical issues, ask tough questions, and have corresponding interpretations on our Web site at www.mhhe.com/kreitner. These Ethical Dilemmas, along with chapter-opening vignettes and chapter-closing cases on the likes of Enron are constant reminders of the importance of ethical management.

Fresh Cases and Features

Our continuing commitment to an up-to-date and relevant textbook is evidenced by the number of new features and cases.

Every chapter opens with a real-name, real-world vignette to provide an interesting and relevant context for the material at hand. All 19 chapter-opening vignettes are new. They highlight male and female role models as well as US and foreign companies.

OB Exercise   What Are the Strategies for Breaking the Glass Ceiling?

Instructions

Read the 13 career strategies shown below that may be used to break the glass ceiling. Next, rank order each strategy in terms of its importance for contributing to the advancement of a woman to a senior management position. Rank the strategies from 1 (most important) to 13 (least important). Once this is completed, compute the gap between your rankings and those provided by the women executives who participated in this research. Their rankings are presented in endnote 30 at the back of the book.[30] In computing the gaps, use the absolute value of the gap. (Absolute values are always positive, so just ignore the sign of your gap.) Finally, compute your total gap score. The larger the gap, the greater the difference in opinion between you and the women executives. What does your total gap score indicate about your recommended strategies?

Strategy	My Rating	Survey Rating	Gap Your Rating	Gap Survey Rating
1. Develop leadership outside office				
2. Gain line management experience				
3. Network with influential colleagues				
4. Change companies				
5. Be able to relocate				
6. Seek difficult or high visibility assignments				
7. Upgrade educational credentials				
8. Consistently exceed performance expectations				
9. Move from one functional area to another				
10. Initiate discussion regarding career aspirations				
11. Have an influential mentor				
12. Develop style that men are comfortable with				
13. Gain international experience				

SOURCE: Strategies and data were taken from B R Ragins, B Townsend, and M Mattis, "Gender Gap in the Executive Suite: CEOs and Female Executives Report on Breaking the Glass Ceiling," *Academy of Management Executive*," February 1998, pp. 28–42.

Twenty-eight **OB Exercises** are distributed throughout the text to foster personal involvement and greater self-awareness. Nine of the built-in OB Exercises are new.

---

http://www.womeninpolitics.org

International OB   The Glass Ceiling Exists around the World

1. Out of 180 countries, only 11 are headed by women.
2. 13% of members of national parliaments worldwide are women.
3. 7% of the world's cabinet ministers are women.
4. 1% of the world's assets are in the name of women.
5. 70% of people in the lowest poverty—living on less than $1 per day—are women.
6. 855,000,000 people in the world are illiterate, and 70% of them are women.
7. There is no country in the world where women's pay is equal to that of men.
8. While women occupy about 33% of all managerial and administrative positions in the developed world, they possess 15% and 13% of these positions in Africa and in Asia and the Pacific.
9. In Silicon Valley, for every 100 shares of stock options owned by a man, one share is owned by a woman.

SOURCES: These statistics were obtained from **www.onlinewomeninpolitics.org/statistics.htm**, updated April 2, 2002, and **www.learningpartnership.org/facts/human.html**, updated January 1, 2002.

All 21 of the **International OB** boxed features are new.

Sixteen of the chapter-closing **OB in Action Case Studies** are new.

Four **new end-of-part video cases,** based on relevant "Manager's Hot Seat" videos, provide structured exercises for incorporating interactive videos into classroom instruction. To achieve a high degree of realism, McGraw-Hill/Irwin created these videos around the concept of having real-life managers deal with challenging hypothetical situations without the aid of a script. Each video has two parts, both of which are followed by the guest manager's view of what went right and wrong in the "hot seat." These video exercises pose the question: "What would you do in the hot seat?"

Pedagogical and Cooperative Learning Features

The Sixth Edition of *Organizational Behavior* is designed to be a complete teaching/learning tool that captures the reader's interest and imparts useful knowledge. Some of the most significant pedagogical features of this text are:

- Classic and modern topics are given balanced treatment in terms of the latest and best available theoretical models, research evidence, and practical applications.

- Several concise learning objectives open each chapter to focus the reader's attention and serve as a comprehension check.

- A colorful and lively art program includes captioned photographs and figures.

- Hundreds of real-world examples involving large and small, public and private organizations have been incorporated into the textual material to make this edition up-to-date, interesting, and relevant.

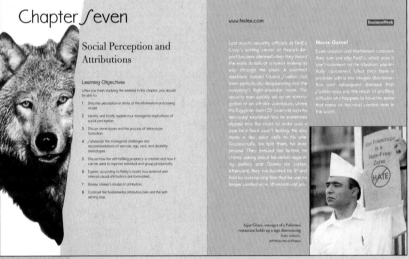

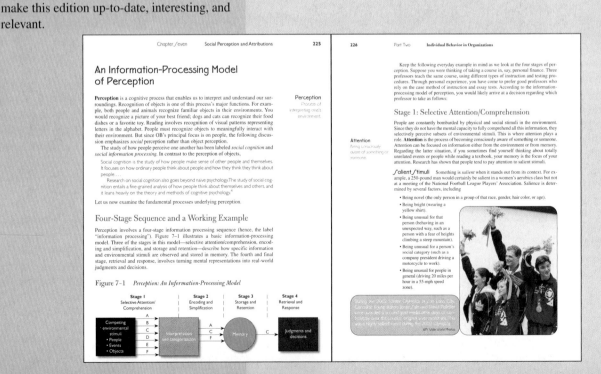

- Women play a prominent role throughout this text, as is befitting their large and growing presence in the workplace. Lots of female role models are included. Special effort has been devoted to uncovering research insights about relevant and important gender-related differences.

- Key terms are emphasized in bold print where they are first defined and featured in the adjacent margins for review purposes.

- A "Summary of Key Concepts" feature at the end of each chapter restates the chapter learning objectives and concisely answers them.

- Ten discussion questions at the end of every chapter challenge the reader to explore the personal and practical implications of what has just been covered. These questions also are useful for classroom discussion and cooperative learning.

- The Internet Exercises found at the end of each chapter have been completely updated for the Sixth Edition, offering more interactivity, variety, and link durability. These exercises encourage and aid students in navigating the Internet to learn more about topics and organizations covered in the text. The Internet Exercises also can serve as a valuable tool for cooperative learning when students team up to track down relevant new information.

- Thirty-eight end-of-chapter exercises foster hands-on experiential and cooperative learning. Every chapter is concluded with a Personal Awareness and Growth Exercise and a Group Exercise. Each exercise has learning objectives, an introduction, clear instructions, and discussion questions to facilitate interaction and learning.

Comprehensive Supplement Package

The **Instructor's Presentation CD** includes an instructor's manual, test bank, computerized test bank, PowerPoint, and video clips.

Prepared by Kim J Wade of Washington State University, each **instructor's manual** chapter includes: chapter summary, lecture outline, discussion questions for international OB boxes, opening case solution, OB in action case solution, personal awareness and growth exercise notes, group exercise notes, list of resources, 1-2 lecturettes, 1-2 additional exercises (including an integrative case featuring fictional manager Roberta), transparency masters and handouts corresponding to lecture materials and exercises. The manual also contains integrative video case teaching notes, video teaching notes, and transparency masters for highlighting key text concepts.

Also prepared by Kim J Wade, the **test bank** contains approximately 1500 questions, with an emphasis on testing concepts rather than memorizing definitions.

A collection of **chapter-by-chapter** videos from NBC News, PBS NewsHour, and the Management Video Library illustrates text concepts and cases, featuring newsworthy people and organizations, such as Pike Place World Famous Fish, and MTV/Viacom China Manager Li Yifei. Programs linked to specific cases and examples in the book are indicated by a video icon. Four **"Manager's Hot Seat"** videos are also available for use with the part-ending OB in Action Video Cases also including Mustang Jeans: Doing Business Across Cultures, A Clash of Styles at Midnight Visions, Group Dynamics at TechBox, and Virtual Disagreement at Saber Union.

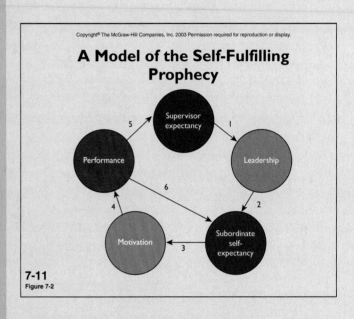

A Model of the Self-Fulfilling Prophecy

7-11
Figure 7-2

Now two sets of **PowerPoint** slides are available for every chapter: one set recaps key concepts, tables, and figures from the text, and another provides supplemental examples, charts, and data from outside sources to enhance lecture presentations.

The Latest in Technology

PageOut is McGraw-Hill's unique point-and-click course Website tool, enabling you to create a full-featured, professional quality course Website without knowing HTML coding. With PageOut you can post your syllabus online, assign McGraw-Hill Online Learning Center or eBook content, add links to important off-site resources, and maintain student results in the online grade book. You can send class announcements, copy your course site to share with colleagues, and upload original files. PageOut is free for every McGraw-Hill/Irwin user and, if you're short on time, we even have a team ready to help you create your site!

You can customize this text. McGraw-Hill/Primis Online's digital database offers you the flexibility to customize your course including material from the largest online collection of textbooks, readings, and cases. Primis leads the way in customized eBooks with hundreds of titles available at prices that save your students over 20% off bookstore prices. Additional information is available at 800-228-0634.

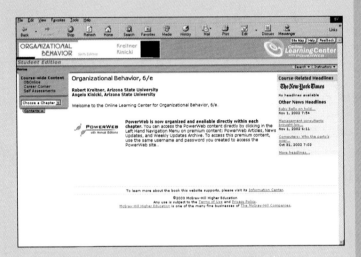

The Online Learning Center (OLC) is a website that follows the text chapter-by-chapter. As students read the book, they can go online to take self-grading quizzes, review material, or work through interactive exercises. OLCs can be delivered multiple ways – professors and students can access them directly through the text-book website, through PageOut, or within a course management system (i.e. WebCT, Blackboard, TopClass, or eCollege.)

For Students

Student Resource CD

With every new copy of the text, students receive a Student Resource CD filled with study aids, enrichment exercises, and reference materials. OB Online Exercises help students learn more about their personal management skills and preferences. The Pike Place Fish Market Video Case illustrates how OB principles helped Pike Place transform itself from an ordinary fish market into a world-renowned tourist destination. Instructors can assign the video case and discussion questions in preparation for classroom discussion.

Other resources include the Career Development Guide; OB Online Exercises; How to Read *BusinessWeek* and Chapter Study, Review, and Research Tools (quizzes, chapter reviews, weblinks).

PowerWeb

Harness the assets of the Web to keep your course current with PowerWeb! Now integrated by chapter into the book's online learning center, PowerWeb provides high quality, peer-reviewed content including up-to-date articles from leading periodicals and journals, current news, weekly updates with assessments, interactive exercises, Web research guide, study tips, and much more! http://www.dushkin.com/powerweb.

BusinessWeek Edition

Your students can subscribe to *BusinessWeek* for a specially priced rate of $8.25 in addition to the price of the text. Students will receive a pass code card shrink-wrapped with their new text. The card directs students to a Website where they enter the code and then gain access to *BusinessWeek's* registration page to enter address info and set up their print and online subscription as well. Passcode ISBN 007-251530-9.

Online Learning Center

Visit our book website at *www.mhhe.com/kreitner* to access self-grading quizzes, chapter review materials, PowerWeb articles, Internet Exercises (from the book), the Specialized Bike Integrative Video Case, and more.

Words of Appreciation

This textbook is the fruit of many people's labor. Our colleagues at Arizona State University have been supportive from the start. Through the years, our organizational behavior students at ASU, the American Graduate School of International Management (Thunderbird), and the University of Tirana (Albania) have been enthusiastic and candid academic "customers." We are grateful for their feedback and we hope we have done it justice in this new edition. Sincere appreciation goes to Kim Wade of Washington State University, for her skillful and dedicated work on the *Instructor's Resource Manual* and *Test Bank*. Thank you to Dale Boroviak for a very professional job of managing our permissions. Thank you to Amanda Gortecki for creating the PowerPoint presentation.

To the manuscript reviewers spanning the prior five editions go our gratitude and thanks. Their feedback was thoughtful, rigorous, constructive, and above all, essential to our goal of *kaizen* (continuous improvement). Our reviewers and focus group participants for this edition were:

Bradley J. Alge
Purdue University

Lynda Allen
Olivet Nazarene University

Abdul Aziz
College of Charleston

Anita D. Bhappu
Southern Methodist University

Byron L. Bissell
University of Arizona South

James H. Browne
University of Southern Colorado

Joel T. Champion
Colorado Christian University

Frank P. DeCaro
Palm Beach Atlantic College

Kathleen Edwards
University of Texas at Austin

Susan Eisner
Ramapo College

James P. Gelatt
University of Maryland University College

Mary Giovannini
Truman State University

Ronald H. Humphrey
Virginia Commonwealth University

Robert C. Liden
University of Georgia

Ty L. Menna, Jr.
University of Arkansas

Linda Morable
Richland College

Rebecca J. Oatsvall
Meredith College

Joy V. Peluchette
University of Southern Indiana

Laura Pohopien
Cal Poly Pomona

Rosemary Shields
University of Texas at El Paso

B. Kay Snavely
Miami University

Christina Stamper
Western Michigan University

Louise Tourigny
University of Wisconsin-Whitewater

Mike Wakefield
University of Southern Colorado

Scott D. Williams
Wright State University

Shirley A. Wilson
Bryant College

Patricia A. Worsham
Cal Poly Pomona

Special thanks go to our dedicated "pack" at Irwin/McGraw-Hill: our editors, John Weimeister and Laura Hurst Spell; our marketing team, Lisa Nicks and Dana Woo; and our design and production team, Matt Baldwin, Sara Evertson, Kimberly Hooker, Rose Hepburn, Judy Kausal, and Betty Hadala.

Finally, we would like to thank our wives, Margaret and Joyce, for being tough and caring "first customers" of our work. This book has been greatly enhanced by their common sense, reality testing, and managerial experience. Thanks in large measure to their love and moral support, this project again was completed on time and it strengthened rather than strained a treasured possession—our friendship.

We hope you enjoy this textbook. Best wishes for success and happiness!

Bob Kreitner
Angelo Kinicki

Brief Contents

Contents

Part Two
Individual Behavior in Organizations   147

Chapter Eight
Motivation through Needs,
Job Design, and Intrinsic
Rewards   256

Chapter Nine
Motivation through Equity,
Expectancy, and Goal
Setting   288

Chapter Ten
Improving Job Performance with Feedback, Extrinsic Rewards, and Positive Reinforcement 322

Part Three
Group and Social Processes 369

Chapter Eleven
Individual and Group Decision Making 370

Chapter Twelve
Group Dynamics 406

Chapter Thirteen
Teams and Teamwork for the 21st Century 444

Chapter Fourteen
Managing Conflict and Negotiation 482

Part Four
Organizational Processes 517

Chapter Sixteen
Influence Tactics, Empowerment, and Politics 556

Chapter Nineteen
Managing Change and Stress
670

Part One

The World of Organizational Behavior

Chapter One

Organizational Behavior: Developing People-Centered Organizations and Skills

Learning Objectives

When you finish studying the material in this chapter, you should be able to:

1. Identify the P's in the 4-P cycle of continuous improvement and define the term *management*.

2. Identify at least 5 of the 11 managerial skills in Wilson's profile of effective managers.

3. Contrast human and social capital and explain why we need to build both.

4. Characterize 21st-century managers.

5. Define the term *organizational behavior*, and explain why OB is a horizontal discipline.

6. Contrast McGregor's Theory X and Theory Y assumptions about employees.

7. Identify the four principles of total quality management (TQM).

8. Define the term *E-business*, and specify five ways the Internet is affecting the management of people at work.

9. Describe the sources of organizational behavior research evidence.

When Herb Kelleher, the legendary co-founder of Southwest Airlines, turned over his CEO title to Jim Parker in 2001, *Harvard Business Review* reported the following question-and-answer session with Southwest's leadership team.

Everybody thinks they understand the Southwest model but few airlines, if any, have been able to replicate it. How do you account for your success?

Colleen Barrett [President] There have been a lot of Southwest wanna-bes, but they have not succeeded. I don't say it with pride because I don't like to see them fail. They have not religiously stuck to what they say they are going to be. People Express forgot who it was going to be and destroyed itself. We don't forget, and we don't let our people forget. You have to talk and talk and talk to your people all the time.

John Denison [Executive VP, Corporate Services] Also, those companies don't understand the distinction between controlling costs and being cheap. There is a need to invest.

Ron Ricks [VP, Government Affairs] We invest in our people. We have competitive, if not superior, wage and benefits packages. That looks like it may pose a high cost up front, but it is cost-effective in the long run, with good people.

Libby Sartain [VP, People] We spend more money to recruit and train than any other airline. We take time to find the right people to hire at all levels within our organization, and we spend time training them. We really believe

(from left to right) Southwest Airlines CEO Jim Parker, President Colleen Barrett, and co-founder and chairman Herb Kelleher. (AP/Wide World Photos)

in the notion of "one bad apple." It's like a religion here. As a result, our turnover is far lower than at other airlines. We want people who are not looking for a job, but rather who are looking for a cause. If we are evenly matched with our competitors on everything else, we will win on customer service.

Barrett For example, United Shuttle took on Southwest; it out-advertised us. Then a year later, United withdrew from Oakland and gave [that territory] back to us. They had a better frequent-flier program, but Herb . . . had 1,400 letters from people who said they had tried United but preferred Southwest's friendliness and service. It all comes back to our people and our delivery of the product.

Observers talk a lot about leadership at Southwest. What has been the role of leadership?

Jim Wimberly [Executive VP, Operations] Organizations take on their leaders' personalities, and there is no other air carrier that has had the same continuity of leadership as Southwest has [led by Kelleher since 1971]. That has shaped this culture, and we are blessed with it.

Donna Conover [Executive VP, Customers] But the most influential leaders in our company—aside from Herb—are the frontline supervisors.

Sartain We are putting even more time and effort now into internal recruitment and training for our frontline supervisors. We bring them in centrally for three months of training. We're only as strong as they are. That's where most organizations break down.

Conover With family structures as they are these days, we often help our young employees grow up. While other airlines are cutting supervisors, we have a large number of supervisors to encourage, guide, and give structure to employees. It lends to the family atmosphere here. We have a ten-to-one employee-to-supervisor ratio.

How can you afford this kind of ratio, which other companies would consider quite extravagant?

Barrett It helps that all of our supervisors are working supervisors—they can do the work of frontline employees, side by side with them.

Observers often wonder how Southwest has been so consistently profitable and operationally effective when its workforce is more unionized than almost any other US airline.

Jim Parker [CEO] We have been successful in negotiations when we go in asking how much we can pay employees rather than how little we can pay. We have been able to reach resolution without work stoppages. We had a landmark 10-year contract in 1994, in which we offered stock options to compensate for a five-year pay freeze for pilots. Union leaders didn't think they could sell it to the members, but the members readily agreed to it.

Then our negotiations focused on how to allocate stock options. The stock-option program has been highly successful. Most labor disputes are not really about money. There is something else at stake—respect. It comes down to personal contact between the company and its employees.

Conover This is one reason our supervisors are so important. It is easier to walk out on people who do not give you respect than to walk out on a friend. And you cannot make up for longstanding problems in the two months before a negotiation. It needs to be consistent.

Barrett We've had one strike—a six-day strike with the mechanics in 1980. We got them temporary jobs with the census during the strike. We are very proud of our employee relationships. We treat people with respect. But we would take a strike if it got down to it—especially if it was about money and we simply couldn't concede without hurting all employees by the decision. We are loving but very realistic and very pragmatic.

Does the respect you give your employees have other benefits besides engendering employee loyalty?

Wimberly I think the respect ripples through our entire business. For example, we have good relations with air-traffic controllers, which is crucial to our reputation for reliability. We make routine visits to control towers in all the airports we serve. We bring the controllers hamburgers. They appreciate our flexibility and our willingness to work with them.

Barrett Most pilots are egomaniacs. We turn pilots and air-traffic-control people into partners. Herb is always told about the civility of Southwest pilots when he makes tower visits, and it pays handsome dividends. The people in the tower are amazed at the civility of our pilots. We practice the golden rule with them just as we do with everyone else.

Can you retain this culture as you continue to expand?

Barrett The naysayers said we could never fly to the Northeast because we wouldn't find employees there who were nice. But we can do it, and we do. Someday, we may go international. And even internationally, we can maintain our culture if we go after people's hearts and grow the Southwest community.

Sartain People are basically good wherever you go. I hate to hear the stereotypes. We do not have a problem with people. We can work with people anywhere.[1]

A re *people* the key to success in today's highly competitive global economy? Southwest Airlines' leadership team certainly would say yes, and prove it with their actions. For instance, when the September 11, 2001, terrorist attacks brought the US airline industry to a complete halt, clear priorities guided Southwest's managers. CEO Jim Parker explains:

> We had to make some decisions very promptly: We had a $180 million profit-sharing payment due on September 14. Because of our limited resources, we had a tough time deciding whether to fund it. In the end, we chose to pay it out, because it was the right thing to do for our employees.
>
> Next on the agenda was deciding not to furlough any employees and to protect all employee jobs. We have a lot of people who have worked hard for more than 30 years so that they can have job security in hard times. It would have been breaking faith with our employees if our first reaction was to cut jobs. Cutting jobs should be the last thing a company does rather than the first thing.[2]

So Parker and his team say people are indeed number one.

But wait a minute. Dilbert cartoonist Scott Adams, who humorously documents managerial lapses of sanity, sees it differently. Adams ranks the often-heard statement "Employees are our most valuable asset" number one on his list of "Great Lies of Management."[3] This raises serious questions. Is Parker the exception, a manager who actually backs up the claim that people are our most valuable resource? Does the typical manager merely pay lip service to the critical importance of people? If so, what are the implications of this hypocrisy for organizational productivity and employee well-being?

Stanford University's Jeffrey Pfeffer and his colleagues recently shed instructive light on this dilemma. Generally, they concluded:

> There is a substantial and rapidly expanding body of evidence, some of it quite methodologically sophisticated, that speaks to the strong connection between how firms manage their people and the economic results achieved.[4]

Their review of research evidence from companies in both the United States and Germany showed *people-centered practices* strongly associated with much higher profits and significantly lower employee turnover. Further analysis uncovered the following seven people-centered practices in successful companies:

1. Job security (to eliminate fear of layoffs).

2. Careful hiring (emphasizing a good fit with the company culture).

3. Power to the people (via decentralization and self-managed teams).

4. Generous pay for performance.

5. Lots of training.

6. Less emphasis on status (to build a "we" feeling).

7. Trust building (through the sharing of critical information).[5]

Importantly, these factors are a *package* deal, meaning they need to be installed in a coordinated and systematic manner—not in bits and pieces.

The dark side of this study is that Scott Adams's cynical assessment is too often true. Managers tend to act counter to their declarations that people are their most important asset. Pfeffer and his colleagues blame a number of modern management trends and practices. For example, undue emphasis on short-term profit precludes long-term efforts to nurture human resources.[6] Also, excessive layoffs, when managers view

SOURCE: DILBERT reprinted by permission of United Feature Syndicate, Inc.

people as a cost rather than an asset, erode trust, commitment, and loyalty.[7] *Only 12% of today's organizations, according to Pfeffer, have the systematic approaches and persistence to qualify as true people-centered organizations, thus giving them a competitive advantage.*[8]

To us, an 88% shortfall in the quest for people-centered organizations represents a tragic loss, both to society and to the global economy. There are profound ethical implications as well. We all need to accept the challenge to do better.[9] Toward that end, the mission of this book is to help increase the number of people-centered managers and organizations around the world.

Our jumping-off point is the 4-P model of strategic results in Figure 1–1 (focusing on *people, products, processes,* and *productivity*). The 4-P model emphasizes the larger strategic context for managing people. Although people indeed are the key to organizational success today, other factors such as planning, technology, and finances also require good management.[10] Further, the 4-P model stresses the importance of day-to-day *continuous improvement* in all aspects of organizational endeavor to cope with more demanding customers and stiffer competition.

The purpose of this first chapter is to explore the manager's job, define and examine organizational behavior and its evolution, and consider how we can learn more about organizational behavior. A topical model for the balance of the book also is introduced.

The Manager's Job: Getting Things Done through Others

Management
Process of working with and through others to achieve organizational objectives efficiently and ethically.

For better or for worse, managers touch our lives in many ways. Schools, hospitals, government agencies, and large and small businesses all require systematic management. Formally defined, **management** is the process of working with and through others to achieve organizational objectives in an efficient and ethical manner. From the standpoint of organizational behavior, the central feature of this definition is "working with and through others." Managers play a constantly evolving role. Today's successful managers are no longer the I've-got-everything-under-control order givers of yesteryear. Rather, they need to creatively envision and actively sell bold new directions in an ethical and sensitive manner. Effective managers are team players empowered by the

Figure 1–1   *Strategic Results: The 4-P Cycle of Continuous Improvement*

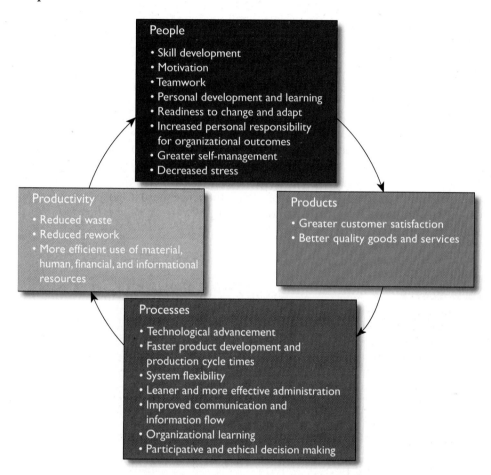

willing and active support of others who are driven by conflicting self-interests. Each of us has a huge stake in how well managers carry out their evolving role. Henry Mintzberg, a respected management scholar, observed: "No job is more vital to our society than that of the manager. It is the manager who determines whether our social institutions serve us well or whether they squander our talents and resources."[11]

Extending our managerial thrust, let us take a closer look at the skills managers need to perform, the concept of human capital, and the future direction of management.

What Do Managers Do? A Skills Profile

Observational studies by Mintzberg and others have found the typical manager's day to be a fragmented collection of brief episodes.[12] Interruptions are commonplace, while large blocks of time for planning and reflective thinking are not. In one particular study, four top-level managers spent 63% of their time on activities lasting less than nine minutes each. Only 5% of the managers' time was devoted to activities lasting more than an hour.[13] But what specific skills do effective managers perform during their hectic and fragmented workdays?

Many attempts have been made over the years to paint a realistic picture of what managers do.[14] Diverse and confusing lists of managerial functions and roles have been suggested. Fortunately, a stream of research over the past 20 years by Clark Wilson and others has given us a practical and statistically validated profile of managerial *skills*[15] (see Table 1–1). Wilson's managerial skills profile focuses on 11 observable categories of managerial behavior. This is very much in tune with today's emphasis on managerial competency.[16] Wilson's unique skills-assessment technique goes beyond the usual self-report approach with its natural bias. In addition to surveying a given manager about his or her 11 skills, the Wilson approach also asks those who report directly to the manager to answer questions about their boss's skills. According to Wilson and his colleagues, the result is an assessment of skill *mastery,* not simply skill awareness.[17] The logic behind Wilson's approach is both simple and compelling. Who better to assess a manager's skills than the people who experience those behaviors on a day-to-day basis—those who report directly to the manager?

Table 1–1   *Skills Exhibited by an Effective Manager**

1. **Clarifies goals and objectives** for everyone involved.
   (See Chs. 6, 7, 9, 15, 17, and 18)
2. **Encourages participation,** upward communication, and suggestions.
   (See Chs. 2, 12, 13, 15, 16, and 17)
3. **Plans and organizes** for an orderly work flow.
   (See Chs. 18 and 19)
4. Has **technical and administrative expertise** to answer organization-related questions.
   (See Chs. 1, 2, 10, 11, 15, and 19)
5. **Facilitates work** through team building, training, coaching, and support.
   (See Chs. 3, 4, 7, 8, 9, 10, 13, 15, 16, 17, 18, and 19)
6. **Provides feedback** honestly and constructively.
   (See Chs. 10, 13, 15, 16, and 17)
7. **Keeps things moving** by relying on schedules, deadlines, and helpful reminders.
   (See Chs. 7, 8, 9, 10, 13, 14, 15, 16, 17, 18, and 19)
8. **Controls details** without being overbearing.
   (See Chs. 2, 4, 5, 6, 10, 11, 15, 17, 18, and 19)
9. Applies reasonable **pressure for goal accomplishment.**
   (See Chs. 1, 4, 5, 6, 7, 8, 9, 10, 11, 12, 14, 15, 16, 17, and 18)
10. **Empowers and delegates** key duties to others while maintaining goal clarity and commitment.
    (See Chs. 2, 3, 11, 13, 16, 17, and 18)
11. **Recognizes good performance** with rewards and positive reinforcement.
    (See Chs. 7, 8, 9, 10, 15, 16, and 17)

*Annotated with relevant chapters in this textbook.

SOURCES: Adapted from material in C Wilson, "Identify Needs with Costs in Mind," *Training and Development Journal,* July 1980, pp. 58–62; and F Shipper, "A Study of the Psychometric Properties of the Managerial Skill Scales of the Survey of Management Practices," *Educational and Psychological Measurement,* June 1995, pp. 468–79.

The Wilson managerial skills research yields four useful lessons:

1. Dealing effectively with *people* is what management is all about. The 11 skills in Table 1–1 constitute a goal creation/commitment/feedback/reward/accomplishment cycle with human interaction at every turn.
2. Managers with high skills mastery tend to have better subunit performance and employee morale than managers with low skills mastery.[18]
3. *Effective* female and male managers *do not* have significantly different skill profiles,[19] contrary to claims in the popular business press in recent years.[20]
4. At all career stages, *derailed* managers (those who failed to achieve their potential) tended to be the ones who *overestimated* their skill mastery (rated themselves higher than their employees did). This prompted the following conclusion from the researcher: "when selecting individuals for promotion to managerial positions, those who are arrogant, aloof, insensitive, and defensive should be avoided."[21]

Welcome to the Age of Human and Social Capital

Management is a lot like juggling. Everything is constantly in motion, with several things up in the air at any given time. Strategically speaking, managers juggle human, financial, material, informational, and technological resources. Each is vital to success in its own way. But jugglers remind us that some objects are rubber and some are glass. Dropped rubber objects bounce; dropped glass objects break. As more and more managers have come to realize, we cannot afford to drop the people factor (referred to in Figure 1–2 as human and social capital).

What Is Human Capital? (Hint: Think BIG)
A team of human resource management authors recently offered this perspective:

> We're living in a time when a new economic paradigm—characterized by speed, innovation, short cycle times, quality, and customer satisfaction—is highlighting the importance of intangible assets, such as brand recognition, knowledge, innovation, and particularly human capital.[22]

Human capital is the productive potential of an individual's knowledge and actions.[23] *Potential* is the operative word in this intentionally broad definition. When you are hungry, money in your pocket is good because it has the potential to buy a meal. Likewise, a present or future employee with the right combination of knowledge, skills, and motivation to excel represents human capital with the potential to give the organization a competitive advantage. Computer chip maker Intel, for example, is a high-tech company whose future depends on innovative engineering. It takes years of math and science studies to make world-class engineers. Not wanting to leave the future supply of engineers to chance, Intel annually spends millions of dollars funding education at all levels. The company encourages youngsters to study math and science and sponsors science competitions with generous scholarships for the winners.[24] Additionally, Intel encourages its employees to volunteer at local schools by giving the schools $200 for every 20 hours contributed.[25] Will all of the students end up working for Intel? No. That's not the point. The point is much bigger—namely, to build the *world's* human capital.

What Is Social Capital?
Our focus now shifts from the individual to social units (e.g., friends, family, company, group or club, nation). Think *relationships*. **Social capital** is productive potential resulting from strong relationships, goodwill, trust, and

Human capital
The productive potential of one's knowledge and actions.

Social capital
The productive potential of strong, trusting, and cooperative relationships.

Figure 1–2   *The Strategic Importance and Dimensions of Human and Social Capital*

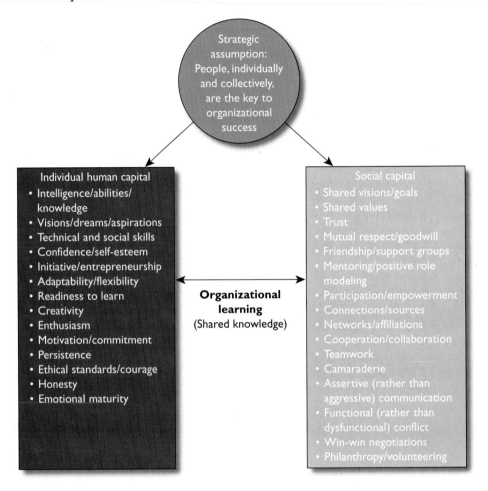

SOURCES: Based on discussions in P S Adler and S Kwon, "Social Capital: Prospects for a New Concept," *Academy of Management Review,* January 2002, pp. 17–40; and C A Bartlett and S Ghoshal, "Building Competitive Advantage through People," *MIT Sloan Management Review,* Winter 2002, pp. 34–41.

cooperative effort.[26] Again, the word *potential* is key. According to experts on the subject: "It's true: the social capital that used to be a given in organizations is now rare and endangered. But the social capital we can build will allow us to capitalize on the volatile, virtual possibilities of today's business environment."[27] Relationships do matter. In a recent general survey, 77% of the women and 63% of the men rated "Good relationship with boss" extremely important. Other factors—including good equipment, resources, easy commute, and flexible hours—received lower ratings.[28]

Building Human and Social Capital   Various dimensions of human and social capital are listed in Figure 1–2. They are a preview of what lies ahead in this book, including our discussion of organizational learning in Chapter 18. Formal organizational learning and *knowledge management* programs, as discussed in Chap-

ſixteen-year-old Walkiria Miranda, a student at Eladio Tirado Lopez High ſchool in Aguada, Puerto Rico, shows off one of her geometrical figures from Intel's 2002 International ſcience and Engineering Fair. By encouraging youngsters from around the world to explore math and science, Intel is helping to build valuable human capital for the global economy.

(Courtesy of Intel Corporation)

ter 11, need social capital to leverage individual human capital for the greater good. It is a straightforward formula for success. Growth depends on the timely sharing of valuable knowledge. After all, what good are bright employees who do not network, teach, and inspire? Moreover, the rich array of factors in Figure 1–2 can be an agenda for progressive people who want to join our quest for more people-centered managers and organizations.

21st-Century Managers

Today's workplace is indeed undergoing immense and permanent changes.[29] Organizations have been "reengineered" for greater speed, efficiency, and flexibility.[30] Teams are pushing aside the individual as the primary building block of organizations.[31] Command-and-control management is giving way to participative management and empowerment.[32] Ego-centered leaders are being replaced by customer-centered leaders. Employees increasingly are being viewed as internal customers. All this creates a mandate for a new kind of manager in the 21st century. Management author and consultant Larry Weber offers this perspective:

> Weber is tired of military metaphors. Not that he's a pacifist. He appreciates the contributions of men and women in the armed forces, especially in times of clear and present danger. He just doesn't think that giving orders is the best way to run a business. . . .
>
> He believes that a new generation of leaders is succeeding in business because they have ditched the military management style personified by a group that he calls "the generals." Instead, Weber sees a new model of leadership: the provocateur. Where generals are rigid and closed, provocateurs are flexible and open. Where generals favor command and control, provocateurs operate through sense and response. Where generals view a company as a pyramid with one person at the top, provocateurs see it as a circle with the customer at its center.[33]

Table 1–2 contrasts the characteristics of past and future managers. As the balance of this book will demonstrate, the managerial shift in Table 1–2 is not just a good idea, it is an absolute necessity in the new workplace.

Table 1–2   *Evolution of the 21st-Century Manager*

	Past Managers	Future Managers
Primary role	Order giver, privileged elite, manipulator, controller	Facilitator, team member, teacher, advocate, sponsor, coach
Learning and knowledge	Periodic learning, narrow specialist	Continuous life-long learning, generalist with multiple specialties
Compensation criteria	Time, effort, rank	Skills, results
Cultural orientation	Monocultural, monolingual	Multicultural, multilingual
Primary source of influence	Formal authority	Knowledge (technical and interpersonal)
View of people	Potential problem	Primary resource
Primary communication pattern	Vertical	Multidirectional
Decision-making style	Limited input for individual decisions	Broad-based input for joint decisions
Ethical considerations	Afterthought	Forethought
Nature of interpersonal relationships	Competitive (win–lose)	Cooperative (win–win)
Handling of power and key information	Hoard and restrict access	Share and broaden access
Approach to change	Resist	Facilitate

The Field of Organizational Behavior: Past and Present

Organizational behavior

Interdisciplinary field dedicated to better understanding and managing people at work.

Organizational behavior, commonly referred to as OB, is an interdisciplinary field dedicated to better understanding and managing people at work. By definition, organizational behavior is both research and application oriented. Three basic levels of analysis in OB are individual, group, and organizational. OB draws upon a diverse array of disciplines, including psychology, management, sociology, organization theory, social psychology, statistics, anthropology, general systems theory, economics, information technology, political science, vocational counseling, human stress management, psychometrics, ergonomics, decision theory, and ethics. This rich heritage has spawned many competing perspectives and theories about human work behavior. By the mid-1980s, one researcher had identified 110 distinct theories about behavior within the field of OB.[34]

Organizational behavior is an academic designation. With the exception of teaching/research positions, OB is not an everyday job category such as accounting, marketing, or finance. Students of OB typically do not get jobs in organizational behavior, per se. This reality in no way demeans OB or lessens its importance in effective organizational management. OB is a *horizontal* discipline cutting across virtually every job category, business function, and professional specialty. Anyone who plans to make a living in a large or small, public or private, organization needs to study organizational behavior.

A historical perspective of the study of people at work helps in studying organizational behavior. According to a management history expert, this is important because:

Historical perspective is the study of a subject in light of its earliest phases and subsequent evolution. Historical perspective differs from history in that the object of historical perspective is to sharpen one's vision of the present, not the past.[35]

In other words, we can better understand where the field of OB is today and where it appears to be headed by appreciating where it has been. Let us examine three significant landmarks in the evolution of understanding and managing people:

1. The human relations movement.
2. The total quality management movement.
3. The Internet revolution.

The Human Relations Movement

A unique combination of factors during the 1930s fostered the human relations movement. First, following legalization of union–management collective bargaining in the United States in 1935, management began looking for new ways of handling employees. Second, behavioral scientists conducting on-the-job research started calling for more attention to the "human" factor. Managers who had lost the battle to keep unions out of their factories heeded the call for better human relations and improved working conditions. One such study, conducted at Western Electric's Chicago-area Hawthorne plant, was a prime stimulus for the human relations movement. Ironically, many of the Hawthorne findings have turned out to be more myth than fact.

The Hawthorne Legacy   Interviews conducted decades later with three subjects of the Hawthorne studies and reanalysis of the original data with modern statistical techniques do not support initial conclusions about the positive effect of supportive supervision. Specifically, money, fear of unemployment during the Great Depression, managerial discipline, and high-quality raw materials—not supportive supervision—turned out to be responsible for high output in the relay assembly test room experiments.[36] Nonetheless, the human relations movement gathered momentum through the 1950s, as academics and managers alike made stirring claims about the powerful effect that individual needs, supportive supervision, and group dynamics apparently had on job performance.

These relay assembly test room employees in the classic Hawthorne Western Electric studies turned in record performance. Why? No one knows for certain, and debate continues to this day. Supportive supervision was long believed to be the key factor. Whatever the reason, Hawthorne gave the budding human relations movement needed research credibility.

(Property of AT&T Archives. Reprinted with permission of AT&T)

The Writings of Mayo and Follett Essential to the human relations movement were the writings of Elton Mayo and Mary Parker Follett. Australian-born Mayo, who headed the Harvard researchers at Hawthorne, advised managers to attend to employees' emotional needs in his 1933 classic, *The Human Problems of an Industrial Civilization.* Follett was a true pioneer, not only as a woman management consultant in the male-dominated industrial world of the 1920s, but also as a writer who saw employees as complex combinations of attitudes, beliefs, and needs. Mary Parker Follett was way ahead of her time in telling managers to motivate job performance instead of merely demanding it, a "pull" rather than "push" strategy. She also built a logical bridge between political democracy and a cooperative spirit in the workplace.[37]

McGregor's Theory Y In 1960, Douglas McGregor wrote a book entitled *The Human Side of Enterprise,* which has become an important philosophical base for the modern view of people at work.[38] Drawing upon his experience as a management consultant, McGregor formulated two sharply contrasting sets of assumptions about human nature (see Table 1–3). His Theory X assumptions were pessimistic and negative and, according to McGregor's interpretation, typical of how managers traditionally perceived employees. To help managers break with this negative tradition, McGregor formulated his **Theory Y,** a modern and positive set of assumptions about people. McGregor believed managers could accomplish more through others by viewing them as self-energized, committed, responsible, and creative beings.[39]

A mid-1990s survey of 10,227 employees from many industries across the United States challenges managers to do a better job of acting on McGregor's Theory Y assumptions. From the employees' perspective, Theory X management practices are the major barrier to productivity improvement and employee well-being. The researcher concluded:

Theory Y

McGregor's modern and positive assumptions about employees being responsible and creative.

Table 1–3 *McGregor's Theory X and Theory Y*

Outdated (Theory X) Assumptions about People at Work	Modern (Theory Y) Assumptions about People at Work
1. Most people dislike work; they avoid it when they can.	1. Work is a natural activity, like play or rest.
2. Most people must be coerced and threatened with punishment before they will work. People require close direction when they are working.	2. People are capable of self-direction and self-control if they are committed to objectives.
3. Most people actually prefer to be directed. They tend to avoid responsibility and exhibit little ambition. They are interested only in security.	3. People generally become committed to organizational objectives if they are rewarded for doing so.
	4. The typical employee can learn to accept and seek responsibility.
	5. The typical member of the general population has imagination, ingenuity, and creativity.

SOURCE: Adapted from D McGregor, *The Human Side of Enterprise* (New York: McGraw-Hill, 1960), Ch 4.

The most noteworthy finding from our survey is that an overwhelming number of American workers—some 97%—desire work conditions known to facilitate high productivity. Workers uniformly reported—regardless of the type of organization, age, gender, pay schedule, or level in the organizational hierarchy—that they needed and wanted in their own workplaces the conditions for collaboration, commitment, and creativity research has demonstrated as necessary for both productivity and health. Just as noteworthy, however, is the finding that the actual conditions of work supplied by management are those conditions that research has identified as *competence suppressors*—procedures, policies, and practices that prevent or punish expressions of competence and most characterize unproductive organizations.[40]

New Assumptions about Human Nature   Unfortunately, unsophisticated behavioral research methods caused the human relationists to embrace some naive and misleading conclusions.[41] For example, human relationists believed in the axiom, "A satisfied employee is a hardworking employee." Subsequent research, as discussed later in this book, shows the satisfaction–performance linkage to be more complex than originally thought.

Despite its shortcomings, the human relations movement opened the door to more progressive thinking about human nature. Rather than continuing to view employees as passive economic beings, managers began to see them as active social beings and took steps to create more humane work environments.

The Total Quality Management Movement

In 1980, NBC aired a television documentary titled "If Japan Can . . . Why Can't We?" It was a wake-up call for North American companies to dramatically improve product quality or continue losing market share to Japanese electronics and automobile companies. A full-fledged movement ensued during the 1980s and 1990s. Much was written, said, and done about improving the quality of both goods and services.[42] Thanks to the concept of *total quality management* (TQM), the quality of much of what we buy today is significantly better than in the past. The underlying principles of TQM are more important than ever given the growth of both E-business on the Internet and the overall service economy.[43] According to one business writer:

> A company stuck in the industrial-age mentality is very likely to get squashed because "zero-defect" quality has become an ante to compete, not a differentiator. Even "zero-time" operations that address customers' expectations for immediate response and gratification are becoming common in today's digital age.[44]

Siebel Systems Inc., the Silicon Valley maker of customer-management software, has gotten the message and taken customer service to a higher level: "No software gets written until customers weigh in. Outside consultants routinely poll clients on their satisfaction, and compensation is heavily based on those reports."[45] TQM principles have profound practical implications for managing people today.[46]

What Is TQM?   Experts on the subject offered this definition of **total quality management:**

> TQM means that the organization's culture is defined by and supports the constant attainment of customer satisfaction through an integrated system of tools, techniques, and training. This involves the continuous improvement of organizational processes, resulting in high-quality products and services.[47]

Total quality management
An organizational culture dedicated to training, continuous improvement, and customer satisfaction.

Quality consultant Richard J Schonberger sums up TQM as "continuous, customer-centered, employee-driven improvement."[48] TQM is necessarily employee driven because product/service quality cannot be continuously improved without the active learning and participation of *every* employee. Thus, in successful quality improvement programs, TQM principles are embedded in the organization's culture. In fact, according to the results of a recent field experiment, bank customers had higher satisfaction after interacting with bank employees who had been trained to provide excellent service.[49]

The Deming Legacy

TQM is firmly established today thanks in large part to the pioneering work of W Edwards Deming.[50] Ironically, the mathematician credited with Japan's post–World War II quality revolution rarely talked in terms of quality. He instead preferred to discuss "good management" during the hard-hitting seminars he delivered right up until his death at age 93 in 1993.[51] Although Deming's passion was the statistical measurement and reduction of variations in industrial processes, he had much to say about how employees should be treated. Regarding the human side of quality improvement, Deming called for the following:

- Formal training in statistical process control techniques and teamwork.
- Helpful leadership, rather than order giving and punishment.
- Elimination of fear so employees will feel free to ask questions.
- Emphasis on continuous process improvements rather than on numerical quotas.
- Teamwork.
- Elimination of barriers to good workmanship.[52]

One of Deming's most enduring lessons for managers is his 85–15 rule.[53] Specifically, when things go wrong, there is roughly an 85% chance the *system* (including management, machinery, and rules) is at fault. Only about 15% of the time is the individual employee at fault. Unfortunately, as Deming observed, the typical manager spends most of his or her time wrongly blaming and punishing individuals for system failures. Statistical analysis is required to uncover system failures.

Principles of TQM

Despite variations in the language and scope of TQM programs, it is possible to identify four common TQM principles:

1. Do it right the first time to eliminate costly rework and product recalls.
2. Listen to and learn from customers and employees.
3. Make continuous improvement an everyday matter.
4. Build teamwork, trust, and mutual respect.[54]

Deming's influence is clearly evident in this list.[55] Once again, as with the human relations movement, we see *people* as the key factor in organizational success.

In summary, TQM advocates have made a valuable contribution to the field of OB by providing a *practical* context for managing people. The case for TQM is strong because, as discovered in two recent comprehensive studies, *it works!*[56] When people are managed according to TQM principles, more of them are likely to get the employment opportunities and high-quality goods and services they demand.[57] As you will see many times in later chapters, this book is anchored to Deming's philosophy and TQM principles.

The Internet Revolution

We can be forgiven if the Internet revolution has left us a bit dizzy (for a brief history of the Internet, see International OB on page 18).[58] In just a few short years, dot-coms exploded onto the scene, with promises of *everything* for sale *cheap* on the Internet. Then, just as suddenly, many dot-coms truly did explode, leaving their overworked employees jobless and their founders telling bizarre riches-to-rags stories.[59] Strange and unforeseen things happened. For example, Pets.com, with a popular and expensive advertising campaign, went broke trying to underprice pet supply stores. Meanwhile, Southwest Airlines, an established company, made the Internet a key feature of its already successful business model. In 2001, "Southwest.com, by far the most successful airline Web site, delivered $2.1 billion in revenue, or 40% of Southwest's passenger revenue."[60]

As we continue to sift through the wreckage of the 2000–2001 dot-com crash looking for winning formulas, one thing is very clear. The **Internet**—the global network of computers, software, cables, servers, switches, and routers—is here to stay as a business tool.[61] *BusinessWeek* framed the situation this way in 2002:

> The latest data . . . show continued growth, even after dot-com shares started to crash in April 2000. The number of Internet users worldwide is still rising—by 48% in 2000 and 27% in 2001, to more than 500 million people. . . . [In 2001,] Internet trade between businesses rose 73%, to $496 billion, and online retail spending rose 56%, to $112 billion, in the worst retail year in a decade.[62]

Apart from these impressive numbers, *BusinessWeek* offered an OB-related Internet challenge: "The real imperative for the next few years, though, will be adapting new technology to people and their work, rather than forcing people to adapt to it."[63]

The purpose of this section is to define *E-business* and identify significant OB implications in the ongoing Internet revolution (as signs of what lies ahead).

E-business Is Much More than E-Commerce

Experts on the subject draw an important distinction between *E-commerce* (buying and selling goods and services over the Internet) and **E-business,** using the Internet to facilitate *every* aspect of running a business.[64] Says one industry observer: "Strip away the highfalutin talk,

Internet

The global system of networked computers.

E-business

Running the *entire* business via the Internet.

Surprise! Southwest Airlines turned out to be a big winner in the feverish dot-com race that ended in ruin for many new economy companies. By 2001, Southwest was booking 40% of its revenue on its Web site, southwest.com. Southwest Airlines skillfully blended the best of both the old and new to come up with a winning E-business formula.

(Courtesy of Southwest Airlines)

Interconnecting computers started out in 1969 with a four-computer hookup. Initially, the researchers concentrated on devising an alternative capability for sustaining and enhancing communications. Developed by the Defense Department's Advanced Research Project Agency (ARPA), the system existed until 1990. By 1971 things hadn't changed much—a mere 15 sites with 24 connected computers in operation.

The milestone event in 1972 was the first electronic mail exchange between two computers by Ray Tomlinson, who also established the @ signage icon.

Because computers available at that time used different operating systems, many of them incompatible, a standard operating protocol was established: TCP/IP, Transmission Control Protocol/Internet Protocol. In 1974, the protocol was upgraded and modified by Vinton Cerf and Jon Postel and evolved into today's common interface. Because the protocol is in the public realm, no license, payment, or permission is required for use.

By 1974, 62 computers were hooked up. Seven years later (1981), there were 200, and 500 computers in 1983, then 28,000 in 1987. The system had grown somewhat. But it still remained the domain of researchers, intellectuals, and academics, facilitating easy and rapid exchange of research materials of mutual interest.

During 1989, the World Wide Web was created at the European Center for Nuclear Research (CERN), a Geneva-based particle physics lab, by [British-born] Tim Berners-Lee. This breakthrough made multimedia available on the Internet in August 1991. During the early 1990s, the Web opened to commercial uses. Fewer than 1 million users were online in 1991.

The foundation for opening up the Web was laid in 1991 when the first Web browser or software was released. During 1993, the National Center for Supercomputing Applications released versions of Mosaic, the first graphical Web browser for Microsoft Windows (developed by Marc Andreessen at the University of Illinois). Now marketed as the Netscape browser, this system facilitated navigating the multimedia offerings. The Netscape Navigator browser was released by Netscape Communications in 1994, and host computers or servers swelled to 3 million.

Worldwide, there were about 130.6 million active Internet users in 1999....Some forecasters believe that the 1-billion-user benchmark will be reached by 2005. One billion, these observers insist, is big enough to dub the virtual world of the Internet as the eighth continent!

SOURCE: G T T Molitor, "A Brief History of the Internet," *The Futurist*, September–October 2001, p. 33.

and at bottom, the Internet is a tool that dramatically lowers the cost of communication. That means it can radically alter any industry or activity that depends heavily on the flow of information."[65] Relevant information includes everything from customer needs and product design specifications to prices, schedules, finances, employee performance data, and corporate strategy. Intel, discussed earlier as a champion of human capital, has taken this broad view of the Internet to heart. The computer-chip giant is striving to become what it calls an E-corporation, one that relies primarily on the Internet to not only buy and sell things, but to facilitate all business functions, exchange knowledge among its employees, and build partnerships with outsiders as well. Intel is on the right track according to this survey finding: "firms that embraced the Internet averaged a 13.4% jump in productivity . . . [in 2000], compared with 4.9% for those that did not."[66] E-business has significant implications for managing people at work because it eventually will seep into every corner of life both on and off the job.

E-business Implications for OB

The following list is intended to open doors and explore possibilities, not serve as a final analysis. It also is a preview of later discussions in this book.

- *E-management*—21st-century managers, profiled earlier in Table 1–2, are needed in the fast-paced Internet age. They are able to create, motivate, and lead teams of far-flung specialists linked by Internet E-mail and project-management software and by fax and phone. Networking skills, applied both inside and outside the organization, are essential today.

- *E-communication*—E-mail has become one of the most used and abused forms of organizational communication. Today's managers need to be masters of concise, powerful E-mail and voice mail messages. Communicating via the Internet's World Wide Web is fast and efficient for those who know how to fully exploit it. Consider the experience of Pietro Senna, a buyer for Nestlé Switzerland:

  > The time savings are immense. Each country's hazelnut buyer, for example, used to visit processing plants in Italy and Turkey. Hazelnuts, a key ingredient in chocolate bars, are prone to wild price swings and uneven quality. But after Senna stopped by some Turkish plants, he posted his report on the Web—and within a week, 73 other Nestlé buyers from around the globe had read it, saving them the trouble of a trip to Turkey. "For the first time, I get to take advantage of Nestlé's size," he says.[67]

  Additionally, employees who "telecommute" from home or report in from remote locations via the Internet present their managers with unique motivational and performance measurement problems. For their part, telecommuters must strike a productive balance between independence and feelings of isolation.

- *Goal setting and feedback*—Abundant research evidence supports the coupling of clear and challenging goals and timely and constructive feedback for keeping employees headed in the right direction. Thanks to Web-based software programs such as *eWorkbench,* managers can efficiently create, align, and track their employee's goals.[68]

- *Organizational structure*—The Internet and modern telecommunications technology have given rise to "virtual teams" and "virtual organizations." Time zones, facilities, and location no longer are hard constraints on getting things accomplished. Got a great product idea but don't have the time to build a factory? No problem, just connect with someone via the Internet who can get the job done. This virtual workplace, with less face-to-face interaction, requires managers and employees who are flexible and adaptable and not bound by slow and rigid bureaucratic structures and methods.

- *Job design*—The *work itself* is a powerful motivator for many employees today, especially those in information technology. A New Economy study by Harvard's Rosabeth Moss Kanter led to this conclusion:

  > [They] are attracted by the chance to take on big responsibility and stretch their skills even further. The "stickiest" work settings (the ones people leave less frequently and more reluctantly) involve opportunity and empowerment. Cutting-edge work with the best tools for the best customers is important in the present because it promises even greater responsibility and rewards in the future.[69]

  Boring and unchallenging and/or dead-end jobs will repel rather than attract top talent in the Internet age.

- *Decision making*—Things indeed are moving faster and faster in the Internet age. Just ask the typical overloaded manager. A recent survey asking 479 managers about their last three years uncovered these findings: 77% reported making more decisions while 43% said they had less time to make decisions.[70] Adding to the pressure, databases linked to the Internet give today's decision makers unprecedented amounts of both relevant and irrelevant data. The trick is to be energized and selective, not overwhelmed. A clear sense of purpose is necessary when sifting for useful information. Moreover, decision makers cannot ignore the trend away from command-and-control tactics and toward employee empowerment and participation. In short, there is more "we" than "me" for Internet-age decision makers.

- *Knowledge management*—Of growing importance today are E-training, E-learning, and distance learning via the Internet.

   [C]orporate spending on e-learning is expected to more than quadruple by 2005, to $18 billion....At IBM, some 200,000 employees received education or training online [in 2000]..., and 75% of the company's Basic Blue course for new managers is online. The move cut IBM's [annual] training bill by $350 million..., because online courses don't require travel.[71]

- *Speed, conflict, and stress*—The name of the popular Internet-age magazine, *Fast Company*, says it all. Unfortunately, conflict and stress are unavoidable by-products of strategic and operational speed. The good news, as you will learn in later chapters, is that conflict and stress can be managed.

- *Change and resistance to change*—As Old Economy companies race to become E-corporations, employees are being asked to digest huge doses of change in every aspect of their worklives. For example, imagine the changes in store for the 198,000 employees at Boeing, the world's largest aircraft maker. As *Fortune* observed:

   talk to Boeing execs and you'll find that everything at the company is being reexamined, from how it interacts with its customers and 15,000 suppliers right down to whether plane-making should be its core business. The goal is to change the entire fabric of the company.[72]

   Inevitable conflict and resistance to change will need to be skillfully managed at Boeing if it is to prosper.[73]

- *Ethics*—Internet-centered organizations are littered with ethical landmines needing to be addressed humanely and responsibly. Among them are around-the-clock work binges, exaggerated promises about rewards, electronic monitoring, questionable antiunion tactics, repetitive-motion injuries from excessive keyboarding, unfair treatment of part-timers, and privacy issues.[74]

Overall, the problems, challenges, and opportunities embodied in the Internet revolution are immense. Skillful management is needed.

The Contingency Approach: Applying Lessons from Theory, Research, and Practice

Contingency approach

Using management tools and techniques in a situationally appropriate manner; avoiding the one-best-way mentality.

Scholars have wrestled for many years with the problem of how best to apply the diverse and growing collection of management tools and techniques. Their answer is the contingency approach. The **contingency approach** calls for using management techniques in a situationally appropriate manner, instead of trying to rely on "one best way." According to a pair of contingency theorists:

[Contingency theories] developed and their acceptance grew largely because they responded to criticisms that the classical theories advocated "one best way" of organizing and managing. Contingency theories, on the other hand, proposed that the appropriate organizational structure and management style were dependent upon a set of "contingency" factors, usually the uncertainty and instability of the environment.[75]

The contingency approach encourages managers to view organizational behavior within a situational context. According to this modern perspective, evolving situations, not hard-and-fast rules, determine when and where various management techniques are appropriate. For example, as discussed in Chapter 17, contingency researchers have determined that there is no single best style of leadership. Organizational behavior specialists embrace the contingency approach because it helps them realistically interrelate individuals, groups, and organizations. Moreover, the contingency approach sends a clear message to managers in today's global economy: Carefully read the situation and then be flexible enough to adapt.[76]

As a human being, with years of interpersonal experience to draw upon, you already know a good deal about people at work. But more systematic and comprehensive understanding is possible and desirable. A working knowledge of current OB theory, research, and practice can help you develop a tightly integrated understanding of why organizational contributors think and act as they do. In order for this to happen, however, prepare yourself for some intellectual surprises from theoretical models, research results, or techniques that may run counter to your current thinking. Research surprises not only make learning fun, they also can improve the quality of our lives both on and off the job. Let us examine the dynamic relationship between OB theory, research, and practice and the value of each.

Figure 1–3 illustrates how theory, research, and practice are related. Throughout the balance of this book, we focus primarily on the central portion, where all three areas

Figure 1–3 *Learning about OB through a Combination of Theory, Research, and Practice*

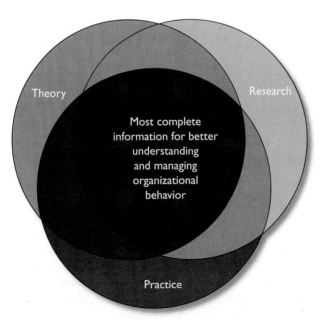

overlap. Knowledge of why people behave as they do and what managers can do to improve performance is greatest within this area of maximum overlap. For each major topic, we build a foundation for understanding with generally accepted theory. This theoretical foundation is then tested and expanded by reviewing the latest relevant research findings. After interpreting the research, we discuss the nature and effectiveness of related practical applications.

Sometimes, depending on the subject matter, it is necessary to venture into the large areas outside the central portion of Figure 1–3. For example, an insightful theory supported by convincing research evidence might suggest an untried or different way of managing. In other instances, an innovative management technique might call for an explanatory theoretical model and exploratory research. Each area—theory, research, and practice—supports and, in turn, is supported by the other two.[77] Each area makes a valuable contribution to our understanding of, and ability to, manage organizational behavior.

Learning from Theory

Theory
A story defining key terms, providing a conceptual framework, and explaining why something occurs.

A respected behavioral scientist, Kurt Lewin, once said there is nothing as practical as a good theory. According to one management researcher, a **theory** is a story that explains "why."[78] Another calls well-constructed theories "disciplined imagination."[79] A good OB theory, then, is a story that effectively explains why individuals and groups behave as they do. Moreover, a good theoretical model

1. *Defines* key terms.
2. Constructs a *conceptual framework* that explains how important factors are interrelated. (Graphic models are often used to achieve this end.)
3. Provides a *departure point* for research and practical application.

Indeed, good theories are a fundamental contributor to improved understanding and management of organizational behavior.[80]

Learning from Research

Because of unfamiliar jargon and complicated statistical procedures, many current and future managers are put off by behavioral research.[81] This is unfortunate because practical lessons can be learned as OB researchers steadily advance the frontier of knowledge. Let us examine the various sources and uses of OB research evidence.

Five Sources of OB Research Insights
To enhance the instructional value of our coverage of major topics, we systematically cite "hard" evidence from five different categories. Worthwhile evidence was obtained by drawing upon the following *priority* of research methodologies:

Meta-analysis
Pools the results of many studies through statistical procedure.

- *Meta-analyses.* A **meta-analysis** is a statistical pooling technique that permits behavioral scientists to draw general conclusions about certain variables from many different studies.[82] It typically encompasses a vast number of subjects, often reaching the thousands. Meta-analyses are instructive because they focus on general patterns of research evidence, not fragmented bits and pieces or isolated studies.[83]

- *Field studies.* In OB, a **field study** probes individual or group processes in an organizational setting. Because field studies involve real-life situations, their results often have immediate and practical relevance for managers.

- *Laboratory studies.* In a **laboratory study,** variables are manipulated and measured in contrived situations. College students are commonly used as subjects. The highly controlled nature of laboratory studies enhances research precision. But generalizing the results to organizational management requires caution.[84]

- *Sample surveys.* In a **sample survey,** samples of people from specified populations respond to questionnaires. The researchers then draw conclusions about the relevant population. Generalizability of the results depends on the quality of the sampling and questioning techniques.

- *Case studies.* A **case study** is an in-depth analysis of a single individual, group, or organization. Because of their limited scope, case studies yield realistic but not very generalizable results.[85]

Three Uses of OB Research Findings

Organizational scholars point out that managers can put relevant research findings to use in three different ways:[86]

1. *Instrumental use.* This involves directly applying research findings to practical problems. For example, a manager experiencing high stress tries a relaxation technique after reading a research report about its effectiveness.

2. *Conceptual use.* Research is put to conceptual use when managers derive general enlightenment from its findings. The effect here is less specific and more indirect than with instrumental use. For example, after reading a meta-analysis showing a negative correlation between absenteeism and age,[87] a manager might develop a more positive attitude toward hiring older people.

3. *Symbolic use.* Symbolic use occurs when research results are relied on to verify or legitimize already held positions. Negative forms of symbolic use involve self-serving bias, prejudice, selective perception, and distortion. For example, tobacco industry spokespersons routinely deny any link between smoking and lung cancer because researchers are largely, but not 100%, in agreement about the negative effects of smoking. A positive example would be managers maintaining their confidence in setting performance goals after reading a research report about the favorable impact of goal setting on job performance.

By systematically reviewing and interpreting research relevant to key topics, this book provides instructive insights about OB. (For more about OB research methods, see Learning Module C at the end of the book.)

Field study

Examination of variables in real-life settings.

Laboratory study

Manipulation and measurement of variables in contrived situations.

Sample survey

Questionnaire responses from a sample of people.

Case study

In-depth study of a single person, group, or organization.

SOURCE: DILBERT reprinted by permission of United Feature Syndicate, Inc.

Learning from Practice

Learning to manage people is like learning to ride a bicycle. You watch others do it. Sooner or later, you get up the courage to try it yourself. You fall off and skin your knee. You climb back on the bike a bit smarter, and so on, until wobbly first attempts turn into a smooth ride. Your chances of becoming a successful manager can be enhanced by studying the theory, research, and practical examples in this textbook. Figuratively speaking, however, you eventually must climb aboard the "managerial bicycle" and learn by doing.

The theory→research→practice sequence discussed in this section will help you better understand each major topic addressed later in this book. Attention now turns to a topical model that provides a road map for what lies ahead.

A Topical Model for Understanding and Managing OB

Figure 1–4 is a topical road map for our journey through this book. Our destination is organizational effectiveness through continuous improvement. Four different criteria for determining whether or not an organization is effective are discussed in Chapter 18.

Figure 1–4   *A Topical Model for What Lies Ahead*

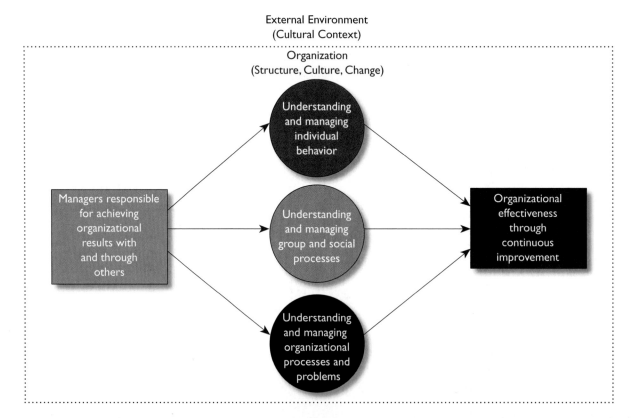

The study of OB can be a wandering and pointless trip if we overlook the need to translate OB lessons into effective and efficient organized endeavor.

At the far left side of our topical road map are managers, those who are responsible for accomplishing organizational results with and through others. The three circles at the center of our road map correspond to Parts Two, Three, and Four of this text. Logically, the flow of topical coverage in this book (following introductory Part One) goes from individuals, to group processes, to organizational processes and problems. Around the core of our topical road map in Figure 1–4 is the organization. Accordingly, we end our journey with organization-related material in Part Four. Organizational structure and design are covered there in Chapter 18 to establish and develop the *organizational* context of organizational behavior. Rounding out our organizational context is a discussion of organizational change in Chapter 19. Chapters 3 and 4 provide a *cultural* context for OB.

The dotted line represents a permeable boundary between the organization and its environment. Energy and influence flow both ways across this permeable boundary. Truly, no organization is an island in today's highly interactive and interdependent world. Relative to the *external* environment, international cultures are explored in Chapter 4. Organization–environment contingencies are examined in Chapter 18.

Chapter 2 examines the OB implications of significant demographic and social trends, and Module A explores important ethical considerations. These discussions provide a realistic context for studying and managing people at work.

Bon voyage! Enjoy your trip through the challenging, interesting, and often surprising world of OB.

Summary of Key Concepts

1. *Identify the P's in the 4-P cycle of continuous improvement and define the term* management. The 4 P's are people, products, processes, and productivity. Management is the process of working with and through others to achieve organizational objectives in an efficient and ethical manner.

2. *Identify at least 5 of the 11 managerial skills in Wilson's profile of effective managers.* According to the Wilson skills profile, an effective manager (a) clarifies goals and objectives, (b) encourages participation, (c) plans and organizes, (d) has technical and administrative expertise, (e) facilitates work through team building and coaching, (f) provides feedback, (g) keeps things moving, (h) controls details, (i) applies reasonable pressure for goals accomplishment, (j) empowers and delegates, and (k) recognizes and rewards good performance.

3. *Contrast human and social capital and explain why we need to build both.* The first involves *individual* characteristics, the second involves *social* relationships. Human capital is the productive potential of an individual's knowledge and actions. Dimensions include such things as intelligence, visions, skills, self-esteem, creativity, motivation, ethics, and emotional maturity. Social capital is productive potential

resulting from strong relationships, goodwill, trust, and cooperative effort. Dimensions include such things as shared visions and goals, trust, mutual respect, friendships, empowerment, teamwork, win–win negotiations, and volunteering. Social capital is necessary to tap individual human capital for the good of the organization through knowledge sharing and networking.

4. *Characterize 21st-century managers.* They will be team players who will get things done cooperatively by relying on joint decision making, their knowledge instead of formal authority, and their multicultural skills. They will engage in life-long learning and be compensated on the basis of their skills and results. They will facilitate rather than resist change, share rather than hoard power and key information, and be multidirectional communicators. Ethics will be a forethought instead of an afterthought. They will be generalists with multiple specialties.

5. *Define the term* organizational behavior *and explain why OB is a horizontal discipline.* Organizational behavior (OB) is an interdisciplinary field dedicated to better understanding and managing people at work. It is both research and application oriented. Except for teaching/research positions, one does not normally get a

job in OB. Rather, because OB is a horizontal discipline, OB concepts and lessons are applicable to virtually every job category, business function, and professional specialty.

6. *Contrast McGregor's Theory X and Theory Y assumptions about employees.* Theory X employees, according to traditional thinking, dislike work, require close supervision, and are primarily interested in security. According to the modern Theory Y view, employees are capable of self-direction, of seeking responsibility, and of being creative.

7. *Identify the four principles of total quality management (TQM).* (a) Do it right the first time to eliminate costly rework. (b) Listen to and learn from customers and employees. (c) Make continuous improvement an everyday matter. (d) Build teamwork, trust, and mutual respect.

8. *Define the term* E-business, *and specify five ways the Internet is affecting the management of people at work.* E-business involves using the Internet to more effectively and efficiently manage every aspect of a business. The Internet is reshaping the management of people in the following areas: E-management (networking), E-communication (E-mail and telecommuting), goal setting and feedback, organizational structure (virtual teams and organizations), job design (desire for more challenge), decision making (greater speed and employee empowerment), knowledge management (E-learning), conflict and stress triggered by increased speed, rapid change and inevitable conflict and resistance, and ethical problems such as overwork and privacy issues.

9. *Describe the sources of organizational behavior research evidence.* Five sources of OB research evidence are meta-analyses (statistically pooled evidence from several studies), field studies (evidence from real-life situations), laboratory studies (evidence from contrived situations), sample surveys (questionnaire data), and case studies (observation of a single person, group, or organization).

Discussion Questions

1. Why do we need people-centered managers and organizations?

2. In your opinion, what are the three or four most important strategic results in Figure 1–1? Why?

3. How would you respond to a fellow student who says, "I have a hard time getting along with other people, but I think I could be a good manager"?

4. Based on either personal experience as a manager or on your observation of managers at work, are the 11 skills in Table 1–1 a realistic portrayal of what managers do?

5. What are you doing to build human and social capital?

6. What is your personal experience with Theory X and Theory Y managers (see Table 1–3)? Which did you prefer? Why?

7. How would you respond to a new manager who made this statement? "TQM is about statistical process control, not about people."

8. How has the Internet changed your life over the past five years?

9. What "practical" theories have you formulated to achieve the things you want in life (e.g., graduating, keeping fit, getting a good job, meeting that special someone)?

10. From a manager's standpoint, which use of research is better: instrumental or conceptual? Explain your rationale.

Internet Exercise

www.businessweek.com/www.intel.com

Keeping Up to Date on the World of Management and OB

BusinessWeek   Managers, particularly those in the business world, have a culture and language of their own. So, too, the world of business has its heroes and villains, intrigue, stories of success and disap- pointments, role models, and innovations. Concepts and definitions covered in your classes and textbooks point you in the direction of greater understanding. But self-study and a faithful reading program are needed to keep you up to date. Seemingly random bits and pieces of information and facts make more sense when integrated within a proper context. Moreover, you might find something useful or interesting that you are *not* expressly looking for (these happy discoveries are called *serendipity*). Thanks to the Internet, you have loads of current information at your fingertips to keep you up to date. The purpose of this exercise is to build bridges between what you read in this chapter and what's going on in the world today.

Go to the home page of *BusinessWeek* magazine (**www.businessweek.com**) and click on "Daily Briefing." Alternatively, depending upon your interests, you may want to start with the headings "Small Business," "Global Business," "Careers," or "Technology." Find an article dealing with one or more of the key topics in this chapter (such as managing people, productivity, building human and social capital, 21st-century managers, product/service quality, TQM, E-business, and management research/practice). *Reminder:* Be sure to make a hard copy of the article if there will be a class discussion.

Questions

1. What prompted you to select that particular article?
2. What is the OB-related linkage between Chapter 1 and your article?
3. What useful or interesting information did you acquire from your selected article? Any serendipitous findings during your search? Explain.
4. What was the practical managerial value of this Internet search?
5. Based on your reading, are you now more (or less) interested in being a manager? Explain.

Building Human Capital

Whether you realize it or not, you are building human capital by going to school, taking classes, attending a training program, reading, or pursuing a program of self-study. The human capital in this case is *you!* As mentioned in this chapter, Intel is an inspiring leader in building human capital because of its deep commitment to improving the quality of education. The purpose of this exercise is to learn more about human capital and what one company is actually doing to build it.

Go to **www.intel.com** and click on "About Intel" in the upper-right corner and then select the menu item "Intel Innovation in Education." Browse the various topical areas and make a list of the various ways Intel is helping education and students.

Questions

1. How many different educational-support programs did you identify? Were you surprised by the extent of Intel's commitment to education? About how much is it costing Intel?
2. How would you respond to this statement? "Intel is wasting its money because very few of the affected students will ever work for Intel."
3. What evidence of *social* capital did you find in this search? Explain.
4. How do we need to improve the nation's human capital to compete successfully in the global economy and Internet age?
5. What changes need to be made in the education system to build better human capital?

OB in Action Case Study

Do Corporate Leaders Have It All Wrong When It Comes to People?[88]

Gallup's Marcus Buckingham thinks that corporate leaders have it all wrong when it comes to fostering talent within their organizations. It may sound like common sense, Buckingham says, but if you are going to succeed, you have to play to your strengths.

"It is intriguing," he says. "All of the best managers we have studied say focus on your strengths and manage your weaknesses. It seems so crushingly obvious. And yet all of the companies we've looked at say the opposite. It's not like they are slightly wrong—they are totally off. They say maintain a person's strengths and focus all of your time on fixing the weaknesses."

For the past 15 years, the 35-year-old Buckingham has studied the connection between workplace performance and bottom-line results for many of Gallup's clients, including Toyota, Wells Fargo, and Disney. Recently, Buckingham completed a Gallup study that helps corporate America measure a culture's impact on company performance. For the study, Buckingham first identified 12 core traits of a healthy work atmosphere (dubbed "Q12") such as workers feeling actively engaged in their work or whether workers have had the opportunity to learn and grow. Then, using more than 30 years of corporate data collected at Gallup, Buckingham measured how these factors contributed to a company's success. So far, corporate America is failing the test.

On average there is an inverse correlation between length of service and a positive Q12 score, according to the study. "What it means is the longer you stay in your job with a company, the less engaged you become," Buckingham says. "So [this study] makes it very specific. Despite all of the money that we are spending on leadership and management development, we actually depreciate our human capital.

"We all say that human capital is one of the few assets that a company has that can generally appreciate," he says. "And yet, according to the humans within that human capital, over time they actually become less clear about their expectations, less cared about, less well-cast in their job."

Corporate America is founded on three flawed assumptions, says Buckingham. First: Everyone who excels at a particular job does it in the same way. A good example of how this assumption is wrong, says Buckingham, is the founding fathers of America, each with their own personal style. "It would have been ludicrous to say, 'John Adams, you need to be less belligerent and more calm like Thomas Jefferson. Thomas Jefferson, you are a terrible public speaker; you need to become like John Adams,' " he says. "The only thing those leaders had in common was they created the same outcome. People followed them."

The second flawed assumption: Everything can be learned. "If you think about it, one of the reasons that current performance management systems are so popular is because of the success of process improvement initiatives like Six Sigma," Buckingham says. "And if you play this out, Six Sigma has a very good reputation because you can take a process and endlessly rework it until all of the kinks are gone. Because a process is endlessly malleable, you can keep playing around with it. The problem is we have

become so enamored with that, we've applied it wholesale to people. And we have forgotten that people and process are made of different things. You aren't endlessly malleable. There are some things about you that you can change, but there are some things about you that you are never going to change."

The third flawed assumption is that corporate America believes fixing weaknesses will lead to success. "Fixing weaknesses will prevent failure," Buckingham says, "but that's a different thing; it's damage control, not development. It gets you from minus six to zero."

Buckingham hopes that his projects will be a call to arms for CEOs to begin actively measuring what really matters. "What we are giving CEOs is a way for them to shine an accurate light within their company to say, 'How strong is our culture? Where is it getting stronger? Where is it getting weaker? What's the range?' "

Buckingham says, "If you want to build a stronger culture, you had better answer one question right: What is the best way to improve one person's performance? If you can answer that question, it will inform everything that you do."

Questions for Discussion

1. Which of the seven people-centered practices discussed at the beginning of this chapter play a role in this case? Explain.

2. For managers who want to do a better job of managing people, what learning points and action items emerge from Buckingham's findings and beliefs?

3. On which points do you most strongly agree with Buckingham? Why?

4. Any points of disagreement? Explain.

Personal Awareness and Growth Exercise

How Strong Is Your Motivation to Manage?

Objectives

1. To introduce a psychological determinant of managerial success.

2. To assess your readiness to manage.

3. To discuss the implications of motivation to manage, from the standpoint of global competitiveness.

Introduction

By identifying personal traits positively correlated with both rapid movement up the career ladder and managerial effectiveness, John B Miner developed a psychometric test for measuring what he calls motivation to manage. The

questionnaire assesses the strength of seven factors relating to the temperament (or psychological makeup) needed to manage others. One word of caution. The following instrument is a shortened and modified version of Miner's original. Our version is for instructional and discussion purposes only. Although we believe it can indicate the *general* strength of your motivation to manage, it is *not* a precise measuring tool.

Instructions

Assess the strength of each of the seven dimensions of *your own* motivation to manage by circling the appropriate numbers on the 1 to 7 scales. Then add the seven circled numbers to get your total motivation to manage score.

Factor	Description	Scale
1. Authority figures	A desire to meet managerial role requirements in terms of positive relationships with superiors.	Weak 1–2–3–4–5–6–7 Strong
2. Competitive games	A desire to engage in competition with peers involving games or sports and thus meet managerial role requirements in this regard.	Weak 1–2–3–4–5–6–7 Strong
3. Competitive situations	A desire to engage in competition with peers involving occupational or work-related activities and thus meet managerial role requirements in this regard.	Weak 1–2–3–4–5–6–7 Strong
4. Assertive role	A desire to behave in an active and assertive manner involving activities that in this society are often viewed as predominantly masculine and thus to meet managerial role requirements.	Weak 1–2–3–4–5–6–7 Strong
5. Imposing wishes	A desire to tell others what to do and to utilize sanctions in influencing others, thus indicating a capacity to fulfill managerial role requirements in relationships with subordinates.	Weak 1–2–3–4–5–6–7 Strong
6. Standing out from group	A desire to assume a distinctive position of a unique and highly visible nature in a manner that is role-congruent for managerial jobs.	Weak 1–2–3–4–5–6–7 Strong
7. Routine administrative functions	A desire to meet managerial role requirements regarding activities often associated with managerial work that are of a day-to-day administrative nature.	Weak 1–2–3–4–5–6–7 Strong
		Total = _____

Scoring and Interpretation

Arbitrary norms for comparison purposes are as follows: Total score of 7–21 = Relatively low motivation to manage; 22–34 = Moderate; 35–49 = Relatively high. How do you measure up? Remember, though, high motivation to manage is only part of the formula for managerial success. The right combination of ability and opportunity is also necessary.

Years of motivation-to-manage research by Miner and others has serious implications for America's future global competitiveness. Generally, in recent years, college students in the United States have not scored highly on motivation to manage.[89] Indeed, compared with samples of US college students, samples of students from Japan, China, Mexico, Korea, and Taiwan consistently scored higher on motivation to manage.[90] Miner believes the United States may consequently lag in developing sufficient managerial talent for a tough global marketplace.[91]

In a study by other researchers, MBA students with higher motivation-to-manage scores tended to earn more money after graduation. But students with a higher motivation to manage did not earn better grades or complete their degree program any sooner than those with a lower motivation to manage.[92]

Questions for Discussion

1. Do you believe our adaptation of Miner's motivation to manage instrument accurately assessed your potential as a manager? Explain.

2. Which of the seven dimensions do you think is probably the best predictor of managerial success? Which is the least predictive? Why?

3. Miner puts heavy emphasis on competitiveness by anchoring two of the seven dimensions of motivation to manage to the desire to compete. Some observers believe the traditional (win–lose) competitive attitude is being pushed aside in favor of a less competitive (win–win) attitude today, thus making Miner's instrument out of date. What is your position on this competitiveness debate? Explain.

4. Do you believe Miner is correct in saying that low motivation to manage hurts the United States's global competitiveness? Explain.

Group Exercise

Timeless Advice

Objectives

1. To get to know some of your fellow students.
2. To put the management of people into a lively and interesting historical context.
3. To begin to develop your teamwork skills.

Introduction

Your creative energy, willingness to see familiar things in unfamiliar ways, and ability to have fun while learning are keys to the success of this warm-up exercise. A 20-minute, small-group session will be followed by brief oral presentations and a general class discussion. Total time required is approximately 40 to 45 minutes.

Instructions

Your instructor will divide your class randomly into groups of four to six people each. Acting as a team, with everyone offering ideas and one person serving as official recorder, each group will be responsible for writing a one-page memo to your current class. Subject matter of your group's memo will be "My advice for managing people today is. . . ." The fun part of this exercise (and its creative element) involves writing the memo from the viewpoint of the person assigned to your group by your instructor.

Among the memo viewpoints your instructor may assign are the following:

• Colleen Barrett (chapter-opening vignette).

• An ancient Egyptian slave master (building the great pyramids).

• Mary Parker Follett.

• Douglas McGregor.

• A Theory X supervisor of a construction crew (see McGregor's Theories X and Y in Table 1–3).

• W Edwards Deming.

• A TQM coordinator at 3M Company.

• A contingency management theorist.

• Marcus Buckingham (end-of-chapter case study).

• A Japanese auto company executive.

• The chief executive officer of IBM in the year 2030.

• Commander of the Starship Enterprise II in the year 3001.

• Others, as assigned by your instructor.

Use your imagination, make sure everyone participates, and try to be true to any historical facts you've encountered. Attempt to be as specific and realistic as possible. Remember, the idea is to provide advice about managing people from another point in time (or from a particular point of view at the present time).

Make sure you manage your 20-minute time limit carefully. A recommended approach is to spend 2 to 3 minutes putting the exercise into proper perspective. Next, take about 10 to 12 minutes brainstorming ideas for your memo, with your recorder jotting down key ideas and phrases. Have your recorder use the remaining time to write your group's one-page memo, with constructive comments and help from the others. Pick a spokesperson to read your group's memo to the class.

Questions for Discussion

1. What valuable lessons about managing people have you heard?
2. What have you learned about how NOT to manage people?
3. From the distant past to today, what significant shifts in the management of people seem to have taken place?
4. Where does the management of people appear to be headed?
5. All things considered, what mistakes are today's managers typically making when managing people?
6. How well did your group function as a "team"?

Ethical Dilemma

Zach Attack![93]

I've always believed that each of us has an innate need to create. Just watch young children at play, and you can see that impulse writ large. But creativity isn't the only impulse you see in children. Lately, after close observation of my seven-year-old son, I've begun to think that each of us also has an innate need to maximize shareholder value.

The evidence comes from a computer game that my son, Zach, has been playing, one called Sim Theme Park, in which participants build and operate an amusement park. The simulated business model is fairly simple. There are revenues (from ticket sales at the entrance to the park), capital investments (the cost of building a ride, for example), and expenses (a payroll that includes janitors, mechanics, security guards, and "researchers"—an R&D team whose job it is to design the next generation of attractions). The game also features some of the headaches involved in running a real-world business, such as disgruntled employees threatening a job action.

Zach has been playing the game on and off for several months now. Until recently, his attitude was similar to that of many first-time technology founders I've known. He couldn't have cared less about his P&L. He just loved the process of invention—choosing the wildest rides, making sure there were plenty of junk-food concessions. His unspoken mission statement was "Build it and they will come, but if they don't, that's OK, 'cause I'm having a very cool time."

Not surprisingly, his theme parks weren't very successful as businesses. He would build one, attract some paying customers, and promptly run out of cash. That never seemed to bother him—until a few weeks ago, when I detected a change in the young founder. Zach had begun paying attention to the numbers.

There was one number in particular that he fixated on. It appears in the upper-left-hand corner of his screen and records how much money a player has at any given time, a kind of cash-flow tracker for the 'N Sync crowd. Clearly, Zach didn't like what he saw. "This is no fun," he announced. "I'm tired of running out of money. I'm going to start a new game, and this time I'm going to make bazillions."

Up to that point, he'd always been a bootstrapper. He'd start building the park with only the $10,000 provided at the beginning of each game. Then he'd open the park to the public before finishing construction so that he could bring additional cash into the business as soon as possible. But the endless challenges of operations had quickly overwhelmed him. Rides had broken down, bathrooms had needed cleaning, employees hadn't performed. Time after time, the start-up would outgrow its inexperienced founder.

With his new determination to make money, Zach adopted a whole new launch strategy. Before installing a single ride, he got a $100,000 loan from "Mike." (Apparently, that's friends-and-family capital; banks don't lend to start-ups, even in the Sim world.) Then Zach refused to open the park to the public until every detail of construction was complete, despite the relentless urging of a little character who appears on the screen offering up one bit of questionable advice after another.

The new strategy was a resounding success, and the park was cash-flow positive from day one. "Congratulations," I said. "You can relax now and start having some fun again."

"Don't bother me, Dad," Zach replied, without taking his eyes off the screen. "I'm making money."

To keep his moneymaking park clean and crime-free, Zach invested in trash cans and surveillance cameras—and promptly laid off his entire crew of janitors and security guards. When I asked him why he'd done that, he gave me the kid-to-parent "Duh!" look and said he was saving money, of course.

"Besides," he said, "the guys I fired were lazy."

"How could you possibly know they were lazy?" I asked. After all, they were just pretend workers. It turned out that Zach had used a "macro" feature of the game to zoom in on his people as they patrolled the park, and he found the janitors walking right past garbage on the ground without stopping to pick it up.

Having discovered the economic advantages of a temporary workforce, Zach proceeded to sack his entire team of mechanics. When a ride broke down, he would rehire the mechanics only for as long as it took to get the ride back in service, whereupon he would simply fire them again. So much for job security in Zachland.

By noon my son had discovered price gouging. Taking advantage of what he says is a glitch in the program, he would lower his ticket prices to build traffic and wait patiently for crowds to surge into the park. Then he'd jack his prices way up, count to 60, and lower them again. He claims it takes a minute or so for the computer to react to higher prices with fewer paying customers.

After several hours of free-market capitalism, Zach finally sat back in his chair, breathed a sigh of entrepreneurial satisfaction, and uttered a line worthy of Andrew Fastow and the Arthur Andersen audit team: "This business is making piles of money."

As for me, I was beginning to question the popular notion that CEO behavior is driven by the merciless demands of Wall Street. Watching Zach play the game of business, I had to wonder whether inside each of us beats the heart of a Jack Welch or, worse, an Al Dunlap.

Zach, on the other hand, wasn't bothered by such thoughts. He knew that his business was just a game. The people weren't real, the rides weren't real, and, above all, the money wasn't real. For him, the real stuff comes in the form of an allowance, and he was ready to get his weekly allotment right at that moment.

My wife, Sara, and I have tried to structure the allowance as an incentive-comp plan of sorts. In theory, Zach does extra chores around the house, for which he gets paid his weekly 25¢. In fact, Zach consistently underperforms but gets paid anyway—just like a real *Fortune* 500 CEO.

So I paid Zach his quarter, and we headed outside to shoot some hoops.

What would you tell your son, Zach? (How would you justify the ethics of your response?)

1. "Nice going, son. You really have a talent for business." (*For discussion:* How do you socialize your child to grow up to be an ethical person/manager?)

2. "I hope you like wearing stripes." (*For discussion:* Does free-enterprise capitalism inevitably bring out the *worst* in people?)

3. "Could we figure out how to create a people-centered business that makes a fair profit?" (*Note:* Get ready to explain the concepts of "people-centered" and "fair profit" to Zach.)

4. Invent other options. Discuss.

For an interpretation of this situation, visit our Web site, **www.mhhe.com/kreitner.**

Learning Module A
Ethics and Organizational Behavior

Renee Hinton says it was hard enough when she was laid off last August from Global Crossing Ltd. after 14 years with the company and its predecessor. But when the former fiber-optic darling declared bankruptcy ... [in 2002], it dragged the systems manager into bankruptcy, too.

Like thousands of other laid-off employees, Ms. Hinton was required to take her severance package in spread-out payments rather than a lump sum. With the company's bankruptcy filing, those payments stopped. Medical benefits also were terminated. Many of the workers' 401(k) retirement plans, loaded with Global Crossing shares, became nearly worthless as the stock price plunged.

But for many Global Crossing executives, the outcome has been quite different. . . . Global Crossing's new chief executive, John Legere, received a $3.5 million signing bonus when he took the job in October [2001]—even though he was already employed as CEO of Asia Global Crossing, a separately traded affiliate. . . . At about the same time, Asia Global Crossing and Global Crossing forgave a $10 million loan to Mr. Legere, and Global Crossing eased the terms of an $8 million loan to Thomas Casey, Global's departing chief executive, according to filings the company made with the government.

The company also moved up its last pay date by a week so that executives and others still employed at Global could get paid before the company declared bankruptcy. . . . Severance payments to the already laid-off workers weren't paid.

Furthermore, in recent months Global Crossing made 11th-hour lump-sum pension payouts totaling $15 million to high-ranking executives, most of them no longer with the company.[1]

> ### For Discussion
> Was Global Crossing acting ethically? Explain your rationale.

The opening vignette highlights the relationship between decision making and ethical behavior. It also underscores the fact that top management's ethical or unethical behavior can significantly affect the lives of employees such as Renee Hinton. Ethics and ethical behavior are receiving greater attention today. This interest is partly due to reported cases of questionable or potentially unethical behavior involving companies like Global Crossing, Enron, Tyco, and Arthur Andersen and the associated costs of unethical behavior.

For instance, US industries lose about $400 billion a year from unethical and criminal behavior. Another nationwide survey revealed that 20% of the respondents were asked to do something that violated their ethical standards: 41% complied.[2] Unethical behavior is a relevant issue for all employees. It occurs from the bottom to the top of an organization. For example, a recent survey of 1,000 senior-level executives revealed that as many as one-third lied on their resumes.[3] Maybe this result should not be surprising because there are more benefits to lying, such as a higher salary and stock options, and the competition for senior management positions is fierce. As you will learn, there are a variety of individual and organizational characteristics that contribute to unethical behavior. OB is an excellent vantage point for better understanding and improving workplace ethics. If OB can provide insights about managing human work behavior, then it can teach us something about avoiding *misbehavior.*

Ethics involves the study of moral issues and choices. It is concerned with right versus wrong, good versus bad, and the many shades of gray in supposedly black-and-white issues. Moral implications spring from virtually every decision, both on and off the job. Managers are challenged to have more imagination and the courage to do the right thing. For example, do you think credit card companies should actively inform consumers that they are charging additional fees on any international transactions? Visa and MasterCard regularly tack on a 1% fee to cover the cost of international purchases.

Ethics
Study of moral issues and choices.

> Now, many of the banks that issue the cards have been quietly adding separate fees of their own. Earlier this month, First USA added a 2% surcharge to all overseas transactions for cards that didn't already have one. That means users of its popular Visa cards will pay an additional 3% on all foreign charges. . . .
>
> In many instances, the credit card fees don't show up separately on travelers' monthly credit card statements. Instead, the surcharges are folded into the cost of each item charged. The fees are disclosed only in the fine print when you first sign up for your card, or sometimes your card issuer will send you an official notice that it's raising the fee. One notable exception is Chase, which discloses the fee on the bill.[4]

Are Visa and MasterCard engaging in sound business practices or unethical behavior? The answer will ultimately be resolved in the courts. *The Wall Street Journal* reports that these hidden charges have instigated a number of lawsuits against both Visa and MasterCard.

To enhance your understanding about ethics and organizational behavior, we discuss (1) a conceptual framework for making ethical decisions, (2) whether moral principles vary by gender, (3) general moral principles for managers, and (4) how to improve an organization's ethical climate.

A Model of Ethical Behavior

Ethical and unethical conduct is the product of a complex combination of influences (see Figure A–1). At the center of the model in Figure A–1 is the individual decision maker. He or she has a unique combination of personality characteristics, values, and moral principles, leaning toward or away from ethical behavior. Personal experience with being rewarded or reinforced for certain behaviors and punished for others also shapes the individual's tendency to act ethically or unethically. Finally, gender plays an important role in explaining ethical behavior. Men and women have different moral orientations toward organizational behavior.[5] This issue is discussed later in this section.

Next, Figure A–1 illustrates two major sources of influence on one's role expectations. People assume many roles in life, including those of employee or manager. One's expectations for how those roles should be played are shaped by a combination of internal and external organizational factors. The International OB, for example, describes how cultural differences between the United States and Europe are forcing American farmers to alter their business practices. This example illustrates how a business practice such as using genetically altered ingredients to grow crops can be viewed as ethi-

Figure A–1   *A Model of Ethical Behavior in the Workplace*

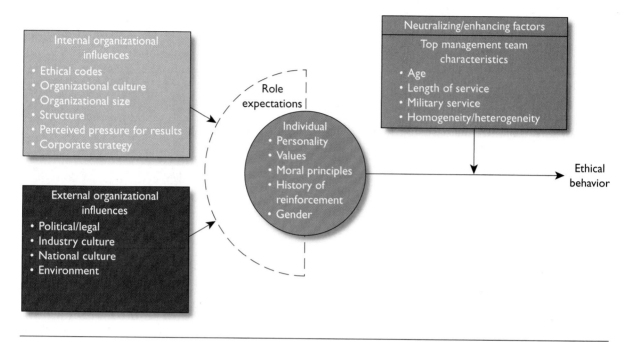

SOURCE: Based in part on A J Daboub, A M A Rasheed, R L Priem, and D A Gray, "Top Management Team Characteristics and Corporate Illegal Activity," *Academy of Management Review,* January 1995, pp. 138–70.

cal and unethical by people with varying cultural backgrounds. Let us now examine how various internal and external organizational influences impact ethical behavior and how these effects are neutralized or enhanced by characteristics possessed by an organization's top management team.

Internal Organizational Influences

Figure A–1 shows six key internal organizational influences on ethical behavior.[6] Corporate ethical codes of conduct and organizational culture, discussed in Chapter 3, clearly contribute to reducing the frequency of unethical behavior. Consider the example of Rudder Finn, the world's largest privately owned public relations agency.

> Rudder Finn established an ethics committee early on in its history because the founders maintain that public relations professionals have a special obligation to believe in what they are doing. David Finn, co-founder and CEO, chairs every ethics committee meeting to demonstrate how seriously he takes this issue. In part, these meetings perform the function of a training program in that all members of staff are invited to participate in an open forum, during which actual ethical problems are freely discussed and an outside adviser provides objectivity. "Employees have to trust that if they go to a line manager to discuss a delicate situation or seek advice, they can do so without fear of repercussions," says Finn.[7]

This example also illustrates the importance of top management support in creating an ethical work environment.

Cultural Differences between Europeans and Americans Influence Farming Practices in the United States

For four years, Michael Aylesworth didn't plant insect-resistant corn on his 2,100-acre [Indiana] farm. The reason: regulations written by bureaucrats 4,000 miles away, in Brussels.

Since many Europeans doubt the safety of such genetically modified crops, the European Union requires any product that contains even 1% of a genetically altered ingredient to say so on its label. It doesn't matter that many Americans don't care one way or another about eating so-called genetically modified organisms, or GMOs. Multina-tional food processors don't want to buy any corn that might create marketing problems in Europe.

By shunning the high-tech seeds, Mr. Aylesworth figures he lost about 7% of last year's crop to a voracious pest called the corn borer. This spring, he took a risk and decided to plant 400 acres with corn that's genetically modified to poison the bug.

SOURCE: Excerpted from B Mitchener, "Standard Bearers: Increasingly, Rules of Global Economy Are Set in Brussels," *The Wall Street Journal*, April 23, 2002, p. A1.

A number of studies have uncovered a positive relationship between organizational size and unethical behavior: Larger firms are more likely to behave illegally. Interestingly, research also reveals that managers are more likely to behave unethically in decentralized organizations. Unethical behavior is suspected to occur in this context because lower-level managers want to "look good" for the corporate office. In support of this conclusion, many studies have found a tendency among middle- and lower-level managers to act unethically in the face of perceived pressure for results. By fostering a pressure-cooker atmosphere for results, managers can unwittingly set the stage for unethical shortcuts by employees who seek to please and be loyal to the company. In contrast, consider how the organizational culture at Timberland reinforces and encourages employees to engage in socially responsible behaviors.

> Everyone gets paid for 40 hours a year of volunteer work. On Timberland's 25th anniversary, the whole place shut down so that employees could work on community projects. One employee described the event as a "religious experience."[8]

Timberland's reward system clearly encourages ethical behavior. Individuals are more likely to behave ethically/unethically when they have incentives to do so.[9] Managers are encouraged to examine their reward systems to ensure that the preferred types of behaviors are being reinforced.

External Organizational Influences

Figure A–1 identifies four key external influences on role expectations and ethical behavior.[10] The political/legal system clearly impacts ethical behavior. The United States, for example, is currently experiencing an increase in the extent to which its political/legal system is demanding and monitoring corporate ethical behavior. Treasury Secretary Paul O'Neill told reporters from *BusinessWeek* in March 2002 that "CEOs should be held accountable not only when they intentionally mislead investors—the legal standard for taking criminal action against them—but also if they fail to stop corporate wrongdoing out of negligence."[11] O'Neill intends to put more emphasis on investigating the ethical behavior of corporate leaders. As a case in point, the Securities and Exchange Commission announced in April 2002 that it was approv-

OB Exercise   How Ethical Are These Behaviors?

Instructions

Evaluate the extent to which you believe the following behaviors are ethical. Circle your responses on the rating scales provided. Compute your average score and compare it to the norms.

	Very Unethical	Unethical	Neither Ethical nor Unethical	Ethical	Very Ethical
Accepting gifts/favors in exchange for preferential treatment	1	2	3	4	5
Giving gifts/favors in exchange for preferential treatment	1	2	3	4	5
Divulging confidential information	1	2	3	4	5
Calling in sick to take a day off	1	2	3	4	5
Using the organization's materials and supplies for personal use	1	2	3	4	5
Doing personal business on work time	1	2	3	4	5
Taking extra personal time (breaks, etc.)	1	2	3	4	5
Using organizational services for personal use	1	2	3	4	5
Passing blame for errors to an innocent co-worker	1	2	3	4	5
Claiming credit for someone else's work	1	2	3	4	5
Not reporting others' violations of organizational policies	1	2	3	4	5
Concealing one's errors	1	2	3	4	5
Average score = _____					

SOURCE: The survey behaviors were taken from T Jackson, "Cultural Values and Management Ethics: A 10-Nation Study," *Human Relations*, October 2001, pp. 1287–88.

Norms (average scores by country)

United States = 1.49

Great Britian = 1.70

Australia = 1.44

France = 1.66

China = 1.46

Average of all 10 countries = 1.67

ing a $10 million fine against Xerox because executives led a four-year scheme to inflate revenue in order to meet Wall Street's growth targets.[12] Past research also uncovered a tendency for firms in certain industries to commit more illegal acts. Researchers partially explained this finding by speculating that an industry's culture, defined as shared norms, values, and beliefs among firms, predisposes managers to act unethically.

Moreover, Figure A–1 shows that national culture affects ethical behavior (national cultures are discussed in Chapter 4). This conclusion was supported in a recent multi-nation study (including United States, Great Britain, France, Germany, Spain, Switzerland, India, China, and Australia) of management ethics. Managers from each country were asked to judge the ethicality of the 12 behaviors used in the OB Exercise. Results revealed significant differences across the 10 nations.[13] That is, managers did not agree about the ethicality of the 12 behaviors. What is your attitude toward these behaviors? (You can find out by completing the OB Exercise.) Finally, the external environment influences ethical behavior. For example, unethical behavior is more likely to occur in environments that are characterized by less generosity and when industry profitability is declining.

Neutralizing/Enhancing Factors

In their search for understanding the causes of ethical behavior, OB researchers uncovered several factors that may weaken or strengthen the relationship between the internal and external influencers shown in Figure A–1 and ethical behavior. These factors all revolve around characteristics possessed by an organization's top management team (TMT): A TMT consists of the CEO and his or her direct reports.[14] The relationship between ethical influencers and ethical behavior is weaker with increasing average age and increasing tenure among the TMT. This result suggests that an older and more experienced group of leaders is less likely to allow unethical behavior to occur. Further, the ethical influencers are less likely to lead to unethical behavior as the number of TMT members with military experience increases and when the TMT possesses heterogenous characteristics (e.g., diverse in terms of gender, age, race, religion, etc.). This conclusion has two important implications.

First, it appears that prior military experience favorably influences the ethical behavior of executives. While OB researchers are uncertain about the cause of this relationship, it may be due to the military's practice of indoctrinating recruits to endorse the values of duty, discipline, and honor. Regardless of the cause, military experience within a TMT is positively related to ethical behavior. Organizations thus should consider the merits of including military experience as one of its selection criteria when hiring or promoting managers. Second, organizations are encouraged to increase the diversity of its TMT if they want to reduce the chances of unethical decision making. Chapter 2 thoroughly discusses how employee diversity can increase creativity, innovation, group problem solving, and productivity.

Do Moral Principles Vary by Gender?

It is interesting to note that two women, Sherron Watkins and Maureen Castaneda, played key roles as whistle-blowers (i.e., when an employee informs others about corporate wrongdoing) in the Enron fiasco. "Watkins, Enron's vice president of corporate development, wrote the prescient memo to Enron's chief executive that warned him the company was in deep financial trouble. Castaneda, Enron's director of foreign exchange, is the one who told authorities that Enron was still shredding documents after its officials were ordered to preserve every piece of paper."[15] Does this suggest that women are more likely to be whistle-blowers because they have different moral principles than men?

A recent study of 300 self-described whistle-blowers revealed that gender was not related to employees' reporting wrongdoing.[16] That said, however, other research suggests that men and women view moral problems and situations differently. Carol Gilligan, a well-known psychologist, proposed one underlying cause of these gender differences. Her research revealed that men and women differed in terms of how they perceived moral problems. Males perceived moral problems in terms of a **justice perspective**, whereas women relied on a **care perspective**. The two perspectives are described as follows:

> A justice perspective draws attention to problems of inequality and oppression and holds up an ideal of reciprocal rights and equal respect for individuals. A care perspective draws attention to problems of detachment or abandonment and holds up an ideal of attention and response to need. Two moral injunctions, not to treat others unfairly and not to turn away from someone in need, capture these different concerns.[17]

This description underscores the point that men are expected to view moral problems in terms of rights, whereas women are predicted to conceptualize moral problems as an issue of care involving empathy and compassion.

A recent meta-analysis of 113 studies tested these ideas by examining whether or not the justice and care orientations varied by gender. Results did not support the expectation that the care perspective was used predominantly by females and the justice orientation predominantly by males.[18] The authors concluded that "although distinct moral orientations may exist, these orientations are not strongly associated with gender."[19] This conclusion suggests that future research is needed to identify the source of moral reasoning differences between men and women.

General Moral Principles

Management consultant and writer Kent Hodgson has helpfully taken managers a step closer to ethical decisions by identifying seven general moral principles (see Table A–1). Hodgson calls them "the magnificent seven" to emphasize their timeless and worldwide relevance. Both the justice and care perspectives are clearly evident in the magnificent seven, which are more detailed and, hence, more practical. Importantly, according to Hodgson, there are no absolute ethical answers for decision makers. The goal for managers should be to rely on moral principles so their decisions are *principled, appropriate,* and *defensible.*[20] Managers require a supportive organizational climate that translates general moral principles into specific dos and don'ts and fosters ethical decisions.

How to Improve the Organization's Ethical Climate

A team of management researchers recommended the following actions for improving on-the-job ethics.[21]

- *Behave ethically yourself.* Managers are potent role models whose habits and actual behavior send clear signals about the importance of ethical conduct. Ethical behavior is a top-to-bottom proposition.

- *Screen potential employees.* Surprisingly, employers are generally lax when it comes to checking references, credentials, transcripts, and other information on applicant

---

Justice perspective
Based on the ideal of reciprocal rights and driven by rules and regulations.

Care perspective
Involves compassion and an ideal of attention and response to need.

Table A–1   *The Magnificent Seven: General Moral Principles for Managers*

1. *Dignity of human life: The lives of people are to be respected.* Human beings, by the fact of their existence, have value and dignity. We may not act in ways that directly intend to harm or kill an innocent person. Human beings have a right to live; we have an obligation to respect that right to life. Human life is to be preserved and treated as sacred.

2. *Autonomy: All persons are intrinsically valuable and have the right to self-determination.* We should act in ways that demonstrate each person's worth, dignity, and right to free choice. We have a right to act in ways that assert our own worth and legitimate needs. We should not use others as mere "things" or only as means to an end. Each person has an equal right to basic human liberty, compatible with a similar liberty for others.

3. *Honesty: The truth should be told to those who have a right to know it.* Honesty is also known as integrity, truth telling, and honor. One should speak and act so as to reflect the reality of the situation. Speaking and acting should mirror the way things really are. There are times when others have the right to hear the truth from us; there are times when they do not.

4. *Loyalty: Promises, contracts, and commitments should be honored.* Loyalty includes fidelity, promise keeping, keeping the public trust, good citizenship, excellence in quality of work, reliability, commitment, and honoring just laws, rules, and policies.

5. *Fairness: People should be treated justly.* One has the right to be treated fairly, impartially, and equitably. One has the obligation to treat others fairly and justly. All have the right to the necessities of life—especially those in deep need and the helpless. Justice includes equal, impartial, unbiased treatment. Fairness tolerates diversity and accepts differences in people and their ideas.

6. *Humaneness.* There are two parts: (1) *Our actions ought to accomplish good,* and (2) *we should avoid doing evil.* We should do good to others and to ourselves. We should have concern for the well-being of others; usually, we show this concern in the form of compassion, giving, kindness, serving, and caring.

7. *The common good: Actions should accomplish the "greatest good for the greatest number" of people.* One should act and speak in ways that benefit the welfare of the largest number of people, while trying to protect the rights of individuals.

SOURCE: *A Rock and a Hard Place: How to Make Ethical Business Decisions When the Choices Are Tough,* © 1992 Kent Hodgson, pp. 69–73. Published by AMACOM, a division of the American Management Association. Used with permission.

résumés. More diligent action in this area can screen out those given to fraud and misrepresentation. Integrity testing is fairly valid but is no panacea.[22]

• *Develop a meaningful code of ethics.* Codes of ethics can have a positive impact if they satisfy these four criteria:

 1. They are *distributed* to every employee.

 2. They are firmly *supported* by top management.

 3. They refer to *specific* practices and ethical dilemmas likely to be encountered by target employees (e.g., salespersons paying kickbacks, purchasing agents receiving payoffs, laboratory scientists doctoring data, or accountants "cooking the books").

 4. They are evenly *enforced* with rewards for compliance and strict penalties for noncompliance.

• *Provide ethics training.* Employees can be trained to identify and deal with ethical issues during orientation and through seminar and video training sessions.

- *Reinforce ethical behavior.* Behavior that is reinforced tends to be repeated, whereas behavior that is not reinforced tends to disappear. Ethical conduct too often is punished while unethical behavior is rewarded.
- *Create positions, units, and other structural mechanisms to deal with ethics.* Ethics needs to be an everyday affair, not a one-time announcement of a new ethical code that gets filed away and forgotten. The Raytheon Company, for example, uses an "Ethics Quick Test" that asks employees to answer a series of questions when faced with ethical dilemmas. The answers help employees determine the best course of action.[23]

Group Exercise

Investigating the Difference in Moral Reasoning between Men and Women

Objectives

1. To determine if men and women resolve moral/ethical problems differently.
2. To determine if males and females use a justice and care perspective, respectively, to solve moral/ethical problems.
3. To improve your understanding about the moral reasoning used by men and women.

Introduction

Men and women view moral problems and situations dissimilarly. This is one reason men and women solve identical moral or ethical problems differently. Researchers believe that men rely on a justice perspective to solve moral problems whereas women are expected to use a care perspective. This exercise presents two scenarios that possess a moral/ethical issue. You will be asked to solve each problem and to discuss the logic behind your decision. The exercise provides you with the opportunity to hear the thought processes used by men and women to solve moral/ethical problems.

Instructions

Your instructor will divide the class into groups of four to six. (An interesting option is to use gender-based groups.) Each group member should first read the scenario alone and then make a decision about what to do. Once this is done, use the space provided to outline the rationale for your decision to this scenario. Next, read the second scenario and follow the same procedure: Make a decision and explain your rationale. Once all group members have completed their analyses for both scenarios, meet as a group to discuss the results. One at a time, each group member should present his or her final decision and the associated reasoning for the first scenario. Someone should keep a running tally of the decisions so that a summary can be turned in to the professor at the end of your discussion. Follow the same procedure for the second scenario.[24]

Scenario 1

You are the manager of a local toy store. The hottest Christmas toy of the year is the new "Peter Panda" stuffed animal. The toy is in great demand and almost impossible to find. You have received your one and only shipment of 12, and they are all promised to people who previously stopped in to place a deposit and reserve one. A woman comes by the store and pleads with you, saying that her six-year-old daughter is in the hospital very ill, and that "Peter Panda" is the one toy she has her heart set on. Would you sell her one, knowing that you will have to break your promise and refund the deposit to one of the other customers? (There is no way you will be able to get an extra toy in time.)

Your Decision: _____

	Would Sell	Would Not Sell	Unsure
Men			
Women			

Rationale for your decision:

Scenario 2

You sell corporate financial products, such as pension plans and group health insurance. You are currently negotiating with Paul Scott, treasurer of a *Fortune* 500 firm, for a sale that could be in the millions of dollars. You feel you are in a strong position to make the sale, but two competitors are also negotiating with Scott, and it could go either way. You have become friendly with Scott, and over lunch one day he confided in you that he has recently been under treatment for manic depression. It so happens that in your office there is a staff psychologist who does employee counseling. The thought has occurred to you that such a trained professional might be able to coach you on how to act with and relate to a personality such as Scott's, so as to persuade and influence him most effectively. Would you consult the psychologist?

Your Decision: _____

	Would Consult	Would Not Consult	Unsure
Men			
Women			

Rationale for your decision:

Questions for Discussion

1. Did males and females make different decisions in response to both scenarios? (Comparative norms can be found in Note 25.)

2. What was the moral reasoning used by women and men to solve the two scenarios?[26]

3. To what extent did males and females use a justice and care perspective, respectively?

4. What useful lessons did you learn from this exercise?

Chapter Two

Managing Diversity: Releasing Every Employee's Potential

Learning Objectives

When you finish studying the material in this chapter, you should be able to:

1 Define diversity.

2 Discuss the four layers of diversity.

3 Explain the differences among affirmative action, valuing diversity, and managing diversity.

4 Demonstrate your familiarity with the demographic trends that are creating an increasingly diverse workforce.

5 Highlight the managerial implications of increasing diversity in the workforce.

6 Review the five reasons managing diversity is a competitive advantage.

7 Identify the barriers and challenges to managing diversity.

8 Discuss the organizational practices used to effectively manage diversity as identified by R Roosevelt Thomas, Jr, and Ann Morrison.

Cristina Banks, PhD, a senior lecturer at Haas Business School at the University of California, Berkeley, thinks she knows why her students have "run screaming to graduate school": Their experience with entry-level jobs, where their needs as employees are habitually ignored, has turned them off of the work world.

"When they leave the undergraduate or graduate program, they're armed with new knowledge and their motivation couldn't be higher to go out and do great things with organizations," she explains. "And within six months, they are discouraged about the opportunities provided to them to actually apply that knowledge and motivation."

Their initial experience is often deflating, say Banks and other industrial/organizational (I/O) psychologists. They're told to pay their dues until they earn enough credit to have a voice—the worst possible management

for young people. "It's a terrible waste," says Banks.

I/O psychologists have studied the types of incentives that build job commitment among today's new generation of workers, Generation X. Born between 1961 and 1981, these workers share certain characteristics, such as independence and a desire for a sense of belonging and meaningfulness of work. I/O psychologists like Banks are now

Generation Xers share certain characteristics and needs. Companies need to focus on providing benefits beyond good pay if they want younger employees to stay.
(c) Farmhouse Productions/Getty Images/The Image Bank

passing what they've learned about this group to employers to help them respond adequately to their younger employees' needs.

"Businesses have to be much more responsive to young people when they say they're not being challenged," says Banks. "A company has to be much more intentional in constructing careers to build those qualities into the worklife experience."

It's More than Money

Retaining the 40-and-under set can be a challenge. Their company loyalty tends to be short-lived. "In their parents' generation, they would have been seen as job-hoppers," says Russell Lobsenz, PhD, of Performa Works in Raleigh, NC. "That mentality is gone."

But, while their tenure at one job may be brief, their on-the-job dedication is often high. "They're not going to stay with an organization for 30 years like their parents did," says Lobsenz, "but while they are there, they will give 110 percent."

To get the young and peripatetic to stay, employers must do more than pay well.

"Pay, for them, is important only to the extent that they are able to do what they want to do outside the workplace," says Lobsenz. "They are not as materialistic as the Baby Boomers."

In fact, financial incentives don't thrill these kids, says Lobsenz, since many watched their sweet stock option packages go sour with the market downturn.[1]

For Discussion

Do you agree that financial incentives do not thrill Generation X employees? Explain.

The opening vignette highlights that the values, needs, and motivations of Generation X employees are not what they are for baby boomers, people born between 1943 and 1960. It also implies that effectively managing diversity requires organizations to adopt a new way of thinking about differences among people. Rather than pitting one group against another, managing diversity entails recognition of the unique contribution every employee can make to an organization. As found at the Container Store, a company that received the 2001 Optimas Award for excellence in people-management, effectively managing diversity can create an infectiously positive work environment.

> In an industry where 100% turnover is common, the Container Store boasts a very low 15 to 20%. Forty-one % of new hires come from employee referrals. But it's the enthusiasm among workers that's so palpable. . . . A stunning 97% of employees agree with the survey statement "People care about each other here." . . . Not long after creating the company, Boone and Tindell [the founders] created innovative parameters called foundation principles. They are a set of humanistic, spiritually based, do-unto-others philosophies. These principles are practiced internally among employees and are reflected in how they treat each other and how the company treats them.[2]

Interestingly, however, some organizations are missing the mark when it comes to managing diversity. Consider the work environments at Ford's New Model Development Center in Allen Park, Michigan, and Rent-A-Center, the nation's largest rent-to-own furniture store, based in Plano, Texas.

An African-American employee at Ford contends that "a co-worker hung hangman's nooses on his forklift, 'mocked what he considered to be African-American styles of speech and manner of walking,' and used 'insulting language.' "[3] The accused employee was suspended without pay for a month and later resigned. A suit filed by the Equal Employment Opportunity Committee for employees at Rent-A-Center alleges that managers, "who took over Rent-A-Center in a 1998 merger, pushed women out and destroyed women's job applications. Sworn statements quote a senior exec as saying: 'women should be home taking care of their husbands and children,' and accuse him of smacking women employees' butts."[4] It is important to note that these things occurred in both companies despite the existence of policies and procedures that prohibited discrimination. As you will learn in this chapter, managing diversity entails much more than creating policies and procedures. Managing diversity is a sensitive, potentially volatile, and sometimes uncomfortable issue. Yet managers are required to deal with it in the name of organizational survival. Accordingly, the purpose of this chapter is to help you get a better understanding of this important context for organizational behavior. We begin by defining diversity. Next, we build the business case for diversity and then discuss the barriers and challenges associated with managing diversity. The chapter concludes by describing the organizational practices used to manage diversity effectively.

Defining Diversity

Diversity represents the multitude of individual differences and similarities that exist among people. This definition underscores three important issues about managing diversity:[5] (1) There are many different dimensions or components of diversity. This implies that diversity pertains to everybody. It is not an issue of age, race, or gender. It is not an issue of being heterosexual, gay, or lesbian or of being Catholic, Jewish, Protestant, or Muslim. Diversity also does not pit white males against all other groups of people. Diversity pertains to the host of individual differences that make all of us unique and different from others. (2) Diversity is not synonymous with differences. Rather, it encompasses both differences and similarities. This means that managing diversity entails dealing with both simultaneously. (3) Diversity includes the collective mixture of differences and similarities, not just the pieces of it. Dealing with diversity requires managers to integrate the collective mixture of differences and similarities that exist within an organization.

This section begins our journey into managing diversity by first reviewing the key dimensions of diversity. Because many people associate diversity with affirmative action, this section compares affirmative action, valuing diversity, and managing diversity. They are not the same.

Diversity
The host of individual differences that make people different from and similar to each other.

Layers of Diversity

Like seashells on a beach, people come in a variety of shapes, sizes, and colors. This variety represents the essence of diversity. Lee Gardenswartz and Anita Rowe, a team of diversity experts, identified four layers of diversity to help distinguish the important ways in which people differ (see Figure 2–1). Taken together, these layers define your personal identity and influence how each of us sees the world.

Figure 2–1 shows that personality is at the center of the diversity wheel. Personality is at the center because it represents a stable set of characteristics that is responsible for a person's identity. The dimensions of personality are discussed later in Chapter 5. The next layer of diversity consists of a set of internal dimensions that are referred to as the primary dimensions of diversity.[6] These dimensions, for the most part, are not within our control, but they strongly influence our attitudes and expectations and assumptions about others, which, in turn, influence our behavior. Take the

Figure 2–1   *The Four Layers of Diversity*

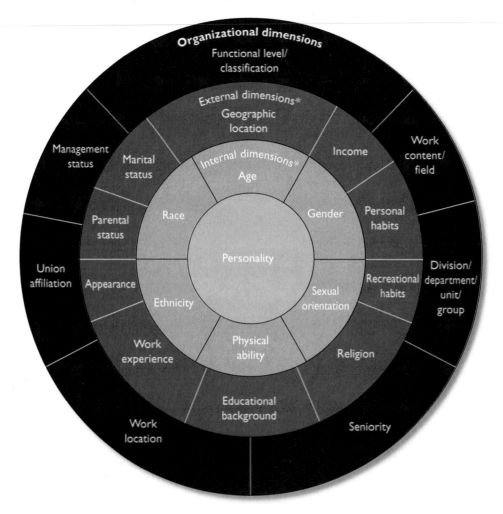

encounter experienced by an African-American woman in middle management while vacationing at a resort:

> While I was sitting by the pool, "a large 50-ish white male approached me and demanded that I get him extra towels. I said, 'Excuse me?' He then said, 'Oh, you don't work here,' with no shred of embarrassment or apology in his voice."[7]

Stereotypes regarding one or more of the primary dimensions of diversity most likely influenced this man's behavior toward the woman.

Figure 2–1 reveals that the next layer of diversity is composed of external influences, which are referred to as secondary dimensions of diversity. They represent individual differences that we have a greater ability to influence or control. Examples include where you grew up and live today, your religious affiliation, whether you are married and have children, and your work experiences. These dimensions also exert a significant influence on our perceptions, behavior, and attitudes.

Consider religion as an illustration. Given that Islam is expected to surpass Judaism as the second-most commonly practiced religion in the United States (Christianity is first), organizations need to consider Muslim employees when implementing their policies, procedures, and programs. Argenbright Security Inc. in Atlanta created problems for itself when management sent home seven Muslim women for wearing Islamic headscarves at their security jobs at Dulles International Airport. Because wearing headscarves in no way affected their job performance, the company had to reimburse the women for back pay and other relief in a settlement negotiated with the Equal Employment Opportunity Commission.[8] In contrast, Ford Motor Co. proactively conducted a series of Islam 101 training sessions in Dearborn, Michigan, after the September 11 terrorist attacks. They did this because the Dearborn area is home to one of the largest Arab-American and Middle Eastern communities in the United States and the company wanted to raise awareness about the Islamic faith.[9]

As you can see from these examples, an organization's level of awareness about the external layer of diversity can cause either negative or positive feelings among employees. The final layer of diversity includes organizational dimensions such as seniority, job title and function, and work location.

Affirmative Action and Valuing Diversity

Valuing diversity and managing diversity require organizations to adopt a new way of thinking about differences among people. Rather than pitting one group against another, valuing diversity and managing diversity strive to recognize the unique contribution every employee can make. This philosophy is much different from that of affirmative action. This section highlights the differences among affirmative action, valuing diversity, and managing diversity. Table 2–1 compares these three approaches to managing employee differences.

Affirmative Action As shown in Table 2–1, affirmative action focuses on achieving equality of opportunity in an organization and is legally mandated in the United States by Equal Opportunity laws. **Affirmative action** is an artificial intervention aimed at giving management a chance to correct an imbalance, an injustice, a mistake, or outright discrimination. Affirmative action does not legitimize quotas. Quotas are illegal. They can only be imposed by judges who conclude that a company has engaged in discriminatory practices. It also is important to note that under no circumstances does affirmative action require companies to hire unqualified people.

Although affirmative action created tremendous opportunities for women and minorities, it does not foster the type of thinking that is needed to effectively manage diversity.[10] For example, affirmative action is resisted more by white males than women and minorities because it is perceived to work against their own self-interest. Affirmative action plans are more successful when employees view them as fair and equitable and when whites are not prejudiced against people of color.[11]

Affirmative action programs also were found to negatively affect the women and minorities expected to benefit from them. Research demonstrated that women and minorities, supposedly hired on the basis of affirmative action, felt negatively stigmatized as unqualified or incompetent. They also experienced lower job satisfaction and more stress than employees supposedly selected on the basis of merit.[12] Another study,

Affirmative action

Focuses on achieving equality of opportunity in an organization.

Table 2–1   *Comparison of Affirmative Action, Valuing Diversity, and Managing Diversity*

Affirmative Action	Valuing Diversity	Managing Diversity
Quantitative. Emphasizes achieving equality of opportunity in the work environment through the changing of organizational demographics. Monitored by statistical reports and analysis.	*Qualitative.* Emphasizes the appreciation of differences and creating an environment in which everyone feels valued and accepted. Monitored by organizational surveys focused on attitudes and perceptions.	*Behavioral.* Emphasizes the building of specific skills and creating policies which get the best from every employee. Monitored by progress toward achieving goals and objectives.
Legally driven. Written plans and statistical goals for specific groups are utilized. Reports are mandated by EEO laws and consent decrees.	*Ethically driven.* Moral and ethical imperatives drive this culture change.	*Strategically driven.* Behaviors and policies are seen as contributing to organizational goals and objectives such as profit and productivity and are tied to rewards and results.
Remedial. Specific target groups benefit as past wrongs are remedied. Previously excluded groups have an advantage.	*Idealistic.* Everyone benefits. Everyone feels valued and accepted in an inclusive environment.	*Pragmatic.* The organization benefits; morale, profit, and productivity increase.
Assimilation model. Assumes that groups brought into system will adapt to existing organizational norms.	*Diversity model.* Assumes that groups will retain their own characteristics and shape the organization as well as be shaped by it, creating a common set of values.	*Synergy model.* Assumes that diverse groups will create new ways of working together effectively in a pluralistic environment.
Opens doors in the organization. Affects hiring and promotion decisions. *Resistance due to* perceived limits to autonomy in decision making and perceived fears of reverse discrimination.	*Opens attitudes, minds, and the culture.* Affects attitudes of employees. *Resistance due to* fear of change, discomfort with differences, and desire for return to "good old days."	*Opens the system.* Affects managerial practices and policies. *Resistance due to* denial of demographic realities, the need for alternative approaches, or benefits associated with change; and the difficulty in learning new skills, altering existing systems, or finding time to work toward synergistic solutions.

SOURCE: L Gardenswartz and A Rowe, *Managing Diversity: A Complete Desk Reference and Planning Guide* (Homewood, IL: Business One Irwin, 1993), p. 405. Reprinted with permission of The McGraw-Hill Companies.

however, showed that these negative consequences were reduced for women when a merit criterion was included in hiring decisions. In other words, women hired under affirmative action programs felt better about themselves and exhibited higher performance when they believed they were hired because of their competence rather than their gender.[13] Moreover, the true valuing and managing of diversity rarely occurs without affirmative action's focus on the hiring and promoting of diverse employees according to a study conducted by the federal Glass Ceiling Commission, a bipartisan group studying diversity in the workplace.[14]

Valuing diversity
Emphasizes the awareness, recognition, understanding, and appreciation of human differences.

Valuing Diversity   Table 2–1 indicates that **valuing diversity** emphasizes the awareness, recognition, understanding, and appreciation of human differences. It revolves around creating an environment in which everyone feels valued and accepted. In essence, valuing diversity entails a cultural change geared toward viewing employee differences as a valuable resource that can contribute to organizational success.[15] This

generally takes place through a series of management education and training programs that attempt to improve interpersonal relationships among diverse employees and to minimize blatant expressions of sexism and racism. For example, a recent study by the Society of Human Resource Management revealed that 75% of *Fortune* 500 firms and 36% of companies of all sizes had implemented some type of initiative aimed at valuing diversity.[16] Simply sending employees to diversity training, however, does not guarantee changes in attitudes or behaviors. Top management support is essential for changing employees' attitudes toward diversity. Consider, for example, the level of top management support provided by Philip Marineau, CEO of Levi Strauss & Co.

> For Phil Marineau, diversity is a personal core value. "It's an expression of what I and Levi Strauss & Co. stand for. It's right for business, our communities, and for our families. It creates greater tolerance." . . . Phil practices accountability with a "zero-tolerance standard for any forms of discrimination." He models accountability by staying personally involved and talking with small groups about issues of diversity. He also monitors his direct reports' results regarding recruitment, retention, and advancement of diverse people, plus the business results of "empathetic marketing."[17]

In addition to top management support, the success of diversity training also was associated with mandatory attendance for all managers, long-term evaluation of training results, and managerial rewards for increasing diversity.[18]

Managing Diversity

Managing diversity entails enabling people to perform up to their maximum potential. It focuses on changing an organization's culture and infrastructure such that people provide the highest productivity possible. Ann Morrison, a diversity expert, conducted a study of 16 organizations that successfully managed diversity. Her results uncovered three key strategies for success: education, enforcement, and exposure. She describes them as follows:

> The education component of the strategy has two thrusts: one is to prepare nontraditional managers for increasingly responsible posts, and the other is to help traditional managers overcome their prejudice in thinking about and interacting with people who are of a different sex or ethnicity. The second component of the strategy, enforcement, puts teeth in diversity goals and encourages behavior change. The third component, exposure to people with different backgrounds and characteristics, adds a more personal approach to diversity by helping managers get to know and respect others who are different.[19]

Managing diversity
Creating organizational changes that enable all people to perform up to their maximum potential.

When it comes to diversity, employees at Levi Strauss have their CEO's full support. Phil Marineau believes diversity is a core value and he monitors the recruitment, retention, and advancement of diverse people. If you were an employee at Levi Strauss, how would top management's support affect your attitudes about working for the company?

(c) Jeff Minton Photography

In summary, both consultants and academics believe that organizations should strive to manage diversity rather than only valuing it or simply using affirmative action. This conclusion was supported by a study of 200 African-American and white males and females employed in retail stores. Results revealed that employees viewed leaders as more accepting of diversity and more desirable to work for when they demonstrated behaviors consistent with managing diversity as opposed to valuing diversity and affirmative action.[20] More is said about managing diversity later in this chapter.

Building the Business Case for Managing Diversity

The rationale for managing diversity goes well beyond legal, social, and moral reasons. Quite simply, the primary reason for managing diversity is the ability to grow and maintain a business in an increasingly competitive marketplace. Verizon, the largest telecommunications company in the United States, believes in this proposition. Ivan Seidenberg, Verizon's CEO,

> views diversity as a strategic business imperative. He believes a multifaceted approach to diversity drives Verizon's success and ability to compete. This strategy includes: acknowledging the unique needs of multicultural employees, customers, and other stakeholders; driving value for the customer; enhancing economic development for many types of businesses and communities; increasing shareholder equity; and winning in a global marketplace.[21]

Organizations cannot use diversity as a strategic advantage if employees fail to contribute their full talents, abilities, motivation, and commitment. It is thus essential for an organization to create an environment or culture that allows all employees to reach their full potential. Managing diversity is a critical component of creating such an organization.

This section explores the business need to manage diversity by first reviewing the demographic trends that are creating an increasingly diverse workforce. We then review the key reasons effective management of diversity creates a competitive advantage.

Increasing Diversity in the Workforce

Workforce demographics

Statistical profiles of adult workers.

Workforce demographics, which are statistical profiles of the characteristics and composition of the adult working population, are an invaluable human-resource planning aid. They enable managers to anticipate and adjust for surpluses or shortages of appropriately skilled individuals. For example, the US labor force is projected to increase by 17 million from 2000 to 2010, and labor force participation rates differ by age, sex, race, and educational attainment.[22] These demographics reveal that organizations should devise strategies to ensure that they can find the number of qualified employees needed to meet their projected demands for labor.

Moreover, general population demographics give managers a preview of the values and motives of future employees. Demographic changes in the US workforce during the last two or three decades have immense implications for organizational behavior. This section explores four demographic trends that are creating an increasingly diverse workforce: (1) women continue to enter the workforce in increasing numbers, (2) people of color (noncaucasian) represent a growing share of the labor force, (3) there is a

critical mismatch between workers' educational attainment and occupational requirements, and (4) the workforce is aging.

Women Entering the Workforce

Table 2–2 shows that approximately
50.4% of the new entrants into the workforce between 2000 and 2010 are expected to
be women. It also shows that women will account for 44.6% of the departures from the
workforce. Men account for the largest share of retirement-bound employees.

In spite of the fact that women constituted 46% of the labor force in 1996 and are
expected to represent 48% by 2010, they continue to encounter the **glass ceiling.**[23] The
glass ceiling represents an invisible barrier that separates women and minorities from
advancing into top management positions. It can be particularly demotivating because
employees can look up and see coveted top management positions through the trans-
parent ceiling but are unable to obtain them. A variety of statistics support the existence
of a glass ceiling.

As of June 2000, women were still underpaid relative to men: Women received 76%
of men's earnings. A General Accounting Office study of 10 industries also found that
female managers working in entertainment and recreations services, finances, insurance and real estate, business and repair services, retail trade, and other professional
services earned less money compared to men in 2000 than they did five years earlier.[24]

Glass ceiling
Invisible barrier
blocking women and
minorities from top
management
positions.

Table 2–2   *Projected Entrants and Departures in the US Workforce
from 2000 to 2010*

	ENTRANTS*		DEPARTURES*	
	2000–2010	Percent	2000–2010	Percent
Total**	41,048	100.0%	24,191	100.0%
Men	20,379	49.6	13,406	55.4
Women	20,669	50.4	10,785	44.6
White non-Hispanic	24,873	60.6	18,717	77.4
Men	12,583	30.7	10,404	43.0
Women	12,290	29.9	8,314	34.4
African-American	5,627	13.7	2,843	11.8
Men	2,463	6.0	1,525	6.3
Women	3,164	7.7	1,318	5.4
Hispanic	7,331	17.9	1,752	7.2
Men	3,820	9.3	1,016	4.2
Women	3,511	8.6	736	3.0
Asian and other races	3,218	7.8	879	3.6
Men	1,513	3.7	461	1.9
Women	1,705	4.2	417	1.7

*Labor force entrants and departures, in thousands, 2000–2010.
*All groups add to total.
Note: Numbers may not add up due to rounding.
SOURCE: Data were taken from Table 9 in H Fullerton Jr and M Toossi, "Labor Force Projections to 2010:
Steady Growth and Changing Composition," *Monthly Labor Review,* November 2001, p. 35.
(www.bls.gov/opub/mlr/2001/11/art2abs.htm)

International OB — The Glass Ceiling Exists around the World

1. Out of 180 countries, only 11 are headed by women.

2. 13% of members of national parliaments worldwide are women.

3. 7% of the world's cabinet ministers are women.

4. 1% of the world's assets are in the name of women.

5. 70% of people in the lowest poverty—living on less than $1 per day—are women.

6. 855,000,000 people in the world are illiterate, and 70% of them are women.

7. There is no country in the world where women's pay is equal to that of men.

8. While women occupy about 33% of all managerial and administrative positions in the developed world, they possess 15% and 13% of these positions in Africa and in Asia and the Pacific.

9. In Silicon Valley, for every 100 shares of stock options owned by a man, one share is owned by a woman.

SOURCES: These statistics were obtained from **www.onlinewomeninpolitics.org/statistics.htm,** updated April 2, 2002; and **www.learningpartnership.org/facts/human.html,** updated January 1, 2002.

Even when women are paid the same as men, they may suffer in other areas of job opportunities. For example, a study of 69 male and female executives from a large multinational financial services corporation revealed no differences in base salary or bonus. However, the women in this sample received fewer stock options than the male executives, even after controlling for level of education, performance, and job function, and reported less satisfaction with future career opportunities.[25] A follow-up study of 13,503 female managers and 17,493 male managers from the same organization demonstrated that women at higher levels in the managerial hierarchy received fewer promotions than males at comparable positions.[26] Would you be motivated if you were a woman working in this organization?

Women still have not broken into the highest echelon of corporate America to any significant extent. Women held 2% of senior management positions in businesses in 2002, and there were only five female CEOs in the *Fortune* 500 corporations. These women were running Xerox, Spherion, Hewlett-Packard, Golden West Financial, and Avon Products.[27] As detailed in the International OB, the glass ceiling also exists around the world. The glass ceiling has been credited as one reason women are increasingly starting their own businesses. For example, the number of women-owned businesses is growing at double the rate of all businesses, and there are 8 million businesses owned by women. These companies employ approximately 25% of the labor force.[28]

Why does the glass ceiling exist for women? A team of researchers attempted to answer this question by surveying 461 executive women who held titles of vice president or higher in *Fortune* 1000 companies and all of the *Fortune* 1000 CEOs. Respondents were asked to evaluate the extent to which they used 13 different career strategies to break through the glass ceiling. The 13 strategies are shown in the OB Exercise.[29] Before discussing the results from this study, we would like you to complete the OB Exercise.

Findings indicated that the top nine strategies were central to the advancement of these female executives. Within this set, however, four strategies were identified as critical toward breaking the glass ceiling: consistently exceeding performance expectations, developing a style with which male managers are comfortable, seeking out difficult or challenging assignments, and having influential mentors. Results further demonstrated that the CEOs and female executives differed in their assessment of the

OB Exercise What Are the Strategies for Breaking the Glass Ceiling?

Instructions

Read the 13 career strategies shown below that may be used to break the glass ceiling. Next, rank order each strategy in terms of its importance for contributing to the advancement of a woman to a senior management position. Rank the strategies from 1 (most important) to 13 (least important). Once this is completed, compute the gap between your rankings and those provided by the women executives who participated in this research. Their rankings are presented in endnote 30 at the back of the book.[30] In computing the gaps, use the absolute value of the gap. (Absolute values are always positive, so just ignore the sign of your gap.) Finally, compute your total gap score. The larger the gap, the greater the difference in opinion between you and the women executives. What does your total gap score indicate about your recommended strategies?

Strategy	My Rating	Survey Rating	Gap |Your − Survey| Rating Rating
1. Develop leadership outside office	_____	_____	_____
2. Gain line management experience	_____	_____	_____
3. Network with influential colleagues	_____	_____	_____
4. Change companies	_____	_____	_____
5. Be able to relocate	_____	_____	_____
6. Seek difficult or high visibility assignments	_____	_____	_____
7. Upgrade educational credentials	_____	_____	_____
8. Consistently exceed performance expectations	_____	_____	_____
9. Move from one functional area to another	_____	_____	_____
10. Initiate discussion regarding career aspirations	_____	_____	_____
11. Have an influential mentor	_____	_____	_____
12. Develop style that men are comfortable with	_____	_____	_____
13. Gain international experience	_____	_____	_____

SOURCE: Strategies and data were taken from B R Ragins, B Townsend, and M Mattis, "Gender Gap in the Executive Suite: CEOs and Female Executives Report on Breaking the Glass Ceiling," *Academy of Management Executive*," February 1998, pp. 28–42.

barriers preventing women from advancing to positions of corporate leadership. CEOs concluded that women do not get promoted because (1) they lack significant general management or line experience and (2) women have not been in the executive talent pool for a long enough period of time to get selected. In contrast, the female executives indicated that (1) male stereotyping and preconceptions and (2) exclusion from informal networks were the biggest inhibitors to their promotability. These findings suggest that it is important to sensitize CEOs to the corporate culture faced by female employees. Breaking the glass ceiling will only occur when senior management has a good understanding of the unique experiences associated with being in the minority.

People of Color in the US Workforce

People of color in the United States are projected to add 39.4% of the new entrants in the workforce from 2000 to 2010 (see Table 2–2). Hispanics are predicted to account for the largest share of this increase

(17.9%). The Hispanic population also continues to grow at a faster rate than other racial groups, and it will surpass the African-American population by 2010.

Unfortunately, four additional trends suggest that people of color are experiencing their own glass ceiling. First, people of color are advancing even less in the managerial and professional ranks than women. For example, African-Americans and Hispanics held 11.3% and 10.9%, respectively, of all managerial and professional jobs in 2001; women held 46.6% of these positions. Second, the number of race-based charges of discrimination that were deemed to show reasonable cause by the US Equal Employment Opportunity Commission increased from 294 in 1995 to 2,397 in 2001. Companies paid a total of $86.5 million to resolve these claims outside of litigation in 2001.[31] Third, people of color also tend to earn less than whites. Median household income in 2000 was $30,400, $33,400, and $44,200 for African-Americans, Hispanics, and whites, respectively. Interestingly, Asians and Pacific Islanders had the highest median income—$55,500.[32]

Finally, a number of studies show that people of color experience more perceived discrimination than whites. For example, a study of 361 first-year students at an Eastern university revealed that whites reported less perceived discrimination than Asians, African-Americans, and Hispanics.[33] Another study of 280 minority executives indicated that 40% believed that they had been denied well-deserved promotions because of discrimination; 52% of these same respondents revealed that they are likely to change jobs for more challenging positions.[34] These findings are consistent with previous studies that indicated that people of color have more negative career experiences, lower upward mobility, lower career satisfaction, decreased job involvement, and greater turnover rates than their white counterparts.[35]

As was true for women, a glass ceiling may be one reason that more people of color are starting their own businesses. For example, minorities owned 15% of all privately held US companies in 2002. They owned less than 7% in 1982.[36] The number of Hispanic-owned businesses partially fueled this growth. These firms grew 30% from 1992 to 1997, a rate that was four times faster than all US companies. Interestingly, 80% of Hispanic firms are one-person operations predominantly located in California, Texas, Florida, New York, and New Jersey.[37]

As was true for women, many people of color encounter the glass ceiling. Rudolpho Lorenzo, who was the recipient of a $5000.00 micro loan to expand his grocery store, escaped the glass ceiling by starting his own business. The number of minority-owned businesses is on the rise, and the number of Hispanic owned businesses partially fueled this growth. Can you recommend other strategies people of color can use to break the glass ceiling?

(c) Tony Savino/The Image Works

Mismatch between Educational Attainment and Occupational Requirements

Approximately 25% of the labor force has a college degree.[38] Unfortunately, many of these people are working in jobs for which they are overqualified. This creates underemployment. **Underemployment** exists when a job requires less than a person's full potential as determined by his or her formal education, training, or skills. Underemployment is associated with higher arrest rates and the likelihood of becoming an unmarried parent for young adults. It also is negatively correlated with job satisfaction, work commitment, job involvement, internal work motivation, life satisfaction, and psychological well-being. Underemployment also is related to higher absenteeism and turnover.[39] On a positive note, however, underemployment is one of the reasons more new college graduates are starting businesses of their own. Moreover, research reveals that over time a college graduate's income ranges from 50% to 100% higher than that obtained by a high-school graduate. For example, the median income in the United States was $28,800 and $46,300 for employees with a high-school diploma and a bachelor's degree, respectively, in 2000.[40] It pays to graduate from college!

> **Underemployment**
> The result of taking a job that requires less education, training, or skills than possessed by a worker.

There is another important educational mismatch. The national high-school dropout rate is approximately 17%, and more than 50% of the US population reads below the eighth-grade level. Further, it is estimated that 90 million adults are functionally illiterate, and this costs corporate America an estimated $60 billion a year in lost productivity.[41] Literacy is defined as "an individual's ability to read, write, and speak in English, compute and solve problems at levels of proficiency necessary to function on the job and in society, to achieve one's goals, and develop one's knowledge and potential."[42] These statistics are worrisome because 70% of on-the-job reading materials are written for ninth-grade to college levels. Also, 43% of illiterate adults live in poverty; thus organizations are having a hard time finding qualified employees.[43] For example, a survey of 300 executives from manufacturing, technology, and finance firms revealed that a shortage of skilled workers limited sales by as much as 33%.[44] In contrast to underemployment, dropouts and illiterate individuals are unlikely to have the skills organizations need to remain competitive.

The Aging Workforce

America's population and workforce are getting older. Between 1995 and 2020, the number of individuals in the United States over age 65 will increase by 60%, the 45- to 64-year-old population by 34%, and those between ages 18 and 44 by 4%.[45] Life expectancy is increasing as well. The number of people living into their 80s is increasing rapidly, and this group disproportionately suffers from chronic illness. The United States is not the only country with an aging population. Japan, Eastern Europe, and former Soviet republics, for example, are expected to encounter significant economic and political problems due to an aging population.

Managerial Implications of Increasing Diversity

Highly skilled women and people of color will be in high demand given future labor shortages. It is estimated that labor shortages will reach 4.8 million workers by 2012, 19.7 million by 2022, and 35.8 million in 30 years. It is essential to close this labor supply gap in order to grow the US economy.[46] To attract and retain the best workers, companies need to adopt policies and programs that meet the needs of women and people of color. Programs such as day care and elder care, flexible work schedules, benefits such as paternal leaves, less rigid relocation policies, and mentoring programs are likely to become more popular. Before implementing such initiatives, however, companies should consider the recommendations derived from Deloitte & Touche's successful women's initiative program (see

Table 2–3   *Deloitte & Touche's Recommendations for Using a Diversity Initiative to Reduce the Turnover of Women*

Recommendations	Supportive Tactics
1. Make sure senior management is front and center.	The CEO actively led the women's initiative.
2. Make an airtight business case for cultural change.	The company documented the business imperative for change before it could justify the investment and effort required by the initiative.
3. Let the world watch you.	The company appointed an external advisory council and informed the press about its plans. The company did not let the initiative become another "program of the year" that led nowhere.
4. Begin with dialogue as the platform for change.	Employees were required to attend intensive workshops to reveal and examine gender-based assumptions in mentoring and client assignments.
5. Use a flexible system of accountability.	Local offices measured their efforts with women professionals. Management worked with office heads to select their focus areas of change under the initiative.
6. Promote work-life balance for men and women.	The company implemented policies for flexible work arrangements and lighter travel schedules.

SOURCE: Excerpted and adapted from D M McCracken, "Winning the Talent War for Women: Sometimes It Takes a Revolution," *Harvard Business Review,* November–December 2000, p. 166.

Table 2–3). The company initiated this program after determining that it was having a problem retaining high-quality women in the firm.

Given the projected increase in the number of Hispanics entering the workforce over the next 20 years, managers should consider progressive methods to recruit, retain, and integrate this segment of the population into their organizations. Consider the examples set by Kmart, the University of North Carolina Health Care System at Chapel Hill, PricewaterhouseCoopers, Chevron, and Pepsi.

> Kmart recruits at colleges and universities that have large numbers of Hispanic students. The company also advertises in Hispanic publications and uses online Hispanic job boards. It also has translated employment and benefit information into Spanish. The University of North Carolina Health Care System at Chapel Hill, NC, has brought in Spanish interpreters at its new-employee orientations and printed part of its job application information in Spanish. . . .
>
> PricewaterhouseCoopers . . . set up employee support and socialization groups where Hispanic managers act as leaders to Hispanic employees, and the company provides scholarships for Hispanic accounting students. Chevron sponsors a Hispanic employee network. . . . Pepsi works with national Hispanic organizations to help with recruiting and is planning a leadership forum for some Hispanic executives. The program will give the executives access to the CEO and other company leaders.[47]

While the above examples highlight the value of progressively recruiting Hispanics, recruiting is not enough to ensure that people of color advance up the organizational hierarchy. Effective mentoring also is needed.

David Thomas, a researcher from Harvard University, conducted a three-year study of mentoring practices at three US corporations: a manufacturer, an electronics company, and a high-tech firm. His results revealed that successful people of color who advanced the furthest had a strong network of mentors and sponsors who nurtured their professional development. Findings also demonstrated that people of color should be mentored differently than their white counterparts. He recommended that organizations

> should provide a range of career paths, all uncorrelated with race, that lead to the executive suite. . . . Achieving this system, however, would require integrating the principles of opportunity, development, and diversity into the fabric of the organization's management practices and human resource systems. And an important element in the process would be to identify potential mentors, train them, and ensure that they are paired with promising professionals of color.[48]

Mismatches between the amount of education needed to perform current jobs and the amount of education possessed by members of the workforce are growing. Underemployment among college graduates threatens to erode job satisfaction and work motivation. As well-educated workers begin to look for jobs commensurate with their qualifications and expectations, absenteeism and turnover likely will increase. This problem underscores the need for job redesign (see the discussion in Chapter 8). In addition, organizations will need to consider interventions, such as realistic job previews and positive reinforcement programs, to reduce absenteeism and turnover. On-the-job remedial skills and literacy training will be necessary to help the growing number of dropouts and illiterates cope with job demands. For example, US organizations spent $57 billion on training in 2001.[49]

Moreover, organizations will continue to be asked to help resolve the educational problems in the United States. Supporting education is good for business and society at large. A better education system not only contributes to the United States' ability to compete internationally, but it facilitates a better quality of life for all its population.

As the baby-boom generation reaches retirement age after the turn of the century, the workforce will be top-heavy with older employees, creating the problem of career plateauing for younger workers. **Career plateauing** is defined "as that point in a career [at] which future hierarchical mobility seems unlikely."[50] Career plateauing is associated with stress and dissatisfaction.[51] Unfortunately, this problem is intensified by the fact that organizations are flattening—and reducing the number of managerial jobs—in order to save costs and increase efficiency. Managers will thus need to find alternatives other than promotions to help employees satisfy their needs and to feel successful, and employees will need to take a much more active role in managing their careers.

Seven managerial initiatives may help organizations to keep older workers engaged and committed and their skills current:[52]

Career plateauing
The end result when the probability of being promoted is very small.

1. Provide challenging work assignments that make a difference to the firm.

2. Give the employee considerable autonomy and latitude in completing a task.

3. Provide equal access to training and learning opportunities when it comes to new technology.

4. Provide frequent recognition for skills, experience, and wisdom gained over the years.

5. Provide mentoring opportunities whereby older workers can pass on accumulated knowledge to younger employees.

6. Ensure that older workers receive sensitive, high-quality supervision.

7. Design a work environment that is both stimulating and fun.

Managing Diversity—A Competitive Advantage

Consultants, academics, and business leaders believe that effectively managing diversity is a competitive advantage. This advantage stems from the process in which the management of diversity affects organizational behavior and effectiveness. Effectively managing diversity can influence an organization's costs and employee attitudes, recruitment of human resources, sales and market share (see International OB on page 61), creativity and innovation, and group problem solving and productivity. This section explores the relationship between managing diversity and each of these outcomes.

Lower Costs and Improved Employee Attitudes   Effectively managing diversity can lower costs in three ways. First, if we assume that adhering to equal employment opportunity laws is a prerequisite to managing diversity, then organizations can reduce the chance of experiencing a costly discrimination lawsuit. For example, the US Equal Employment Opportunity Commission negotiated nonlitigated settlements of $94 million for sex-based discrimination, $53 million for sexual harassment, $45.2 million for age discrimination, and $42.2 million for disability discrimination in 2001.[53] Second, diversity initiatives can reduce health care expenses and absenteeism. Consider the effect of supporting a lactation or breast-feeding program. Research shows that breast-fed babies have fewer allergies, respiratory infections, ear infections, and serious disease. Other studies show that one-day absences from work due to a baby's illness are twice as high among mothers who use formula as opposed to breast-feeding. CIGNA Corp. offers a good illustration of the benefits associated with a lactation program. The company realized savings of $300,000 a year in health costs and a 77% reduction in lost work time.[54] Finally, employee recruiting and training expenses can be reduced by effectively managing diversity. These savings occur through reductions in turnover by women and people of color. NationsBank and Aetna Life & Casualty were able to reduce turnover of diverse employees by implementing targeted diversity programs:

> At NationsBank, two-thirds of employees on flexible schedules said they would have left without these policies.
>
> Aetna Life & Casualty dramatically demonstrated the effect employer policies can have on retention. By modifying company policy to allow part-time return after family leave, the company cut attrition by more than 50%—resulting in an 88% to 91% retention rate of leave-takers over the past five years. Aetna calculated that reduction in turnover represents more than $1 million in annual savings.[55]

Diversity also was related to employee attitudes.

Past research revealed that people who were different from their work units in racial or ethnic background were less psychologically committed to their organizations, less satisfied with their careers, and perceived less autonomy to make decisions on their jobs. African-Americans also were found to receive lower performance ratings than whites.[56] Organizational surveys further demonstrated that between 25% and 66% of gay and lesbian employees experienced discrimination at work. Gay and lesbian employees also reported higher levels of stress than heterosexual employees, and gay and bisexual male workers earned from 11% to 27% less than heterosexual peers with similar experience and education.[57]

How important is the issue of sexual preference? An analysis conducted by the Human Rights Campaign Foundation revealed that gay and lesbian families totaled 601,209 in 2000. Assuming that both individuals involved in these families work, then

New Disney Theme Park Outside Paris Is Designed around Cultural Considerations

When visitors take a tram ride through the new Walt Disney Studios theme park here, their virtual tour guides won't be Hollywood stars like Bruce Willis. Instead, European actors like Jeremy Irons, Isabella Rossellini and Natassja Kinski will be speaking—and in their native tongues.

A decade after being slammed for its alleged ignorance of European ways with Disneyland Paris, Disney is trying to prove it's gotten things right the second time around. . . . Their first venture, Disneyland Paris (originally called Euro Disney), was considered a flop for years after its 1992 opening. Disney was taken to task for creating a mere outpost of American cultural imperialism, even failing to mind such basic local customs as serving wine with meals. . . .

Over time, Disney added more local flourishes and food options that seem to have quieted critics and improved business. Indeed, visitor numbers show that Disneyland Paris today is Europe's biggest tourist attraction—even more popular than the Eiffel Tower—a turnaround that showed the park operators' ability to learn from their mistakes. . . .

But elements here and there remind guests that this is Europe, rather than the US. A show celebrating the history of animation involves a montage of Disney characters speaking six different languages. A big stunt show, designed by French stuntman Remy Julienne, features cars and motorcycles that race through a village modeled after the French resort town of St. Tropez.

Francois Confino, a Swiss architect and set designer who worked as a consultant in planning the park, says he wasn't sure at first whether Disney would be open to many of the ideas he deemed necessary to make a park more European. But he says he was happy to find that Disney planners in California were open to his suggestions, such as including. "Les Enfants de Paradis," a French film from the 1940s, as a staple for CineMagique, the park's retrospective film attraction. . . .

Paul Pressler, who oversees all of Disney's theme-park empire as chairman of Disney Parks and Resorts, says small details reflect the cultural lessons learned. "We made sure that all of our food venues have covered seating," he says, recalling that open-air restaurants when Disneyland Paris first opened offered no protection from the rainy weather that ails the park for long stretches of the year.

On the food front, Disneyland Paris offered only a French sausage, drawing complaints from the English, Germans, Italians and everyone else about why their local sausages weren't available. This time around, Mr. Pressler says, the park will cater to "the multiple indigenous cultures throughout Europe"—which includes a wider selection of sausages.

Actress Geraldine Chaplin's smile, as she poses at the entrance of the Walt Disney Studios in Disneyland Paris, seems reflective of the park's newfound success. For years after its 1992 opening, Disneyland Paris was considered a flop—a mere outpost of American culture and customs. Over time however, Disney learned its lesson and with new culturally sensitive improvements in place, Disneyland Paris is now Europe's biggest tourist attraction. Why do you think it was so important for Disneyland Paris to become more culturally aware?

AP/Wide World Photos

SOURCE: Excerpted from P Prada and B Orwall, "A Certain 'Je Ne Sais Quoi' at Disney's New Park," *The Wall Street Journal*, March 12, 2002, pp. B1, B4.

there are approximately 1.2 million gay or lesbian employees in the United States. Some organizations appear to recognize the importance of accommodating sexual preference, as the number of companies that cover domestic partner benefits increased from 2,856 in 1999 to 4,285 in 2001, and 59% of *Fortune* 500 companies include sexual orientation in their nondiscrimination policies—this represents a 17% increase from the previous year.[58]

Employees' mental/physical abilities and characteristics are another dimension of diversity that needs to be effectively managed. Data from the 2001 US census indicate that approximately 25% of the labor force has a work disability. Although two out of three individuals with disabilities want to work, roughly 75% are unemployed.[59] Individuals with disabilities also tend to be employed in part-time, low-status jobs offering little chance for advancement, and they earn up to 35% less than their nondisabled counterparts.[60] These statistics prompted the passage of the **Americans with Disabilities Act** in 1992. This law bans discrimination against the disabled in the United States and requires organizations to reasonably accommodate an individual's disabilities. Despite the fact that most job accommodations are relatively inexpensive (e.g., nearly 20% of accommodations cost nothing, and 50% cost less than $500), disabled workers are still finding it difficult to obtain employment.[61] Do you think this segment of the population is being underutilized?

Americans with Disabilities Act

Prohibits discrimination against the disabled.

Improved Recruiting Efforts

Attracting and retaining competent employees is a competitive advantage. This is particularly true given the workforce demographics discussed in the preceding section. Organizations that effectively manage diversity are more likely to meet this challenge because women and people of color are attracted to such companies. Moreover, recruiting diverse employees helps organizations to provide better customer service. Former IBM chairman Louis Gerstner came to the following conclusion about recruiting diverse workers:

> Our commitment to build a workforce as broad and diversified as the customer base we serve in more than 160 countries isn't an option; it's a business imperative as fundamental as delivering superior technologies to the marketplace.[62]

Increased Sales, Market Share, and Corporate Profits

Workforce diversity is the mirror image of consumer diversity. It is thus important for companies to market their products so that they appeal to diverse customers and markets. McDonald's Corp. and Wal-Mart Stores are good examples of companies that followed this advice.

> Both organizations, realizing that the US Hispanic market grew at a tremendous rate in the 1990s, decided to attempt to improve their marketing to the Hispanic community. Because of an increased understanding of the importance of the extended family in Hispanic cultures, McDonald's has reconfigured the seating in many of its restaurants to provide larger group areas where extended families can sit together. Similarly, Wal-Mart has begun to advertise heavily in Hispanic areas during the period between Christmas and Three Kings Day (January 6) in recognition of the tradition of Hispanics exchanging gifts on Three Kings Day.[63]

Researchers are beginning to examine the effects of a top management team's (TMT's) demographic characteristics on an organization's financial performance. For example, a study of 1,000 companies conducted by the American Management Association and the Business & Professional Women's Foundation suggests that a diverse TMT can contribute to corporate profits. Results revealed that sales growth averaged 22.9%, 20.2%, and 13% for companies whose senior management team contained a majority of women, included people of color, and consisted of a majority of white men, respectively.[64] Given these impressive results, other researchers are trying to identify the exact process or manner in which a TMT's diversity positively impacts corporate success. The current thinking is that diversity promotes the sharing of unique ideas and a variety of perspectives, which, in turn, leads to more effective decision making.[65]

Increased Creativity and Innovation

Preliminary research supports the idea that workforce diversity promotes creativity and innovation. This occurs through the sharing of diverse ideas and perspectives. Rosabeth Moss-Kanter, a management expert, was one of the first to investigate this relationship. Her results indicated that innovative companies deliberately used heterogeneous teams to solve problems, and they employed more women and people of color than less innovative companies. She also noted that innovative companies did a better job of eliminating racism, sexism, and classism.[66] A recent summary of 40 years of diversity research supported Moss-Kanter's conclusion that diversity can promote creativity and improve a team's decision making.[67]

Increased Group Problem Solving and Productivity

Because diverse groups possess a broader base of experience and perspectives from which to analyze a problem, they can potentially improve problem solving and performance. Research findings based on short-term groups that varied in terms of values, attitudes, educational backgrounds, and experience supported this conclusion. Heterogeneous groups produced better-quality decisions and demonstrated higher productivity than homogeneous groups. Nevertheless, these results must be interpreted cautiously because the experimental samples, tasks, time frames, and environmental situations bear very little resemblance to actual ongoing organizational settings.[68] Additional research has attempted to control these problems.

More recent studies do not clearly support the proposed benefits of diversity. A study of culturally homogeneous and diverse groups over a period of 17 weeks showed higher performance among homogeneous groups for the first 9 weeks due to the fact that heterogeneous groups experienced less effective group processes than homogeneous groups. Over weeks 10 through 17, however, homogeneous and heterogeneous groups demonstrated similar performance.[69] Additional studies found that work group diversity was associated with less cooperation among team members and more negative impressions toward people who were demographically different.[70]

In summary, research shows that diversity can improve creativity and innovation, but these positive benefits may not influence productivity because diverse groups generally experience more negative group dynamics. How then do managers capitalize on the positive benefits of diversity? One lesson seems to be that organizations should not simply assemble a diverse group and then let group dynamics take care of themselves. Rather, training should be used to help group members become aware of cultural and attitudinal differences of other group members. This training should be conducted at the beginning of a group's formation because conflict is likely to be highest at this point and this conflict negatively influences subsequent group processes.[71] A second lesson revolves around the fact that the group processes and performance of diverse groups are enhanced when group members share common values and norms that promote the pursuit of common goals.[72] Managers and organizations thus are encouraged to identify ways of enhancing group members' sense of shared values and a common fate. Increasing shared values can be facilitated through an organization's culture, which is discussed in Chapter 3, and common fate can be created by making group members accountable for group or team-level performance goals. Team goals and team rewards are discussed in Chapter 13.

Barriers and Challenges to Managing Diversity

We introduced this chapter by noting that diversity is a sensitive, potentially volatile, and sometimes uncomfortable issue. It is therefore not surprising that organizations encounter significant barriers when trying to move forward with managing diversity. The following is a list of the most common barriers to implementing successful diversity programs;[73]

1. *Inaccurate stereotypes and prejudice.* This barrier manifests itself in the belief that differences are viewed as weaknesses. In turn, this promotes the view that diversity hiring will mean sacrificing competence and quality.

2. *Ethnocentrism.* The ethnocentrism barrier represents the feeling that one's cultural rules and norms are superior or more appropriate than the rules and norms of another culture. This barrier is thoroughly discussed in Chapter 4.

3. *Poor career planning.* This barrier is associated with the lack of opportunities for diverse employees to get the type of work assignments that qualify them for senior management positions.

4. *An unsupportive and hostile working environment for diverse employees.* Diverse employees are frequently excluded from social events and the friendly camaraderie that takes place in most offices.

5. *Lack of political savvy on the part of diverse employees.* Diverse employees may not get promoted because they do not know how to "play the game" of getting along and getting ahead in an organization. Research reveals that women and people of color are excluded from organizational networks.[74]

6. *Difficulty in balancing career and family issues.* Women still assume the majority of the responsibilities associated with raising children. This makes it harder for women to work evenings and weekends or to frequently travel once they have children. Even without children in the picture, household chores take more of a woman's time than a man's time.

7. *Fears of reverse discrimination.* Some employees believe that managing diversity is a smoke screen for reverse discrimination. This belief leads to very strong resistance because people feel that one person's gain is another's loss.

8. *Diversity is not seen as an organizational priority.* This leads to subtle resistance that shows up in the form of complaints and negative attitudes. Employees may complain about the time, energy, and resources devoted to diversity that could have been spent doing "real work."

9. *The need to revamp the organization's performance appraisal and reward system.* Performance appraisals and reward systems must reinforce the need to effectively manage diversity. This means that success will be based on a new set of criteria. Employees are likely to resist changes that adversely affect their promotions and financial rewards.

10. *Resistance to change.* Effectively managing diversity entails significant organizational and personal change. As discussed in Chapter 19, people resist change for many different reasons.

In summary, managing diversity is a critical component of organizational success. Case studies and limited research inform us that this effort is doomed to failure unless top management is truly committed to managing diversity. The next section examines the variety of ways organizations are attempting to manage diversity.

Organizational Practices Used to Effectively Manage Diversity

Many organizations throughout the United States are unsure of what it takes to effectively manage diversity. This is partly due to the fact that top management only recently became aware of the combined need and importance of this issue.

So what are organizations doing to effectively manage diversity? Answering this question requires that we provide a framework for categorizing organizational initiatives. Researchers and practitioners have developed relevant frameworks. One was developed by R Roosevelt Thomas, Jr, a diversity expert. He identified eight generic action options that can be used to address any type of diversity issue. A second was proposed by another diversity expert, Ann Morrison. She empirically identified the specific diversity initiatives used by 16 organizations that successfully managed diversity. This section reviews these frameworks in order to provide you with both a broad and specific understanding about how organizations are effectively managing diversity.

R Roosevelt Thomas, Jr's Generic Action Options

Thomas identified eight basic responses for handling any diversity issue. After describing each action option, we discuss relationships among them.[75]

Option 1: Include/Exclude
This choice is an outgrowth of affirmative action programs. Its primary goal is to either increase or decrease the number of diverse people at all levels of the organizations. Shoney's restaurant represents a good example of a company that attempted to include diverse employees after settling a discrimination lawsuit. The company subsequently hired African-Americans into positions of dining-room supervisors and vice presidents, added more franchises owned by African-Americans, and purchased more goods and services from minority-owned companies.[76]

Option 2: Deny
People using this option deny that differences exist. Denial may manifest itself in proclamations that all decisions are color, gender, and age blind and that success is solely determined by merit and performance. Consider State Farm Insurance, for example. "Although it was traditional for male agents and their regional managers to hire male relatives, State Farm Insurance avoided change and denied any alleged effects in a nine-year gender-bias suit that the company lost."[77]

Option 3: Assimilate
The basic premise behind this alternative is that all diverse people will learn to fit in or become like the dominant group. It only takes time and reinforcement for people to see the light. Organizations initially assimilate employees through their recruitment practices and the use of company orientation programs. New hires generally are put through orientation programs that aim to provide employees with the organization's preferred values and a set of standard operating procedures. Employees then are encouraged to refer to the policies and procedure manual when they are confused about what to do in a specific situation. These practices create homogeneity among employees.

Option 4: Suppress
Differences are squelched or discouraged when using this approach. This can be done by telling or reinforcing others to quit whining and complaining about issues. The old "you've got to pay your dues" line is another frequently used way to promote the status quo.

Option 5: Isolate
This option maintains the current way of doing things by setting the diverse person off to the side. In this way the individual is unable to influence organizational change. Managers can isolate people by putting them on special projects. Entire work groups or departments are isolated by creating functionally independent entities, frequently referred to as "silos." Shoney Inc.'s employees commented to a *Wall Street Journal* reporter about isolation practices formerly used by the company:

> White managers told of how Mr Danner [previous chairman of the company] told them to fire blacks if they became too numerous in restaurants in white neighborhoods; if they refused, they would lose their jobs, too. Some also said that when Mr Danner was expected to visit their restaurant, they scheduled black employees off that day or, in one case, hid them in the bathroom. Others said blacks' applications were coded and discarded.[78]

Option 6: Tolerate
Toleration entails acknowledging differences but not valuing or accepting them. It represents a live-and-let-live approach that superficially allows organizations to give lip service to the issue of managing diversity. Toleration is different from isolation in that it allows for the inclusion of diverse people. However, differences are not really valued or accepted when an organization uses this option.

Option 7: Build Relationships
This approach is based on the premise that good relationships can overcome differences. It addresses diversity by fostering quality relationships—characterized by acceptance and understanding—among diverse groups. R R Donnelley is a good example of a company attempting to use this diversity option. "R R Donnelley sponsors an exchange program where counterparts in two nations swap positions for several weeks to learn about each other's countries and customs."[79]

Julia Steward, president of the Applebee's division of Applebee's International, also uses this diversity action option. She spends five minutes each day talking with each of the nine managers reporting to her about such down-home topics as where they ate over the weekend or whether a spouse passed the real estate exam. 'It's important to establish what's important to them,' she says.[80]

Option 8: Foster Mutual Adaptation
In this option, people are willing to adapt or change their views for the sake of creating positive relationships with others. This implies that employees and management alike must be willing to accept differences, and most important, agree that everyone and everything is open for change. Companies can foster mutual adaptation through their recruitment and retention strategies. Consider the approach used by the SAS Institute, a privately held software company:

> The company encourages movement from within, posting jobs internally to gauge interest, then soliciting outside applicants only if no qualified internal candidates exist. . . . The Cary, NC–based company enjoys a turnover rate among its 7,000 worldwide employees that never exceeds 5% a year. When asked to elaborate on how SAS keeps its employees, [Jack] Dornan [a company spokesperson] points to several amenities: on-site child care and health care, gymnasium facilities, a flexible workplace where trust between employees and managers is not only expected but is also demanded, and a corporate climate that encourages employees to have a life outside of work.[81]

This example illustrates that mutual adaptation requires a unique organizational culture or climate that supports the accommodation and acceptance of diverse people.

Conclusions about Action Options

Although the action options can be used alone or in combination, some are clearly better than others. Exclusion, denial, assimilation, suppression, isolation, and toleration are among the least preferred options. Inclusion, building relationships, and mutual adaptation are the preferred strategies. That said, Thomas reminds us that mutual adaptation is the only approach that unquestionably endorses the philosophy behind managing diversity. In closing this discussion, it is important to note that choosing how to best manage diversity is a dynamic process that is determined by the context at hand. For instance, some organizations are not ready for mutual adaptation. The best one might hope for in this case is the inclusion of diverse people.

Ann Morrison Identifies Specific Diversity Initiatives

As previously mentioned, Ann Morrison conducted a landmark study of the diversity practices used by 16 organizations that successfully managed diversity. Her results uncovered 52 different practices, 20 of which were used by the majority of the companies sampled. She classified the 52 practices into three main types: accountability, development, and recruitment.[82] The top 10 practices associated with each type are shown in Table 2–4. They are discussed next in order of relative importance.

Table 2–4   *Common Diversity Practices*

Accountability Practices	Development Practices	Recruitment Practices
1. Top management's personal intervention	1. Diversity training programs	1. Targeted recruitment of nonmanagers
2. Internal advocacy groups	2. Networks and support groups	2. Key outside hires
3. Emphasis on EEO statistics, profiles	3. Development programs for all high-potential managers	3. Extensive public exposure on diversity (AA)
4. Inclusion of diversity in performance evaluation goals, ratings	4. Informal networking activities	4. Corporate image as liberal, progressive, or benevolent
5. Inclusion of diversity in promotion decisions, criteria	5. Job rotation	5. Partnerships with educational institutions
6. Inclusion of diversity in management succession planning	6. Formal mentoring program	6. Recruitment incentives such as cash supplements
7. Work and family policies	7. Informal mentoring program	7. Internships (such as INROADS)
8. Policies against racism, sexism	8. Entry development programs for all high-potential new hires	8. Publications or PR products that highlight diversity
9. Internal audit or attitude survey	9. Internal training (such as personal safety or language)	9. Targeted recruitment of managers
10. Active AA/EEO committee, office	10. Recognition events, awards	10. Partnership with nontraditional groups

SOURCE: Abstracted from Tables A.10, A.11, and A.12 in A M Morrison, *The New Leaders: Guidelines on Leadership Diversity in America* (San Francisco: Jossey-Bass, 1992).

Accountability practices

Focus on treating diverse employees fairly.

Accountability Practices

Accountability practices relate to managers' responsibility to treat diverse employees fairly. Table 2–4 reveals that companies predominantly accomplish this objective by creating administrative procedures aimed at integrating diverse employees into the management ranks (practices number 3, 4, 5, 6, 8, 9, and 10). In contrast, work and family policies, practice 7, focuses on creating an environment that fosters employee commitment and productivity. Both IBM and Fannie Mae use a variety of accountability practices in their attempts to manage diversity.

> At IBM, 38% of the worldwide management council (the company's top management team) consists of women, minorities, and non-US-born people. Ted Childs, vice president of diversity, says that women hold top spots in Peru, Indonesia, France, Spain, Portugal, Singapore, Hong Kong, and Latin America. IBM's executive sourcing process, which focuses on leadership development and succession planning, specifically targets women and minorities....Fannie Mae has also established clear goals to increase the ratio of minorities at the officer and director levels, and it ties compensation to the promotion of diversity as a business value.[83]

Development Practices

The use of development practices to manage diversity is relatively new compared with the historical use of accountability and recruitment practices. **Development practices** focus on preparing diverse employees for greater responsibility and advancement. These activities are needed because most nontraditional employees have not been exposed to the type of activities and job assignments that develop effective leadership and social networks.[84] Table 2–4 indicates that diversity training programs, networks and support groups, and mentoring programs are among the most frequently used developmental practices. Consider the networking practices used by Xerox and Fannie Mae.

Development practices

Focus on preparing diverse employees for greater responsibility and advancement.

> Many years ago when Xerox was trying to ensure more participation from blacks in its workforce, a caucus established among black employees had the blessing of then-CEO David Kearns, who encouraged black employees to get together periodically to talk about their challenges in moving through the organization and to get help from other managers. After that, there arose a women's caucus, and Hispanic caucus, and so on. Fannie Mae has taken the idea of employee caucus groups a step further. It has 14 Employee Networking Groups for African-Americans, Hispanics, Native Americans, Catholics, Christians, Muslims, older workers, gays, lesbians, veterans, and so forth. The groups serve as social and networking hubs, and they foster workplace communication about diversity issues among all employees, including senior managers.[85]

There is one particular developmental practice that more and more organizations are confronting: Teaching English to non-English-speaking workers. Successfully teaching English and learning to communicate in multiple languages will become increasingly important as employers continue to hire people for whom English is not their first language. Imagine the situation faced by Doubletree Hotels Corporation when it had to communicate about its revamped employee benefits to a workforce of 30,000 people who speak 20 different languages:

> Instead of being daunted by the prospect of explaining benefits in multiple languages and to many employees with limited educations, Doubletree launched an outreach program that spoke to virtually all employees in their own tongues, on their own terms. The main tools were audio cassette tapes, shipped to each work site and made available for employees to use with loaned tape players. The tapes explained changes in the benefits program, such as a greater selection of health maintenance organizations and the debut of flexible benefits.

Multi-ethnic employee caucuses serve as social and networking hubs, fostering workplace communication about diversity issues among employees as well as senior managers. Do you think support groups such as diversity caucuses are an effective way to develop employees? Why or why not?

(c) Mark Richards/ PhotoEdit

The tapes were recorded in 14 languages, including Spanish, Somali, Tongan, Creole, Mandarin, and Russian, and became very popular with employees, some of whom are illiterate and would not have understood written materials, said Lenny Sanicola, benefits manager of Phoenix-based Doubletree. The company decided to communicate in native languages with any group of at least 25 employees.[86]

Recruitment Practices

Recruitment practices focus on attracting job applicants at all levels who are willing to accept challenging work assignments. This focus is critical because people learn the leadership skills needed for advancement by successfully accomplishing increasingly challenging and responsible work assignments. As shown in Table 2–4, targeted recruitment of nonmanagers (practice 1) and managers (practice 9) are commonly used to identify and recruit women and people of color. The McGraw-Hill Companies, for example, is noted for relying on targeted recruiting:

> The McGraw-Hill Companies emphasizes diverse talent management. One example of its talent management strategy is the Associate Development Program (ADP). Since the program began in 1993, it has attracted talented individuals from top MBA business schools who are diverse in race, ethnicity, experience, and perspective. The McGraw-Hill Companies has recruited, developed, and promoted many outstanding new managers from the ADP program. . . . Attracting, retaining, and developing the best talent for the company will continue to be an area of focus in the near term and the long term. The McGraw-Hill Companies' talent management strategy includes building a talent pipeline by enhancing recruitment efforts in the Hispanic, African-American, and Asian communities.[87]

Recruitment practices

Attempts to attract qualified, diverse employees at all levels.

ſummary of Key Concepts

1. *Define diversity.* Diversity represents the host of individual differences that make people different from and similar to each other. Diversity pertains to everybody. It is not simply an issue of age, race, gender, or sexual orientation.

2. *Discuss the four layers of diversity.* The layers of diversity define an individual's personal identity and constitute a perceptual filter that influences how we interpret the world. Personality is at the center of the diversity wheel.

The second layer of diversity consists of a set of internal dimensions that are referred to as the primary dimensions of diversity. The third layer is composed of external influences and are called secondary dimensions of diversity. The final layer of diversity includes organizational dimensions.

3. *Explain the differences among affirmative action, valuing diversity, and managing diversity.* Affirmative action focuses on achieving equality of opportunity in an organization. It represents an artificial intervention aimed at giving management a chance to correct an imbalance, an injustice, a mistake, or outright discrimination. Valuing diversity emphasizes the awareness, recognition, understanding, and appreciation of human differences. Training programs are the dominant method used to accomplish this objective. Managing diversity entails creating a host of organizational changes that enable all people to perform up to their maximum potential.

4. *Demonstrate your familiarity with the demographic trends that are creating an increasingly diverse workforce.* There are four key demographic trends: (a) half of the new entrants into the workforce between 1990 and 2010 will be women, (b) people of color will account for more than a third of the new entrants into the workforce between 1990 and 2010, (c) a mismatch exists between workers' educational attainment and occupational requirements, and (d) the workforce is aging.

5. *Highlight the managerial implications of increasing diversity in the workforce.* There are seven broad managerial implications: (a) To attract the best workers, companies need to adopt policies and programs that particularly meet the needs of women and people of color; (b) managers should consider progressive methods to recruit, retain, and integrate Hispanic workers into their organizations; (c) mentoring programs are needed to help people of color advance within the organizational hierarchy; (d) remedial skills training is necessary to help the growing number of dropouts and illiterates cope with job demands; (e) organizations will need to tangibly support education if the United States is to remain globally competitive; (f) the problem of career plateauing needs to be managed; and (g) seven separate managerial

initiatives can help organizations to keep older workers engaged and committed and their skills current.

6. *Review the five reasons managing diversity is a competitive advantage.* (a) Managing diversity can lower costs and improve employee attitudes. (b) Managing diversity can improve an organization's recruiting efforts. (c) Managing diversity can increase sales, market share, and corporate profits. (d) Managing diversity can increase creativity and innovation. (e) Managing diversity can increase group problem solving and productivity.

7. *Identify the barriers and challenges to managing diversity.* There are 10 barriers to successfully implementing diversity initiatives: (a) inaccurate stereotypes and prejudice, (b) ethnocentrism, (c) poor career planning, (d) an unsupportive and hostile working environment for diverse employees, (e) lack of political savvy on the part of diverse employees, (f) difficulty in balancing career and family issues, (g) fears of reverse discrimination, (h) diversity is not seen as an organizational priority, (i) the need to revamp the organization's performance appraisal and reward system, and (j) resistance to change.

8. *Discuss the organizational practices used to effectively manage diversity as identified by R Roosevelt Thomas, Jr, and Ann Morrison.* There are many different practices organizations can use to manage diversity. R Roosevelt Thomas, Jr, identified eight basic responses for handling any diversity issue: include/exclude, deny, assimilate, suppress, isolate, tolerate, build relationships, and foster mutual adaptation. Exclusion, denial, assimilation, suppression, isolation, and toleration are among the least preferred options. Inclusion, building relationships, and mutual adaptation are the preferred strategies. Ann Morrison's study of diversity practices identified three main types or categories of activities. Accountability practices relate to a manager's responsibility to treat diverse employees fairly. Development practices focus on preparing diverse employees for greater responsibility and advancement. Recruitment practices emphasize attracting job applicants at all levels who are willing to accept challenging work assignments. Table 2–4 presents a list of activities that are used to accomplish each main type.

Discussion Questions

1. Whom do you think would be most resistant to accepting the value or need to manage diversity? Explain.

2. What role does communication play in effectively managing diversity?

3. Does diversity suggest that managers should follow the rule "Do unto others as you would have them do unto you"?

4. What can be done to break the glass ceiling for women and people of color?

5. What can be done to facilitate the career success of the disabled? Explain.

6. Why is underemployment a serious human resource management problem? If you have ever been underemployed, what were your feelings about it?

7. How can interpersonal conflict be caused by diversity? Explain your rationale.

8. Have you seen any examples that support the proposition that diversity is a competitive advantage?

9. Which of the barriers to managing diversity would be most difficult to reduce? Explain.

10. How can Thomas's generic action options and Morrison's specific diversity initiatives be helpful in overcoming the barriers and challenges to managing diversity?

Internet Exercise

www.bls.gov

This chapter discussed a variety of demographic statistics that underlie the changing nature of the US workforce. We discussed how a glass ceiling is affecting the promotional opportunities and pay for women and people of color. We also reviewed the mismatch between educational attainment and occupational requirements. We did not, however, discuss the employment opportunities within your chosen field of study. The purpose of this exercise is for you to conduct a more thorough examination of statistics related to the workforce as a whole and for statistics pertaining to your career goals. Visit the Web site for the Bureau of Labor Statistics at **www.bls.gov,** and review information pertaining to the "US Economy at a Glance" and "Occupations." In particular, look at reports and tables pertaining to average hourly earnings, unemployment, and statistics shown in the occupational outlook handbook.

Questions

1. To what extent are income levels rising? Determine whether differences exist by race and gender.

2. Do unemployment rates vary by race? Identify which racial groups are advantaged and disadvantaged.

3. What occupational categories are projected to experience the greatest growth in employment opportunities?

4. What are the employment prospects for your chosen field of study or targeted job? Be sure to identify job opportunities and projected wages. Are you happy with your career choice?

OB in Action Case Study

Marathon Oil Company Actively Manages Diversity[88]

BusinessWeek Marathon Oil Company (MOC) is a large US integrated oil firm where diversity is an important element of its business strategy and is integrated into every facet of its human resource planning. Although an integrated company, Marathon's refining and marketing activities are operated through an affiliate, Marathon Ashland Petroleum (MAP), a venture with Ashland in which Marathon has a 62% interest. MOC and its affiliate, MAP have both been successful at driving diversity synergies by linking and insuring consistency in their approaches to formulating diversity business cases and strategies, plus implementing common diversity initiatives. While aligned, each company has autonomy in implementation of diversity programs.

The presidents of each of these affiliated companies, Gary Heminger (MAP) and Clarence Cazalot (MOC), have committed resources (time, money, and people) to insure that diversity drives business success. The head of each diversity organization partners with the respective senior leadership diversity team and meets frequently to search and reapply diversity best practices, identify natural synergies between the two companies, and troubleshoot common challenges.

During the last two years, both companies have committed to an inclusive diversity strategy and many corporatewide diversity initiatives, including (1) customized diversity business case for their respective business; (2) diversity training for over 10,000 employees; (3) a mentoring program; and (4) multicultural recruiting. Each company tailored these four initiatives to address their business needs and the unique culture of their organization.

An example of the company's approach to diversity can be seen through a closer look at its refining and retailing business. Marathon Ashland Petroleum's successful implementation of several diversity initiatives demonstrates how focused leadership commitment, a diversity strategy that complements business objectives, and a practical plan creates significant results in a short period of time. In fact, diversity is one of MAP's five core values, which are diversity, ethics, environmental stewardship, safety, and premier employer, for which its senior leadership and employees are held accountable.

Minority Recruiting

Faye Gerard's (MAP's diversity manager) positive professional experiences as an African-American female chemical engineer, intensifies her commitment to achieve MAP's goal to increase representation of minorities and women in technical positions. The declining number of minorities, particularly minority women, and the increased competition for technical talent makes this a daunting task. MAP's senior executives, partnering with Faye, have created a six component recruiting strategy that focuses on (1) corporatewide, cross-functional recruiting; (2) relationship-based recruiting with first- and second-tiered schools; (3) internships; (4) scholarships; (5) informal mentoring; and (6) organizational affiliations.

Diversity Awareness Training

The senior leadership felt it was important for each employee to understand diversity's relationship to MAP's business strategies, corporate success and expectations for their behavior. Therefore, MAP required its 6,000 employees to attend diversity training. Managers and supervisors attended an eight-hour in-class session, nonmanagement spent four hours at in-class training, and the hourly workforce had computer-based diversity training. In less than 1.5 years, 95% of MAP's workforce has been trained.

Mentoring

Over the last year, MAP has implemented Knowledge Enhancement Exchange Program, (KEEP), a mentoring program that targets all employees. Its objective is to increase retention and contributions to the business, expand individual knowledge bases, and further instill MAP's five core values by driving supportive work relationships. There are two target populations: new hires and experienced employees. New hires are paired with experienced MAP employees and experienced employees are paired with senior, more experienced employees. Informal and formal feedback (employee surveys) have indicated that KEEP has been extremely effective.

Phase II Diversity at MAP

MAP is now in the design and implementation of its Phase II diversity initiative. This Phase focuses on (1) increasing diversity skill sets and tools for managers and supervisors; (2) work-life balance; (3) accelerated join-up for new hires; and (4) on-going senior executive leadership for diversity.

Questions for Discussion

1. Which layers of diversity is Marathon Oil targeting in its recruiting and mentoring initiatives?

2. Compare and contrast the extent to which Marathon is using principles from affirmative action, valuing diversity, and managing diversity. Explain your rationale.

3. Which of R Roosevelt Thomas, Jr's eight generic diversity options is Marathon Oil using to manage diversity? Explain.

4. Using Table 2–4 as a point of reference, identify the various accountability, development, and recruitment practices used by Marathon Oil.

Personal Awareness and Growth Exercise

How Does Your Diversity Profile Affect Your Relationships with Other People?

Objectives

1. To identify the diversity profile of yourself and others.

2. To consider the implications of similarities and differences across diversity profiles.

Introduction

People vary along four layers of diversity: personality, internal dimensions, external dimensions, and organizational dimensions. Differences across these four layers are likely to influence interpersonal relationships and the ability or willingness to work with others. You will be asked to compare yourself with a group of other people you interact with and then to examine the quality of the relationships between yourself and these individuals. This enables you to gain a better understanding of how similarities and differences among people influence attitudes and behavior.

Instructions

Complete the diversity profile by first selecting five current or past co-workers/work associates or fellow students.[89] Alternatively, you can select five people you interact with in order to accomplish your personal goals (e.g., team members on a class project). Write their names on the diagonal lines at the top of the worksheet. Next, determine whether each person is similar to or different from you with respect to each diversity dimension. Mark an "S" if the person is the same or a "D" if the person is different from yourself. Finally, answer the questions for discussion.

Questions for Discussion

1. To whom are you most similar and different?

2. Which diversity dimensions have the greatest influence with respect to whom you are drawn to and whom you like the best?

3. Which dimensions of diversity seem relatively unimportant with respect to the quality of your interpersonal relationships?

4. Consider the individual that you have the most difficult time working with or getting along with. Which dimensions are similar and different? Which dimensions seem to be the source of your difficulty?

5. If you choose co-workers for this exercise, discuss the management actions, policies, or programs that could be used to increase inclusiveness, reduce turnover, and increase job satisfaction.

Diversity Worksheet

Work Associates

Diversity Dimensions					
Personality					
e.g., Loyalty					
Internal Dimensions					
Age					
Gender					
Sexual orientation					
Physical ability					
Ethnicity					
Race					

continued

Work Associates

Diversity Dimensions

External Dimensions					
Geographic location					
Income					
Personal habits					
Recreational habits					
Religion					
Educational background					
Work experience					
Appearance					
Parental status					
Marital status					
Organizational Dimensions					
Functional level/classification					
Work content/field					
Division/department/unit/group					
Seniority					
Work location					
Union affiliation					
Management status					

Group Exercise

Managing Diversity-Related Interactions

Objectives

1. To improve your ability to manage diversity-related interactions more effectively.

2. To explore different approaches for handling diversity interactions.

Introduction

The interpersonal component of managing diversity can be awkward and uncomfortable. This is partly due to the fact that resolving diversity interactions requires us to deal with situations we may never have encountered before. The purpose of this exercise is to help you manage diversity-related interactions more effectively. To do so, you will be asked to read three scenarios and then decide how you will handle each situation.

Instructions

Presented here are three scenarios depicting diversity-related interactions. Please read the first scenario, and then answer the three questions that follow it. Follow the same procedure for the next two scenarios. Next, divide into groups of three. One at a time, each person should present his or her responses to the three questions for the first scenario. The groups should then discuss the various approaches that were proposed to resolve the diversity interaction and try to arrive at a consensus recommendation. Follow the same procedure for the next two scenarios.

Scenario 1

Dave, who is one of your direct reports, comes to you and says that he and Scott are having a special commitment ceremony to celebrate the beginning of their lives together. He has invited you to the ceremony. Normally the department has a party and cake for special occasions. Mary, who is one of Dave's peers, has just walked into your office and asks you whether you intend to have a party for Dave.

A. How would you respond?

_____
_____

B. What is the potential impact of your response?

_____
_____
_____

C. If you choose not to respond, what is the potential impact of your behavior?

_____
_____
_____

Scenario 2

You have an open position for a supervisor, and your top two candidates are an African-American female and a white female. Both candidates are equally qualified. The position is responsible for five white team leaders. You hire the white female because the work group likes her. The team leaders said that they felt more comfortable with the white female. The vice president of human resources has just called you on the phone and asks you to explain why you hired the white female.

A. How would you respond?

_____
_____

B. What is the potential impact of not hiring the African-American?

_____
_____

C. What is the potential impact of hiring the African-American?

_____
_____
_____

Scenario 3

> While attending an off-site business meeting, you are waiting in line with a group of team leaders to get your lunch at a buffet. Without any forewarning, one of your peers in the line loudly says, "Thank goodness Terry is at the end of the line. With his size and appetite there wouldn't be any food left for the rest of us." You believe Terry may have heard this comment, and you feel the comment was more of a "weight-related" slur than a joke.
>
> A. How would you respond?
>
> _____
>
> _____
>
> B. What is the potential impact of your response?
>
> _____
>
> _____
>
> _____
>
> C. If you choose not to respond, what is the potential impact of your behavior?
>
> _____
>
> _____
>
> _____

Questions for Discussion

1. What was the recommended response for each scenario?

2. Which scenario generated the most emotion and disagreement? Explain why this occurred.

3. What is the potential impact of a manager's lack of response to Scenarios 1 and 3? Explain.

Ethical Dilemma

An Employee Sues Georgia Power for Race Discrimination[90]

In more than a quarter century as an African-American lineman at one of the South's biggest electric companies, Cornelius Cooper says he abided a stream of racial indignities. He says he was passed over for promotions, subjected to racial slurs, and repeatedly spray-painted in his genital area by white employees. Worse, co-workers made light of lynchings, tied hangman's nooses in his presence, and often left such knots displayed in company facilities.

"You didn't do anything but smile, even though it was intimidating to the max," Mr Cooper said in an interview last week.

In July, Mr Cooper and two others filed a lawsuit alleging that managers at Georgia Power Co. and its parent, Southern Co., unfairly denied promotions to African-American workers, gave lower pay to black employees than to similarly qualified whites, and were indifferent to overt harassment of blacks. Attached to the charges, which the companies vigorously deny, was an 8-by-10 color photograph of a noose hanging inside a company building in Cornelia, Ga.

Executives at Georgia Power and its parent company were taken aback. But their surprise wasn't at finding a noose on the premises; it was in discovering that African-Americans could be offended by one.

"I had no earthly idea that anybody today would consider that to be a racial symbol. None whatsoever," testified former Southern Chairman and Chief Executive Officer A. W. "Bill" Dahlberg in a deposition given for the case on January 30. . . .

An internal investigation conducted by the company in response to the suit discovered a total of 13 ropes tied as nooses of varying types in eight Georgia Power facilities, according to court filings. The company said it couldn't account for the origins of all the nooses, some of which had been displayed for several years, but insists that only one of the nooses it found appeared to have been an intentional effort to intimidate a black worker. . . .

Mr Cooper's decision to challenge his employer of 27 years came early in 2000, after his ninth try at being promoted to a mid-level management job since becoming a full-fledged lineman in the mid-1970s. Utility linemen repair or install electric power cables running on poles and underground. Mr Cooper, 49 years old and graying at the temples, had long hoped to move into a job training other linemen—which would have boosted his annual earnings to about $60,000 from the approximately $43,000 he makes currently. Every time he was turned down, managers told him he needed another training class or should polish a particular skill. At the suggestion of a supervisor, Mr Cooper, who continues to work at Georgia Power, took a company-organized class on interview techniques. Told by the instructor "you have to sell yourself," he decided to be "more confident" in his next job interview. He still didn't get the job. Mr Cooper says he later was told that one of the managers in the session thought he acted like he "could walk on water."

What would you do if you were the chief executive officer at Georgia Power?

1. Fight the discrimination case and do not implement any special diversity training.

2. Fight the case and implement diversity awareness training and internal network and support groups.

3. Admit wrongdoing, settle the suit, and implement diversity awareness training and internal network and support groups.

4. Invent other options. Discuss.

For an interpretation of this situation, visit our Web site, **www.mhhe.com/kreitner.**

Chapter Three

Organizational Culture, Socialization, and Mentoring

Learning Objectives

When you finish studying the material in this chapter, you should be able to:

1 Define organizational culture and discuss its three layers.

2 Discuss the difference between espoused and enacted values.

3 Describe the manifestations and functions of an organization's culture.

4 Discuss the three general types of organizational culture and their associated normative beliefs.

5 Explain the three perspectives proposed to explain the type of cultures that enhance an organization's financial performance.

6 Discuss the process of developing an adaptive culture.

7 Summarize the methods used by organizations to embed their cultures.

8 Describe the three phases in Feldman's model of organizational socialization.

9 Discuss the various socialization tactics used to socialize employees.

10 Explain the four developmental networks associated with mentoring.

www.yahoo.com

They were the most successful sextet [Jerry Yang, David Filo, Tim Brady, Ellem Siminoff, Anil Singh, and Jeff Mallett] of the Internet boom. . . . Their company, Yahoo! Inc., rocketed to a market value of $134 billion, and the young leaders became legends, defining Silicon Valley start-up life. . . . On Wednesday [March 7, 2001] the game abruptly ended. With its stock down 92% from its peak and advertising sales plunging, Yahoo said it would launch a search for a new chief executive from outside the company. . . . The unexpected move amounted to a humbling acknowledgment of something people close to Yahoo have increasingly been saying: that the tight-knit, us-against-the-world management style that fueled Yahoo's astronomical rise may also have exacerbated its decline.

"Their culture helped them build a superb site and a really edgy brand, but it also held them back from making forward-looking business decisions," says Holly Becker, an analyst at Lehman Brothers. "The culture that served them so incredibly well until the middle of last year is now letting them down."

Business partners and former executives say the small group's intense closeness made it hard for Yahoo to retain or attract experienced managers. Over a long acquisition spree, Yahoo spent billions to buy GeoCities Inc., Broadcast.com, and numerous smaller companies—yet many of the

David Filo and Jerry Yang, founders of Yahoo! circa 1998 before the company's insular management style exacerbated its future decline.
(c) 1998 Ed Kashi/CORBIS

targets' top executives wound up leaving Yahoo, unable to penetrate its inner sanctum. Yahoo's top European and Asian executives and a slew of middle managers also left, amid complaints that the top team wouldn't delegate authority.

"They're very insular," says Stephen Hansen, former chief financial officer at GeoCities, a company acquired by Yahoo in 1999. "They see the world through the Yahoo lens.". . .

When the dot-com boom arrived, Yahoo was besieged by companies begging to advertise on its site. It went on a hiring binge. From 386 employees in 1997, it went to 803 in 1998 and 1,992 in 1999.

That's when Yahoo's management style began to look like a liability, some advertisers say. A sense developed that

decisions always had to go to the top. New employees, often fresh out of school and sometimes ill-informed, were always having to check with higher-ups before agreeing to terms.

"You can't run a 3,000-person company, a $2 billion company, with a core management team of four or five people," says Bill Bishop, co-founder and executive vice president of CBS Marketwatch Inc., a Yahoo advertiser. "It doesn't work."[1]

For Discussion
How would you describe the organizational culture at Yahoo?

The opening vignette highlights the role of organizational culture in contributing to organizational effectiveness. At Yahoo, the organizational culture was an asset as the company formed and grew. Over time, however, the culture became a liability because it fostered a bureaucratic environment in which senior management failed to delegate and empower employees. This example also underscores that an organization's culture originates from the values and beliefs of its founders and it can be very difficult, if not impossible to change.

Much has been written and said about organizational culture in recent years. This interest grew from the acknowledgment that an organization's culture could significantly influence an organization's short- and long-term success. Carol Lavin Bernick, president of Alberto-Culver North America, for example, speculated about this possibility. She believed her company's organizational culture was contributing to flattened sales, slipping profit margins, and a turnover rate twice the industry average.

> It wasn't our people who were to blame; Culver employees have always been decent, and hardworking. It was our culture. We needed people to have a sense of ownership and urgency around the business, to welcome innovation and take risks. But in the existing culture, people dutifully waited for marching orders and thought of their bosses' needs before their customers'. Through long-standing practice, rooted in good intentions, we had sheltered our people from our detailed operating results and all the business realities that drove them. In doing so, we had denied them the knowledge and perspective that could make them our true business partners in growing the business.[2]

Bernick was correct. Alberto-Culver's organization culture subtly and systematically led to decreased innovation and risk taking over time. The good news, however, is that a negative or inappropriate culture can be changed or modified. Bernick was able to turn the company around by implementing significant cultural change. This example reinforces how important it is for present and future managers to become aware of the dynamics associated with organizational culture. Organizational culture is not something to be taken for granted. As noted by Herb Kelleher, former CEO of Southwest Airlines, "culture is one of the most precious things a company has so you must work harder at it than anything else."[3]

This chapter will help you better understand how managers can use organizational culture as a competitive advantage. After defining and discussing the context of organizational culture, we examine (1) the dynamics of organizational culture, (2) the development of a high-performance culture, (3) the organization socialization process, and (4) the embedding of organizational culture through mentoring.

Organizational Culture: Definition and Context

Organizational culture is "the set of shared, taken-for-granted implicit assumptions that a group holds and that determines how it perceives, thinks about, and reacts to its various environments."[4] This definition highlights three important characteristics of organizational culture. First, organizational culture is passed on to new employees through the process of socialization, a topic discussed later in this chapter. Second, organizational culture influences our behavior at work. Finally, organizational culture operates at different levels.

Figure 3–1 provides a conceptual framework for reviewing the widespread impact organizational culture has on organizational behavior.[5] It also shows the linkage between this chapter—culture, socialization, and mentoring—and other key topics in this book. Figure 3–1 reveals organizational culture is shaped by four key components: the founders' values, the industry and business environment, the national culture, and the senior leaders' vision and behavior. In turn, organizational culture influences the type of organizational structure adopted by a company and a host of practices, policies, and procedures implemented in pursuit of organizational goals. These organizational characteristics then affect a variety of group and social processes. This sequence ultimately affects employees' attitudes and behavior and a variety of organizational outcomes. All told, Figure 3–1 reveals that organizational culture is a contextual variable influencing individual, group, and organizational behavior.

Organizational culture
Shared values and beliefs that underlie a company's identity.

Figure 3–1   *A Conceptual Framework for Understanding Organizational Culture*

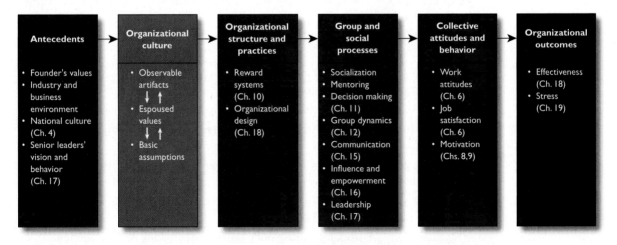

SOURCE: Adapted in part from C Ostroff, A Kinicki, and M Tamkins, "Organizational Culture and Climate," in *Comprehensive Handbook of Psychology*, vol 12, eds WC Burman, DR Ilgen, and RJ Klimoski (New York: Wiley and Sons, in press).

Dynamics of Organizational Culture

To gain a better understanding of how organizational culture is formed and used by employees, this section begins by discussing the layers of organizational culture. We then review the manifestation of organizational culture, the four functions of organizational culture, types of organizational culture, and research on organizational culture.

Layers of Organizational Culture

Figure 3–1 shows the three fundamental layers of organizational culture: observable artifacts, espoused values, and basic assumptions. Each level varies in terms of outward visibility and resistance to change, and each level influences another level.

Observable Artifacts   At the more visible level, culture represents observable artifacts. Artifacts consist of the physical manifestation of an organization's culture. Organizational examples include acronyms, manner of dress, awards, myths and stories told about the organization, published lists of values, observable rituals and ceremonies, special parking spaces, decorations, and so on. This level also includes visible behaviors exhibited by people and groups. Artifacts are easier to change than the less visible aspects of organizational culture.

Values

Enduring belief in a mode of conduct or end-state.

Espoused Values   Values possess five key components. "**Values** (1) are concepts or beliefs, (2) pertain to desirable end-states or behaviors, (3) transcend situations, (4) guide selection or evaluation of behavior and events, and (5) are ordered by relative importance."[6] It is important to distinguish between values that are espoused versus those that are enacted.

Espoused values

The stated values and norms that are preferred by an organization.

Espoused values represent the explicitly stated values and norms that are preferred by an organization. They are generally established by the founder of a new or small company and by the top management team in a larger organization. For example, executives from AOL Time Warner met shortly after the two companies merged in January 2001 to establish a new set of values for the combined company. The AOL Time Warner values are as follows:

- *Creativity.* We strive on initiative and originality—encouraging risk taking and divergent voices.
- *Customer focus.* We value all of our customers—putting their needs and interests at the center of everything we do.
- *Agility.* We move quickly—embracing change and seizing new opportunities.
- *Teamwork.* We treat each other with respect—creating value by working together and across our businesses.
- *Integrity.* We rigorously uphold editorial independence and artistic expression—earning the trust of our readers, viewers, listeners, members, and subscribers.
- *Diversity.* We attract and develop the world's best talent—seeking to include the broadest range of people and perspectives.
- *Responsibility.* We work to improve our communities—taking pride in serving the public interest as well as the interest of our shareholders.[7]

Because espoused values such as those at AOL Time Warner represent aspirations that are explicitly communicated to employees, managers hope that espoused values will directly influence employee behavior. Unfortunately, aspirations do not automatically produce the desired behaviors because people do not always "walk the talk."

Enacted values, on the other hand, represent the values and norms that actually are exhibited or converted into employee behavior. Let us consider the difference between these two types of values. Home Depot, for instance, has espoused that it values customer service and safety. If the organization displays customer service and safety through its store layouts and behavior of employees, then the espoused value is enacted and individual behavior is being influenced by the values of customer service and safety. Unfortunately, Home Depot appears to have a discrepancy between its espoused and enacted values:

> "Home Depot advertises having the best customer service, but it seems like everybody is so busy," says Priscilla High, a customer shopping in Atlanta recently for a rug and kitchen sink. "Lowe's [a Home Depot rival] has more customer service." . . . [A]s sales volumes soared and product lines expanded in recent years, that busy warehouse action became a liability. Shoppers complained that pallets of merchandise cluttered the aisles. Injuries from falling merchandise grabbed headlines. And the company says many employees became more concerned with stocking socket wrenches than helping customers. . . . On a recent morning at a Home Depot near Stone Mountain, [Georgia], assistant manager Jill Roberts found three pallets of space heaters clogging an aisle of kitchen sinks and plumbing supplies. . . . Another priority for Home Depot is improved store safety in the wake of three deaths last year [2000] and other injuries caused by falling merchandise.[8]

It is important to reduce gaps between espoused and enacted values because they can significantly influence employee attitudes and organizational performance. For example, a study of 312 British rail drivers revealed that employees were more cynical about safety when they believed that senior managers' behaviors were inconsistent with the stated values regarding safety.[9] Home Depot is aware of this important issue and has instituted a program labeled Service Performance Improvement, or SPI, to reduce the gap between espoused and enacted values regarding customer service and safety. Preliminary results from six test stores indicated increases in store sales and the amount of time store employees spent helping customers.[10]

Basic Assumptions
Basic underlying assumptions are unobservable and represent the core of organizational culture. They constitute organizational values that have become so taken for granted over time that they become assumptions that guide organizational behavior. They thus are highly resistant to change. When basic assumptions are widely held among employees, people will find behavior based on an inconsistent value inconceivable. Southwest Airlines, for example, is noted for operating according to basic assumptions that value employees' welfare and providing high-quality service. Employees at Southwest Airlines would be shocked to see management act in ways that did not value employees' and customers' needs.

Practical Application of Research on Values
Organizations subscribe to a constellation of values rather than to only one and can be profiled according to their values.[11] This enables managers to determine whether or not the organization's values are consistent and supportive of its corporate goals and initiatives. Organizations are less likely to accomplish their corporate goals when employees perceive an inconsistency between espoused values (e.g., honesty) and the behaviors needed to accomplish the goals (e.g., shredding financial documents). Similarly, organizational change is unlikely to succeed if it is based on a set of values highly inconsistent with employees' individual values.[12]

Enacted values

The values and norms that are exhibited by employees.

OB Exercise   Manifestations of Organizational Culture at Setpoint

Instructions

Read the following description and answer the discussion questions. Answers can be found following the Endnotes for this chapter at the end of the book.

> Setpoint's CEO, Joe Knight, met them [Steve Petersen and Ted Johnstun, president and chief financial officer at Petersen Inc.] in the lobby and took them on a tour of the facility.... Petersen says he was standing there surveying the scene, when he happened to notice a large whiteboard off to one side, on a wall next to a canteen area in a corner of the shop. Scribbled across the board were about 20 rows and 10 columns of numbers forming a table of sort, with a few dollar signs sprinkled here and there.
>
> "What's that?" he asked.
>
> "That's our board," Knight said. "It's how we track our projects and figure out whether or not we're making money." ...
>
> For one thing, almost half of its [Setpoint] workforce—including its two founders—are dirt-bike fanatics, and they regularly go riding together in the mountains around Ogden, Utah, where Setpoint is located. On the bulletin board in the shop are photographs of various employees flying through the air on their motorcycles....
>
> Somehow it [Setpoint] has built a culture that has everyone involved in the process of controlling cash. The process begins with Setpoint's management system, which allows people throughout the company to track their progress on specific projects with an extraordinarily high degree of accuracy....
>
> Life at Setpoint has changed, everyone agrees, since the introduction of the board and the weekly huddle. "Before that, we had monthly meetings to go over the numbers, but it was too little, too late," says Ken Waudby, the shop manager.
>
> Now there's a huddle every Monday at 11 A.M. "[But] we don't just look at the budget and the hours on Monday," says Brad Stryker, a project engineer. "We monitor them throughout the week, and we make decisions based on them." ...
>
> When it comes to leveraging resources, moreover, the technicians on the shop floor are as focused as the engineers. "I watch GP [gross profit] per hour," says Johnny Lane, a technician.... But do people actually talk about their GP per hour while they're working? "Oh, yeah, sure," says Lane. "We discuss it all the time."
>
> That's true, says Waudby, "Like someone will say, 'I worked my butt off, and we only made $50 an hour.' People are always talking about the hours."
>
> That's the most interesting part: the process itself serves as a motivator. "It keeps you involved and lets you understand your impact," says Lyman Houston, a project engineer. "I like to know what condition jobs are in, and why, and what I can do about it. That totally interests and motivates me."

Discussion Questions

1. Identify the shared things, sayings, doings, and feelings at Setpoint.

2. Does Setpoint's culture attempt to control employees or does it allow them freedom to act as they see fit? Explain.

SOURCE: Excerpted from B Burlingham, "What's Your Culture Worth?" *Inc.*, September 2001, pp 126, 128, 130.

Manifestations of Organizational Culture

When is an organization's culture most apparent? In addition to the physical artifacts of organizational culture that were previously discussed, cultural assumptions assert themselves through socialization of new employees, subculture clashes, and top management behavior. Consider these three situations, for example: A newcomer who shows up late for an important meeting is told a story about someone who was fired for repeated tardiness. Conflict between product design engineers who emphasize a product's function and marketing specialists who demand a more stylish product reveals an underlying clash of subculture values. Top managers, through the behavior they model and the administrative and reward systems they create, prompt a significant improvement in the quality of a company's products. These examples illustrate that an organization's culture can show itself in a variety of ways.

Vijay Sathe, a Harvard researcher, identified four general manifestations or evidence of organizational culture. They are shared things (objects), shared sayings (talk), shared doings (behavior), and shared feelings (emotion).[13] One can begin collecting cultural information within an organization by asking, observing, reading, and feeling.

The OB Exercise on page 84 provides you with the opportunity to practice identifying the manifestations of organizational culture at Setpoint, a custom-manufacturing company with 30 employees and $6 million in sales.

Four Functions of Organizational Culture

As illustrated in Figure 3–2, an organization's culture fulfills four functions. To help bring these functions to life, let us consider how each of them has taken shape at Southwest Airlines. Southwest is a particularly instructive example because it has grown to become the fourth-largest US airline since its inception in 1971 and has achieved 30 consecutive years of profitability. Since 1997, *Fortune* has ranked Southwest Airlines in the top five of the best companies to work for in America. Southwest also was ranked

Figure 3–2   *Four Functions of Organizational Culture*

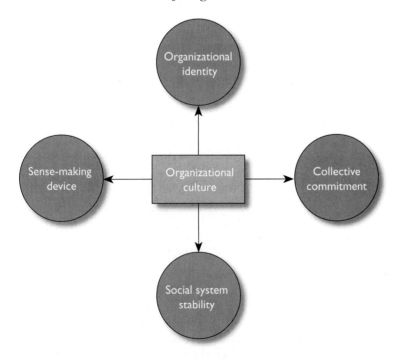

SOURCE: Adapted from discussion in L Smircich, "Concepts of Culture and Organizational Analysis," *Administrative Science Quarterly,* September 1983, pp 339–58. Reproduced by permission of John Wiley & Sons, Limited.

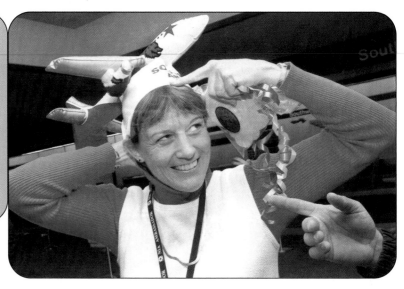

as the second most admired company in the United States by *Fortune* in 2002, partly due to its strong and distinctive culture.[14]

1. *Give members an organizational identity.* Southwest Airlines is known as a fun place to work that values employee satisfaction and customer loyalty over corporate profits. Herb Kelleher, former CEO and current chairman of the board, commented on this issue.

   > Who comes first? The employees, customers, or shareholders? That's never been an issue to me. The employees come first. If they're happy, satisfied, dedicated, and energetic, they'll take real good care of the customers. When the customers are happy, they come back. And that makes the shareholders happy.[15]

   The company also has a catastrophe fund based on voluntary contributions for distribution to employees who are experiencing serious personal difficulties. Southwest's people-focused identity is reinforced by the fact that it is an employer of choice. For example, Southwest received 194,821 resumes and hired 6,406 new employees in 2001. The company also was noted as an employer of choice among college students by *Fortune,* and a survey of MBA students by consulting firm Universum revealed that Southwest Airlines was among the top 50 most coveted employers.

2. *Facilitate collective commitment.* The mission of Southwest Airlines "is dedication to the highest quality of Customer Service delivered with a sense of warmth, friendliness, individual pride, and Company Spirit."[16] Southwest's more than 35,000 employees are committed to this mission. The Department of Transportation's Air Travel Consumer Report reported Southwest was ranked number one in fewest customer complaints for the last 11 consecutive years.[17]

3. *Promote social system stability.* Social system stability reflects the extent to which the work environment is perceived as positive and reinforcing, and conflict and change are managed effectively. Southwest is noted for its philosophy of having fun, having parties, and celebrating. For example, each city in which the firm operates is given a budget for parties. Southwest also uses a variety of performance-based awards and service awards to reinforce employees. The company's positive

and enriching environment is supported by the lowest turnover rates in the airline industry and the employment of 1,000 married couples.

4. *Shape behavior by helping members make sense of their surroundings.* This function of culture helps employees understand why the organization does what it does and how it intends to accomplish its long-term goals. Keeping in mind that Southwest's leadership originally viewed ground transportation as their main competitor in 1971, employees come to understand why the airline's primary vision is to be the best primarily short-haul, low-fare, high-frequency, point-to-point carrier in the United States. Employees understand they must achieve exceptional performance, such as turning a plane in 20 minutes, because they must keep costs down in order to compete against Greyhound and the use of automobiles. In turn, the company reinforces the importance of outstanding customer service and high performance expectations by using performance-based awards and profit sharing. Employees own about 10% of the company stock.

Types of Organizational Culture

Researchers have attempted to identify and measure various types of organizational culture in order to study the relationship between types of culture and organizational effectiveness. This pursuit was motivated by the possibility that certain cultures were more effective than others. Unfortunately, research has not uncovered a universal typology of cultural styles that everyone accepts.[18] Just the same, there is value in providing an example of various types of organizational culture. Table 3–1 is thus presented as an illustration rather than a definitive conclusion about the types of organizational culture that exist. Awareness of these types provides you with greater understanding about the manifestations of culture.

Table 3–1 shows that there are three general types of organizational culture—constructive, passive–defensive, and aggressive–defensive—and that each type is associated with a different set of normative beliefs.[19] **Normative beliefs** represent an individual's thoughts and beliefs about how members of a particular group or organization are expected to approach their work and interact with others. A *constructive culture* is one in which employees are encouraged to interact with others and to work on tasks and projects in ways that will assist them in satisfying their needs to grow and develop. This type of culture endorses normative beliefs associated with achievement, self-actualizing, humanistic-encouraging, and affiliative. In contrast, a *passive–defensive culture* is characterized by an overriding belief that employees must interact with others in ways that do not threaten their own job security. This culture reinforces the normative beliefs associated with approval, conventional, dependent, and avoidance (see Table 3–1). Finally, companies with an *aggressive–defensive culture* encourage employees to approach tasks in forceful ways in order to protect their status and job security. This type of culture is more characteristic of normative beliefs reflecting oppositional, power, competitive, and perfectionist.

Although an organization may predominately represent one cultural type, it still can manifest normative beliefs and characteristics from the others. Research demonstrates that organizations can have functional subcultures, hierarchical subcultures based on one's level in the organization, geographical subcultures, occupational subcultures based on one's title or position, social subcultures derived from social activities such as a bowling or golf league and a reading club, and countercultures.[20] It is important

Normative beliefs
Thoughts and beliefs about expected behavior and modes of conduct.

Table 3–1 *Types of Organizational Culture*

General Types of Culture	Normative Beliefs	Organizational Characteristics
Constructive	Achievement	Organizations that do things well and value members who set and accomplish their own goals. Members are expected to set challenging but realistic goals, establish plans to reach these goals, and pursue them with enthusiasm. (Pursuing a standard of excellence)
Constructive	Self-actualizing	Organizations that value creativity, quality over quantity, and both task accomplishment and individual growth. Members are encouraged to gain enjoyment from their work, develop themselves, and take on new and interesting activities. (Thinking in unique and independent ways)
Constructive	Humanistic-encouraging	Organizations that are managed in a participative and person-centered way. Members are expected to be supportive, constructive, and open to influence in their dealings with one another. (Helping others to grow and develop)
Constructive	Affiliative	Organizations that place a high priority on constructive interpersonal relationships. Members are expected to be friendly, open, and sensitive to the satisfaction of their work group. (Dealing with others in a friendly way)
Passive–defensive	Approval	Organizations in which conflicts are avoided and interpersonal relationships are pleasant—at least superficially. Members feel that they should agree with, gain the approval of, and be liked by others. ("Going along" with others)
Passive–defensive	Conventional	Organizations that are conservative, traditional, and bureaucratically controlled. Members are expected to conform, follow the rules, and make a good impression. (Always following policies and practices)
Passive–defensive	Dependent	Organizations that are hierarchically controlled and nonparticipative. Centralized decision making in such organizations leads members to do only what they are told and to clear all decisions with superiors. (Pleasing those in positions of authority)
Passive–defensive	Avoidance	Organizations that fail to reward success but nevertheless punish mistakes. This negative reward system leads members to shift responsibilities to others and avoid any possibility of being blamed for a mistake. (Waiting for others to act first)
Aggressive–defensive	Oppositional	Organizations in which confrontation and negativism are rewarded. Members gain status and influence by being critical and thus are reinforced to oppose the ideas of others. (Pointing out flaws)
Aggressive–defensive	Power	Nonparticipative organizations structured on the basis of the authority inherent in members' positions. Members believe they will be rewarded for taking charge, controlling subordinates and, at the same time, being responsive to the demands of superiors. (Building up one's power base)
Aggressive–defensive	Competitive	Winning is valued and members are rewarded for outperforming one another. Members operate in a "win–lose" framework and believe they must work against (rather than with) their peers to be noticed. (Turning the job into a contest)
Aggressive–defensive	Perfectionistic	Organizations in which perfectionism, persistence, and hard work are valued. Members feel they must avoid any mistake, keep track of everything, and work long hours to attain narrowly defined objectives. (Doing things perfectly)

SOURCE: Reproduced with permission of authors and publisher from R A Cooke and J L Szumal, "Measuring Normative Beliefs and Shared Behavioral Expectations in Organizations: The Reliability and Validity of the Organizational Culture Inventory," *Psychological Reports*, 1993, vol 72, pp 1299–330. © *Psychological Reports*, 1993.

for managers to be aware of the possibility that conflict between subgroups that form subcultures can undermine an organization's overall performance.

Research on Organizational Cultures

Because the concept of organizational culture is a relatively recent addition to OB, the research base is incomplete. Studies to date are characterized by inconsistent definitions and varied methodologies. Quantitative treatments are sparse because there is little agreement on how to measure cultural variables. As a matter of convenience, we review two streams of organizational culture research in this section. One stream has been reported in best-selling books and the other in research journal articles.[21]

Anecdotal Evidence from Best-Selling Books about Organizational Culture   Initial widespread interest in organizational cultures was stirred by William Ouchi's 1981 best-seller, *Theory Z: How American Business Can Meet the Japanese Challenge.* From a research standpoint, Ouchi's two main contributions were (1) focusing attention on internal culture as a key determinant of organizational effectiveness and (2) developing an instructive typology of organizations based in part on cultural variables.[22]

Close on the heels of Ouchi's book came two 1982 best-sellers: Deal and Kennedy's *Corporate Cultures: The Rites and Rituals of Corporate Life*[23] and Peters and Waterman's *In Search of Excellence.*[24] Both books drew upon interviews and the authors' consulting experience. Each team of authors relied on abundant anecdotal evidence to make the point that successful companies tend to have strong cultures. For example, Peters and Waterman observed:

> Without exception, the dominance and coherence of culture proved to be an essential quality of the excellent companies. Moreover, the stronger the culture and the more it was directed toward the marketplace, the less need was there for policy manuals, organization charts, or detailed procedures and rules. In these companies, people way down the line know what they are supposed to do in most situations because the handful of guiding values is crystal clear.[25]

These best-sellers generated excitement about cultural factors such as heroes and stories. They also generated the impression that organizations have one distinct culture. As previously discussed, few people accept this generic conclusion. Finally, these best-sellers failed to break any new ground in the measurement and evaluation of organizational cultures.

Evidence from Research Articles and Management Implications
Both managers and academic researchers believe that organizational culture can be a driver of employee attitudes and organizational effectiveness and performance. To test this possibility, various measures of organizational culture have been correlated with a variety of individual and organizational outcomes.[26] We have learned four key conclusions from this research. First, several studies demonstrated that organizational culture was significantly correlated with employee attitudes and behavior. For example, a constructive culture (see the description in Table 3–1) was positively related with motivation, job satisfaction, teamwork, considerate leadership, quality of customer service, and performance and was negatively associated with work avoidance, stress, and a supervisor's use of criticism. In contrast, passive–defensive and aggressive–defensive cultures (see Table 3–1) were negatively correlated with motivation, job satisfaction,

teamwork, participation in goal setting, autonomy, and quality of work relations and positively with a supervisor's use of criticism and centralized decision making.[27] These results suggest that employees seem to prefer organizations that encourage people to interact and work with others in ways that assist them in satisfying their needs to grow and develop.

Second, results from several studies revealed the congruence between an individual's values and the organization's values was significantly associated with organizational commitment, job satisfaction, intentions to quit, and turnover.[28] These results should encourage you to consider the similarity between your values and those possessed by potential employers when you apply for future jobs. Everything else equal, select the company with which your values are most aligned.

Third, a summary of 10 quantitative studies showed that organizational culture did not predict an organization's financial performance.[29] This means that there is not one type of organizational culture that fuels financial performance. That said, however, a study of 207 companies for an 11-year period demonstrated that financial performance was higher among companies that had adaptive and flexible cultures.[30] The explanation for this important relationship is discussed in the next section on developing high-performance cultures.

Finally, studies of mergers indicated they frequently failed due to incompatible cultures. Due to the increasing number of corporate mergers around the world, and the conclusion that 7 out of 10 mergers and acquisitions failed to meet their financial promise, managers within merged companies would be well advised to consider the role of organizational culture in creating a new organization.[31]

In summary, these results underscore the significance of organizational culture. They also reinforce the need to learn more about the process of cultivating and changing an organization's culture. An organization's culture is not determined by fate. It is formed and shaped by the combination and integration of everyone who works in the organization. As a case in point, a longitudinal study of 322 employees working in a governmental organization revealed that managerial intervention successfully shifted the organizational culture toward greater participation and employee involvement. This change in organizational culture was associated with improved job satisfaction and communication across all hierarchical levels.[32] This study further highlights the interplay between organizational culture and organizational change. Successful organizational change is highly dependent on an organization's culture.[33] A change-resistant culture, for instance, can undermine the effectiveness of any type of organizational change. Although it is not an easy task to change an organization's culture, the next section provides a preliminary overview of how this might be done.

Developing High-Performance Cultures

An organization's culture may be strong or weak, depending on variables such as cohesiveness, value consensus, and individual commitment to collective goals. Contrary to what one might suspect, a strong culture is not necessarily a good thing. The nature of the culture's central values is more important than its strength. For example, a strong but change-resistant culture may be worse, from the standpoint of profitability and competitiveness, than a weak but innovative culture. This section discusses the type of organizational cultures that enhance an organization's financial performance and the process by which cultures are embedded in an organization and learned by employees.

What Type of Cultures Enhance an Organization's Financial Performance?

Three perspectives have been proposed to explain the type of cultures that enhance an organization's economic performance. They are referred to as the strength, fit, and adaptive perspectives, respectively:

1. The **strength perspective** predicts a significant relationship between strength of corporate culture and long-term financial performance. The idea is that strong cultures create goal alignment, employee motivation, and needed structure and controls to improve organizational performance.[34] Critics of this perspective believe that companies with a strong culture can become arrogant, inwardly focused, and bureaucratic after they achieve financial success because financial success reinforces the strong culture. This reinforcement can blind senior managers to the need for new strategic plans and may result in a general resistance to change.

2. The **fit perspective** is based on the premise that an organization's culture must align with its business or strategic context. For example, a culture that promotes standardization and planning might work well in a slow-growing industry but be totally inappropriate for Internet companies that work in a highly volatile and changing environment. Consider how Ed Siciliano described the difference between working at Xerox and at Applied Theory, an Internet service provider based on Long Island, New York:

   > "At Xerox, you're following a well-defined process for just about everything," he says. At Applied Theory, "you don't have time to haul out the guidebook." At Xerox, for example, he held monthly sales reviews with each salesperson. At his new job [at Applied Theory], "you grab people in the hallway, the lunchroom, or on the weekend and that's where you have your discussion of sales prospects," he says. He also dropped the lengthy, Xerox-style sales reports he prepared for superiors each month because nobody read them.[35]

   Likewise, a culture in which individual performance is valued might help a sales organization but would undermine performance in an organization where people work in teams. Accordingly, there is no one best culture. A culture is predicted to facilitate economic performance only if it "fits" its context.

3. The **adaptive perspective** assumes that the most effective cultures help organizations anticipate and adapt to environmental changes. A team of management experts defined this culture as follows:

   > An adaptive culture entails a risk-taking, trusting, and proactive approach to organizational as well as individual life. Members actively support one another's efforts to identify all problems and implement workable solutions. There is a shared feeling of confidence: The members believe, without a doubt, that they can effectively manage whatever new problems and opportunities will come their way. There is widespread enthusiasm, a spirit of doing whatever it takes to achieve organizational success. The members are receptive to change and innovation.[36]

Strength perspective
Assumes that the strength of corporate culture is related to a firm's financial performance.

Fit perspective
Assumes that culture must align with its business or strategic context.

Adaptive perspective
Assumes that adaptive cultures enhance a firm's financial performance.

This proactive adaptability is expected to enhance long-term financial performance.

The International OB discusses the struggles occurring within Deutsche Bank as it attempts to become more adaptable. Contrary to this example, adaptability requires senior leaders to cooperate and collaborate among themselves.

Deutsche Bank's Attempt to Adapt Creates Internal Conflict

Late last year, Deutsche Bank's 40 top managers met in a castle-turned-hotel near here [Frankfurt]. The stage was set for the traditional elements of corporate retreats in Germany: long dry speeches, and due respect for the Vorstand, a management council dedicated to consensus.

Josef Ackermann, head of Deutsche Bank is attempting to turn around the company's decreasing net income. Part of his challenge involves internal struggles associated with changing Deutsche Bank's culture. What steps should Ackermann take in order to develop and preserve an adaptable culture?

(c) Sean Gallup/Getty Images

Not this time. Michael Philipp, a boisterous former Merrill Lynch banker who heads Deutsche's fund-management business, launched a tirade against the way the bank was run. The Vorstand should be scrapped, he said, according to people present at the meeting. All council members including himself should resign to make way for a clear, US-style hierarchical leadership, where the boss makes the decisions and takes the rap.

The outburst was just one sign of a struggle under way inside the world's second-biggest bank as it takes big steps to shed its German past....

The traditionalists haven't gone quietly. Vorstand member Thomas Fischer, who once challenged Mr Ackermann for the top job but lost, campaigned inside the bank against Mr Ackermann's plan to downgrade the Vorstand and hand yet more power to the investment bankers.

At the New York Stock Exchange last September when Deutsche Bank listed its shares, Mr Fischer wore a stars-and-stripes waistcoat and bow tie, but he showed his true colors a few months later. In internal meetings last month, Mr Fischer defended Deutsche's German culture and attacked its creeping Americanization, according to colleagues.

Source: M Walker, "Making Its Mark: Deutsche Bank Finds That It Has to Cut German Roots to Grow," *The Wall Street Journal*, February 14, 2002, pp A1, A10.

A Test of the Three Perspectives   John Kotter and James Heskett tested the three perspectives on a sample of 207 companies from 22 industries for the period 1977 to 1988. After correlating results from a cultural survey and three different measures of financial performance, results partially supported the strength and fit perspectives. However, findings were completely consistent with the adaptive culture perspective. Long-term financial performance was highest for organizations with an adaptive culture.[37]

Developing an Adaptive Culture   Figure 3–3 illustrates the process of developing and preserving an adaptive culture. The process begins with leadership; that is, leaders must create and implement a business vision and associated strategies that fit the organizational context. A **vision** represents a long-term goal that describes "what" an organization wants to become. Consider how Medtronic Inc. has successfully modified its vision and adapted through the years. When William George, chairman and CEO of Medtronic, joined the company in 1989 it was a $1 billion company, with the majority of sales coming from pacemakers. Today, the company has $5 billion in sales and is worth $63 billion.

Vision

Long-term goal describing "what" an organization wants to become.

> During the 12 years I have been with Medtronic, we have used a dynamic business strategy that is adaptable to changing business conditions. Around the company, we use the

Figure 3–3   *Developing and Preserving an Adaptive Culture*

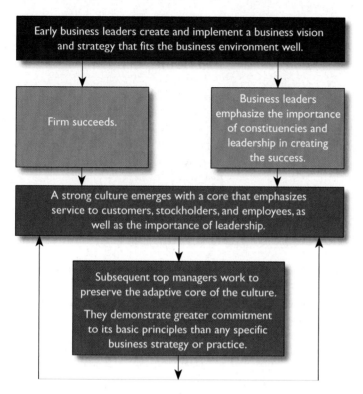

SOURCE: Adapted with permission of the Free Press, an imprint of Simon & Schuster Adult Publishing Group, from *Corporate Culture and Performance* by John P Kotter and James L Heskett. Copyright © 1992 by Kotter Associates, Inc and James L Heskett.

phrase "reinventing Medtronic" to describe this process. Every five years, Medtronic is completely reinvented in terms of our business and our strategies, such that the business does not look anything like it did five years before.

From the time I joined Medtronic in 1989 until 1994, we saw a complete transformation from the pacemaker company of the first 40 years to a broadly based cardiovascular company.... Within the next five years, we introduced revolutionary new therapies for cardiac surgery, aortic aneurysms, spasticity, essential tremor, spinal and neurological surgery, and ear, nose, and throat surgery. Thus, by 1999, we could legitimately claim to be the world's leading medical technology company.

By 2004, Medtronic will be transformed once again, thanks to the dramatic innovations and treatments we will be introducing as part of our unmet-medical-needs strategy. These innovations will provide multiple treatments for heart failure, atrial fibrillation, diabetes, and Parkinson's disease, just to name a few. By 2010, Medtronic will be transformed into a chronic-disease-management company, providing lifelong solutions for people with chronic disease. This is the basis of Medtronic Vision 2010, which includes Internet-based patient-management systems linking patients at home with their specialty physicians.[38]

This example highlights that an adaptive culture is promoted over time by a combination of organizational success and a specific leadership focus.

Medtronic Inc. uses a dynamic business strategy adaptable to changing business conditions. The company, with its majority of past sales coming from pacemakers such as the one Sung Lee, Dick Cheney's doctor implanted in 2001, reinvents itself every five years in terms of its business and strategies. Why do you think a clear vision is important in terms of creating an adaptive culture?

(c) Reuters NewMedia Inc./CORBIS

Figure 3–3 shows that leaders must get employees to buy into a timeless philosophy or set of values that emphasizes service to the organization's key constituents—customers, stockholders, and employees—and also emphasizes the improvement of leadership. An infrastructure must then be created to preserve the organization's adaptiveness. Management does this by consistently reinforcing and supporting the organization's core philosophy or values of satisfying constituency needs and improving leadership. This is precisely what Herb Kelleher, former CEO of Southwest Airlines, did at Southwest Airlines.

> Long before "empowerment" became a management buzzword, Ms Barrett [the number two executive at Southwest] was giving employees freedom from centralized policies. She constantly reinforces the company's message that employees should be treated like customers and continually celebrates workers who go above and beyond the call of duty. And when she sensed the carrier was outgrowing its personality-kid-among-the-impersonal-giants image, she created a "culture committee" of employees charged with preserving Southwest's spirit. . . .
>
> Southwest employees are well-paid compared with counterparts at other airlines. Celebrations are an important part of work, from spontaneous "fun sessions" to Christmas parties beginning in September to a lavish annual awards banquet, where the individual's contribution to the whole is glorified.
>
> At the same time, employees work like crazy between festivities. With that formula, the airline has avoided bureaucracy and mediocrity that infect other companies when they outgrow their entrepreneurial roots.[39]

How Cultures Are Embedded in Organizations

An organization's initial culture is an outgrowth of the founder's values and business philosophy. For example, an achievement culture is likely to develop if the founder is an achievement-oriented individual driven by success. Over time, the original culture is either embedded as is or modified to fit the current environmental situation. Edgar Schein, a well-known OB scholar, notes that embedding a culture involves a teaching process. That is, organizational members teach each other about the organization's preferred values, beliefs, expectations, and behaviors. This is accomplished by using one or more of the following mechanisms:[40]

1. *Formal statements of organizational philosophy, mission, vision, values, and materials used for recruiting, selection, and socialization.* Texas Instruments, for example, published a list of corporate values that includes integrity, innovation, and commitment.[41]

2. *The design of physical space, work environments and buildings.* Consider how Acordia Inc. attempted to create a more entrepreneurial culture by building a new one-floor facility.

    The building facilitated interactive workflow procedures. Interactions among new-venture team members and among independent teams became grounded in forming and sharing tacit knowledge. Positive feelings surfacing from these interactions and the knowledge they fostered created positive morale in individuals and between employees and their vice president.[42]

    Entrepreneurial activity ultimately increased as a result of Acordia's new building.

3. *Slogans, language, acronyms, and sayings.* For example, Bank One promotes its desire to provide excellent client service through the slogan "whatever it takes." Employees are encouraged to do whatever it takes to exceed customer expectations.

4. *Deliberate role modeling, training programs, teaching, and coaching by managers and supervisors.* General Semiconductor implemented the "People Plus" program. It is an in-house leadership development and problem-solving training program that uses the company's mission and values as the springboard for creating individual development plans.[43]

5. *Explicit rewards, status symbols (e.g., titles), and promotion criteria.* Consider how Jack Welch, former CEO of General Electric, describes the reward system at General Electric.

    "The top 20% should be rewarded in the soul and wallet because they are the ones who make magic happen. Losing one of these people must be held up as a leadership sin," Welch says. The middle 70% should be energized to improve; the rest should be shown the door. Not getting rid of the 10% early "is not only a management failure, but false kindness as well—a form of cruelty," Welch says. They will wind up being fired eventually and "stranded" in midcareer.[44]

6. *Stories, legends, or myths about key people and events.* Imagine how the following story might be used to reinforce PepsiCo's commitment to its employees.

    Four years ago, the then-chairman and chief executive officer of PepsiCo, Roger A. Enrico, decided that rather than pocket his $900,000 annual salary, he would ask the company's board to use the money to fund scholarships for children of employees who earn less than $60,000 a year. PepsiCo's foundation already was offering scholarships, but Mr Enrico—who is the son of an iron worker and went to college on a scholarship—wanted to enlarge the fund. "I wanted to do something personal to say thanks to front-line employees who make, sell and move our products," he says.[45]

7. *The organizational activities, processes, or outcomes that leaders pay attention to, measure, and control.* Dick Brown, CEO at Electronic Data Systems, believes that leaders get the behavior they tolerate. He thus instituted a monthly "performance

A leader's reaction to organizational crises is important in terms of embedding culture in organizations. In 2002, Enron's leaders continuously passed blame during investigations into the company's attempts to hide debt. What cultural message do you think former CEO Jeffrey Skilling sent when he denied awareness of Enron's precarious financial situation?

A/P Wide World Photos

call" with the top 100 executives to review the past month's numbers and critical activities in detail. "Everyone knows who is on target for the year, who is ahead of projections, and who is behind. Those who are behind must explain the shortfall—and how they plan to get back on track."[46]

8. *Leader reactions to critical incidents and organizational crises.* Consider the cultural message sent by former Enron leaders as they passed the blame for the financial crises of 2002.

> At a time when former leaders Kenneth L Lay and Jeffrey K Skilling are trying to blame the company's problems on a small group of rogue financial execs, the details of Enron's investment portfolio indicate the company's problems went well beyond the CFO's office—and well beyond its controversial off-balance-sheet partnerships.[47]

Do you think that this leader behavior would instill an accountability-based culture?

9. *The workflow and organizational structure.* Hierarchical structures are more likely to embed an orientation toward control and authority than a flatter organization. Leaders from many organizations are increasingly reducing the number of organizational layers in an attempt to empower employees (see Chapter 16) and increase employee involvement.

10. *Organizational systems and procedures.* Capital One, for example, is using a variety of procedures to reinforce a culture that focuses on self-development.

> And like most development plans, Capital One's program highlights key areas in which associates [employees] might want or need to develop and helps them identify specific ways to reach those goals. But the DAP [development action plan] program goes a step farther and is supported with a performance management process in which an individual's objectives are strategically aligned with company objectives to develop core competencies, maximize individual performance, and provide appropriate rewards for performance. The competency planning and development team accomplishes this through an ongoing cycle of setting objec-

tives, DAPs, ongoing feedback, coaching, mentoring, and, of course, 360-degree performance evaluations at least twice a year.[48]

11. *Organizational goals and the associated criteria used for recruitment, selection, development, promotion, layoffs, and retirement of people.* PepsiCo reinforces a high-performance culture by setting challenging goals. Executives strive to achieve a 15% increase in revenue per year.[49]

The Organizational Socialization Process

Organizational socialization is defined as "the process by which a person learns the values, norms, and required behaviors which permit him to participate as a member of the organization."[50] As previously discussed, organization socialization is a key mechanism used by organizations to embed their organizational cultures. In short, organizational socialization turns outsiders into fully functioning insiders by promoting and reinforcing the organization's core values and beliefs. This section introduces a three-phase model of organizational socialization and examines the practical application of socialization research.

Organizational socialization
Process by which employees learn an organization's values, norms, and required behaviors.

A Three-Phase Model of Organizational Socialization

One's first year in a complex organization can be confusing. There is a constant swirl of new faces, strange jargon, conflicting expectations, and apparently unrelated events. Some organizations treat new members in a rather haphazard, sink-or-swim manner. More typically, though, the socialization process is characterized by a sequence of identifiable steps.[51]

Organizational behavior researcher Daniel Feldman has proposed a three-phase model of organizational socialization that promotes deeper understanding of this important process. As illustrated in Figure 3–4, the three phases are (1) anticipatory socialization, (2) encounter, and (3) change and acquisition. Each phase has its associated perceptual and social processes. Feldman's model also specifies behavioral and affective outcomes that can be used to judge how well an individual has been socialized. The entire three-phase sequence may take from a few weeks to a year to complete, depending on individual differences and the complexity of the situation.

Phase 1: Anticipatory Socialization   **Anticipatory socialization** occurs before an individual actually joins an organization. It is represented by the information people have learned about different careers, occupations, professions, and organizations. For example, anticipatory socialization partially explains the different perceptions you might have about working for the US government versus a high-technology company like Intel or Microsoft. Anticipatory socialization information comes from many sources. US Marine recruiting ads, for instance, prepare future recruits for a rough-and-tumble experience. Widely circulated stories about the fast- and ever-changing environments within Internet companies probably deter those who would prefer working in a more stable environment from applying.

All of this information—whether formal or informal, accurate or inaccurate—helps the individual anticipate organizational realities. Unrealistic expectations about the nature of the work, pay, and promotions are often formulated during phase I.

Anticipatory socialization
Occurs before an individual joins an organization, and involves the information people learn about different careers, occupations, professions, and organizations.

Figure 3–4   *A Model of Organizational Socialization*

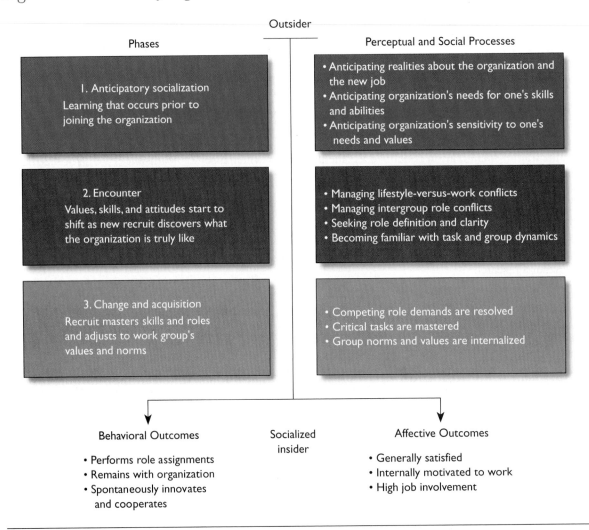

Outsider

Phases

1. Anticipatory socialization
Learning that occurs prior to joining the organization

Perceptual and Social Processes

• Anticipating realities about the organization and the new job
• Anticipating organization's needs for one's skills and abilities
• Anticipating organization's sensitivity to one's needs and values

2. Encounter
Values, skills, and attitudes start to shift as new recruit discovers what the organization is truly like

• Managing lifestyle-versus-work conflicts
• Managing intergroup role conflicts
• Seeking role definition and clarity
• Becoming familiar with task and group dynamics

3. Change and acquisition
Recruit masters skills and roles and adjusts to work group's values and norms

• Competing role demands are resolved
• Critical tasks are mastered
• Group norms and values are internalized

Behavioral Outcomes

• Performs role assignments
• Remains with organization
• Spontaneously innovates and cooperates

Socialized insider

Affective Outcomes

• Generally satisfied
• Internally motivated to work
• High job involvement

SOURCE: Adapted from material in D C Feldman, "The Multiple Socialization of Organization Members," *Academy of Management Review,* April 1981, pp 309–18.

Realistic job preview

Presents both positive and negative aspects of a job.

Because employees with unrealistic expectations are more likely to quit their jobs in the future, organizations may want to use realistic job previews.[52] A **realistic job preview** (RJP) involves giving recruits a realistic idea of what lies ahead by presenting both positive and negative aspects of the job. RJPs may be verbal, in booklet form, audiovisual, or hands-on. Research supports the practical benefits of using RJPs. A meta-analysis of 40 studies revealed that RJPs were related to higher performance and to lower attrition from the recruitment process. Results also demonstrated that RJPs lowered job applicants' initial expectations and led to lower turnover among those applicants who were hired.[53]

Encounter phase

Employees learn what the organization is really like and reconcile unmet expectations.

Phase 2: Encounter   This second phase begins when the employment contract has been signed. During the **encounter phase** employees come to learn what the organization is really like. It is a time for reconciling unmet expectations and making sense of a new work environment. Behavioral scientists warn that reality shock can occur during the encounter phase. **Reality shock** reflects a newcomer's feeling of surprise after experiencing unexpected situations or events. Jack Welch, former CEO of GE, for example, experienced reality shock after starting his first job with GE.

> When it [GE] recruited me, the company had laid out a cushy red carpet. They convinced me I was just the person they were looking for to help develop a new plastic called PPO. When Carolyn and I arrived in Pittsfield, MA, in October 1960, I was expecting at least a little of that seductive treatment to continue. We had driven 950 miles from Illinois in my fading black Volkswagen. We came with little more than the change in our pockets.
>
> Quickly, my new boss, Burt Coplan, made it clear that the wooing was over. A thin 40-something development manager, Coplan asked if my wife and I had already found an apartment in town. When I told him we were staying at the local hotel, he said, "Well, we don't cover that, you know." I couldn't believe it.[54]

A realistic job preview may have reduced Welch's unrealistic expectations.

Many companies use a combination of orientation and training programs to socialize employees during the encounter phase. Consider the combination used at Capital One.

> On their first day as a Capital One associate, new hires can literally hit the ground running thanks to a recruiting process that identifies the required competencies for each position and incorporates job simulation into the pre-hire evaluation process. Candidates for a customer contact position, for example, can experience the job before a position is offered or accepted. Once on board, orientation includes a departmental new hire training program, which, depending on the job, can range anywhere from two to six weeks. After training but before phone associates join permanent teams, they spend time "nesting," taking customer calls in a controlled environment with many experienced associates to coach them.[55]

Phase 3: Change and Acquisition

The **change and acquisition** phase requires employees to master important tasks and roles and to adjust to their work group's values and norms. Table 3–2 presents a list of socialization processes or tactics used by organizations to help employees through this adjustment process. Trilogy, for example, uses a variety of these tactics in its renowned socialization program. The three-month program takes place at the organization's corporate university, called Trilogy University.

Month One. When you arrive at Trilogy University, you are assigned to a section and to an instruction track. Your section, a group of about 20, is your social group for the duration of TU. . . . Tracks are designed to be microcosms of future work life at Trilogy. . . . The technical challenges in such exercises closely mimic real customer engagements, but the time frames are dramatically compressed. The assignments pile up week after week for the first month, each one successively more challenging than the last. During that time, you're being constantly measured and evaluated, as assignment grades and comments are entered into a database monitoring your progress. . . .

Month Two. Month two is TU project month. . . . In teams of three to five people, they have to come up with an idea, create a business model for it, build the product, and develop the marketing plan. In trying to launch bold new ideas in a hyperaccelerated time frame, they gain a deep appreciation of the need to set priorities, evaluate probabilities, and measure results. Mind you, these projects are not hypothetical—they're the real thing. . . .

Month Three. Month three at Trilogy University is all about finding your place and having a broader impact in the larger organization. A few students continue with their TU projects, but most move on to "graduation projects," which generally are assignments within various Trilogy business units. People leave TU on a rolling basis as they find sponsors out in the company who are willing to take them on.[56]

Reality shock
A newcomer's feeling of surprise after experiencing unexpected situations or events.

Change and acquisition
Requires employees to master tasks and roles and to adjust to work group values and norms.

Table 3–2   *Socialization Tactics*

Tactic	Description
Collective vs. individual	Collective socialization consists of grouping newcomers and exposing them to a common set of experiences rather than treating each newcomer individually and exposing him or her to more or less unique experiences.
Formal vs. informal	Formal socialization is the practice of segregating a newcomer from regular organization members during a defined socialization period versus not clearly distinguishing a newcomer from more experienced members. Army recruits must attend boot camp before they are allowed to work alongside established soldiers.
Sequential vs. random	Sequential socialization refers to a fixed progression of steps that culminate in the new role, compared to an ambiguous or dynamic progression. The socialization of doctors involves a lock-step sequence from medical school, to internship, to residency before they are allowed to practice on their own.
Fixed vs. variable	Fixed socialization provides a timetable for the assumption of the role, whereas a variable process does not. American university students typically spend one year apiece as freshmen, sophomores, juniors, and seniors.
Serial vs. disjunctive	A serial process is one in which the newcomer is socialized by an experienced member, whereas a disjunctive process does not use a role model.
Investiture vs. divestiture	Investiture refers to the affirmation of a newcomer's incoming global and specific role identities and attributes. Divestiture is the denial and stripping away of the newcomer's existing sense of self and the reconstruction of self in the organization's image. During police training, cadets are required to wear uniforms and maintain an immaculate appearance, they are addressed as "officer," told they are no longer ordinary citizens but are representatives of the police force.

SOURCE: Descriptions were taken from B E Ashforth, *Role Transitions in Organizational Life: An Identity-Based Perspective* (Mahwah, NJ: Lawrence Erlbaum Associates, 2001), pp 149–83.

The change and acquisition phase at Trilogy is stressful, exhilarating, and critical for finding one's place within the organization. How would you like to work there? Returning to Table 3–2, can you identify the socialization tactics used by Trilogy?

Practical Application of Socialization Research

Past research suggests five practical guidelines for managing organizational socialization.[57]

1. Managers should avoid a haphazard, sink-or-swim approach to organizational socialization because formalized socialization tactics positively affect new hires. A formalized orientation program positively influenced 116 new employees in a variety of occupations.[58]

2. Managers play a key role during the encounter phase. Studies of newly hired accountants demonstrated that the frequency and type of information obtained during their first six months of employment significantly affected their job performance, their role clarity, and the extent to which they were socially integrated.[59] Managers need to help new hires integrate within the organizational culture.

3. Support for stage models is mixed. Although there are different stages of socialization, they are not identical in order, length, or content for all people or jobs.[60] Managers are advised to use a contingency approach toward organizational socialization. In other words, different techniques are appropriate for different people at different times.

4. The organization can benefit by training new employees to use proactive socialization behaviors. A study of 154 entry-level professionals showed that effectively using proactive socialization behaviors reduced the newcomers' general anxiety and stress during the first month of employment and increased their motivation and anxiety six months later.[61]

5. Managers should pay attention to the socialization of diverse employees. Research demonstrated that diverse employees, particularly those with disabilities, experienced different socialization activities than other newcomers. In turn, these different experiences affected their long-term success and job satisfaction.[62]

Embedding Organizational Culture through Mentoring

The modern word *mentor* derives from Mentor, the name of a wise and trusted counselor in Greek mythology. Terms typically used in connection with mentoring are *teacher, coach, sponsor,* and *peer.* **Mentoring** is defined as the process of forming and maintaining intensive and lasting developmental relationships between a variety of developers (i.e., people who provide career and psychosocial support) and a junior person (the protégé, if male; or protégée, if female).[63] Mentoring can serve to embed an organization's culture when developers and the protégé/protégée work in the same organization for two reasons. First, mentoring contributes to creating a sense of oneness by promoting the acceptance of the organization's core values throughout the organization. Second, the socialization aspect of mentoring also promotes a sense of membership.

Mentoring
Process of forming and maintaining developmental relationships between a mentor and a junior person.

A mentee, an Associate Program Manager, looks to her mentor, Director of Training and Development during a Fannie Mae employee mentor program. Mentoring promotes the acceptance of the organization's core values and a sense of membership. How might a formal mentoring program help a new employee learn the organization's culture?

(c) Steven Rubin/The Image Works

Not only is mentoring important as a tactic for embedding organizational culture, but research suggests it can significantly influence the protégé/protégée's future career. For example, mentored employees performed better on the job and experienced more rapid career advancement than nonmentored employees. Mentored employees also reported higher job and career satisfaction and working on more challenging job assignments.[64] With this information in mind, this section focuses on how people can use mentoring to their advantage. We discuss the functions of mentoring, the developmental networks underlying mentoring, and the personal and organizational implications of mentoring.

Functions of Mentoring

Kathy Kram, a Boston University researcher, conducted in-depth interviews with both members of 18 pairs of senior and junior managers. As a by-product of this study, Kram identified two general functions—career and psychosocial—of the mentoring process. Five *career functions* that enhanced career development were sponsorship, exposure-and-visibility, coaching, protection, and challenging assignments. Four *psychosocial functions* were role modeling, acceptance-and-confirmation, counseling, and friendship. The psychosocial functions clarified the participants' identities and enhanced their feelings of competence.[65]

Developmental Networks Underlying Mentoring

Historically, it was thought that mentoring was primarily provided by one person who was called a mentor. Today, however, the changing nature of technology, organizational structures, and marketplace dynamics requires that people seek career information and support from many sources. Mentoring is currently viewed as a process in which protégés and protégées seek developmental guidance from a network of people, who are referred to as developers. This implies that the diversity and strength of a person's network of relationships is instrumental in obtaining the type of career assistance needed to manage his or her career. Figure 3–5 presents a developmental network typology based on integrating the diversity and strength of developmental relationships.[66]

Diversity of developmental relationships
The variety of people in a network used for developmental assistance.

The **diversity of developmental relationships** reflects the variety of people within the network an individual uses for developmental assistance. There are two subcomponents associated with network diversity: (1) the number of different people the person is networked with and (2) the various social systems from which the networked relationships stem (e.g., employer, school, family, community, professional associations, and religious affiliations). As shown in Figure 3–5, developmental relationship diversity ranges from low (few people or social systems) to high (multiple people or social systems). **Developmental relationship strength** reflects the quality of relationships among the individual and those involved in his or her developmental network. For example, strong ties are reflective of relationships based on frequent interactions, reciprocity, and positive affect. Weak ties, in contrast, are based more on superficial relationships. Together, the diversity and strength of developmental relationships results in four types of developmental networks (see Figure 3–5): receptive, traditional, entrepreneurial, and opportunistic.

Developmental relationship strength
The quality of relationships among people in a network.

A *receptive* developmental network is composed of a few weak ties from one social system such as an employer or a professional association. The single oval around D1 and D2 in Figure 3–5 is indicative of two developers who come from one social system. In contrast, a *traditional* network contains a few strong ties between an employee

Figure 3–5   *Developmental Networks Associated with Mentoring*

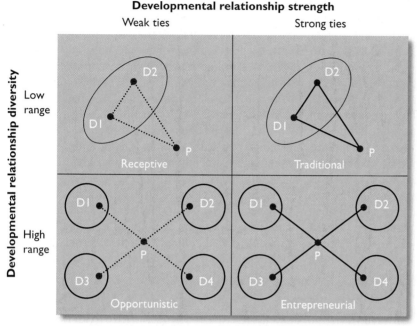

Key: D, developer; P, protégé

SOURCE: M Higgins and K Kram, "Reconceptualizing Mentoring at Work: A Developmental Network Perspective," *Academy of Management Review*, April 2001, p 270.

and developers coming from one social system. TDIndustries, a company in the construction industry, uses a traditional network to assist employees' career development.

> TDI's mentoring program was developed to give all new hires a positive start at the company. A mentor adopts a new employee for the first six months of employment, and the relationship continues as long as both employees work together on the same job site. If, and ultimately when, the new hire changes job sites a different mentor is assigned.
>
> New hires are not the only recipients of TDI's development initiatives, however. In fact, many personal development efforts begin at the top. For example, TDI's board of directors developed "Learning Partners," a program in which participants in every training class select a "learning partner" from among their classmates. The idea is to encourage employees to not only use what was taught in the class and apply it to their jobs, but also to share that continued learning with their partners.[67]

An *entrepreneurial* network, which is the strongest type of developmental network, is made up of strong ties among several developers (D1–D4) who come from four different social systems. Finally, an *opportunistic* network is associated with having weak ties with multiple developers from different social systems.

Personal and Organizational Implications

There are two key personal implications to consider. First, job and career satisfaction are likely to be influenced by the consistency between an individual's career goals and the type of developmental network at his or her disposal. For example, people with an entrepreneurial developmental network are more likely to experience change in their careers and to benefit from personal learning than people with receptive, traditional, and opportunistic networks. If this sounds attractive to you, you should try to increase the diversity and strength of your developmental relationships. In contrast, lower levels of job satisfaction are expected when employees have receptive developmental networks and they desire to experience career advancement in multiple organizations. Receptive developmental networks, however, can be satisfying to someone who does not desire to be promoted up the career ladder.[68] Second, a developer's willingness to provide career and psychosocial assistance is a function of the protégé/protégée's ability, potential, and the quality of the interpersonal relationship.[69] This implies that you must take ownership for enhancing your skills, abilities, and developmental networks if you desire to experience career advancement throughout your life.

Research also supports the organizational benefits of mentoring. In addition to the obvious benefit of employee development, mentoring enhances the effectiveness of organizational communication. Specifically, mentoring increases the amount of vertical communication both up and down an organization, and it provides a mechanism for modifying or reinforcing organizational culture. Consider the benefits derived by the approach used at Network Management, a $10 million health care consultancy in Minneapolis:

> The company, which added 65 employees in 1998, urges all newcomers to lunch individually with each member of its 10-person management team. "When new hires meet the CEO and have a discussion about the company from his perspective, they can really get infected by that," says Scott Ofstead, director of human resources.[70]

These informal lunches sound like a good vehicle to increase vertical communication and to reinforce the organization's preferred values and beliefs.

Summary of Key Concepts

1. **Define organizational culture and discuss its three layers.** Organizational culture represents the shared assumptions that a group holds. It influences employees' perceptions and behavior at work. The three layers of organizational culture include observable artifacts, espoused values, and basic assumptions. Artifacts are the physical manifestations of an organization's culture. Espoused values represent the explicitly stated values and norms that are preferred by an organization. Basic underlying assumptions are unobservable and represent the core of organizational culture.

2. **Discuss the difference between espoused and enacted values.** Espoused values represent the explicitly stated values and norms that are preferred by an organization. Enacted values, in contrast, reflect the values and norms that actually are exhibited or converted into employee behavior. Employees become cynical when management espouses one set of values and norms and then behaves in an inconsistent fashion.

3. **Describe the manifestations and functions of an organization's culture.** General manifestations of an organization's culture are shared objects, talk, behavior, and emotion. Four functions of organization culture are organizational identity, collective commitment, social system stability, and sense-making device.

4. **Discuss the three general types of organizational culture and their associated normative beliefs.** The three general types of organizational culture are constructive, passive–defensive, and aggressive–defensive. Each type is grounded in different normative beliefs. Normative beliefs represent an individual's thoughts and beliefs about how members of a particular group or organization are expected to approach their work and interact with others. A constructive culture is associated with the beliefs of achievement, self-actualizing, humanistic-encouraging, and affiliative. Passive–defensive organizations tend to endorse the beliefs of approval, conventional, dependent, and

avoidance. Aggressive–defensive cultures tend to endorse the beliefs of oppositional, power, competitive, and perfectionistic.

5. *Explain the three perspectives proposed to explain the type of cultures that enhance an organization's financial performance.* The three perspectives are referred to as the strength, fit, and adaptive perspective. The strength perspective assumes that the strength of corporate culture is related to a firm's financial performance. The fit perspective is based on the premise that an organization's culture must align with its business or strategic context. The adaptive perspective assumes that the most effective cultures help organizations anticipate and adapt to environmental changes.

6. *Discuss the process of developing an adaptive culture.* The process begins with charismatic leadership that creates a business vision and strategy. Over time, adaptiveness is created by a combination of organizational success and leaders' ability to get employees to buy into a philosophy or set of values of satisfying constituency needs and improving leadership. Finally, an infrastructure is created to preserve the organization's adaptiveness.

7. *Summarize the methods used by organizations to embed their cultures.* Embedding a culture amounts to teaching employees about the organization's preferred values, beliefs, expectations, and behaviors. This is accomplished by using one or more of the following 11 mechanisms: (a) formal statements of organizational philosophy, mission, vision, values, and materials used for recruiting, selection, and socialization; (b) the design of physical space, work environments, and buildings; (c) slogans, language, acronyms, and sayings; (d) deliberate role modeling, training programs, teaching, and coaching by managers and supervisors; (e) explicit rewards, status symbols, and promotion criteria; (f) stories, legends, and myths about key people and events; (g) the organizational activities, processes, or outcomes that

leaders pay attention to, measure, and control; (h) leader reactions to critical incidents and organizational crises; (i) the workflow and organizational structure; (j) organizational systems and procedures; and (k) organizational goals and associated criteria used for recruitment, selection, development, promotion, layoffs, and retirement of people.

8. *Describe the three phases in Feldman's model of organizational socialization.* The three phases of Feldman's model are anticipatory socialization, encounter, and change and acquisition. Anticipatory socialization begins before an individual actually joins the organization. The encounter phase begins when the employment contract has been signed. Phase 3 involves the period in which employees master important tasks and resolve any role conflicts.

9. *Discuss the various socialization tactics used to socialize employees.* There are six key socialization tactics. They are collective versus individual, formal versus informal, sequential versus random, fixed versus variable, serial versus disjunctive, and investiture versus divestiture (see Table 3–2). Each tactic provides organizations with two opposing options for socializing employees.

10. *Explain the four developmental networks associated with mentoring.* The four developmental networks are based on integrating the diversity and strength of an individual's developmental relationships. The four resulting developmental networks are receptive, traditional, entrepreneurial, and opportunistic. A receptive network is composed of a few weak ties from one social system. Having a few strong ties with developers from one social system is referred to as a traditional network. An entrepreneurial network is made up of strong ties among several developers; and a opportunistic network is associated with having weak ties from different social systems.

Discussion Questions

1. How would you respond to someone who made the following statement? "Organizational cultures are not important as far as managers are concerned."

2. What are the enacted values within your current classroom? Provide examples to support your evaluation.

3. Have you ever worked for a company that endorsed values that were inconsistent with your own? Explain and discuss what you did to reconcile this inconsistency.

4. What type of organizational culture exists within your current or most recent employer? Explain.

5. Can you think of any organizational heroes who have influenced your work behavior? Describe them, and explain how they affected your behavior.

6. Do you know of any successful companies that do not have a positive adaptive culture? Why do you think they are successful?

7. Why is socialization essential to organizational success?

8. Which of the socialization tactics shown in Table 3–2 have you experienced? Discuss whether or not they were effective in the context you experienced them.

9. Have you ever had a mentor? Explain how things turned out.

10. Using Figure 3–5 as a point of reference, what type of developmental networks do you possess? Discuss whether or not your developmental network is consistent with your career goals.

Internet Exercise

This chapter focused on the role of values and beliefs in forming an organization's culture. We also discussed how cultures are embedded and reinforced through socialization and mentoring. The topic of organizational culture is big business on the Internet. Many companies use their Web pages to describe their mission, vision, and corporate values and beliefs. There also are many consulting companies that advertise how they help organizations to change their cultures. The purpose of this exercise is for you to obtain information pertaining to the organizational culture for two different companies. You can go about this task by very simply searching on the key words "organizational culture" or "corporate vision and values." This search will identify numerous companies for you to use in answering the following questions. You may want to select a company for this exercise that you would like to work for in the future.

Questions

1. What are the organization's espoused values and beliefs?

2. Using Table 3–1 as a guide, how would you classify the organization's culture? Be sure to provide supporting evidence.

OB in Action Case Study

Enron's Organizational Culture Contributed to Its Financial and Legal Problems[71]

BusinessWeek For most of the 1990s, CEOs at Old Economy companies struggled to turn slow-moving organizations into nimbler, more flexible outfits. Failure cost chieftains their jobs at General Motors, Eastman Kodak, Westinghouse, and a host of other behemoths. Truth is, real transformations are the exception rather than the rule. Changing the core values, the attitudes, the fundamental relationships of a vast organization is overwhelmingly difficult. General Electric Co.'s John F. Welch and IBM's Louis V. Gerstner Jr have been lionized for having led two of the very few successful makeovers.

That's why an army of academics and consultants descended on Enron in the late 1990s and held it up as a paragon of management virtue. Enron seemed to have transformed itself from a stodgy regulated utility to a fast-moving enterprise where performance was paramount. The Harvard case study put it simply enough: "Enron's transformation: From gas pipelines to New Economy powerhouse."

If only that were true. Many of the same academics are now scurrying to distill the cultural and leadership lessons from the debacle. Their conclusion so far: Enron didn't fail just because of improper accounting or alleged corruption at the top. It also failed because of its entrepreneurial culture—the very reason Enron attracted so much attention and acclaim. The unrelenting emphasis on earnings growth and individual initiative, coupled with a shocking absence of the usual corporate checks and balances, tipped the culture from one that rewarded aggressive strategy to one that increasingly relied on unethical corner-cutting. In the end, too much leeway was given to young, inexperienced managers without the necessary controls to minimize failures. This was a company that simply placed a lot of bad bets on businesses that weren't so promising to begin with. . . .

Skilling's [Jeff Skilling, Enron's former CEO] recipe for changing the company was right out of the New Economy playbook. Layers of management were wiped out. Hundreds of outsiders were recruited and encouraged to bring new thinking to a tradition-bound business. The company abolished seniority-based salaries in favor of more highly leveraged compensation that offered huge cash bonuses and stock option grants to top performers. Young people, many just out of undergraduate or MBA programs, were handed extraordinary authority, able to make $5 million decisions without higher approval.

In the new culture, success or failure came remarkably fast. . . .

At Enron, however, the pressure to make the numbers often overwhelmed the pretext of "tight" controls. "The environment was ripe for abuse," says a former manager in Enron's energy services unit. "Nobody at corporate was asking the right questions. It was completely hands-off management. A situation like that requires tight controls. Instead, it was a runaway train."

The train was supposed to be kept on the tracks partly by an internal risk management group with a staff of 180 employees to screen proposals and review deals. Many of the unit's employees were MBAs with little perspective and every reason to sign off on deals: Their own performance reviews were partially done by the people whose deals they were approving. The process made honest evaluations virtually impossible. "If your boss was [fudging], and you have never worked anywhere else, you just assume that everybody fudges earnings," says one young Enron control person. "Once you get there and you realized how it was, do you stand up and lose your job? It was scary. It was easy to get into 'Well, everybody else is doing it, so maybe it isn't so bad.' " . . .

Central to forging a new Enron culture was an unusual performance review system that Skilling adapted from his days at McKinsey. Under this peer-review process, a select group of 20 people were named to a performance review committee (PRC) to rank more than 400 vice presidents, then all the directors, and finally all of Enron's managers. The stakes were high because all the rewards were linked to ranking decisions by the PRC, which had to unanimously agree on each person. Managers judged "superior"—the top 5%—got bonuses 66% higher than those who got an "excellent" rating, the next 30%. They also got much larger stock option grants.

Although Skilling told Harvard researchers that the system "stopped most of the game playing since it was impossible to kiss 20 asses," other Enron managers say it had the opposite effect. In practice, the system bred a culture in which people were afraid to get crossways with someone who could screw up their reviews. How did managers ensure they passed muster? "You don't object to anything," says one former Enron executive. "The whole culture at the vice-president level and above just became a yes-man culture."

Several former and current Enron execs say that Andrew S. Fastow, the ex-chief financial officer who is at the center of Enron's partnership controversy, had a reputation for exploiting the review system to get back at people who expressed disagreement or criticism. "Andy was such a cut-throat bastard that he would use it against you in the PRC," says one manager. He could filibuster and hold up the group for days, the exec adds, because every decision had to be unanimous. A spokesman for Fastow declined comment.

Although managers were supposed to be graded on teamwork, Enron was actually far more reflective of a survival-of-the-fittest mind-set. The culture was heavily built around star players, such as [Lynda] Clemmons, with little value attached to team-building. The upshot: The organization rewarded highly competitive people who were less likely to share power, authority, or information.

Indeed, some believe the extreme focus on individual ambition undermined any teamwork or institutional commitment. At other companies, by contrast, an emphasis on individual achievement is balanced by a strong focus on process and metrics or a set of guiding values.

Questions for Discussion

1. Using Figure 3–1, explain how Enron's culture influenced organizational structure and practices, group and social processes, collective attitudes and behavior, and ultimately organizational outcomes.

2. How would you describe the type of organizational culture that existed at Enron? Be sure to provide examples about the extent to which Enron displayed the 12 types of normative beliefs shown in Table 3–1.

3. What were the shared things, sayings, doings, and feelings at Enron? Discuss.

4. Which of the techniques for embedding organizational culture were used at Enron? Explain.

5. How were employees socialized to act entrepreneurial? Provide examples.

6. How would you change the culture at Enron if you were its new CEO? Provide specific recommendations.

Personal Awareness and Growth Exercise

Have You Been Adequately Socialized?

Objectives

1. To determine whether or not your current employer has properly socialized you.

2. To promote deeper understanding of organizational socialization processes.

Introduction

Organizations use a variety of socialization tactics to help employees learn their new jobs, work roles, and adjust to work group values and norms. The effectiveness of this process has been found to affect employees' job satisfaction, job performance, and role clarity. The questionnaire[72] in this exercise is designed to help you gauge how well you have been socialized by your current or a past employer.

Instructions

Complete the following survey items by considering either your current job or one you held in the past. If you have never worked, identify a friend who is working and ask that individual to complete the questionnaire for his or her organization. Read each item and circle your response by using the rating scale shown below. Remember, there are no right or wrong answers. Upon completion, compute your total score by adding up your responses and compare it to the scoring norms.

	Strongly Disagree	Disagree	Neutral	Agree	Strongly Agree
1. I have been through a set of training experiences that are specifically designed to give newcomers a thorough knowledge of job-related skills.	1	2	3	4	5
2. This organization puts all newcomers through the same set of learning experiences.	1	2	3	4	5
3. I did not perform any of my normal job responsibilities until I was thoroughly familiar with departmental procedures and work methods.	1	2	3	4	5
4. There is a clear pattern in the way one role leads to another, or one job assignment leads to another, in this organization.	1	2	3	4	5
5. I can predict my future career path in this organization by observing other people's experiences.	1	2	3	4	5
6. Almost all of my colleagues have been supportive of me personally.	1	2	3	4	5
7. My colleagues have gone out of their way to help me adjust to this organization.	1	2	3	4	5
8. I received much guidance from experienced organizational members as to how I should perform my job.	1	2	3	4	5
9. In the last several months, I have been extensively involved with other new recruits in common, job-related activities.	1	2	3	4	5
10. I am gaining a clear understanding of my role in this organization from observing my senior colleagues.	1	2	3	4	5

Total score = _____

Scoring Norms

10–20 = Low socialization

21–39 = Moderate socialization

40–50 = High socialization

Questions for Discussion

1. How strongly have you been socialized? Do you agree with this assessment?

2. What does your degree of socialization suggest about your job satisfaction and performance? Do you agree with this conclusion? Explain.

3. If your socialization score was low or moderate, what can you do to enhance your socialization within the organization? Discuss.

4. How important is socialization to your success within the organization under consideration? Explain.

Group Exercise

Assessing the Organizational Culture at Your School

Objectives

1. To provide you with a framework for assessing organizational culture.

2. To conduct an evaluation of the organizational culture at your school.

3. To consider the relationship between organizational culture and organizational effectiveness.

Introduction

Academics and consultants do not agree about the best way to measure an organization's culture. Some people measure culture with surveys, while others use direct observation or information obtained in interviews/workshops with employees. This exercise uses an informal group-based approach to assess the three levels of organizational culture discussed in this chapter. This approach has successfully been used to measure organizational culture at a variety of organizations.[73]

Instructions

Your instructor will divide the class into groups of four to six people. Each group member should then complete the Cultural Assessment Worksheet by him- or herself. It asks you to identify the artifacts, espoused values, and basic assumptions that are present at your current school: You may find it useful to reread the material on layers of organizational culture discussed earlier. When everyone is done, meet as a group and share the information contained on your individual worksheets. Create a summary worksheet based on a consensus of the cultural characteristics contained at each level of culture. Next, compare the information contained on the summary worksheet with the cultural descriptions contained in Table 3–1 and discuss what type of culture your school possesses. Again, strive to obtain a consensus opinion. Finally, the group should answer the discussion questions that follow the Cultural Assessment Worksheet.

Culture Assessment Worksheet

Artifacts (physical or visible manifestations of culture; they include jargon, heroes, stories, language, ritual, dress, material objects, mascots, physical arrangements, symbols, traditions, and so forth)	Espoused Values (the stated values and norms preferred by the organization)	Basic Assumptions (taken-for-granted beliefs about the organization that exist on an unconscious level)

Questions for Discussion

1. What are the group's consensus artifacts, espoused values, and basic assumptions? Are you surprised by anything on this list? Explain.

2. What type of culture does your school possess? Do you like this organizational culture? Discuss why or why not.

3. Do you think the organizational culture identified in question 2 is best suited for maximizing your learning? Explain your rationale.

4. Is your school in need of any cultural change? If yes, discuss why and recommend how the school's leaders might create this change. The material on embedding organizational culture would help answer this question.

Ethical Dilemma

Arthur Andersen's Pursuit of Consulting Income Created Ethical Challenges in Its Auditing Operations[74]

Andersen realized long ago that no one was going to get rich doing just audits. So for partners to share in hundreds of thousands of dollars of firm profits each year, Andersen would have to boost its lucrative consulting business. That quest for revenue is how the firm lost sight of its obligation to cast a critical eye on its clients' accounting practices, some critics say. . . .

The problems with focusing on consulting are evident in Andersen's biggest accounting blowups. Consider Waste Management Inc., which generated millions of dollars in consulting fees for Andersen. Last year, securities regulators alleged that Andersen bent the accounting rules so far the firm committed fraud. Time and again, starting in 1988 up through 1997, when Waste Management announced what at the time was the biggest financial restatement in US history, Andersen auditors knew the company was violating generally accepted accounting principles, the Securities and Exchange Commission said in a settled complaint filed in a Washington, DC, federal court.

Throughout the late 1990s, Andersen proposed hundreds of millions of dollars of accounting adjustments to rectify the situation, the SEC said in its suit. But when Waste Management refused to follow their recommendations, to the auditors' disappointment, they caved in. Those decisions were backed at the highest levels of Andersen's Chicago office, the SEC suit says.

Before taking over Waste Management's audit in 1991, Andersen partner Robert Allgyer had been in charge of coordinating the Chicago office's efforts to cross-sell nonaudit services to Andersen's audit clients. Indeed, for Andersen, nonaudit services were the only potential source of revenue growth from the trash hauler. That year, Waste Management had capped the amount of audit fees it would pay Andersen. The company, however, allowed Andersen to earn additional fees for "special work."

What would you have done if you were auditing Waste Management's financial statements?

1. Vigorously challenge Waste Management employees to correct their accounting practices.

2. Go to your manager when you first realize Waste Management was not following generally accepted accounting principles and tell him or her that you will not work on this account until Waste Management changes its ways.

3. Complete the work as best you can because your efforts contribute to Andersen's financial goals.

4. Invent other options. Discuss.

For an interpretation of this situation, visit our Web site, **www.mhhe.com/kreitner.**

Chapter Four

International OB: Managing across Cultures

Learning Objectives

When you finish studying the material in this chapter, you should be able to:

1 Define the term *culture,* and explain how societal culture and organizational culture combine to influence on-the-job behavior.

2 Define *ethnocentrism,* and distinguish between high-context and low-context cultures.

3 Identify and describe the nine cultural dimensions from Project GLOBE.

4 Distinguish between individualistic and collectivist cultures, and explain the difference between monochronic and polychronic cultures.

5 Outline the practical lessons from the Hofstede–Bond cross-cultural studies.

6 Explain what Project GLOBE researchers discovered about leadership.

7 Specify why US managers have a comparatively high failure rate on foreign assignments.

8 Summarize the research findings about North American women on foreign assignments, and tell how to land a foreign assignment.

9 Identify four stages of the foreign assignment cycle and the OB trouble spot associated with each stage.

It's the ſuit vs. the Tattoo ſet. Foggy Bottom and the Hip Hop Crowd. The General and the Veejay. It's, it's . . . well, it's another weird but fascinating cultural moment on MTV, the Viacom-owned music network that supplements its core mission of delivering 150-decibel music to the world's teens with straight-talking programs on issues such as AIDſ, drugs, and racism. . . .

Media moguls can babble on about the global village, about how C/V/V or BBC can reach out and touch the world. But those news shows are bush league operations compared with MTV's clout. Thanks to the roaring success of its subsidiary, MTV /Vetworks International, the music channel and its sister operations, VHI and /Vickelodeon, reach 1 billion people in 18 different languages in 164 countries. Eight out of ten MTV viewers live outside the Uſ. C/V/V reaches an international audience less than half the size of MTV's. Its impressive global reach has earned

MTV membership in that elite of such globally transcendent brands as Coke and Levi's. . . .

MTV /Vetworks International owes its success to a lot of factors. First, demographics: There were 2.7 billion people between the ages of 10 and 34 in 2000. By 2010, there will be 2.8 billion. Increasingly, this age group is acquiring the bucks to buy CDs, jeans, acne cream—whatever brands are hot in

Tough job, but somebody's got to do it. MTV's Bill Roedy is surrounded by regional MTV stars from Taiwan and Russia.
©2002 Brad Trent

each country. That means advertisers increasingly love MTV International. Second, music: All that stuff about music being a universal language is true, and rock is the universal language for Planet Teen. What MTV does is customize the offering in a brilliant way. Third, television: The number of sets in the world's living rooms—especially in such places as China, Brazil, Russia, and India—is exploding. So are the globe's cable networks. "Everyone who has a TV knows there's something called MTV," says Chantara Kapahi, a 17-year-old student at Jai Hind College in Bombay. The fourth reason: Bill Roedy.

Roedy, a 53-year-old West Point grad, is president of MTV Networks International and, theoretically, is based in London. Theoretically, since his real office is more of a semi-perpetual airborne state involving him, his trademark army green pen and paper, and a business-class round-trip ticket to wherever. To give kids their dose of rock, he has break-fasted with former Israeli Prime Minister Shimon Peres, dined with Singapore founder Lee Kuan Yew, and chewed the fat with Chinese leader Jiang Zemin. Roedy even met with El Caudillo himself—Cuban leader Fidel Castro, who wondered if MTV could teach Cuban kids English. Says Roedy: "We've had very little resistance once we explain that we're not in the business of exporting American culture."

Roedy & Co. are shrewd enough to realize that while the world's teens want American music, they really want the local stuff, too. So, MTV's producers and veejays scour their local markets for the top talent. The result is an endless stream of overnight sensations that keep MTV's global offerings fresh.[1]

> **For Discussion**
> What is the managerial significance of calling MTV a global business based in the United States, versus calling it a US business that exports its product?

MTV's Bill Roedy does a good job of "thinking globally, but acting locally." MTV Networks International is one of Viacom's crown jewels because, according to *BusinessWeek,* it "makes buckets of money year after year from a potent combination of cable subscriber fees, advertising, and increasingly, new media."[2] More specifically, MTV Networks International made $135 million in profits on $600 million in sales in 2001.[3] This sort of opportunity in today's global economy challenges virtually all employees to become more internationally aware and cross-culturally adept. The path to the top typically winds through one or more foreign assignments today. A prime example is Samir Gibara, chief executive officer of Goodyear Tire & Rubber, who spent 27 of his 36 years with the company on foreign assignments in Canada, France, Morocco, and Belgium.[4] In fact, according to a recent study, US multinational companies headed by CEOs with international assignments on their résumés tended to outperform the competition.[5] Even managers and employees who stay in their native country will find it hard to escape today's global economy. Many will be thrust into international relationships by working for foreign-owned companies or by dealing with foreign suppliers, customers, and co-workers. *Management Review* offered this helpful perspective:

> It's easy to think that people who have lived abroad or who are multilingual have global brains, while those who still live in their hometowns are parochial. But both notions are fallacies. Managers who have never left their home states can have global brains if they are interested in the greater world around them, make an effort to learn about other people's perspectives, and integrate those perspectives into their own way of thinking.[6]

The global economy is a rich mix of cultures, and the time to prepare to work in it is now.[7] Accordingly, the purpose of this chapter is to help you take a step in that direction by exploring the impacts of culture in today's increasingly internationalized organization. This chapter draws upon the area of cultural anthropology. We begin with a model that shows how societal culture and organizational culture (covered in Chapter 3) combine to influence work behavior. Next, we examine key dimensions of societal culture with the goal of enhancing cross-cultural awareness. Practical lessons from cross-cultural management research are then reviewed. The chapter concludes by exploring the challenge of accepting a foreign assignment.

Culture and Organizational Behavior

How would you, as a manager, interpret the following situations?

> An Asian executive for a multinational company, transferred from Taiwan to the Midwest, appears aloof and autocratic to his peers.
>
> A West Coast bank embarks on a "friendly teller" campaign, but its Filipino female tellers won't cooperate.
>
> A white manager criticizes a black male employee's work. Instead of getting an explanation, the manager is met with silence and a firm stare.[8]

If you attribute the behavior in these situations to personalities, three descriptions come to mind: arrogant, unfriendly, and hostile. These are reasonable conclusions. Unfortunately, they are probably wrong, being based more on prejudice and stereotypes than on actual fact. However, if you attribute the behavioral outcomes to *cultural* differences, you stand a better chance of making the following more valid interpretations: "As it turns out, Asian culture encourages a more distant managing style, Filipinos associate overly friendly behavior in women with prostitution, and blacks as a group act more deliberately, studying visual cues, than most white men."[9] One cannot afford to overlook relevant cultural contexts when trying to understand and manage organizational behavior.

Societal Culture Is Complex and Multilayered

In Chapter 3, we discussed *organizational* culture. Here, the focus is more broadly on *societal* culture. "**Culture** is a set of beliefs and values about what is desirable and undesirable in a community of people, and a set of formal or informal practices to support the values."[10] So culture has both prescriptive (what people should do) and descriptive (what they actually do) elements. Culture is passed from one generation to the next by family, friends, teachers, and relevant others. Most cultural lessons are learned by observing and imitating role models as they go about their daily affairs or as observed in the media.[11]

Culture is difficult to grasp because it is multilayered. International management experts Fons Trompenaars (from the Netherlands) and Charles Hampden-Turner (from Britain) offered this instructive analogy in their landmark book, *Riding the Waves of Culture:*

> Culture comes in layers, like an onion. To understand it you have to unpeel it layer by layer.
>
> On the outer layer are the products of culture, like the soaring skyscrapers of Manhattan, pillars of private power, with congested public streets between them. These are expressions of deeper values and norms in a society that are not directly visible (values such as upward mobility, "the more-the-better," status, material success). The layers of values and norms are deeper within the "onion," and are more difficult to identify.[12]

Consequently, the September 11, 2001, destruction of the New York World Trade Center towers by terrorists was as much an attack on American culture as it was on lives and

Culture

Beliefs and values about how a community of people should and do act.

property.[13] That deepened the hurt and made the anger more profound for Americans and their friends around the world. In both life and business, culture is a serious matter.

Culture Is a Subtle but Pervasive Force

Culture generally remains below the threshold of conscious awareness because it involves *taken-for-granted assumptions* about how one should perceive, think, act, and feel. Cultural anthropologist Edward T Hall put it this way:

> Since much of culture operates outside our awareness, frequently we don't even know what we know. We pick . . . [expectations and assumptions] up in the cradle. We unconsciously learn what to notice and what not to notice, how to divide time and space, how to walk and talk and use our bodies, how to behave as men or women, how to relate to other people, how to handle responsibility, whether experience is seen as whole or fragmented. This applies to all people. The Chinese or the Japanese or the Arabs are as unaware of their assumptions as we are of our own. We each assume that they're part of human nature. What we think of as "mind" is really internalized culture.[14]

In sum, it has been said: "you are your culture, and your culture is you." As part of the growing sophistication of marketing practices in the global economy, companies are hiring anthropologists to decipher the cultural roots of customer needs and preferences.

Ellen Brown, an anthropologist employed by Exxon, greets local inhabitants in the Central African nation of Chad. As explained in the OB in Action Case Study at the end of this chapter, the giant oil company hired Brown to handle cross-cultural relations during a recent 660-mile pipeline project from Chad to Cameroon's Atlantic coast. After all, Exxon's managers weren't as well equipped as Brown to deal with ceremonial chicken sacrifices.

(c) Tom Stoddart-IPG/Matrix

Culture Overrides National Boundaries

The term *societal* culture is used here instead of national culture because the boundaries of many nation-states were not drawn along cultural lines. Instead, they evolved through conquest, treaties, and geopolitics. The former Soviet Union, for example, included 15 republics and more than 100 ethnic nationalities, many with their own distinct language.[15] Also, English-speaking Canadians in Vancouver are culturally closer to Americans in Seattle than to their French-speaking compatriots in Quebec.

If we could redraw the world map along cultural lines instead of along geographical and political lines, we would end up with something very strange and different. That is precisely what researchers at the University of Michigan's Institute for Social Research have done with their World Values Survey, an ongoing study of 65 societies around the world.[16] Their cultural map in Figure 4–1 cross-references two different cultural dimensions: traditional versus secular-rational values and survival versus self-expression values. This odd-looking cultural map includes religious, political, language, and annual income overlays. To a cultural anthropologist, the map in Figure 4–1 says a lot more than an ordinary map of the world. For example, notice how Spain and Argentina, although separated by the Atlantic Ocean on a standard map, actually are close neighbors on this cultural map. Meanwhile, physically close Britain and Ireland are distanced from each other by religion on the cultural map. And former East and West Germany may be politically reunited, but a cultural gulf remains.

More than a decade after reunification, Germany remains a nation divided. Many western Germans resent the fact that billions of marks—their future pensions—were transferred to their poorer cousins. Some view the easterners as lazy. Citizens in the east regard their richer counterparts as arrogant know-it-alls who are out to rip them off.[17]

Cultural variables other than the ones in Figure 4–1 would likely produce very different maps. The point is, when preparing to live and work in a different country, be sure to consider more than national boundaries—study the culture.

More than a decade after the political reunification of Germany, a cultural gulf lingers between former East and West Germans. Some East Germans have found the transition from Communism to free-market capitalism difficult. As these Berlin school children enjoying an outdoor drawing lesson at the feet of Karl Marx and Friedrich Engels will come to appreciate, history matters when it comes to culture.

AP/Wide World Photos

Figure 4–1   *Redrawing the World Map along Cultural Lines*

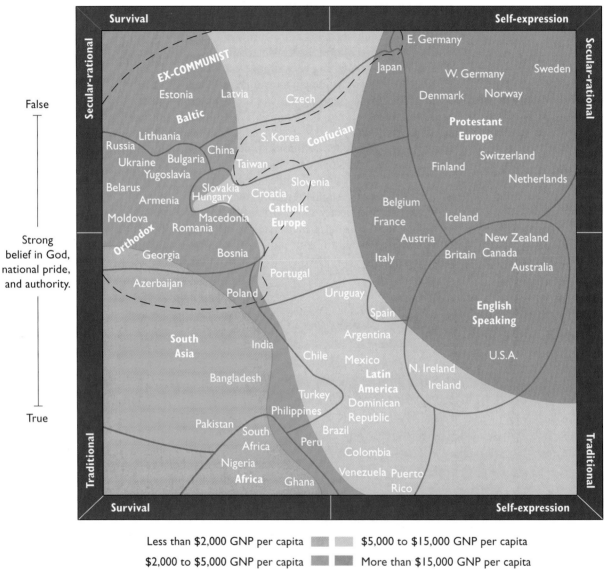

SOURCE: Adapted from R Inglehart and W E Baker, "Modernization's Challenges to Traditional Values: Who's Afraid of Ronald McDonald?" *The Futurist,* March–April 2001, p 19.

A Model of Societal and Organizational Cultures

As illustrated in Figure 4–2, culture influences organizational behavior in two ways. Employees bring their societal culture to work with them in the form of customs and language. Organizational culture, a by-product of societal culture, in turn affects the

Figure 4–2 *Cultural Influences on Organizational Behavior*

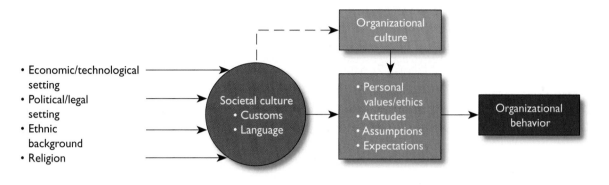

individual's values/ethics, attitudes, assumptions, and expectations. Societal culture is shaped by the various environmental factors listed in the left-hand side of Figure 4–2.

Once inside the organization's sphere of influence, the individual is further affected by the *organization's* culture. Mixing of societal and organizational cultures can produce interesting dynamics in multinational companies. For example, with French and American employees working side by side at General Electric's medical imaging production facility in Waukesha, Wisconsin, unit head Claude Benchimol has witnessed some culture shock:

> The French are surprised the American parking lots empty out as early as 5 PM; the Americans are surprised the French don't start work at 8 AM. Benchimol feels the French are more talkative and candid. Americans have more of a sense of hierarchy and are less likely to criticize. But they may be growing closer to the French. Says Benchimol: "It's taken a year to get across the idea that we are all entitled to say what we don't like to become more productive and work better."[18]

Same company, same company culture, yet GE's French and American co-workers have different attitudes about time, hierarchy, and communication. They are the products of different societal cultures.[19]

When managing people at work, the individual's societal culture, the organizational culture, and any interaction between the two need to be taken into consideration. For example, American workers' cultural orientation toward quality improvement differs significantly from the Japanese cultural pattern.

> Unlike Japanese workers, Americans aren't interested in making small step-by-step improvements to increase quality. They want to achieve the breakthrough, the impossible dream. The way to motivate them: Ask for the big leap, rather than for tiny steps.[20]

Ethnocentrism: A Cultural Roadblock in the Global Economy

Ethnocentrism, the belief that one's native country, culture, language, and modes of behavior are superior to all others, has its roots in the dawn of civilization. First identified as a behavioral science concept in 1906, involving the tendency of groups to reject outsiders,[21] the term *ethnocentrism* generally has a more encompassing (national

Ethnocentrism
Belief that one's native country, culture, language, and behavior are superior.

or societal) meaning today. Worldwide evidence of ethnocentrism is plentiful. For example, when a congressman said, "It is the English language which unites us,"[22] during a 1996 debate on an English-only bill for US federal agencies, charges of ethnocentrism were made by civil rights groups worried about the loss of bilingual ballots for non-English-speaking citizens. Militant ethnocentrism led to deadly "ethnic cleansing" in Bosnia and Kosovo and genocide in the African nations of Rwanda and Burundi.

Less dramatic, but still troublesome, is ethnocentrism within managerial and organizational contexts. Experts on the subject framed the problem this way:

> [Ethnocentric managers have] a preference for putting home-country people in key positions everywhere in the world and rewarding them more handsomely for work, along with a tendency to feel that this group is more intelligent, more capable, or more reliable. . . . Ethnocentrism is often not attributable to prejudice as much as to inexperience or lack of knowledge about foreign persons and situations. This is not too surprising, since most executives know far more about employees in their home environments. As one executive put it, "At least I understand why our own managers make mistakes. With our foreigners, I never know. The foreign managers may be better. But if I can't trust a person, should I hire him or her just to prove we're multinational?"[23]

Research suggests ethnocentrism is bad for business. A survey of 918 companies with home offices in the United States (272 companies), Japan (309), and Europe (337) found ethnocentric staffing and human resource policies to be associated with increased personnel problems. Those problems included recruiting difficulties, high turnover rates, and lawsuits over personnel policies. Among the three regional samples, Japanese companies had the most ethnocentric human resource practices and the most international human resource problems.[24]

Current and future managers can effectively deal with ethnocentrism through education, greater cross-cultural awareness, international experience, and a conscious effort to value cultural diversity.

Toward Greater Cross-Cultural Awareness and Competence

This section explores basic ways of describing and comparing cultures. As a foundation, we discuss cultural stereotyping and paradoxes. Next we contrast high-context and low-context cultures and introduce nine cultural dimensions identified in the new GLOBE project. Then our attention turns to examining cross-cultural differences in terms of individualism, time, space, and religion.

Caution: Be Alert for Cultural Paradoxes

An important qualification needs to be offered at this juncture. All of the cultural differences in this chapter and elsewhere need to be viewed as *tendencies* and *patterns* rather than as absolutes. As soon as one falls into the trap of assuming *all* Italians are this, and *all* Koreans will do that, and so on, potentially instructive generalizations become mindless stereotypes. A pair of professors with extensive foreign work experience advises: "As teachers, researchers, and managers in cross-cultural contexts, we need to recognize that our original characterizations of other cultures are best guesses that we need to modify as we gain more experience."[25] Consequently, they contend, we will be better prepared to deal with inevitable *cultural paradoxes.* By paradox, they mean there are always exceptions to the rule; individuals who do not fit the expected cultural pattern. A good example is the head of Canon. "By Japanese CEO standards, Canon Inc.'s Fujio Mitarai is something of an anomaly. For starters, he's fast and decisive—a far cry from the consensus builders who typically run Japan Inc."[26] One also encounters lots of cultural paradoxes in large and culturally diverse nations such as the United States and Brazil.[27] As in all human interaction, there is no adequate substitute for having extensive personal knowledge of the other person.

High-Context and Low-Context Cultures

This is a broadly applicable and useful cultural distinction[28] (see Figure 4–3). People from **high-context cultures**—including China, Korea, Japan, Vietnam, Mexico, and Arab cultures—rely heavily on situational cues for meaning when perceiving and communicating with others. Nonverbal cues such as one's official position, status, or family connections convey messages more powerfully than do spoken words. Thus, we come to better understand the ritual of exchanging *and reading* business cards in Japan. Japanese culture is relatively high context. One's business card, listing employer and official position, conveys vital silent messages about one's status to members of Japan's homogeneous society. Also, people from high-context cultures who are not especially talkative during a first encounter with a stranger are not necessarily being unfriendly; they are simply taking time to collect "contextual" information.[29]

High-context cultures
Primary meaning derived from nonverbal situational cues.

Reading the Fine Print in Low-Context Cultures   In **low-context cultures,** written and spoken words carry the burden of shared meanings. Low-context cultures include those found in Germany, Switzerland, Scandinavia, North America,

Low-context cultures
Primary meaning derived from written and spoken words.

Figure 4–3 *Contrasting High-Context and Low-Context Cultures*

High-Context
- Establish social trust first
- Value personal relations and goodwill
- Agreement by general trust
- Negotiations slow and ritualistic

Low-Context
- Get down to business first
- Value expertise and performance
- Agreement by specific, legalistic contract
- Negotiations as efficient as possible

SOURCE: M Munter, "Cross-Cultural Communication for Managers." Reprinted with permission from *Business Horizons*, May–June 1993, Figure 3, p 72. Copyright © 1993 by the Board of Trustees at Indiana University, Kelley School of Business.

and Great Britain. True to form, Germany has precise written rules for even the smallest details of daily life.[30] In *high*-context cultures, agreements tend to be made on the basis of someone's word or a handshake, after a rather prolonged get-acquainted and trust-building period. Low-context Americans and Canadians, who have cultural roots in Northern Europe, see the handshake as a signal to get a signature on a detailed, lawyer-approved, ironclad contract.

Avoiding Cultural Collisions
Misunderstanding and miscommunication often are problems in international business dealings when the parties are from high- versus low-context cultures. A Mexican business professor recently made this instructive observation:

> Over the years, I have noticed that across cultures there are different opinions on what is expected from a business report. US managers, for instance, take a pragmatic, get-to-the-point approach, and expect reports to be concise and action-oriented. They don't have time to read long explanations: "Just the facts, ma'am."
>
> Latin American managers will usually provide long explanations that go beyond the simple facts. . . .
>
> I have a friend who is the Latin America representative for a United States firm and has been asked by his boss to provide regular reports on sales activities. His reports are long, including detailed explanations on the context in which the events he is reporting on occur and the possible interpretations that they might have. His boss regularly answers these reports with very brief messages, telling him to "cut the crap and get to the point!"[31]

Awkward situations such as this can be avoided when those on both sides of the context divide make good-faith attempts to understand and accommodate their counterparts. Here are some practical tips:

- People on both sides of the context barrier must be trained to make adjustments.
- A new employee should be greeted by a group consisting of his or her boss, several colleagues who have similar duties, and an individual located near the newcomer.
- Background information is essential when explaining anything. Include the history and personalities involved.
- Do not assume the newcomer is self-reliant. Give explicit instructions not only about objectives, but also about the process involved.
- High-context workers from abroad need to learn to ask questions outside their department and function.
- Foreign workers must make an effort to become more self-reliant.[32]

Nine Cultural Dimensions from the GLOBE Project

Project GLOBE (Global Leadership and Organizational Behavior Effectiveness) is the brainchild of University of Pennsylvania professor Robert J House.[33] It is a massive and ongoing attempt to "develop an empirically based theory to describe, understand, and predict the impact of specific cultural variables on leadership and organizational processes and the effectiveness of these processes."[34] GLOBE has evolved into a network of more than 150 scholars from 62 countries since the project was launched in Calgary, Canada, in 1994. Most of the researchers are native to the particular cultures they study, thus greatly enhancing the credibility of the project. During the first two phases of the GLOBE project, a list of nine basic cultural dimensions was developed and statistically validated. Translated questionnaires based on the nine dimensions were administered to thousands of managers in the banking, food, and telecommunications industries around the world to build a database. Results are being published on a regular basis.[35] Much work and many years are needed if the project's goal, as stated above, is to be achieved. In the meantime, we have been given a comprehensive, valid, and up-to-date tool for better understanding cross-cultural similarities and differences.

The nine cultural dimensions from the GLOBE project are:

- *Power distance:* How much unequal distribution of power should there be in organizations and society?
- *Uncertainty avoidance:* How much should people rely on social norms and rules to avoid uncertainty and limit unpredictability?
- *Societal collectivism:* How much should leaders encourage and reward loyalty to the social unit, as opposed to the pursuit of individual goals?
- *In-group collectivism:* How much pride and loyalty should individuals have for their family or organization?
- *Gender egalitarianism:* How much effort should be put into minimizing gender discrimination and role inequalities?
- *Assertiveness:* How confrontational and dominant should individuals be in social relationships?
- *Future orientation:* How much should people delay gratification by planning and saving for the future?
- *Performance orientation:* How much should individuals be rewarded for improvement and excellence?
- *Humane orientation:* How much should society encourage and reward people for being kind, fair, friendly, and generous?[36]

What about *Your* Culture?   Take a short break from your reading to complete the OB Exercise on page 124. It will help you better comprehend the nine GLOBE cultural dimensions. Can you trace your cultural profile to family history and country of origin of your ancestors? For example, one of your author's German roots are evident in his cultural profile. What are the personal implications of any cultural "gaps" that surfaced?

Country Profiles and Practical Implications   How do different countries score on the GLOBE cultural dimensions? Data from 18,000 managers yielded the profiles in Table 4–1. A quick overview shows a great deal of cultural diversity around the world. But thanks to the nine GLOBE dimensions, we have more precise understanding of *how* cultures vary. Closer study reveals telling cultural *patterns,* or cultural fingerprints for nations. The US managerial sample, for instance, scored high on assertiveness and performance orientation. Accordingly, Americans are widely perceived as pushy and hardworking. Switzerland's high scores on uncertainty avoidance and future orientation help explain its centuries of political neutrality and world-renowned banking industry. Singapore is known as a great place to do business because it is clean and safe and its people are well educated and hardworking. This is no surprise, considering Singapore's high scores on social collectivism, future orientation, and performance orientation. In contrast, Russia's low scores on future orientation and performance orientation could foreshadow a slower than hoped for transition from a centrally planned

OB Exercise What Is Your Cultural Profile?

Instructions

Take two trips through this questionnaire, both times rating your degree of agreement with each statement. In the first round, rate the people in your native culture as you perceive them to be (by putting an X through the appropriate response). In the second round, indicate how *you* think people in general should behave (by circling the appropriate response). There are no right or wrong answers. *Note:* This particular instrument has *not* been validated and is for instructional purposes only.

Power Distance

1. Followers are (should be) expected to obey their leaders without question.

Disagree   Agree
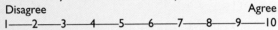
1—2—3—4—5—6—7—8—9—10

Uncertainty Avoidance

2. Most people lead (should lead) structured lives with few unexpected events.

Disagree   Agree
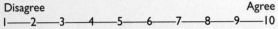
1—2—3—4—5—6—7—8—9—10

Societal Collectivism

3. Leaders encourage (should encourage) group loyalty even if individual goals suffer.

Disagree   Agree
1—2—3—4—5—6—7—8—9—10

In-Group Collectivism

4. Employees feel (should feel) great loyalty toward the organization.

Disagree   Agree
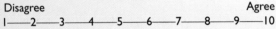
1—2—3—4—5—6—7—8—9—10

Gender Egalitarianism

5. Both women and men have (should have) equal educational and career opportunities.

Disagree   Agree
1—2—3—4—5—6—7—8—9—10

Assertiveness

6. People are (should be) generally dominant in their relationships with each other.

Disagree   Agree
1—2—3—4—5—6—7—8—9—10

Future Orientation

7. People live, plan, and save (should live, plan, and save) for the future.

Disagree   Agree
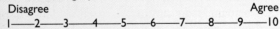
1—2—3—4—5—6—7—8—9—10

Performance Orientation

8. Students are encouraged (should be encouraged) to strive for continuously improved performance.

Disagree   Agree
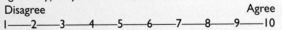
1—2—3—4—5—6—7—8—9—10

Humane Orientation

9. People are generally (should be generally) very tolerant of mistakes.

Disagree   Agree
1—2—3—4—5—6—7—8—9—10

Scoring

Draw one vertical line connecting the Xs from your first pass. Draw another vertical line connecting the circles from your second pass. The connected Xs indicate your prescribed cultural values. The connected circles indicate your personal values. The width of the gaps between the two lines indicate how well aligned you are with your native culture.

SOURCE: Based on and seven survey items excerpted from R House, M Javidan, P Hanges, and P Dorfman, "Understanding Cultures and Implicit Leadership Theories across the Globe: An Introduction to Project GLOBE," *Journal of World Business*, Spring 2002, Table 1, p 6.

Table 4–1   *Countries Ranking Highest and Lowest on the GLOBE Cultural Dimensions*

Dimension	Highest	Lowest
Power distance	Morocco, Argentina, Thailand, Spain, Russia	Denmark, Netherlands, South Africa—black sample, Israel, Costa Rica
Uncertainty avoidance	Switzerland, Sweden, German—former West, Denmark, Austria	Russia, Hungary, Bolivia, Greece, Venezuela
Societal collectivism	Sweden, South Korea, Japan, Singapore, Denmark	Greece, Hungary, Germany—former East, Argentina, Italy
In-group collectivism	Iran, India, Morocco, China, Egypt	Denmark, Sweden, New Zealand, Netherlands, Finland
Gender egalitarianism	Hungary, Poland, Slovenia, Denmark, Sweden	South Korea, Egypt, Morocco, India, China
Assertiveness	Germany—former East, Austria, Greece, US, Spain	Sweden, New Zealand, Switzerland, Japan, Kuwait
Future orientation	Singapore, Switzerland, Netherlands, Canada—English speaking, Denmark	Russia, Argentina, Poland, Italy, Kuwait
Performance orientation	Singapore, Hong Kong, New Zealand, Taiwan, US	Russia, Argentina, Greece, Venezuela, Italy
Humane orientation	Philippines, Ireland, Malaysia, Egypt, Indonesia	Germany—former West, Spain, France, Singapore, Brazil

SOURCE: Adapted from M Javidan and R J House, "Cultural Acumen for the Global Manager: Lessons from Project GLOBE," *Organizational Dynamics*, Spring 2001, pp 289–305.

economy to free enterprise capitalism. These illustrations bring us to an important practical lesson: *knowing the cultural tendencies of foreign business partners and competitors can give you a strategic competitive advantage.*

Individualism versus Collectivism

Have you ever been torn between what you personally wanted and what the group, organization, or society expected of you? If so, you have firsthand experience with a fundamental and important cultural distinction: individualism versus collectivism. This source of cultural variation—represented by two of the nine GLOBE dimensions—deserves a closer look. As might be expected with an extensively researched topic, individualism–collectivism has many interpretations.[37] Let us examine the basic concept for greater cultural awareness.

Individualistic cultures, characterized as "I" and "me" cultures, give priority to individual freedom and choice. **Collectivist cultures,** oppositely called "we" and "us" cultures, rank shared goals higher than individual desires and goals. People in collectivist cultures are expected to subordinate their own wishes and goals to those of the relevant social unit. A worldwide survey of 30,000 managers by Trompenaars and Hampden-Turner, who prefer the term *communitarianism* to collectivism, found the highest degree of individualism in Israel, Romania, Nigeria, Canada, and the United States. Countries ranking lowest in individualism—thus qualifying as collectivist cultures—were Egypt, Nepal, Mexico, India, and Japan. Brazil, China, and France also ended up toward the collectivist end of the scale.[38]

Individualistic culture

Primary emphasis on personal freedom and choice.

Collectivist culture

Personal goals less important than community goals and interests.

A Business Success Factor   Of course, one can expect to encounter both individualists and collectivists in culturally diverse countries such as the United States. For example, imagine the frustration of Dave Murphy, a Boston-based mutual fund salesperson, when he tried to get Navajo Indians in Arizona interested in saving money for their retirement. After several fruitless meetings with groups of Navajo employees, he was given this cultural insight by a local official: "If you come to this environment, you have to understand that money is different. It's there to be spent. If you have some, you help your family."[39] (This suggests Navajos would score high on in-group collectivism and low on future orientation on the GLOBE scale.) To traditional Navajos, enculturated as collectivists, saving money is an unworthy act of selfishness. Subsequently, the sales pitch was tailored to emphasize the *family* benefits of individual retirement savings plans.

Allegiance to Whom?   The Navajo example brings up an important point about collectivist cultures. Specifically, which unit of society predominates? For the Navajos, family is the key reference group. But, as Trompenaars and Hampden-Turner observe, important differences exist among collectivist (or communitarian) cultures:

> For each single society, it is necessary to determine the group with which individuals have the closest identification. They could be keen to identify with their trade union, their family, their corporation, their religion, their profession, their nation, or the state apparatus. The French tend to identify with *la France, la famille, le cadre*; the Japanese with the corporation; the former eastern bloc with the Communist Party; and Ireland with the Roman Catholic Church. Communitarian goals may be good or bad for industry depending on the community concerned, its attitude and relevance to business development.[40]

This observation validates GLOBE's distinction between societal and in-group collectivism.

Cultural Perceptions of Time

In North American and Northern European cultures, time seems to be a simple matter. It is linear, relentlessly marching forward, never backward, in standardized chunks. To the American who received a watch for his or her third birthday, time is like money. It is spent, saved, or wasted.[41] Americans are taught to show up 10 minutes early for appointments. When working across cultures, however, time becomes a very complex matter.[42] Imagine a New Yorker's chagrin when left in a waiting room for 45 minutes, only to find a Latin American government official dealing with three other people at once. The North American resents the lack of prompt and undivided attention. The Latin American official resents the North American's impatience and apparent self-centeredness.[43] This vicious cycle of resentment can be explained by the distinction between **monochronic time** and **polychronic time:**

> The former is revealed in the ordered, precise, schedule-driven use of public time that typifies and even caricatures efficient Northern Europeans and North Americans. The latter is seen in the multiple and cyclical activities and concurrent involvement with different people in Mediterranean, Latin American, and especially Arab cultures.[44]

A Matter of Degree   Monochronic and polychronic are relative rather than absolute concepts. Generally, the more things a person tends to do at once, the more polychronic that person is.[45] Thanks to the Internet and advanced telecommunications systems, highly polychronic managers can engage in "multitasking."[46] For example, it is

Monochronic time
Preference for doing one thing at a time because time is limited, precisely segmented, and schedule driven.

Polychronic time
Preference for doing more than one thing at a time because time is flexible and multidimensional.

possible to talk on the telephone, read and respond to E-mail, print a report, check an instant message, *and* eat a stale sandwich all at the same time. Unfortunately, this extreme polychronic behavior too often is not as efficient as hoped and, as discussed in Chapter 19, can be very stressful. Monochronic people prefer to do one thing at a time. What is your attitude toward time?

Practical Implications   Low-context cultures, such as that of the United States, tend to run on monochronic time, while high-context cultures, such as that of Mexico, tend to run on polychronic time. People in polychronic cultures view time as flexible, fluid, and multidimensional. The Germans and Swiss have made an exact science of monochronic time. In fact, a radio-controlled watch made by a German company, Junghans, is "guaranteed to lose no more than one second in 1 million years."[47] Many a visitor has been a minute late for a Swiss train, only to see its taillights leaving the station. Time is more elastic in polychronic cultures. During the Islamic holy month of Ramadan in Middle Eastern nations, for example, the faithful fast during daylight hours, and the general pace of things markedly slows. Managers need to reset their mental clocks when doing business across cultures (see International OB on page 128).

Interpersonal Space

Anthropologist Edward T Hall noticed a connection between culture and preferred interpersonal distance. People from high-context cultures were observed standing close when talking to someone. Low-context cultures appeared to dictate a greater amount of interpersonal space. Hall applied the term **proxemics** to the study of cultural expectations about interpersonal space.[48] He specified four interpersonal distance zones. Some call them space bubbles. They are *intimate* distance, *personal* distance, *social* distance, and *public* distance. Ranges for the four interpersonal distance zones are illustrated in Figure 4–4, along with selected cultural differences.

Proxemics

Hall's term for the study of cultural expectations about interpersonal space.

Figure 4–4 *Interpersonal Distance Zones for Business Conversations Vary from Culture to Culture*

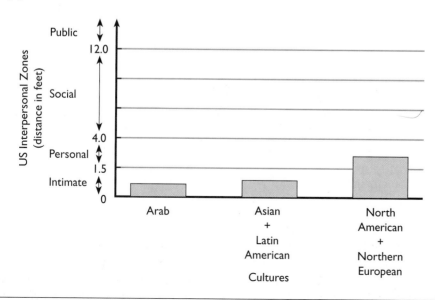

Afghans Heap on the Hospitality

Mullahs and milk chocolate, warlords and wafers: not the kind of imagery associated with the War on Terrorism.

But the truth is that all this hype about Afghan hospitality—remember the Taliban assertion that Osama bin Laden was their "guest"—may not all be, well, hype.

Truth be told, Pashtuns take about as much pride in their hospitality as they do in their Kalishnikovs. On a recent war-covering assignment in Pakistan, I found that you can't drop into the home of an Afghan warlord, particularly the Pashtuns of the south, without being offered a steaming cup of green tea or hot chocolate, and usually a plate—a heaping plate in some cases—of sweet biscuits, cookies and pastries.

And with the sweets there may be, from the server, a wary eye curious to see if this offering is accepted or rejected by a guest. After all, the art of graciousness cuts both ways.

Afghans make a mean cookie. Called a kulchi, or sweet biscuit, it is this wonderful mound of dough with a crunchy soft center covered by a fluffy, powdered-sugar coating. You don't eat them. You inhale them.

Walk down a rutted, dirt street in an Afghan refugee neighborhood of Peshawar, Pakistan, and amid the fly-strewn carcasses hanging in butcher shops and the open sewers of the roadside ditches, the pungent aroma of freshly baked kulchi inevitably brings a smile to a visitor's face.

From the fortress-like upper floor of a warlord's home in Quetta, Pakistan, to a mullah's reception room in Peshawar, to the lavishly wood-paneled dining room of a wealthy Pashtun landowner near the Afghan border, any discussion or interview I had required polite stages. There was the greeting, the handshake and the invariable moment of silence as a relative or associate or servant carried in hot liquid drinks and something sweet to nibble.

Patience was a prerequisite, deadlines be damned.

If the moment was within two or three hours of lunch or dinner, invariably there was the offer—or more accurately, the insistence—to stay and eat a full meal of naan, roast lamb, rice and yogurt. Refusals were not taken lightly or easily.

This may be a land of violence and turmoil. But there was always time for one important question—do you take sugar in your green tea?

SOURCE: G Zoroya, "Afghans Heap on the Hospitality," *USA Today,* December 21, 2001, p 1D.

(c) Michael Yamashita

North American business conversations normally are conducted at about a three- to four-foot range, within the personal zone in Figure 4–4. A range of approximately one foot is common in Latin American and Asian cultures, uncomfortably close for Northern Europeans and North Americans. Some Arabs like to get even closer. Mismatches in culturally dictated interpersonal space zones can prove very distracting for the unprepared. Hall explains:

> Arabs tend to get very close and breathe on you. It's part of the high sensory involvement of a high-context culture. . . .
>
> The American on the receiving end can't identify all the sources of his discomfort but feels that the Arab is pushy. The Arab comes close, the American backs up. The Arab follows, because he can only interact at certain distances. Once the American learns that Arabs handle space differently and that breathing on people is a form of communication, the situation can sometimes be redefined so the American relaxes.[49]

Asian and Middle-Eastern hosts grow weary of having to seemingly chase their low-context guests around at social gatherings to maintain what they feel is proper conversational range. Backing up all evening to keep conversational partners at a proper distance is an awkward experience as well. Awareness of cultural differences, along with skillful accommodation, are essential to productive intercultural business dealings.

Religion

Religious beliefs and practices can have a profound effect on cross-cultural relations. A comprehensive treatment of different religions is beyond the scope of our current discussion.[50] However, we can examine the relationship between religious affiliation and work-related values. A study of 484 international students at a midwestern US university uncovered wide variability. The following list gives the most important work-related value for each of five religious affiliations:

Catholic—Consideration ("Concern that employees be taken seriously, be kept informed, and that their judgments be used.")

Protestant—Employer effectiveness ("Desire to work for a company that is efficient, successful, and a technological leader.")

Buddhist—Social responsibility ("Concern that the employer be a responsible part of society.")

Muslim—Continuity ("Desire for stable environment, job longevity, reduction of uncertainty.")

No religious preference—Professional challenge ("Concern with having a job that provides learning opportunities and opportunities to use skills well.")[51]

Thus, there was virtually *no agreement* across religions about the primary work value. This led the researchers to conclude: "Employers might be wise to consider the impact that religious differences (and more broadly, cultural factors) appear to have on the values of employee groups."[52] Of course, in the United States and other selected countries, equal employment opportunity laws forbid managers from basing employment-related decisions on an applicant's religious preference.

Practical Insights from Cross-Cultural Management Research

Nancy Adler, an international OB specialist at Canada's McGill University, has offered the following introductory definition: "**Cross-cultural management** explains the behavior of people in organizations around the world and shows people how to work in organizations with employee and client populations from many different cultures."[53] Historically, cross-cultural management research has focused almost exclusively on cultural differences.[54] But GLOBE researchers Mansour Javidan and Robert J House recommend studying *similarities* as well. They believe tracking cultural similarities will help us judge how applicable specific management practices are in foreign cultures. "For example, leadership theories developed in the US are probably more easily generalizable to UK managers (another member of the Anglo cluster) than to managers in an Arab country."[55] In this section we will examine two different streams of

Cross-cultural management
Understanding and teaching behavioral patterns in different cultures.

cross-cultural management research—one emphasizing differences, the other emphasizing similarities. Both offer useful lessons for today's managers.

The Hofstede–Bond Stream of Research

Instructive insights surfaced in the mid-1980s when the results of two very different
cross-cultural management studies were merged. The first study was conducted under
the guidance of Dutch researcher Geert Hofstede. Canadian Michael Harris Bond, at
the Chinese University of Hong Kong, was a key researcher in the second study. What
follows is a brief overview of each study, a discussion of the combined results, and a
summary of important practical implications.

The Two Studies   Hofstede's study is a classic in the annals of cross-cultural
management research.[56] He drew his data for that study from a collection of 116,000
attitude surveys administered to IBM employees worldwide between 1967 and 1973.
Respondents to the attitude survey, which also asked questions on cultural values and
beliefs, included IBM employees from 72 countries. Fifty-three cultures eventually
were analyzed and contrasted according to four cultural dimensions. Hofstede's database was unique, not only because of its large size, but also because it allowed him to
isolate cultural effects. If his subjects had not performed *similar jobs* in *different countries* for the *same company,* no such control would have been possible. Cross-cultural
comparisons were made along the first four dimensions listed in Table 4–2, power distance, individualism–collectivism, masculinity–femininity, and uncertainty avoidance.

Bond's study was much smaller, involving a survey of 100 (50% women) students
from 22 countries and five continents. The survey instrument was the Chinese Value
Survey (CVS), based on the Rokeach Value Survey.[57] The CVS also tapped four cultural dimensions. Three corresponded to Hofstede's first three in Table 4–2. Hofstede's
fourth cultural dimension, uncertainty avoidance, was not measured by the CVS.
Instead, Bond's study isolated the fifth cultural dimension in Table 4–2. It eventually
was renamed *long-term versus short-term orientation* to reflect how strongly a person

Table 4–2   *Key Cultural Dimensions in the Hofstede–Bond Studies*

Power distance: How much do people expect inequality in social institutions (e.g., family, work organizations, government)?
Individualism–collectivism: How loose or tight is the bond between individuals and societal groups?
Masculinity–femininity: To what extent do people embrace competitive masculine traits (e.g., success, assertiveness and performance) or nurturing feminine traits (e.g., solidarity, personal relationships, service, quality of life)?
Uncertainty avoidance: To what extent do people prefer structured versus unstructured situations?
Long-term versus short-term orientation (Confucian values): To what extent are people oriented toward the future by saving and being persistent versus being oriented toward the present and past by respecting tradition and meeting social obligations?

SOURCE: Adapted from discussion in G Hofstede, "Cultural Constraints in Management Theories,"
Academy of Management Executive, February 1993, pp 81–94.

believes in the long-term thinking promoted by the teachings of the Chinese philoso-pher Confucius (551–479 BC). According to an update by Hofstede: "On the long-term side one finds values oriented towards the future, like thrift (saving) and persistence. On the short-term side one finds values rather oriented towards the past and present, like respect for tradition and fulfilling social obligations."[58] Importantly, one may embrace Confucian long-term values without knowing a thing about Confucius.[59]

East Meets West   By merging the two studies, a serious flaw in each was cor-rected. Namely, Hofstede's study had an inherent Anglo-European bias, and Bond's study had a built-in Asian bias. How would cultures compare if viewed through the overlapping lenses of the two studies? Hofstede and Bond were able to answer that question because 18 countries in Bond's study overlapped the 53 countries in Hofstede's sample.[60] Table 4–3 lists the countries scoring highest on each of the five cultural dimensions. (Countries earning between 67 and 100 points on a 0 to 100 rela-tive ranking scale qualified as "high" for Table 4–3.) The United States scored the high-est in individualism, moderate in power distance, masculinity, and uncertainty avoid-ance, and low in long-term orientation.

Practical Lessons   Individually, and together, the Hofstede and Bond studies yielded the following useful lessons for international managers:

1. Due to varying cultural values, management theories and practices need to be adapted to the local culture. This is particularly true for made-in-America management theories (e.g., Maslow's need hierarchy theory) and Japanese management practices.[61] *There is no one best way to manage across cultures,* according to the Hofstede–Bond school of thought.

2. High long-term orientation was the only one of the five cultural dimensions to correlate positively with national economic growth. (Note how the four Asian countries listed under high long-term orientation in Table 4–3 have been among the

Table 4–3   *Countries Scoring the Highest in the Hofstede–Bond Studies*

High Power Distance	High Individualism	High Masculinity	High Uncertainty Avoidance	High Long-Term Orientation*
Philippines	United States	Japan	Japan	Hong Kong***
India	Australia		Korea	Taiwan
Singapore	Great Britain		Brazil	Japan
Brazil	Netherlands		Pakistan	Korea
Hong Kong***	Canada		Taiwan	
	New Zealand			
	Sweden			
	Germany**			

*Originally called Confucian Dynamism.
**Former West Germany.
***Reunited with China.

SOURCE: Adapted from Exhibit 2 in G Hofstede and M H Bond, "The Confucius Connection: From Cultural Roots to Economic Growth," *Organizational Dynamics,* Spring 1988, pp 12–13.

world's economic growth leaders over the past 30 years, with the exception of the Asian currency crisis in 1997–1998.) In the long term, this correlation may not bode well for countries scoring lowest on this dimension: Pakistan, Philippines, Canada, Great Britain, and the United States. (Oddly, as indicated back in Table 4–1, English-speaking Canadians scored high on GLOBE's future orientation dimension.)

3. Industrious cultural values are a necessary but insufficient condition for economic growth. Markets and a supportive political climate also are required to create the right mix.[62] (It remains to be seen if Hong Kong can achieve long-term economic vitality following the 1997 takeover by China and if Japan can pull out of its long recession.)

4. Cultural arrogance is a luxury individuals and nations can no longer afford in a global economy.

Leadership Lessons from the GLOBE Project

In direct contrast to the Hofstede tradition of searching for cultural differences, researchers from the GLOBE project set out to discover which, if any, attributes of leadership were universally liked or disliked. They surveyed 15,022 middle managers from 60 societies/cultures.[63] The responding managers worked for a total of 779 different organizations. Twenty-two leader attributes were found to be universally liked, 8 were universally disliked, and 35 received mixed reviews. Table 4–4 highlights the findings by listing the most liked, most disliked, and most disputed leader attributes.

This study represents a refreshing redirection in cross-cultural management research. Specifically, it stakes out some *common* cultural ground in the important area of leadership. Among the practical implications:

Table 4–4   *Leadership Attributes Universally Liked, Universally Disliked, and Most Strongly Disputed across 60 Cultures Worldwide*

Leader Attributes Universally Liked*	Leader Attributes Universally Disliked**	Most Disputed Leader Attributes***
• Trustworthy	• Noncooperative	• Subdued
• Dynamic	• Irritable	• Intragroup conflict avoider
• Motive arouser	• Egocentric	• Cunning
• Decisive	• Ruthless	• Sensitive
• Intelligent	• Dictatorial	• Provocateur
• Dependable	• Loner/self-centered	• Self-effacing
• Plans ahead		• Willful
• Excellence oriented		
• Team builder		
• Encouraging		

Selection criteria for this table:
*Mean score of 6.14 or higher on 1–7 scale.
**Mean score of 2.06 or lower on 1–7 scale.
***Standard deviation of .84 or higher.

SOURCE: Adapted from Den Hartog et al., "Emics and Etics of Culturally-Endorsed Implicit Leadership Theories: Are Attributes of Charismatic/Transformational Leadership Universally Endorsed?" *Leadership Quarterly*, in press.

- According to the researchers, leader attributes associated with the charismatic/transformational leadership style, discussed in depth in Chapter 17, are globally applicable.
- Certain leader attributes, listed in the middle column of Table 4–4, should be avoided in all cultures.
- Leader attributes that are widely disputed across cultures need to be used (or avoided) on a culture-by-culture basis. In other words, the contingency approach applies.[64]

Preparing Employees for Successful Foreign Assignments

As the reach of global companies continues to grow, many opportunities for living and working in foreign countries will arise. Imagine, for example, the opportunities for foreign duty and cross-cultural experiences at Siemens, the German electronics giant. "While Siemens' corporate headquarters is near Munich, nearly 80% of the firm's business is international. Worldwide the company has 470,000 employees, including 75,000 in the United States and 25,000 in China."[65] Siemens and other global players need a vibrant and growing cadre of employees who are willing and able to do business across cultures. Thus, the purpose of this final section is to help you prepare yourself and others to work successfully in foreign countries.

Why Do US Expatriates Fail On Foreign Assignments?

As we use the term here, **expatriate** refers to anyone living and/or working outside their home country. Hence, they are said to be *expatriated* when transferred to another country and *repatriated* when transferred back home. US expatriate managers, now at more than 300,000,[66] usually are characterized as culturally inept and prone to failure

Expatriate
Anyone living or working in a foreign country.

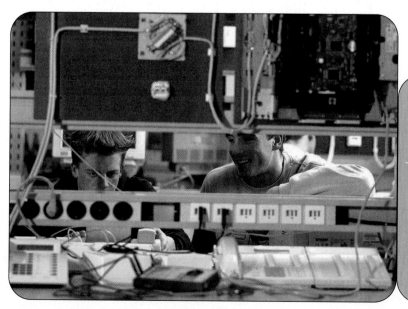

In today's global economy, there are many opportunities for cross-cultural work experiences and foreign assignments. Germany's Siemens, the electronics company with 470,000 employees worldwide, has 75,000 employees in the United States and 25,000 in China. Here trainees team up on an electrical engineering problem at Siemens' Professional Education Center in Munich.

Courtesy of Siemens AG

on international assignments. Sadly, research supports this view. A pair of international management experts offered this assessment:

> Over the past decade, we have studied the management of expatriates at about 750 US, European, and Japanese companies. We asked both the expatriates themselves and the executives who sent them abroad to evaluate their experiences. In addition, we looked at what happened after expatriates returned home. . . .
>
> Overall, the results of our research were alarming. We found that between 10% and 20% of all US managers sent abroad returned early because of job dissatisfaction or difficulties in adjusting to a foreign country. Of those who stayed for the duration, nearly one-third did not perform up to the expectations of their superiors. And perhaps most problematic, one-fourth of those who completed an assignment left their company, often to join a competitor, within one year after repatriation. That's a turnover rate double that of managers who did not go abroad.[67]

Because of the high cost of sending employees and their families to foreign countries for extended periods, significant improvement is needed.

Research has uncovered specific reasons for the failure of US expatriate managers. Listed in decreasing order of frequency, the seven most common reasons are as follows:

1. The manager's spouse cannot adjust to new physical or cultural surroundings.
2. The manager cannot adapt to new physical or cultural surroundings.
3. Family problems.
4. The manager is emotionally immature.
5. The manager cannot cope with foreign duties.
6. The manager is not technically competent.
7. The manager lacks the proper motivation for a foreign assignment.[68]

Collectively, *family and personal adjustment problems,* not technical competence, are the main stumbling block for American managers working in foreign countries.

This conclusion is reinforced by the results of a survey that asked 72 human resource managers at multinational corporations to identify the most important success factor in a foreign assignment. "Nearly 35% said cultural adaptability: patience, flexibility, and tolerance for others' beliefs. Only 22% of them listed technical and management skills."[69] US multinational companies clearly need to do a better job of preparing employees and their families for foreign assignments.

A Bright Spot: North American Women on Foreign Assignments

Historically, a woman from the United States or Canada on a foreign assignment was a rarity. Things are changing, albeit slowly. A review of research evidence and anecdotal accounts uncovered these insights:

- The proportion of corporate women from North America on foreign assignments grew from about 3% in the early 1980s to between 11% and 15% in the late 1990s.
- Self-disqualification and management's assumption that women would not be welcome in foreign cultures—not foreign prejudice, itself—are the primary barriers for potential female expatriates.

- Expatriate North American women are viewed first and foremost by their hosts as being foreigners, and only secondarily as being female.
- North American women have a very high success rate on foreign assignments.[70]

Considering the rapidly growing demand for global managers today,[71] self-disqualification by women and management's prejudicial policies are counterproductive. For their part, women and others who desire a foreign assignment need to take affirmative steps (see Table 4–5).

Avoiding OB Trouble Spots in Foreign Assignments

Finding the right person (often along with a supportive and adventurous family) for a foreign position is a complex, time-consuming, and costly process.[72] For our purposes, it is sufficient to narrow the focus to common OB trouble spots in the foreign assignment cycle. As illustrated in Figure 4–5, the first and last stages of the cycle occur at home. The middle two stages occur in the foreign or host country. Each stage hides an OB-related trouble spot that needs to be anticipated and neutralized. Otherwise, the bill for another failed foreign assignment will grow.

Avoiding Unrealistic Expectations with Cross-Cultural Training

Realistic job previews (RJPs) have proven effective at bringing people's unrealistic expectations about a pending job assignment down to earth by providing a realistic balance of good and bad news. People with realistic expectations tend to quit less often and be more satisfied than those with unrealistic expectations. RJPs are a must for future expatriates. In addition, cross-cultural training is required.

Cross-cultural training is any type of structured experience designed to help departing employees adjust to a foreign culture. The trend is toward more such training in the

Cross-cultural training
Structured experiences to help people adjust to a new culture/country.

Table 4–5   *Tips for Women (and Men) for Landing a Foreign Assignment*

- While still in school, pursue foreign study opportunities and become fluent in one or more foreign languages.
- Starting with the very first job interview, clearly state your desire for a foreign assignment.
- Become very knowledgeable about foreign countries where you would like to work (take vacations there).
- Network with expatriates (both men and women) in your company to uncover foreign assignment opportunities.
- Make sure your family fully supports a foreign assignment.
- Get your boss's support by building trust and a strong working relationship.
- Be visible: make sure upper management knows about your relevant accomplishments and unique strengths.
- Stay informed about your company's international strategies and programs.
- Polish your cross-cultural communication skills daily with foreign-born co-workers.

SOURCE: Based on discussions in A Varma, L K Stroh, and L B Schmitt, "Women and International Assignments: The Impact of Supervisor-Subordinate Relationships," *Journal of World Business*, Winter 2001, pp 380–88; and T Wilen, "Women Working Overseas," *Training and Development*, May 2001, pp 120–22.

Figure 4–5   *The Foreign Assignment Cycle (with OB Trouble Spots)*

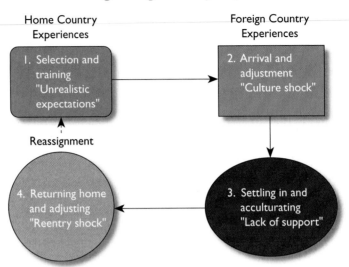

United States. But there is a great deal of room for improvement, as indicated by the results of a recent *Training* magazine survey. Only 12% rated cross-cultural/diversity training as "very important" for preparing employees for international assignments.[73] Experts believe that cross-cultural training, although costly, is less expensive than failed foreign assignments. Programs vary widely in type and also in rigor. Of course, the greater the difficulty, the greater the time and expense:

- *Easiest.* Predeparture training is limited to informational materials, including books, lectures, films, videos, and internet searches.
- *Moderately difficult.* Experiential training is conducted through case studies, role playing, assimilators (simulated intercultural incidents), and introductory language instruction.
- *Most difficult.* Departing employees are given some combination of the preceding methods plus comprehensive language instruction and field experience in the target culture. As an example of the latter, PepsiCo Inc. transfers "about 25 young foreign managers a year to the US for one-year assignments in bottling plants."[74]

Which approach is the best? Research to date does not offer a final answer. One study involving US employees in South Korea led the researcher to recommend a *combination* of informational and experiential predeparture training.[75] As a general rule of thumb, the more rigorous the cross-cultural training, the better. Our personal experience with teaching OB to foreign students both in the United States and abroad reminds us that there really is no substitute for an intimate knowledge of the local language and culture.

Culture shock
Anxiety and doubt caused by an overload of new expectations and cues.

Avoiding Culture Shock   Have you ever been in a totally unfamiliar situation and felt disoriented and perhaps a bit frightened? If so, you already know something about culture shock. According to anthropologists, **culture shock** involves anxiety and doubt caused by an overload of unfamiliar expectations and social cues.[76] College freshmen often experience a variation of culture shock. An expatriate manager, or family member, may be thrown off balance by an avalanche of strange sights, sounds, and behaviors. Among them may be unreadable road signs, strange-tasting food, inability to use your left hand for social activities (in Islamic countries, the left hand is the toilet hand), or failure to get a laugh with your sure-fire joke. For the expatriate manager trying to concentrate on the fine details of a business negotiation, culture shock is more than an embarrassing inconvenience. It is a disaster! Like the confused college freshman who quits and goes home, culture-shocked employees often panic and go home early.

The best defense against culture shock is comprehensive cross-cultural training, including intensive language study. Once again, the best way to pick up subtle—yet important—social cues is via the local language.

Support during the Foreign Assignment

Especially during the first six months, when everything is so new to the expatriate, a support system needs to be in place.[77] *Host-country sponsors,* assigned to individual managers or families, are recommended because they serve as "cultural seeing-eye dogs." In a foreign country, where even the smallest errand can turn into an utterly exhausting production, sponsors can get things done quickly because they know the cultural and geographical territory. Honda's Ohio employees, for example, enjoyed the help of family sponsors when training in Japan:

> Honda smoothed the way with Japanese wives who once lived in the US. They handled emergencies such as when Diana Jett's daughter Ashley needed stitches in her chin. When Task Force Senior Manager Kim Smalley's daughter, desperate to fit in at elementary school, had to have a precisely shaped bag for her harmonica, a Japanese volunteer stayed up late to make it.[78]

Avoiding Reentry Shock

Strange as it may seem, many otherwise successful expatriate managers encounter their first major difficulty only after their foreign assignment is over. Why? Returning to one's native culture is taken for granted because it seems so routine and ordinary. But having adjusted to another country's way of doing things for an extended period of time can put one's own culture and surroundings in a strange new light. Three areas for potential reentry shock are work, social activities, and general environment (e.g., politics, climate, transportation, food). Ira Caplan's return to New York City exemplifies reentry shock:

> During the past 12 years, living mostly in Japan, he and his wife had spent their vacations cruising the Nile or trekking in Nepal. They hadn't seen much of the US. They are getting an eyeful now. . . .
>
> Prices astonish him. The obsession with crime unnerves him. What unsettles Mr Caplan more, though, is how much of himself he has left behind.
>
> In a syndrome of return no less stressful than that of departure, he feels displaced, disregarded, and diminished. . . .
>
> In an Italian restaurant, crowded at lunchtime, the waiter sets a bowl of linguine in front of him. Mr Caplan stares at it. "In Asia, we have smaller portions and smaller people," he says.
>
> Asia is on his mind. He has spent years cultivating an expertise in a region of huge importance. So what? This is New York.[79]

Work-related adjustments were found to be a major problem for samples of repatriated Finnish, Japanese, and American employees.[80] Upon being repatriated, a 12-year veteran of one US company said: "Our organizational culture was turned upside down. We now have a different strategic focus, different 'tools' to get the job done, and different buzzwords to make it happen. I had to learn a whole new corporate 'language.' "[81]

Reentry shock can be reduced through employee career counseling and home-country sponsors. Simply being aware of the problem of reentry shock is a big step toward effectively dealing with it.[82]

Overall, the key to a successful foreign assignment is making it a well-integrated link in a career chain rather than treating it as an isolated adventure.

Summary of Key Concepts

1. *Define the term* culture, *and explain how societal culture and organizational culture combine to influence on-the-job behavior.* Culture is a set of beliefs and values about what is desirable and undesirable in a community of people, and a set of formal or informal practices to support the values. Culture has both prescriptive and descriptive elements and involves taken-for-granted assumptions about how to think, act, and feel. Culture overrides national boundaries. Key aspects of societal culture, such as customs and language, are brought to work by the individual. Working together, societal and organizational culture influence the person's values, ethics, attitudes, and expectations.

2. *Define* ethnocentrism, *and distinguish between high-context and low-context cultures.* Ethnocentrism is the belief that one's native culture, language, and ways of doing things are superior to all others. People from low-context cultures infer relatively less from situational cues and extract more meaning from spoken and written words. In high-context cultures such as China and Japan, managers prefer slow negotiations and trust-building meetings, which tends to frustrate low-context Northern Europeans and North Americans who prefer to get right down to business.

3. *Identify and describe the nine cultural dimensions from Project GLOBE.* (1) *Power distance*—How equally should power be distributed? (2) *Uncertainty avoidance*—How much should social norms and rules reduce uncertainty and unpredictability? (3) *Societal collectivism*—How much should loyalty to the social unit override individual interests? (4) *In-group collectivism*—How strong should one's loyalty be to family or organization? (5) *Gender egalitarianism*—How much should gender discrimination and role inequalities be minimized? (6) *Assertiveness*—How confrontational and dominant should one be in social relationships? (7) *Future orientation*—How much should one delay gratification by planning and saving for the future? (8) *Performance orientation*—How much should individuals be rewarded for improvement and excellence? (9) *Humane orientation*—How much should individuals be rewarded for being kind, fair, friendly, and generous?

4. *Distinguish between individualistic and collectivist cultures, and explain the difference between monochronic and polychronic cultures.* People in individualistic cultures think primarily in terms of "I" and "me" and place a high value on freedom and personal choice. Collectivist cultures teach people to be "we" and "us" oriented and to subordinate personal wishes and goals to the interests of the relevant social unit (such as family, group, organization, or society). People in monochronic cultures are schedule driven and prefer to do one thing at a time. To them, time is like money; it is spent wisely or wasted. In polychronic cultures, there is a tendency to do many things at once and to perceive time as flexible and multidimensional. Polychronic people view monochronic people as being too preoccupied with time.

5. *Outline the practical lessons from the Hofstede–Bond cross-cultural studies.* According to the Hofstede–Bond cross-cultural management studies, caution needs to be exercised when transplanting management theories and practices from one culture to another. Also, long-term orientation was the only one of five cultural dimensions in the Hofstede–Bond studies to correlate positively with national economic growth.

6. *Explain what Project GLOBE researchers discovered about leadership.* Across 60 cultures, they identified three categories of leader attributes: universally liked, universally disliked, and disputed. The universally liked leader attributes—including trustworthy, dynamic, motive arouser, decisive, and intelligent—are associated with the charismatic/transformational leadership style that is widely applicable. Universally disliked leader attributes—such as noncooperative, irritable, egocentric, and dictatorial—should be avoided in all cultures. Disputed leader attributes need to be used or avoided on a culture-by-culture contingency basis.

7. *Specify why US managers have a comparatively high failure rate on foreign assignments.* American expatriates are troubled by family and personal adjustment problems. These problems center on cultural awareness and adaptability, not technical skills.

8. *Summarize the research findings about North American women on foreign assignments, and tell how to land a foreign assignment.* The number of North American women on foreign assignments is still small, but growing. Self-disqualification and prejudicial home-country supervisors and staffing policies are largely to blame. Foreigners tend to view North American women primarily as foreigners and secondarily as women. North American women have a high success rate on foreign assignments. Foreign language skills, a strong and formally announced desire, foreign experience, networking, family and supervisory support, and visibility with upper management can increase the chances of getting a desired foreign assignment for both women and men.

9. *Identify four stages of the foreign assignment cycle and the OB trouble spot associated with each stage.* Stages of the foreign assignment cycle (with OB trouble spots) are (1) *Selection and training* (unrealistic expectations); (2) *Arrival and adjustment* (culture shock); (3) *Settling in and acculturating* (lack of support); and (4) *Returning home and adjusting* (reentry shock).

Discussion Questions

1. Regarding your cultural awareness, how would you describe the prevailing culture in your country to a stranger from another land?

2. What are your personal experiences with ethnocentrism and cross-cultural dealings? What lessons have you learned?

3. Why are people from high-context cultures such as China and Japan likely to be misunderstood by low-context Westerners?

4. What are the managerial implications of your GLOBE cultural profile in the OB Exercise?

5. Culturally speaking, are you individualistic or collectivist? How does that cultural orientation affect how you run your personal and/or business affairs?

6. In your view, what is the most important lesson for global managers from the Hofstede–Bond studies? Explain.

7. Do you personally agree with the lists of universally liked and disliked leader attributes in Table 4–4? Explain.

8. What needs to be done to improve the success rate of US managers in foreign assignments?

9. How strong is your desire for a foreign assignment? Why? If it is strong, where would you like to work? Why? How prepared are you for a foreign assignment? What do you need to do to be better prepared?

10. What is your personal experience with culture shock? Which of the OB trouble spots in Figure 4–5 do you believe is the greatest threat to expatriate employee success? Explain.

Internet Exercise   **www.lonelyplanet.com**

Thanks to the power of the Internet, you can take a trip to a far-flung corner of the world without ever leaving your chair. The purpose of this exercise is to enhance your cross-cultural awareness by using the Internet to learn about a foreign country of your choice. Our primary resource is the Internet site **www.lonelyplanet.com** based on the popular, highly readable, and somewhat off-beat Lonely Planet travel guides available in bookstores. (This is our favorite, but if you prefer another online travel guide, use it and tell others.) At the Lonely Planet Online home page, select "Worldguide" and then click on "Destinations." Use the geographic menus on the Destinations page to *select a foreign country where your native language is not the primary language.* Explore the map of your selected country and then read the material in the "Introduction" and "Facts for the Traveler" and "Culture" sections. If you have the time and interest, read some of the other relevant sections such as "History."

A second important stop on your Internet trip is **www.travlang.com** to start building your language skills for your selected country. At the home page, scroll to the bottom and select "Foreign Languages for Travelers" and then follow steps 1 and 2. Next, select "Basic Words" from the language page you picked in step 2. Practice essential words such as "Hello," "Yes," "No," "Thank you," and any others you deem necessary. Take the language *quiz* if you have time.

Questions

1. How strong is your interest in taking a foreign assignment in your selected country? Explain.

2. Culturally, does your focus country seem to be high-context or low-context, individualistic or collectivist, and monochronic or polychronic? Cite specific clues from your Internet research.

3. How do you say "Hello" and "Thank you" in the primary language of your chosen country? (Perhaps you have a classmate who can help you with your pronunciation.)

4. What is the likelihood of experiencing "culture shock" in this country? How could you avoid or minimize it?

OB in Action Case Study

Exxon Goes to Africa for Oil and Gets Chicken Sacrifices[83]

BusinessWeek When he first heard that Exxon Mobil would be drilling for oil a mile beneath his village of Mbanga, in southern Chad, Patrice Matangarti's head swam with expectations. Perhaps his village would finally get the things it so desperately needed: a health clinic, a proper school, clean water, electricity. Maybe Exxon would even build him a house, something better than his one-room mud hut.

But today, the village chief is plainly unhappy with a visiting Exxon representative. "Nobody here has been hired for the project," he complains, sitting in the shade of a fig tree, while dozens of villagers look on silently. "And [Exxon] has cut those big trees that make it rain. The wind passes, the clouds pass, but it doesn't rain."

The power disparity could not be wider—a poor villager in the world's fifth-poorest country lecturing the world's second-largest corporation—and in a different day and age, Exxon could easily have shrugged off the complaints. Today it cannot afford to. That's why Ellen Brown is careful to hear the chief out, politely leaving a gift of tea and sugar.

Brown is Exxon's anthropologist, an odd job to find on an oil company payroll. But in its bid to build a 660-mile pipeline from the oil fields of Chad, in the geographic heart of Africa, to the coast of Cameroon, Exxon has had to turn itself into something more than an oil company. Under pressure from activists, who have made the pipeline a focus of their campaign against globalization, Exxon has been forced to take on the unlikely role of development agency, human-rights promoter, de facto local government, and even (don't laugh) environmental watchdog. It's an unfamiliar way of doing business for a company used to having its way around the globe. But if the experiment succeeds, observers say, it could rewrite the rule book for how multinationals operate worldwide. "It's a whole new ball game for Big Oil," says Terry Lynn Karl, a Stanford political scientist who studies oil and development. "The traditional way of doing business—getting the oil out of the ground without getting involved in politics, human rights, and the environment—just isn't tenable anymore."

Even before pipeline construction began in December [2001], the $3.5 billion project was one of the most scrutinized in history. Oil projects have historically been a curse for Africa, and critics were convinced this one would only despoil the environment while enriching Chad's President Idriss Déby, a former warlord whose regime has a flair for human-rights abuses. But others considered the pipeline Chad's last, best hope for development: At war for much of its four decades of independence, it is a land of subsistence farming and pre-industrial villages, where a plow is the rare luxury. Annual per capita income is $230. Life expectancy is 47. Three-quarters of the population lacks access to health care, sanitation, or safe water. By carrying some 225,000 barrels of oil a day to a marine terminal for export, the pipeline could bring the landlocked nation more than $2 billion over 25 years, boosting the government's annual budget by half. "The critics forget that this is the opportunity of the century," says Nassour G. Ouaidou, a former prime minister of Chad and now the government's coordinator for the project.

The solution: a complex, four-way agreement between Exxon, the host governments, activists, and the World Bank. In exchange for the privilege of making money on the project—Exxon and its partners, Chevron Texaco and Petronas, stand to earn as much as $5.7 billion over the project's 25-year life—Exxon would carry out many of the activists' demands. And so began an unusual experiment in the multinational as missionary.

"The first thing people ask me is, 'What's an anthropologist doing working for an oil company?'" says Brown, 57, who came to Chad with the Peace Corps in 1968 and has remained, off and on, ever since. "I tell them that there's a lot of oil in the ground, but there's a lot of people living on top of it too." Since joining the project in 1995, she has spent hundreds of hours in villages like Mbanga, consulting with locals about what the pipeline would and would not bring. "In the beginning," she recalls, "people were saying, 'If you drill for oil, won't there be a big hole in the ground and a big earthquake and everything will collapse in the hole?'"

While reassuring people on that score, Brown has helped oversee a $1.5 million initiative in which Exxon has built schools, funded health clinics, dug wells, advised local entrepreneurs, fielded an AIDS-education van, and distributed 32,000 anti-malarial mosquito nets. It has also paid for prostitute focus groups, gorilla habitat studies, even ritual chicken sacrifices.

That's right. When a sacred tree stands in the pipeline's right of way, villagers must coax the spirits inside to decamp to a new locale. This requires a ceremony involving live poultry. To make sure cultural sensitivities aren't ruffled, Brown foots the bill, making for a memorable expense report and earning herself the local *nom de guerre* "Madame Sacrifice."

Meanwhile, Exxon has compiled a database of every mango tree, bean plant, and cotton field in the pipeline's path. Their cultivators are entitled to compensation based on a plant's life expectancy, annual yield, local fruit prices, and so forth; Exxon says it has paid out $7 million to 7,000 people so far. (Recipients can either take cash or select goods from a glossy catalog of plows, carts, sewing machines, bicycles, water pumps, and other items.) Hexes are another business challenge. When Cameroonian workers went to clear mahogany trees from one farmer's land, they came face to face with a wood-and-bark symbol—and refused to go a step farther. The symbol meant the farmer wasn't satisfied with the compensation he was receiving for his trees. "I think we ended up paying him another half-million francs [$675]" to take it down, says Grant Batterham, an environmental consultant. . . .

While Exxon hasn't exactly gotten religion, it has gotten wise to the perils of what Harvard Business School professor Debora Spar has dubbed the "spotlight phenomenon." Using the Internet and mass media as cudgels, nongovernmental organizations (NGOs) such as Greenpeace, Human Rights Watch, and Friends of the Earth have grown increasingly adept at singling out multinationals for their misdeeds. And oil companies offer a particularly ripe target. They are big, which NGOs readily translate as "bad." They have highly visible brands, making them vulnerable to boycotts at the pump. They cannot choose where oil deposits are located, meaning they increasingly operate in countries with unsavory rulers, sensitive environments, and impoverished populations. And their power tends to dwarf that of their host countries: Exxon's 2001 revenues were $191.6 billion, compared with Chad's GDP of $1.4 billion. . . .

To complicate matters for Exxon, the demands of Western NGOs often conflict directly with the wishes of locals. The NGOs want Cameroon's rain forests untouched; local farmers plead for Exxon to clear them with chain saws. The NGOs want roads routed around villages; villagers sneak out at night to move road markers closer to their homes and shops.

Other times, Exxon is torn between appeasing the NGOs and maintaining its own internal standards. Activists, for instance, berate the company for not hiring enough local contractors. Yet Exxon insists, perhaps not unreasonably, that any trucks it hires must have brakes. It also balks at buying food from local farmers who lack hygienic standards—though it's now helping organize growers into cooperatives that can sell in bulk. (It has also sent Chadians abroad for technical training in petroleum production.)

Especially thorny is the issue of compensation for the land that Exxon commandeers. In the village of Mbanga, Djimadem Pierre describes how he received $1,250 for the four acres of land he used to farm. "The first thing I did was buy some grain so we could eat," he says. The rest went for clothing, a sewing machine, a cart, a plough, and six oxen. "I was very happy to get [the money], and I invested it," he says, "but now it's all gone." His uncle has since given him a smaller plot of land, but Pierre says that's not enough to support his two wives, eight children, an aged mother, and the widow and family of his dead brother. "I'm in a bind. Maybe I'll take up goat farming."

Another villager, Cecile Yossanguem, received $875 for lost land, but because it was the "hungry season," when the previous year's crop is mostly eaten and the new one not ready for harvest, she spent it on food for herself and her four grandchildren. "I've eaten all the compensation," she laments. "What do I do now?" Exxon has encouraged villagers to invest the money for the long haul, distributing comic books that depict a couple saving it for their children's education. But Brown, the anthropologist, acknowledges that there's a fine line between a helping hand and a meddling one. "How far should the corporation go?" she wonders. "Where should you draw the line?". . .

Today construction is passing through the home of the Bakola Pygmy people, an ethnic minority who eke out a marginal existence at the bottom of Cameroon's social ladder. A half-mile path through dense rain forest leads to a Pygmy settlement—small huts of wood and thatch, children playing in the dust, women preparing strong-smelling manioc. A diminutive man, the local healer, emerges with the spear he uses to hunt porcupines and rats.

"Where have you been?" he asks, addressing George Koppert, a Dutch anthropologist and nutritionist who works with Exxon. "Why have you forgotten me?" At the insistence of NGOs, Exxon took pains to steer the pipeline clear of the Pygmies' hunting grounds and settlements. Yet that left some Pygmies feeling excluded. With Cameroon's government all but nonexistent on the ground here, Exxon is the first real authority they have known. That left Exxon scrambling to distribute gifts of machetes, axes, and hoes. "I was very happy with the machete and the axe," says the healer. "But I want a big dog to go hunting with. Will you bring me a big dog?"

"It's not the hand of the white man that must feed the Pygmies," Koppert says, obviously picking up a long-running discussion. "It's the hand of the Pygmies that must feed the Pygmies."

"I want a road so people can come see me by car," the healer persists, motioning to several patients who have journeyed here on foot. "I'm in favor of the pipeline, but I asked you to build a road from the pipeline to my settlement, and you've done nothing. Nothing!"

Later, a project official heaves a sigh. "We go through all this trouble to keep the pipeline away from these people, and what do they want? They want it at their back door."

Questions for Discussion

1. What are the benefits for Exxon of having cultural anthropologists on the payroll? Any drawbacks? Explain.

2. What evidence can you find in this case of any of the GLOBE project's nine cultural dimensions? Explain your selections.

3. What potential cross-cultural value conflicts are evident in this case? How can they be resolved?

4. Using anthropologist Ellen Brown's words, where should Exxon draw the line between offering a helping hand and a meddling one to local inhabitants?

5. Has anyone made any major cross-cultural blunders in this case? Explain.

6. Would you like to work as an on-site manager for a foreign project of this magnitude? What would be the major positives and negatives? Explain.

7. What potential ethical traps do you see in this case?

Personal Awareness and Growth Exercise

How Do Your Work Goals Compare Internationally?

Objectives

1. To increase your cross-cultural awareness.
2. To see how your own work goals compare internationally.

Introduction

In today's multicultural global economy, it is a mistake to assume everyone wants the same things from the job as you do. This exercise provides a "window" on the world of work goals.

Instructions

Below is a list of 11 goals potentially attainable in the workplace. In terms of your own personal preferences, rank the goals from 1 to 11 (1 = Most important; 11 = Least important). After you have ranked all 11 work goals, compare your list with the national samples under the heading *Survey Results*. These national samples represent cross sections of employees from all levels and all major occupational groups. (Please complete your ranking now, before looking at the national samples.) How important are the following in your work life?

Rank	Work Goals
_____	A lot of opportunity to *learn* new things
_____	Good *interpersonal relations* (supervisors, co-workers)
_____	Good opportunity for upgrading or *promotion*
_____	*Convenient* work *hours*
_____	A lot of *variety*
_____	*Interesting* work (work that you really like)
_____	Good *job security*
_____	A good *match* between your job requirements and your abilities and experience
_____	Good *pay*
_____	Good physical working *conditions* (such as light, temperature, cleanliness, low noise level)
_____	A lot of *autonomy* (you decide how to do your work)[84]

Questions for Discussion

1. Which national profile of work goals most closely matches your own? Is this what you expected, or not?

2. Are you surprised by any of the rankings in the four national samples? Explain.

3. What sorts of motivational/leadership adjustments would a manager have to make when moving among the four countries?

Survey Results[85]

Ranking of Work Goals by Country

(1 = MOST IMPORTANT; 11 = LEAST IMPORTANT)

Work Goals	United States	Britain	Germany*	Japan
Interesting work	1	1	3	2
Pay	2	2	1	5
Job security	3	3	2	4
Match between person and job	4	6	5	1
Opportunity to learn	5	8	9	7
Variety	6	7	6**	9
Interpersonal relations	7	4	4	6
Autonomy	8	10	8	3
Convenient work hours	9	5	6**	8
Opportunity for promotion	10	11	10	11
Working conditions	11	9	11	10

*Former West Germany.
**Tie.

Group Exercise

Looking into a Cultural Mirror

Objectives

1. To generate group discussion about the impact of societal culture on managerial style.
2. To increase your cultural awareness.
3. To discuss the idea of a distinct American style of management.
4. To explore the pros and cons of the American style of management.

Introduction

A time-tested creativity technique involves "taking something familiar and making it strange." This technique can yield useful insights by forcing us to take a close look at things we tend to take for granted. In the case of this group exercise, the focus of your attention will be mainstream cultural tendencies in the United States (or any other country you or your instructor may select) and management. A 15-minute, small-group session will be followed by brief oral presentations and a general class discussion. Total time required is about 35 to 45 minutes.

Instructions

Your instructor will divide your class randomly into small groups of five to eight. Half of the teams will be designated "red" teams, and half will be "green" teams. Each team will assign someone the role of recorder/presenter, examine the cultural traits listed below, and develop a cultural profile of the "American management style." Members of each red team will explain the *positive* implications of each trait in their cultural profile. Green team members will explain the *negative* implications of the traits in their profiles.

During the brief oral presentations by the various teams, the instructor may jot down on the board or flip chart a composite cultural profile of American managers. A general class discussion of positive and negative implications will follow. *Note:* Special effort should be made to solicit comments and observations from foreign students and students who have traveled or worked in other countries. Discussion needs to focus on the appropriateness or inappropriateness of the American cultural style of management in other countries and cultures.

As "seed" for group discussion, here is a list of American cultural traits identified by researchers[86] (feel free to supplement this short list):

- Individualistic
- Independent
- Aggressive/assertive/blunt
- Competitive
- Informal
- Pragmatic/practical

- Impatient
- Materialistic
- Unemotional/rational/objective
- Hard working

Questions for Discussion

1. Are you surprised by anything you have just heard? Explain.

2. Is there a distinct American management style? Explain.

3. Can the American management style be exported easily? If it needs to be modified, how?

4. What do American managers need to do to be more effective at home and in foreign countries?

Ethical Dilemma

3M Tries to Make a Difference in Russia[87]

Russian managers aren't inclined . . . to reward people for improved performance. They spurn making investments for the future in favor of realizing immediate gains. They avoid establishing consistent business practices that can reduce uncertainty. Add in the country's high political risk and level of corruption, and it's no wonder that many multinationals have all but given up on Russia. . . .

The Russian business environment can be corrupt and dangerous; bribes and protection money are facts of life. But unlike many international companies, which try to distance themselves from such practices by simply banning them, 3M Russia actively promotes not only ethical behavior but also the personal security of its employees. . . .

3M Russia also strives to differentiate itself from competitors by being an ethical leader. For example, it holds training courses in business ethics for its customers.

Should 3M export its American ethical standards to Russia?

1. If 3M doesn't like the way things are done in Russia, it shouldn't do business there. Explain your rationale.

2. 3M should do business in Russia but not meddle in Russian culture. "When in Russia, do things the Russian way." Explain your rationale.

3. 3M has a basic moral responsibility to improve the ethical climate in foreign countries where it does business. Explain your rationale.

4. 3M should find a practical middle ground between the American and Russian ways of doing business. How should that happen?

5. Invent other options. Discuss.

For an interpretation of this situation, visit our Web site,**www.mhhe.com/kreitner.**

OB in Action Video Case

Mustang Jeans: Doing Business across Cultures

Total run time for both parts: 15 minutes.

About the Manager's Hot Seat video series: To achieve a high degree of realism, McGraw-Hill/Irwin created these videos around the concept of having real-life managers deal with challenging hypothetical situations without the aid of a script. Each Manager's Hot Seat video has two parts. Both parts are followed by the guest manager's view of what went right and wrong in the "hot seat." What would *you* do in the manager's hot seat?

Characters: Guest manager Michael Sokolow, founder of PropertyRover, Inc., is the American sales manager at Mustang Jeans. Norio Tokunaka, the VP of merchandise at Pop-Wear, has spent his entire career at the Japanese clothing retailer.

Situation: Sokolow, a successful get-to-the-point guy who has been with Mustang Jeans for two years, took over the Pop-Wear account in a recent reorganization. He believes his predecessor did all the necessary groundwork to get Tokunaka to sign the contract. Part 1 of the video is the first meeting ever between Sokolow and Tokunaka. Part 2 is a follow-up meeting a week later. Both meetings take place in Sokolow's office at Mustang Jeans' corporate headquarters in the United States.

Links to textual material: Chapter 1: 21st-century managers. Chapter 2: managing diversity. Chapter 3: organizational cultures. Chapter 4: cross-cultural awareness and competence.

For Class Discussion (following Part 1)

1. What were the two men's apparent objectives for this meeting?
2. In terms of high-context and low-context cultures, what is the cultural collision here?
3. Using the nine GLOBE cultural dimensions as a guide, what are the major cultural differences here?
4. Do monochronic and polychronic time play a role in this case? Explain.
5. What are the chances of Tokunaka signing the contract during this visit to the United States? Explain.
6. What did Sokolow do wrong in this first meeting? What should he have done?
7. What approach should Sokolow take in the second meeting?

For Class Discussion (following Part 2)

1. Are you surprised about how things turned out? Explain.
2. What cross-cultural mistakes did Sokolow make in Part 2? How should he have handled things?
3. Is Tokunaka guilty of exploiting the American's cultural tendencies to gain a business advantage? Explain.

Part Two

Individual Behavior in Organizations

Chapter Five

Individual Differences: Self-Concept, Personality, and Emotions

Learning Objectives

When you finish studying the material in this chapter, you should be able to:

1 Define self-esteem, and explain how it can be improved with Branden's six pillars of self-esteem.

2 Define self-efficacy, and explain its sources.

3 Contrast high and low self-monitoring individuals, and discuss the ethical implications of organizational identification.

4 Explain the social learning model of self-management.

5 Identify and describe the Big Five personality dimensions, and specify which one is correlated most strongly with job performance.

6 Describe the proactive personality, and explain the difference between an internal and an external locus of control.

7 Distinguish between positive and negative emotions, and explain how they can be judged.

8 Identify the four key components of emotional intelligence, and discuss the practical significance of emotional contagion and emotional labor.

How badly did Phyllis Anzalone want to work for Enron? In January 1996, at the start of energy deregulation, she interviewed with two Enron executives and issued an ultimatum: "I said, 'You can either hire me or compete against me.'"

What did working at Enron do for Anzalone? For one thing, it made her a lot of money, so much that the company's failure cost her about $1 million. More important, it made *her*. It took her from being a reasonably successful facilities-management salesperson from rural Louisiana and propelled her into the ranks of sales superstars. It changed her view of herself; it confirmed what she thought she could achieve. "Enron had a profound effect on my life," she says. "As devastating as it was, I'm glad I did it. It was like being on steroids every day."

And what does Anzalone think of the executives who ran Enron—and then ran it into the ground? "They are scum," she says. "They are crooks, and they are traitors. They betrayed many people's trust, including mine. Jeff Skilling is lying. Every single employee at Enron knows he's lying."

All of which makes Anzalone a true believer. "Working for Enron was a commitment," she says. . . .

Four months after Enron hired her, Anzalone went to San Francisco to crack California's retail-electricity market. She was an "originator"—she

Phyllis Anzalone has strong mixed feelings about her former employer Enron.
(c) Len Irish

"originated," or sold, energy-supply contracts. "I concentrated on Silicon Valley and health care. Those were critical operating environments that used a lot of energy," Anzalone says. "My goal was to show businesses how they could improve on the 'do nothing' position. That was our biggest competitor—companies who decided to do nothing, to just keep getting electricity from the utility."

Eventually, she had Applied Materials, Sutter Health, and all of Kaiser Permanente's sprawling California facilities among her customers. "It was a brand-new industry doing things that had never been done before. It was the most fun I've ever had." . . .

Enron Energy Services (EES), Anzalone says, "was an entrepreneurial culture. If you met your goals, you could double your salary. I was always doubling my goals—or more. In the first five months of 2001, I quadrupled my goals." In 2000 and 2001, she earned an annual salary well into six figures.

That was the part of Enron that Anzalone thrived on. Then there was the part of Enron that she shunned: the culture of Enron's Houston headquarters. She disliked it so much that she managed to avoid being stationed there for four of her five years at the company. "I wanted to produce and be left alone," she says. "I didn't like the politics of Houston."

The problem was that Anzalone didn't fit the Enron pedigree. Much of her appeal is her high-energy, up-by-the-bootstraps hustle. Much of Enron's cachet was built on its ability to attract the polished graduates of the nation's leading business schools. "The arrogance of the leadership always offended me," she says. "I always had a great boss at EES. But I always said, 'I like the people I work *with*. I hate the people I work *for*.'" . . .

More than anything, because she believed so deeply in Enron, Anzalone feels deeply betrayed. "Emotionally," she says, "I'll feel a sense of loss for a long time. I'm incredibly disappointed in senior management. They lied to the shareholders, they lied to the employees, and they lied to the people at Enron who were making things happen." She pauses. "You know, if you were at Enron, you loved it."[1]

For Discussion

Do you feel badly for Anzalone, or do you believe she got what she deserved? Explain.

What makes you *you?* What characteristics do you share with others? Which ones set you apart? Perhaps you have a dynamic personality and dress accordingly, while a low-key friend dresses conservatively and avoids crowds. People's values, attitudes, abilities, and emotions also vary, as in the case of Enron's Phyllis Anzalone. Some computer buffs would rather surf the Internet than eat; other people suffer from computer phobia. A lunchtime debate finds one manager equating success with wealth, another says life is all about meaningful relationships. Sometimes students who skim their reading assignments at the last moment get higher grades than those who study for days. People standing patiently in a long line watch an angry customer shout at a store clerk. One employee consistently does more than asked while another equally skilled employee barely does the job. A job satisfaction survey yields polar opposite scores for two co-workers doing identical work. Thanks to a vast array of individual differences such as these, modern organizations have a rich and interesting human texture. On the other hand, individual differences make the manager's job endlessly challenging. In fact, according to research, "variability among workers is substantial at all levels but increases dramatically with job complexity. In life insurance sales, for example, variability in performance is around six times as great as in routine clerical jobs."[2]

Growing workforce diversity compels managers to view individual differences in a fresh new way. The case for this new perspective was presented in Britain's *Journal of Managerial Psychology:*

For many years America's businesses sought homogeneity—a work force that believed in, supported, and presented a particular image. The notion of the company man dressed for success in the banker's blue or corporation's grey flannel suit was *de riguer*. Those able to move into leadership positions succeeded to the extent they behaved and dressed according to a rather narrowly defined standard.

To compete today, and in preparation for the work force of tomorrow, successful businesses and organisations are adapting to both internal and external changes. New operational styles, language, customs, values, and even dress, are a real part of this adaptation. We now hear leaders talking about "valuing differences," and learning to "manage diversity."[3]

So rather than limiting diversity, as in the past, today's managers need to better understand and accommodate employee diversity and individual differences.[4]

Both this chapter and the next explore the various dimensions of individual differences portrayed in Figure 5–1. Figure 5–1 is an instructional road map showing linkages between self-concept (how you view yourself), personal values (which of life's means and ends are important to you), personality (how you appear to others), and key forms of self-expression. This chapter focuses on self-concept, personality, and emotions. Personal values, attitudes, abilities, and job satisfaction are covered in Chapter 6. Taken as an integrated whole, all these factors provide a foundation for better understanding each organizational contributor as a unique and special individual.

From Self-Concept to Self-Management

Self is the core of one's conscious existence. Awareness of self is referred to as one's self-concept. The relevance of this topic surfaced in a recent survey. People ages 16 to 70 were asked what they would do differently if they could live life over again; 48%

Figure 5–1   *An Instructional Road Map for the Study of Individual Differences in OB*

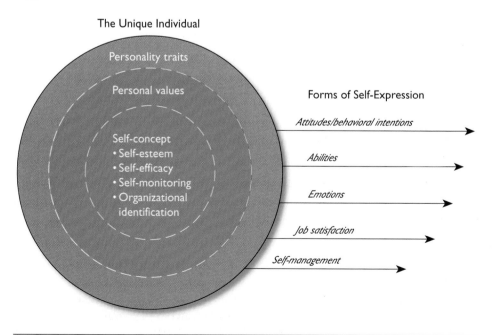

∫elf-concept

Person's self-perception as a physical, social, spiritual being.

Cognitions

A person's knowledge, opinions, or beliefs.

chose the response category "Get in touch with self."[5] Sociologist Viktor Gecas defines **self-concept** as "the concept the individual has of himself as a physical, social, and spiritual or moral being."[6] In other words, because you have a self-concept, you recognize yourself as a distinct human being. A self-concept would be impossible without the capacity to think. This brings us to the role of cognitions. **Cognitions** represent "any knowledge, opinion, or belief about the environment, about oneself, or about one's behavior."[7] Among many different types of cognitions, those involving anticipation, planning, goal setting, evaluating, and setting personal standards are particularly relevant to OB. Several cognition-based topics are discussed in later chapters. Differing cognitive styles are introduced in the next chapter. Cognitions play a central role in social perception, as will be discussed in Chapter 7. Also, as we will see in Chapters 8 and 9, modern motivation theories and techniques are powered by cognitions. Successful self-management, covered at the end of this section, requires cognitive support.

Importantly, ideas of self and self-concept vary from one historical era to another, from one socioeconomic class to another, and from culture to culture. How well one detects and adjusts to different cultural notions of self can spell the difference between success and failure in international dealings. For example, as detailed in the International OB on page 153, Japanese–US communication and understanding is often hindered by significantly different degrees of self-disclosure. With a comparatively large public self, Americans pride themselves in being open, honest, candid, and to the point. Meanwhile, Japanese, who culturally discourage self-disclosure, typically view Americans as blunt, prying, and insensitive to formalities. For their part, Americans tend to see Japanese as distant, cold, and evasive.[8] One culture is not right and the other wrong. They are just different, and a key difference involves culturally rooted conceptions of self and self-disclosure.

Keeping this cultural qualification in mind, let us explore three topics invariably mentioned when behavioral scientists discuss self-concept. They are self-esteem, self-efficacy, and self-monitoring.[9] We also consider the ethical implications of organizational identification, a social aspect of self. A social learning model of self-management is presented as a practical capstone for this section. Each of these areas deserves a closer look by those who want to better understand and effectively manage themselves and others.

Self-Esteem: A Controversial Topic

∫elf-esteem

One's overall self-evaluation.

Self-esteem is a belief about one's own self-worth based on an overall self-evaluation.[10] Self-esteem is measured by having survey respondents indicate their agreement or disagreement with both positive and negative statements. A positive statement on one general self-esteem survey is: "I feel I am a person of worth, the equal of other people."[11] Among the negative items is: "I feel I do not have much to be proud of."[12] Those who agree with the positive statements and disagree with the negative statements have high self-esteem. They see themselves as worthwhile, capable, and acceptable. People with low self-esteem view themselves in negative terms. They do not feel good about themselves and are hampered by self-doubts.[13]

The Battle over ∫elf-Esteem

The subject of self-esteem has generated a good deal of controversy in recent years, particularly among educators and those seeking to help the disadvantaged.[14] While both sides generally agree that positive self-esteem is a good thing for students and youngsters, disagreement rages over how to im-

Culture Dictates the Degree of Self-Disclosure in Japan and the United States

Japanese Public and Private Self

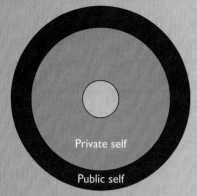

American Public and Private Self

Private self (the self not revealed to others)
Public self (the self made accessible to others)

Survey research in Japan and the United States uncovered the following *distinct contrasts* in Japanese versus American self-disclosure:

- Americans disclosed nearly as much to strangers as the Japanese did to their own fathers.

- Americans reported two to three times greater physical contact with parents and twice greater contact with friends than the Japanese.

- The Japanese may be frightened at the prospect of being communicatively invaded (because of the unexpected spontaneity and bluntness of the American); the American is annoyed at the prospect of endless formalities and tangential replies.

- American emphasis on self-assertion and talkativeness cultivates a communicator who is highly self-oriented and expressive; the Japanese emphasis on "reserve" and "sensitivity" cultivates a communicator who is other-oriented and receptive.

SOURCE: Adapted from D C Barnlund, "Public and Private Self in Communicating with Japan," *Business Horizons*, March–April 1989, pp 32–40.

prove self-esteem. Consider, for example, how the battle lines have been drawn in one Boston school:

> The students at Mather School in Boston start the day with a pledge: They'll work hard and learn from their mistakes. They don't chant "I am special because I'm me" mantras. Weaknesses have to be faced, praise has to be earned.
>
> Their pledge is in stark contrast to the principles of the "self-esteem movement," which tries to build kids' self-worth through lots of praise, love-yourself maxims, and easy-to-achieve goals.
>
> Kim Marshall, principal of Mather, never bought into that movement. And though the concept has been embraced by parents and become firmly entrenched in school curricula, he doesn't think kids ever really bought it, either. "Praise (from teachers) needs to be specific, genuine, and believable," he says. "When you talk to kids in a phony way, they see right through it."[15]

Feelings of self-esteem are, in fact, shaped by our circumstances and how others treat us. Researchers who tracked 654 young adults (192 male, 462 female) for eight years found higher self-esteem among those in school or working full-time than among those with part-time jobs or unemployed.[16]

Surprising Research Insights

Is high self-esteem always a good thing? Research evidence provides both expected and surprising answers. A pair of studies confirmed that people with high self-esteem (HSE) handle failure better than those with low self-esteem (LSE). Specifically, when confronted with failure, HSEs drew upon their strengths and emphasized the positive whereas LSEs focused on their weaknesses and had primarily negative thoughts.[17] But in another study, HSEs tended to become egotistical and boastful when faced with pressure situations.[18] Other researchers found high levels of self-esteem associated with aggressive and even violent behavior. Indeed, contrary to the common belief that low self-esteem and criminality go hand in hand, youth gang members and criminals often score highly on self-esteem and become violent when their inflated egos are threatened.[19] Our conclusion is that high self-esteem *can* be a good thing, but only *if*—like many other human characteristics such as creativity, intelligence, and persistence—it is nurtured and channeled in constructive and ethical ways. Otherwise, it can become antisocial and destructive.

Self-Esteem across Cultures

What are the cross-cultural implications for self-esteem, a concept that has been called uniquely Western? In a survey of 13,118 students from 31 countries worldwide, a moderate positive correlation was found between self-esteem and life satisfaction. But the relationship was stronger in individualistic cultures (e.g., United States, Canada, New Zealand, Netherlands) than in collectivist cultures (e.g., Korea, Kenya, Japan). The researchers concluded that individualistic cultures socialize people to focus more on themselves, while people in collectivist cultures "are socialized to fit into the community and to do their duty. Thus, how a collectivist feels about him- or herself is less relevant to . . . life satisfaction."[20] Global managers need to remember to deemphasize self-esteem when doing business in collectivist ("we") cultures, as opposed to emphasizing it in individualistic ("me") cultures.

Can General Self-Esteem Be Improved?

The short answer is *yes* (see Table 5–1). More detailed answers come from research. In one study, youth-league baseball coaches who were trained in supportive teaching techniques had a positive effect on the self-esteem of young boys. A control group of untrained coaches had no such positive effect.[21] Another study led to this conclusion: "Low self-esteem can be raised more by having the person think of *desirable* characteristics *possessed* rather than of undesirable characteristics from which he or she is free."[22] This approach can help neutralize the self-defeating negative thoughts of LSEs, discussed earlier.

Self-Efficacy

Have you noticed how those who are confident about their ability tend to succeed, while those who are preoccupied with failing tend to fail? Perhaps that explains the comparative golfing performance of your authors! One consistently stays in the fairways and hits the greens. The other spends the day thrashing through the underbrush, wading in water hazards, and blasting out of sand traps. At the heart of this performance mismatch is a specific dimension of self-esteem called self-efficacy. **Self-efficacy**

self-efficacy
Belief in one's ability to do a task.

Table 5–1   *Branden's Six Pillars of Self-Esteem*

What nurtures and sustains self-esteem in grown-ups is not how others deal with us but how we ourselves operate in the face of life's challenges—the choices we make and the actions we take.

This leads us to the six pillars of self-esteem.

1. *Live consciously:* Be actively and fully engaged in what you do and with whom you interact.
2. *Be self-accepting:* Don't be overly judgmental or critical of your thoughts and actions.
3. *Take personal responsibility:* Take full responsibility for your decisions and actions in life's journey.
4. *Be self-assertive:* Be authentic and willing to defend your beliefs when interacting with others, rather than bending to their will to be accepted or liked.
5. *Live purposefully:* Have clear near-term and long-term goals and realistic plans for achieving them to create a sense of control over your life.
6. *Have personal integrity:* Be true to your word and your values.

Between self-esteem and the practices that support it, there is reciprocal causation. This means that the behaviors that generate good self-esteem are also expressions of good self-esteem.

SOURCE: Excerpted and adapted from Nathaniel Branden, *Self-Esteem at Work: How Confident People Make Powerful Companies* (San Francisco: Jossey-Bass, 1998), pp 33–36.

is a person's belief about his or her chances of successfully accomplishing a specific task. According to one OB writer, "Self-efficacy arises from the gradual acquisition of complex cognitive, social, linguistic, and/or physical skills through experience."[23] Childhood experiences have a powerful effect on a person's self-efficacy. Whoopi Goldberg, for example, attributes much of her success as a performing artist to her mother's guidance. Says Goldberg, who grew up in New York City as Caryn Johnson,

> My mom encouraged me to explore the city, get on the bus and go watch Leonard Bernstein conduct the young people's concerts, go to the museums and planetarium, Central Park and Coney Island. There were always things for me to investigate, and she encouraged me to ask a lot of questions.
>
> As kids, my mom instilled in both my brother [Clyde] and me an ideal of what life could and should be, and how we could participate in it. It was never intimated to me that I couldn't be exactly what I wanted to be.[24]

The relationship between self-efficacy and performance is a cyclical one. Efficacy→ performance cycles can spiral upward toward success or downward toward failure.[25] Researchers have documented strong linkages between high self-efficacy expectations and success in widely varied physical and mental tasks, anxiety reduction, addiction control, pain tolerance, illness recovery, avoidance of seasickness in naval cadets, and stress avoidance.[26] Oppositely, those with low self-efficacy expectations tend to have low success rates. Chronically low self-efficacy is associated with a condition called **learned helplessness,** the severely debilitating belief that one has no control over one's environment.[27] Although self-efficacy sounds like some sort of mental magic, it operates in a very straightforward manner, as a model will show.

What Are the Mechanisms of Self-Efficacy?
A basic model of self-efficacy is displayed in Figure 5–2. It draws upon the work of Stanford psychologist

Learned helplessness
Debilitating lack of faith in one's ability to control the situation.

Figure 5–2   *A Model of How Self-Efficacy Beliefs Can Pave the Way for Success or Failure*

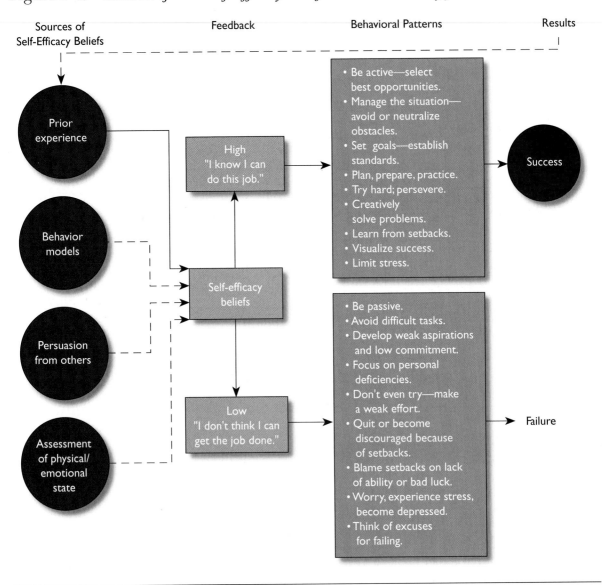

SOURCES: Adapted from discussion in A Bandura, "Regulation of Cognitive Processes through Perceived Self-Efficacy." *Developmental Psychology*, September 1989, pp 729–35; and R Wood and A Bandura, "Social Cognitive Theory of Organizational Management," *Academy of Management Review*, July 1989, pp 361–84.

Albert Bandura. Let us explore this model with a simple illustrative task. Imagine you have been told to prepare and deliver a 10-minute talk to an OB class of 50 students on the workings of the self-efficacy model in Figure 5–2. Your self-efficacy calculation would involve cognitive appraisal of the interaction between your perceived capability and situational opportunities and obstacles.

As you begin to prepare for your presentation, the four sources of self-efficacy beliefs would come into play. Because prior experience is the most potent source, according to Bandura, it is listed first and connected to self-efficacy beliefs with a solid line.[28] Past success in public speaking would boost your self-efficacy. But bad experiences with delivering speeches would foster low self-efficacy. Regarding behavior models as a source of self-efficacy beliefs, you would be influenced by the success or failure of your classmates in delivering similar talks. Their successes would tend to bolster you (or perhaps their failure would if you were very competitive and had high self-esteem). Likewise, any supportive persuasion from your classmates that you will do a good job would enhance your self-efficacy. Physical and emotional factors also might affect your self-confidence. A sudden case of laryngitis or a bout of stage fright could cause your self-efficacy expectations to plunge. Your cognitive evaluation of the situation then would yield a self-efficacy belief—ranging from high to low expectations for success. Importantly, self-efficacy beliefs are not merely boastful statements based on bravado; they are deep convictions supported by experience.

Moving to the *behavioral patterns* portion of Figure 5–2, we see how self-efficacy beliefs are acted out. In short, if you have high self-efficacy about giving your 10-minute speech you will work harder, more creatively, and longer when preparing for your talk than will your low-self-efficacy classmates. The results would then take shape accordingly. People program themselves for success or failure by enacting their self-efficacy expectations. Positive or negative results subsequently become feedback for one's base of personal experience. Bob Schmonsees, a software entrepreneur, is an inspiring example of the success pathway through Figure 5–2:

> A contender in mixed-doubles tennis and a former football star, Mr Schmonsees was standing near a ski lift when an out-of-control skier rammed him. His legs were paralyzed. He would spend the rest of his life in a wheelchair.
>
> Fortunately, he discovered a formula for his different world: Figure out the new rules for any activity, then take as many small steps as necessary to master those rules. After learning the physics of a tennis swing on wheels and the geometry of playing a second bounce (standard rules), he became the world's top wheelchair player over age 40.[29]

Self-Efficacy Implications for Managers

On-the-job research evidence encourages managers to nurture self-efficacy, both in themselves and in others. In fact, a meta-analysis encompassing 21,616 subjects found a significant positive correlation between self-efficacy and job performance.[30] Self-efficacy requires constructive action in each of the following managerial areas:

1. *Recruiting/selection/job assignments.* Interview questions can be designed to probe job applicants' general self-efficacy as a basis for determining orientation and training needs. Pencil-and-paper tests for self-efficacy are not in an advanced stage of development and validation. Care needs to be taken not to hire solely on the basis of self-efficacy because studies have detected below-average self-esteem and self-efficacy among women and protected minorities.[31]

2. *Job design.* Complex, challenging, and autonomous jobs tend to enhance perceived self-efficacy.[32] Boring, tedious jobs generally do the opposite.

3. *Training and development.* Employees' self-efficacy expectations for key tasks can be improved through guided experiences, mentoring, and role modeling.[33]

4. *Self-management.* Systematic self-management training, as discussed later, involves enhancement of self-efficacy expectations.[34]

5. *Goal setting and quality improvement.* Goal difficulty needs to match the individual's perceived self-efficacy.[35] As self-efficacy and performance improve, goals and quality standards can be made more challenging.

6. *Coaching.* Those with low self-efficacy and employees victimized by learned helplessness need lots of constructive pointers and positive feedback.[36]

7. *Leadership and mentoring.* Needed leadership talent surfaces when top management gives high self-efficacy managers a chance to prove themselves under pressure.[37]

8. *Rewards.* Small successes need to be rewarded as stepping-stones to a stronger self-image and greater achievements.

Self-Monitoring

Consider these contrasting scenarios:

1. You are rushing to an important meeting when a co-worker pulls you aside and starts to discuss a personal problem. You want to break off the conversation, so you glance at your watch. He keeps talking. You say, "I'm late for a big meeting." He continues. You turn and start to walk away. The person keeps talking as if they never received any of your verbal and nonverbal signals that the conversation was over.

2. Same situation. Only this time, when you glance at your watch, the person immediately says, "I know, you've got to go. Sorry. We'll talk later."

In the first all-too-familiar scenario, you are talking to a "low self-monitor." The second scenario involves a "high self-monitor." But more is involved here than an irritating situation. A significant and measurable individual difference in self-expression behavior, called self-monitoring, is highlighted. **Self-monitoring** is the extent to which a person observes their own self-expressive behavior and adapts it to the demands of the situation. Experts on the subject offer this explanation:

Self-monitoring
Observing one's own behavior and adapting it to the situation.

> Individuals high in self-monitoring are thought to regulate their expressive self-presentation for the sake of desired public appearances, and thus be highly responsive to social and interpersonal cues of situationally appropriate performances. Individuals low in self-monitoring are thought to lack either the ability or the motivation to so regulate their expressive self-presentations. Their expressive behaviors, instead, are thought to functionally reflect their own enduring and momentary inner states, including their attitudes, traits, and feelings.[38]

In organizational life, both high and low monitors are subject to criticism. High self-monitors are sometimes called *chameleons,* who readily adapt their self-presentation to their surroundings. Low self-monitors, on the other hand, often are criticized for being on their own planet and insensitive to others. Former US housing secretary and 1996 vice presidential candidate, Jack Kemp, frustrated his political handlers with his low self-monitoring ways:

> Bush administration veterans recall windy lectures on US urban policy during cabinet meetings, and friends say Kemp will debate anything with anyone, any time. "We used to laugh at him for going to Iowa, where he'd wind up talking the gold standard with two farmers, three hogs, and two dogs," a former staffer says. "Everyone else had left."[39]

Importantly, within an OB context, self-monitoring is like any other individual difference—not a matter of right or wrong or good versus bad, but rather a source of diversity that needs to be adequately understood by present and future managers.

A Matter of Degree
Self-monitoring is not an either-or proposition. It is a matter of degree; a matter of being relatively high or low in terms of related patterns of self-expression. The OB Exercise on page 159 is a self-assessment of your self-monitoring

OB Exercise — What Are Your Self-Monitoring Tendencies?

Instructions

In an honest self-appraisal, mark each of the following statements as true (T) or false (F), and then consult the scoring key.

_____ 1. I guess I put on a show to impress or entertain others.

_____ 2. In a group of people I am rarely the center of attention.

_____ 3. In different situations and with different people, I often act like very different persons.

_____ 4. I would not change my opinions (or the way I do things) in order to please someone or win their favor.

_____ 5. I have considered being an entertainer.

_____ 6. I have trouble changing my behavior to suit different people and different situations.

_____ 7. At a party I let others keep the jokes and stories going.

_____ 8. I feel a bit awkward in public and do not show up quite as well as I should.

_____ 9. I can look anyone in the eye and tell a lie with a straight face (if for a right end).

_____ 10. I may deceive people by being friendly when I really dislike them.

Scoring Key

Score one point for each of the following answers:

1. T; 2. F; 3. T; 4. F; 5. T; 6. F; 7. F; 8. F; 9. T; 10. T

Score: _____

1–3 = Low self-monitoring

4–5 = Moderately low self-monitoring

6–7 = Moderately high self-monitoring

8–10 = High self-monitoring

SOURCE: Excerpted and adapted from M Snyder and S Gangestad, "On the Nature of Self-Monitoring: Matters of Assessment, Matters of Validity," *Journal of Personality and Social Psychology*, July 1986, p 137.

tendencies. It can help you better understand your*self*. Take a short break from your reading to complete the 10-item survey. Does your score surprise you in any way? Are you unhappy with the way you present yourself to others? What are the ethical implications of your score (particularly with regard to items 9 and 10)?

Research Findings and Practical Recommendations

A recent meta-analysis encompassing 23,191 subjects in 136 samples found self-monitoring to be relevant and useful when dealing with job performance and emerging leaders.[40] According to field research, there is a positive relationship between high self-monitoring and career success. Among 139 MBA graduates who were tracked for five years, high self-monitors enjoyed more internal and external promotions than did their

SOURCE: DILBERT reprinted by permission of United Feature Syndicate, Inc.

low self-monitoring classmates.[41] Another study of 147 managers and professionals found that high self-monitors had a better record of acquiring a mentor (someone to act as a personal career coach and professional sponsor).[42] These results mesh well with an earlier study that found managerial success (in terms of speed of promotions) tied to political savvy (knowing how to socialize, network, and engage in organizational politics).[43]

The foregoing evidence and practical experience lead us to make these practical recommendations:

For high, moderate, and low self-monitors: Become more consciously aware of your self-image and how it affects others (the OB Exercise is a good start).

For high self-monitors: Don't overdo it by evolving from a successful chameleon into someone who is widely perceived as insincere, dishonest, phoney, and untrustworthy. You cannot be everything to everyone.

For low self-monitors: You can bend without breaking, so try to be a bit more accommodating while being true to your basic beliefs. Don't wear out your welcome when communicating. Practice reading and adjusting to nonverbal cues in various public situations. If your conversation partner is bored or distracted, stop—because they are not really listening.

Organizational Identification: A *Social* Aspect of Self-Concept with Ethical Implications

Organizational identification

Organizational values or beliefs become part of one's self-identity.

The dividing line between self and others is not a neat and precise one. A certain amount of blurring occurs, for example, when an employee comes to define him- or herself with a *specific* organization—a psychological process called *organizational identification.* According to an expert on this emerging OB topic, "**organizational identification** occurs when one comes to integrate beliefs about one's organization into one's identity."[44] Organizational identification goes to the heart of organizational culture and socialization (recall our discussion in Chapter 3).

Managers put a good deal of emphasis today on organizational mission, philosophy, and values with the express intent of integrating the company into each employee's self-identity. Hopefully, as the logic goes, employees who identify closely with the organization will be more loyal, more committed, and harder working.[45] Some companies, such as consultant McKinsey & Company, go so far as to cultivate organizational identification among *former* employees through corporate alumni networks. Former employees who still identify strongly with the company are potential customers, as well as informal marketers and goodwill ambassadors.[46] As an extreme case in point, organizational identification among employees at Harley-Davidson's motorcycle factories is so strong many have had the company logo tattooed on their bodies.[47] Working at Harley is not just a job, it is a lifestyle. (Somehow, your authors have a hard time imagining an employee with a Pepsi or Burger King tattoo!)

A company tattoo may be a bit extreme, but the ethical implications of identifying too closely with one's employer are profound. Phyllis Anzalone, the former Enron employee profiled in the opening vignette for this chapter, is a good case in point. She admitted that Enron *was* her self-identity and she ended up with emotional scars. She seems to have distanced herself from Enron's most unsavory characters during her years with the company. But some of her colleagues, with equally strong organizational identification, evidently turned their backs on their personal ethical standards and values when working on clearly illegal deals. When employees suspend their critical thinking and lose their objectivity, unhealthy groupthink can occur and needed constructive conflict does *not* occur. (Groupthink is covered in Chapter 12 and functional conflict is discussed in Chapter 14.) Company loyalty and dedication are one thing, blind obedience is quite another.

Self-Management: A Social Learning Model

Albert Bandura, the Stanford psychologist introduced earlier, extended his self-efficacy concept into a comprehensive model of human learning. According to Bandura's *social learning theory,* an individual acquires new behavior through the interplay of environmental cues and consequences and cognitive processes.[48] When you consciously control this learning process yourself, you are engaging in self-management. Bandura explains:

> [A] distinguishing feature of social learning theory is the prominent role it assigns to self-regulatory capacities. By arranging environmental inducements, generating cognitive supports, and producing consequences for their own actions people are able to exercise some measure of control over their own behavior.[49]

In other words, to the extent that you can control your environment and your cognitive representations of your environment, you are the master of your own behavior. The practical model displayed in Figure 5–3 is derived from social learning theory. The two-headed arrows reflect dynamic interaction among all factors in the model. Each of the four major components of this self-management model requires a closer look. Since the focal point of this model is *behavior change,* let us begin by discussing the behavior component in the center of the triangle.[50]

An Agenda for Self-Improvement   In today's fast-paced Internet age, corporate hand-holding is pretty much a thing of the past when it comes to career management. Employees are told such things as "You own your own employability." They must make the best of themselves and any opportunities that may come along. A brochure at one large US company tells employees: "No one is more interested or qualified when it comes to evaluating your individual interests, values, skills, and goals than you are."[51] The new age of *career self-management* challenges you to do a better job of setting personal goals, having clear priorities, being well organized, skillfully managing your time, and developing a self-learning program.[52]

Fortunately, Stephen R Covey, in his best-selling book *The 7 Habits of Highly Effective People,* has given managers a helpful agenda for improving themselves (see Table 5–2). Covey refers to the seven habits, practiced by truly successful people, as

Figure 5–3   *A Social Learning Model of Self-Management*

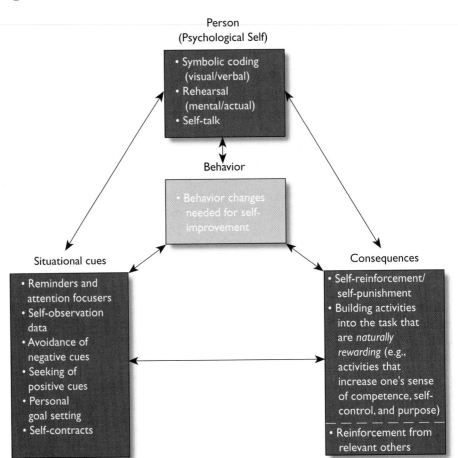

Person
(Psychological Self)

- Symbolic coding
  (visual/verbal)
- Rehearsal
  (mental/actual)
- Self-talk

Behavior

- Behavior changes
  needed for self-
  improvement

Situational cues

- Reminders and
  attention focusers
- Self-observation
  data
- Avoidance of
  negative cues
- Seeking of
  positive cues
- Personal
  goal setting
- Self-contracts

Consequences

- Self-reinforcement/
  self-punishment
- Building activities
  into the task that
  are *naturally
  rewarding* (e.g.,
  activities that
  increase one's sense
  of competence, self-
  control, and purpose)

- Reinforcement from
  relevant others

"principle-centered, character-based."[53] The first step for putting the model in Figure 5–3 to work is to pick one or more of the seven habits that are personal trouble spots and translate them to specific behaviors. For example, "think win/win" might remind a conflict-prone manager to practice cooperative teamwork behaviors with co-workers. Habit number five might prompt another manager to stop interrupting others during conversations. Next, a supportive environment is needed for the target behavior.

Managing Situational Cues
When people try to give up a nagging habit such as smoking, the cards are stacked against them. Many people (friends who smoke) and situations (after dinner, when under stress at work, or when relaxing) serve as subtle yet powerful cues telling the individual to light up. If the behavior is to be changed, the cues need to be rearranged so as to trigger the alternative behavior. Six techniques for managing situational cues are listed in the left column of Figure 5–3.

Reminders and attention focusers do just that. For example, many students and managers cue themselves about deadlines and appointments with Post-it™ notes stuck all over their work areas, refrigerators, and dashboards. Self-observation data, when com-

Table 5–2   *Covey's Seven Habits: An Agenda for Managerial Self-Improvement*

1. *Be proactive.* Choose the right means and ends in life, and take personal responsibility for your actions. Make timely decisions and make positive progress.
2. *Begin with the end in mind.* When all is said and done, how do you want to be remembered? Be goal oriented.
3. *Put first things first.* Establish firm priorities that will help you accomplish your mission in life. Strike a balance between your daily work and your potential for future accomplishments.
4. *Think win/win.* Cooperatively seek creative and mutually beneficial solutions to problems and conflicts.
5. *Seek first to understand, then to be understood.* Strive hard to become a better listener.
6. *Synergize.* Because the whole is greater than the sum of its parts, you need to generate teamwork among individuals with unique abilities and potential. Value interpersonal differences.
7. *Sharpen the saw.* "This is the habit of self-renewal, which has four elements. The first is mental, which includes reading, visualizing, planning, and writing. The second is spiritual, which means value clarification and commitment, study, and meditation. Third is social/emotional, which involves service, empathy, synergy, and intrinsic security. Finally, the physical element includes exercise, nutrition, and stress management."

SOURCE: Adapted from discussion in S R Covey, *The 7 Habits of Highly Effective People* (New York: Simon & Schuster, 1989). Excerpt from "Q & A with Stephen Covey," *Training*, December 1992, p 38.

pared against a goal or standard, can be a potent cue for improvement. Those who keep a weight chart near their bathroom scale will attest to the value of this tactic. Successful self-management calls for avoiding negative cues while seeking positive cues. Managers in Northwestern Mutual Life Insurance Company's new business department appreciate the value of avoiding negative cues: "On Wednesdays, the department shuts off all incoming calls, allowing workers to speed processing of new policies. On those days, the unit averages 23% more policies than on other days."[54]

Goals, as repeatedly mentioned in this text, are the touchstone of good management. So it is with challenging yet attainable personal goals and effective self-management. Goals simultaneously provide a target and a measuring stick of progress. Finally, a self-contract is an "if-then" agreement with oneself. For example, if you can define all the key terms in this chapter, treat yourself to something special.

Arranging Cognitive Supports
Referring to the *person* portion of the self-management model in Figure 5–3, three cognitive supports for behavior change are symbolic coding, rehearsal, and self-talk. These amount to psychological, as opposed to environmental, cues. Yet, according to Bandura, they prompt appropriate behavior in the same manner. Each requires brief explanation:

- *Symbolic coding.* From a social learning theory perspective, the human brain stores information in visual and verbal codes. For example, a sales manager could use the visual picture of a man chopping down a huge tree to remember Woodman, the name of a promising new client. In contrast, people commonly rely on acronyms to recall names, rules for behavior, and other information. An acronym (or verbal code) that is often heard in managerial circles is the KISS principle, standing for "Keep It Simple, Stupid."

- *Rehearsal.* While it is true that practice often makes perfect, mental rehearsal of challenging tasks also can increase one's chances of success. Importantly, experts draw a clear distinction between systematic visualization of how one should proceed and daydreaming about success:

> The big difference between daydreaming and visualizing is that "visualizing is much more specific and detailed," says Philadelphia consultant Judith Schuster. "A daydream typically has gaps in it—we jump immediately to where we want to wind up. In visualization, we use building blocks and, step-by-step, construct the result we want."[55]

This sort of visualization has been recommended for use in managerial planning.

Managers stand to learn a great deal about mental rehearsal and visualization from successful athletes. Kim Woodring, Wittenberg University's two-time All-American volleyball player, is a good example. She effectively combines visualization and self-talk:

> "I'm always positive," she says. "Even if I'm losing. I talk positively to myself. I go on with the next play and don't worry about the last one. When I visualize, I always see the perfect pass, perfect hit, perfect set, perfect kill, perfect result."[56]

Job-finding seminars are very popular on college campuses today because they typically involve mental and actual rehearsal of tough job interviews. This sort of manufactured experience can build the confidence and self-efficacy necessary for real-world success.[57]

ſelf-talk

Evaluating thoughts about oneself and one's circumstances.

- *Self-talk.* According to an expert on the subject, "**self-talk** is the set of evaluating thoughts that you give yourself about facts and events that happen to you."[58] Personal experience tells us that self-talk tends to be a self-fulfilling prophecy. Negative self-talk tends to pave the way for failure, whereas positive self-talk often facilitates success. Replacing negative self-talk ("I'll never get a raise") with positive self-talk ("I deserve a raise and I'm going to get it") is fundamental to better self-management. One business writer, while urging salespeople to be their own cheerleaders, offered this advice for handling difficult situations:

> Tell yourself there's a positive side to everything and train yourself to focus on it. At first your new self-talk will seem forced and unnatural, but stick with it. Use mental imagery to help you concentrate on the benefits of what you think is a bad situation. If you don't like cold calling, for example, think of how good you'll feel when you're finished, knowing you have a whole list of new selling opportunities. Forming a new habit isn't easy, but the effort will pay off.[59]

ſelf-Reinforcement   The completion of self-contracts and other personal achievements calls for self-reinforcement. According to Bandura, three criteria must be satisfied before self-reinforcement will work:

1. The individual must have *control over desired reinforcers.*

2. Reinforcers must be *self-administered on a conditional basis.* Failure to meet the performance requirement must lead to self-denial.

3. *Performance standards must be adopted* to establish the quantity and quality of target behavior required for self-reinforcement.[60]

In view of the following realities, self-reinforcement strategies need to be resourceful and creative:

Self-granted rewards can lead to self-improvement. But as failed dieters and smokers can attest, there are short-run as well as long-run influences on self-reinforcement. For the overeater, the immediate gratification of eating has more influence than the promise of a new wardrobe. The same sort of dilemma plagues procrastinators. Consequently, one needs to weave a powerful web of cues, cognitive supports, and internal and external consequences to win the tug-of-war with status-quo payoffs. Primarily because it is so easy to avoid, self-punishment tends to be ineffectual. As with managing the behavior of others, positive instead of negative consequences are recommended for effective self-management.[61]

In addition, it helps to solicit positive reinforcement for self-improvement from supportive friends, co-workers, and relatives.

Research and Managerial Implications   There is a modest body of evidence showing that the social learning approach to self-management works. For example, in one controlled study of 20 college students, 17 were able to successfully modify their own behavior problems involving smoking, lack of assertiveness, poor study habits, overeating, sloppy housekeeping, lack of exercise, and moodiness.[62] In a workplace study, 31 out of 33 employees who had received self-management training reported positive results.[63] Other job-related problems helped by self-management training include overdependence on the boss, ignoring paperwork, leaving the office without notifying anyone, failing to fill out expense reports, and absenteeism.[64]

More comprehensive research is needed to discover how, why, and under what conditions the social learning approach to self-management works and does not work. In the meantime, present and future managers can fine-tune their own behavior by taking lessons from proven self-management techniques.

Continuing our quest for greater understanding of individual differences, our attention now turns to personality traits and dynamics.

Personality: Concepts and Controversy

Individuals have their own way of thinking and acting, their own unique style or *personality*. **Personality** is defined as the combination of stable physical and mental characteristics that give the individual his or her identity.[65] These characteristics or traits—including how one looks, thinks, acts, and feels—are the product of interacting genetic and environmental influences. In this section, we introduce the Big Five personality dimensions, explore the proactive personality, issue some cautions about workplace personality testing, and examine an important personality factor called locus of control.

Personality
Stable physical and mental characteristics responsible for a person's identity.

The Big Five Personality Dimensions

Long and confusing lists of personality dimensions have been distilled in recent years to the Big Five.[66] They are extraversion, agreeableness, conscientiousness, emotional stability, and openness to experience (see Table 5–3 for descriptions). Standardized personality tests determine how positively or negatively a person scores on each of the Big Five. For example, someone scoring negatively on extraversion would be an introverted person prone to shy and withdrawn behavior. Someone scoring negatively on emotional security would be nervous, tense, angry, and worried. Appropriately, the

Table 5–3   *The Big Five Personality Dimensions*

Personality Dimension	Characteristics of a Person Scoring Positively on the Dimension
1. Extraversion	Outgoing, talkative, sociable, assertive
2. Agreeableness	Trusting, good natured, cooperative, soft hearted
3. Conscientiousness	Dependable, responsible, achievement oriented, persistent
4. Emotional stability	Relaxed, secure, unworried
5. Openness to experience	Intellectual, imaginative, curious, broad minded

SOURCE: Adapted from M R Barrick and M K Mount, "Autonomy as a Moderator of the Relationships between the Big Five Personality Dimensions and Job Performance," *Journal of Applied Psychology*, February 1993, pp 111–18.

negative end of the emotional stability scale is labeled neuroticism. A person's scores on the Big Five reveal a personality profile as unique as his or her fingerprints. Yet one important question lingers: Are personality models ethnocentric or unique to the culture in which they were developed? At least as far as the Big Five model goes, recent cross-cultural research evidence points in the direction of "no." Specifically, the Big Five personality structure held up very well in one study of women and men from Russia, Canada, Hong Kong, Poland, Germany, and Finland and a second study (85% male) of South Korean managers and stockbrokers.[67]

Those interested in OB want to know the connection between the Big Five and job performance. Ideally, Big Five personality dimensions that correlate positively and strongly with job performance would be helpful in the selection, training, and appraisal of employees. A meta-analysis of 117 studies involving 23,994 subjects from many professions offers guidance.[68] Among the Big Five, *conscientiousness* had the strongest positive correlation with job performance and training performance. According to the researchers, "those individuals who exhibit traits associated with a strong sense of purpose, obligation, and persistence generally perform better than those who do not."[69] Another recent finding: Extraversion (an outgoing personality) correlated positively with promotions, salary level, and career satisfaction. And, as one might expect, neuroticism (low emotional stability) was associated with low career satisfaction.[70]

The Proactive Personality

As suggested by the above discussion, someone who scores high on the Big Five dimension of conscientiousness is probably a good worker. Thomas S Bateman and J Michael Crant took this important linkage an additional step by formulating the concept of the proactive personality. They define and characterize the **proactive personality** in these terms: "someone who is relatively unconstrained by situational forces and who effects environmental change. Proactive people identify opportunities and act on them, show initiative, take action, and persevere until meaningful change occurs."[71] In short, people with proactive personalities are "hardwired" to change the status quo. In a review of relevant studies, Crant recently found the proactive personality to be positively associated with individual, team, and organizational success.[72]

Successful entrepreneurs exemplify the proactive personality. Take this dynamic duo, for example:

Proactive personality

Action-oriented person who shows initiative and perseveres to change things.

A dynamic duo. Like their well-educated parents, sisters Alka (on the left) and Mona Srivastava planned to pursue post-graduate degrees. That was until they were bitten by the entrepreneurial bug. They launched their new business career by moving to Los Angeles and starting Florentyna Intima, a lingerie company. Thanks to their proactive personalities and lots of hard work, over 200 stores and boutiques now carry their products.

(c) 2002, USA TODAY. Reprinted with permission

A few years ago, sisters Alka and Mona Srivastava planned to follow in their family's highly educated footsteps—Alka, 30, planned to get a PhD in economics and Mona, 31, a law degree.

But instead, they gave it all up, and in 1995, quit their jobs and moved from the power suit world of New York to the beaches of Los Angeles to start Florentyna Intima, a lingerie firm. Now, their bras, underwear and camisoles are sold in more than 200 specialty shops and catalogs, and sales have grown about 30% each year since the first item was shipped in 1999. . . .

"You are talking about two girls who had no idea about anything to do with manufacturing, except for the fact that we knew that we liked to shop," Mona says. "We had to learn everything as we went along."[73]

People with proactive personalities truly are valuable *human capital,* as defined in Chapter 1. Those wanting to get ahead would do well to cultivate the initiative, drive, and perseverance of someone with a proactive personality, and managers would do well to hire them.

Issue: What about Personality Testing in the Workplace?

Personality testing as a tool for making decisions about hiring, training, and promotion is questionable for three reasons. First is the issue of *predictive validity.* Can personality tests actually predict job performance? In the Big Five meta-analysis discussed earlier, conscientiousness may have been the best predictor of job performance, but it was *not a strong* predictor. Moreover, the most widely used personality test, the Minnesota Multiphasic Personality Inventory (MMPI), does not directly measure conscientiousness. No surprise that the MMPI and other popular personality tests historically have been poor predictors of job performance.[74]

Second is the issue of *differential validity,* relative to race. Do personality tests measure whites and minority races differently? We still do not have a definitive answer to this important and difficult question. Respected Big Five researchers concluded, "To date, the evidence indicates that differential validity is not typically associated with personality measures. Caution is required in interpreting this conclusion, however, in light of the small number of studies available."[75] Meanwhile, personality testing remains a lightening rod for controversy on the job.[76] In police departments, where psychological testing is routinely used supposedly to weed out racists, critics claim the opposite actually occurs. According to *The Wall Street Journal,* "many black police officers in particular remain skeptical, contending that the psychological evaluations are so subjective that they have been used to discriminate against minorities."[77]

A third issue involves faking. Both those who favor and disapprove of personality testing in the workplace generally agree that faking occurs. Faking involves intentionally misrepresenting one's true beliefs on a personality test. For instance, a test taker with knowledge of the proactive personality might want to improve her or his chances of landing a job by pretending to be a proactive person. The crux of the faking issue is this: To what extent does faking alter a personality test's *construct validity* (the degree to which the test actually measures what it is supposed to measure)? Recent research suggests faking is a threat to the construct validity of personality tests.[78]

The practical tips in Table 5–4 can help managers avoid abuses and costly discrimination lawsuits when using personality and psychological testing for employment-related decisions. Another alternative for employers is to eliminate personality testing altogether. At Microsoft, where 12,000 résumés stream in every month, recruits are screened with challenging interviews, but no psychological tests. When *Fortune* magazine asked David Pritchard, Microsoft's director of recruiting, about the standard practice of screening recruits with psychological tests, Pritchard replied, "It doesn't

Table 5–4   *Advice and Words of Caution about Personality Testing in the Workplace*

Researchers, test developers, and organizations that administer personality assessments offer the following suggestions for getting started or for evaluating whether tests already in use are appropriate for forecasting job performance:

- Determine what you hope to accomplish. If you are looking to find the best fit of job and applicant, analyze the aspects of the position that are most critical for it.
- Look for outside help to determine if a test exists or can be developed to screen applicants for the traits that best fit the position. Industrial psychologists, professional organizations, and a number of Internet sites provide resources.
- Insist that any test recommended by a consultant or vendor be validated scientifically for the specific purpose that you have defined. Vendors should be able to cite some independent, credible research supporting a test's correlation with job performance.
- Ask the test provider to document the legal basis for any assessment: Is it fair? Is it job-related? Is it biased against any racial or ethnic group? Does it violate an applicant's right to privacy under state or federal laws? Vendors should provide a lawyer's statement that a test does not adversely affect any protected class, and employers may want to get their own lawyer's opinion, as well.
- Make sure that every staff member who will be administering tests or analyzing results is educated about how to do so properly and keeps results confidential. Use the scores on personality tests in tandem with other factors that you believe are essential to the job—such as skills and experience—to create a comprehensive evaluation of the merits of each candidate, and apply those criteria identically to each applicant.

SOURCE: S Bates, "Personality Counts," *HR Magazine,* February 2002, p 34.

really interest me much. In the end, you end up with a bunch of people who answer the questions correctly, and that's not always what you want. How can a multiple-choice test tell whether someone is creative or not?"[79] The growing use of job-related skills testing and behavioral interviewing is an alternative to personality testing.

Issue: Why Not Just Forget about Personality?

Personality testing problems and unethical applications do not automatically cancel out the underlying concepts. Present and future managers need to know about personality traits and characteristics, despite the controversy over personality testing. Rightly or wrongly used, the term *personality* is routinely encountered both on and off the job. Knowledge of the Big Five and the proactive personality encourages more precise understanding of the rich diversity among today's employees. Good management involves taking the time to get to know *each* employee's *unique combination* of personality, abilities, and potential and then creating a productive and satisfying person-job fit.

Let us take a look at locus of control, another important job-related personality factor.

Locus of Control: Self or Environment?

Individuals vary in terms of how much personal responsibility they take for their behavior and its consequences. Julian Rotter, a personality researcher, identified a dimension of personality he labeled *locus of control* to explain these differences. He proposed that people tend to attribute the causes of their behavior primarily to either themselves or environmental factors.[80] This personality trait produces distinctly different behavior patterns.

People who believe they control the events and consequences that affect their lives are said to possess an **internal locus of control.** For example, such a person tends to attribute positive outcomes, such as getting a passing grade on an exam, to her or his own abilities. Similarly, an "internal" tends to blame negative events, such as failing an exam, on personal shortcomings—not studying hard enough, perhaps. Many entrepreneurs eventually succeed because their *internal* locus of control helps them overcome setbacks and disappointments. They see themselves as masters of their own fate and not simply lucky. But, as *Fortune*'s Jaclyn Fierman humorously noted, luck is a matter of interpretation and not always a bad thing:

> For those of us who believe we are the masters of our fate, the captains of our soul, the notion that a career might hinge on random events is unthinkable. Self-made men and women are especially touchy on this subject. If they get all the breaks, it's because they're smarter and harder working than everyone else. If they know the right people, it's because they network the nights away. Luck? Many successful people think it diminishes them.
>
> Hard workers do get ahead, no doubt about it. . . . But then there are folks like Ringo Starr. One day he was an obscure drummer of limited talent from Liverpool; the next day he was a Beatle.
>
> Nobody demonstrates better than Ringo that true luck is accidental, not inevitable.[81]

On the other side of this personality dimension are those who believe their performance is the product of circumstances beyond their immediate control. These individuals are said to possess an **external locus of control** and tend to attribute outcomes to environmental causes, such as luck or fate. Unlike someone with an internal locus of

Internal locus of control
Attributing outcomes to one's own actions.

External locus of control
Attributing outcomes to circumstances beyond one's control.

OB Exercise   Where Is Your Locus of Control?

Circle one letter for each pair of items, in accordance with your beliefs:

1. A. Many of the unhappy things in people's lives are partly due to bad luck.
   B. People's misfortunes result from the mistakes they make.
2. A. Unfortunately, an individual's worth often passes unrecognized no matter how hard he tries.
   B. In the long run, people get the respect they deserve.
3. A. Without the right breaks one cannot be an effective leader.
   B. Capable people who fail to become leaders have not taken advantage of their opportunities.
4. A. I have often found that what is going to happen will happen.
   B. Trusting to fate has never turned out as well for me as making a decision to take a definite course of action.
5. A. Most people don't realize the extent to which their lives are controlled by accidental happenings.
   B. There really is no such thing as "luck."
6. A. In the long run, the bad things that happen to us are balanced by the good ones.
   B. Most misfortunes are the result of lack of ability, ignorance, laziness, or all three.
7. A. Many times I feel I have little influence over the things that happen to me.
   B. It is impossible for me to believe that chance or luck plays an important role in my life.

Note: In determining your score, A = 0 and B = 1.

Arbitrary norms for this shortened version are: External locus of control = 1–3; Balanced internal and external locus of control = 4; Internal locus of control = 5–7.

SOURCE: Excerpted from J B Rotter, "Generalized Expectancies for Internal versus External Control of Reinforcement," *Psychological Monographs,* vol. 80 (Whole no. 609, 1966), pp 11–12. Copyright © 1966 by the American Psychological Association. Reprinted with permission.

control, an "external" would attribute a passing grade on an exam to something external (an easy test or a good day) and attribute a failing grade to an unfair test or problems at home. A shortened version of an instrument Rotter developed to measure one's locus of control is presented in the OB Exercise above. Where is your locus of control: internal, external, or a combination?

Research Findings on Locus of Control   Researchers have found important behavioral differences between internals and externals:

- Internals display greater work motivation.
- Internals have stronger expectations that effort leads to performance.
- Internals exhibit higher performance on tasks involving learning or problem solving, when performance leads to valued rewards.
- There is a stronger relationship between job satisfaction and performance for internals than externals.
- Internals obtain higher salaries and greater salary increases than externals.
- Externals tend to be more anxious than internals.[82]

Implications of Locus of Control Differences for Managers   The preceding summary of research findings on locus of control has important implications for managing people at work. Let us examine two of them.

First, since internals have a tendency to believe they control the work environment through their behavior, they will attempt to exert control over the work setting. This can be done by trying to influence work procedures, working conditions, task assignments, or relationships with peers and supervisors. As these possibilities imply, internals may resist a manager's attempts to closely supervise their work. Therefore, management may want to place internals in jobs requiring high initiative and low compliance. Externals, on the other hand, might be more amenable to highly structured jobs requiring greater compliance. Direct participation also can bolster the attitudes and performance of externals. This conclusion comes from a field study of 85 computer system users in a wide variety of business and government organizations. Externals who had been significantly involved in designing their organization's computer information system had more favorable attitudes toward the system than their external-locus co-workers who had not participated.[83]

Second, locus of control has implications for reward systems. Given that internals have a greater belief that their effort leads to performance, internals likely would prefer and respond more productively to incentives such as merit pay or sales commissions.[84]

Emotions: An Emerging OB Topic

In the ideal world of management theory, employees pursue organizational goals in a logical and rational manner. Emotional behavior seldom is factored into the equation.[85] Yet day-to-day organizational life shows us how prevalent and powerful emotions can be. Anger and jealousy, both potent emotions, often push aside logic and rationality in the workplace. Managers use fear and other emotions to both motivate and intimidate. For example, consider Microsoft CEO Steve Ballmer's management style prior to his recent efforts to become a kinder, gentler leader: "Ballmer shouts when he gets excited or angry—his voice rising so suddenly that it's like an electric shock. . . . By the early 1990s, Ballmer had to have throat surgery to fix problems brought on by shouting."[86]

Less noisy, but still emotion laden, is John Chambers's tightrope act as CEO of Cisco Systems:

> Any company that thinks it's utterly unbeatable is already beaten. So when I begin to think we're getting a little bit too confident, you'll see me emphasizing the paranoia side. And then when I feel that there's a little bit too much fear and apprehension, I'll just jump back to the other side. My job is to keep those scales perfectly balanced.[87]

These admired corporate leaders would not have achieved what they have without the ability to be logical and rational decision makers *and* be emotionally charged. Too much emotion, however, could have spelled career and organizational disaster for either of them.

In this final section, our examination of individual differences turns to defining emotions, reviewing a typology of 10 positive and negative emotions, exploring emotional intelligence and maturity, and focusing on the management of anger, a potentially destructive and dangerous emotion.

Positive and Negative Emotions

Emotions

Complex human reactions to personal achievements and setbacks that may be felt and displayed.

Richard S Lazarus, a leading authority on the subject, defines **emotions** as "complex, patterned, organismic reactions to how we think we are doing in our lifelong efforts to survive and flourish and to achieve what we wish for ourselves."[88] The word *organismic* is appropriate because emotions involve the *whole* person—biological, psychological, and social. Importantly, psychologists draw a distinction between *felt* and *displayed* emotions.[89] For example, a person might feel angry (felt emotion) at a rude co-worker but not make a nasty remark in return (displayed emotion). As discussed in Chapter 19, emotions play roles in both causing and adapting to stress and its associated biological and psychological problems. The destructive effect of emotional behavior on social relationships is all too obvious in daily life.[90]

Lazarus's definition of emotions centers on a person's goals. Accordingly, his distinction between positive and negative emotions is goal oriented. Some emotions are triggered by frustration and failure when pursuing one's goals. Lazarus calls these *negative* emotions. They are said to be goal incongruent. For example, which of the six negative emotions in Figure 5–4 are you likely to experience if you fail the final exam in a required course? Failing the exam would be incongruent with your goal of graduating on time. On the other hand, which of the four *positive* emotions in Figure 5–4 would you probably experience if you graduated on time and with honors? The emotions you would experience in this situation are positive because they are congruent (or consistent) with an important lifetime goal. The individual's goals, it is important to note, may or may not be socially acceptable. Thus, a positive emotion, such as

Figure 5–4   *Positive and Negative Emotions*

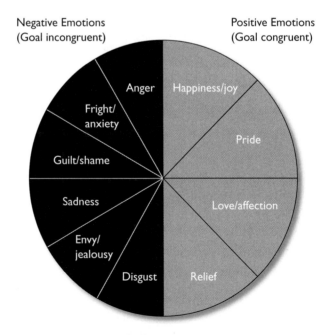

SOURCE: Adapted from discussion in R S Lazarus, *Emotion and Adaptation* (New York: Oxford University Press, 1991), Chs 6, 7.

Talk about baptism by fire. Just 10 months after being named CEO of American Express, Kenneth I. Chenault addressed 5,000 of his coworkers in an emotional meeting to begin the healing process following the September 11, 2001 terrorists attacks. The tragedy claimed the lives of 11 AmEx employees and closed the firm's New York headquarters for eight months of repairs. Chenault, seen here presiding over AmEx's May 13, 2002 headquarters homecoming celebration, reportedly handled the post-9/11 meeting with great skill and compassion.

AP/Wide World Photos

love/affection, may be undesirable if associated with sexual harassment. Oppositely, slight pangs of guilt, anxiety, and envy can motivate extra effort. On balance, the constructive or destructive nature of a particular emotion must be judged in terms of both its intensity and the person's relevant goal.

For a dramatic real-life example of the interplay between negative and positive emotions, consider the situation Kenneth I Chenault faced just 10 months after becoming CEO of American Express. The September 11, 2001, terrorist attacks claimed the lives of 11 employees, and the firm's headquarters building, across the street from ground zero in Lower Manhattan, had to be abandoned for what turned out to be eight months of repairs.

> Chenault gathered 5,000 American Express employees at the Paramount Theater in New York on September 20 for a highly emotional "town hall meeting." During the session, Chenault demonstrated the poise, compassion, and decisiveness that vaulted him to the top. He told employees that he had been filled with such despair, sadness, and anger that he had seen a counselor. Twice, he rushed to spontaneously embrace grief-stricken employees. Chenault said he would donate $1 million of the company's profits to the families of the AmEx victims. "I represent the best company and the best people in the world," he concluded. "In fact, you are my strength, and I love you."[91]

Thus, Chenault masterfully used positive emotions to cope with profound negative emotions.

Emotional Intelligence and Maturity in the Age of Global Terrorism

The post-9/11 era has been an emotional roller-coaster ride, complete with anthrax-tainted mail, nerve-wracking security checks, and a steady diet of terrorist threats and alerts. All this has left Americans, accustomed to feeling safe and secure, a bit frayed

International OB — ## History Says Fear Is Not an Effective Weapon

Today in America, fear is a weapon. It is the knife that would sever our faith in each other, the club that would beat us into resignation, the gun that would stop us from flying and buying.

Fear would make us hoard antibiotics and seek needless tests. It would blind us to reassuring odds on the safety of air travel and the danger of anthrax. It would make us shun the skyscraper, flee the subway and stop the mail.

Fear would make us suspect anyone who wears a turban or buys too much Halloween candy. It would induce a national nervous breakdown.

But those who study fear agree: Frightening civilians in any kind of war is a loser's hand.

"Terrorism doesn't seem to work very well," says Roy Licklider, a Rutgers University political scientist who studies the subject. "It's the weapon of the weak. It's hard to find any functioning society that ever became unglued because of terrorism."

... [I]n practice, fear is a bomb that usually blows up in a terrorist's face. "Fear hasn't had the impact its wielders have hoped," says Col. Thomas Dempsey of the U.S. Army War College in Carlisle, Pa. "It usually will rebound on you."

Fear didn't win for the Germans who bombed civilians in London in 1941. It didn't overthrow the czar or drive the British out of Northern Ireland. It hasn't created a Palestinian state or a Basque nation.

Fear, experts say, has two main flaws as a weapon against society:

- Fear mostly unites people, makes them more resolute and just plain ticks them off....

- Fear gets old fast. Studies show that no matter how much you scare people, they get back into routines before very long.

Londoners learned to sleep in the subway during the Blitz. Most survivors of Hiroshima moved back to the city within three months. Bakers in Beirut whose windows were shattered by car bombs in the 1980s were back in business the same day. Residents in areas of Belfast learned not to stand by a window.

SOURCE: Excerpted from R Hampson, "Terrorist Tactics Rarely Triumph," *USA Today*, November 1, 2001, pp 1A–2A.

around the edges. Truth is, most of the world's 6.2 billion people face fearful conditions daily and have learned to live with them (see the International OB above). Fear is a core emotion. If we can learn to better handle fear, then we can readily deal with all the other emotions.

Keeping Things in Perspective

One proven way to deal with fear is to consider specific threats in broader perspective. President Franklin D Roosevelt, who knew the fear of waking one morning paralyzed from the neck down by polio, told a Depression-ravaged nation that the thing they had to fear most was fear itself.[92] In 2001, more than 13 times as many people (41,730) died in crashes on America's highways as were killed in the September 11 attacks (3,056).[93] About 40% (16,692) of those traffic deaths were alcohol-related.[94] In perspective, on a day-to-day basis which is a bigger threat to you and your family's safety: foreign terrorists or your neighborhood drunk driver?

Developing Emotional Intelligence

Another way to deal more effectively with fear and other emotions is to become more emotionally mature by developing emotional intelligence. In 1995, Daniel Goleman, a psychologist turned journalist, created a stir in education and management circles with the publication of his book *Emotional Intelligence*. Hence, an obscure topic among psychologists became mainstream. According to Goleman, traditional models of intelligence (IQ) are too narrow, failing to consider interpersonal competence. Goleman's broader agenda includes "abilities such as being able to motivate oneself and persist in the face of frustrations; to control impulse and delay gratification; to regulate one's moods and keep distress from swamping the ability to think; to empathize and to hope."[95] Thus, **emotional intelligence** is the ability to manage oneself and one's relationships in mature and constructive ways. Referred to by some as EI and others as EQ, emotional intelligence is said to have four key components: self-awareness, self-management, social awareness, and relationship management. The first two constitute *personal competence;* the second two feed into *social competence* (see Table 5–5).

Emotional intelligence
Ability to manage oneself and interact with others in mature and constructive ways.

Table 5–5   *Developing Personal and Social Competence through Emotional Intelligence*

Personal Competence: These capabilities determine how we manage ourselves.

Self-Awareness
- *Emotional self-awareness:* Reading one's own emotions and recognizing their impact; using "gut sense" to guide decisions.
- *Accurate self-assessment:* Knowing one's strengths and limits.
- *Self-confidence:* A sound sense of one's self-worth and capabilities.

Self-Management
- *Emotional self-control:* Keeping disruptive emotions and impulses under control.
- *Transparency:* Displaying honesty and integrity; trustworthiness.
- *Adaptability:* Flexibility in adapting to changing situations or overcoming obstacles.
- *Achievement:* The drive to improve performance to meet inner standards of excellence.
- *Initiative:* Readiness to act and seize opportunities.
- *Optimism:* Seeing the upside in events.

Social Competence: These capabilities determine how we manage relationships.

Social Awareness
- *Empathy:* Sensing others' emotions, understanding their perspective, and taking active interest in their concerns.
- *Organizational awareness:* Reading the currents, decision networks, and politics at the organizational level.
- *Service:* Recognizing and meeting follower, client, or customer needs.

Relationship Management
- *Inspirational leadership:* Guiding and motivating with a compelling vision.
- *Influence:* Wielding a range of tactics for persuasion.
- *Developing others:* Bolstering others' abilities through feedback and guidance.
- *Change catalyst:* Initiating, managing, and leading in a new direction.
- *Conflict management:* Resolving disagreements.
- *Building bonds:* Cultivating and maintaining a web of relationships.
- *Teamwork and collaboration:* Cooperation and team building.

SOURCE: D Goleman, R Boyatzis, and A McKee, *Primal Leadership: Realizing the Power of Emotional Intelligence* (Boston: Harvard Business School Press, 2002), p 39.

As an integrated package, Covey's seven habits in Table 5–2, the proactive personality discussed earlier, and the characteristics listed in Table 5–5 constitute a challenging self-development agenda for each of us. Indeed, Goleman and his followers believe greater emotional intelligence can boost individual, team, and organizational effectiveness.[96]

Practical OB Research Insights about Emotions

Two streams of OB research on emotions are beginning to yield interesting and instructive insights:

- *Emotional contagion.* Have you ever had someone's bad mood sour your mood? That person could have been a parent, supervisor, co-worker, friend, or someone serving you in a store or restaurant. Appropriately, researchers call this *emotional contagion.* We, quite literally, can catch another person's bad mood or displayed negative emotions. This effect was documented in a recent study of 131 bank tellers (92% female) and 220 exit interviews with their customers. Tellers who expressed positive emotions tended to have more satisfied customers.[97] Two field studies with nurses and accountants as subjects found a strong linkage between the work group's collective mood and the individual's mood.[98] Both foul moods and good moods turned out to be contagious. Perhaps more managers should follow the lead of this German executive:

    After arriving at his Munich office in the morning, Ulrich Schumacher likes to pop a CD into a player on his desk and blast a track by singer James Brown. Nothing like the godfather of soul shouting "I feel good!" to get a manager psyched up for the day ahead, says Schumacher, 43, CEO of German semiconductor maker Infineon Technologies.[99]

- *Emotional labor.* Although they did not have the benefit of a catchy label or a body of sophisticated research, generations of managers have known about the power of emotional contagion in the marketplace. "Smile, look happy for the customers" employees are told over and over. But what if the employee is having a rotten day? What if they have to mask their true feelings and emotions? What if they have to fake it? Researchers have begun studying the dynamics of what they call *emotional labor.* A pair of authors, one from Australia the other from the United States, recently summarized the research lessons to date:

    Emotional labor can be particularly detrimental to the employee performing the labor and can take its toll both psychologically and physically. Employees . . . may bottle up feelings of frustration, resentment, and anger, which are not appropriate to express. These feelings result, in part, from the constant requirement to monitor one's negative emotions and express positive ones. If not given a healthy expressive outlet, this emotional repression can lead to a syndrome of emotional exhaustion and burnout.[100]

Interestingly, a pair of laboratory studies with US college students as subjects found no gender difference in *felt* emotions. But the women were more emotionally *expressive* than the men.[101] This stream of research on emotional labor has major practical implications for productivity and job satisfaction, as well as for workplace anger, aggression, and violence (see Table 5–6). Clearly, managers need to be attuned to (and responsive to) the emotional states and needs of their people. This requires emotional intelligence.

Table 5–6   *How to Manage Anger in Yourself and Others*

Reducing Chronic Anger (in Yourself)	Responding to Angry Provocation
Guides for Action	**Guides for Action**
• Appreciate the potentially valuable lessons from anger.	• Expect angry people to exaggerate.
• Use mistakes and slights to learn.	• Recognize the other's frustrations and pressures.
• Recognize that you and others can do well enough without being perfect.	• Use the provocation to develop your abilities.
	• Allow the other to let off steam.
• Trust that most people want to be caring, helpful family members and colleagues.	• Begin to problem solve when the anger is at moderate levels.
• Forgive others and yourself.	• Congratulate yourself on turning an outburst into an opportunity to find solutions.
• Confront unrealistic, blame-oriented assumptions.	
• Adopt constructive, learning-oriented assumptions.	• Share successes with partners.
Pitfalls to Avoid	**Pitfalls to Avoid**
• Assume every slight is a painful wound.	• Take every word literally.
• Equate not getting what you want with catastrophe.	• Denounce the most extreme statements and ignore more moderate ones.
• See every mistake and slip as a transgression that must be corrected immediately.	• Doubt yourself because the other does.
• Attack someone for your getting angry.	• Attack because you have been attacked.
• Attack yourself for getting angry.	• Forget the experience without learning from it.
• Try to be and have things perfect.	
• Suspect people's motives unless you have incontestable evidence that people can be trusted.	
• Assume any attempt to change yourself is an admission of failure.	
• Never forgive.	

Summary of Key Concepts

1. *Define self-esteem, and explain how it can be improved with Branden's six pillars of self-esteem.* Self-esteem is how people perceive themselves as physical, social, and spiritual beings. Branden's six pillars of self-esteem are live consciously, be self-accepting, take personal responsibility, be self-assertive, live purposefully, and have personal integrity.

2. *Define self-efficacy, and explain its sources.* Self-efficacy involves one's belief about his or her ability to accomplish specific tasks. Those extremely low in self-efficacy suffer from learned helplessness. Four sources of self-efficacy beliefs are prior experience, behavior models, persuasion from others, and assessment of one's physical and emotional states. High self-efficacy beliefs foster constructive and goal-oriented action, whereas low self-

efficacy fosters passive, failure-prone activities and emotions.

3. *Contrast high and low self-monitoring individuals, and discuss the ethical implications of organizational identification.* A high self-monitor strives to make a good public impression by closely monitoring his or her behavior and adapting it to the situation. Very high self-monitoring can create a "chameleon" who is seen as insincere and dishonest. Low self-monitors do the opposite by acting out their momentary feelings, regardless of their surroundings. Very low self-monitoring can lead to a one-way communicator who seems to ignore verbal and nonverbal cues from others. People who supplant their own identity with that of their organization run the risk of blind obedience and groupthink because of a failure to engage in critical

thinking and not being objective about what they are asked to do.

4. *Explain the social learning model of self-management.* Behavior results from interaction among four components: (a) situational cues, (b) the person's psychological self, (c) the person's behavior, and (d) consequences. Behavior, such as Covey's seven habits of highly effective people, can be developed by relying on supportive cognitive processes such as mental rehearsal and self-talk. Carefully arranged cues and consequences also help in the self-improvement process.

5. *Identify and describe the Big Five personality dimensions, and specify which one is correlated most strongly with job performance.* The Big Five personality dimensions are extraversion (social and talkative), agreeableness (trusting and cooperative), conscientiousness (responsible and persistent), emotional stability (relaxed and unworried), and openness to experience (intellectual and curious). Conscientiousness is the best predictor of job performance.

6. *Describe the proactive personality, and explain the difference between an internal and an external locus of control.* Someone with a proactive personality shows initiative, takes action, and perseveres to bring about change. People with an internal locus of control, such as entrepreneurs, believe they are masters of their own fate. Those with an external locus of control attribute their behavior and its results to situational factors and forces.

7. *Distinguish between positive and negative emotions, and explain how they can be judged.* Positive emotions—happiness/joy, pride, love/affection, and relief—are personal reactions to circumstances congruent with one's goals. Negative emotions—anger, fright/anxiety, guilt/shame, sadness, envy/jealousy, and disgust—are personal reactions to circumstances incongruent with one's goals. Both types of emotions need to be judged in terms of intensity and the appropriateness of the person's relevant goal.

8. *Identify the four key components of emotional intelligence, and discuss the practical significance of emotional contagion and emotional labor.* Goleman's model says the four components are self-awareness, self-management, social awareness, and relationship management. People can, in fact, catch another person's good or bad moods and expressed emotions, much as they would catch a contagious disease. Managers and others in the workplace need to avoid spreading counterproductive emotions. People in service jobs who are asked to suppress their own negative emotions and display positive emotions, regardless of their true feelings at the time, pay a physical and mental price for their emotional labor. Managers who are not mindful of emotional labor may experience lower productivity, reduced job satisfaction, and possibly aggression and even violence.

Discussion Questions

1. How should the reality of a more diverse workforce affect management's approach to dealing with individual differences?

2. What is your personal experience with high and low self-esteem people?

3. How is someone you know with low self-efficacy, relative to a specified task, "programming themselves for failure?" What could be done to help that individual develop high self-efficacy?

4. What are the career implications of your self-monitoring score in the OB Exercise on page 159?

5. Why is organizational identification both a good and bad thing in today's workplace?

6. Do you agree with the assumption that managers need to do a good job with self-management before they can effectively manage others? Explain.

7. What importance would you attach to self-talk in self-management? Explain.

8. On scales of low = 1 to high = 10, how would you rate yourself on the Big Five personality dimensions? Is your personality profile suitable for a managerial position?

9. How would you respond to the following statement? "Whenever possible, managers should hire people with an external locus of control."

10. What are your personal experiences with negative emotions being positive and positive emotions being negative?

Internet Exercise

Lots of interactive questionnaires can be found on the Internet to help you learn more about yourself. *Note:* This self-test is for instructional and entertainment purposes only. It is not intended to replace rigorously validated and properly administered psychometric tests and should not be used to establish qualifications or make personnel decisions. Still, it can provide useful insights and stimulate discussion. The purpose of this exercise is to learn more about emotional intelligence (EQ), as discussed in this chapter.

A Free Online Interactive Emotional Intelligence (EQ) Test

Go to *Fortune* magazine's Internet site (**www.fortune.com**) and select "Careers" from the main menu. Then scroll down the middle column to the subheading "Quizzes," and select "What's Your EQ at Work?" Read the instructions and complete the 25 test items. (*Note:* This is a very quick-and-easy test.) Follow the prompt to submit your answers to auto-

matic scoring. You may want to explore some of *Fortune*'s other career resources while you are there, or bookmark the site for later reference.

Questions

1. Do you believe this sort of so-called pencil-and-paper psychological testing has any merit? Explain your rationale.

2. Could self-serving bias, discussed at the end of Chapter 7, influence the way people evaluate psychometric tests? Briefly, self-serving bias involves taking personal responsibility for your successes and blaming your failures on other factors. For example, "I scored high, so I think it's a good test." "I scored low, so it's an unfair or invalid test." Explain.

3. Do you agree with psychologist Daniel Goleman that EQ can be more important and more powerful than IQ? Explain.

OB in Action Case Study

Learning-Disabled Kids Who Made It to the Top[102]

Consider the following four dead-end kids.

One was spanked by his teachers for bad grades and a poor attitude. He dropped out of school at 16. Another failed remedial English and came perilously close to flunking out of college. The third feared he'd never make it through school—and might not have without a tutor. The last finally learned to read in third grade, devouring Marvel comics, whose pictures provided clues to help him untangle the words.

These four losers are, respectively, Richard Branson, Charles Schwab, John Chambers, and David Boies. Billionaire Branson developed one of Britain's top brands with Virgin Records and Virgin Atlantic Airways. Schwab virtually created the discount brokerage business. Chambers is CEO of Cisco. Boies is a celebrated trial attorney, best known as the guy who beat Microsoft.

In one of the stranger bits of business trivia, they have something in common: They are all dyslexic. So is billionaire Craig McCaw, who pioneered the cellular industry; John Reed, who led Citibank to the top of banking; Donald Winkler, who until recently headed Ford Financial; Gaston Caperton, former governor of West Virginia and now head of the College Board; Paul Orfalea,

founder of Kinko's; Diane Swonk, chief economist of Bank One. The list goes on. . . . Many of these adults seemed pretty hopeless as kids. All have been wildly successful in business. Most have now begun to talk about their dyslexia as a way to help children and parents cope with a condition that is still widely misunderstood. "This is very painful to talk about, even today," says Chambers. "The only reason I am talking about it is 100% for the kids and their parents."

What exactly is dyslexia? The Everyman definition calls it a reading disorder in which people jumble letters, confusing dog with god, say, or box with pox. The exact cause is unclear; scientists believe it has to do with the way a developing brain is wired. Difficulty reading, spelling, and writing are typical symptoms. But dyslexia often comes with one or more other learning problems as well, including trouble with math, auditory processing, organizational skills, and memory. No two dyslexics are alike—each has his own set of weaknesses and strengths. About 5% to 6% of American public school children have been diagnosed with a learning disability; 80% of the diagnoses are dyslexia-related. But some studies indicate that up to 20% of the population may have some degree of dyslexia. . . .

A generation ago this was a problem with no name. Boies, Schwab, and Bill Samuels Jr, the president of Maker's Mark, did not realize they were dyslexic until some of their own children were diagnosed with the disorder, which is often inherited. . . .

Most of the adults *Fortune* talked to had diagnosed themselves. Says Branson: "At some point, I think I decided that being dyslexic was better than being stupid."

Stupid. Dumb. Retard. Dyslexic kids have heard it all. According to a March 2000 Roper poll, almost two-thirds of Americans still associate learning disabilities with mental retardation. That's probably because dyslexics find it so difficult to learn through conventional methods. "It is a disability in learning," says Boies. "It is not an intelligence disability. It doesn't mean you can't think."

He's right. Dyslexia has nothing to do with IQ; many smart, accomplished people have it, or are thought to have had it, including Winston Churchill and Albert Einstein. Sally Shaywitz, a leading dyslexia neuroscientist at Yale, believes the disorder can carry surprising talents along with its well-known disadvantages. "Dyslexics are overrepresented in the top ranks of people who are unusually insightful, who bring a new perspective, who think out of the box," says Shaywitz. She is co-director of the Center for Learning and Attention at Yale, along with her husband, Dr. Bennett Shaywitz, a professor of pediatrics and neurology.

Dyslexics don't outgrow their problems—reading and writing usually remain hard work for life—but with patient teaching and deft tutoring, they do learn to manage. Absent that, dyslexia can snuff out dreams at an early age, as children lose their way in school, then lose their self-esteem and drive. "The prisons are filled with kids who can't read," says Caperton. "I suspect a lot of them have learning disabilities."

Dyslexia is a crucible, particularly in a high-pressure society that allows so little room for late bloomers. "People are either defeated by it or they become much more tenacious," says McCaw. Don Winkler, a top financial services executive at Bank One and then at Ford Motor, remembers coming home from school bloodied by fights he'd had with kids who called him dumb. Kinko's founder, Paul Orfalea, failed second grade and spent part of third in a class of mentally retarded children. He could not learn to read, despite the best efforts of parents who took him to testers, tutors, therapists, special reading groups, and eye doctors. As young classmates read aloud, Orfalea says it was as if "angels whispered words in their ears."

In his unpublished autobiography, Orfalea says that to a dyslexic, a sentence is worse than Egyptian hieroglyphics. "It's more like a road map with mouse holes or coffee stains in critical places. You're always turning into blind alleys and ending up on the wrong side of town." He finally graduated, but not before being "invited to leave . . . practically every high school in Los Angeles." One principal coun-

seled his mother to enroll him in trade school, suggesting that Orfalea could become a carpet layer. His mother went home and tearfully told her husband, "I just know he can do more than lay carpet." . . .

Until about five years ago Chambers kept his dyslexia a secret. As CEO, he says, "you don't want people to see your weaknesses." One day a little girl at Cisco's Bring Your Children to Work Day forced him out of the closet. Chambers had called on her, and she was trying to ask a question before a crowd of 500 kids and parents. But she couldn't get the words out. "I have a learning disability," she said tearfully.

Chambers cannot tell this story without choking up himself. "You could immediately identify with what that was like," he says. "You know that pain. She started to leave, and you knew how hurt she was in front of the group and her parents." Chambers threw her a lifeline. "I have a learning disability too," he said. In front of the crowd, he began talking to her as if they were the only two people in the room. "You've just got to learn your way through it," Chambers told her. "Because there are some things you can do that others cannot, and there are some things others can do you're just not going to be able to do, ever. Now my experience has been that what works is to go a little bit slower. . . ."

Better than most people, dyslexics learn humility and how to get along with others. It's probably no accident that Kinko's, Cisco, and Schwab have all been on *Fortune*'s list of the best places to work. "I never put people down, because I know what that feels like," says Branson, who seldom asks for a résumé either, "because I haven't got one myself."

By the time these guys got into business, they had picked themselves up so many times that risk taking was second nature. . . .

If, as kids, the dyslexic executives had learned the downside of their disorder inside out, as adults they began to see its upside: a distinctly different way of processing information that gave them an edge in a volatile, fast-moving world. Bill Dreyer, an inventor and a biologist at Caltech, recalls a dinner-party conversation years ago in which he told a colleague how his dyslexic brain works: "I think in 3-D Technicolor pictures instead of words." "You what?" replied the incredulous colleague. The two argued the rest of the night about how that was possible.

Dreyer believes that thinking in pictures enabled him to develop groundbreaking theories about how antibodies are made, and then to invent one of the first protein-sequencing machines, which helped to launch the human genome revolution. "I was able to see the machine in my head and rotate valves and actually see the instrumentation," he says. "I don't think of dyslexia as a deficiency. It's like having CAD [computer-aided design] in your brain. I bet these other guys see business in 3-D too. I bet they see graphs and charts of how trends will unfold."

In his office, Chambers goes from wounded to animated as he heads to the dry-erase board to show that's exactly what he does. "I can't explain why, but I just approach problems differently," he says. "It's very easy for me to jump conceptually from A to Z. I picture a chess game on a multiple-layer dimensional cycle and almost play it out in my mind. But it's not a chess game. It's business. I don't make moves one at a time. I can usually anticipate the potential outcome and where the Y's in the road will occur." As he's talking, he's scrawling a grid depicting how Cisco diversified into switches, fiber optics, and wireless by acquisition, internal development, or partnering. It was a picture he used to explain his vision to the board of directors back in 1993, when he was an executive vice president and Cisco was a one-product company. It became a road map. "All we did was fill in the chart," he says. . . .

Diane Swonk's former boss and mentor at Bank One always thought Swonk had a "third eye." Swonk, an economist, says it's dyslexia. Although she has worked in the same building for 16 years, she still has a hard time figuring out which track her commuter train is on and which way to turn when she leaves the office elevator. She can't dial telephone numbers. She has a hard time with arithmetic, reversing and transposing numbers.

But she revels in higher-level math concepts, and in January 1999, when almost everyone was bemoaning the global financial crisis and fretting about the stock market—then trading at around 9300—she told the Executives Club of Chicago that the Dow would break 11,000 by year-end. The prediction seemed so surprising that the moderator made her repeat it. She was right then and right again last year, when she insisted—even after September 11—that the economic downturn would not be as bad as feared. Why not? Because consumers would keep spending. Which they did. "I'm not in the consensus a lot," says Swonk. "In fact, being in the consensus makes me really uncomfortable." . . .

For years, Orfalea says, "I was a closet bad reader. . . I never showed anybody my handwriting until I was in my 40s." He cultivated a casual, can't-be-bothered-with-it management style that allowed him to avoid the written word. If he received a long letter, for instance, "I'd just hand it to somebody else and say, 'Here, read it.' " He mostly avoided the corporate office and instead went from Kinko's to Kinko's, observing, talking to customers, making changes. He wasn't goofing off; he was vacuuming up information in his own way—orally, visually, multisensorily.

For most dyslexic business leaders, reading is still not easy. They tend to like newspapers, short magazine articles, summaries. Says Chambers: "Short reading is fine. But long reading I just really labor over." His staff knows to deliver summaries in three pages or less, the major points highlighted in yellow. McCaw says he can read and write. "But to do either requires a lot of energy and concentration." He and the others are information grazers. "You learn for self-preservation to grasp the maximum amount of meaning out of the minimal amount of context," says McCaw. . . .

Researchers used to think that many more boys than girls were dyslexic. (Schools were identifying four times as many boys as girls a decade ago.) But an ongoing study at Yale of 400 Connecticut children indicates that the numbers are about equal. . .

Despite all the unknowns, dyslexia is clearly better understood and treated today than it was a generation ago. Yet in a high-pressure society where straight A's and high test scores count for so much, the disorder still carries a heavy penalty. Boies says nothing has been harder for him than watching the struggles of two of his own children who are dyslexic. "It is awful. Awful. The most difficult thing I've ever done," he says. . . . Boies wishes that society allowed more room and more time for late bloomers. "In this environment," he says, "you get children who think they are masters of the universe, and children who think they are failures, when they're 10 years old. They're both wrong. And neither is well served by that misconception."

Questions for Discussion

1. How can the parent of a child with a learning disability build the youngster's self-esteem and self-efficacy? Could learned helplessness be a problem? Explain.

2. If you or one of your adult classmates is still battling a learning disability, how can the social learning model of self-management help? Explain.

3. What evidence of the proactive personality do you find in this case? Explain.

4. Do you think standardized personality and intelligence tests discriminate against people with learning disabilities? Explain your position. Any suggestions for improvement?

5. Is it possible that a learning disability sometimes can be a blessing in disguise?

6. Why did the dyslexics profiled in this case, especially Cisco Systems' CEO John Chambers, seem to develop superior emotional intelligence?

7. What practical lessons about dealing more effectively with individual differences in the workplace emerge from this case?

Personal Awareness and Growth Exercise

How Do You Score on the Big Five Personality Factors?

Objectives

1. To learn more about yourself.
2. To learn more about the Big Five personality dimensions, as introduced in this chapter.

Introduction

Personality is an extremely complex subject. There are many ways of measuring personality, as a quick Internet search will reveal. While the Big Five model is not universally accepted as the best way of understanding personal-

ity, it is well established and is accompanied by abundant research. *Note:* The Big Five personality profile presented here is for instructional purposes only; it has not been validated and should not be used for personnel selection or evaluation purposes.

Instructions

Please circle one number on the scale for each pair of adjectives, reflecting your personality. Add the three circled numbers for each Big Five dimension to obtain subscores.

Personality Profile[103]

Introversion–Extraversion

Quiet	1——2——3——4——5——6——7——8——9——10	Talkative
Shy	1——2——3——4——5——6——7——8——9——10	Outgoing
Retiring	1——2——3——4——5——6——7——8——9——10	Sociable
	Subscore = _____	

Agreeableness

Critical	1——2——3——4——5——6——7——8——9——10	Trusting
Aggressive	1——2——3——4——5——6——7——8——9——10	Amiable
Cold	1——2——3——4——5——6——7——8——9——10	Affectionate
	Subscore = _____	

Conscientiousness

Careless	1——2——3——4——5——6——7——8——9——10	Organized
Negligent	1——2——3——4——5——6——7——8——9——10	Self-disciplined
Inconsistent	1——2——3——4——5——6——7——8——9——10	Reliable
	Subscore = _____	

Neuroticism–Emotional Stability

Anxious	1——2——3——4——5——6——7——8——9——10	Calm
Insecure	1——2——3——4——5——6——7——8——9——10	Self-reliant
Temperamental	1——2——3——4——5——6——7——8——9——10	Poised
	Subscore = _____	

Openness to Experience

Narrow interests	1——2——3——4——5——6——7——8——9——10	Wide interests
Unimaginative	1——2——3——4——5——6——7——8——9——10	Imaginative
Imperceptive	1——2——3——4——5——6——7——8——9——10	Insightful
	Subscore = _____	

Scoring

There are no right or wrong answers on this personality test. There is only an infinite variety of individual differences. You may want to take two passes through this profile. The first indicating how you are now and the second plotting how you would like to be. Any gaps would represent self-improvement challenges. Alternatively, if you have the courage, rate yourself and then have a close acquaintance rate you, for comparison purposes (and probably lively discussion).

Questions for Discussion

1. Any surprises? Explain.

2. What important aspects of personality are overlooked in this particular profile?

3. What other adjective pairings could you use for each of the five dimensions?

4. Why do you have your particular personality traits? Nature (genetics)? Nurture (family traditions, culture, schooling, etc.)? Some combination of nature and nurture (in what proportion)?

5. Why is it supposedly so difficult to alter an individual's personality?

Group Exercise

Anger Control Role Play

Objectives

1. To demonstrate that emotions can be managed.

2. To develop your interpersonal skills for managing both your own and someone else's anger.

Introduction

Personal experience and research tell us that anger begets anger. People do not make their best decisions when angry. Angry outbursts often inflict unintentional interpersonal damage by triggering other emotions (e.g., disgust in observers and subsequent guilt and shame in the angry person). Effective managers know how to break the cycle of negative emotions by defusing anger in themselves and others. This is a role-playing exercise for groups of four. You will have a chance to play two different roles. All the roles are generic, so they can be played as either a woman or a man.

Instructions

Your instructor will divide the class into groups of four. Everyone should read all five roles described. Members of each foursome will decide among themselves who will play which roles. All told, you will participate in two rounds of role playing (each round lasting no longer than eight minutes). In round one, one person will play Role 1 and another will play Role 3; the remaining two group members will play Role 5. In round two, those who played Role 5 in the first round will play Roles 2 and 4. The other two will switch to Role 5.

ROLE 1: THE ANGRY (OUT-OF-CONTROL) SHIFT SUPERVISOR

You work for a leading electronics company that makes computer chips and other computer-related equipment. Your factory is responsible for assembling and testing the company's most profitable line of computer microprocessors. Business has been good, so your factory is working three shifts. The day shift, which you are now on, is the most desirable one. The night shift, from 11 PM to 7:30 AM is the least desirable and least productive. In fact, the night shift is such a mess that your boss, the factory manager, wants you to move to the night shift next week. Your boss just broke this bad news as the two of you are having lunch in the company cafeteria. You are shocked and angered because you are one of the most senior and highly rated shift supervisors in the factory. Thanks to your leadership, your shift has broken all production records during the past year. As the divorced single parent of a 10-year-old child, the radical schedule change would be a major lifestyle burden. Questions swirl through your head. "Why me?" "What kind of reliable child-care will be available when I sleep during the day and work at night?" "Why should I be 'punished' for being a top supervisor?" "Why don't they hire someone for the position?" Your boss asks what you think.

When playing this role, be as realistic as possible without getting so loud that you disrupt the other groups. Also, if anyone in your group would be offended by foul language, please refrain from cursing during your angry outburst.

ROLE 2: THE ANGRY (UNDER-CONTROL) SHIFT SUPERVISOR

Same situation as in Role 1. But this role will require you to read and act according to the tips for reducing chronic anger in the left side of Table 5–6. You have plenty of reason to be frustrated and angry, but you realize the importance of maintaining a good working relationship with the factory manager.

ROLE 3: THE (HARD-DRIVING) FACTORY MANAGER

You have a reputation for having a "short fuse." When someone gets angry with you, you attack. When playing this role, be as realistic as possible. Remember, you are responsible for the entire factory with its 1,200 employees and hundreds of millions of dollars of electronics products. A hiring freeze is in place, so you have to move one of your current supervisors. You have chosen your best supervisor because the night shift is your biggest threat to profitable operations. The night-

shift supervisor gets a 10% pay premium. Ideally, the move will only be for six months.

ROLE 4: THE (MELLOW) FACTORY MANAGER

Same general situation as in Role 3. However, this role will require you to read and act according to the tips for responding to angry provocation in the right side of Table 5–6. You have a reputation for being results-oriented but reasonable. You are good at taking a broad, strategic view of problems and are a good negotiator.

ROLE 5: SILENT OBSERVER

Follow the exchange between the shift supervisor and the factory manager without talking or getting actively involved. Jot down some notes (for later class discussion) as you observe whether the factory manager did a good job of managing the supervisor's anger.

Questions for Discussion

1. Why is uncontrolled anger a sure road to failure?
2. Is it possible to express anger without insulting others? Explain.
3. Which is more difficult, controlling anger in yourself or defusing someone else's anger? Why?
4. What useful lessons did you learn from this role-playing exercise?

Ethical Dilemma

Hot Heads!

Situation

You are the human resources vice president at a leading overnight express company. After lunch today, one of your top trainers excitedly plopped down in your office and said "Read this short section I marked in a *Business 2.0* article." You took it and read the following:

> Thrown any good lamps lately? Of course, you're probably too professional and well-bred to show anger at work. Just be aware: Being restrained may not be doing your career any good.
>
> For some years, Larissa Tiedens, an assistant professor of organizational behavior at Stanford Business School, has been studying the effects of anger in the workplace. Her research has revealed that employers have a bias toward promoting employees who get mad now and again. "I don't think we're cognizant of this," Tiedens says. "We make inferences about people

all the time, and we don't always know where the information has come from."

> Tiedens began testing her hypothesis at a software firm in Palo Alto. She gave 24 of the employees a list of 10 or so emotions and asked them to rate how often their colleagues expressed each one. At the same time, the group managers filled out a questionnaire about how likely they would be to promote each of the employees. Those who were rated high on the anger scale were more likely to be on the promotion list. In a separate experiment, Tiedens had MBA students watch video clips of mock job interviews. In one tape the applicant shows visible signs of anger when discussing a presentation that went wrong, and in the other the candidate is fairly restrained. Most of the MBAs said they would have slotted the angry candidate for the higher-paying position.[104]

As you handed the reading back, you remarked "Let me see if I get this. You want to teach our managers *how* to get angry, or get angry *more often?*" An ethical flag went up in your mind.

What would you do?

1. Kill the idea on the spot. Explain how.

2. Take an immediate cue from what you just read and angrily tell the trainer that some research shouldn't be taken so literally. How would you do that?

3. Make an appointment with the trainer to discuss and refine the concept to make it an acceptable part of your management training program. Explain how.

4. Without hurting the trainer's feelings or discouraging creativity, take a few minutes to review the ethical implications of what you just read.

5. Invent other options. Discuss.

For an interpretation of this situation, visit our Web site, **www.mhhe.com/kreitner.**

Chapter *f*ix

Values, Attitudes, Abilities, and Job Satisfaction

Learning Objectives

When you finish studying the material in this chapter, you should be able to:

1   Distinguish between instrumental and terminal values, and describe three types of value conflict.

2   Describe the values model of work/family conflict, and specify at least three practical lessons from work/family conflict research.

3   Define attitudes, explain how they differ from values, and identify the three components of attitudes.

4   Explain how attitudes affect behavior in terms of Ajzen's theory of planned behavior.

5   Define the key work attitudes of job satisfaction, organizational commitment, and job involvement.

6   Describe Carl Jung's cognitive styles typology.

7   Identify and briefly describe five alternative causes of job satisfaction.

8   Identify seven important correlates/ consequences of job satisfaction, and summarize how each one relates to job satisfaction.

"There is a loyalty crisis in America today," says Frederick Reichheld, a leading corporate loyalty expert, "because so few senior business leaders really have any idea of what it means to be loyal and why loyalty is relevant to business success."

Most managers and employees understand that greener pastures sprout up during tight labor markets, while periods of economic uncertainty make ambitious workers less likely to leap the corporate fence. On the other hand, leaders who grasp the value of employee relationships, reward initiatives, vigorous and open communica-tion, measurement programs and sub-stantial training investments engender a brand of loyalty that bears little resemblance to the job-for-life mental-ity of yesteryear. . . .

And just because the recent tight labor market has slackened, managers still need to remain focused on reten-tion and not neglect employee loyalty, says Diane Downey, president of Downey Associates International, New York, in her book, *Assimilating New Leaders: The Key to Executive Retention* (Amacom, 2001).

"There isn't much turnover now because of the business climate,"

Topping *Fortune's* "Best Company to Work For" list two years in a row, The Container Store keeps its employees loyal and satisfied while generating bottom-line results.
Courtesy The Container Store

Downey says, "But that view focuses on a lagging indicator, after the person is out the door. People mentally tune out much sooner than that. I'm finding that a lot of people have begun to turn over mentally but because the market isn't good, they're not leaving yet. Right now, businesses have an enormous opportunity to solidify the commitment of their key players." . . .

Among loyalty leaders, that solidification process has deep and lasting roots in the corporate culture. Consider The Container Store, a Dallas-based retailer that has topped *Fortune*'s "Best Companies to Work For" list for two consecutive years. When the retailer opened a Houston outlet in the late 1980s, the financial results were at least three times what the company expected. Despite the retail success, CEO Kip Tindell says it marked the first time that he had ever observed the workforce operate in disharmony. Rather than accepting workforce discord as the price for higher revenues, Tindell chose to nourish employee loyalty as a means of generating bottom-line success.

Consequently Tindell developed foundation principles; a set of underlying business philosophies that the company's employees use to guide their activities and decisions. "The original premise of our foundation principles is that we're not smart enough to tell employees how to act in every situation," Tindell says. "We agree upon what we're trying to do as an organization and then how we get there is up to your individual genius. Life is too situational, and certainly retail is too situational, for someone to try to get there with a big rule and policy book." That approach has led to financial and cultural harmony at The Container Store.

Tindell and executives at other companies recognized for outstanding employee loyalty tend to use touchy-feely phrases like "harmony," "individual genius," "sense of community" and "fiercely proud" when discussing employee relationship management, yet they ground their language in organizational performance—the clear link between loyalty and the bottom line. . . .

To attract and retain employees, some companies are investing heavily in internal promotions and incentive plans. The Container Store pours about 10% of its sales revenues into training expenditures each year, nearly double the retail industry average range of 4.3 to 6%, according to the National Retail Federation. The executive team also keeps tabs on average sale value per customer visit, a retail metric that Tindell believes links to loyalty. "I've been working hard the past couple of years to make sure the people in our organization understand industry average metrics and where we stand," he says, noting that the positive comparisons help engender loyalty. "I mean, the guy who is happiest that they bother to count home runs is [the leading home run hitter]. . . . It's very reinforcing for us to emphasize these metrics."

Customer and employee retention rates are a widely used, if imperfect, loyalty metric. "Loyalty leaders have voluntary attrition rates about 10 percent better than the rest of their industry," says Reichheld. "Businesses that measure employee and customer retention have a pretty good sense of whether they are earning loyalty." And high employee retention rates can boost a company's bottom line.

Customer retention is directly influenced by employee retention. Reichheld has discovered that a 5% improvement in customer retention can result in a 25% or more increase in profits in some industries. But he stresses that retention is an inexact loyalty metric. "Sometimes, employees stay simply because they're lazy," he says. "And they're dead wood."

Reichheld suggests that loyalty-challenged enterprises can begin to address employee relations by measuring satisfaction. The key question in the loyalty acid test he [proposes] is a simple one: Does this organization deserve your loyalty? "That's the bottom-line question," he says. "The greatest companies I have found will have 70 to 80% of their people agree with that statement. The average company is lucky if half of their employees agree that the organization is worth their loyalty."[1]

For Discussion

What does an employer need to do to win *your* loyalty? What do you need to do to win an *employer's* loyalty?

Some may think employee loyalty is a quaint, out-of-date idea. But at successful companies such as The Container Store, it is a major competitive advantage. When The Container Store once again made *Fortune*'s list of the 100 best companies to work for in 2002, in the number two spot, researchers uncovered a telltale fact. Among The Container Store employees surveyed, an incredible 94% said they believed they made a difference for the company.[2] Every single *individual* counts at The Container Store, and it shows! The company reaps the benefits of faithfully

Figure 6–1   *Individual Differences Impact Job Performance and Job Satisfaction*

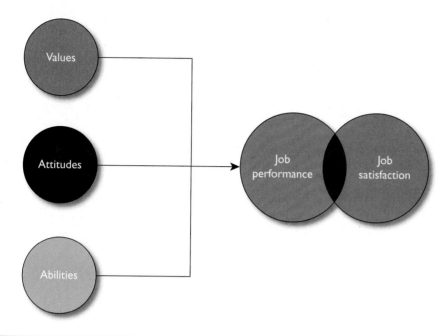

investing in human and social capital. In this chapter, we continue our study of individual differences by exploring the impact of personal values, attitudes, and abilities on job performance and satisfaction (see Figure 6–1). Special attention is devoted to the dynamics of job satisfaction, as it relates to job performance and other important work outcomes.

Personal Values

When discussing organizational culture in Chapter 3, we defined *values* as desired ways of behaving or desired end-states. Accordingly, pioneering values researcher Milton Rokeach defined a person's **value system** as an "enduring organization of beliefs concerning preferable modes of conduct or end-states of existence along a continuum of relative importance."[3] Our focus in Chapter 3 was on collective or shared values; here the focus shifts to *personal* values. Your organization and your co-workers may or may not share your key personal values. Lifelong behavior patterns are dictated by values that are fairly well set by the time people are in their early teens. However, significant life-altering events—such as having a child, business failure, death of a loved one, going to war, or surviving a serious accident or disease—can reshape an adult's value system.

Extensive research supports Rokeach's contention that differing value systems go a long way toward explaining individual differences in behavior. Value → behavior connections have been documented for a wide variety of behaviors, ranging from weight loss, shopping selections, and political party affiliation to religious involvement and

Value system

The organization of one's beliefs about preferred ways of behaving and desired end-states.

In China, young students receive a Confucian education while reciting and memorizing moral precepts as a way of improving character. The sixth-century B.C. philosopher Confucius believed in maintaining a strict social order and provided advice on governing China. Now many Chinese seek a return to "traditional values" and Confucian teachings are making a comeback. Critics of the system say that despite the moral lessons, Confucianism can be used to create docile, obedient citizens in service only to the communist state. Can children be taught instrumental or terminal values by reciting words they don't understand?

(c) Paul Mooney

choice of a college major.[4] As with the GLOBE study in Chapter 4, researchers have found both differences and similarities across cultures. Regarding the similarities, respondents from 62 nations had a very high degree of agreement about the relative importance of values relating to three key life domains. The high value-consensus domains were "cooperative and supportive primary relations, productive and innovative task performance, and gratification of self-oriented needs and desires."[5] As with all individual differences, both commonality and uniqueness matter. Generalizations need to be made with research support and caution.

Let us learn more about personal values by distinguishing between instrumental and terminal values, discussing three types of value conflict, and examining the timely value-related topic of work versus family life conflicts.

Instrumental and Terminal Values

Instrumental values

Personally preferred ways of behaving.

In line with his distinction between modes of conduct and end-states, Rokeach distinguished between instrumental values and terminal values. **Instrumental values** are alternative behaviors or means by which we achieve desired ends. Sample instrumental values from Rokeach's original list of 18 are ambitious, honest, independent, loving, and obedient.[6] Someone who ranks the instrumental value "honest" highly, relative to the other instrumental values, is likely to be more honest than someone who gives it a low ranking.

Highly ranked **terminal values**—such as a sense of accomplishment, happiness, pleasure, salvation, and wisdom—are desired end-states or life goals. Some would say terminal values are what life is all about. History is full of examples of people who were persecuted or put to death for their passionately held terminal values. Longitudinal evidence from value surveys during the 1960s, 1970s, and 1980s showed relative stability of terminal values among Americans, despite turbulent social and economic times. Six terminal values consistently ranked in the top one-third were family security, a world at peace, freedom, self-respect, happiness, and wisdom.[7]

Terminal values
Personally preferred end-states of existence.

Value Conflicts

There are three types of value conflict of which we must be aware. Knowing how to recognize and deal effectively with them are major quality-of-life issues. They are *intra*personal value conflict, *inter*personal value conflict, and individual–organization value conflict. These sources of conflict are, respectively, from inside the person, between people, and between the person and the organization.

Intrapersonal Value Conflict
Inner conflict and resultant stress typically are experienced when highly ranked instrumental and terminal values pull the individual in different directions. This is somewhat akin to role conflict, as discussed in Chapter 12. The main difference is locus of influence: Role conflict involves *outside* social expectations; intrapersonal value conflict involves *internal* priorities. For employees who want balance in their lives, a stressful conflict arises when one values, for example, "being ambitious" (instrumental value) and "ending up happy" (terminal value). As the experience of Intel's director of new business development, Kirby Dyess, attests, it takes discipline to achieve balance in the face of intrapersonal value conflict.

> I can tell that I've hit the wall at work, and that I need to recalibrate my life, when I can no longer empathize with others, when I'm focused only on results, when I ignore other people's goals, and when I become frustrated with life's interruptions. Or when my daughter has to tell me, "It'll be all right, Kirby."
>
> To reorient my life, I take several important steps: Every day, I do something that's totally for myself. I constantly look for ways to simplify my life. And when I start to run out of creative juices, I avoid the temptation to work harder. Instead, I do something recreational, like gardening.[8]

Interpersonal Value Conflict
This type of value conflict often is at the core of personality conflicts. Just as people have different styles that may or may not mesh, they also embrace unique combinations of instrumental and terminal values that inevitably spark disagreement. Consider, for example, the situation of Chad Myers, a Peace Corps volunteer who spent his two-year tour of duty building latrines in Bolivia:

> "A lot of my friends were going into high-paying, good jobs," said Chad, a recent graduate of North Carolina State. "They look at me in shock and disgust and ask, 'Why are you working for free when you could be making $50,000 a year?' "
>
> Chad's rationale for joining the Peace Corps was apparent a few minutes later when he explained: "I've set a goal, and this is pretty high. If I can get 20 kids to wash their hands after going to the bathroom, I will have accomplished something that will have changed their lives and someday those of their children."[9]

Chad's goal would seem laughable to classmates acting out more selfish and materialistic values. But his unconventional value-driven behavior certainly means a lot to the health of his Bolivian friends.

Individual–Organization Value Conflict
As we saw in Chapter 3, companies actively seek to embed certain values into their corporate cultures. Conflict can occur when values espoused and enacted by the organization collide with employees' personal values. This is a very common and persistent problem. For example, a culture shift at Time Warner, the huge entertainment company, hit some bumps just prior to its merger with AOL. Time Warner began a program to shed its reputation for internal warfare and get everyone to embrace "what the company calls its 'core values and guiding principles'—among them 'diversity,' 'respect,' and 'integrity.' "[10] One thousand executives were slated to attend two-day seminars to acquaint them with the "new" corporate values. As *The Wall Street Journal* reported at the time, it was not love at first sight:

> Not surprisingly for a company filled with cynical journalists and media executives, the program has met with some initial derision. For all the expensive management talent involved in the process, the values strike some employees as a bit obvious. In addition to diversity, respect, and integrity, other central values are "creativity," "community," and "teamwork."
>
> One senior executive who has attended innumerable meetings involved in the process describes the company's values statement as "The Boy Scout's oath. No nuclear bombs." (Even though the values statement says that Time Warner welcomes "divergent voices even if we risk controversy or loss," none of the internal critics of the program would allow their names to be used.)[11]

Like personalities, personal values are resistant to change.

Handling Value Conflicts through Values Clarification
For intrapersonal conflict, a Toronto management writer and consultant recommends getting out of what she calls "the busyness trap" by asking these questions:

- Is your work really meeting your most important needs?
- Are you defining yourself purely in terms of your accomplishments?
- Why are you working so hard? To what personal ends?
- Are you making significant sacrifices in favor of your work?
- Is your work schedule affecting other people who are important in your life?[12]

Meanwhile, a New Jersey management consultant tells us to fight interpersonal and individual-organization conflict by being value-centered leaders who consistently role model positive personal values.[13]

Yet another approach for dealing with all forms of value conflict is a career-counseling and team-building technique called *values clarification*. To gain useful hands-on experience, take a break from your reading and complete the OB Exercise on page 193. Our key learning point is to get you and others to identify and talk about personal values to establish common ground as a basis for teamwork and conflict avoidance/resolution (as discussed in Chapters 13 and 14).

Work versus Family Life Conflict

A complex web of demographic and economic factors makes the balancing act between job and life very challenging for most of us. Demographically, there are more women

OB Exercise Personal Values Clarification

Instructions for Individuals Working Alone
Review the following list of 30 values and then rank your top 6 values (1 = most important; 6 = least important). What *intra*personal value conflicts can you detect? How can you resolve them? Which, if any, of your cherished values likely conflict with those deemed important by your family, friends, co-workers, and employer? What could be done to reduce this interpersonal and individual-organizational value conflict?

Instructions for Teams
Each team member should begin by ranking their top six personal values, as specified above. Have someone record each team member's top-ranked value on a flip chart or chalkboard (no names attached). Then spend a few minutes discussing both differences and commonalities. Try to find common ground among seemingly different values. If your group is a task team, an additional step could be to derive four or more consensus values to guide the team's work. (Do not short-cut consensus seeking by voting.) How do your personal values align with your teammates' values and the team's consensus values? What needs to be done to reduce actual or threatened value conflict?

_____ Responsibility (joint and/or individual)	_____ Accomplishment
_____ Involvement in decision making	_____ Satisfying relationships
_____ Competence	_____ Creativity
_____ Meaning	_____ Self-worth
_____ Autonomy	_____ Self-expression
_____ Recognition	_____ Leadership opportunities
_____ Personal and professional growth	_____ Financial security
_____ New and different experiences	_____ Diversity
_____ Collaboration on common tasks	_____ Career mobility
_____ Harmony or an absence of conflict	_____ A sense of belonging
_____ Competition	_____ Shared fun and experiences
_____ Meeting deadlines in a timely manner	_____ Peace and serenity
_____ A high standard of excellence	_____ Good health
_____ Status, position	_____ Loyalty
_____ Stimulation from challenge and change	_____ Duty to family
	_____ Other _____

SOURCE: List of values from L Gardenswartz and A Rowe, *Diverse Teams at Work: Capitalizing on the Power of Diversity* (New York: McGraw-Hill, 1994), p. 85. © 1994. Reproduced with permission of The McGraw-Hill Companies.

in the workforce, more dual-income families, more single working parents, and an aging population that gives mid-career employees day care or elder care responsibilities, or both.[14] On the economic front, years of downsizing and corporate cost-cutting have given employees heavier workloads. Meanwhile, an important trend was recently documented in a unique 25-year study of values in the United States: "employees have become less convinced that work should be an important part of one's life or that working hard makes one a better person."[15] Something has to give in this collision of trends.

Too often family life suffers. The experience of executive Jeri Rosenbaum and her lawyer husband, Keith, parents of three youngsters, is a sign of the times:

"He kept saying he was gonna, he was gonna, he was gonna," she says, but time for her kept getting shoved aside.

Finally, she insisted he schedule a weekly lunch with her on his calendar—just as if she were a client. Keith hesitated. It seemed cold, somehow, to book time with your wife. "Before we start putting it on the calendar ..." he began. Jeri interrupted. Tears in her eyes, she insisted, "I'm waiting for you to punch a hole in your schedule for me!"

Keith complied, and the two now lunch weekly. "I know it sounds bad to treat the family like a client," he says, but booking time together has eased the tension.[16]

In this section, we seek to better understand work versus family life conflict by introducing a values-based model and discussing practical research insights. Importantly, our goal here is to get a firmer grasp on this difficult area, not offer quick-and-easy solutions with little chance of success.

A Values-Based Model of Work/Family Conflict

Building upon the work of Rokeach, Pamela L Perrewé and Wayne A Hochwarter constructed the model in Figure 6–2. On the left, we see one's general life values feeding into one's family-related values and work-related values. Family values involve enduring beliefs about the importance of family and who should play key family roles (e.g., child rearing, housekeeping, and income earning). Work values center on the relative importance of work and career goals in one's life. *Value similarity* relates to the degree of consensus among family members about family values. When a housewife launches a business

Figure 6–2   *A Values Model of Work/Family Conflict*

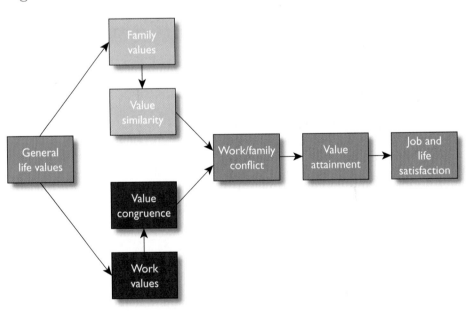

SOURCE: Pamela L Perrewé and Wayne A Hochwarter, "Can We Really Have It All? The Attainment of Work and Family Values," *Current Directions in Psychological Science*, February 2001, p. 30. Published by Blackwell Publishers, Inc. © American Psychological Society.

venture despite her husband's desire to be the sole breadwinner, lack of family value similarity causes work/family conflict. *Value congruence,* on the other hand, involves the amount of value agreement between employee and employer. If, for example, refusing to go on a business trip to stay home for a child's birthday is viewed as disloyalty to the company, lack of value congruence can trigger work/family conflict.

In turn, "work-family conflict can take two distinct forms: work interference with family and family interference with work."[17] For example, suppose two managers in the same department have daughters playing on the same soccer team. One manager misses the big soccer game to attend a last-minute department meeting; the other manager skips the meeting to attend the game. Both may experience work/family conflict, but for different reasons.

The last two boxes in the model—value attainment and job and life satisfaction—are a package deal. Satisfaction tends to be higher for those who live according to their values and lower for those who do not. Overall, this model reflects much common sense. How does *your* life track through the model? Sadly, it is a painful trip for many these days.

Practical Research Insights about Work/Family Conflict
This is a new but very active area of OB research. Typically, the evidence comes from field surveys of real people in real jobs, rather than from contrived laboratory studies. Recent practical findings include

- *Gender inequality begins at home.* Despite their growing presence in the workforce, women continue to shoulder most of the standard household chores. In a recent study of professionally successful men and women, 50% of the women and 9% of the men prepared meals. Data for other chores: shopping for groceries (51% women, 7% men); organizing childrens' activities (61% women, 3% men); cleaning the house (45% women, 5% men); taking time off for sick child (51% women, 9% men).[18] Conceivably, men who performed this poorly in the workplace would be fired on the spot!

- *An employer's family-supportive philosophy is more important than specific programs.* Many employers offer family-friendly programs today, including child and elder day care assistance, parental leave, telecommuting, and flexible work schedules. However, if employees are afraid or reluctant to take advantage of those programs because the organization's culture values hard work and long hours above all else, families will inevitably suffer. To be truly family-friendly, the organization needs to provide programs and back them up with a family-supportive philosophy and culture[19] (see the OB Exercise on page 196). Arbitron, the Columbia, Maryland, radio station research company, is an interesting case in point. Each year it hosts a Winterfest party at which its employees can ship their holiday packages to family and friends. "Arbitron pays for shipping and employees donate the shipping equivalent to a local women's shelter."[20] This is not just a program, it is *a way of thinking* about families and community. It is an investment in social capital, as defined in Chapter 1.

- *Work flexibility is more important than time flexibility in promoting work-family balance.* Research suggests management should give a higher priority to job redesign (giving people more control over what they do and how they do it) than to flexible work schedules (such as flextime and job-sharing).[21]

- *Mentors can help.* A field survey of 502 graduates of a US university (63% men), yielded this result: "The results indicate that having a mentor is significantly related

OB Exercise   How Family-Supportive Is Your Employer?

Instructions

Rate the organization where you work by circling one number for each of the following dimensions. Remember, you are rating the *organization's* philosophy or what is really important to the organization as conveyed through its culture and reinforced values. You are *not* rating your personal beliefs. If you are presently unemployed, you can rate a past employer or interview someone who is employed. (*Note:* The higher the score, the more family-supportive the organization.)

	Strongly Disagree				Strongly Agree*
1. Work should be the primary priority in a person's life.	5 — 4 — 3 — 2 — 1
2. It is best to keep family matters separate from work.	5 — 4 — 3 — 2 — 1
3. Expressing involvement and interest in nonwork matters is viewed as healthy.	1 — 2 — 3 — 4 — 5
4. Attending to personal needs, such as taking time off for sick children is frowned upon.	5 — 4 — 3 — 2 — 1
5. Employees should keep their personal problems at home.	5 — 4 — 3 — 2 — 1
6. Employees are given ample opportunity to perform both their job and their personal responsibilities well.	1 — 2 — 3 — 4 — 5
7. Offering employees flexibility in completing their work is viewed as a strategic way of doing business.	1 — 2 — 3 — 4 — 5
8. The way to advance is to keep nonwork matters out of the workplace.	5 — 4 — 3 — 2 — 1

Arbitrary norms: 8–18 = Low family-supportiveness; 19–29 = Moderate family-supportiveness; 30–40 = High family supportiveness
*Items 1, 2, 4, 5, and 8 are reverse weighted.

SOURCE: Adapted from and eight survey items excerpted from T D Allen, "Family-Supportive Work Environments: The Role of Organizational Perceptions," *Journal of Vocational Behavior*, June 2001, p. 423.

to lower levels of work-family conflict. . . . Such findings suggest another potential benefit of mentoring: a source of social support to reduce employee stress caused by conflicts between the work and family domains."[22]

- *Being your own boss is no panacea.* Self-employment turns out to be a good news/bad news proposition, when compared to standard organizational employment. Among the benefits of being self-employed are a stronger sense of autonomy, a higher level of job involvement, and greater job satisfaction. But self-employed people report higher levels of work/family conflict and lower levels of family satisfaction.[23]

A Vision of Work/Family Integration, Not Just Balance   A team of researchers recently advanced the work/family agenda a significant step by calling for *integration* rather than balance. Balance is needed for opposites. They believe work and family are not opposites but instead should be a well-integrated whole. They envision a world in which important life functions—such as income production, child rearing, and homemaking—are performed by women and men alike, based on their talents, values, and preferences. They explain:

Gendered assumptions and stereotypes based in the separation of [occupational and family] spheres constrain the choices of both women and men. Our vision of gender equity is to relax these social norms about separation so that men and women are free to experience these

Conflict between our personal life and work life affects our performance at work and the overall quality of our lives. Some companies such as Synovus recognize this relationship and attempt to help employees cope with these competing demands. Synovus's "Right Choice" benefit program enables employees to take time off to spend with their children at school. Is Synovus's program one of "Work/Family Integration" or "Work/Family Balance?"

Courtesy of Synovus

two parts of their lives as integrated rather than as separate domains that need to be "balanced." Integration would make it possible for both women and men to perform up to their capabilities and find satisfaction in both work and personal life, no matter how they allocate their time commitment between the two. To convey this goal, we speak of integrating work and personal life rather than balancing. This terminology expresses our belief in the need to diminish the separation between these two spheres of life in ways that will *change both,* rather than merely reallocating—or "balancing"—time between them as they currently exist.[24]

Attitudes

Hardly a day goes by without the popular media reporting the results of another attitude survey. The idea is to take the pulse of public opinion. What do we think about candidate X, the war on drugs, gun control, or abortion? In the workplace, meanwhile, managers conduct attitude surveys to monitor such things as job and pay satisfaction. All this attention to attitudes is based on the assumption that attitudes somehow influence behavior such as voting for someone, working hard, or quitting one's job. In this section, we examine the connection between attitudes and behavior and explore the important work attitudes of job satisfaction, organizational commitment, and job involvement.

The Nature of Attitudes

An **attitude** is defined as "a learned predisposition to respond in a consistently favorable or unfavorable manner with respect to a given object."[25] Attitudes affect behavior at a different level than do values. While values represent global beliefs that influence behavior across *all* situations, attitudes relate only to behavior directed toward *specific* objects, persons, or situations.[26] Values and attitudes generally, but not always, are in harmony. A manager who strongly values helpful behavior may have a negative attitude toward helping an unethical co-worker. The difference between attitudes and values is

Attitude
Learned predisposition toward a given object.

clarified by considering the three components of attitudes: affective, cognitive, and behavioral.[27]

Affective component

The feelings or emotions one has about an object or situation.

Affective Component   The **affective component** of an attitude contains the feelings or emotions one has about a given object or situation. For example, how do you *feel* about people who talk on cell phones in restaurants? If you feel annoyed or angry with such people you are expressing negative affect or feelings toward people who talk on cell phones in restaurants. In contrast, the affective component of your attitude is neutral if you are indifferent about people talking on cell phones in restaurants.

Cognitive Component   What do you *think* about people who talk on cell phones in restaurants? Do you believe this behavior is inconsiderate, productive, completely acceptable, or rude? Your answer represents the cognitive component of your attitude toward people talking on cell phones in restaurants. The **cognitive component** of an attitude reflects the beliefs or ideas one has about an object or situation.

Cognitive component

The beliefs or ideas one has about an object or situation.

Behavioral component

How one intends to act or behave toward someone or something.

Behavioral Component   The **behavioral component** refers to how one intends or expects to act toward someone or something. For example, how would you intend to respond to someone talking on a cell phone during dinner at a restaurant if this individual were sitting in close proximity to you and your guest? Attitude theory suggests that your ultimate behavior in this situation is a function of all three attitudinal components. You are unlikely to say anything to someone using a cell phone in a restaurant if you are not irritated by this behavior (affective), if you believe cell phone use helps people to manage their lives (cognitive), and you have no intention of confronting this individual (behavioral).

How Stable Are Attitudes?

In one landmark study, researchers found the *job* attitudes of 5,000 middle-aged male employees to be very stable over a five-year period. Positive job attitudes remained positive; negative ones remained negative. Even those who changed jobs or occupations tended to maintain their prior job attitudes.[28] More recent research suggests the foregoing study may have overstated the stability of attitudes because it was restricted to a middle-aged sample. This time, researchers asked: What happens to attitudes over the entire span of adulthood? *General* attitudes were found to be more susceptible to change during early and late adulthood than during middle adulthood. Three factors accounted for middle-age attitude stability: (1) greater personal certainty, (2) perceived abundance of knowledge, and (3) a need for strong attitudes. Thus, the conventional notion that general attitudes become less likely to change as the person ages was rejected. Elderly people, along with young adults, can and do change their general attitudes because they are more open and less self-assured.[29]

Because our cultural backgrounds and experiences vary, our attitudes and behavior vary. Attitudes are translated into behavior via behavioral intentions. Let us examine an established model of this important process.

Attitudes Affect Behavior via Intentions

Over the years, Icek Ajzen and his colleagues developed and refined a model focusing on *intentions* as the key link between attitudes and actual behavior. Ajzen's theory of planned behavior in Figure 6–3 shows three separate but interacting determinants of

Figure 6–3   *Ajzen's Theory of Planned Behavior*

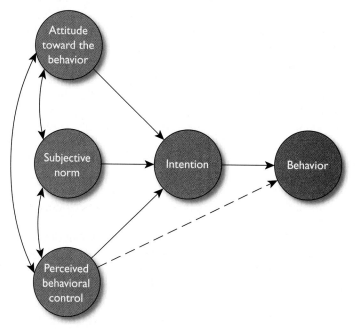

SOURCE: Reprinted from *Organizational Behavior and Human Decision Processes,* I. Aizen, "The Theory of Planned Behavior," Figure 1, p. 182, Copyright 1991, with permission from Elsevier Science.

one's intention (planned behavior) to do something (actual behavior). Importantly, this model only predicts behavior under the individual's control, not behavior due to circumstances beyond one's control. For example, this model can predict the likelihood of someone skipping work if the person says his intention is to stay in bed tomorrow morning. But it would be a poor model for predicting getting to work on time, because uncontrolled circumstances such as traffic delays or an accident could intervene.

Determinants of Intention   Ajzen has explained the nature and roles of the three determinants of intention as follows:

> The first is the *attitude toward the behavior* and refers to the degree to which a person has a favorable or unfavorable evaluation or appraisal of the behavior in question. The second predictor is a social factor termed *subjective norm;* it refers to the perceived social pressure to perform or not to perform the behavior. The third antecedent of intention is the degree of *perceived behavior control,* which . . . refers to the perceived ease or difficulty of performing the behavior and it is assumed to reflect past experience as well as anticipated impediments and obstacles.[30]

To bring these three determinants of intention to life, let us return to our lazy soul who chose to stay in bed rather than go to work. He feels overworked and underpaid and thus has a favorable attitude about skipping work occasionally. His perceived subjective norm is favorable because he sees his co-workers skipping work with no ill effects (in fact, they collect sick pay). Regarding perceived behavior control, he is completely in charge of acting on his intention to skip work today. So he turns off the alarm clock and pulls the covers over his head. Sweet dreams!

Intentions and Behavior Research Lessons and Implications

According to the model of planned behavior, someone's intention to engage in a given behavior is a strong predictor of that behavior. For example, the quickest and possibly most accurate way of determining whether an individual will quit his or her job is to have an objective third party ask if he or she intends to quit. A meta-analysis of 34 studies of employee turnover involving more than 83,000 employees validated this direct approach. The researchers found stated behavioral intentions to be a better predictor of employee turnover than job satisfaction, satisfaction with the work itself, or organizational commitment.[31]

Research has demonstrated that Ajzen's model accurately predicted intentions to buy consumer products, have children, and choose a career versus becoming a home-maker. Weight loss intentions and behavior, voting for political candidates, attending on-the-job training sessions, managers' use of structured interviews, and reenlisting in the National Guard also have been predicted successfully by the model.[32] In fact, the model correctly identified 82% of the 225 National Guard personnel in the study who actually reenlisted.[33]

From a practical management standpoint, the behavioral intention model we have just reviewed has important implications. First, managers need to appreciate the dynamic relationships between attitudes, subjective norms, and behavioral intentions when attempting to foster productive behavior. For example, the negative attitudes among 349 Florida college students toward affirmative action plans often were based on incorrect beliefs.[34] Although attitudes often are resistant to change, they can be influenced *indirectly* through education and training experiences that change underlying beliefs. A case in point is a study documenting how men's beliefs about gender differences can be reduced by taking a women's studies course.[35] Another tactic involves redirecting subjective norms through clear and credible communication, organizational culture values, and role models. Finally, regular employee-attitude surveys can let managers know if their ideas and changes go with or against the grain of popular sentiment.[36]

Key Work Attitudes

What is your attitude toward work? Is it something meaningful that defines and fulfills you, or is it just a way to pay the bills? Interestingly, attitudes toward work have changed significantly throughout recorded history (see Figure 6–4). Note the difference between the early Greeks' attitude toward work and the current perspective. Having fun at work clearly beats slavery! While everyone does not agree about having fun at work, organizations such as Southwest Airlines have turned it into a strategic competitive advantage. Key employee selection factors at Southwest Airlines are a keen sense of humor and a general positive attitude. Consider how CEO Bob Pike's positive attitude toward work would set the tone for his employees at Creative Training Techniques International, Inc.:

> It is not a choice between fun and work, it is a choice for fun and work. I find it depressing that so many people spend 8 hours a day at work and 16 hours trying to forget that they did! It's time for us to replace the common definition of work: if it is not dull and boring then it can't be work! Work should be about passion, it should have a sense of purpose, it should be about involvement and participation. High-performing teams who do challenging work also know how to have fun. They have an attitude that says they enjoy what they do and that they belong to a diverse group of committed individuals who know the mission, values, and vision of the team. And they look forward to making a contribution.

Figure 6–4   *Timeline of Work Values and Attitudes*

Ben Franklin
Advocates work as a virtue;
not a means to amass wealth
but as a contribution of self.
America is the land of opportunity.
Work becomes the key to wealth.

Calvin & Luther
Work as a commandment
and moral obligation. The
evolution of the Protestant
Work Ethic.

The trades
Working with your
hands as a skilled artisan
is highly prized. Payment
provided for work.
With the onset of the
Renaissance, work and
art are merged.

Early Greeks
Focus not on work but on
personal development.
Work was completed by
those enslaved. The
emergence of the
concept of 'liberal arts,'
and the pursuit of
knowledge.

Craftsmen vs Professionals
Separation between people who
work with their hands and
professionals who work with
their heads. The bias is that
working with your head is
a more esteemed vocation.

Industrial Age
The birth of Scientific Management Theory.

Unions
Unions help workers
defend their ability to
earn a livelihood against
managers and owners
who see employees as
objects.

1950s
The beginning of understanding
of the culture of work in terms
of Theory X and Theory Y.
Loyalty to the organization
becomes the expected norm.

1970s
Democracy comes to the
workplace. Sexes and races
begin to assume more equal
roles in all aspects of work
environments.

1980s
Gurus abound. How to
make work meaningful.
TQM becomes the newest
program of the corporate
culture.

1990s
Empowerment,
Building the Team,
and Reengineering
begin the decade.
Downsizing at the
end of the decade
completes the near
total loss of loyalty
as an organizational
value.

2000s
Because we
spend more
time at work
than at any
other activity,
we begin to
question
whether we live
to work or
work to live.
The beginning
of the Fun/Work
Fusion.

SOURCE: Reprinted with permission of the publisher. From *Fun Works: Creating Places Where People Love to Work*, copyright© 2001 by L. Yerkes, Berrett-Koehler Publishers, Inc., San Francisco, CA. All rights reserved. www.bkconnection.com.

OB Exercise   How Satisfied Are You with Your Present Job?

	Very Dissatisfied				Very Satisfied
1. The way I am noticed when I do a good job	1 —	2 —	3 —	4 —	5
2. The recognition I get for the work I do	1 —	2 —	3 —	4 —	5
3. The praise I get for doing a good job	1 —	2 —	3 —	4 —	5
4. How my pay compares with that for similar jobs in other companies	1 —	2 —	3 —	4 —	5
5. My pay and the amount of work I do	1 —	2 —	3 —	4 —	5
6. How my pay compares with that of other workers	1 —	2 —	3 —	4 —	5
7. The way my boss handles employees	1 —	2 —	3 —	4 —	5
8. The way my boss takes care of complaints brought to him/her by employees	1 —	2 —	3 —	4 —	5
9. The personal relationship between my boss and his/her employees	1 —	2 —	3 —	4 —	5

Total score for satisfaction with recognition (add questions 1–3), compensation (add questions 4–6), and supervision (add questions 7–9).

Comparative norms for each dimension of job satisfaction are: Total score of 3–6 = Low job satisfaction; 7–11 = Moderate satisfaction; 12 and above = High satisfaction.

SOURCE: Adapted from DJ Weiss, RV Dawis, GW England, and LH Lofquist, *Manual for the Minnesota Satisfaction Questionnaire,* (Minneapolis: Industrial Relations Center, University of Minnesota, 1967). Used with permission.

Understand that there will always be both fun-loving and fun-killing people. Fun-killers don't actually object to the fun; they feel that the fun isn't relevant to the work and therefore not important.[37]

How would you like to work for Bob Pike?

People have a multitude of attitudes about things that happen to them at work, but OB researchers have focused on a limited number of them. This section specifically examines three work attitudes—job satisfaction, organizational commitment, and job involvement—that have important practical implications.

Job Satisfaction   Job satisfaction essentially reflects the extent to which an individual likes his or her job. Formally defined, **job satisfaction** is an affective or emotional response toward various facets of one's job. This definition implies job satisfaction is not a unitary concept. Rather, a person can be relatively satisfied with one aspect of his or her job and dissatisfied with one or more other aspects. For example, researchers at Cornell University developed the Job Descriptive Index (JDI) to assess one's satisfaction with the following job dimensions: work, pay, promotions, co-workers, and supervision.[38] Researchers at the University of Minnesota concluded there are 20 different dimensions underlying job satisfaction. Selected Minnesota Satisfaction Questionnaire (MSQ) items measuring satisfaction with recognition, compensation, and supervision are listed in the OB Exercise above. Please take a moment now to determine how satisfied you are with these three aspects of your present or most recent job, and then use the norms to compare your score.[39] How do you feel about your job?

Research revealed that job satisfaction varied across countries. A recent study of 9,300 adults in 39 countries identified the percentage of workers who said they were

Job satisfaction

An affective or emotional response to one's job.

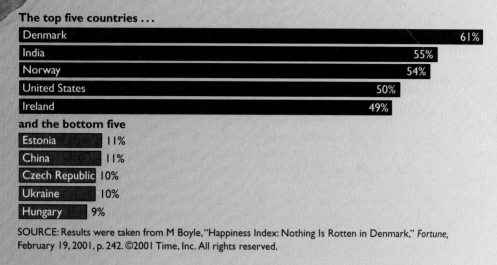

Job Satisfaction Varies around the Globe

The top five countries . . .

Denmark	61%
India	55%
Norway	54%
United States	50%
Ireland	49%

and the bottom five

Estonia	11%
China	11%
Czech Republic	10%
Ukraine	10%
Hungary	9%

SOURCE: Results were taken from M Boyle, "Happiness Index: Nothing Is Rotten in Denmark," *Fortune*, February 19, 2001, p. 242. ©2001 Time, Inc.

"very satisfied with their job." Results are shown in the International OB above. Why do you think Hungarian employees indicate the lowest job satisfaction? An average monthly salary of $302 and poor labor–management relations are two possible causes.

Job satisfaction is one of the most frequently studied work attitudes by OB researchers. For example, more than 12,000 job satisfaction studies were published by the early 1990s.[40] We thoroughly examine the causes and consequences of job satisfaction in the final section of this chapter due to its importance in understanding a variety of employee attitudes and behavior.

Organizational Commitment

Organizational commitment reflects the extent to which an individual identifies with an organization and is committed to its goals. It is an important work attitude because committed individuals are expected to display a willingness to work harder to achieve organizational goals and a greater desire to stay employed at an organization. In this day and age of corporate scandals, layoffs, and the associated distrust in management, managers are very interested in fostering organizational commitment. Interestingly, companies use a variety of method to increase employees' organizational commitment. Consider the different approaches used by Jeff Skilling, former Enron CEO, and George David, CEO of United Technologies Corp.

> Skilling hired some 250 bright young MBAs each year, all desperate to prove themselves so they, too, could hit the jackpot. Around Houston, a Porsche was seen as the Enron company car. "Skilling would say all that matters is money: You buy loyalty with money," says an ex-exec.[41]
>
> Six years ago, some of George David's subordinates at United Technologies Corp. thought he was nuts.
>
> But he is the CEO. So they acquiesced to his demand that the big manufacturer turn its undistinguished go-back-to-college program into one of the most generous in corporate America. . . .
>
> UTC pays all tuition and fees upfront for any credit course, no matter what the subject. . . . To lure workers to the classroom, UTC also offers up to three hours off each

Organizational commitment

Extent to which an individual identifies with an organization and its goals.

week—with pay—to study. . . . UTC also gives $5,000 worth of stock to employees who finish an associate's degree and $10,000 worth to those who finish higher degrees. At current market prices, the company has awarded $87 million of stock to 7,457 employees.[42]

While organizations such as Enron might attempt to "buy loyalty," we prefer the long-term, human capital approach used by UTC. UTC builds organizational commitment by investing in its employees. Anecdotal evidence from UTC supports the effectiveness of this method. For example, there is a greater percentage of employees from UTC taking college courses than is typical throughout other US corporations. Further, UTC's employee turnover is lower among employees participating in the educational program (4%) than it is among nonparticipating employees (8–10%).[43] Let us now consider the relationship between organizational commitment and other employee attitudes and performance.

A meta-analysis of 68 studies and 35,282 individuals uncovered a significant and strong relationship between organizational commitment and job satisfaction.[44] This finding encourages managers to increase job satisfaction in order to elicit higher levels of commitment. In turn, a recent meta-analysis involving 26,344 individuals revealed organizational commitment was significantly correlated with job performance.[45] This is an important finding because it implies managers can increase productivity by enhancing employees' organizational commitment. Finally, a recent study showed that employees had lower intentions to quit their jobs when they were committed to their respective organizations.[46] In summary, managers are encouraged to focus on improving employees' organizational commitment. To do this, however, it is important for managers to set the stage by encouraging positive social interactions among people. Providing opportunities for employees from different work areas to interact both socially and professionally can help.[47]

Job Involvement

Job involvement

Extent to which an individual is immersed in his or her present job.

Job involvement is defined as "the degree to which one is cognitively preoccupied with, engaged in, and concerned with one's present job."[48] This work attitude manifests itself through the extent to which people are immersed in their job tasks. Take Vinton Studios' animator/directors Sean Burns and Doug Aberle for example. (Vinton Studios trademarked an animation process known as Claymation.® The process has been used in television commercials involving the California Raisins and M&Ms and the television series *The PJs*.) Sean says, "This is a great place to work. We work on truly interesting and cutting-edge stuff. Plus I get to work on things that interest me. Each project is a new situation every time. We suggest interesting twists, new ideas."[49] Doug also is involved in his work. "At the end of the day, you've never been so tired—or had so much fun! There's a lot of variety in working on a TV show. There's something different every day."[50] This suggests it is important for managers to understand the causes and consequences of job involvement because of its association with motivation and satisfaction. Let us now consider results from a meta-analytic study involving thousands of people, to learn more about job involvement.[51]

Job involvement was positively associated with job satisfaction, organizational commitment, and intrinsic motivation, and negatively related to intentions to quit. There are three key managerial implications associated with these results. First, managerial attempts to improve any one of the three key work attitudes discussed in this section—job satisfaction, organizational commitment, and job involvement—are likely to positively affect the other two work attitudes. Second, managers can increase employees' job involvement by providing work environments that fuel intrinsic motivation.[52] Spe-

Although this little Claymation® character seems a bit skeptical, the artists at Vinton Studios exhibit high job involvement. They love working on creative projects that hold their interest and turn hard work into fun. Task variety also is a big plus. An added bonus: their uncooperative subjects can be tossed back into the clay bucket.

Courtesy of Vinton Studios

cific recommendations for doing this are discussed in the section on intrinsic motivation in Chapter 8. Third, improving job involvement can reduce employee turnover.

Past results pertaining to the relationship between job involvement and performance are controversial. While the original meta-analysis failed to uncover a significant relationship between job involvement and performance, poor measures of job involvement used in past studies may have biased the results. A recent study corrected this problem and found a positive relationship between job involvement and performance.[53] Managers thus are encouraged to increase employees' job involvement as a viable strategy for improving job performance.

Abilities and Performance

Individual differences in abilities and accompanying skills are a central concern for managers because nothing can be accomplished without appropriately skilled personnel. An **ability** represents a broad and stable characteristic responsible for a person's maximum—as opposed to typical—performance on mental and physical tasks. A **skill,** on the other hand, is the specific capacity to physically manipulate objects. Consider this difference as you imagine yourself being the only passenger on a small commuter airplane in which the pilot has just passed out. As the plane nose-dives, your effort and

Ability
Stable characteristic responsible for a person's maximum physical or mental performance.

Skill
Specific capacity to manipulate objects.

Figure 6–5   *Performance Depends on the Right Combination of Effort, Ability, and Skill*

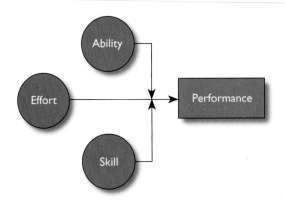

abilities will not be enough to save yourself and the pilot if you do not possess flying skills. As shown in Figure 6–5, successful performance (be it landing an airplane or performing any other job) depends on the right combination of effort, ability, and skill.

Abilities and skills are getting a good deal of attention in management circles these days. The more encompassing term *competencies* is typically used. According to the head of a New Jersey consulting firm,

> In the past decade, thousands of organizations throughout the world have joined the quest for competencies. Often, they spend a year or more conducting competency studies—identifying "clusters" of knowledge, attitudes, and skills needed to perform various jobs. The competencies turned up by these studies become the basis for decisions about hiring, training, promotions, and other human resource issues.[54]

Among the many desirable competencies are oral communication, initiative, decisiveness, tolerance, problem solving, adaptability, and resilience.[55] Importantly, our cautions about on-the-job personality testing in Chapter 5 extend to ability, intelligence, and competency testing and certification.

Before moving on, we need to say something about a modern-day threat to abilities, skills, and general competence. That threat, according to public health officials, is *sleep deprivation*[56] (take a short break for the OB Exercise on page 207). If you are routinely short-changing your basic sleep needs, you are likely to be less effective and more stressed (see Chapter 19) than you should be. Habitually sleep-deprived people need to be aware of this stunning fact: "Staying awake 24 hours impairs cognitive psychomotor performance to the same degree as having a 0.1 percent blood alcohol level. . . . That is above many states' legal driving limits, which range from 0.4 percent to 0.1 percent."[57]

The balance of this section explores important abilities and cognitive styles related to job performance.

Intelligence
Capacity for constructive thinking, reasoning, problem solving.

Intelligence and Cognitive Abilities

Although experts do not agree on a specific definition, **intelligence** represents an individual's capacity for constructive thinking, reasoning, and problem solving.[58] Historically, intelligence was believed to be an innate capacity, passed genetically from one

OB Exercise Wake Up! Are Your Abilities and Skills Being Eroded by a Lack of Sleep?

Background

During the past three decades, Americans have put in longer hours at the office and packed ever more into their pre-bedtime hours: working at home on laptop computers, surfing the Internet and E-mailing friends, flipping among ever-expanding choices on television.

The result: Nearly two-thirds of adults get less than the eight hours of sleep a night during the week that the average American adult requires. . . . And nearly one-third of Americans make due with 61/2 hours or less sleep a night during the work week. . . .

The upshot of this mass sleep deprivation? Many Americans are yawning their way through life. According to . . . [sleep experts;] about 62% of adults have driven while drowsy during the past year and 27% have, alarmingly, dozed off behind the wheel. About 40% of adults are so sleepy during the day that it interferes with their jobs, family duties, and other daily activities.*

Instructions

Realizing that the optimum amount of sleep is a very individualized thing, rate your daily sleep needs and habits with the following unscientific index. Are you compromising your health, potential, and effectiveness with lack of adequate sleep?

I feel refreshed and up to my full potential after _____ hours of sleep.

My performance starts to decline with less than _____ hours of sleep.

My performance seriously declines with less than _____ hours of sleep.

I can go for _____ days without getting adequate sleep before I "crash."

I am a complete "zombie" when I get less than _____ hours of sleep.

During the last month, I have averaged _____ hours of sleep per 24-hour period.

I view quality sleep as a resource that I carefully manage. True? False?

SOURCE: *Excerpted from NA Jeffrey, "Sleep: The New Status Symbol," *The Wall Street Journal*, April 2, 1999, pp. W1, W12.

generation to the next. Research since has shown, however, that intelligence (like personality) also is a function of environmental influences.[59] Organic factors have more recently been added to the formula as a result of mounting evidence of the connection between alcohol and drug abuse by pregnant women and intellectual development problems in their children.[60]

Researchers have produced some interesting findings about abilities and intelligence in recent years. A unique five-year study documented the tendency of people to "gravitate into jobs commensurate with their abilities."[61] This prompts the vision of the labor market acting as a giant sorting or sifting machine, with employees tumbling into various ability bins. Meanwhile, a steady and significant rise in average intelligence among those in developed countries has been observed over the last 70 years. Why? Experts at an American Psychological Association conference concluded, "Some combination of better schooling, improved socioeconomic status, healthier nutrition, and a more technologically complex society might account for the gains in IQ scores."[62] So if you think you're smarter than your parents and your teachers, you're probably right!

Two Types of Abilities

Human intelligence has been studied predominantly through the empirical approach. By examining the relationships between measures of mental abilities and behavior, researchers have statistically isolated major components of intelligence. Using this empirical procedure, pioneering psychologist Charles Spearman proposed in 1927 that all cognitive performance is determined by two types of abilities. The first can be characterized as a general mental ability needed for *all* cognitive tasks. The second is unique to the task at hand.[63] For example, an individual's ability to complete crossword puzzles is a function of his or her broad mental abilities as well as the specific ability to perceive patterns in partially completed words.

Seven Major Mental Abilities

Through the years, much research has been devoted to developing and expanding Spearman's ideas on the relationship between cognitive abilities and intelligence. One research psychologist listed 120 distinct mental abilities. Table 6–1 contains definitions of the seven most frequently cited mental abilities. Of the seven abilities, personnel selection researchers have found verbal ability, numerical ability, spatial ability, and inductive reasoning to be valid predictors of job performance for both minority and majority applicants.[64]

Jung's Cognitive Styles Typology

Cognitive style

A perceptual and judgmental tendency, according to Jung's typology.

Within the context of Jung's theory, the term **cognitive style** refers to mental processes associated with how people perceive and make judgments from information. Although the landmark work on cognitive styles was completed in the 1920s by the noted Swiss psychoanalyst Carl Jung, his ideas did not catch on in the United States until the 1940s. That was when the mother–daughter team of Katharine C Briggs and Isabel Briggs

Table 6–1   *Mental Abilities Underlying Performance*

Ability	Description
1. Verbal comprehension	The ability to understand what words mean and to readily comprehend what is read.
2. Word fluency	The ability to produce isolated words that fulfill specific symbolic or structural requirements (such as all words that begin with the letter *b* and have two vowels).
3. Numerical	The ability to make quick and accurate arithmetic computations such as adding and subtracting.
4. Spatial	Being able to perceive spatial patterns and to visualize how geometric shapes would look if transformed in shape or position.
5. Memory	Having good rote memory for paired words, symbols, lists of numbers, or other associated items.
6. Perceptual speed	The ability to perceive figures, identify similarities and differences, and carry out tasks involving visual perception.
7. Inductive reasoning	The ability to reason from specifics to general conclusions.

SOURCE: Adapted from MD Dunnette, "Aptitudes, Abilities, and Skills," in *Handbook of Industrial and Organizational Psychology,* ed MD Dunnette (Skokie, IL: RandMcNally, 1976), pp. 478–83.

Myers developed the Myers-Briggs Type Indicator (MBTI), an instrument for measuring Jung's cognitive styles. Today, the MBTI is a widely used (and abused) personal growth and development tool in schools and businesses.[65]

Four Different Cognitive Styles

According to Jung, two dimensions influence perception and two others affect individual judgment. Perception is based on either *sensation,* using one's physical senses to interpret situations, or *intuition,* relying on past experience. In turn, judgments are made by either *thinking* or *feeling.* Finally, Jung proposed that an individual's cognitive style is determined by the pairing of one's perception and judgment tendencies. The resulting four cognitive styles are as follows:

- Sensation/thinking (ST)
- Intuition/thinking (NT)
- Sensation/feeling (SF)
- Intuition/feeling (NF)

Characteristics of each style are presented in Figure 6–6.[66] (The Personal Awareness and Growth Exercise at the end of this chapter, patterned after the MBTI, will help you determine your cognitive style.)

An individual with an ST style uses senses for perception and rational thinking for judgment. The ST-style person uses facts and impersonal analysis and develops greater abilities in technical areas involving facts and objects. A successful engineer could be

Figure 6–6 *People Have Different Cognitive Styles and Corresponding Characteristics*

	Decision Style			
	ST Sensation/Thinking	**NT** Intuition/Thinking	**SF** Sensation/Feeling	**NF** Intuition/Feeling
Focus of attention	Facts	Possibilities	Facts	Possibilities
Method of handling things	Impersonal analysis	Impersonal analysis	Personal warmth	Personal warmth
Tendency to become	Practical and matter-of-fact	Logical and ingenious	Sympathetic and friendly	Enthusiastic and insightful
Expression of abilities	Technical skills with facts and objects	Theoretical and technical developments	Practical help and services for people	Understanding and communicating with people
Representative occupation	Technician	Planner	Teacher	Artist
		Manager		

SOURCE: W Taggart and D Robey, "Minds and Managers: On the Dual Nature of Human Information Processing and Management," *Academy of Management Review,* April 1981, p. 190. Used with permission.

expected to exhibit this cognitive style. In contrast, a person with an NT style focuses on possibilities rather than facts and displays abilities in areas involving theoretical or technical development. This style would enhance the performance of a research scientist. Although an SF person likely is interested in gathering facts, he or she tends to treat others with personal warmth, sympathy, and friendliness. Successful counselors or teachers probably use this style. Finally, an individual with an NF style tends to exhibit artistic flair while relying heavily on personal insights rather than objective facts (see Figure 6–6).

Practical Research Findings If Jung's cognitive styles typology is valid, then individuals with different cognitive styles should seek different kinds of information when making a decision. A study of 50 MBA students found that those with different cognitive styles did in fact use qualitatively different information while working on a strategic planning problem.[67] Research also has shown that people with different cognitive styles prefer different careers. For example, people who rely on intuition prefer careers in psychology, advertising, teaching, and the arts.

Findings have further shown that individuals who make judgments based on the "thinking" approach have higher work motivation and quality of work life than those who take a "feeling" approach. In addition, individuals with a sensation mode of perception have higher job satisfaction than those relying on intuition.[68] Small business owner/managers with a "thinking" style made more money than their "feeling" counterparts. But no correlation was found between the four Jungian styles and small business owner/manager success.[69] The following conclusion from an exhaustive review of management-oriented MBTI studies makes us cautious about these findings: "It is clear that efforts to detect simplistic linkages between type preferences and managerial effectiveness have been disappointing. Indeed, given the mixed quality of research and the inconsistent findings, no definitive conclusions regarding these relationships can be drawn."[70] On balance, we believe Jung's cognitive styles typology and the MBTI are useful for diversity training and management development purposes,[71] but inappropriate for making personnel decisions such as hiring and promotions.

Job Satisfaction

We introduced the topic of job satisfaction earlier in our discussion of key work attitudes. It was noted that job satisfaction reflects the extent to which an individual likes his or her job, and it is the most frequently studied outcome variable by OB researchers.[72] We now want to examine this employee attitude in more detail by focusing on the causes and consequences of job satisfaction.

The Causes of Job Satisfaction

Five predominant models of job satisfaction focus on different causes. They are need fulfillment, discrepancy, value attainment, equity, and dispositional/genetic components. A brief review of these models will provide insight into the complexity of this seemingly simple concept.[73]

Need Fulfillment These models propose that satisfaction is determined by the extent to which the characteristics of a job allow an individual to fulfill his or her needs. For example, a survey of 30 Massachusetts law firms revealed that 35% to 50% of law-firm associates left their employers within three years of starting because the firms did not accommodate family needs. This example illustrates that unmet needs can affect both satisfaction and turnover.[74] Although these models generated a great degree of controversy, it is generally accepted that need fulfillment is correlated with job satisfaction.[75]

Discrepancies   These models propose that satisfaction is a result of met expectations. **Met expectations** represent the difference between what an individual expects to receive from a job, such as good pay and promotional opportunities, and what he or she actually receives. When expectations are greater than what is received, a person will be dissatisfied. In contrast, this model predicts the individual will be satisfied when he or she attains outcomes above and beyond expectations. A meta-analysis of 31 studies that included 17,241 people demonstrated that met expectations were significantly related to job satisfaction.[76] Many companies use employee attitude or opinion surveys to assess employees' expectations and concerns. Consider the Charles Schwab Corp. for example.

> Four years ago the company started surveying its employees; now it quizzes the entire workforce annually. The questions ask about workloads, benefits, office culture, and career development. . . . Schwab uses the information it gathers to gauge concerns about companywide issues. More important (on the retention front, anyway), it narrows the replies to individual departments and holds front-line managers responsible for addressing any serious problems that surface. Managers meet individually with each subordinate and develop plans to address the concerns. Mentoring programs, specialized training tracks, flexible schedules, and a host of other changes have been initiated as a result.
>
> Perhaps the most significant outcome of all this, however, is the coaching and training of department heads themselves. . . . If, for instance, a manager's interpersonal skills are criticized, Schwab may enroll him in a communications seminar or have him shadow a senior colleague.[77]

Value Attainment   The idea underlying **value attainment** is that satisfaction results from the perception that a job allows for fulfillment of an individual's important work values.[78] In general, research consistently supports the prediction that value fulfillment is positively related to job satisfaction.[79] Managers can thus enhance employee satisfaction by structuring the work environment and its associated rewards and recognition to reinforce employees' values.

Equity   In this model, satisfaction is a function of how "fairly" an individual is treated at work. Satisfaction results from one's perception that work outcomes, relative to inputs, compare favorably with a significant other's outcomes/inputs. A meta-analysis involving 190 studies and 64,757 people supported this model. Employees' perceptions of being treated fairly at work were highly related to overall job satisfaction.[80] Managers thus are encouraged to monitor employees' fairness perceptions and to interact with employees in such a way that they feel equitably treated. Chapter 9 explores this promising model in more detail.

Dispositional/Genetic Components   Have you ever noticed that some of your co-workers or friends appear to be satisfied across a variety of job circumstances, whereas others always seem dissatisfied? This model of satisfaction attempts to explain this pattern.[81] Specifically, the dispositional/genetic model is based on the belief that job satisfaction is partly a function of both personal traits and genetic factors. As such, this model implies that stable individual differences are just as important in explaining job satisfaction as are characteristics of the work environment. Although only a few

Met expectations
The extent to which one receives what he or she expects from a job.

Value attainment
The extent to which a job allows fulfillment of one's work values.

People can be like sunny days and rainy days. Sunny-day people tend to find satisfaction in all aspects of their lives. Rainy-day people generally express dissatisfaction with everything. Pete and Laura Wakeman, founders of Great Harvest Bread Company, have tried to hire people with positive dispositions for the past 25 years. Here, franchisee Dave Scheel, owner of a Great Harvest store in Missoula, Montana, gets down to business. The Wakemans are on the right track because it surely takes an optimist to face mountains of bread dough at 5 am.

Courtesy of Great Harvest Bread Company

studies have tested these propositions, results support a positive, significant relationship between personal traits and job satisfaction over time periods ranging from 2 to 50 years.[82] Genetic factors also were found to significantly predict life satisfaction, well-being, and general job satisfaction.[83] Overall, researchers estimate that 30% of an individual's job satisfaction is associated with dispositional and genetic components.[84] Pete and Laura Wakeman, founders of Great Harvest Bread Company, have used this model of job satisfaction while running their company for over 25 years.

Our hiring ads say clearly that we need people with "strong personal loves as important as their work." This is not a little thing. You can't have a great life unless you have a buffer of like-minded people all around you. If you want to be nice, you can't surround yourself with crabby people and expect it to work. You might stay nice for a while, just because— but it isn't sustainable over years. If you want a happy company, you can do it only by hiring naturally happy people. You'll never build a happy company by "making people happy"—you can't really "make" people any way that they aren't already. Laura and I want to be in love with life, and our business has been a good thing for us in that journey.[85]

Although Pete and Laura's hiring approach is consistent with the dispositional and genetic model of job satisfaction, it is important to note that hiring "like-minded" people can potentially lead to discriminatory decisions. Managers are advised not to discriminate on the basis of race, gender, religion, color, national origin, and age.

Major Correlates and Consequences of Job Satisfaction

This area has significant managerial implications because thousands of studies have examined the relationship between job satisfaction and other organizational variables. Because it is impossible to examine them all, we will consider a subset of the more important variables from the standpoint of managerial relevance.

Table 6–2 summarizes the pattern of results. The relationship between job satisfaction and these other variables is either positive or negative. The strength of the rela-

Table 6–2   *Correlates of Job Satisfaction*

Variables Related with Satisfaction	Direction of Relationship	Strength of Relationship
Motivation	Positive	Moderate
Organizational citizenship behavior	Positive	Moderate
Absenteeism	Negative	Weak
Tardiness	Negative	Weak
Withdrawal cognitions	Negative	Strong
Turnover	Negative	Moderate
Heart disease	Negative	Moderate
Perceived stress	Negative	Strong
Pro-union voting	Negative	Moderate
Job performance	Positive	Moderate
Life satisfaction	Positive	Moderate
Mental health	Positive	Moderate

tionship ranges from weak (very little relationship) to strong. Strong relationships imply that managers can significantly influence the variable of interest by increasing job satisfaction. Let us now consider seven key correlates of job satisfaction.

Motivation   A recent meta-analysis of nine studies and 1,739 workers revealed a significant positive relationship between motivation and job satisfaction. Because satisfaction with supervision also was significantly correlated with motivation managers are advised to consider how their behavior affects employee satisfaction.[86] Managers can potentially enhance employees' motivation through various attempts to increase job satisfaction.

Organizational Citizenship Behavior   **Organizational citizenship behaviors (OCBs)** consist of employee behaviors that are beyond the call of duty. Examples include "such gestures as constructive statements about the department, expression of personal interest in the work of others, suggestions for improvement, training new people, respect for the spirit as well as the letter of housekeeping rules, care for organizational property, and punctuality and attendance well beyond standard or enforceable levels."[87] Managers certainly would like employees to exhibit these behaviors. A meta-analysis covering 7,100 people and 22 separate studies revealed a significant and moderately positive correlation between organizational citizenship behaviors and job satisfaction.[88] Moreover, additional research demonstrated that employees' citizenship behaviors were determined more by leadership and characteristics of the work environment than by an employee's personality.[89] It thus appears that managerial behavior significantly influences an employee's willingness to exhibit citizenship behaviors. This relationship is important to recognize because employees' OCBs were positively correlated with their conscientiousness at work, organizational commitment, and performance ratings.[90] Another recent study demonstrated a broader impact of OCBs on organizational effectiveness. Results revealed that the amount of OCBs exhibited by employees working in 28 regional restaurants was significantly associated with each restaurant's corporate profits one year later.[91] Because employees' perceptions of being treated fairly at work are related to their willingness to engage in

Organizational citizenship behaviors (OCBs)
Employee behaviors that exceed work-role requirements.

OCBs, managers are encouraged to make and implement employee-related decisions in an equitable fashion.

Absenteeism   Absenteeism is costly, and managers are constantly on the lookout for ways to reduce it. One recommendation has been to increase job satisfaction. If this is a valid recommendation, there should be a strong negative relationship (or negative correlation) between satisfaction and absenteeism. In other words, as satisfaction increases, absenteeism should decrease. A researcher tracked this prediction by synthesizing three separate meta-analyses containing a total of 74 studies. Results revealed a weak negative relationship between satisfaction and absenteeism.[92] It is unlikely, therefore, that managers will realize any significant decrease in absenteeism by increasing job satisfaction.

Withdrawal Cognitions   Although some people quit their jobs impulsively or in a fit of anger, most go through a process of thinking about whether or not they should quit.[93] **Withdrawal cognitions** encapsulate this thought process by representing an individual's overall thoughts and feelings about quitting. What causes an individual to think about quitting his or her job? Job satisfaction is believed to be one of the most significant contributors. For example, a recent study of managers, salespersons, and auto mechanics from a national automotive retail store chain demonstrated that job dissatisfaction caused employees to begin the process of thinking about quitting. In turn, withdrawal cognitions had a greater impact on employee turnover than job satisfaction in this sample.[94] Results from this study imply that managers can indirectly help to reduce employee turnover by enhancing employee job satisfaction.

Withdrawal cognitions

Overall thoughts and feelings about quitting a job.

Turnover   Turnover is important to managers because it both disrupts organizational continuity and is very costly. For example, turnover increases the direct costs of recruiting and training new employees (see the example in Table 6–3) and the indirect costs associated with impaired service quality, lost business to competitors, loss of technical knowledge and human capital, and decreased morale and increased turnover among remaining workers.[95] Although there are many different things a manager can do to reduce employee turnover, many of them revolve around attempts to improve employees' job satisfaction.[96] This trend is supported by results from a meta-analysis of 67 studies covering 24,556 people. Job satisfaction obtained a moderate negative relationship with employee turnover.[97] Given the strength of this relationship, managers are advised to try to reduce employee turnover by increasing employee job satisfaction.

Perceived Stress   Stress can have very negative effects on organizational behavior and an individual's health. Stress is positively related to absenteeism, turnover, coronary heart disease, and viral infections.[98] Based on a meta-analysis of seven studies covering 2,659 individuals, Table 6–2 reveals that perceived stress has a strong, negative relationship with job satisfaction.[99] It is hoped that managers would attempt to reduce the negative effects of stress by improving job satisfaction.

Job Performance   One of the biggest controversies within OB research centers on the relationship between job satisfaction and job performance. Although researchers have identified seven different ways in which these variables are related, the dominant beliefs are either that satisfaction causes performance or performance causes satisfaction.[100] A team of researchers recently attempted to resolve this controversy through a meta-analysis of data from 312 samples involving 54,417 individuals.[101] There were two key findings from this study. First, job satisfaction and performance are moderately

Table 6–3   *An Illustrative Example of the Direct Costs of Employee Turnover*

Below are the expected activities and estimated costs to conduct a national search for a mid-level manager at a large company.

Activity	Estimated Costs
Newspaper ads (run several months in local and national papers)	$ 8,000
Search firm fees (including commission for a prestigious national headhunter)	10,000
Interview costs (factoring in coach airline fare, standard hotels, and meals for several out-of-town candidates)	4,000
Managerial time (hourly value of four managers spending 25 hours each reading résumés and interviewing)	4,000
Work put on hold (minimal projects set aside for less than a month)	2,000
Overload on team (overtime for one employee and compensation for a temp)	4,000
Training for new employee (assuming one- to two-month learning curve)	6,000
Lost contracts, customers, and/or accounts (loss of some customers, but not key clients)	8,000
Lowered office morale (employees' hourly rate spent complaining at the water cooler or surfing online classifieds)	2,000
Loss of other employees (one other employee starting to look for a new job)	3,000
Signing bonus and other perks (minimal bonus)	6,000
Relocation expenses (moving van, temporary housing for out-of-town hire)	7,000
The final tab	$64,000

SOURCE: Excerpted from M Littman, "Best Bosses Tell All," *Working Woman*, October 2000, p. 56.

related. This is an important finding because it supports the belief that employee job satisfaction is a key work attitude managers should consider when attempting to increase employees' job performance. Second, the relationship between job satisfaction and performance is much more complex than originally thought. It is not as simple as satisfaction causing performance or performance causing satisfaction. Rather, researchers now believe both variables indirectly influence each other through a host of individual differences and work-environment characteristics.[102] There is one additional consideration to keep in mind regarding the relationship between job satisfaction and job performance.

Researchers believe the relationship between satisfaction and performance is understated due to incomplete measures of individual-level performance. For example, if performance ratings used in past research did not reflect the actual interactions and interdependencies at work, inaccurate measures of performance served to lower the reported correlations between satisfaction and performance. Examining the relationship between *aggregate* measures of job satisfaction and organizational performance is one solution to correct this problem.[103] In support of these ideas, a team of researchers conducted a recent meta-analysis of 7,939 business units in 36 companies. Results uncovered significant positive relationships between business-unit-level employee satisfaction and business-unit outcomes of customer satisfaction, productivity, profit, employee turnover, and accidents.[104] It thus appears managers can positively affect a variety of important organizational outcomes, including performance, by increasing employee job satisfaction.

Summary of Key Concepts

1. *Distinguish between instrumental and terminal values, and describe three types of value conflict.* An instrumental value is an enduring belief about how one should behave (e.g., obedient). A terminal is an enduring belief about a desired end-state (e.g., happiness). Three types of value conflict are intrapersonal, interpersonal, and individual-organization.

2. *Describe the values model of work/family conflict, and specify at least three practical lessons from work/family conflict research.* General life values determine one's values about family and work. Work/family conflict can occur when there is a lack of value similarity with family members. Likewise, work/family conflict can occur when one's own work values are not congruent with the company's values. When someone does not attain his or her values because of work/family conflicts, job or life satisfaction, or both, can suffer. Five practical lessons from work/family conflict research are (1) gender inequality begins at home, (2) an employer's family-supportive philosophy is key, (3) work flexibility is more important than time flexibility, (4) a mentor can help, and (5) self-employment has its rewards, but it is associated with higher work/family conflict and lower family satisfaction.

3. *Define attitudes, explain how they differ from values, and identify the three components of attitudes.* An attitude is a learned predisposition to respond in a favorable or unfavorable way toward an object. Attitudes relate only to behavior directed toward specific objects, persons, or situations. In contrast, values represent global beliefs that influence behavior across all situations. The affective component represents the feelings or emotions one has about a given object or situation. The cognitive component reflects the beliefs or ideas one has about an object or situation. The behavioral component refers to how one intends or expects to act toward someone or something.

4. *Explain how attitudes affect behavior in terms of Ajzen's theory of planned behavior.* Intentions are the key link between attitudes and behavior in Ajzen's model. Three determinants of the strength of an intention are one's attitude toward the behavior, subjective norm (social expectations and role models), and the perceived degree of one's control over the behavior. Intentions, in turn, are powerful determinants of behavior.

5. *Define the key work attitudes of job satisfaction, organizational commitment, and job involvement.* Job satisfaction reflects how much people like or dislike their jobs. Organizational commitment reflects how strongly the person identifies with an organization and is committed to its goals. Job involvement is the extent to which a person is preoccupied with, immersed in, and concerned with their job.

6. *Describe Carl Jung's cognitive styles typology.* By combining two dimensions of perception (sensation and intuition) with two dimensions of judgment (thinking and feeling), Jung identified four cognitive styles. They are sensation/thinking (practical and matter-of-fact), intuition/thinking (logical and ingenious), sensation/feeling (sympathetic and friendly), and intuition/feeling (enthusiastic and insightful).

7. *Identify and briefly describe five alternative causes of job satisfaction.* They are need fulfillment (the degree to which one's own needs are met), discrepancies (satisfaction depends on the extent to which one's expectations are met), value attainment (satisfaction depends on the degree to which one's work values are fulfilled), equity (perceived fairness of input/outcomes determines one's level of satisfaction), and dispositional/genetic (job satisfaction is dictated by one's personal traits and genetic makeup).

8. *Identify seven important correlates/consequences of job satisfaction, and summarize how each one relates to job satisfaction.* Seven major correlates/consequences of job satisfaction are motivation (moderate positive relationship), organizational citizenship behavior (moderate positive), absenteeism (weak negative), withdrawal cognitions/thoughts about quitting (strong negative), turnover/quitting (moderate negative), perceived stress (strong negative), and job performance (moderate positive).

Discussion Questions

1. Which type of value conflict have you found most troublesome? Why?

2. What is your experience with work/family conflict, and what useful lessons did you learn from our discussion of it?

3. Is it easier to change an employee's attitudes or values? Explain.

4. How could a specific intention you have at this time be explained with Ajzen's model of planned behavior?

5. In your own life, how would you rank the three work attitudes—job satisfaction, organizational commitment, and job involvement—in terms of relative importance? Explain.

6. Is habitual sleep deprivation eroding your abilities? Explain. Aside from "just getting a good night's sleep," what corrective actions do you need to take?

7. Which of the seven major mental abilities in Table 6–1 are your strengths? Which need improvement? Would your mental ability profile be an asset or liability as a manager? Explain.

8. What do you think your cognitive style is, relative to Jung's typology? (Try the Personal Awareness and Growth Exercise at the end of the chapter to check.) Any surprises?

9. Do you believe that job satisfaction is partly a function of both personal traits and genetic factors? Explain.

10. Do you think job satisfaction leads directly to better job performance? Provide your rationale.

Internet Exercise

www.fortune.com

This chapter covers a lot of positive things about jobs and workplaces. Among them are loyalty, family-supportive company philosophy, job satisfaction, organizational commitment, and job involvement. So where do you find this good stuff in real life? A great place to begin looking is *Fortune* magazine's Web site. Go to **www.fortune.com** and click on "Best to Work For" under the heading "Companies." First, read the section titled "How We Pick the 100 Best." You will discover how a company's ranking on the list depends on how randomly selected employees respond to a survey about the company's culture. From the most recent annual list of 100 companies, select 10 companies (randomly or based on selection criteria of your own). Click on each one and survey the brief sketches, with the questions below in mind.

(Take some notes for later reference.) Be sure to check the voluntary turnover data and summary comments for each company.

Questions

1. What common denominators, if any, did you detect?

2. What did these companies do to build employee loyalty?

3. How did these companies enact a family-supportive philosophy?

4. How was job satisfaction increased and turnover reduced?

5. Would you like to work for any of the companies you researched? Which ones? Why?

OB in Action Case Study

A US Navy Commander Saves the Ship by Winning Hearts and Minds[105]

Commander D Michael Abrashoff, US Navy, Captain, USS Benfold:

If employee retention is a headache for business, it's a migraine for the US Navy. Forty percent of the navy's new recruits will wash out of the service before their four-year tours are up. That's not just bad for the military's effectiveness, it's expensive: it costs taxpayers about $35,000 to recruit one sailor and send him through nine weeks of boot camp. Of those who make it through their first hitch, only 30% sign on for a second term.

When I took command of the destroyer USS *Benfold* in June 1997, the navy's retention problem, which I had observed all through my 16 years in the service, became mine to endure or to solve. Although the *Benfold* is a technological wonder—for instance, its radar system can track a bird-sized object from 50 miles away—virtually all its 310 sailors were deeply demoralized. In fact, they were so unhappy with their lives on board, they literally cheered when my predecessor left the ship for the last time. Watching that scene in shock, I vowed that would never happen to me. I wanted sailors so engaged with their work, they would perform better than ever, willingly stick around for their entire tours, and possibly even respect me in the process. The only problem: I had no idea how to make that dream come true.

Over the next 21 months, I found out. Retaining people sometimes requires redeeming them—changing their lives. But first, I had to redeem myself. I had to become an entirely different type of leader. A different type of person, really. Only then was I able to redeem my sailors, one at a time. Together we learned a different way to think and act. All in all, it was an enormous undertaking; I ran the risk of never getting promoted again. But I realized that the only way to achieve my goals—combat readiness, retention, and trust—was to make my people grow. It worked. The *Benfold* has set all-time records for performance and retention, and the waiting list of officers and enlisted personnel who want to transfer to the *Benfold* is pages long. It's a long wait because very few aboard the *Benfold* want to leave. . . .

My first step, then, was rejecting the 225-year-old US Navy way of running things. That was hard, but I had a strong sense that the time had come. The command-and-control style may have worked when ships and warfare were less complex and technology-intensive. But it wasn't going to work on an 8,300-ton, 505-foot-long ship like the *Benfold*. Loaded with state-of-the-art computers and radar gear, it can detect and destroy enemy submarines, surface craft, and airplanes while at the same time launching computer-guided missiles at land-based targets. No single person could hope to manage all the information and make all the split-second decisions that those operations entail.

Besides, I had come to realize over the course of my career that no commanding officer has a monopoly on a ship's skills and brainpower. There's an astonishing amount of creativity and know-how below decks, just waiting to be unleashed. To set it loose and make it flourish, a leader should neither command nor control; he should provide vision and values and then guide, coach, and even follow his people. . . .

Shortly after I took command of the *Benfold,* I vowed to treat every encounter with every person on the ship as the most important thing in my world at that moment. It wasn't easy for me, and I didn't do it perfectly, but my crew's enthusiasm and bright ideas kept me going when I was tempted to turn back to the dark side. One day, just a few weeks into my command, I asked a seaman what he would like to change on the *Benfold*. He came back with a question of his own. "Captain," he asked, "have you ever painted your home?"

"Sure," I replied.

"It's no fun, is it?" the sailor asked.

"No, it's not," I said warily. "What's your point?"

The point, the sailor explained, was that the *Benfold*'s bolts and fittings were made of ferrous metals, which quickly oxidized and streaked the ship with rust stains that needed to be painted over every two months. Why didn't we invest in fittings made of nonferrous metals? I implemented the idea immediately. The ship now gets painted once a year instead of every other month. The money saved on paint funds a shipboard learning center, where sailors can use the time they've saved to take college-level distance learning courses. And those who think they can't change the course of their organizations might be interested to know that nonferrous bolts and fittings are now standard throughout the navy.

That idea came from one of the get-to-know-you sessions I held when I first took command. I met individually in my cabin with every sailor on the *Benfold* and asked each the same set of questions: Where are you from? Why did you join the navy? What's your family situation? Is there anything the navy can do to help your family? What do you like most about the *Benfold?* What do you like least? What would you change if you could? Is there sexual harassment on the ship? Is there racial prejudice? Getting to know my crew as individuals did more than generate innovations and process improvements. It was also an important discipline for me. Getting to know someone as an individual prevents you from zoning out when they're talking. It forces you to listen. You can't ignore or shut down people you know and respect.

Questions for Discussion

1. Did Commander Abrashoff view the *Benfold*'s crew as government property or as human capital? Explain the managerial significance of your answer.

2. What, in your view, was Abrashoff's secret to success?

3. Based on what you learned in this chapter, what are the key linkages between Abrashoff's approach and the sailors' values and attitudes, loyalty, organizational commitment, job satisfaction, turnover, and job performance? (*Hint:* It may help to draw a graphical model.)

4. Would you like to work for a boss like Abrashoff? Why or why not?

5. Do you think Abrashoff's unconventional management style will be widely imitated in the US Navy? Why or why not?

Personal Awareness and Growth Exercise

What Is Your Cognitive Style?

Objectives

1. To identify your cognitive style, according to Carl Jung's typology.[106]

2. To consider the managerial implications of your cognitive style.

Instructions

Please respond to the next 16 items. There are no right or wrong answers. After you have completed all the items, refer to the scoring key, and follow its directions.

Questionnaire

Part I. Circle the response that comes closest to how you usually feel or act.

1. Are you more careful about:
   A. People's feelings
   B. Their rights

2. Do you usually get along better with:
   A. Imaginative people
   B. Realistic people

3. Which of these two is the higher compliment:
   A. A person has real feeling
   B. A person is consistently reasonable

4. In doing something with many other people, does it appeal more to you:
   A. To do it in the accepted way
   B. To invent a way of your own

5. Do you get more annoyed at:
   A. Fancy theories
   B. People who don't like theories

6. It is higher praise to call someone:
   A. A person of vision
   B. A person of common sense

7. Do you more often let:
   A. Your heart rule your head
   B. Your head rule your heart

8. Do you think it is worse:
   A. To show too much warmth
   B. To be unsympathetic

9. If you were a teacher, would you rather teach:
   A. Courses involving theory
   B. Fact courses

Part II. Which word in each of the following pairs appeals to you more? Circle A or B.

10. A. Compassion
    B. Foresight

11. A. Justice
    B. Mercy

12. A. Production
    B. Design

13. A. Gentle
    B. Firm

14. A. Uncritical
    B. Critical

15. A. Literal
    B. Figurative

16. A. Imaginative
    B. Matter of fact

Scoring Key

To categorize your responses to the questionnaire, count one point for each response on the following four scales, and total the number of points recorded in each column. Instructions for classifying your scores are indicated below.

Sensation	Intuition	Thinking	Feeling
2B _____	2A _____	1B _____	1A _____
4A _____	4B _____	3B _____	3A _____
5A _____	5B _____	7B _____	7A _____
6B _____	6A _____	8A _____	8B _____
9B _____	9A _____	10B _____	10A _____
12A _____	12B _____	11A _____	11B _____
15A _____	15B _____	13B _____	13A _____
16B _____	16A _____	14B _____	14A _____
Totals = _____	_____	_____	_____

Classifying Total Scores

Write *intuitive* if your intuition score is equal to or greater than your sensation score.

Write *sensation* if sensation is greater than intuition.

Write *feeling* if feeling is greater than thinking.

Write *thinking* if thinking is greater than feeling.

When *thinking* equals feeling, you should write feeling if a male and thinking if a female.

Questions for Discussion

1. What is your cognitive style?

   Sensation/thinking (ST) _____

   Intuition/thinking (NT) _____

   Sensation/feeling (SF) _____

   Intuition/feeling (NF) _____

2. Do you agree with this assessment? Why or why not?

3. Will your cognitive style, as determined in this exercise, help you achieve your career goal(s)?

4. Would your style be an asset or liability for a managerial position involving getting things done through others?

Group Exercise

The Paper Airplane Contest

Objectives

1. To consider how individual abilities influence group performance.

2. To examine the role of attitudes in completing a group-based task.

3. To determine the impact of job satisfaction and job involvement on task performance.

Introduction

In this chapter, we discussed the impact of an individual's values, attitudes, and abilities on a variety of outcomes such as performance and turnover. We did not consider, however, that these same concepts apply in the context of working on a team project. The purpose of this exercise is to examine the role of abilities and attitudes when working on a team project to build a paper airplane. The quality of the team's work will be assessed by measuring three aspects of your team's airplane: (1) how far it flies, (2) how far it flies with a payload, and (3) design characteristics.[107]

Instructions

Your instructor will divide the class into groups of three to six people. Each team should pick a team name. Once formed, begin to plan what type of plane you want to design and actually construct. Keep in mind that the quality of your work will be measured through the three criteria noted above. You will be provided with one 8.5-by-11-inch sheet of blank paper and adhesive tape. Try not to make mistakes, as you will not be given more than one piece of paper. Use these materials to construct one airplane. Decorate your plane as you see fit. It is recommended that you decorate your plane before actually building it. Once all groups complete their work, a contest will be held to determine the best overall plane. There will be three rounds to complete this assessment. In the first round, each team will be asked to launch their plane and distance flown will be measured. The second round entails adding a payload—a paperclip—to your plane and then flying it once again. Distance flown will be measured. The final round entails a subjective evaluation by the entire class of the plane's design. Each team's overall performance will be assessed and posted.

Questions for Discussion

1. How did the group decide to design the plane?

2. Did the team consider each member's abilities when designing and flying the plane? Explain.

3. Were all team members equally involved in the task and equally satisfied with the team's final product? Discuss why or why not.

4. How could the team have increased its members' job involvement and task performance? Provide specific recommendations.

Ethical Dilemma

What Is the Impact of the Old College Grind on Personal Values?[108]

BusinessWeek Does an MBA change a person's values? According to a new study, the answer is yes—and perhaps not for the better. The nonprofit Aspen Institute found that students enter B-school with relatively idealistic ambitions, such as creating quality products. By the time they graduate, these goals have taken a backseat to such priorities as boosting share prices.

Sound a lot like MBAs Jeffrey Skilling (Harvard, 1979) and Andrew Fastow (Northwestern, 1987) at Enron? Indeed. The study included 1,978 MBAs who graduated in 2001 from 13 leading B-schools. It asked what a company's priorities should be: 75% said maximizing shareholder value; 71% chose satisfying customers; 33% said producing high-quality goods and services. Only 5% thought environmentalism should be a top goal; just 25% said creating value for their communities.

But two years earlier, when the students started B-school, 68% cited shareholder value; 75%, customer satisfaction; and 43%, quality goods and services.

MBAs also said they would leave companies whose values they can't stomach rather than stay and try to change them. "The Enron fiasco is showing that there are going to be serious cases where an organization's values are disputed, or disregarded," says Jennifer Welsh, Oxford University lecturer and manager of the research project. "We want them to stick up for their values and try to resolve the conflict."

One sure way to get MBAs keen on ethics: Put a number on how much good values add to earnings. Priscilla Wisner, a professor at Thunderbird who links corporate responsibility to profitability, says until that happens, B-schools are unlikely to go beyond the stray ethics course. That means the philosophy MBAs live by is less likely to be "Doing well by doing good" than "Show me the money."

Are your values for sale?

1. Yes, show me the money! What are the broader implications of this approach?

2. No, I have been true to my values through college and will continue to be. Explain.

3. No, I think it's possible to be true to your values and still make a good living. Explain.

4. Maybe, it depends on the situation. Explain.

5. I'm not sure, because I'm not as idealistic as I was when I started college. Explain.

6. Invent other options. Discuss.

For an interpretation of this situation, visit our Web site, **www.mhhe.com/kreitner.**

Chapter Seven

Social Perception and Attributions

Learning Objectives

When you finish studying the material in this chapter, you should be able to:

1 Describe perception in terms of the information-processing model.

2 Identify and briefly explain four managerial implications of social perception.

3 Discuss stereotypes and the process of stereotype formation.

4 Summarize the managerial challenges and recommendations of sex-role, age, race, and disability stereotypes.

5 Discuss how the self-fulfilling prophecy is created and how it can be used to improve individual and group productivity.

6 Explain, according to Kelley's model, how external and internal causal attributions are formulated.

7 Review Weiner's model of attribution.

8 Contrast the fundamental attribution bias and the self-serving bias.

Last month, security officials at FedEx Corp.'s sorting center at Newark Airport became alarmed when they heard the eerie details of a rumor making its way through the plant: A contract mechanic named Osama Sweilan had been periodically disappearing into the company's flight-simulator room. The security men quickly set up an interrogation at an off-site warehouse, where the Egyptian-born 35-year-old says he nervously explained how he sometimes slipped into the room to make sure a pipe he'd fixed wasn't leaking. He also made a few quick calls to his wife. Occasionally, he told them, he even prayed. They pressed him further, he claims, asking about his beliefs regarding politics and Osama bin Laden. Afterward, they confiscated his ID and told his outsourcing firm that he was no longer wanted in his 16-month-old job.

Name Game?

Even staunch civil libertarians concede they can see why FedEx, which says it can't comment on the situation, was initially concerned. What they have a problem with is the alleged discrimination and subsequent dismissal that Sweilan says was the result of profiling a Muslim who happens to have the same first name as the most wanted man in the world.

Aijaz Ghani, manager of a Pakistani restaurant holds up a sign denouncing hate crimes.
AP/Wide World Photos

Sweilan is one of a growing number of Arab Americans who allege they are victims of a new, post–September 11 wave of workplace discrimination, one they claim is legitimizing privacy violations and unfair firings under the rubric of corporate security. Some say they have lost their jobs after being questioned—and cleared—by the FBI, while others complain of being turned away by recruiters or informed that they can no longer count on their companies' support in getting H1B visas.

This heightened wariness of anyone who is or appears to be from the Arab world is yet another new feature of the post-attack workplace. Arab American advocacy groups report as many as 1,000 complaints of September 11–related discrimination and harassment, with the most recent batch of which originated on the job. "We have people being targeted at work who have lived in this country for 25 years with no record of any violation," says Imad Hamad, the Detroit-based regional director of the American-Arab Anti-Discrimination Committee. The Equal Employment Opportunity Commission is investigating 100 such cases and has created a special category for the claims and a new task force. "We're beginning to see a backlash," says EEOC chair Cari M. Dominguez.[1]

For Discussion
How are negative stereotypes affecting the lives of Arab Americans?

Perception, stereotypes, and attributions, three topics discussed in this chapter, play a central role in the opening vignette. Osama Sweilan probably was interrogated because of perceptions associated with his behavior of disappearing into the company's flight-simulator room and he is from Egyptian descent. Perceptions and interpretations of Sweilan's behavior clearly influenced the manner in which he was treated at FedEx. Although FedEx's actions can be questioned, the underlying interpretive process that influenced Sweilan's treatment is not surprising. As human beings, we constantly strive to make sense of our surroundings. The resulting knowledge influences our behavior and helps us navigate our way through life. Think of the perceptual process that occurs when meeting someone for the first time. Your attention is drawn to the individual's physical appearance, mannerisms, actions, and reactions to what you say and do. You ultimately arrive at conclusions based on your perceptions of this social interaction. The brown-haired, green-eyed individual turns out to be friendly and fond of outdoor activities. You further conclude that you like this person and then ask him or her to go to a concert, calling the person by the name you stored in memory.

This reciprocal process of perception, interpretation, and behavioral response also applies at work. A field study illustrates this relationship. Researchers wanted to know whether employees' perceptions of how much an organization valued them affected their behavior and attitudes. The researchers asked samples of high school teachers, brokerage-firm clerks, manufacturing workers, insurance representatives, and police officers to indicate their perception of the extent to which their organization valued their contributions and their well-being. Employees who perceived that their organization cared about them reciprocated with reduced absenteeism, increased performance, innovation, and positive work attitudes.[2] This study illustrates the importance of employees' perceptions. Employees are more committed to an organization and work harder in support of its goals when they perceive the organization cares about them.[3] Let us now begin our exploration of the perceptual process and its associated outcomes.

In this chapter we focus on (1) an information processing model of perception, (2) stereotypes, (3) the self-fulfilling prophecy, and (4) how causal attributions are used to interpret behavior.

An Information-Processing Model of Perception

Perception is a cognitive process that enables us to interpret and understand our surroundings. Recognition of objects is one of this process's major functions. For example, both people and animals recognize familiar objects in their environments. You would recognize a picture of your best friend; dogs and cats can recognize their food dishes or a favorite toy. Reading involves recognition of visual patterns representing letters in the alphabet. People must recognize objects to meaningfully interact with their environment. But since OB's principal focus is on people, the following discussion emphasizes *social* perception rather than object perception.

The study of how people perceive one another has been labeled *social cognition* and *social information processing.* In contrast to the perception of objects,

> Social cognition is the study of how people make sense of other people and themselves. It focuses on how ordinary people think about people and how they think they think about people....
>
> Research on social cognition also goes beyond naive psychology. The study of social cognition entails a fine-grained analysis of how people think about themselves and others, and it leans heavily on the theory and methods of cognitive psychology.[4]

Let us now examine the fundamental processes underlying perception.

> **Perception**
> Process of interpreting one's environment.

Four-Stage Sequence and a Working Example

Perception involves a four-stage information processing sequence (hence, the label "information processing"). Figure 7–1 illustrates a basic information-processing model of perception. Three of the stages in this model—selective attention/comprehension, encoding and simplification, and storage and retention—describe how specific information and environmental stimuli are observed and stored in memory. The fourth and final stage, retrieval and response, involves turning mental representations into real-world judgments and decisions.

Figure 7–1   *Perception: An Information-Processing Model*

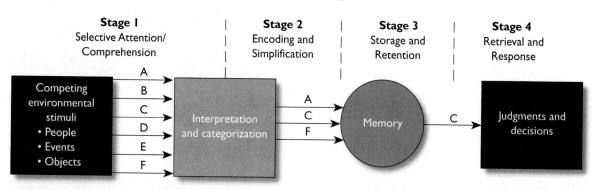

Keep the following everyday example in mind as we look at the four stages of perception. Suppose you were thinking of taking a course in, say, personal finance. Three professors teach the same course, using different types of instruction and testing procedures. Through personal experience, you have come to prefer good professors who rely on the case method of instruction and essay tests. According to the information-processing model of perception, you would likely arrive at a decision regarding which professor to take as follows:

Stage 1: Selective Attention/Comprehension

People are constantly bombarded by physical and social stimuli in the environment. Since they do not have the mental capacity to fully comprehend all this information, they selectively perceive subsets of environmental stimuli. This is where attention plays a role. **Attention** is the process of becoming consciously aware of something or someone. Attention can be focused on information either from the environment or from memory. Regarding the latter situation, if you sometimes find yourself thinking about totally unrelated events or people while reading a textbook, your memory is the focus of your attention. Research has shown that people tend to pay attention to salient stimuli.

Attention

Being consciously aware of something or someone.

Salient Stimuli   Something is *salient* when it stands out from its context. For example, a 250-pound man would certainly be salient in a women's aerobics class but not at a meeting of the National Football League Players' Association. Salience is determined by several factors, including

- Being novel (the only person in a group of that race, gender, hair color, or age).
- Being bright (wearing a yellow shirt).
- Being unusual for that person (behaving in an unexpected way, such as a person with a fear of heights climbing a steep mountain).
- Being unusual for a person's social category (such as a company president driving a motorcycle to work).
- Being unusual for people in general (driving 20 miles per hour in a 55-mph speed zone).

During the 2002 Winter Olympics in Salt Lake City, Canadian figure skaters Jamie Sale and David Pelletier were awarded a second gold medal after days of controversy over the couples' original silver medal win. This was a highly salient event during the 2002 Olympics.

AP/Wide World Photos

- Being extremely positive (a noted celebrity) or negative (the victim of a bad traffic accident).
- Being dominant in the visual field (sitting at the head of the table).[5]

One's needs and goals often dictate which stimuli are salient. For a driver whose gas gauge is on empty, an Exxon or Mobil sign is more salient than a McDonald's or Burger King sign. The reverse would be true for a hungry driver with a full gas tank. Moreover, research shows that people have a tendency to pay more attention to negative than positive information. This leads to a negativity bias.[6] This bias helps explain the gawking factor that slows traffic to a crawl following a car accident.

Back to Our Example   You begin your search for the "right" personal finance professor by asking friends who have taken classes from the three professors. You also may interview the various professors who teach the class to gather still more relevant information. Returning to Figure 7–1, all the information you obtain represents competing environmental stimuli labeled A through F. Because you are concerned about the method of instruction (e.g., line A in Figure 7–1), testing procedures (e.g., line C), and past grade distributions (e.g., line F), information in those areas is particularly salient to you. Figure 7–1 shows that these three salient pieces of information thus are perceived, and you then progress to the second stage of information processing. Meanwhile, competing stimuli represented by lines B, D, and E in Figure 7–1 fail to get your attention and are discarded from further consideration.

Stage 2: Encoding and Simplification

Observed information is not stored in memory in its original form. Encoding is required; raw information is interpreted or translated into mental representations. To accomplish this, perceivers assign pieces of information to **cognitive categories.** "By *category* we mean a number of objects that are considered equivalent. Categories are generally designated by names, e.g., *dog, animal.*"[7] People, events, and objects are interpreted and evaluated by comparing their characteristics with information contained in schemata (or schema in singular form).

Schemata   A **schema** represents a person's mental picture or summary of a particular event or type of stimulus. For example, what is your mental picture of the sequence of events that occur when you go out to dinner in a restaurant? Your memory probably is quite similar to the restaurant schema shown in Table 7–1.

Cognitive-category labels are needed to make schemata meaningful. The OB Exercise on page 229 illustrates this by having you rate the comprehensiveness of a schema both without and with its associated category label.[8] Take a moment now to complete this exercise.

Encoding Outcomes   We use the encoding process to interpret and evaluate our environment. Interestingly, this process can result in differing interpretations and evaluations of the same person or event. The International OB on page 230, for example, illustrates how residents of Aniane, France, perceived Robert Mondavi Corp.'s desire to start a winery very differently from the company's intentions. Mondavi ultimately canceled its vineyard project due to the negative perceptions. Varying interpretations of what we observe occur due to four key reasons.

Cognitive categories
Mental depositories for storing information.

Schema
Mental picture of an event or object.

Table 7–1 *Restaurant Schema*

Schema: Restaurant.
Characters: Customers, hostess, waiter, chef, cashier.
Scene 1: Entering.
    Customer goes into restaurant.
    Customer finds a place to sit.
      He may find it himself.
      He may be seated by a hostess.
        He asks the hostess for a table.
        She gives him permission to go to the table.
Scene 2: Ordering.
    Customer receives a menu.
    Customer reads it.
    Customer decides what to order.
    Waiter takes the order.
      Waiter sees the customer.
      Waiter goes to the customer.
      Customer orders what he wants.
    Chef cooks the meal.
Scene 3: Eating.
    After some time the waiter brings the meal from the chef.
    Customer eats the meal.
Scene 4: Exiting.
    Customer asks the waiter for the check.
    Waiter gives the check to the customer.
    Customer leaves a tip.
      The size of the tip depends on the goodness of the service.
    Customer pays the cashier.
    Customer leaves the restaurant.

SOURCE: From D Rumelhart, *Introduction to Human Information Processing* (New York: John Wiley & Sons, Inc., 1977. Reprinted by permission of John Wiley & Sons, Inc.)

First, people possess different information in the schemata used for interpretation. For instance, a recent meta-analysis of 62 studies revealed women and men had different opinions about what type of behaviors constituted sexual harassment. Women defined a broader range of behaviors as harassing.[9] Second, our moods and emotions influence our focus of attention and evaluations of others.[10] Third, people tend to apply recently used cognitive categories during encoding. For example, you are more likely to interpret a neutral behavior exhibited by a professor as positive if you were recently thinking about positive categories and events.[11] Fourth, individual differences influence encoding. Pessimistic or depressed individuals, for instance, tend to interpret their surroundings more negatively than optimistic and happy people.[12] The point is that we should not be surprised when people interpret and evaluate the same situation or event differently. Researchers are currently trying to identify the host of factors that influence the encoding process.

Back to Our Example   Having collected relevant information about the three personal finance professors and their approaches, you compare this information with

OB Exercise   Does a Schema Improve the Comprehension of Written Material?

Instructions

The purpose of this exercise is to demonstrate the role of schema in encoding. First read the passage shown below. Once done, rate the comprehensiveness of what you read using the scale provided. Next, examine the schema label presented in note 8 in the Endnotes section at the end of the book. With this label in mind, reread the passage, and rate its comprehensiveness. Now think about the explanation for why your ratings changed. You just experienced the impact of schema in encoding.

Read This Passage

The procedure is actually quite simple. First you arrange things into different groups. Of course, one pile may be sufficient depending on how much there is to do. If you have to go somewhere else due to lack of facilities, that is the next step; otherwise you are pretty well set. It is important not to overdo things. That is, it is better to do too few things at once than too many. In the short run this may not seem important, but complications can easily arise. A mistake can be expensive as well. At first the whole procedure will seem complicated. Soon, however, it will become just another facet of life. It is difficult to foresee any end to the necessity for this task in the immediate future, but then you never can tell. After the procedure is completed, you arrange the materials into different groups again. Then they can be put into their appropriate places. Eventually they will be used once more, and the whole cycle will then have to be repeated. However, that is part of life.

Comprehensive Scale

Very Uncomprehensive		Neither		Very Comprehensive
	1——2——3——4——5			

SOURCE: J D Bransford and M K Johnson, "Contextual Prerequisite for Understanding: Some Investigations of Comprehension and Recall," *Journal of Verbal Learning and Verbal Behavior*, December 1972, p. 722. Copyright © 1972 by Academic Press. Reproduced by permission of the publisher.

other details contained in schemata. This leads you to form an impression and evaluation of what it would be like to take a course from each professor. In turn, the relevant information contained on paths A, C, and F in Figure 7–1 are passed along to the third stage of information processing.

Stage 3: Storage and Retention

This phase involves storage of information in long-term memory. Long-term memory is like an apartment complex consisting of separate units connected to one another. Although different people live in each apartment, they sometimes interact. In addition, large apartment complexes have different wings (such as A, B, and C). Long-term memory similarly consists of separate but related categories. Like the individual apartments inhabited by unique residents, the connected categories contain different types of information. Information also passes among these categories. Finally, long-term memory is made up of three compartments (or wings) containing categories of information about events, semantic materials, and people.[13]

Residents of Aniane, France, Perceive Robert Mondavi Corp. in a Negative Light

BusinessWeek David Pearson loves wine and France. The San Diego native studied oenology [the science or study of wines and winemaking] at the University of California and spent a year after graduation working as an intern on French wine estates. So when Robert Mondavi Corp. asked him in 1998 to head up its Vichon Mediterranean subsidiary, the fresh-faced, French-speaking 39-year-old Pearson crossed the Atlantic and settled in Southern France. . . . Pearson spent his first two years conducting geological surveys to locate top-quality wine real estate. He needed a large tract to produce 260,000 bottles a year, the minimum number that made economic sense for a giant such as Mondavi. He finally settled on a swath of hillside above the 2,000-person village of Aniane, about 15 miles northwest of the regional center of Montpellier. . . . A violent backlash ensued. Hunters worried that planting vineyards would frighten away wild boar. Environmentalists railed against razing a forest. Pearson sipped pastis with the locals, reassuring them that the company intended to plant small "islands" of vines and leave much of the natural scrubland untouched. Hunters, he promised, still could roam the hillside during autumn. But the American couldn't shake off one far-reaching charge—that the invading Anglo-Saxons would destroy the village's social cohesion and deform traditional winemaking methods, imposing an alien, money-grubbing industrial model.

SOURCE: Excerpted from W Echikson, "How Mondavi's French Venture Went Sour," *BusinessWeek*, September 3, 2001, p. 60.

Event Memory This compartment is composed of categories containing information about both specific and general events. These memories describe appropriate sequences of events in well-known situations, such as going to a restaurant (refer back to Table 7–1), going on a job interview, going to a food store, or going to a movie.

Semantic Memory Semantic memory refers to general knowledge about the world. In so doing, it functions as a mental dictionary of concepts. Each concept contains a definition (e.g., a good leader) and associated traits (outgoing), emotional states (happy), physical characteristics (tall), and behaviors (works hard). Just as there are schemata for general events, concepts in semantic memory are stored as schemata. Given our previous discussion of managing diversity in Chapter 2 and International OB in Chapter 4, it should come as no surprise that there are cultural differences in the type of information stored in semantic memory.

Person Memory Categories within this compartment contain information about a single individual (your supervisor) or groups of people (managers).

Back to Our Example As the time draws near for you to decide which personal finance professor to take, your schemata of them are stored in the three categories of long-term memory. These schemata are available for immediate comparison or retrieval.

Stage 4: Retrieval and Response

People retrieve information from memory when they make judgments and decisions. Our ultimate judgments and decisions are either based on the process of drawing on, interpreting, and integrating categorical information stored in long-term memory or on retrieving a summary judgment that was already made.

Concluding our example, it is registration day and you have to choose which professor to take for personal finance. After retrieving from memory your schemata-based impressions of the three professors, you select a good one who uses the case method and gives essay tests (line C in Figure 7–1). In contrast, you may choose your preferred professor by simply recalling the decision you made two weeks ago.

Managerial Implications

Social cognition is the window through which we all observe, interpret, and prepare our responses to people and events. A wide variety of managerial activities, organizational processes, and quality-of-life issues are thus affected by perception. Consider, for example, the following implications.

Hiring   Interviewers make hiring decisions based on their impression of how an applicant fits the perceived requirements of a job. Inaccurate impressions in either direction produce poor hiring decisions. Moreover, interviewers with racist or sexist schemata can undermine the accuracy and legality of hiring decisions. Those invalid schemata need to be confronted and improved through coaching and training. Failure to do so can lead to poor hiring decisions. For example, a study of 46 male and 66 female financial-institution managers revealed that their hiring decisions were biased by the physical attractiveness of applicants. More attractive men and women were hired over less attractive applicants with equal qualifications.[14] On the positive side, however, another study demonstrated that interviewer training can reduce the use of invalid schema. Training improved interviewers' ability to obtain high-quality, job-related information and to stay focused on the interview task. Trained interviewers provided more balanced judgments about applicants than did nontrained interviewers.[15]

Performance Appraisal   Faulty schemata about what constitutes good versus poor performance can lead to inaccurate performance appraisals, which erode work motivation, commitment, and loyalty. For example, a study of 166 production employees indicated that they had greater trust in management when they perceived that the performance appraisal process provided accurate evaluations of their performance.[16] Therefore, it is important for managers to accurately identify the behavioral characteristics and results indicative of good performance at the beginning of a performance review cycle. These characteristics then can serve as the standards for evaluating employee performance. The importance of using objective rather than subjective measures of employee performance was highlighted in a meta-analysis involving 50 studies and 8,341 individuals. Results revealed that objective and subjective measures of employee performance were only moderately related. The researchers concluded that objective and subjective measures of performance are not interchangeable.[17] Managers are thus advised to use more objectively based measures of performance as much as possible because subjective indicators are prone to bias and inaccuracy. In those cases where the job does not possess objective measures of performance, however, managers should still use subjective evaluations. Furthermore, because memory for specific instances of employee performance deteriorates over time, managers need a mechanism for accurately recalling employee behavior.[18] Research reveals that individuals can be trained to be more accurate raters of performance.[19]

Leadership   Research demonstrates that employees' evaluations of leader effectiveness are influenced strongly by their schemata of good and poor leaders. A leader will have a difficult time influencing employees when he or she exhibits behaviors contained in employees' schemata of poor leaders. A team of researchers investigated the behaviors contained in our schemata of good and poor leaders. Good leaders were perceived as exhibiting the following behaviors: (1) assigning specific tasks to group members, (2) telling others that they had done well, (3) setting specific goals for the group, (4) letting other group members make decisions, (5) trying to get the group to work as a team, and (6) maintaining definite standards of performance. In contrast, poor leaders were perceived to exhibit these behaviors: (1) telling others that they had performed poorly, (2) insisting on having their own way, (3) doing things without explaining themselves, (4) expressing worry over the group members' suggestions, (5) frequently changing plans, and (6) letting the details of the task become overwhelming.[20]

Communication Managers need to remember that social perception is a screening process that can distort communication, both coming and going. Messages are interpreted and categorized according to schemata developed through past experiences and influenced by one's age, gender, and ethnic, geographic, and cultural orientations.

Consider how investors of Conseco, a Carmel, Indiana, insurer, perceived and responded to the announcement that Charles Chokel, the company's chief financial officer, had left the company "to pursue other interests."

> That explanation stirred concern among shareholders already worried about Conseco's financial performance and its ability to meet its 2002 debt obligations. Some speculated that Mr Chokel had no confidence in Conseco's financial strategy, and had therefore left in the middle of the company's audit. Investors began dumping the stock. By the end of the day, the company's shares had fallen 15% in trading.
>
> The next day, Conseco CEO Gary Wendt announced in a memo to investors that the 48-year-old Mr Chokel didn't resign but was fired. "I let him go because I did not believe he was up to the job," Mr Wendt wrote in his memo....
>
> Adds Mark Lubbers, executive vice president of corporate affairs: "It wasn't legal issues that caused us to announce Chuck's departure the way we did. Gary liked Chuck and he didn't want to embarrass him."[21]

Wendt clearly underestimated the investors' perceptions and response to Conseco's announcement of Chokel's departure. That said, however, Wendt quickly noticed the drop in stock price and took corrective action by writing a second memo to investors. Effective communicators try to tailor their messages to the receiver's perceptual schemata. This requires well-developed listening and observations skills and cross-cultural sensitivity.

∫tereotypes: Perceptions about Groups of People

While it is often true that beauty is in the eye of the beholder, perception does result in some predictable outcomes. Managers aware of the perception process and its outcomes enjoy a competitive edge. The Walt Disney Company, for instance, takes full advantage of perceptual tendencies to influence customers' reactions to waiting in long lines at its theme parks:

> In Orlando, at Disney-MGM Studios, visitors waiting to get into a Muppet attraction watch tapes of Kermit the Frog on TV monitors. At the Magic Kingdom, visitors to the ExtraTer-

Table 7–2   *Commonly Found Perceptual Errors*

Perceptual Error	Description	Example
Halo	A rater forms an overall impression about an object and then uses that impression to bias ratings about the object.	Rating a professor high on the teaching dimensions of ability to motivate students, knowledge, and communication because we like him or her.
Leniency	A personal characteristic that leads an individual to consistently evaluate other people or objects in an extremely positive fashion.	Rating a professor high on all dimensions of performance regardless of his or her actual performance. The rater that hates to say negative things about others.
Central tendency	The tendency to avoid all extreme judgments and rate people and objects as average or neutral.	Rating a professor average on all dimensions of performance regardless of his or her actual performance.
Recency effects	The tendency to remember recent information. If the recent information is negative, the person or object is evaluated negatively.	Although a professor has given good lectures for 12 to 15 weeks, he or she is evaluated negatively because lectures over the last 3 weeks were done poorly.
Contrast effects	The tendency to evaluate people or objects by comparing them with characteristics of recently observed people or objects.	Rating a good professor as average because you compared his or her performance with three of the best professors you have ever had in college. You are currently taking courses from the three excellent professors.

restrial Alien Encounter attraction are entertained by a talking robot before the show. At some rides, the company uses simple toys, like blocks, to help parents keep small children busy and happy during the wait.[22]

This example illustrates how the focus of one's attention influences the perception of standing in long lines.

Likewise, managers can use knowledge of perceptual outcomes to help them interact more effectively with employees. For example, Table 7–2 describes five common perceptual errors. Since these perceptual errors often distort the evaluation of job applicants and of employee performance, managers need to guard against them. This section examines one of the most important and potentially harmful perceptual outcomes associated with person perception: stereotypes. After exploring the process of stereotype formation and maintenance, we discuss sex-role stereotypes, age stereotypes, race stereotypes, disability stereotypes, and the managerial challenge to avoid stereotypical biases.

Stereotype Formation and Maintenance

"A **stereotype** is an individual's set of beliefs about the characteristics or attributes of a group."[23] Stereotypes are not always negative. For example, the belief that engineers are good at math is certainly part of a stereotype. Stereotypes may or may not be accurate. Engineers may in fact be better at math than the general population. In general, stereotypic characteristics are used to differentiate a particular group of people from other groups.[24]

Stereotype
Beliefs about the characteristics of a group.

Unfortunately, stereotypes can lead to poor decisions, can create barriers for women, older individuals, people of color, and people with disabilities, and can undermine loyalty and job satisfaction. For example, a recent study of 44 African-American managers and 80 white managers revealed that African-American managers experienced slower rates of promotion and less psychological support than white managers.[25] Another sample of 69 female executives and 69 male executives indicated women reported greater promotional barriers and fewer overseas assignments, and had more assignments with no authority than men.[26]

Stereotyping is a four-step process. It begins by categorizing people into groups according to various criteria, such as gender, age, race, and occupation. Next, we infer that all people within a particular category possess the same traits or characteristics (e.g., all women are nurturing, older people have more job-related accidents, all African-Americans are good athletes, all professors are absentminded). Then, we form expectations of others and interpret their behavior according to our stereotypes. Finally, stereotypes are maintained by (1) overestimating the frequency of stereotypic behaviors exhibited by others, (2) incorrectly explaining expected and unexpected behaviors, and (3) differentiating minority individuals from oneself.[27] Although these steps are self-reinforcing, there are ways to break the chain of stereotyping.

Research shows that the use of stereotypes is influenced by the amount and type of information available to an individual and his or her motivation to accurately process information.[28] People are less apt to use stereotypes to judge others when they encounter salient information that is highly inconsistent with a stereotype. For instance, you are unlikely to assign stereotypic "professor" traits to a new professor you have this semester if he or she rides a Harley-Davidson, wears leather pants to class, and has a pierced nose. People also are less likely to rely on stereotypes when they are motivated to avoid using them. That is, accurate information processing requires mental effort. Stereotyping is generally viewed as a less effortful strategy of information processing. Let us now take a look at different types of stereotypes and consider additional methods for reducing their biasing effects.

Sex-Role Stereotypes

/ex-role stereotype
Beliefs about appropriate roles for men and women.

A **sex-role stereotype** is the belief that differing traits and abilities make men and women particularly well suited to different roles. A recent Gallup poll sheds light on the sex-role stereotypes held by adults within the United States. Results revealed the majority of respondents viewed women as more emotional, affectionate, talkative, patient, and creative than men.[29] Men, on the other hand, were perceived as more aggressive, courageous, easygoing, and ambitious than women.[30] Although research demonstrates that men and women do not systematically differ in the manner suggested by traditional stereotypes,[31] these stereotypes still persist. A study compared sex-role stereotypes held by men and women from five countries: China, Japan, Germany, the United Kingdom, and the United States. Males in all five countries perceived that successful managers possessed characteristics and traits more commonly ascribed to men in general than to women in general. Among the females, the same pattern of managerial sex typing was found in all countries except the United States. US females perceived that males and females were equally likely to possess traits necessary for managerial success.[32] The key question now becomes whether these stereotypes influence the hiring, evaluation, and promotion of people at work.

A meta-analysis of 19 studies comprising 1,842 individuals found no significant relationships between applicant gender and hiring recommendations.[33] A second meta-analysis of 24 experimental studies revealed that men and women received similar performance ratings for the same level of task performance. Stated differently, there was no pro-male bias. These experimental results were further supported in a field study of female and male professors.[34] Unfortunately, results pertaining to promotion decisions are not as promising. A field study of 682 employees in a multinational *Fortune* 500 company revealed that gender was significantly related to promotion potential ratings. Men received more favorable evaluations than women in spite of controlling for age, education, organizational tenure, salary grade, and type of job.[35] Another study of 100 male and female US Army commissioned officers at the rank of captain unfortunately produced similar results. Men were consistently judged to be better leaders than women.[36] The existence of sex-role stereotypes may partially explain this finding.

Age Stereotypes

Age stereotypes reinforce age discrimination because of their negative orientation. For example, long-standing age stereotypes depict older workers as less satisfied, not as involved with their work, less motivated, not as committed, less productive than their younger co-workers, and more apt to be absent from work. Older employees are also perceived as being more accident prone. As with sex-role stereotypes, these age stereotypes are based more on fiction than fact.

OB researcher Susan Rhodes sought to determine whether age stereotypes were supported by data from 185 different studies. She discovered that as age increases so do employees' job satisfaction, job involvement, internal work motivation, and organizational commitment. Moreover, older workers were not more accident prone.[37] Consistent results also were found in a more recent study conducted by the National Council on Aging. A survey of 240 employers from 27 states indicated that respondents viewed older workers as thorough and reliable in their work, flexible and willing to change, and interested in learning new tasks.[38]

Results are not as clear-cut regarding job performance. A meta-analysis of 96 studies representing 38,983 people and a cross section of jobs revealed that age and job performance were unrelated.[39] Some OB researchers, however, believe that this finding does not reflect the true relationship between age and performance. They propose that the relationship between age and performance changes as people grow older.[40] This idea was tested on data obtained from 24,219 individuals. In support of this hypothesis, results revealed that age was positively related to performance for younger employees (25 to 30 years of age) and then plateaued: Older employees were not less productive. Age and experience also predicted performance better for more complex jobs than other jobs, and job experience had a stronger relationship with performance than age.[41] Another study examined memory, reasoning, spatial relations, and dual tasking for 1,000 doctors, ages 25 to 92, and 600 other adults. The researchers concluded "that a large proportion of older individuals scored as well or better on aptitude tests as those in the prime of life. We call these intellectually vigorous individuals 'optimal agers' "[42] Robbie Eisenberg is a good example. He worked for Zabin Industries when he was 102.

Like most people, Eisenberg tried retirement. Didn't like it. . . . Eisenberg was bored, and when he received a call to go back to work at Zabin as a consultant in 1979, he jumped at it.

Zabin Industries manufactures and distributes zippers and notions for the garment industry, a field often thought of as a game for the young. It is a fast-paced business where the demands and products change seasonally. It might be tempting to think that Eisenberg, who was a co-founder of the business in 1954, was brought back as a figurehead, but he's not about to be put on a pedestal. Alan Failoa, president of Zabin, says, "He wants to be

At Vita Needle Company in Needham, Massachusetts, the workers' average age is 73. The workers manufacture veterinary, human, and industrial needles. Knowing the average age of the employees, what was your initial reaction to what the employees manufacture? What age stereotypes might exist for the workers at Vita Needle Co.?

AP/ Wide World Photos

treated as a friend, not an icon. If you don't let him be involved, it doesn't make much difference. He'll get involved."[43]

What about turnover and absenteeism? A meta-analysis containing 45 samples and a total of 21,656 individuals revealed that age and turnover were negatively related.[44] That is older employees quit less often than did younger employees. Similarly, another meta-analysis of 34 studies encompassing 7,772 workers indicated that age was inversely related to both voluntary (a day at the beach) and involuntary (sick day) absenteeism.[45] Contrary to stereotypes, older workers are ready and able to meet their job requirements. Moreover, results from the two meta-analyses suggest managers should focus more attention on the turnover and absenteeism among younger workers than among older workers.

Race Stereotypes

There are many different racial stereotypes that exist. For instance, African-Americans have been viewed as athletic and aggressive; Asians as quiet, introverted, smarter, and more quantitatively oriented; and Hispanics as family oriented and religious.[46]

Unfortunately, negative stereotypes such as some of those just listed are still apparent in many organizations. Consider the evidence presented in the following paragraphs.

There is not a large percentage of African-American, Hispanic, and Asian managers in the United States. African-Americans and Hispanics held 11.3% and 10.9%, respectively, of all managerial and professional jobs in 2001.[47] Furthermore, a study examined the relationship of race to employee attitudes across 814 African-American managers and 814 white managers. Results demonstrated that African-Americans, when compared with whites, felt less accepted by peers, perceived lower managerial discretion on their jobs, reached career plateaus more frequently, noted lower levels of career satisfaction, and received lower performance ratings.[48] Negative findings such as these prompted researchers to investigate if race stereotypes actually bias hiring decisions, performance ratings, and promotion decisions.

A meta-analysis of interview decisions from 31 studies with total samples of 4,169 African-Americans and 6,307 whites revealed that whites received higher interviewer evaluations. Another study of 2,805 interviews uncovered a same-race bias for Hispanics and African-Americans, but not for whites. That is, Hispanics and African-American interviewers evaluated applicants of their own race more favorably than applicants of other races. White interviewers did not exhibit any such bias.[49] Performance ratings were found to be unbiased in two studies that used large samples of 21,547 and 39,537 rater-ratee pairs of African-American and white employees, respectively, from throughout the United States. These findings revealed that African-American and white managers did not differentially evaluate their employees based on race.[50] Finally, a study of 153 police officers' promotion decisions by panel interviews indicated a same-race rating effect. That is, candidates received higher evaluations when they were racially similar to the interviewers.[51] Given the increasing number of people of color that will enter the workforce over the next 10 years (recall our discussion in Chapter 2), employers should focus on nurturing and developing women and people of color as well as increasing managers' sensitivities to invalid racial stereotypes.

Disability Stereotypes

People with disabilities not only face negative stereotypes that affect their employability, but they also can be stigmatized by the general population. Consider Paul Stephen Miller's experience after he graduated from Harvard Law School near the top of his class:

> He looked forward to a future full of possibilities, having graduated from arguably the top law school in the country, a virtual guarantee of a high-paying job in an elite law firm. While his classmates snared those prestigious jobs, over 40 firms with whom he interviewed rejected him. Miller is a dwarf. He prefers to call himself "short stature." Most employers simply explained that there were other "more qualified" candidates. A Philadelphia firm explained, however, that while impressed with his credentials, they feared their clients might see Miller in the hallway and "think we were running some sort of circus freak show."[52]

Unfortunately, Miller's experience is not atypical. Although two out of three individuals with disabilities can and want to work, roughly 75% are unemployed.[53] In addition, disabled employees make less money on average than people without disabilities. People with disabilities are more likely to live in poverty than people without disabilities.[54] Moreover, people with disabilities face stereotypes that depict them as more likely to miss work, less capable, needy or helpless, bitter, and antisocial.[55] So what do you know about the performance and costs of employing people with disabilities?

Unfortunately, there have not been any rigorous scientific studies comparing the performance of disabled and able-bodied employees performing the same job. There are, however, other data suggesting that disabled employees are highly effective at work. A Harris poll found that almost 90% of disabled workers received "good" or "excellent" performance ratings. They also were found to perform their jobs just as well as employees without disabilities, and they were not more difficult to manage. Another Harris poll indicated that employers supported policies to increase the employment of disabled people because they were so pleased with the performance of their disabled employees. DuPont, for example, found that disabled employees had higher safety ratings than their nondisabled counterparts. The stereotypes about disabled employees being expensive to accommodate also is untrue. Nearly 20% of accommodations cost nothing, and 50% cost less than $500.[56]

Managerial Challenges and Recommendations

The key managerial challenge is to make decisions that are blind to gender, age, race, and disabilities. To do so, organizations first need to educate themselves about the problem of stereotyping through employee training. Training also can be used to equip managers with the skills needed to handle unique situations associated with managing employees with mental disabilities. The next step entails engaging in a broad effort to reduce stereotypes throughout the organization. Social scientists believe that "quality" interpersonal contact among mixed groups is the best way to reduce stereotypes because it provides people with more accurate data about the characteristics of other groups of people. As such, organizations should create opportunities for diverse employees to meet and work together in cooperative groups of equal status.

Another recommendation is for managers to identify valid individual differences (discussed in Chapter 5) that differentiate between successful and unsuccessful performers. As previously discussed, for instance, research reveals experience is a better predictor of performance than age. Research also shows that managers can be trained to use these valid criteria when hiring applicants and evaluating employee performance.[57]

Removing promotional barriers for men and women, people of color, and for persons with disabilities is another viable solution to alleviating the stereotyping problem. This can be accomplished by minimizing the differences in job experience across groups of people. Similar experience, coupled with the accurate evaluation of performance, helps managers to make decisions that are blind to gender, age, race, and disability.

There are several recommendations that can be pursued based on the documented relationship between age and performance:

1. Because performance plateaus with age for noncomplex jobs, organizations may use the variety of job design techniques discussed in Chapter 8 to increase employees' intrinsic motivation.

2. Organizations may need to consider using incentives to motivate employees to upgrade their skills and abilities. This will help avoid unnecessary plateaus.

3. It may be advisable to hire older people in order to acquire their accumulated experience. This is especially useful for highly complex jobs. Moreover, hiring older workers is a good solution for reducing turnover, providing role models for younger employees, and coping with the current shortage of qualified entry-level workers.

It is important to obtain top management's commitment and support to eliminate the organizational practices that support or reinforce stereotyping and discriminatory decisions. Research clearly demonstrates that top management support is essential to successful implementation of the types of organizational changes being recommended.

∫elf-Fulfilling Prophecy: The Pygmalion Effect

Historical roots of the self-fulfilling prophecy are found in Greek mythology. According to mythology, Pygmalion was a sculptor who hated women yet fell in love with an ivory statue he carved of a beautiful woman. He became so infatuated with the statue

that he prayed to the goddess Aphrodite to bring her to life. The goddess heard his prayer, granted his wish, and Pygmalion's statue came to life. The essence of the **self-fulfilling prophecy,** or Pygmalion effect, is that people's expectations or beliefs determine their behavior and performance, thus serving to make their expectations come true. In other words, we strive to validate our *perceptions* of reality, no matter how faulty they may be. Thus, the self-fulfilling prophecy is an important perceptual outcome we need to better understand.

/elf-fulfilling prophecy
People's expectations determine behavior and performance.

Research and an Explanatory Model

The self-fulfilling prophecy was first demonstrated in an academic environment. After giving a bogus test of academic potential to students from grades 1 to 6, researchers informed teachers that certain students had high potential for achievement. In reality, students were randomly assigned to the "high potential" and "control" (normal potential) groups. Results showed that children designated as having high potential obtained significantly greater increases in both IQ scores and reading ability than did the control students.[58] The teachers of the supposedly high potential group got better results because their high expectations caused them to give harder assignments, more feedback, and more recognition of achievement. Students in the normal potential group did not excel because their teachers did not expect outstanding results.

Research similarly has shown that by raising instructors' and managers' expectations for individuals performing a wide variety of tasks, higher levels of achievement/productivity can be obtained. Results from a meta-analysis of 17 studies involving 2,874 people working in a variety of industries and occupations demonstrated the Pygmalion effect was quite strong.[59] This finding implies that higher levels of achievement and productivity can be obtained by raising managers' performance expectations of their employees. Further, the performance enhancing Pygmalion effect was stronger in the military, with men, and for people possessing low performance expectations.[60] It is important to note, however, that no study has determined whether or not female leaders can produce the self-fulfilling prophecy among subordinate men. Given the number of women in managerial roles, future research is needed to determine if the Pygmalion effect works in this context.[61]

Figure 7–2 presents a model of the self-fulfilling prophecy that helps explain these results. This model attempts to outline how supervisory expectations affect employee

Figure 7–2   *A Model of the Self-Fulfilling Prophecy*

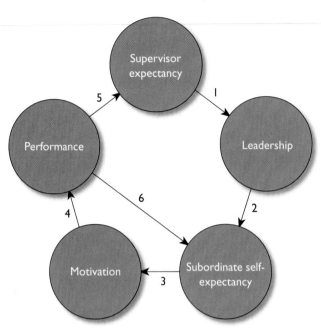

SOURCE: D Eden, "Self-Fulfilling Prophecy as a Management Tool: Harnessing Pygmalion," *Academy of Management Review*, January 1984, p. 67. Used with permission.

performance. As indicated, high supervisory expectancy produces better leadership (linkage 1), which subsequently leads employees to develop higher self-expectations (linkage 2). Higher expectations motivate workers to exert more effort (linkage 3), ultimately increasing performance (linkage 4) and supervisory expectancies (linkage 5). Successful performance also improves an employee's self-expectancy for achievement (linkage 6). Researchers coined the term *Golem effect* to represent the negative side of the performance enhancing process depicted in Figure 7–2. The **Golem effect** is a loss in performance resulting from low leader expectations.[62] Let us consider how it works.

Golem effect

Loss in performance due to low leader expectations.

Say that an employee makes a mistake such as losing notes during a meeting or exhibits poor performance on a task—turning in a report a day late. A manager then begins to wonder if this person has what it takes to be successful in the organization. This doubt leads the manager to watch this person more carefully. The employee of course notices this doubt and begins to sense a loss of trust. The suspect employee then responds in one of two ways. He or she may doubt his or her own judgment and competence. This in turn leads the individual to become more risk averse and to decrease the amount of ideas and suggestions for the manager's critical review. The manager notices this behavior and interprets it as an example of less initiative. Oppositely, the employee may take on more and more responsibility so that he or she can demonstrate his or her competence and worth. This is likely to cause the employee to screw up on something, which in turn reinforces the manager's suspicions. You can see that this process results in a destructive relationship that is fueled by negative expectations. The point to remember is that the self-fulfilling prophecy works in both directions. The next section discusses ideas for enhancing the Pygmalion effect and reducing the Golem effect.

Putting the Self-Fulfilling Prophecy to Work

Largely due to the Pygmalion effect, managerial expectations powerfully influence employee behavior and performance. Consequently, managers need to harness the Pygmalion effect by building a hierarchical framework that reinforces positive performance expectations throughout the organization.

Employees' self-expectations are the foundation of this framework. In turn, positive self-expectations improve interpersonal expectations by encouraging people to work toward common goals. This cooperation enhances group-level productivity and promotes positive performance expectations within the work group. At Microsoft Corporation, for example, employees routinely put in 75-hour weeks, especially when work groups are trying to meet shipment deadlines for new products. Because Microsoft is known for meeting its deadlines, positive group-level expectations help create and reinforce an organizational culture of high expectancy for success. This process then excites people about working for the organization, thereby reducing turnover.[63]

Because positive self-expectations are the foundation for creating an organization-wide Pygmalion effect, let us consider how managers can create positive performance expectations. This task may be accomplished by using various combinations of the following:

1. Recognize that everyone has the potential to increase his or her performance.
2. Instill confidence in your staff.
3. Set high performance goals.
4. Positively reinforce employees for a job well done.
5. Provide constructive feedback when necessary.
6. Help employees advance through the organization.
7. Introduce new employees as if they have outstanding potential.
8. Become aware of your personal prejudices and nonverbal messages that may discourage others.
9. Encourage employees to visualize the successful execution of tasks.
10. Help employees master key skills and tasks.[64]

Causal Attributions

Attribution theory is based on the premise that people attempt to infer causes for observed behavior. Rightly or wrongly, we constantly formulate cause-and-effect explanations for our own and others' behavior. Attributional statements such as the following are common: "Joe drinks too much because he has no willpower; but I need a couple of drinks after work because I'm under a lot of pressure." Formally defined, **causal attributions** are suspected or inferred causes of behavior. Even though our causal attributions tend to be self-serving and are often invalid, it is important to understand how people formulate attributions because they profoundly affect organizational behavior. For example, a supervisor who attributes an employee's poor performance to a lack of effort might reprimand that individual. However, training might be deemed necessary if the supervisor attributes the poor performance to a lack of ability.

Generally speaking, people formulate causal attributions by considering the events preceding an observed behavior. This section introduces and explores two different

> **Causal attributions**
> Suspected or inferred causes of behavior.

Figure 7–3   *Performance Charts Showing Low and High Consensus, Distinctiveness, and Consistency Information*

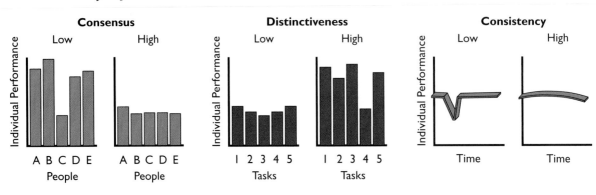

SOURCE: K A Brown, "Explaining Group Poor Performance: An Attributional Analysis," *Academy of Management Review*, January 1984, p. 56. Used with permission.

widely cited attribution models proposed by Harold Kelley and Bernard Weiner. Attributional tendencies, research, and related managerial implications also are discussed.

Kelley's Model of Attribution

Current models of attribution, such as Kelley's, are based on the pioneering work of the late Fritz Heider. Heider, the founder of attribution theory, proposed that behavior can be attributed either to **internal factors** within a person (such as ability) or to **external factors** within the environment (such as a difficult task). This line of thought parallels the idea of an internal versus external locus of control, as discussed in Chapter 5. Building on Heider's work, Kelley attempted to pinpoint major antecedents of internal and external attributions. Kelley hypothesized that people make causal attributions after gathering information about three dimensions of behavior: consensus, distinctiveness, and consistency.[65] These dimensions vary independently, thus forming various combinations and leading to differing attributions.

Figure 7–3 presents performance charts showing low versus high consensus, distinctiveness, and consistency. These charts are now used to help develop a working knowledge of all three dimensions in Kelley's model.

- *Consensus* involves a comparison of an individual's behavior with that of his or her peers. There is high consensus when one acts like the rest of the group and low consensus when one acts differently. As shown in Figure 7–3, high consensus is indicated when persons A, B, C, D, and E obtain similar levels of individual performance. In contrast, person C's performance is low in consensus because it significantly varies from the performance of persons A, B, D, and E.

- *Distinctiveness* is determined by comparing a person's behavior on one task with his or her behavior on other tasks. High distinctiveness means the individual has performed the task in question in a significantly different manner than he or she has performed other tasks. Low distinctiveness means stable performance or quality from one task to another. Figure 7–3 reveals that the employee's performance on task 4 is highly distinctive because it significantly varies from his or her performance on tasks 1, 2, 3, and 5.

• *Consistency* is determined by judging if the individual's performance on a given task is consistent over time. High consistency implies that a person performs a certain task the same, time after time. Unstable performance of a given task over time would mean low consistency. The downward spike in performance depicted in the consistency graph of Figure 7–3 represents low consistency. In this case, the employee's performance on a given task varied over time.

It is important to remember that consensus relates to other *people*, distinctiveness relates to other *tasks*, and consistency relates to *time*. The question now is: How does information about these three dimensions of behavior lead to internal or external attributions?

Kelley hypothesized that people attribute behavior to *external* causes (environmental factors) when they perceive high consensus, high distinctiveness, and low consistency. *Internal* attributions (personal factors) tend to be made when observed behavior is characterized by low consensus, low distinctiveness, and high consistency. So, for example, when all employees are performing poorly (high consensus), when the poor performance occurs on only one of several tasks (high distinctiveness), and the poor performance occurs during only one time period (low consistency), a supervisor will probably attribute an employee's poor performance to an external source such as peer pressure or an overly difficult task. In contrast, performance will be attributed to an employee's personal characteristics (an internal attribution) when only the individual in question is performing poorly (low consensus), when the inferior performance is found across several tasks (low distinctiveness), and when the low performance has persisted over time (high consistency). Many studies supported this predicted pattern of attributions.[66]

Weiner's Model of Attribution

Bernard Weiner, a noted motivation theorist, developed an attribution model to explain achievement behavior and to predict subsequent changes in motivation and performance. Figure 7–4 presents a modified version of his model. Weiner believes that the attribution process begins after an individual performs a task. A person's performance leads him or her to judge whether it was successful or unsuccessful. This evaluation then produces a causal analysis to determine if the performance was due to internal or external factors. Figure 7–4 shows that ability and effort are the primary internal causes of performance and task difficulty, luck, and help from others the key external causes. These attributions for success and failure then influence how individuals feel about themselves. For instance, a meta-analysis of 104 studies involving almost 15,000 individuals found that people who attributed failure to their lack of ability (as opposed to bad luck) experienced psychological depression. The exact opposite attributions (to good luck rather than to high ability) tended to trigger depression in people experiencing positive events. In short, perceived bad luck took the sting out of a negative outcome, but perceived good luck reduced the joy associated with success.[67]

Returning to Figure 7–4, note that the psychological consequences can either increase or decrease depending on the causes of performance. For example, your self-esteem is likely to increase after achieving an "A" on your next exam if you believe that your performance was due to your ability or effort. In contrast, this same grade can either increase or decrease your self-esteem if you believe that the test was easy. Finally, the feelings that people have about their past performance influences future performance. Figure 7–4 reveals that future performance is higher when individuals attribute success to internal causes and lower when failure is attributed to external factors. Future performance is more uncertain when individuals attribute either their success or failure to external causes.

Figure 7–4   *A Modified Version of Weiner's Attribution Model*

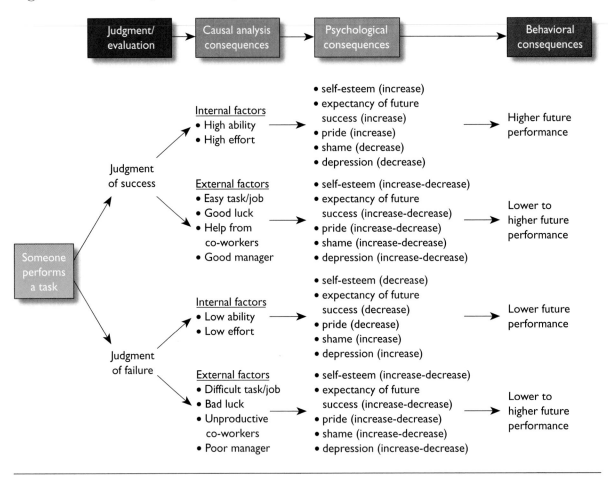

SOURCES: Based in part on B Weiner, "An Attributional Theory of Achievement Motivation and Emotion," *Psychological Review,* October 1985, pp. 548–73; and T S Bateman, G R Ferris, and S Strasser, "The 'Why' behind Individual Work Performance," *Management Review,* October 1984, p. 71.

In further support of Weiner's model, a study of 130 male salespeople in the United Kingdom revealed that positive, internal attributions for success were associated with higher sales and performance ratings.[68] A second study examined the attributional processes of 126 employees who were permanently displaced by a plant closing. Consistent with the model, as the explanation for job loss was attributed to internal and stable causes, life satisfaction, self-esteem, and expectations for reemployment diminished.[69] Furthermore, research also shows that when individuals attribute their success to internal rather than external factors, they (1) have higher expectations for future success, (2) report a greater desire for achievement, and (3) set higher performance goals.[70]

Attributional Tendencies

Researchers have uncovered two attributional tendencies that distort one's interpretation of observed behavior—*fundamental attribution bias* and *self-serving bias.*

Fundamental Attribution Bias   The **fundamental attribution bias** reflects one's tendency to attribute another person's behavior to his or her personal characteristics, as opposed to situational factors. This bias causes perceivers to ignore important environmental forces that often significantly affect behavior. For example, a study of 1,420 employees of a large utility company demonstrated that supervisors tended to make more internal attributions about worker accidents than did the workers. Interestingly, research also shows that people from Westernized cultures tend to exhibit the fundamental attribution bias more than individuals from East Asia.[71]

Self-Serving Bias   The **self-serving bias** represents one's tendency to take more personal responsibility for success than for failure. Referring again to Figure 7–4, the self-serving bias suggests employees will attribute their success to internal factors (high ability or hard work) and their failures to uncontrollable external factors (tough job, bad luck, unproductive co-workers, or an unsympathetic boss). For example, after losing to the US hockey team in the 2002 winter Olympics, Russian hockey coach Slava Fetisov blamed the referees and the disparity in penalties for his team's loss. He also "leveled charges of conspiracy, saying the tournament was 'designed to have a final with Canada and the US, and you have this final.' "[72]

Much research has investigated the self-serving bias. Two studies, for instance, examined whether or not senior executives fell prey to the self-serving bias when communicating with stockholders in their annual Letter to Shareholders. Results revealed executives in the United States and Singapore took credit for themselves when their companies did well and blamed negative outcomes on the environment.[73] Overall, however, research on the self-serving bias has produced inconsistent results. Two general patterns of attributions have been observed in past research. The first reveals that individuals make internal attributions for success as predicted by a self-serving bias. In contrast, people make both internal and external attributions for failure.[74] This means people do not automatically blame failure on external factors as originally expected from a self-serving bias. A team of researchers concluded, "When highly self-focused people feel that failure can be rapidly remedied, they will attribute failure to self; when the likelihood of improvement seems low, however, failure will be attributed externally."[75]

Managerial Application and Implications

Attribution models can be used to explain how managers handle poorly performing employees. One study revealed that managers gave employees more immediate, frequent, and negative feedback when they attributed their performance to low effort. This reaction was even more pronounced when the manager's success was dependent on an employee's performance. A second study indicated that managers tended to transfer employees whose poor performance was attributed to a lack of ability. These same managers also decided to take no immediate action when poor performance was attributed to external factors beyond an individual's control.[76]

The preceding situations have several important implications for managers. First, managers tend to disproportionately attribute behavior to *internal* causes.[77] This can result in inaccurate evaluations of performance, leading to reduced employee motivation. No one likes to be blamed because of factors they perceive to be beyond their control. Further, because managers' responses to employee performance vary according to their attributions, attributional biases may lead to inappropriate managerial actions,

Fundamental attribution bias
Ignoring environmental factors that affect behavior.

Self-serving bias
Taking more personal responsibility for success than failure.

including promotions, transfers, layoffs, and so forth. This can dampen motivation and performance. Attributional training sessions for managers are in order. Basic attributional processes can be explained, and managers can be taught to detect and avoid attributional biases. Finally, an employee's attributions for his or her own performance have dramatic effects on subsequent motivation, performance, and personal attitudes such as self-esteem. For instance, people tend to give up, develop lower expectations for future success, and experience decreased self-esteem when they attribute failure to a lack of ability. Fortunately, attributional retraining can improve both motivation and performance. Research shows that employees can be taught to attribute their failures to a lack of effort rather than to a lack of ability.[78] This attributional realignment paves the way for improved motivation and performance. It also is important to remember the implications of the self-serving bias. If managers want employees to accept personal responsibility for failure and correspondingly modify their effort and behavior, it is essential for employees to believe that they can improve upon their performance in the future. Otherwise, employees are likely to attribute failure to external causes and they will not change their behavior.

Summary of Key Concepts

1. *Describe perception in terms of the information-processing model.* Perception is a mental and cognitive process that enables us to interpret and understand our surroundings. Social perception, also known as social cognition and social information processing, is a four-stage process. The four stages are selective attention/comprehension, encoding and simplification, storage and retention, and retrieval and response. During social cognition, salient stimuli are matched with schemata, assigned to cognitive categories, and stored in long-term memory for events, semantic materials, or people.

2. *Identify and briefly explain four managerial implications of social perception.* Social perception affects hiring decisions, performance appraisals, leadership perceptions, and communication processes. Inaccurate schemata or racist and sexist schemata may be used to evaluate job applicants. Similarly, faulty schemata about what constitutes good versus poor performance can lead to inaccurate performance appraisals. Invalid schemata need to be identified and replaced with appropriate schemata through coaching and training. Further, managers are advised to use objective rather than subjective measures of performance. With respect to leadership, a leader will have a difficult time influencing employees when he or she exhibits behaviors contained in employees' schemata of poor leaders. Finally, communication is influenced by schemata used to interpret any message. Effective communicators try to tailor their messages to the receiver's perceptual schemata.

3. *Discuss stereotypes and the process of stereotype formation.* Stereotypes represent grossly oversimplified beliefs or expectations about groups of people. Stereotyping is a four-step process that begins by categorizing people into groups according to various criteria. Next, we infer that all people within a particular group possess the same traits or characteristics. Then, we form expectations of others and interpret their behavior according to our stereotypes. Finally, stereotypes are maintained by (a) overestimating the frequency of stereotypic behaviors exhibited by others, (b) incorrectly explaining expected and unexpected behaviors, and (c) differentiating minority individuals from oneself. The use of stereotypes is influenced by the amount and type of information available to an individual and his or her motivation to accurately process information.

4. *Summarize the managerial challenges and recommendations of sex-role, age, race, and disability stereotypes.* The key managerial challenge is to make decisions that are blind to gender, age, race, and disabilities. Training can be used to educate employees about the problem of stereotyping and to equip managers with the skills needed to handle unique situations associated with managing employees with mental disabilities. Because mixed-group contact reduces stereotyping, organizations should create opportunities for diverse employees to meet and work together in cooperative groups of equal status. Hiring decisions should be based on valid individual differences, and managers can be trained to use valid criteria when evaluating employee performance. Minimizing differences in job opportunities and experiences across groups of people can help alleviate promotional barriers. Job design techniques can be used to reduce performance plateaus associated with age. Organizations also may need to use incentives to motivate employees to upgrade their skills and abilities, and hiring older workers has many potential organizational benefits. It is critical to obtain top management's commitment and support to eliminate stereotyping and discriminatory decisions.

5. *Discuss how the self-fulfilling prophecy is created and how it can be used to improve individual and group productivity.* The self-fulfilling prophecy, also known as the Pygmalion effect, describes how people behave so their expectations come true. High managerial expectations foster high employee self-expectations. These, in turn, lead to greater effort and better performance, and yet higher expectations. Conversely, the Golem effect represents the negative side of the self-fulfilling prophecy. Managers are encouraged to harness the Pygmalion effect by building a hierarchical framework that reinforces positive performance expectations throughout the organization.

6. *Explain, according to Kelley's model, how external and internal causal attributions are formulated.* Attribution theory

attempts to describe how people infer causes for observed behavior. According to Kelley's model of causal attribution, external attributions tend to be made when consensus and distinctiveness are high and consistency is low. Internal (personal responsibility) attributions tend to be made when consensus and distinctiveness are low and consistency is high.

7. *Review Weiner's model of attribution.* Weiner's model of attribution predicts achievement behavior in terms of causal attributions. Attributions of ability, effort, task difficulty, luck, and help from others affect how individuals feel about themselves. In turn, these feelings directly influence subsequent achievement-related performance.

8. *Contrast the fundamental attribution bias and the self-serving bias.* Fundamental attribution bias involves emphasizing personal factors more than situational factors while formulating causal attributions for the behavior of others. Self-serving bias involves personalizing the causes of one's successes and externalizing the causes of one's failures.

Discussion Questions

1. Why is it important for managers to have a working knowledge of perception and attribution?

2. When you are sitting in class, what stimuli are salient? What is your schema for classroom activity?

3. Have you ever been stereotyped by someone else? Discuss.

4. Which type of stereotype (sex-role, age, race, or disability) do you believe is more pervasive in organizations? Why?

5. What evidence of self-fulfilling prophecies have you seen lately?

6. How might your professor use the process outlined in Figure 7–2 to improve the overall performance of the students in your class?

7. How would you formulate an attribution, according to Kelley's model, for the behavior of a classmate who starts arguing in class with your professor?

8. In what situations do you tend to attribute your successes/failures to luck? How well does Weiner's attributional model in Figure 7–4 explain your answers? Explain.

9. Are poor people victimized by a fundamental attribution bias? Explain.

10. What evidence of the self-serving bias have you observed lately?

Internet Exercise   **www.adl.org**

This chapter examined the process of stereotype formation and discussed stereotypes pertaining to gender, age, race, and disabilities. The purpose of this exercise is to explore the issue of stereotypes in more detail. Go to the Internet home page for the Anti-Defamation League (ADL) at **www.adl.org,** and select the subheading "About ADL." After reading this material, go back to the home page and look under the section titled "Issues." Select the options for "Anti-Semitism" and "Combating Hate." Under the Combating Hate topic, explore the item regarding "101 Ways to Combat Prejudice." Finally, conduct a search within the ADL's database on the term *stereotypes.*

Questions

1. Who founded the ADL? What is the purpose of the ADL and how has it evolved?

2. What are the differences among stereotypes, prejudice, discrimination, and scapegoating?

3. How prevalent are anti-Semitic views? Who is most likely to hold anti-Semitic views?

4. How can organizations reduce the use of stereotypes and prejudice at work?

OB In Action Case Study

Do the Skills That Come with Age Count for Less and Less in Today's Organizations?[79]

America is no place to age gracefully. Of course, basketball players, dancers, and fashion models are finished young; mathematicians and chess players peak early too. So do construction workers and coal miners. Once you're 55, it's almost impossible to find a job in business. But a new trend is emerging: In corporate America, 40 is starting to look and feel old.

Since the early 1980s big companies have been getting rid of people. For a long time, though, seniority mattered. Hierarchy was respected too. If people had to be fired, the younger, junior people were usually the first to go. That's no longer true. The working world has changed. It has become faster and more efficient and, for many people, crueler. . . .

Companies today have less and less tolerance for people they believe are earning more than their output warrants. Such intolerance, or pragmatism, hits older workers hardest. The older an employee, the more likely it is he can be replaced by someone younger who earns half as much. "For my salary the company could hire two twenty-somethings," says a 41-year-old we spoke to. "I'm good at what I do. But am I better than two people? Even I know that's not true." Today, for many people, the longer you've been at one company, the more disposable you are. . . .

Perhaps technology is to blame. Maybe in this "new" economy, the old ways of doing business are indeed anachronistic—if the economy is new, who needs experience? Whatever the reason, in America today the skills that come with age and experience appear to count for less and less. It's hard to demonstrate with numbers, but a lot of people over 40 sense it: Youth, with its native optimism, is what companies want now. . . .

That so many workers are over 40 compounds the problem. In just four years, for the first time ever, there will be more workers over 40 than there are workers under 40. . . . All those people—the 78 million baby-boomers—are competing for a limited number of top jobs. For those who have made it (status, money, fan mail, a title, a corner office), there's no problem; but for the millions who are just decent, everyday performers, it's another story. These people are

squeezed: They can't rise to the top (there's no room), and right behind, ready to overtake them, is another generation. In years gone by, executives in this position spoke of reaching a plateau—if their path no longer led upward, at least they were in a stable, safe place. Now the plateau is a narrow ledge. Suddenly, at an age when they expected to be at the peak of their careers, growing numbers of fortysomethings are slipping backward.

Debbie Brown is a software engineer who recently lost her job after 14 years at Northrop Grumman. Since last June, when Brown first knew she'd lose her job, she has sent out about 300 résumés. Her yield so far: four phone interviews, one in-person interview, and not a single job offer. Brown is 44. She earned a master's degree in software engineering from the University of California at Irvine in 1983 and has 23 years of industry experience. According to headhunters, however, she's obsolete—not because she's worked in the defense business (although that probably doesn't help), but largely because she moved into management in an era when forty-something middle managers are a dime a dozen. As for her technical skills, well, people half her age are better qualified. To get a job offer, she must be prepared to cut her $88,500 salary in half, headhunters advise. Either that or go back to school. "I came to Northrop thinking that I'd retire here," she says. "And now here I am, at 44, out of work and useless."

It's not only high-tech firms that are slamming the door on people over 40. In older industries, too, as the lives of products get shorter and as the speed of change gets faster, it can be awfully hard to keep up unless you have the stamina of a 25-year-old. . . .

There are advantages to age. Older employees have more experience than younger workers; they also have better judgment, have a greater commitment to quality, are more likely to show up on time, and are less likely to quit—that's what a recent study commissioned by the American Association of Retired Persons found. Younger workers, by contrast (in this case defined as under 50), were found to be more flexible, more adaptable, more accepting of new technology, and better at learning new skills. It may seem that there are as many advantages in hiring older workers as in hiring younger ones. But as the AARP study discovered, increasingly what matters to companies is potential, not experience; street smarts, not wisdom. "The traits most commonly desired for the new world of work are flexibility, acceptance of change, and the ability to solve problems independently—performance attributes on which managers generally did not rate older workers highly," notes the AARP study. "The message is consistent: Managers generally view older workers as less suitable for the future work environment than other segments of the work force."

To discover, after years of being promoted, that all of a sudden you are "less suitable" for your job than people younger than you is not easy. . . . FedEx delivered letters to the homes of 389 Gerber Products salespeople telling them they were out of work. Of those 389 employees, nearly 70% were over 40. One of them was Tom Johnson. He had been selling Gerber baby food for 27 years; he started with the company when he was 21. Shouldn't he have known he was vulnerable? "Right up until D-day, I was convinced I wouldn't be hit, what with me calling on national accounts and all," Johnson says.

It's human nature that causes us to be blind-sided: No matter how often we hear stories of corporate ruthlessness, of 45-year-olds being replaced by 28-year-olds, we believe it won't happen to us. Sitting in his living room in Mesquite, Texas, in his La-Z-Boy, Johnson opened up that FedEx letter and felt sick. "I sat in my chair and read it eight times and couldn't believe it, I just couldn't believe it. It was like someone grabbed me and hit me as hard as they could right in the stomach. I thought, 'God, all I've done and all I've worked, and it doesn't mean a thing.'" His unemployment insurance checks, at $476 every two weeks, ran out months ago. When we last spoke to him, he had sent out about 400 résumés, and still he hadn't found a job. If truth be told, his chance of finding anything that comes close to paying what he earned at Gerber is probably zero. . . .

"The market is so fast moving that for some reason it's reduced the premium these [older] guys have," notes a New Yorker who runs a hedge fund. Callously, but realistically, he explains his preference for younger employees this way (and for obvious reasons he won't let his name be used): "The way I look at it, for $40,000 or $50,000, I can get a smart, raw kid right out of undergrad who's going to work seven days a week for me for the next two years. I'll train him the way I want him, he'll grow with me, and I'll pay him long-term options so I own him, for lack of a better word. He'll do exactly what I want—and if he doesn't, I'll fire him. . . . The alternative is to pay twice as much for some 40-year-old who does half the amount of work, has been trained improperly, and doesn't listen to what I say." . . .

What unnerves these forty-somethings is that in a world increasingly dominated by information technology, people in their 20s and early 30s (Generation X) are more technically savvy than most baby-boomers. Even more, many Gen Xers work 60 or 70 hours a week, mostly because their job is their whole life. But so what? From the perspective of an employer, such single-mindedness, such devotion to the company, makes Gen Xers all the more valuable. It also makes for unflattering comparisons to the forty-something employee who leaves the office right at 6 P.M. to pick up the children from day care. As one highly placed human resources manager put it, "The attitude is, Why not hire someone who's young and idealistic and will work 80 hours a week?" . . .

In an economy where the rules seem to shift every day, it's the risk takers, the people who believe they can do anything, who are being rewarded. And after all, who's more likely to take risks—a 46-year-old with a mortgage and two kids in college, or a 30-year-old with nothing to lose? (Freedom may be just another word for not having a mortgage.) Robert Michlewicz is the president of one of Consolidated Graphics' biggest plants, Houston-based Chas P Young Co., with sales of $20 million. He's 30, oversees a staff of 150 people, and works 70 hours a week. When he started with the company, just out of Texas A&M, Michlewicz wouldn't be constrained by the printing industry's traditional ways of doing business. "When I got into sales here, there was this rule of thumb that once you sold $1 million worth of printing, you were an established, veteran salesperson," he explains. "I did $500,000 in my first year, $1.5 million in my second year, and $6.1 million in 1995. . . . I had no preconceived notions. That million-dollar threshold didn't mean anything to me."

The harder Gen Xers work, the more they tend to resent all those 44-year-olds who put in half as many hours and earn more money. "A large percentage [of us] have decided not to buy into a corporate system clogged with entrenched boomers who won't make way for people who are more efficient and have better ideas," writes 28-year-old "Delsyn" in an Internet posting on the Boomer Board chat room. Younger generations may have always felt thus; what's different now is that Delsyn, or someone like her, may be your next boss.

"You have to do more for young people because they are likely to turn over more quickly than older workers. Consequently, a lot of companies are putting young people on the fast track, so you have 28-year-olds running entire departments that 20 years ago were run by 55-year-olds," explains Joe Gibbons, a human resources consultant at William M Mercer. "That's a big change—it's a sea change." . . .

Older employees don't just earn more. Granting more vacation time costs money. The costs of medical benefits and insurance, too, rise with age. And the older an employee, and the longer he's been with the firm, the more expensive it becomes to support his pension plan. If length of work experience really counted for something, these extra costs wouldn't be an issue; but several studies have shown that differences in job performance between some-one with 20 years' experience and someone with just five years are often negligible. That is to say that a 28-year-old with six years on the job may perform as well as a 48-year-old with 26 years on the job. The 28-year-old, however, earns $45,000, while the 48-year-old makes $120,000 (assuming a 5% raise every year). . . .

If companies discard older workers because they're earn-ing more than they deserve, then perhaps the solution is to change the way people are being paid: Pay them what they're worth. It's self-evident, but it's rarely the way companies compensate people. "The solution is to develop compensa-tion plans that pay for ideas, not tenure; that pay for contri-bution, not hierarchy," declares George Bailey, who until recently was head of Watson Wyatt's human-capital group.

Implementing performance-based compensation plans isn't easy. The key is figuring out how to value the per-formance of every employee ("If you can't find a way to measure [a job's value], you can probably eliminate it," declares Bailey). How many new ideas did she think up this year? How much money did she save? What did she do to help meet our goals? Did she accomplish the goals we set for her? It's a lot of work, but it beats rewarding people just because they've been with the firm for a long time.

Questions for Discussion

1. Do the skills that come with age and experience count for less in today's organizations? Explain.
2. What examples of age stereotypes did you observe in the case? Discuss.
3. To what extent is Debbie Brown being influenced by the self-fulfilling prophecy?
4. Use Weiner's model to assess how Debbie Brown and Tom Johnson are reacting to being laid off by their respective companies. Be sure to identify the perceived causes of the layoff and the associated psychological and behavioral consequences that are apparent in the case.
5. Do you agree with the theme that organizations are better off to replace forty-somethings with younger employees? Explain your rationale.
6. What advice would you give to people who are either twenty-something or forty-something based on this case?

Personal Awareness and Growth Exercise

How Do Diversity Assumptions Influence Team Member Interactions?

Objectives

1. To identify diversity assumptions.
2. To consider how diversity assumptions impact team members' interactions.

Introduction

Assumptions can be so ingrained that we do not even know that we are using them. Negative assumptions can limit our relationships with others because they influence how we perceive and respond to those we encounter in our daily lives. This exercise is designed to help identify the assump-tions that you have about groups of people. Although this exercise may make you uncomfortable because it asks you to identify stereotypical assumptions, it is a positive first step at facing and examining the assumptions we make about other people. This awareness can lead to positive behavioral change.

Instructions

Complete the diversity assumptions worksheet.[80] The first column contains various dimensions of diversity. For each dimension, the second column asks you to identify the assumptions held by the general public about people with this characteristic. Use the third column to determine how each assumption might limit team members' ability to effectively interact with each other. Finally, answer the questions for discussion.

Questions for Discussion

1. Where do our assumptions about others come from?
2. Is it possible to eliminate negative assumptions about others? How might this be done?
3. What most surprised you about your answers to the diversity assumption worksheet?

Diversity Assumption Worksheet[81]

Dimension of Diversity	Assumption That Might Be Made	Impact on Team Members' Interactions
Age	Example: You can't teach an old dog new tricks. Older people are closed to new ideas. Example: Younger people haven't had the proper experience to come up with good solutions.	Example: Older people are considered to be resistant to change. Example: Input from younger employee is not solicited.
Ethnicity (e.g., Mexican)		
Gender		
Race		
Physical ability (e.g., hard of hearing)		
Sexual orientation		
Marital/parental status (e.g., single parent with children)		
Religion (e.g., Buddhist)		
Recreational habits (e.g., hikes on weekends)		
Educational background (e.g., college education)		
Work experience (e.g., union)		
Appearance (e.g., overweight)		
Geographic location (e.g., rural)		
Personal habits (e.g., smoking)		
Income (e.g., well-to-do)		

Group Exercise

Using Attribution Theory to Resolve Performance Problems

Objectives

1. To gain experience determining the causes of performance.
2. To decide on corrective action for employee performance.

Introduction

Attributions are typically made to internal and external factors. Perceivers arrive at their assessments by using various informational cues or antecedents. To determine the types of antecedents people use, we have developed a case containing various informational cues about an individual's performance. You will be asked to read the case and make attributions about the causes of performance. To assess the impact of attributions on managerial behavior, you will also be asked to recommend corrective action.

Instructions

Presented on the following page is a case that depicts the performance of Mary Martin, a computer programmer. Please read the case to the right and then identify the causes of her behavior by answering the questions following the case. Then determine whether you made an internal or external attribution. After completing this task, decide on the appropriateness of various forms of corrective action. A list of potential recommendations has been developed. The list is divided into four categories. Read each action, and evaluate its appropriateness by using the scale provided. Next, compute a total score for each of the four categories.

Causes of Performance

To what extent was each of the following a cause of Mary's performance? Use the following scale:

Very little			Very much	
1 ——	2 ——	3 ——	4 ——	5

a. High ability		1	2	3	4	5
b. Low ability		1	2	3	4	5
c. Low effort		1	2	3	4	5
d. Difficult job		1	2	3	4	5
e. Unproductive co-workers	1	2	3	4	5
f. Bad luck		1	2	3	4	5

Internal attribution (total score for causes a, b, and c) _____
External attribution (total score for causes d, e, and f) _____

THE CASE OF MARY MARTIN

Mary Martin, 30, received her baccalaureate degree in computer science from a reputable state school in the Midwest. She also graduated with above-average grades. Mary is currently working in the computer support/analysis department as a programmer for a nationally based firm. During the past year, Mary has missed 10 days of work. She seems unmotivated and rarely has her assignments completed on time. Mary is usually given the harder programs to work on.

Past records indicate Mary, on the average, completes programs classified as "routine" in about 45 hours. Her co-workers, on the other hand, complete "routine" programs in an average time of 32 hours. Further, Mary finishes programs considered "major problems," on the average, in about 115 hours. Her co-workers, however, finish these same "major problem" assignments, on the average, in about 100 hours. When Mary has worked in programming teams, her peer performance reviews are generally average to negative. Her male peers have noted she is not creative in attacking problems and she is difficult to work with.

The computer department recently sent a questionnaire to all users of its services to evaluate the usefulness and accuracy of data received. The results indicate many departments are not using computer output because they cannot understand the reports. It was also determined that the users of output generated from Mary's programs found the output chaotic and not useful for managerial decision making.

Appropriateness of Corrective Action

Evaluate the following courses of action by using the scale below:

	Very Inappropriate				**Very Appropriate**
	1 —— 2 —— 3 —— 4 —— 5				

Coercive Actions

		1	2	3	4	5
a.	Reprimand Mary for her performance	1	2	3	4	5
b.	Threaten to fire Mary if her performance does not improve	1	2	3	4	5

Change Job

		1	2	3	4	5
c.	Transfer Mary to another job	1	2	3	4	5
d.	Demote Mary to a less demanding job	1	2	3	4	5

Nonpunitive Actions

		1	2	3	4	5
e.	Work with Mary to help her do the job better	1	2	3	4	5
f.	Offer Mary encouragement to help her improve	1	2	3	4	5

No Immediate Actions

		1	2	3	4	5
g.	Do nothing	1	2	3	4	5
h.	Promise Mary a pay raise if she improves	1	2	3	4	5

Compute a score for the four categories:
Coercive actions = a + b =
Change job = c + d =
Nonpunitive actions = e + f =
No immediate actions = g + h =

Questions for Discussion

1. How would you evaluate Mary's performance in terms of consensus, distinctiveness, and consistency?

2. Is Mary's performance due to internal or external causes?

3. What did you identify as the top two causes of Mary's performance? Are your choices consistent with Weiner's classification of internal and external factors? Explain.

4. Which of the four types of corrective action do you think is most appropriate? Explain. Can you identify any negative consequences of this choice?

Ethical Dilemma

Enron Employees Try to Alter the Perceptions of Wall Street Analysts[82]

Some current and former employees of Enron's retail-energy unit say the company asked them to pose as busy electricity and natural-gas sales representatives one day in 1998 so the unit could impress Wall Street analysts visiting its Houston headquarters.

Enron rushed 75 employees of Enron Energy Services—including secretaries and actual sales representatives—to an empty trading floor and told them to act as if they were trying to sell energy contracts to businesses over the phone, the current and former employees say.

"When we went down to the sixth floor, I remember we had to take the stairs so the analysts wouldn't see us," said Kim Garcia, who at the time was an administrative assistant for Enron Energy Services and was laid off in December.

"We brought some of our personal stuff, like pictures, to make it look like the area was lived in," Ms Garcia said in an interview. "There were a bunch of trading desks on the sixth floor, but the desks were totally empty. Some of the computers didn't even work, so we worked off of our laptops. When the analysts arrived, we had to make believe we were on the phone buying and selling electricity and natural gas. The whole thing took like 10 minutes."

Penny Marksberry—who also worked as an Enron Energy Services administrative assistant in 1998 and was laid off in December—and two employees who still work at the unit also say they were told to act as if they were trying to sell contracts.

"They actually brought in computers and phones and they told us to act like we were typing or talking on the phone when the analysts were walking through," Ms Marksberry said. "They told us it was very important for us to make a good impression and if the analysts saw that the operation was disorganized, they wouldn't give the company a good rating."

What would you do if you were asked to act busy in front of the analysts?

1. Follow the company's instructions by going to the sixth floor and acting busy in front of the analysts.

2. Explain to your manager that this behavior is inconsistent with your personal values and that you will not participate.

3. Go to the sixth floor in support of the company's request, but do not act busy or bring personal artifacts to create a false impression.

4. Invent other options. Discuss.

For an interpretation of this situation, visit our Web site,**www.mhhe.com/kreitner.**

Chapter Eight

Motivation through Needs, Job Design, and Intrinsic Rewards

Learning Objectives

When you finish studying the material in this chapter, you should be able to:

1 Define the term *motivation*.

2 Discuss the job performance model of motivation.

3 Review the historical roots of modern motivation theories.

4 Contrast Maslow's, Alderfer's, and McClelland's need theories.

5 Describe the mechanistic, motivational, biological, and perceptual-motor approaches to job design.

6 Explain the practical significance of Herzberg's distinction between motivators and hygiene factors.

7 Describe how intrinsic motivation is increased by using the job characteristics model.

8 Review the four intrinsic rewards underlying intrinsic motivation.

9 Discuss how managers cultivate intrinsic motivation in others.

Not far from the steady blatt-blatt of the rivet guns on its 757 assembly line just outside Seattle sits what Boeing Co. calls its moonshine shop: The people here distill work-saving ideas into contraptions that make it easier to build jets.

Consider the hay loader next to an almost-completed 757. Normally, this cross between a ladder and a metal-spiked conveyor belt would be dumping bales of hay onto waiting trucks. But to veteran mechanic Robert Harms, the hay loader is the perfect way to get bulky passenger seats from the factory floor up 13 feet to the door of a plane without having to use an overhead crane. "It might look funny, but when you see it work, you wonder why we didn't do it this way all along," he says.

Moonshine shops—so named because they work outside traditional channels and use whatever materials are available—are the essence of Boeing Chairman Phil Condit's campaign to boost profits by driving out costly manufacturing techniques and the decades-old thinking behind them. . . .

Boeing has been gradually adopting "lean" manufacturing techniques since

Boeing Chairman, Phil Condit, launched a campaign to speed up the time it takes to assemble a plane in order to cut costs and increase profits. Boeing's use of "lean" manufacturing techniques was instrumental in accomplishing Condit's goals.
(c) The Boeing Company

the early 1990s—a decade after the US auto industry began emulating the Japanese approach. The basic philosophy: Everything from the design of a component to the machine used to build it is examined with the goal of making it as easy as possible for workers to boost output using less space and fewer movements.

Since late 1998, when the company began applying lean activities on its newest model, the 777, the time it takes to assemble the major components into a finished aircraft has dropped to 37 days from 71. And just since April [2001], the company has trimmed two days out of what was a 20-day final assembly of its best-selling plane, the 737. . . .

Seattle-area workers got their strongest taste yet of where Boeing is going in April. That's when the company began converting one of its three 737 assembly lines in Renton to a moving line from the traditional bays in which planes are parked among fixed catwalks and other machinery for days at a time. Now, once the wings and landing gear are attached, each plane is dragged by a giant tug toward the door at two inches a minute for two shifts a day. The goal is to shove an aircraft out the door in about five days, down from the 11 days it now takes.

The workers move with the airplane on a float-like contraption. Rather than having mechanics waste time walking back and forth to retrieve tools or parts, specific items for each job are wheeled to waiting spots along the line.

"The moving line adds a sense of urgency because you can look at the airplane and tell when the work is even just a few minutes behind schedule," says Carolyn Corvi, 737 program manager. At several places along the line, devices resembling emergency call boxes with traffic lights on top have been set up so that workers can alert support departments to problems that might slow or stop the line. In one engineering group, the flashing light is accompanied by a recording of Aretha Franklin's "Rescue Me" to bring help running.[1]

For Discussion

What are the pros and cons of using job redesign at Boeing? Explain.

Effective employee motivation has long been one of management's most difficult and important duties. Success in this endeavor is becoming more challenging in light of pressures to increase productivity and customer satisfaction while reducing costs. As revealed in the chapter-opening vignette, Boeing implemented a variety of work redesign techniques to meet this challenge. Boeing found that employees were more motivated and productive when their work environments were positively redesigned. In turn, this motivation and efficiency significantly reduced Boeing's costs to produce an airplane. The purpose of this chapter, as well as the next, is to provide you with a foundation for understanding the complexities of employee motivation.

Specifically, this chapter provides a definitional and theoretical foundation for the topic of motivation so that a rich variety of motivation theories and techniques can be introduced and discussed. Coverage of employee motivation extends to Chapter 9.

After providing a conceptual model for understanding motivation, this chapter focuses on (1) need theories of motivation, (2) an overview of job design methods used to motivate employees, and (3) the process of leading others toward intrinsic motivation. In the next chapter, our attention turns to equity, expectancy, and goal-setting theory.

What Does Motivation Involve?

Motivation

Psychological processes that arouse and direct goal-directed behavior.

The term *motivation* derives from the Latin word *movere*, meaning "to move." In the present context, **motivation** represents "those psychological processes that cause the arousal, direction, and persistence of voluntary actions that are goal directed."[2] Managers need to understand these psychological processes if they are to successfully guide employees toward accomplishing organizational objectives. This section thus provides a conceptual framework for understanding motivation and examines the historical roots of motivational concepts.

A Job Performance Model of Motivation

Terence Mitchell, a well-known OB researcher, proposed a broad conceptual model that explains how motivation influences job behaviors and performance. This model, which is shown in Figure 8–1, integrates elements from several of the theories we discuss in this book. It identifies the causes and consequences of motivation.[3]

Figure 8–1 shows that individual inputs and job context are the two key categories of factors that influence motivation. As discussed in Chapter 5, employees bring ability, job knowledge, dispositions and traits, emotions, moods, beliefs, and values to the work setting. The job context includes the physical environment, the tasks one completes, the organization's approach to recognition and rewards, the adequacy of supervisory support and coaching, and the organization's culture (recall our discussion in Chapter 3). These two categories of factors influence each other as well as the motivational processes of arousal, direction, and persistence. Consider the motivational implications associated with the job context at Great Plains Software in Fargo, ND:

> All employees get stock options. An expansive cafeteria offers a sweeping view of the 48-acre prairie campus. Casual dress is the standard. Daily extracurricular classes are offered in

Figure 8–1   *A Job Performance Model of Motivation*

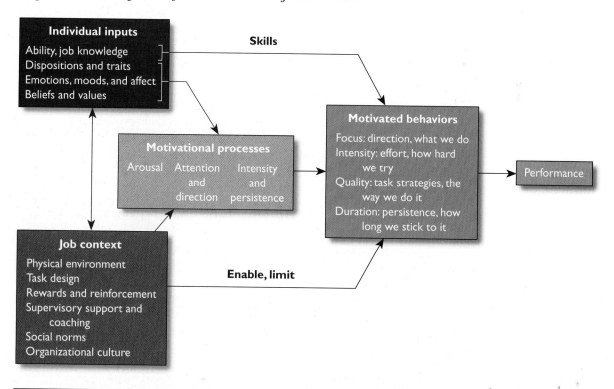

SOURCE: Adapted from T R Mitchell, "Matching Motivational Strategies with Organizational Contexts," in *Research in Organizational Behavior*, vol 19, eds L L Cummings and B M Staw (Greenwich, CT: JAI Press, 1997), p. 63.

everything from aerobics and yoga to parenting and personal finance. And next year will bring an onsite day care facility.…What does make Great Plains such a great place to work is its commitment to the development of its people. Simply stroll down the hallways of Horizon, the company's main building, and you'll see that commitment evidenced in the posters promoting scores of training and educational opportunities available to team members.[4]

In support of the idea that job context influences employee motivation and commitment, Great Plains turnover rate is 5%, which is well below the information technology industry average of 18 to 25%.[5]

Figure 8–1 further reveals that *motivated behaviors* are directly affected by an individual's ability and job knowledge (skills), motivation, and a combination of enabling and limiting job context factors. For instance, it would be difficult to persist on a project if you were working with defective raw materials or broken equipment. In contrast, motivated behaviors are likely to be enhanced when managers supply employees with adequate resources to get the job done and provide effective coaching. This coaching might entail furnishing employees with successful role models, showing employees how to complete complex tasks, and helping them maintain high self-efficacy and self-esteem (recall the discussion in Chapter 5). Performance is, in turn, influenced by motivated behavior.

There are four important conclusions to remember about Figure 8–1. First, motivation is different from behavior. Motivation involves a host of psychological processes that culminate in an individual's desire and intentions to behave in a particular way. Behavior reflects something that we can see or hear. The outcomes of motivation are generally assessed in terms of the behaviors actually exhibited, the amount of effort exerted, or the choice of strategies used to complete a job or task. Actual effort or persistence is the most direct behavioral outcome of motivation. Second, behavior is influenced by more than just motivation. Behavior is affected by individual inputs, job context factors, and motivation. For example, the amount of time you spend studying for your next exam (behavior) is influenced by your motivation in combination with your ability and personal goals (individual inputs) and the quality of your lecture notes (enabling/limiting job context variable). Kenneth Lewis, CEO at Bank of America, also is aware of this relationship. He is trying to improve customer service (motivated behaviors) by changing components of individual inputs (improved teller training programs) and job context (tying executive salaries to sales targets). Thus far his efforts have helped to improve the bank's financial performance.[6] These examples illustrate that behavior is due to a combination of factors rather than simply motivation.

Third, behavior is different from performance. Performance represents an accumulation of behaviors that occur over time and across contexts and people. Performance also reflects an external standard that is typically set by the organization and assessed by an employee's manager. Consider the final grade a student might receive for accumulating a final course average of 88%. While this average is based on behaviors exhibited over an entire class, the student's final grade or performance might range from an A to a B. The final grade depends on the specific professor's standards and the grade distribution of the class under consideration. Fourth, motivation is a necessary but insufficient contributor to job performance. This conclusion reveals that performance problems are due to a combination of individual inputs, job context factors, motivation, and appropriate motivated behaviors. Drawing a distinction between motivation and performance has its advantages. According to one motivation expert,

> The implication is that there probably are some jobs for which trying to influence motivation will be irrelevant for performance. These circumstances can occur in a variety of ways.

There may be situations in which ability factors or role expectation factors are simply more important than motivation. For example, the best predictor of high school grades typically is intellectual endowment, not hours spent studying. . . .

Another circumstance may occur in which performance is controlled by technological factors. For example, on an assembly line, given that minimally competent and attentive people are there to do the job, performance may not vary from individual to individual. Exerting effort may be irrelevant for performance.[7]

Managers are better able to identify and correct performance problems when they recognize that poor performance is not due solely to inadequate motivation. This awareness can foster better interpersonal relations in the workplace.

Historical Roots of Modern Motivation Theories

Five methods of explaining behavior—needs, reinforcement, cognition, job characteristics, and feelings/emotions—underlie the evolution of modern theories of human motivation. As we proceed through this review, remember the objective of each alternative motivation theory is to explain and predict purposeful or goal-directed behavior. As will become apparent, the differences between theoretical perspectives lie in the causal mechanisms used to explain behavior.

Needs   Needs theories are based on the premise that individuals are motivated by unsatisfied needs. Dissatisfaction with your social life, for example, should motivate you to participate in more social activities. Henry Murray, a 1930s psychologist, was the first behavioral scientist to propose a list of needs thought to underlie goal-directed behavior. From Murray's work sprang a wide variety of need theories, some of which remain influential today. Recognized need theories of motivation are explored in the next section of this chapter.

Reinforcement   Reinforcement theorists, such as Edward L Thorndike and B F Skinner, proposed that behavior is controlled by its consequences, not by the result of hypothetical internal states such as instincts, drives, or needs. This proposition is based on research data demonstrating that people repeat behaviors followed by favorable consequences and avoid behaviors resulting in unfavorable consequences. Few would argue with the statement that organizational rewards have a motivational impact on job behavior. However, behaviorists and cognitive theorists do disagree over the role of internal states and processes in motivation. Reinforcement theory is discussed in Chapter 10.

Cognitions   Uncomfortable with the idea that behavior is shaped completely by environmental consequences, cognitive motivation theorists contend that behavior is a function of beliefs, expectations, values, and other mental cognitions. Behavior is therefore viewed as the result of rational and conscious choices among alternative courses of action. In Chapter 9, we discuss cognitive motivation theories involving equity, expectancies, and goal setting.

Job Characteristics   This theoretical approach is based on the idea that the task itself is the key to employee motivation. Specifically, a boring and monotonous job stifles motivation to perform well, whereas a challenging job enhances motivation. Three ingredients of a more challenging job are variety, autonomy, and decision authority.

Two popular ways of adding variety and challenge to routine jobs are job enrichment (or job redesign) and job rotation. These techniques are discussed later in this chapter.

Feelings/Emotions

This most recent addition to the evolution of motivation theory is based on the idea that workers are whole people who pursue goals outside of becoming a high performer.[8] For example, you may want to be an A student, a loving boyfriend or girlfriend, a caring parent, a good friend, a responsible citizen, or a happy person. Work motivation is thus thought to be a function of your feelings and emotions toward the multitude of interests and goals that you have. You are likely to study long and hard if your only interest in life is to enter graduate school and become a doctor. In contrast, a highly motivated professor is likely to quit lecturing and dismiss class upon receiving a message that his or her child was seriously hurt in an accident.

A Motivational Puzzle

Motivation theory presents managers with a psychological puzzle composed of alternative explanations and recommendations. There is not any one motivation theory that is appropriate in all situations. Rather, managers need to use a contingency framework to pick and choose the motivational techniques best suited to the people and situation involved. The matrix in Figure 8–2 was created to help managers make these decisions.

Because managers face a variety of motivational problems that can be solved with different theories of motivation, the matrix crosses outcomes of interest with six major motivation theories. Entries in the matrix indicate which theories are best suited for explaining each outcome. For instance, each motivation theory can help managers determine how to increase employee effort. In contrast, need, equity, and job characteristics theories are most helpful in developing programs aimed at increasing employees' job satisfaction. Managers faced with high turnover are advised to use the reinforcement, equity, expectancy, or job characteristics theory to correct the problem.

You will be better able to apply this matrix after reading the material in this chapter and Chapters 9 and 10. This chapter covers theories related to needs and job characteristics, Chapter 9 focuses on equity, expectancy, and goal setting, and reinforcement theory is reviewed in Chapter 10.

Figure 8–2   *Motivation Theories and Workplace Outcomes: A Contingency Approach*

Outcome of Interest	Motivation Theories					
	Need	Reinforcement	Equity	Expectancy	Goal Setting	Job Characteristics
• Choice to pursue a course of action				X		
• Effort	X	X	X	X	X	X
• Performance		X	X		X	X
• Satisfaction	X		X			X
• Absenteeism		X	X			X
• Turnover		X	X	X		X

SOURCE: Adapted and extended from F J Landy and W S Becker, "Motivation Theory Reconsidered," in *Research in Organizational Behavior,* vol. 9, eds L L Cummings and B M Staw (Greenwich, CT: JAI Press, 1987), p. 33.

Need Theories of Motivation

Need theories attempt to pinpoint internal factors that energize behavior. **Needs** are physiological or psychological deficiencies that arouse behavior. They can be strong or weak and are influenced by environmental factors. Thus, human needs vary over time and place. Three popular need theories are discussed in this section: Maslow's need hierarchy theory, Alderfer's ERG theory, and McClelland's need theory.

Needs
Physiological or psychological deficiencies that arouse behavior.

Maslow's Need Hierarchy Theory

In 1943, psychologist Abraham Maslow published his now-famous **need hierarchy theory** of motivation. Although the theory was based on his clinical observation of a few neurotic individuals, it has subsequently been used to explain the entire spectrum of human behavior. Maslow proposed that motivation is a function of five basic needs. These needs are:

Need hierarchy theory
Five basic needs—physiological, safety, love, esteem, and self-actualization—influence behavior.

1. *Physiological.* Most basic need. Entails having enough food, air, and water to survive.
2. *Safety.* Consists of the need to be safe from physical and psychological harm.
3. *Love.* The desire to be loved and to love. Contains the needs for affection and belonging.
4. *Esteem.* Need for reputation, prestige, and recognition from others. Also contains need for self-confidence and strength.
5. *Self-actualization.* Desire for self-fulfillment—to become the best one is capable of becoming.

Maslow said these five needs are arranged in the prepotent hierarchy shown in Figure 8–3. In other words, he believed human needs generally emerge in a predictable stair-step fashion. Accordingly, when one's physiological needs are relatively satisfied,

Figure 8–3   *Maslow's Need Hierarchy*

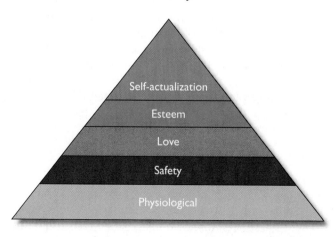

one's safety needs emerge, and so on up the need hierarchy, one step at a time. Once a need is satisfied it activates the next higher need in the hierarchy. This process continues until the need for self-actualization is activated.[9]

Although research does not clearly support this theory of motivation, there is one key managerial implication of Maslow's theory worth noting. That is, a satisfied need may lose its motivational potential. Therefore, managers are advised to motivate employees by devising programs or practices aimed at satisfying emerging or unmet needs. Many companies have responded to this recommendation by offering employees flexible scheduling and benefit plans:

> At Accenture, the large consulting company based in Chicago, staffers can put in their 40 hours in four days instead of five, getting an extra day. Some companies also allow trading of benefits. For instance, workers might be able to forfeit their health insurance if they are covered by a spouse's plan and instead get an educational loan for the same amount. At Mellon Bank in Pittsburgh, employees get "credits" that can be used for a variety of benefits such as health, vision, and dental care—or extra days off.[10]

Other companies are beginning to offer "specialized" benefits aimed at satisfying the needs of unique employees. Consider the case of Tom Tyler:

> With two job offers in hand, mechanical engineer Tom Tyler knew he'd be moving from suburban Detroit to the San Francisco area. The only question was, which employer would get his services? "The only difference between what [his eventual employer] offered me and the other company was the housing assistance," Tyler says. "The other company even offered $5,000 more per year in salary. But, when all was said and done, the house buying and selling assistance was worth somewhere in the neighborhood of $30,000...." The benefit that swayed Tyler's job decision was mortgage help through an employer-assisted housing (EAH) program.[11]

In conclusion, managers are more likely to fuel employee motivation by offering benefits and rewards that meet individual needs.

Alderfer's ERG Theory

ERG theory
Three basic needs—existence, relatedness, and growth—influence behavior.

Clayton Alderfer developed an alternative theory of human needs in the late 1960s. Alderfer's theory differs from Maslow's in three major respects. First, a smaller set of core needs is used to explain behavior. From lowest to highest level they are *existence needs* (E)—the desire for physiological and materialistic well-being; *relatedness needs* (R)—the desire to have meaningful relationships with significant others; and *growth needs* (G)—the desire to grow as a human being and to use one's abilities to their fullest potential; hence, the label **ERG theory.** Second, ERG theory does not assume needs are related to each other in a stairstep hierarchy as does Maslow. Alderfer believes that more than one need may be activated at a time. Finally, ERG theory contains a frustration-regression component. That is, frustration of higher-order needs can influence the desire for lower-order needs.[12] For example, employees may demand higher pay or better benefits (existence needs) when they are frustrated or dissatisfied with the quality of their interpersonal relationships (relatedness needs) at work.

Research on ERG theory has provided mixed support for some of the theory's key propositions.[13] That said, however, there are two key managerial implications associated with ERG. The first revolves around the frustration-regression aspect of the theory. Managers should keep in mind that employees may be motivated to pursue lower-level needs because they are frustrated with a higher-order need. For instance, the solution for a stifling work environment may be a request for higher pay or better benefits. Second, ERG theory is consistent with the finding that individual and cultural differences influence our need states (see International OB on page 266).[14] People are motivated by different needs at different times in their lives. For example, a recent survey of 1,250 women by the AFL-CIO, an umbrella organization for US unions, revealed that respondents were more concerned about health benefits than about receiving child care, elder care, and additional training or developmental opportunities.[15] This implies that managers should customize their reward and recognition programs to meet employees' varying needs. Consider how Marc Albin, CEO of a $12 million high-tech staffing firm in Sunnyvale, California, handles this recommendation.

> To identify which parts of individual employees' egos need scratching, Albin takes an unconventional approach. "My experience in managing people is, they're all different," says Albin. "Some people want to be recognized for their cheerful attitude and their ability to spread their cheerful attitude. Some want to be recognized for the quality of their work, some for the quantity of their work. Some like to be recognized individually; others want to be recognized in groups." Consequently, at the end of each employee-orientation session Albin E-mails his new hires and asks them how and in what form they prefer their strokes. "It helps me understand what they think of themselves and their abilities, and I make a mental note to pay special attention to them when they're working in that particular arena," he says. "No one has ever said, 'Just recognize me for anything I do well.' "[16]

McClelland's Need Theory

David McClelland, a well-known psychologist, has been studying the relationship between needs and behavior since the late 1940s. Although he is most recognized for his research on the need for achievement, he also investigated the needs for affiliation and power. Let us consider each of these needs.

The Need for Achievement
Achievement theories propose that motivation and performance vary according to the strength of one's need for achievement. For example, a field study of 222 life insurance brokers found a positive correlation between the number of policies sold and the brokers' need for achievement. McClelland's research supported an analogous relationship for societies as a whole. His results revealed that a country's level of economic development was positively related to its overall achievement motivation.[17] The **need for achievement** is defined by the following desires:

Need for achievement
Desire to accomplish something difficult.

> To accomplish something difficult. To master, manipulate, or organize physical objects, human beings, or ideas. To do this as rapidly and as independently as possible. To overcome obstacles and attain a high standard. To excel one's self. To rival and surpass others. To increase self-regard by the successful exercise of talent.[18]

Achievement-motivated people share three common characteristics. One is a preference for working on tasks of *moderate* difficulty. The high achiever's preference for moderately difficult tasks reinforces achievement behavior by reducing the frequency of failure and increasing the satisfaction associated with successfully

Cultural Differences Influence Need States

BusinessWeek Observers have long remarked on the sharp disparity between American and European work habits. Americans not only put in considerably more time on the job, but their yearly tally of work hours has actually risen in recent decades. In contrast, most Europeans work fewer hours and have enjoyed a steady decline on annual work time.

A common view is that this difference reflects cultural factors: Europeans, who tend to regard Americans as workaholics, simply prefer leisure to labor. Surveys indicate, for example, that many Europeans would like to reduce their work time, while many more Americans would like to increase theirs and earn more despite the fact that they already clock a lot more hours.

In a recent National Bureau of Economic Research study, however, economists Linda A Bell and Richard B Freeman suggest that the difference is related less to cultural values than to the wider range of wages within US companies and the overall economy. In essence, they argue that America's greater pay disparity creates incentives for employees to work harder.

As evidence, the authors cite data on German and US labor markets and workers' attitudes. In both countries, they note, workers in occupations with greater wage inequality tend to put in longer hours at work. But in America, where such inequality is more pervasive, they report that a much larger percentage of workers believes that their chances for advancement are high and that their work effort will pay off in pay hikes and promotions....

In sum, workers in both nations appear to log more time on the job when pay scales are unequal, but the impact is much weaker in Germany, where wages are far less variable and where greater job security, high jobless benefits, and a national health system cushion the adverse effects of layoffs. Americans work longer hours mainly because of the lure of big wage gains, the authors suggest, they're also responding to the higher risk of losing income and health coverage if the boss lets them go.

SOURCE: Excerpted from G Koretz, "Why Americans Work So Hard," *Business Week*, June 11, 2001, p 34.

This employee working in a German brewery is likely to work less hours than his American counterpart. What do you think is the primary cause of this difference in work attitudes between Americans and Europeans?

(c) Bonn-/equenz/ Imapress/ The Image Works

completing challenging tasks. Achievers also like situations in which their performance is due to their own efforts rather than to other factors, such as luck. A third identifying characteristic of high achievers is that they desire more feedback on their successes and failures than do low achievers.[19] Given these characteristics, McClelland proposed that high achievers are more likely to be successful entrepreneurs. A recent review of research on the "entrepreneurial" personality supported this conclusion. Entrepreneurs were found to have a higher need for achievement than nonentrepreneurs.[20]

The Need for Affiliation

Researchers believe that people possess a basic desire to form and maintain a few lasting, positive, and important interpersonal relationships. Research supports this proposition in both our personal and work lives. For example, psychological and physical health problems were higher among people lacking social attachments.[21] The need to affiliate also predicted employees' desire to stay with the same employer in a national random survey of 1,000 US workers. Further, the Gallup organization's survey of 105,000 employees similarly revealed that "having a best friend at work" was associated with employees' being more engaged and productive at work.[22] Just the same, not everyone has a high need to affiliate.

People with a high **need for affiliation** prefer to spend more time maintaining social relationships, joining groups, and wanting to be loved. Individuals high in this need are not the most effective managers or leaders because they have a hard time making difficult decisions without worrying about being disliked.

The Need for Power

The **need for power** reflects an individual's desire to influence, coach, teach, or encourage others to achieve. People with a high need for power like to work and are concerned with discipline and self-respect. There is a positive and negative side to this need. The negative face of power is characterized by an "if I win, you lose" mentality. In contrast, people with a positive orientation to power focus on accomplishing group goals and helping employees obtain the feeling of competence. More is said about the two faces of power in Chapter 16.

Because effective managers must positively influence others, McClelland proposes that top managers should have a high need for power coupled with a low need for affiliation. He also believes that individuals with high achievement motivation are *not* best suited for top management positions. Several studies support these propositions.[23]

Managerial Implications

Given that adults can be trained to increase their achievement motivation,[24] organizations should consider the benefits of providing achievement training for employees. Moreover, achievement, affiliation, and power needs can be considered during the selection process, for better placement. For example, a study revealed that individuals' need for achievement affected their preference to work in different companies. People with a high need for achievement were more attracted to companies that had a pay-for-performance environment than were those with a low achievement motivation.[25] Finally, managers should create challenging task assignments or goals because the need for achievement is positively correlated with goal commitment, which, in turn, influences performance.[26] Moreover, challenging goals should be accompanied with a more autonomous work environment and employee empowerment to capitalize on the characteristics of high achievers.

Motivating Employees through Job Design

Job design is used when a manager suspects that the type of work an employee performs or characteristics of the work environment are causing motivational problems. **Job design,** also referred to as job redesign, "refers to any set of activities that involve the alteration of specific jobs or interdependent systems of jobs with the intent of improving the quality of employee job experience and their on-the-job productivity."[27] A team of researchers examined the various methods for conducting job design and

Need for affiliation
Desire to spend time in social relationships and activities.

Need for power
Desire to influence, coach, teach, or encourage others to achieve.

Job design
Changing the content or process of a specific job to increase job satisfaction and performance.

integrated them into an interdisciplinary framework that contains four major approaches: mechanistic, motivational, biological, and perceptual-motor.[28] As you will learn, each approach to job design emphasizes different outcomes.[29] This section discusses these four approaches to job design and focuses most heavily on the motivational methods.

The Mechanistic Approach

The mechanistic approach draws from research in industrial engineering and scientific management and is most heavily influenced by the work of Frederick Taylor. Taylor, a mechanical engineer, developed the principles of scientific management while working at both Midvale Steel Works and Bethlehem Steel in Pennsylvania. He observed very little cooperation between management and workers and found that employees were underachieving by engaging in output restriction, which Taylor called "systematic soldiering." Taylor's interest in scientific management grew from his desire to improve upon this situation.

Scientific management is "that kind of management which conducts a business or affairs by *standards* established by facts or truths gained through *systematic* observation, experiment, or reasoning."[30] Taylor's approach focused on using research and experimentation to determine the most efficient way to perform jobs. The application of scientific management involves the following five steps: (1) develop standard methods for performing jobs by using time and motion studies, (2) carefully select employees with the appropriate abilities, (3) train workers to use the standard methods and procedures, (4) support workers and reduce interruptions, and (5) provide incentives to reinforce performance.[31] Because jobs are highly specialized and standardized when they are designed according to the principles of scientific management, this approach to job design targets efficiency, flexibility, and employee productivity.

Designing jobs according to the principles of scientific management has both positive and negative consequences. Positively, employee efficiency and productivity are increased. On the other hand, research reveals that simplified, repetitive jobs also lead to job dissatisfaction, poor mental health, higher levels of stress, and low sense of accomplishment and personal growth.[32] These negative consequences paved the way for the motivational approach to job design.

∫cientific management
Using research and experimentation to find the most efficient way to perform a job.

Motivational Approaches

The motivational approaches to job design attempt to improve employees' affective and attitudinal reactions such as job satisfaction and intrinsic motivation as well as a host of behavioral outcomes such as absenteeism, turnover, and performance.[33] We discuss three key motivational techniques: job enlargement, job enrichment, and a contingency approach called the job characteristics model.

Job Enlargement
This technique was first used in the late 1940s in response to complaints about tedious and overspecialized jobs. **Job enlargement** involves putting more variety into a worker's job by combining specialized tasks of comparable difficulty. Some call this *horizontally loading* the job. Consider how Westinghouse Air Brake Company in Chicago enlarged Jeffrey Byrom's job:

Job enlargement
Putting more variety into a job.

In traditional factories, workers often are assigned to run single machines, churning out huge batches of parts. But this is no traditional plant. Mr Byrom's job requires him to juggle the operation of three different machines simultaneously while also checking regularly for defects in finished items. . . . Mr Byrom works on a line that produces "slack adjusters," big pogo-stick-like devices used to keep the distance steady between the brakes and wheels on trains, and his job is an elaborate juggling act. Operating in a tight U-shaped area known as a "cell," he first uses a big blue metal-cutting device to shape both ends of a long bar, which he then puts into a second machine that cuts a threading into one end. From there, he places the bar in a third machine that welds a metal ring onto it.[34]

Although Byrom's job is hectic and a bit stressful, he says that he enjoys the pace because it makes the day go by faster. Westinghouse also reports that Byrom's line now produces 10 times more per day than in 1991.[35]

Proponents of job enlargement claim it can improve employee satisfaction, motivation, and quality of production. Unfortunately, research reveals that job enlargement, by itself, does not have a significant and lasting positive impact on job performance. Researchers recommend using job enlargement as part of a broader approach that uses multiple job design techniques.[36]

Job Rotation

As with job enlargement, job rotation's purpose is to give employees greater variety in their work. **Job rotation** calls for moving employees from one specialized job to another. Rather than performing only one job, workers are trained and given the opportunity to perform two or more separate jobs on a rotating basis. By rotating employees from job to job, managers believe they can stimulate interest and motivation while providing employees with a broader perspective of the organization.

Other proposed advantages of job rotation include increased worker flexibility and easier scheduling because employees are cross trained to perform different jobs. In turn, this cross training requires employees to learn new skills, which can assist them in upward or lateral mobility. Many companies also use job rotation as part of their career development process. Wellpoint Health Networks, a *Fortune* 500 health insurance company, is a good example.

Job rotation

Moving employees from one specialized job to another.

At the peak of Wellpoint's hierarchy, the board of directors annually evaluates the top 500 people to identify future leaders and create custom career development plans that include training, job rotations and coaching. The plans are reviewed quarterly with managers to ensure that the employees are on track to achieve development goals and that the goals remain relevant.... Rotational assignments are key to Wellpoint's succession planning program, ensuring that new executives are prepared to handle the far-reaching responsibilities of upper-echelon positions.[37]

Although this example supports the use of job rotation, the promised benefits associated with job rotation programs have not been adequately researched. It is thus difficult to draw any empirical conclusions about their effectiveness.

Job Enrichment   Job enrichment is the practical application of Frederick Herzberg's motivator–hygiene theory of job satisfaction. Herzberg's theory is based on a landmark study in which he interviewed 203 accountants and engineers.[38] These interviews sought to determine the factors responsible for job satisfaction and dissatisfaction. Herzberg found separate and distinct clusters of factors associated with job satisfaction and dissatisfaction. Job satisfaction was more frequently associated with achievement, recognition, characteristics of the work, responsibility, and advancement. These factors were all related to outcomes associated with the *content* of the task being performed. Herzberg labeled these factors **motivators** because each was associated with strong effort and good performance. He hypothesized that motivators cause a person to move from a state of no satisfaction to satisfaction (see Figure 8–4). Therefore, Herzberg's theory predicts managers can motivate individuals by incorporating "motivators" into an individual's job.

Motivators

Job characteristics associated with job satisfaction.

Figure 8–4   *Herzberg's Motivator–Hygiene Model*

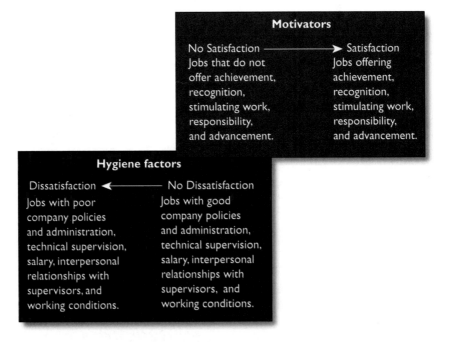

SOURCE: Adapted in part from D A Whitsett and E K Winslow, "An Analysis of Studies Critical of the Motivator–Hygiene Theory," *Personnel Psychology*, Winter 1967, pp. 391–415.

Herzberg found job *dissatisfaction* to be associated primarily with factors in the work *context* or environment. Specifically, company policy and administration, technical supervision, salary, interpersonal relations with one's supervisor, and working conditions were most frequently mentioned by employees expressing job dissatisfaction. Herzberg labeled this second cluster of factors **hygiene factors.** He further proposed that they were not motivational. At best, according to Herzberg's interpretation, an individual will experience no job dissatisfaction when he or she has no grievances about hygiene factors (refer to Figure 8–4).

The key to adequately understanding Herzberg's motivator–hygiene theory is recognizing that he believes that satisfaction is not the opposite of dissatisfaction. Herzberg concludes that "the opposite of job satisfaction is not job dissatisfaction, but rather no job satisfaction; and similarly, the opposite of job dissatisfaction is not job satisfaction, but no dissatisfaction."[39] Herzberg thus asserts that the dissatisfaction–satisfaction continuum contains a zero midpoint at which dissatisfaction and satisfaction are absent. Conceivably, an organization member who has good supervision, pay, and working conditions but a tedious and unchallenging task with little chance of advancement would be at the zero midpoint. That person would have no dissatisfaction (because of good hygiene factors) and no satisfaction (because of a lack of motivators).

Herzberg's theory generated a great deal of research and controversy. Although research does not support the two-factor aspect of his theory, it does support many of the theory's implications for job design.[40] Job enrichment is based on the application of Herzberg's ideas. Specifically, **job enrichment** entails modifying a job such that an employee has the opportunity to experience achievement, recognition, stimulating work, responsibility, and advancement. These characteristics are incorporated into a job through vertical loading. Rather than giving employees additional tasks of similar difficulty (horizontal loading), *vertical loading* consists of giving workers more responsibility. In other words, employees take on chores normally performed by their supervisors. Managers are advised to follow seven principles when vertically loading jobs (see Table 8–1).

Hygiene factors
Job characteristics associated with job dissatisfaction.

Job enrichment
Building achievement, recognition, stimulating work, responsibility, and advancement into a job.

Table 8–1   *Principles of Vertically Loading a Job*

Principle	Motivators Involved
A. Removing some controls while retaining accountability	Responsibility and personal achievement
B. Increasing the accountability of individuals for their own work	Responsibility and recognition
C. Giving a person a complete natural unit of work (module, division, area, and so on)	Responsibility, achievement, and recognition
D. Granting additional authority to an employee in his activity; job freedom	Responsibility, achievement, and recognition
E. Making periodic reports directly available to the worker himself rather than to the supervisor	Internal recognition
F. Introducing new and more difficult tasks not previously handled	Growth and learning
G. Assigning individuals specific or specialized tasks, enabling them to become experts	Responsibility, growth, and advancement

SOURCE: Reprinted by permission of the *Harvard Business Review.* An exhibit from "One More Time: How Do You Motivate Employees?" by F Herzberg (January–February 1968). Copyright © 1968 by the President and Fellows of Harvard College; all rights reserved.

The Job Characteristics Model

The Job Characteristics Model   Two OB researchers, J Richard Hackman and Greg Oldham, played a central role in developing the job characteristics approach. These researchers tried to determine how work can be structured so that employees are intrinsically motivated. (Intrinsic motivation is thoroughly discussed in the next section of this chapter.) **Intrinsic motivation** occurs when an individual is "turned on to one's work because of the positive internal feelings that are generated by doing well, rather than being dependant on external factors (such as incentive pay or compliments from the boss) for the motivation to work effectively."[41] These positive feelings power a self-perpetuating cycle of motivation. As shown in Figure 8–5, internal work motivation is determined by three psychological states. In turn, these psychological states are fostered by the presence of five core job dimensions. As you can see in Figure 8–5, the object of this approach is to promote high internal motivation by designing jobs that possess the five core job characteristics shown in Figure 8–5. Let us examine the core job dimensions.

In general terms, **core job dimensions** are common characteristics found to a varying degree in all jobs. Three of the job characteristics shown in Figure 8–5 combine to determine experienced meaningfulness (i.e., feeling that one's job is important and worthwhile) of work:

- *Skill variety.* The extent to which the job requires an individual to perform a variety of tasks that require him or her to use different skills and abilities.

- *Task identity.* The extent to which the job requires an individual to perform a whole or completely identifiable piece of work. In other words, task identity is

Intrinsic motivation
Motivation caused by positive internal feelings.

Core job dimensions
Job characteristics found to various degrees in all jobs.

Figure 8–5   *The Job Characteristics Model*

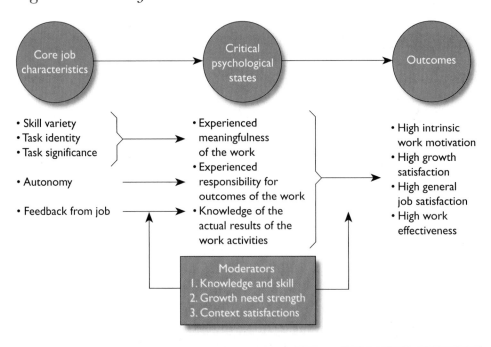

SOURCE: J R Hackman and G R Oldham, *Work Redesign,* © 1980, Addison-Wesley Publishing Co., Reading, MA, p. 90. Reprinted with permission.

high when a person works on a product or project from beginning to end and sees a tangible result.

- *Task significance.* The extent to which the job affects the lives of other people within or outside the organization.

Experienced responsibility (i.e., believing that one is accountable for work outcomes) is elicited by the job characteristic of autonomy, defined as follows:

- *Autonomy.* The extent to which the job enables an individual to experience freedom, independence, and discretion in both scheduling and determining the procedures used in completing the job.

Finally, knowledge of results is fostered by the job characteristic of feedback, defined as follows:

- *Feedback.* The extent to which an individual receives direct and clear information about how effectively he or she is performing the job.[42]

Hackman and Oldham recognized that everyone does not want a job containing high amounts of the five core job characteristics. They incorporated this conclusion into their model by identifying three attributes that affect how individuals respond to job enrichment. These attributes are concerned with the individual's knowledge and skill, growth need strength (representing the desire to grow and develop as an individual), and context satisfactions (see the box labeled Moderators in Figure 8–5). Context satisfactions represent the extent to which employees are satisfied with various aspects of their job, such as satisfaction with pay, co-workers, and supervision.

There are several practical implications associated with using the job characteristics model to enhance intrinsic motivation: Steps for applying this model are shown in Table 8–2. Because research overwhelmingly demonstrates a moderately strong relationship between job characteristics and satisfaction,[43] managers can use this model to increase employees' job satisfaction. Sun Microsystems, for example, used drop-in centers to redesign the work environment of its employees in order to enhance employee satisfaction:

Called alternative drop-in, hoteling, or telework locations, Sun's satellite work centers are comfortable but no-frills operations, little more than a series of cubicles, each quipped with

Table 8–2   *Steps for Applying the Job Characteristics Model*

1. Diagnose the work environment to determine if a performance problem is due to demotivating job characteristics. Hackman and Oldham developed a self-report instrument for managers to use called the job diagnostic survey: It is shown and used in the Group Exercise at the end of this chapter. Diagnosis begins by determining whether the core job characteristics are low or high. If the job characteristics are lower than desired, a manager proceeds to step 2. If the performance problem is not due to low job characteristics, then a manager looks to apply another model of motivation or human behavior to solve the performance problem.
2. Determine whether job redesign is appropriate for a given group of employees. Job redesign is most likely to work in a participative environment in which employees have the necessary knowledge and skills to perform the enriched tasks and their job satisfaction is average to high.
3. Determine how to best redesign the job. The focus of this effort is to increase those core job characteristics that are low. Employee input is essential during this step to determine the details of a redesign initiative.

a computer workstation and a telephone. . . . Sun opened its first three drop-in centers almost three years ago at the suggestion of a group of engineers who were tired of wasting so much time getting to and from work on the ever-more-congested Silicon Valley highway system. . . . Sun, which is very aware that its success depends on a happy workforce, has made giving its 40,000 employees worksite options a top priority, said Sun workspace architect Scott Ekman. "This initiative is part of our overall effort to keep Sun a competitive place to work. In today's tight labor market, employees are able to exert more control on where they live and work."[44]

Unfortunately, job redesign appears to reduce the quantity of output just as often as it has a positive effect. Caution and situational appropriateness are advised. For example, one study demonstrated that job redesign works better in less complex organizations (small plants or companies).[45] Nonetheless, managers are likely to find noticeable increases in the quality of performance after a job redesign program. Results from 21 experimental studies revealed that job redesign resulted in a median increase of 28% in the quality of performance.[46] Moreover, two separate meta-analyses support the practice of using the job characteristics model to help managers reduce absenteeism and turnover.[47] Athleta Corp., a sports apparel company in Petaluma, California, for instance, helped reduce employee turnover to less than 1% by using the job characteristic of autonomy to allow employees to set their own schedules and handle personal matters during the workday.[48]

Job characteristics research also underscores an additional implication for companies undergoing reengineering. Reengineering potentially leads to negative work outcomes because it increases job characteristics beyond reasonable levels. This occurs for two reasons: (1) reengineering requires employees to use a wider variety of skills to perform their jobs, and (2) reengineering typically results in downsizing and short-term periods of understaffing.[49] The unfortunate catch is that understaffing was found to produce lower levels of group performance, and jobs with either overly low or high levels of job characteristics were associated with higher stress.[50] Managers are advised to carefully consider the level of perceived job characteristics when implementing reengineering initiatives.

Biological and Perceptual-Motor Approaches

The biological approach to job design is based on research from biomechanics, work physiology, and ergonomics and focuses on designing the work environment to reduce employees' physical strain, fatigue, and health complaints.[51] An attempt is made to redesign jobs so that they eliminate or reduce the amount of repetitive motions from a worker's job. Intel, for example, has implemented the biological approach to job design.

At Intel, the most common types of workplace injuries are musculoskeletal disorders. That's one reason the company has stepped up efforts to prevent and treat repetitive-motion injuries. When employees change offices, Intel will tear down and rebuild their workstations if needed so that they are ergonomically customized. They've created an ergonomics-profile database for their Santa Clara, CA, facility which includes information on workers' heights, preferred chairs, mouse arrangement, ideal desk heights, and whether employees are left- or right-handed. A companywide database is under development.[52]

The perceptual-motor approach is derived from human factors engineering, perceptual and cognitive skills, and information processing. This approach to job design emphasizes the reliability of work outcomes by examining error rates, accidents, and workers' feedback about facilities and equipment.[53] IBM and Steelcase are jointly

IBM and Steelcase are developing an interactive office system called BlueSpace based on the perceptual-motor approach to job design. The system features a touch screen, which puts users in control of their heat, cooling, ventilation, and light, and other features putting workers in control of their environment. How might companies with programs such as BlueSpace and other ergonomic features improve employees' job satisfaction and motivation?

Photo by Paul L. Newby II, (c) The Grand Rapids Press

developing a new interactive office system, labeled BlueSpace, that is based on this method of job design. Its features include[54]

- *BlueScreen:* A touch screen that sits next to a user's computer monitor and puts users in control of their heat or cooling, ventilation, and light.
- *Everywhere Display:* A video projector that displays information on walls, floors, desktops, and other surfaces.
- *Monitor rail:* A moving rail that consists of a work surface that travels the length of a work space and a dual monitor arm that rotates to nearly a complete circle, letting users be positioned almost anywhere.
- *Threshold:* An L-shaped partial ceiling and wall on wheels that provides on-demand visual and territorial privacy to a user.

The frequency of using both the biological and perceptual-motor approaches to job redesign is increasing in light of the number of workers who experience injuries related to overexertion or repetitive motion. A study conducted by the National Research Council and the Institute of Medicine revealed "Musculoskeletal disorders cause about 1 million employees to miss work each year and cost the nation $45 billion to $54 billion in compensation costs, lost wages and decreased productivity."[55] Moreover, the Occupational Safety and Health Administration (OSHA) implemented a new set of guidelines regarding ergonomic standards in the workplace due to this trend. The standards went into effect on October 14, 2001.[56]

Leading Others toward Intrinsic Motivation

In Chapter 1 we discussed how 21st century managers would rely less on a command and control style of leadership and more on a participatory and empowering approach. While most of us can identify situations or organizations in which this transformation has not yet taken place, several workplace trends are reinforcing the need for these leadership styles. For example, today's flatter organizational structures require managers to supervise more people. This results in managers having less time to closely supervise employees and ensure they are doing their jobs and following organizational policies and procedures. Technological developments also have led to situations where many managers supervise people geographically dispersed around the globe, thereby forcing managers to manage virtually. Virtual management, which is discussed in detail in Chapter 13, reflects the practice of using electronic means to supervise people from different locations, different organizations, and different time zones. Managers are better able to manage in these circumstances when they create an environment in which employees are more self-managing. In other words, managerial effectiveness is increased when employees take responsibility for partially managing themselves.

Managers play a major role in encouraging employees to self-manage. Quite simply, employees tend to engage in self-management when they are intrinsically motivated by their work.[57] It thus is important to have an understanding of how managers can influence employees' intrinsic motivation.

We begin our exploration of intrinsic motivation by discussing the difference between intrinsic and extrinsic motivation and then presenting a model of intrinsic motivation. We conclude by focusing on how managers can cultivate intrinsic motivation in others.

The Foundation of Intrinsic Motivation

Intrinsic motivation was defined earlier as being driven by positive feelings associated with doing well on a task or job. Intrinsically motivated people are driven to act for the fun or challenge associated with a task rather than because of external rewards, pressures, or requests. Motivation comes from the psychological rewards associated with doing well on a task that one enjoys. It is important to note that individual differences exist when it comes to intrinsic motivation. People are intrinsically motivated for some activities and not others, and everyone is not intrinsically motivated by the same tasks.[58] For example, while the authors of this book are intrinsically motivated to write, we do not jump for joy when asked to proofread hundreds of pages. In contrast, someone else may hate to write but love the task of finding typos in a document.

Extrinsic motivation

Motivation caused by the desire to attain specific outcomes.

In contrast to completing tasks for the joy of doing them, **extrinsic motivation** drives people's behavior when they do things in order to attain a specific outcome. In other words, extrinsic motivation is fueled by a person's desire to avoid or achieve some type of consequence for his or her behavior.[59] For example, a student who completes homework because he or she wants to avoid the embarrassment of being called on in class without knowing the answer is extrinsically motivated because he or she is doing it to avoid the negative outcome of being embarrassed. Similarly, a student who does homework because he or she believes it will help him or her obtain a job also is extrinsically motivated because he or she is studying for its instrumental value rather than because of pure interest. As you can see, extrinsic motivation is related to the receipt of extrinsic rewards. *Extrinsic rewards* do not come from the work itself; they are given by others (e.g., teachers, managers, parents, friends, or customers). At work, they include things like salaries, bonuses, promotions, benefits, awards, and titles.

There has been an extensive amount of research on the topic of intrinsic motivation. The majority of this research relied on students performing tasks in laboratory experiments to determine whether or not the use of extrinsic rewards dampened their intrinsic motivation. Unfortunately, the overall pattern of results has created controversy and debate among researchers.[60] Nonetheless, this conclusion does not detract from the value of focusing on the positive application of intrinsic motivation at work.

A Model of Intrinsic Motivation

Kenneth Thomas proposed the most recent model of intrinsic motivation. He developed his model by integrating research on empowerment, which is discussed in Chapter 16, with two previous models of intrinsic motivation.[61] Thomas specifically linked components of the job characteristics model of job design discussed in the last section with Edward Deci and Richard Ryan's cognitive evaluation theory. Deci and Ryan proposed people must satisfy their needs for autonomy and competence when completing a task for it to be intrinsically motivating.[62] Thomas's model is shown in Figure 8–6.

Figure 8–6 illustrates the four key intrinsic rewards underlying an individual's level of intrinsic motivation. Looking across the rows, rewards of meaningfulness and progress are derived from the purpose for completing various tasks, while the sense of choice and sense of competence come from the specific tasks one completes. Looking down the columns, the sense of choice and meaningfulness are related to the opportunity to use one's own judgment and to pursue a worthwhile purpose. In contrast, accomplishment rewards—a sense of competence and progress—are derived from the extent to which individuals feel competent in completing tasks and successful in attaining their original task purpose, respectively. Thomas believes intrinsic motivation is a direct result of the extent to which an individual experiences these four intrinsic rewards while working. Let us examine these intrinsic rewards in more detail.

ſense of Meaningfulness   "A **sense of meaningfulness** is the opportunity you feel to pursue a worthy task purpose. The feeling of meaningfulness is the feeling that you are on a path that is worth your time and energy—that you are on a valuable mission, that your purpose matters in the larger scheme of things."[63] This description reveals that it is not the task itself that drives intrinsic motivation, but rather the overall

ſense of meaningfulness
The task purpose is important and meaningful.

Figure 8–6   *A Model of Intrinsic Motivation*

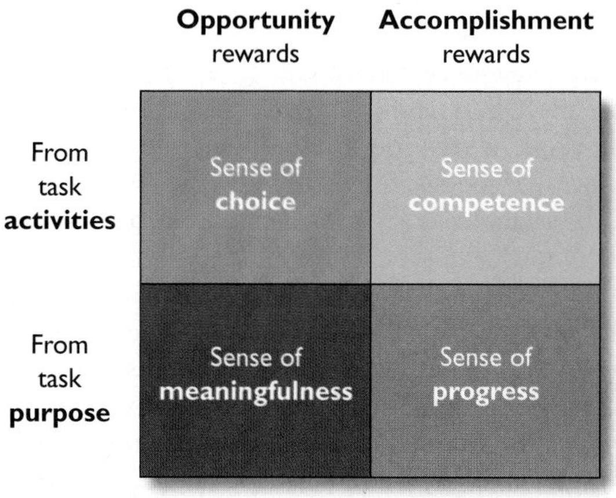

SOURCE: Reprinted with permission of the publisher. From *Intrinsic Motivation at Work: Building Energy and Commitment,* copyright© 2000 by K. Thomas, Berrett-Koehler Publishers, Inc., San Francisco, CA. All rights reserved, www.bkconnection.com.

purpose for completing tasks. People have a desire to do meaningful work, work that makes a difference. This conclusion was supported by results from a recent national survey of employees. Results revealed that the primary contributor to workplace pride was that employees were doing work that mattered.[64]

ʃense of choice

The ability to use judgment and freedom when completing tasks.

ʃense of Choice   "A **sense of choice** is the opportunity you feel to select task activities that make sense to you and to perform them in ways that seem appropriate. The feeling of choice is the feeling of being free to choose—of being able to use your own judgment and act out of your own understanding of the task."[65] Athleta Corp., a sports apparel company in Petaluma, California, for example, significantly reduced employee turnover and increased employee loyalty by allowing employees more choice in setting their schedules and handling personal matters during the workday.[66]

ʃense of competence

Feelings of accomplishment associated with doing high-quality work.

ʃense of Competence   "A **sense of competence** is the accomplishment you feel in skillfully performing task activities you have chosen. The feeling of competence involves the sense that you are doing good, high-quality work on a task."[67] A sense of competence also is related to the level of challenge associated with completing tasks. In general, people feel a greater sense of competence by completing challenging tasks. Unfortunately, large-scale surveys conducted by the Gallup organization suggest that intrinsic motivation is being undermined by a lack of challenging work. Only 15% of Gallup's respondents indicated that they had the opportunity to use their skills on a daily basis; 69% revealed they did not even get to use their strengths once a week.[68] These underutilized employees more likely posses lower intrinsic motivation.

ʃense of progress

Feeling that one is accomplishing something important.

ʃense of Progress   "A **sense of progress** is the accomplishment you feel in achieving the task purpose. The feeling of progress involves the sense that the task is moving forward, that your activities are really accomplishing something."[69] A sense of progress promotes intrinsic motivation because it reinforces the feeling that one is wisely spending his or her time. A low sense of progress leads to discouragement. Over time, a low sense of progress can lower enthusiasm and lead to feelings of being stuck or helpless.

Cultivating Intrinsic Motivation in Others

Before discussing how managers can lead others toward intrinsic motivation, we would like you to complete the OB Exercise on page 279. It assesses the level of intrinsic motivation in your current or past job. How did you stack up? Does your job need a dose of intrinsic rewards? If it does, the following discussion outlines how you or your manager might attempt to increase your intrinsic motivation.

Building blocks of intrinsic motivation

Essential work environment characteristics needed for intrinsic motivation.

Managers enhance intrinsic motivation by increasing the amount of intrinsic rewards employees derive from their work. This requires managers to create a set of conditions necessary to allow each reward to flourish. Thomas labeled this set of conditions the **building blocks of intrinsic rewards.** He used the term *building blocks* because they represent the essential ingredients of intrinsic motivation. Stated differently, the building blocks represent a host of work environment characteristics managers should strive to provide their employees. The building blocks for the intrinsic rewards are shown in Figure 8–7.

There are four diverse sets of managerial behaviors needed to establish the building blocks of intrinsic rewards. Not surprisingly, different managerial behaviors are needed for each intrinsic reward.

OB Exercise   Are You Intrinsically Motivated at Work?

Instructions

The following survey was designed to assess the extent to which you are deriving intrinsic rewards from your current job: If you are not working, use a past job or your role as a student to complete the survey. There are no right or wrong answers to the statements. Circle your answer by using the rating scale provided. After evaluating each of the survey statements, complete the scoring guide.

	Strongly Disagree	Disagree	Neither Agree nor Disagree	Agree	Strongly Agree
1. I am passionate about my work.	1	2	3	4	5
2. I can see how my work tasks contribute to my organization's corporate vision.	1	2	3	4	5
3. I have significant autonomy in determining how I do my job.	1	2	3	4	5
4. My supervisor/manager delegates important projects/tasks to me that significantly impact my department's overall success.	1	2	3	4	5
5. I have mastered the skills necessary for my job.	1	2	3	4	5
6. My supervisor/manager recognizes when I competently perform my job.	1	2	3	4	5
7. Throughout the year, my department celebrates its progress toward achieving its goals.	1	2	3	4	5
8. I regularly receive evidence/information about my progress toward achieving my overall performance goals.	1	2	3	4	5

Scoring Key

Sense of meaningfulness (add items 1–2)   _____

Sense of choice (add items 3–4)   _____

Sense of competence (add items 5–6)   _____

Sense of progress (add items 7–8)   _____

Overall score (add all items)   _____

Arbitrary Norms

For each intrinsic reward, a score of 2–4 indicates low intrinsic motivation, 5–7 represents moderate intrinsic motivation, and 8–10 indicates high intrinsic motivation. For the overall score, 8–19 is low, 20–30 is moderate, and 31–40 is high.

Figure 8–7 *Building Blocks for Intrinsic Rewards*

Choice:	**Competence:**
• Delegated authority • Trust in workers • Security (no punishment) for honest mistakes • A clear purpose • Information	• Knowledge • Positive feedback • Skill recognition • Challenge • High, non-comparative standards
Meaningfulness:	**Progress:**
• A non-cynical climate • Clearly identified passions • An exciting vision • Relevant task purposes • Whole tasks	• A collaborative climate • Milestones • Celebrations • Access to customers • Measurement of improvement

SOURCE: K Thomas, *Intrinsic Motivation at Work: Building Energy and Commitment* (San Francisco: Berrett-Koehler, 2000), p. 49.

Leading for Meaningfulness

Managers lead for meaningfulness by *inspiring* their employees and *modeling* desired behaviors. Figure 8–7 reveals managers can accomplish this by helping employees to identify their passions at work and creating an exciting organizational vision employees feel connected to. In support of this recommendation, results from Gallup poll surveys show that employees are more engaged and productive at work when they see the connection between their work and the organization's vision.[70] This connection creates a sense of purpose for employees.

Leading for Choice

Managers lead for choice by *empowering* employees and *delegating* meaningful assignments and tasks. Consider how Gail Evans, an executive vice president at Atlanta-based CNN, and Judy Lewent, senior vice president and chief financial officer for pharmaceutical giant Merck & Co., feel about leading for choice.

> Gail Evans . . . says delegating is essential. If you refuse to let your staff handle their own projects, you're jeopardizing their advancement—because they aren't learning new skills and adding successes to their resume—and you're wasting your precious hours doing someone else's work. . . . For Lewent, delegating the responsibility of running staff meetings to one of her team members means she can sit back and observe her employees, an activity that helps her make decisions about their career development. It also lets her subordinates hone their leadership skills—a must as they move up the ladder. In fact, when asked for her single definition of a good boss, Lewent says, "someone who understands the true art of teamwork and delegation."[71]

Leading for Competence

Managers lead for competence by *supporting* and *coaching* their employees. Figure 8–7 provides several examples of how this might be done. Managers first need to make sure employees have the knowledge needed to successfully perform their jobs. Deficiencies can be handled through training and mentoring. Providing positive feedback and sincere recognition can also be coupled with the assignment of a challenging task to fuel employees' intrinsic motivation.

Leading for Progress   Managers lead for progress by *monitoring* and *rewarding* others. Julie Stewart, president of the Applebee's division of Applebee's International, a $670 million chain of more than 1,000 restaurants, makes it a point to use some of the building blocks listed in Figure 8–7 to create a sense of progress.

> Every night, Applebee's Stewart uses a trick she learned from a previous boss. After everyone is gone, she leaves a sealed note on the chair of an employee, explaining how critical that person's work is or how much she appreciates the completion of a recent project. Sometimes she leaves voice mail; other times she might send flowers. "For a lot of people, it means more than any raise," Stewart says. "I do not leave the office without doing this."[72]

Research and Recommendations

Thomas's model of intrinsic motivation has not been subjected to much research at this point in time. This is partly due to its newness in the field of organizational behavior and the fact the model is based on integrating theories—the job characteristics model and cognitive evaluation theory—that have been supported by past research. This leads us to conclude that the basic formulation of the model appears to be on solid ground, and future research is needed to study the specific recommendations for leading others toward intrinsic motivation. In the meantime, managers are encouraged to use the building blocks of intrinsic rewards as a way to increase employees' intrinsic motivation.

Summary of Key Concepts

1. *Define the term* motivation. Motivation is defined as those psychological processes that cause the arousal, direction, and persistence of voluntary, goal-oriented actions. Managers need to understand these psychological processes if they are to successfully guide employees toward accomplishing organizational objectives.

2. *Discuss the job performance model of motivation.* Individual inputs and job context variables are the two key categories of factors that influence motivation. In turn, motivation leads to motivated behaviors, which then affect performance. The model highlights four key issues: (1) Motivation is different from behavior. (2) Behavior is influenced by more than just motivation. (3) Behavior is different from performance. (4) Motivation is a necessary but insufficient contributor to job performance.

3. *Review the historical roots of modern motivation theories.* Five ways of explaining behavior—needs, reinforcement, cognition, job characteristics, and feelings/emotions— underlie the evolution of modern theories of human motivation. Some theories of motivation focus on internal energizers of behavior such as needs, satisfaction, and feelings/emotions. Other motivation theories, which deal in terms of reinforcement, cognitions, and job characteristics, focus on more complex

person–environment interactions. There is no single, universally accepted theory of motivation.

4. *Contrast Maslow's, Alderfer's, and McClelland's need theories.* Maslow proposed that motivation is a function of five basic needs arranged in a prepotent hierarchy. The concept of a stair-step hierarchy has not stood up well under research. Alderfer concluded that three core needs explain behavior—existence, relatedness, and growth. He proposed that more than one need can be activated at a time and frustration of higher-order needs can influence the desire for lower-level needs. McClelland argued that motivation and performance vary according to the strength of an individual's need for achievement. High achievers prefer tasks of moderate difficulty, situations under their control, and a desire for more performance feedback than low achievers. Top managers should have a high need for power coupled with a low need for affiliation.

5. *Describe the mechanistic, motivation, biological, and perceptual-motor approaches to job design.* The mechanistic approach is based on industrial engineering and scientific management and focuses on increasing efficiency, flexibility, and employee productivity. Motivational approaches aim to improve employees' affective and

attitudinal reactions and behavioral outcomes. Job enlargement, job enrichment, and a contingency approach called the job characteristics model are motivational approaches to job design. The biological approach focuses on designing the work environment to reduce employees' physical strain, fatigue, and health complaints. The perceptual-motor approach emphasizes the reliability of work outcomes.

6. *Explain the practical significance of Herzberg's distinction between motivators and hygiene factors.* Herzberg believes job satisfaction motivates better job performance. His *hygiene* factors, such as policies, supervision, and salary, erase sources of dissatisfaction. On the other hand, his *motivators,* such as achievement, responsibility, and recognition, foster job satisfaction. Although Herzberg's motivator–hygiene theory of job satisfaction has been criticized on methodological grounds, it has practical significance for job enrichment.

7. *Describe how intrinsic motivation is increased by using the job characteristics model.* The psychological states of experienced meaningfulness, experienced responsibility, and knowledge of results produce internal work motivation. These psychological states are fostered by the presence of five core job characteristics. People respond positively to jobs containing these core job characteristics when they have the knowledge and skills necessary to perform the job, high growth needs, and high context satisfactions.

8. *Review the four intrinsic rewards underlying intrinsic motivation.* Intrinsic motivation is driven by the opportunity rewards of a sense of meaningfulness and a sense of choice, and the accomplishment rewards of a sense of competence and a sense of progress. A sense of meaningfulness and progress are driven by the purpose underlying task completion, whereas a sense of choice and competence revolve around the tasks one performs at work.

9. *Discuss how managers cultivate intrinsic motivation in others.* Managers begin by trying to create a set of conditions necessary to allow intrinsic rewards to flourish. This set of conditions is labeled the building blocks of intrinsic rewards. Managers specifically lead for meaningfulness, choice, competence, and progress by inspiring and modeling, empowering and delegating, supporting and coaching, and monitoring and rewarding, respectively.

Discussion Questions

1. Why should the average manager be well versed in the various motivation theories?

2. From a practical standpoint, what is a major drawback of theories of motivation based on internal factors such as needs, satisfaction, and feelings/emotions?

3. Are you a high achiever? How can you tell? How will this help or hinder your path to top management?

4. How have hygiene factors and motivators affected your job satisfaction and performance?

5. Which of the four types of job design is most likely to be used in the future? Explain your rationale.

6. How might the job characteristics model be used to increase your internal motivation to study?

7. Do you know anyone who would not respond positively to an enriched job? Describe this person.

8. To what extent is your behavior and performance a function of intrinsic and extrinsic motivation? Explain.

9. How might your professor use the building blocks of intrinsic rewards to increase students' intrinsic motivation?

10. What are the three most valuable lessons about employee motivation that you have learned from this chapter?

Internet Exercise   **www.fed.org**

This chapter discussed a variety of approaches for motivating employees. We noted that there is not one best theory of motivation and that managers can use different theories to solve various types of performance problems. The purpose of this exercise is for you to identify motivational techniques or programs that are being used at different companies. Begin by visiting the Web site for the Foundation for Enterprise Development at **www.fed.org.** The Foundation is a nonprofit organization that helps managers to implement equity-based compensation and broad-based participation programs aimed at improving corporate performance. To begin your search, select the resource library and follow up by choosing to view the library by subject. You will be given a variety of categories to choose from. Use the categories of "case studies of private companies" or "case studies of public companies," and then pick two companies that you would like to analyze.

Questions

1. In what ways are these companies using the theories and models discussed in this chapter?

2. To what extent is employee motivation related to these organizations' cultures?

3. What motivational methods are these companies using that were not discussed in this chapter?

OB in Action Case Study

Technology Professionals Corp. (TPC) Uses a Variety of Techniques to Motivate Employees[73]

Linda Connor is a high-school-yearbook editor at heart. The vice-president of corporate culture at Technology Professionals Corp. (TPC), a $6.6-million technology staffing and services company in Grand Rapids, MI, is constantly amassing and recording lively tidbits about the organization's almost 90 employees. She then takes that information, runs it through her imagination, and pulls out ingenious—occasionally audacious—ideas for customized rewards.

"I sit down at employees' 30-day reviews and ask specific questions about hobbies and interests for each member of their families," says Connor, who has, among other things, arranged for a staffer to fly on an F17 bomber. "I ask about the spouse, children, and even pets, so that if an event occurs that I know has been a drain on the family, I can do something special just for the spouse or kids." Connor updates her profiles over time with information and insights gleaned from routine interaction, "so we are prepared to do things that are very timely for their current interests or needs," she explains. "Every time I meet an employee or I hear about a meeting someone else has had, I take mental notes."

Collecting information about individuals and transforming it into tailored offerings is the stuff of one-to-one marketing, a seed planted in 1993 by Don Peppers and Martha Rogers that has since grown into the mighty oak of customer-relationship management (CRM). But in a new twist, TPC and companies like it are taking that concept and focusing it on their own employees. . . .

One-to-one-management companies are run—in a timely inversion of John Adams's ideal—as organizations of men (and women), not of laws. Nonetheless, a few laws, or at least cultural traits, appear to govern many such organizations. Together those traits create an environment where employees' needs are known, sometimes anticipated, and served, just as customers' needs are known, sometimes anticipated, and served in CRM-focused organizations. . . .

TPC's Connor doesn't need a good memory—she simply consults her extensive notes about employees' peeves and preferences. Connor's entry about consultant Phil Mayrose, for example, reveals that he loves college football, oldies music, and—above all else—golf. "Loves to try different courses. Send him out with either his wife, teammates, or a friend and he's in heaven," reads Connor's Mayrose entry. Last year she used that information to reward the hardworking Mayrose with a weekend getaway at a dude ranch that included several rounds of golf.

Connor doesn't focus exclusively on rewards. She also wants to understand employees' personal lives so that she can help when things spin out of balance. Her comments about one employee read more like a page torn from a therapist's notebook than something from a human-resources file: "During stressful periods [she] loses confidence in her ability as a mom, housekeeper, sister, daughter, friend, and aunt," Connor observes. "Ideas during high-stress times: lawn-mowing service, housekeeping, hot meals, day away with her son."

Connor's dedicated chronicling of employees' passions manifests the philosophy of TPC's founder and CEO, Steven Lassig, whose own ballooning workload makes it impossible for him to keep up with every member of his fast-growing staff. Back when TPC was just starting up, hiring someone was a little like making a new friend, says Lassig. "I used to take not only the people we were hiring but also their spouse or significant other to dinner," says the CEO. "We'd talk about families, hobbies, kids."

Lassig no longer has the time even to meet every new hire, so he schedules informal lunches several times a month with groups of no more than six employees, just to chat. "Eventually, everyone attends," says Lassig. "It helps me get to know them and gives me ideas on how to reward them when they do something well.". . .

At TPC employees are consulted about more substantive things—including their own compensation. The employee-owned staffing company—whose products are, in essence, its people—opens its books to its staff, sharing financial information down to the CEO's salary. Individuals know both their target and actual margins for each assignment. Once a year Connor asks the company's programmers for hire to research the market value for their skill sets and experience, and then to use that information, together with knowledge of their own margins, to propose annual raises. (Connor uses the same method when determining compensation for sales, recruitment, and office-support staff, although information on margins, in those cases, does not apply.) She accepts their numbers without question 95% of the time, she says, and occasionally assents to a larger-than-warranted increase if an employee's personal circumstances recommend it.

"It's silly for me to slide a piece of paper across the table saying, 'This is what you're worth this year,' without any input from them," says Connor. "If there's a year that they have to be a little less fair to the corporation because of something that's going on in their lives—a sickness in the family, for example—I don't have any issue with that because I know these people are committed to the TPC family. And if they take a little more this year, next year when the new bill rate [for their services] comes in, they'll choose to take slightly less."

TPC has gone so far as to solicit input into company culture. In 1999, Lassig staged a contest he called "Programmers' Paradise," which invited employees to describe their ideal work environment. First prize, for the best answer, was $5,000; second and third prizes were a couple of PCs.

Many of the suggestions Lassig received migrated into company policy: for example, performance awards can be monetary or—if an employee chooses—in the form of free housecleaning services or airline tickets. When TPC raises the rate at which an employee is billed out, the employee can choose additional vacation days in lieu of a raise. To keep those ideas flowing, TPC eschews traditional end-of-year performance reviews and instead asks employees to fill out extensive surveys on how they feel the company is doing and how their work lives can be improved. "We ask if the organization is serving their needs and if not, why not," says Lassig. "Instead of us reviewing them, it's them reviewing us."

Questions for Discussion

1. To what extent is the concept of one-to-one management consistent with recommendations derived from need theories of motivation? Explain.

2. How is TPC using the principles of job enrichment? Discuss.

3. Using the model of intrinsic motivation shown in Figure 8–6, describe how TPC fosters the four intrinsic rewards.

4. How does management at TPC lead for meaningfulness, choice, competence, and progress? Discuss.

5. Do you think Linda Connor's approach for motivating employees would work at larger companies? Explain your rationale.

Personal Awareness and Growth Exercise

What Is Your Work Ethic?

Objectives

1. To measure your work ethic.
2. To determine how well your work ethic score predicts your work habits.

Introduction

The work ethic reflects the extent to which an individual values work. A strong work ethic involves the belief that hard work is the key to success and happiness. In recent years, there has been concern that the work ethic is dead or dying. This worry is based on findings from observational studies and employee attitude surveys.

People differ in terms of how much they believe in the work ethic. These differences influence a variety of behavioral outcomes. What better way to gain insight into the work ethic than by measuring your own work ethic and seeing how well it predicts your everyday work habits?

Instructions

To assess your work ethic, complete the eight-item instrument developed by a respected behavioral scientist. Being honest with yourself, circle your responses on the rating scales following each of the eight items. There are no right or wrong answers. Add up your total score for the eight items, and record it in the space provided. *The higher your total score, the stronger your work ethic.*

Following the work ethic scale is a short personal-work-habits questionnaire. Your responses to this questionnaire will help you determine whether your work ethic score is a good predictor of your work habits.

Work Ethic Scale

		Agree completely				Disagree completely

1. When the workday is finished, people should forget their jobs and enjoy themselves.   1 — 2 — 3 — 4 — 5
2. Hard work does not make an individual a better person.   1 — 2 — 3 — 4 — 5
3. The principal purpose of a job is to provide a person with the means for enjoying his or her free time.   1 — 2 — 3 — 4 — 5
4. Wasting time is not as bad as wasting money.   1 — 2 — 3 — 4 — 5
5. Whenever possible, a person should relax and accept life as it is, rather than always striving for unreachable goals.   1 — 2 — 3 — 4 — 5
6. A person's worth should not be based on how well he or she performs a job.   1 — 2 — 3 — 4 — 5
7. People who do things the easy way are the smart ones.   1 — 2 — 3 — 4 — 5
8. If all other things are equal, it is better to have a job with little responsibility than one with a lot of responsibility.   1 — 2 — 3 — 4 — 5

Total = _____

Personal Work Habits Questionnaire

1. How many unexcused absences from classes did you have last semester or quarter?
   _____ absences
2. How many credit hours are you taking this semester or quarter?
   _____ hours
3. What is your overall grade point average?
   _____ GPA
4. What percentage of your school expenses are you earning through full- or part-time employment?
   _____ %
5. In terms of percent, how much effort do you typically put forth at school and/or work?
   School = _____%   Work = _____%

Questions for Discussion

1. How strong is your work ethic?
   Weak = 8–18 Moderate = 19–29
   Strong = 30–40
2. How would you rate your work habits/results?
   Below average _____ Average _____
   Above average _____
3. How well does your work ethic score predict your work habits or work results?
   Poorly _____ Moderately well _____
   Very well _____

Group Exercise

Applying the Job Characteristics Model

Objectives

1. To assess the motivating potential score (MPS) of several jobs.
2. To determine which core job characteristics need to be changed for each job.
3. To explore how you might redesign one of the jobs.

Introduction

The first step in applying the job characteristics model is to diagnose the work environment to determine if a perfor- mance problem is due to de-motivating job characteristics. This can be accomplished by having employees complete the job diagnostic survey (JDS).[74] The JDS is a self-report instrument that assesses the extent to which a specific job possesses the five core job characteristics. With this instru- ment, it also is possible to calculate a motivating potential score for a job. The motivating potential score (MPS) is a summary index that represents the extent to which the job characteristics foster internal work motivation. Low scores indicate that an individual will not experience high intrin- sic motivation from the job. Such a job is a prime candidate for job redesign. High scores reveal that a job is capable of stimulating intrinsic motivation and suggest that a performance problem is not due to de-motivating job characteristics. The MPS is computed as follows:

$$MPS = \frac{\left(\dfrac{Skill}{variety} + \dfrac{Task}{identity} + \dfrac{Task}{significance}\right)}{3}$$
$$\times \; Autonomy \times Feedback$$

Judging from this equation, which core job characteristic do you think is relatively more important in determining the motivational potential of a job? Because autonomy and feedback are not divisible by another number, low amounts of autonomy and feedback have a greater chance of lowering MPS than the job characteristics of skill variety, task identity, and task significance.

Since the JDS is a long questionnaire, we would like you to complete a subset of the instrument. This will enable you to calculate the MPS and to identify deficient job characteristics.

Instructions

Your instructor will divide the class into groups of four to six. Each group member will first assess the MPS of his or her current job and then will identify which core job characteristics need to be changed. Once each group member completes these tasks, the group will identify the job with the lowest MPS and devise a plan for redesigning it. The following steps should be used.

You should first complete the 12 items from the JDS. For each item, indicate whether it is an accurate or inaccurate description of your current or most recent job by selecting one number from the scale provided. Write your response in the space provided next to each item. After completing the JDS, use the scoring key to compute a total score for each of the core job characteristics.

1 = Very inaccurate   5 = Slightly accurate
2 = Mostly inaccurate   6 = Mostly accurate
3 = Slightly inaccurate   7 = Very accurate
4 = Uncertain

_____ 1. Supervisors often let me know how well they think I am performing the job.

_____ 2. The job requires me to use a number of complex or high-level skills.

_____ 3. The job is arranged so that I have the chance to do an entire piece of work from beginning to end.

_____ 4. Just doing the work required by the job provides many chances for me to figure out how well I am doing.

_____ 5. The job is not simple and repetitive.

_____ 6. This job is one where a lot of other people can be affected by how well the work gets done.

_____ 7. The job does not deny me the chance to use my personal initiative or judgment in carrying out the work.

_____ 8. The job provides me the chance to completely finish the pieces of work I begin.

_____ 9. The job itself provides plenty of clues about whether or not I am performing well.

_____ 10. The job gives me considerable opportunity for independence and freedom in how I do the work.

_____ 11. The job itself is very significant or important in the broader scheme of things.

_____ 12. The supervisors and co-workers on this job almost always give me "feedback" about how well I am doing in my work.

Scoring Key

Compute the *average* of the two items that measure each job characteristic.

Skill variety (2 and 5) _____

Task identity (3 and 8) _____

Task significance (6 and 11) _____

Autonomy (7 and 10) _____

Feedback from job itself (4 and 9) _____

Feedback from others (1 and 12) _____

Now you are ready to calculate the MPS. First, you need to compute a total score for the feedback job characteristic. This is done by computing the average of the job characteristics entitled "feedback from job itself" and "feedback from others." Second, use the MPS formula presented earlier to compute the MPS. Finally, use the JDS norms provided to interpret the relative status of the MPS and each individual job characteristic.[75]

Once all group members have finished these activities, convene as a group to complete the exercise. Each group member should present his or her results and interpretations of the strengths and deficiencies of the job characteristics. Next, pick the job within the group that has the lowest MPS. Prior to redesigning this job, however, each group member needs more background information. The individual who works in the lowest MPS job should thus provide a thorough description of the job, including its associated tasks, responsibilities, and reporting relationships. A brief overview of the general working environment is also useful. With this information in hand, the group should now devise a detailed plan for how it would redesign the job.

Norms

TYPE OF JOB			
	Professional/ Technical	Clerical	Sales	Service
Skill variety	5.4	4.0	4.8	5.0
Task identity	5.1	4.7	4.4	4.7
Task significance	5.6	5.3	5.5	5.7
Autonomy	5.4	4.5	4.8	5.0
Feedback from job itself	5.1	4.6	5.4	5.1
Feedback from others	4.2	4.0	3.6	3.8
MPS	135	90	106	114

Questions for Discussion

1. Using the norms, which job characteristics are high average, or low for the job being redesigned?

2. Which job characteristics did you change? Why?

3. How would you specifically redesign the job under consideration?

4. What would be the difficulties in implementing the job characteristics model in a large organization?

Ethical Dilemma

Should Part-Time Workers Get Special Considerations?[76]

After a 15-year trend toward workplace flexibility, most big employers now offer setups aimed at allowing people to jam more roles and responsibilities into their day. But the idea of allowing people simply to cut back to a good, permanent part-time job has been a nonstarter at most companies. . . .

Many who ask to reduce their hours meet strong resistance. When a corporate strategist for a New Jersey financial-services firm asked to switch to the part-time status offered in his employer's written policies, the response from a manager was, 'You've got to be kidding!' the strategist says. He was so stunned he dropped the idea. He has since left the company.

Tracy Wilson, of Richmond, VA, part of a top-producing bond-sales team at a banking concern, laid the groundwork for a part-time position. She had an agreement from her partners and a plan for meeting goals. Then, she asked her boss to test a reduced-hours schedule, with periodic evaluations. Her boss refused, saying he didn't want to set a precedent, she says. At her boss's suggestion, she found a job-share partner. Again, the boss said no, that he had changed his mind, Ms Wilson says. "It was something I couldn't understand," she says. . . .

From employers' standpoint, most of the costs of part-timers are manageable. Part-timers tend to pay a larger share of health insurance, while life insurance, pensions and payroll taxes tend to cost their employers less. Part-timers, however, often need full-time office space. A bigger hurdle is inconvenience. Managing more bodies can be complex. And work hours in many jobs are so open-ended that it can be hard to figure out a part-timer's pay, says Hewitt's Carol Sladek.

What would you have done if you were Tracy Wilson's boss?

1. I would not allow Tracy to work part-time because it would set a bad precedent. Tracy works in a team and the company needs the full team at work in order to succeed.

2. In order to allow Tracy some flexibility, I would ask her to work 20 hours on-site and 20 at home. Explain why this is the best option.

3. I would allow Tracy to job share. Job sharing allows Tracy's job to be completed by two people. Tracy would work 20 hours on-site, and I would hire someone else to work the other 20 hours. Explain your rationale.

4. Invent other options. Discuss.

For an interpretation of this situation, visit our Web site, **www.mhhe.com/kreitner.**

Chapter Nine

Motivation through Equity, Expectancy, and Goal Setting

Learning Objectives

When you finish studying the material in this chapter, you should be able to:

1 Discuss the role of perceived inequity in employee motivation.

2 Explain the differences among distributive, procedural, and interactional justice.

3 Describe the practical lessons derived from equity theory.

4 Explain Vroom's expectancy theory.

5 Discuss Porter and Lawler's expectancy theory of motivation.

6 Describe the practical implications of expectancy theory of motivation.

7 Explain how goal setting motivates an individual.

8 Identify five practical lessons to be learned from goal-setting research.

9 Specify issues that should be addressed before implementing a motivational program.

Ed Ossie, a former executive at Texas Instruments, is president and CEO of MTW Corporation. MTW provides Web-based software and services mainly to insurance companies and state governments. MTW's sales have jumped from $7 million in 1996 to nearly $40 million in 2000 under Ossie's leadership. Ossie has grown the company from 50 to 215 employees, with a turnover rate that is approximately 20% of the industry norm, by creating a people-first culture.

Ed Ossie believes that the bedrock of MTW's success is the "expectations agreements" that he and [Dick] Mueller [founder of MTW] exchanged when Ossie joined the company. . . . It involves the articulation of both professional and personal goals dear to each party. In Ossie's case they included his making significant time in his life to be a good parent to his son. They also included a mandate to grow MTW's value by shifting its focus from simply providing technology services to also developing proprietary software that would fetch higher margins.

Performance is enhanced when employees and managers have consistent performance expectations. Ed Ossie [on the right], president and CEO of MTW Corporation, used this knowledge to help MTW's sales grow from $7 million in 1996 to nearly $4 million in 2000.
Tim Pott (left); Scott Cunningham/Stone (Right)

Ossie explains that the value of an expectations agreement is that it involves "empathic listening," in which each party articulates his or her goals and then has them repeated back by the other person. "People want to be heard, and if you can communicate to someone that you not only heard him but you understood what he said, that's the greatest affirmation you can give another person," says Ossie. "If we hadn't done this, we'd just end up guessing what matters to each other."

Every employee that joins MTW writes an expectations agreement, for a simple reason. "A lot of people are here because their expectations were not met somewhere else," says Ossie. At MTW, new hires

are encouraged to put it all out on the table. Ossie says the process allows employees to name what's most important to them. Sometimes people want flexibility to handle special family situations, be it an aging parent or a child with special needs.

The expectations agreement is a two-way, ever evolving document that follows an employee throughout his or her career at MTW. It's reviewed, and potentially revised, about every six months. Sandy Clark, who came from Zurich Personal Insurance, a large insurance company that was once a customer of MTW's, says that in a large company "a lot of time you put your heart and soul into something, and then it doesn't get implemented." She says that doesn't happen at MTW, where there is a clearer sense of mission. "The company is aware of where you want to go, and you are aware of where it's heading." . . .

John Van Blaricum, who works in marketing, says that his expectations agreement, like most at MTW, is a mix of general and specific goals. In his case he had no trouble articulating a handful of the latter. He wanted support from the company in broadening his experience in software marketing, he wanted to find a mentor to help him grow professionally, he wanted to get involved in a number of professional trade associations to increase his knowledge of the industry, and he wanted more exposure to business operations in order "to learn more about the business, and not just marketing."

MTW's management assented and then responded in equally concrete terms. It wanted him and his team to redesign and redeploy the company's Web site by a certain date. It wanted him to write three articles about MTW and get them published within a six-month period. And it wanted him to go to a certain number of industry conferences to ramp up promotion for a new market. Writing an agreement with that level of detail, recalls Van Blaricum, "helped me plan and focus my efforts for the coming year. It gets you to reflect on what you've been doing, as well as project what you should be doing."

Though an employee's expectations agreement is intended to be reviewed every six months, MTW builds flexibility into the process by trying to time the update to occur at the end of a particular project. Similarly, the review isn't a meeting between a boss and a worker; rather, it involves the employee's sitting down with the team leader of that particular project over lunch. "We want someone you've been working with doing this, because they know what you're up to," Ossie explains.[1]

> **For Discussion**
> How would you like to work at MTW? Explain.

The opening vignette highlights how employee productivity, turnover, and corporate profits are related to the use of "expectation agreements." You should not be surprised by this finding in light of our discussion of met expectations in the last chapter. Recall that job satisfaction is higher when an employee's expectations are met at work. This chapter provides a more thorough explanation for the success of Ed Ossie's expectation agreements by exploring three cognitive theories of work motivation: equity, expectancy, and goal setting. Each theory is based on the premise that employees' cognitions are the key to understanding their motivation. To help you apply what you have learned in Chapter 8 and this chapter, we conclude by highlighting the prerequisites of successful motivational programs.

Equity theory
Holds that motivation is a function of fairness in social exchanges.

Adams's Equity Theory of Motivation

Defined generally, **equity theory** is a model of motivation that explains how people strive for *fairness* and *justice* in social exchanges or give-and-take relationships. Equity theory is based on cognitive dissonance theory, developed by social psychologist Leon Festinger in the 1950s.[2]

According to Festinger's theory, people are motivated to maintain consistency between their cognitive beliefs and their behavior. Perceived inconsistencies create cognitive dissonance (or psychological discomfort), which, in turn, motivates corrective action. For example, a cigarette smoker who sees a heavy-smoking relative die of lung cancer probably would be motivated to quit smoking if he or she attributes the death to smoking. Accordingly, when victimized by unfair social exchanges, our resulting cognitive dissonance prompts us to correct the situation. Corrective action may range from a slight change in attitude or behavior to stealing to the extreme case of trying to harm someone. For example, researchers have demonstrated that people attempt to "get even" for perceived injustices by using either direct (e.g., theft or sabotage) or indirect (e.g., intentionally working slowly, giving a co-worker the silent treatment) retaliation.[3] Consider the form of direct retaliation used by Donald McNeese against Prudential Insurance Company.

> Not long after Donald McNeese had a falling-out with a boss at Prudential Insurance Co., he supposedly settled on a scheme to exact revenge.
>
> McNeese worked in the tax department of Prudential's Jacksonville, FL, office and was frustrated at what he felt was unfairly low pay. US prosecutors say he took out his anger by stealing computerized personnel files for more than 60,000 company employees.
>
> McNeese sold some of that information over the Internet, prosecutors say, and sent E-mail to workers designed to incriminate his former supervisor in the theft.... Investigators say it may amount to one of the largest identity-theft cases ever.[4]

Psychologist J Stacy Adams pioneered application of the equity principle to the workplace. Central to understanding Adams's equity theory of motivation is an awareness of key components of the individual–organization exchange relationship. This relationship is pivotal in the formation of employees' perceptions of equity and inequity.

The Individual–Organization Exchange Relationship

Adams points out that two primary components are involved in the employee–employer exchange, *inputs* and *outcomes*. An employee's inputs, for which he or she expects a just return, include education, experience, skills, and effort. On the outcome side of the exchange, the organization provides such things as pay, fringe benefits, and recognition. These outcomes vary widely, depending on one's organization and rank. Table 9–1 presents a list of on-the-job inputs and outcomes employees consider when making equity comparisons.

Negative and Positive Inequity

On the job, feelings of inequity revolve around a person's evaluation of whether he or she receives adequate rewards to compensate for his or her contributive inputs. People perform these evaluations by comparing the perceived fairness of their employment exchange to that of relevant others. This comparative process, which is based on an equity norm, was found to generalize across countries.[5] People tend to compare themselves to other individuals with whom they have close interpersonal ties—such as

Table 9–1   *Factors Considered When Making Equity Comparisons*

Inputs	Outcomes
Time	Pay/bonuses
Education/training	Fringe benefits
Experience	Challenging assignments
Past performance	Time off with pay
Ability and skill	Job security
Creativity	Career advancement/promotions
Seniority	Status symbols
Loyalty to organization	Pleasant/safe working environment
Age	Opportunity for personal growth/development
Personality traits	Supportive supervision
Effort expended	Recognition
Personal appearance	Participation in important decisions

SOURCE: Based in part on J S Adams, "Toward an Understanding of Inequity," *Journal of Abnormal and Social Psychology,* November 1963, pp. 422–36.

friends—or to similar others—such as people performing the same job or individuals of the same gender or educational level—rather than dissimilar others.[6]

Three different equity relationships are illustrated in Figure 9–1: equity, negative inequity, and positive inequity. Assume the two people in each of the equity relationships in Figure 9–1 have equivalent backgrounds (equal education, seniority, and so forth) and perform identical tasks. Only their hourly pay rates differ. Equity exists for an individual when his or her ratio of perceived outcomes to inputs is equal to the ratio of outcomes to inputs for a relevant co-worker (see part A in Figure 9–1). Since equity is based on comparing *ratios* of outcomes to inputs, inequity will not necessarily be perceived just because someone else receives greater rewards. If the other person's additional outcomes are due to his or her greater inputs, a sense of equity may still exist. However, if the comparison person enjoys greater outcomes for similar inputs, **negative inequity** will be perceived (see part B in Figure 9–1). On the other hand, a person will experience **positive inequity** when his or her outcome to input ratio is greater than that of a relevant co-worker (see part C in Figure 9–1).

Negative inequity
Comparison in which another person receives greater outcomes for similar inputs.

Positive inequity
Comparison in which another person receives lesser outcomes for similar inputs.

Equity sensitivity
An individual's tolerance for negative and positive equity.

Dynamics of Perceived Inequity

Managers can derive practical benefits from Adams's equity theory by recognizing that (1) negative inequity is less tolerable than positive inequity and (2) inequity can be reduced in a variety of ways.

Thresholds of Equity and Inequity
Have you ever noticed that some people become very upset over the slightest inequity whereas others are not bothered at all? Research has shown that people respond differently to the same level of inequity due to an individual difference called equity sensitivity. **Equity sensitivity** reflects an individual's "different preferences for, tolerances for, and reactions to the level of equity

Figure 9–1   *Negative and Positive Inequity*

A. An Equitable Situation   **B. Negative Inequity**

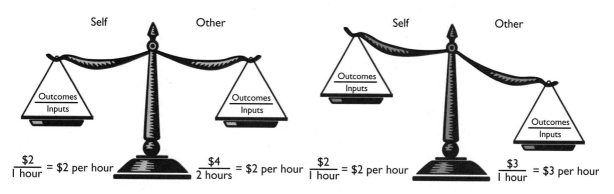

$\dfrac{\$2}{1 \text{ hour}}$ = $2 per hour $\dfrac{\$4}{2 \text{ hours}}$ = $2 per hour $\dfrac{\$2}{1 \text{ hour}}$ = $2 per hour $\dfrac{\$3}{1 \text{ hour}}$ = $3 per hour

C. Positive inequity

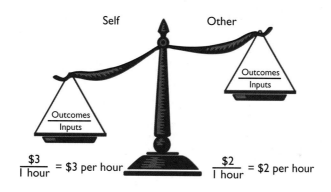

$\dfrac{\$3}{1 \text{ hour}}$ = $3 per hour $\dfrac{\$2}{1 \text{ hour}}$ = $2 per hour

---

associated with any given situation."[7] Equity sensitivity spans a continuum ranging from benevolents to sensitives to entitled.

Benevolents are people who have a higher tolerance for negative inequity. They are altruistic in the sense that they prefer their outcome/input ratio to be lower than ratios from comparison others. In contrast, equity *sensitives* are described as individuals who adhere to a strict norm of reciprocity and are quickly motivated to resolve both negative and positive inequity. Finally, *entitleds* have no tolerance for negative inequity. They actually expect to obtain greater output/input ratios than comparison others and become upset when this is not the case.[8]

Although researchers have not investigated whether or not *equity sensitivity* varies by gender, a meta-analysis of 64,757 individuals demonstrated that males and females had equal reactions to negative inequity. There were no gender differences in response to inequitable situations.[9]

Reducing Inequity   Equity ratios can be changed by attempting to alter one's outcomes or adjusting one's inputs. Table 9–2 lists eight possible ways to reduce inequity. For example, negative inequity might be resolved by asking for a raise or a promotion

Table 9–2   *Eight Ways to Reduce Inequity*

Methods	Examples
1. Person can increase his or her inputs.	Work harder; attend school or a specialized training program.
2. Person can decrease his or her inputs.	Don't work as hard; take longer breaks.
3. Person can attempt to increase his or her outcomes.	Ask for a raise; ask for a new title; seek outside intervention.
4. Person can decrease his or her outcomes.	Ask for less pay.
5. Leave the field.	Absenteeism and turnover.
6. Person can psychologically distort his or her inputs and outcomes.	Convince self that certain inputs are not important; convince self that he or she has a boring and monotonous job.
7. Person can psychologically distort the inputs or outcomes of comparison other.	Conclude that other has more experience or works harder; conclude that other has a more important title.
8. Change comparison other.	Pick a new comparison person; compare self to previous job.

SOURCE: Adapted from J S Adams, "Toward an Understanding of Inequity," *Journal of Abnormal and Social Psychology*, November 1963, pp. 422–36.

(i.e., raising outputs) or by reducing inputs (i.e., working fewer hours or exerting less effort). It also is important to note that equity can be restored by altering one's equity ratios behaviorally or cognitively. A cognitive strategy entails psychologically distorting perceptions of one's own or one's comparison person's outcomes and inputs (e.g., conclude that comparison other has more experience or works harder).

Expanding the Concept of Equity: Organizational Justice

Distributive justice
The perceived fairness of how resources and rewards are distributed.

Procedural justice
The perceived fairness of the process and procedures used to make allocation decisions.

Interactional justice
Extent to which people feel fairly treated when procedures are implemented.

Beginning in the later 1970s, researchers began to expand the role of equity theory in explaining employee attitudes and behavior. This led to a domain of research called *organizational justice*. Organizational justice reflects the extent to which people perceive that they are treated fairly at work. This, in turn, led to the identification of three different components of organizational justice: distributive, procedural, and interactional.[10] **Distributive justice** reflects the perceived fairness of how resources and rewards are distributed or allocated. **Procedural justice** is defined as the perceived fairness of the process and procedures used to make allocation decisions. Research shows that positive perceptions of distributive and procedural justice are enhanced by giving employees a "voice" in decisions that affect them. Voice represents the extent to which employees who are affected by a decision can present relevant information about the decision to others. Voice is analogous to asking employees for their input into the decision-making process.

The last justice component, **interactional justice,** relates to the "quality of the interpersonal treatment people receive when procedures are implemented."[11] This form of justice does not pertain to the outcomes or procedures associated with decision making, but rather it focuses on whether or not people feel they are treated fairly when decisions are implemented. Fair interpersonal treatment necessitates that managers communicate truthfully and treat people with courtesy and respect. Consider the role of interactional justice in how a manager of information-management systems responded to being laid off by a New Jersey chemical company. The man gained access to the company's computer systems from home by using another executive's password and deleted critical inventory and personnel files. The sabotage ultimately caused $20 million in damage and postponed a public stock offering that had been in the works. Why would a former employee do something like this?

> An anonymous note that he wrote to the company president sheds light on his motive. "I have been loyal to the company in good and bad times for over 30 years," he wrote. "I was expecting a member of top management to come down from his ivory tower to face us with the layoff announcement, rather than sending the kitchen supervisor with guards to escort us off the premises like criminals. You will pay for your senseless behavior."[12]

This employee's direct retaliation against the company was caused by the insensitive manner—interactional justice—in which employees were notified about the layoffs.

Equity Research Findings

Different managerial insights have been gained from laboratory and field studies.

Insights from Laboratory Studies
The basic approach used in laboratory studies is to pay an experimental subject more (overpayment) or less (underpayment) than the standard rate for completing a task. People are paid on either an hourly or piece-rate basis. Research findings supported equity theory. Overpaid subjects on a piece-rate system lowered the quantity of their performance and increased the quality of their performance. In contrast, underpaid subjects increased the quantity and decreased the quality of their performance.[13] A study extended this stream of research by examining the effect of underpayment inequity on ethical behavior. A total of 102 undergraduate students were either equitably paid or underpaid for performing a clerical task. Results indicated that underpaid students stole money to compensate for their negative inequity.[14]

Insights from Field Studies
Many studies of organizational justice have been conducted over the last two decades. Fortunately, two recent meta-analyses of over 190 studies help summarize what has been learned from this research.[15] The following trends were uncovered: (1) job performance was positively associated with both distributive and procedural justice, but procedural justice was the best predictor of this outcome, (2) all three forms of justice were positively correlated with job satisfaction, organizational commitment, organizational citizenship behaviors, and employees' trust, and negatively with employees' withdrawal cognitions and turnover, and (3) distributive and procedural injustice were negatively related to negative emotions such as anger. All told, these results reinforce the management philosophy of Joe Lee, CEO and chairman of the board of Darden Restaurants, Inc., the largest casual-dining restaurant company in the world.

> I have a lot of thoughts about management, but at the core of my thoughts is to operate with integrity and fairness. Treat people fairly and give them an environment that they can work in and trust. If you do that, you then can take care of your business objectives and your employees' needs and everybody can win.[16]

Feelings of Injustice Cause Chinese Employees to Protest

BusinessWeek Four and a half months ago, the run-down Ferro Alloy Factory shut its doors after a half-century of cranking out metal plates for industry in the grim Chinese city of Liaoyang. When the state-owned enterprise closed, 5,000 people lost their jobs. The workers, accustomed to cradle-to-grave security, were promised pensions and back wages for the previous year. But little or nothing materialized. Meanwhile, say workers, their erstwhile bosses busied themselves selling off factory equipment and pocketing the cash.

The workers were outraged. So, every day for the past few weeks, they have marched through Liaoyang, finishing up on Democracy Road outside the factory. There, the protesters—often joined by workers from other local factories—noisily demand the money owed them and the arrest of their former bosses. One typical worker—let's call him Li Feng—is owed $240 in back wages, enough to keep him and his family going for four months. For now Li, 55, has a job shoveling coal into a city furnace—but that will end when the weather warms up. None of this sits well with Li's wife, a retired hand at a paper factory. So she has joined the protests. "Life is so hard" for the common people, she says. "But the officials—their salaries keep rising."

SOURCE: Excerpted from D Roberts, B Einhorn, and F Balfour, "Days of Rage," *BusinessWeek*, April 8, 2002, p. 50.

In efforts to boost efficiency and reduce costs, 10,000 Chinese railway workers were involuntarily retired. This decision surprised and angered workers. As pictured here, many of these workers protested outside the Railway Ministry in Beijing. How are the workers' reactions and decision to protest consistent or inconsistent with Equity Theory?

AP/ Wide World Photos

Practical Lessons from Equity Theory

Equity theory has at least eight important practical implications. First, equity theory provides managers with yet another explanation of how beliefs and attitudes affect job performance. According to this line of thinking, the best way to manage job behavior is to adequately understand underlying cognitive processes. Indeed, we are motivated powerfully to correct the situation when our ideas of fairness and justice are offended.

Second, research on equity theory emphasizes the need for managers to pay attention to employees' perceptions of what is fair and equitable. No matter how fair management thinks the organization's policies, procedures, and reward system are, each employee's *perception* of the equity of those factors is what counts. People respond negatively when they perceive organizational and interpersonal injustices; the same is true in China (see the International OB shown above). Managers thus are encouraged to make hiring and promotion decisions on merit-based, job-related information. Moreover, because justice perceptions are influenced by the extent to which managers explain their decisions, managers are encouraged to explain the rationale behind their decisions.

Third, managers benefit by allowing employees to participate in making decisions about important work outcomes. In general, employees' perceptions of procedural justice are enhanced when they have a "voice" in the decision-making process.[17] For example, employees were more satisfied with their performance appraisals and resultant outcomes when they had a voice during the appraisal review.[18] Fourth, employees should be given the opportunity to appeal decisions that affect their welfare. Being able to appeal a decision fosters perceptions of distributive and procedural justice. In turn, perceptions of distributive and procedural justice promote job performance, job satisfaction, organizational commitment, and organizational citizenship behavior, and help reduce counterproductive work behavior, psychological distress, absenteeism, and turnover.[19]

Fifth, employees are more likely to accept and support organizational change when they believe it is implemented fairly and when it produces equitable outcomes.[20]

Sixth, managers can promote cooperation and teamwork among group members by treating them equitably. Research reveals that people are just as concerned with fairness in group settings as they are with their own personal interests.[21] Seventh, treating employees inequitably can lead to litigation and costly court settlements. Employees denied justice at work are more likely to turn to arbitration and the courts.[22] Finally, managers need to pay attention to the organization's climate for justice. For example, an organization's climate for justice was found to significantly influence employees' job satisfaction.[23] Researchers also believe a climate of justice can significantly influence the type of customer service provided by employees. In turn, this level of service is likely to influence customers' perceptions of "fair service" and their subsequent loyalty and satisfaction.[24]

Managers can attempt to follow these practical implications by monitoring equity and justice perceptions through informal conversations, interviews, or attitude surveys. For example, researchers have developed and validated a host of surveys that can be used for this purpose. Please take a moment now to complete the OB Exercise on page 298. It contains part of a survey that was developed to measure employees' perceptions of fair interpersonal treatment. If you perceive your work organization as interpersonally unfair, you are probably dissatisfied and have contemplated quitting. In contrast, your organizational loyalty and attachment are likely greater if you believe you are treated fairly at work.

Expectancy Theory of Motivation

Expectancy theory holds that people are motivated to behave in ways that produce desired combinations of expected outcomes. Perception plays a central role in expectancy theory because it emphasizes cognitive ability to anticipate likely consequences of behavior. Embedded in expectancy theory is the principle of hedonism. Hedonistic people strive to maximize their pleasure and minimize their pain. Generally, expectancy theory can be used to predict behavior in any situation in which a choice between two or more alternatives must be made. For example, it can be used to predict whether to quit or stay at a job; whether to exert substantial or minimal effort at a task; and whether to major in management, computer science, accounting, marketing, psychology, or communication.

This section introduces and explores two expectancy theories of motivation: Vroom's expectancy theory and Porter and Lawler's expectancy theory. Understanding these cognitive process theories can help managers develop organizational policies and practices that enhance rather than inhibit employee motivation.

Expectancy
theory
Holds that people are
motivated to behave
in ways that produce
valued outcomes.

OB Exercise   Measuring Perceived Fair Interpersonal Treatment

Instructions

Indicate the extent to which you agree or disagree with each of the following statements by considering what your organization is like most of the time. Then compare your overall score with the arbitrary norms that are presented.

	Strongly Disagree	Disagree	Neither	Agree	Strongly Agree
1. Employees are praised for good work.	1	2	3	4	5
2. Supervisors do not yell at employees.	1	2	3	4	5
3. Employees are trusted.	1	2	3	4	5
4. Employees' complaints are dealt with effectively.	1	2	3	4	5
5. Employees are treated with respect.	1	2	3	4	5
6. Employees' questions and problems are responded to quickly.	1	2	3	4	5
7. Employees are treated fairly.	1	2	3	4	5
8. Employees' hard work is appreciated.	1	2	3	4	5
9. Employees' suggestions are used.	1	2	3	4	5
10. Employees are told the truth.	1	2	3	4	5
			Total score = _____		

Arbitrary Norms

Very fair organization = 38–50

Moderately fair organization = 24–37

Unfair organization = 10–23

SOURCE: Adapted in part from M A Donovan, F Drasgow, and L J Munson, "The Perceptions of Fair Interpersonal Treatment Scale: Development and Validation of a Measure of Interpersonal Treatment in the Workplace," *Journal of Applied Psychology*, October 1998, pp. 683–92.

Vroom's Expectancy Theory

Victor Vroom formulated a mathematical model of expectancy theory in his 1964 book *Work and Motivation*.[25] Vroom's theory has been summarized as follows:

> The strength of a tendency to act in a certain way depends on the strength of an expectancy that the act will be followed by a given consequence (or outcome) and on the value or attractiveness of that consequence (or outcome) to the actor.[26]

Motivation, according to Vroom, boils down to the decision of how much effort to exert in a specific task situation. This choice is based on a two-stage sequence of expectations (effort→performance and performance→outcome). First, motivation is affected by an individual's expectation that a certain level of effort will produce the intended performance goal. For example, if you do not believe increasing the amount of time you spend studying will significantly raise your grade on an exam, you probably will not study any harder than usual. Motivation also is influenced by the employee's perceived chances of getting various outcomes as a result of accomplishing his or her performance goal. Finally, individuals are motivated to the extent that they value the outcomes received. Consider how employee motivation is likely to be influenced by compensation practices being instituted in 2002 in response to the the poor economy.

> This quarter [February 2002], for example, is turning into the bloodiest ever for bonuses. Salaries aren't immune, either. Nearly 30% of companies have cut or frozen pay, says Steven E Gross of compensation consultant William M Mercer Cos.—a number he projects could rise to 50% this year if the economy stays weak. That's not to mention the overwhelming majority of employee stock options that are deep underwater. What's more, almost half of the companies polled by Mercer, for example, said they plan on shifting greater portions of their health-care costs onto workers in the coming years. Kenneth R Jacobsen, a consultant with benefits expert Segal Co., estimates that the percentage of an employee's paycheck going toward health care could spiral—in the worst-case scenario—to as much as 8.2% by 2005, up from 3.4% today.[27]

Based on expectancy theory, employee motivation is likely to decrease due to a drop in extrinsic rewards—pay, bonuses, stock options—and an increase in the amount paid for health benefits.

Vroom used a mathematical equation to integrate the above concepts into a predictive model of motivational force or strength. For our purposes however, it is sufficient to define and explain the three key concepts within Vroom's model—*expectancy, instrumentality,* and *valence.*

Expectancy

An **expectancy,** according to Vroom's terminology, represents an individual's belief that a particular degree of effort will be followed by a particular level of performance. In other words, it is an effort→ performance expectation. Expectancies take the form of subjective probabilities. As you may recall from a course in statistics, probabilities range from zero to one. An expectancy of zero indicates effort has no anticipated impact on performance.

For example, suppose you have not memorized the keys on a keyboard. No matter how much effort you exert, your perceived probability of typing 30 error-free words per minute likely would be zero. An expectancy of one suggests that performance is totally dependent on effort. If you decided to memorize the letters on a keyboard as well as practice a couple of hours a day for a few weeks (high effort), you should be able to type 30 words per minute without any errors. In contrast, if you do not memorize the letters on a keyboard and only practice an hour or two per week (low effort), there is a very low probability (say, a 20% chance) of being able to type 30 words per minute without any errors.

The following factors influence an employee's expectancy perceptions:

- Self-esteem.
- Self-efficacy.
- Previous success at the task.
- Help received from a supervisor and subordinates.
- Information necessary to complete the task.
- Good materials and equipment to work with.[28]

Instrumentality

An **instrumentality** is a performance→ outcome perception. It represents a person's belief that a particular outcome is contingent on accomplishing a specific level of performance. Performance is instrumental when it leads to something else. For example, passing exams is instrumental to graduating from college.

Expectancy
Belief that effort leads to a specific level of performance.

Instrumentality
A performance→ outcome perception.

Instrumentalities range from −1.0 to 1.0. An instrumentality of 1.0 indicates attainment of a particular outcome is totally dependent on task performance. An instrumentality of zero indicates there is no relationship between performance and outcome. For example, most companies link the number of vacation days to seniority, not job performance. Finally, an instrumentality of −1.0 reveals that high performance reduces the chance of obtaining an outcome while low performance increases the chance. For example, the more time you spend studying to get an A on an exam (high performance), the less time you will have for enjoying leisure activities. Similarly, as you lower the amount of time spent studying (low performance), you increase the amount of time that may be devoted to leisure activities.

The concept of instrumentality can be seen in practice by considering the reward program used by Don Clark, Net2000's chief financial officer. Net2000 is an integrated communication provider located in Herndon, Virginia.

> Learning of an Atlanta company that was giving a BMW Z-3 to every one of its new hires, Clark linked the idea to retention and performance. "The theory was to give something to our employees that they wouldn't typically buy for themselves, and use it to motivate them."
>
> An employee who's been around for two years and met a designated performance rating can earn a three-year lease on a BMW, Dodge Durango or Audi TT. Failure to maintain the necessary performance ranking sends the vehicle back to the dealer and the employee also has to pay any early lease termination penalties. But with 70 cars awarded since the program began, Clark says, "We've never had to take one away."[29]

The incentive program clearly makes performance instrumental for receiving a leased car.

Valence

The value of a reward or outcome.

Valence   As Vroom used the term, **valence** refers to the positive or negative value people place on outcomes. Valence mirrors our personal preferences.[30] For example, most employees have a positive valence for receiving additional money or recognition. In contrast, job stress and being laid off would likely result in negative valence for most individuals. In Vroom's expectancy model, *outcomes* refer to different consequences that are contingent on performance, such as pay, promotions, or recognition. An outcome's valence depends on an individual's needs and can be measured for research purposes with scales ranging from a negative value to a positive value. For example, an individual's valence toward more recognition can be assessed on a scale ranging from −2 (very undesirable) to 0 (neutral) to +2 (very desirable).

How would you like a new BMW Z3 Roadster? Employees at Net2000 earn a three-year lease on a new BMW after they have been at the company for two years and met a designated performance rating. Net2000's rating program clearly makes performance instrumental to receiving a roadster.

(c) 2002 BMW of North America. Used with permissions. The BMW name and logo are registered trademarks

Vroom's Expectancy Theory in Action   Vroom's expectancy model of motivation can be used to analyze a real-life motivation program. Consider the following performance problem described by Frederick W Smith, founder and chief executive officer of Federal Express Corporation:

> [W]e were having a helluva problem keeping things running on time. The airplanes would come in, and everything would get backed up. We tried every kind of control mechanism that you could think of, and none of them worked. Finally, it became obvious that the underlying problem was that it was in the interest of the employees at the cargo terminal—they were college kids, mostly—to run late, because it meant that they made more money. So what we did was give them all a minimum guarantee and say, "Look, if you get through before a certain time, just go home, and you will have beat the system." Well, it was unbelievable. I mean, in the space of about 45 days, the place was way ahead of schedule. And I don't even think it was a conscious thing on their part.[31]

How did Federal Express get its college-age cargo handlers to switch from low effort to high effort? According to Vroom's model, the student workers originally exerted low effort because they were paid on the basis of time, not output. It was in their best interest to work slowly and accumulate as many hours as possible. By offering to let the student workers *go home early if and when they completed their assigned duties,* Federal Express prompted high effort. This new arrangement created two positively valued outcomes: guaranteed pay plus the opportunity to leave early. The motivation to exert high effort became greater than the motivation to exert low effort.

Judging from the impressive results, the student workers had both high effort→performance expectancies and positive performance→outcome instrumentalities. Moreover, the guaranteed pay and early departure opportunity evidently had strongly positive valences for the student workers.

Porter and Lawler's Extension

Two OB researchers, Lyman Porter and Edward Lawler III, developed an expectancy model of motivation that extended Vroom's work. This model attempted to (1) identify the source of people's valences and expectancies and (2) link effort with performance and job satisfaction. The model is presented in Figure 9–2.[32]

Predictors of Effort   Effort is a function of the perceived value of a reward (box 1 in Figure 9–2), which represents the reward's valence, and the perceived effort→ reward probability (box 2, which reflects an expectancy). Employees should exhibit more effort when they believe they will receive valued rewards for task accomplishment.

Predictors of Performance   Performance is determined by more than effort. Figure 9–2 indicates that the relationship between effort and performance is contingent on an employee's abilities and traits (box 4) and role perceptions (box 5). That is, employees with higher abilities attain higher performance for a given level of effort than employees with less ability. Similarly, effort results in higher performance when employees clearly understand and are comfortable with their roles. This occurs because effort is channeled into the most important job activities or tasks.

Predictors of Satisfaction   Employees receive both intrinsic (circle 7A in Figure 9–2) and extrinsic (circle 7B) rewards for performance. We discussed four key

Figure 9–2   *Porter and Lawler's Expectancy Model*

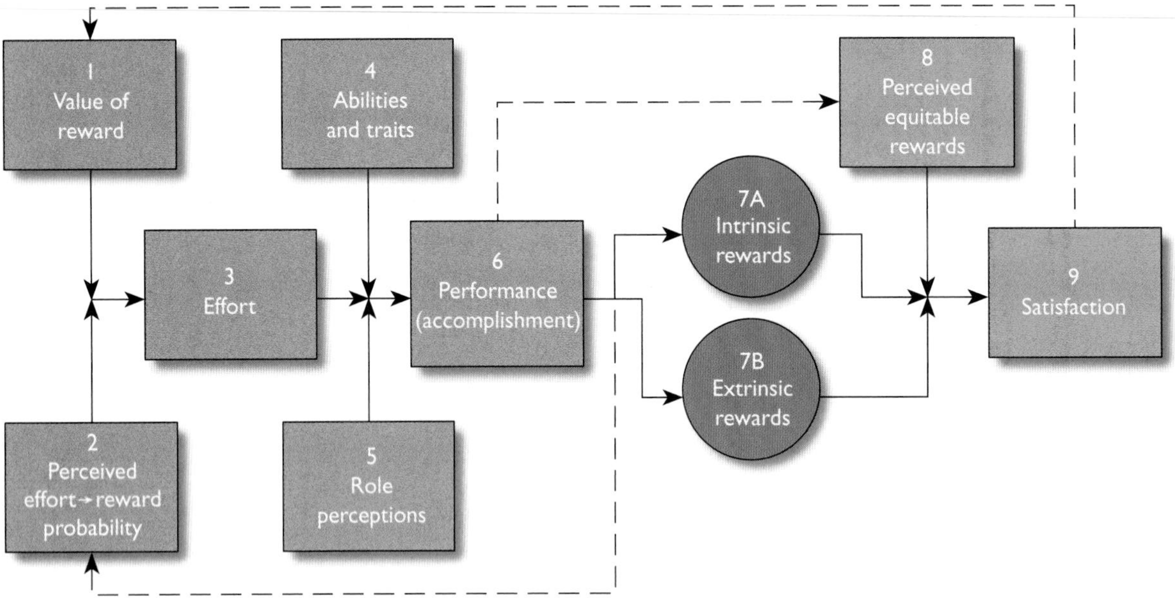

SOURCE: L W Porter and E E Lawler III, *Managerial Attitudes and Performance* (New York: McGraw-Hill/Irwin, 1968), p. 165.

intrinsic rewards in the last chapter: meaningfulness, choice, competence, and progress. Extrinsic rewards are tangible outcomes such as pay and public recognition. In turn, job satisfaction is determined by employees' perceptions of the equity of the rewards received (box 8 in Figure 9–2). Employees are more satisfied when they feel equitably rewarded. Figure 9–2 further shows that job satisfaction affects employees' subsequent valence of rewards. Finally, employees' future effort→ reward probabilities are influenced by past experience with performance and rewards.

Research on Expectancy Theory and Managerial Implications

Many researchers have tested expectancy theory. In support of the theory, a meta-analysis of 77 studies indicated that expectancy theory significantly predicted performance, effort, intentions, preferences, and choice.[33] Another summary of 16 studies revealed that expectancy theory correctly predicted occupational or organizational choice 63.4% of the time; this was significantly better than chance predictions.[34] Further, components of expectancy theory accurately predicted employee theft, perceptions of procedural justice, organizational citizenship behaviors (OCBs), task persistence, achievement, employment status of previously unemployed people, job satisfaction, decisions to retire (80% accuracy), voting behavior in union representation elections (over 75% accuracy), reenlistment in the National Guard (66% accuracy), and the frequency of drinking alcohol.[35]

Nonetheless, expectancy theory has been criticized for a variety of reasons. For example, the theory is difficult to test, and the measures used to assess expectancy, instrumentality, and valence have questionable validity.[36] In the final analysis, how-

Table 9–3   *Managerial and Organizational Implications of Expectancy Theory*

Implications for Managers	Implications for Organizations
Determine the outcomes employees value.	Reward people for desired performance; and do not keep pay decisions secret.
Identify good performance so appropriate behaviors can be rewarded.	Design challenging jobs.
Make sure employees can achieve targeted performance levels.	Tie some rewards to group accomplishments to build teamwork and encourage cooperation.
Link desired outcomes to targeted levels of performance.	Reward managers for creating, monitoring, and maintaining expectancies, instrumentalities, and outcomes that lead to high effort and goal attainment.
Make sure changes in outcomes are large enough to motivate high effort.	Monitor employee motivation through interviews or anonymous questionnaires.
Monitor the reward system for inequities.	Accommodate individual differences by building flexibility into the motivation program.

ever, expectancy theory has important practical implications for individual managers and organizations as a whole (see Table 9–3).

Managers are advised to enhance effort→performance expectancies by helping employees accomplish their performance goals. Managers can do this by providing support and coaching and by increasing employees' self-efficacy. A management expert suggests that managers can effectively coach for success by (1) establishing both individual and team goals, (2) holding individuals and team members accountable for goals, (3) showing employees how to complete difficult assignments and tasks, (4) advising employees on how to overcome performance roadblocks, (5) verbally expressing support, (6) listening to employees and fostering two-way communication, and (7) sharing and recognizing progress.[37]

It also is important for managers to influence employees' instrumentalities and to monitor valences for various rewards. This raises the issue of whether organizations should use monetary rewards as the primary method to reinforce performance. Although the reward of money certainly has a positive valence for most people, there are three issues to consider when deciding on the relative balance between monetary and nonmonetary rewards.

First, research shows that some workers value interesting work and recognition more than money.[38] Second, extrinsic rewards can lose their motivating properties over time and may undermine intrinsic motivation.[39] This conclusion, however, must be balanced by the fact that performance is related to the receipt of financial incentives. A recent meta-analysis of 39 studies involving 2,773 people showed that financial incentives were positively related to performance quantity but not to performance quality.[40] Third, monetary rewards must be large enough to generate motivation. For example, Steven Kerr, chief learning officer at General Electric, estimates that monetary awards must be at least 12% to 15% above employees' base pay to truly motivate people.[41]

Although this percentage is well above the typical salary increase received by most employees, some organizations have designed their incentive systems with this recommendation in mind. For example, Egon Zehnder International (EZI), an executive search firm, pays its partners substantial monetary rewards based on a combination of overall corporate performance and tenure.

> For partners, compensation comes in three ways: salary, equity stake in EZI, and profit shares. . . . To begin with, each partner has an equal number of shares in the firm's equity, whether he has been a partner for 30 years or one year. The shares rise in value each year, because we put 10% to 20% of our profits back into the firm. . . . The remaining 80% to 90% of the profit is distributed among the partners in two ways. Sixty percent is divided equally among all the partners, and the remaining 40% is allocated according to years of seniority. . . . So a 15-year partner gets 15 times more from this portion of the profit pool than a one-year partner.[42]

EZI's annual turnover rate among partners of 2% suggests the incentive system is working: The industry average is 30%. In summary, there is not one best type of reward. Individual differences and need theories tell us that people are motivated by different rewards. Managers should therefore focus on linking employee performance to valued rewards regardless of the type of reward used to enhance motivation.

There are four prerequisites to linking performance and rewards:

1. Managers need to develop and communicate performance standards to employees.

2. Managers need valid and accurate performance ratings with which to compare employees. Inaccurate ratings create perceptions of inequity and thereby erode motivation.

3. Managers need to determine the relative mix of individual versus team contribution to performance and then reward accordingly. For example, pharmaceutical giant Pharmacia designed its reward system around its belief in creating an organizational culture that reinforced collaboration, customer focus, and speed. "The company's reward system reinforced this collaborative model by explicitly linking compensation to the actions of the group. Every member's compensation would be based on the time to bring the drug to market, the time for the drug to reach peak profitable share, and total sales. The system gave group members a strong incentive to talk openly with one another and to share information freely."[43]

4. Managers should use the performance ratings to differentially allocate rewards among employees. That is, it is critical that managers allocate significantly different amounts of rewards for various levels of performance.

SOURCE: *Dilbert* reprinted by permission of United Feature Syndicate, Inc.

Motivation through Goal Setting

Regardless of the nature of their specific achievements, successful people tend to have one thing in common. Their lives are goal oriented. This is as true for politicians seeking votes as it is for rocket scientists probing outer space. In Lewis Carroll's delightful tale of *Alice's Adventures in Wonderland,* the smiling Cheshire cat advised the bewildered Alice, "If you don't know where you're going, any road will take you there." Goal-oriented managers tend to find the right road because they know where they are going. Within the context of employee motivation, this section explores the theory, research, and practice of goal setting.

Goals: Definition and Background

Edwin Locke, a leading authority on goal setting, and his colleagues define a **goal** as "what an individual is trying to accomplish; it is the object or aim of an action."[44] Expanding this definition, they add:

> The concept is similar in meaning to the concepts of purpose and intent. . . . Other frequently used concepts that are also similar in meaning to that of goal include performance standard (a measuring rod for evaluating performance), quota (a minimum amount of work or production), work norm (a standard of acceptable behavior defined by a work group), task (a piece of work to be accomplished), objective (the ultimate aim of an action or series of actions), deadline (a time limit for completing a task), and budget (a spending goal or limit).[45]

Goal
What an individual is trying to accomplish.

The motivational impact of performance goals and goal-based reward plans has been recognized for a long time. As discussed in the last chapter, Frederick Taylor attempted to scientifically establish how much work of a specified quality an individual should be assigned each day. He proposed that bonuses be based on accomplishing those output standards. More recently, goal setting has been promoted through a widely used management technique called management by objectives (MBO). **Management by objectives** is a management system that incorporates participation in decision making, goal setting, and objective feedback.[46] A meta-analysis of MBO programs showed productivity gains in 68 of 70 different organizations. Specifically, results uncovered an average gain in productivity of 56% when top-management commitment was high. The average gain was only 6% when commitment was low. A second meta-analysis of 18 studies further demonstrated that employees' job satisfaction was significantly related to top management's commitment to an MBO implementation.[47] These impressive results highlight the positive benefits of implementing MBO and setting goals. To further understand how MBO programs can increase both productivity and satisfaction, let us examine the process by which goal setting works.

Management by objectives
Management system incorporating participation in decision making, goal setting, and feedback.

How Does Goal Setting Work?

Despite abundant goal-setting research and practice, goal-setting theories are surprisingly scarce. An instructive model was formulated by Locke and his associates (see Figure 9–3). According to Locke's model, goal setting has four motivational mechanisms.

Figure 9–3   *Locke's Model of Goal Setting*

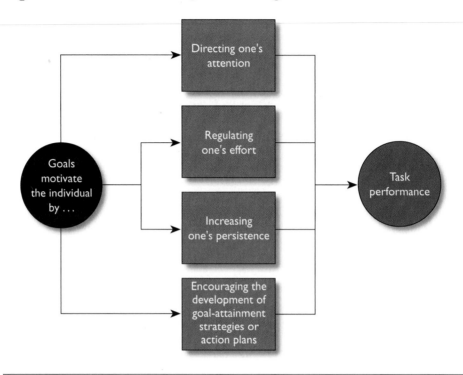

SOURCE: E A Locke and G P Latham, *A Theory of Goal Setting and Task Performance* (Englewood Cliffs, NJ: Prentice Hall, 1990). © 1990. Adapted and reprinted by permission of Prentice Hall, Inc.

Goals Direct Attention
Goals that are personally meaningful tend to focus one's attention on what is relevant and important. If, for example, you have a term project due in a few days, your thoughts tend to revolve around completing that project. Similarly, the members of a home appliance salesforce who are told they can win a trip to Hawaii for selling the most refrigerators will tend to steer customers toward the refrigerator display.

Goals Regulate Effort
Not only do goals make us selectively perceptive, they also motivate us to act. The instructor's deadline for turning in your term project would prompt you to complete it, as opposed to going out with friends, watching television, or studying for another course. Generally, the level of effort expended is proportionate to the difficulty of the goal.

Persistence

Extent to which effort is expended on a task over time.

Goals Increase Persistence
Within the context of goal setting, **persistence** represents the effort expended on a task over an extended period of time. It takes effort to run 100 meters; it takes persistence to run a 26-mile marathon. Persistent people tend to see obstacles as challenges to be overcome rather than as reasons to fail. A difficult goal that is important to an individual is a constant reminder to keep exerting effort in the appropriate direction. Steven Spielberg is a great example of someone who persisted at his goal to be a filmmaker:

> As the most popular and successful filmmaker ever, the 56-year-old Spielberg has directed nine of the 50 top-grossing films of all time. All totaled, films he has directed have brought in more than $5 billion worldwide, and films he's produced have brought in another $4 bil-

lion. . . . Spielberg identified his dream early in life and tenaciously pursued it. He allowed himself to imagine and trusted his imagination in his art. . . . Spielberg started making movies at age 11 when he learned how to use his father's eight-millimeter windup camera. . . . Having defined his ambition to direct movies from a young age, Spielberg suffered a setback when the prestigious UCLA and USC film schools rejected him because of low high school grades. Instead, because it was near Hollywood, he enrolled as an English major at California State University at Long Beach.

The summer before college, Spielberg took the Universal Studios Tour, and when the tour guides weren't watching, he broke away from the group to wander the giant movie-making factory.

"I went back there every day for three months," says Spielberg in Frank Sanello's *Spielberg: The Man, the Movies, the Mythology.* "I walked past the guard every day, waved at him and he waved back. I always wore a suit and carried a briefcase, and he assumed I was some kid related to some mogul."

He took over an unused office and put his name in the building directory with plastic letters: Steven Spielberg, room 23C. He immersed himself in film production at the industry's epicenter, wandering the Universal property to watch directors at work, and once got to see one of his heroes, Alfred Hitchcock, direct scenes for *Torn Curtain.*

Hanging out with directors, writers, and editors, Spielberg learned that to get the attention of studio executives he had to demonstrate his directing ability on the professional film width of 35 millimeters. A friend who wished to become a producer fronted $15,000 for Spielberg to make the short film *Amblin,* which caught the eye of Universal executive Sid Sheinberg, who offered Spielberg a contract to direct television shows. Still several months short of graduating from college, Spielberg hesitated. In a now famous retort, Sheinberg shot back "Kid, do you want to go to college or do you want to direct?" Spielberg dropped out and took the job.[48]

Goals Foster Strategies and Action Plans

If you are here and your goal is out there somewhere, you face the problem of getting from here to there. For example, the person who has resolved to lose 20 pounds must develop a plan for getting from "here" (his or her present weight) to "there" (20 pounds lighter). Goals can help because they encourage people to develop strategies and action

Steven Spielberg is a great example of someone who persisted at his goal to be a filmmaker. Spielberg identified his dream early in life and tenaciously pursued it, overcoming several obstacles along the way, such as being rejected by the UCLA and USC film schools because of low high school grades. Ironically, Spielberg went on to become the most popular and successful filmmaker ever. How do you think Spielberg's persistence affected his career?

Westenberger/The Liaison Agency/ Getty Images

plans that enable them to achieve their goals.[49] By virtue of setting a weight-reduction goal, the dieter may choose a strategy of exercising more, eating less, or some combination of the two. For a work-related example, consider the goals, strategies, and plans being used by Monica Luechtefeld, the executive vice president heading up Office Depot Inc.'s online business:

> Under her leadership, the Delray Beach (FL)–based company has quietly become the second-largest E-tailer in the world behind Amazon.com. . . . And this year [2001], online sales are expected to nearly double, to $1.5 billion, representing 20% of the company's overall sales. Now, she aims to push to 50% from 40% the number of Office Depot customers ordering online by year end. . . . To do that, she plans to offer them more than just office supplies. "I want us to serve them both as coach and trusted adviser," she says. To Luechtefeld that means expanding to include online services such as tax preparation and bookkeeping. Office Depot has no expertise in this area, so Luechtefeld is making alliances with those that do, including software giant Microsoft Corp.[50]

Insights from Goal-Setting Research

Research consistently has supported goal setting as a motivational technique. Setting performance goals increases individual, group, and organizational performance. Further, the positive effects of goal setting were found in six other countries or regions: Australia, Canada, the Caribbean, England, West Germany, and Japan. Goal setting works in different cultures. Reviews of the many goal-setting studies conducted over the past few decades have given managers five practical insights:

Goal difficulty

The amount of effort required to meet a goal.

1. *Difficult goals lead to higher performance.* **Goal difficulty** reflects the amount of effort required to meet a goal. It is more difficult to sell nine cars a month than it is to sell three cars a month. A meta-analysis spanning 4,000 people and 65 separate studies revealed that goal difficulty was positively related to performance.[51] As illustrated in Figure 9–4 , however, the positive relationship between goal difficulty and performance breaks down when goals are perceived to be impossible. Figure 9–4 reveals that performance goes up when employees are given hard goals as opposed to easy or moderate goals (section A). Performance then plateaus (section B) and drops (section C) as the difficulty of a goal goes from challenging to impossible.[52]

Goal specificity

Quantifiability of a goal.

2. *Specific, difficult goals lead to higher performance for simple rather than complex tasks.* **Goal specificity** pertains to the quantifiability of a goal. For example, a goal of selling nine cars a month is more specific than telling a salesperson to do his or her best. In an early review of goal-setting research, 99 of 110 studies (90%) found that specific, hard goals led to better performance than did easy, medium, do-your-best, or no goals. This result was confirmed in a meta-analysis of 70 studies conducted between 1966 and 1984, involving 7,407 people.[53]

   In contrast to these positive effects; several recent studies demonstrated that setting specific, difficult goals leads to poorer performance under certain circumstances. For example, a meta-analysis of 125 studies indicated that goal-setting effects were strongest for easy tasks and weakest for complex tasks.[54] There are two explanations for this finding. First, employees are not likely to put forth increased effort to achieve complex goals unless they "buy in" or support them.[55] Thus, it is important for managers to obtain employee commitment to the goal-setting process. Second, novel and complex tasks take employees longer to complete. This occurs because employees spend more time thinking about how to approach and solve these tasks. In contrast, employees do not have to spend much time thinking about solutions for easy

Figure 9–4   *Relationship between Goal Difficulty and Performance*

A Performance of committed individuals with adequate ability
B Performance of committed individuals who are working at capacity
C Performance of individuals who lack commitment to high goals

SOURCE: E A Locke and G P Latham, *A Theory of Goal Setting and Task Performance* (Englewood Cliffs, NJ: Prentice Hall, 1990). © 1990. Adapted and reprinted by permission of Prentice Hall.

tasks. Specific difficult goals thus impair performance on novel, complex tasks when employees do not have clear strategies for solving these types of problems. On a positive note, however, a recent study demonstrated that goal setting led to gradual improvements in performance on complex tasks when people were encouraged to explicitly solve the problem at hand.[56]

Finally, positive effects of goal setting also were reduced when people worked on interdependent tasks.[57] Managers need to encourage cooperation and efficient work flow in these situations.

3. *Feedback enhances the effect of specific, difficult goals.* Feedback plays a key role in all of our lives. For example, consider the role of feedback in bowling. Imagine going to the bowling lanes only to find that someone had hung a sheet from the ceiling to the floor in front of the pins. How likely is it that you would reach your goal score or typical bowling average? Not likely, given your inability to see the pins. Regardless of your goal, you would have to guess where to throw your second ball if you did not get a strike on your first shot. The same principles apply at work.

Feedback lets people know if they are headed toward their goals or if they are off course and need to redirect their efforts. Goals plus feedback is the recommended approach.[58] Goals inform people about performance standards and expectations so that they can channel their energies accordingly. In turn, feedback provides the information needed to adjust direction, effort, and strategies for goal accomplishment.

4. *Participative goals, assigned goals, and self-set goals are equally effective.* Both managers and researchers are interested in identifying the best way to set goals. Should goals be participatively set, assigned, or set by the employee him- or herself? A summary of goal-setting research indicated that no single approach was consistently more effective than others in increasing performance.[59]

Managers are advised to use a contingency approach by picking a method that seems best suited for the individual and situation at hand. For example, employees' preferences for participation should be considered. Some employees desire to participate in the process of setting goals, whereas others do not. Employees are also more likely to respond positively to the opportunity to participate in goal setting when they have greater task information, higher levels of experience and training, and greater levels of task involvement. Finally, a participative approach helps reduce employees' resistance to goal setting.

Goal commitment

Amount of commitment to achieving a goal.

5. *Goal commitment and monetary incentives affect goal-setting outcomes.* **Goal commitment** is the extent to which an individual is personally committed to achieving a goal. In general, an individual is expected to persist in attempts to accomplish a goal when he or she is committed to it. Researchers believe that goal commitment moderates the relationship between the difficulty of a goal and performance. That is, difficult goals lead to higher performance only when employees are committed to their goals. Conversely, difficult goals are hypothesized to lead to lower performance when people are not committed to their goals. A meta-analysis of 21 studies based on 2,360 people supported these predictions.[60] It also is important to note that people are more likely to commit to difficult goals when they have high self-efficacy about successfully accomplishing their goals.[61] Managers thus are encouraged to consider employees' self-efficacy when setting goals. Take a moment now to complete the goal commitment scale and the study habits questions contained in the OB Exercise on page 311. Is your goal commitment related to the behaviors associated with your study habits? If not, what is the cause of the discrepancy?[62]

Like goal setting, the use of monetary incentives to motivate employees is seldom questioned. Unfortunately, recent research uncovered some negative consequences when goal achievement is linked to individual incentives. Case studies, for example, reveal that pay should not be linked to goal achievement unless (1) performance goals are under the employees' control; (2) goals are quantitative and measurable; and (3) frequent, relatively large payments are made for performance achievement.[63] Goal-based incentive systems are more likely to produce undesirable effects if these three conditions are not satisfied.

Moreover, empirical studies demonstrated that goal-based bonus incentives produced higher commitment to easy goals and lower commitment to difficult goals. People were reluctant to commit to difficult goals that were tied to monetary incentives. People with high goal commitment also offered less help to their co-workers when they received goal-based bonus incentives to accomplish difficult individual goals. Individuals also neglected aspects of the job that were not covered in the performance goals.[64] For example, a sales consultant who works for a national retail store and is paid an hourly rate plus a commission tied to achieving sales goals indicates that the salespeople who make the most sales and receive the greatest commissions are those who focus on their own self-interests. So, rather than engaging in behaviors that promote outstanding customer service (e.g., keeping the floor straightened up and clean, taking the time to ring up small dollar sales, writing up sales for salespeople who are missing from the floor, following up with customers to ensure that they received their merchandise in a timely manner, and sending thank-you notes), these individuals focus on maximizing their personal monetary sales at the expense of customer service for the store at large. As another case in point, several studies revealed that quality suffered when employees were given quantity goals.[65]

These findings underscore some of the dangers of using goal-based incentives, particularly for employees in complex, interdependent jobs requiring cooperation. Managers need to consider the advantages, disadvantages, and dilemmas of goal-based incentives prior to implementation.

OB Exercise
Is Your Commitment to Achieving Your Performance Goal for This Course Related to Your Behavior?

Instructions

Begin by identifying your performance goal (desired grade) for this class. My desired grade is _____. Next, use the rating scale shown below to circle the answer that best represents how you feel about each of the following statements. After computing a total score for the goal commitment items, answer the questions related to your study habits for this course.

1 = Strongly disagree

2 = Disagree

3 = Neither agree nor disagree

4 = Agree

5 = Strongly agree

1. I am trying hard to reach my performance goal.	1	2	3	4	5
2. I am exerting my maximum effort (100%) in pursuit of my performance goal.	1	2	3	4	5
3. I am committed to my performance goal.	1	2	3	4	5
4. I am determined to reach my performance goal.	1	2	3	4	5
5. I am enthusiastic about attempting to achieve my performance goal.	1	2	3	4	5
6. I am striving to attain my performance goal.	1	2	3	4	5

Total score _____

Arbitrary Norms

Low goal commitment = 6–15

Moderate goal commitment = 15–23

High goal commitment = 24–30

Study Habits

How many hours have you spent studying for this class? _____ hours

What is your grade at this point in the course? _____

How many times have you missed class? _____ absences

SOURCE: Items were adapted from those presented in R W Renn, C Danehower, P M Swiercz, and M L Icenogle, "Further Examination of the Measurement Properties of Leifer and McGannon's (1986) Goal Acceptance and Goal Commitment Scales," *Journal of Occupational and Organizational Psychology*, March 1999, pp. 107–13.

Practical Application of Goal Setting

There are three general steps to follow when implementing a goal-setting program. Serious deficiencies in one step cannot make up for strength in the other two. The three steps need to be implemented in a systematic fashion.

Step 1: Set Goals   A number of sources can be used as input during this goal-setting stage. Time and motion studies are one source. Goals also may be based on the average past performance of job holders. Third, the employee and his or her manager may set the goal participatively, through give-and-take negotiation. Fourth, goals can be set by conducting external or internal benchmarking. Benchmarking is used when an organization wants to compare its performance or internal work processes to those of other organizations (external benchmarking) or to other internal units, branches, departments, or divisions within the organization (internal benchmarking). For example, a company might set a goal to surpass the customer service levels or profit of a benchmarked competitor. Finally, the overall strategy of a company (e.g., become the lowest-cost producer) may affect the goals set by employees at various levels in the organization.

In accordance with available research evidence, goals should be "SMART." SMART is an acronym that stands for specific, measurable, attainable, results oriented, and time bound. Table 9–4 contains a set of guidelines for writing SMART goals. There are two

Table 9–4   *Guidelines for Writing SMART Goals*

Specific	Goals should be stated in precise rather than vague terms. For example, a goal that provides for 20 hours of technical training for each employee is more specific than stating that a manager should send as many people as possible to training classes. Goals should be quantified when possible.
Measurable	A measurement device is needed to assess the extent to which a goal is accomplished. Goals thus need to be measurable. It also is critical to consider the quality aspect of the goal when establishing measurement criteria. For example, if the goal is to complete a managerial study of methods to increase productivity, one must consider how to measure the quality of this effort. Goals should not be set without considering the interplay between quantity and quality of output.
Attainable	Goals should be realistic, challenging, and attainable. Impossible goals reduce motivation because people do not like to fail. Remember, people have different levels of ability and skill.
Results oriented	Corporate goals should focus on desired end-results that support the organization's vision. In turn, an individual's goals should directly support the accomplishment of corporate goals. Activities support the achievement of goals and are outlined in action plans. To focus goals on desired end-results, goals should start with the word *to*, followed by verbs such as *complete, acquire, produce, increase,* and *decrease.* Verbs such as *develop, conduct, implement,* or *monitor* imply activities and should not be used in a goal statement.
Time bound	Goals specify target dates for completion.

SOURCE: A J Kinicki, *Performance Management Systems* (Superstition Mt., AZ: Kinicki and Associates Inc., 1992), pp. 2–9. Reprinted with permission; all rights reserved.

additional recommendations to consider when setting goals. First, for complex tasks, managers should train employees in problem-solving techniques and encourage them to develop a performance action plan. Action plans specify the strategies or tactics to be used in order to accomplish a goal.

Second, because of individual differences (recall our discussion in Chapter 5), it may be necessary to establish different goals for employees performing the same job. For example, a study of 103 undergraduate business students revealed that individuals high in conscientiousness had higher motivation, had greater goal commitment, and obtained higher grades than students low in conscientiousness.[66] An individual's goal orientation is another important individual difference to consider when setting goals. There are two types of goal orientations: a learning goal orientation and a performance goal orientation. A team of researchers described the differences and implications for goal setting in the following way:

> Individuals with a learning goal orientation are primarily concerned with developing their skills and ability. Given this focus, a difficult goal should be of interest because it provides a challenging opportunity that can lead to personal growth. In contrast, individuals with a performance goal orientation are concerned with obtaining positive evaluations about their ability. Given this focus, a difficult goal should be of lower interest because it provides a greater potential for failure. As goal difficulty increases, the probability of obtaining a positive evaluation through goal attainment decreases.[67]

A series of studies demonstrated that people set higher goals, exerted more effort, engaged in more performance planning, achieved higher performance, and responded more positively to performance feedback when they possessed a learning orientation toward goal setting than a performance orientation.[68] In conclusion, managers should consider individual differences when setting goals.

Step 2: Promote Goal Commitment

Obtaining goal commitment is important because employees are more motivated to pursue goals they view as reasonable, obtainable, and fair. Goal commitment may be increased by using one or more of the following techniques:

1. Provide an explanation for why the organization is implementing a goal-setting program.
2. Present the corporate goals, and explain how and why an individual's personal goals support them.
3. Have employees establish their own goals and action plans. Encourage them to set challenging, stretch goals. Goals should be difficult, but not impossible.
4. Train managers in how to conduct participative goal-setting sessions, and train employees in how to develop effective action plans.
5. Be supportive, and do not use goals to threaten employees.
6. Set goals that are under the employees' control, and provide them with the necessary resources.
7. Provide monetary incentives or other rewards for accomplishing goals.

Step 3: Provide Support and Feedback

Step 3 calls for providing employees with the necessary support elements or resources to get the job done. This includes ensuring that each employee has the necessary abilities and information to reach his or her goals. As a pair of goal-setting experts succinctly stated, "Motivation without knowledge is useless."[69] Training often is required to help employees achieve difficult goals. Moreover, managers should pay attention to employees' perceptions of effort→performance expectancies, self-efficacy, and valence of rewards. Finally, as we discuss in detail in Chapter 10, employees should be provided with timely, specific feedback (knowledge of results) on how they are doing.

Putting Motivational Theories to Work

Successfully designing and implementing motivational programs is not easy. Managers cannot simply take one of the theories discussed in this book and apply it word for word. Dynamics within organizations interfere with applying motivation theories in "pure" form. According to management scholar Terence Mitchell,

> There are situations and settings that make it exceptionally difficult for a motivational system to work. These circumstances may involve the kinds of jobs or people present, the technology, the presence of a union, and so on. The factors that hinder the application of motivational theory have not been articulated either frequently or systematically.[70]

With Mitchell's cautionary statement in mind, this section uses Figure 8–1 (see page 259 in Chapter 8) to raise issues that need to be addressed before implementing a motivational program. Our intent is not to discuss all relevant considerations but rather to highlight a few important ones.

Assuming a motivational program is being considered to improve productivity, quality, or customer satisfaction, the first issue revolves around the difference between motivation and performance. As pointed out in Chapter 8, motivation and performance are not one and the same. Motivation is only one of several factors that influence performance. For example, poor performance may be more a function of outdated or inefficient materials and machinery, not having goals to direct one's attention, a monotonous job, feelings of inequity, a negative work environment characterized by political behavior and conflict, poor supervisory support and coaching, or poor work flow. Motivation cannot make up for a deficient job context (see Figure 8–1). Managers, therefore, need to carefully consider the causes of poor performance and employee misbehavior.

Importantly, managers should not ignore the individual inputs identified in Figure 8–1. As discussed in this chapter as well as Chapters 5 and 6, individual differences are an important input that influence motivation and motivated behavior. Managers are advised to develop employees so that they have the ability and job knowledge to effectively perform their jobs. In addition, attempts should be made to nurture positive employee characteristics, such as self-esteem, self-efficacy, positive emotions, a learning goal orientation, and need for achievement.

Because motivation is goal directed, the process of developing and setting goals should be consistent with our previous discussion. Moreover, the method used to evaluate performance also needs to be considered. Without a valid performance appraisal system, it is difficult, if not impossible, to accurately distinguish good and poor performers.[71] Consider the motivational effect of using a performance rating system in which managers are required to rank employees against each other according to some specified distribution:

> At GE, which has used the system for several years, this means that 20% of salaried, managerial, and executive employees are rated outstanding each year, 70% "high-performance middle," and 10% in need of improvement. At Enron, where some have nicknamed the sys-

tem "rank and yank," employees are put in one of five categories: 5% are identified as superior, 30% excellent, 30% strong, 20% satisfactory, and 15% "needs improvement." And Ford, which began using rating systems last year, dictates that 10% of the auto maker's 18,000 managers will get A grades, 85% Bs, and 5% Cs. (Initially, it asked for 10% Cs.) Those who receive a second consecutive C can be fired.[72]

The problem with ranking systems is that they are based on subjective judgments. Motivation thus is decreased to the extent these judgments are inaccurate. Managers need to keep in mind that both equity theory and expectancy theory suggest that employee motivation is squelched by inaccurate performance ratings. Not only can inaccurate performance rating systems negatively influence motivation, but they can lead to lawsuits: For example, employees and former employees with Microsoft, Ford, and Conoco have filed lawsuits claiming that ranking systems are biased toward some groups over others.[73]

Managers also should keep in mind the distinction between intrinsic and extrinsic motivation. Both forms of motivation influence performance and are fueled by different factors. As discussed in Chapter 8, managers can increase intrinsic motivation by creating work environments that provide a sense of meaningfulness, a sense of choice, a sense of competence, and a sense of progress. In contrast, extrinsic motivation is affected by the link between performance and the receipt of extrinsic rewards such as pay, bonuses, awards, and promotions.

Consistent with expectancy theory, managers should make extrinsic rewards contingent on performance. In doing so, however, it is important to consider two issues. First, managers need to ensure that performance goals are directed to achieve the "right" end-results. For example, health insurers and medical groups wrestle over the relative focus on cost savings versus patient satisfaction. Consider the case of Oakland-based Kaiser Permanente.

Telephone clerks at California's largest HMO received bonuses for keeping calls with patients brief and limiting the number of doctor visits they set up....The California Nurses Association, the union representing Kaiser's registered nurses, derided the program as deceitful and harmful to patients with serious medical problems.

"Patients don't understand they're talking to a high school graduate with no nursing background," [Jim] Anderson said.

The clerks, who generally have little to no medical training, answer phone calls from customers wanting to set up doctor appointments or asking simple medical questions.

Cash bonuses were paid to those who made appointments for fewer than 35% of callers and spent less than an average of three minutes, 45 seconds on the phone with each patient. Clerks were also encouraged to transfer fewer than 50% of the calls to registered nurses for further evaluation.[74]

Interestingly, incentives based on quality care and patient satisfaction are twice as common as cost-cutting incentives among health insurers across the United States.[75] Second, the promise of increased rewards will not prompt higher effort and good performance unless those rewards are clearly tied to performance and they are large enough to gain employees' interests or attention. Dennis Kozlowski, former CEO of Tyco International, adhered to this recommendation.

Tyco executives don't receive bonuses unless they come close to meeting the aggressive earnings targets set by Kozlowski, typically about 15%. If they hit the target, they'll get a bonus at least equal to their salary. And if they blow past the target, the sky's the limit.[76]

Moreover, equity theory tells us that motivation is influenced by employee perceptions about the fairness of reward allocations. Motivation is decreased when employees believe rewards are inequitably allocated. Rewards also need to be integrated appropriately into the appraisal system. If performance is measured at the individual level, individual achievements need to be rewarded. On the other hand, when performance is the result of group effort, rewards should be allocated to the group.

Feedback also should be linked with performance. Feedback provides the information and direction needed to keep employees focused on relevant tasks, activities, and goals. Managers should strive to provide specific, timely, and accurate feedback to employees.

Finally, we end this chapter by noting that an organization's culture significantly influences employee motivation and behavior. A positive self-enhancing culture such as that at Rhino Foods, for example, is more likely to engender higher motivation and commitment than a culture dominated by suspicion, faultfinding, and blame.

Summary of Key Concepts

1. *Discuss the role of perceived inequity in employee motivation.* Equity theory is a model of motivation that explains how people strive for fairness and justice in social exchanges. On the job, feelings of inequity revolve around a person's evaluation of whether he or she receives adequate rewards to compensate for his or her contributive inputs. People perform these evaluations by comparing the perceived fairness of their employment exchange with that of relevant others. Perceived inequity creates motivation to restore equity.

2. *Explain the differences among distributive, procedural, and interactional justice.* Distributive, procedural, and interactional justice are the three key components underlying organizational justice. Distributive justice reflects the perceived fairness of how resources and rewards are distributed. Procedural justice represents the perceived fairness of the process and procedures used to make allocation decisions. Interactional justice entails the perceived fairness of a decision maker's behavior in the process of decision making.

3. *Describe the practical lessons derived from equity theory.* Equity theory has at least eight practical implications. First, because people are motivated to resolve perceptions of inequity, managers should not discount employees' feelings and perceptions when trying to motivate workers. Second, managers should pay attention to employees' feelings and perceptions when trying to motivate workers. Second, managers should pay attention to employees' *perceptions* of what is fair and equitable. It is the employee's view of reality that counts when trying to motivate someone, according to equity theory. Third, employees should be given a voice in decisions that affect

them. Fourth, employees should be given the opportunity to appeal decisions that affect their welfare. Fifth, employees are more likely to accept and support organizational change when they believe it is implemented fairly and when it produces equitable outcomes. Sixth, managers can promote cooperation and teamwork among group members by treating them equitably. Seventh, treating employees inequitably can lead to litigation and costly court settlements. Finally, managers need to pay attention to the organization's climate for justice because it influences employee attitudes and behavior.

4. *Explain Vroom's expectancy theory.* Expectancy theory assumes motivation is determined by one's perceived chances of achieving valued outcomes. Vroom's expectancy model of motivation reveals how effort→performance expectancies and performance→outcome instrumentalities influence the degree of effort expended to achieve desired (positively valent) outcomes.

5. *Discuss Porter and Lawler's expectancy theory of motivation.* Porter and Lawler developed a model of expectancy that expanded upon the theory proposed by Vroom. This model specifies (a) the source of people's valences and expectancies and (b) the relationship between performance and satisfaction.

6. *Describe the practical implications of expectancy theory of motivation.* Managers are advised to enhance effort→performance expectancies by helping employees accomplish their performance goals. With respect to instrumentalities and valences, managers should attempt

to link employee performance and valued rewards. There are four prerequisites to linking performance and rewards: (1) Managers need to develop and communicate performance standards to employees, (2) managers need valid and accurate performance ratings, (3) managers need to determine the relative mix of individual versus team contribution to performance and then reward accordingly, and (4) managers should use performance ratings to differentially allocate rewards among employees.

7. *Explain how goal setting motivates an individual.* Four motivational mechanisms of goal setting are as follows: (1) Goals direct one's attention, (2) goals regulate effort, (3) goals increase one's persistence, and (4) goals encourage development of goal-attainment strategies and action plans.

8. *Identify five practical lessons to be learned from goal-setting research.* Difficult goals lead to higher performance than easy or moderate goals: goals should not be impossible to achieve. Specific, difficult goals lead to higher performance for simple rather than complex tasks. Third, feedback enhances the effect of specific, difficult goals.

Fourth, participative goals, assigned goals, and self-set goals are equally effective. Fifth, goal commitment and monetary incentives affect goal-setting outcomes.

9. *Specify issues that should be addressed before implementing a motivational program.* Managers need to consider the variety of causes of poor performance and employee misbehavior. Undesirable employee performance and behavior may be due to a host of deficient individual inputs (e.g., ability, dispositions, emotions, and beliefs) or job context factors (e.g., materials and machinery, job characteristics, reward systems, supervisory support and coaching, and social norms). The method used to evaluate performance as well as the link between performance and rewards must be examined. Performance must be accurately evaluated and rewards should be equitably distributed. Managers also should keep in mind the distinction between intrinsic and extrinsic motivation, as both forms of motivation influence performance and are fueled by different factors. Finally, managers should recognize that employee motivation and behavior are influenced by organizational culture.

Discussion Questions

1. Have you experienced positive or negative inequity at work? Describe the circumstances in terms of the inputs and outcomes of the comparison person and yourself.

2. Could a manager's attempt to treat his or her employees equally lead to perceptions of inequity? Explain.

3. What work outcomes (refer to Table 9–1) are most important to you? Do you think different age groups value different outcomes? What are the implications for managers who seek to be equitable?

4. Relative to Table 9–2, what techniques have you relied on recently to reduce either positive or negative inequity?

5. What is your definition of studying hard? What is your expectancy for earning an A on the next exam in this course? What is the basis of this expectancy?

6. If someone who reported to you at work had a low expectancy for successful performance, what could you do to increase this person's expectancy?

7. Do goals play an important role in your life? Explain.

8. How would you respond to a manager who said, "Goals must be participatively set?"

9. Goal-setting research suggests that people should be given difficult goals. How does this prescription mesh with expectancy theory? Explain.

10. How could a professor use equity, expectancy, and goal-setting theory to motivate students?

Internet Exercise

www.ge.com

This chapter discussed how employee motivation is influenced by goal setting and the relationship between performance and rewards. We also reviewed the variety of issues that managers should con-sider when implementing motivational programs. The purpose of this exercise is for you to examine the motivational techniques used by General Electric (GE). GE is one of the most successful companies in the world. The company is well known for establishing clear corporate goals and then creating the infrastructure (e.g., rewards) to achieve them. Begin by visiting GE's home page at **www.ge.com.** Begin your search by locating GE's corporate values and corporate goals in the most recent annual report. Then expand your search by looking through the compensation committee report to obtain information that discusses the different incentives GE uses to motivate its employees.

Questions

1. How will the company's values influence goal-setting and motivation?

2. Based on the values and goals, what type of behavior is the organization trying to motivate?

3. What rewards does GE use to reinforce desired behavior and performance?

4. To what extent are GE's practices consistent with the material covered in this chapter?

OB in Action Case Study

How Long Can Employers Ask Workers to Do More with Less?[77]

BusinessWeek   On his recent family vacation in Arizona, Peter Spina spent much of his time camped out under a palm tree while his kids splashed around in the Scottsdale Princess Hotel's luxurious pool. Spina wasn't lounging. He was working—hammering out deals on his cell phone in a mad dash to break new accounts at Vulcan Ventures Inc., where he's publisher of *The Sporting News*. Spina says the downturn has forced him to work even longer hours than he did during the boom—about 15% more. Ditto for his sales force. Whereas once he had lots of bonus money to throw around, he now tries to make up for the tough slog by bringing popsicles to the office on hot days. The added hustling is one reason his team has racked up revenue gains of 46% this year in an abysmal ad market. "They're working longer and harder," says Spina.

Much has been made of the recent upsurge in productivity. Although recessions usually bring slides in this efficiency measure, the fourth quarter's astounding 5% gain gave more credibility to the idea that technology has made the economy more productive than ever before. But tell that to white-collar workers, and you're likely to hear that the gains have come on their backs. Rather than bring relief, layoff survivors say, the downturn has only socked it to them more. They complain about managing the orphaned workloads of downsized colleagues, scouring new avenues for business, and fighting for high-profile posts so if the ax falls, it won't hit them. "What we're discovering is that in this early stage of recovery, not only are companies making people work harder, but, believe me, some people want to," says J P Morgan Chase & Co. senior economist James E. Glassman. "They're trying to protect their job security." . . .

But it's not just fear that's motivating today's workplace. A number of other structural changes are also helping bosses to extract maximum productivity from their ranks. From the increased use of temps, to the reclassification of hourly workers into salaried employees ineligible for overtime pay, to the rise in variable pay that puts part of workers' paychecks at risk, companies are now able to get more out of less. . . .

Still, whatever the numbers say, there's no doubt that right now employees feel they have little choice but to accept the grueling loads. Despite some evidence of a rebound, the job market in many quarters is still weak. In April [2002], the specter of layoffs revived when General Electric Capital Services Inc. announced cuts of 7,000 jobs and Lucent Technologies Inc. eliminated an additional 6,000 positions. Job cuts are no longer a last resort-in hard times but an ongoing tool for matching supply with demand. . . .

Already, companies are looking first to bring in contract workers that they can quickly tap and zap without paying any benefits or severance. In fact, the temps have been the fastest growing sector of employment this year. And they aren't accounted for as regular employees. This helps companies that use a lot of them, like Cisco Systems Inc., to drive up revenue per employee.

The growing use of the just-in-time workforce is not the only means by which companies are priming the productivity pump. Workers complain that many employers are taking advantage of outdated labor laws by misclassifying them as salaried-exempt so they can skirt overtime pay. Already, Wal-Mart Stores, Taco Bell, Starbucks, and U-Haul, among others, have been slapped with class actions. In the case of General Dynamics Corp., this resulted in a $100 million award that is now on appeal. At Farmer's Insurance, employees got $90 million. Some employers are so worried about the issue that they are now doing wage-and-hour audits.

Another potential productivity enhancer: incentive pay, which enables bosses to motivate people to work harder during tough times to make up for lost wages. General

Electric Co. will soon start factoring customer performance into employee pay, putting an even greater chunk of compensation at risk. Under this system, if a customer's business suffers, so does the GE employee's paycheck.

Yet even as they push existing employees, companies also have to think about what's down the road—the likely return of tight labor markets and a replay of the 1990s' battle for talent. Demographers and labor experts note that the recession merely masked the deep skills shortages lurking within the labor force. "It will be even worse than it was in 2000," predicts Texas Instruments Inc. Chairman, CEO, and President Tom Engibous, who says the sequel could come as early as 2003.

Like many CEOs, Engibous faces the tough job of balancing the need to juice profits right now with the longer term goal of cultivating his choice employees. That's why he has launched a "rerecruiting initiative" at TI, asking workers what they need—days off, new assignments, a different boss—to keep them satisfied right now. He figures if he waits until the rebound is in full bloom, it could be too late. For companies that squeeze too hard, it probably already is.

Questions for Discussion

1. What methods or techniques were used by companies profiled in this case to increase productivity? Discuss the details.

2. To what extent are the productivity enhancement strategies used consistent with equity and expectancy theory? Explain.

3. What are the drawbacks of the productivity enhancement strategies being used by companies? Discuss.

4. Based on Chapters 8 and 9, how would you attempt to motivate employees within the current economic environment? Explain.

Personal Awareness and Growth Exercise

What Outcomes Motivate Employees?

Objectives

1. To determine how accurately you perceive the outcomes that motivate nonmanagerial employees.

2. To examine the managerial implications of inaccurately assessing employee motivators.

Introduction

One thousand employees were given a list of 10 outcomes people want from their work. They were asked to rank these items from most important to least important. We are going to have you estimate how you think these workers ranked the various outcomes. This will enable you to compare your perceptions with the average rankings documented by a researcher. The survey results are presented in Endnote 78 at the end of this book. Please do not read them until indicated.

Instructions

Below is a list of 10 outcomes people want from their work. Read the list, and then rank each item according to how you think the typical nonmanagerial employee would rank them. Rank the outcomes from 1 to 10; 1 = most important and 10 = least important. (Please do this now before reading the rest of these instructions.) After you have completed your ranking, calculate the discrepancy between your perceptions and the actual results. Take the absolute value of the difference between your ranking and the actual ranking for each item, and then add them to get a total discrepancy score. For example, if you gave job security a ranking of 1, your discrepancy score would be 3 because the actual ranking was 4. The lower your discrepancy score, the more accurate your perception of the typical employee's needs. The actual rankings are shown in Endnote 78.

How do you believe the typical nonmanagerial employee would rank these outcomes?

_____ Full appreciation of work done

_____ Job security

_____ Good working conditions

_____ Feeling of being in on things

_____ Good wages

_____ Tactful discipline

_____ Personal loyalty to employees

_____ Interesting work

_____ Sympathetic help with personal problems

_____ Promotion and growth in the organization

Questions for Discussion

1. Were your perceptions accurate? Why or why not?

2. What would Vroom's expectancy theory suggest you should do?

3. Based on the size of your discrepancy, what does Porter and Lawler's expectancy model suggest will happen to satisfaction?

4. Would you generalize the actual survey results to all nonmanagerial employees? Why or why not?

Group Exercise

The Case of the Missing Form

Objectives

1. To give you practice at diagnosing the causes of a performance problem by using the job performance model of motivation presented in Figure 8–1.
2. To apply one of the motivation models discussed in Chapters 8 and 9 in order to solve a performance problem.

Introduction

Managers frequently encounter performance problems. These problems might represent incidents such as missed deadlines, poor quality, inadequate levels of performance, excessive time off, cynical or negative behavior, and lack of cooperation with team members. As we discussed in both this chapter and Chapter 8, motivation is only one factor in these types of performance problems. As such, managers must learn how to diagnose the cause(s) of performance problems prior to trying to solve them. The following case provides you this opportunity. After diagnosing the cause(s) of the performance problem, you will be asked to solve it. The models of motivation presented in Chapters 8 and 9 provide useful frameworks for generating solutions.

Instructions

Your instructor will divide the class into groups of four to six. You should first read the case provided. Once all group members are finished, meet as a group to discuss the case. Begin your discussion by brainstorming a list of potential causes of the performance problem. Use the job perform-ance model of motivation presented in Figure 8–1 to con-duct this brainstorming activity. Be sure to consider whether each and every individual input and job context factor are possible causes of the problem. Once the group has identi-fied the causes of the performance problem, the group should answer the discussion questions that follow the case.

THE CASE OF THE MISSING FORM[79]

S	M	T	W	T	F	S		S	M	T	W	T	F	S
			MAY								JUNE			
		1	2	3	4									1
5	6	7	8	9	10	11		2	3	4	5	6	7	8
12	13	14	15	16	17	18		9	10	11	12	13	14	15
19	20	21	22	23	24	25		16	17	18	19	20	21	22
26	27	28	29	30	31			23	24	25	26	27	28	29
								30						

Ann Anders has been manager of Training and Development at TYCO Financial Services for 3 years.

(Ann has been with TYCO 21 years.) She has 10 professional level training employees reporting to her.

Her boss, Joyce Davis, director of training, asked Ann to put together a new cost benefit analysis package on a project Ann had completed. This was not a requirement for Ann by her previous boss; training has never been measured in terms of dollars and cents.

Joyce explained that she wanted Ann to document the savings that the "Customer Dispute Resolution" training program had produced so she could share it with her peers in the other divisions of TYCO. She wanted to formalize the practice of preparing a cost benefit analysis (CBA) format because this was something no one else had done. She directed Ann to further research the numbers' to validate the findings and put it into a form (Joyce's idea of a form was a page with lines and boxes). It was Wednesday, May 15; Joyce was leaving for a meeting in New York at 8:00 AM Monday, May 20. She wanted to take this assignment with her. Joyce asked Ann to see her Friday with her progress.

On Thursday, Ann met with the Performance. Engineering department at TYCO and shared with Joyce a format they were currently using on their projects. Ann agreed to apply that process to her training project. Joyce was pleased with the progress.

Ann returned to Joyce on Friday, May 17, with the formula for the training CBA typed on a plain white page. Joyce acknowledged the work to prepare the calculations and again asked if Ann could create a form. Joyce had to catch her airplane first thing Monday morning and knew she would not have time to review a second document. Joyce took the work Ann had completed; however, she decided to stall until the next monthly meeting in June to present the idea.

The following week, on May 27, Joyce explained to Ann that there was not enough time to discuss her CBA so she would do it next month. Joyce asked Ann for additional information that needed to be gathered to effectively document the project and set a new completion date, June 10: only one week prior to the June 17 meeting.

Ann returned on June 10 with more calculations that were thoroughly documented. Joyce was happy to see the additional research. However, she was disappointed because the format had not yet been put into a professional "form." Joyce then took out a piece of paper and wrote the sections for Ann so she could better understand what she wanted.

Joyce felt confident that Ann understood what she wanted. Joyce, in order to give Ann the maximum time to get it right this time, said she needed the document no later than the end of the day Friday, June 14.

The end of the day Friday, June 14, Ann walked into Joyce's office proudly displaying this neatly typed document. However, there were no lines or boxes as you would see on a traditional business form. Joyce said "This is not in a form! I'll take it home over the weekend and bring you the revision Monday morning, you can then fax me the changes at the meeting."

Joyce then took 15 to 20 minutes Sunday to draw out the lines and reformat the information for ease of reading and to create a professional image for the product. On Monday morning Joyce stopped by and gave the changes to her secretary to finish. Ann faxed the changes. Joyce presented "the form" at the meeting, and it had the positive impact she expected.

After the meeting, Joyce reflected on Ann's problem. After 21 years with this company and 3 years as a manager, why couldn't Ann create something as simple as a business form? Joyce is trying to determine the root cause(s) of Ann's poor performance.

Questions for Discussion

1. What are the causes of Ann's poor performance? Explain your rationale.

2. Based on the causes you identified, how would you keep the problem from happening again?

3. Which of the motivation models discussed in Chapters 8 and 9 are most relevant for solving this problem? Why?

4. How would you use the model identified in question 3 to improve Ann's future performance? Be sure to specifically discuss how you would apply the model.

Ethical Dilemma

A High School Teacher Must Deal with Plagiarizing Students[80]

High school teacher Christine Pelton wasted no time after discovering that nearly a fifth of her biology students had plagiarized their semester projects from the Internet.

She had received her rural Kansas district's backing before when she accused students of cheating, and she expected it again this time after failing the 28 sophomores.

Her principal and superintendent agreed: It was plagiarism, and the students should get a zero for the assignment.

But after parents complained, the Piper School Board ordered her to go easier on the guilty. . . . The board ordered her to give the students partial credit and to decrease the project's value from 50% of the final course grade to 30%.

One of the complaining parents, Theresa Woolley, told the *Kansas City Star* that her daughter did not plagiarize but was not sure how much she needed to rewrite research material.

But Pelton said the course syllabus, which she required students to sign, warned of the consequences of cheating and plagiarism. . . .

What is worse, McCabe said [Donald McCabe is a professor of management at Rutgers University], is that toler-

ance of dishonesty disheartens other students, who have to compete with the cheaters to get into college.

"If they see teachers looking the other way, students feel compelled to participate even though it makes them uncomfortable," McCabe said.

What would you do if you were Christine Pelton?

1. Resign your position in protest over the school board's lack of support. Explain your rationale.

2. Do what the school board ordered. Discuss the impact of this choice on the students who plagiarized and those who did not?

3. Ignore the school board's order and give the failing grades. Explain your rationale.

4. Invent other options. Discuss.

For an interpretation of this situation, visit our Web site, **www.mhhe.com/kreitner.**

Chapter Ten

Improving Job Performance with Feedback, Extrinsic Rewards, and Positive Reinforcement

Learning Objectives

When you finish studying the material in this chapter, you should be able to:

1　Specify the two basic functions of feedback and three sources of feedback, and summarize at least three practical lessons from feedback research.

2　Define upward feedback and 360-degree feedback, and summarize the general tips for giving good feedback.

3　Identify and briefly explain the four different organizational reward norms.

4　Summarize the reasons why extrinsic rewards often fail to motivate employees.

5　Discuss how managers can generally improve extrinsic reward and pay-for-performance plans.

6　State Thorndike's "law of effect," and explain Skinner's distinction between respondent and operant behavior.

7　Define positive reinforcement, negative reinforcement, punishment, and extinction, and distinguish between continuous and intermittent schedules of reinforcement.

8　Demonstrate your knowledge of behavior shaping.

www.hinda.com

When John Wilhelm became manager of benefits administration at beauty products company L'Oreal USA, he was shocked by the company's time-consuming and complicated service award program.

"It was ridiculous," he recalls. "We had a person on staff who spent a significant amount of her time tracking down gifts, finding missing orders, sending reminders to employees and helping them make returns. I knew there had to be a better way."

That's when Wilhelm contracted with a vendor to provide the company with an online program. Now, the company hands in a list of people eligible for service awards at the beginning of the year, and the vendor handles the rest.

But isn't L'Oreal USA paying a premium for such service? "It's actually less expensive than the paper program when you factor in the zero amount of time anyone here spends administering this," Wilhelm explains. "The lost work time was really the hidden cost in the old program."

As more HR [human resource] functions go online, there's an increased interest in bringing awards programs online, says Bill Termini, national sales manager for Hinda Incentives Inc. in Chicago, a longtime industry vendor that began offering Web-based awards programs in 1999.

Online awards systems can be connected with HR management systems, payroll systems or the company's

Chicago's Hinda Incentives, Inc. is one of a growing number of vendors specializing in online incentives for employees.

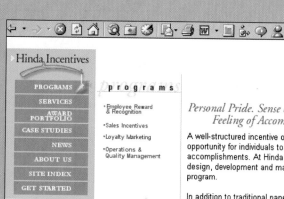

Hinda Incentives

PROGRAMS
SERVICES
AWARD PORTFOLIO
CASE STUDIES
NEWS
ABOUT US
SITE INDEX
GET STARTED

programs

• Employee Reward & Recognition
• Sales Incentives
• Loyalty Marketing
• Operations & Quality Management

Personal Pride. Sense of Ownership.
Feeling of Accomplishment.

A well-structured incentive or recognition program is one that provides an opportunity for individuals to achieve specific goals and to be rewarded for their accomplishments. At Hinda, we have the tools and resources to assist in the design, development and management of a financially sound and motivational program.

In addition to traditional paper-based programs, Hinda offers Web-based recognition and incentive programs, as well as online actions, quizzes and games that are sure to motivate employees!

enterprise resource planning system, says Kevin Jorgensen, president and CEO of Beyond Work Inc., a provider of incentive and recognition programs based in San Jose, CA. . . .

One of the biggest benefits is that online programs offer an immediacy that offline programs just can't match, proponents say.

"Managers can send immediate recognition for a job well done, which has a big impact," says Peter Fornal, vice president of HR for Log On America Inc., a regional telecommunications services provider in Providence, RI, who studies the online awards industry. "You can recognize people in ways you couldn't before. Think about companies with employees who telecommute or work from satellite offices."

Online programs also enable organizations to recognize and motivate a variety of employees by running multiple programs at once.

One caveat: To reach everyone, everyone must be wired. While that's rapidly becoming a reality, some companies have employees on factory floors, in the field and at cash registers across the country who cannot readily tap into PCs. Most online vendors continue to offer supplemental paper materials for these employees. Meanwhile, many companies are making the investment to give all employees computer access.

"Dismiss any myths about online programs not working when some employees are not online. We have one client who is a manufacturer with 13 locations," says Hinda Incentives' Termini. "The money they saved in administrative costs enabled them to invest in kiosks so all employees have access.". . .

One of the biggest drawbacks to an online system is the impersonal nature of presenting an award via computer. For 71% of companies with incentives programs whose managers have personally presented awards, the idea of acknowledging people through E-mail can seem a bit cold.

It's not just old-economy businesses that find online presentation lacking. "One of our high-tech clients, a networking services provider, asked that we implement a rule in their recognition system that prevented awards from being presented online," Jorgensen says. "They felt that their computer-based culture was becoming too impersonal and they wanted to use recognition as a way of boosting the people factor on the job."

Most companies use the online system to notify managers of important anniversaries (for service awards) or provide a spot for managers to log performance awards, but the actual congratulations is done in person.

"The online program shouldn't take the place of personal contact, but should be a supplement to it," says Fornal.[1]

For Discussion

From a managerial perspective, what are the positives and negatives of online recognition and reward programs? What about the nonmanagerial employee's perspective?

Productivity and total quality experts tell us we need to work smarter, not harder. While it is true that a sound education and appropriate skill training are needed if one is to work smarter, the process does not end there. Today's employees, such as those at L'Oreal USA, need instructive and supportive feedback and desired rewards if they are to translate their knowledge into improved productivity and superior quality. This point was reinforced by a recent survey of 612 employees in the United States. When asked about the changes top management needs to make to attract and keep good people, these two items headed the list: "improving salaries and benefits" (72%) and "recognizing and rewarding good employee performance" (69%).[2] Figure 10–1 illustrates a learning- and development-focused cycle in which feedback enhances ability, encourages effort, and acknowledges results. Rewards and positive reinforcement, in turn, motivate effort and compensate results. Learning and personal development, according to the authors of the book, *Working Wisdom,* are the key to success at all levels:

[W]ork can be an enriching experience, a way of developing mastery in the world, a source of valued relationships, and for some—however high-minded this may sound—a path to self-realization. Combining work and learning to promote personal development, as well

Figure 10–1   *Feedback and Rewards Are Important Links in the Job Performance Cycle*

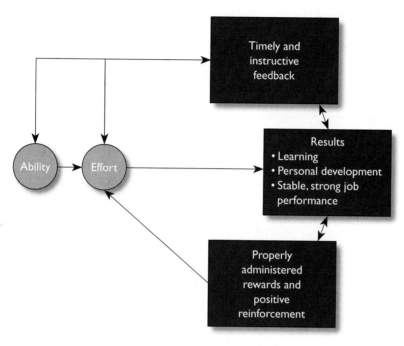

as a profitable enterprise, is the key. As the pace of change quickens, individuals, companies, and countries that fail to continually learn and adapt to change will be left behind.[3]

Properly administered feedback and rewards can guide, teach, and motivate people in the direction of positive change.

This chapter continues our discussion of individual behavior by discussing the effect of feedback and rewards on behavior and by integrating those insights with what you have learned about individual differences, perception, and various motivational tools such as goal setting.

Understanding the Feedback Process

Numerous surveys and studies tell us employees have a hearty appetite for feedback.[4] So also do achievement-oriented students. Following a difficult exam, for instance, students want to know two things: how they did and how their peers did. By letting students know how their work measures up to grading and competitive standards, an instructor's feedback permits the students to adjust their study habits so they can reach their goals. Likewise, managers in well-run organizations follow up goal setting with a feedback program to provide a rational basis for adjustment and improvement. For example, consider the following remarks by Fred Smith, the founder and CEO of Federal Express, the overnight delivery pioneer with $20 billion in annual revenues and nearly 180,000 employees.[5] Smith's experience as a US Marine company commander during the Vietnam War helped shape his leadership style.

My leadership philosophy is a synthesis of the principles taught by the marines and every organization for the past 200 years.

When people walk in the door, they want to know: What do you expect out of me? What's in this deal for me? What do I have to do to get ahead? Where do I go in this organization to get justice if I'm not treated appropriately? They want to know how they're doing. They want some feedback. And they want to know that what they are doing is important.

If you take the basic principles of leadership and answer those questions over and over again, you can be successful dealing with people.[6]

Feedback

Objective information about performance.

As the term is used here, **feedback** is objective information about individual or collective performance. Subjective assessments such as, "You're doing a poor job," "You're too lazy," or "We really appreciate your hard work" do not qualify as objective feedback. But hard data such as units sold, days absent, dollars saved, projects completed, customers satisfied, and quality rejects are all candidates for objective feedback programs. Management consultants Chip Bell and Ron Zemke offered this perspective of feedback:

Feedback is, quite simply, any information that answers those "How am I doing?" questions. *Good* feedback answers them truthfully and productively. It's information people can use either to confirm or correct their performance.

Feedback comes in many forms and from a variety of sources. Some is easy to get and requires hardly any effort to understand. The charts and graphs tracking group and individual performance that are fixtures in many workplaces are an example of this variety. Performance feedback—the numerical type at least—is at the heart of most approaches to total quality management.

Some feedback is less accessible. It's tucked away in the heads of customers and managers. But no matter how well-hidden the feedback, if people need it to keep their performance on track, we need to get it to them—preferably while it's still fresh enough to make an impact.[7]

Two Functions of Feedback

Experts say feedback serves two functions for those who receive it, one is *instructional* and the other *motivational*. Feedback instructs when it clarifies roles or teaches new behavior. For example, an assistant accountant might be advised to handle a certain entry as a capital item rather than as an expense item. On the other hand, feedback motivates when it serves as a reward or promises a reward.[8] Having the boss tell you that a grueling project you worked on earlier has just been completed can be a rewarding piece of news. As documented by researchers, the motivational function of feedback can be significantly enhanced by pairing *specific*, challenging goals with *specific* feedback about results.[9] We expand upon these two functions in this section by analyzing a cognitive model of feedback, and reviewing the practical implications of recent feedback research.

A Cognitive-Processing Model of Performance Feedback

Giving and receiving feedback on the job are popular ideas today. Conventional wisdom says the more feedback organizational members get, the better. An underlying assumption is that feedback works automatically. Managers simply need to be moti-

Figure 10–2   *A Cognitive-Processing Model of Feedback*

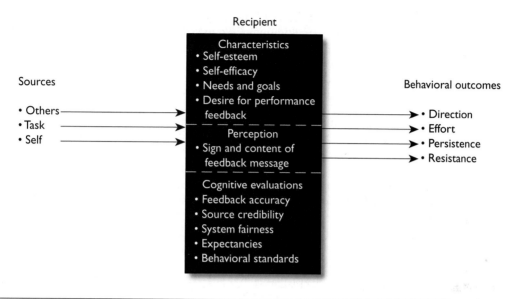

SOURCES: Based in part on discussion in M S Taylor, C D Fisher, and D R Ilgen, "Individuals' Reactions to Performance Feedback in Organizations: A Control Theory Perspective," in *Research in Personnel and Human Resources Management,* vol. 2, eds K M Rowland and G R Ferris (Greenwich, CT: JAI Press, 1984), pp. 81–124; and A N Kluger and A DeNisi, "The Effects of Feedback Interventions on Performance: A Historical Review, a Meta-Analysis, and a Preliminary Feedback Intervention Theory," *Psychological Bulletin,* March 1996, pp. 254–84.

vated to give it. According to a meta-analysis of 23,663 feedback incidents, however, feedback is far from automatically effective. While feedback did, in fact, have a generally positive impact on performance, performance actually *declined* in more than 38% of the feedback incidents.[10] Feedback also can be warped by nontask factors, such as race. A laboratory study at Stanford University focused on cross-race feedback on the content (subjective feedback) and writing mechanics (objective feedback) of written essays. White students gave African-American students *less* critical *subjective* feedback than they did to white students. This positive racial bias disappeared with objective feedback.[11] These results are a bright caution light for those interested in improving job performance with feedback. Subjective feedback is easily contaminated by situational factors. Moreover, if objective feedback is to work as intended, managers need to understand the interaction between feedback recipients and their environment.[12] A fuller understanding of how employees cognitively or mentally process feedback is an important first step in the right direction. This complex process is illustrated in Figure 10–2. Immediately obvious is the fact that feedback must successfully clear many hurdles if the desired behavioral outcomes are to be achieved.

A lighthearted case in point is Scott Adams, the former telephone company employee who draws the popular cartoon strip, Dilbert. According to *The Wall Street Journal,*

he can thank feedback from his readers, who flooded him with comments—about 200 a day—after he published his E-mail address in 1993. They persuaded him to concentrate on workplace issues, which had been a smaller part of the strip, and Dilbert's popularity soared. "There was this huge vein of discontent and nobody was talking about it from the employees' perspective," he says.

Thanks to his experiences in the trenches, and his E-mail army, Mr Adams has become a walking database of workplace foibles and career frustrations.[13]

If you've ever gotten a good laugh from a Dilbert cartoon, you can thank the feedback process. Feedback—from customers, in this case—was effective because cartoonist Adams (1) wanted feedback, (2) actively sought feedback, and (3) acted on the feedback. A step-by-step exploration of the model in Figure 10–2 can help us better understand this sort of feedback-performance relationship.

Sources of Feedback

It almost goes without saying that employees receive objective feedback from others such as peers, supervisors, subordinates, and outsiders. Perhaps less obvious is the fact that the task itself is a ready source of objective feedback.[14] Anyone who has spent hours on a "quick" Internet search can appreciate the power of task-provided feedback. Similarly, skilled tasks such as computer programming or landing a jet airplane provide a steady stream of feedback about how well or poorly one is doing. A third source of feedback is oneself, but self-serving bias and other perceptual problems can contaminate this source. Those high in self-confidence tend to rely on personal feedback more than those with low self-confidence. Although circumstances vary, an employee can be bombarded by feedback from all three sources simultaneously. This is where the gatekeeping functions of perception and cognitive evaluation are needed to help sort things out.

The Recipient of Feedback

Listed in the center portion of Figure 10–2 are three aspects of the recipient requiring our attention. They are the individual's characteristics, perceptions, and cognitive evaluations. As characterized earlier, each recipient variable is a hurdle intended feedback must clear if it is to be effective. Knowing about these recipient hurdles is a big step in the right direction.

The Recipient's Characteristics   Personality characteristics such as self-esteem and self-efficacy can help or hinder one's readiness for feedback.[15] Those having low self-esteem and low self-efficacy generally do not actively seek feedback that, unfortunately, would tend to confirm those problems. Needs and goals also influence one's openness to feedback. In a laboratory study, Japanese psychology students who scored high on need for achievement responded more favorably to feedback than did their classmates who had low need for achievement.[16] This particular relationship likely exists in Western cultures as well. For example, 331 employees in the marketing department of a large public utility in the United States were found to seek feedback on important issues or when faced with uncertain situations. Long-tenured employees from this sample also were less likely to seek feedback than employees with little time on the job.[17] High self-monitors, those chameleonlike people we discussed in Chapter 5, are also more open to feedback because it helps them adapt their behavior to the situation. Recall from Chapter 5 that high self-monitoring employees were found to be better at initiating relationships with mentors (who typically provide feedback).[18] Low self-monitoring people, in contrast, are tuned into their own internal feelings more than they are to external cues. For example, someone observed that talking to media kingpin Ted Turner, a very low self-monitor, was like having a conversation with a radio!

Researchers have started to focus more directly on the recipient's actual desire for feedback, as opposed to indirectly on personality characteristics, needs, and goals.

OB Exercise   How Strong Is Your Desire for Performance Feedback?

Instructions

Circle one number indicating the strength of your agreement or disagreement with each statement. Total your responses, and compare your score with our arbitrary norms.

	Disagree				Agree
1. As long as I think that I have done something well, I am not too concerned about how other people think I have done.	5	4	3	2	1
2. How other people view my work is not as important as how I view my own work.	5	4	3	2	1
3. It is usually better not to put much faith in what others say about your work, regardless of whether it is complimentary or not.	5	4	3	2	1
4. If I have done something well, I know it without other people telling me so.	5	4	3	2	1
5. I usually have a clear idea of what I am trying to do and how well I am proceeding toward my goal.	5	4	3	2	1
6. I find that I am usually a pretty good judge of my own performance.	5	4	3	2	1
7. It is very important to me to know what people think of my work.	1	2	3	4	5
8. It is a good idea to get someone to check on your work before it's too late to make changes.	1	2	3	4	5
9. Even though I may think I have done a good job, I feel a lot more confident of it after someone else tells me so.	1	2	3	4	5
10. Since one cannot be objective about their own performance, it is best to listen to the feedback provided by others.	1	2	3	4	5

Total score = _____

Arbitrary Norms

10–23 = Low desire for feedback   24–36 = Moderate desire for feedback   37–50 = High desire for feedback

SOURCE: Excerpted and adapted from D M Herold, C K Parsons, and R B Rensvold, "Individual Differences in the Generation and Processing of Performance Feedback," *Educational and Psychological Measurement*, February 1996, Table 1, p. 9. Copyright © 1996 by Sage Publications. Reprinted by permission of Sage Publications, Inc.

Everyday experience tells us that not everyone really wants the performance feedback they supposedly seek. Restaurant servers who ask, "How was everything?" while presenting the bill, typically are not interested in a detailed reply. A study of 498 supervisors yielded an instrument for measuring desire for performance feedback[19] (see the OB Exercise above, for a shortened version). Such desire involves *self-reliance* (items 1–3), *self-assessment ability* (items 4–6), and a *preference for external information* (items 7–10). The general contingency approach to management would require different strategies for giving feedback to employees scoring low versus high on the OB Exercise.

The Recipient's Perception of Feedback   The *sign* of feedback refers to whether it is positive or negative. Generally, people tend to perceive and recall positive feedback more accurately than they do negative feedback.[20] But feedback with a

negative sign (e.g., being told your performance is below average) can have a *positive* motivational impact. In fact, in one study, those who were told they were below average on a creativity test subsequently outperformed those who were led to believe their results were above average. The subjects apparently took the negative feedback as a challenge and set and pursued higher goals. Those receiving positive feedback apparently were less motivated to do better.[21] Nonetheless, feedback with a negative sign or threatening content needs to be administered carefully to avoid creating insecurity and defensiveness. Self-efficacy also can be damaged by negative feedback, as discovered in a pair of experiments with business students. The researchers concluded, "To facilitate the development of strong efficacy beliefs, managers should be careful about the provision of negative feedback. Destructive criticism by managers which attributes the cause of poor performance to internal factors reduces both the beliefs of self-efficacy and the self-set goals of recipients."[22]

The Recipient's Cognitive Evaluation of Feedback   Upon receiving feedback, people cognitively evaluate factors such as its accuracy, the credibility of the source, the fairness of the system (e.g., performance appraisal system), their performance-reward expectancies, and the reasonableness of the standards. Any feedback that fails to clear one or more of these cognitive hurdles will be rejected or downplayed. Personal experience largely dictates how these factors are weighed. For instance, you would probably discount feedback from someone who exaggerates or from someone who performed poorly on the same task you have just successfully completed. In view of the "trust gap," discussed in Chapter 13, managerial credibility is an ethical matter of central importance today. According to the authors of the book *Credibility: How Leaders Gain and Lose It, Why People Demand It,* "without a solid foundation of personal credibility, leaders can have no hope of enlisting others in a common vision."[23] Managers who have proven untrustworthy and not credible have a hard time improving job performance through feedback.[24]

Feedback from a source who apparently shows favoritism or relies on unreasonable behavior standards would be suspect.[25] Also, as predicted by expectancy motivation theory, feedback must foster high effort→performance expectancies and performance→reward instrumentalities if it is to motivate desired behavior. For example, many growing children have been cheated out of the rewards of athletic competition because they were told by respected adults that they were too small, too short, too slow, too clumsy, and so forth. Feedback can have a profound and lasting impact on behavior.

Behavioral Outcomes of Feedback

In Chapter 9, we discussed how goal setting gives behavior direction, increases expended effort, and fosters persistence. Because feedback is intimately related to the goal-setting process, it involves the same behavioral outcomes: direction, effort, and persistence. However, while the fourth outcome of goal setting involves formulating goal-attainment strategies, the fourth possible outcome of feedback is *resistance*. Feedback schemes, that smack of manipulation or fail one or more of the perceptual and cognitive evaluation tests just discussed, breed resistance. Steve Jobs, the co-founder of Apple Computer (and once again its CEO), left the firm amid controversy in 1985 partly because his uneven and heavy-handed feedback bred resistance:

> According to several insiders, Jobs, a devout believer that new technology should super-sede the old, couldn't abide the success of the venerable Apple II. Nor did he hide his feel-ings. He once addressed the Apple II marketing staff as members of the "dull and boring

product division." As chairman and largest stockholder, with an 11.3% block, Jobs was a disproportionately powerful general manager. And he had disproportionate enthusiasm for the [Macintosh] staff. Says one of them: "He was so protective of us that whenever we complained about somebody outside the division, it was like unleashing a Doberman. Steve would get on the telephone and chew the guy out so fast your head would spin."[26]

Practical Lessons from Feedback Research

After reviewing dozens of laboratory and field studies of feedback, a trio of OB researchers cited the following practical implications for managers:

- The acceptance of feedback should not be treated as a given; it is often misperceived or rejected. This is especially true in intercultural situations.
- Managers can enhance their credibility as sources of feedback by developing their expertise and creating a climate of trust.
- Negative feedback is typically misperceived or rejected.
- Although very frequent feedback may erode one's sense of personal control and initiative, feedback is too *infrequent* in most work organizations.
- Feedback needs to be tailored to the recipient.
- While average and below-average performers need extrinsic rewards for performance, high performers respond to feedback that enhances their feelings of competence and personal control.[27]

More recent research insights about feedback include the following:

- Computer-based performance feedback leads to greater improvements in performance when it is received directly from the computer system rather than via an immediate supervisor.[28]
- Recipients of feedback perceive it to be more accurate when they actively participate in the feedback session versus passively receiving feedback.[29]
- Destructive criticism tends to cause conflict and reduce motivation.[30]
- "The higher one rises in an organization the less likely one is to receive quality feedback about job performance."[31]

Managers who act on these research implications and the trouble signs in Table 10–1 can build credible and effective feedback systems.

Table 10–1   *Six Common Trouble Signs for Organizational Feedback Systems*

1. Feedback is used to punish, embarrass, or put down employees.
2. Those receiving the feedback see it as irrelevant to their work.
3. Feedback information is provided too late to do any good.
4. People receiving feedback believe it relates to matters beyond their control.
5. Employees complain about wasting too much time collecting and recording feedback data.
6. Feedback recipients complain about feedback being too complex or difficult to understand.

SOURCE: Adapted from C Bell and R Zemke, "On-Target Feedback," *Training*, June 1992, pp. 36–44.

Our discussion to this point has focused on traditional downward feedback. Let us explore a couple of new and interesting approaches to feedback in the workplace.

Nontraditional Feedback: Upward and 360-Degree

Traditional top-down feedback programs have given way to some interesting variations in recent years. Two newer approaches, discussed in this section, are upward feedback and so-called 360-degree feedback. Aside from breaking away from a strict superior-to-subordinate feedback loop, these newer approaches are different because they typically involve *multiple sources* of feedback. Instead of getting feedback from one boss, often during an annual performance appraisal, more and more managers are getting structured feedback from superiors, subordinates, peers, and even outsiders such as customers. Nontraditional feedback is growing in popularity for at least six reasons:

1. Traditional performance appraisal systems have created widespread dissatisfaction.

2. Team-based organization structures are replacing traditional hierarchies. This trend requires managers to have good interpersonal skills that are best evaluated by team members.

3. Multiple-rater systems are said to make feedback more valid than single-source feedback.[32]

4. Advanced computer network technology (the Internet and company intranets) greatly facilitates multiple-rater systems.[33]

5. Bottom-up feedback meshes nicely with the trend toward participative management and employee empowerment.

6. Co-workers and subordinates are said to know more about a manager's strengths and limitations than the boss.[34]

Together, these factors make a compelling case for looking at better ways to give and receive performance feedback.

Upward Feedback

Upward feedback
Subordinates evaluate their boss.

Upward feedback stands the traditional approach on its head by having subordinates provide feedback on a manager's style and performance. This type of feedback is generally anonymous. Most students are familiar with upward feedback programs from years of filling out anonymous teacher evaluation surveys. Early adopters of upward evaluations include AT&T, General Mills, Motorola, and Procter & Gamble.[35]

Managers typically resist upward feedback programs because they believe it erodes their authority. Other critics say anonymous upward feedback can become little more than a personality contest or, worse, be manipulated by managers who make promises or threats. What does the research literature tell us about upward feedback?

Research Insights   Studies with diverse samples have given us these useful insights:

• The question of whether upward feedback should be *anonymous* was addressed by a study at a large US insurance company. All told, 183 employees rated the skills and effectiveness of 38 managers. Managers who received anonymous upward feedback received *lower* ratings and liked the process *less* than did those receiving feedback from identifiable employees. This finding confirmed the criticism that employees will tend to go easier on their boss when not protected by confidentiality.[36]

- In another study, 83 supervisors employed by a US government agency were divided into three feedback groups: (1) feedback from both superiors and subordinates, (2) feedback from superiors only, and (3) feedback from subordinates only. Group 1 was most satisfied with the overall evaluation process and responded more positively to upward feedback. "Group 3 expressed more concern that subordinate appraisals would undermine supervisors' authority and that supervisors would focus on pleasing subordinates."[37]

- A large-scale study at the US Naval Academy, where student leaders and followers live together day and night, discovered a positive impact of upward feedback on leader behavior.[38]

- In a field study of 238 corporate managers, upward feedback had a positive impact on the performance of low to moderate performers.[39]

General Recommendations for Using Upward Feedback   These research findings suggest the practical value of *anonymous* upward feedback used in *combination* with other sources of performance feedback and evaluation. Because of managerial resistance and potential manipulation, using upward feedback as the primary determinant for promotions and pay decisions is *not* recommended. Carefully collected upward feedback is useful for management development programs.

360-Degree Feedback

The concept of giving a manager collective feedback from different levels and categories of co-workers is not new. Training and development specialists have used multirater, multilevel feedback for 25 years. Aggressively marketed 360-degree feedback software programs have mushroomed in recent years. A 1999 product review identified 30 different 360-degree packages for sale.[40] Consequently, according to a broad survey by the Society for Human Resource Management, 32% of companies were using 360-degree feedback programs in 2000.[41] Whether 360-degree feedback goes down in history as just another passing fad or an established practice remains to be seen.[42] An unfortunate by-product of sudden popularity is that enthusiastic sellers of 360-degree feedback systems are more interested in advocacy than objective evaluation. Importantly, our goal here is not to provide cookbook instructions in how to administer complex 360-degree reviews. Rather, our purpose is to see if the concept is sound and deserves managerial time and money.

The concept of **360-degree feedback** involves letting individuals compare their own perceived performance with behaviorally specific (and usually anonymous) performance information from their manager, subordinates, and peers. Even outsiders may be involved in what is sometimes called full-circle feedback (see Figure 10–3). *Fortune* offered this humorous yet instructive explanation:

> Here's how it works. Everyone from the office screwup to your boss, including your crackerjack assistant and your rival across the hall, will fill out lengthy, anonymous questionnaires about you. You'll complete one too. Are you crisp, clear, and articulate? Abrasive? Spreading yourself too thin? Trustworthy? Off-the-cuff remarks may be gathered too. A week or

360-degree feedback
Comparison of anonymous feedback from one's superior, subordinates, and peers with, self-perceptions.

Figure 10–3   *Sources and Types of Feedback in the 360-Degree Approach*

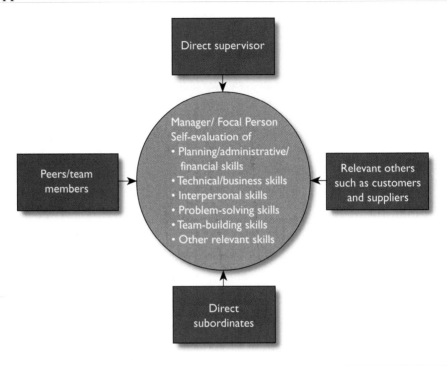

two later you'll get the results, all crunched and graphed by a computer. Ideally, all this will be explained by someone from your human-resources department or the company that handled the questionnaires, a person who can break bad news gently. You get to see how your opinion of yourself differs from those of the group of subordinates who participated, your peer group, and the boss.[43]

The idea is to let the individual know how their behavior affects others, with the goal of motivating change. In a 360-degree feedback program, a given manager will play different roles, including focal person, superior, subordinate, and peer. Of course, the focal person role is played only once. The other roles are played more than once for various other focal persons.[44]

Relevant Research Evidence   Because upward feedback is a part of 360-degree feedback programs, the evidence reviewed earlier applies here as well. As with upward feedback, peer- and self-evaluations, central to 360-degree feedback programs, also are a significant affront to tradition. But advocates say co-workers and managers themselves are appropriate performance evaluators because they are closest to the action. Generally, research builds a stronger case for peer appraisals than for self-appraisals.[45] Self-serving bias, discussed in Chapter 7, is a problem.

A body of rigorous research evidence of 360-degree feedback programs is being built. Among the significant findings: A two-year study of 48 managers given 360-degree feedback in a large US public utility company led to these somewhat promising results. According to the researchers, "The group as a whole developed its skills, but there was substantial variability among individuals in how much change occurred."[46] As with any feedback, individuals vary in their response to 360-degree feedback. Indeed, a recent study found a tendency among people who got *unfavorable* 360-degree ratings to question the accuracy of the feedback and to react negatively. The researchers concluded: "The results question widely held assumptions about 360° feedback that negative and discrepant feedback motivates positive change."[47]

Practical Recommendations for 360-Degree Feedback Programs

Our recommendations for upward feedback, *favoring* anonymity and *discouraging* linkage to pay and promotion decisions, apply as well to 360-degree feedback programs. According to one expert, *trust* is the issue:

> Trust is at the core of using 360-degree feedback to enhance productivity. Trust determines how much an individual is willing to contribute for an employer. Using 360 confidentially, for developmental purposes, builds trust; using it to trigger pay and personnel decisions puts trust at risk.[48]

We agree that 360-degree feedback has a place in the development of managerial skills, especially in today's team-based organizations. However, it is important to remember that this complex feedback process is only as strong as its various components:

• Process design and planning.

• Instrument development.

• Instrument design.

• Administration.

• Feedback processing and reporting.

• Action planning as a result of feedback.[49]

It is not a quick-and-easy fix for performance problems, as some advocates would have us believe. General Electric's recently retired CEO, Jack Welch, offered this blunt assessment:

> We led the charge into "360-degree evaluations"—reviews that take into account the judgments of peers and subordinates. We loved the idea; for a few years it helped us locate the "horse's asses" who "kissed up and kicked down." But like anything driven by peer input, the system is capable of being gamed over the long haul—people began saying nice things about one another so they all would come out with good ratings. The 360s are now used only in special situations.[50]

Some Concluding Tips for Giving Good Feedback

Managers need to keep the following tips in mind when giving feedback:

• Relate feedback to existing performance *goals* and clear *expectations.*

• Give *specific* feedback tied to observable behavior or measurable results.

• Channel feedback toward *key result areas.*

• Give feedback as *soon* as possible.[51]

• Give positive feedback for *improvement,* not just final results.

• Focus feedback on *performance,* not personalities.

• Base feedback on *accurate* and *credible* information.

Extrinsic Reward Systems

Rewards are an ever-present and always controversial feature of organizational life.[52] Some employees see their jobs as the source of a paycheck and little else. Others derive great pleasure from their jobs and association with co-workers. Even volunteers who donate their time to charitable organizations, such as the Red Cross, walk away with rewards in the form of social recognition and pride of having given unselfishly of their time. Hence, the subject of organizational rewards includes, but goes far beyond, monetary compensation.[53] This section examines key components of organizational reward systems to provide a conceptual background for discussing the timely topics of pay for performance and team-based pay.

Despite the fact that reward systems vary widely, it is possible to identify and interrelate some common components. The model in Figure 10–4 focuses on four important components: (1) types of rewards, (2) reward norms, (3) distribution criteria, and (4) desired outcomes. Let us examine these components.

Types of Rewards

Including the usual paycheck, the variety and magnitude of organizational rewards boggles the mind—from subsidized day care to college tuition reimbursement to stock

Figure 10–4   *A General Model of Organizational Reward Systems*

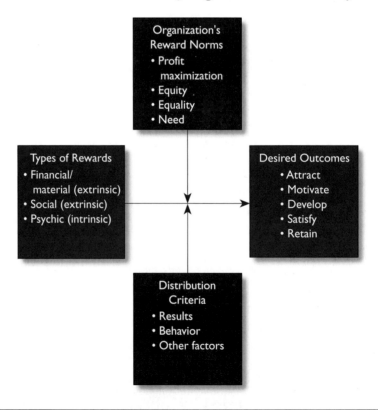

options.[54] A US Bureau of Labor Statistics economist offered the following historical perspective of employee compensation:

> One of the more striking developments . . . over the past 75 years has been the growing complexity of employee compensation. Limited at the outbreak of World War I largely to straight-time pay for hours worked, compensation now includes a variety of employer-financed benefits, such as health and life insurance, retirement income, and paid time off. Although the details of each vary widely, these benefits are today standard components of the compensation package, and workers generally have come to expect them.[55]

Today, it is common for nonwage benefits to be 50% or more of total compensation.

In addition to the obvious pay and benefits, there are less obvious social and psychic rewards. Social rewards include praise and recognition from others both inside and outside the organization. Psychic rewards come from personal feelings of self-esteem, self-satisfaction, and accomplishment.

In line with our discussion of intrinsic motivation in Chapter 8 is the distinction between extrinsic and intrinsic rewards. Financial, material, and social rewards qualify as **extrinsic rewards** because they come from the environment. Psychic rewards, however, are **intrinsic rewards** because they are self-granted. An employee who works to obtain extrinsic rewards, such as money or praise, is said to be extrinsically motivated. One who derives pleasure from the task itself or experiences a sense of competence or self-determination is said to be intrinsically motivated. The relative importance of extrinsic and intrinsic rewards is a matter of culture and personal tastes. Our focus in this chapter is on *extrinsic* rewards.

Extrinsic rewards
Financial, material, or social rewards from the environment.

Intrinsic rewards
Self-granted, psychic rewards.

Organizational Reward Norms

As discussed in Chapter 9 under the heading of equity theory, the employer–employee linkage can be viewed as an exchange relationship. Employees exchange their time and talent for rewards. Ideally, four alternative norms dictate the nature of this exchange. In pure form, each would lead to a significantly different reward distribution system. They are as follows:

- *Profit maximization.* The objective of each party is to maximize its net gain, regardless of how the other party fares. A profit-maximizing company would attempt to pay the least amount of wages for maximum effort. Conversely, a profit-maximizing employee would seek maximum rewards, regardless of the organization's financial well-being, and leave the organization for a better deal.

- *Equity.* According to the **reward equity norm,** rewards should be allocated proportionate to contributions. Those who contribute the most should be rewarded the most. A cross-cultural study of American, Japanese, and Korean college students led the researchers to the following conclusion: "Equity is probably a phenomenon common to most cultures, but its strength will vary."[56] Basic principles of fairness and justice, evident in most cultures, drive the equity norm. However, pay equity between women and men in the United States remains an unresolved issue.[57]

Reward equity norm
Rewards should be tied to contributions.

- *Equality.* The **reward equality norm** calls for rewarding all parties equally, regardless of their comparative contributions. Because absolute equality does not exist in today's hierarchical organizations, researchers explored the impact of pay *inequality.* They looked at *pay dispersion* (the pay gap between high-level and low-level employees). Result: The smaller the pay gap, the better the individual and organizational performance.[58] Thus, the outlandish compensation packages for many

Reward equality norm
Everyone should get the same rewards.

of today's top executives is not only a widely debated moral issue, it is a productivity issue as well.[59]

- *Need.* This norm calls for distributing rewards according to employees' needs rather than their contributions.[60]

A pair of researchers concluded that these contradictory norms are typically intertwined:

> We propose that employer–employee exchanges are governed by the contradictory norms of profit maximization, equity, equality, and need. These norms can coexist; what varies is the extent to which the rules for correct application of a norm are clear and the relative emphasis different managements will give to certain norms in particular allocations.[61]

Conflict and ethical debates often arise over the perceived fairness of reward allocations because of disagreement about reward norms. Stockholders might prefer a profit-maximization norm, while technical specialists would like an equity norm, and unionized hourly workers would argue for a pay system based on equality. A reward norm anchored to need might prevail in a family owned and operated business. Effective reward systems are based on clear and consensual exchange norms.

Reward Distribution Criteria

According to one expert on organizational reward systems, three general criteria for the distribution of rewards are as follows:

- *Performance: results.* Tangible outcomes such as individual, group, or organization performance; quantity and quality of performance.

SOURCE: © Steve Lindstrom, *Duluth* (MN) *News Tribune.*

International OB

Carlos Ghosn, the French CEO Who Turned around Japan's Nissan, Put the Brakes on Seniority-Based Pay

Our most fundamental challenge was cultural. Like other Japanese companies, Nissan paid and promoted its employees based on their tenure and age. The longer employees stuck around, the more power and money they received, regardless of their actual performance. Inevitably, that practice bred a certain degree of complacency, which undermined Nissan's competitiveness. What car buyers want, after all, is performance, performance, performance. They want well-designed, high-quality products at attractive prices, delivered on time. They don't care how the company does that or who in the company does it. It's only logical, then, to build a company's reward and incentive systems around performance, irrespective of age, gender, or nationality.

So we decided to ditch the seniority rule. Of course, that didn't mean we systematically started selecting the youngest candidates for promotion. In fact, the senior vice presidents that I've nominated over the past two years all have had long records of service, though they were usually not the most senior candidates. We looked at people's performance records, and if the highest performer was also the most senior, fine. But if the second or third or even the fifth most senior had the best track record, we did not hesitate to pass over those with longer service. As expected when changing longstanding practices, we've had some

problems. When you nominate a younger person to a job in Japan, for example, he sometimes suffers for being younger—in some cases, older people may not be willing to cooperate with him as fully as they might. Of course, it's also true that an experience like that can be a good test of the quality of leadership a manager brings to the job.

We also revamped our compensation system to put the focus on performance. In the traditional Japanese compensation system, managers receive no share options, and hardly any incentives are built into the manager's pay packet. If a company's average pay raise is, say, 4%, then good performers can expect a 5% or 6% raise, and poor performers get 2% or 2.5%. The system extends to the upper reaches of management, which means that the people whose decisions have the greatest impact on the company have little incentive to get them right. We changed all that. High performers today can expect cash incentives that amount to more than a third of their annual pay packages, on top of which employees receive company stock options. Here, too, other Japanese companies are making similar changes.

SOURCE: Excerpted from C Ghosn, "Saving the Business without Losing the Company," *Harvard Business Review,* January 2002, pp. 39–40.

- *Performance: actions and behaviors.* Such as teamwork, cooperation, risk taking, creativity.
- *Nonperformance considerations.* Customary or contractual, where the type of job, nature of the work, equity, tenure, level in hierarchy, and so forth are rewarded.[62]

The trend today is toward performance criteria and away from nonperformance criteria such as seniority (see the International OB above). NBC *Tonight Show* host Jay Leno's surprise for his staff of nearly 200 on April 1, 2002, was a generous exception to this trend.

> [W]ith his 10th anniversary approaching on May 25, [he] told them he wanted to show his appreciation for all their hard work. Holding a stack of personal checks, he explained that each of the stunned staffers would receive $1,000 for every year of service, regardless of salary or position. An April Fool's Day joke? Nope. Leno, who makes about $15 million a year, handed out about $1.5 million of his own money.[63]

Dream on!

Desired Outcomes of the Reward System

As listed in Figure 10–4, a good reward system should attract talented people and moti-vate and satisfy them once they have joined the organization. Further, a good reward system should foster personal growth and development and keep talented people from leaving. A prime example is Worthington Industries, the profitable steel processing firm in Columbus, Ohio, where the usual time clocks are not to be found. "Workers get profit-sharing payouts ranging from 40% to 70% of base pay, and the company pays 100% of health insurance premiums for employees and family members."[64] Worthing-ton enjoys an industry-low turnover rate of 12% and a long line of job applicants.

Why Do Extrinsic Rewards Fail to Motivate?

Despite huge investments of time and money for organizational reward systems, the desired motivational impact often is not achieved. A management consultant/writer recently offered these eight reasons:

1. Too much emphasis on monetary rewards.

2. Rewards lack an "appreciation effect."

3. Extensive benefits become entitlements.

4. Counterproductive behavior is rewarded. (For example, "a pizza delivery company focused its rewards on the on-time performance of its drivers, only to discover that it was inadvertently rewarding reckless driving."[65])

5. Too long a delay between performance and rewards.

6. Too many one-size-fits-all rewards.

7. Use of one-shot rewards with a short-lived motivational impact.

8. Continued use of demotivating practices such as layoffs, across-the-board raises and cuts, and excessive executive compensation.[66]

These stubborn problems have fostered a growing interest in more effective reward and compensation practices. Although we cannot engage in a comprehensive discussion of modern compensation practices in the balance of this chapter, a subject requiring an entire book,[67] we can explore general approaches to boosting the motivational impact of monetary rewards. This is where pay for performance and team-based pay enter the picture.

Pay for Performance

Pay for performance
Monetary incentives tied to one's results or accomplishments.

Pay for performance is the popular term for monetary incentives linking at least some portion of the paycheck directly to results or accomplishments. Many refer to it simply as *incentive pay,* while others call it *variable pay.*[68] The general idea behind pay-for-performance schemes—including but not limited to merit pay, bonuses, and profit sharing—is to give employees an incentive for working harder or smarter. Pay for performance is something extra, compensation above and beyond basic wages and salaries. Proponents of incentive compensation say something extra is needed because hourly wages and fixed salaries do little more than motivate people to show up at work and put in the required hours.[69] The most basic form of pay for performance is the tra-ditional piece-rate plan, whereby the employee is paid a specified amount of money for

These folks not only make really cool picnic baskets, they actually work *inside* one! Longaberger's headquarters building in Frazeyburg, Ohio, is a giant replica of the firm's famous maple wood baskets. Each day, 2,500 employees who are paid on a piece-rate basis weave 40,000 hand-crafted baskets. This team of Longaberger employees recently won a prestigious quality award for cutting waste and improving productivity.

Michael A Foley (c) 2002 Rycus Associates Photography LLC

each unit of work. For example, 2,500 artisans at Longaberger's, in Frazeyburg, Ohio, are paid a fixed amount for each handcrafted wooden basket they weave. Together, they produce 40,000 of the prized maple baskets daily.[70] Sales commissions, whereby a salesperson receives a specified amount of money for each unit sold, is another long-standing example of pay for performance. Today's service economy is forcing management to creatively adapt and go beyond piece rate and sales commission plans to accommodate greater emphasis on product and service quality, interdependence, and teamwork.

Table 10–2   *The Use and Effectiveness of Modern Incentive Pay Plans*

Plan Type	Have	Plan to Have	Highly Effective	Moderately Effective	Not at All Effective
Annual bonus	74%	4%	20%	63%	5%
Special one-time spot awards (after the fact)	42	2	38	52	3
Individual incentives	39	4	27	57	2
Long-term incentives (executive level)	32	1	44	44	4
Lump-sum merit pay	28	1	19	51	21
Competency-based pay	22	5	31	51	—
Profit-sharing (apart from retirement program)	22	1	43	46	9
Profit-sharing (as part of retirement program)	22	—	46	37	9
ESOP* stock plan	21	2	33	33	18
Suggestion/proposal programs	17	1	19	44	11
Team-based pay	15	4	29	50	4
Long-term incentives (below executive levels)	13	2	43	38	—
Skill-/knowledge-based pay	12	2	58	37	—
Group incentives (not team-based)	11	2	24	59	6
Pay for quality	9	9	29	36	14
Gainsharing	8	1	38	31	15
Special key-contributor programs (before the fact)	7	1	55	27	—

*Employee stock ownership plan.

SOURCE: "Incentive Pay Plans: Which Ones Work . . . and Why," *HR Focus*, April 2001, p. 3.

Current Practices   For an indication of current practices, see Table 10–2, which is based on a survey of 156 US executives. The lack of clear patterns in Table 10–2 is indicative of the still experimental nature of incentive compensation today. Much remains to be learned from research and practice.

Research Insights   According to available expert opinion and research results, pay for performance too often falls short of its goal of improved job performance. "Experts say that roughly half the incentive plans they see don't work, victims of poor design and administration."[71] In fact, one recent study documented how incentive pay had a *negative* effect on the performance of 150,000 managers from 500 financially distressed companies.[72] A meta-analysis of 39 studies found only a modest positive correlation between financial incentives and performance *quantity* and no impact on performance *quality*.[73] Other researchers have found only a weak statistical link between large executive bonuses paid out in good years and subsequent improvement in corporate profitability.[74] Also, in a survey of small business owners, more than half said their commission plans failed to motivate extra effort from their salespeople.[75] Linking teachers' merit pay to student performance, an exciting school reform idea, turned out to be a big disappointment: "The bottom line is that despite high hopes, none of the 13 districts studied was able to use teacher pay incentives to achieve significant, lasting gains in student performance."[76] Clearly, the pay-for-performance area is still very much up in the air.

Team-Based Pay

One very clear trend in today's workplace is the move toward teams (see Chapter 13). There are permanent work teams and temporary project teams. There are cross-functional teams with specialists from different areas such as engineering, production, marketing, and finance. There are self-managed teams, where employees take turns handling traditional managerial tasks including staffing, scheduling, training, and recordkeeping. Most recently, there are *virtual* teams where people from different geographic locations collaborate via computer networks, often with little or no face-to-face contact. While the move toward team structure certainly is a promising one, there are many loose ends, a major one being how to reward team members and teamwork. *Training* magazine's Beverly Geber puts things into context by noting:

> It's a struggle trying to persuade many employees that working cooperatively with others is in their best interest. It's an epic battle teaching them *how* to collaborate, especially when it means they must resist a lifetime of seeking personal glory. And it's truly exasperating trying to get nonteamed parts of the organization, as well as customers and suppliers, to work harmoniously with the teams.
>
> Unfortunately, there's another bugaboo waiting just around the corner. It is the issue of compensation. To wit: Now that people are working closely together to produce a product jointly, how do you pay them in a way that encourages collaboration and spurs the team to produce its utmost, but does not ignore the individual's innate desire for personal recognition?[77]

Team-based pay is defined as incentive compensation that rewards individuals for teamwork and/or rewards teams for collective results. This definition highlights an important distinction between individual *behavior* and team *results*. Stated another way, it takes team players to get team results. Any team-oriented pay plan that ignores this distinction almost certainly will fail.

Team-based pay
Linking pay to teamwork behavior and/or team results.

Problems

The biggest single barrier to effective team-based pay is *cultural*, especially in highly individualistic cultures such as the United States, Canada, Norway, and Australia.[78] Individual competition for pay and pay raises has long been the norm in the United States. Entrenched grading schemes in schools and colleges, focused on individual competition and not group achievement, are a good preview of the traditional American workplace. Team-based pay is a direct assault on the cultural tradition of putting the individual above the group. Indeed, a recent scientific poll of nearly 1,500 full-time employees across the United States found little support for team-based rewards and a strong preference for permanent pay increases for individual performance. This led the researchers to conclude: "Workers' lack of interest in team pay implies that employers are simply not rewarding teams as effectively as they could."[79]

Another culturally rooted problem is a general *lack of teamwork skills.* Members of high-performance teams are skilled communicators, conflict handlers, and negotiators; they are flexible, adaptable, and open to change. Employees accustomed to being paid for personal achievements tend to resent having their pay dependent upon others' performance and problems. The combination of poor interpersonal skills and an individualistic work ethic can breed conflict and excessive peer pressure, as Levi Strauss & Co. learned at its El Paso, Texas, pants factory. The El Paso plant was one of 27 sewing operations in the United States, where Levi's switched from traditional assembly lines to 20- to 30-worker multitask teams responsible for complete batches of pants, from start to finish. Eighteen months into the new team structure, orders were being processed in only three days, as opposed to a seven-day turnaround under the old system. But Levi's got more than improved productivity:

> Under the team system, a worker's incentive pay is tied to team performance. A poor performer or absent worker affects everybody's paycheck. When someone is perceived to be faking sick days or lollygagging on a sewing machine, tempers flare. Says [team member Salvador] Salas: "Somebody's fooling around, and somebody else calls attention to that, and the first guy will just flip him off." Supervisor Gracie Cortez says that "it gets tough out there." She finds herself intervening to prevent "big fights." Says plant manager Edward Alvarez: "Peer pressure can be vicious and brutal."[80]

Levi's officials eventually realized that only two weeks of "group dynamics" training for plant workers, prior to the shift to teams, was insufficient.

Research Evidence   Research evidence to date is not encouraging. A recent comprehensive review of studies that examined team-based rewards in the workplace led to this conclusion: "The field-based empirical evidence is limited and inconclusive."[81]

Recommendations   The state of the art in team-based pay is very primitive today. Given the many different types of teams, we can be certain there is no single best approach. However, based on anecdotal evidence from the general management literature and case studies,[82] we can make these five recommendations:

- *Prepare employees* for team-based systems with as much interpersonal skills training as possible. This ongoing effort should include diversity training and skill training in communication, conflict resolution, trust building, group problem solving, and negotiating.
- *Establish teams* and get them running smoothly before introducing team-based pay incentives to avoid overload and frustration.
- Create a pay plan that *blends* individual achievement and team incentives.
- Begin by rewarding teamwork *behaviors* (such as mutual support, cooperation, and group problem solving), and then phase in pay incentives for team *results*.
- When paying for team results, make sure individual team members see a clear connection between their own work and team results. Compensation specialists call this *a clear line of sight.*

Getting the Most out of Extrinsic Rewards and Pay for Performance

Based on what we have learned to date,[83] here is a workable plan for maximizing the motivational impact of extrinsic rewards.

- Tie praise, recognition, and noncash awards to *specific* results.
- Make pay for performance an integral part of the organization's basic strategy (e.g., pursuit of best-in-the-industry product or service quality).
- Base incentive determinations on objective performance data.
- Have all employees actively participate in the development, implementation, and revision of the performance-pay formulas.
- Encourage two-way communication so problems with the incentive plan will be detected early.

- Build pay-for-performance plans around participative structures such as suggestion systems or quality circles.
- Reward teamwork and cooperation whenever possible.
- Actively sell the plan to supervisors and middle managers who may view employee participation as a threat to their traditional notion of authority.
- If annual cash bonuses are granted, pay them in a lump sum to maximize their motivational impact.
- Remember that money motivates when it comes in significant amounts, not occasional nickels and dimes.

Positive Reinforcement

Feedback and extrinsic reward programs all too often are ineffective because they are administered in haphazard ways. For example, consider these scenarios:

- A young programmer stops E-mailing creative suggestions to his boss because she never responds.
- The office politician gets a great promotion while her more skilled co-workers scratch their heads and gossip about the injustice.

In the first instance, a productive behavior faded away for lack of encouragement. In the second situation, unproductive behavior was unwittingly rewarded. Feedback and rewards need to be handled more precisely. Fortunately, the field of behavioral psychology can help. Thanks to the pioneering work of Edward L Thorndike, B F Skinner, and many others, a behavior modification technique called *positive reinforcement* helps managers achieve needed discipline and desired effect when providing feedback and granting extrinsic rewards.[84]

Thorndike's Law of Effect

During the early 1900s, Edward L Thorndike observed in his psychology laboratory that a cat would behave randomly and wildly when placed in a small box with a secret trip lever that opened a door. However, once the cat accidentally tripped the lever and escaped, the animal would go straight to the lever when placed back in the box. Hence, Thorndike formulated his famous **law of effect,** which says *behavior with favorable consequences tends to be repeated, while behavior with unfavorable consequences tends to disappear.*[85] This was a dramatic departure from the prevailing notion a century ago that behavior was the product of inborn instincts.

Law of effect
Behavior with favorable consequences is repeated; behavior with unfavorable consequences disappears.

Skinner's Operant Conditioning Model

Skinner refined Thorndike's conclusion that behavior is controlled by its consequences. Skinner's work became known as *behaviorism* because he dealt strictly with observable behavior.[86] As a behaviorist, Skinner believed it was pointless to explain behavior in terms of unobservable inner states such as needs, drives, attitudes, or thought processes.[87] He similarly put little stock in the idea of self-determination.

In his 1938 classic, *The Behavior of Organisms,* Skinner drew an important distinction between the two types of behavior: respondent and operant behavior.[88] He labeled

Renowned behavioral psychologist B. F. Skinner and your co-author Bob Kreitner met and posed for a snapshot at an Academy of Management meeting in Boston. As a behaviorist, Skinner preferred to deal with observable behavior and its antecedents and consequences in the environment rather than with inner states such as attitudes and cognitive processes. The late professor Skinner was a fascinating man who left a permanent mark on modern psychology.

Courtesy of the author

Respondent behavior

Skinner's term for unlearned stimulus–response reflexes.

unlearned reflexes, or stimulus–response (S–R) connections, **respondent behavior.** This category of behavior was said to describe a very small proportion of adult human behavior. Examples of respondent behavior would include shedding tears while peeling onions and reflexively withdrawing one's hand from a hot stove.[89] Skinner attached the label **operant behavior** to behavior that is learned when one "operates on" the environment to produce desired consequences. Some call this the response–stimulus (R–S) model. Years of controlled experiments with pigeons in "Skinner boxes" helped Skinner develop a sophisticated technology of behavior control, or operant conditioning. For example, he taught pigeons how to pace figure-eights and how to bowl by reinforcing the underweight (and thus hungry) birds with food whenever they more closely approximated target behaviors. Skinner's work spawned the field or behavior modification and has significant implications for OB because the vast majority of organizational behavior falls into the operant category.[90]

Operant behavior

Skinner's term for learned, consequence-shaped behavior.

Contingent Consequences

Contingent consequences, according to Skinner's operant theory, control behavior in four ways: positive reinforcement, negative reinforcement, punishment, and extinction. The term *contingent* means there is a systematic if-then linkage between the target behavior and the consequence. Remember Mom (and Pink Floyd) saying something to this effect: "If you don't finish your dinner, you don't get dessert" (see Figure 10–5)? To avoid the all-too-common mislabeling of these consequences, let us review some formal definitions.

Positive reinforcement

Making behavior occur more often by contingently presenting something positive.

Positive Reinforcement Strengthens Behavior
Positive reinforcement is the process of strengthening a behavior by contingently presenting something pleasing. (Importantly, a behavior is strengthened when it increases in frequency and weakened when it decreases in frequency.) A design engineer who works overtime because of praise and recognition from the boss is responding to positive reinforcement.[91]

Figure 10–5   *Contingent Consequences in Operant Conditioning*

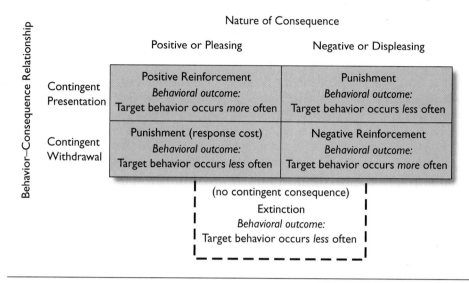

Similarly, people tend to return to businesses where they are positively reinforced with high-quality service. For example, Commerce Bank, based in Cherry Hill, New Jersey, owes part of its success and rapid growth to a culture based on positive reinforcement. Commerce tries hard to "wow" its customers with service innovations such as Sunday banking hours.

> Employees are praised for being "wowy." And every March, [CEO Vernon] Hill recognizes top performers at the companywide Wow Awards. " 'Wow' is more than a word around here," says John Manning, vice president of—that's right—the Wow Department. "It's a feeling that you give and get."
>
> That type of obsessive service culture starts with hiring the right people. "This is not the job for someone who's interested in being cool or indifferent," Manning says. And instead of the usual humdrum orientation class, every new employee attends a one-day course at Commerce University called Traditions. It's part game show, part training session, part common sense. Banks do all sorts of stupid things to customers, Manning tells new hires. That's why the company has a "Kill a Stupid Rule" program. "If you identify a rule that prevents you from wowing customers," Manning says, "we'll pay you 50 bucks."[92]

Negative Reinforcement Also Strengthens Behavior
Negative reinforcement is the process of strengthening a behavior by contingently withdrawing something displeasing. For example, an army sergeant who stops yelling when a recruit jumps out of bed has negatively reinforced that particular behavior. Similarly, the behavior of clamping our hands over our ears when watching a jumbo jet take off is negatively reinforced by relief from the noise. Negative reinforcement is often confused with punishment. But the two strategies have opposite effects on behavior. Negative reinforcement, as the word *reinforcement* indicates, strengthens a behavior because it provides relief from an unpleasant situation.

Punishment Weakens Behavior
Punishment is the process of weakening behavior through either the contingent presentation of something displeasing or the contingent withdrawal of something positive. A manager assigning a tardy employee to a dirty

Negative reinforcement
Making behavior occur more often by contingently withdrawing something negative.

Punishment
Making behavior occur less often by contingently presenting something negative or withdrawing something positive.

job exemplifies the first type of punishment. Docking a tardy employee's pay is an example of the second type of punishment, called "response cost" punishment. Legal fines involve response cost punishment. Salespeople who must make up any cash register shortages out of their own pockets are being managed through response cost punishment. Ethical questions can and should be raised about this type of on-the-job punishment.[93]

Extinction

Making behavior occur less often by ignoring or not reinforcing it.

Extinction Also Weakens Behavior   **Extinction** is the weakening of a behavior by ignoring it or making sure it is not reinforced. Getting rid of a former boyfriend or girlfriend by refusing to answer their phone calls is an extinction strategy. A good analogy for extinction is to imagine what would happen to your houseplants if you stopped watering them. Like a plant without water, a behavior without occasional reinforcement eventually dies. Although very different processes, both punishment and extinction have the same weakening effect on behavior.

Schedules of Reinforcement

As just illustrated, contingent consequences are an important determinant of future behavior. The *timing* of behavioral consequences can be even more important. Based on years of tedious laboratory experiments with pigeons in highly controlled environments, Skinner and his colleagues discovered distinct patterns of responding for various schedules of reinforcement.[94]

Although some of their conclusions can be generalized to negative reinforcement, punishment, and extinction, it is best to think only of positive reinforcement when discussing schedules.

Continuous reinforcement

Reinforcing every instance of a behavior.

Continuous Reinforcement   As indicated in Table 10–3, every instance of a target behavior is reinforced when a **continuous reinforcement** (CRF) schedule is in effect. For instance, when your television set is operating properly, you are reinforced with a picture every time you turn it on (a CRF schedule). But, as with any CRF schedule of reinforcement, the behavior of turning on the television will undergo rapid extinction if the set breaks.

Intermittent reinforcement

Reinforcing some but not all instances of behavior.

Intermittent Reinforcement   Unlike CRF schedules, **intermittent reinforcement** involves reinforcement of *some* but not all instances of a target behavior. Four subcategories of intermittent schedules, described in Table 10–3, are fixed and variable ratio schedules and fixed and variable interval schedules. Reinforcement in *ratio* schedules is contingent on the number of responses emitted. *Interval* reinforcement is tied to the passage of time. Some common examples of the four types of intermittent reinforcement are as follows:

- *Fixed ratio*—piece-rate pay; bonuses tied to the sale of a fixed number of units.
- *Variable ratio*—slot machines that pay off after a variable number of lever pulls; lotteries that pay off after the purchase of a variable number of tickets.
- *Fixed interval*—hourly pay; annual salary paid on a regular basis.
- *Variable interval*—random supervisory praise and pats on the back for employees who have been doing a good job. (See the OB Exercise on page 350).

Scheduling Is Critical   The schedule of reinforcement can more powerfully influence behavior than the magnitude of reinforcement. Although this proposition grew

Table 10–3   *Schedules of Reinforcement*

Schedule	Description	Probable Effects on Responding
Continuous (CRF)	Reinforcer follows every response.	Steady high rate of performance as long as reinforcement continues to follow every response. High frequency of reinforcement may lead to early satiation. Behavior weakens rapidly (undergoes extinction) when reinforcers are withheld. Appropriate for newly emitted, unstable, or low-frequency responses.
Intermittent	Reinforcer does not follow every response.	Capable of producing high frequencies of responding. Low frequency of reinforcement precludes early satiation. Appropriate for stable or high-frequency responses.
Fixed ratio (FR)	A fixed number of responses must be emitted before reinforcement occurs.	A fixed ratio of 1:1 (reinforcement occurs after every response); the same as a continuous schedule. Tends to produce a high rate of response, which is vigorous and steady.
Variable ratio (VR)	A varying or random number of responses must be emitted before reinforcement occurs.	Capable of producing a high rate of response, which is vigorous, steady, and resistant to extinction.
Fixed interval (FI)	The first response after a specific period of time has elapsed is reinforced.	Produces an uneven response pattern varying from a very slow, unenergetic response immediately following reinforcement to a very fast, vigorous response immediately preceding reinforcement.
Variable interval (VI)	The first response after varying or random periods of time have elapsed is reinforced.	Tends to produce a high rate of response, which is vigorous, steady, and resistant to extinction.

SOURCE: F Luthans and R Kreitner, *Organizational Behavior Modification and Beyond: An Operant and Social Learning Approach* (Glenview, IL Scott, Foresman, 1985), p. 58. Used with authors' permission.

out of experiments with pigeons, subsequent on-the-job research confirmed it. Consider, for example, a field study of 12 unionized beaver trappers employed by a lumber company to keep the large rodents from eating newly planted tree seedlings.[95]

The beaver trappers were randomly divided into two groups that alternated weekly between two different bonus plans. Under the first schedule, each trapper earned his regular $7 per hour wage plus $1 for each beaver caught. Technically, this bonus was paid on a CRF schedule. The second bonus plan involved the regular $7 per hour wage plus a one-in-four chance (as determined by rolling the dice) of receiving $4 for each beaver trapped. This second bonus plan qualified as a variable ratio (VR-4) schedule. In the long run, both incentive schemes averaged out to a $1-per-beaver bonus. Surprisingly, however, when the trappers were under the VR-4 schedule, they were 58% more productive than under the CRF schedule, despite the fact that the net amount of pay averaged out the same for the two groups during the 12-week trapping season.

Work Organizations Typically Rely on the Weakest ∫chedule

Generally, variable ratio and variable interval schedules of reinforcement produce the strongest behavior that is most resistant to extinction. As gamblers will attest, variable schedules hold the promise of reinforcement after the next target response. For example, the following drama at a Laughlin, Nevada, gambling casino is one more illustration of the potency of variable ratio reinforcement:

> An elderly woman with a walker had lost her grip on the slot [machine] handle and had collapsed on the floor.
> "Help," she cried weakly.
> The woman at the machine next to her interrupted her play for a few seconds to try to help her to her feet, but all around her the army of slot players continued feeding coins to the machines.
> A security man arrived to soothe the woman and take her away.
> "Thank you," she told him appreciatively.
> "But don't forget my winnings."[97]

Organizations without at least some variable reinforcement are less likely to prompt this type of dedication to task. Consider this approach:

> One global telecommunications firm recently created a rewards bank on its intranet. Managers are given a "points budget" and encouraged to give worthy employees just-in-time compensation for their performance. Employees can redeem these points for time off, cash, and assorted goods.[98]

Despite the trend toward this sort of pay-for-performance, time-based pay schemes such as hourly wages and yearly salaries that rely on the weakest schedule of reinforcement (fixed interval) are still the rule in today's workplaces.

Behavior Shaping

Have you ever wondered how trainers at aquarium parks manage to get bottle-nosed dolphins to do flips, killer whales to carry people on their backs, and seals to juggle balls? The results are seemingly magical. Actually, a mundane learning process called shaping is responsible for the animals' antics.

Two-ton killer whales, for example, have a big appetite, and they find buckets of fish very reinforcing. So if the trainer wants to ride a killer whale, he or she reinforces very basic behaviors that will eventually lead to the whale being ridden. The killer whale is contingently reinforced with a few fish for coming near the trainer, then for being touched, then for putting its nose in a harness, then for being straddled, and eventually for swimming with the trainer on its back. In effect, the trainer systematically raises the behavioral requirement for reinforcement. Thus, **shaping** is defined as the process of reinforcing closer and closer approximations to a target behavior.

Shaping works very well with people, too, especially in training and quality programs involving continuous improvement. Praise, recognition, and instructive and credible feedback cost managers little more than moments of their time. Yet, when used in conjunction with a behavior-shaping program, these consequences can efficiently foster significant improvements in job performance. The key to successful behavior shaping lies in reducing a complex target behavior to easily learned steps and then faithfully (and patiently) reinforcing any improvement. For example, Continental Airlines used a cash bonus program to improve its on-time arrival record from one of the worst in the industry to one of the best. Employees originally were promised a $65 bonus each month Continental earned a top-five ranking. Now it takes a second- or third-place ranking to earn the $65 bonus and a $100 bonus awaits employees when they achieve a number one ranking.[99] (Table 10–4 lists practical tips on shaping.)

Shaping
Reinforcing closer and closer approximations to a target behavior.

Table 10–4   *Ten Practical Tips for Shaping Job Behavior*

1. *Accommodate the process of behavioral change.* Behaviors change in gradual stages, not in broad, sweeping motions.
2. *Define new behavior patterns specifically.* State what you wish to accomplish in explicit terms and in small amounts that can be easily grasped.
3. *Give individuals feedback on their performance.* A once-a-year performance appraisal is not sufficient.
4. *Reinforce behavior as quickly as possible.*
5. *Use powerful reinforcement.* To be effective, rewards must be important to the employee—not to the manager.
6. *Use a continuous reinforcement schedule.* New behaviors should be reinforced every time they occur. This reinforcement should continue until these behaviors become habitual.
7. *Use a variable reinforcement schedule for maintenance.* Even after behavior has become habitual, it still needs to be rewarded, though not necessarily every time it occurs.
8. *Reward teamwork—not competition.* Group goals and group rewards are one way to encourage cooperation in situations in which jobs and performance are interdependent.
9. *Make all rewards contingent on performance.*
10. *Never take good performance for granted.* Even superior performance, if left unrewarded, will eventually deteriorate.

SOURCE: Adapted from A T Hollingsworth and D Tanquay Hoyer, "How Supervisors Can Shape Behavior," *Personnel Journal,* May 1985, pp. 86, 88.

Summary of Key Concepts

1. *Specify the two basic functions of feedback and three sources of feedback, and summarize at least three practical lessons from feedback research.* Feedback, in the form of *objective* information about performance, both instructs and motivates. According to the cognitive-processing model, individuals receive feedback from others, the task, and from themselves.

   Feedback is not automatically accepted as intended, especially negative feedback. Managerial credibility can be enhanced through expertise and a climate of trust. Feedback must not be too frequent or too scarce and must be tailored to the individual. Feedback directly from computers is effective. Active participation in the feedback session helps people perceive feedback as more accurate. The quality of feedback received decreases as one moves up the organizational hierarchy.

2. *Define upward feedback and 360-degree feedback, and summarize the general tips for giving good feedback.* Lower-level employees provide upward feedback (usually anonymous) to their managers. A focal person receives 360-degree feedback from subordinates, the manager, peers, and selected others such as customers or suppliers. Good feedback is tied to performance *goals* and clear *expectations,* linked with *specific* behavior or results, reserved for *key result areas,* given as soon as possible, provided for *improvement* as well as for final results, focused on *performance* rather than on personalities, and based on *accurate* and *credible* information.

3. *Identify and briefly explain the four different organizational reward norms.* Maximizing individual gain is the object of the *profit maximization* reward norm. The *equity* norm calls for distributing rewards proportionate to contributions (those who contribute the most should earn the most). Everyone is rewarded equally when the *equality* reward norm is in force. The *need* reward norm involves distributing rewards based on employees' needs.

4. *Summarize the reasons why extrinsic rewards often fail to motivate employees.* Extrinsic reward systems can fail to motivate employees for these reasons: overemphasis on money, no appreciation effect, benefits become entitlements, wrong behavior is rewarded, rewards are delayed too long, use of one-size-fits-all rewards, one-

shot rewards with temporary impact, and demotivating practices such as layoffs.

5. *Discuss how managers can generally improve extrinsic reward and pay-for-performance plans.* They need to be strategically anchored, based on quantified performance data, highly participative, actively sold to supervisors and middle managers, and teamwork oriented. Annual bonuses of significant size are helpful.

6. *State Thorndike's "law of effect," and explain Skinner's distinction between respondent and operant behavior.* According to Edward L Thorndike's law of effect, behavior with favorable consequences tends to be repeated, while behavior with unfavorable consequences tends to disappear. B F Skinner called unlearned stimulus–response reflexes respondent behavior. He applied the term *operant behavior* to all behavior learned through experience with environmental consequences.

7. *Define positive reinforcement, negative reinforcement, punishment, and extinction, and distinguish between continuous and intermittent schedules of reinforcement.* Positive and negative reinforcement are consequence management strategies that strengthen behavior, whereas punishment and extinction weaken behavior. These strategies need to be defined objectively in terms of their actual impact on behavior frequency, not subjectively on the basis of intended impact.

   Every instance of a behavior is reinforced with a continuous reinforcement (CRF) schedule. Under intermittent reinforcement schedules—fixed and variable ratio or fixed and variable interval—some, rather than all, instances of a target behavior are reinforced. Variable schedules produce the most extinction-resistant behavior.

8. *Demonstrate your knowledge of behavior shaping.* Behavior shaping occurs when closer and closer approximations of a target behavior are reinforced. In effect, the standard for reinforcement is made more difficult as the individual learns. The process begins with continuous reinforcement, which gives way to intermittent reinforcement when the target behavior becomes strong and habitual.

Discussion Questions

1. How can feedback, extrinsic rewards, and positive reinforcement be combined to improve job performance?

2. How has feedback instructed or motivated you lately?

3. Relative to your school work, which of the three sources of feedback—others, task, self—has the greatest impact on your performance? If you have a job, which source of feedback is most potent in that situation?

4. Which of the five cognitive evaluation criteria for feedback—feedback accuracy, source credibility, system fairness, expectancies, behavioral standards—do you think ranks as most important? Explain.

5. How would you summarize the practical benefits and drawbacks of 360-degree feedback?

6. Which of the four organizational reward norms do you prefer? Why?

7. How would you respond to a manager who said, "Employees cannot be motivated with money"?

8. What real-life examples of positive reinforcement, negative reinforcement, both forms of punishment, and extinction can you draw from your recent experience? Were these strategies appropriately or inappropriately used?

9. From a schedule of reinforcement perspective, why do people find gambling so addictive?

10. What sort of behavior shaping have you engaged in lately? Explain your success or failure.

Internet Exercise

www.panoramicfeedback.com

As discussed in this chapter, 360-degree feedback is getting a good deal of attention these days. Our purpose here is to introduce you to a sample 360-degree evaluation from an innovative Internet-based program marketed by Panoramic Feedback. (*Note:* Our use of this sample is for instructional purposes only and does not constitute an endorsement of the program, which may or may not suit your needs.)

Go to the Internet home page (**www.panoramicfeedback.com**), and select "Samples: Questionnaire" from the main menu. The sample evaluation is for a hypothetical supervisor named Terry Smith. For our purposes, substitute the name of *your manager* from your present or past job. The idea is to do an *upward* evaluation of someone you actually know. Read the brief background piece, and proceed to Part One of the questionnaire. Read and follow the instructions for the eight performance dimensions. All responses you click and any comments you type into the two boxes in Part One will show up on your printed copy, if you choose to make one. Move to Part Two and type your personal evaluations of your manager in the box provided.

These comments also will be on any printed copy you may make.

Questions

1. How would you rate the eight performance dimensions in this brief sample? Relevant? Important? Good basis for constructive feedback?

2. If you were to expand this evaluation, what other performance scales would you add?

3. Is this a *fair* evaluation, as far as it goes? Explain.

4. How comfortable would you be evaluating the following people with this type of *anonymous* 360-degree instrument: Boss? Peers? Self? People reporting directly to you?

5. Would you like to be the focal person in a 360-degree review? Under what circumstances? Explain.

6. Results of anonymous 360-degree reviews should be used for which of the following purposes: Promotions? Pay raises? Job assignments? Feedback for personal growth and development? Explain.

OB in Action Case Study

Lantech's Revolving Pay Plans[100]

Corporate culture sometimes doesn't mix well with team-based pay, no matter how much you try to align goals with pay. Lantech, a machinery manufacturer based in Louisville, KY, experimented with two types of team-based compensation, and ultimately it chose a non-team-based pay strategy after both systems prompted employee behavior that was counterproductive to achieving the company's goals.

Lantech is a privately held, family-owned business that has 285 employees in the United States, primarily at the firm's Louisville plant, and had $65 million in sales last year. The company manufactures stretch-wrap machinery, which is used to apply stretch wrap over pallets of products. The company was founded in 1972 on the philosophy that "it is possible to have commercial success as well as human success," says Jean Cunningham, vice president of company services and chief financial officer. Cunningham oversees the firm's compensation system.

Lantech first tried a team-based concept in the early 1980s, using small teams built along work-group lines, such as a group of welders or a group of field service engineers. Company management was exploring whether employees, grouped in small teams and with an understanding of the company mission, "could make good decisions about who is the best to lead that team and who is making the best contribution," Cunningham says. "We actually went so far as to give those teams the ability to decide within the team how much different members would be paid."

She acknowledges that this approach seems "pretty extreme." But, she says, "we went into it with a very pure, very positive expectation and a very high ideal of how people could rise above their own personal needs."

Unfortunately, this ideal turned out to be unrealistic. "It was just too hard to be objective and manage the team," she says. The structure prompted some employees to try to get their friends or relatives on the same team to exert more influence on decisions about raises. "We really started to see some negative behavior," Cunningham notes.

This system was set aside. Then, in the late 1980s, Lantech tried another team-based compensation structure, one based on its three strategic business units. Employees' compensation consisted of three parts: base salary, an individual discretionary bonus based on performance and a team-based bonus based on the profitability of the business unit.

This system also turned out to have glitches. Lantech management was finding that it was "not compensating the right behaviors," Cunningham says.

For example, Cunningham recalls bumping into an employee on the shop floor and encouraging him to pursue a good job opportunity in another business unit. He told her he was hesitant because the other unit's bonus program was not as successful as his current unit's. "This would have been a good career move for this individual. But because of the system that we had, it was a barrier to good decisions being made," she says.

The system also encouraged a competitive feeling among business units that was not always productive. Lantech's units buy equipment from each other, and how these items are priced internally was affecting how profitable individual units were, a key consideration within the team-based compensation system. Cunningham says the situation would become so acrimonious that a third party, such as the company's controller, would be called in to resolve internal pricing disputes.

"It really came to a head in the early '90s," she notes. Lantech's balance sheet overall was in the red, but one of the company's business units was profitable, and thus paid out bonuses. Lantech's management realized that the team-based compensation system was not sending the right message or supporting the company's efforts to focus on customer satisfaction. "This just did not make sense," Cunningham says. "It wasn't focusing on the external world."

The company scrapped the system, but not without "great pains. Any time you change compensation systems, it's very painful," she notes. "We started thinking about why you want an incentive system in the first place."

Lantech now uses a companywide bonus program based on profitability. "We want to share the results of us working together to satisfy the customer." Cunningham says. Through monthly companywide meetings, employees are kept apprised of Lantech's financial outlook. Lantech also uses frequent nonmonetary rewards and recognition, such as celebrations for receiving patents, to give employees a sense of belonging and appreciation.

Questions for Discussion

1. Why did team-based pay fail at Lantech?

2. What would Lantech need to do to have a successful team-based pay plan?

3. Is the newest pay plan likely to succeed? Explain.

4. How could feedback and positive reinforcement be used to strengthen the present companywide profit-sharing program?

5. Why is employee compensation such a troublesome area today?

Personal Awareness and Growth Exercise

What Kind of Feedback Are You Getting?

Objectives

1. To provide actual examples of on-the-job feedback from three primary sources: organization/supervisor, co-workers, and self/task.

2. To provide a handy instrument for evaluating the comparative strength of positive feedback from these three sources.

Introduction

A pair of researchers from Georgia Tech developed and tested a 63-item feedback questionnaire to demonstrate the importance of both the sign and content of feedback messages.[101] Although their instrument contains both positive and negative feedback items, we have extracted 18 positive items for this self-awareness exercise.

Instructions

Thinking of your current job (or your most recent job), circle one number for each of the 18 items. Alternatively, you could ask one or more other employed individuals to complete the questionnaire. Once the questionnaire has been completed, calculate subtotal and total scores by adding the circled numbers. Then try to answer the discussion questions.

Instrument

How frequently do you experience each of the following outcomes in your present (or past) job?

ORGANIZATIONAL/SUPERVISORY FEEDBACK

	Rarely	Occasionally	Very Frequently
1. My supervisor complimenting me on something I have done.	1 — 2 — 3 — 4 — 5		
2. My supervisor increasing my responsibilities.	1 — 2 — 3 — 4 — 5		
3. The company expressing pleasure with my performance.	1 — 2 — 3 — 4 — 5		
4. The company giving me a raise.	1 — 2 — 3 — 4 — 5		
5. My supervisor recommending me for a promotion or raise.	1 — 2 — 3 — 4 — 5		
6. The company providing me with favorable data concerning my performance.	1 — 2 — 3 — 4 — 5		

Subscore = _____

CO-WORKER FEEDBACK

7. My co-workers coming to me for advice.	1 — 2 — 3 — 4 — 5		
8. My co-workers expressing approval of my work.	1 — 2 — 3 — 4 — 5		
9. My co-workers liking to work with me.	1 — 2 — 3 — 4 — 5		
10. My co-workers telling me that I am doing a good job.	1 — 2 — 3 — 4 — 5		
11. My co-workers commenting favorably on something I have done.	1 — 2 — 3 — 4 — 5		
12. Receiving a compliment from my co-workers.	1 — 2 — 3 — 4 — 5		

Subscore = _____

SELF/TASK FEEDBACK

13. Knowing that the way I go about my duties is superior to most others.	1 — 2 — 3 — 4 — 5		
14. Feeling I am accomplishing more than I used to.	1 — 2 — 3 — 4 — 5		
15. Knowing that I can now perform or do things which previously were difficult for me.	1 — 2 — 3 — 4 — 5		
16. Finding that I am satisfying my own standards for "good work."	1 — 2 — 3 — 4 — 5		
17. Knowing that what I am doing "feels right."	1 — 2 — 3 — 4 — 5		
18. Feeling confident of being able to handle all aspects of my job.	1 — 2 — 3 — 4 — 5		

Subscore = _____

Total score = _____

Questions for Discussion

1. Which items on this questionnaire would you rate as primarily instructional in function? Are all of the remaining items primarily motivational? Explain.

2. In terms of your own feedback profile, which of the three types is the strongest (has the highest subscore)? Which is the weakest (has the lowest subscore)? How well does your feedback profile explain your job performance and/or satisfaction?

3. How does your feedback profile measure up against those of your classmates? (Arbitrary norms, for comparative purposes, are as follows: deficient feedback = 18–42; moderate feedback = 43–65; abundant feedback = 66–90.)

4. Which of the three sources of feedback is most critical to your successful job performance or job satisfaction or both? Explain.

Group Exercise

Rewards, Rewards, Rewards

Objectives

1. To tap the class's collective knowledge of organizational rewards.
2. To appreciate the vast array of potential rewards.
3. To contrast individual and group perceptions of rewards.
4. To practice your group creativity skills.

Introduction

Rewards are a centerpiece of organizational life. Both extrinsic and intrinsic rewards motivate us to join and continue contributing to organized effort. But not all rewards have the same impact on work motivation. Individuals have their own personal preferences for rewards. The best way to discover people's reward preferences is to ask them, both individually and collectively. This group brainstorming and class discussion exercise requires about 20 to 30 minutes.

Instructions

Your instructor will divide your class randomly into teams of five to eight people. Each team will go through the following four-step process:

1. Each team will have a six-minute brainstorming session, with one person acting as recorder. The objective of this brainstorming session is to list as many different organizational rewards as the group can think of. Your team might find it helpful to think of rewards by category (such as rewards from the work itself, rewards you can spend, rewards you can eat and drink, rewards you can feel, rewards you can wear, rewards you can share, rewards you cannot see, etc.). Remember, good brainstorming calls for withholding judgments about whether ideas are good or not. Quantity is wanted. Building upon other people's ideas also is encouraged.

2. Next, each individual will take four minutes to write down, in decreasing order of importance, 10 rewards they want from the job. *Note:* These are your *personal* preferences; your "top 10" rewards that will motivate you to do your best.

3. Each team will then take five minutes to generate a list of "today's 10 most powerful rewards." List them in decreasing order of their power to motivate job performance. Voting may be necessary.

4. A general class discussion of the questions listed below will conclude the exercise.

Questions for Discussion

1. How did your personal top 10 list compare with your group's top 10 list? If there is a serious mismatch, how would it affect your motivation? (To promote discussion, the instructor may have several volunteers read their personal top 10 lists to the class.)

2. Which team had the most productive brainstorming session? (The instructor may request each team to read its brainstormed list of potential rewards and top 10 list to the class.)

3. Were you surprised to hear certain rewards getting so much attention? Why?

4. How can managers improve the incentive effect of the rewards most frequently mentioned in class?

5. What is the likely future of organizational reward plans? Which of today's compensation trends will probably thrive, and which are probably passing fads?

Ethical Dilemma

CEO Pay: Welcome to the Twilight Zone between Need and Greed

As a matter of basic fairness, Plato posited that no one in a community should earn more than five times the wages of the ordinary worker. Management guru Peter F. Drucker has long warned that the growing pay gap between CEOs and workers could threaten the very credibility of leadership. He argued in the mid-1980s that no leader should earn more than 20 times the company's lowest-paid employee. His reasoning: If the CEO took too large a share of the rewards, it would make a mockery of the contributions of all the other employees in a successful organization.

After massive increases in compensation, Drucker's suggested standard looks quaint. CEOs of large corporations last year [2001] made 411 times as much as the average factory worker. In the past decade, as rank-and-file wages increased 36%, CEO pay climbed 340%, to $11 million.[102]

What is your ethical interpretation of this situation?

1. CEO pay these days is obscene and unethical. Explain why?

2. CEOs deserve whatever they get because of the pressures and demands of their jobs and their many years of dedication and hard work. Explain.

3. CEOs should be paid no more than _____ times the company's lowest-paid employee. Explain your choice. How will this limit be enforced?

4. Like top athletes and Hollywood actors, CEOs should be paid whatever the market dictates. Explain.

5. CEOs should voluntarily cap their compensation at reasonable and fair levels? What's reasonable and fair?

6. Something needs to be done to curb CEO compensation because it is eroding employee trust and loyalty. Suggestions?

7. Invent other options (but not stock options). Discuss.

For an interpretation of this situation, visit our Web site, **www.mhhe.com/kreitner.**

Learning Module B
Performance Appraisal

Performance appraisal, when done properly and fairly, is supposed to be an energizing growth experience for everyone involved. Unfortunately, as Tammy Galvin, executive editor of *Training* magazine, recently observed, the area of employee performance appraisal tends to be short on results and long on controversy these days:

> The annual performance review process, touted by some as the gateway to future prosperity, is, in reality for many companies, nothing more than a fill-in-the-blank, form-completing task that plots an individual's performance against a sanitized list of often generic corporate expectations and required competencies.
>
> There are many areas of debate surrounding performance reviews. When should they be held? How frequently? Should pay be linked to performance?[1]

In fact, 75% of the managers responding to one survey expressed significant dissatisfaction with their company's performance appraisal system.[2] Legal problems can surface, as well.

The purpose of this module is to explore the foundation concepts of fair and effective performance appraisals. Complete books are devoted to performance appraisal theory, research, and practice.[3] Our more restricted goal in this module is to give you a basic set of tools for understanding and evaluating the diverse array of appraisal techniques you will encounter in the years ahead. Those techniques, some of which do not even exist today, no doubt will range from excellent to bizarre.

Definition and Components

Performance appraisal

Judgmental evaluation of one's traits, behavior, or accomplishments as basis for personnel decisions and development plans.

In everyday life, it is hard to escape being on the receiving end of some sort of performance appraisal. There are report cards all through school, win–loss records in organized sports, and periodic meetings with one's boss. For managers, who are in the position of both giving and receiving them, performance appraisals are an especially important consideration. As used here, **performance appraisal** involves the judgmental evaluation of a jobholder's traits, behavior, or accomplishments as a basis for making important personnel decisions and development plans. A survey of 106 industrial psychologists identified the top 10 uses for performance appraisal data. In diminishing order of importance, they are used for

1. Salary administration.
2. Performance feedback.
3. Identifying individual strengths and weaknesses.
4. Documenting personnel decisions.
5. Recognition of individual performance.
6. Identifying poor performance.

7. Assisting in goal identification.

8. Promotion decisions.

9. Retention or termination of personnel.

10. Evaluating goal achievement.

Also, performance appraisal information was typically used for *multiple* purposes, rather than for a single purpose.[4] Economic efficiency, the principle of fairness, and applicable laws dictate that these decisions be made on the basis of valid and reliable evidence, rather than as the result of prejudice and guesswork.

Components of the Performance Appraisal Process

Although formal performance appraisals are practically universal in the managerial ranks, few express satisfaction with them, as mentioned above. Appraisers and appraisees alike are unhappy with the process. Much of the problem stems from the complexity of the appraisal process. One writer has captured this issue with the following example:

> If you wonder why evaluating an employee's performance can be so difficult, consider a simpler appraisal: one made by the barroom fan who concludes that his team's quarterback is a bum because several of his passes have been intercepted. An objective appraisal would raise the following questions: Were the passes really that bad, or did the receivers run the wrong patterns? Did the offensive line give the quarterback adequate protection? Did he call those plays himself, or were they sent in by the coach? Was the quarterback recovering from an injury?
>
> And what about the fan? Has he ever played football himself? How good is his vision? Did he have a good view of the TV set through the barroom's smoky haze? Was he talking to his friends at the bar during the game? How many beers did he down during the game?[5]

Further complicating things are Equal Employment Opportunity laws and guidelines that constrain managers' actions during the appraisal process.[6] Let us begin to sort out the complex appraisal process by examining its key components. Four key components, as shown in Figure B–1, are the appraiser, the appraisee, the appraisal method, and the outcomes.

The Appraiser

Managers generally express discomfort with playing the role of performance appraiser. Human resource (HR) experts tell us why:

> Busy managers have little incentive to devote precious time and energy to a process they consider difficult and filled with paperwork, says David Dell, research director of The Conference Board, a business research organization in New York.
>
> "A lot of people find that the methodology itself is cumbersome," Dell says. The Conference Board surveyed HR directors and executives and found that 90% of respondents felt that their performance measures and management approaches needed reform. And if

Figure B–1   *Components of the Performance Appraisal Process*

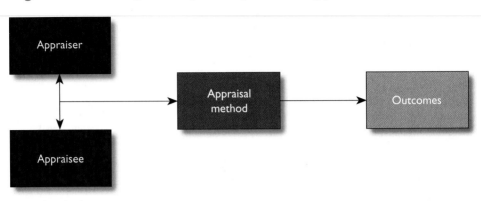

HR and executives—who do fewer reviews than many managers—don't like their performance systems, they can't convey a positive message about performance appraisal to the managers.

Managers also may feel that they lack control over the process because higher-ups dictate the results the system should give, says Lynda Ford, SPHR, president of The Ford Group, an HR consulting firm in Lee Center, NY. When that happens, managers get jaded.[7]

Charges of racism, sexism, and perceptual distortion also have been leveled at appraisers. In a survey of 267 corporations, 62% of the respondents reported that leniency was their number one appraisal problem.[8] Everyday experience and research evidence show how stereotyping and bias can contaminate the appraisal process. For example, combined evidence from a laboratory study and a field study documented how women professors tended to get lower ratings from students with traditional stereotypes of women.[9] Another study monitored the fates of 173 unionized employees who had filed grievances against their supervisors over an eight-year period. Those who had filed grievances tended to receive lower performance ratings from their supervisors than did their co-workers who had not filed grievances. This was especially true when the grievances had been settled in favor of the employee.[10] Thus, in this study at least, supervisors were shown to use performance appraisals as a weapon to get even with disliked subordinates. The ethical implications of this practice are obvious. Moreover, because performance appraisers engage in social perception (see Chapter 7), problems can occur in comprehending, encoding, retaining, or retrieving performance-related information.

Finally, managers typically lack the necessary performance appraisal skills. In fact, according to one study, only 25% of the managers doing performance appraisals had actually been trained for the task. The researchers added: "When there is training it often goes little further than to explain how to use the form, administrative procedures, and deadlines for submitting and getting the forms approved."[11] Experts on the subject have specified four criteria for a willing and able performance appraiser:

The person doing the assessment must: (1) be in a position to observe the behavior and performance of the individual of interest; (2) be knowledgeable about the dimensions or features of performance; (3) have an understanding of the scale format and the instrument itself; and (4) must be motivated to do a conscientious job of rating.[12]

Managers need to ensure that all four criteria are satisfied if performance appraisals are to be conducted properly.

SOURCE: DILBERT reprinted by permission of United Feature Syndicate, Inc.

The Appraisee

Employees play a characteristically passive listening and watching role when their own performance is being appraised. This experience can be demeaning and often threatening. According to a pair of human resource consultants:

> Whatever method is used, performance appraisals are always manager-driven. Managers are in charge of the schedule, the agenda, and the results, and managers are the ones that receive any training and/or rewards concerning performance appraisals. Subordinates generally are given no responsibility or particular preparation for their roles in the process beyond attending the appraisal meetings.[13]

Consequently, these consultants recommend four *proactive* roles (see Table B–1) for appraisees. They suggest formal *appraisee* training so analyzer, influencer, planner,

Table B–1   *Proactive Appraisee Roles during Performance Appraisal*

Role	Description
Analyzer	Performs self-assessment of goal achievement. Identifies performance strengths and weaknesses. Makes suggestions for performance improvement. Takes personal responsibility for solving performance problems.
Influencer	Improves communication skills (e.g., negotiations, advocating, providing information, advising, soliciting feedback, listening). Questions old assumptions and organizational roadblocks. Strives for collaborative relationship with boss.
Planner	Develops a clear vision of why his or her job exists. Identifies quality-of-service goals relative to "customers" or "clients." Understands what his or her job contributes (or does not contribute) to the organization.
Protégé	Learns from high-performing role models without compromising personal uniqueness. Learns through personal initiative rather than by waiting for instructions from others.

SOURCE: Adapted from B Jacobson and B L Kaye, "Career Development and Performance Appraisal: It Takes Two to Tango," *Personnel*, January 1986, pp. 26–32.

and protégé roles can be performed skillfully. This represents a marked departure from the usual practice of training appraisers only. The goal of this promising approach is to marry performance appraisal and career development through enhanced communication and greater personal commitment.

The Appraisal Method

Three distinct approaches to appraising job performance have emerged over the years—the trait approach, the behavioral approach, and the results approach. Figure B–2 displays examples of these three approaches. Controversy surrounds the question of which of these three approaches (and a suggested contingency approach) is best.

- *Trait approach*—This approach involves rating an individual's personal traits or characteristics. Commonly assessed traits are initiative, decisiveness, and dependability. Although the trait approach is widely used by managers, it is generally considered by experts to be the weakest. Trait ratings are deficient because they are ambiguous relative to actual performance. For instance, rating someone low on initiative tells him or her nothing about how to improve job performance. Also,

Figure B–2   *Three Basic Approaches to Appraising Job Performance*

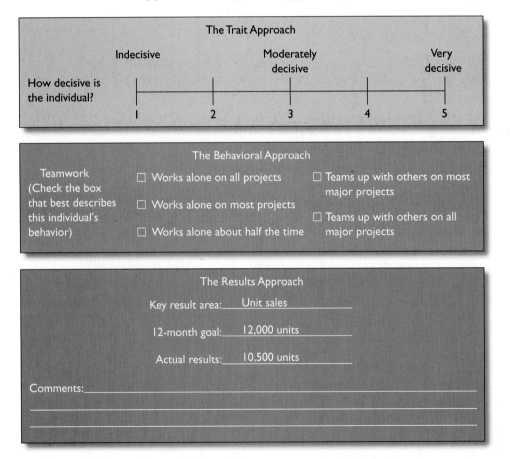

employees tend to react defensively to feedback about their personality (who or what they are).[14]

- *Behavioral approach*—How the person actually behaves, rather than his or her personality, matters in the behavioral approach.[15] As indicated in Figure B–3, the legal defensibility (in the United States) of performance appraisals is enhanced when performance ratings are supported with behavioral examples of performance.

- *Results approach*—Whereas the trait approach focuses on the "person" and the behavioral approach focuses on the "process," the results approach focuses on the "product" of one's efforts. In other words, what has the individual accomplished? *Management by objectives* (MBO) is the most common format for the results approach.[16]

Figure B–3 *Six Criteria of Legally Defensible Performance Appraisal Systems*

Based on an analysis of 51 employment discrimination cases, a performance appraisal system has a better chance of standing up in court if it satisfies these six criteria:

A *job analysis* is used to develop the appraisal system

Definitive *standards* of performance are developed, written, and provided to all raters regardless of the type of rating methods used

Raters are *trained* to properly use the rating instrument

Formal *appeal* mechanisms are developed and performance ratings are reviewed by upper-level management

Performance ratings are supported with documented examples of *behavior*

Employees are given a chance to improve their performance by provision of performance *counseling* or corrective *guidance*

SOURCE: Adapted from G V Barret and M C Kernan, "Performance Appraisal and Terminations: A Review of Court Decisions since *Brito v. Zia* with Implications for Personnel Practice," *Personnel Psychology*, Autumn 1987, pp. 489–503.

Table B–2   *A Contingency Approach to Performance Appraisals*

Function of Appraisal	Appraisal Method	Comments
Promotion decisions	Trait	Appropriate when competing appraisees have *dissimilar* jobs.
	Behavioral	Appropriate when competing appraisees have *similar* jobs.
	Results	Same as above.
Development decisions	Trait	Tends to cause defensiveness among low self-esteem employees.
	Behavioral	Pinpoints specific performance improvement needs.
	Results	Identifies deficient results, but does not tell why.
Pay decisions	Trait	Weak performance–reward linkage.
	Behavioral	Enhances performance–reward linkage.
	Results	Same as above.
Layoff decisions	Trait	Inappropriate, potentially discriminatory.
	Behavioral	Weighted combination of behaviors, results, and seniority is recommended.
	Results	Same as above.

SOURCE: Adapted from K N Wexley and R Klimoski, "Performance Appraisal: An Update," in *Research in Personnel and Human Resources Management*, vol. 2, eds K M Rowland and G R Ferris (Greenwich, CT: JAI press, 1984), pp. 35–79.

- *Contingency approach*—A pair of performance appraisal experts has called the trait-behavioral-results controversy a "pseudo issue."[17] They contend that each approach has its appropriate use, depending on the demands of the situation. Thus, they recommend a contingency approach (see Table B–2). Note how the poorly regarded trait approach is appropriate when a promotion decision needs to be made for candidates with dissimilar jobs. Although it has widespread applicability, the results approach is limited by its failure to specify why the appraisee's objectives have not been met. Overall, the behavioral approach emerges as the strongest. But it too is subject to situational limitations, such as when employees with dissimilar jobs are being evaluated for a promotion.

Outcomes of the Appraisal

According to a researcher from the Center for Creative Leadership, there are three indicators of a useful performance appraisal:

- Timely feedback on performance.
- Input for key personnel decisions.
- Individual and organizational planning tool.[18]

To this list, we would add "human resource development tool." These four appraisal outcomes cannot be left to chance. They need to be forethoughts rather than afterthoughts.

Performance Appraisal Research Insights and Practical Implications

Researchers have probed many facets of the appraisal process. Resulting insights include the following:

Table B–3   *The Essential Elements of a Good Performance Appraisal*

Elements to consider include
1. Objectives set by the employee and manager at the last appraisal.
2. List of specific competencies or skills being measured, with examples of successful behaviors.
3. Ratings scale appropriate to the organization.
4. Space for employee's self-appraisal.
5. Space for supervisor's appraisal.
6. Space for specific comments from the supervisor about the employee's performance.
7. Suggestions for employee development.
8. Objectives to meet by the next appraisal date.

SOURCE: C Joinson, "Making Sure Employees Measure Up," *HR Magazine*, March 2001, p. 39.

- Appraisers typically rate same-race appraisees higher. A meta-analysis of 74 studies and 17,159 individuals revealed that white superiors tended to favor white subordinates. Similarly, African-American superiors tended to favor African-American subordinates in a meta-analysis of 14 studies and 2,248 people.[19]

- A field study found a higher degree of trust for management when employees approved of the performance appraisal system.[20]

- In a meta-analysis of 32 field samples, researchers discovered the more employees participated in the design and implementation of the appraisal process, the more satisfied they were.[21]

- In two studies involving university administrators and state government managers, managers who saw themselves as victims of unfair discrimination during performance appraisal tended to react favorably to a "procedurally just system." The researchers concluded: "Organizations may gain a great deal by providing vivid examples of system unfairness and its results both during training and afterward."[22]

- Although a great deal of effort has been devoted to creating more precise rating formats, formats account for very little difference (4% to 8%) in ratings.

- Performance appraisers tend to give poor performers significantly higher ratings when they have to give the appraisees face-to-face feedback as opposed to anonymous written feedback or no feedback.

- More experienced appraisers tend to render higher quality appraisals. This finding suggests that comprehensive appraiser training and practice can reduce rater errors.[23]

These research insights, along with evidence of rater bias discussed earlier, constitute a bad news–good news situation for management. The *bad* news: Performance appraisals can be contaminated by racism, sexism, personal bias, and fear of conflict. The *good* news: Managers can be sensitized to discrimination and trained to improve their performance appraisal skills. Progress can be made if managers embrace the basic elements or a good performance appraisal listed in Table B–3.

OB in Action Video Case

A Clash of Styles at Midnight Visions?

Total run time for both parts: 14 minutes, 10 seconds.

About the Manager's IIot Seat video series: To achieve a high degree of realism, McGraw-Hill/Irwin created these videos around the concept of having real-life managers deal with challenging hypothetical situations without the aid of a script. Each Manager's IIot Seat video has two parts. Both parts are followed by the guest manager's view of what went right and wrong in the "hot seat." What would *you* do in the manager's hot seat?

Characters: Guest manager Pilar Grimault's real-life job as marketing director for the Spanish Broadcasting System serves her well in her "hot seat" role as senior account manager at Midnight Visions, a New York–based advertising agency. Grimault moved into upper management two years ago after a successful stint as creative director at the company's London office. She is a strong manager who is well liked by most and feared by some. Miguel Valentino, 26, has been a rapidly rising star during his four years with the company. He was promoted to senior creative designer a year and a half ago and is perceived as creative, energetic, and sometimes arrogant. The two have had an uneven working relationship, sometimes great and other times rocky.

Situation: In Part 1, Grimault has a meeting with Valentino to review his performance on the large and important accounts he is handling. Grimault feels she needs to watch Valentino more closely because his zealous style goes over the top sometimes. For example, the Jezebel account was a creative success, but the client complained about budget overruns. Grimault wants to help Valentino mature into a more effective manager without stifling his creative energy.

Links to textual material: Chapter 5: self-concept, personality, and emotions. Chapters 8 and 9: motivation. Chapter 10: feedback and positive reinforcement. Learning Module B: performance appraisal.

For Class Discussion (following Part 1)

1. What did Grimault do right (and wrong) in this review meeting?

2. How would you rate Valentino on self-monitoring? Explain. What effect did it have on the meeting?

3. In terms of the Big Five personality dimensions, what is the potential for a personality clash between these two people?

4. Using the "Personal Values Clarification" in the Chapter 6 OB Exercise (page 193) as a guide, what appear to be the most important three or four values for Grimault and Valentino? Could value differences be a source of conflict? Explain.

5. What seems to motivate Valentino and how can Grimault motivate him?

6. What feedback, positive reinforcement, and performance appraisal tips would you offer Grimault for the Part 2 meeting?

For Class Discussion (following Part 2)

1. How would you rate Valentino's emotional maturity in the two meetings? Explain. What impact did it have on the meetings?

2. What did Grimault do right (and wrong) in the follow-up meeting?

Part Three

Group and Social Processes

Chapter Eleven

Individual and Group Decision Making

Learning Objectives

When you finish studying the material in this chapter, you should be able to:

1 Compare and contrast the rational model of decision making and Simon's normative model.

2 Discuss knowledge management and techniques used by companies to increase knowledge sharing.

3 Explain the model of decision-making styles.

4 Describe the model of escalation of commitment.

5 Summarize the pros and cons of involving groups in the decision-making process.

6 Explain how participative management affects performance.

7 Contrast brainstorming, the nominal group technique, the Delphi technique, and computer-aided decision making.

8 Describe the stages of the creative process.

9 Explain the model of organizational creativity and innovation.

BusinessWeek While Enron's culture emphasized risk-taking and entrepreneurial thinking, it also valued personal ambition over teamwork, youth over wisdom, and earnings growth at any cost. What's more, the very ideas Enron embraced were corrupted in their execution. Risk-taking without oversight resulted in failures. Youth without supervision resulted in chaos. And an almost unrelenting emphasis on earnings, without a system of checks and balances, resulted in ethical lapses that ultimately led to the company's downfall. While Enron is the extreme case, many other companies show the same symptoms.

If the challenge for executives in the 1990s was to transform corporate behemoths into nimble competitors, the challenge in coming years will be to create corporate cultures that encourage and reward integrity as much as creativity and entrepreneurship. To do that, executives need to start at the top, becoming not only exemplary managers but also the moral compass for the company. CEOs must set the tone by publicly embracing the organization's values. How? They need to be

An Enron employee wipes her eyes as she leaves the company's headquarters in Houston. Enron's culture encouraged risk-taking, entrepreneurial thinking, and valued personal ambition over teamwork, youth over wisdom, and earnings growth at any cost. Unfortunately, this strategy led to the company's demise. Enron filed for Chapter 11 protection and laid off thousands of workers.
AP/Wide World Photos

forthright in taking responsibility for shortcomings, whether an earnings shortfall, product failure, or a flawed strategy and show zero tolerance for those who fail to do the same.

The best insurance against crossing the ethical divide is a roomful of skeptics. CEOs must actively encourage dissent among senior managers by creating decision-making processes, reporting relationships, and incentives that encourage opposing viewpoints. At too many companies, the performance review system encourages a "yes-man culture" that subverts the organization's checks and balances. By advocating dissent, top executives can create a climate where wrongdoing will not go unchallenged.

None of these proposals can guarantee that another Enron, Cendant, or Sunbeam will never surface. No one can legislate or mandate ethical behavior. But leadership must create an environment where honesty and fairness is paramount. If integrity is to be the foundation for competitiveness it has to begin at the top.[1]

For Discussion
How can decision makers encourage a healthy dose of dissension when making decisions? Explain.

Decision making is one of the primary responsibilities of being a manager. The quality of a manager's decisions is important for two principal reasons. First, the quality of a manager's decisions directly affects his or her career opportunities, rewards, and job satisfaction. Second, managerial decisions contribute to the success or failure of an organization.

In Part Two, we studied individual and personal factors within organizational settings. Now, in Part Three, our attention turns to the collective or social dimensions of organizational behavior. We begin this new focus by examining individual and group decision making.

The chapter-opening vignette is a good illustration of how performance appraisals, reward systems, and organizational culture influence ethical decision making. It also highlights that decision making is a means to an end. Specifically, the vignette encourages managers to include opposing viewpoints into the decision-making process as a means to reduce unethical decisions.

Decision making
Identifying and choosing solutions that lead to a desired end result.

Decision making entails identifying and choosing alternative solutions that lead to a desired state of affairs. The process begins with a problem and ends when a solution has been chosen. To gain an understanding of how managers can make better decisions, this chapter focuses on (1) models of decision making, (2) the dynamics of decision making, (3) group decision making, and (4) creativity.

Models of Decision Making

There are two fundamental models of decision making. The first, the rational model, identifies the process that *should* be used when making decisions. As we all know, however, decision making does not always follow an orderly plan. This awareness led to the development of a normative model of decision making. The normative model outlines the process *actually* used to make decisions. Each model is based on a different set of assumptions and offers unique insight into the decision-making process. Let us begin our exploration of decision-making models by examining the most orderly or rational explanation of managerial decision making.

The Rational Model

The **rational model** proposes that managers use a rational, four-step sequence when making decisions: (1) identifying the problem, (2) generating alternative solutions, (3) selecting a solution, and (4) implementing and evaluating the solution. According to this model, managers are completely objective and possess complete information to make a decision. Despite criticism for being unrealistic, the rational model is instructive because it analytically breaks down the decision-making process and serves as a conceptual anchor for newer models.[2] Let us now consider each of these four steps.

Identifying the Problem
A **problem** exists when the actual situation and the desired situation differ. For example, a problem exists when you have to pay rent at the end of the month and don't have enough money. Your problem is not that you have to pay rent. Your problem is obtaining the needed funds. Consider the situation faced by General Motors Corporation as it attempts to slash more than $1 billion from its annual warranty repair expenses.

> GM manufactures about 25,000 cars and trucks a day, which means little glitches can rapidly become epidemics. And behind every sick car is an unhappy customer. GM handles 22.5 million warranty claims a year, ranging from minor tweaks most customers barely notice to catastrophes such as engine failure. GM has made it a top priority for the entire company, from designers to dealers to reduce warranty repairs with improved design and quality and early detection of problems. The goal is to eliminate some nine million claims and to save $1.6 billion.... Detecting problems early also is critical to avoiding costly recalls like the one of about a million trucks that GM announced last month, in which it will foot the bill to fix a switch miswired during manufacturing.[3]

General Motors' problem is the amount of warranty expenses the company is incurring: The company is spending far too much on repairing cars that are under warranty. Potential causes of the problem include poor design, defective parts, and manufacturing glitches.

How do companies like General Motors know when a problem exists or is going to occur in the near future? One expert proposed that managers use one of three methods to identify problems: historical cues, planning, and other people's perceptions:[4]

1. Using historical cues to identify problems assumes that the recent past is the best estimate of the future. Thus, managers rely on past experience to identify discrepancies (problems) from expected trends. For example, a sales manager may conclude that a problem exists because the first-quarter sales are less than they were a year ago. This method is prone to error because it is highly subjective.

2. A planning approach is more systematic and can lead to more accurate results. This method consists of using projections or scenarios to estimate what is expected to occur in the future. A time period of one or more years is generally used. The **scenario technique** is a speculative, conjectural forecast tool used to identify future states, given a certain set of environmental conditions. Once different scenarios are developed, companies devise alternative strategies to survive in the various situations. This process helps to create contingency plans far into the future. Companies such as Royal Dutch/Shell, Fleet Financial Group, IBM, and Pfizer are increasingly using the scenario technique as a planning tool.[5]

3. A final approach to identifying problems is to rely on the perceptions of others. A restaurant manager may realize that his or her restaurant provides poor service

Rational model
Logical four-step approach to decision making.

Problem
Gap between an actual and desired situation.

ʃcenario technique
ʃpeculative forecasting method.

when a large number of customers complain about how long it takes to receive food after placing an order. In other words, customers' comments signal that a problem exists. Interestingly, companies frequently compound their problems by ignoring customer complaints or feedback.

Generating Solutions   After identifying a problem, the next logical step is generating alternative solutions. For repetitive and routine decisions such as deciding when to send customers a bill, alternatives are readily available through decision rules. For example, a company might routinely bill customers three days after shipping a product. This is not the case for novel and unstructured decisions. Because there are no cut-and-dried procedures for dealing with novel problems, managers must creatively generate alternative solutions. Managers can use a number of techniques to stimulate creativity. Techniques to increase creativity are discussed later in this chapter.

Selecting a Solution   Optimally, decision makers want to choose the alternative with the greatest value. Decision theorists refer to this as maximizing the expected utility of an outcome. This is no easy task. First, assigning values to alternatives is complicated and prone to error. Not only are values subjective, but they also vary according to the preferences of the decision maker. Research demonstrates that people vary in their preferences for safety or risk when making decisions.[6] For example, a meta-analysis summarizing 150 studies revealed that males displayed more risk taking than females.[7] Further, evaluating alternatives assumes they can be judged according to some standards or criteria. This further assumes that (1) valid criteria exist, (2) each alternative can be compared against these criteria, and (3) the decision maker actually uses the criteria. As you know from making your own key life decisions, people frequently violate these assumptions. Finally, the ethics of the solution should be considered.

Implementing and Evaluating the Solution   Once a solution is chosen, it needs to be implemented. Before implementing a solution, though, managers need to do their homework. For example, three ineffective managerial tendencies have been observed frequently during the initial stages of implementation (see Table 11–1). Skillful managers try to avoid these tendencies. Table 11–1 indicates that to promote necessary understanding, acceptance, and motivation, managers should involve implementators in the choice-making step.

After the solution is implemented, the evaluation phase assesses its effectiveness. If the solution is effective, it should reduce the difference between the actual and desired states that created the problem. If the gap is not closed, the implementation was not suc-

Table 11–1   *Three Managerial Tendencies Reduce the Effectiveness of Implementation*

Managerial Tendency	Recommended Solution
The tendency not to ensure that people understand what needs to be done.	Involve the implementators in the choice-making step. When this is not possible, a strong and explicit attempt should be made to identify any misunderstanding, perhaps by having the implementor explain what he or she thinks needs to be done and why.
The tendency not to ensure the acceptance or motivation for what needs to be done.	Once again, involve the implementators in the choice-making step. Attempts should also be made to demonstrate the payoffs for effective implementation and to show how completion of various tasks will lead to successful implementation.
The tendency not to provide appropriate resources for what needs to be done.	Many implementations are less effective than they could be because adequate resources, such as time, staff, or information, were not provided. In particular, the allocations of such resources across departments and tasks are assumed to be appropriate because they were appropriate for implementing the previous plan. These assumptions should be checked.

SOURCE: Modified from G P Huber, *Managerial Decision Making* (Glenview, IL: Scott, Foresman, 1980), p. 19.

cessful, and one of the following is true: Either the problem was incorrectly identified, or the solution was inappropriate. Assuming the implementation was unsuccessful, management can return to the first step, problem identification. If the problem was correctly identified, management should consider implementing one of the previously identified, but untried, solutions. This process can continue until all feasible solutions have been tried or the problem has changed.[8]

ſummarizing the Rational Model   The rational model is based on the premise that managers optimize when they make decisions. **Optimizing** involves solving problems by producing the best possible solution and is based on the fundamental assumptions listed in Figure 11–1. Practical experience, of course, tells us the assumptions outlined in the figure are unrealistic. As noted by Herbert Simon, a decision theorist who in 1978 earned the Nobel prize for his work on decision making, "The assumptions of perfect rationality are contrary to fact. It is not a question of approximation; they do not even remotely describe the processes that human beings use for making decisions in complex situations."[9] Thus, the rational model is at best an instructional tool. Since decision makers do not follow these rational procedures, Simon proposed a normative model of decision making.

Optimizing
Choosing the best possible solution.

Simon's Normative Model

This model attempts to identify the process that managers actually use when making decisions. The process is guided by a decision maker's bounded rationality. **Bounded rationality** represents the notion that decision makers are "bounded" or restricted by a variety of constraints when making decisions. These constraints include any personal or environmental characteristics that reduce rational decision making. Examples are

Bounded rationality
Constraints that restrict rational decision making.

Figure 11–1   *Assumptions of Rational Decision Making*

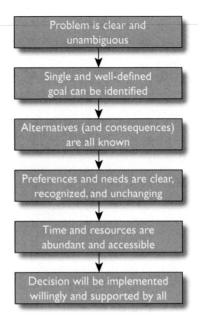

SOURCE: S W Williams, *Making Better Business Decisions* (Thousand Oaks, CA: Sage Publications, 2002), p. 15, copyright © 2002 by Sage Publications, Inc. Reprinted by permission of Sage Publications, Inc.

the limited capacity of the human mind, problem complexity and uncertainty, amount and timeliness of information at hand, criticality of the decision, and time demands.[10]

As opposed to the rational model, Simon's normative model suggests that decision making is characterized by (1) limited information processing, (2) the use of judgmental heuristics, and (3) satisficing. Each of these characteristics is now explored.

Limited Information Processing

Managers are limited by how much information they process because of bounded rationality. This results in the tendency to acquire manageable rather than optimal amounts of information. In turn, this practice makes it difficult for managers to identify all possible alternative solutions. In the long run, the constraints of bounded rationality cause decision makers to fail to evaluate all potential alternatives.

Judgmental heuristics

Rules of thumb or shortcuts that people use to reduce information-processing demands.

Judgmental Heuristics

Judgmental heuristics represent rules of thumb or shortcuts that people use to reduce information processing demands.[11] We automatically use them without conscious awareness. The use of heuristics helps decision makers to reduce the uncertainty inherent within the decision making process. Because these shortcuts represent knowledge gained from past experience, they can help decision makers evaluate current problems. But they also can lead to systematic errors that erode the quality of decisions. Consider the role of judgmental heuristics in how people invest in the stock market.

> Behaviorists say investors tend to latch on to extremes.... Down or up trends are etched in their minds as certainties, rather than mere probabilities. Take Cisco Systems, Inc. The stock zoomed for years, delivering double-digit returns. Investors got used to it, and expected history to repeat itself.... when the stock began to fall as evidence emerged

that business was shaky, many investors went into denial, refusing to let go. "Investors have extrapolated Cisco's past performance too far into the future," says Josef Lakonishok, chief investment officer of LSV Asset Management. . . .

Far too often, analysts—and investors who follow them—exhibit "anchoring" behavior. They get attached to inaccurate price targets and ignore evidence that they might be wrong.[12]

There are two common categories of heuristics that are important to consider: the availability heuristic and the representative heuristic.

The **availability heuristic** represents a decision maker's tendency to base decisions on information that is readily available in memory. Information is more accessible in memory when it involves an event that recently occurred, when it is salient (e.g., a plane crash), and when it evokes strong emotions (e.g., a high school student shooting other students). This heuristic is likely to cause people to overestimate the occurrence of unlikely events such as a plane crash or a high school shooting. This bias also is partially responsible for the recency effect discussed in Chapter 7. For example, a manager is more likely to give an employee a positive performance evaluation if the employee exhibited excellent performance over the last few months.

The **representativeness heuristic** is used when people estimate the probability of an event occurring. It reflects the tendency to assess the likelihood of an event occurring based on one's impressions about similar occurrences. A manager, for example, may hire a graduate from a particular university because the past three people hired from this university turned out to be good performers. In this case, the "school attended" criterion is used to facilitate complex information processing associated with employment interviews. Unfortunately, this shortcut can result in a biased decision. Similarly, an individual may believe that he or she can master a new software package in a short period of time because a different type of software was easy to learn. This estimate may or may not be accurate. For example, it may take the individual a much longer period of time to learn the new software because it involves learning a new programming language.

ſatisficing   People satisfice because they do not have the time, information, or ability to handle the complexity associated with following a rational process. This is not necessarily undesirable. **Satisficing** consists of choosing a solution that meets some minimum qualifications, one that is "good enough." Satisficing resolves problems by producing solutions that are satisfactory, as opposed to optimal. Finding a radio station to listen to in your car is a good example of satisficing. You cannot optimize because it is impossible to listen to all stations at the same time. You thus stop searching for a station when you find one playing a song you like or do not mind hearing.

A recent survey of 479 managers from medium and large companies underscores the existence of satisficing: 77% of the respondents indicated the number of decisions they made had increased over the last three years and 42% revealed the average amount of time to make these decisions had correspondingly decreased.[13] We can generalize from these results that managers are being asked to make more decisions in less and less time.

Dynamics of Decision Making

Decision making is part science and part art. Accordingly, this section examines three dynamics of decision making—knowledge management, decision-making styles, and the problem of escalation of commitment—that affect the "science" component. An understanding of these dynamics can help managers make better decisions.

Availability heuristic

Tendency to base decisions on information readily available in memory.

Representativeness heuristic

Tendency to assess the likelihood of an event occurring based on impressions about similar occurrences.

ſatisficing

Choosing a solution that meets a minimum standard of acceptance.

Improving Decision Making through Effective Knowledge Management

Have you ever had to make a decision without complete information? If you have, then you know the quality of a decision is only as good as the information used to make the decision. The same is true for managerial decision making. In this case, however, managers frequently need information or knowledge possessed by people working in other parts of the organization. This realization has spawned a growing interest in the concept of knowledge management. **Knowledge management** (KM) is "the development of tools, processes, systems, structures, and cultures explicitly to improve the creation, sharing, and use of knowledge critical for decision making."[14] The effective use of KM helps organizations improve the quality of their decision making and correspondingly reduce costs and increase efficiency.[15] Consider the case of British Telecommunication.

> British Telecommunication's global effort to expand product lines and services was hampered because all of its six industry sectors were acting as silos. Employees in one industry sector were not aware of the knowledge and expertise of employees in the other sectors. To overcome this lack of awareness, they introduced virtual communities of practice that were connected through the Knowledge Interchange Network (KIN). This increased awareness of experts via the distributed technology and improved cross-sector collaboration.[16]

This section explores the fundamentals of KM so that you can use them to improve your decision making.

Knowledge management

Implementing systems and practices that increase the sharing of knowledge and information throughout an organization.

Knowledge Comes in Different Forms

There are two types of knowledge that impact the quality of decisions: tacit knowledge and explicit knowledge. **Tacit knowledge** "entails information that is difficult to express, formalize, or share. It . . . is unconsciously acquired from the experiences one has while immersed in an environment."[17] Many skills, for example, such as swinging a golf club or writing a speech, are difficult to describe in words because they involve tacit knowledge. Tacit knowledge is intuitive and is acquired by having considerable experience and expertise at some task or job. Although some people joke about the role of intuition or gut feelings when making decisions, executive testimonies and research results increasingly reveal that the intuitive component of tacit knowledge is a key component of effective decision making. Consider the opinions of Ralph Larsen, former chair and CEO of Johnson & Johnson, and Richard Abdoo, chair and CEO of Wisconsin Energy Corporation, for example.

Tacit knowledge

Information gained through experience that is difficult to express and formalize.

> "Often there is absolutely no way that you could have the time to thoroughly analyze every one of the options or alternatives available to you," says Larsen. "So you have to rely on your business judgment." Richard Abdoo . . . agrees. . . . "We now have to make decisions in a timely manner. And that means that we process the best information that's available and infer from it and use our intuition to make a decision." . . . Larsen says that one thing his experience has taught him is to listen to his instincts. "Ignoring them has led to some bad decisions," he notes. Adds Abdoo, "You end up consuming more Rolaids, but you have to learn to trust your intuition. Otherwise, at the point when you've gathered enough data to be 99.99% certain that the decision you're about to make is the correct one, that decision has become obsolete."[18]

Larsen and Abdoo reinforce the importance of intuition in decision making. Don't underestimate its value.

www.ispat.com

Ispat International Promotes Knowledge Sharing

Senior executives at this London-based global steel maker have institutionalized several simple mechanisms for sharing knowledge across their far-flung units that could easily be implemented in companies from many other industries. One is Ispat's policy of cross-directorships, which requires the general manager of every operating unit to sit on the board of at least one other unit. The managing directors of Germany and Trinidad, for instance, sit on each other's boards because they both produce "long" steel products, such as rods and other structural materials. This peer oversight encourages units to adopt best practices from other units—for instance, Germany's successful downsizing initiative. Managing directors of each operating unit also join together every week for a phone meeting that lasts no longer than two hours. Managers report exceptions, non-routine activities, and things that, in company parlance, "keep them awake at night." In one recent call, the managing director in Trinidad mentioned problems he was having with a transformer that repeatedly failed. As it turned out, managers in Mexico and Canada had similar transformers and were having similar problems. The three units ended up cooperating on both troubleshooting and buying the expertise to perform repairs.

SOURCE: Reprinted by permission of Harvard Business Review. From "Introducing T-Shaped Managers: Knowledge Management's Next Generation," by M T Hansen and B von Oetinger, March 2001. Copyright © 2001 by Harvard Business School Publishing Corporation; all rights reserved.

In contrast, **explicit knowledge** can easily be put into words and explained to others. This type of knowledge is shared verbally or in written documents or numerical reports. In summary, tacit knowledge represents private information that is difficult to share, whereas explicit knowledge is external or public and is more easily communicated. Although both types of knowledge affect decision making, experts suggest competitive advantages are created when tacit knowledge is shared among employees.[19] Let us now examine how companies foster this type of information sharing.

Knowledge Sharing Organizations increasingly rely on sophisticated KM software to share explicit knowledge. This software allows companies to amass large amounts of information that can be accessed quickly from around the world. In contrast, tacit knowledge is shared most directly by observing, participating, or working with experts or coaches. Mentoring, which was discussed in Chapter 3, is another method for spreading tacit knowledge. Finally, informal networking, periodic meetings (see the International OB above), and the design of office space can be used to facilitate KM. Alcoa, for example, designed its headquarters with the aim of increasing information sharing among its executives.

> Alcoa, the world's leading producer of aluminum, wanted to improve access between its senior executives. When designing their new headquarters they focused on open offices, family-style kitchens in the center of each floor, and plenty of open spaces. Previously, top executives would only interact with a couple of people in the elevator and those they had scheduled meetings with. Now, executives bump into each other more often and are more accessible for serendipitous conversations. This change in space has increased general accessibility as well as narrowed the gap between top executives and employees.[20]

It is important to remember that the best-laid plans for increasing KM are unlikely to succeed without the proper organizational culture. Effective KM requires a knowledge-sharing culture that both encourages and reinforces the spread of tacit knowledge. IBM Global Services has taken this recommendation to heart.

> IBM Global Services has incorporated knowledge creation, sharing, and reuse measurements into performance metrics. Performance metrics and incentives, particularly at the

Explicit knowledge
Information that can be easily put into words and shared with others.

executive rank, have driven collaborative behavior into the day-to-day work practices of executive networks. Further, knowledge sharing has been incorporated into personal business commitments, which are required for certification and affect promotion decisions. This encourages employees at all levels to be collaborative with and accessible to each other.[21]

General Decision-Making Styles

It should come as no surprise to learn that personal characteristics influence the manner in which we make decisions. For example, a recent meta-analysis involving 14 studies and 3,338 individuals revealed that entrepreneurs had higher risk-taking propensities when making decisions than did managers.[22] This finding underscores the value of investigating the relationship between individual differences and decision making. This section therefore focuses on how an individual's decision-making style affects his or her approach to decision making. We believe this awareness can help you make better decisions.

Decision-making style

A combination of how individuals perceive and respond to information.

A **decision-making style** reflects the combination of how an individual perceives and comprehends stimuli and the general manner in which he or she chooses to respond to such information.[23] A team of researchers developed a model of decision-making styles that is based on the idea that styles vary along two different dimensions: value orientation and tolerance for ambiguity.[24] *Value orientation* reflects the extent to which an individual focuses on either task and technical concerns or people and social concerns when making decisions. Some people, for instance, are very task focused at work and do not pay much attention to people issues, whereas others are just the opposite. The second dimension pertains to a person's *tolerance for ambiguity*. This individual difference indicates the extent to which a person has a high need for structure or control in his or her life. Some people desire a lot of structure in their lives (a low tolerance for ambiguity) and find ambiguous situations stressful and psychologically uncomfortable. In contrast, others do not have a high need for structure and can thrive in uncertain situations (a high tolerance for ambiguity). Ambiguous situations can energize people with a high tolerance for ambiguity. When the dimensions of value orientation and tolerance for ambiguity are combined, they form four styles of decision making (see Figure 11–2): directive, analytical, conceptual, and behavioral.

Directive   People with a *directive* style have a low tolerance for ambiguity and are oriented toward task and technical concerns when making decisions. They are efficient, logical, practical, and systematic in their approach to solving problems. People with this style are action oriented and decisive and like to focus on facts. In their pursuit of speed and results, however, these individuals tend to be autocratic, exercise power and control, and focus on the short run. Consider how Mario Monti's directive style influences his behavior and the administrative practices he recommends as the head of the European Union's antitrust department.

> EU antitrust agents can walk without warning into any company doing business in the 15-nation union to look for whatever they think might be proof of illegal activity. Then they can use the evidence to levy fines as steep as 10% of a company's worldwide revenue.... Now Mr Monti is taking big steps to expand this controversial practice [dawn raids in which investigators show up unannounced]. Currently, his investigators are limited to searching corporate offices for evidence of price fixing and abuse of market power, but he is pushing to extend raids to executive's homes. He is also seeking the power to interrogate employees about antitrust violations without guaranteeing they would be entitled to

Figure 11–2   *Decision-Making Styles*

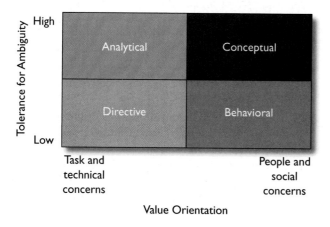

SOURCE: Based on discussion contained in A J Rowe and R O Mason, *Managing with Style: A Guide to Understanding, Assessing, and Improving Decision Making* (San Francisco: Jossey-Bass, 1987), pp. 1–17.

consult a lawyer. "We must make the commission's inspection powers more biting," the 58-year-old former economics professor said in a speech in Stockholm.[25]

Right or wrong, Monti clearly leans toward an autocratic approach that uses his powers to the fullest.

Analytical   This style has a much higher tolerance for ambiguity and is characterized by the tendency to overanalyze a situation. People with this style like to consider more information and alternatives than do directives. Analytic individuals are careful decision makers who take longer to make decisions but who also respond well to new or uncertain situations. They can often be autocratic.

European Union Commissioner for Competition, Mario Monti, is taking big steps to expand the powers of EU antitrust. Monti's aggressive approach is characteristic of a directive decision making style. What ethical concerns might be associated with Monti's directive decision making style?

AP/Wide World Photos

Conceptual

Conceptual   People with a conceptual style have a high tolerance for ambiguity and tend to focus on the people or social aspects of a work situation. They take a broad perspective to problem solving and like to consider many options and future possibilities. Conceptual types adopt a long-term perspective and rely on intuition and discussions with others to acquire information. They also are willing to take risks and are good at finding creative solutions to problems. On the downside, however, a conceptual style can foster an idealistic and indecisive approach to decision making.

Behavioral   This style is the most people oriented of the four styles. People with this style work well with others and enjoy social interactions in which opinions are openly exchanged. Behavioral types are supportive, receptive to suggestions, show warmth, and prefer verbal to written information. Although they like to hold meetings, people with this style have a tendency to avoid conflict and to be too concerned about others. This can lead behavioral types to adopt a wishy-washy approach to decision making and to have a hard time saying no to others and to have difficulty making difficult decisions.

Research and Practical Implications   Research shows that very few people have only one dominant decision-making style. Rather, most managers have characteristics that fall into two or three styles. Studies also show that decision-making styles vary across occupations, job level, and countries.[26] You can use knowledge of decision-making styles in three ways. First, knowledge of styles helps you to understand yourself. Awareness of your style assists you in identifying your strengths and weaknesses as a decision maker and facilitates the potential for self-improvement. (You can assess your decision-making style by completing the Personal Awareness and Growth Exercise located at the end of this chapter.) Second, you can increase your ability to influence others by being aware of styles. For example, if you are dealing with an analytical person, you should provide as much information as possible to support your ideas. This same approach is more likely to frustrate a directive type. Finally, knowledge of styles gives you an awareness of how people can take the same information and yet arrive at different decisions by using a variety of decision-making strategies. Different decision-making styles represent one likely source of interpersonal conflict at work (conflict is thoroughly discussed in Chapter 14). It is important to conclude with the caveat that there is not a best decision-making style that applies in all situations.

Escalation of Commitment

Escalation of commitment

Sticking to an ineffective course of action too long.

Escalation situations involve circumstances in which things have gone wrong but where the situation can possibly be turned around by investing additional time, money, or effort. **Escalation of commitment** refers to the tendency to stick to an ineffective course of action when it is unlikely that the bad situation can be reversed. Personal examples include investing more money into an old or broken car, waiting an extremely long time for a bus to take you somewhere when you could have walked just as easily, or trying to save a disruptive interpersonal relationship that has lasted 10 years. Case studies also indicate that escalation of commitment is partially responsible for some of the worst financial losses experienced by organizations. For example, from 1966 to 1989 the Long Island Lighting Company's investment in the Shoreham nuclear power plant escalated from $65 million to $5 billion, despite a steady flow of negative feedback. The plant was never opened.[27]

Figure 11–3   *A Model of Escalation of Commitment*

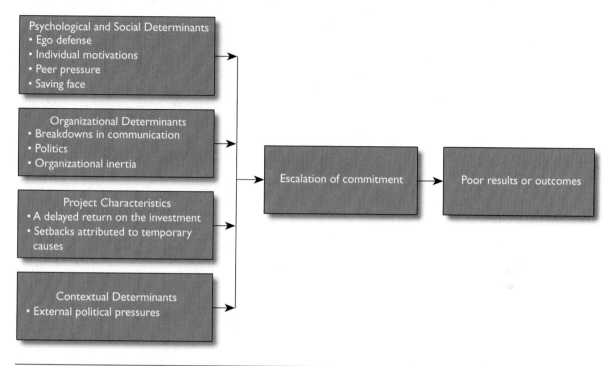

SOURCE: Based on discussion in J Ross and B M Staw, "Organizational Escalation and Exit: Lessons from the Shoreham Nuclear Power Plant," *Academy of Management Journal,* August 1993, pp. 701–32.

OB researchers Jerry Ross and Barry Staw identified four reasons for escalation of commitment (see Figure 11–3). They involve psychological and social determinants, organizational determinants, project characteristics, and contextual determinants.[28]

Psychological and Social Determinants

Ego defense and individual motivations are the key psychological contributors to escalation of commitment. Individuals "throw good money after bad" because they tend to (1) bias facts so that they support previous decisions, (2) take more risks when a decision is stated in negative terms (to recover losses) rather than positive ones (to achieve gains), and (3) get too ego-involved with the project. Because failure threatens an individual's self-esteem or ego, people tend to ignore negative signs and push forward.[29]

Social pressures can make it difficult for a manager to reverse a course of action. For instance, peer pressure makes it difficult for an individual to drop a course of action when he or she publicly supported it in the past. Further, managers may continue to support bad decisions because they don't want their mistakes exposed to others. For example, a study involving 102 students working on a computer-simulated competition revealed that they engaged in less escalation of commitment when their performance was being monitored.[30]

Organizational Determinants

Breakdowns in communication, workplace politics, and organizational inertia cause organizations to maintain bad courses of action.

Project Characteristics
Project characteristics involve the objective features of a project. They have the greatest impact on escalation decisions. For example, because most projects do not reap benefits until some delayed time period, decision makers are motivated to stay with the project until the end.[31] Thus, there is a tendency to attribute setbacks to temporary causes that are correctable with additional expenditures. Moreover, escalation is related to whether the project has clearly defined goals and whether people receive clear feedback about performance. One study, for instance, revealed that escalation was fueled by ambiguous performance feedback and the lack of performance standards.[32]

Contextual Determinants
These causes of escalation are due to forces outside an organization's control. For instance, a recent study showed that a manager's national culture influenced the amount of escalation in decision making. Samples of decision makers in Mexico and the United States revealed that Mexican managers exhibited more escalation than US managers.[33]

External political forces also represent a contextual determinant. The continuance of the previously discussed Shoreham nuclear power plant, for example, was partially influenced by pressures from other public utilities interested in nuclear power, representatives of the nuclear power industry, and people in the federal government pushing for the development of nuclear power.[34]

Reducing Escalation of Commitment
It is important to reduce escalation of commitment because it leads to poor decision making for both individuals and groups.[35] Barry Staw and Jerry Ross, the researchers who originally identified the phenomenon of escalation, recommended several ways to reduce it:

- Set minimum targets for performance, and have decision makers compare their performance with these targets.
- Have different individuals make the initial and subsequent decisions about a project.
- Encourage decision makers to become less ego-involved with a project.
- Provide more frequent feedback about project completion and costs.
- Reduce the risk or penalties of failure.
- Make decision makers aware of the costs of persistence.[36]

Group Decision Making

Groups such as committees, task forces, project teams, or review panels often play a key role in the decision-making process. Are two or more heads always better than one? Do all employees desire to have a say in the decision-making process? To what extent are managers involving employees in the decision-making process? What techniques do groups use to improve their decision making? Are face-to-face meetings more effective than computer-aided decision making? This section provides the background for answering these questions. We discuss (1) group involvement in decision making, (2) advantages and disadvantages of group-aided decision making, (3) participative management, and (4) group problem-solving techniques. A broader examination of group dynamics and the problems associated with group decision making is discussed in Chapter 12.

Group Involvement in Decision Making

Whether groups assemble in face-to-face meetings or rely on other technologically based methods to communicate, they can contribute to each stage of the decision-making process. In order to maximize the value of group-aided decision making, however, it is important to create an environment in which group members feel free to participate and express their opinions. A recent study sheds light on how managers can create such an environment.

A team of researchers conducted two studies to determine whether a group's innovativeness was related to *minority dissent,* defined as the extent to which group members feel comfortable disagreeing with other group members, and a group's level of participation in decision making. Results showed that the most innovative groups possessed high levels of both minority dissent and participation in decision making.[37] These findings encourage managers to seek divergent views from group members during decision making. They also support the practice of not seeking compliance from group members or punishing group members who disagree with majority opinion. Take a moment now to complete the OB Exercise on page 386. It assesses the amount of minority dissent and participation in group decision making for a group project you have completed or are currently working on in school or on the job. Is your satisfaction with the group related to minority dissent and participation in decision making? If not, what might explain this surprising result?

The above study reinforces the notion that the quality of group decision making varies across groups. This in turn raises the issue of how to best assess a group's decision-making effectiveness. Although experts do not agree on the one "best" criterion, there is agreement that groups need to work through various aspects of decision making in order to be effective. One expert proposed that decision-making effectiveness in a group is dependent on successfully accomplishing the following:[38]

1. Developing a clear understanding of the decision situation.
2. Developing a clear understanding of the requirements for an effective choice.
3. Thoroughly and accurately assessing the positive qualities of alternative solutions.
4. Thoroughly and accurately assessing the negative qualities of alternative solutions.

To increase the probability of groups making high-quality decisions, managers, team leaders, and individual group members are encouraged to focus on satisfying these four requirements.[39]

Advantages and Disadvantages of Group-Aided Decision Making

Including groups in the decision-making process has both pros and cons (see Table 11–2). On the positive side, groups contain a greater pool of knowledge, provide more varied perspectives, create more comprehension of decisions, increase decision acceptance, and create a training ground for inexperienced employees. These advantages must be balanced, however, with the disadvantages listed in Table 11–2. In doing so, managers need to determine the extent to which the advantages and disadvantages apply to the decision situation. The following three guidelines may then be applied to help decide whether groups should be included in the decision-making process.

OB Exercise Assessing Participation in Group Decision Making

Instructions

The following survey measures minority dissent, participation in group decision making, and satisfaction with a group. For each of the items, use the rating scale shown below to circle the answer that best represents your feelings based on a group project you were or currently are involved in. Next, use the scoring key to compute scores for the levels of minority dissent, participation in decision making, and satisfaction with the group.

1 = Strongly disagree
2 = Disagree
3 = Neither agree nor disagree
4 = Agree
5 = Strongly agree

1. Within my team, individuals disagree with one another.	1	2	3	4	5
2. Within my team, individuals do not go along with majority opinion.	1	2	3	4	5
3. Within my team, individuals voice their disagreement of majority opinion.	1	2	3	4	5
4. Within my team, I am comfortable voicing my disagreement of the majority opinion	1	2	3	4	5
5. Within my team, individuals do not immediately agree with one another.	1	2	3	4	5
6. As a team member, I have a real say in how work is carried out.	1	2	3	4	5
7. Within my team, most members have a chance to participate in decisions.	1	2	3	4	5
8. My team is designed so that everyone has the opportunity to participate in decisions.	1	2	3	4	5
9. I am satisfied with my group.	1	2	3	4	5
10. I would like to work with this group on another project.	1	2	3	4	5

Scoring Key

Minority dissent (add scores for items 1, 2, 3, 4, 5): _____

Participation in decision making (add scores for items 6, 7, 8): _____

Satisfaction (add scores for items 9, 10): _____

Arbitrary Norms

Low minority dissent = 5–15

High minority dissent = 16–25

Low participation in decision making = 3–8

High participation in decision making = 9–15

Low satisfaction = 2–5

High satisfaction = 6–10

SOURCE: The items in the survey were developed from C K W De Dreu and M A West "Minority Dissent and Team Innovation: The Importance of Participation in Decision Making," *Journal of Applied Psychology*, December 2001, pp. 1191–201.

Table 11–2   *Advantages and Disadvantages of Group-Aided Decision Making*

Advantages	Disadvantages
1. **Greater pool of knowledge.** A group can bring much more information and experience to bear on a decision or problem than can an individual acting alone.	1. **Social pressure.** Unwillingness to "rock the boat" and pressure to conform may combine to stifle the creativity of individual contributors.
2. **Different perspectives.** Individuals with varied experience and interests help the group see decision situations and problems from different angles.	2. **Domination by a vocal few.** Sometimes the quality of group action is reduced when the group gives in to those who talk the loudest and longest.
3. **Greater comprehension.** Those who personally experience the give-and-take of group discussion about alternative courses of action tend to understand the rationale behind the final decision.	3. **Logrolling.** Political wheeling and dealing can displace sound thinking when an individual's pet project or vested interest is at stake.
4. **Increased acceptance.** Those who play an active role in group decision making and problem solving tend to view the outcome as "ours" rather than "theirs."	4. **Goal displacement.** Sometimes secondary considerations such as winning an argument, making a point, or getting back at a rival displace the primary task of making a sound decision or solving a problem.
5. **Training ground.** Less experienced participants in group action learn how to cope with group dynamics by actually being involved.	5. **Groupthink.** Sometimes cohesive in-groups let the desire for unanimity override sound judgment when generating and evaluating alternative courses of action. (Groupthink is discussed in Chapter 12.)

SOURCE: R Kreitner, *Management*, 8th ed (Boston: Houghton Mifflin, 2001), p. 243.

1. If additional information would increase the quality of the decision, managers should involve those people who can provide the needed information.

2. If acceptance is important, managers need to involve those individuals whose acceptance and commitment are important.

3. If people can be developed through their participation, managers may want to involve those whose development is most important.[40]

Group versus Individual Performance

Before recommending that managers involve groups in decision making, it is important to examine whether groups perform better or worse than individuals. After reviewing 61 years of relevant research, a decision-making expert concluded that "Group performance was generally qualitatively and quantitatively superior to the performance of the average individual."[41] Although subsequent research of small-group decision making generally supported this conclusion, there are five important issues to consider when using groups to make decisions:

1. Groups were less efficient than individuals. Consider how long it took a team of Nokia executives to decide whether or not to license its software to other phone

makers. "Nokia executives, who prize consensus, debated the issue for nine months from mid-2000 to early 2001. At eight successive monthly meetings of the company's nine-person executive board, members raised questions and stalled the project."[42] This example highlights that time constraints are an important consideration when determining whether to involve groups in decision making.

2. Groups were more confident about their judgments and choices than individuals. Because group confidence is not a surrogate for group decision quality, this overconfidence can fuel groupthink—groupthink is discussed in Chapter 12—and a resistance to consider alternative solutions proposed by individuals outside the group.

3. Group size affected decision outcomes. Decision quality was negatively related to group size.[43]

4. Decision-making accuracy was higher when (*a*) groups knew a great deal about the issues at hand and (*b*) group leaders possessed the ability to effectively evaluate the group members' opinions and judgments. Groups need to give more weight to relevant and accurate judgments while downplaying irrelevant or inaccurate judgments made by its members.[44]

5. The composition of a group affects its decision-making processes and ultimately performance. For example, groups of familiar people are more likely to make better decisions when members share a lot of unique information. In contrast, unacquainted group members should outperform groups of friends when most group members possess common knowledge.[45]

Additional research suggests that managers should use a contingency approach when determining whether to include others in the decision-making process. Let us now consider these contingency recommendations.

Practical Contingency Recommendations   If the decision occurs frequently, such as deciding on promotions or who qualifies for a loan, use groups because they tend to produce more consistent decisions than do individuals. Given time constraints, let the most competent individual, rather than a group, make the decision. In the face of environmental threats such as time pressure and potential serious effects of a decision, groups use less information and fewer communication channels. This increases the probability of a bad decision. This conclusion underscores a general recommendation that managers should keep in mind: Because the quality of communication strongly affects a group's productivity, on complex tasks it is essential to devise mechanisms to enhance communication effectiveness.

Participative Management

An organization needs to maximize its workers' potential if it wants to successfully compete in today's global economy. Participative management and employee empowerment, which is discussed in Chapter 16, are highly touted methods for meeting this productivity challenge. Interestingly, employees also seem to desire or recognize the need for participative management. A nationwide survey of 2,408 employees, for example, revealed that almost 66% desired more influence or decision-making power in their jobs.[46]

Confusion exists about the exact meaning of participative management (PM). One management expert clarified this situation by defining **participative management** as

Participative management

Involving employees in various aspects of decision making.

the process whereby employees play a direct role in (1) setting goals, (2) making decisions, (3) solving problems, and (4) making changes in the organization. Without question, participative management entails much more than simply asking employees for their ideas or opinions.

Advocates of PM claim employee participation increases employee satisfaction, commitment, and performance. To get a fuller understanding of how and when participative management works, we begin by discussing a model of participative management.

A Model of Participative Management

Consistent with our discussion of Maslow's need theory and intrinsic motivation (see Chapter 8), participative management is predicted to increase motivation because it helps employees fulfill three basic needs: (1) autonomy, (2) meaningfulness of work, and (3) interpersonal contact. Satisfaction of these needs enhances feelings of acceptance and commitment, security, challenge, and satisfaction. In turn, these positive feelings supposedly lead to increased innovation and performance.[47]

Participative management does not work in all situations. The design of work, the level of trust between management and employees, and the employees' competence and readiness to participate represent three factors that influence the effectiveness of PM. With respect to the design of work, individual participation is counterproductive when employees are highly interdependent on each other, as on an assembly line. The problem with individual participation in this case is that interdependent employees generally do not have a broad understanding of the entire production process. Participative management also is less likely to succeed when employees do not trust management. Finally, PM is more effective when employees are competent, prepared, and interested in participating.[48]

Research and Practical Suggestions for Managers

Participative management can significantly increase employee job involvement, organizational commitment, creativity, and perceptions of procedural justice and personal control.[49] Two meta-analyses provided additional support for the value of participative management. Results from a meta-analysis involving 27 studies and 6,732 individuals revealed that employee participation in the performance appraisal process was positively related to an employee's satisfaction with his or her performance review, perceived value of the appraisal, motivation to improve performance following a performance review, and perceived fairness of the appraisal process.[50] A second meta-analysis of 86 studies involving 18,872 people further demonstrated that participation had a small but significant effect on job performance and a moderate relationship with job satisfaction.[51] This later finding questions the widespread conclusion that participative management should be used to increase employee performance.

So what is a manager to do? We believe that PM is not a quick-fix solution for low productivity and motivation, as some enthusiastic supporters claim. Nonetheless, because participative management is effective in certain situations, managers can increase their chances of obtaining positive results by using once again a contingency-approach.[52] For example, the effectiveness of participation depends on the type of interactions between managers and employees as they jointly solve problems. Effective participation requires a constructive interaction that fosters cooperation and respect, as opposed to competition and defensiveness.[53] Managers are advised not to use participative programs when they have destructive interpersonal interactions with their employees.

Experiences of companies implementing participative management programs suggest three additional practical recommendations. First, supervisors and middle managers tend to resist participative management because it reduces their power and authority. It thus is important to gain the support and commitment from employees who have managerial responsibility. This conclusion was supported by results from a 15-year study of 41,000 middle and upper-level managers: 35% of the managers surveyed between 1985 and 1987 preferred to make decisions autocratically versus 31% between 1997 and 1999.[54] Second, a longitudinal study of *Fortune* 1000 firms in 1987, 1990, and 1993 indicated that employee involvement was more effective when it was implemented as part of a broader total quality management program.[55] This study suggests that organizations should use participative management and employee involvement as vehicles to help them meet their strategic and operational goals as opposed to using these techniques as ends in and of themselves. Third, the process of implementing participative management must be firmly supported and monitored by top management.[56]

Group Problem-Solving Techniques

Consensus

Presenting opinions and gaining agreement to support a decision.

Using groups to make decisions generally requires that they reach a consensus. According to a decision-making expert, a **consensus** "is reached when all members can say they either agree with the decision or have had their 'day in court' and were unable to convince the others of their viewpoint. In the final analysis, everyone agrees to support the outcome."[57] This definition indicates that consensus does not require unanimous agreement because group members may still disagree with the final decision but are willing to work toward its success.

Groups can experience roadblocks when trying to arrive at a consensus decision. For one, groups may not generate all relevant alternatives to a problem because an individual dominates or intimidates other group members. This can be overt or subtle. For instance, group members who possess power and authority, such as a CEO, can be intimidating, regardless of interpersonal style, simply by being present in the room. Moreover, shyness inhibits the generation of alternatives. Shy or socially anxious individuals may withhold their input for fear of embarrassment or lack of confidence. Satisficing is another hurdle to effective group decision making. As previously noted, groups satisfice due to limited time, information, or ability to handle large amounts of information. A management expert offered the following dos and don'ts for successfully achieving consensus: Groups should use active listening skills, involve as many members as possible, seek out the reasons behind arguments, and dig for the facts. At the same time, groups should not horse trade (I'll support you on this decision because you supported me on the last one), vote, or agree just to avoid "rocking the boat."[58] Voting is not encouraged because it can split the group into winners and losers.[59]

Decision-making experts have developed three group problem-solving techniques—brainstorming, the nominal group technique, and the Delphi technique—to reduce the above roadblocks. Knowledge of these techniques can help current and future managers to more effectively use group-aided decision making. Further, the advent of computer aided decision making enables managers to use these techniques to solve complex problems with large groups of people.

Brainstorming

Process to generate a quantity of ideas.

Brainstorming   Brainstorming was developed by A F Osborn, an advertising executive, to increase creativity.[60] **Brainstorming** is used to help groups generate multiple ideas and alternatives for solving problems. This technique is effective because it helps reduce interference caused by critical and judgmental reactions to one's ideas from other group members.

When brainstorming, a group is convened, and the problem at hand is reviewed. Individual members then are asked to silently generate ideas/alternatives for solving the problem. Silent idea generation is recommended over the practice of having group members randomly shout out their ideas because it leads to a greater number of unique ideas. Next, these ideas/alternatives are solicited and written on a board or flip chart. A recent study suggests that managers or team leaders may want to collect the brainstormed ideas anonymously. Results demonstrated that more controversial ideas and more nonredundant ideas were generated by anonymous than nonanonymous brainstorming groups.[61] Finally, a second session is used to critique and evaluate the alternatives. Managers are advised to follow four rules for brainstorming:[62]

1. *Stress quantity over quality.* Managers should try to generate and write down as many ideas as possible. Encouraging quantity encourages people to think beyond their pet ideas.

2. *Freewheeling should be encouraged; do not set limits.* Group members are advised to offer any and all ideas they have. The wilder and more outrageous, the better.

3. *Suspend judgment.* Don't criticize during the initial stage of idea generation. Phrases such as "we've never done it that way," "it won't work," "it's too expensive," and "the boss will never agree" should not be used.

4. *Ignore seniority.* People are reluctant to freewheel when they are trying to impress the boss or when their ideas are politically motivated. The facilitator of a brainstorming session should emphasize that everyone has the same rank. No one is given veto power when brainstorming.

Brainstorming is an effective technique for generating new ideas/alternatives. It is not appropriate for evaluating alternatives or selecting solutions.

The Nominal Group Technique
The **nominal group technique** (NGT) helps groups generate ideas and evaluate and select solutions. NGT is a structured group meeting that follows this format:[63]

A group is convened to discuss a particular problem or issue. After the problem is understood, individuals silently generate ideas in writing. Each individual, in roundrobin fashion, then offers one idea from his or her list. Ideas are recorded on a blackboard or flip chart; they are not discussed at this stage of the process. Once all ideas are elicited, the group discusses them. Anyone may criticize or defend any item. During this step, clarification is provided as well as general agreement or disagreement with the idea. The "30-second soap box" technique, which entails giving each participant a maximum of 30 seconds to argue for or against any of the ideas under consideration, can be used to facilitate this discussion. Finally, group members anonymously vote for their top choices with a weighted voting procedure (e.g., 1st choice = 3 points; 2nd choice = 2 points; 3rd choice = 1 point). The group leader then adds the votes to determine the group's choice. Prior to making a final decision, the group may decide to discuss the top ranked items and conduct a second round of voting.

The nominal group technique reduces the roadblocks to group decision making by (1) separating brainstorming from evaluation, (2) promoting balanced participation among group members, and (3) incorporating mathematical voting techniques in order to reach consensus. NGT has been successfully used in many different decision-making situations.

The Delphi Technique
This problem-solving method was originally developed by the Rand Corporation for technological forecasting.[64] It now is used as a

Nominal group technique
Process to generate ideas and evaluate solutions.

Delphi technique

Process to generate ideas from physically dispersed experts.

multipurpose planning tool. The **Delphi technique** is a group process that anonymously generates ideas or judgments from physically dispersed experts. Unlike the NGT, experts' ideas are obtained from questionnaires or via the Internet as opposed to face-to-face group discussions.

A manager begins the Delphi process by identifying the issue(s) he or she wants to investigate. For example, a manager might want to inquire about customer demand, customers' future preferences, or the effect of locating a plant in a certain region of the country. Next, participants are identified and a questionnaire is developed. The questionnaire is sent to participants and returned to the manager. In today's computer-networked environments, this often means that the questionnaires are E-mailed to participants. The manager then summarizes the responses and sends feedback to the participants. At this stage, participants are asked to (1) review the feedback, (2) prioritize the issues being considered, and (3) return the survey within a specified time period. This cycle repeats until the manager obtains the necessary information.

The Delphi technique is useful when face-to-face discussions are impractical, when disagreements and conflict are likely to impair communication, when certain individuals might severely dominate group discussion, and when groupthink is a probable outcome of the group process.[65]

Computer-Aided Decision Making

The purpose of computer-aided decision making is to reduce consensus roadblocks while collecting more information in a shorter period of time. There are two types of computer-aided decision making systems: chauffeur driven and group driven.[66] Chauffeur-driven systems ask participants to answer predetermined questions on electronic keypads or dials. Live television audiences on shows such as "Who Wants to Be a Millionaire" and "Whose Line Is It Anyway?" are frequently polled with this system. The computer system tabulates participants' responses in a matter of seconds.

Group-driven electronic meetings are conducted in one of two major ways. First, managers can use E-mail systems, which are discussed in Chapter 15, or the Internet to collect information or brainstorm about a decision that must be made. For example, MedPanel, a Cambridge, MASS., medical consulting company, uses E-mail to obtain information and feedback from medical doctors around the country about new and existing drugs. Consider how MedPanel's system works:

> A client contracts with MedPanel for a research project—looking for, perhaps, advice on how to structure clinical trials for a cancer drug. MedPanel consults its database of participating physicians and E-mails invitations to the most appropriate doctors. The doctors who sign up (earning a fee for their time) log onto **www.medpanel.com,** type in a password, and call up a screen that looks a lot like a bulletin-board-style discussion group. Individual messages are listed in chronological order. A moderator poses questions and helps guide the discussion. Doctors drop in whenever they can, catch up on recent postings, and type their own messages. It's simple technology, but the results can be powerful.[67]

MedPanel has found that it can collect information faster and cheaper using its electronic system of data collection.

The second method of computer-aided, group-driven meetings is conducted in special facilities equipped with individual workstations that are networked to each other. Instead of talking, participants type their input, ideas, comments, reactions, or evaluations on their keyboards. The input simultaneously appears on a large projector screen at the front of the room, thereby enabling all participants to see all input. This computer-driven process reduces consensus roadblocks because input is anonymous, everyone gets a chance to contribute, and no one can dominate the process. Research demonstrated that computer-aided decision making produced greater quality and quantity of ideas than either traditional brainstorming or the nominal group technique for both small and large groups of people.[68]

Interestingly, however, another recent study suggests caution when determining what forms of computer-aided decision making to use. This meta-analysis of 52 studies compared the effectiveness of face-to-face decision-making groups with "chat" groups. Results revealed that the use of chat groups led to decreased group effectiveness and member satisfaction and increased time to complete tasks compared to face-to-face groups.[69] These findings underscore the need to use a contingency approach for selecting the best method of computer-aided decision making in a given situation. Our discussion of a contingency model for selecting communication media in Chapter 15 can help in this process.

Creativity

In light of today's need for fast-paced decisions, an organization's ability to stimulate the creativity and innovation of its employees is becoming increasingly important. Some organizations believe that creativity and innovation are the seeds of success. Consider 3M, for example.

> Throughout its 100-year history, 3M has had a surefire formula for growth: hire top-notch scientists in every field, give each an ample endowment, then stand back and let them do their thing. That anything-goes approach has yielded thousands of new products over the decades, from sandpaper and magnetic audio tape to Post-it Notes and Thinsulate insulation. Indeed, 3M generated $5.6 billion in sales in 2000—fully one-third of its revenues—from goods that didn't exist just four years earlier.[70]

To gain further insight into managing the creative process, we begin by defining creativity and highlighting the stages underlying individual creativity. This section then presents a model of organizational creativity and innovation.

Definition and Stages

Although many definitions have been proposed, **creativity** is defined here as the process of using imagination and skill to develop a new or unique product, object, process, or thought.[71] It can be as simple as locating a new place to hang your car keys or as complex as developing a pocket-size microcomputer. This definition highlights three broad types of creativity. One can create something new (creation), one can combine or synthesize things (synthesis), or one can improve or change things (modification).

Early approaches to explaining creativity were based on differences between the left and right hemispheres of the brain. Researchers thought the right side of the brain was responsible for creativity. More recently, however, researchers have questioned this explanation:

> "The left brain/right brain dichotomy is simplified and misleading," says Dr John C Mazziotta, a researcher at the University of California at Los Angeles School of Medicine.
>
> What scientists have found instead is that creativity is a feat of mental gymnastics engaging the conscious and subconscious parts of the brain. It draws on everything from knowledge, logic, imagination, and intuition to the ability to see connections and distinctions between ideas and things.[72]

Creativity
Process of developing something new or unique.

Let us now examine the stages underlying the creativity process.

Researchers are not absolutely certain how creativity takes place. Nonetheless, we do know that creativity involves "making remote associations" between unconnected events, ideas, information stored in memory (recall our discussion in Chapter 7), or physical objects. Consider how remote associations led to a creative idea that ultimately increased revenue for Japan Railways (JR) East, the largest rail carrier in the world:

> While JR East was building a new bullet-train line, water began to cause problems in the tunnel being dug through Mount Tanigawa. As engineers drew up plans to drain it away, some of the workers had found a use for the water—they were drinking it. A maintenance worker, whose job was to check the safety of the tunneling equipment, thought it tasted so good that he proposed that JR East should bottle and market it as premium mineral water. This past year, "Oshimizu" water generated some $60 million of sales for JR East.[73]

The maintenance worker obviously associated the tunnel water with bottled water, and this led to the idea of marketing the water as a commercial product. Figure 11–4 depicts five stages underlying the creative process.[74]

The *preparation* stage reflects the notion that creativity starts from a base of knowledge. Experts suggest that creativity involves a convergence between tacit and explicit knowledge. During the *concentration* stage, an individual focuses on the problem at hand. Interestingly, Japanese companies are noted for encouraging this stage as part of a quality improvement process more so than American companies. For example, the average number of suggestions per employee for improving quality and productivity is significantly lower in the typical US company than in comparable Japanese firms.[75]

Incubation is done unconsciously. During this stage, people engage in daily activities while their minds simultaneously mull over information and make remote associations. These associations ultimately are generated in the *illumination* stage. Finally, *verification* entails going through the entire process to verify, modify, or try out the new idea.

Let us examine the stages of creativity to determine why Japanese organizations propose and implement more ideas than do American companies. To address this issue, a creativity expert visited and extensively interviewed employees from five major Japanese companies. He observed that Japanese firms have created a management infrastructure that encourages and reinforces creativity. People were taught to identify problems (discontents) on their first day of employment. In turn, discontents were referred to as "golden eggs" to reinforce the notion that it is good to identify problems.

These organizations also promoted the stages of incubation, illumination, and verification through teamwork and incentives. For example, some companies posted the golden eggs on large wall posters in the work area; employees were then encouraged to interact with each other to execute the final three stages of the creative process. Employees eventually received monetary awards for any suggestions that passed all

Figure 11–4   *Stages of the Creative Process*

five phases of this process.[76] This research underscores the conclusion that creativity can be enhanced by effectively managing the creativity process. Hallmark cards does a good job of managing the creativity process:

> It takes 740 creative people to produce 18,000 new Hallmark greeting cards each year. To manage that creative energy, CEO Irv Hockaday says, "We have the largest creative staff in the world. If you mismanage, it's like a sack full of cats. You have to strike a balance between defining for them generally what you want and then giving them a lot of running room to try ways to respond to it. You don't overmanage, but you anchor them in well-articulated consumer needs. Then allow them exposure to all kinds of trends going on. We encourage them to travel and we support their traveling. They follow fashion trends, go to museums, look at what the automative industry is doing in terms of design and color pallets. We have a wonderful pastoral environment, a retreat where they can go and reflect."[77]

A Model of Organizational Creativity and Innovation

Organizational creativity and innovation are relatively new topics within the field of OB despite their importance for organizational success. Rather than focus on group and organizational creativity, researchers historically examined the predictors of individual creativity. This final section examines a process model of organizational creativity. Knowledge of its linkages can help you to facilitate and contribute to organizational creativity.

Figure 11–5 illustrates the process underlying organizational creativity and innovation. It shows that organizational creativity is directly influenced by organizational characteristics and the amount of creative behavior that occurs within work groups. In turn, a group's creative behavior is influenced by group characteristics and the individual creative behavior/performance of its members. Individual creative behavior is directly affected by a variety of individual characteristics. The double-headed arrows between individual and group and between group and organizational characteristics indicate that the various characteristics all influence each other. Let us now consider the model's major components.

Individual Characteristics   Creativity requires motivation. In other words, people make a decision whether or not they want to apply their knowledge and capabilities to create new ideas, things, or products.[78] Consider the amount of creativity that was unleashed after September 11, 2001, when the Pentagon issued the following plea for help:

> Please, America, send us your ideas for combating terrorism. The request prompted derision from late-night TV comics, while newspapers in Poland and Germany marveled how the world's most powerful military force had been reduced to advertising for advice on how to fight its enemies.
>
> No matter. America's techno-wizards responded with a massive outpouring of ideas. Normally, the Pentagon's Technical Support Working Group (TSWG), which trolls for new technologies to help the military, gets about 900 proposals a year. But the October appeal garnered 12,500 brainstorms in just two months.[79]

In addition to motivation, creative people typically march to the beat of a different drummer. They are highly motivated individuals who spend considerable time developing both tacit and explicit knowledge about their field of interest or occupation. But contrary to stereotypes, creative people are not necessarily geniuses or introverted

Figure 11–5   *A Model of Organizational Creativity and Innovation*

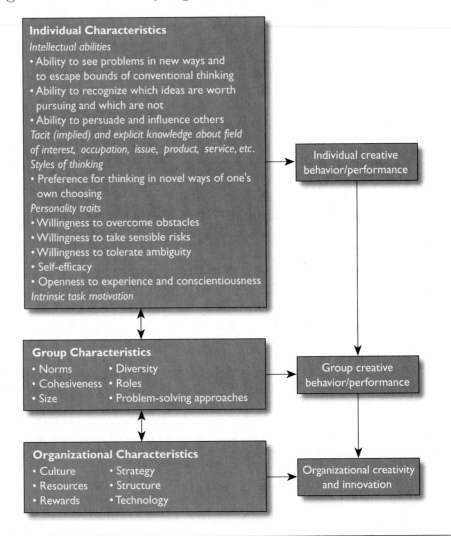

Individual Characteristics
Intellectual abilities
• Ability to see problems in new ways and to escape bounds of conventional thinking
• Ability to recognize which ideas are worth pursuing and which are not
• Ability to persuade and influence others
Tacit (implied) and explicit knowledge about field of interest, occupation, issue, product, service, etc.
Styles of thinking
• Preference for thinking in novel ways of one's own choosing
Personality traits
• Willingness to overcome obstacles
• Willingness to take sensible risks
• Willingness to tolerate ambiguity
• Self-efficacy
• Openness to experience and conscientiousness
Intrinsic task motivation

Individual creative behavior/performance

Group Characteristics
• Norms   • Diversity
• Cohesiveness   • Roles
• Size   • Problem-solving approaches

Group creative behavior/performance

Organizational Characteristics
• Culture   • Strategy
• Resources   • Structure
• Rewards   • Technology

Organizational creativity and innovation

SOURCES: Based on discussion in R J Sternberg and R I Lubart, "Investing in Creativity," *American Psychologist,* July 1996, pp. 677–88; and R W Woodman, J E Sawyer, and R W Griffin, "Toward a Theory of Organizational Creativity," *Academy of Management Review,* April 1993, pp. 293–321.

nerds. In addition, they are not *adaptors.* "Adaptors are those who . . . prefer to resolve difficulties or make decisions in such a way as to have the least impact upon the assumptions, procedures, and values of the organization."[80] In contrast, creative individuals are dissatisfied with the status quo. They look for new and exciting solutions to problems. Because of this, creative organizational members can be perceived as disruptive and hard to get along with.[81] Further, research indicates that male and female managers do not differ in levels of creativity, and there are a host of personality characteristics that are associated with creativity.[82] These characteristics include, but are not limited to, those shown in Figure 11–5. This discussion comes to life by considering the following example.

After the attacks on September 11, 2001, the Pentagon issued a plea for Americans to submit ideas for combating terrorism. Dr. Joseph Atick, President and CEO of Visionics Corp., submitted his innovative high-tech face scanner in hopes that America's airports would use the scanners to look for international terrorists. The scanner is being tested at a Florida airport. What are the pros and cons of using face scanners to detect potential terrorists?

AP/Wide World Photos

The Post-it Notes story represents a good illustration of how the individual characteristics shown in Figure 11–5 promote creative behavior/performance. Post-it Notes are a \$200 million-a-year product for 3M Corporation:

> The idea originated with Art Fry, a 3M employee who used bits of paper to mark hymns when he sat in his church choir. These markers kept falling out of the hymn books. He decided that he needed an adhesive-backed paper that would stick as long as necessary but could be removed easily. He soon found what he wanted in the 3M laboratory, and the Post-it Note was born.
>
> Fry saw the market potential of his invention, but others did not. Market-survey results were negative; major office-supply distributors were skeptical. So he began giving samples to 3M executives and their secretaries. Once they actually used the little pieces of adhesive paper, they were hooked. Having sold 3M on the project, Fry used the same approach with other executives throughout the United States.[83]

Notice how Fry had to influence others to try out his idea. Figure 11–5 shows that creative people have the ability to persuade and influence others.

Group Characteristics

Figure 11–5 also lists six characteristics that influence the level of creative behavior/performance exhibited by a work group. In general, group creativity is fueled by a cohesive environment that supports open interactions, diverse viewpoints, and playful surroundings.[84] The work environment at E Ink is a good example.

> E Ink CEO Jim Juliano tries to infuse his company's core values into everything it does. When designing the work environment at E Ink, Juliano wanted to encourage a community feeling. He wanted the feeling of sitting at an Italian family's dinner table where "anyone can overhear multiple conversations. When people hear things, cross-fertilization occurs." So E Ink's workplace is without walls, with the exception of several conference rooms.
>
> Juliano also wanted the work environment to resemble an Italian piazza, so the office spaces are built around a central square. This piazza is the company's Chill Center, with toys, games such as Foosball, and free vending machines. Juliano feels the center encourages people to float freely.[85]

Table 11–3 *Suggestions for Improving Employee Creativity*

Develop an environment that supports creative behavior.
Try to avoid using an autocratic style of leadership.
Encourage employees to be more open to new ideas and experiences.
Keep in mind that people use different strategies, like walking around or listening to music, to foster their creativity.
Provide employees with stimulating work that creates a sense of personal growth.
Allow employees to have fun and play around.
Encourage an open environment that is free from defensive behavior.
Treat errors and mistakes as opportunities for learning.
Let employees occasionally try out their pet ideas. Provide a margin of error.
Avoid using a negative mind-set when an employee approaches you with a new idea.
Reward creative behavior.

SOURCE: Adapted from discussion in E Raudsepp, "101 Ways to Spark Your Employees' Creative Potential," *Office Administration and Automation*, September 1985, pp. 38, 39–43, 56.

Organizational Characteristics   Research and corporate examples clearly support the importance of organizational characteristics in generating organizational creativity. Organizations such as Rubbermaid, 3M, Microsoft, The Body Shop, DuPont, and Rich Products Corp. are all known as innovative companies that encourage creativity via the organizational characteristics shown in Figure 11–5. Rich Products Corp., for example, has built a culture that links rewards to creativity.

> Part of creating the right culture and fostering creativity involves encouraging top leaders to put goals in place around innovation. As at Rich Products, the business managers at financial holding company, BB&T Corp., have specific objectives to meet each year, which require them to capitalize on their teams' innate ingenuity.
>
> That creativity is reinforced "constantly," says Tim Davis, executive vice president of the Human Systems Division at the company's headquarters in Winston-Salem, NC. "We talk about it from the office of the CEO right through the organization." BB&T provides training that links creative initiatives to the business plan and sets incentives around that in order to reward the appropriate behaviors. "One of the company's corporate values is 'independent thinking,' and each functional area is encouraged to approach the concept of creativity and innovation in its own way," he says.[86]

This example illustrates the point that organizational creativity requires resources, commitment, and a reinforcing organizational culture. Table 11–3 presents a number of suggestions that may be used to help create this type of culture.

Summary of Key Concepts

1. *Compare and contrast the rational model of decision making and Simon's normative model.* The rational decision-making model consists of identifying the problem, generating alternative solutions, evaluating and selecting a solution, and implementing and evaluating the solution. Research indicates that decision makers do not follow the series of steps outlined in the rational model.

   Simon's normative model is guided by a decision maker's bounded rationality. Bounded rationality means that decision makers are bounded or restricted by a variety of constraints when making decisions. The normative model suggests that decision making is characterized by *(a)* limited information processing, *(b)* the use of judgmental heuristics, and *(c)* satisficing.

2. *Discuss knowledge management and techniques used by companies to increase knowledge sharing.* Knowledge management involves the implementation of systems and practices that increase the sharing of knowledge and information throughout an organization. There are two types of knowledge that impact the quality of decisions: tacit knowledge and explicit knowledge. Organizations use computer systems to share explicit knowledge. Tacit knowledge is shared by observing, participating, or working with experts or coaches. Mentoring, informal networking, meetings, and design of office space also influence knowledge sharing.

3. *Explain the model of decision-making styles.* The model of decision-making styles is based on the idea that styles vary along two different dimensions: value orientation and tolerance for ambiguity. When these two dimensions are combined, they form four styles of decision making: directive, analytical, conceptual, and behavioral. People with a directive style have a low tolerance for ambiguity and are oriented toward task and technical concerns. Analytics have a higher tolerance for ambiguity and are characterized by a tendency to overanalyze a situation. People with a conceptual style have a high threshold for ambiguity and tend to focus on people or social aspects of a work situation. This behavioral style is the most people oriented of the four styles.

4. *Describe the model of escalation of commitment.* Escalation of commitment refers to the tendency to stick to an ineffective course of action when it is unlikely that a bad situation can be reversed. Psychological and social determinants, organizational determinants, project characteristics, and contextual determinants cause managers to exhibit this decision-making error.

5. *Summarize the pros and cons of involving groups in the decision-making process.* There are both pros and cons to involving groups in the decision-making process. Although research shows that groups typically outperform the average individual, there are five important issues to consider when using groups to make decisions. (1) Groups are less efficient than individuals. (2) A group's overconfidence can fuel groupthink. (3) Decision quality is negatively related to group size. (4) Groups are more accurate when they know a great deal about the issues at hand and when the leader possesses the ability to effectively evaluate the group members' opinions and judgments. (5) The composition of a group affects its decision-making processes and performance. In the final analysis, managers are encouraged to use a contingency approach when determining whether to include others in the decision-making process.

6. *Explain how participative management affects performance.* Participative management reflects the extent to which employees participate in setting goals, making decisions, solving problems, and making changes in the organization. Participative management is expected to increase motivation because it helps employees fulfill three basic needs: (1) autonomy, (2) meaningfulness of work, and (3) interpersonal contact. Participative management does not work in all situations. The design of work and the level of trust between management and employees influence the effectiveness of participative management.

7. *Contrast brainstorming, the nominal group technique, the Delphi technique, and computer-aided decision making.* Group problem-solving techniques facilitate better decision making within groups. Brainstorming is used to help groups generate multiple ideas and alternatives for solving problems. The nominal group technique assists groups both to generate ideas and to evaluate and select solutions. The Delphi technique is a group process that anonymously generates ideas or judgments from physically dispersed experts. The purpose of computer-aided decision making is to reduce consensus roadblocks while collecting more information in a shorter period of time.

8. *Describe the stages of the creative process.* Creativity is defined as the process of using imagination and skill to develop a new or unique product, object, process, or thought. It is not adequately explained by differences between the left and right hemispheres of the brain. There are five stages of the creative process: preparation, concentration, incubation, illumination, and verification.

9. *Explain the model of organizational creativity and innovation.* Organizational creativity is directly influenced by organizational characteristics and the creative behavior that occurs within work groups. In turn, a group's creative behavior is influenced by group characteristics and the individual creative behavior/performance of its members. Individual creative behavior is directly affected by a variety of individual characteristics. Finally, individual, group, and organizational characteristics all influence each other within this process.

Discussion Questions

1. What role do emotions play in decision making?

2. Do you think people are rational when they make decisions? Under what circumstances would an individual tend to follow a rational process?

3. Describe a situation in which you satisficed when making a decision. Why did you satisfice instead of optimize?

4. Do you think knowledge management will become more important in the future? Explain your rationale.

5. Why would decision-making styles be a source of interpersonal conflict?

6. Describe a situation in which you exhibited escalation of commitment. Why did you escalate a losing situation?

7. Do you prefer to solve problems in groups or by yourself? Why?

8. Given the intuitive appeal of participative management, why do you think it fails as often as it succeeds? Explain.

9. Do you think you are creative? Why or why not?

10. What advice would you offer a manager who was attempting to improve the creativity of his or her employees? Explain.

Internet Exercise

www.brainstorming.co.uk

There are countless brainstorming sessions conducted by individuals and groups within organizations on a daily basis. We do not expect this trend to stop. To help you successfully facilitate and participate in a brainstorming session, this chapter provided a set of guidelines for conducting a brainstorming session. We did not, however, discuss different techniques that can be used to enhance individual and group creativity while brainstorming. The purpose of this exercise is for you to learn two techniques that can be used to enhance creative idea generation and to complete two creativity puzzles.

Begin the exercise by going to the following Internet site: **www.brainstorming.co.uk.** Then select their home page. Once at the home page, click on the option for "training on creative techniques." After a brief discussion about creativity, you will be given the option to learn more about a variety of different techniques that can be used to enhance creativity. Choose any two techniques and then answer questions 1 and 2 below.

Now return to the home page, and select the option for creativity puzzles. Follow the instructions and attempt to complete two puzzles. Don't peek ahead to see the answers until you have tried to finish the activity. Based on your experience with these creativity puzzles, answer questions 3, 4, and 5.

Questions

1. How might you use these techniques in a class project?

2. Should different techniques be used in different situations? Explain.

3. To what extent were the puzzles hard to complete?

4. Why do these puzzles help people to think outside of the box?

5. How might these puzzles be used during a brainstorming session?

OB in Action Case Study

www.sb.com

SmithKline Beecham Uses a Three-Step Process to Make Resource-Allocation Decisions[87]

In 1993, SmithKline Beecham was spending more than half a billion dollars per year on R&D, the lifeblood of any pharmaceuticals company. Ever since the 1989 merger that created the company, however, SB believed that it had been spending too much time arguing about how to value its R&D projects—and not enough time figuring out how to make them more valuable. . . .

Major resource-allocation decisions are never easy. For a company like SB, the problem is this: How do you make good decisions in a high-risk, technically complex business when the information you need to make those decisions comes largely from the project champions who are competing against one another for resources? A critical company process can become politicized when strong-willed, charismatic project leaders beat out their less competitive colleagues for resources. That in turn leads to the cynical view that your project is as good as the performance you can put on at funding time. . . .

Most organizations think of decision making as an event, not a process. They attach great importance to key decision meetings. But in most cases, and SB is no exception, the real problems occur before those meetings ever take place. And so the process that SB designed—a three-phase dialogue between the project teams and the company's decision makers—focused on the inputs to the resource-allocation decision and the role of the organization in preparing those inputs.

Phase I: Generating Alternatives

One of the major weaknesses of most resource-allocation processes is that project advocates tend to take an all-or-nothing approach to budget requests. At SB, that meant that project leaders would develop a single plan of action and present it as the *only* viable approach. Project teams rarely took the time to consider meaningful alternatives—especially if they suspected that doing so might mean a cutback in funding.

And so we insisted that each team develop at least four alternatives: the *current plan* (the team would follow the existing plan of activity), a *"buy-up" option* (the team would be given more to spend on the project), a *"buy-down" option* (the team would be given less to spend on the project), and a *minimal plan* (the team would abandon the project while preserving as much of the value earned to date as possible). Working with a facilitator, a team would begin by describing a project's objective, which usually was to develop a particular chemical entity targeted at one or more diseases. Then it would brainstorm about what it would do under each of the four funding alternatives. . . .

Near the end of this phase, the project alternatives were presented to a peer review board for guidance before any significant evaluation of the alternatives had been performed. Members of the review board, who were managers from key functions and major product groups within the pharmaceuticals organization, tested the fundamental assumptions of each alternative by asking probing questions: In the buy-down alternative, which trial should we eliminate? Should a once-a-day formulation be part of our buy-up alternative? Couldn't we do better by including Japan earlier in the current plan? The discussion session improved the overall quality of the project alternatives and helped build consensus about their feasibility and completeness.

The project teams then revised their alternatives where appropriate and submitted them again for review, this time to the group of senior managers who would, at a later point in the process, make the final investment decisions on all the projects. . . .

Phase II: Valuing Alternatives

Once we had engineered the process that took us through phase I, we needed a consistent methodology to value each one of the project alternatives. We chose to use decision analysis because of its transparency and its ability to capture the technical uncertainties and commercial risks of drug development. For each alternative, we constructed a decision tree; using the most knowledgeable experts to help structure the tree and assess the major uncertainties facing each project. . . .

We developed six requirements for achieving credibility and buy-in to the valuation of each alternative:

- First, the same information set must be provided for every project. . . .

- Second, the information must come from reliable sources. . . .

- Third, the sources of information must be clearly documented. . . .

- Fourth, the assessments must undergo peer review by experienced managers across functions and therapeutic areas. . . .

- Fifth, the valuations must be compared with those done by external industry observers and market analysts to establish that the numbers are realistic.

- Sixth, the impact of each variable on the project's expected value must be identified. . . .

We increased transparency and consistency in yet another way by having a specially designated group of analysts process the valuation information and draw preliminary insights. Having this work done by a neutral group was a relief to many project team members, who were rarely satisfied with the previous approaches to valuation, as well as to the top management group, who were tired of trying to make sense of widely disparate types of analysis. As the company's CFO for pharmaceuticals put it, "Inconsistent valuations are worse than none."

Once the alternatives had been valued, a second peer-review meeting was held to make sure that all the participants had a chance to question and understand the results. This step was designed to ensure that no surprises would emerge when the decisions were being made. And again, the peer review was followed by a senior management review that provided an opportunity to challenge, modify, and agree on the underlying assumptions driving the valuations. During the meeting, however, the senior managers were explicitly asked *not* to begin discussing which alternatives to invest in; instead, they were asked only to confirm that they understood and believed the valuations. And if they didn't, why not? What seemed out of line? . . .

Phase III: Creating a Portfolio and Allocating Resources

The goal of this phase was to create the highest-value portfolio based on all the project alternatives that had been developed. This was no easy task: with 20 major projects—each of which had four well-conceived alternatives—the number of possible configurations was enormous. We appointed a neutral analytic team, rather than the project advocates, to carry out a systematic approach to identifying the highest-value portfolio based on return on investment.

The portfolio could then be examined along a number of strategic dimensions, including stability under different scenarios, balance across therapeutic areas and stages in the development pipeline, and feasibility of success given SB's technical and commercial resources. Because the senior managers had already agreed—and vigorously debated—the underlying project descriptions (phase I) and valuations (phase II) for each alternative they now focused their complete attention on the portfolio decisions. . . .

The first 14 project decisions, which involved increasing or maintaining funding levels, were made without controversy. However, when it came time to discuss the first project whose funding would be cut, the manager of the relevant therapeutic area challenged the decision. The meeting's chairman listened to his case for maintaining the current funding and then asked whether that case was reflected in the project valuations. The manager agreed that it was, but repeated the argument that SB would lose value by terminating the project. The chairman agreed that value would be lost but pointed out that the funds originally scheduled for the project would create more value when applied elsewhere. That ended a potentially explosive discussion.

The new process not only reduced the controversy in the resource-allocation process, it also led the company to change its investment strategy. Although top management had set out to cut back on the company's development budget, they now saw their investment decision in a new light: they believed the new portfolio to be 30% more valuable than the old one—without any additional investment. Furthermore, the marginal return on additional investment had tripled from 5:1 to 15:1. To exploit this opportunity, the company ultimately decided to increase development spending by more than 50%.

Questions for Discussion

1. Is SmithKline Beecham's resource-allocation decision-making process more characteristic of the rational or normative model of decision making? Discuss your rationale.

2. How does SmithKline Beecham's approach attempt to control for escalation of commitment?

3. Does SmithKline Beecham effectively use groups in the decision-making process? Explain how.

4. To what extent does SmithKline Beecham promote organizational creativity and innovation? Explain your answer by applying Figure 11–5 to the case.

5. Why do you think the three-step decision-making process has been such a success? Discuss your rationale.

Personal Awareness and Growth Exercise

What Is Your Decision-Making Style?

Objectives

1. To assess your decision-making style.
2. To consider the managerial implications of your decision-making style.

Introduction

Earlier in the chapter we discussed a model of decision-making styles that is based on the idea that styles vary along the dimensions of an individual's value orientation and tolerance for ambiguity. In turn, these dimensions combine to form four styles of decision making (see Figure 11–2): directive, analytical, conceptual, and behavioral. Alan Rowe, an OB researcher, developed an instrument called the Decision Style Inventory to measure these four styles. This exercise provides you the opportunity to assess and interpret your decision-making style using this measurement device.

Instructions

The Decision Style Inventory consists of 20 questions, each with four responses.[88] You must consider each possible response for a question and then rank them according to how much you prefer each response. There are no right or wrong answers, so respond with what first comes to mind. Because many of the questions are anchored to how individuals make decisions at work, you can feel free to use your student role as a frame of reference to answer the questions. For each question, use the space on the survey to rank the four responses with either a 1, 2, 4, or 8. Use the number 8 for the responses that are **most** like you, a 4 for those that are **moderately** like you, a 2 for those that are **slightly** like you, and a 1 for the responses that are **least** like you. For instance, a question could be answered as follows: [8], [4], [2], [1]. Notice that each number was used only once to answer a question. Do not repeat any number when answering a given question. These numbers are placed in the spaces next to each of the answers. Once all of the responses for the 20 questions have been ranked, total the scores in each of the four columns. The total score for column one represents your score for the directive style, column two your analytical style, column three your conceptual style, and column four your behavioral style.

Questions for Discussion

1. In terms of your decision-making profile, which of the four styles best represents your decision-making style (has the highest subscore)? Which is the least reflective of your style (has the lowest subscore)?

2. Do you agree with this assessment? Explain.

3. How do your scores compare with the following norms: directive (75), analytical (90), conceptual (80), and behavioral (55)? What do the differences between your scores and the survey norms suggest about your decision-making style?

4. What are the advantages and disadvantages of your decision-making profile?

5. Which of the other decision-making styles is most inconsistent with your style? How would this difference affect your ability to work with someone who has this style?

1. My prime objective in life is:	to have a position with status	be the best in whatever I do	be recognized for my work	feel secure in my job
2. I enjoy work that:	is clear and well defined	is varied and challenging	lets me act independently	involves people
3. I expect people to be:	productive	capable	committed	responsive
4. My work lets me:	get things done	find workable approaches	apply new ideas	be truly satisfied
5. I communicate best by:	talking with others	putting things in writing	being open with others	having a group meeting
6. My planning focuses on:	current problems	how best to meet goals	future opportunities	needs of people in the organization
7. I prefer to solve problems by:	applying rules	using careful analysis	being creative	relying on my feelings
8. I prefer information:	that is simple and direct	that is complete	that is broad and informative	that is easily understood
9. When I'm not sure what to do:	I rely on my intuition	I search for alternatives	I try to find a compromise	avoid making a decision
10. Whenever possible, I avoid:	long debates	incomplete work	technical problems	conflict with others
11. I am really good at:	remembering details	finding answers	seeing many options	working with people
12. When time is important, I:	decide and act quickly	apply proven approaches	look for what will work	refuse to be pressured
13. In social settings, I:	speak with many people	observe what others are doing	contribute to the conversation	want to be part of the discussion
14. I always remember:	people's names	places I have been	people's faces	people's personalities
15. I prefer jobs where I:	receive high rewards	have challenging assignments	can reach my personal goals	am accepted by the group
16. I work best with people who:	are energetic and ambitious	are very competent	are open minded	are polite and understanding
17. When I am under stress, I:	speak quickly	try to concentrate on the problem	become frustrated	worry about what I should do
18. Others consider me:	aggressive	disciplined	imaginative	supportive
19. My decisions are generally:	realistic and direct	systematic and logical	broad and flexible	sensitive to the other's needs
20. I dislike:	losing control	boring work	following rules	being rejected
Total score				

SOURCE: © Alan J Rowe, Professor Emeritus. Revised December 18, 1998. Reprinted by permission.

Group Exercise

Ethical Decision Making

Objectives

1. To apply the rational model of decision making.

2. To examine the ethical implications of a managerial decision.

Introduction

In this chapter we learned there are four steps in the rational model of decision making. The third stage involves evaluating alternatives and selecting a solution. Part of this evaluation entails deciding whether or not a solution is ethical. The purpose of this exercise is to examine the steps in decision making and to consider the issue of ethical decision making. You may want to examine Learning Module A on ethics and organizational behavior.

Instructions

Break into groups of five or six people and read the following case. As a group, discuss the decision made by the company and answer the questions for discussion at the end of the case. Before answering questions 4 and 5, however, brainstorm alternative decisions the managers at TELE-COMPROS could have made. Finally, the entire class can reconvene and discuss the alternative solutions that were generated.

THE CASE OF TELECOMPROS

For large cellular service providers, maintaining their own customer service call center can be very expensive. Many have found they can save money by outsourcing their customer service calls to outside companies.

TELECOMPROS is one such company. It specializes in cellular phone customer service. TELECOMPROS saves large cellular companies money by eliminating overhead costs associated with building a call center, installing additional telephone lines, and so forth. Once TELECOMPROS is hired by large cellular service providers, TELECOMPROS employees are trained on the cellular service providers' systems, policies, and procedures. TELECOMPROS' income is derived from charging a per hour fee for each employee.

Six months ago, TELECOMPROS acquired a contract with Cell2u, a large cellular service provider serving the western United States. In the beginning of the contract, Cell2U was very pleased. As a call center,

TELECOMPROS has a computer system in place that monitors the number of calls the center receives and how quickly the calls are answered. When Cell2U received its first report, the system showed that TELECOMPROS was a very productive call center and it handled the call volume very well. A month later however, Cell2U launched a nationwide marketing campaign. Suddenly, the call volume increased and TELECOMPROS' customer service reps were unable to keep up. The phone monitoring system showed that some customers were on hold for 45 minutes or longer, and at any given time throughout the day there were as many as 50 customers on hold. It was clear to Cell2U that the original number of customer service reps it had contracted for was not enough. It renegotiated with upper management at TELECOMPROS and hired additional customer service reps. TELECOMPROS was pleased because it was now receiving more money from Cell2U for the extra employees, and Cell2U was happy because the call center volume was no longer overwhelming and its customers were happy with the attentive customer service.

Three months later though, TELECOMPROS' customer service supervisors noticed a decrease in the number of customer service calls. It seemed that the reps had done such a good job that Cell2U customers had fewer problems. There were too many people and not enough calls. With little to do, some reps were playing computer games or surfing the Internet while waiting for calls to come in.

Knowing that if Cell2U analyzed its customer service needs, it would want to decrease the reps to save money, TELECOMPROS' upper management made a decision. Rather than decrease its staff and lose the hourly pay from Cell2U, the upper management told customer service supervisors to call the customer service line. Supervisors called in and spent enough time on the phone with reps to ensure that the computer registered the call and the time it took to "resolve" the call. Then they would hang up and call the call center again. TELECOMPROS did not have to decrease its customer service reps, and Cell2U continued to pay for the allotted reps until the end of the contract.

Questions for Discussion

1. Was the decision made by TELECOMPROS an ethical one? Why or why not?

2. If you were a manager at TELECOMPROS, what would you have done when your manager asked you to call the customer service line? What are the ramifications of your decision? Discuss.

3. Where did the decision-making process at TELECOMPROS break down? Explain.

4. What alternative solutions to the problem at hand did you identify? What is your recommended solution? Explain why you selected this alternative.

5. How would you implement your preferred solution? Describe in detail.

Ethical Dilemma

Are Lawyers at Vinson & Elkins Partly Responsible for Enron's Collapse?[89]

Early in the morning . . . [on] October 23, [2001,] Ronald Astin, a partner at the Houston law firm Vinson & Elkins, joined Enron Corp. executives in a meeting room next to Chairman Kenneth Lay's office. A conference call with analysts was about to begin, and the group needed to script an explanation for Enron's unfolding troubles, which included mysterious partnerships that appeared to be keeping big chunks of debt hidden away.

The tense mood soon grew worse. Mr Astin had drafted a section saying that Enron Chief Financial Officer Andrew Fastow initially presented the idea of the partnerships to the board. According to people at the meeting, Mr Fastow began shouting that he wasn't responsible for forming the partnerships.

It was the climax of a beneath-the-surface struggle between the outside lawyer and the Enron executive. Over five years, as Mr Fastow structured ever-more-complex deals for the big energy and trading company, Mr Astin and other Vinson & Elkins lawyers sometimes objected, saying the deals posed conflicts of interest or weren't in Enron's best interests.

But Vinson & Elkins didn't blow the whistle. Again and again, its lawyers backed down when rebuffed by Mr Fastow or his lieutenants, expressing their unease to Enron's in-house attorneys but not to its most senior executives or to its board. And when asked to assess Enron manager Sherron Watkins' warning to Mr Lay last summer of potential accounting scandals, Vinson & Elkins delivered to Enron a report that largely downplayed the risks.

Now, deals that troubled some Vinson & Elkins lawyers are central to investigations of the collapse of Enron. But while the mantle of heroine has fallen on Ms Watkins, Vinson & Elkins is on the defensive. One of the country's most powerful law firms, with some 850 lawyers in nine cities, Vinson & Elkins now faces lawsuits from Enron shareholders and Enron employees. And a report of a special investigation done for Enron's board has criticized the law firm for an "absence" of "objective and critical professional advice."

The firm's bind casts a stark light on the central issue law firms face when they represent large corporations: Just what are their obligations to the client and the client's shareholders? In terms of legal ethics, outside lawyers have a clear ethical duty to withdraw from transactions in which clients are obviously breaking the law. But many situations are murkier. At what point should the lawyers speak up, and to whom, when the legality of planned corporate moves is merely questionable? And what about when individual executives are planning steps that appear not in the interests of the client company itself?

Vinson & Elkins' managing partner, Joseph Dilg, has told a congressional panel probing Enron that so long as a transaction isn't illegal and has been approved by the client company's management, outside lawyers may advise on the transaction. "In doing so, the lawyers are not approving the business decisions that were made by their clients," he said.

But others, such as Boston University law professor Susan Koniak, say lawyers must do more. They have a duty to make sure a client's managers aren't "breaching their duties to the corporation," says Ms Koniak, who testified before a Senate hearing on Enron and accountability issues in February [2002]. She believes Vinson & Elkins lawyers should have taken their concerns to Enron directors.

What should lawyers at Vinson & Elkins have done in this case?

1. The lawyers are not responsible for the acts of Enron's management. Lawyers are paid to advise their clients, and it is up to the clients to take or ignore this advice.

2. Blow the whistle and let legal authorities know about Enron's mysterious partnerships. Explain your rationale and discuss the ramifications of this choice.

3. Take your concerns to Enron's board of directors. Explain your rationale and discuss the ramifications of this choice.

4. Invent other options. Discuss.

For an interpretation of this situation, visit our Web site, **www.mhhe.com/kreitner.**

Chapter Twelve

Group Dynamics

Learning Objectives

When you finish studying the material in this chapter, you should be able to:

1 Identify the four sociological criteria of a group and explain the role of equity in the Workplace Social Exchange Network (WSEN) model.

2 Describe the five stages in Tuckman's theory of group development, and discuss the threat of group decay.

3 Distinguish between role conflict and role ambiguity.

4 Contrast roles and norms, and specify four reasons norms are enforced in organizations.

5 Distinguish between task and maintenance functions in groups.

6 Summarize the practical contingency management implications for group size.

7 Discuss why managers need to carefully handle mixed-gender task groups.

8 Describe groupthink, and identify at least four of its symptoms.

9 Define social loafing, and explain how managers can prevent it.

Networking is a powerful way to meet people and get things done. Unfortunately, it's one of those important but not urgent things that don't always get the attention they deserve. For women in particular—who may also be running households and raising children (and who almost always shoulder most of the responsibility for those things, according to recent reality checks)—there isn't enough time to attend a formal networking meeting. And the more informal contacts one makes could be more helpful by being more specific and less guarded about giving advice and sharing information. It's easier to ask a friend about salary negotiation than to ask someone sitting across from you at a luncheon meeting.

Many women have risen to the challenge by forming their own small groups—Girl Gangs—that get together regularly in person, by phone, or via email to talk about life and career. These buddies share ideas and con-

tacts, celebrate personal and professional successes, and help their members get more done. The power they represent is as awesome as that of any of the Powerpuff Girls on Saturday morning TV.

No less a personage than Oprah Winfrey says she relies on informal networks. . . .

In this era of multitasking, Oprah isn't the only woman who is mingling her personal and professional lives with the

Oprah Winfrey, seen here hugging singer/actress Jennifer Lopez, enjoys the support of an informal network of friends.
AP/ Wide World Photos

help of an informal network of likeminded people. Given the demands faced by the average American woman juggling work, family, and life in general, an informal group offers a great way to harness the energy of different people dealing with similar situations. . . .

The Corporate Manager

In a big company, one needs to network just to navigate efficiently. In fact, it's as important to network within a company as it is to network outside of it.

Daimler-Chrysler has 13,000 people working in its Auburn Hills, Michigan, headquarters. Kathryn Lee, staff labor programs administrator, is proud that her company supports a Women's Network Group and provides a number of opportunities for after-hours networking, including guest speakers and presentations. But as a working mother of two young children, formal networking is a low priority for her right now.

"Being perfectly candid, I would rather spend my evenings with my family and pass on the optional business gatherings," she says. Intentionally or not, her company has provided a networking opportunity for women in the exact same circumstance.

After her second child was born, Lee started spending her lunches and breaks in Daimler-Chrysler's lactation room, where she met a lot of other women.

"You could spot us a mile away," she says, "with the sweater or suit jacket to cover up leaks and the oversized Pump-N-Style bag. Since we were all on a schedule, we got to know each other pretty well. It felt like we were in a secret club."

In part because they didn't work together, these women would use their pumping sessions to share ideas for work as well as to talk about kids. Lee credits the group for helping her stick to nursing for a year, which isn't easy. She says she's also grateful for the opportunity to meet others in her company without taking extra time to attend meetings after work.

"I learned which areas in the company have great bosses, which departments have a lot of international travel, and other information that I can use on my job," she says. And her companion nursing mothers formed a cross-departmental network as strong as any within the company.

The Academic

Universities are hardly free from the political and career-management demands of corporate life. Marita Golden is a writer and professor in the MFA Graduate Creative Writing Program at Virginia Commonwealth University in Richmond. She often meets with a group of other African American women teaching at colleges in the Washington, DC, area.

"The group has helped us feel that we are supported in the trenches, even though we're not all at the same university," she says. "It's very good to know that you're not alone and that your experiences are valid."

Golden believes these groups are vitally important. "Even in a university, there are very few situations where we get together to talk about what we are doing creatively," she says.

In Golden's experience, an informal group gives members a better chance to talk about their research or their articles in progress than in an organized faculty forum, which often degenerates into discussions about students, grading, and university policies. Her group finds that exchanging ideas informally leads to better formal academic work in the long run. They also enjoy discussing their lives in general with colleagues who have become friends.

"One woman in the group was a grandmother who provided great wisdom about life that we came to rely on," says Golden.

That powerful combination of the personal and the professional is one reason that members come to rely on their girl gangs.[1]

> **For Discussion**
> What would you say to a manager who doesn't like informal networks because they are not "under control?"

B ecause the management of organizational behavior is above all else a social endeavor, managers need a strong working knowledge of *interpersonal* behavior. Research consistently reveals the importance of social skills for both individual and organizational success. An ongoing study by the Center for Creative Leadership (involving diverse samplings from Belgium, France, Germany, Italy, the United Kingdom, the United States, and Spain) found four stumbling blocks that tend to derail executives' careers. According to the researchers, "A derailed executive is one who, having reached the general manager level, finds that there is little chance of future advancement due to a misfit between job requirements and personal skills."[2] The four stumbling blocks, consistent across the cultures studied, are as follows:

Table 12–1   *Key Social Skills Managers Need for Building Social Capital*

Social Skill	Description	Topical Linkages in This Text
Social perception	Ability to perceive accurately the emotions, traits, motives, and intentions of others	• Individual differences, Chapters 5 and 6 • Emotional intelligence, Chapter 5 • Social perception, Chapter 7 • Employee motivation, Chapters 8 and 9
Impression management	Tactics designed to induce liking and a favorable first impression by others	• Impression management, Chapter 16
Persuasion and social influence	Ability to change others' attitudes or behavior in desired directions	• Influence tactics and social power, Chapter 16 • Leadership, Chapter 17
Social adaptability	Ability to adapt to, or feel comfortable in, a wide range of social situations	• Emotional intelligence, Chapter 5 • Managing change, Chapter 19

SOURCE: Columns 1 and 2 excerpted from R A Baron and G D Markman, "Beyond Social Capital: How Social Skills Can Enhance Entrepreneurs' Success," *Academy of Management Executive,* February 2000, table 1, p. 110.

1. Problems with interpersonal relationships.
2. Failure to meet business objectives.
3. Failure to build and lead a team.
4. Inability to change or adapt during a transition.[3]

Notice how both the first and third career stumbling blocks involve social skills—the ability to get along and work effectively with others. Managers with interpersonal problems typically were described as manipulative and insensitive. Interestingly, two-thirds of the derailed European managers studied had problems with interpersonal relationships. That same problem reportedly plagued one-third of the derailed US executives. Management, as defined in Chapter 1, involves getting things done with and through others. Experts say managers need to build social capital with four key social skills: social perception, impression management, persuasion and social influence, and social adaptability (see Table 12–1).[4] How polished are your social skills? Where do you need improvement?

Let us begin by defining the term *group* as a prelude to examining types of groups, functions of group members, social exchanges in the workplace, and the group development process. Our attention then turns to group roles and norms, the basic building blocks of group dynamics. Effects of group structure and member characteristics on group outcomes are explored next. Finally, three serious threats to group effectiveness are discussed. (This chapter serves as a foundation for our discussion of teams and teamwork in the following chapter.)

Groups and Social Exchanges

Groups and teams are inescapable features of modern life. College students are often teamed with their peers for class projects. Parents serve on community advisory boards at their local high school. Managers find themselves on product planning committees and productivity task forces. Productive organizations simply cannot function without gathering individuals into groups and teams. But as personal experience shows, group effort can bring out both the best and the worst in people. A marketing department meeting, where several people excitedly brainstorm and refine a creative new advertising campaign, can yield results beyond the capabilities of individual contributors. Conversely, committees have become the butt of jokes (e.g., a committee is a place where they take minutes and waste hours; a camel is a horse designed by a committee) because they all too often are plagued by lack of direction and by conflict. Modern managers need a solid understanding of groups and group processes so as to both avoid their pitfalls and tap their vast potential. Moreover, the huge and growing presence of the Internet—with its own unique network of informal and formal social relationships—is a major challenge for profit-minded business managers.

Group

Two or more freely interacting people with shared norms and goals and a common identity.

Although other definitions of groups exist, we draw from the field of sociology and define a **group** as two or more freely interacting individuals who share collective norms and goals and have a common identity.[5] Figure 12–1 illustrates how the four criteria in this definition combine to form a conceptual whole. Organizational psychologist Edgar Schein shed additional light on this concept by drawing instructive distinctions between a group, a crowd, and an organization:

> The size of a group is thus limited by the possibilities of mutual interaction and mutual awareness. Mere aggregates of people do not fit this definition because they do not interact and do not perceive themselves to be a group even if they are aware of each other as, for instance, a crowd on a street corner watching some event. A total department, a union, or a whole organization would not be a group in spite of thinking of themselves as "we," because they generally do not all interact and are not all aware of each other. However, work teams, committees, subparts of departments, cliques, and various other informal associations among organizational members would fit this definition of a group.[6]

Take a moment now to think of various groups of which you are a member. Does each of your groups satisfy the four criteria in Figure 12–1?

Figure 12–1   *Four Sociological Criteria of a Group*

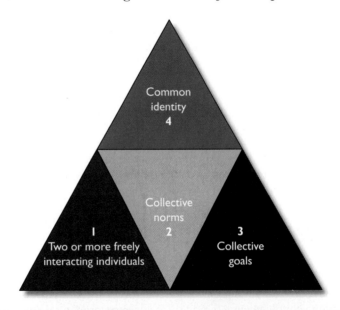

Formal and Informal Groups

Individuals join groups, or are assigned to groups, to accomplish various purposes. If the group is formed by a manager to help the organization accomplish its goals, then it qualifies as a **formal group.** Formal groups typically wear such labels as work group, team, committee, quality circle, or task force. An **informal group** exists when the members' overriding purpose of getting together is friendship or common interests.[7] Although formal and informal groups often overlap, such as a team of corporate auditors heading for the tennis courts after work, some employees are not friends with their co-workers. The desirability of overlapping formal and informal groups is problematic. Some managers firmly believe personal friendship fosters productive teamwork on the job while others view workplace "bull sessions" as a serious threat to productivity. Both situations are common, and it is the manager's job to strike a workable balance, based on the maturity and goals of the people involved.

Formal group
Formed by the organization.

Informal group
Formed by friends or those with common interests.

Functions of Formal Groups

Researchers point out that formal groups fulfill two basic functions: *organizational* and *individual.* The various functions are listed in Table 12–2. Complex combinations of these functions can be found in formal groups at any given time.

For example, consider what Mazda's new American employees experienced when they spent a month working in Japan before the opening of the firm's Flat Rock, Michigan, plant:

> After a month of training in Mazda's factory methods, whipping their new Japanese buddies at softball and sampling local watering holes, the Americans were fired up....[A maintenance manager] even faintly praised the Japanese practice of holding group calisthenics at the start of each working day:"I didn't think I'd like doing exercises every morning, but I kind of like it."[8]

Table 12–2   *Formal Groups Fulfill Organizational and Individual Functions*

Organizational Functions	Individual Functions
1. Accomplish complex, interdependent tasks that are beyond the capabilities of individuals.	1. Satisfy the individual's need for affiliation.
2. Generate new or creative ideas and solutions.	2. Develop, enhance, and confirm the individual's self-esteem and sense of identity.
3. Coordinate interdepartmental efforts.	3. Give individuals an opportunity to test and share their perceptions of social reality.
4. Provide a problem-solving mechanism for complex problems requiring varied information and assessments.	4. Reduce the individual's anxieties and feelings of insecurity and powerlessness.
5. Implement complex decisions.	5. Provide a problem-solving mechanism for personal and interpersonal problems.
6. Socialize and train newcomers.	

SOURCE: Adapted from E H Schein, *Organizational Psychology,* 3rd ed (Englewood Cliffs, NJ: Prentice Hall, 1980), pp. 149–51.

While Mazda pursued the organizational functions it wanted—interdependent team-work, creativity, coordination, problem solving, and training—the American workers benefited from the individual functions of formal groups. Among those benefits were affiliation with new friends, enhanced self-esteem, exposure to the Japanese social reality, and reduction of anxieties about working for a foreign-owned company. In short, Mazda created a workable blend of organizational and individual group functions by training its newly hired American employees in Japan.

Social Exchanges in the Workplace

Social relationships are complex, alive, and dynamic. Accordingly, we need dynamic models for realistic understanding. A team of researchers from Auburn University recently proposed the instructive model shown in Figure 12–2. They call it the Workplace Social Exchange Network (WSEN) because it captures multilevel social

Figure 12–2   *The Workplace Social Exchange Network Model*

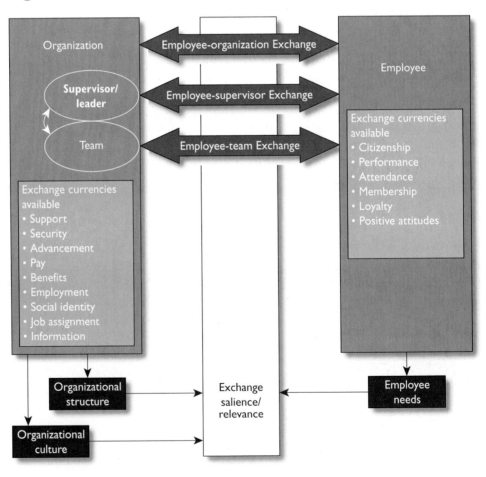

SOURCE: Adapted from M S Cole, W S Schaninger Jr, and S G Harris, "The Workplace Social Exchange Network: A Multilevel, Conceptual Examination," *Group & Organization Management,* March 2002, figure 1, p. 148, Copyright © 2002 by Sage Publication, Inc. Reprinted by permission of Sage Publications, Inc.

exchanges within organizations, along with the complex *network* of variables affecting those exchanges.[9]

The Exchange of Currencies   The economic notion of exchange is at the heart of this model. In starkest economic terms, people exchange their time and labor for money when they take a job. But as this model realistically shows, there is much more at stake than just the exchange of time and labor for money. Individuals, organizations, and teams have many "currencies" they can grant or withhold.

Notably, the only social exchange currency that is not self-explanatory is "citizenship." *Organizational citizenship* involves going above and beyond what is expected (e.g., voluntarily working late to finish an important project)—in short, being a good citizen.

Three Types of Social Exchange   According to the WSEN model, every employee has social exchanges on three levels: with the organization, with the boss, and with the work team as a whole. From the individual's perspective, exchanges at the various levels can be favorable or unfavorable. They can be motivating or demotivating, depending on the perceived equity of the exchange. (Recall our discussion of equity motivation theory in Chapter 9.) For example, someone may have high-quality exchanges with his or her supervisor and work team, and thus want to be around them, be motivated to work hard for them, and be loyal to them. However, because the organization has a reputation for massive layoffs, the employee–organization exchange would be perceived unfavorably, thus fostering dissatisfaction and possibly poor performance and turnover.

Situational Factors   The WSEN model includes three intervening factors: organizational structure, organizational culture, and employee needs. Structure—in the form of reporting relationships, policies, and work rules—shapes the individual's expectations about what is fair and what is unfair. So, too, cultural norms and traditions create a context for judging the fairness of social exchanges. The individual's need profile, as discussed in Chapter 8, will determine which of the organization's exchange currencies are motivating and which are not. People are motivated when they have a realistic chance of having their needs satisfied.

Is the Social Exchange Relevant?   Finally, at the bottom center of the WSEN model is the individual's perceptual filter. Is the particular social exchange salient or relevant? Recall from the discussion of social perception in Chapter 7 that salient stimuli tend to capture and dominate one's attention. An exchange between the employee and his or her organization, leader, or team needs to be salient if it is to influence behavior. If, say, a marketing assistant is indifferent to her teammates on a special project, that particular exchange would not be salient or relevant for her.

Overall, the WSEN model does a good job of building a conceptual bridge between motivation theories and group dynamics. Also, it realistically indicates the multilevel nature of social relationships within organizations.

The Group Development Process

Groups and teams in the workplace go through a maturation process, such as one would find in any life-cycle situation (e.g., humans, organizations, products). While there is general agreement among theorists that the group development process occurs

Figure 12–3   *Tuckman's Five-Stage Theory of Group Development*

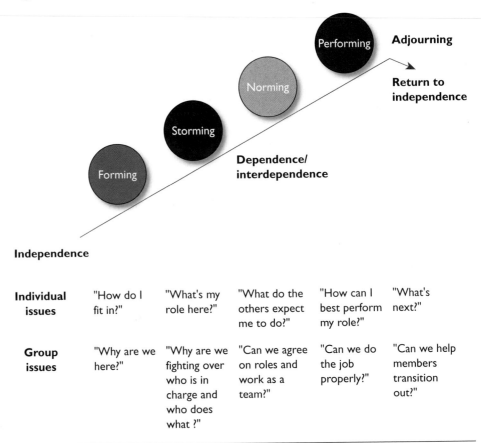

Individual issues	"How do I fit in?"	"What's my role here?"	"What do the others expect me to do?"	"How can I best perform my role?"	"What's next?"
Group issues	"Why are we here?"	"Why are we fighting over who is in charge and who does what ?"	"Can we agree on roles and work as a team?"	"Can we do the job properly?"	"Can we help members transition out?"

in identifiable stages, they disagree about the exact number, sequence, length, and nature of those stages.[10] One oft-cited model is the one proposed in 1965 by educational psychologist Bruce W Tuckman. His original model involved only four stages (forming, storming, norming, and performing). The five-stage model in Figure 12–3 evolved when Tuckman and a doctoral student added "adjourning" in 1977.[11] A word of caution is in order. Somewhat akin to Maslow's need hierarchy theory, Tuckman's theory has been repeated and taught so often and for so long that many have come to view it as documented fact, not merely a theory. Even today, it is good to remember Tuckman's own caution that his group development model was derived more from group therapy sessions than from natural-life groups. Still, many in the OB field like Tuckman's five-stage model of group development because of its easy-to-remember labels and common-sense appeal.[12]

Five Stages

Let us briefly examine each of the five stages in Tuckman's model. Notice in Figure 12–3 how individuals give up a measure of their independence when they join and participate in a group. Also, the various stages are not necessarily of the same duration or intensity. For instance, the storming stage may be practically nonexistent or painfully long, depending on the goal clarity and the commitment and maturity of the members. You can make this process come to life by relating the various stages to your own experiences with work groups, committees, athletic teams, social or religious groups, or class project teams. Some group happenings that surprised you when they occurred may now make sense or strike you as inevitable when seen as part of a natural development process.

Stage 1: Forming

During this ice-breaking stage, group members tend to be uncertain and anxious about such things as their roles, who is in charge, and the group's goals. Mutual trust is low, and there is a good deal of holding back to see who takes charge and how. If the formal leader (e.g., a supervisor) does not assert his or her authority, an emergent leader will eventually step in to fulfill the group's need for leadership and direction. Leaders typically mistake this honeymoon period as a mandate for permanent control. But later problems may force a leadership change.

Stage 2: Storming

This is a time of testing. Individuals test the leader's policies and assumptions as they try to determine how they fit into the power structure. Subgroups take shape, and subtle forms of rebellion, such as procrastination, occur. Many groups stall in stage 2 because power politics erupts into open rebellion.[13]

Stage 3: Norming

Groups that make it through stage 2 generally do so because a respected member, other than the leader, challenges the group to resolve its power struggles so something can be accomplished. Questions about authority and power are resolved through unemotional, matter-of-fact group discussion. A feeling of team spirit is experienced because members believe they have found their proper roles. **Group cohesiveness,** defined as the "we feeling" that binds members of a group together, is the principal by-product of stage 3.[14] (For a good laugh, see the golfing explanation below the photo on page 416.)

Group cohesiveness
A "we feeling" binding group members together.

Stage 4: Performing

Activity during this vital stage is focused on solving task problems. As members of a mature group, contributors get their work done without hampering others. (See the Personal Awareness and Growth Exercise at the end of this chapter for a way to measure group maturity.) There is a climate of open communication, strong cooperation, and lots of helping behavior. Conflicts and job boundary disputes are handled constructively and efficiently. Cohesiveness and personal commitment to group goals help the group achieve more than could any one individual acting alone. According to a pair of group development experts,

> the group structure can become flexible and adjust to fit the requirements of the situation without causing problems for the members. Influence can shift depending on who has the particular expertise or skills required for the group task or activity. Subgroups can work on special problems or subproblems without posing threats to the authority or cohesiveness of the rest of the group.[15]

Stage 5: Adjourning

The work is done; it is time to move on to other things. Having worked so hard to get along and get something done, many members feel a compelling sense of loss. The return to independence can be eased by rituals celebrating "the end" and "new beginnings." Parties, award ceremonies, graduations, or mock

A recent *Fortune* article examined the question, Why do people love to mix golf and business? (Hint: It's all about group dynamics.):

Ask people why they golf with business associates, and the answer is always the same: It's a great way to build relationships. They say this far more about golf than about going to dinner or attending a baseball game, and for good reason. Indeed, this may be the central fact about corporate golf, though it's rarely said: When people golf together, they see one another humiliated. At least 95% of all golfers are terrible, which means that in 18 holes everyone in the foursome will hit a tree, take three strokes in one bunker, or four-putt, with everyone else watching. Bonding is simply a matter of people jointly going through adversity, and a round of golf will furnish plenty of it. Of course it's only a game, but of course it isn't, so the bonds can be surprisingly strong. And what's that worth?

SOURCE: G Colvin, "Why Execs Love Golf," *Fortune*, April 30, 2001, p 46.

(c) George Shelly/Corbis StockMarket

funerals can provide the needed punctuation at the end of a significant group project. Leaders need to emphasize valuable lessons learned in group dynamics to prepare everyone for future group and team efforts.

Group Development: Research and Practical Implications

A growing body of group development research provides managers with some practical insights.

Extending the Tuckman Model: Group Decay
An interesting study of 10 software development teams, ranging in size from 5 to 16 members, enhanced the practical significance of Tuckman's model.[16] Unlike Tuckman's laboratory groups who worked together only briefly, the teams of software engineers worked on projects lasting *years*. Consequently, the researchers discovered more than simply a five-stage group development process. Groups were observed actually shifting into reverse once

Tuckman's "performing" stage was reached, in what the researchers called *group decay*. In keeping with Tuckman's terminology, the three observed stages of group decay were labeled "de-norming," "de-storming," and "de-forming." These additional stages take shape as follows:

- *De-norming*. As the project evolves, there is a natural erosion of standards of conduct. Group members drift in different directions as their interests and expectations change.

- *De-storming*. This stage of group decay is a mirror opposite of the storming stage. Whereas disagreements and conflicts arise rather suddenly during the storming stage, an undercurrent of discontent slowly comes to the surface during the destorming stage. Individual resistance increases and cohesiveness declines.

- *De-forming*. The work group literally falls apart as subgroups battle for control. Those pieces of the project that are not claimed by individuals or subgroups are abandoned. "Group members begin isolating themselves from each other and from their leaders. Performance declines rapidly because the whole job is no longer being done and group members little care what happens beyond their self-imposed borders."[17]

The primary management lesson from this study is that group leaders should not become complacent upon reaching the performing stage. According to the researchers: "The performing stage is a knife edge or saddle point, not a point of static equilibrium."[18] Awareness is the first line of defense. Beyond that, constructive steps need to be taken to reinforce norms, bolster cohesiveness, and reaffirm the common goal—*even when work groups seem to be doing their best.*

Feedback

Feedback   Another fruitful study was carried out by a pair of Dutch social psychologists. They hypothesized that interpersonal feedback would vary systematically during the group development process. "The unit of feedback measured was a verbal message directed from one participant to another in which some aspect of behavior was addressed."[19] After collecting and categorizing 1,600 instances of feedback from four different eight-person groups, they concluded the following:

- Interpersonal feedback increases as the group develops through successive stages.

- As the group develops, positive feedback increases and negative feedback decreases.

- Interpersonal feedback becomes more specific as the group develops.

- The credibility of peer feedback increases as the group develops.[20]

These findings hold important lessons for managers. The content and delivery of interpersonal feedback among work group or committee members can be used as a gauge of whether the group is developing properly. For example, the onset of stage 2 (storming) will be signaled by a noticeable increase in *negative* feedback. Effort can then be directed at generating specific, positive feedback among the members so the group's development will not stall. The feedback model discussed in Chapter 10 is helpful in this regard.

Deadlines

Deadlines   Field and laboratory studies found uncertainty about deadlines to be a major disruptive force in both group development and intergroup relations. The practical implications of this finding were summed up by the researcher as follows:

Uncertain or shifting deadlines are a fact of life in many organizations. Interdependent organizational units and groups may keep each other waiting, may suddenly move deadlines forward or back, or may create deadlines that are known to be earlier than is necessary in efforts to control erratic workflows. The current research suggests that the consequences of such uncertainty may involve more than stress, wasted time, overtime work, and intergroup conflicts. Synchrony in group members' expectations about deadlines may be critical to groups' abilities to accomplish successful transitions in their work.[21]

Thus, effective group management involves clarifying not only tasks and goals, but deadlines as well. When group members accurately perceive important deadlines, the pacing of work and timing of interdependent tasks tend to be more efficient.

Leadership Styles

Along a somewhat different line, experts in the area of leadership contend that different leadership styles are needed as work groups develop.

In general, it has been documented that leadership behavior that is active, aggressive, directive, structured, and task-oriented seems to have favorable results early in the group's history. However, when those behaviors are maintained throughout the life of the group, they seem to have a negative impact on cohesiveness and quality of work. Conversely, leadership behavior that is supportive, democratic, decentralized, and participative seems to be related to poorer functioning in the early group development stages. However, when these behaviors are maintained throughout the life of the group, more productivity, satisfaction, and creativity result.[22]

The practical punch line here is that managers are advised to shift from a directive and structured leadership style to a participative and supportive style as the group develops.[23]

Roles and Norms: Social Building Blocks for Group and Organizational Behavior

Work groups transform individuals into functioning organizational members through subtle yet powerful social forces.[24] These social forces, in effect, turn "I" into "we" and "me" into "us." Group influence weaves individuals into the organization's social fabric by communicating and enforcing both role expectations and norms. We need to understand roles and norms if we are to effectively manage group and organizational behavior.

Roles

Roles

Expected behaviors for a given position.

Four centuries have passed since William Shakespeare had his character Jaques speak the following memorable lines in Act II of *As You Like It:* "All the world's a stage, And all the men and women merely players; They have their exits and their entrances; And one man in his time plays many parts." This intriguing notion of all people as actors in a universal play was not lost on 20th-century sociologists who developed a complex theory of human interaction based on roles. According to an OB scholar, "**roles** are sets of behaviors that persons expect of occupants of a position."[25] Role theory attempts to explain how these social expectations influence employee behavior. This section explores role theory by analyzing a role episode and defining the terms *role overload,* *role conflict,* and *role ambiguity.*

Role Episodes

A role episode, as illustrated in Figure 12–4, consists of a snapshot of the ongoing interaction between two people. In any given role episode, there is a role sender and a focal person who is expected to act out the role. Within a broader

Figure 12–4   *A Role Episode*

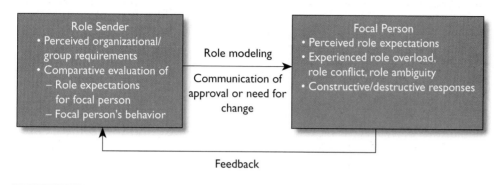

SOURCE: Adapted in part from R L Kohn, D M Wolfe, R P Quinn, and J D Snoek, *Organizational Stress: Studies in Role Conflict and Ambiguity*, 1981 ed. (Malabar, FL: Robert E Krieger Publishing, 1964), p. 26.

context, one may be simultaneously a role sender and a focal person. For the sake of social analysis, however, it is instructive to deal with separate role episodes.

Role episodes begin with the role sender's perception of the relevant organization's or group's behavioral requirements. Those requirements serve as a standard for formulating expectations for the focal person's behavior. The role sender then cognitively evaluates the focal person's actual behavior against those expectations. Appropriate verbal and behavioral messages are then sent to the focal person to pressure him or her into behaving as expected.[26] Consider how Westinghouse used a carrot-and-stick approach to communicate role expectations:

> The carrot is a plan, that . . . rewarded 134 managers with options to buy 764,000 shares of stock for boosting the company's financial performance.
>
> The stick is quarterly meetings that are used to rank managers by how much their operations contribute to earnings per share. The soft-spoken . . . [chairman of the board] doesn't scold. He just charts in green the results of the sectors that have met their goals and charts the laggards in red. Peer pressure does the rest. Shame "is a powerful tool," says one executive.[27]

On the receiving end of the role episode, the focal person accurately or inaccurately perceives the communicated role expectations and modeled behavior. Various combinations of role overload, role conflict, and role ambiguity are then experienced. (These three outcomes are defined and discussed in the following sections.) The focal person then responds constructively by engaging in problem solving, for example, or destructively because of undue tension, stress, and strain.[28]

Role Overload
According to organizational psychologist Edgar Schein, **role overload** occurs when "the sum total of what role senders expect of the focal person far exceeds what he or she is able to do."[29] Students who attempt to handle a full course load and maintain a decent social life while working 30 or more hours a week know full well the consequences of role overload. As the individual tries to do more and more in less and less time, stress mounts and personal effectiveness slips.

Role Conflict
Have you ever felt like you were being torn apart by the conflicting demands of those around you? If so, you were a victim of role conflict. **Role conflict** is experienced when "different members of the role set expect different things of

Role overload
Others' expectations exceed one's ability.

Role conflict
Others have conflicting or inconsistent expectations.

the focal person."[30] Managers often face conflicting demands between work and family, as discussed in Chapter 6. Women experience greater role conflict between work and family than men because women continue to perform the majority of the household duties and child-care responsibilities.[31] Employees in single-person households have their own version of role conflict between work and outside interests. This is the situation Liz Dolan faced prior to quitting her job as Nike's global marketing chief and becoming a part-time consultant:

> It's hard to admit that your work life is out of control. I loved my job at Nike, but it was all-consuming. I had no life. My housekeeper was spending more time at my house than I was. I reached a point where I could not remember the last time I had slept in my own bed. I love summers in Oregon, but I was never there long enough to enjoy one. But the real indicator that my life was out of whack came when I got a call from my brother, Brendan. He'd been trying to reach me for several weeks. I was always too "busy" to call him back. When we finally connected, he told me that he'd had to do a Lexis-Nexis search on me to figure out where I was that week. I was being Lexis-Nexised by my own brother! That really made me stop and think.[32]

Role conflict also may be experienced when internalized values, ethics, or personal standards collide with others' expectations. For instance, an otherwise ethical production supervisor may be told by a superior to "fudge a little" on the quality control reports so an important deadline will be met. The resulting role conflict forces the supervisor to choose between being loyal but unethical or ethical but disloyal. Tough ethical choices such as this mean personal turmoil, interpersonal conflict, and even resignation.[33] Consequently, experts say business schools should do a better job of weaving ethics training into their course requirements.

Role Ambiguity   Those who experience role conflict may have trouble complying with role demands, but they at least know what is expected of them. Such is not the case with **role ambiguity,** which occurs when "members of the role set fail to communicate to the focal person expectations they have or information needed to perform the role, either because they do not have the information or because they deliberately withhold it."[34] In short, people experience role ambiguity when they do not know what is expected of them. Organizational newcomers often complain about unclear job descriptions and vague promotion criteria. According to role theory, prolonged role ambiguity can foster job dissatisfaction, erode self-confidence, and hamper job performance.

As might be expected, role ambiguity varies across cultures. In a 21-nation study, people in individualistic cultures were found to have higher role ambiguity than people in collectivist cultures.[35] In other words, people in collectivist or "we" cultures had a clearer idea of others' expectations. Collectivist cultures make sure everyone knows their proper place in society. People in individualistic "me" cultures, such as the United States, may enjoy more individual discretion, but comparatively less input from others has its price—namely, greater role ambiguity.

As mentioned earlier, these role outcomes typically are experienced in some combination, usually to the detriment of the individual and the organization. In fact, a study in Israel documented lower job performance when employees experienced a combination of role conflict and role ambiguity.[36]

Take a moment now to complete the self-assessment exercise in the OB Exercise on page 421. See if you can distinguish between sources of role conflict and sources of role ambiguity, as they affect your working life.

Role ambiguity
Others' expectations
are unknown.

OB Exercise Measuring Role Conflict and Role Ambiguity

Instructions

Step 1. While thinking of your current (or last) job, circle one response for each of the following statements. Please consider each statement carefully because some are worded positively and some negatively.

Step 2. In the space in the far right column, label each statement with either a "C" for role conflict or an "A" for role ambiguity. (See Chapter 12 footnote 37 for a correct categorization.)

Step 3. Calculate separate totals for role conflict and role ambiguity, and compare them with these arbitrary norms: 5–14 = low; 15–25 = moderate; 26–35 = high.

		Very False	**Very True**	
1. I feel certain about how much authority I have.		7 — 6 — 5 — 4 — 3 — 2 — 1		_____
2. I have to do things that should be done differently.		1 — 2 — 3 — 4 — 5 — 6 — 7		_____
3. I know that I have divided my time properly.		7 — 6 — 5 — 4 — 3 — 2 — 1		_____
4. I know what my responsibilities are.		7 — 6 — 5 — 4 — 3 — 2 — 1		_____
5. I have to buck a rule or policy in order to carry out an assignment.		1 — 2 — 3 — 4 — 5 — 6 — 7		_____
6. I feel certain how I will be evaluated for a raise or promotion.		7 — 6 — 5 — 4 — 3 — 2 — 1		_____
7. I work with two or more groups who operate quite differently.		1 — 2 — 3 — 4 — 5 — 6 — 7		_____
8. I know exactly what is expected of me.		7 — 6 — 5 — 4 — 3 — 2 — 1		_____
9. I do things that are apt to be accepted by one person and not accepted by others.		1 — 2 — 3 — 4 — 5 — 6 — 7		_____
10. I work on unnecessary things.		1 — 2 — 3 — 4 — 5 — 6 — 7		_____

Role conflict score = _____
Role ambiguity score = _____

SOURCE: Adapted from J R Rizzo, R J House, and S I Lirtzman, "Role Conflict and Ambiguity in Complex Organizations," *Administrative Science Quarterly*, June 1970, p. 156.

Norms

Norms are more encompassing than roles. While roles involve behavioral expectations for specific positions, norms help organizational members determine right from wrong and good from bad (see the International OB on page 422). According to one respected team of management consultants: "A **norm** is an attitude, opinion, feeling, or action— shared by two or more people—that guides their behavior."[38] Although norms are typically unwritten and seldom discussed openly, they have a powerful influence on group and organizational behavior.[39] PepsiCo Inc., for instance, has evolved a norm that equates corporate competitiveness with physical fitness. According to observers,

> Leanness and nimbleness are qualities that pervade the company. When Pepsi's brash young managers take a few minutes away from the office, they often head straight for the company's physical fitness center or for a jog around the museum-quality sculptures outside of PepsiCo's Purchase, New York, headquarters.[40]

At PepsiCo and elsewhere, group members positively reinforce those who adhere to current norms with friendship and acceptance. On the other hand, nonconformists experience criticism and even **ostracism,** or rejection by group members. Anyone who

Norm
Shared attitudes, opinions, feelings, or actions that guide social behavior.

Ostracism
Rejection by other group members.

International OB   Cooperative Norms Drive South African Philosophy of *Ubuntu*

The dismantling of apartheid in the 1990s was a watershed of historic development for South Africa. The world watched as the country charted its course toward the establishment of a democratic, nonracial, nonsexist system of government. With democratic processes now firmly in place, the spotlight has shifted to economic revitalization. South Africa has shown steady economic progress since the days of apartheid, and stands 42nd in the 2001 IMD world competitiveness rankings. This recovery is a welcome sign that South Africa has turned the corner. Now it can focus on those practices that will allow it to excel domestically and globally. An important step will be to understand the culture, values, norms, and beliefs held by the largest segment of the population, the Africans....

Observable workplace behavior is strongly influenced by latent, unobservable social attitudes. Such social attitudes manifest the philosophical thought system of the group from which the individual comes. The philosophical thought system itself is a product of various factors including history, folklore, mythology, culture, norms, values, and religious beliefs....

There are important lessons to be learned from understanding the philosophical thought system known as *ubuntu*, which embodies the beliefs, values, and behaviors of a large majority of the South African population. Whether it is a critical issue that needs to be interpreted or a problem that needs to be solved, *ubuntu* is invariably invoked as a scale for weighing good versus bad, right versus wrong, just versus unjust....

Ubuntu can be defined as humaneness—a pervasive spirit of caring and community, harmony and hospitality, respect and responsiveness—that individuals and groups display for one another. *Ubuntu* is the foundation for the basic values that manifest themselves in the ways African people think and behave toward each other and everyone else they encounter. One of the most important attributes of *ubuntu* is the high degree of harmony and continuity throughout the system. Unfortunately, with all the talk about *ubuntu,* the philosophy has not been fully embraced in the workplace since its strategic advantages are not fully appreciated by managers. Traditional management systems are guided by misapplied economic assumptions about human nature: that self-interest is the ultimate determinant of behavior, and it is maximized when employees earn as much as possible from contributing as little as possible....

An organizing concept of *ubuntu* is human interdependence. The driving norms are reciprocity, suppression of self-interest, and the virtue of symbiosis. Hence it is often repeated that *umntu ngumntu ngabanye* (a person is a person through others). This statement conveys the notion that a person becomes a person only through his/her relationship with and recognition by others. This recognition has far-reaching implications for day-to-day interactions among people and for an individual's status in society....

An equally important aspect of relationships with others is teamwork. The solidarity spirit of *ubuntu* simultaneously supports cooperation and competitiveness by allowing individuals to contribute their best efforts for the betterment of the entire team. Everyone understands that together the team can accomplish more than if each individual worked alone. The notion of synergy, i.e., the creation of a whole that is larger than the sum of the individual parts, is an integral part of *ubuntu*. Organizations can ensure that individuals continue to uphold this spirit, by linking their reward systems to team performance.

SOURCE: Excerpted from M P Mangaliso, "Building Competitive Advantage from *Ubuntu*: Management Lessons from South Africa," *Academy of Management Executive*, August 2001, pp. 23–33.

has experienced the "silent treatment" from a group of friends knows what a potent social weapon ostracism can be. Norms can be put into proper perspective by understanding how they develop and why they are enforced.

How Norms Are Developed   Experts say norms evolve in an informal manner as the group or organization determines what it takes to be effective. Generally speaking, norms develop in various combinations of the following four ways:

I. *Explicit statements by supervisors or co-workers.* For instance, a group leader might explicitly set norms about not drinking (alcohol) at lunch.

2. *Critical events in the group's history.* At times there is a critical event in the group's history that establishes an important precedent. (For example, a key recruit may have decided to work elsewhere because a group member said too many negative things about the organization. Hence, a norm against such "sour grapes" behavior might evolve.)

3. *Primacy.* The first behavior pattern that emerges in a group often sets group expectations. If the first group meeting is marked by very formal interaction between supervisors and employees, then the group often expects future meetings to be conducted in the same way.

4. *Carryover behaviors from past situations.* Such carryover of individual behaviors from past situations can increase the predictability of group members' behaviors in new settings and facilitate task accomplishment. For instance, students and professors carry fairly constant sets of expectations from class to class.[41]

We would like you to take a few moments and think about the norms that are currently in effect in your classroom. List the norms on a sheet of paper. Do these norms help or hinder your ability to learn? Norms can affect performance either positively or negatively.[42]

Why Norms Are Enforced

Norms tend to be enforced by group members when they

- Help the group or organization survive.
- Clarify or simplify behavioral expectations.
- Help individuals avoid embarrassing situations.
- Clarify the group's or organization's central values and/or unique identity.[43]

Working examples of each of these four situations are presented in Table 12–3.

Table 12–3   *Four Reasons Norms Are Enforced*

Norm	Reason for Enforcement	Example
"Make our department look good in top management's eyes."	Group/organization survival	After vigorously defending the vital role played by the Human Resources Management Department at a divisional meeting, a staff specialist is complimented by her boss.
"Success comes to those who work hard and don't make waves."	Clarification of behavioral expectations	A senior manager takes a young associate aside and cautions him to be a bit more patient with co-workers who see things differently.
"Be a team player, not a star."	Avoidance of embarrassment	A project team member is ridiculed by her peers for dominating the discussion during a progress report to top management.
"Customer service is our top priority."	Clarification of central values/unique identity	Two sales representatives are given a surprise Friday afternoon party for having received prestigious best-in-the-industry customer service awards from an industry association.

Relevant Research Insights and Managerial Implications

Although instruments used to measure role conflict and role ambiguity have questionable validity,[44] two separate meta-analyses indicated that role conflict and role ambiguity negatively affected employees. Specifically, role conflict and role ambiguity were associated with job dissatisfaction, tension and anxiety, lack of organizational commitment, intentions to quit, and, to a lesser extent, poor job performance.[45]

The meta-analyses results hold few surprises for managers. Generally, because of the negative association reported, it makes sense for management to reduce both role conflict and role ambiguity. In this endeavor, managers can use feedback, formal rules and procedures, directive leadership, setting of specific (difficult) goals, and participation. Managers also can use the mentoring process discussed in Chapter 3 to reduce role conflict and ambiguity.

Regarding norms, a recent set of laboratory studies involving a total of 1,504 college students as subjects has important implications for workplace diversity programs. Subjects in groups where the norm was to express prejudices, condone discrimination, and laugh at hostile jokes tended to engage in these undesirable behaviors. Conversely, subjects tended to disapprove of prejudicial and discriminatory conduct when exposed to groups with more socially acceptable norms.[46] So, once again, Mom and our teachers were right when they warned us about the dangers of hanging out with "the wrong crowd." Managers who want to build strong diversity programs need to cultivate favorable role models and group norms. Poor role models and antisocial norms need to be identified and weeded out.

Group Structure and Composition

Work groups of varying size are made up of individuals with varying ability and motivation. Moreover, those individuals perform different roles, on either an assigned or voluntary basis. No wonder some work groups are more productive than others. No wonder some committees are tightly knit while others wallow in conflict. In this section, we examine three important dimensions of group structure and composition: (1) functional roles of group members, (2) group size, and (3) gender composition. Each of these dimensions alternatively can enhance or hinder group effectiveness, depending on how it is managed.

Functional Roles Performed by Group Members

Task roles

Task-oriented group behavior.

As described in Table 12–4, both task and maintenance roles need to be performed if a work group is to accomplish anything.[47]

Maintenance roles

Relationship-building group behavior.

Task versus Maintenance Roles   **Task roles** enable the work group to define, clarify, and pursue a common purpose. Meanwhile, **maintenance roles** foster supportive and constructive interpersonal relationships. In short, task roles keep the group *on track* while maintenance roles keep the group *together*. A project team member is performing a task function when he or she stands at an update meeting and says, "What is the real issue here? We don't seem to be getting anywhere." Another individual who

Table 12–4   *Functional Roles Performed by Group Members*

Task Roles	Description
Initiator	Suggests new goals or ideas.
Information seeker/giver	Clarifies key issues.
Opinion seeker/giver	Clarifies pertinent values.
Elaborator	Promotes greater understanding through examples or exploration of implications.
Coordinator	Pulls together ideas and suggestions.
Orienter	Keeps group headed toward its stated goal(s).
Evaluator	Tests group's accomplishments with various criteria such as logic and practicality.
Energizer	Prods group to move along or to accomplish more.
Procedural technician	Performs routine duties (e.g., handing out materials or rearranging seats).
Recorder	Performs a "group memory" function by documenting discussion and outcomes.
Maintenance Roles	**Description**
Encourager	Fosters group solidarity by accepting and praising various points of view.
Harmonizer	Mediates conflict through reconciliation or humor.
Compromiser	Helps resolve conflict by meeting others half way.
Gatekeeper	Encourages all group members to participate.
Standard setter	Evaluates the quality of group processes.
Commentator	Records and comments on group processes/dynamics.
Follower	Serves as a passive audience.

SOURCE: Adapted from discussion in K D Benne and P Sheats, "Functional Roles of Group Members," *Journal of Social Issues,* Spring 1948, pp. 41–49.

says, "Let's hear from those who oppose this plan," is performing a maintenance function. Importantly, each of the various task and maintenance roles may be played in varying combinations and sequences by either the group's leader or any of its members.

Checklist for Managers   The task and maintenance roles listed in Table 12–4 can serve as a handy checklist for managers and group leaders who wish to ensure proper group development. Roles that are not always performed when needed, such as those of coordinator, evaluator, and gatekeeper, can be performed in a timely manner by the formal leader or assigned to other members. The task roles of initiator, orienter, and energizer are especially important because they are *goal-directed* roles. Research studies on group goal setting confirm the motivational power of challenging goals. As with individual goal setting (in Chapter 9), difficult but achievable goals are associated with better group results.[48] Also in line with individual goal-setting theory and research, group goals are more effective if group members clearly understand them and are both individually and collectively committed to achieving them. Initiators, orienters, and energizers can be very helpful in this regard.

International managers need to be sensitive to cultural differences regarding the relative importance of task and maintenance roles. In Japan, for example, cultural tradition calls for more emphasis on maintenance roles, especially the roles of harmonizer and compromiser:

> Courtesy requires that members not be conspicuous or disputatious in a meeting or classroom. If two or more members discover that their views differ—a fact that is tactfully taken to be unfortunate—they adjourn to find more information and to work toward a stance that all can accept. They do not press their personal opinions through strong arguments, neat logic, or rewards and threats. And they do not hesitate to shift their beliefs if doing so will preserve smooth interpersonal relations. (To lose is to win.)[49]

Group Size

How many group members is too many? The answer to this deceptively simple question has intrigued managers and academics for years. Folk wisdom says "two heads are better than one" but that "too many cooks spoil the broth." So where should a manager draw the line when staffing a committee? At 3? At 5 or 6? At 10 or more? Researchers have taken two different approaches to pinpointing optimum group size: mathematical modeling and laboratory simulations. Let us briefly review research evidence from these two approaches.

The Mathematical Modeling Approach   This approach involves building a mathematical model around certain desired outcomes of group action such as decision quality. Due to differing assumptions and statistical techniques, the results of this research are inconclusive. Statistical estimates of optimum group size have ranged from 3 to 13.[50]

The Laboratory Simulation Approach   This stream of research is based on the assumption that group behavior needs to be observed firsthand in controlled laboratory settings. A laboratory study by respected Australian researcher Philip Yetton and his colleague, Preston Bottger, provides useful insights about group size and performance.[51]

A total of 555 subjects (330 managers and 225 graduate management students, of whom 20% were female) were assigned to task teams ranging in size from 2 to 6. The teams worked on the National Aeronautics and Space Administration moon survival exercise. (This exercise involves the rank ordering of 15 pieces of equipment that would enable a spaceship crew on the moon to survive a 200-mile trip between a crash-landing site and home base.)[52] After analyzing the relationships between group size and group performance, Yetton and Bottger concluded the following:

> It would be difficult, at least with respect to decision quality, to justify groups larger than five members. . . . Of course, to meet needs other than high decision quality, organizations may employ groups significantly larger than four or five.[53]

More recent laboratory studies exploring the brainstorming productivity of various size groups (2 to 12 people), in face-to-face versus computer-mediated situations, proved fruitful. In the usual face-to-face brainstorming sessions, productivity of ideas did not increase as the size of the group increased. But brainstorming productivity increased as the size of the group increased when ideas were typed into networked computers.[54] These results suggest that computer networks are helping to deliver on the promise of productivity improvement through modern information technology.

Managerial Implications   Within a contingency management framework, there is no hard-and-fast rule about group size. It depends on the manager's objective for the group. If a high-quality decision is the main objective, then a three- to five-member group would be appropriate. However, if the objective is to generate creative ideas, encourage participation, socialize new members, engage in training, or communicate policies, then groups much larger than five could be justified. But even in this developmental domain, researchers have found upward limits on group size. According to a meta-analysis, the positive effects of team-building activities diminished as group size increased.[55] Managers also need to be aware of *qualitative* changes that occur when group size increases. A meta-analysis of eight studies found the following relationships: as group size increased, group leaders tended to become more directive, and group member satisfaction tended to decline slightly.[56]

Odd-numbered groups (e.g., three, five, seven members) are recommended if the issue is to be settled by a majority vote. Voting deadlocks (e.g., 2–2, 3–3) too often hamper effectiveness of even-numbered groups. For example, as outlined in this recent news clipping, a voting deadlock paved the way for inept government oversight of business:

> Pepsi got the go-ahead for its $13.4 billion acquisition of Quaker Oats after the Federal Trade Commission deadlocked Wednesday on whether to try to block the deal.
>
> In a closed meeting, FTC commissioners split 2–2 on whether to go to court to oppose Pepsi's bid for Quaker and its powerhouse Gatorade sports-drink brand. FTC staff investigating the deal had recommended that the agency try to block it because of the increased clout Pepsi would get in the $56 billion soft-drink industry.
>
> The move to go to court required a majority. After the failed vote, commissioners voted unanimously to close the probe begun after the deal was announced in December. That vote allows Pepsi and Quaker to close the deal without regulatory conditions. Pepsi said it expects to do so before the weekend.[57]

A five-member FTC panel might well have rendered the same outcome, but in a more decisive manner.

Effects of Men and Women Working Together in Groups

As pointed out in Chapter 2, the female portion of the US labor force has grown significantly in recent decades. This demographic shift brought an increase in the number of organizational committees and teams composed of both men and women. Some profound effects on group dynamics might be expected.[58] Let us see what researchers have found in the way of group gender composition effects and what managers can do about them.

Women Face an Uphill Battle in Mixed-Gender Task Groups

Laboratory and field studies paint a picture of inequality for women working in mixed-gender groups. Both women and men need to be aware of these often subtle but powerful group dynamics so corrective steps can be taken.

In a laboratory study of six-person task groups, a clear pattern of gender inequality was found in the way group members interrupted each other. Men interrupted women significantly more often than they did other men. Women, who tended to interrupt less frequently and less successfully than men, interrupted men and women equally.[59]

One study suggests that females entering male-dominated fields, such as law enforcement, face greater challenges than do males entering female-dominated fields.

A. Ramey/Stock Boston

A field study of mixed-gender police and nursing teams in the Netherlands found another group dynamics disadvantage for women. These two particular professions—police work and nursing—were fruitful research areas because men dominate the former while women dominate the latter. As women move into male-dominated police forces and men gain employment opportunities in the female-dominated world of nursing, who faces the greatest resistance? The answer from this study was the women police officers. As the representation of the minority gender (either female police officers or male nurses) increased in the work groups, the following changes in attitude were observed:

> The attitude of the male majority changes from neutral to resistant, whereas the attitude of the female majority changes from favorable to neutral. In other words, men increasingly want to keep their domain for themselves, while women remain willing to share their domain with men.[60]

Again, managers are faced with the challenge of countering discriminatory tendencies in group dynamics.

The Issue of Sexual Harassment
Social-sexual behavior was the focus of a random survey of 1,232 working men ($n = 405$) and women ($n = 827$) in the Los Angeles area.[61] Both harassing and nonharassing sexual conduct were investigated. One-third of the female employees and one-fourth of the male employees reported being sexually harassed in their current job. Nonharassing sexual behavior was much more common, with 80% of the total sample reporting experience with such behavior. Indeed, according to the researchers, increased social contact between men and women in work groups and organizations had led to increased sexualization (e.g., flirting and romance) in the workplace.

From an OB research standpoint, sexual harassment is a complex and multifaceted problem. For example, a recent meta-analysis of 62 studies found women perceiving a broader range of behaviors as sexual harassment (see Table 12–5), as opposed to what men perceived. Women and men tended to agree that sexual propositions and coercion qualified as sexual harassment, but there was less agreement about other aspects of a hostile work environment.[62]

Table 12–5   *Behavioral Categories of Sexual Harassment*

Category	Description	Behavioral Examples
Derogatory attitudes—impersonal	Behaviors that reflect derogatory attitudes about men or women in general	Obscene gestures not directed at target Sex-stereotyped jokes
Derogatory attitudes—personal	Behaviors that are directed at the target that reflect derogatory attitudes about the target's gender	Obscene phone calls Belittling the target's competence
Unwanted dating pressure	Persistent requests for dates after the target has refused	Repeated requests to go out after work or school
Sexual propositions	Explicit requests for sexual encounters	Proposition for an affair
Physical sexual contact	Behaviors in which the harasser makes physical sexual contact with the target	Embracing the target Kissing the target
Physical nonsexual contact	Behaviors in which the harasser makes physical nonsexual contact with the target	Congratulatory hug
Sexual coercion	Requests for sexual encounters or forced encounters that are made a condition of employment or promotion	Threatening punishment unless sexual favors are given Sexual bribery

SOURCE: M Rotundo, D Nguyen, and P R Sackett, "A Meta-Analytic Review of Gender Differences in Perceptions of Sexual Harassment," *Journal of Applied Psychology*, October 2001, Article 914–922, copyright © 2001 by the American Psychological Association. Reprinted with permission.

Constructive Managerial Action   Male and female employees can and often do work well together in groups.[63] A survey of 387 male US government employees sought to determine how they were affected by the growing number of female co-workers. The researchers concluded, "Under many circumstances, including intergender interaction in work groups, frequent contact leads to cooperative and supportive social relations."[64] Still, managers need to take affirmative steps to ensure that the documented sexualization of work environments does not erode into sexual harassment. Whether perpetrated against women or men, sexual harassment is demeaning, unethical, and appropriately called "work environment pollution." Moreover, the US Equal Employment Opportunity Commission holds employers legally accountable for behavior it considers sexually harassing. An expert on the subject explains:

> What exactly is sexual harassment? The Equal Employment Opportunity Commission (EEOC) says that unwelcome sexual advances, requests for sexual favors, and other verbal or physical conduct of a sexual nature constitute sexual harassment when submission to such conduct is made a condition of employment; when submission to or rejection of sexual advances is used as a basis for employment decisions; or when such conduct creates an intimidating, hostile, or offensive work environment. These EEOC guidelines interpreting Title VII of the Civil Rights Act of 1964 further state that employers are responsible for the actions of their supervisors and agents and that employers are responsible for the actions of other employees if the employer knows or should have known about the sexual harassment.[65]

Training magazine's 2001 survey of 1,652 US companies with at least 100 employees found 91% conducting some sort of sexual harassment training, and 68% doing so at least annually.[66] Given the disagreement between women and men about what constitutes sexual harassment, this type of education is very important.

Beyond avoiding lawsuits by establishing and enforcing antidiscrimination and sexual harassment policies, managers need to take additional steps. Workforce diversity training is a popular approach today. Gender-issue workshops are another option. "Du Pont Co., for example, holds monthly workshops to make managers aware of gender-related attitudes."[67] Phyllis B Davis, a senior vice president at Avon Corporation, has framed the goal of such efforts by saying: "It's a question of consciously creating an environment where everyone has an equal shot at contributing, participating, and most of all advancing."[68]

Importantly, this embracing of organizational and work group diversity goes beyond gender, race, ethnicity, and culture. A laboratory study of US college students found a stronger positive relationship between group effectiveness and *value* diversity (as opposed to demographic diversity).[69] Once again we see the importance of managers recognizing and accommodating individual differences rather than relying on stereotypes.

Threats to Group Effectiveness

Even when managers carefully staff and organize task groups, group dynamics can still go haywire. Forehand knowledge of three major threats to group effectiveness—the Asch effect, groupthink, and social loafing—can help managers take necessary preventive steps. Because the first two problems relate to blind conformity, some brief background work is in order.

Very little would be accomplished in task groups and organizations without conformity to norms, role expectations, policies, and rules and regulations. After all, deadlines, commitments, and product/service quality standards have to be established and adhered to if the organization is to survive. But as pointed out by management consultants Robert Blake and Jane Srygley Mouton, conformity is a two-edged sword:

> Social forces powerful enough to influence members to conform may influence them to perform at a very high level of quality and productivity. All too often, however, the pressure to conform stifles creativity, influencing members to cling to attitudes that may be out of touch with organizational needs and even out of kilter with the times.[70]

Moreover, excessive or blind conformity can stifle critical thinking, the last line of defense against unethical conduct. Almost daily accounts in the popular media of executive misdeeds, insider trading scandals, price fixing, illegal dumping of hazardous wastes, and other unethical practices make it imperative that future managers understand the mechanics of blind conformity.

The Asch Effect

Fifty years ago, social psychologist Solomon Asch conducted a series of laboratory experiments that revealed a negative side of group dynamics.[71] Under the guise of a "perception test," Asch had groups of seven to nine volunteer college students look at 12 pairs of cards such as the ones in Figure 12–5. The object was to identify the line that was the same length as the standard line. Each individual was told to announce his or her choice to the group. Since the differences among the comparison lines were obvious, there should have been unanimous agreement during each of the 12 rounds. But that was not the case.

A Minority of One   All but one member of each group were Asch's confederates who agreed to systematically select the wrong line during seven of the rounds (the other five rounds were control rounds for comparison purposes). The remaining individual

Figure 12–5   *The Asch Experiment*

Standard Line Card

Comparison Lines Card

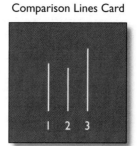

was the naive subject who was being tricked. Group pressure was created by having the naive subject in each group be among the last to announce his or her choice. Thirty-one subjects were tested. Asch's research question was: "How often would the naive subjects conform to a majority opinion that was obviously wrong?"

Only 20% of Asch's subjects remained entirely independent; 80% yielded to the pressures of group opinion at least once! Fifty-eight percent knuckled under to the "immoral majority" at least twice. Hence, the **Asch effect,** the distortion of individual judgment by a unanimous but incorrect opposition, was documented. (Do you ever turn your back on your better judgment by giving in to group pressure?)

A Managerial Perspective   Asch's experiment has been widely replicated with mixed results. Both high and low degrees of blind conformity have been observed with various situations and subjects. Replications in Japan and Kuwait have demonstrated that the Asch effect is not unique to the United States.[72] A 1996 meta-analysis of 133 Asch-line experiments from 17 countries found a *decline* in conformity among US subjects since the 1950s. Internationally, collectivist countries, where the group prevails over the individual, produced higher levels of conformity than individualistic countries.[73] The point is not precisely how great the Asch effect is in a given situation or culture, but rather, managers committed to ethical conduct need to be concerned that the Asch effect exists.

For Jeffrey Skilling, the disgraced former CEO of Enron, the Asch effect was something to cultivate and nurture. Consider this organizational climate for blind obedience:

> Skilling was filling headquarters with his own troops. He was not looking for "fuzzy skills," a former employee recalls. His recruits talked about a socialization process called "Enronizing." Family time? Quality of life? Forget it. Anybody who did not embrace the elbows-out culture "didn't get it." They were "damaged goods" and "shipwrecks," likely to be fired by their bosses at blistering annual job reviews known as rank-and-yank sessions. The culture turned paranoid: former CIA and FBI agents were hired to enforce security. Using "sniffer" programs, they would pounce on anyone E-mailing a potential competitor. The "spooks," as the former agents were called, were known to barge into offices and confiscate computers.[74]

Even isolated instances of blind, unthinking conformity seriously threaten the effectiveness and integrity of work groups and organizations. Functional conflict and assertiveness, discussed in Chapters 14 and 15, can help employees respond appropriately when they find themselves facing an immoral majority. Ethical codes mentioning specific practices also can provide support and guidance.

Asch effect
Giving in to a unanimous but wrong opposition.

Groupthink

Why did President Lyndon B Johnson and his group of intelligent White House advisers make some very *unintelligent* decisions that escalated the Vietnam War? Those fateful decisions were made despite obvious warning signals, including stronger than expected resistance from the North Vietnamese and withering support at home and abroad. Systematic analysis of the decision-making processes underlying the war in Vietnam and other US foreign policy fiascoes prompted Yale University's Irving Janis to coin the term *groupthink*.[75] Modern managers can all too easily become victims of groupthink, just like President Johnson's staff, if they passively ignore the danger.

Groupthink

Janis's term for a cohesive in-group's unwillingness to realistically view alternatives.

Definition and Symptoms of Groupthink   Janis defines **groupthink** as "a mode of thinking that people engage in when they are deeply involved in a cohesive in-group, when members' strivings for unanimity override their motivation to realistically appraise alternative courses of action."[76] He adds, "Groupthink refers to a deterioration of mental efficiency, reality testing, and moral judgment that results from in-group pressures."[77] Unlike Asch's subjects, who were strangers to each other, members of groups victimized by groupthink are friendly, tightly knit, and cohesive.

The symptoms of groupthink listed in Figure 12–6 thrive in the sort of climate outlined in the following critique of corporate directors in the United States:

> Many directors simply don't rock the boat. "No one likes to be the skunk at the garden party," says [management consultant] Victor H. Palmieri. . . . "One does not make friends and influence people in the boardroom or elsewhere by raising hard questions that create embarrassment or discomfort for management."[78]

In short, policy- and decision-making groups can become so cohesive that strong-willed executives are able to gain unanimous support for poor decisions.

Figure 12–6   *Symptoms of Groupthink Lead to Defective Decision Making*

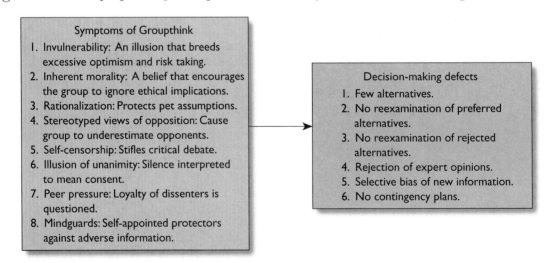

Symptoms of Groupthink

1. Invulnerability: An illusion that breeds excessive optimism and risk taking.
2. Inherent morality: A belief that encourages the group to ignore ethical implications.
3. Rationalization: Protects pet assumptions.
4. Stereotyped views of opposition: Cause group to underestimate opponents.
5. Self-censorship: Stifles critical debate.
6. Illusion of unanimity: Silence interpreted to mean consent.
7. Peer pressure: Loyalty of dissenters is questioned.
8. Mindguards: Self-appointed protectors against adverse information.

Decision-making defects

1. Few alternatives.
2. No reexamination of preferred alternatives.
3. No reexamination of rejected alternatives.
4. Rejection of expert opinions.
5. Selective bias of new information.
6. No contingency plans.

SOURCES: Symptoms adapted from I L Janis, *Groupthink*, 2nd ed (Boston: Houghton Mifflin, 1982), pp. 174–75. Defects excerpted from G Moorhead. "Groupthink: Hypothesis in Need of Testing," *Group & Organization Studies*, December 1982, p. 434. Copyright © 1982 by Sage Publications. Reprinted by permission of Sage Publications, Inc.

Groupthink Research and Prevention   Laboratory studies using college students as subjects validate portions of Janis's groupthink concept. Specifically, it has been found that

- Groups with a moderate amount of cohesiveness produce better decisions than low- or high-cohesive groups.
- Highly cohesive groups victimized by groupthink make the poorest decisions, despite high confidence in those decisions.[79]

Janis believes prevention is better than cure when dealing with groupthink. He recommends the following preventive measures:

1. Each member of the group should be assigned the role of critical evaluator. This role involves actively voicing objections and doubts.

2. Top-level executives should not use policy committees to rubber-stamp decisions that have already been made.

3. Different groups with different leaders should explore the same policy questions.

4. Subgroup debates and outside experts should be used to introduce fresh perspectives.

5. Someone should be given the role of devil's advocate when discussing major alternatives. This person tries to uncover every conceivable negative factor.

6. Once a consensus has been reached, everyone should be encouraged to rethink their position to check for flaws.[80]

These antigroupthink measures can help cohesive groups produce sound recommendations and decisions. When *Business Week* recently tackled the issue of corporate governance, this was one of the recommendations:

> The best insurance against crossing the ethical divide is a roomful of skeptics. CEOs must actively encourage dissent among senior managers by creating decision-making processes, reporting relationships, and incentives that encourage opposing viewpoints. At too many companies, the performance review system encourages a "yes-man culture" that subverts the organization's checks and balances. By advocating dissent, top executives can create a climate where wrongdoing will not go unchallenged.[81]

Groupthink also will be less likely.

The OB in Action Case Study at the end of this chapter explores the possible role of groupthink in the 1986 Challenger Space Shuttle disaster.

Social Loafing

Is group performance less than, equal to, or greater than the sum of its parts? Can three people, for example, working together accomplish less than, the same as, or more than they would working separately? An interesting study conducted more than a half century ago by a French agricultural engineer named Ringelmann found the answer to be "less than."[82] In a rope-pulling exercise, Ringelmann reportedly found that three people pulling together could achieve only two and a half times the average individual rate. Eight pullers achieved less than four times the individual rate. This tendency for individual effort to decline as group size increases has come to be called **social loafing.**[83] Let us briefly analyze this threat to group effectiveness and synergy with an eye toward avoiding it.

∫ocial loafing
Decrease in individual effort as group size increases.

ʃocial Loafing Theory and Research   Among the theoretical explanations for the social loafing effect are (1) equity of effort ("Everyone else is goofing off, so why shouldn't I?"), (2) loss of personal accountability ("I'm lost in the crowd, so who cares?"), (3) motivational loss due to the sharing of rewards ("Why should I work harder than the others when everyone gets the same reward?"), and (4) coordination loss as more people perform the task ("We're getting in each other's way.").

Laboratory studies refined these theories by identifying situational factors that moderated the social loafing effect. Social loafing occurred when

- The task was perceived to be unimportant, simple, or not interesting.[84]
- Group members thought their individual output was not identifiable.[85]
- Group members expected their co-workers to loaf.[86]

But social loafing did *not* occur when group members in two laboratory studies expected to be evaluated.[87] Also, research suggests that self-reliant "individualists" are more prone to social loafing than are group-oriented "collectivists." But individualists can be made more cooperative by keeping the group small and holding each member personally accountable for results.[88]

Practical Implications   These findings demonstrate that social loafing is not an inevitable part of group effort. Management can curb this threat to group effectiveness by making sure the task is challenging and perceived as important. Additionally, it is a good idea to hold group members personally accountable for identifiable portions of the group's task. One way to do this is with the *stepladder technique,* a group decision-making process proven effective by researchers (see Table 12–6). Compared with conventional groups, stepladder groups produced significantly better decisions in the same

Table 12–6   *How to Avoid Social Loafing in Groups and Teams: The Stepladder Technique*

The stepladder technique is intended to enhance group decision making by structuring the entry of group members into a core group. Increasing or decreasing the number of group members alters the number of steps. In a four-person group, the stepladder technique has three steps. Initially, two group members (the initial core group) work together on the problem at hand. Next, a third member joins the core group and presents his or her preliminary solutions for the same problem. The entering member's presentation is followed by a three-person discussion. Finally, the fourth group member joins the core group and presents his or her preliminary solutions. This is followed by a four-person discussion, which has as its goal the rendering of a final group decision.

The stepladder technique has four requirements. First, each group member must be given the group's task and sufficient time to think about the problem before entering the core group. Second, the entering member must present his or her preliminary solutions before hearing the core group's preliminary solutions. Third, with the entry of each additional member to the core group, sufficient time to discuss the problem is necessary. Fourth, a final decision must be purposely delayed until the group has been formed in its entirety.

SOURCE: Excerpted from S G Rogelberg, J L Barnes-Farrell, and C A Lowe, "The Stepladder Technique: An Alternative Group Structure Facilitating Effective Group Decision Making," *Journal of Applied Psychology,* 77 (October 1992), p. 731. Copyright © 1992 by the American Psychological Association. Reprinted with permission.

amount of time. "Furthermore, stepladder groups' decisions surpassed the quality of their best individual members' decisions 56% of the time. In contrast, conventional groups' decisions surpassed the quality of their best members' decisions only 13% of the time."[89] The stepladder technique could be a useful tool for organizations relying on self-managed or total quality management (TQM) teams.

Summary of Key Concepts

1. *Identify the four sociological criteria of a group, and explain the role of equity in the Workplace Social Exchange Network (WSEN) model.* Sociologically, a *group* is defined as two or more freely interacting individuals who share collective norms and goals and have a common identity. The WSEN model identifies three levels of social exchange: employee–organization, employee–supervisor, and employee–team. Individuals judge each type of social exchange in terms of perceived equity or fairness. The greater the perceived fairness, the more loyal, motivated, and hard-working the individual will be. Lack of perceived fairness is demotivating.

2. *Describe the five stages in Tuckman's theory of group development, and discuss the threat of group decay.* The five stages in Tuckman's theory are *forming* (the group comes together), *storming* (members test the limits and each other), *norming* (questions about authority and power are resolved as the group becomes more cohesive), *performing* (effective communication and cooperation help the group get things done), and *adjourning* (group members go their own way). According to recent research, group decay occurs when a work group achieves the "performing" stage and then shifts into reverse. Group decay occurs through *de-norming* (erosion of standards), *de-storming* (growing discontent and loss of cohesiveness), and *de-forming* (fragmentation and break-up of the group).

3. *Distinguish between role conflict and role ambiguity.* Organizational *roles* are sets of behaviors persons expect of occupants of a position. One may experience role overload (too much to do in too little time), role conflict (conflicting role expectations), or role ambiguity (unclear role expectations).

4. *Contrast roles and norms, and specify four reasons norms are enforced in organizations.* While roles are specific to the person's position, norms are shared attitudes that differentiate appropriate from inappropriate behavior in a variety of situations. Norms evolve informally and are enforced because they help the group or organization survive, clarify behavioral expectations, help people avoid embarrassing situations, and clarify the group's or organization's central values.

5. *Distinguish between task and maintenance functions in groups.* Members of formal groups need to perform both task (goal-oriented) and maintenance (relationship-oriented) roles if anything is to be accomplished.

6. *Summarize the practical contingency management implications for group size.* Laboratory simulation studies suggest decision-making groups should be limited to five or fewer members. Larger groups are appropriate when creativity, participation, or socialization are the main objectives. If majority votes are to be taken, odd-numbered groups are recommended to avoid deadlocks.

7. *Discuss why managers need to carefully handle mixed-gender task groups.* Women face special group dynamics challenges in mixed-gender task groups. Steps need to be taken to make sure increased sexualization of work environments does not erode into illegal sexual harassment.

8. *Describe groupthink, and identify at least four of its symptoms.* Groupthink plagues cohesive in-groups that shortchange moral judgment while putting too much emphasis on unanimity. Symptoms of groupthink include invulnerability, inherent morality, rationalization, stereotyped views of opposition, self-censorship, illusion of unanimity, peer pressure, and mindguards. Critical evaluators, outside expertise, and devil's advocates are among the preventive measures recommended by Irving Janis, who coined the term *groupthink*.

9. *Define social loafing, and explain how managers can prevent it.* Social loafing involves the tendency for individual effort to decrease as group size increases. This problem can be contained if the task is challenging and important, individuals are held accountable for results and group members expect everyone to work hard. The stepladder technique, a structured approach to group decision making, can reduce social loafing by increasing personal effort and accountability.

Discussion Questions

1. Which of the following would qualify as a sociological group? A crowd watching a baseball game? One of the baseball teams? Explain.

2. What is your opinion about employees being friends with their co-workers (overlapping formal and informal groups)?

3. What is your personal experience with groups that failed to achieve stage 4 of group development? At which stage did they stall? Why? Have you observed group decay? Explain.

4. Considering your current lifestyle, how many different roles are you playing? What sorts of role conflict and role ambiguity are you experiencing?

5. What norms do college students usually enforce in class? How are they enforced?

6. Which roles do you prefer to play in work groups: task or maintenance? How could you do a better job in this regard?

7. How would you respond to a manager who made the following statement? "When it comes to the size of work groups, the bigger the better."

8. Are women typically at a disadvantage in mixed-gender work groups? Give your rationale.

9. Have you ever been a victim of either the Asch effect or groupthink? Explain the circumstances.

10. Have you observed any social loafing recently? What were the circumstances and what could be done to correct the problem?

Internet Exercise

www.queendom.com
www.de.psu.edu/harass/intro.htm

Social skills are a central theme in this chapter, as well as in Chapters 13 through 17. Sexual harassment, in mixed-gender work groups, is a related topic of great importance today. The purpose of this exercise is to assess your basic social and communication skills and build your understanding of sexual harassment.

Free Self-Assessment Questionnaire for Social Skills

Managers, who are responsible for getting things accomplished with and through others, simply cannot be effective if they are unable to interact skillfully in social settings. As with any skill development program, you need to know *where you are* before constructing a learning agenda for *where you want to be.* Go to the Internet home page for Body-Mind Queendom (**www.queendom.com**), and select the category "Tests & Profiles." (*Note:* Our use of this site is for instructional purposes only and does not constitute an endorsement of any products that may or may not suit your needs. There is no obligation to buy anything.) Next, choose "Relationships" and select the "Communication Skills Test." Read the brief instructions, complete all 34 items, and click on the "score" button for automatic scoring. It is possible, if you choose, to print a personal copy of your completed questionnaire and results.

If you have time, some of the other relationships tests are interesting and fun. We recommend trying the follow-

ing ones: Arguing Style Test; Assertiveness Test; Conflict Management Test; and Emotional IQ Test.

Free Tutorial about Sexual Harassment

As discussed in this chapter, sexual harassment can be a problem when women and men work together in groups. Professor Nancy Wyatt, from the Pennsylvania State University's Delaware County campus, has compiled a comprehensive and instructive Internet site on the topic of sexual harassment (**www.de.psu.edu/harass/intro.htm**). Explore this resource for insights.

Questions

1. Possible scores on the self-assessment questionnaire range from 0 to 100. How did you score? Are you pleasantly (or unpleasantly) surprised by your score?

2. What is your strongest social/communication skill?

3. Reviewing the questionnaire item by item, can you find obvious weak spots in your social/communication skills? For instance, are you a poor listener? Do you interrupt too often? Do you need to be more aware of others, both verbally and nonverbally? Do you have a hard time tuning into others' feelings or expressing your own feelings? How do you handle disagreement?

4. Based on the results of this questionnaire, what is your learning agenda for improving your social and

communication skills. (*Note:* You will find lots of good ideas and practical tips in Chapters 13 through 17.)

5. What insights did you pick up from the sexual harassment website? What is your personal

experience with sexual harassment in the workplace? Is the problem getting better or worse, in your estimation? What constructive steps need to be taken by today's managers and employees?

OB in Action Case Study

www.hq.nasa.gov

A 10-Year Retrospective of the Challenger Space Shuttle Disaster: Was It Groupthink?

A Fateful Decision

The debate over whether to launch on January 28, 1986, unfolded as follows, according to the report of the Presidential Commission on the Space Shuttle Challenger Accident:

Shortly after 1 PM ET on January 27, NASA's [the National Aeronautic and Space Administration's] booster rocket manager in Cape Canaveral, Larry Wear, asks officials of rocket maker Morton Thiokol in Utah whether cold weather on the 28th would present a problem for launch.

By 2 PM, NASA's top managers are discussing how temperatures in the 30s at the launch pad might affect the shuttle's performance. In Utah, an hour later, Thiokol engineer Roger Boisjoly learns of the forecast for the first time.

By late afternoon, midlevel NASA managers at the Cape are on the phone with Thiokol managers, who point out that the booster's rubbery O-rings, which seal in hot gases, might be affected by cold.

That concern brings in officials from NASA's Marshall Space Flight Center in Huntsville, Alabama, which buys the rockets from Thiokol and readies them for launch.

Marshall managers decide that a three-way telephone conference call is needed, linking NASA and Thiokol engineers and managers in Alabama, Florida, and Utah.

The first conference call begins about 5:45 PM, and Thiokol tells NASA it believes launch should be delayed until noon or afternoon, when the weather turns warmer. It is decided a second conference call would be needed later that evening.

Marshall deputy project manager Judson Lovingood tells shuttle projects manager Stan Reinartz at the Cape that if Thiokol persists, NASA should not launch. Top NASA managers at Marshall are told of Thiokol's concern.

At 8:45 PM, the second conference call begins, involving 34 engineers and managers from NASA and Thiokol at the three sites.

Thiokol engineers Boisjoly and Arnie Thompson present charts showing a history of leaking O-ring joints from tests and previous flights.

The data show that the O-rings perform worse at lower temperatures and that the worst leak of hot gases came in

January 1985, when a shuttle launched with the temperature at 53 degrees. Thiokol managers recommend not flying Challenger at temperatures colder than that.

NASA's George Hardy says he's "appalled" at Thiokol's recommendation. Larry Mulloy, Marshall's booster rocket manager, complains that Thiokol is setting down new launch criteria and exclaims, "My God, Thiokol, when do you want me to launch, next April?"

Thiokol Vice President Joe Kilminster asks for five minutes to talk in private. The debate continues for 30 minutes. Boisjoly, Thompson, engineer Bob Ebeling, and others are overruled by Thiokol management, who decide to approve the launch.

At 11 PM, Kilminster tells NASA that Thiokol has changed its mind: Temperature is still a concern but the data are inconclusive. He recommends launch.

Thiokol's concerns that cold weather could hurt the booster joints are not passed up NASA's chain of command beyond officials at the Marshall Space Flight Center.

Challenger is launched at 11:38 AM January 28 in a temperature of 36 degrees.[90]

Shortly after launch on January 28, 1986, Challenger was engulfed in a fiery explosion that led to the deaths of six astronauts and teacher-in-space Christa McAuliffe. As a shocked world watched great billows of smoke trail over the Atlantic, it was clear to those involved that launching Challenger in 36-degree weather was a catastrophic decision.[91]

Ten Years Later

Two who argued the longest and loudest against launch were Thiokol engineers Roger Boisjoly and Arnie Thompson. But their lives took widely differing paths after the accident.

Boisjoly remembers the prelaunch debate this way: "When NASA created the pressure, they all buckled."

He became nationally known as the primary whistle-blower. Thiokol removed Boisjoly from the investigation team and sent him home after he testified before a presidential commission that the company ignored evidence that the booster rocket seals would fail in cold weather.

Boisjoly, 57, says he was blackballed by the industry and run out of town by Thiokol.

For a time, he sought psychiatric help. "It just became unbearable to function," says Boisjoly, who now lives with his wife and daughter in a small mountain town in Utah. He spoke on condition that the town not be named because he fears for his family's safety.

Boisjoly is convinced he is a marked man because some former co-workers believe his testimony contributed to resulting layoffs at Thiokol.

After the accident, he says, drivers would try to run him off the road when he was out on a walk. He got threatening phone calls. Someone tried to break into his house.

"It became so uncomfortable for me that I went out and bought a .38 revolver," he says.

Now retired, Boisjoly earns $1,500 for speeches to universities and business groups. He also runs his own engineering company and teaches Sunday school in the Mormon church, something he says he never would have dreamed of doing before the accident.

Says Thompson, the other voice against launch: "There were the two of us that didn't want to fly and we were defeated. A lot of my top managers were not happy with me."

Yet, with longer ties to Thiokol than Boisjoly, Thompson was promoted to manager and stayed on through the shuttle's redesign.

He retired three years ago at the end of a 25-year-career. Now 66, he spends his time building a small office building in Brigham City, Utah.

"My attitude was, I wanted to stay on and redesign the bird and get back into the air," says Thompson. "I had a personal goal to get flying again." . . .

Thiokol's Bob Ebeling was so sure that Challenger was doomed, he asked his daughter, Leslie, then 33, to his office to watch "a super colossal disaster" unfold on live TV.

When it exploded, "I was in the middle of a prayer for the Lord to do his will and let all these things come to a happy ending and not let this happen," says Ebeling, who managed the rocket ignition system for Thiokol. "We did our level best but it wasn't good enough."

The fact that he foresaw disaster and could not stop it has tortured him since.

Ebeling, 69, says that within a week of the accident he became impotent and suffered high stress and constant headaches, problems he still has today. After 40 years of engineering experience, Thiokol "put me out to pasture on a medical" retirement, he says.

Ebeling still feels "the decision to recommend a launch was pre-ordained by others, by NASA leaning on our upper management. The deck was stacked."

One of those who overruled Ebeling and the others was Jerry Mason, the senior Thiokol manager on the conference call. He took an early retirement from Thiokol five months after the disaster, ending a 25-year career in aerospace.

"I was basically responsible for the operation the day it happened," says Mason, 69. "It was important to the company to put that behind them and get going on the recovery and it would be hard to do that with me sitting there. So I left."

In Mason's case, that meant going abruptly from corporate chieftain to unpaid volunteer. He helped set up a local economic development board and now chairs the Utah Wildlife Federation.

"I had a pretty successful career, and would liked to have gone out with the feeling that I really had done very well all the time instead of having to go out feeling I'd made a mistake at the end."

For Judson Lovingood, the loss was more personal.

Formerly one of NASA's deputy managers for the shuttle project, he wonders still if Challenger contributed to the breakup of his marriage.

"I think (Challenger) had an effect on my personal life," says Lovingood, "a long-term effect."

After the accident, he went to work for Thiokol in Huntsville and retired as director of engineering in 1993. Now remarried, he spends his time puttering in the yard of his Gurley, Alabama, home.

"Sometimes when I think about the seven people (aboard the shuttle), it's pretty painful," says Lovingood.

Besides McAuliffe, on board Challenger were commander Dick Scobee, pilot Mike Smith, and astronauts Ron McNair, Ellison Onizuka, Judy Resnik, and Greg Jarvis.

Their families settled with the government and Thiokol for more than $1.5 billion. Still, "I think people should hold us collectively responsible as a group," Lovingood says. "Every person in that meeting the night before the launch shared in the blame." . . .

Investigations of the Challenger explosion placed much of the blame on NASA's George Hardy, a senior engineering manager.

By saying he was "appalled" by Thiokol's fears of flying in cold weather, critics charged, Hardy pressured Thiokol into approving the launch.

But Hardy refuses to shoulder the blame. "If Thiokol had stuck to their position, there wasn't any way we were going to launch," he says.

Hardy left NASA four months after the accident. Now 65, he runs a small aerospace consulting company in Athens, Alabama.

Whatever else the last decade brought, many of the recollections return to that pressure-packed conference call on the eve of launch.

Questions for Discussion

1. Which task and maintenance roles in Table 12–4 should have been performed or performed better? By whom?

2. Using Figure 12–6 as a guide, which *symptoms* of groupthink are evident in this case?

3. Using Figure 12–6 as a guide, which *decision-making defects* can you identify in this case?

4. Do you think groupthink was a major contributor to the Challenger disaster? Explain.

5. All things considered, who was most to blame for the catastrophic decision to launch? Why?

Personal Awareness and Growth Exercise

Is This a Mature Work Group or Team?

Objectives

1. To increase your knowledge of group processes and dynamics.

2. To give you a tool for assessing the maturity of a work group or task team as well as a diagnostic tool for pinpointing group problems.

3. To help you become a more effective group leader or contributor.

Introduction

Group action is so common today that many of us take it for granted. But are the groups and teams to which we con-tribute much of our valuable time mature and hence more likely to be effective? Or do they waste our time? How can they be improved? We can and should become tough critical evaluators of group processes.

Instructions

Think of a work group or task team with which you are very familiar (preferably one you worked with in the past or are currently working with). Rate the group's maturity on each of the 20 dimensions.[92] Then add your circled responses to get your total group maturity score. The higher the score, the greater the group's maturity.

	Very False (or Never)				Very True (or Always)
1. Members are clear about group goals.	1	2	3	4	5
2. Members agree with the group's goals.	1	2	3	4	5
3. Members are clear about their roles.	1	2	3	4	5
4. Members accept their roles and status.	1	2	3	4	5
5. Role assignments match member abilities.	1	2	3	4	5
6. The leadership style matches the group's developmental level.	1	2	3	4	5
7. The group has an open communication structure in which all members participate.	1	2	3	4	5
8. The group gets, gives, and uses feedback about its effectiveness and productivity.	1	2	3	4	5
9. The group spends time planning how it will solve problems and make decisions.	1	2	3	4	5
10. Voluntary conformity is high.	1	2	3	4	5
11. The group norms encourage high performance and quality.	1	2	3	4	5
12. The group expects to be successful.	1	2	3	4	5
13. The group pays attention to the details of its work.	1	2	3	4	5
14. The group accepts coalition and subgroup formation.	1	2	3	4	5
15. Subgroups are integrated into the group as a whole.	1	2	3	4	5
16. The group is highly cohesive.	1	2	3	4	5
17. Interpersonal attraction among members is high.	1	2	3	4	5
18. Members are cooperative.	1	2	3	4	5
19. Periods of conflict are frequent but brief.	1	2	3	4	5
20. The group has effective conflict-management strategies.	1	2	3	4	5

Total score = _____

Arbitrary Norms

20–39   "When in doubt, run in circles, scream and shout!"
40–59   A long way to go
60–79   On the right track
80–100   Ready for group dynamics graduate school

Questions for Discussion

1. Does your evaluation help explain why the group or team was successful or not? Explain.

2. Was (or is) there anything *you* could have done (or can do) to increase the maturity of this group? Explain.

3. How will this evaluation instrument help you be a more effective group member or leader in the future?

Group Exercise

A Committee Decision

Objectives

1. To give you firsthand experience with work group dynamics through a role-playing exercise.[93]

2. To develop your ability to evaluate group effectiveness.

Introduction

Please read the following case before going on.

THE JOHNNY ROCCO CASE

Johnny has a grim personal background. He is the third child in a family of seven. He has not seen his father for several years, and his recollection is that his father used to come home drunk and beat up every member of the family; everyone ran when his father came staggering home.

His mother, according to Johnny, wasn't much better. She was irritable and unhappy, and she always predicted that Johnny would come to no good end. Yet she worked when her health allowed her to do so in order to keep the family in food and clothing. She always decried the fact that she was not able to be the kind of mother she would like to be.

Johnny quit school in the seventh grade. He had great difficulty conforming to the school routine—he misbehaved often, was truant frequently, and fought with schoolmates. On several occasions he was picked up by the police and, along with members of his group, questioned during several investigations into cases of both petty and grand larceny. The police regarded him as "probably a bad one."

The juvenile officer of the court saw in Johnny some good qualities that no one else seemed to sense. Mr O'Brien took it on himself to act as a "big brother" to Johnny. He had several long conversations with Johnny,

during which he managed to penetrate to some degree Johnny's defensive shell. He represented to Johnny the first semblance of personal interest in his life. Through Mr O'Brien's efforts, Johnny returned to school and obtained a high school diploma. Afterwards, Mr O'Brien helped him obtain a job.

Now 20, Johnny is a stockroom clerk in one of the laboratories where you are employed. On the whole Johnny's performance has been acceptable, but there have been glaring exceptions. One involved a clear act of insubordination on a fairly unimportant matter. In another, Johnny was accused, on circumstantial grounds, of destroying some expensive equipment. Though the investigation is still open, it now appears the destruction was accidental.

Johnny's supervisor wants to keep him on for at least a trial period, but he wants "outside" advice as to the best way of helping Johnny grow into greater responsibility. Of course, much depends on how Johnny behaves in the next few months. Naturally, his supervisor must follow personnel policies that are accepted in the company as a whole. It is important to note that Johnny is not an attractive young man. He is rather weak and sickly, and he shows unmistakable signs of long years of social deprivation.

A committee is formed to decide the fate of Johnny Rocco. The chairperson of the meeting is Johnny's supervisor and should begin by assigning roles to the group members. These roles [shop steward (representing the union), head of production, Johnny's co-worker, director of personnel, and social worker who helped Johnny in the past] represent points of view the chairperson believes should be included in this meeting. (Johnny is not to be included.) Two observers should also be assigned. Thus, each group will have eight members.

Instructions

After roles have been assigned, each role player should complete the personal preference part of the work sheet, ranking from 1 to 11 the alternatives according to their appropriateness from the vantage point of his or her role.

Once the individual preferences have been determined, the chairperson should call the meeting to order. The following rules govern the meeting: (1) The group must reach a consensus ranking of the alternatives; (2) the group cannot use a statistical aggregation, or majority vote, decision-making process; (3) members should stay "in character" throughout the discussion. Treat this as a committee meeting consisting of members with different backgrounds, orientation, and interests who share a problem.

After the group has completed the assignment, the observers should conduct a discussion of the group process, using the Group Effectiveness Questions here as a guide. Group members should not look at these questions until after the group task has been completed.

Group Effectiveness Questions

A. Referring to Table 12–4, what task roles were performed? By whom?

B. What maintenance roles were performed? By whom?

C. Were any important task or maintenance roles ignored? Which?

D. Was there any evidence of the Asch effect, groupthink, or social loafing? Explain.

Questions for Discussion

1. Did your committee do a good job? Explain.

2. What, if anything, should have been done differently?

3. How much similarity in rankings is there among the different groups in your class? What group dynamics apparently were responsible for any variations in rankings?

Worksheet

Personal Preference	Group Discussion	
_____	_____	Warn Johnny that at the next sign of trouble he will be fired.
_____	_____	Do nothing, as it is unclear if Johnny did anything wrong.
_____	_____	Create strict controls (dos and don'ts) for Johnny with immediate strong punishment for any misbehavior.
_____	_____	Give Johnny a great deal of warmth and personal attention and affection (overlooking his present behavior) so he can learn to depend on others.
_____	_____	Fire him. It's not worth the time and effort spent for such a low-level position.
_____	_____	Talk over the problem with Johnny in an understanding way so he can learn to ask others for help in solving his problems.
_____	_____	Give Johnny a well-structured schedule of daily activities with immediate and unpleasant consequences for not adhering to the schedule.
_____	_____	Do nothing now, but watch him carefully and provide immediate punishment for any future behavior.
_____	_____	Treat Johnny the same as everyone else, but provide an orderly routine so he can learn to stand on his own two feet.
_____	_____	Call Johnny in and logically discuss the problem with him and ask what you can do to help him.
_____	_____	Do nothing now, but watch him so you can reward him the next time he does something good.

Ethical Dilemma

Can "Social Norming" Make the Grade on College Campuses?

Situation

You're the dean of students at a major university and you've been getting a lot of pressure from parents and state legislators lately about curbing out-of-control alcohol and tobacco use among students. At a meeting today, a colleague gave you this newspaper article to read.

Nine out of every 10 college students have never damaged property because they were drunk or high. Three out of four have never blown an exam or school project because of drugs or alcohol. Ninety-nine percent of students who drink do not have unwanted sex.

Most kids don't go out and get trashed every night.

Each year, more students choose to abstain from alcohol. Fewer choose to smoke and do drugs.

Death by alcohol-related accidents or suicide is rare.

The widespread impression that the norm for today's young people is drunken debauchery simply isn't true. Most kids are OK. It's the best-kept secret on college campuses, and a growing number of experts believe that keeping all this good news quiet is doing far more harm than good.

Parents are often the most unaware, and they fear the worst when they send kids off to college, says Michael Haines, a substance-abuse expert at Northern Illinois University in DeKalb. Students today take very seriously the risks of drinking, he says, "yet parents are being sold a bill of goods, with kids portrayed in number-crunching stories as drunken, reckless, careless boozers."

Haines is the father of a grassroots movement among prevention educators called "social norming," and it's gaining fast favor on college campuses. The premise is quite simple, but completely at odds with today's accepted practice of scaring teens away from risky behaviors.

Social norming operates on this notion: If the general impression is that most kids don't drink alcohol, then those who *do* drink will drink less, and fewer will start drinking in the first place. The key is to not overreport the incidences of dangerous drinking that occur, and to broadly promote the general good health of students so that it is perceived as normal not to drink.

At least 30 college campuses nationwide, including the universities of Arizona, North Carolina, Oregon, and Missouri, Rutgers University, and 23 campuses of the California State University system, have joined the social norming bandwagon to curb drinking among students. Dartmouth, home of the *Animal House* legend, is currently in the market to hire an educator with social norming experience.

The philosophy has begun trickling down to high schools and middle schools and has been expanded to target other risky behaviors, including smoking. . . .

Campuses in general have seen little change in student drinking patterns, despite comprehensive and consistent antidrinking programs, [student health and safety expert Drew] Hunter says. The social norming effort is showing results "by promoting health, not death and destruction." . . .

The social norming program works by simply reframing the same data that traditionally highlights the minority of students who are boozing up heavily and presenting it with a focus on the majority who aren't. The statistics most often used on a national level are those from the ongoing Harvard School of Public Health College Alcohol Study, National College Health Assessment and the Core Alcohol and Drug Survey, all of which look at college drinking patterns. . . .

Campuses develop their own norming programs by polling students and feeding back to them—in the form of posters, pencils, Frisbees, and bumper stickers—data about the majority who aren't drinking, smoking, or engaging in other risky behavior.

Funny thing, though, is that most students are surprised, since most students—like most parents—think most kids are drinking and smoking. That simply fuels the problem, says Lydia Gerzel Short, who is behind the nation's first social norming program for high school students. Her three-year program in two DeKalb County high schools has seen drinking and smoking drop significantly faster than the national trends. . . .

"Misperceptions create a silent majority," says Jan Gascoigne, director of health promotions with Bacchus & Gamma, which last fall launched a six-campus project with the Centers for Disease Control and Prevention to study how social norming might curb college smoking. When the University of Washington in Seattle polled students in 1999, it found that students believed nearly 95% of the student body smoked. In reality, about one-third were smokers.

"Social norming breaks down that perception," says Gascoigne. "If I'm a student, and I think 95% of everybody smokes, there's a perception that that's what people do here. Potentially that becomes my behavior because I want to fit in."

The drop in the rate of student smoking at the University of Wisconsin–Oshkosh after last year's social-norm marketing campaign was so astonishing, officials are reluctant to release the data nationally because some population quirk may have skewed the numbers. The results: a 29% drop in student smoking, or one out of three smokers quit. . . .

Like many colleges and universities that try social norming, Wisconsin–Oshkosh turned to it as a "last resort" because nothing else was making a dent in student drinking and smoking, [psychologist Mike] Altekruse says. "We well-meaning health educators . . . just keep giving them knowledge that it's unhealthy, and we hope they'll quit drinking. But they don't."[94]

How Should You Respond to This New Information about Social Norming? (Discuss the ethical implications for your answer.)

1. Read the article at home after work while relaxing with a glass of wine and a cigarette.

2. Deny that your university has any problems with alcohol or tobacco abuse. Toss the article.

3. Dismiss the idea as just another fad that, at best, might work for a semester and then become irrelevant.

4. Arrange a fact-finding meeting with one of your school's sociology professors who has published research articles on social norming. (What then?)

5. Decide to implement a social norming program on your campus. (How would you proceed?)

6. Invent other options. Discuss.

For an interpretation of this situation, visit our Web site, **www.mhhe.com/kreitner.**

Chapter Thirteen

Teams and Teamwork for the 21st Century

Learning Objectives

When you finish studying the material in this chapter, you should be able to:

1   Explain how a work group becomes a team, and identify and describe the four types of work teams.

2   Explain the ecological model of work team effectiveness.

3   Discuss why teams fail.

4   Identify the five essential KSAs (knowledge, skills, and abilities) for team players.

5   List at least three things managers can do to build trust.

6   Distinguish two types of group cohesiveness, and summarize cohesiveness research findings.

7   Define quality circles, virtual teams, and self-managed teams.

8   Discuss what must be done to set the stage for self-managed teams.

9   Describe high-performance teams.

Most people who consider using virtual-collaboration tools assume that, even at their best, they are a second-best solution. If companies had unlimited travel budgets and if teams had endless amounts of time, then face-to-face meetings would be the best way to work, right? Not so fast. A team of product developers at Texas Instruments has discovered that virtual meetings work better than their face-to-face alternative.

A case in point: TI's efforts to develop the next generation of wireless communications devices. The company's Dallas-based mobility and collaboration team recently delivered a crucial strategy presentation to employees and business partners in Europe, Japan, and the United States. The format was pretty standard: 45 minutes of PowerPoint slides followed by an extended Q&A. Not so long ago, TI would have flown in participants from all over the globe. This time, managers conducted the meeting over WebEx, the Internet-based virtual-meeting platform. Participants followed the slides using their laptops and instant-messaged their questions and comments throughout the presentation.

The virtual meeting reduced travel costs and saved time. But over the course of the session, the team discovered that the virtual presentation was

Computer-aided meetings bring a world of information to the table.
(c) Ronnie Kaufman/Corbis

also more effective at soliciting feedback from attendees than any of the face-to-face meetings that they had conducted with international participants. "So many of our international partners are not comfortable with English," says Evan Miller, team manager. "On a conference call, or even in person, accents can be tricky—especially when you gather a group from Europe, Japan, and the United States. With WebEx's chat feature, we found that many people could type English better than they could speak it. It made everything so much smoother."

Smoother, even, for meeting participants who were already in Dallas. During the same presentation, Miller's colleague Lisa Maestas was connected via WebEx from TI's South Campus, about five miles across the traffic-choked city. Says Maestas: "I got to stay at my desk, listen in, and participate, but I could still keep an eye on my other projects."

In fact, *local* group interaction is quickly becoming one of the most valuable uses of WebEx for this TI team—even among people who are sitting in the same room. Portions of both of the company's Dallas facilities are outfitted for wireless network connectivity. So these days, when Miller, Maestas, and other local members of the mobility team gather for a meeting, they bring their laptops, make their wireless connections, power up WebEx, and take a personal view of the document under discussion. "It's usually so hard to crowd around a screen to see what people are talking about," says Maestas. "With four laptops, everyone can see the screen. We can share control of the screen and annotate as we go along. At the end of the meeting, everyone has the same version of what we worked on. There's no more confusion."[1]

For Discussion

What are the pros and cons of virtual meetings, where people interact electronically rather than face to face?

eams and *teamwork* are popular terms in management circles these days. Cynics might dismiss teamwork as just another management fad or quick-fix gimmick. But a closer look reveals a more profound and durable trend. People are teaming up in new and different ways. Modern computer and telecommunications technologies, as illustrated at Texas Instruments, have made it possible for people to attend globe-spanning meetings without leaving their desks. The team approach to managing organizations is having diverse and substantial impacts on organizations and individuals.[2] Teams promise to be a cornerstone of progressive management for the foreseeable future. According to management expert Peter Drucker, tomorrow's organizations will be flatter, information based, and organized around teams.[3] This means virtually all employees will need to polish their team skills. Southwest Airlines, a company that credits a strong team spirit for its success, puts team skills above all else. Case in point:

> Southwest rejected a top pilot from another airline who did stunt work for movie studios because he was rude to a receptionist. Southwest believes that technical skills are easier to acquire than a teamwork and service attitude.[4]

Fortunately, the trend toward teams has a receptive audience today. Both women and younger employees, according to recent studies, thrive in team-oriented organizations.[5]

Emphasis in this chapter is on tapping the full and promising potential of work groups and teams. We will (1) identify different types of work teams, (2) introduce a model of team effectiveness, (3) discuss keys to effective teamwork, such as trust, (4) explore applications of the team concept, and (5) review team-building techniques.

Work Teams: Types, Effectiveness, and Stumbling Blocks

Jon R Katzenbach and Douglas K Smith, management consultants at McKinsey & Company, say it is a mistake to use the terms *group* and *team* interchangeably. After studying many different kinds of teams—from athletic to corporate to military—they concluded that successful teams tend to take on a life of their own. Katzenbach and Smith define a **team** as "a small number of people with complementary skills who are committed to a common purpose, performance goals, and approach for which they hold themselves mutually accountable."[6] Relative to Tuckman's theory of group development in Chapter 12— forming, storming, norming, performing, and adjourning—teams are task groups that have matured to the *performing* stage (but not slipped into decay). Because of conflicts over power and authority and unstable interpersonal relations, many work groups never qualify as a real team.[7] Katzenbach and Smith clarified the distinction this way: "The essence of a team is common commitment. Without it, groups perform as individuals; with it, they become a powerful unit of collective performance."[8] (See Table 13–1.)

When Katzenbach and Smith refer to "a small number of people" in their definition, they mean between 2 and 25 team members. They found effective teams to typically have fewer than 10 members. This conclusion was echoed in a survey of 400 workplace team members in the United States and Canada: "The average North American team consists of 10 members. Eight is the most common size."[9]

Team

Small group with complementary skills who hold themselves mutually accountable for common purpose, goals, and approach.

A General Typology of Work Teams

Work teams are created for various purposes and thus face different challenges. Managers can deal more effectively with those challenges when they understand how teams differ. A helpful way of sorting things out is to consider a typology of work teams developed by Eric Sundstrom and his colleagues.[10] Four general types of work teams listed in Table 13–2 are (1) advice, (2) production, (3) project, and (4) action. Each of these labels identifies a basic *purpose*. For instance, advice teams generally make recommendations for managerial decisions. Less commonly do they actually make final decisions. In contrast, production and action teams carry out management's decisions.

Table 13–1   *The Evolution of a Team*

A work group becomes a team when
1. *Leadership* becomes a shared activity.
2. *Accountability* shifts from strictly individual to both individual and collective.
3. The group develops its own *purpose* or mission.
4. *Problem solving* becomes a way of life, not a part-time activity.
5. *Effectiveness* is measured by the group's collective outcomes and products.

SOURCE: Condensed and adapted from J R Katzenbach and D K Smith, *The Wisdom of Teams: Creating the High-Performance Organization* (New York: HarperBusiness, 1999), p. 214.

Table 13–2   *Four General Types of Work Teams and Their Outputs*

Types and Examples	Degree of Technical Specialization	Degree of Coordination with Other Work Units	Work Cycles	Typical Outputs
Advice Committees Review panels, boards Quality circles Employee involvement groups Advisory councils	Low	Low	Work cycles can be brief or long; one cycle can be team life span.	Decisions Selections Suggestions Proposals Recommendations
Production Assembly teams Manufacturing crews Mining teams Flight attendant crews Data processing groups Maintenance crews	Low	High	Work cycles typically repeated or continuous process; cycles often briefer than team life span.	Food, chemicals Components Assemblies Retail sales Customer service Equipment repairs
Project Research groups Planning teams Architect teams Engineering teams Development teams Task forces	High	Low (for traditional units) or High (for cross-functional units)	Work cycles typically differ for each new project; one cycle can be team life span.	Plans, designs Investigations Presentations Prototypes Reports, findings
Action Sports teams Entertainment groups Expeditions Negotiating teams Surgery teams Cockpit crews Military platoons and squads Police and fire teams	High	High	Brief performance events, often repeated under new conditions, requiring extended training or preparation.	Combat missions Expeditions Contracts, lawsuits Concerts Surgical operations Competitive events Disaster assistance

SOURCE: Excerpted and adapted from E Sundstrom, K P De Meuse, and D Futrell, "Work Teams," *American Psychologist,* February 1990, p. 125.

Four key variables in Table 13–2 deal with technical specialization, coordination, work cycles, and outputs. Technical specialization is low when the team draws upon members' general experience and problem-solving ability. It is high when team members are required to apply technical skills acquired through higher education or extensive training. The degree of coordination with other work units is determined by the team's relative independence (low coordination) or interdependence (high coordination). Work cycles are the amount of time teams need to discharge their missions. The various outputs listed in Table 13–2 are intended to illustrate real-life impacts. A closer look at each type of work team is in order.[11]

Advice Teams   As their name implies, advice teams are created to broaden the information base for managerial decisions. Quality circles, discussed later, are a prime example because they facilitate suggestions for quality improvement from volunteer production or service workers. Advice teams tend to have a low degree of technical specialization. Coordination also is low because advice teams work pretty much on their own. Ad hoc committees (e.g., the annual picnic committee) have shorter life cycles than standing committees (e.g., the grievance committee).

Production Teams   This second type of team is responsible for performing day-to-day operations. Minimal training for routine tasks accounts for the low degree of technical specialization. But coordination typically is high because work flows from one team to another. For example, railroad maintenance crews require fresh information about needed repairs from train crews, and the train crews, in turn, need to know exactly where maintenance crews are working.

Project Teams   Projects require creative problem solving, often involving the application of specialized knowledge. For example, Boeing's 777 jumbo jet was designed by project teams consisting of engineering, manufacturing, marketing, finance, and customer service specialists. State-of-the-art computer modeling programs allowed the teams to assemble three-dimensional computer models of the new aircraft. Design and assembly problems were ironed out in project team meetings before production workers started cutting any metal for the first 777. Boeing's 777 design teams required a high degree of coordination among organizational subunits because they were cross functional.[12] A pharmaceutical research team of biochemists, on the other hand, would interact less with other work units because it is relatively self-contained. Also, project teams can be a useful tool for training and management development programs (see the International OB on page 450).

Action Teams   This last type of team is best exemplified by a baseball team. High specialization is combined with high coordination. Nine highly trained athletes play

Randy Johnson, the 6' 10" left-handed pitching ace for the Arizona Diamondbacks, enjoys a good laugh with his teammates during the ring ceremony honoring their 2001 World Series championship. Thanks to the leadership of veterans such as Johnson and Mark Grace (third from right) and great teamwork, the D-Backs exceeded everyone's expectations by winning the big prize after just four years of existence.

(c) Reuters NewMedia Inc./CORBIS

International OB

Germany's Siemens Develops Its Managers with Project Teams

A start-up company that needs entrepreneurial managers can go out and hire them as it builds its organization. By contrast, established companies like Siemens, a worldwide provider of everything from mobile phones to gas turbines, already have tens of thousands of managers around the world and have no choice but to find ways to make its old managers into new ones. So collaboration became the central goal of an in-house management development program at Siemens. The program was created for all managers in the late 1990s.

Many companies have established "active learning" curricula focused on the study of cases and other real-life problems. But we realized that changing people's behavior is less about intellectual learning than it is about blasting them loose from nearly impenetrable, self-imposed—and often company-rewarded—boundaries. We started our people off with some classroom teaching, but the bulk of the program put them in teams working on actual projects.

These "business impact projects" had to show measurable results and typically lasted about four months. It wasn't enough for a team to recommend a new marketing strategy or propose a new procedure for product development. We didn't want the end result to be a paper no one would read. Instead, we wanted people to get their hands dirty in the real work of organizational maneuvering and achievement.

Once a team settled on an opportunity to pursue, they had to recruit a "coach," usually a high-level executive in the business area that the team was focusing on. Executives were free to decline these requests; some teams had to try several times before landing their coaches....

In each case, it helped that the teams consisted of people from different product areas, functions, and geographies. But diverse teammates and their existing contact networks weren't enough; the projects wouldn't work without each team figuring out how to win support from people who had little interest in—or who even felt threatened by—the team's efforts.

In interviews after the projects ended, nearly all the participants reported a new perspective on their organizational comfort zones.

At first, they said, they had felt liberated by their status in the program—as though they were immune from risk. But in retrospect, they came to understand that the program conferred no special status on them at all; their previous hesitation toward risk-taking had been largely self-imposed. The management program had given them the unique sense of "permission" to venture that they had actually had all along.

SOURCE: Reprinted by permission of *Harvard Business Review.* From "Freeing Managers to Innovate" by M. Bellmann and R.H. Schaffer, June 2001. Copyright © 2001 by the Harvard Business School Publishing Corporation; all rights reserved.

specialized defensive positions. But good defensive play is not enough because effective hitting is necessary. Moreover, coordination between the manager, base runners, base coaches, and the bull pen needs to be precise. So it is with airline cockpit crews, firefighters, hospital surgery teams, mountain-climbing expeditions, rock music groups, labor contract negotiating teams, and police SWAT teams, among others. A unique challenge for action teams is to exhibit peak performance on demand.[13]

This four-way typology of work teams is dynamic and changing, not static. Some teams evolve from one type to another. Other teams represent a combination of types. For example, consider the work of a team at General Foods: "The company launched a line of ready-to-eat desserts by setting up a team of nine people with the freedom to operate like entrepreneurs starting their own business. The team even had to oversee construction of a factory with the technology required to manufacture their product."[14] This particular team was a combination advice-project-action team. In short, the General Foods team did everything but manufacture the end product themselves (that was done by production teams).

Figure 13–1   *An Ecological Model of Work Team Effectiveness*

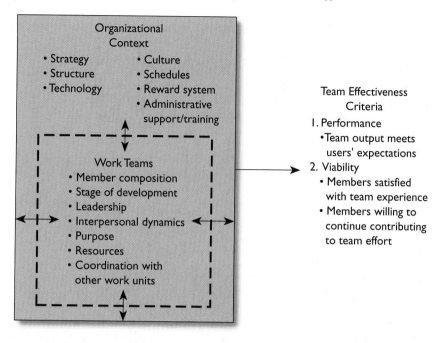

SOURCES: Adapted in part from E Sundstrom, K P DeMeuse, and D Futrell, "Work Teams," *American Psychologist*, February 1990, pp. 120–33; and J N Choi, "External Activities and Team Effectiveness: Review and Theoretical Development," *Small Group Research*, April 2002, pp. 181–208.

Work Team Effectiveness: An Ecological Model

The effectiveness of athletic teams is a straightforward matter of wins and losses. Things become more complicated, however, when the focus shifts to work teams in today's organizations.[15] Figure 13–1 lists two effectiveness criteria for work teams: performance and viability. According to Sundstrom and his colleagues: *"Performance* means acceptability of output to customers within or outside the organization who receive team products, services, information, decisions, or performance events (such as presentations or competitions)."[16] While the foregoing relates to satisfying the needs and expectations of outsiders such as clients, customers, and fans, another team-effectiveness criterion arises. Namely, **team viability,** defined as team member satisfaction and continued willingness to contribute. Are the team members better or worse off for having contributed to the team effort?[17] A work team is not truly effective if it gets the job done but self-destructs in the process or burns everyone out.

Figure 13–1 is an *ecological* model because it portrays work teams within their organizational environment. In keeping with the true meaning of the word *ecology*— the study of interactions between organisms and their environments—this model emphasizes that work teams need an organizational life-support system. Seven critical organizational context variables are listed in Figure 13–1. Work teams have a much greater chance of being effective if they are nurtured and facilitated by the organization. The team's purpose needs to be in concert with the organization's strategy.

Team viability

Team members satisfied and willing to contribute.

Table 13–3   *Characteristics of an Effective Team*

1. Clear purpose	The vision, mission, goal, or task of the team has been defined and is now accepted by everyone. There is an action plan.
2. Informality	The climate tends to be informal, comfortable, and relaxed. There are no obvious tensions or signs of boredom.
3. Participation	There is much discussion, and everyone is encouraged to participate.
4. Listening	The members use effective listening techniques such as questioning, paraphrasing, and summarizing to get out ideas.
5. Civilized disagreement	There is disagreement, but the team is comfortable with this and shows no signs of avoiding, smoothing over, or suppressing conflict.
6. Consensus decisions	For important decisions, the goal is substantial but not necessarily unanimous agreement through open discussion of everyone's ideas, avoidance of formal voting, or easy compromises.
7. Open communication	Team members feel free to express their feelings on the tasks as well as on the group's operation. There are few hidden agendas. Communication takes place outside of meetings.
8. Clear roles and work assignments	There are clear expectations about the roles played by each team member. When action is taken, clear assignments are made, accepted, and carried out. Work is fairly distributed among team members.
9. Shared leadership	While the team has a formal leader, leadership functions shift from time to time depending on the circumstances, the needs of the group, and the skills of the members. The formal leader models the appropriate behavior and helps establish positive norms.
10. External relations	The team spends time developing key outside relationships, mobilizing resources, and building credibility with important players in other parts of the organization.
11. Style diversity	The team has a broad spectrum of team-player types including members who emphasize attention to task, goal setting, focus on process, and questions about how the team is functioning.
12. Self-assessment	Periodically, the team stops to examine how well it is functioning and what may be interfering with its effectiveness.

SOURCE: G M Parker, *Team Players and Teamwork: The New Competitive Business Strategy* (San Francisco: Jossey-Bass, 1990), table 2, p. 33. Copyright © 1990 by Jossey-Bass Inc., Publishers. Reprinted by permission of John Wiley & Sons, Inc.

Similarly, team participation and autonomy require an organizational culture that values those processes. Team members also need appropriate technological tools, *reasonable* schedules, and training. Teamwork needs to be reinforced by the organizational reward system. Such is not the case when pay and bonuses are tied solely to individual output.

Regarding the internal processes of work teams, seven important factors are listed in Figure 13–1. Table 13–3 contains an expanded list of characteristics of effective teams that can be useful for evaluating task teams both in school and on the job.[18]

Why Do Work Teams Fail?

Advocates of the team approach to management paint a very optimistic and bright picture. Yet there is a dark side to teams.[19] While exact statistics are not available, they can and often do fail. Anyone contemplating the use of team structures in the workplace needs a balanced perspective of advantages and limitations. One dissenting opinion comes from Gerald A Kraines, head of a major management consulting company, who "denounces trends toward employee empowerment and work teams."[20] In an exchange with *The Wall Street Journal,* Kraines offered this unconventional view:

Q: Isn't hierarchy a dirty word these days?

A: This is the greatest disservice that business schools and the business media have perpetrated on the public. They say hierarchies stifle initiative, creativity, and job fulfillment. They say work groups should form and dissolve flexibly, and without regard to accountability.

The assumption is that employees would be so relieved to be freed from their chains of enslavement that they will act very responsibly and creatively. But they have been so discouraged, beaten, and demoralized that they essentially give up. Then the CEO says, "Poof, you're empowered." What people say, under their breath, is, "I haven't been empowered, I've been poofed."[21]

Team advocates may find these words harsh, but they remind us to reject the myth that teams can magically replace traditional authority and accountability links. If teams are to be effective, both management and team members must make a concerted effort to think and do things differently.

Common Management Mistakes with Teams

The main threats to team effectiveness, according to the center of Figure 13–2, are *unrealistic expectations* leading to *frustration.* Frustration, in turn, encourages people to abandon teams. Both managers and team members can be victimized by unrealistic expectations.[22]

On the left side of Figure 13–2 is a list of common management mistakes. These mistakes generally involve doing a poor job of creating a supportive environment for teams and teamwork. Recalling our discussion of team-based rewards in Chapter 10, reward plans that encourage individuals to compete with one another erode teamwork. As mentioned earlier, teams need a good organizational life-support system.

Problems for Team Members

The lower-right portion of Figure 13–2 lists common problems for team members. Contrary to critics' Theory X contention about employees lacking the motivation and creativity for real teamwork, it is common for teams to take on too much too quickly and to drive themselves too hard for fast results. Important group dynamics and team skills get lost in the rush for results. Consequently, team members' expectations need to be given a reality check by management and team members themselves. Also, teams need to be counseled against quitting when they run into an unanticipated obstacle. Failure is part of the learning process with teams, as it is elsewhere in life. Comprehensive training in interpersonal skills can prevent many common teamwork problems.

Identifying and Developing Good Team Players

Anyone who is familiar with wilderness hiking and camping knows the folly of heading for the wilds without proper gear and skills. One's life can depend on being able to conserve fluids, prevent hypothermia, and avoid dangerous situations. So, too, managers need to make sure teams are staffed with appropriately skilled people. Michael J Stevens and Michael A Campion developed a very useful model

Figure 13–2   *Why Work Teams Fail*

Mistakes typically made by management

- Teams cannot overcome weak strategies and poor business practices.
- Hostile environment for teams (command-and-control culture; competitive/individual reward plans; management resistance).
- Teams adopted as a fad, a quick-fix; no long-term commitment.
- Lessons from one team not transferred to others (limited experimentation with teams).
- Vague or conflicting team assignments.
- Inadequate team skills training.
- Poor staffing of teams.
- Lack of trust.

Unrealistic expectations resulting in frustration

Problems typically experienced by team members

- Team tries to do too much too soon.
- Conflict over differences in personal work styles (and/or personality conflicts).
- Too much emphasis on results, not enough on team processes and group dynamics.
- Unanticipated obstacle causes team to give up.
- Resistance to doing things differently.
- Poor interpersonal skills (aggressive rather than assertive communication, destructive conflict, win-lose negotiation).
- Poor interpersonal chemistry (loners, dominators, self-appointed experts do not fit in).
- Lack of trust.

SOURCES: Adapted from discussion in S R Rayner, "Team Traps: What They Are, How to Avoid Them," *National Productivity Review*, Summer 1996, pp. 101–15: L Holpp and R Phillips, "When Is a Team Its Own Worst Enemy?" *Training*, September 1995, pp. 71–82: B Richardson, "Why Work Teams Flop—and What Can Be Done about It," *National Productivity Review*, Winter 1994/95, pp. 9–13; and C O Longenecker and M Neubert, "Barriers and Gateways to Management Cooperation and Teamwork," *Business Horizons*, September–October 2000, pp. 37–44.

for assessing one's readiness for teamwork.[23] It lists the knowledge, skills, and abilities (KSAs) needed for both team-member and team success (see Table 13–4). Three of the KSAs are interpersonal: conflict resolution, collaborative problem solving, and communication. Two KSAs involve self-management: goal setting and performance management, and planning and task coordination. As an integrated package, these five KSAs are a template for the team players we need today. Managers in team-oriented organizations need to be mindful of these KSAs when recruiting, hiring, staffing, and training. How do you measure up? Where do you need improvement?

Table 13-4   *Good Team Players Have the Right Knowledge, Skills, and Abilities*

Interpersonal KSAs
1. *Conflict resolution KSAs.* Recognizing types and sources of conflict; encouraging desirable conflict but discouraging undesirable conflict; and employing integrative (win–win) negotiation strategies rather than distributive (win–lose) strategies.
2. *Collaborative problem-solving KSAs.* Identifying situations requiring participative group problem solving and using the proper degree of participation; and recognizing obstacles to collaborative group problem solving and implementing appropriate corrective actions.
3. *Communication KSAs.* Understanding effective communication networks and using decentralized networks where possible; recognizing open and supportive communication methods; maximizing the consistency between nonverbal and verbal messages; recognizing and interpreting the nonverbal messages of others; and engaging in and understanding the importance of small talk and ritual greetings.

Self-management KSAs
4. *Goal-setting and performance management KSAs.* Establishing specific, challenging, and accepted team goals; and monitoring, evaluating, and providing feedback on both overall team performance and individual team-member performance.
5. *Planning and task coordination KSAs.* Coordinating and synchronizing activities, information, and tasks between team members, as well as aiding the team in establishing individual task and role assignments that ensure the proper balance of workload between team members.

SOURCE: D L Miller, "Reexamining Teamwork KSAs and Team Performance," *Small Group Research,* December 2001, table 1, p. 748, as adapted from M J Stevens and M A Campion, "The Knowledge, Skill, and Ability Requirements for Teamwork: Implications for Human Resource Management," *Journal of Management,* Summer 1994, table 1, p. 505. Copyright © 1994 by Sage Publications Inc. Reprinted by permission of Sage Publications, Inc.

Effective Teamwork through Cooperation, Trust, and Cohesiveness

As competitive pressures intensify, experts say organizational success increasingly will depend on teamwork rather than individual stars. No where is this more true than in hospitals. Imagine yourself or a loved one being in this terrible situation:

> A 67-year-old woman was admitted to the hospital for treatment of cerebral aneurysms— weakened blood vessels in the brain. Doctors examined her and sent her to her room.
>
> The next day, she was wheeled into cardiology, of all places, where a doctor had threaded a catheter into her heart before someone noticed he had the wrong patient. The procedure was stopped; the patient recovered.[24]

Analysis of this case by researchers revealed the need for better communication and teamwork.

Whether in hospitals or the world of business, three components of teamwork receiving the greatest attention are cooperation, trust, and cohesiveness. Let us explore the contributions each can make to effective teamwork.

Cooperation

Individuals are said to be cooperating when their efforts are systematically *integrated* to achieve a collective objective. The greater the integration, the greater the degree of cooperation.

Want more cooperation and spontaneous teamwork in your office? Put everything on wheels. Flexible office-design modules fit the facilities to the people, rather than vise versa.

(c) Mark Richards/ PhotoEdit

Cooperation versus Competition

A widely held assumption among American managers is that "competition brings out the best in people." From an economic standpoint, business survival depends on staying ahead of the competition. But from an interpersonal standpoint, critics contend competition has been overemphasized, primarily at the expense of cooperation.[25] According to Alfie Kohn, a strong advocate of greater emphasis on cooperation in our classrooms, offices, and factories,

> My review of the evidence has convinced me that there are two ... important reasons for competition's failure. First, success often depends on sharing resources efficiently, and this is nearly impossible when people have to work against one another. Cooperation takes advantage of all the skills represented in a group as well as the mysterious process by which that group becomes more than the sum of its parts. By contrast, competition makes people suspicious and hostile toward one another and actively discourages this process. . . .
>
> Second, competition generally does not promote excellence because trying to do well and trying to beat others simply are two different things. Consider a child in class, waving his arm wildly to attract the teacher's attention, crying, "Oooh! Oooh! Pick me!" When he is finally recognized, he seems befuddled. "Um, what was the question again?" he finally asks. His mind is focused on beating his classmates, not on the subject matter.[26]

Research Support for Cooperation

After conducting a meta-analysis of 122 studies encompassing a wide variety of subjects and settings, one team of researchers concluded that

1. Cooperation is superior to competition in promoting achievement and productivity.
2. Cooperation is superior to individualistic efforts in promoting achievement and productivity.
3. Cooperation without intergroup competition promotes higher achievement and productivity than cooperation with intergroup competition.[27]

Given the size and diversity of the research base, these findings strongly endorse cooperation in modern organizations. Cooperation can be encouraged by reward systems that reinforce teamwork, along with individual achievement.

Interestingly, cooperation can be encouraged by quite literally tearing down walls, or not building them in the first place. A recent study of 229 managers and professionals employed by eight small businesses proved insightful:

> The researchers looked at the effects of private offices, shared private offices, cubicles, and team-oriented open offices on productivity, and found to their initial surprise that the small team, open-office configuration (desks scattered about in a small area with no partitions) to be significantly correlated with superior performance. In addition, they found that the open-office configuration was particularly favored by the youngest employees, who believe open offices provide them greater access to colleagues and the opportunity to learn from their more seasoned senior compatriots.[28]

There is a movement among architects and urban planners to design and build structures that encourage spontaneous interaction, cooperation, and teamwork.[29] Sorry about that private corner office you might have had in mind!

A study involving 84 male US Air Force trainees uncovered an encouraging link between cooperation and favorable race relations. After observing the subjects interact in three-man teams during a management game, the researchers concluded: "[Helpful] teammates, both black and white, attract greater respect and liking than do teammates who have not helped. This is particularly true when the helping occurs voluntarily."[30] These findings suggest that managers can enhance equal employment opportunity and diversity programs by encouraging *voluntary* helping behavior in interracial work teams. Accordingly, it is reasonable to conclude that voluntary helping behavior could build cooperation in mixed-gender teams and groups as well.

Another study involving 72 health care professionals in a US Veterans Affairs Medical Center found a negative correlation between cooperation and team size. In other words, cooperation diminished as the health care team became larger.[31] Managers thus need to restrict the size of work teams if they desire to facilitate cooperation.

Trust

These have not been good times for trust in the corporate world. Years of mergers, downsizings, layoffs, bloated executive bonuses, corporate scandals, and broken promises have left many employees justly cynical about trusting management.[32] In fact, a recent *USA Today*/CNN/Gallup poll found "only 10% of adults surveyed think corporations can be trusted a great deal to look out for the interests of their employees."[33] About 13% chose the response category, "Not at all." Those who might be tempted to say "So what?" to these findings need to consider the results of another recent survey: "In a study of 500 business professionals, conducted by MasterWorks, Annandale, Virginia, 95% said the main factor in deciding to stay or leave their job was whether they had a trusting relationship with their manager."[34] Clearly, remedial action is needed to close the huge trust gap.

In this section, we examine the concept of trust and introduce six practical guidelines for building trust.

A Cognitive Leap   **Trust** is defined as reciprocal faith in others' intentions and behavior.[35] Experts on the subject explain the reciprocal (give-and-take) aspect of trust as follows:

> When we see others acting in ways that imply that they trust us, we become more disposed to reciprocate by trusting in them more. Conversely, we come to distrust those whose actions appear to violate our trust or to distrust us.[36]

Trust
Reciprocal faith in others' intentions and behavior.

**Propensity
to trust**

A personality trait
involving one's general
willingness to trust
others.

In short, we tend to give what we get: trust begets trust; distrust begets distrust.

A newer model of organizational trust includes a personality trait called **propensity to trust.** The developers of the model explain:

> Propensity might be thought of as the *general willingness to trust others*. Propensity will influence how much trust one has for a trustee prior to data on that particular party being available. People with different developmental experiences, personality types, and cultural backgrounds vary in their propensity to trust. . . . An example of an extreme case of this is what is commonly called blind trust. Some individuals can be observed to repeatedly trust in situations that most people would agree do not warrant trust. Conversely, others are unwilling to trust in most situations, regardless of circumstances that would support doing so.[37]

What is your propensity to trust? How did you develop that personality trait? (See the trust questionnaire in the Personal Awareness and Growth Exercise at the end of this chapter.)

Trust involves "a cognitive 'leap' beyond the expectations that reason and experience alone would warrant"[38] (see Figure 13–3). For example, suppose a member of a newly formed class project team works hard, based on the assumption that her teammates also are working hard. That assumption, on which her trust is based, is a cognitive leap that goes beyond her actual experience with her teammates. When you trust someone, you have *faith* in their good intentions. The act of trusting someone, however, carries with it the inherent risk of betrayal.[39] Progressive managers believe that the benefits of interpersonal trust far outweigh any risks of betrayed trust. For example, Michael Powell, who founded the chain of bookstores bearing his name more than 25 years ago, built his business around the principles of open-book management, empowerment, and trust. Powell's propensity to trust was sorely tested when one of his employees stole more than $60,000 in a used-book purchasing scheme. After putting in some accounting safeguards, Powell's propensity to trust remains intact. He observed:

> The incident was a watershed for me and my staff, dispelling any naïveté we may have had about crime. We realized that not only *can* theft happen; it *will* happen. At the same time, dealing with the matter forced us to revisit our basic values and managerial philosophies. We believe that the modern demands of business call for an empowered and fully flexible staff, and we know that such a staff will often have to handle valuable commodities and money. We also believe that most people are not going to abuse our trust if they are put in a position with a reasonable amount of review and responsibility.[40]

Figure 13–3   *Interpersonal Trust Involves a Cognitive Leap*

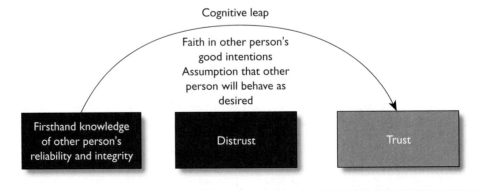

How to Build Trust   Management professor/consultant Fernando Bartolomé offers the following six guidelines for building and maintaining trust:

1. *Communication.* Keep team members and employees informed by explaining policies and decisions and providing accurate feedback. Be candid about one's own problems and limitations. Tell the truth.[41]

2. *Support.* Be available and approachable. Provide help, advice, coaching, and support for team members' ideas.

3. *Respect.* Delegation, in the form of real decision-making authority, is the most important expression of managerial respect. Actively listening to the ideas of others is a close second. (Empowerment is not possible without trust.)[42]

4. *Fairness.* Be quick to give credit and recognition to those who deserve it. Make sure all performance appraisals and evaluations are objective and impartial.

5. *Predictability.* As mentioned previously, be consistent and predictable in your daily affairs. Keep both expressed and implied promises.

6. *Competence.* Enhance your credibility by demonstrating good business sense, technical ability, and professionalism.[43]

Trust needs to be earned; it cannot be demanded.

Cohesiveness

Cohesiveness is a process whereby "a sense of 'we-ness' emerges to transcend individual differences and motives."[44] Members of a cohesive group stick together. They are reluctant to leave the group. Cohesive group members stick together for one or both of the following reasons: (1) because they enjoy each others' company or (2) because they need each other to accomplish a common goal. Accordingly, two types of group cohesiveness, identified by sociologists, are socio-emotional cohesiveness and instrumental cohesiveness.[45]

> **Cohesiveness**
> A sense of "we-ness" helps group stick together.

Socio-Emotional and Instrumental Cohesiveness   **Socio-emotional cohesiveness** is a sense of togetherness that develops when individuals derive emotional satisfaction from group participation. Most general discussions of group cohesiveness are limited to this type. However, from the standpoint of getting things accomplished in task groups and teams, we cannot afford to ignore instrumental cohesiveness. **Instrumental cohesiveness** is a sense of togetherness that develops when group members are mutually dependent on one another because they believe they could not achieve the group's goal by acting separately. A feeling of "we-ness" is *instrumental* in achieving the common goal. Team advocates generally assume both types of cohesiveness are essential to productive teamwork. But is this really true?

> **Socio-emotional cohesiveness**
> Sense of togetherness based on emotional satisfaction.

> **Instrumental cohesiveness**
> Sense of togetherness based on mutual dependency needed to get the job done.

Lessons from Group Cohesiveness Research   What is the connection between group cohesiveness and performance? A landmark meta-analysis of 49 studies involving 8,702 subjects provided these insights:

- There is a small but statistically significant cohesiveness→performance effect.
- The cohesiveness→performance effect was stronger for smaller and real groups (as opposed to contrived groups in laboratory studies).

- The cohesiveness→performance effect becomes stronger as one moves from nonmilitary real groups to military groups to sports teams.
- Commitment to the task at hand (meaning the individual sees the performance standards as legitimate) has the most powerful impact on the cohesiveness→performance linkage.
- The *performance→cohesiveness* linkage is stronger than the cohesiveness→ performance linkage. Thus, success tends to bind group or team members together rather than closely knit groups being more successful.
- Contrary to the popular view, cohesiveness is not "a 'lubricant' that minimizes friction due to the human 'grit' in the system."[46]
- All this evidence led the researchers to this practical conclusion: "Efforts to enhance group performance by fostering interpersonal attraction or 'pumping up' group pride are not likely to be effective."[47]

A second meta-analysis found no significant relationship between cohesiveness and the quality of group decisions. However, support was found for Janis's contention that *groupthink* tends to afflict cohesive in-groups with strong leadership. Groups whose members liked each other a great deal tended to make poorer quality decisions.[48]

Getting ſome Positive Impact from Group Cohesiveness

Research tells us that group cohesiveness is no secret weapon in the quest for improved group or team performance. The trick is to keep task groups small, make sure performance standards and goals are clear and accepted, achieve some early successes, and follow the tips in Table 13–5. A good example is Westinghouse's highly automated military radar electronics plant in College Station, Texas. Compared with their counterparts at a traditional factory in Baltimore, each of the Texas plant's 500 employees produces eight times more, at half the per-unit cost:

> The key, says Westinghouse, is not the robots but the people. Employees work in teams of 8 to 12. Members devise their own solutions to problems. Teams measure daily how each person's performance compares with that of other members and how the team's performance compares with the plant's. Joseph L Johnson, 28, a robotics technician, says that

Table 13–5   *Steps Managers Can Take to Enhance the Two Types of Group Cohesiveness*

Socio-Emotional Cohesiveness
Keep the group relatively small.
Strive for a favorable public image to increase the status and prestige of belonging.
Encourage interaction and cooperation.
Emphasize members' common characteristics and interests.
Point out environmental threats (e.g., competitors' achievements) to rally the group.

Instrumental Cohesiveness
Regularly update and clarify the group's goal(s).
Give every group member a vital "piece of the action."
Channel each group member's special talents toward the common goal(s).
Recognize and equitably reinforce every member's contributions.
Frequently remind group members they need each other to get the job done.

is a big change from a previous hourly factory job where he cared only about "picking up my paycheck." Here, peer pressure "makes sure you get the job done."[49]

Self-selected work teams (in which people pick their own teammates) and off-the-job social events can stimulate socio-emotional cohesiveness.[50] The fostering of socio-emotional cohesiveness needs to be balanced with instrumental cohesiveness. The latter can be encouraged by making sure everyone in the group recognizes and appreciates each member's vital contribution to the group goal. While balancing the two types of cohesiveness, managers need to remember that groupthink theory and research cautions against too much cohesiveness.

Teams in Action: Quality Circles, Virtual Teams, and ʃelf-Managed Teams

All sorts of interesting approaches to teams and teamwork can be found in the workplace today. A great deal of experimentation is taking place as organizations struggle to be more flexible and responsive. New information technologies also have spurred experimentation with team formats. This section profiles three different approaches to teams: quality circles, virtual teams, and self-managed teams. We have selected these particular types of teams for three reasons: (1) They have recognizable labels, (2) They have at least some research evidence, (3) They range from low to mixed to high degrees of empowerment (refer to Figure 16–2 in Chapter 16).

As indicated in Table 13–6, the three types of teams are distinct but not totally unique. Overlaps exist. For instance, computer-networked virtual teams may or may not have volunteer members and may or may not be self-managed. Another point of overlap involves the fifth variable in Table 13–6: relationship to organization structure. Quality circles are called *parallel* structures because they exist outside normal channels of authority and communication.[51] Self-managed teams, on the other hand, are

Table 13–6   *Basic Distinctions among Quality Circles, Virtual Teams, and Self-Managed Teams*

	Quality Circles	Virtual Teams	Self-Managed Teams
Type of team (see Table 13–2)	Advice	Advice or project (usually project)	Production, project, or action
Type of empowerment (see Figure 16–2)	Consultation	Consultation, participation, or delegation	Delegation
Members	Production/service personnel	Managers and technical specialists	Production/service, technical specialists
Basis of membership	Voluntary	Assigned (some voluntary)	Assigned
Relationship to organization structure	Parallel	Parallel or integrated	Integrated
Amount of face-to-face communication	Strictly face to face	Periodic to none	Varies, depending on use of information technology

integrated into the basic organizational structure. Virtual teams vary in this regard, although they tend to be parallel because they are made up of functional specialists (engineers, accountants, marketers, etc.) who team up on temporary projects. Keeping these basic distinctions in mind, let us explore quality circles, virtual teams, and self-managed teams.

Quality Circles

Quality circles
Small groups of volunteers who strive to solve quality-related problems.

Quality circles are small groups of people from the same work area who voluntarily get together to identify, analyze, and recommend solutions for problems related to quality, productivity, and cost reduction. Some prefer the term *quality control circles*. With an ideal size of 10 to 12 members, they typically meet for about 60 to 90 minutes on a regular basis. Some companies allow meetings during work hours, others encourage quality circles to meet after work on employees' time. Once a week or twice a month are common schedules. Management facilitates the quality circle program through skills training and listening to periodic presentations of recommendations. Monetary rewards for suggestions tend to be the exception rather than the rule. Intrinsic motivation, derived from learning new skills and meaningful participation, is the primary payoff for quality circle volunteers.

The Quality Circle Movement
American quality control experts helped introduce the basic idea of quality circles to Japanese industry soon after World War II. The idea eventually returned to the United States and reached fad proportions during the 1970s and 1980s. Proponents made zealous claims about how quality circles were the key to higher productivity, lower costs, employee development, and improved job attitudes. At its zenith during the mid-1980s, the quality circle movement claimed millions of employee participants around the world.[52] Hundreds of US companies and government agencies adopted the idea under a variety of labels.[53] Dramatic growth of quality circles in the United States was attributed to (1) a desire to replicate Japan's industrial success, (2) America's penchant for business fads, and (3) the relative ease of installing quality circles without restructuring the organization.[54] All too often, however, early enthusiasm gave way to disappointment, apathy, and abandonment.[55]

But quality circles, if properly administered and supported by management, can be much more than a management fad seemingly past its prime. According to USC researchers Edward E Lawler and Susan A Mohrman, "quality circles can be an important first step toward organizational effectiveness through employee involvement."[56]

Insights from Field Research on Quality Circles
There is a body of objective field research on quality circles. Still, much of what we know comes from testimonials and case histories from managers and consultants who have a vested interest in demonstrating the technique's success. Although documented failures are scarce, one expert concluded that quality circles have failure rates of more than 60%.[57] Poor implementation is probably more at fault than the quality circle concept itself.[58]

To date, field research on quality circles has been inconclusive. Lack of standardized variables is the main problem, as it typically is when comparing the results of field studies.[59] Team participation programs of all sizes and shapes have been called quality circles. Here's what we have learned to date. A case study of military and civilian personnel at a US Air Force base found a positive relationship between quality circle participation and desire to continue working for the organization. The observed effect on job performance was slight. A longitudinal study spanning 24 months revealed that quality circles had only a marginal impact on employee attitudes but had a positive impact on productivity. In a more recent study, utility company employees who participated in quality circles received significantly better job performance ratings and were promoted more frequently than nonparticipants. This suggests that quality circles live up to their billing as a good employee development technique.[60]

Overall, quality circles are a promising participative management tool, *if they are carefully implemented and supported by all levels of management.*

Virtual Teams

Virtual teams are a product of modern times. They take their name from *virtual reality* computer simulations, where "it's almost like the real thing." Thanks to evolving information technologies such as the Internet, E-mail, instant messaging, videoconferencing, groupware, and fax machines, you can be a member of a work team without really being there.[61] Traditional team meetings are location specific. Team members are either physically present or absent. Virtual teams, in contrast, convene electronically with members reporting in from different locations, different organizations, and even different time zones.

Because virtual teams are relatively new, there is no consensual definition. Our working definition of a **virtual team** is a physically dispersed task group that conducts its business through modern information technology.[62] Advocates say virtual teams are very flexible and efficient because they are driven by information and skills, not by time and location. People with needed information or skills can be team members, regardless of where or when they actually do their work. On the negative side, lack of face-to-face interaction can weaken trust, communication, and accountability.

Research Insights   As one might expect with a new and ill-defined area, research evidence to date is a bit spotty. Here is what we have learned so far from recent studies of computer-mediated groups:

- Virtual groups formed over the Internet follow a group development process similar to that for face-to-face groups.[63] (Recall our discussion of Tuckman's model in Chapter 12.)

- Internet chat rooms create more work and yield poorer decisions than face-to-face meetings and telephone conferences.[64]

- Successful use of groupware (software that facilitates interaction among virtual group members) requires training and hands-on experience.[65]

- Inspirational leadership has a positive impact on creativity in electronic brainstorming groups.[66]

- Conflict management is particularly difficult for *asynchronous* virtual teams (those not interacting in real time) that have no opportunity for face-to-face interaction.[67]

Practical Considerations   Virtual teams may be in fashion, but they are not a cure-all. In fact, they may be a giant step backward for those not well versed in modern information technology. Managers who rely on virtual teams agree on one point: *Meaningful face-to-face contact, especially during early phases of the group development process, is absolutely essential.* Virtual group members need "faces" in their minds to go with names and electronic messages. Periodic face-to-face interaction not

Virtual team
Information technology allows group members in different locations to conduct business.

Table 13–7   *How to Manage Virtual Teams*

Establishing trust and commitment, encouraging communication, and assessing team members pose tremendous challenges for virtual team managers. Here are a few tips to make the process easier:

- Establish regular times for group interaction.
- Set up firm rules for communication.
- Use visual forms of communication where possible.
- Emulate the attributes of co-located teams. For example, allow time for informal chitchat and socializing, and celebrate achievements.
- Give and receive feedback and offer assistance on a regular basis. Be persistent with people who aren't communicating with you or each other.
- Agree on standard technology so all team members can work together easily.
- Consider using 360-degree feedback to better understand and evaluate team members.
- Provide a virtual meeting room via intranet, Web site or bulletin board.
- Note which employees effectively use E-mail to build team rapport.
- Smooth the way for an employee's next assignment if membership on the team, or the team itself, is not permanent.
- Be available to employees, but don't wait for them to seek you out.
- Encourage informal, off-line conversation between team members.

SOURCE: C Joinson, "Managing Virtual Teams," *HR Magazine*, June 2002, p. 71.

only fosters social bonding among virtual team members, it also facilitates conflict resolution. Additionally, virtual teams cannot succeed without some old-fashioned factors such as top-management support, hands-on training, a clear mission and specific objectives, effective leadership, and schedules and deadlines. (See the additional practical tips listed in Table 13–7.)

Self-Managed Teams

Have you ever thought you could do a better job than your boss? Well, if the trend toward self-managed work teams continues to grow as predicted, you just may get your chance. Entrepreneurs and artisans often boast of not having a supervisor. The same generally cannot be said for employees working in organizational offices and factories. But things are changing. In fact, an estimated half of the employees at *Fortune* 500 companies are working on teams.[68] A growing share of those teams are self-managing, as exemplified by the following situation:

> At a General Mills cereal plant in Lodi, California, teams . . . schedule, operate, and maintain machinery so effectively that the factory runs with no managers present during the night shift.[69]

At Texas Instruments' electronics factory near Kuala Lumpur, Malaysia, quality circles have evolved into a system made up almost entirely of self-managing teams:

> Daily administration, explains A Subramaniam, [the factory's] . . . training manager, involves teams taking on routine activities formerly performed by supervisors. "Now," he says, "they are expected to take care of the daily operations like marking attendance, setup, control of material usage, quality control, monitoring cycle time, safety, and line audits." . . .

Low Say Sun, training and development administrator, adds, "They [team members] are expected in daily management to detect abnormality and take corrective action as well as make improvements in their work area using problem-solving techniques and quality control tools. It will be just like running a business company. Of course," he adds, "there will be facilitators or managers whom they can turn to for help. In other words, there will be somebody to take care of the team. Training will be provided to enable them to manage their operation and process well."[70]

General Mills has found that, when it comes to management, less can mean more. At the Lodi plant, some of the self-managed teams have set higher production goals for themselves than those formerly set by management. Self-managed teamwork does have its price tag, however. Each team member at Texas Instruments' Malaysian facility undergoes 50 hours of intensive training in everything from quality control tools to problem solving to team building and communication.

This section explores self-managed teams by looking at their past, present, and future.

What Are ∫elf-Managed Teams?

Something much more complex is involved than this apparently simple label suggests. The term *self-managed* does not mean simply turning workers loose to do their own thing. Indeed, as we will see, an organization embracing self-managed teams should be prepared to undergo revolutionary changes in management philosophy, structure, staffing and training practices, and reward systems. Moreover, the traditional notions of managerial authority and control are turned on their heads. Not surprisingly, many managers strongly resist giving up the reins of power to people they view as subordinates. They see self-managed teams as a threat to their job security.[71] Texas Instruments has constructively dealt with this problem at its Malaysian factory by making former production supervisors part of the all-important training function.

Self-managed teams are defined as groups of workers who are given administrative oversight for their task domains. Administrative oversight involves delegated activities such as planning, scheduling, monitoring, and staffing. These are chores normally performed by managers. In short, employees in these unique work groups act as their own supervisor.[72] Self-managed teams are variously referred to as semiautonomous work groups, autonomous work groups, and superteams. A common feature of self-managed teams, particularly among those above the shop-floor or clerical level, is **cross-functionalism**.[73] In other words, specialists from different areas are put on the same team. Amgen, a biotechnology company in Thousand Oaks, California, is literally run by cross-functional, self-managed teams:

> There are two types: product development teams, known as PDTs, which are concerned with everything that relates to bringing a new product to market, and task forces, which do everything else. The members of both come from all areas of the company, including marketing and finance as well as the lab bench. The groups range from five or six employees up to 80 and usually report directly to senior management. In a reversal of the normal process, department heads called facilitators don't run teams; they work for them, making sure they have the equipment and money they need. Teams may meet weekly, monthly, or whenever the members see fit.[74]

As indicated in Table 13–8, self-managed teams can be empowered in many different ways, producing countless variations.

Among companies with self-managed teams, according to one survey, the most commonly delegated tasks are work scheduling and dealing directly with outside

∫elf-managed teams
Groups of employees granted administrative oversight for their work.

Cross-functionalism
Team made up of technical specialists from different areas.

Table 13–8   *There Are Many Ways to Empower Self-Managed Teams*

External Leader Behavior
1. Make team members responsible and accountable for the work they do.
2. Ask for and use team suggestions when making decisions.
3. Encourage team members to take control of their work.
4. Create an environment in which team members set their own team goals.
5. Stay out of the way when team members attempt to solve work-related problems.
6. Generate high team expectations.
7. Display trust and confidence in the team's abilities.

Production/Service Responsibilities
1. The team sets its own production/service goals and standards.
2. The team assigns jobs and tasks to its members.
3. Team members develop their own quality standards and measurement techniques.
4. Team members take on production/service learning and development opportunities.
5. Team members handle their own problems with internal and external customers.
6. The team works with a whole product or service, not just a part.

Human Resource Management System
1. The team gets paid, at least in part, as a team.
2. Team members are cross-trained on jobs within their team.
3. Team members are cross-trained on jobs in other teams.
4. Team members are responsible for hiring, training, punishment, and firing.
5. Team members use peer evaluations to formally evaluate each other.

Social Structure
1. The team gets support from other teams and departments when needed.
2. The team has access to and uses important and strategic information.
3. The team has access to and uses the resources of other teams.
4. The team has access to and uses resources inside and outside the organization.
5. The team frequently communicates with other teams.
6. The team makes its own rules and policies.

SOURCE: Reprinted from *Organizational Dynamics*, B L Kirkman and B Rosen, "Powering Up Teams," *Organizational Dynamics*, Winter 2000, exhibit 3, p. 56, © 2000, with permission from Elsevier Science.

customers. The least common team chores are hiring and firing.[75] Most of today's self-managed teams remain bunched at the shop-floor level in factory settings. Experts predict growth of the practice in the technical and professional ranks and in service operations.

Historical and Conceptual Roots of Self-Managed Teams   Self-managed teams are an outgrowth of a blend of behavioral science and management practice. Group dynamics research of variables such as cohesiveness initially paved the way. A later stimulus was the socio-technical systems approach in which first British, and then American researchers, tried to harmonize social and technical factors. Their goal was to simultaneously increase productivity and employees' quality of work life. More recently, the idea of self-managed teams has gotten a strong boost from job design and participative management advocates. Recall our discussion of Hackman and Oldham's job characteristics model in Chapter 8. According to their model, internal

OB Exercise   Measuring Work Group Autonomy

Instructions

Think of your current (or past) job and work groups. Characterize the group's situation by choosing one number on the following scale for each statement. Add your responses for a total score:

Strongly Disagree						Strongly Agree
1 —— 2 —— 3 —— 4 —— 5 —— 6 —— 7						

Work Method Autonomy

1. My work group decides how to get the job done. _____

2. My work group determines what procedures to use. _____

3. My work group is free to choose its own methods when carrying out its work. _____

Work Scheduling Autonomy

4. My work group controls the scheduling of its work. _____

5. My work group determines how its work is sequenced. _____

6. My work group decides when to do certain activities. _____

Work Criteria Autonomy

7. My work group is allowed to modify the normal way it is evaluated so some of our activities are emphasized and some deemphasized. _____

8. My work group is able to modify its objectives (what it is supposed to accomplish). _____

9. My work group has some control over what it is supposed to accomplish. _____

Total score = _____

Norms

9–26 = Low autonomy

27–45 = Moderate autonomy

46–63 = High autonomy

SOURCE: Adapted from an individual autonomy scale in J A Breaugh, "The Work Autonomy Scales: Additional Validity Evidence," Human Relations, November 1989, pp. 1033–56.

motivation, satisfaction, and performance can be enhanced through five core job characteristics. Of those five core factors, increased *autonomy* is a major benefit for members of self-managed teams. Three types of autonomy are method, scheduling, and criteria autonomy (see the OB Exercise above). Members of self-managed teams score high on group autonomy. Autonomy empowers those who are ready and able to handle added responsibility. How did you score? Finally, the social learning theory of self-management, as discussed in Chapter 5, has helped strengthen the case for self-managed teams.

The net result of this confluence is the continuum in Figure 13–4. The traditional clear-cut distinction between manager and managed is being blurred as nonmanagerial employees are delegated greater authority and granted increased autonomy. Importantly, self-managed teams do not eliminate the need for all managerial control (see the

Figure 13–4   *The Evolution of Self-Managed Work Teams*

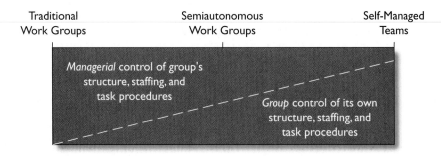

upper-right corner of Figure 13–4). Semiautonomous work teams represent a balance between managerial and group control.

Are Self-Managed Teams Effective? Research Evidence   As with quality circles and virtual teams, much of what we know about self-managed teams comes from testimonials and case studies. Fortunately, a body of higher-quality field research is slowly developing. A review of three meta-analyses covering 70 individual studies concluded that self-managed teams had

- A positive impact on productivity.
- A positive impact on specific attitudes relating to self-management (e.g., responsibility and control).
- No significant impact on general attitudes (e.g., job satisfaction and organizational commitment).
- No significant impact on absenteeism or turnover.[76]

Other recent research insights about self-managed teams include

- Disciplinary actions should be handled by group consensus because individual team members tend to be too lenient.[77]
- Group cohesiveness (a positive "we" feeling) is associated with higher performance ratings.[78]
- When implementing self-managed teams in multinational companies, societal values need to be taken into consideration because some cultures are more resistant to the practice than others. In fact, "teams-related resistance is apparently greater for employees in the United States than for those in Finland or the Philippines."[79]

Although encouraging, these results do not qualify as a sweeping endorsement of self-managed teams. Nonetheless, experts say the trend toward self-managed work teams will continue. Managers need to be prepared for the resulting shift in organizational administration.

Setting the Stage for Self-Managed Teams   Experience shows that it is better to build a new production or service facility around self-managed teams than to attempt to convert an existing one. The former approach involves so-called green-field

sites. General Foods, for example, pioneered the use of autonomous work teams in the United States in 1971 by literally building its Topeka, Kansas, Gravy Train pet food plant around them.[80] Green-field sites give management the advantage of selecting appropriate technology and carefully screening job applicants likely to be good team players.

But the fact is, most organizations are not afforded green-field opportunities. They must settle for introducing self-managed teams into an existing organization structure.[81]

Making the Transition to Self-Managed Teams

Extensive *management training and socialization* are required to deeply embed Theory Y and participative management values into the organization's culture. This new logic necessarily has to start with top management and filter down. Otherwise, resistance among middle- and lower-level managers will block the transition to teams. Some turnover can be expected among managers who refuse to adjust to broader empowerment. Both *technical and organizational redesign* are necessary. Self-managed teams may require special technology. Volvo's team-based auto assembly plant, for example, relies on portable assembly platforms rather than traditional assembly lines. Structural redesign of the organization must take place because self-managed teams are an integral part of the organization, not patched onto it as in the case of quality circles. For example, in one of Texas Instruments' computer chip factories a hierarchy of teams operates within the traditional structure. Four levels of teams are responsible for different domains. Reporting to the steering team that deals with strategic issues are quality-improvement, corrective-action, and effectiveness teams. TI's quality-improvement and corrective-action teams are cross-functional teams made up of middle managers and functional specialists such as accountants and engineers. Production workers make up the effectiveness teams. The corrective-action teams are unique because they are formed to deal with short-term problems and are disbanded when a solution is found. All the other teams are long-term assignments.[82]

In turn, *personnel, goal setting, and reward systems* need to be adapted to encourage teamwork. Staffing decisions may shift from management to team members who hire their own co-workers. A study of 60 self-managing teams involving 540 employees suggests how goal setting should be reoriented. Teams with highly *cooperative* goals functioned more smoothly and had better results than teams with competitive goals.[83] Accordingly, individual bonuses must give way to team bonuses. *Supervisory development workshops* are needed to teach managers to be facilitators rather than order givers.[84] Finally, extensive *team training* is required to help team members learn more about technical details, the business as a whole, and how to be team players. This is where team building enters the picture.

Team Building

Team building is a catch-all term for a whole host of techniques aimed at improving the internal functioning of work groups. Whether conducted by company trainers or outside consultants, team-building workshops strive for greater cooperation, better communication, and less dysfunctional conflict. Experiential learning techniques such as interpersonal trust exercises, conflict-handling role-play sessions, and interactive games are common. For example, Germany's Opel uses Lego blocks to teach its autoworkers the tight teamwork necessary for just-in-time production.[85] In the mountains of British

Team building

Experiential learning aimed at better internal functioning of groups.

The University of Chicago Business School promotes "hands-on" learning through team-building exercises. These blindfolded students can accomplish their task only with the help of their teammates. The message is clear: today's business leaders cannot do the job alone.

(c) Marc Pokempner/Getty Images/Stone

Columbia, Canada, DowElanco employees try to overcome fear and build trust as they help each other negotiate a difficult tree-top rope course.[86] Meanwhile, in the United States, the Target department store chain has its salesclerks learn cooperation and teamwork with this exercise: "employees linked in a human chain must each wriggle through two Hula-Hoops moving in opposite directions, without breaking the chain or letting the hoops touch the ground."[87] And in Prescott, Arizona, trainees at Motorola's Advanced Leadership Academy polish their teamwork skills by trying to make music with an odd assortment of percussion instruments.[88]

Rote memorization and lectures/discussions are discouraged by team-building experts who prefer *active* versus passive learning. Greater emphasis is placed on *how* work groups get the job done than on the job itself.

Complete coverage of the many team-building techniques would require a separate book. Consequently, the scope of our current discussion is limited to the goal of team building and the day-to-day development of self-management skills. This foundation is intended to give you a basis for selecting appropriate team-building techniques from the many you are likely to encounter in the years ahead.[89]

The Goal of Team Building: High-Performance Teams

Team building allows team members to wrestle with simulated or real-life problems. Outcomes are then analyzed by the group to determine what group processes need improvement. Learning stems from recognizing and addressing faulty group dynamics. Perhaps one subgroup withheld key information from another, thereby hampering group progress. With cross-cultural teams becoming commonplace in today's global economy, team building is more important than ever (see the International OB on page 471).

A nationwide survey of team members from many organizations, by Wilson Learning Corporation, provides a useful model or benchmark of what we should expect of teams. The researchers' question was simply: "What is a high-performance team?"[90] The respondents were asked to describe their peak experiences in work teams. Analy-

International OB — This London Company Has Turned Corporate Team Building into a Circus

Are you ready to take your corporate team to new heights? Prepare yourself, because the next department meeting may cover the flying trapeze, acrobatic balancing and tight-wire walking, that is if the next meeting takes place at Circus Space.

Besides being one of Europe's top circus facilities, London's Circus Space offers programs designed to help corporate groups learn the circus way when it comes to teamwork, leadership, communication, and trust. While many companies claim these values, incorporating them into the workplace can be tricky.

"When an acrobatic or flying trapeze troupe works with a director on a new act for the show, they are inherently creating a successful team that trusts and relies on each other to create an end result," says Adult Program Manager Rob Colbert. "Likewise in business, you need a productive team that works well together."

The tailor-made classes, which attempt to teach a different view of simple goals, have attracted a word-of-mouth-based audience with companies like U B S Warburg, Disney, Microsoft, International Distillers, and Unilever.

Colbert attributes Circus Space's success to its unusual method of training.

"The main criticism of other team-building workshops from our clients is that they are either too dull or competitive, and this is where the circus training has come in," Colbert says. "Our courses offer a shared physical experience where participants can directly gain new ways of learning and a real sense of achievement, develop a mutual support and respect for each other, and have the opportunity to use the skills as a powerful management metaphor."

Colbert says just by coming to Circus Space, companies are stepping in the right direction. "If companies employ us to be creative with their new recruits, then companies are sending a powerful message about their expectations and how they want their new employees to work," he explains. "Whereas with managers and directors, the companies are saying, 'We want you to open up and look at new possibilities, take risks and be creative.' "

SOURCE: "Training on the Tight Wire," *Training*, November 2001, p. 31.

---

sis of the survey results yielded the following eight attributes of high-performance teams:

1. *Participative leadership.* Creating an interdependency by empowering, freeing up, and serving others.

2. *Shared responsibility.* Establishing an environment in which all team members feel as responsible as the manager for the performance of the work unit.

3. *Aligned on purpose.* Having a sense of common purpose about why the team exists and the function it serves.

4. *High communication.* Creating a climate of trust and open, honest communication.

5. *Future focused.* Seeing change as an opportunity for growth.

6. *Focused on task.* Keeping meetings focused on results.

7. *Creative talents.* Applying individual talents and creativity.

8. *Rapid response.* Identifying and acting on opportunities.[91]

These eight attributes effectively combine many of today's most progressive ideas on management, among them being participation, empowerment, service ethic, individual responsibility and development, self-management, trust, active listening, and envisioning. But patience and diligence are required. According to a manager familiar with work teams, "high-performance teams may take three to five years to build."[92] Let us keep this inspiring model of high-performance teams in mind as we conclude our discussion of team building.

Developing Team Members' Self-Management Skills

A promising dimension of team building has emerged in recent years. It is an extension of the self-management approach discussed in Chapter 5. Proponents call it **self-management leadership,** defined as the process of leading others to lead themselves. An underlying assumption is that self-managed teams likely will fail if team members are not expressly taught to engage in self-management behaviors. This makes sense because it is unreasonable to expect employees who are accustomed to being managed and led to suddenly manage and lead themselves. Transition training is required, as discussed in the prior section. A key transition to self-management involves *current managers* engaging in self-management leadership behaviors. This is team building in the fullest meaning of the term.

Six self-management leadership behaviors were isolated in a field study of a manufacturing company organized around self-managed teams. The observed behaviors were

1. *Encourages self-reinforcement* (e.g., getting team members to praise each other for good work and results).
2. *Encourages self-observation/evaluation* (e.g., teaching team members to judge how well they are doing).
3. *Encourages self-expectation* (e.g., encouraging team members to expect high performance from themselves and the team).
4. *Encourages self-goal-setting* (e.g., having the team set its own performance goals).
5. *Encourages rehearsal* (e.g., getting team members to think about and practice new tasks).
6. *Encourages self-criticism* (e.g., encouraging team members to be critical of their own poor performance).[93]

According to the researchers, Charles Manz and Henry Sims, this type of leadership is a dramatic departure from traditional practices such as giving orders or making sure everyone gets along. Empowerment, not domination, is the overriding goal.

ſummary of Key Concepts

1. *Explain how a work group becomes a team, and identify and describe the four types of work teams.* A team is a mature group where leadership is shared, accountability is both individual and collective, the members have developed their own purpose, problem solving is a way of life, and effectiveness is measured by collective outcomes. Four general types of work teams are advice, production, project, and action teams. Each type has its characteristic degrees of specialization and coordination, work cycle, and outputs.

2. *Explain the ecological model of work team effectiveness.* According to the ecological model, two effectiveness criteria for work teams are performance and viability. The performance criterion is met if the group satisfies its

clients/customers. A work group is viable if its members are satisfied and continue contributing. An ecological perspective is appropriate because work groups require an organizational life-support system. For instance, group participation is enhanced by an organizational culture that values employee empowerment.

3. *Discuss why teams fail.* Teams fail because unrealistic expectations cause frustration and failure. Common management mistakes include weak strategies, creating a hostile environment for teams, faddish use of teams, not learning from team experience, vague team assignments, poor team staffing, inadequate training, and lack of trust. Team members typically try too much too soon, experience conflict over differing work styles and

personalities, ignore important group dynamics, resist change, exhibit poor interpersonal skills and chemistry, and display a lack of trust.

4. *Identify the five essential KSAs (knowledge, skills, and abilities) for team players.* Three interpersonal KSAs are conflict resolution, collaborative problem solving, and communication. The other two KSAs, centered on self-management, are goal setting and performance management, and planning and task coordination. Together, these five KSAs are a template for the team players we need today.

5. *List at least three things managers can do to build trust.* Six recommended ways to build trust are through communication, support, respect (especially delegation), fairness, predictability, and competence.

6. *Distinguish two types of group cohesiveness, and summarize cohesiveness research findings.* Cohesive groups have a shared sense of togetherness or a "we" feeling. Socio-emotional cohesiveness involves emotional satisfaction. Instrumental cohesiveness involves goal-directed togetherness. There is a small but significant relationship between cohesiveness and performance. The effect is stronger for smaller groups. Commitment to task among group members strengthens the cohesiveness→ performance linkage. Success can build group cohesiveness. Cohesiveness is not a cure-all for group problems. Too much cohesiveness can lead to groupthink.

7. *Define quality circles, virtual teams, and self-managed teams.* Quality circles are small groups of volunteers who meet regularly to solve quality-related problems in their work area. Virtual teams are physically dispersed work groups that conduct their business via modern information technologies such as the Internet, E-mail, and videoconferences. Self-managed teams are work groups that perform their own administrative chores such as planning, scheduling, and staffing.

8. *Discuss what must be done to set the stage for self-managed teams.* Management must embed a new Theory Y logic in the organization's culture. Technology and the organization need to be redesigned to accommodate self-managed teams. Personnel changes, goals, and reward systems that reinforce cooperation and teamwork are necessary. Supervisory training helps managers learn to be facilitators rather than traditional order givers. Team members need lots of training and team building to make them cooperative team players.

9. *Describe high-performance teams.* Eight attributes of high-performance teams are (1) participative leadership, (2) shared responsibility, (3) aligned on purpose, (4) high communication, (5) future focused for growth, (6) focused on task, (7) creative talents applied, and (8) rapid response.

Discussion Questions

1. Do you agree or disagree with Drucker's vision of more team-oriented organizations? Explain your assumptions and reasoning.

2. Which of the factors listed in Table 13–1 is most crucial to a successful team? Explain.

3. Why bother taking an ecological perspective of work team effectiveness?

4. In your personal friendships, how do you come to trust someone? How fragile is that trust? Explain.

5. Why is delegation so important to building organizational trust?

6. Why should a group leader strive for both socio-emotional and instrumental cohesiveness?

7. Are virtual teams likely to be just a passing fad? Why or why not?

8. Would you like to work on a self-managed team? Explain.

9. How would you respond to a manager who said, "Why should I teach my people to manage themselves and work myself out of a job?"

10. Have you ever been a member of a high-performing team? If so, explain the circumstances and success factors.

Internet Exercise

As covered in this chapter, teams are the organizational unit of choice today. Auto companies have design and production teams. Hospitals have patient care teams. Team policing is practiced by many law enforcement agencies. Airlines have ground crew teams. Current and future managers (indeed, all employees) need to know as much as possible about teams and teamwork. The purpose of this exercise is to continue building your knowledge of workplace teams and to assess your readiness for Internet-age teamwork.

Instructive Updates on Teams and Teamwork

For interesting and useful material on teams and teamwork, go to *Fast Company* magazine's Web site (**www.fastcompany.com**) and click on "Themes" under the main menu tab "Magazine." Select the "Teamwork" heading and browse the listed articles with the objective of finding three *useful insights* about teams and teamwork. Try to find at least one article about either virtual teams or self-managed teams. (*Note*: Another alternative is to click on "Dynamic Archives" under the "Magazine" tab and browse the contents of recent issues of *Fast Company* magazine for articles on teams, teamwork, virtual teams, and self-managed teams.)

Assess Your Teamwork Skills

Want to know how ready you are for today's team-based organizations? Here are a couple of free self-assessment tests. Go to **www.project-manager.com** and click on the box "Direct to P-M's Site Map." Scroll down the site map page and select the heading "3.0) PERSONAL SKILLS." The link "Quiz 1" will take you to a quick eight-question quiz, complete with instructions and scoring procedure. If you have the time and interest, go back and click on the "Quiz 2" link for a 24-item test that assesses your leadership, teamwork, and project management skills.

Questions

1. What three useful insights did you pick up from your *Fast Company* search? How could each of those ideas help you be a good team leader?

2. What are your main concerns about today's rush to adopt team-based organizations?

3. What are the main pros and cons of virtual teams and self-managed teams?

4. How did you score on the team skills quiz? Any surprises? What are the managerial implications of your scoring category?

OB in Action Case Study

Trilogy University—A Corporate Boot Camp

Welcome to Trilogy[94]

Trilogy University is the orientation program of Austin, Texas–based Trilogy, designed to turn the company's raw recruits—hired straight off the campuses of MIT, Stanford, University of Michigan, and the like—into highly productive contributors. Started in 1995, it is the brainchild of Trilogy's president and CEO, Joe Liemandt, and its vice president of marketing, John Price.

The company has a pressing need for new-employee orientation because its growth has been extremely rapid, and the biggest drag on growth has been the difficulty of recruiting and bringing new talent up to speed. Trilogy started fast out of the gate in 1989 when Liemandt nailed a market opportunity to create "configuration software" for large manufacturers like Hewlett-Packard and Boeing. The products these companies sell have innumerable variants, as alternative components are assembled to suit each buyer's highly specific preferences. Trilogy's software solves a huge problem traditionally faced in the selling process by allowing a salesperson with a laptop to translate a customer's needs into a workable specification. The software spots where components are incompatible, for instance, or where one part requires another, and it configures a system that will work. Then—and this is really important to those salespeople—it produces an accurate price quote on the spot.

Trilogy's breakthrough allowed it to do something most small software companies only dream of: sign up brand-name accounts like Hewlett-Packard while the product was still in its infancy. Since then, Trilogy has expanded on its original offering to launch E-commerce applications for both the buying and selling of products, and its revenues have grown to about $200 million. Along the way, its employee base has grown 35% annually. In 2000, the company brought 450 new hires into an existing organization of 1,000.

Joe Liemandt realized early on that, as each influx of new hires came through the doors, the company needed to equip them with not only the skills required for their jobs but also the vision and values with which they should align their work. But because each new group represented a fair proportion of the whole organization, assimilation wasn't going to happen in some natural, organic way. It would have to be deliberately managed. Having to compress a great deal of learning and acculturation into a short time frame, Liemandt decided he needed a boot camp.

Three High-Pressure Months

"The first day, Joe walks in. And, like, his very few first words are, 'You're going to be the future of Trilogy—the company is relying on you—and everybody's waiting on you.'"

The speaker is Vince Mallet, a computer science master's grad who was wearing a Java T-shirt, his long hair in a neat ponytail, and a broad grin as he recently gave me the student's view of TU. Liemandt's message was apparently hitting home. Mallet told me, "I just want to go out in the company and be able to have that impact." It would be a tough several weeks before he got that chance.

Trilogy University is run twice a year. In the summer, it currently includes 170 to 200 hires, and in the winter about 60, all coming straight from campus. A class typically has a sprinkling of freshly minted master's and PhDs, and a fair number of liberal arts majors, but it's mostly drawn from undergraduate computer science departments. The program generally lasts 12 weeks. It's structured to take students through a well-thought-out process to develop skills, relationships, and values, which they then apply in intense R&D projects before they're ultimately introduced as a positive new force into the rest of the organization.

Month One   When you arrive at Trilogy University, you are assigned to a section and to an instruction track. Your section, a group of about 20, is your social group for the duration of TU. You share a section leader (an experienced person from Trilogy who serves as a mentor) and virtually all of your time with these people. Tracks are designed to be microcosms of future work life at Trilogy. For example, as a future developer or consultant, you might learn about technologies like XML and JSP one week by building a customizable sales analysis Web site for a fictional company. The technical challenges in such exercises closely mimic real customer engagements, but the time frames are dramatically compressed. The assignments pile up week after week for the first month, each one successively more challenging than the last.

During that time, you're being constantly measured and evaluated, as assignment grades and comments are entered into a database monitoring your progress. The functional training is so intense it would be easy to assume that it is the most important goal of TU. But Allan Drummond, the Trilogy vice president who runs TU, says that's not the case. "If people don't learn Java in TU, I don't care. They're very bright—they can pick up what they need. But if they

don't develop nearly unbreakable bonds with fellow TUers, if they don't learn to prioritize and make smart decisions, if they don't leave charged up, then TU is a failure."

The goals Drummond is emphasizing are the focus of the sections. Unlike tracks, sections continue past the first month. In a sense, they last for life. Effectiveness at Trilogy depends on having trusting relationships with co-workers, and sections are designed to prime that process. That's why Vince Mallet explained to me, "on the second day, we were all asked to tell the most significant emotional experience of our lives." Vince says some of the students' first reactions were cynical: "Yeah, we're going to tell stories about us. Whatever." But the technique worked its magic as people began to talk and listen. Before long, he says, "some people were crying; some people were making other people cry. And I thought, whoa—this is totally unusual." People were getting deeply acquainted, not incidentally but intentionally. The individuals in each section represent a cross section of functions; upon graduation from TU, the students will disperse to all corners of Trilogy, and the trust and bonds they develop will form horizontal networks linking them to people throughout the company for the rest of their careers.

Beyond developing skills and relationships, month one of Trilogy University also begins to instill values. Humility is one of the values Liemandt wants to see, and that's one reason the tracks deliberately stretch students beyond the point of failure. Other values are introduced through what people at Trilogy refer to as "big talks," which Liemandt or other Trilogy stars have with the whole TU class, usually in a Socratic style, and which are further discussed and debated in sections. Students learn early that Trilogy values creativity, innovation, and being a force for positive change in the workplace. They learn that Trilogy wants to see teamwork and a strong belief that success means solving the customer's problem. More than anything, they learn that Trilogy values risk taking. Along with the skills and relationships forged in month one, these values will be sorely tested in month two.

Month Two   Month two is TU project month. This is when the TUers, most of them 22 years old and employees for all of a month, take on the responsibility of inventing the company's future. "We tell them that, in order for the company to survive, they have to come up with a frame-breaking great new business idea," says Liemandt. "And they believe it because I really believe it."

Liemandt's learned, he says, "the hard way" that taking risks and suffering the consequences is a crucial part of any business. When he decided to launch Trilogy, he was in his senior year at Stanford. Rather than miss what might be a narrow window of opportunity, he decided to drop out and dedicate himself full-time to it. At least one very accomplished businessman, a former GE senior executive (who also happened to be his father), told him: "You're a moron."

The TU project is Liemandt's way of giving new recruits his own experience all over again. In teams of three to five people, they have to come up with an idea, create a business model for it, build the product, and develop the marketing plan. In trying to launch bold new ideas in a hyperaccelerated time frame, they gain a deep appreciation of the need to set priorities, evaluate probabilities, and measure results. Mind you, these projects are not hypothetical—they're the real thing. But even more important, when each team presents its innovation, Liemandt is there, deciding whether or not to put up the money to launch it. It's exhausting but it's also energizing, because Trilogy's best and most senior people are in the mix. New employees know they're getting noticed and that their ideas have a chance of being taken up.

How big is that chance? About 15% of the projects survive beyond the month that's allocated to them in TU. It's that humility thing again. Drummond describes the reaction of recruits who think their ideas are brilliant but then see them fail. "They're like, 'We stink. Not near good enough.' Actually, we never want that feeling to end. Because the minute you get arrogant, someone comes and beats you."

At the same time, the seriousness with which Liemandt and all the rest of Trilogy take the projects builds confidence. "We encourage them to go for the fence with their ideas and, while we don't reward failure around here, we don't punish them for it either," says Liemandt. "So, when people leave TU, most of them are thinking, 'I know I can make a difference, and I am not afraid to try'—which is exactly what we want them to think."

Month Three   Month three at Trilogy University is all about finding your place and having a broader impact in the larger organization. A few students continue with their TU projects, but most move on to "graduation projects," which generally are assignments within the various Trilogy business units. People leave TU on a rolling basis as they find sponsors out in the company who are willing to take them on.

The graduation process is a meeting between the graduate, the new manager, and the section leader. Before the meeting, each has been asked to evaluate the TUer on his or her various abilities. At the meeting, the three of them discuss the evaluation to resolve disagreements. "We don't just want understanding; we want agreement," Drummond says. "On all of the rankings where there is a disparity, they have to reach an agreement." The TUers have also written lists of objectives and their thoughts on how they want their careers to unfold. The manager responds to these with a list of specific goals that the TUer must agree to. Typically, the

manager will set three to five year-long goals that include a skill development goal, a mainline execution goal, and an organizational development goal. In addition, the manager creates another plan focused on creating the job assignments and coaching opportunities that will help the TUer reach his or her longer-term career goals.

"We want everyone here to be a star. We won't graduate TUers until they have found positions they want and where the new manager will take responsibility for helping them become a star," explains former TU head Danielle Rios. The TU faculty sometimes help persuade managers who are reluctant to take a risk, but a TUer who ultimately can't find a sponsor is out of the company.

It's the rare TU graduate who can't find a home within Trilogy because, clearly, Trilogy University succeeds at the basics of basic training. Graduates emerge from it prepared—by their skills, their relationships, and their values—to hit the ground running. But what really sets this boot camp apart from others I know is that it contributes much more to Trilogy than that. First, thanks to the energy and attention devoted to the TU projects, TU has become the company's primary research and development engine. Second, it has become the setting for Trilogy's leadership development. Third, it provides a great context and impetus for management to revisit and communicate strategic direction. And fourth, it serves as a constant source of organizational renewal and transformation.

Questions for Discussion

1. Based on what you have read about group dynamics and teamwork in Chapters 12 and 13, what is Trilogy University doing *right*?

2. What would you say is the key success factor in this program?

3. Which of the team player KSAs, discussed in this chapter, would be most beneficial for a person attending Trilogy University? Explain.

4. What actual or potential problems can you spot in this case? Explain.

5. Would you like to attend Trilogy University? Why or why not?

Personal Awareness and Growth Exercise

How Trusting Are You?

Objectives

1. To introduce you to different dimensions of interpersonal trust.
2. To measure your trust in another person.
3. To discuss the managerial implications of your propensity to trust.

Introduction

The trend toward more open and empowered organizations where teamwork and self-management are vital requires heightened interpersonal trust. Customers need to be able to trust organizations producing the goods and services they buy, managers need to trust nonmanagers to carry out the organization's mission, and team members need to trust each other in order to get the job done. As with any other interpersonal skill, we need to be able to measure and improve our ability to trust others. This exercise is a step in that direction.

Instructions[95]

Think of a specific individual who currently plays an important role in your life (e.g., current or future spouse, friend, supervisor, co-worker, team member, etc.), and rate his or her trustworthiness for each statement according to the following scale. Total your responses, and compare your score with the arbitrary norms provided.

Strongly Disagree		**Strongly Agree**

$$1 — 2 — 3 — 4 — 5 — 6 — 7 — 8 — 9 — 10$$

Overall Trust   **Score**

1. I can expect this person to play fair.   _____
2. I can confide in this person and know she/he desires to listen.   _____
3. I can expect this person to tell me the truth.   _____
4. This person takes time to listen to my problems and worries.   _____

Emotional Trust

5. This person would never intentionally misrepresent my point of view to other people.
6. I can confide in this person and know that he/she will not discuss it with others.   _____
7. This person responds constructively and caringly to my problems.   _____
                                                                                                                                                        _____

Reliableness

8. If this person promised to do me a favor, she/he would carry out that promise.
9. If I had an appointment with this person, I could count on him/her showing up.   _____
10. I could lend this person money and count on getting it back as soon as possible.   _____
11. I do not need a backup plan because I know this person will come through for me.   _____
Total score = _____

Trustworthiness Scale

77–110 = High (Trust is a precious thing.)
45–76 = Moderate (Be careful; get a rearview mirror.)
11–44 = Low (Lock up your valuables!)

Questions for Discussion

1. Which particular items in this trust questionnaire are most central to your idea of trust? Why?

2. Does your score accurately depict the degree to which you trust (or distrust) the target person?

3. Why do you trust (or distrust) this individual?

4. If you trust this person to a high degree, how hard was it to build that trust? Explain. What would destroy that trust?

5. Based on your responses to this questionnaire, how would you rate your "propensity to trust"? Low? Moderate? High?

6. What are the managerial implications of your propensity to trust?

Group Exercise

Student Team Development Project

Objectives

1. To help you better understand the components of teamwork.

2. To give you a practical diagnostic tool to assess the need for team building.

3. To give you a chance to evaluate and develop an actual group/team.

Introduction

Student teams are very common in today's college classrooms. They are an important part of the move toward cooperative and experiential learning. In other words, learning by doing. Group dynamics and teamwork are best learned by doing. Unfortunately, many classroom teams wallow in ambiguity, conflict, and ineffectiveness. This team development questionnaire can play an important role in the life cycle of your classroom team or group. All members of your team can complete this evaluation at one or more of the following critical points in your team's life cycle: (1) when the team reaches a crisis point and threatens to break up, (2) about halfway through the life of the team, and (3) at the end of the team's life cycle. Discussion of the results by all team members can enhance the group's learning experience.

Instructions

Either at the prompting of your instructor or by group consensus, decide at what point in your team's life cycle this exercise should be completed. *Tip:* Have each team member write their responses to the 10 items on a sheet of paper with no names attached. This will permit the calculation of a group mean score for each item and for all 10 items. Attention should then turn to the discussion questions provided to help any team development problems surface and to point the way toward solutions.

(An alternative to these instructions is to evaluate a team or work group you are associated with in your current job. You may also draw from a group experience in a past job.)

Questionnaire[96]

1. To what extent do I feel a real part of the team?

5	4	3	2	1
Completely a part all the time.	A part most of the time.	On the edge—sometimes in, sometimes out.	Generally outside except for one or two short periods.	On the outside, not really a part of the team.

2. How safe is it in this team to be at ease, relaxed, and myself?

5	4	3	2	1
I feel perfectly safe to be myself; they won't hold mistakes against me.	I feel most people would accept me if I were completely myself, but there are some I am not sure about.	Generally one has to be careful what one says or does in this team.	I am quite fearful about being completely myself in this team.	I am not a fool; I would never be myself in this team.

3. To what extent do I feel "under wraps," that is, have private thoughts, unspoken reservations, or unexpressed feelings and opinions that I have not felt comfortable bringing out into the open?

1	2	3	4	5
Almost completely under wraps.	Under wraps many times.	Slightly more free and expressive than under wraps.	Quite free and expressive much of the time.	Almost completely free and expressive.

4. How effective are we, in our team, in getting out and using the ideas, opinions, and information of all team members in making decisions?

1	2	3	4	5
We don't really encourage everyone to share their ideas, opinions, and information with the team in making decisions.	Only the ideas, opinions, and information of a few members are really known and used in making decisions.	Sometimes we hear the views of most members before making decisions, and sometimes we disregard most members.	A few are sometimes hesitant about sharing their opinions, but we generally have good participation in making decisions.	Everyone feels his or her ideas, opinions, and information are given a fair hearing before decisions are made.

5. To what extent are the goals the team is working toward understood, and to what extent do they have meaning for you?

5	4	3	2	1
I feel extremely good about the goals of our team.	I feel fairly good, but some things are not too clear or meaningful.	A few things we are doing are clear and meaningful.	Much of the activity is not clear or meaningful to me.	I really do not understand or feel involved in the goals of the team.

6. How well does the team work at its tasks?

1	2	3	4	5
Coasts, loafs, makes no progress.	Makes a little progress, but most members loaf.	Progress is slow; spurts of effective work.	Above average in progress and pace of work.	Works well; achieves definite progress.

7. Our planning and the way we operate as a team are largely influenced by:

1	2	3	4	5
One or two team members.	A clique.	Shifts from one person or clique to another.	Shared by most of the members, but some are left out.	Shared by all members of the team.

8. What is the level of responsibility for work in our team?

5	4	3	2	1
Each person assumes personal responsibility for getting work done.	A majority of the members assume responsibility for getting work done.	About half assume responsibility; about half do not.	Only a few assume responsibility for getting work done.	Nobody (except perhaps one) really assumes responsibility for getting work done.

9. How are differences or conflicts handled in our team?

1	2	3	4	5
Differences or conflicts are denied, suppressed, or avoided at all costs.	Differences or conflicts are recognized but remain mostly unresolved.	Differences or conflicts are recognized, and some attempts are made to work them through by some members, often outside the team meetings.	Differences and conflicts are recognized, and some attempts are made to deal with them in our team.	Differences and conflicts are recognized, and the team usually is working them through satisfactorily.

10. How do people relate to the team leader, chairperson, or "boss"?

1	2	3	4	5
The leader dominates the team, and people are often fearful or passive.	The leader tends to control the team, although people generally agree with the leader's direction.	There is some give and take between the leader and the team members.	Team members relate easily to the leader and usually are able to influence leader decisions.	Team members respect the leader, but they work together as a unified team, with everyone participating and no one dominant.

Total score = _____

Questions for Discussion

1. Have any of the items on the questionnaire helped you better understand why your team has had problems? What problems?

2. Based on Table 13–1, are you part of a group or team? Explain.

3. How do your responses to the items compare with the average responses from your group? What insights does this information provide?

4. Refer back to Tuckman's five-stage model of group development in Figure 12–3. Which stage is your team at? How can you tell? Did group decay set in?

5. If you are part way through your team's life cycle, what steps does your team need to take to become more effective?

6. If this is the end of your team's life cycle, what should your team have done differently?

7. What lasting lessons about teamwork have you learned from this exercise?

Ethical Dilemma

Sexy but Sexless Relationships?

Situation

You're the ground crew manager in Chicago for a major commercial airline company. During lunchtime in your office, you run across a curious article while browsing *Fast Company* magazine's Web archives. You begin to read:

> "You're intensely together on a project, things are going well, and the adrenaline gets pumping," says David R Eyler. "The chemistry feels right, but you don't want to mess up your personal or professional relationships by having an affair. You recognize that you've got something good here, and you set limits on your behavior."
>
> Can you have a sexy but sexless relationship? Researchers are embracing a new notion that sexual attraction between co-workers may not be bad. It may, in fact, be beneficial.
>
> Eyler and Andrea P Baridon, authors of three books on men and women in the workplace and senior staff members of the National Center for Higher Education in Washington, propose an unconventional alternative to an illicit affair. Instead of giving in to sexual attraction, you manage it. They call the relationship *More than Friends, Less than Lovers*—the title of a book they published in 1991.[97]

The article goes on to say researchers have found men and women using "sexual synergy" to achieve goals in the workplace. Five tips are offered for keeping these close, but not too close, relationships within bounds.

What is your reaction? (Explain the ethical reasoning for your choice.)

1. Hmmm. A little harmless flirting might boost productivity and be good for morale.

2. This is a surefire invitation to sexual harassment abuses and charges. What a stupid idea! (*Tip:* Refer back to Table 12–5, Behavioral Categories of Sexual Harassment.)

3. I should discuss this with our human resource department to check our stance on workplace romances and their relationship to our sexual harassment policy.

4. I could pass a copy of this article around to see if we have a problem with sexual harassment.

5. Invent other options. Discuss.

For an interpretation of this situation, visit our Web site, **www.mhhe.com/kreitner.**

Chapter Fourteen

Managing Conflict and Negotiation

Learning Objectives

When you finish studying the material in this chapter, you should be able to:

1 Define the term *conflict*, and put the three metaphors of conflict into proper perspective for the workplace.

2 Distinguish between functional and dysfunctional conflict, and identify three desired conflict outcomes.

3 Define *personality conflicts*, and explain how managers should handle them.

4 Discuss the role of in-group thinking in intergroup conflict, and explain what management can do about intergroup conflict.

5 Discuss what can be done about cross-cultural conflict.

6 Explain how managers can stimulate functional conflict, and identify the five conflict-handling styles.

7 Explain the nature and practical significance of conflict triangles and alternative dispute resolution for third-party conflict intervention.

8 Explain the difference between distributive and integrative negotiation, and discuss the concept of added-value negotiation.

Margaret Boitano, *Fortune Magazine*

It's Monday, 11 A.M., and I'm in the boss' office thinking I'm finally going to get that long-awaited promotion. "I want to tell you that we think you have great potential," she says with a stern face. "But you really need to do something about your style." My mind races as I try to figure out what she could possibly mean. I make a mental note never to trust people who start conversations with compliments. "Well . . . ah . . . it's nice to know that I'm appreciated," I stammer, stomach churning. "But I have to be honest. I don't know what you're talking about." She leans forward and says, "You need to dress more conservatively." Apparently I've been coming to work looking like Erin Brockovich, and that's considered inappropriate for a manager. I don't know whether to laugh or scream, and I briefly toy with the idea of simply storming out of her office. This can't be happening.

It isn't.

My "boss" isn't really a boss at all. She designs exhibits for a science museum. Surrounding us in the lobby of the Marriott hotel in Cambridge, Massachusetts, are 120 other people having similar conversations. We're all here for

Conflict is unavoidable and not necessarily a bad thing in today's high-pressure and fast-paced workplaces.
(c) Michael Newman/PhotoEdit

a two-day seminar on Managing the Difficult Business Conversation, and if the subject sounds overly touchie-feelie, like a grown-up version of *Barney*, stop smirking. The seminar is run by Harvard Law School's Program on Negotiation, an applied-research center that studies dispute resolution around the world.

"Conflict is a growth industry," says Bruce Patton, an associate director of the Program on Negotiation who worked with the US and Iranian governments to end the hostage crisis in 1980. "Most companies aim to minimize it, but the best companies learn to harness it to spur creativity." In fact, difficult conversations are increasingly common these days, as companies move to flattened management structures and the economy grinds through a painful slowdown. If you run a small business, chances are you're on one end of just about every difficult conversation that takes place—plus all those that don't take place but should. . . .

The 120 attendees of this class are from small businesses and from giant corporations like Procter & Gamble, McDonald's, Pfizer, and Bayer. For Paige Ireland of Canal Bridge Consulting, a private company in Bethesda, Maryland, with 16 employees, just getting into the course elicited an uncomfortable exchange. She found a flier on her desk one morning with the word "Interested?" scribbled on it by her boss. "Is there something you're trying to tell me?" she asked. Fortunately, he laughed it off. One CEO, Pablo Figueroa, flew in from Puerto Rico to attend, leaving his No. 2 in charge of the architectural design firm he founded 14 years ago. Even two people from the IRS showed up—one, appropriately enough, from the audit department.

Most attendees brought along a specific problem they hoped to resolve. "How do I tell employees that their bonus is going to be much smaller than expected?" asked one woman. Another wanted tips on how to soften a customer's expectations when you know there's no chance you can meet them.

Admittedly, some of the course materials were written in language you might find in a marriage-counseling manual. The second morning, for example, we covered Managing Your Feelings and Getting Straight on Purposes, or how to get what you want from employees without letting emotions overwhelm the discussion. However, we picked up some concrete guidance as well. One of the first rules: Erase the word "but" from your vocabulary and replace it with "and." (As in, "I understand how you could feel that way, and . . .") According to the instructors, saying "but" creates an either/or situation, which can put subordinate employees on the defensive.

As elementary as instructions like these sound, they're surprisingly difficult to put into practice, even in role-playing sit-

uations. Though I'd never met the woman playing my boss, I still somehow resented her for taking issue with my hypothetical attire. (For the record, I don't dress all that much like Erin Brockovich.) At the cocktail reception that evening, I learned I wasn't alone in my feelings. A number of people—mainly women, who made up about 40% of the attendees—were still stewing from the conversations they'd had that morning. One, a portfolio manager at a small New York bank, grew flustered when she realized that her partner wasn't merely acting the part of a mean boss but actually was one. "I'm bad at role-playing, so I'm just going to be myself," he told her before lashing out. (Translation: I'm going to be a jerk.) We decided that he must have been sent by his company for mandatory sensitivity training. Another woman's partner actually called her a slut. So much for "getting straight on purposes."

The next morning, we discussed the "F" word (feelings, that is) and learned that feelings are the biggest factor preventing people from having difficult conversations at work. They're certainly what stopped me from reconciling with my "boss"—we politely avoided each other for the rest of the seminar. "People assume that you check your feelings at the door when you go to work," says Sheila Heen, a Harvard Law School lecturer who has worked with corporations and helped the Citadel military college in South Carolina go coed.

During the discussion on feelings, one small-business owner said he often became overwhelmed at work but was reluctant to tell employees for fear they'd lose faith in him. A woman who heads an education company said she didn't voice her feelings because she didn't want to be considered too emotional. Others said being candid about your feelings at work can have negative repercussions.

The professors didn't have sure-fire solutions for any of these issues. They offered us some Zen-like advice—for example, learn to recognize the difference between "expressing emotions" and "being emotional"—and they listed the five things you should never say when someone is upset: "Calm down"; "What did you expect?"; "It's not so bad"; "What you need to understand is . . ."; and "I see your point, but . . ." (there's that "but" again). Then they showed us how to map out both our feelings and what we think the other person might be feeling. Don't assume the worst about things you don't know, they cautioned. If you feel you don't have enough information, try bouncing your thoughts off a co-worker. . . .

Back in our seats, we talked about making the toughest decision of all: whether a situation even warrants a difficult conversation. The short answer: only if there's a compelling business need and you have a constructive purpose. (Telling somebody they're an idiot and wrong doesn't cut it.) Whatever you decide, it won't be easy. "The first time you try to use this stuff, assume it won't go well," cautioned Douglas Stone, a Harvard Law School lecturer who has worked as a consultant in Cyprus helping leaders from Greece and Turkey communicate. "If you do it every day, though, you'll get better at it."

So the next time you get a call from the IRS and hear something strange like "I imagine how awful you must feel, and I'm terribly sorry for any inconvenience this may cause.

You're being audited," don't take it so hard. At least you'll know somebody is trying.[1]

For Discussion
How do you handle difficult work-related conversations? How effectively do you deal with conflict?

H ow would you handle this situation?

Your name is Annie and you are a product development manager for Amazon.com. As you were eating lunch today in your cubicle, Laura, a software project manager with an office nearby, asked if she could talk to you for a few minutes. You barely know Laura and you have heard both good and bad things about her work habits. Although your mind was more on how to meet Friday's deadline than on lunch, you waved her in.

She proceeded to pour out her woes about how she is having an impossible time partnering with Hans on a new special project. He is regarded as a top-notch software project manager, but Laura has found him to be ill-tempered and uncooperative. Laura thought you and Hans were friends because she has seen the two of you talking in the cafeteria and parking lot. You told Laura you have a good working relationship with Hans, but he's not really a friend. Still, Laura pressed on. "Would you straighten Hans out for me?" she asked. "We've got to get moving on this special project."

"Why this?" "Why now?" "Why me?!!" you thought as your eyes left Laura and drifted back to your desk.

Write down some ideas about how to handle this all-too-common conflict situation. Set it aside. We'll revisit your recommendation later in the chapter. In the meantime, we need to explore the world of conflict because, as indicated in the opening vignette, conflict is an ever-present feature of modern life. After discussing a modern view of conflict and four major types of conflict, we learn how to manage conflict both as a participant and as a third party. The related topic of negotiation is examined next. We conclude with a contingency approach to conflict management and negotiation.

Conflict: A Modern Perspective

Make no mistake about it. Conflict is an unavoidable aspect of organizational life. These major trends conspire to make *organizational* conflict inevitable:

- Constant change.
- Greater employee diversity.
- More teams (virtual and self-managed).

- Less face-to-face communication (more electronic interaction).
- A global economy with increased cross-cultural dealings.

Dean Tjosvold, from Canada's Simon Fraser University, notes that "Change begets conflict, conflict begets change"[2] and challenges us to do better with this sobering global perspective:

> Learning to manage conflict is a critical investment in improving how we, our families, and our organizations adapt and take advantage of change. Managing conflicts well does not insulate us from change, nor does it mean that we will always come out on top or get all that we want. However, effective conflict management helps us keep in touch with new developments and create solutions appropriate for new threats and opportunities.
>
> Much evidence shows we have often failed to manage our conflicts and respond to change effectively. High divorce rates, disheartening examples of sexual and physical abuse of children, the expensive failures of international joint ventures, and bloody ethnic violence have convinced many people that we do not have the abilities to cope with our complex interpersonal, organizational, and global conflicts.[3]

But respond we must. As outlined in this chapter, tools and solutions are available, if only we develop the ability and will to use them persistently. The choice is ours: Be active managers of conflict, or be managed by conflict.

A comprehensive review of the conflict literature yielded this consensus definition: "**conflict** is a process in which one party perceives that its interests are being opposed or negatively affected by another party."[4] The word *perceives* reminds us that sources of conflict and issues can be real or imagined. The resulting conflict is the same. Conflict can escalate (strengthen) or deescalate (weaken) over time. "The conflict process unfolds in a context, and whenever conflict, escalated or not, occurs the disputants or third parties can attempt to manage it in some manner."[5] Consequently, current and future managers need to understand the dynamics of conflict and know how to handle it effectively (both as disputants and as third parties).

Conflict

One party perceives its interests are being opposed or set back by another party.

The Language of Conflict: Metaphors and Meaning

Conflict is a complex subject for several reasons. Primary among them is the reality that conflict often carries a lot of emotional luggage. Fear of losing or fear of change quickly raises the emotional stakes in a conflict. Conflicts also vary widely in magnitude. Conflicts have both participants and observers. Some observers may be interested and active, others disinterested and passive. Consequently, the term *conflict* can take on vastly different meanings, depending on the circumstances and one's involvement. For example, consider these three metaphors and accompanying workplace expressions:

- *Conflict as war:* "We shot down that idea."
- *Conflict as opportunity:* "What are all the possibilities for solving this problem?"
- *Conflict as journey:* "Let's search for common ground."[6]

Anyone viewing a conflict as war will try to win at all costs and wipe out the enemy. Alternatively, those seeing a conflict as an opportunity and a journey will tend to be more positive, open-minded, and constructive. In a hostile world, combative and destructive warlike thinking too often prevails. But workplace conflicts are *not* war. So when dealing with organizational conflicts, we are challenged to rely less on the metaphor and language of war and more on the metaphors and language of *opportunity* and *journey*. We need to monitor our choice of words in conflict situations carefully.

While explaining the three metaphors, conflict experts Kenneth Cloke and Joan Goldsmith made this instructive observation that we want to keep in mind for the balance of this chapter:

> Conflict gives you an opportunity to deepen your capacity for empathy and intimacy with your opponent. Your anger transforms the "Other" into a stereotyped demon or villain. Similarly, defensiveness will prevent you from communicating openly with your opponents, or listening carefully to what they are saying. On the other hand, once you engage in dialogue with that person, you will resurrect the human side of their personality—and express your own as well.
>
> Moreover, when you process your conflicts with integrity, they lead to growth, increased awareness, and self-improvement. Uncontrolled anger, defensiveness, and shame defeat these possibilities. Everyone feels better when they overcome their problems and reach resolution, and worse when they succumb and fail to resolve them. It is a bitter truth that victories won in anger lead to long-term defeat. Those defeated turn away, feeling betrayed and lost, and carry this feeling with them into their next conflict.
>
> Conflict can be seen simply as a way of learning more about what is not working and discovering how to fix it. The usefulness of the solution depends on the depth of your understanding of the problem. This depends on your ability to listen to the issue as you would to a teacher, which depends on halting the cycle of escalation and searching for opportunities for improvement.[7]

In short, win–win beats win–lose in both conflict management and negotiation.

A Conflict Continuum

Ideas about managing conflict underwent an interesting evolution during the 20th century. Initially, scientific management experts such as Frederick W Taylor believed all conflict ultimately threatened management's authority and thus had to be avoided or quickly resolved. Later, human relationists recognized the inevitability of conflict and advised managers to learn to live with it. Emphasis remained on resolving conflict whenever possible, however. Beginning in the 1970s, OB specialists realized conflict had both positive and negative outcomes, depending on its nature and intensity. This perspective introduced the revolutionary idea that organizations could suffer from *too little* conflict. Figure 14–1 illustrates the relationship between conflict intensity and outcomes.

Work groups, departments, or organizations experiencing too little conflict tend to be plagued by apathy, lack of creativity, indecision, and missed deadlines. Excessive conflict, on the other hand, can erode organizational performance because of political infighting, dissatisfaction, lack of teamwork, and turnover. Workplace aggression and violence can be manifestations of excessive conflict.[8] Appropriate types and levels of conflict energize people in constructive directions.[9]

Functional versus Dysfunctional Conflict

The distinction between **functional conflict** and **dysfunctional conflict** pivots on whether the organization's interests are served. According to one conflict expert,

> Some [types of conflict] support the goals of the organization and improve performance; these are functional, constructive forms of conflict. They benefit or support the main purposes of the organization. Additionally, there are those types of conflict that hinder

Functional conflict
Serves organization's interests.

Dysfunctional conflict
Threatens organization's interests.

Figure 14–1   *The Relationship between Conflict Intensity and Outcomes*

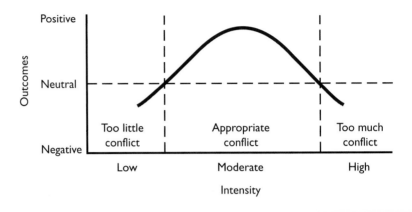

SOURCE: LD Brown, *Managing Conflict of Organizational Interfaces*, (Reading; MA, Addison-Wesley Publishing, 1986), figure 1.1, p. 8 © 1986, Addison-Wesley Publishing Co. Reprinted with permission.

organizational performance; these are dysfunctional or destructive forms. They are undesirable and the manager should seek their eradication.[10]

Functional conflict is commonly referred to in management circles as constructive or cooperative conflict.[11]

Often, a simmering conflict can be defused in a functional manner or driven to dysfunctional proportions, depending on how it is handled. For example, consider these two very different outcomes at Southwest Airlines and Gateway, the computer maker with the familiar black-and-white cow shipping boxes:

> Recently tensions broke out between flight attendants and their schedulers (the ones with the sorry job of telling flight attendants they have to work on a day off). The flight attendants believed the schedulers were overworking them; the schedulers claimed the attendants were hostile and uncooperative. The solution was very, well, Southwest: Both sides had to switch jobs for a day and see how difficult the other side had it. For now, at least, the tactic has eased tensions.[12]

Meanwhile, trouble was brewing at Gateway, where sales were off sharply. Company founder Ted Waitt had retired one year earlier when his handpicked successor, Jeff Weitzen, took over after being hired from AT&T. *Fortune* magazine followed the action:

> It all came to a head at Gateway's January 17 [2001] board meeting. In a hostile and combative proceeding, insiders say, Waitt and the board interrogated Weitzen relentlessly. At one point, after Weitzen had finished talking about his plans to improve customer service, one board member snapped, "Why should we believe you?"
>
> After the meeting Weitzen was furious. Stewing all weekend, he confronted Waitt the following Monday. High-level insiders say they argued for hours behind locked doors over how and by whom Gateway should be run. Waitt told Weitzen that he wanted him to stay on as CEO while Waitt took a more active role as chairman. For Weitzen, this arrangement—effectively a demotion—was unacceptable. Weitzen delivered an ultimatum: Back off or he was quitting.
>
> Taking a day to think about it, Waitt decided he wasn't backing off.[13]

A few days later, Weitzen and most of his top-management team were gone and Waitt's brief retirement was over.

Antecedents of Conflict

Certain situations produce more conflict than others. By knowing the antecedents of conflict, managers are better able to anticipate it and take steps to resolve it if it becomes dysfunctional. Among the situations tending to produce either functional or dysfunctional conflict are

- Incompatible personalities or value systems.
- Overlapping or unclear job boundaries.
- Competition for limited resources.
- Interdepartment/intergroup competition.
- Inadequate communication.
- Interdependent tasks (e.g., one person cannot complete his or her assignment until others have completed their work).
- Organizational complexity (conflict tends to increase as the number of hierarchical layers and specialized tasks increase).
- Unreasonable or unclear policies, standards, or rules.
- Unreasonable deadlines or extreme time pressure.
- Collective decision making (the greater the number of people participating in a decision, the greater the potential for conflict).
- Decision making by consensus.
- Unmet expectations (employees who have unrealistic expectations about job assignments, pay, or promotions are more prone to conflict).
- Unresolved or suppressed conflicts.[14]

Proactive managers carefully read these early warnings and take appropriate action.

Desired Conflict Outcomes

Within organizations, conflict management is more than simply a quest for agreement. If progress is to be made and dysfunctional conflict minimized, a broader agenda is in order. Tjosvold's cooperative conflict model calls for three desired outcomes:

1. *Agreement.* But at what cost? Equitable and fair agreements are best. An agreement that leaves one party feeling exploited or defeated will tend to breed resentment and subsequent conflict.

2. *Stronger relationships.* Good agreements enable conflicting parties to build bridges of goodwill and trust for future use. Moreover, conflicting parties who trust each other are more likely to keep their end of the bargain.

3. *Learning.* Functional conflict can promote greater self-awareness and creative problem solving. Like the practice of management itself, successful conflict handling is learned primarily by doing. Knowledge of the concepts and techniques in this chapter is a necessary first step, but there is no substitute for hands-on practice. In a contentious world, there are plenty of opportunities to practice conflict management.[15]

Types of Conflict

Certain antecedents of conflict, highlighted earlier, deserve a closer look. This section probes the nature and organizational implications of three basic types of conflict: personality conflict, intergroup conflict, and cross-cultural conflict. Our discussion of each type of conflict includes some practical tips and techniques.

Personality Conflict

We visited the topic of personalities in our Chapter 2 discussion of diversity. Also, recall the Big Five personality dimensions introduced in Chapter 5. Once again, your *personality* is the package of stable traits and characteristics creating your unique identity. According to experts on the subject:

> Each of us has a unique way of interacting with others. Whether we are seen as charming, irritating, fascinating, nondescript, approachable, or intimidating depends in part on our personality, or what others might describe as our style.[16]

Personality conflict

Interpersonal opposition driven by personal dislike or disagreement.

Given the many possible combinations of personality traits, it is clear why personality conflicts are inevitable. We define a **personality conflict** as interpersonal opposition based on personal dislike, disagreement, and/or different styles. For example, imagine the potential for a top-level personality conflict at EMC Corp., a leading maker of data storage equipment. Michael C Ruettgers, executive chairman of the Massachusetts-based firm, gave up his CEO position in January 2001 after running the company for nine years.

> In a January [2002] interview, Ruettgers gave CEO Joseph M Tucci A's in innovation and strategic management, but F's in stock-price performance and financial management because the company lost $508 million in 2001. Ruettgers added that he was disappointed Tucci has attracted so little outside talent during his year at the helm. . . .
>
> At the same time, some former execs say, Tucci has wanted to move faster to cut costs, make acquisitions, and introduce new software but Ruettgers and EMC have slowed the pace of change. And Ruettgers, who had planned to be less active in daily affairs, has continued to attend weekly meetings to review operations. This has analysts and insiders speculating that Tucci could soon take the fall for EMC's poor performance. "In that culture, someone must fail," says a former EMC executive. "There will be a scapegoat." . . .
>
> The personal and management styles of Tucci, a salesman, and Ruettgers, who started at EMC as an operations expert, couldn't be more different. Tucci likes to build one-on-one relationships, while Ruettgers is more aloof. Tucci seems to be more willing than Ruettgers to make tough decisions quickly. Bill Scannell, EMC's senior vice president for global sales, says Tucci gives him an answer immediately when he asks for advice. Ruettgers tends to chew on things awhile. And Tucci praises and thanks his troops regularly, while Ruettgers once told a former executive that saying thank-you is a sign of weakness.[17]

Any way you look at it, Tucci is in a tough spot, and personalities can only make matters worse.

Workplace Incivility: The Seeds of Personality Conflict   Somewhat akin to physical pain, chronic personality conflicts often begin with seemingly insignificant irritations. For instance, a manager can grow to deeply dislike someone in the next cubicle who persistently whistles off-key while drumming their foot on the

side of a filing cabinet. Sadly, grim little scenarios such as this are all too common to-day, given the steady erosion of civility in the workplace. Researchers have noted how increased informality, pressure for results, and employee diversity have fostered an "anything goes" atmosphere in today's workplaces. They view incivility as a self-perpetuating vicious cycle that can end in violence.[18] A new study indicates the extent of workplace incivility: "71% of 1,100 workers surveyed said they'd experienced put-downs or condescending and outright rude behavior on the job."[19] What is your experience with workplace incivility (both give and take)?

Vicious cycles of incivility need to be avoided, or broken early, with an organizational culture that places a high value on respect for co-workers. This requires managers and leaders to act as caring and courteous role models. A positive spirit of cooperation, as opposed to one based on negativism and aggression, also helps. Some organizations have resorted to workplace etiquette training. More specifically, constructive feedback or skillful behavior shaping can keep a single irritating behavior from precipitating a full-blown personality conflict (or worse).

Dealing with Personality Conflicts   Personality conflicts are a potential minefield for managers. Let us frame the situation. Personality traits, by definition, are stable and resistant to change. Moreover, according to the American Psychiatric Association's *Diagnostic and Statistical Manual of Mental Disorders,* there are 410 psychological disorders that can and do show up in the workplace.[20] This brings up legal issues. Employees in the United States suffering from psychological disorders such as depression and mood-altering diseases such as alcoholism are protected from discrimination by the Americans with Disabilities Act.[21] (Other nations have similar laws.) Also, sexual harassment and other forms of discrimination can grow out of apparent personality conflicts.[22] Finally, personality conflicts can spawn workplace aggression and violence.[23]

Traditionally, managers dealt with personality conflicts by either ignoring them or transferring one party. In view of the legal implications, just discussed, both of these options may be open invitations to discrimination lawsuits. Table 14–1 presents practical tips for both nonmanagers and managers who are involved in or affected by personality conflicts. Our later discussions of handling dysfunctional conflict and alternative dispute resolution techniques also apply.[24]

Intergroup Conflict

Conflict among work groups, teams, and departments is a common threat to organizational competitiveness. For example, when Michael Volkema became CEO of Herman Miller in the mid-1990s, he found an inward-focused company with divisions fighting over budgets. He has since curbed intergroup conflict at the Michigan-based furniture maker by emphasizing collaboration and redirecting everyone's attention outward, to the customer.[25] Managers who understand the mechanics of intergroup conflict are better equipped to face this sort of challenge.

In-Group Thinking: The ʃeeds of Intergroup Conflict   As we discussed in previous chapters, *cohesiveness*—a "we feeling" binding group members together—can be a good or bad thing. A certain amount of cohesiveness can turn a group of individuals into a smooth-running team. Too much cohesiveness, however, can breed groupthink because a desire to get along pushes aside critical thinking. The

Table 14–1   *How to Deal with Personality Conflicts*

Tips for Employees Having a Personality Conflict	Tips for Third-Party Observers of a Personality Conflict	Tips for Managers Whose Employees Are Having a Personality Conflict
• Communicate directly with the other person to resolve the perceived conflict (emphasize problem solving and common objectives, not personalities). • Avoid dragging co-workers into the conflict. • If dysfunctional conflict persists, seek help from direct supervisors or human resource specialists.	• Do not take sides in someone else's personality conflict. • Suggest the parties work things out themselves in a constructive and positive way. • If dysfunctional conflict persists, refer the problem to parties' direct supervisors.	• Investigate and document conflict. • If appropriate, take corrective action (e.g., feedback or behavior shaping). • If necessary, attempt informal dispute resolution. • Refer difficult conflicts to human resource specialists or hired counselors for formal resolution attempts and other interventions.

Note: All employees need to be familiar with and *follow* company policies for diversity, antidiscrimination, and sexual harassment.

study of ingroups by small group researchers has revealed a whole package of changes associated with increased group cohesiveness. Specifically,

- Members of in-groups view themselves as a collection of unique individuals, while they stereotype members of other groups as being "all alike."
- In-group members see themselves positively and as morally correct, while they view members of other groups negatively and as immoral.
- In-groups view outsiders as a threat.
- In-group members exaggerate the differences between their group and other groups. This typically involves a distorted perception of reality.[26]

In-group thinking is a major cause of conflict in work organizations. It is divisive and thrives on stereotypes. Fanatical sports fans, such as these Brazilians celebrating their 2002 World Cup soccer championship, illustrate an extreme form of in-group thinking. Managers cannot eliminate in-group thinking, but they can strive to keep it within reasonable bounds. Otherwise, our workplaces would resemble this Sao Paulo mob scene.

AP/Wide World Photos

Avid sports fans who simply can't imagine how someone would support the opposing team exemplify one form of in-group thinking. Also, this pattern of behavior is a form of ethnocentrism, discussed as a cross-cultural barrier in Chapter 4. Reflect for a moment on evidence of in-group behavior in your life. Does your circle of friends make fun of others because of their race, gender, nationality, sexual preference, weight, or major in college?[27]

In-group thinking is one more fact of organizational life that virtually guarantees conflict. Managers cannot eliminate in-group thinking, but they certainly should not ignore it when handling intergroup conflicts.

Research Lessons for Handling Intergroup Conflict   Sociologists have long recommended the contact hypothesis for reducing intergroup conflict. According to the *contact hypothesis,* the more the members of different groups interact, the less intergroup conflict they will experience. Those interested in improving race, international, and union-management relations typically encourage cross-group interaction. The hope is that *any* type of interaction, short of actual conflict, will reduce stereotyping and combat in-group thinking. But recent research has shown this approach to be naive and limited. For example, one study of 83 health center employees (83% female) at a midwest US university probed the specific nature of intergroup relations and concluded:

> The number of *negative* relationships was significantly related to higher perceptions of intergroup conflict. Thus, it seems that negative relationships have a salience that overwhelms any possible positive effects from friendship links across groups.[28]

Intergroup friendships are still desirable, as documented in many studies,[29] but they are readily overpowered by negative intergroup interactions. Thus, *priority number one for managers faced with intergroup conflict is to identify and root out specific negative linkages among groups.* A single personality conflict, for instance, may contaminate the entire intergroup experience. The same goes for an employee who voices negative opinions or spreads negative rumors about another group. Our updated contact model in Figure 14–2 is based on this and other recent research insights, such as the need to foster positive attitudes toward other groups.[30] Also, notice how conflict within the group and negative gossip from third parties are threats that need to be neutralized if intergroup conflict is to be minimized.[31]

Cross-Cultural Conflict

Doing business with people from different cultures is commonplace in our global economy where cross-border mergers, joint ventures, and alliances are the order of the day.[32] Because of differing assumptions about how to think and act, the potential for cross-cultural conflict is both immediate and huge.[33] Success or failure, when conducting business across cultures, often hinges on avoiding and minimizing actual or perceived conflict. For example, consider this cultural mismatch:

> Mexicans place great importance on saving face, so they tend to expect any conflicts that occur during negotiations to be downplayed or kept private. The prevailing attitude in the [United States], however, is that conflict should be dealt with directly and publicly to prevent hard feelings from developing on a personal level.[34]

This is not a matter of who is right and who is wrong; rather it is a matter of accommodating cultural differences for a successful business transaction. Awareness of the

Figure 14–2   *An Updated Contact Model for Minimizing Intergroup Conflict*

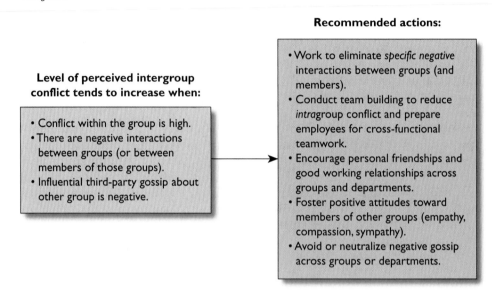

Level of perceived intergroup conflict tends to increase when:

- Conflict within the group is high.
- There are negative interactions between groups (or between members of those groups).
- Influential third-party gossip about other group is negative.

Recommended actions:

- Work to eliminate *specific negative interactions* between groups (and members).
- Conduct team building to reduce *intragroup* conflict and prepare employees for cross-functional teamwork.
- Encourage personal friendships and good working relationships across groups and departments.
- Foster positive attitudes toward members of other groups (empathy, compassion, sympathy).
- Avoid or neutralize negative gossip across groups or departments.

SOURCES: Based on research evidence in G Labianca, D J Brass, and B Gray, "Social Networks and Perceptions of Intergroup Conflict: The Role of Negative Relationships and Third Parties," *Academy of Management Journal,* February 1998, pp. 55–67; C D Batson et al., "Empathy and Attitudes: Can Feeling for a Member of a Stigmatized Group Improve Feelings toward the Group?" *Journal of Personality and Social Psychology,* January 1997, pp. 105–18; and S C Wright et al., "The Extended Contact Effect: Knowledge of Cross-Group Friendships and Prejudice," *Journal of Personality and Social Psychology,* July 1997, pp. 73–90.

GLOBE project's cross-cultural dimensions, discussed in Chapter 4, is an important first step. Stereotypes also need to be identified and neutralized (see the International OB on page 495). Beyond that, cross-cultural conflict can be moderated by using international consultants and building cross-cultural relationships.

International Consultants
In response to broad demand, there is a growing army of management consultants specializing in cross-cultural relations. Competency and fees vary widely, of course. But a carefully selected cross-cultural consultant can be helpful, as this illustration shows:

> [W]hen electronics-maker Canon planned to set up a subsidiary in Dubai through its Netherlands division, it asked consultant Sahid Mirza of Glocom, based in Dubai, to find out how the two cultures would work together.
>
> Mirza sent out the test questionnaires and got a sizeable response. "The findings were somewhat surprising," he recalls. "We found that, at the bedrock level, there were relatively few differences. Many of the Arab businessmen came from former British colonies and viewed business in much the same way as the Dutch."
>
> But at the level of behavior, there was a real conflict. "The Dutch are blunt and honest in expression, and such expression is very offensive to Arab sensibilities." Mirza offers the example of a Dutch executive who says something like, "We can't meet the deadline." Such a negative expression—true or not—would be gravely offensive to an Arab. As a result of Mirza's research, Canon did start the subsidiary in Dubai, but it trained both the Dutch and the Arab executives first.[35]

International OB

Researchers Probe the Linkage between Negative Stereotypes and Aggressive Behavior among Immigrant Boys

When it comes to schooling, the Herrera boys are no match for the Herrera girls. Last week, four years after she arrived from Honduras, Martha, 20, graduated from Fairfax High School in Los Angeles. She managed decent grades while working 36 hours a week at a Kentucky Fried Chicken. Her sister, Marlin, 22, attends a local community college and will soon be a certified nurse assistant. The brothers are a different story. Oscar, 17, was expelled two years ago from Fairfax for carrying a knife and later dropped out of a different school. The youngest, Jonathan, 15, is now in a juvenile boot camp after running into trouble with the law. "The boys get sidetracked more," says the kids' mother, Suyapa Landaverde. "The girls are more confident."

This is no aberration. Immigrant girls consistently outperform boys, according to the preliminary findings of a just-completed, five-year study of immigrant children—the largest of its kind, including Latino, Chinese, and Haitian kids—by Marcelo and Carola Suárez-Orozco of the Harvard Graduate School of Education. Though that trend holds for US-born kids as well, the reasons for the discrepancy among immigrants are different. The study found that immigrant girls are more adept at straddling cultures than boys. "The girls are able to retain some of the protective features of [their native] culture" because they're kept closer to the hearth, says Marcelo Suárez-Orozco, "while they maximize their acquisition of skills in the new culture" by helping their parents navigate it.

Consider the kids' experiences in school. The study found that boys face more peer pressure to adopt American youth culture—the dress, the slang, the disdain for education. They're disciplined more often and, as a result, develop more adversarial relationships with teachers—and the wider society. They may also face more debilitating prejudices. One teacher interviewed for the study said that the "cultural awareness training" she received as part of her continuing education included depictions of Latino boys as "aggressive" and "really macho" and of the girls as "pure sweetness."

Gender shapes immigrant kids' experiences outside school as well. Often hailing from traditional cultures, the girls face greater domestic obligations. They also frequently act as "cultural ambassadors," translating for parents and mediating between them and the outside world, says Carola Suárez-Orozco. An unintended consequence: "The girls get foisted into a responsible role more than the boys do." Take Christina Im, 18, a junior at Fairfax who arrived from South Korea four years ago. She ranks ninth in a class of 400 students and still finds time to fix dinner for the family and work on Saturdays at her mother's clothing shop. Her brother? "He plays computer games," says Im.

The Harvard study bears a cautionary note: If large numbers of immigrant boys continue to be alienated academically—and to be clear, plenty perform phenomenally—they risk sinking irretrievably into an economic underclass. Oscar Herrera, Martha's dropout brother, may be realizing that. "I'm thinking of returning to school," he recently told his mother. He ought to look to his sisters for guidance.

SOURCE: A Campo-Flores, " 'Macho' or 'Sweetness'?" *Newsweek,* July 1, 2002, p. 51.

Demographers tell us that 25% of the U.S. population will be Hispanic/Latino by the year 2050. This trend is part of a general pattern of more racial and ethnic diversity in our classrooms and workplaces. Cross-cultural conflict can be minimized or avoided by appreciating how peoples' cultural backgrounds affect their values, perceptions, and behavior. Teachers and managers need to know where people are "coming from" before helping them get where they want to go.

(c) Spencer Grant/PhotoEdit

Table 14–2   *Ways to Build Cross-Cultural Relationships*

Behavior	Rank
Be a good listener	1
Be sensitive to needs of others	2
Be cooperative, rather than overly competitive	2
Advocate inclusive (participative) leadership	3
Compromise rather than dominate	4
Build rapport through conversations	5
Be compassionate and understanding	6
Avoid conflict by emphasizing harmony	7
Nurture others (develop and mentor)	8

(Ranks 2 and 2 marked with a bracket: > Tie)

SOURCE: Adapted from R L Tung, "American Expatriates Abroad: From Neophytes to Cosmopolitans," *Journal of World Business,* Summer 1998, table 6, p. 136.

Consultants also can help untangle possible personality, and intergroup conflicts from conflicts rooted in differing national cultures. *Note:* Although we have discussed these three basic types of conflict separately, they typically are encountered in complex, messy bundles.

Building Cross-Cultural Relationships to Avoid Dysfunctional Conflict   Rosalie L Tung's study of 409 expatriates from US and Canadian multinational firms, mentioned in Chapter 4, is very instructive.[36] Her survey sought to pinpoint success factors for the expatriates (14% female) who were working in 51 different countries worldwide. Nine specific ways to facilitate interaction with host-country nationals, as ranked from most useful to least useful by the respondents, are listed in Table 14–2. Good listening skills topped the list, followed by sensitivity to others and cooperativeness rather than competitiveness. Interestingly, US managers are culturally characterized as just the opposite: poor listeners, blunt to the point of insensitivity, and excessively competitive. Some managers need to add self-management to the list of ways to minimize cross-cultural conflict.

Managing Conflict

As we have seen, conflict has many faces and is a constant challenge for managers who are responsible for reaching organizational goals. Our attention now turns to the active management of both functional and dysfunctional conflict. We discuss how to stimulate functional conflict, how to handle dysfunctional conflict, and how third parties can deal effectively with conflict. Relevant research lessons also are examined.

Stimulating Functional Conflict

Sometimes committees and decision-making groups become so bogged down in details and procedures that nothing substantive is accomplished. Carefully monitored functional conflict can help get the creative juices flowing once again. Managers basically have two options. They can fan the fires of naturally occurring conflict—but this approach can be unreliable and slow. Alternatively, managers can resort to programmed conflict. Experts in the field define **programmed conflict** as "conflict that raises different opinions *regardless of the personal feelings of the managers*."[37] The trick is to get contributors to either defend or criticize ideas based on relevant facts rather than on the basis of personal preference or political interests. This requires disciplined role playing. Two programmed conflict techniques with proven track records are devil's advocacy and the dialectic method. Let us explore these two ways of stimulating functional conflict.

Devil's Advocacy

This technique gets its name from a traditional practice within the Roman Catholic Church. When someone's name came before the College of Cardinals for elevation to sainthood, it was absolutely essential to ensure that he or she had a spotless record. Consequently, one individual was assigned the role of *devil's advocate* to uncover and air all possible objections to the person's canonization. In accordance with this practice, **devil's advocacy** in today's organizations involves assigning someone the role of critic.[38] Recall from Chapter 12, Irving Janis recommended the devil's advocate role for preventing groupthink.

In the left half of Figure 14–3, note how devil's advocacy alters the usual decision-making process in steps 2 and 3. This approach to programmed conflict is intended to generate critical thinking and reality testing.[39] It is a good idea to rotate the job of devil's advocate so no one person or group develops a strictly negative reputation. Moreover, periodic devil's advocacy role-playing is good training for developing analytical and communication skills and emotional intelligence.

The Dialectic Method

Like devil's advocacy, the dialectic method is a time-honored practice. This particular approach to programmed conflict traces back to the dialectic school of philosophy in ancient Greece. Plato and his followers attempted to synthesize truths by exploring opposite positions (called *thesis* and *antithesis*). Court systems in the United States and elsewhere rely on directly opposing points of view for determining guilt or innocence. Accordingly, today's **dialectic method** calls for managers to foster a structured debate of opposing viewpoints prior to making a decision.[40] Steps 3 and 4 in the right half of Figure 14–3 set the dialectic approach apart from the normal decision-making process. Here is how Anheuser-Busch's corporate policy committee uses the dialectic method:

> When the policy committee . . . considers a major move—getting into or out of a business, or making a big capital expenditure—it sometimes assigns teams to make the case for each side of the question. There may be two teams or even three. Each is knowledgeable about the subject; each has access to the same information. Occasionally someone in favor of the project is chosen to lead the dissent, and an opponent to argue for it. Pat Stokes, who heads the company's beer empire, describes the result: "We end up with decisions and alternatives we hadn't thought of previously," sometimes representing a synthesis of the opposing views. "You become a lot more anticipatory, better able to see what might happen, because you have thought through the process."[41]

A major drawback of the dialectic method is that "winning the debate" may overshadow the issue at hand. Also, the dialectic method requires more skill training than does devil's advocacy. Regarding the comparative effectiveness of these two approaches to stimulating functional conflict, however, a laboratory study ended in a

---

Programmed conflict

Encourages different opinions without protecting management's personal feelings.

Devil's advocacy

Assigning someone the role of critic.

Dialectic method

Fostering a debate of opposing viewpoints to better understand an issue.

Figure 14–3 *Techniques for Stimulating Functional Conflict: Devil's Advocacy and the Dialectic Method*

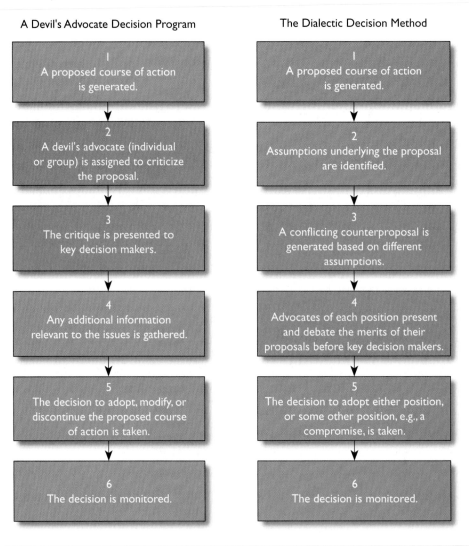

A Devil's Advocate Decision Program

1
A proposed course of action is generated.

2
A devil's advocate (individual or group) is assigned to criticize the proposal.

3
The critique is presented to key decision makers.

4
Any additional information relevant to the issues is gathered.

5
The decision to adopt, modify, or discontinue the proposed course of action is taken.

6
The decision is monitored.

The Dialectic Decision Method

1
A proposed course of action is generated.

2
Assumptions underlying the proposal are identified.

3
A conflicting counterproposal is generated based on different assumptions.

4
Advocates of each position present and debate the merits of their proposals before key decision makers.

5
The decision to adopt either position, or some other position, e.g., a compromise, is taken.

6
The decision is monitored.

SOURCE: R A Cosier and C R Schwenk, "Agreement and Thinking Alike: Ingredients for Poor Decisions," *Academy of Management Executive,* February 1990, pp. 72–73. Used with permission.

tie. Compared with groups that strived to reach a consensus, decision-making groups using either devil's advocacy or the dialectic method yielded equally higher quality decisions.[42] But, in a more recent laboratory study, groups using devil's advocacy produced more potential solutions and made better recommendations for a case problem than did groups using the dialectic method.[43]

In light of this mixed evidence, managers have some latitude in using either devil's advocacy or the dialectic method for pumping creative life back into stalled deliberations.[44] Personal preference and the role players' experience may well be the deciding factors in choosing one approach over the other. The important thing is to actively stim-

Figure 14–4   *Five Conflict-Handling Styles*

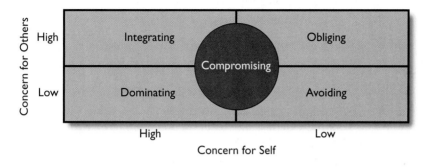

SOURCE: M. A. Rahim, "A Strategy for Managing Conflict in Complex Organizations, *Human Relations*, January 1985, p. 84. Used with author's permission of Plenum Publishing.

ulate functional conflict when necessary, such as when the risk of blind conformity or groupthink is high. Joseph M Tucci, the CEO of EMC introduced earlier, fosters functional conflict by creating a supportive climate for dissent:

> Good leaders always leave room for debate and different opinions. . . .
> The team has to be in harmony. But before you move out, there needs to be a debate. Leadership is not a right. You have to earn it.
> . . . [E]very company needs a healthy paranoia. It's the CEO's job to keep it on the edge, to put tension in the system. You have to do the right thing for the right circumstances.[45]

This meshes well with the results of a pair of recent laboratory studies that found a positive relationship between the degree of minority dissent and team innovation, *but only when participative decision making was used.*[46]

Alternative Styles for Handling Dysfunctional Conflict

People tend to handle negative conflict in patterned ways referred to as *styles.* Several conflict styles have been categorized over the years. According to conflict specialist Afzalur Rahim's model, five different conflict-handling styles can be plotted on a 2 × 2 grid. High to low concern for *self* is found on the horizontal axis of the grid, while low to high concern for *others* forms the vertical axis (see Figure 14–4). Various combinations of these variables produce the five different conflict-handling styles: integrating, obliging, dominating, avoiding, and compromising.[47] There is no single best style; each has strengths and limitations and is subject to situational constraints.

Integrating (Problem Solving)
In this style, interested parties confront the issue and cooperatively identify the problem, generate and weigh alternative solutions, and select a solution. Integrating is appropriate for complex issues plagued by misunderstanding. However, it is inappropriate for resolving conflicts rooted in opposing value systems. Its primary strength is its longer lasting impact because it deals with the underlying problem rather than merely with symptoms. The primary weakness of this style is that it is very time consuming.

Obliging (*J*moothing)

"An obliging person neglects his or her own concern to satisfy the concern of the other party."[48] This style, often called *smoothing,* involves playing down differences while emphasizing commonalities. Obliging may be an appropriate conflict-handling strategy when it is possible to eventually get something in return. But it is inappropriate for complex or worsening problems. Its primary strength is that it encourages cooperation. Its main weakness is that it's a temporary fix that fails to confront the underlying problem.

Dominating (Forcing)

High concern for self and low concern for others encourages "I win, you lose" tactics. The other party's needs are largely ignored. This style is often called *forcing* because it relies on formal authority to force compliance. Dominating is appropriate when an unpopular solution must be implemented, the issue is minor, or a deadline is near. It is inappropriate in an open and participative climate. Speed is its primary strength. The primary weakness of this domineering style is that it often breeds resentment. Interestingly, the National Center for Women and Policing cites this particular conflict-handling style as a reason for hiring more women.

> Women are 12.7% of the personnel in large police departments but account for 2% of excessive-force cases that are upheld. . . . the findings support their contention that women's negotiating and communication skills should prompt police departments to hire more women.[49]

Avoiding

This tactic may involve either passive withdrawal from the problem or active suppression of the issue. Avoidance is appropriate for trivial issues or when the costs of confrontation outweigh the benefits of resolving the conflict. It is inappropriate for difficult and worsening problems. The main strength of this style is that it buys time in unfolding or ambiguous situations. The primary weakness is that the tactic provides a temporary fix that sidesteps the underlying problem.

Compromising

This is a give-and-take approach involving moderate concern for both self and others. Compromise is appropriate when parties have opposite goals or possess equal power. But compromise is inappropriate when overuse would lead to inconclusive action (e.g., failure to meet important deadlines). The primary strength of this tactic is that the democratic process has no losers, but it's a temporary fix that can stifle creative problem solving.

Third-Party Interventions

In a perfect world, people would creatively avoid conflict and handle actual conflicts directly and positively. Dream on! Organizational politics being what they are, we can find ourselves as unwilling (and often unready) third parties to someone else's conflict. Thus, a working knowledge of conflict triangles and alternative dispute resolution techniques, the focus of this section, is essential to effective management today.

Conflict triangle

Conflicting parties involve a third person rather than dealing directly with each other.

Conflict Triangles

Remember Annie, the Amazon.com manager at the start of this chapter? Her busy day was interrupted by her co-worker Laura's tale of a conflict situation. Laura was recruiting Annie to help settle the situation. This is a classic conflict triangle. A **conflict triangle** "occurs when two people are having a problem and, instead of addressing the problem directly with each other, one of them gets a third

Figure 14–5 *Third-Party Intervention Options for Handling Conflict Triangles*

Detriangling
(least political; low
risk of dysfunctional
conflict)

1. Reroute complaints by coaching the sender to find ways to constructively bring up the matter with the receiver. Do not carry messages for the sender.
2. Facilitate a meeting with the sender and receiver to coach them to speak directly and constructively with each other.
3. Transmit verbatim messages with the sender's name included and coach the receiver on constructive ways to discuss the message with the sender.
4. Carry the message verbatim but protect the sender's name.
5. Soften the message to protect the sender.
6. Add your spin to the message to protect the sender.
7. Do nothing. The participants will triangle in someone else.
8. Do nothing and spread the gossip. You will triangle in others.

More triangling
(most political; high
risk of dysfunctional
conflict)

SOURCE: List of options excerpted from P Ruzich, "Triangles: Tools for Untangling Interpersonal Messes," *HR Magazine,* July 1999, p. 134.

person involved."[50] As discussed under the heading of organizational politics, in Chapter 16, employees tend to form political *coalitions* because there is power in numbers. In Annie's case, Laura was engaged in a not-so-subtle attempt to gang up against her adversary, Hans. Moreover, Laura was using Annie to vent her pent-up frustrations. This is a common and often very disruptive situation in today's organizations. The question is, What to do?

Those finding themselves in conflict triangles have a wide range of options, according to experts on the subject. Figure 14–5 shows how responses can promote either functional or dysfunctional conflict. Preferred options 1 and 2, called *detriangling,* involve the third party channeling the disputants' energy in a direct and positive manner, toward each other. Importantly, the third party avoids becoming part of a political coalition in options 1 and 2. Options 3 through 8 can be a slippery slope toward further counterproductive triangling. Also, political and ethical implications multiply as the third party progresses to option 3 and beyond.

Alternative Dispute Resolution (ADR)

Disputes between employees, between employees and their employer, and between companies too often end up in lengthy and costly court battles. A more constructive, less expensive approach called *alternative dispute resolution* has enjoyed enthusiastic growth in recent years.[51] In fact, the widely imitated People's Court–type television shows operating outside the formal judicial system are part of this trend toward what one writer calls "do-it-yourself justice."[52] **Alternative dispute resolution** (ADR), according to a pair of Canadian labor lawyers, "uses faster, more user-friendly methods of dispute resolution, instead of traditional, adversarial approaches (such as unilateral decision making or litigation)."[53] The following ADR techniques represent a progression of steps third parties can take to resolve organizational conflicts.[54] They are ranked from easiest and least expensive to most difficult and costly. A growing number of organizations have

Alternative dispute resolution
Avoiding costly lawsuits by resolving conflicts informally or through mediation or arbitration.

formal ADR policies involving an established sequence of various combinations of these techniques:

- *Facilitation.* A third party, usually a manager, informally urges disputing parties to deal directly with each other in a positive and constructive manner. This can be a form of detriangling, as discussed earlier.

- *Conciliation.* A neutral third party informally acts as a communication conduit between disputing parties. This is appropriate when conflicting parties refuse to meet face to face. The immediate goal is to establish direct communication, with the broader aim of finding common ground and a constructive solution.

- *Peer review.* A panel of trustworthy co-workers, selected for their ability to remain objective, hears both sides of a dispute in an informal and confidential meeting. Any decision by the review panel may or may not be binding, depending on the company's ADR policy. Membership on the peer review panel often is rotated among employees.

- *Ombudsman.* Someone who works for the organization, and is widely respected and trusted by his or her co-workers, hears grievances on a confidential basis and attempts to arrange a solution. This approach, more common in Europe than North America, permits someone to get help from above without relying on the formal hierarchy chain.

- *Mediation.* "The mediator—a trained, third-party neutral—actively guides the disputing parties in exploring innovative solutions to the conflict. Although some companies have in-house mediators who have received ADR training, most also use external mediators who have no ties to the company."[55] Unlike an arbitrator, a mediator does *not* render a decision. It is up to the disputants to reach a mutually acceptable decision.

- *Arbitration.* Disputing parties agree ahead of time to accept the decision of a neutral arbitrator in a formal courtlike setting, often complete with evidence and witnesses. Participation in this form of ADR can be voluntary or mandatory, depending upon company policy or union contracts.[56] Statements are confidential. Decisions are based on legal merits. Trained arbitrators, typically from outside agencies such as the American Arbitration Association, are versed in relevant laws and case precedents.

Practical Lessons from Conflict Research

Laboratory studies, relying on college students as subjects, uncovered the following insights about organizational conflict:

- People with a high need for affiliation tended to rely on a smoothing (obliging) style while avoiding a forcing (dominating) style.[57] Thus, personality traits affect how people handle conflict.

- Disagreement expressed in an arrogant and demeaning manner produced significantly more negative effects than the same sort of disagreement expressed in a reasonable manner.[58] In other words, *how* you disagree with someone is very important in conflict situations.

- Threats and punishment, by one party in a disagreement, tended to produce intensifying threats and punishment from the other party.[59] In short, aggression breeds aggression.

- As conflict increased, group satisfaction decreased. An integrative style of handling conflict led to higher group satisfaction than did an avoidance style.[60]
- Companies with mandatory or binding arbitration policies were viewed *less* favorably than companies without such policies.[61] Apparently, mandatory or binding arbitration policies are a turn-off for job applicants who dislike the idea of being forced to do something.

Field studies involving managers and real organizations have given us the following insights:

- Both intradepartmental and interdepartmental conflict decreased as goal difficulty and goal clarity increased. Thus, challenging and clear goals can defuse conflict.
- Higher levels of conflict tended to erode job satisfaction and internal work motivation.[62]
- Men and women at the same managerial level tended to handle conflict similarly. In short, there was no gender effect.[63]
- Conflict tended to move around the organization in a case study of a public school system.[64] Thus, managers need to be alerted to the fact that conflict often originates in one area or level and becomes evident somewhere else. Conflict needs to be traced back to its source if there is to be lasting improvement.
- Samples of Japanese, German, and American managers who were presented with the same conflict scenario preferred different resolution techniques. Japanese and German managers did not share the Americans' enthusiasm for integrating the interests of all parties. The Japanese tended to look upward to management for direction, whereas the Germans were more bound by rules and regulations. In cross-cultural conflict resolution, there is no one best approach. Cultural-specific preferences need to be taken into consideration prior to beginning the conflict resolution process.[65]

As we transition from conflict to negotiation, take a few minutes to complete the OB Exercise on page 504. What better way to reinforce what you have learned about managing conflict than to apply it to your own life?

Negotiation

Formally defined, **negotiation** is a give-and-take decision-making process involving interdependent parties with different preferences.[66] Common examples include labor-management negotiations over wages, hours, and working conditions and negotiations between supply chain specialists and vendors involving price, delivery schedules, and credit terms. Self-managed work teams with overlapping task boundaries also need to rely on negotiated agreements. Negotiating skills are more important today than ever.[67]

Negotiation
Give-and-take process between conflicting interdependent parties.

Two Basic Types of Negotiation

Negotiation experts distinguish between two types of negotiation—*distributive* and *integrative.* Understanding the difference requires a change in traditional fixed-pie thinking:

A *distributive* negotiation usually involves a single issue—a "fixed-pie"—in which one person gains at the expense of the other. For example, haggling over the price of a rug in a bazaar is a distributive negotiation. In most conflicts, however, more than one issue is at stake, and each party values the issues differently. The outcomes available are no longer a

OB Exercise   The Conflict Iceberg

Instructions
This is a useful tool for understanding the full context of an interpersonal or intergroup conflict. First, identify a conflict situation that has involved and perhaps frustrated you lately (such as a broken friendship, a disagreement at school or work, or a family feud). Next, work your way down the conflict iceberg by writing some brief notes about the apparent issue, the personalities involved, relevant emotions, and so forth. The goal is to achieve "awareness of interconnection." In the spirit of functional or cooperative conflict, see if the other party to the conflict would be willing to complete this exercise from his or her perspective. Use the information gathered from one or both parties to move toward some sort of resolution. Importantly, be very honest with yourself because *you* may be a major obstacle or problem in the conflict situation. How can a similar conflict be avoided in the future?

SOURCE: Figure from K Cloke and J Goldsmith, *Resolving Conflicts at Work: A Complete Guide for Everyone on the Job* (San Francisco: Jossey-Bass, 2000), p. 114.

fixed-pie divided among all parties. An agreement can be found that is better for both parties than what they would have reached through distributive negotiation. This is an *integrative* negotiation.

However, parties in a negotiation often don't find these beneficial trade-offs because each *assumes* its interests *directly* conflict with those of the other party. "What is good for the other side must be bad for us" is a common and unfortunate perspective that most people have. This is the mind-set we call the *mythical* "fixed-pie."[68]

Distributive negotiation involves traditional win–lose thinking. Integrative negotiation calls for a progressive win–win strategy,[69] such as the one in Figure 14–6. In a laboratory study of joint venture negotiations, teams trained in integrative tactics achieved better outcomes for *both* sides than did untrained teams.[70] However, another study involving 700 employees from 11 cultures discovered the integrative (or problem-solving) approach to negotiation was *not* equally effective across cultures.[71] North American negotiators generally are too short-term oriented and poor relationship builders when negotiating in Asia, Latin America, and the Middle East.[72]

Figure 14–6   *An Integrative Approach: Added-Value Negotiation*

Separately   **Jointly**

Step 1: Clarify interests.

- Identify tangible and intangible needs.

- Discuss respective needs.
- Find *common ground* for negotiation.

Step 2: Identify options.

- Identify *elements of value* (e.g., property, money, behavior, rights, risks).

- Create a *marketplace of value* by discussing respective elements of value.

Step 3: Design alternative deal packages.

- Mix and match *elements of value* in various workable combinations.
- Think in terms of *multiple deals.*

Step 4: Select a deal.

- Analyze deal packages proposed by other party.

- Discuss and select from feasible deal packages.
- Think in terms of *creative agreement.*

Step 5: Perfect the deal.

- Discuss unresolved issues.
- Develop written agreement.
- *Build relationships* for future negotiations.

SOURCE: Adapted from K Albrecht and S Albrecht, "Added Value Negotiating," *Training,* April 1993, pp. 26–29.

Ethical Pitfalls in Negotiation

The success of integrative negotiation, such as added-value negotiation, hinges to a large extent on the *quality* of information exchanged, as researchers have recently documented.[73] Telling lies, hiding key facts, and engaging in the other potentially unethical tactics listed in Table 14–3 erode trust and goodwill, both vital in win–win negotiations.[74] An awareness of these dirty tricks can keep good faith bargainers from being unfairly exploited.[75] Unethical negotiating tactics need to be factored into organizational codes of ethics.

Practical Lessons from Negotiation Research

Recent laboratory and field studies have yielded these insights:

- Negotiators with fixed-pie expectations produced poor joint outcomes because they restricted and mismanaged information.[76]

Table 14–3   *Questionable/Unethical Tactics in Negotiation*

Tactic	Description/Clarification/Range
Lies	Subject matter for lies can include limits, alternatives, the negotiator's intent, authority to bargain, other commitments, acceptability of the opponent's offers, time pressures, and available resources.
Puffery	Among the items that can be puffed up are the value of one's payoffs to the opponent, the negotiator's own alternatives, the costs of what one is giving up or is prepared to yield, importance of issues, and attributes of the products or services.
Deception	Acts and statements may include promises or threats, excessive initial demands, careless misstatements of facts, or asking for concessions not wanted.
Weakening the opponent	The negotiator here may cut off or eliminate some of the opponent's alternatives, blame the opponent for his own actions, use personally abrasive statements to or about the opponent, or undermine the opponent's alliances.
Strengthening one's own position	This tactic includes building one's own resources, including expertise, finances, and alliances. It also includes presentations of persuasive rationales to the opponent or third parties (e.g., the public, the media) or getting mandates for one's position.
Nondisclosure	Includes partial disclosure of facts, failure to disclose a hidden fact, failure to correct the opponents' misperceptions or ignorance, and concealment of the negotiator's own position or circumstances.
Information exploitation	Information provided by the opponent can be used to exploit his weaknesses, close off his alternatives, generate demands against him, or weaken his alliances.
Change of mind	Includes accepting offers one had claimed one would not accept, changing demands, withdrawing promised offers, and making threats one promised would not be made. Also includes the failure to behave as predicted.
Distraction	These acts or statements can be as simple as providing excessive information to the opponent, asking many questions, evading questions, or burying the issue. Or they can be more complex, such as feigning weakness in one area so that the opponent concentrates on it and ignores another.
Maximization	Includes demanding the opponent make concessions that result in the negotiator's gain and the opponent's equal or greater loss. Also entails converting a win–win situation into win–lose.

SOURCE: H J Reitz, J A Wall, Jr, and M S Love, "Ethics in Negotiation: Oil and Water or Good Lubrication?" *Business Horizons,* May–June 1998, p. 6. Reprinted with permission. Copyright © 1998 by the Board of Trustees at Indiana University, Kelley School of Business.

- A meta-analysis of 62 studies found a *slight* tendency for women to negotiate more cooperatively than men. But when faced with a tit-for-tat bargaining strategy (equivalent countermoves), women were significantly more competitive than men.[77]

- Personality characteristics can affect negotiating success. Negotiators who scored high on the Big Five personality dimensions of extraversion and agreeableness (refer back to Table 5–3) tended to do poorly with distributive (fixed-pie; win–lose) negotiations.[78]

- Good and bad moods can have positive and negative effects, respectively, on negotiators' plans and outcomes.[79] So wait until both you and your boss are in a good mood before you ask for a raise.

- Studies of negotiations between Japanese, between Americans, and between Japanese and Americans found less productive joint outcomes across cultures than

"Here's an offer you can't refuse on this sweet little buggy." Although there are many honest and fair-minded car dealers today, slick used-car salesmen have given negotiation a bad name. But the "I win, you lose" approach is being pushed aside by a more progressive and mutually satisfying win-win negotiating style. There are many ethical pitfalls to avoid in any type of negotiation.

(c) Susan Van Etten/PhotoEdit

within cultures.[80] Less understanding of the other party makes cross-cultural negotiation more difficult than negotiations at home.

Conflict Management and Negotiation: A Contingency Approach

Three realities dictate how organizational conflict should be managed. First, various types of conflict are inevitable because they are triggered by a wide variety of antecedents. Second, too little conflict may be as counterproductive as too much. Third, there is no single best way of avoiding or resolving conflict. Consequently, conflict specialists recommend a contingency approach to managing conflict. Antecedents of conflict and actual conflict need to be monitored. If signs of too little conflict such as apathy or lack of creativity appear, then functional conflict needs to be stimulated. This can be done by nurturing appropriate antecedents of conflict or programming conflict with techniques such as devil's advocacy and the dialectic method. On the other hand, when conflict becomes dysfunctional, the appropriate conflict-handling style needs to be enacted. Realistic training involving role playing can prepare managers to try alternative conflict styles.

Third-party interventions are necessary when conflicting parties are unwilling or unable to engage in conflict resolution or integrative negotiation. Integrative or added-value negotiation is most appropriate for intergroup and interorganizational conflict. The key is to get the conflicting parties to abandon traditional fixed-pie thinking and their win–lose expectations.

Managers can keep from getting too deeply embroiled in conflict by applying four lessons from recent research: (1) establish challenging and clear goals, (2) disagree in a constructive and reasonable manner, (3) do not get caught up in conflict triangles, and (4) refuse to get caught in the aggression-breeds-aggression spiral.

Summary of Key Concepts

1. *Define the term* conflict, *and put the three metaphors of conflict into proper perspective for the workplace.* Conflict is a process in which one party perceives that its interests are being opposed or negatively affected by another party. Conflict is inevitable but not necessarily destructive. Metaphorically, conflict can be viewed as *war* (win at all costs), an *opportunity* (be creative, grow, and improve), or a *journey* (a search for common ground and a better way). Within organizations, we are challenged to see conflicts as win–win opportunities and journeys rather than as win–lose wars.

2. *Distinguish between functional and dysfunctional conflict, and identify three desired conflict outcomes.* Functional conflict enhances organizational interests while dysfunctional conflict is counterproductive. Three desired conflict outcomes are agreement, stronger relationships, and learning.

3. *Define* personality conflicts, *and explain how managers should handle them.* Personality conflicts involve interpersonal opposition based on personal dislike or disagreement (or as an outgrowth of workplace incivility). Care needs to be taken with personality conflicts in the workplace because of the legal implications of diversity, anti-discrimination, and sexual harassment. Managers should investigate and document personality conflict, take corrective actions such as feedback or behavior modification if appropriate, or attempt informal dispute resolution. Difficult or persistent personality conflicts need to be referred to human resource specialists or counselors.

4. *Discuss the role of in-group thinking in intergroup conflict, and explain what management can do about intergroup conflict.* Members of in-groups tend to see themselves as unique individuals who are more moral than outsiders, whom they view as a threat and stereotypically as all alike. In-group thinking is associated with ethnocentric behavior. According to the updated contact model, managers first must strive to eliminate negative relationships between conflicting groups. Beyond that, they need to provide team building, encourage personal friendships across groups, foster positive attitudes about other groups, and minimize negative gossip about groups.

5. *Discuss what can be done about cross-cultural conflict.* International consultants can prepare people from different cultures to work effectively together. Cross-cultural conflict can be minimized by having expatriates build strong cross-cultural relationships with their hosts (primarily by being good listeners, being sensitive to others, and being more cooperative than competitive).

6. *Explain how managers can stimulate functional conflict, and identify the five conflict-handling styles.* There are many antecedents of conflict—including incompatible personalities, competition for limited resources, and unrealized expectations—that need to be monitored. Functional conflict can be stimulated by permitting antecedents of conflict to persist or programming conflict during decision making with devil's advocates or the dialectic method. The five conflict-handling styles are integrating (problem solving), obliging (smoothing), dominating (forcing), avoiding, and compromising. There is no single best style.

7. *Explain the nature and practical significance of conflict triangles and alternative dispute resolution for third-party conflict intervention.* A conflict triangle occurs when one member of a conflict seeks the help of a third party rather than facing the opponent directly. Detriangling is advised, whereby the third-party redirects the disputants' energy toward each other in a positive and constructive manner. Alternative dispute resolution involves avoiding costly court battles with more informal and user-friendly techniques such as facilitation, conciliation, peer review, ombudsman, mediation, and arbitration.

8. *Explain the difference between distributive and integrative negotiation, and discuss the concept of added-value negotiation.* Distributive negotiation involves fixed-pie and win–lose thinking. Integrative negotiation is a win–win approach to better results for both parties. The five steps in added value negotiation are as follows: step 1, clarify interests; step 2, identify options; step 3, design alternative deal packages; step 4, select a deal; and step 5, perfect the deal. Elements of value, multiple deals, and creative agreement are central to this approach.

Discussion Questions

1. What is your experience with people viewing conflict as war, versus seeing it as an opportunity or a journey? How did things turn out?

2. What examples of functional and dysfunctional conflict have you observed lately?

3. Which of the antecedents of conflict do you think are most common (or most troublesome) in today's workplaces?

4. Have you ever been directly involved in a personality conflict? Explain. Was it handled well? Explain. What could have been done differently?

5. How could in-group thinking affect the performance of a manager living and working in a foreign country?

6. Which of the five conflict-handling styles is your strongest? Your weakest? How can you improve your ability to handle conflict?

7. What is your personal experience with conflict triangles? Based on what you have learned in this chapter, do you think you could do a better job of handling conflict triangles in the future? Explain.

8. Which of the six ADR techniques appeals the most to you? Why?

9. Has your concept of negotiation, prior to reading this chapter, been restricted to fixed-pie thinking? Explain.

10. How could added-value negotiation make your life a bit easier? Explain in terms of a specific problem, conflict, or deadlock.

Internet Exercise

www.ncpc.org/1safe5dc.htm
www.adrr.com

A great deal of interesting and useful material about conflict and negotiation can be found on the Internet. This is a good thing because the more than six billion people on this planet have a lot to learn about getting along. The purpose of this exercise is to help develop your conflict-handling skills and broaden your understanding of alternative dispute resolution and negotiation.

Practical Tips on Managing Conflict and Preventing Violence and Crime

The National Crime Prevention Council (NCPC), with help from its familiar mascot McGruff the Crime Dog®, has a Web site offering sound advice for people of all ages. Go to the home page (**www.ncpc.org/1safe5dc.htm**), and follow your personal interests to relevant sections. For instance, if you're a parent, click on "Help your children manage conflict" or "stopping school violence." A good general category is the NCPC main menu heading "self, home, family." There you will find lots of useful information and guidelines about "Protecting Yourself," "Safeguarding Your Family," and "Business and Workplace Safety." Under the heading "You Can Do More," be sure to read "10 Things Adults Can Do to Stop Violence" and "10 Things Kids Can Do to Stop Violence."

Background Information on ADR

Stephen R Marsh, a lawyer and mediator from Dallas, Texas, has compiled an extensive and user-friendly Internet site on alternative dispute resolution (**www.adrr.com**). In volume one of the Mediation Essays, read the material under the headings "What Is Mediation?", "Preparing for Mediation," "Negotiation in Mediation," and "Ethical and Practical Considerations." In volumes three and four of the Mediation Essays, the section "Defining Conflict" presents an instructive perspective. You will find many other good readings, depending on your interests and circumstances. Also, pay a quick visit to **www.cybersettle.com** to get an idea of how the power and scope of the Internet is being used to avoid costly lawsuits with ADR.

Cutting-Edge Ideas about Negotiation

Harvard Law School, in cooperation with other leading universities, hosts the Web site "Program on Negotiation" (**www.pon.harvard.edu**). Under the main menu heading "Research," select the subheading "The Research Projects," and browse some or all of the projects. Focus on concepts and practices relevant to managing organizational behavior.

Questions

1. What are the three best pieces of advice about handling conflict and preventing crime you picked up at the NCPC site? Any other useful ideas or approaches?

2. How important is it to "walk in the other person's shoes" when trying to avoid or resolve a conflict? Explain.

3. Why is there so much interest in ADR these days? Are you presently involved in a dispute or conflict that could be mediated? Explain. What do you think of Cybersettle.com? Does it seem practical?

4. What useful new insights about conflict handling and negotiation did you pick up from the Program on Negotiation research projects?

OB in Action Case Study

Pulp Friction at Weyerhaeuser[81]

BusinessWeek Things got ugly in a hurry for Steven R Rogel, CEO of Weyerhaeuser Co. In November 2000, he sent a letter to William Swindells, chairman of Willamette Industries Inc., letting him know that Weyerhaeuser was making a run at his company. This was not the usual takeover attempt, however. Call it a homecoming of sorts: Rogel, 59, had been Swindells' protégé at Willamette in Portland, Oregon—in fact, he had worked there for 25 years, running the place in the final two.

When Rogel left Willamette in 1997 to head up its much hated, far larger, and somewhat troubled rival, it was as if the favorite son had grown up, taken a job at the local bank, and then returned to repossess the family farm. Indeed, one reason Weyerhaeuser board members recruited Rogel was precisely because they believed he could mount a successful hostile takeover if necessary. Weyerhaeuser executives had never formally made an offer, but they knew Swindells was not likely to be receptive. He had flatly rejected friendly overtures from several other companies. So when Rogel's message arrived, Swindells, 71, had a few choice words for the courier: "You can take this letter back to Steve and tell him where to put it."

It was the first of many angry words in what became one of the most contentious buyouts in recent history. Ultimately, Rogel prevailed. But it took him another year to complete the acquisition of Willamette, and the price was steep—in more ways than one. He had to extend his buyout offer 12 times and paid a final price of $6.2 billion, $825 million more than he originally offered. And he endured a welter of personal attacks. Willamette executives, who considered him a traitor, taped a picture of him to a voodoo doll and jabbed pins into its face. Many of the nearly 15,000 Willamette employees sported "Just Say No Wey" buttons. And last summer, Rogel had to walk past Willamette workers picketing their company's annual meeting and carrying signs that read: "Rogue'l: You're looking for love in all the wrong faces."

Rogel knew what he was getting into with the folks at Willamette: The 85-year-old company had a reputation for fierce independence. That was what drew Rogel, a chemical engineer who grew up in a small wheat-farming town in eastern Washington, to Willamette in the first place. It was also a company that prided itself on the loyalty of its employees. When Rogel resigned as chief executive, Swindells insisted he leave the company that very day. The two haven't spoken since: Rogel clinched the deal in conversations with Willamette CEO Duane C McDougall. "I knew [the hostile bid] would be upsetting to them and come back on me personally," Rogel says. What kept him going through those 12 months was his certainty about the benefits of the deal: "I slept well at night. I was doing the right thing not just for Weyerhaeuser but for good friends at Willamette," he says. "Nevertheless, you're human, and it impacts you."

Integrating Weyerhaeuser and Willamette will require considerable finesse. In addition to the usual challenges of merging two companies, Rogel has to overcome the hostilities of his new employees. . . .

Rogel figures the best thing he can do is to get through the integration quickly. So far, he has appointed two Willamette executives to senior positions in Weyerhaeuser's operations and has vowed that those laid off won't all be Willamette employees. He has set up toll-free phone numbers for merger-related questions and promised to post all relevant information on the company intranet. And he is leading forums with Willamette employees to articulate his vision for the new company. "Everyone has to know fairly and honestly what's going on," he says.

Back when he was rising to the top at Willamette, Rogel was respected for his nitty-gritty understanding of the business. Some employees are even welcoming him back. Bob Banister, a Willamette technical analyst who attended one of Rogel's meetings, says: "Steve came across very well and genuine." Putting the bitter fight aside won't be easy for everybody, though. Swindells, who resigned with the rest of the board . . . , declined to comment. And as one senior Willamette executive says: "Were this a friendly, amicable situation, it would probably be different. But it's not." Rogel may be picking voodoo pins out for some time.

Questions for Discussion

1. What evidence of dysfunctional conflict can you find in this case?

2. What antecedents of conflict can you detect in this case? Which one(s) present Rogel with the greatest challenge? Explain.

3. How big a problem was in-group thinking in this case? Explain.

4. Which of the cross-cultural skills in Table 14–2 would serve Rogel well while integrating the two companies? Explain.

5. Which conflict-handling style in Figure 14–4 should Rogel rely most heavily upon during the integration process? Explain.

Personal Awareness and Growth Exercise

What Is Your Primary Conflict-Handling Style?

Objectives

1. To continue building your self-awareness.

2. To assess your approach to conflict.

3. To provide a springboard for handling conflicts more effectively.

Introduction

Professor Afzalur Rahim, developer of the five-style conflict model in Figure 14–4, created an assessment instrument upon which the one in this exercise is based. The original instrument was validated through a factor analysis of responses from 1,219 managers from across the United States.[82]

Instructions

For each of the 15 items, indicate how often you rely on that tactic by circling the appropriate number.

Conflict-Handling Tactics	Rarely				Always
1. I argue my case with my co-workers to show the merits of my position.	1	2	3	4	5
2. I negotiate with my co-workers so that a compromise can be reached.	1	2	3	4	5
3. I try to satisfy the expectations of my co-workers.	1	2	3	4	5
4. I try to investigate an issue with my co-workers to find a solution acceptable to us.	1	2	3	4	5
5. I am firm in pursuing my side of the issue.	1	2	3	4	5
6. I attempt to avoid being "put on the spot" and try to keep my conflict with my co-workers to myself.	1	2	3	4	5
7. I hold on to my solution to a problem.	1	2	3	4	5
8. I use "give and take" so that a compromise can be made.	1	2	3	4	5
9. I exchange accurate information with my co-workers to solve a problem together.	1	2	3	4	5
10. I avoid open discussion of my differences with my co-workers.	1	2	3	4	5
11. I accommodate the wishes of my co-workers.	1	2	3	4	5
12. I try to bring all our concerns out in the open so that the issues can be resolved in the best possible way.	1	2	3	4	5
13. I propose a middle ground for breaking deadlocks.	1	2	3	4	5
14. I go along with the suggestions of my co-workers.	1	2	3	4	5
15. I try to keep my disagreements with my co-workers to myself in order to avoid hard feelings.	1	2	3	4	5

Scoring and Interpretation

Enter your responses, item by item, in the five categories below, and then add the three scores for each of the styles. Note: There are no right or wrong answers, because individual differences are involved.

Integrating		Obliging		Dominating	
Item	Score	Item	Score	Item	Score
4.	_____	3.	_____	1.	_____
9.	_____	11.	_____	5.	_____
12.	_____	14.	_____	7.	_____
Total =	_____	Total =	_____	Total =	_____

Avoiding		Compromising	
Item	Score	Item	Score
6.	_____	2.	_____
10.	_____	8.	_____
15.	_____	13.	_____
Total =	_____	Total =	_____

Your primary conflict-handling style is: _____

(The category with the highest total.)

Your backup conflict-handling style is: _____

(The category with the second highest total.)

Questions for Discussion

1. Are the results what you expected? Explain.

2. Is there a clear gap between your primary and backup styles, or did they score about the same? If they are about the same, does this suggest indecision about handling conflict on your part? Explain.

3. Will your primary conflict-handling style carry over well to many different situations? Explain.

4. What is your personal learning agenda for becoming a more effective conflict handler?

Group Exercise

Bangkok Blowup—A Role-Playing Exercise

Objectives

1. To further your knowledge of interpersonal conflict and conflict-handling styles.

2. To give you a firsthand opportunity to try the various styles of handling conflict.

Introduction

This is a role-playing exercise intended to develop your ability to handle conflict. There is no single best way to resolve the conflict in this exercise. One style might work for one person, while another gets the job done for someone else.

Instructions

Read the following short case, "Can Larry Fit In?" Pair up with someone else and decide which of you will play the role of Larry and which will play the role of Melissa, the office manager. Pick up the action from where the case leaves off. Try to be realistic and true to the characters in the case. The manager is primarily responsible for resolving this conflict situation. Whoever plays Larry should resist any unreasonable requests or demands and cooperate with any personally workable solution. *Note:* To conserve time, try to resolve this situation in less than 15 minutes.

CAN LARRY FIT IN?[83]

Melissa, Office Manager

You are the manager of an auditing team sent to Bangkok, Thailand, to represent a major international accounting firm headquartered in New York. You and Larry, one of your auditors, were sent to Bangkok to set up an auditing operation. Larry is about seven years older than you and has five more years seniority in the firm. Your relationship has become very strained since you were recently designated as the office manager. You feel you were given the promotion because you have established an excellent working relationship with the Thai staff as well as a broad range of international clients.

In contrast, Larry has told other members of the staff that your promotion simply reflects the firm's heavy emphasis on affirmative action. He has tried to isolate you from the all-male accounting staff by focusing discussions on sports, local night spots, and so forth.

You are sitting in your office reading some complicated new reporting procedures that have just arrived from the home office. Your concentration is suddenly interrupted by a loud knock on your door. Without waiting for an invitation to enter, Larry bursts into your office. He is obviously very upset, and it is not difficult for you to surmise why he is in such a nasty mood.

You recently posted the audit assignments for the coming month, and you scheduled Larry for a job you knew he wouldn't like. Larry is one of your senior auditors, and the company norm is that they get the choice assignments. This particular job will require him to spend two weeks away from Bangkok in a remote town, working with a company whose records are notoriously messy.

Unfortunately, you have had to assign several of these less-desirable audits to Larry recently because you are short of personnel. But that's not the only reason. You have received several complaints from the junior staff (all Thais) recently that Larry treats them in a condescending manner. They feel he is always looking for an opportunity to boss them around, as if he were their supervisor instead of an experienced, supportive mentor. As a result, your whole operation works more smoothly when you can send Larry out of town on a solo project for several days. It keeps him from coming into your office and telling you how to do your job, and the morale of the rest of the auditing staff is significantly higher.

Larry slams the door and proceeds to express his anger over this assignment.

Larry, Senior Auditor

You are really ticked off! Melissa is deliberately trying to undermine your status in the office. She knows that the company norm is that senior auditors get the better jobs. You've paid your dues, and now you expect to be treated with respect. And this isn't the first time this has happened. Since she was made the office manager, she has tried to keep you out of the office as much as possible. It's as if she doesn't want her rival for leadership of the office around. When you were asked to go to Bangkok, you assumed that you would be made the office manager because of your seniority in the firm. You are certain that the decision to pick Melissa is yet another indication of reverse discrimination against white males.

In staff meetings, Melissa has talked about the need to be sensitive to the feelings of the office staff as well as the clients in this multicultural setting. "Where does she come off preaching about sensitivity! What about my feelings, for heaven's sake?" you wonder. This is nothing more than a straightforward power play. She is probably feeling insecure about being the only female accountant in the office and being promoted over someone with more experience. "Sending me out of town," you decide, "is a clear case of 'out of sight, out of mind.' "

Well, it's not going to happen that easily. You are not going to roll over and let her treat you unfairly. It's time for a showdown. If she doesn't agree to change this assignment and apologize for the way she's been treating you, you're going to register a formal complaint with her boss in the New York office. You are prepared to submit your resignation if the situation doesn't improve.

Questions for Discussion

1. What antecedents of conflict appear to be present in this situation? What can be done about them?

2. Having heard how others handled this conflict, did one particular style seem to work better than the others?

3. Did emotions cloud your conflict-handling ability? If so, reread the material on emotional intelligence in Chapter 5.

Ethical Dilemma

A Matter of Style at German Software Giant SAP[84]

While [co-CEO Hasso] Plattner believes in obtaining consensus among his lieutenants, he doesn't care how much he irritates people along the way. In fact, his confrontational style is deliberate. "He creates stressful situations. He fuels the discussions with provocative statements. Sometimes he's rigid, even rude. But it's about getting people engaged so they can be creative," says Wolfgang Kemna, CEO of SAP America, a 13-year SAP veteran. Co-CEO Henning Kagermann, whom Plattner elevated to work alongside him in 1998, is his counterweight in the organization—calm and efficient.

Is Plattner's Heavy-handed Management Style an Ethical Issue?

1. No, not if he effectively stimulates creativity and functional conflict. Explain.

2. Yes, his abrasive personality will intimidate some co-workers and possibly even promote blind obedience or groupthink. Explain.

3. Yes, his intimidating management style could create a hostile work environment where sexual harassment might thrive. Explain.

4. Maybe. It depends upon the circumstances and individuals involved. Explain.

5. Not in this situation, because his tough ways are counterbalanced by his co-CEO's calm style. Explain.

6. Invent other options. Discuss.

For an interpretation of this situation, visit our Web site, **www.mhhe.com/kreitner.**

OB in Action Video Case

Group Dynamics at TechBox

Total run time for both parts: 17 minutes, 21 seconds.

About the Manager's Hot Seat video series: To achieve a high degree of realism, McGraw-Hill/Irwin created these videos around the concept of having real-life managers deal with challenging hypothetical situations without the aid of a script. Each Manager's Hot Seat video has two parts. Both parts are followed by the guest manager's view of what went right and wrong in the "hot seat." What would *you* do in the manager's hot seat?

Characters: Guest manager Patrick Bennett takes on the role of the young hot-shot managing supervisor of production at TechBox, a high-end computer chip maker. In real life, Bennett is design director at Goodspeed & Associates. Sam Adelson is the up-from-the-bottom VP of operations. Lucinda Bergen, TechBox's only woman executive, is director of product management. Wise-cracking Morgan Baincs is VP of distribution.

Situation: Three months ago, Bennett was put in charge of a top-priority and costly project to improve product quality with a new computerized tracking system. Now the time has come (in Part 1) for an executive-level update meeting on the project. Bennett thinks things are going great and is proud of what he has accomplished. Troubling questions are raised by the others. The meeting in Part 2 takes place a week later with the same cast of characters.

Links to textual material: Chapter 11: group decision making. Chapter 12: group dynamics. Chapter 13: teams and teamwork. Chapter 14: managing conflict.

For Class Discussion (following Part 1)

1. Was this meeting doomed to failure from the very start? Why or why not?

2. What did Bennett do right (and wrong) in this meeting?

3. Which of the advantages and disadvantages of group-aided decision making covered in Chapter 11 are evident in this case?

4. At which stage of Tuckman's model of development is this group? Explain.

5. Which of the group task and maintenance roles covered in Chapter 12 are evident in this case? Who performed them? Which roles were *not* performed and should have been? By whom?

6. What does this group need to do to evolve into a high-performance team?

7. Was trust an issue in this first meeting? Explain. What does Bennett need to do to build trust?

For Class Discussion (following Part 2)

1. Did Bennett do a better job of handling this second meeting? Explain.

2. What would you have done in Bennett's situation, in either meeting?

Part Four

Organizational Processes

Chapter Fifteen

Organizational Communication in the Internet Age

Learning Objectives

When you finish studying the material in this chapter, you should be able to:

1 Describe the perceptual process model of communication.

2 Describe the process, personal, physical, and semantic barriers to effective communication.

3 Contrast the communication styles of assertiveness, aggressiveness, and nonassertiveness.

4 Discuss the primary sources of both nonverbal communication and listener comprehension.

5 Review the 10 keys to effective listening.

6 Describe the communication differences between men and women, and explain the source of these differences.

7 Explain the contingency approach to media selection.

8 Discuss patterns of hierarchical communication and the grapevine.

9 Demonstrate your familiarity with four antecedents of communication distortion between managers and employees.

10 Explain the information technology of Internet/intranet/extranet, E-mail, videoconferencing, and collaborative computing, and explain the related use of telecommuting.

Instant messaging isn't just for the under-20 set. It's now booming among an older group: office employees. The number of folks instant messaging at work grew 26% from October [2001] to April [2002], to 16.9 million, according to Jupiter Media Metrix. They're spending more time doing it, too: 7.2 billion minutes in April [2002], up 74% from November [2001].

Problem is, the finger-snap-fast communication among employees often doesn't propel productivity. True, some auto makers negotiate with suppliers using chat windows. And about 80% of real-time customer service by Lands' End, for instance, occurs via online chat. But employers fear that most cyber-yakking has nothing to do with work. Technicians at port management firm Virginia International Terminals in Norfolk, for example, had to install snooping software to block certain employees from gossiping up to two hours a day. Technical Div. manager Lung Cheng says 99% of employee IM use was personal and was "beginning to impact productivity."

As instant messaging invades the workplace in a big way, employers are sounding alarm bells.

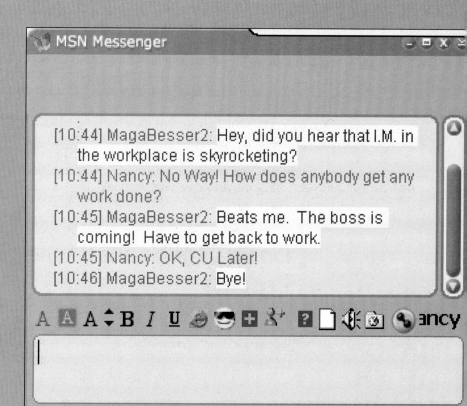

*S*ecurity is another concern. Instant messages are easily broken into, letting hackers delve into corporate systems. Doug Fowler, chief executive of cyber monitor *S*pector*S*oft, calls IM "a security disaster waiting to happen."[1]

Management is communication. Every managerial function and activity involves some form of direct or indirect communication. Whether planning and organizing or directing and leading, managers find themselves communicating with and through others. Importantly, effective communication is critical for both managerial and organizational success. For example, a study of 2,011 employees from three organizations revealed that a climate of positive communication—open, participative, and supportive—was associated with employees' organizational identification (see Chapter 5).[2] Another study involving 65 savings and loan employees and 110 manufacturing employees revealed that employee satisfaction with organizational communication was positively and significantly correlated with both job satisfaction and performance.[3] Finally, a survey of 300 executives underscored the importance of communication. Results demonstrated that 71% and 68% of the respondents believed that written communication skills and interpersonal communication skills, respectively, were critical competencies that needed enhancement via training. These executives believed the lack of communication skills had resulted in increased costs.[4]

Moreover, the chapter-opening vignette highlights how organizational communication has been dramatically affected by the introduction and explosive use of computers and information technology. Who would have guessed that employees might spend two hours a day gossiping on the Internet? Managers need more than good interpersonal skills to effectively communicate in today's workplace. They also need to understand the pros and cons of different types of communication media and information technology. As you will learn in this chapter, the best way to communicate depends on the situation at hand.

This chapter will help you to better understand how managers can both improve their communication skills and design more effective communication programs. We discuss (1) basic dimensions of the communication process, focusing on a perceptual process model and barriers to effective communication; (2) interpersonal communication; (3) organizational communication; and (4) communicating in the computerized information age.

Basic Dimensions of the Communication Process

Communication

Interpersonal exchange of information and understanding.

Communication is defined as "the exchange of information between a sender and a receiver, and the inference (perception) of meaning between the individuals involved."[5] Analysis of this exchange reveals that communication is a two-way process consisting of consecutively linked elements (see Figure 15–1). Managers who understand this

Figure 15–1   *A Perceptual Model of Communication*

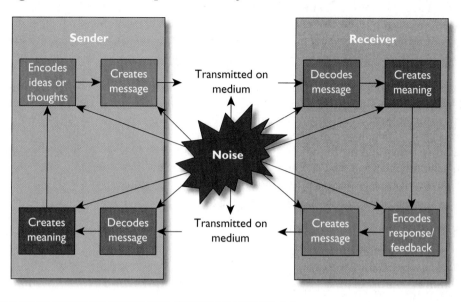

process can analyze their own communication patterns as well as design communication programs that fit organizational needs. This section reviews a perceptual process model of communication and discusses a contingency approach to choosing communication media.

A Perceptual Process Model of Communication

The communication process historically has been described in terms of a *conduit* model. This traditional model depicts communication as a pipeline in which information and meaning are transferred from person to person. Recently, however, communication scholars have criticized the conduit model for being based on unrealistic assumptions. For example, the conduit model assumes communication transfers *intended meanings* from person to person.[6] If this assumption was true, miscommunication would not exist and there would be no need to worry about being misunderstood. We could simply say or write what we want and assume the listener or reader accurately understands our intended meaning.

As we all know, communicating is not that simple or clear-cut. Communication is fraught with miscommunication. In recognition of this, researchers have begun to examine communication as a form of social information processing (recall the discussion in Chapter 7) in which receivers interpret messages by cognitively processing information. This view led to development of a **perceptual model of communication** that depicts communication as a process in which receivers create meaning in their own minds. Let us briefly examine the elements of the perceptual process model shown in Figure 15–1.

Sender   The sender is an individual, group, or organization that desires or attempts to communicate with a particular receiver. Receivers may be individuals, groups, or organizations.

Perceptual model of communication
Process in which receivers create their own meaning.

Encoding

Communication begins when a sender encodes an idea or thought. Encoding translates mental thoughts into a code or language that can be understood by others. Managers typically encode using words, numbers, gestures, nonverbal cues such as facial expressions, or pictures. Moreover, different methods of encoding can be used to portray similar ideas. The following short exercise highlights this point.

On a piece of paper, draw a picture of the area currently surrounding you. Now, write a verbal description of the same area. Does the pictorial encoding portray the same basic message as the verbal description? Which mode was harder to use and which more effective? Interestingly, a growing number of companies and management consultants recommend using visual communication, such as drawings, to analyze and improve group interaction and problem solving and to reduce stress. Consider how Rosenbluth International, a Philadelphia-based company that specializes in global travel services, uses drawings to improve employee satisfaction:

> In addition to annual associate satisfaction surveys, the company asks employees to draw them a picture. "We send out crayons and paper and ask them to draw how they feel about the company," says [Diane McFerrin Peters, the former chief communications officer]. "Most of the pictures are happy—a lot of salmon flopping around because the salmon is our mascot, but when we see a storm cloud in a corner that indicates a problem, we call the 'artist' to discuss it."[7]

The Message

The output of encoding is a message. There are two important points to keep in mind about messages. First, they contain more than meets the eye. Messages may contain hidden agendas as well as trigger affective or emotional reactions. For example, comparisons of internal and external documents within the forest products industry over a 10-year period demonstrated that executives' private and public evaluative statements about events and situations were inconsistent. These executives apparently wanted to convey different messages to the public and to internal employees.[8] The second point to consider about messages is that they need to match the medium used to transmit them. How would you evaluate the match between the message of letting someone know he was being let go and the communication medium used in the following example?

> Six months ago [January 2002], Tower Snow was chairman of Brobeck, Phleger & Harrison, one of the nation's premier law firms. Late Friday, as he got off a United Airlines flight in San Francisco, a gate agent handed him an envelope. Inside: notice that Brobeck had fired him.[9]

How would you feel if this happened to you? Surely there is a better way to let someone know he or she is being fired. This example illustrates how thoughtless managers can be when they do not carefully consider the interplay between a message and the medium used to convey it. More is said about this issue later in this chapter.

Selecting a Medium

Managers can communicate through a variety of media. Potential media include face-to-face conversations, telephone calls, electronic mail, voice mail, videoconferencing, written memos or letters, photographs or drawings, meetings, bulletin boards, computer output, and charts or graphs. Choosing the appropriate media depends on many factors, including the nature of the message, its intended purpose, the type of audience, proximity to the audience, time horizon for disseminating the message, and personal preferences.

All media have advantages and disadvantages. Face-to-face conversations, for instance, are useful for communicating about sensitive or important issues and those

Clearly today's managers have many choices of communication media, each having various pros and cons. Choosing the right medium depends on several factors, such as the nature of the message, purpose, type of audience, and so on. Many people tend to use one method more than another. Do you have a preferred communication medium? What are its limitations?

(c) David Samuel Robbins/CORBIS Sygma

requiring feedback and intensive interaction. Telephones are convenient, fast, and private, but lack nonverbal information. Although writing memos or letters is time consuming, it is a good medium when it is difficult to meet with the other person, when formality and a written record are important, and when face-to-face interaction is not necessary to enhance understanding. More is said later in this chapter about choosing media.

Decoding   Decoding is the receiver's version of encoding. Decoding consists of translating verbal, oral, or visual aspects of a message into a form that can be interpreted. Receivers rely on social information processing to determine the meaning of a message during decoding. Decoding is a key contributor to misunderstanding in interracial and intercultural communication because decoding by the receiver is subject to social values and cultural values that may not be understood by the sender.[10]

Creating Meaning   In contrast to the conduit model's assumption that meaning is directly transferred from sender to receiver, the perceptual model is based on the belief that a receiver creates the meaning of a message in his or her mind. A receiver's interpretation of a message often will differ from that intended by the sender. In turn, receivers act according to their own interpretations, not the communicator's. Consider how this issue created problems for Arthur Andersen.

> Two Houston employees of Arthur Andersen LLP said they believed they were following the firm's policy when they, and other auditors and personnel, destroyed documents related to the firm's audits of Enron Corp. in the weeks leading up to Andersen's receipt of a subpoena from the Securities and Exchange Commission for Enron-related documents.
>
> Andersen's policy for retaining and destroying documents requires that its auditors retain only those documents "needed to support or defend our work" and "eliminate or destroy" all other documents when they are no longer needed. "Only essential information to support our conclusions should be retained," the policy says.[11]

A spokesperson for the company offered a different interpretation of these policies.

> Andersen spokesman Charlie Leonard said the firm's policy tells firm auditors to "save the documents that support your conclusions" and that the policy doesn't instruct auditors to destroy documents that contradict the firm's audit conclusions.[12]

It appears that Andersen's policies were interpreted differently within the company. A communication expert concluded the following after considering this element of the communication process:

> Miscommunication and unintentional communication are to be expected, for they are the norm. Organizational communicators who take these ideas seriously would realize just how difficult successful communication truly is. Presumably, they would be conscious of the constant effort needed to communicate in ways most closely approximating their intentions. . . . Communication is fraught with unintentionality and, thereby, great difficulty for communicators.[13]

Managers are encouraged to rely on *redundancy* of communication to reduce this unintentionality. This can be done by transmitting the message over multiple media. For example, a production manager might follow up a phone conversation about a critical schedule change with a memo or E-mail.

Feedback   Once a receiver decodes a message, he or she encodes a response and then transmits it to the original sender. This new message is then decoded and interpreted. This process repeats itself when further communication is needed. As you can see from this discussion, feedback is used as a comprehension check. It gives senders an idea of how accurately their message is understood.

Noise

Interference with the transmission and understanding of a message.

Noise   **Noise** represents anything that interferes with the transmission and understanding of a message. It affects all linkages of the communication process. Noise includes factors such as a speech impairment, poor telephone connections, illegible handwriting, inaccurate statistics in a memo or report, poor hearing and eyesight, and physical distance between sender and receiver. Managers can improve communication by reducing noise.

Barriers to Effective Communication

Communication noise is a barrier to effective communication because it interferes with the accurate transmission and reception of a message. Management awareness of these barriers is a good starting point to improve the communication process. There are four key barriers to effective communication: (1) process barriers, (2) personal barriers, (3) physical barriers, and (4) semantic barriers.

Process Barriers   Every element of the perceptual model of communication shown in Figure 15–1 is a potential process barrier. Consider the following examples:

1. *Sender barrier.* A customer gets incorrect information from a customer service agent because he or she was recently hired and lacks experience.
2. *Encoding barrier.* An employee for whom English is a second language has difficulty explaining why a delivery was late.
3. *Message barrier.* An employee misses a meeting for which he or she never received a confirmation E-mail.
4. *Medium barrier.* A salesperson gives up trying to make a sales call when the potential customer fails to return three previous phone calls.
5. *Decoding barrier.* An employee does not know how to respond to a manager's request to stop exhibiting passive aggressive behavior.

www.vivendiuniversal.com

Jean-Marie Messier's Communication Style Causes Problems for Vivendi Universal

BusinessWeek [Former] Vivendi Universal CEO Jean-Marie Messier looked shell-shocked, and no wonder. As his corporate jet touched down in Paris on April 16, [2002,] *Le Monde* hit the newsstands with a front-page story outlining a supposed boardroom plot to oust him. While aides rushed to scuttle that rumor, Messier headed to a meeting where he fired Pierre Lescure, the popular founder of Vivendi's Canal+ pay-TV unit. Outraged Canal+ employees promptly interrupted regular programming, put a tearful Lescure on the air to denounce Messier, and urged the station's French viewers to cancel their subscriptions. Meanwhile, at a hastily convened press conference, Messier defended his decision but issued a rare mea culpa for the turbulence that has sent Vivendi stock tumbling 35% since January [2002]. "Have I sometimes communicated too often and out of provocation? Yes," he said. . . .

What's most troubling is that the Canal+ blowup could have been avoided if Messier had curbed his tongue. Canal+ is Vivendi's chief media asset in Europe, and it clearly needs attention. It turned in a $330 million operating loss last year—the only major Vivendi unit to run in the red. Messier had to do something—but why did he have to trumpet the nasty details in the press? In March, he told French business daily *La Tribune* of his ultimatum to Lescure and Canal+ Chief Operating Officer Denis Olivennes to reach breakeven in two years. After a furious Olivennes defended himself in an E-mail to employees, Messier upbraided him and Lescure in front of 400 Vivendi execs. "It was appalling," says one. "Messier does not know how to manage people."

SOURCE: Excerpted from C Matlack, J Rossant, and R Grover, "Messier's Mess: Vivendi's Outspoken Boss Is Trying Board Members' Nerves," *Business Week*, April 29, 2002, 1pp. 54–55.

---

6. *Receiver barrier.* A student who is talking to his or her friend during a lecture asks the professor the same question that was just answered.

7. *Feedback barrier.* The nonverbal head nodding of an interviewer leads an interviewee to think that he or she is doing a great job answering questions.

Barriers in any of these process elements can distort the transfer of meaning. Reducing these barriers is essential but difficult given the current diversity of the workforce.

Personal Barriers   There are many personal barriers to communication. We highlight eight of the more common ones. The first is our *ability to effectively communicate.* People possess varying levels of communication skills. The International OB above highlights how Jean-Marie Messier's communication style caused problems for both himself and Vivendi Universal. In fact, he left the company soon after this incident. The *way people process and interpret information* is a second barrier. Chapter 6 highlighted the fact that people use different frames of reference and experiences to interpret the world around them. We also learned that people selectively attend to various stimuli. All told, these differences affect both what we say and what we think we hear. Third, the *level of interpersonal trust between people* can either be a barrier or enabler of effective communication. Communication is more likely to be distorted when people do not trust each other. *Stereotypes and prejudices* are a fourth barrier. They can powerfully distort what we perceive about others. Our *egos* are a fifth barrier. Egos can cause political battles, turf wars, and pursuit of power, credit, and resources. Egos influence how people treat each other as well as our receptiveness to being influenced by others. *Poor listening skills* are a sixth barrier.

Carl Rogers, a renowned psychologist, identified the seventh and eighth barriers that interfere with interpersonal communication.[14] The seventh barrier is a *natural tendency to evaluate or judge a sender's message.* To highlight the natural tendency to evaluate, consider how you might respond to the statement "I like the book you are reading." What would you say? Your likely response is to approve or disapprove the statement. You may say, "I agree," or alternatively, "I disagree, the book is boring." The point is that we all tend to evaluate messages from our own point of view or frame of reference. The tendency to evaluate messages is greatest when one has strong feelings or emotions about the issue being discussed. An *inability to listen with understanding* is the eighth personal barrier to effective communication. Listening with understanding occurs when a receiver can "see the expressed idea and attitude from the other person's point of view, to sense how it feels to him, to achieve his frame of reference in regard to the thing he is talking about."[15] Listening with understanding reduces defensiveness and improves accuracy in perceiving a message.

Physical Barriers
The distance between employees can interfere with effective communication. Communication can be distorted when employees work in close confinement or when they are miles apart. The following example highlights the impact of modern day office design on communication, job satisfaction, and performance.

> Every couple of weeks, Michael McKay, a 33-year-old business analyst with a Santa Clara, California, Internet services company, finds his concentration totally disrupted when three colleagues who sit near his workstation hop onto the same conference call—all on speakerphones.
>
> "You get this stereophonic effect of hearing one person's voice live, and then hearing it coming out of someone else's speakerphone two or three cubes over," fumes Mr McKay.
>
> Incessant phone-ringing, very personal conversations, chitchat about weekend exploits, laughing at bad jokes—day in and day out, office employees hear it all. The modern workplace got so loud in part after the New Economy's forward thinkers surmised that open-office designs would foster creativity, communication, and collaboration among workers. Older-line companies picked up the concept and kicked workers and many managers out of private offices and into cubicles and pods.[16]

Time zone differences around the world represent physical barriers. The quality of telephone lines or crashed computers also represents physical barriers that affect our ability to communicate with information technology.

In spite of the general acceptance of physical barriers, they can be reduced. For example, offices can be redesigned, and employees on the U.S. East Coast can agree to call their West Coast peers prior to leaving for lunch. It is important that managers attempt to manage this barrier by choosing a medium that optimally reduces the physical barrier at hand.

Semantic Barriers
Semantics is the study of words. Semantic barriers show up as encoding and decoding errors because these phases of communication involve transmitting and receiving words and symbols. These barriers are partially fueled by the use of jargon and unnecessarily complex words.[17] Consider the following statement: Crime is ubiquitous. Do you understand this message? Even if you do, would it not be simpler to say that "crime is all around us" or "crime is everywhere"? Choosing our words more carefully is the easiest way to reduce semantic barriers. This barrier can also be decreased by attentiveness to mixed messages and cultural diversity. Mixed messages occur when a person's words imply one message while his or her actions or nonverbal cues suggest something different. Obviously, understanding is enhanced when a person's actions and nonverbal cues match the verbal message.

Interpersonal Communication

The quality of interpersonal communication within an organization is very important. People with good communication skills helped groups to make more innovative decisions and were promoted more frequently than individuals with less developed abilities.[18] Although there is no universally accepted definition of **communication competence,** it is a performance-based index of an individual's abilities to effectively use communication behaviors in a given context.[19] Business etiquette, for example, is one component of communication competence. At this time we would like you to complete the business etiquette test in the OB Exercise on page 528. How did you score?

Communication competence is determined by three components: communication abilities and traits, situational factors, and the individuals involved in the interaction (see Figure 15–2). Cross-cultural awareness, for instance, is an important communication ability/trait. Individuals involved in an interaction also affect communication competence. People are likely to withhold information and react emotionally or defensively when interacting with someone they dislike or do not trust. You can improve your communication competence through five communication styles/abilities/traits under your control: assertiveness, aggressiveness, nonassertiveness, nonverbal communication, and active listening. We conclude this section by discussing gender differences in communication.

> **Communication competence**
>
> Ability to effectively use communication behaviors in a given context.

Assertiveness, Aggressiveness, and Nonassertiveness

The saying "You can attract more flies with honey than with vinegar" captures the difference between using an assertive communication style and an aggressive style.

Figure 15–2   *Communication Competence Affects Upward Mobility*

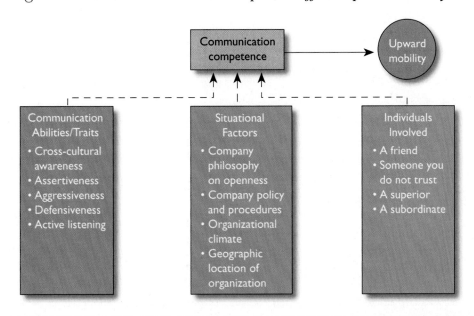

OB Exercise   What Is Your Business Etiquette?

Instructions

Business etiquette is one component of communication competence. Test your business etiquette by answering the following questions. After circling your response for each item, calculate your score by reviewing the correct answers listed in note 20 in the Endnotes section of the book. Next, use the norms at the end of the test to interpret your results.

1. The following is an example of a proper introduction: "Ms Boss, I'd like you to meet our client, Mr Smith."

   True   False

2. If someone forgets to introduce you, you shouldn't introduce yourself you should just let the conversation continue.

   True   False

3. If you forget someone's name, you should keep talking and hope no one will notice. This way you don't embarrass yourself or the person you are talking to.

   True   False

4. When shaking hands, a man should wait for a woman to extend her hand.

   True   False

5. Who goes through a revolving door first?

   a. Host   *b.* Visitor

6. It is all right to hold private conversations, either in person or on a cell phone in office bathrooms, elevators, and other public spaces.

   True   False

7. When two U.S. businesspeople are talking to one another, the space between them should be approximately

   a. 1.5 feet   *b.* 3 feet   *c.* 7 feet

8. Business casual attire requires socks for men and hose for women.

   True   False

9. To signal that you do not want a glass of wine, you should turn your wine glass upside down.

   True   False

10. If a call is disconnected, it's the caller's responsibility to redial.

    True   False

11. When using a speakerphone, you should tell the caller if there is anyone else in the room.

    True   False

12. You should change your voicemail message if you are going to be out of the office.

    True   False

Arbitrary Norms

Low business etiquette (0–4 correct): Consider buying an etiquette book or hiring a coach to help you polish your professional image.

Moderate business etiquette (5–8 correct): Look for a role model or mentor, and look for ways you can improve your business etiquette.

High business etiquette (9–12 correct): Good for you. You should continue to practice good etiquette and look for ways to maintain your professional image.

SOURCE: This test was adapted from material contained in M Brody, "Test Your Etiquette," *Training & Development*, February 2002, pp. 64–66.

Research studies indicate that assertiveness is more effective than aggressiveness in both work-related and consumer contexts.[21] An **assertive style** is expressive and self-enhancing and is based on the "ethical notion that it is not right or good to violate our own or others' basic human rights, such as the right to self-expression or the right to be treated with dignity and respect."[22] In contrast, an **aggressive style** is expressive and self-enhancing and strives to take unfair advantage of others. A **nonassertive style** is characterized by timid and self-denying behavior. Nonassertiveness is ineffective because it gives the other person an unfair advantage.

Managers may improve their communication competence by trying to be more assertive and less aggressive or nonassertive. Chaim Fortgang, for example, failed to heed this advice.

> Bankruptcy lawyers are a notoriously combative bunch. But many in the profession say Chaim J Fortgang is in a class by himself.
>
> During his 30-year career as one of the nation's preeminent corporate bankruptcy attorneys, he has hurled food at adversaries. He has called the judgment of a federal bankruptcy trustee "moronic." He even once threatened to pull out a rival lawyer's tongue, that lawyer says.
>
> Now he may have become a rare example of a bankruptcy attorney who's too combative even for his thick-skinned peers. Late last year, the elite New York law firm of Wachtell, Lipton, Rosen & Kratz announced Mr Fortgang was resigning as a partner. People familiar with the matter now say he was pressured to leave, although others say he was ready to go anyway because he didn't feel the firm was helping him expand his practice.[23]

Managers like Fortgang can improve their communication competence by using the appropriate nonverbal and verbal behaviors listed in Table 15–1. For instance, managers should attempt to use the nonverbal behaviors of good eye contact, a strong, steady, and audible voice, and selective interruptions. They should avoid nonverbal behaviors such as glaring or little eye contact, threatening gestures, slumped posture, and a weak or whiny voice. Appropriate verbal behaviors include direct and unambiguous language and the use of "I" messages instead of "you" statements. For example, when you say, "Mike, I was disappointed with your report because it contained typographical errors," rather than "Mike, your report was poorly done," you reduce defensiveness. "I" statements describe your feelings about someone's performance or behavior instead of laying blame on the person.

Remember that nonverbal and verbal behaviors should complement and reinforce each other. James Waters, a communication expert, further recommends that assertiveness can be enhanced by using various combinations of the following assertiveness elements:

1. *Describe* the situation or the behavior of people to which you are reacting.

2. *Express* your feelings, or *explain* what impact the other's behavior has on you.

3. *Empathize* with the other person's position in the situation.

4. *Specify* what changes you would like to see in the situation or in another's behavior, and offer to *negotiate* those changes with the other person.

5. *Indicate,* in a nonthreatening way, the possible consequences that will follow if change does not occur.[24]

Waters offers managers the following situational advice when using the various assertiveness elements: (1) *empathize* and *negotiate* with superiors or others on whom you are dependent, (2) *specify* with friends and peers, and (3) *describe* to strangers.

Assertive style
Expressive and self-enhancing, but does not take advantage of others.

Aggressive style
Expressive and self-enhancing, but takes unfair advantage of others.

Nonassertive style
Timid and self-denying behavior.

Table 15–1   *Communication Styles*

Communication Style	Description	Nonverbal Behavior Pattern	Verbal Behavior Pattern
Assertive	Pushing hard without attacking; permits others to influence outcome; expressive and self-enhancing without intruding on others	Good eye contact Comfortable but firm posture Strong, steady, and audible voice Facial expressions matched to message Appropriately serious tone Selective interruptions to ensure understanding	Direct and unambiguous language No attributions or evaluations of other's behavior Use of "I" statements and cooperative "we" statements
Aggressive	Taking advantage of others; expressive and self-enhancing at other's expense	Glaring eye contact Moving or leaning too close Threatening gestures (pointed finger; clenched fist) Loud voice Frequent interruptions	Swear words and abusive language Attributions and evaluations of other's behavior Sexist or racist terms Explicit threats or put-downs
Nonassertive	Encouraging others to take advantage of us; inhibited; self-denying	Little eye contact Downward glances Slumped posture Constantly shifting weight Wringing hands Weak or whiny voice	Qualifiers ("maybe"; "kind of") Fillers ("uh," "you know," "well") Negaters ("It's not really that important"; "I'm not sure")

SOURCE: Adapted in part from J A Waters, "Managerial Assertiveness," *Business Horizons*, September–October 1982, pp. 24–29.

Sources of Nonverbal Communication

Nonverbal communication

Messages sent outside of the written or spoken word.

Nonverbal communication is "Any message, sent or received independent of the written or spoken word . . . [It] includes such factors as use of time and space, distance between persons when conversing, use of color, dress, walking behavior, standing, positioning, seating arrangement, office locations and furnishing."[25]

Communication experts estimate that 65 to 90% of every conversation is partially interpreted through nonverbal communication.[26] It thus is important to ensure that your nonverbal signals are consistent with your intended verbal messages. Inconsistencies create noise and promote miscommunications.[27] Because of the prevalence of nonverbal communication and its significant impact on organizational behavior (including, but not limited to, perceptions of others, hiring decisions, work attitudes, and turnover),[28] it is important that managers become consciously aware of the sources of nonverbal communication.

Body Movements and Gestures   Body movements, such as leaning forward or backward, and gestures, such as pointing, provide additional nonverbal information that can either enhance or detract from the communication process. A study, for example, showed that the use of appropriate hand gestures increased listeners' pragmatic understanding of a message.[29] Open body positions such as leaning forward, communicate *immediacy,* a term used to represent openness, warmth, closeness, and availability for communication. *Defensiveness* is communicated by gestures such as folding arms,

Communication experts estimate that 65 to 90% of every conversation is partially interpreted through nonverbal communication. Thus, it is important to ensure that your nonverbal signals are consistent with your intended verbal messages. Here, participants in Dr. Madan Kataria's laughter seminar in New York City try the "cocktail laugh," a friendly disagreeing chuckle accompanied by wagging index fingers, one of a variety of laughs Kataria teaches.

(c) Monika Graff/The Image Works

crossing hands, and crossing one's legs. Judith Hall, a communication researcher, conducted a meta-analysis of gender differences in body movements and gestures. Results revealed that women nodded their heads and moved their hands more than men. Leaning forward, large body shifts, and foot and leg movements were exhibited more frequently by men than women.[30] Although it is both easy and fun to interpret body movements and gestures, it is important to remember that body-language analysis is subjective, easily misinterpreted, and highly dependent on the context and cross-cultural differences. Thus, managers need to be careful when trying to interpret body movements. Inaccurate interpretations can create additional noise in the communication process.

Touch   Touching is another powerful nonverbal cue. People tend to touch those they like. A meta-analysis of gender differences in touching indicated that women do more touching during conversations than men.[31] Of particular note, however, is the fact that men and women interpret touching differently. Sexual harassment claims might be reduced by keeping this perceptual difference in mind.

Moreover, norms for touching vary significantly around the world. Consider the example of two males walking across campus holding hands. In the Middle East, this behavior would be quite normal for males who are friends or have great respect for each other. In contrast, this behavior is not commonplace in the United States.

Facial Expressions   Facial expressions convey a wealth of information. Smiling, for instance, typically represents warmth, happiness, or friendship, whereas frowning conveys dissatisfaction or anger. Do you think these interpretations apply to different cross-cultural groups? If you said yes, it supports the view that there is a universal recognition of emotions from facial expressions. If you said no, this indicates you believe the relationship between facial expressions and emotions varies across cultures. A summary of relevant research revealed that the association between facial expressions and emotions varies across cultures.[32] A smile, for example, does not convey the same emotion in different countries. Therefore, managers need to be careful in interpreting facial expressions among diverse groups of employees.

Eye Contact   Eye contact is a strong nonverbal cue that serves four functions in communication. First, eye contact regulates the flow of communication by signaling the beginning and end of conversation. There is a tendency to look away from others when beginning to speak and to look at them when done. Second, gazing (as opposed to glaring) facilitates and monitors feedback because it reflects interest and attention. Third, eye contact conveys emotion. People tend to avoid eye contact when discussing bad news or providing negative feedback. Fourth, gazing relates to the type of relationship between communicators.

As is also true for body movements, gestures, and facial expressions, norms for eye contact vary across cultures. Westerners are taught at an early age to look at their parents when spoken to. In contrast, Asians are taught to avoid eye contact with a parent or superior in order to show obedience and subservience.[33] Once again, managers should be sensitive to different orientations toward maintaining eye contact with diverse employees.

Practical Tips   It is important to have good nonverbal communication skills in light of the fact that they are related to the development of positive interpersonal relationships. A communication expert offers the following advice to improve nonverbal communication skills:[34]

Positive Nonverbal Actions That Help Communication

• Maintaining eye contact.

• Occasionally nodding the head in agreement.

• Smiling and showing animation.

• Leaning toward the speaker.

• Speaking at a moderate rate, in a quiet, assuring tone. . . .

Actions to Avoid

• Looking away or turning away from the speaker.

• Closing your eyes.

• Using an unpleasant voice tone.

• Speaking too quickly or too slowly.

• Yawning excessively.

Practice these tips by turning the sound off while watching television and then trying to interpret emotions and interactions. Honest feedback from your friends about your nonverbal communication style also may help.

Active Listening

Some communication experts contend that listening is the keystone communication skill for employees involved in sales, customer service, or management. In support of this conclusion, listening effectiveness was positively associated with customer satisfaction and negatively associated with employee intentions to quit. Poor communication between employees and management also was cited as a primary cause of employee discontent.[35] Listening skills are particularly important for all of us because we spend a great deal of time listening to others. Estimates suggest the average person typically spends about 40% of a working day listening, 35% talking, 16% reading, and 9% writing.[36]

Unfortunately, research evidence suggests that most people are not very good at listening. For example, communication experts estimate that people generally comprehend about 35% of a typical verbal message. Interestingly, this problem is partly due to the fact that people can process information faster than most speakers talk. The average speaker communicates 125 words per minute while people can process 500 words per minute. Poor listeners use this information processing gap to daydream and think about other things, thereby missing important parts of what is being communicated.[37]

Listening involves much more than hearing a message. Hearing is merely the physical component of listening. **Listening** is the process of *actively* decoding and interpreting verbal messages. Listening requires cognitive attention and information processing; hearing does not. With these distinctions in mind, we will examine a model of listener comprehension and some practical advice for becoming a more effective listener.

<aside>
Listening
Actively decoding and interpreting verbal messages.
</aside>

Listener Comprehension Model

Listener comprehension represents the extent to which an individual can recall factual information and draw accurate conclusions and inferences from a verbal message. It is a function of listener, speaker, message, and environmental characteristics (see Figure 15–3). Communication researchers Kittie Watson and Larry Barker conducted a global review of listening behavior research and arrived at the following conclusions. Listening comprehension is positively related to high mental and reading abilities, academic achievements, a large vocabulary, being ego-involved with the speaker, having energy, being female, extrinsic motivation to pay attention, and being able to take good notes. Speakers who talk too fast or too slow, possess disturbing accents or speech patterns, are not visible to the audience, lack credibility, or are disliked have a negative impact on listening comprehension. In contrast, clear messages stated in the active voice increase listening comprehension. The same is true of messages containing viewpoints similar to the listener's or those that disconfirm expectations. Finally, comfortable environmental characteristics and compact seating arrangements enhance listening comprehension.[38]

Becoming a More Effective Listener

Effective listening is a learned skill that requires effort and motivation. That's right, it takes energy and desire to really listen to others. Unfortunately, it may seem like there are no rewards for listening, but there are negative consequences when we don't. Think of a time, for example, when someone did not pay attention to you by looking at his or her watch or doing some other activity such as typing on a keyboard? How did you feel? You may have felt put down, unimportant, or offended. In turn, such feelings can erode the quality of interpersonal relationships as well as fuel job dissatisfaction, lower productivity, and poor customer service. Listening is an important skill that can be improved by avoiding the 10 habits of bad listeners while cultivating the 10 good listening habits (see Table 15–2). Stephen Covey, author of the bestseller *The 7 Habits of Highly Effective People,* offers another good piece of advice about becoming a more effective listener. He concludes that we should "seek first to understand, then to be understood."[39] In conclusion, it takes awareness, effort, and practice to improve one's listening comprehension. Listening is not a skill that will improve on its own. Is anyone listening?

Figure 15–3   *Listener Comprehension Model*

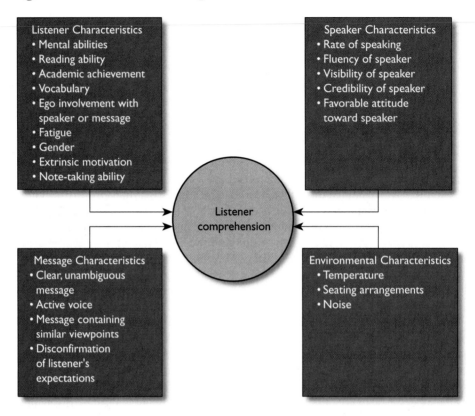

SOURCE: Adapted from discussion in K W Watson and L L Barker, "Listening Behavior: Definition and Measurement," in *Communication Yearbook* 8, ed R N Bostrom (Beverly Hills, CA: Sage Publications, 1984), pp. 178–97.

Women and Men Communicate Differently

Women and men have communicated differently since the dawn of time. These differences can create communication problems that undermine productivity and interpersonal communication. For example, surveys identified five common communication problems between women and men: (1) men were too authoritarian, (2) men did not take women seriously, (3) women were too emotional, (4) men did not accept women as co-workers or bosses, and (5) women did not speak up enough.[40]

Gender-based differences in communication are partly caused by linguistic styles commonly used by women and men. Deborah Tannen, a communication expert, defines **linguistic style** as follows:

Linguistic style

A person's typical speaking pattern.

> Linguistic style refers to a person's characteristic speaking pattern. It includes such features as directness or indirectness, pacing and pausing, word choice, and the use of such elements as jokes, figures of speech, stories, questions, and apologies. In other words, linguistic style is a set of culturally learned signals by which we not only communicate what we mean but also interpret others' meaning and evaluate one another as people.[41]

Linguistic style not only helps explain communication differences between women and men, but it also influences our perceptions of others' confidence, competence, and

Table 15-2   *The Keys to Effective Listening*

Keys to Effective Listening	The Bad Listener	The Good Listener
1. Capitalize on thought speed	Tends to daydream	Stays with the speaker, mentally summarizes the speaker, weighs evidence, and listens between the lines
2. Listen for ideas	Listens for facts	Listens for central or overall ideas
3. Find an area of interest	Tunes out dry speakers or subjects	Listens for any useful information
4. Judge content, not delivery	Tunes out dry or monotone speakers	Assesses content by listening to entire message before making judgments
5. Hold your fire	Gets too emotional or worked up by something said by the speaker and enters into an argument	Withholds judgment until comprehension is complete
6. Work at listening	Does not expend energy on listening	Gives the speaker full attention
7. Resist distractions	Is easily distracted	Fights distractions and concentrates on the speaker
8. Hear what is said	Shuts out or denies unfavorable information	Listens to both favorable and unfavorable information
9. Challenge yourself	Resists listening to presentations of difficult subject matter	Treats complex presentations as exercise for the mind
10. Use handouts, overheads, or other visual aids	Does not take notes or pay attention to visual aids	Takes notes as required and uses visual aids to enhance understanding of the presentation

SOURCES: Derived from N Skinner, "Communication Skills," *Selling Power*, July–August 1999, pp. 32–34; and G Manning, K Curtis, and S McMillen, *Building the Human Side of Work Community* (Cincinnati: Thomson Executive Press, 1996), pp. 127–54.

abilities. Increased awareness of linguistic styles can thus improve communication accuracy and your communication competence. This section strives to increase your understanding of interpersonal communication between women and men by discussing alternative explanations for differences in linguistic styles, various communication differences between women and men, and recommendations for improving communication between the sexes.

Why Do Linguistic Styles Vary between Women and Men?

Although researchers do not completely agree on the cause of communication differences between women and men, there are two competing explanations that involve the well-worn debate between *nature* and *nurture.* Some researchers believe that interpersonal differences between women and men are due to inherited biological differences between the sexes. More specifically, this perspective, which also is called the *Darwinian perspective* or *evolutionary psychology,* attributes gender differences in communication to drives, needs, and conflicts associated with reproductive strategies used by women and men. For example, proponents would say that males communicate more aggressively, interrupt others more than women, and hide their emotions because they have an inherent desire to possess features attractive to females in order to compete with other males for purposes of mate selection. Although males may not be competing for mate selection during a business meeting, evolutionary psychologists propose that men cannot turn off their biologically based determinants of behavior.[42]

Table 15–3 *Communication Differences between Women and Men*

1. Men are less likely to ask for information or directions in a public situation that would reveal their lack of knowledge.
2. In decision making, women are more likely to downplay their certainty; men are more likely to downplay their doubts.
3. Women tend to apologize even when they have done nothing wrong. Men tend to avoid apologies as signs of weakness or concession.
4. Women tend to accept blame as a way of smoothing awkward situations. Men tend to ignore blame and place it elsewhere.
5. Women tend to temper criticism with positive buffers. Men tend to give criticism directly.
6. Women tend to insert unnecessary and unwarranted thank-you's in conversations. Men may avoid thanks altogether as a sign of weakness.
7. Women tend to ask "What do you think?" to build consensus. Men often perceive that question to be a sign of incompetence and lack of confidence.
8. Women tend to give directions in indirect ways, a technique that may be perceived as confusing, less confident, or manipulative by men.
9. Men tend to usurp [take] ideas stated by women and claim them as their own. Women tend to allow this process to take place without protest.
10. Women use softer voice volume to encourage persuasion and approval. Men use louder voice volume to attract attention and maintain control.

SOURCE: Excerpted from D M Smith, *Women at Work: Leadership for the Next Century* (Upper Saddle River, NJ: Prentice Hall, 2000), pp 26–32.

In contrast, social role theory is based on the idea that females and males learn ways of speaking as children growing up. Research shows that girls learn conversational skills and habits that focus on rapport and relationships, whereas boys learn skills and habits that focus on status and hierarchies. Accordingly, women come to view communication as a network of connections in which conversations are negotiations for closeness. This orientation leads women to seek and give confirmation and support more so than men. Men, on the other hand, see conversations as negotiations in which people try to achieve and maintain the upper hand. It thus is important for males to protect themselves from others' attempts to put them down or push them around. This perspective increases a male's need to maintain independence and avoid failure.[43]

Gender Differences in Communication

Research demonstrates that women and men communicate differently in a number of ways.[44] Table 15–3 illustrates 10 different communication patterns that vary between women and men. There are two important issues to keep in mind about the trends identified in Table 15–3. First, the trends identified in the table cannot be generalized to include all women and men. Some men are less likely to boast about their achievements, and some women are less likely to share the credit. The point is that there are always exceptions to the rule. Second, your linguistic style influences perceptions about your confidence, competence, and authority. These judgments may, in turn, affect your future job assignments and subsequent promotability. Consider, for instance, linguistic styles displayed by Greg and Mindy. Greg downplays any uncertainties he has about issues and asks very few questions. He does this even when he is unsure about an issue being discussed. In contrast, Mindy is more forthright at admitting when she does not understand something, and she tends to ask a lot of questions. Some people may perceive Greg as more competent than Mindy because he displays confidence and acts as if he understands the issues being discussed.

Improving Communication between the Sexes   Author Judith Tingley suggests that women and men should learn to genderflex. **Genderflex** entails the temporary use of communication behaviors typical of the other gender in order to increase the potential for influence.[45] For example, a female manager might use sports analogies to motivate a group of males. She believes that this approach increases understanding and sensitivity between the sexes. Research has not yet investigated the effectiveness of this approach.

In contrast, Deborah Tannen recommends that everyone needs to become aware of how linguistic styles work and how they influence our perceptions and judgments. She believes that knowledge of linguistic styles helps to ensure that people with valuable insights or ideas get heard. Consider how gender-based linguistic differences affect who gets heard at a meeting:

> Those who are comfortable speaking up in groups, who need little or no silence before raising their hands, or who speak out easily without waiting to be recognized are far more likely to get heard at meetings. Those who refrain from talking until it's clear that the previous speaker is finished, who wait to be recognized, and who are inclined to link their comments to those of others will do fine at a meeting where everyone else is following the same rules but will have a hard time getting heard in a meeting with people whose styles are more like the first pattern. Given the socialization typical of boys and girls, men are more likely to have learned the first style and women the second, making meetings more congenial for men than for women.[46]

Knowledge of these linguistic differences can assist managers in devising methods to ensure that everyone's ideas are heard and given fair credit both in and out of meetings. Furthermore, it is useful to consider the organizational strengths and limitations of your linguistic style. You may want to consider modifying a linguistic characteristic that is a detriment to perceptions of your confidence, competence, and authority. In conclusion, communication between the sexes can be improved by remembering that women and men have different ways of saying the same thing.

Organizational Communication

Examining the broader issue of organizational communication is a good way to identify factors contributing to effective and ineffective management. For example, research reveals that employees do not receive enough information from their immediate supervisors. It is therefore no surprise to learn that a lot of employees use the grapevine as a source for information. This section promotes a working knowledge of four important aspects of organizational communication: a contingency approach to choosing communication media, hierarchical communication, the grapevine, and communication distortion.

Choosing Media: A Contingency Perspective

Employees increasingly note they are being overwhelmed with the high volume of information being transmitted over different communication media (telephone, E-mail, voicemail, fax, pagers, cell phone, express mail, memos, and so forth).[47] Fortunately, managers can help reduce this information overload and improve communication effectiveness through their choice of communication media. If an inappropriate medium is used, managerial decisions may be based on inaccurate information, important messages may not reach the intended audience, and employees may become dissatisfied and unproductive. Consider Marnie Puritz Stone's reaction to the inappropriate use of E-mail.

> "All communications regarding hiring and firings were sent via E-mail," Stone explains. Her managers may have felt they were being efficient, but she and her colleagues thought the managers were rude. "I think that callousness with which [some] E-mail delivers news—good or bad—is a poor way to show leadership," she says. "And it creates a lot of resentment."
>
> Stone's manager created even more resentment when it came to providing feedback, which was done mostly through E-mail. "I was reprimanded via E-mail, which was really bad," she recalls. "Criticism via E-mail leaves you very belittled since you can't respond."[48]

This example illustrates that media selection is a key component of communication effectiveness. The following section explores a contingency model designed to help managers select communication media in a systematic and effective manner. Media selection in this model is based on the interaction between information richness and complexity of the problem/situation at hand.

Information Richness

Respected organizational theorists Richard Daft and Robert Lengel define **information richness** in the following manner:

> Richness is defined as the potential information-carrying capacity of data. If the communication of an item of data, such as a wink, provides substantial new understanding, it would be considered rich. If the datum provides little understanding, it would be low in richness.[49]

Information richness
Information-carrying capacity of data.

As this definition implies, alternative media possess levels of information richness that vary from rich to lean.

Information richness is based on four factors: (1) feedback (ranging from fast to very slow), channel (ranging from the combined visual and audio characteristics of a video conference to the limited visual aspects of a computer report), (3) type of communication (ranging from personal to impersonal), and (4) language source (ranging from the natural body language and speech contained in a face-to-face conversation to the numbers contained in a financial statement).

Face-to-face is the richest form of communication. It provides immediate feedback and allows for the observation of multiple language cues such as body language and tone of voice. Although high in richness, the telephone and video conferencing are not as informative as the face-to-face medium. In contrast, newsletters, computer reports, and general E-mail are lean media because feedback is very slow, the channels involve only limited visual information, and the information provided is generic or impersonal.

Complexity of the Managerial Problem/Situation

Managers face problems and situations that range from low to high in complexity. Low-complexity situations are routine, predictable, and managed by using objective or standard procedures. Calculating an employee's paycheck is an example of low complexity. Highly complex situations, like a corporate reorganization, are ambiguous, unpredictable, hard to analyze, and often emotionally laden. Managers spend considerably more time analyzing these situations because they rely on more sources of information during their deliberations. There are no set solutions to complex problems or situations.

Contingency Recommendations   The contingency model for selecting media is graphically shown in Figure 15–4. As shown, there are three zones of communication effectiveness. Effective communication occurs when the richness of the medium is matched appropriately with the complexity of the problem or situation. Media low in richness—impersonal static and personal static—are better suited for simple problems; media high in richness—interactive media and face-to-face—are appropriate for complex problems or situations. DaimlerChrysler's CEO followed this recommendation when communicating with employees about layoffs.

> Since DaimlerChrysler announced big workforce cuts in January [2001], Chief Executive Dieter Zetsche has held town hall–style meetings with employees at several plants, with plans to visit all three dozen North American plants. He fielded questions and rallied the troops at each site.[50]

Conversely, ineffective communication occurs when the richness of the medium is either too high or too low for the complexity of the problem or situation. For example, a district sales manager would fall into the *overload zone* if he or she communicated monthly sales reports through richer media. Conducting face-to-face meetings or telephoning each salesperson would provide excessive information and take more time than necessary to communicate monthly sales data. The *oversimplification zone* represents another ineffective choice of communication medium. In this situation, media with inadequate richness are used to communicate about complicated or emotional issues. An example would be an executive who uses a general E-mail message

Figure 15–4   *A Contingency Model for Selecting Communication Media*

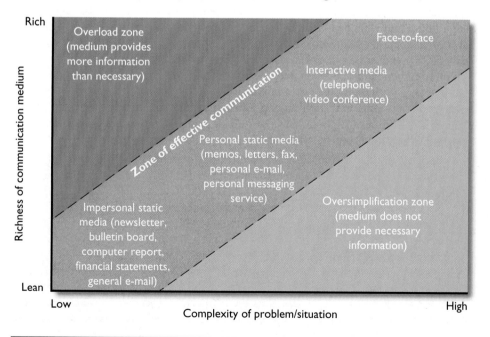

SOURCES: Adapted from R Lengel and R L Daft, "The Selection of Communication Media as an Executive Skill," *Academy of Management Executive,* August 1988, pp. 226, 22; and R L Daft and R H Lengel, "Information Richness: A New Approach to Managerial Behavior and Organization Design," *Research in Organizational Behavior,* eds B M Staw and L L Cummings (Greenwich, CT: JAI Press, 1984), p. 199.

to communicate about a merger or a major reorganization. This choice of medium is ineffective because employees are likely to be nervous and concerned about how a merger or reorganization will affect their futures.

Research Evidence   The relationship between media richness and problem/ situation complexity has not been researched extensively because the underlying theory is relatively new. Available evidence indicates that managers used richer sources when confronted with ambiguous and complicated events, and miscommunication was increased when rich media were used to transmit information that was traditionally communicated through lean media.[51] Moreover, a meta-analysis of more than 40 studies revealed that media usage was significantly different across organizational levels. Upper-level executives/managers spent more time in face-to-face meetings than did lower-level managers.[52] This finding is consistent with recommendations derived from the contingency model just discussed.

Hierarchical Communication

Hierarchical communication

Exchange of information between managers and employees.

Hierarchical communication is defined as "those exchanges of information and influence between organizational members, at least one of whom has formal (as defined by official organizational sources) authority to direct and evaluate the activities of other organizational members."[53] This communication pattern involves information exchanged downward from manager to employee and upward from employee to manager. Managers provide five types of information through downward communication: job instructions, job rationale, organizational procedures and practices, feedback about performance, and indoctrination of goals. Employees, in turn, communicate information upward about themselves, co-workers and their problems, organizational practices and policies, and what needs to be done and how to do it. Timely and valid hierarchical communication can promote individual and organizational success. For example, a study of 24 branches of a large East Coast bank revealed that those with a two-way pattern of communication between managers and employees were 70% more profitable than branches with a one-way communication pattern.[54] Managers are encouraged to foster two-way communication among all employees, particularly when faced with tough times. Thomas Corcoran, CEO of FelCor Lodging Trust, is a good example of someone who follows this recommendation.

> At Felcor Lodging Trust, the Irving, Texas, hotel real-estate investment trust, Chief Executive Thomas J Corcoran cites open and frank communication with employees as "the best motivator."
>
> FelCor, owner of the largest number of Embassy Suites, Crowne Plaza and Holiday-Inn branded hotels in the US, has been hurt by the travel slump since September 11 and canceled merge plans with MeriStar Hospitality. As a result, "bonuses were thin in January," Mr Corcoran says, and stress at work and home is higher than a year ago.
>
> He has responded by trying to keep his staff of about 65 employees informed. Since last year, for example, he has shared with staffers the monthly report he used to give only to company directors. . . . "I've always hated bosses who keep their doors closed. When you do that, your staff is going to get paranoid and worried about what is going on, even when there's no cause."[55]

Unfortunately, not all managers have the desire or skills to create an open communication environment like Corcoran. If that is the case, management needs to devise alternative methods for obtaining employee feedback. Some companies use anonymous E-mail addresses or suggestion boxes to obtain this feedback.

The Grapevine

The term *grapevine* originated from the Civil War practice of stringing battlefield telegraph lines between trees. Today, the **grapevine** represents the unofficial communication system of the informal organization. Information traveling along the grapevine supplements official or formal channels of communication. Although the grapevine can be a source of inaccurate rumors, it functions positively as an early warning signal for organizational changes, a medium for creating organizational culture, a mechanism for fostering group cohesiveness, and a way of informally bouncing ideas off others.[56] Evidence indicates that the grapevine is alive and well in today's workplaces.

A national survey of the readers of *Industry Week,* a professional management magazine, revealed that employees used the grapevine as their most frequent source of information.[57] Contrary to general opinion, the grapevine is not necessarily counterproductive. Plugging into the grapevine can help employees, managers, and organizations alike achieve desired results. To enhance your understanding of the grapevine, we will explore grapevine patterns and research and managerial recommendations for monitoring this often-misunderstood system of communication.

Grapevine Patterns   Communication along the grapevine follows predictable patterns (see Figure 15–5). The most frequent pattern is not a single strand or gossip chain, but the cluster pattern. Although the probability and cluster patterns look similar, the process by which information is passed is very different between these two grapevine structures. People *randomly* gossip to others in a probability structure. For instance, Figure 15–5 shows that person A tells persons F and D a piece of information but ignores co-workers B and J. Person A may have done this simply because he or she ran into co-workers F and D in the hallway. In turn, persons F and D randomly discuss

> **Grapevine**
> Unofficial communication system of the informal organization.

Figure 15–5   *Grapevine Patterns*

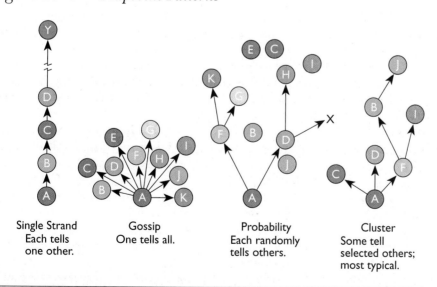

Single Strand
Each tells
one other.

Gossip
One tells all.

Probability
Each randomly
tells others.

Cluster
Some tell
selected others;
most typical.

SOURCE: K Davis and J W Newstrom, *Human Behavior at Work: Organizational Behavior,* 7th ed (New York: McGraw-Hill, 1985), p. 317. Used with permission. Copyright © 1985. Reproduced with permission of the McGraw-Hill Companies.

this information with others in their work environments. In contrast, the cluster pattern is based on the idea that information is *selectively* passed from one person to another. People tend to selectively communicate because they know that certain individuals tend to leak or pass information to others, and they actually want the original piece of information to be spread around. For example, Figure 15–5 shows that person A selectively discusses a piece of information with three people, one of whom—person F—tells two others, and then one of those two—person B—tells one other. Only certain individuals repeat what they hear when the probability or cluster patterns are operating. People who consistently pass along grapevine information to others are called **liaison individuals** or "gossips":

Liaison individuals

Those who consistently pass along grapevine information to others.

> About 10% of the employees on an average grapevine will be highly active participants. They serve as liaisons with the rest of the staff members who receive information but spread it to only a few other people. Usually these liaisons are friendly, outgoing people who are in positions that allow them to cross departmental lines. For example, secretaries tend to be liaisons because they can communicate with the top executive, the janitor, and everyone in between without raising eyebrows.[58]

Effective managers monitor the pulse of work groups by regularly communicating with known liaisons.

Organizational moles

Those who use the grapevine to enhance their power and status.

In contrast to liaison individuals, **organizational moles** use the grapevine for a different purpose. They obtain information, often negative, in order to enhance their power and status. They do this by secretly reporting their perceptions and hearsay about the difficulties, conflicts, or failure of other employees to powerful members of management. This enables a mole to divert attention away from him- or herself and to position him- or herself as more competent than others. Management should attempt to create an open, trusting environment that discourages mole behavior because moles can destroy teamwork, create conflict, and impair productivity.[59]

Research and Practical Implications
Although research activity on this topic has slowed in recent years, past research about the grapevine provided the following insights: (1) it is faster than formal channels; (2) it is about 75% accurate; (3) people rely on it when they are insecure, threatened, or faced with organizational changes; and (4) employees use the grapevine to acquire the majority of their on-the-job information.[60]

The key managerial recommendation is to *monitor* and *influence* the grapevine rather than attempt to control it. Effective managers accomplish this by openly sharing relevant information with employees. This is precisely what managers at Shaw's Supermarkets did after acquiring another organization.

> When Shaw's Supermarkets acquired another company, rumors ran rampant. How many stores would be closed? How many people would be laid off? Controlling the rumor mill is never easy, especially for a company with 32,000 employees in seven New England states. The solution: introduction of *The Rumor Buster*, a newsletter published on an as-needed—but at least weekly—basis during the merger, says Ruth Bramson, senior vice president of human resources in East Bridgewater, Massachusetts.
>
> "Communication is the major stumbling block to a successful merger," says Bramson. *The Rumor Buster* "addressed whatever horrendous rumors were going around at the moment. We found it to be an incredibly successful tool."
>
> HR discovered just how useful the newsletter was when employees of the newly acquired company were polled; they indicated that the newsletter had been an important and positive part of the integration.[61]

Communication Distortion between Managers and Employees

Communication distortion occurs when an employee purposely modifies the content of a message, thereby reducing the accuracy of communication between managers and employees. Employees tend to engage in this practice because of workplace politics, a desire to manage impressions, or fear of how a manager might respond to a message.[62] Communication experts point out the organizational problems caused by distortion:

> Distortion is an important problem in organizations because modifications to messages cause misdirectives to be transmitted, nondirectives to be issued, incorrect information to be passed on, and a variety of other problems related to both the quantity and quality of information.[63]

Knowledge of the antecedents or causes of communication distortion can help managers avoid or limit these problems.

Studies have identified four situational antecedents of distortion in upward communication (see Figure 15–6). Distortion tends to increase when supervisors have high upward influence or power. Employees also tend to modify or distort information when they aspire to move upward or when they do not trust their supervisors.[64] Because managers generally do not want to reduce their upward influence or curb their direct reports' desire for upward mobility, they can reduce distortion in several ways:

1. Managers can deemphasize power differences between themselves and their direct reports.

2. They can enhance trust through a meaningful performance review process that rewards actual performance.

3. Managers can encourage staff feedback by conducting smaller, more informal meetings.

Communication distortion
Purposely modifying the content of a message.

Figure 15–6   *Sources of Distortion in Upward Communication*

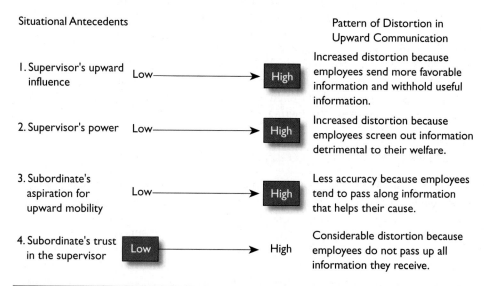

Situational Antecedents — Pattern of Distortion in Upward Communication

1. Supervisor's upward influence   Low ⟶ High   Increased distortion because employees send more favorable information and withhold useful information.

2. Supervisor's power   Low ⟶ High   Increased distortion because employees screen out information detrimental to their welfare.

3. Subordinate's aspiration for upward mobility   Low ⟶ High   Less accuracy because employees tend to pass along information that helps their cause.

4. Subordinate's trust in the supervisor   Low ⟶ High   Considerable distortion because employees do not pass up all information they receive.

SOURCE: Adapted in part from J Fulk and S Mani, "Distortion of Communication in Hierarchical Relationships," in *Communication Yearbook* 9, ed M L McLaughlin (Beverly Hills, CA: Sage Publications, 1986).

4. They can establish performance goals that encourage employees to focus on problems rather than personalities.

5. Distortion can be limited by encouraging dialogue between those with opposing viewpoints.

Communication in the Computerized Information Age

As discussed in Chapter 1, the use of computers and information technology is dramatically affecting many aspects of organizational behavior. Consider, for example, how Mike Bouissey is using information technology to change his immediate work environment.

> Mike Bouissey already works on the top floor of a seven-story building in Philadelphia's Center City. But on warm, sunny days, he slips his notebook computer under his arm and heads up one more flight.
>
> Whenever weather permits, Bouissey, a project manager for Web-design company WebLinc, works on the building's flat asphalt-topped roof. He's never out of touch. He forwards calls from his desk to his cell phone, and—although there's not a cord or a cable in sight—he remains logged on to the company's local area network (LAN), using radio waves rather than wires. He can send and receive E-mail, build Web pages, track his team's progress, and do anything else he'd do downstairs in the office, all while sitting on a blanket in the sun.[65]

While many of us cannot or do not want to work on a rooftop like Mike Bouissey, the electronic age is radically changing communication patterns in both our personal and work lives.[66] For example, U.S. Census Bureau data revealed that more than 50% of all households and all Americans were connected to the Internet in 2002. An estimated 143 million Americans used the Net in 2002.[67] Interestingly, some people use the Internet with such frequency that they become dependent on it. For example, a recent study of 1,300 students at eight colleges revealed that nearly 10% were dependent on the Internet and that their Internet usage affected their academics, ability to meet new people, and sleep patterns.[68] This section explores five key components of information technology that influence communication patterns and management within a computerized workplace: Internet/intranet/extranet, electronic mail, videoconferencing, collaborative computing, and telecommuting.

Internet/Intranet/Extranet

Internet
A global network of computer networks.

Intranet
An organization's private internet.

The Internet, or more simply, the Net, is more than a computer network. It is a network of computer networks. The **Internet** is a global network of independently operating, but interconnected computers. It links more than 140,000 smaller networks in more than 200 countries. The Internet connects everything from supercomputers, to large mainframes contained in businesses, government, and universities, to the personal computers in our homes and offices. An **intranet** is nothing more than an organization's private Internet. Intranets also have *firewalls* that block outside Internet users from accessing internal information. This is done to protect the privacy and confidentiality of company documents. More than half of companies with more than 500 employees have corporate intranets according to Information Data Corporation.[69] In contrast to the internal focus of an intranet, an **extranet** is an extended intranet in that it connects internal employees with selected customers, suppliers, and other strategic partners. Ford Motor Company, for instance, has an extranet that connects its dealers worldwide. Ford's extranet was set up to help support the sales and servicing of cars and to enhance customer satisfaction.

> **Extranet**
> Connects internal employees with selected customers, suppliers, and strategic partners.

The primary benefit of the Internet, intranets, and extranets is that they can enhance the ability of employees to find, create, manage, and distribute information. The effectiveness of these systems, however, depends on how organizations set up and manage their intranet/extranet and how employees use the acquired information because information by itself cannot solve or do anything; information is knowledge or a thing. For example, communication effectiveness actually can decrease if a corporate intranet becomes a dumping ground of unorganized information. In this case, employees will find themselves flailing in a sea of information. To date, however, no rigorous research studies have been conducted that directly demonstrate productivity increases from using the Internet, intranets, or extranets. But there are case studies that reveal other organizational benefits. For example, Cisco Systems uses the Internet to recruit potential employees: The company has hired 66% of its people and received 81% of its resumes from the Net. This translated into reduced costs because the company was able to employ fewer in-house recruiters as it grew from 2,000 to 8,000 people.[70]

IBM also saved $1 million in costs in 2000 by asking 140,000 employees located in Armonk, New York, to enroll for employee benefits on the company's intranet: 80% enrolled electronically.[71] General Mills similarly used the Internet to reduce costs:

> It used to be that General Mills Inc. had to send researchers across the country to conduct focus groups or hire marketing companies to poll consumers on a new kind of cereal or yet another variety of Hamburger Helper. Now the Minneapolis food company conducts 60% of its consumer research online, reducing costs by 50%. . . . The company also makes purchases from Transora, an electronic-marketplace consortium. And it shares trucking services through an online network—expecting to shave 7% off shipping costs.[72]

In contrast to these positive case studies, a survey conducted by Vault.com revealed that one out of every eight workers spent more than two hours a day corresponding via E-mail, shopping on the Web, or searching for information related to personal interests. All told, International Data Corp. estimated personal use of the Internet during work hours contributes to a 30 to 40% decrease in productivity.[73] Organizations are taking these statistics to heart and are attempting to root out cyberslackers by tracking employee behavior with electronic monitoring. A 2001 study by the American Management Association showed that nearly 80% of all major US companies checked employees' use of E-mail, the Internet, or phone connections, and 25% of these organizations fired an employee for misuse of the Internet or office E-mail.[74] Only the future will tell whether the Internet is more useful as a marketing/sales tool, a device to conduct personal transactions such as banking or ordering movies, or a management vehicle that enhances employee motivation and productivity.

Electronic Mail

> **Electronic mail**
> Uses the Internet/intranet to send computer-generated text and documents.

Electronic mail, or E-mail, uses the Internet/intranet to send computer-generated text and documents between people. The use of E-mail is on the rise throughout the world. For example, recent surveys reveal that US employees receive somewhere between 20 to 30 E-mail messages per day.[75] Further, another survey of executives by the administrative staffing firm Office Team showed that 73% of the respondents believed that E-mail would be the leading form of business communication for employees by 2005.[76] E-mail is becoming a major communication medium because of four key benefits:

1. E-mail reduces the cost of distributing information to a large number of employees.

2. E-mail is a tool for increasing teamwork. It enables employees to quickly send messages to colleagues on the next floor, in another building, or in another country.

3. E-mail reduces the costs and time associated with print duplication and paper distribution. One management expert estimated that these savings can total $9,000 a year per employee.[77]

4. E-mail fosters flexibility. This is particularly true for employees with a portable computer because they can log onto E-mail whenever and wherever they want.

In spite of these positive benefits, there are four key drawbacks to consider. First, sending and receiving E-mail can lead to a lot of wasted time and effort, or it can distract employees from completing critical job duties. For example, a recent national survey of US workers indicated that between 33% and 50% of their E-mail messages were unimportant.[78] Second, the system itself may be cumbersome and ineffective. Consider what happened at AOL Time Warner when the company adopted a new E-mail system.

> In a humbling reversal, AOL Time Warner Inc. is retreating from a top-level directive that required the divisions of the old Time Warner to convert to an E-mail system based on AOL software and run by America Online's giant public server computers in Virginia. . . .
>
> Instead, management got months of complaints from both senior and junior executives in the divisions involved, who said the E-mail system, initially designed for consumers, wasn't appropriate for business use. Among the problems cited: The E-mail software frequently crashed, staffers weren't able to send messages with large attachments, they were often kicked offline without warning, and if they tried to send messages to large groups of users they were labeled as spammers and locked out of the system. Sometimes, E-mails were just plain lost in the AOL etherworld and never found. And if there was an out-of-office reply function, most people couldn't find it.[79]

Information overload is the third problem associated with the increased use of E-mail. People tend to send more messages to others, and there is a lot of "spamming" going on: sending junk mail, bad jokes, or irrelevant memos (e.g., the "cc" of E-mail). The Federal Trade Commission, for example, reported receiving 15,000 complaints about spam every day in the first quarter of 2002.[80]

Finally, preliminary evidence suggests that people are using electronic mail to communicate when they should be using other media. This practice can result in reduced communication effectiveness. A four-year study of communication patterns within a university demonstrated that the increased use of electronic mail was associated with decreased face-to-face interactions and with a drop in the overall amount of organizational communication. Employees also expressed a feeling of being less connected and less cohesive as a department as the amount of E-mails increased.[81] This interpersonal "disconnection" may be caused by the trend of replacing everyday face-to-face interactions with electronic messages. It is important to remember that employees' social needs are satisfied through the many different interpersonal interactions that occur at work.

There are three additional issues to consider when using E-mail: (1) E-mail only works when the party you desire to communicate with also uses it. E-mail may not be a viable communication medium in all cases. (2) The speed of getting a response to an E-mail message is dependent on how frequently the receiver examines his or her messages. It is important to consider this issue when picking a communication medium. (3) Many companies do not have policies for using E-mail, which can lead to misuse and potential legal liability. For instance, four female employees working at Chevron filed a suit claiming that they were sexually harassed through E-mail. The company settled for $2.2 million, plus legal fees and court costs. Do not assume that your E-mail messages are private and confidential. Organizations are advised to develop policies regarding the use of E-mail.[82]

Videoconferencing

Videoconferencing, also known as teleconferencing, uses video and audio links along with computers to enable people in different locations to see, hear, and talk with one another. This enables people from many locations to conduct a meeting without having to travel. Consider the following applications of videoconferencing.

> At Harken Energy Corp., an oil and gas exploration company in Houston, engineers use video capabilities to share seismic graphs and other geological displays and data from offices in Latin America. The Department of Labor uses videoconferencing to impart basic computer, financial, and résumé-writing skills to citizens. The potential uses of the technology seem even brighter, particularly in marketing and community outreach efforts. . . . Video also is a critical component of eGetgoing's virtual therapy offering. "Treatment requires the participants to see the reaction of the counselor in order to create an emotional bond," says [Barry] Karlin, who notes that the one-way streaming video eGetgoing uses contains the benefit of maintaining anonymity among the 10 patients in each single-group session.[83]

Videoconferencing thus can significantly reduce an organization's travel expenses. Many organizations set up special videoconferencing rooms or booths with specially equipped television cameras. More recent equipment enables people to attach small cameras and microphones to their desks or computer monitors. This enables employees to conduct long-distance meetings and training classes without leaving their office or cubicle.

Collaborative Computing

Collaborative computing entails using state-of-the-art computer software and hardware to help people work better together. Collaborative systems enable people to share information without the constraints of time and space. This is accomplished by utilizing computer networks to link people across a room or across the globe. Collaborative applications include messaging and E-mail systems, calendar management, videoconferencing, computer teleconferencing, electronic whiteboards, and the type of computer-aided decision-making systems discussed in Chapter 11.

Corporate applications of collaborative computing have demonstrated increased productivity and cost savings.

> The new tools are barely out of the box, but some early experiments are showing solid results. By using the Web to coordinate auto design by internal engineers and external suppliers, General Motors Corp. can get a car into production in 18 months, down from the 42 months it took in the mid-1990s. Land O'Lakes Inc. has saved $40,000 a month since

Collaborative computing
Using computer software and hardware to help people work better together.

September by using the Web to stuff butter and cheese into trucks it shares with companies such as Georgia-Pacific Corp. And Deloitte Consulting says it can bring a new team member up to speed on a project in a day or two, down from three weeks, by keeping everything they need to know on a Web site.[84]

Organizations that use full-fledged collaborative systems have the ability to create virtual teams or to operate as a virtual organization. Virtual organizations are discussed in Chapter 18. You may recall from Chapter 13 that a virtual team represents a physically dispersed task group that conducts its business by using the types of information technology currently being discussed. Specifically, virtual teams tend to use Internet/intranet systems, collaborative software systems, and videoconferencing systems. These real-time systems enable people to communicate with anyone at anytime.

It is important to keep in mind that modern-day information technology only enables people to interact virtually; it doesn't guarantee effective communications. Interestingly, there are a whole host of unique communication problems associated with using the information technology needed to operate virtually.[85]

Telecommuting

Telecommuting

Doing work that is generally performed in the office away from the office using different information technologies.

Telecommuting is a work practice in which an employee does part of his or her job in a remote location using a variety of information technologies. Examples include "wireless E-mail from Starbucks, videoconferencing from Kinko's and home, and even telework centers in remote villages in India, served by wireless computer links."[86] As you can see from these examples, telecommuting involves receiving and sending work from a remote location via some form of information technology such as wireless devices, fax, or a home computer that is linked via modem to an office computer. Telecommuting is more common for jobs involving computer work, writing, and phone work that require concentration and limited interruptions. The International Telework Association and Council estimated that 23.6 million US workers telecommuted in 2002.[87] Proposed benefits of telecommuting include:

Do you ever have days when you wish you could just stay home and work in your pajamas? If yes, telecommuting may be just what you need. Telecommuting allows employees to complete their work away from the office using different information technologies.

(c) G&M David DeLossy/Getty Images/The Image Bank

1. *Reduction of capital costs.* Merrill Lynch and IBM reported lower costs by letting employees work at home.

2. *Increased flexibility and autonomy for workers.*

3. *Competitive edge in recruitment.*

4. *Lower turnover.* Employees like telecommuting because it helps resolve work-family conflicts. Merrill Lynch's turnover fell significantly after it implemented a telework program.

5. *Increased productivity.* Telecommuting resulted in productivity increases of 25% and 35% for FourGen Software and Continental Traffic Services, respectively.

6. *Tapping nontraditional labor pools* (such as prison inmates and homebound disabled persons).[88]

Although telecommuting represents an attempt to accommodate employee needs and desires, it requires adjustments and is not for everybody. Many people thoroughly enjoy the social camaraderie that exists within an office setting. These individuals probably would not like to telecommute. Others lack the self-motivation needed to work at home. Finally, organizations must be careful to implement telecommuting in a nondiscriminatory manner. Organizations can easily and unknowingly violate one of several antidiscrimination laws.

Summary of Key Concepts

1. *Describe the perceptual process model of communication.* Communication is a process of consecutively linked elements. Historically, this process was described in terms of a conduit model. Criticisms of this model led to development of a perceptual process model of communication that depicts receivers as information processors who create the meaning of messages in their own mind. Because receivers' interpretations of messages often differ from those intended by senders, miscommunication is a common occurrence.

2. *Describe the process, personal, physical, and semantic barriers to effective communication.* Every element of the perceptual model of communication is a potential process barrier. There are eight personal barriers that commonly influence communication: (1) the ability to effectively communicate, (2) the way people process and interpret information, (3) the level of interpersonal trust between people, (4) the existence of stereotypes and prejudices, (5) the egos of the people communicating, (6) the ability to listen, (7) the natural tendency to evaluate or judge a sender's message, and (8) the inability to listen with understanding. Physical barriers pertain to distance, physical objects, time, and work and office noise. Semantic barriers show up as encoding and decoding errors because these phases of communication involve transmitting and receiving words and symbols.

3. *Contrast the communication styles of assertiveness, aggressiveness, and nonassertiveness.* An assertive style is expressive and self-enhancing but does not violate others' basic human rights. In contrast, an aggressive style is expressive and self-enhancing but takes unfair advantage of others. A nonassertive style is characterized by timid and self-denying behavior. An assertive communication style is more effective than either an aggressive or nonassertive style.

4. *Discuss the primary sources of both nonverbal communication and listener comprehension.* There are several identifiable sources of nonverbal communication effectiveness. Body movements and gestures, touch, facial expressions, and eye contact are important nonverbal cues. The interpretation of these nonverbal cues significantly varies across cultures. Listening is the process of actively decoding and interpreting verbal messages. Listener characteristics, speaker characteristics, message characteristics, and environmental characteristics influence listener comprehension.

5. *Review the 10 keys to effective listening.* Good listeners use the following 10 listening habits: (1) capitalize on thought speed by staying with the speaker and listening between the lines, (2) listen for ideas rather than facts, (3) identify areas of interest between the speaker and

listener, (4) judge content and not delivery, (5) do not judge until the speaker has completed his or her message, (6) put energy and effort into listening, (7) resist distractions, (8) listen to both favorable and unfavorable information, (9) read or listen to complex material to exercise the mind, and (10) take notes when necessary and use visual aids to enhance understanding.

6. *Describe the communication differences between men and women, and explain the source of these differences.* Men and women vary in terms of how they ask for information, express certainty, apologize, accept blame, give criticism and praise, say thank you, build consensus, give directions, claim ownership of ideas, and use tone of voice. There are two competing explanations for these differences. The biological perspective attributes gender differences in communication to inherited drives, needs, and conflicts associated with reproductive strategies used by women and men. The second explanation, which is based on social role theory, is based on the idea that females and males learn different ways of speaking as children growing up.

7. *Explain the contingency approach to media selection.* Selecting media is a key component of communication effectiveness. Media selection is based on the interaction between the information richness of a medium and the complexity of the problem/situation at hand. Information richness ranges from low to high and is a function of four factors: speed of feedback, characteristics of the channel, type of communication, and language source. Problems/situations range from simple to complex. Effective communication occurs when the richness of the medium matches the complexity of the problem/situation. From a contingency perspective, richer media need to be used as problems/situations become more complex.

8. *Discuss the patterns of hierarchical communication and the grapevine.* Hierarchical communication patterns describe exchanges of information between managers and the employees they supervise. Managers provide five types of downward communication: job instructions, job rationale, organizational procedures and practices, feedback about performance, and indoctrination of goals. Employees communicate information upward about themselves, co-workers and their problems, organizational practices and policies, and what needs to be done and how to do it.

The grapevine is the unofficial communication system of the informal organization. Communication along the grapevine follows four predictable patterns: single strand, gossip, probability, and cluster. The cluster pattern is the most common.

9. *Demonstrate your familiarity with four antecedents of communication distortion between managers and employees.* Communication distortion is a common problem that consists of modifying the content of a message. Employees distort upward communication when their supervisor has high upward influence or power. Distortion also increases when employees aspire to move upward or when they do not trust their supervisor.

10. *Explain the information technology of Internet/intranet/ extranet, E-mail, videoconferencing, and collaborative computing, and explain the related use of telecommuting.* The Internet is a global network of computer networks. An intranet is an organization's private Internet. It contains a firewall that blocks outside Internet users from accessing private internal information. An extranet connects an organization's internal employees with selected customers, suppliers, and strategic partners. The primary benefit of these "nets" is that they can enhance the ability of employees to find, create, manage, and distribute information. E-mail uses the Internet/intranet/extranet to send computer-generated text and documents between people. Videoconferencing uses video and audio links along with computers to enable people located at different locations to see, hear, and talk with one another. Collaborative computing entails using state-of-the-art computer software and hardware to help people work better together. Information is shared across time and space by linking people with computer networks. Telecommuting involves doing work that is generally performed in the office away from the office using different information technologies.

Discussion Questions

1. Describe a situation where you had trouble decoding a message. What caused the problem?

2. What are some sources of noise that interfere with communication during a class lecture, an encounter with a professor in his or her office, or a movie?

3. Which barrier to effective communication is more difficult to reduce? Explain.

4. Would you describe your prevailing communication style as assertive, aggressive, or nonassertive? How can you tell? Would your style help or hinder you as a manager?

5. Are you good at reading nonverbal communication? Give some examples.

6. Which of the keys to effective listening are most difficult to follow when listening to a class lecture? Explain.

7. Describe a miscommunication that occurred between you and someone of the opposite sex. Now, explain how genderflexing might have been used to improve this interaction.

8. Which of the three zones of communication in Figure 15–4 (overload, effective, oversimplification) do you think is most common in today's large organizations? What is your rationale?

9. What is your personal experience with the grapevine? Do you see it as a positive or negative factor in the workplace? Explain.

10. Have you ever distorted upward communication? What was your reason? Was it related to one of the four antecedents of communication distortion? Explain.

Internet Exercise

www.queendom.com

As covered in this chapter, communication styles vary from nonassertive to aggressive. We recommended that you strive to use an assertive style while avoiding the tendencies of being nonassertive or aggressive. In trying to be assertive, however, keep in mind that too much of a good thing is bad. That is, the use of an assertive style can transform to an aggressive one if it is taken too far.

A Free Self-Assessment Questionnaire for Assertiveness

The purpose of this exercise is to provide you with feedback on the extent to which you use an assertive communication style. Go to the Internet home page for Body-Mind Queendom (**www.queendom.com**), and click on the box "Tests & Profiles." (*Note:* Our use of this site is for instructional purposes only and does not constitute an endorsement of any products that may or may not suit your needs. There is no obligation to buy anything.) Next, select "Tests, Tests, Tests. . ." and then click on the "Relationships" category. Under the heading "Classic Tests," choose "Assertiveness Test-

Abridged." Complete the quick 10-item questionnaire and hit the scoring button. Read the interpretation of your results. (*Note:* Queendom frequently updates its collection of tests, but the site always has good communication-related questionnaires such as the "Communication Skills Test." You may need to do some browsing, but it will be well worth the effort.)

Questions

1. How did you score? Are you surprised by the results? Do you agree with the interpretation of your score?

2. Reviewing the questionnaire item by item, can you find aspects of communication in which you are either nonassertive or possibly too assertive? Do you think that your communication style can be improved by making adjustments within these areas of communication?

3. Based on the results of this questionnaire, develop an action plan for improving your communication style. Table 15–1 is a helpful source.

OB in Action Case Study

Information Technology Dramatically Affects Communication, Productivity, and Customer Service[89]

BusinessWeek Three years ago, US Fleet Services considered building a wireless network for its drivers, but soon decided against it. Customizing mobile devices and developing software was too hard, and the company didn't have computer systems robust enough to make it worth the hassle. Then, last year, US

Fleet revisited the technology—and this time it put the pedal to the metal.

The reason? These days, wireless is cheaper and easier to deploy—and it's already paying off. In September, US Fleet, which refuels vehicles for customers such as Coca-Cola and Nabisco, began equipping its 200 trucks with mobile devices and wireless connections to its corporate intranet. The price: $1.5 million, a quarter of what it would have cost three years earlier. Now, managers can check drivers' locations online, letting them rearrange routes on the fly—and increase the average number of daily deliveries per truck from six to seven. As soon as drivers fill a client's vehicle, the information is scanned into their handheld computers and zapped off to the network. That lets customers check deliveries immediately on US Fleet's Web site, two days faster than before the system was installed. Wireless "makes good business sense and doesn't cost an arm and a leg," says Saul Cohen, vice president of information technology at US Fleet.

Once written off as overhyped and underperforming, wireless is enjoying a resurgence in Corporate America. Thanks to plunging equipment prices, new standards for radio links, and increased cellular coverage, even small companies can afford wireless systems once available only to deep-pocketed giants such as United Parcel Service Inc. . . .

The biggest action is in reaching out to field personnel. In years past, Pepsi Bottling Group Inc.'s 700 soda fountain technicians spent too much time on the phone instead of time fixing the company's 1.3 million vending and fountain machines. Customers called in problems, then a call-center employee paged a technician, who would ring for details about the job. At the end of the day, repair workers would fax in forms detailing their visits—with results not available on Pepsi's intranet until five days later.

That system is on its way to the trash heap. Pepsi's technicians now have off-the-shelf handheld devices from Armonk (New York)-based Melard Technologies Inc. Dispatchers today retrieve from Pepsi's intranet everything the technicians need to know about a job and zap it off to the paperback-sized handheld. When the job's done, the technician sends an electronic bill to headquarters. At the same time, the handheld automatically tells the stockroom which parts were used, so when the technician stops in for supplies, replacements are waiting for pick-up.

The payoff? Pepsi answers calls 20% faster than it used to and has saved $7 million—meaning the project will pay for itself in just two years. And parts replenishment requests are now nearly 100% accurate, versus 85% in the past, when legibility was a big issue. "We sell soda," says Gary K Wandschneider, senior vice president for opera-

tions of Pepsi Bottling Group. "When we tried to figure out why customers switched to our competitors, part of the answer was customer service and equipment failure."

Field workers aren't the only ones going wireless. In warehouses, offices, and hospitals, wireless technology gives mobile workers instant access to data. St. Luke's Episcopal Hospital in Houston spent $2.5 million on computers and a WiFi network for three of its 22 floors. Nurses and doctors bring laptops on their rounds, entering treatment info and zapping it to the hospital's intranet. Staff in the departments with wireless have cut data-entry time by 30%, says Gene Gretzer, the hospital's wireless project leader. The respiratory therapy group alone was able to shave staff by 20%, saving $1.5 million while handling 13% more patients.

Increasingly, companies are using wireless devices that talk to each other, cutting out humans entirely. Thermo King Corp., which makes cooling units for trucks and shipping containers, is selling self-monitoring equipment. When a truck returns from a delivery, a radio connected to the Net contacts sensors on the vehicle that track the performance of the cooling machinery. If there's a problem, an alert is sent to a Web site monitored by technicians. That can mean savings of up to $1,000 per truck annually by reducing spoilage and cutting maintenance staff.

Sure, the wireless Web hasn't lived up to expectations for consumers. For businesses though, the mobility of wireless combined with the wealth of data on the Internet are creating a one-two punch.

Questions for Discussion

1. Why is wireless technology being used by more and more companies? Explain your rationale.

2. What are the pros and cons of using wireless technology? Discuss results obtained by the various companies profiled in the case.

3. Is Pepsi's use of wireless technology consistent with the contingency model for selecting media? Discuss your rationale.

4. What types of communication noise are associated with the use of wireless technology? Explain.

5. How might US Fleet's and Pepsi's use of wireless technology affect the grapevine and communication distortion? Discuss your logic.

Personal Awareness and Growth Exercise

Assessing Your Listening Skills

Objectives

1. To assess your listening skills.
2. To develop a personal development plan aimed at increasing your listening skills.

Introduction

Listening is a critical component of effective communication. Unfortunately, research and case studies suggest that many of us are not very good at actively listening. This is particularly bad in light of the fact that managers spend more time listening than they do speaking or writing. This exercise provides you the opportunity to assess your listening skills and develop a plan for improvement.

Instructions

The following statements reflect various habits we use when listening to others. For each statement, indicate the extent to which you agree or disagree with it by selecting one number from the scale provided. Circle your response for each statement. Remember, there are no right or wrong answers. After completing the survey, add up your total score for the 17 items, and record it in the space provided.

Listening Skills Survey

1 = Strongly disagree
2 = Disagree
3 = Neither agree nor disagree
4 = Agree
5 = Strongly agree

1. I daydream or think about other things when listening to others.   1 — 2 — 3 — 4 — 5
2. I do not mentally summarize the ideas being communicated by a speaker.   1 — 2 — 3 — 4 — 5
3. I do not use a speaker's body language or tone of voice to help interpret what he or she is saying.   1 — 2 — 3 — 4 — 5
4. I listen more for facts than overall ideas during classroom lectures.   1 — 2 — 3 — 4 — 5
5. I tune out dry speakers.   1 — 2 — 3 — 4 — 5
6. I have a hard time paying attention to boring people.   1 — 2 — 3 — 4 — 5
7. I can tell whether someone has anything useful to say before he or she finishes communicating a message.   1 — 2 — 3 — 4 — 5
8. I quit listening to a speaker when I think he or she has nothing interesting to say.   1 — 2 — 3 — 4 — 5
9. I get emotional or upset when speakers make jokes about issues or things that are important to me.   1 — 2 — 3 — 4 — 5
10. I get angry or distracted when speakers use offensive words.   1 — 2 — 3 — 4 — 5
11. I do not expend a lot of energy when listening to others.   1 — 2 — 3 — 4 — 5
12. I pretend to pay attention to others even when I'm not really listening.   1 — 2 — 3 — 4 — 5
13. I get distracted when listening to others.   1 — 2 — 3 — 4 — 5
14. I deny or ignore information and comments that go against my thoughts and feelings.   1 — 2 — 3 — 4 — 5
15. I do not seek opportunities to challenge my listening skills.   1 — 2 — 3 — 4 — 5
16. I do not pay attention to the visual aids used during lectures.   1 — 2 — 3 — 4 — 5
17. I do not take notes on handouts when they are provided.   1 — 2 — 3 — 4 — 5

Total score = _____

Preparing a Personal Development Plan

1. Use the following norms to evaluate your listening skills:
   17–34 = Good listening skills
   35–53 = Moderately good listening skills
   54–85 = Poor listening skills
   How would you evaluate your listening skills?

2. Do you agree with the assessment of your listening skills? Why or why not?

3. The 17-item listening skills survey was developed to assess the extent to which you use the keys to effective listening presented in Table 15–2. Use Table 15–2 and the development plan format shown on the following page to prepare your development plan. First, identify the five statements from the listening skills survey that received your highest ratings—high ratings represent low skills. Record the survey numbers in the space provided in the development plan. Next, compare the content of these survey items to the descriptions of bad and good listeners shown in Table 15–2. This comparison will help you identify the keys to effective listening being measured by each survey item. Write down the keys to effective listening that correspond to each of the five items you want to improve. Finally, write down specific actions or behaviors that you can undertake to improve the listening skill being considered.

Development Plan

Survey Items	Key to Effective Listening I Want to Improve	Action Steps Required (What Do You Need to Do to Build Listening Skills for This Listening Characteristic?)
#		
#		
#		
#		
#		

Group Exercise

Practicing Different Styles of Communication

Objectives

1. To demonstrate the relative effectiveness of communicating assertively, aggressively, and nonassertively.
2. To give you hands-on experience with different styles of communication.

Introduction

Research shows that assertive communication is more effective than either an aggressive or nonassertive style. This *role-playing exercise* is designed to increase your ability to communicate assertively. Your task is to use different communication styles while attempting to resolve the work-related problems of a poor performer.

Instructions

Divide into groups of three, and read the "Poor Performer" and "Store Manager" roles provided here. Then decide who will play the poor performer role, who will play the managerial role, and who will be the observer. The observer will be asked to provide feedback to the manager after each role play. When playing the managerial role, you should first attempt to resolve the problem by using an aggressive communication style. Attempt to achieve your objective by using the nonverbal and verbal behavior patterns associated with the aggressive style shown in Table 15–1. Take about four to six minutes to act out the instructions. The observer should give feedback to the manager after completing the role play. The observer should comment on how the employee responded to the aggressive behaviors displayed by the manager.

After feedback is provided on the first role play, the person playing the manager should then try to resolve the problem with a nonassertive style. Observers once again should provide feedback. Finally, the manager should confront the problem with an assertive style. Once again, rely on the relevant nonverbal and verbal behavior patterns presented in Table 15–1, and take four to six minutes to act out each scenario. Observers should try to provide detailed feedback on how effectively the manager exhibited nonverbal and verbal assertive behaviors. Be sure to provide positive and constructive feedback.

After completing these three role plays, switch roles: manager becomes observer, observer becomes poor performer, and poor performer becomes the manager. When these role plays are completed, switch roles once again.

ROLE: POOR PERFORMER

You sell shoes full-time for a national chain of shoe stores. During the last month you have been absent three times without giving your manager a reason. The quality of your work has been slipping. You have a lot of creative excuses when your boss tries to talk to you about your performance.

When playing this role, feel free to invent a personal problem that you may eventually want to share with your manager. However, make the manager dig for information about this problem. Otherwise, respond to your manager's comments as you normally would.

ROLE: STORE MANAGER

You manage a store for a national chain of shoe stores. In the privacy of your office, you are talking to one of your salespeople who has had three unexcused absences from work during the last month. (This is excessive, according to company guidelines, and must be corrected.) The quality of his or her work has been slipping. Customers have complained that this person is rude, and co-workers have told you this individual isn't carrying his or her fair share of the work. You are fairly sure this person has some sort of personal problem. You want to identify that problem and get him or her back on the right track.

Questions for Discussion

1. What drawbacks of the aggressive and nonassertive styles did you observe?
2. What were major advantages of the assertive style?
3. What were the most difficult aspects of trying to use an assertive style?
4. How important was nonverbal communication during the various role plays? Explain with examples.

Ethical Dilemma

Waddell & Reed Financial Inc. Attempts to Keep the Clients of a Fired Employee[90]

On February 3, 1997, Waddell & Reed Financial Inc. asked star broker Stephen Sawtelle to chair an elite club made up of the firm's top 12 producers. "Your distinguished service to your clients and our company is unmeasurable," the mutual fund company wrote in a note. Tucked in the envelope was a check for $5,000.

Seven days later, Waddell & Reed fired him for "personality conflicts."

What followed was an extraordinary struggle for control of Mr Sawtelle's 2,800 clients. Waddell hired a telemarketing firm to place rapid-fire calls to the customers. The firm sent letters saying Mr Sawtelle, a 47-year-old former Green Beret, was "not authorized" to handle their accounts. Mr Sawtelle says some clients were told that if they filed complaints against him they could get a lower-fee mutual fund. One client was so alarmed that he asked the police to find out if the broker "had been reported missing or if there were any outstanding warrants" for his arrest.

Waddell lost the battle: Mr Sawtelle, a 17-year veteran of the firm, retained 2,600 of his clients. Then it lost the war: An arbitration panel ruled this month that the firm must pay $27.6 million in damages to Mr Sawtelle for "reprehensible conduct" in smearing the broker's reputation. . . .

Questionable tactics long have been common on Wall Street in the behind-the-scenes scuffles that erupt over investor accounts when brokers leave their firms. Remaining brokers start making their pitches to get the business—and sometimes they are less than upfront about their former colleagues. . . .

After the firing, things got really nasty. Mr Sawtelle says many of his clients received a letter from Waddell on February 10, 1997—the day he was fired—saying: "You may

be aware that your representative, Steve Sawtelle, is no longer with our firm, and therefore not authorized to service your accounts with Waddell & Reed." The letter added that investors could face tax penalties if they transferred money from Waddell, a tactic Mr Sawtelle believes was used to prevent customers from changing firms. Letters such as these are common in the securities industry when a broker leaves a firm. . . .

Waddell brought out big guns. In addition to the letters, Waddell hired Adecco SA, a staffing company to provide telemarketers, which contacted hundreds of customers. About 10 temporary workers set up camp in a Waddell conference room telling clients Mr Sawtelle was gone and a new broker had been assigned to them.

What would you do to prevent this situation from happening again at Waddell & Reed?

1. Aggressively pursue the clients of a fired broker, but do not use false statements in letters or phone conversations. Explain your rationale.
2. Send clients a letter informing them that the broker no longer worked in the firm, and ask them if they would like to be reassigned to another broker. Why is this a better choice?
3. Let the fired employee retain his or her clients.
4. Invent other options. Discuss.

For an interpretation of this situation, visit our Web site, **www.mhhe.com/kreitner**.

Chapter Sixteen

Influence Tactics, Empowerment, and Politics

Learning Objectives

When you finish studying the material in this chapter, you should be able to:

1 Explain the concept of mutuality of interest.

2 Name at least three "soft" and two "hard" influence tactics, and summarize the practical lessons from influence research.

3 Identify and briefly explain Cialdini's six principles of influence and persuasion.

4 Identify and briefly describe French and Raven's five bases of power, and discuss the responsible use of power.

5 Define the term *empowerment*, and discuss the realities of open-book management.

6 Explain why delegation is the highest form of empowerment, and discuss the connections among delegation, trust, and personal initiative.

7 Define *organizational politics*, and explain what triggers it.

8 Distinguish between favorable and unfavorable impression management tactics.

9 Explain how to manage organizational politics.

Backward thinking usually gets companies in trouble. But for Wes-Tex Printing, [in Brownwood, Texas,] looking at the production process in reverse led to changes that cut delivery times in half.

Quick turnaround is a huge advantage in the high-volume, low-profit-margin world of business card printing. And Wes-Tex President Steve Blake was getting frustrated that his edicts to cut the time it took to deliver orders, up to seven days, didn't seem to work.

"I knew what needed to be done, but it was me having to do everything," Blake says.

So he took a radical approach. He turned the task of speeding up production to his 130 employees. That led to the formation of interdisciplinary teams. . . .

"Here was an owner who probably three or four years ago didn't let anyone buy a pencil without his approval, who found the wherewithal to stand aside and let people choose their own destiny," says [consultant] Chuck

Blevins of Chuck Blevins & Associates in Vienna, Virginia.

Here's how Wes-Tex did it:

- A team of workers in each step of the production process was brought together to try to pinpoint the bottlenecks.
- Team leader Shirley Stovall, with help from Dutch Hoekstra, set out to chart the production process to find sticky points—going backward.

Empowered teamwork is vital to success in the time-sensitive printing business.
(c) PhotoDisc

They started at the loading dock where finished boxes of business cards are picked up by United Parcel Service at 6 PM weekdays to be shipped to neighborhood printing shops around the country. They traced every step back to the time that orders arrive in the morning mail.

The verdict: By ironing out the wrinkles in the system, repeat orders could be shipped in two days, and all products could go within four days. "I was ecstatic," Stovall recalls.

- The team was consulted. In order to achieve the two-day/four-day goal, some employees would have to work different hours. Three platemakers, for instance, volunteered to change their shifts from days to evenings. The diemakers agreed to arrive every workday at 3:30 AM instead of the usual 7:30 AM starting time. The press operators started coming in at 5:30 AM

As a result Wes-Tex has made its customers—the stationers and others who subcontract their business card orders—happy.

"It used to take four days, and now it takes two days," says Catherine Dounies of the Hall Letter Shop in Bakersfield, California, a Wes-Tex customer.

But Wes-Tex isn't finished. The turnaround-time team recommended a new team to improve workflow. The new team decided to try an experiment in which three workers from different but related departments were thrown together to teach each other their jobs and jointly solve problems. They were seen around the plant together so often that they became known as "the triplets."

Now, orders that used to sit in baskets going back and forth between departments for changes or fixes could be acted on immediately.

The increased variety made the jobs more enjoyable, giving a boost to morale.

By July, the company will have six teams in action—one pilot and five regular operating units.

"It's been a 180-degree turn in culture and thought processes," Blake says.

And it's paying off: Wes-Tex expects to see another 5% increase in its more than $7 million in annual revenue this year, the same increase it saw last year.[1]

For Discussion

Why isn't this sort of employee empowerment more widespread? What changes would make it more common?

At the very heart of interpersonal dealings in today's work organizations is a constant struggle between individual and collective interests. For example, Sid wants a raise, but his company doesn't make enough money to both grant raises and buy needed capital equipment. Preoccupation with self-interest is understandable. After all, each of us was born, not as a cooperating organization member, but as an individual with instincts for self-preservation. It took socialization in family, school, religious, sports, recreation, and employment settings to introduce us to the notion of mutuality of interest. Basically, **mutuality of interest** involves win–win situations in which one's self-interest is served by cooperating actively and creatively with potential adversaries. A pair of organization development consultants offered this managerial perspective of mutuality of interest:

Mutuality of interest

Balancing individual and organizational interests through win–win cooperation.

> Nothing is more important than this sense of mutuality to the effectiveness and quality of an organization's products and services. Management must strive to stimulate a strong sense of shared ownership in every employee, because otherwise an organization cannot do its best in the long run. Employees who identify their own personal self-interest with the quality of their organization's output understand mutuality and strive to maintain it in their jobs and work relations.[2]

Figure 16–1 graphically portrays the constant tug-of-war between employees' self-interest and the organization's need for mutuality of interest. It also shows the linkage between this chapter—influence, empowerment, and politics—and other key topics in this book. Managers need a complete tool kit of techniques to guide diverse individu-

Figure 16–1   *The Constant Tug-of-War between Self-Interest and Mutuality of Interest Requires Managerial Action*

als, who are often powerfully motivated to put their own self-interests first, to pursue common objectives. At stake in this tug-of-war between individual and collective interests is no less than the ultimate survival of the organization.

Organizational Influence Tactics: Getting One's Way at Work

How do you get others to carry out your wishes? Do you simply tell them what to do? Or do you prefer a less direct approach, such as promising to return the favor? Whatever approach you use, the crux of the issue is *social influence.* A large measure of interpersonal interaction involves attempts to influence others, including parents, bosses, coworkers, spouses, teachers, friends, and children. All of us need to sharpen our influence skills. A good starting point is familiarity with the following research insights.

Nine Generic Influence Tactics

A particularly fruitful stream of research, initiated by David Kipnis and his colleagues in 1980, reveals how people influence each other in organizations. The Kipnis methodology involved asking employees how they managed to get either their bosses, coworkers, or subordinates to do what they wanted them to do.[3] Statistical refinements and replications by other researchers over a 13-year period eventually yielded nine influence tactics. The nine tactics, ranked in diminishing order of use in the workplace are as follows:

1. *Rational persuasion.* Trying to convince someone with reason, logic, or facts.

2. *Inspirational appeals.* Trying to build enthusiasm by appealing to others' emotions, ideals, or values.

3. *Consultation.* Getting others to participate in planning, making decisions, and changes.

4. *Ingratiation.* Getting someone in a good mood prior to making a request; being friendly, helpful, and using praise or flattery.

International OB   Appealing to Emotions Gets Results for
Disabled People in Israel

The organization of registered disabled people in Israel initiated during 2000 a program to change what it saw as the inadequate and unjust state benefits package to which the disabled are entitled. In an attempt to radically change government policy toward disabled people, the organization presented its demands to government officials and tried to persuade them to increase their benefits. The plan was strongly opposed by all government officials, who argued that if would cost too much and would break the financial balance of the country, as other sectors would jump on the bandwagon and demand more money. Organized protests and struggles to change the policy were ignored. The cause seemed hopeless, and the protesters appeared to have no means of exerting pressure on the government. Facing this situation, they decided to change their persuasion tactics. The daily protests continued, but with widespread media coverage. Leaders and others, all in their wheelchairs, appeared on television, explaining their difficulties, and painting in colorful and vivid details the everyday hardships they faced. Some of them were sobbing during interviews. The widespread media coverage of the protest caused an upsurge of public support for the disabled protesters, and officials were seen as cruel and callous. Continued coverage of the negotiations with government officials granted the protesters much leverage throughout the talks, and eventually led to the attainment of their goals. It was widely accepted that the emotions the disabled aroused were the main cause for the change in government policy.

SOURCE: Excerpted from S Fox and Y Amichai-Hamburger, "The Power of Emotional Appeals in Promoting Organizational Change Programs," *Academy of Management Executive*, November 2001, p. 84.

5. *Personal appeals.* Referring to friendship and loyalty when making a request.

6. *Exchange.* Making express or implied promises and trading favors.

7. *Coalition tactics.* Getting others to support your effort to persuade someone.

8. *Pressure.* Demanding compliance or using intimidation or threats.

9. *Legitimating tactics.* Basing a request on one's authority or right, organizational rules or policies, or express or implied support from superiors.[4]

These approaches can be considered *generic* influence tactics because they characterize social influence in all directions and in a wide variety of settings. For example, consider the effective use of emotions (inspirational appeal) in the International OB above. Researchers have found this ranking to be fairly consistent regardless of whether the direction of influence is downward, upward, or lateral.[5]

Some call the first five influence tactics—rational persuasion, inspirational appeals, consultation, ingratiation, and personal appeals—"soft" tactics because they are friendlier and not as coercive as the last four tactics. Exchange, coalition, pressure, and legitimating tactics accordingly are called "hard" tactics because they involve more overt pressure.

Three Possible Influence Outcomes

Put yourself in this familiar situation. It's Wednesday and a big project you've been working on for your project team is due Friday. You're behind on the preparation of your computer graphics for your final report and presentation. You catch a friend who is great at computer graphics as he heads out of the office at quitting time. You try this *exchange tactic* to get your friend to help you out: "I'm way behind. I need your help. If you could come back in for two to three hours tonight and help me with these graphics, I'll complete those spreadsheets you've been complaining about." According to researchers, your friend will engage in one of three possible influence outcomes:

1. *Commitment.* Your friend enthusiastically agrees and will demonstrate initiative and persistence while completing the assignment.

2. *Compliance.* Your friend grudgingly complies and will need prodding to satisfy minimum requirements.

3. *Resistance.* Your friend will say no, make excuses, stall, or put up an argument.[6]

The best outcome is commitment because the target person's intrinsic motivation will energize good performance. However, managers often have to settle for compliance in today's hectic workplace. Resistance means a failed influence attempt.

Practical Research Insights

Laboratory and field studies have taught us useful lessons about the relative effectiveness of influence tactics along with other instructive insights:

• Commitment is more likely when people rely on consultation, strong rational persuasion, and inspirational appeals and *do not* rely on pressure and coalition tactics.[7] Interestingly, in one study, managers were not very effective at *downward* influence. They relied most heavily on inspiration (an effective tactic), ingratiation (a moderately effective tactic), and pressure (an ineffective tactic).[8]

• A meta-analysis of 69 studies suggests ingratiation (making the boss feel good) can slightly improve your performance appraisal results and make your boss like you significantly more.[9]

• Commitment is more likely when the influence attempt involves something *important* and *enjoyable* and is based on a *friendly* relationship.[10]

• In a survey, 214 employed MBA students (55% female) tended to perceive their superiors' "soft" influence tactics as fair and "hard" influence tactics as unfair. *Unfair* influence tactics were associated with greater *resistance* among employees.[11]

• Another study probed male-female differences in influencing work group members. Many studies have found women to be perceived as less competent and less influential in work groups than men. The researchers had male and female work group leaders engage in either task behavior (demonstrating ability and task competence) or dominating behavior (relying on threats). For both women and men, task behavior was associated with perceived competence and effective influence. Dominating behavior was not effective. The following conclusion by the researchers has important practical implications for all current and future managers who desire to successfully influence others: "The display of task cues is an effective means to enhance one's status in groups and . . . the attempt to gain influence in task groups through dominance is an ineffective and poorly received strategy for both men and women."[12]

• After reviewing relevant studies, a team of researchers concluded: "Each tactic includes a broad variety of behaviors; when planning an influence attempt, it is important to consider not only what tactics to use but also what forms of each tactic are most appropriate for the situation."[13]

• Interpersonal influence is culture bound. The foregoing research evidence on influence tactics has a bias in favor of European–North Americans. Much remains to be learned about how to effectively influence others (without unintended insult) in today's diverse labor force and cross-cultural economy.

Finally, Barbara Moses, consultant and author from Toronto, Canada, offers this advice on influencing your boss:

> If your boss doesn't understand the need for change, this might be partly your fault. You can't make change; you have to sell it. And the key to selling anything is to understand where the other person is coming from—rather than to assume that your boss is a complete jerk. But most of us communicate from an egocentric place. We construct an idea or a project mainly in terms of what makes sense to us. Instead, ask yourself: "What's most important to my boss?" "What are his greatest concerns?" Go forward only after you've answered these questions.[14]

How to Do a Better Job of Influencing and Persuading Others

Because of a string of corporate scandals and executive misdeeds at the likes of Enron, Andersen, Tyco, ImClone, and WorldCom, the trust and credibility gap between management and workers remains sizable.[15] According to a recent survey, "more than 20 percent of American workers say their company's senior managers don't act in a manner consistent with their words."[16] Aside from being a siren call for better ethics,[17] this trend makes managerial attempts at influence and persuasion more challenging than ever. Skill development in this area is essential.

Practical, research-based advice has been offered by Robert B Cialdini, a respected expert at Arizona State University (see the Internet Exercise at the end of this chapter). Based on many years of research by himself and others, Cialdini (pronounced Chaldee-knee) derived the following six principles of influence and persuasion:[18]

1. *Liking.* People tend to like those who like them. Learning about another person's likes and dislikes through informal conversations builds friendship bonds. So do sincere and timely praise, empathy, and recognition.

2. *Reciprocity.* The belief that both good and bad deeds should be repaid in kind is virtually universal. Managers who act unethically and treat employees with contempt can expect the same in return. Worse, those employees, in turn, are likely to treat each other and their customers unethically and with contempt. Managers need to be positive and constructive role models and fair-minded to benefit from the principle of reciprocity.

3. *Social proof.* People tend to follow the lead of those most like themselves. Role models and peer pressure are powerful cultural forces in social settings. Managers are advised to build support for workplace changes by first gaining the enthusiastic support of informal leaders who will influence their peers.

4. *Consistency.* People tend to do what they are personally committed to do. A manager who can elicit a verbal commitment from an employee has taken an important step toward influence and persuasion. (Recall the importance of attitudes and intentions in our discussion of Ajzen's theory of planned behavior in Chapter 6.)

5. *Authority.* People tend to defer to and respect credible experts. According to Cialdini, too many managers and professionals take their expertise for granted, as in the case of a hospital where he consulted:

The physical therapy staffers were frustrated because so many of their stroke patients abandoned their exercise routines as soon as they left the hospital. No matter how often the staff emphasized the importance of regular home exercise—it is, in fact, crucial to the process of regaining independent function—the message just didn't sink in.

Interviews with some of the patients helped us pinpoint the problem. They were familiar with the background and training of their physicians, but the patients knew little about the credentials of the physical therapists who were urging them to exercise. It was a simple matter to remedy that lack of information: We merely asked the therapy director to display all the awards, diplomas, and certifications of her staff on the walls of the therapy rooms. The result was startling: Exercise compliance jumped 34% and has never dropped since.[19]

6. *Scarcity.* People want items, information, and opportunities that have limited availability. Special opportunities and privileged information are influence builders for managers.

Importantly, Cialdini recommends using these six principles in combination, rather than separately, for maximum impact. Because of major ethical implications, one's goals need to be worthy and actions need to be sincere and genuine when using these six principles.

By demonstrating the rich texture of social influence, the foregoing research evidence and practical advice whet our appetite for learning more about how today's managers can and do reconcile individual and organizational interests. Let us focus on social power.

Social Power

The term *power* evokes mixed and often passionate reactions. Citing recent instances of government corruption and corporate misconduct, many observers view power as a sinister force. To these skeptics, Lord Acton's time-honored statement that "power corrupts and absolute power corrupts absolutely" is as true as ever. However, OB specialists remind us that, like it or not, power is a fact of life in modern organizations. According to one management writer:

> Power must be used because managers must influence those they depend on. Power also is crucial in the development of managers' self-confidence and willingness to support subordinates. From this perspective, power should be accepted as a natural part of any organization. Managers should recognize and develop their own power to coordinate and support the work of subordinates; it is powerlessness, not power, that undermines organizational effectiveness.[20]

Thus, power is a necessary and generally positive force in organizations. As the term is used here, **social power** is defined as "the ability to marshal the human, informational, and material resources to get something done."[21]

Importantly, the exercise of social power in organizations is not necessarily a downward proposition. Employees can and do exercise power upward and laterally. An example of an upward power play occurred at Alberto-Culver Company, the personal care products firm. Leonard Lavin, founder of the company, was under pressure to revitalize the firm because key employees were departing for more innovative competitors

Social power
Ability to get things done with human, informational, and material resources.

such as Procter & Gamble. Lavin's daughter Carol Bernick, and her husband Howard, both long-time employees, took things into their own hands:

> Even the Bernicks were thinking of jumping ship. Instead, in September 1994, they marched into Lavin's office and presented him with an ultimatum: Either hand over the reins as CEO or run the company without them. It was a huge blow for Lavin, forcing him to face selling his company to outsiders or ceding control to the younger generation. Unwilling to sell, he reluctantly stepped down, though he remains chairman.
>
> How does it feel to push aside your own father and wrest operating control of the company he created? "It isn't an easy thing to do with the founder of any company, whether he's your father or not," says Carol Bernick, 46, now vice chairman and president of Alberto-Culver North America.[22]

Howard Bernick became CEO, the firm's top-down management style was scrapped in favor of a more open culture, and Lavin reportedly is happy with how things have turned out.[23]

Dimensions of Power

While power may be an elusive concept to the casual observer, social scientists view power as having reasonably clear dimensions. Two dimensions of power that deserve our attention are (1) socialized versus personalized power and (2) the five bases of power.

Two Types of Power
Behavioral scientists such as David McClelland contend that one of the basic human needs is the need for power (n Pwr), as discussed in Chapter 8. Because this need is learned and not innate, the need for power has been extensively studied. Historically, need for power was said to be high when subjects interpreted TAT pictures in terms of one person attempting to influence, convince, persuade, or control another. More recently, however, researchers have drawn a distinction between **socialized power** and **personalized power.**

Socialized power
Directed at helping others.

Personalized power
Directed at helping oneself.

> There are two subscales or "faces" in n Pwr. One face is termed "socialized" (s Pwr) and is scored in the Thematic Apperception Test (TAT) as "plans, self-doubts, mixed outcomes and concerns for others, . . ." while the second face is "personalized" power (p Pwr), in which expressions of power for the sake of personal aggrandizement become paramount.[24]

This distinction between socialized and personalized power helps explain why power has a negative connotation for many people.[25] Managers and others who pursue personalized power for their own selfish ends give power a bad name. But a series of interviews with 25 American women elected to public office found a strong preference for socialized power. The following comments illustrate their desire to wield power effectively and ethically:

- "Power in itself means nothing. . . . I think power is the opportunity to really have an impact on your community."
- "My goal is to be a powerful advocate on the part of my constituents."[26]

Five Bases of Power
A popular classification scheme for social power traces back more than 40 years ago to the work of John French and Bertram Raven. They proposed that power arises from five different bases: reward power, coercive power, legitimate power, expert power, and referent power.[27] Each involves a different approach to influencing others:

- *Reward power.* A manager has **reward power** to the extent that he or she obtains compliance by promising or granting rewards. On-the-job behavior shaping, for example, relies heavily on reward power.
- *Coercive power.* Threats of punishment and actual punishment give an individual **coercive power.** A sales manager who threatens to fire any salesperson who uses a company car for family vacations is relying on coercive power.
- *Legitimate power.* This base of power is anchored to one's formal position or authority. Thus, individuals who obtain compliance primarily because of their formal authority to make decisions have **legitimate power.** Legitimate power may express itself in either a positive or negative manner in managing people. Positive legitimate power focuses constructively on job performance. Negative legitimate power tends to be threatening and demeaning to those being influenced. Its main purpose is to build the power holder's ego.
- *Expert power.* Valued knowledge or information gives an individual **expert power** over those who need such knowledge or information. The power of supervisors is enhanced because they know about work schedules and assignments before their employees do. Skillful use of expert power played a key role in the effectiveness of team leaders in a study of three physician medical diagnosis teams.[28] Knowledge *is* power in today's high-tech workplaces.
- *Referent power.* Also called charisma, **referent power** comes into play when one's personality becomes the reason for compliance. Role models have referent power over those who identify closely with them.

To further your understanding of these five bases of power and to assess your self-perceived power, please take a moment to complete the questionnaire in the OB Exercise on page 566. Think of your present job or your most recent job when responding to the various items. What is your power profile?

Research Insights about Social Power

In one study, a sample of 94 male and 84 female nonmanagerial and professional employees in Denver, Colorado, completed TAT tests. The researchers found that the male and female employees had similar needs for power (n Pwr) and personalized power (p Pwr). But the women had a significantly higher need for socialized power (s Pwr) than did their male counterparts.[29] This bodes well for today's work organizations where women are playing an ever greater administrative role. Unfortunately, as women gain power in the workplace, greater tension between men and women has been observed. *Training* magazine offered this perspective:

> [O]bservers view the tension between women and men in the workplace as a natural outcome of power inequities between the genders. Their argument is that men still have most of the power and are resisting any change as a way to protect their power base. [Consultant Susan L] Webb asserts that sexual harassment has far more to do with exercising power in an unhealthy way than with sexual attraction. Likewise, the glass ceiling, a metaphor for the barriers women face in climbing the corporate ladder to management and executive positions, is about power and access to power.[30]

Accordingly, "powerful women were described more positively by women than by men" in a study of 140 female and 125 male college students in Sydney, Australia.[31]

A reanalysis of 18 field studies that measured French and Raven's five bases of power uncovered "severe methodological shortcomings."[32] After correcting for these

Reward power

Obtaining compliance with promised or actual rewards.

Coercive power

Obtaining compliance through threatened or actual punishment.

Legitimate power

Obtaining compliance through formal authority.

Expert power

Obtaining compliance through one's knowledge or information.

Referent power

Obtaining compliance through charisma or personal attraction.

OB Exercise   What Is Your Self-Perceived Power?

Instructions

Score your various bases of power for your current (or former) job, using the following scale:

1 = Strongly disagree   4 = Agree
2 = Disagree   5 = Strongly agree
3 = Slightly agree

Reward Power Score = _____
1. I can reward persons at lower levels. _____
2. My review actions affect the rewards gained at lower levels. _____
3. Based on my decisions, lower level personnel may receive a bonus. _____

Coercive Power Score = _____
1. I can punish employees at lower levels. _____
2. My work is a check on lower level employees. _____
3. My diligence reduces error. _____

Legitimate Power Score = _____
1. My position gives me a great deal of authority. _____
2. The decisions made at my level are of critical importance. _____
3. Employees look to me for guidance. _____

Expert Power Score = _____
1. I am an expert in this job. _____
2. My ability gives me an advantage in this job. _____
3. Given some time, I could improve the methods used on this job. _____

Referent Power Score = _____
1. I attempt to set a good example for other employees. _____
2. My personality allows me to work well in this job. _____
3. My fellow employees look to me as their informal leader. _____

Arbitrary Norms

3–6 = Weak power base
7–11 = Moderate power base
12–15 = Strong power base

SOURCE: Adapted and excerpted in part from D L Dieterly and B Schneider, "The Effect of Organizational Environment on Perceived Power and Climate: A Laboratory Study," *Organizational Behavior and Human Performance*, June 1974, pp. 316–37.

problems, the researchers identified the following relationships between power bases and work outcomes such as job performance, job satisfaction, and turnover:

• Expert and referent power had a generally positive impact.

• Reward and legitimate power had a slightly positive impact.

• Coercive power had a slightly negative impact.

The same researcher, in a follow-up study involving 251 employed business seniors, looked at the relationship between influence styles and bases of power. This was a bottom-up study. In other words, employee perceptions of managerial influence and power were examined. Rational persuasion was found to be a highly acceptable managerial influence tactic. Why? Because employees perceived it to be associated with the three bases of power they viewed positively: legitimate, expert, and referent.[33]

In summary, expert and referent power appear to get the best *combination* of results and favorable reactions from lower-level employees.[34]

Using Power Responsibly and Ethically

As democracy continues to spread around the world, one reality stands clear. Leaders who do not use their power responsibly risk losing it. This holds for corporations and non-profit organizations as well as for governments. A key to success in this regard is understanding the difference between commitment and mere compliance.

Responsible managers strive for socialized power while avoiding personalized power. In fact, in a survey, organizational commitment was higher among US federal government executives whose superiors exercised socialized power than among colleagues with "power-hungry" bosses. The researchers used the appropriate terms *uplifting power* versus *dominating power.*[35] How does this relate to the five bases of power? As with influence tactics, managerial power has three possible outcomes: commitment, compliance, or resistance. Reward, coercive, and negative legitimate power tend to produce *compliance* (and sometimes, resistance). On the other hand, positive legitimate power, expert power, and referent power tend to foster *commitment.* Once again, commitment is superior to compliance because it is driven by internal or intrinsic motivation.[36] Employees who merely comply require frequent "jolts" of power from the boss to keep them headed in a productive direction. Committed employees tend to be self-starters who do not require close supervision—a key success factor in today's flatter, team-oriented organizations.

Abigail Johnson, president of Fidelity, the financial services giant with $1.4 trillion in mutual funds and other assets under management, is a good example of a manager who responsibly avoids the use of dominating power while building commitment. Abby, as she is known within the company, is the founder's granddaughter and the CEO's daughter. Despite being a billionaire by birth, she worked her way up through the ranks at Fidelity, starting as a customer-service telephone representative after completing high school. She is characterized as self-effacing, committed, and hardworking. Moreover, she does not "share her father's tendency to obsess over details, such as choosing lighting fixtures for a new building. 'It's a mistake for a

Here's a tough question. How would you spend your time if you were a billionaire by birth? If you're Abigail Johnson, granddaughter of the founder of financial services powerhouse Fidelity, you diligently work your way up from the bottom to become president of the company. Even more impressive, Abby wields her considerable power with a light hand. She gives her mutual fund managers room to run.

(c) Pier Nicola D-Amico

manager to delve into the details on everything,' she says."[37] Accordingly, she has given her mutual fund managers more flexibility in their stockpicking.

According to research cited earlier, expert and referent power have the greatest potential for improving job performance and satisfaction and reducing turnover. Formal education, training, and self-development can build a manager's expert power. At the same time, one's referent power base can be strengthened by building and maintaining strong internal and external networks.

Empowerment: From Power Sharing to Power Distribution

Empowerment

Sharing varying degrees of power with lower-level employees to tap their full potential.

An exciting trend in today's organizations centers on giving employees a greater say in the workplace. This trend wears various labels, including "high-involvement management," "participative management," and "open-book management." Regardless of the label one prefers, it is all about empowerment. Management consultant and writer W Alan Randolph offers this definition: "**empowerment** is recognizing and releasing into the organization the power that people already have in their wealth of useful knowledge, experience, and internal motivation."[38] A core component of this process is pushing decision-making authority down to progressively lower levels. The chairman of AOL Time Warner, Steve Case, believes in employee empowerment. He recently said in an interview: "The only way to be successful, particularly in a rapidly growing, rapidly changing market, is to hire terrific people and point them generally in the right direction. And let them go."[39]

Steve Kerr, the chief learning officer at General Electric, a pioneer in employee empowerment, adds this important qualification: "We say empowerment is moving decision making down to the lowest level *where a competent decision can be made.*"[40] Of course, it is naive and counterproductive to hand power over to unwilling or unprepared employees.

No Information Sharing, No Empowerment

According to an informal poll of *HR Magazine*'s readers, 47% of the respondents' companies use open-book management. An additional 15% plan to adopt it in the near future.[41] To us, this indicates a mainstream trend. Open-book management breaks down the traditional organizational caste system made up of information haves (managers) and information have-nots (nonmanagers). Managers historically were afraid to tell their employees about innovations, company finances, and strategic plans for fear of giving the advantage to unions and competitors. To varying extents, those threats persist today. But in the larger scheme of things, organizations with unified and adequately informed employees have a significant competitive advantage. The problematic question then becomes: How much information sharing is enough (or too much)? As demonstrated in the large- and small-company case studies in Table 16–1, there is no exact answer. Empowerment-oriented managers need to learn from experience, be careful in what they share, and let employees know when certain information requires secrecy. Make no mistake, however, empowerment through open-book management carries some risk of betrayal, like any act of trust. Advocates of empowerment believe the rewards (more teamwork and greater competitiveness) outweigh the risks.

Table 16–1 *How Much Information Should Be Shared? Two Cases*

Large Company

www.campbellsoup.com

When Ron Ferner first joined Campbell's Soup, in the 1960s, none of the company's executives believed in sharing any kind of information with anybody. By the time he retired, in 1996, Ferner and his colleagues had started sharing everything—goals, financials, product news—with employees.

"At first I was very skeptical about sharing information with employees, but now I'm a believer. I saw the power of the thing. But we always drew the line at salaries. And if we had a supersecret project that we were not sure we would actually launch, we may not have told. But everything else was fair game. Even with the hourly employees that ran the filling machines, putting soup in the cans, we shared the financials.

"At one point Campbell's had a philosophy of meeting with all employees every quarter. I had 1,800 people in my plant. It took three days to hold the meetings. It was quite a chore, but worth it. The employees got very comfortable. It was a real change from the old days, when we would stand behind a post and peek out to watch them work.

"That approach doesn't work overnight. If you don't talk to employees for 10 years and then show up and say that today we start talking, you'll be really disappointed. You have to pick where to draw the line very carefully. You're building trust and don't want to backtrack. It took us years to talk to employees and make them comfortable. Once they were, we started getting their ideas and finding out what the real problems were. A lot of things amazed us.

"One time a packaging team in Sacramento was having problems with boxes breaking. Some of us managers started talking to them about what the problems were and realized they really had a good handle on what was wrong. So we said 'Why don't you guys call the supplier?' Then we called the supplier to tell them they would be hearing from our crew, and they said, 'Why not have them talk directly to our hourly employees?'

"If the managers alone had tried to solve this problem, it would have gone on forever. Instead, we rented a van, sent our people over, and solved the whole thing. Afterward, we had a party. It gave the workers great confidence. That never would have happened in the days when Campbell's had a policy of not telling anybody anything that wasn't written down for them."

Small Company

www.sapient.com

Adjacency CEO Andrew Sather and his partner, Chris DeVore, figured that for their four-year-old [Internet service] company to become a powerhouse, they would have to tap into the entrepreneurial instincts of every staffer. That meant treating all employees as if they were partners. All were given equity stakes. "I tried to set up the kind of company where I'd like to work," Sather says.

Last year, Sather and DeVore gathered their 25 workers together every week to discuss the most intimate details of their company, including cash flow and potential customers. The partners could tell that workers appreciated the honest communication. At meetings, employees would pepper the partners with loads of questions. But it quickly became apparent that there were some things employees would rather not know. For instance, they didn't want to hear about Adjacency's close calls with missing payroll—not an uncommon syndrome in the entrepreneurial world, but one that employees find quite unnerving. "We overestimated our employees' desire to be entrepreneurs, and sometimes we scared them," Sather says.

Sather and DeVore also overestimated their staff's ability to keep secrets. Last summer they told employees about a huge, potentially lucrative deal with a hot new client. One worker left the meeting so pumped that he bragged to a friend at a competing company. Bad move. The "friend" relayed the news to his bosses, who promptly tried to persuade the coveted customer to dump Adjacency and go with them. "We almost lost the client," DeVore says. "The client was livid, and rightfully so."

The partners considered shutting down the flow of sales information but decided against it. Now they're careful to identify what information is top secret.

"We've learned to get a lot more explicit about how information can be used," Sather says. In fact, the partners still divulge just as much confidential information as they did before the incident, conveying to employees that they trust them more than ever. There is one topic though, that Sather and DeVore are careful to avoid: the nitty-gritty details of cash flow. "We've learned to filter some information that employees find disconcerting," Sather admits.

[Now that Adjacency has fully integrated its business with Sapient, an innovative E-services consultancy, it will be interesting to observe how much of its open-book management style persists.]

SOURCES: Thea Singer, "Share It All with Employees, Soup to Nuts," *Inc.*, Tech 1999, no. 1, p. 48; and S Greco and M Ballon, "Too Hot To Handle," *Inc.*, February 1999, p. 52.

A Matter of Degree

The concept of empowerment requires some adjustments in traditional thinking. First, power is not a zero-sum situation where one person's gain is another's loss. Social power is unlimited. This requires win–win thinking. Frances Hesselbein, the woman credited with modernizing the Girl Scouts of the USA, put it this way: "The more power you give away, the more you have."[42] Authoritarian managers who view employee empowerment as a threat to their personal power are missing the point because of their win–lose thinking.[43]

The second adjustment to traditional thinking involves seeing empowerment as *a matter of degree* not as an either–or proposition.[44] Figure 16–2 illustrates how power can be shifted to the hands of nonmanagers step by step. The overriding goal is to increase productivity and competitiveness in leaner organizations. Each step in this evolution increases the power of organizational contributors who traditionally had little or no legitimate power. Consider this example of midrange empowerment involving a combination of influence sharing (consultation) and power sharing (participation):

> Long ladders don't seem to have much to do with saving jet fuel. But when United Airlines Inc. brought together its pilots, ramp workers, and managers for the first time to brainstorm about fuel conservation, the answer was just that simple. The idea was to use electricity instead of jet fuel to power planes idling at gates. But ramp workers couldn't plug cables into the aircraft because their ladders were often too short. "In the past, we would have sent out an edict and nothing would have changed," [said a United Airlines executive]. . . . Now, equipped with taller ladders, the carrier will save $20 million in fuel costs [annually].[45]

Figure 16–2   *The Evolution of Power: From Domination to Delegation*

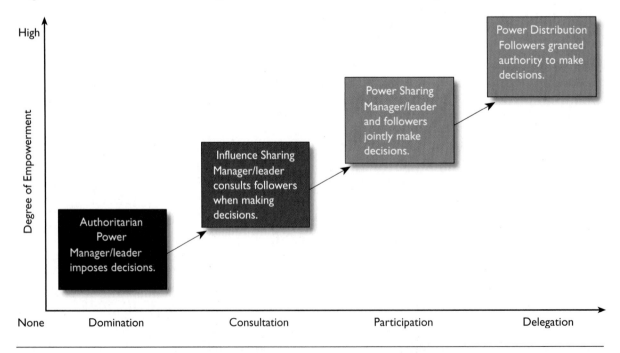

Delegation

The highest degree of empowerment is **delegation,** the process of granting decision-making authority to lower-level employees.[46] This amounts to *power distribution.* Delegation has long been the recommended way to lighten the busy manager's load while at the same time developing employees' abilities.[47] Importantly, delegation gives non-managerial employees more than simply a voice in decisions. It empowers them to make their own decisions. A prime example is the Ritz-Carlton Hotel chain:

> At Ritz-Carlton, every worker is authorized to spend up to $2,000 to fix any problem a guest encounters. Employees do not abuse the privilege. "When you treat people responsibly, they act responsibly," said Patrick Mene, the hotel chain's director of quality.[48]

Not surprising, then, that Ritz-Carlton has won national service quality awards.

Delegation

Granting decision-making authority to people at lower levels.

Barriers to Delegation   Delegation is easy to talk about, but many managers find it hard to actually do. A concerted effort to overcome these common barriers to delegation needs to be made.

- Belief in the fallacy, "If you want it done right, do it yourself."
- Lack of confidence and trust in lower-level employees.
- Low self-confidence.
- Fear of being called lazy.
- Vague job definition.
- Fear of competition from those below.
- Reluctance to take the risks involved in depending on others.
- Lack of controls that provide early warning of problems with delegated duties.
- Poor example set by bosses who do not delegate.[49]

Delegation Research and Implications for Trust and Personal Initiative   Researchers at the State University of New York at Albany surveyed pairs of managers and employees and did follow-up interviews with the managers concerning their delegation habits. Their results confirmed some important common sense notions about delegation. Greater delegation was associated with the following factors:

1. Competent employee.
2. Employee shared manager's task objectives.
3. Manager had a long-standing and positive relationship with employee.
4. The lower-level person also was a supervisor.[50]

This delegation scenario boils down to one pivotal factor, *trust.*[51]

Managers prefer to delegate important tasks and decisions to the people they trust. As discussed in Chapter 13, it takes time and favorable experience to build trust. Of course, trust is fragile; it can be destroyed by a single remark, act, or omission. Ironically, managers cannot learn to trust someone without, initially at least, running the risk of betrayal. This is where the empowerment evolution in Figure 16–2 represents a three-step ladder to trust: consultation, participation, and delegation. In other words, managers need to start small and work up the empowerment ladder. They need to delegate small tasks and decisions and scale up as competence, confidence, and trust grow. Employees need to work on their side of the trust equation as well. One of the best ways

Figure 16–3   *Personal Initiative: The Other Side of Delegation*

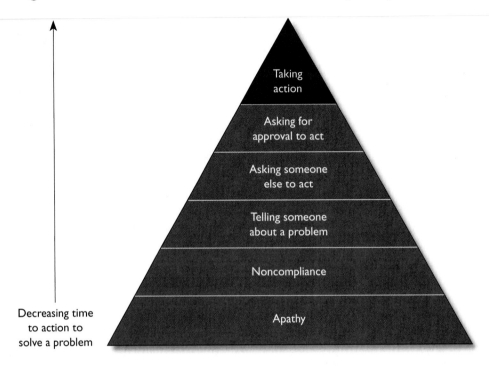

Decreasing time
to action to
solve a problem

SOURCES: Figure from A L Frohman, "Igniting Organizational Change from Below: The Power of Personal Initiative," *Organizational Dynamics*, Winter 1997, p. 46, © 1997, with permission from Elsevier Science.

to earn a manager's trust is to show *initiative* (see Figure 16–3). Researchers in the area offer this instructive definition and characterization:

Personal initiative

Going beyond formal job requirements and being an active self-starter.

Personal initiative is a behavior syndrome resulting in an individual's taking an active and self-starting approach to work and going beyond what is formally required in a given job. More specifically, personal initiative is characterized by the following aspects: it (1) is consistent with the organization's mission, (2) has a long-term focus, (3) is goal-directed and action-oriented, (4) is persistent in the face of barriers and setbacks, and (5) is self-starting and proactive.[52]

Recall our discussion of the *proactive personality* in Chapter 5.

Empowerment: The Research Record and Practical Advice

Like other widely heralded techniques—such as TQM, 360-degree reviews, teams, and learning organizations—empowerment has its fair share of critics and suffers from unrealistic expectations.[53] Research results to date are mixed, with a recent positive uptrend:

- According to a field study of 26 insurance claims supervisors, employees who enjoyed a greater degree of delegation processed more insurance claims at lower cost.[54]
- A study of 297 service employees led the researchers to conclude: "Empowerment may contribute to an employee's job satisfaction, but not as profoundly shape work effort and performance."[55]
- When the job performance of 81 empowered employees at the home office of a Canadian life insurance company was compared with a control group of 90 employees, the researchers found "minimal support" for empowerment.[56]
- Among 612 nurses, skilled professionals, and administrators (21% male), at a US hospital, higher perceived empowerment was associated with higher rank, longer tenure with the organization, approachable leaders, effective and worthwhile task groups, higher job satisfaction, and lower propensity to quit. No gender or race effects were found.[57]
- Another study at an insurance company, two textile makers, and a high-tech company in the United States focused on 111 empowered teams. More empowered teams tended to be more productive and render better customer service than less empowered teams. Empowered team members also tended to be more satisfied with (and committed to) their job, team, and employer.[58]
- Most recently, a study of 164 New Zealand companies employing at least 100 people found a positive correlation between high-involvement management practices and employee retention and company productivity.[59]

We believe empowerment has good promise if managers go about it properly. Empowerment is a sweeping concept with many different definitions. Consequently, researchers use inconsistent measurements, and cause-effect relationships are fuzzy. Managers committed to the idea of employee empowerment need to follow the path of continuous improvement, learning from their successes and failures. Eight years of research with 10 "empowered" companies led Randolph to formulate the three-pronged empowerment plan in Figure 16–4. Notice how open-book management and active information sharing are needed to build the necessary foundation of trust. Beyond that, clear goals and lots of relevant training are needed. While noting that the empowerment process can take several years to unfold, Randolph offered this perspective:

> While the keys to empowerment may be easy to understand, they are hard to implement. It takes tremendous courage to start sharing sensitive information. It takes true strength to build more structure just at the point when people want more freedom of action. It takes real growth to allow teams to take over the management decision-making process. And above all, it takes perseverance to complete the empowerment process.[60]

Organizational Politics and Impression Management

Most students of OB find the study of organizational politics intriguing. Perhaps this topic owes its appeal to the antics of Hollywood's corporate villains who get their way by stepping on anyone and everyone. As we will see, however, organizational politics includes, but is not limited to, dirty dealing. Organizational politics is an ever-present and sometimes annoying feature of modern work life. "Executives say that they spend 19%

Figure 16–4 *Randolph's Empowerment Model*

The Empowerment Plan

Share Information

- Share company performance information.
- Help people understand the business.
- Build trust through sharing sensitive information.
- Create self-monitoring possibilities.

Create Autonomy through Structure

- Create a clear vision and clarify the little pictures.
- Create new decision-making rules that support empowerment.
- Clarify goals and roles collaboratively.
- Establish new empowering performance management processes.
- Use heavy doses of training.

Let Teams Become The Hierarchy

- Provide direction and training for new skills.
- Provide encouragement and support for change.
- Gradually have managers let go of control.
- Work through the leadership vacuum stage.
- Acknowledge the fear factor.

Remember: Empowerment is not magic; it consists of a few simple steps and a lot of persistence.

SOURCE: "Navigating the Journey to Empowerment," by W Alan Randolph. Reprinted from *Organizational Dynamics,* Spring 1995. © 1995 American Management Association International. Reprinted by permission of the American Management Association International, New York. All rights reserved. www.amanet.org.

of their time dealing with political infighting with their staffs, according to a survey by OfficeTeam, a staffing services firm."[61] One expert recently observed, "Many 'new economy' companies use the acronym 'WOMBAT'—or waste of money, brains, and time—to describe office politics."[62] On the other hand, organizational politics can be a positive force in modern work organizations. Skillful and well-timed politics can help you get your point across, neutralize resistance to a key project, or get a choice job assignment.

Roberta Bhasin, a telephone company district manager, put organizational politics into perspective by observing the following:

> Most of us would like to believe that organizations are rationally structured, based on reasonable divisions of labor, a clear hierarchical communication flow, and well-defined lines of authority aimed at meeting universally understood goals and objectives.
>
> But organizations are made up of *people* with personal agendas designed to win power and influence. The agenda—the game—is called corporate politics. It is played by avoiding the rational structure, manipulating the communications hierarchy, and ignoring established lines of authority. The rules are never written down and seldom discussed.
>
> For some, corporate politics are second nature. They instinctively know the unspoken rules of the game. Others must learn. Managers who don't understand the politics of their organizations are at a disadvantage, not only in winning raises and promotions, but even in getting things *done.*[63]

We explore this important and interesting area by (1) defining the term *organizational politics,* (2) identifying three levels of political action, (3) discussing eight specific political tactics, (4) considering a related area called *impression management,* and (5) examining relevant research and practical implications.

Definition and Domain of Organizational Politics

"**Organizational politics** involves intentional acts of influence to enhance or protect the self-interest of individuals or groups."[64] An emphasis on *self-interest* distinguishes this form of social influence. Managers are constantly challenged to achieve a workable balance between employees' self-interests and organizational interests, as discussed at the beginning of this chapter. When a proper balance exists, the pursuit of self-interest may serve the organization's interests. Political behavior becomes a negative force when self-interests erode or defeat organizational interests. For example, researchers have documented the political tactic of filtering and distorting information flowing up to the boss. This self-serving practice put the reporting employees in the best possible light.[65]

Organizational politics
Intentional enhancement of self-interest.

Uncertainty Triggers Political Behavior   Political maneuvering is triggered primarily by *uncertainty.* Five common sources of uncertainty within organizations are

1. Unclear objectives.

2. Vague performance measures.

3. Ill-defined decision processes.

4. Strong individual or group competition.[66]

5. Any type of change.

"ONE OF LIFE'S IRONIES IS THAT OBNOXIOUS, BROWNNOSING OVERACHIEVERS DON'T ALWAYS GET AHEAD."

Source: (c) Harley L. Schwadron

Regarding this last source of uncertainty, organization development specialist Anthony Raia noted, "Whatever we attempt to change, the political subsystem becomes active. Vested interests are almost always at stake and the distribution of power is challenged."[67]

Thus, we would expect a field sales representative, striving to achieve an assigned quota, to be less political than a management trainee working on a variety of projects. While some manage-

For better or for worse, Hollywood has provided lots of role models for dysfunctional organizational politics and impression management. Michael Douglas's character in the hit movie *Wall Street* was a particularly nasty guy who put himself first.

Getty Images

ment trainees stake their career success on hard work, competence, and a bit of luck, many do not. These people attempt to gain a competitive edge through some combination of the political tactics discussed below. Meanwhile, the salesperson's performance is measured in actual sales, not in terms of being friends with the boss or taking credit for others' work. Thus, the management trainee would tend to be more political than the field salesperson because of greater uncertainty about management's expectations.

Because employees generally experience greater uncertainty during the earlier stages of their careers, are junior employees more political than more senior ones? The answer is yes, according to a survey of 243 employed adults in upstate New York. In fact, one senior employee nearing retirement told the researcher: "I used to play political games when I was younger. Now I just do my job."[68]

Three Levels of Political Action
Although much political maneuvering occurs at the individual level, it also can involve group or collective action. Figure 16–5 illustrates three different levels of political action: the individual level, the coalition level, and the network level.[69] Each level has its distinguishing characteristics. At the individual level, personal self-interests are pursued by the individual. The political aspects of coalitions and networks are not so obvious, however.

People with a common interest can become a political coalition by fitting the following definition. In an organizational context, a **coalition** is an informal group bound together by the *active* pursuit of a *single* issue. Coalitions may or may not coincide with formal group membership. When the target issue is resolved (a sexual-harassing supervisor is fired, for example), the coalition disbands. Experts note that political coalitions have "fuzzy boundaries," meaning they are fluid in membership, flexible in structure, and temporary in duration.[70]

Coalitions are a potent political force in organizations. Consider the situation Charles J Bradshaw faced in a finance committee meeting at Transworld Corporation. Bradshaw, president of the company, opposed the chairman's plan to acquire a $93 million nursing home company:

Coalition

Temporary groupings of people who actively pursue a single issue.

Figure 16–5   *Levels of Political Action in Organizations*

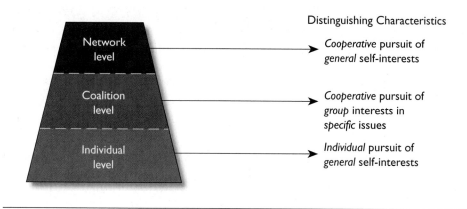

Distinguishing Characteristics

Network level → *Cooperative* pursuit of *general* self-interests

Coalition level → *Cooperative* pursuit of *group* interests in *specific* issues

Individual level → *Individual* pursuit of *general* self-interests

[The senior vice president for finance] kicked off the meeting with a battery of facts and figures in support of the deal. "Within two or three minutes, I knew I had lost," Bradshaw concedes. "No one was talking directly to me, but all statements addressed my opposition. I could tell there was a general agreement around the board table." . . .

Then the vote was taken. Five hands went up. Only Bradshaw voted no.[71]

After the meeting, Bradshaw resigned his $530,000-a-year position, without as much as a handshake or good-bye from the chairman. In Bradshaw's case, the finance committee was a formal group that temporarily became a political coalition aimed at sealing his fate at Transworld. During the 1990s, coalitions on the corporate boards of American Express, IBM, and General Motors ousted the heads of those giant companies.

A third level of political action involves networks.[72] Unlike coalitions, which pivot on specific issues, networks are loose associations of individuals seeking social support for their general self-interests. Politically, networks are people oriented, while coalitions are issue oriented. Networks have broader and longer term agendas than do coalitions. For instance, Avon's Hispanic employees have built a network to enhance the members' career opportunities.

Political Tactics

Anyone who has worked in an organization has firsthand knowledge of blatant politicking. Blaming someone else for your mistake is an obvious political ploy. But other political tactics are more subtle. Researchers have identified a range of political behavior.

One landmark study, involving in-depth interviews with 87 managers from 30 electronics companies in southern California, identified eight political tactics. Top-, middle-, and low-level managers were represented about equally in the sample. According to the researchers: "Respondents were asked to describe organizational political tactics and personal characteristics of effective political actors based upon their accumulated experience in *all* organizations in which they had worked."[73] Listed in descending order of occurrence, the eight political tactics that emerged were

1. Attacking or blaming others.

2. Using information as a political tool.

Table 16-2   *Eight Common Political Tactics in Organizations*

Political Tactic	Percentage of Managers Mentioning Tactic	Brief Description of Tactic
1. Attacking or blaming others	54%	Used to avoid or minimize association with failure. Reactive when scapegoating is involved. Proactive when goal is to reduce competition for limited resources.
2. Using information as a political tool	54	Involves the purposeful withholding or distortion of information. Obscuring an unfavorable situation by overwhelming superiors with information.
3. Creating a favorable image (impression management)	53	Dressing/grooming for success. Adhering to organizational norms and drawing attention to one's successes and influence. Taking credit for others' accomplishments.
4. Developing a base of support	37	Getting prior support for a decision. Building others' commitment to a decision through participation.
5. Praising others (ingratiation)	25	Making influential people feel good ("apple polishing").
6. Forming power coalitions with strong allies	25	Teaming up with powerful people who can get results.
7. Associating with influential people	24	Building a support network both inside and outside the organization.
8. Creating obligations (reciprocity)	13	Creating social debts ("I did you a favor, so you owe me a favor").

SOURCE: Adapted from R W Allen, D L Madison, L W Porter, P A Renwick, and B T Mayes, "Organizational Politics: Tactics and Characteristics of Its Actors," *California Management Review,* Fall 1979, pp. 77–83.

3. Creating a favorable image. (Also known as *impression management.*)

4. Developing a base of support.

5. Praising others (ingratiation).

6. Forming power coalitions with strong allies.

7. Associating with influential people.

8. Creating obligations (reciprocity).

Table 16–2 describes these political tactics and indicates how often each reportedly was used by the interviewed managers.

The researchers distinguished between reactive and proactive political tactics. Some of the tactics, such as scapegoating, were *reactive* because the intent was to *defend* one's self-interest. Other tactics, such as developing a base of support, were *proactive* because they sought to *promote* the individual's self-interest.

What is your attitude toward organizational politics? How often do you rely on the various tactics in Table 16–2? You can get a general indication of your political tendencies by comparing your behavior with the characteristics in Table 16–3. Would you characterize yourself as politically *naive,* politically *sensible,* or a political *shark?* How do you think others view your political actions? What are the career, friendship, and

Table 16–3   *Are You Politically Naive, Politically Sensible, or a Political Shark?*

Characteristics	Naive	Sensible	Sharks
Underlying attitude	Politics is unpleasant.	Politics is necessary.	Politics is an opportunity.
Intent	Avoid at all costs.	Further departmental goals.	Self-serving and predatory.
Techniques	Tell it like it is.	Network; expand connections; use system to give and receive favors.	Manipulate; use fraud and deceit when necessary.
Favorite tactics	None—the truth will win out.	Negotiate, bargain.	Bully; misuse information; cultivate and use "friends" and other contacts.

SOURCE: Reprinted with permission from J K Pinto and O P Kharbanda, "Lessons for an Accidental Profession," *Business Horizons*, March–April 1995, p. 45. Copyright © 1995 by the Indiana University Board of Trustees at Indiana University, Kelley School of Business.

ethical implications of your political tendencies?[74] (For a more detailed analysis of your political tendencies, see the Personal Awareness and Growth Exercise at the end of this chapter.)

Impression Management

Impression management is defined as "the process by which people attempt to control or manipulate the reactions of others to images of themselves or their ideas."[75] This encompasses how one talks, behaves, and looks. Most impression management attempts are directed at making a *good* impression on relevant others. But, as we will see, some employees strive to make a *bad* impression. For purposes of conceptual clarity, we will focus on *upward* impression management (trying to impress one's immediate supervisor) because it is most relevant for managers. Still, it is good to remember that *anyone* can be the intended target of impression management. Parents, teachers, peers, employees, and customers are all fair game when it comes to managing the impressions of others.

Impression management

Getting others to see us in a certain manner.

A Conceptual Crossroads   Impression management is an interesting conceptual crossroads involving self-monitoring, attribution theory, and organizational politics.[76] Perhaps this explains why impression management has gotten active research attention in recent years. High self-monitoring employees ("chameleons" who adjust to their surroundings) are likely to be more inclined to engage in impression management than would low self-monitors. Impression management also involves the systematic manipulation of attributions. For example, a bank president will look good if the board of directors is encouraged to attribute organizational successes to her efforts and attribute problems and failures to factors beyond her control. Impression management definitely fits into the realm of organizational politics because of an overriding focus on furthering one's *self-interests*.

Making a Good Impression   If you "dress for success," project an upbeat attitude at all times, and have polished a 15-second elevator speech for top executives, you are engaging in favorable impression management—particularly so if your motive is to improve your chances of getting what you want in life.[77] There are questionable ways to create a good impression, as well. For instance, Stewart Friedman, director of the University of Pennsylvania's Leadership Program, offered this gem:

> Last year, I was doing some work with a large bank. The people there told me a story that astounded me: After 7 PM, people would open the door to their office, drape a spare jacket on the back of their chair, lay a set of glasses down on some reading material on their desk—and then go home for the night. The point of this elaborate gesture was to create the illusion that they were just out grabbing dinner and would be returning to burn the midnight oil.[78]

Impression management often strays into unethical territory.

A statistical factor analysis of the influence attempts reported by a sample of 84 bank employees (including 74 women) identified three categories of favorable upward impression management tactics.[79] As labeled in the OB Exercise on page 581, favorable upward impression management tactics can be *job-focused* (manipulating information about one's job performance), *supervisor-focused* (praising and doing favors for one's supervisor), and *self-focused* (presenting oneself as a polite and nice person). Take a short break from your studying to complete the OB Exercise. How did you do? A moderate amount of upward impression management is a necessity for the average employee today. Too little, and busy managers are liable to overlook some of your valuable contributions when they make job assignment, pay, and promotion decisions. Too much, and you run the risk of being branded a "schmoozer," a "phony," and other unflattering things by your co-workers.[80] Excessive flattery and ingratiation can backfire by embarrassing the target person and damaging one's credibility. Also, the risk of unintended insult is very high when impression management tactics cross gender, racial, ethnic, and cultural lines.[81] International management experts warn:

> The impression management tactic is only as effective as its correlation to accepted norms about behavioral presentation. In other words, slapping a Japanese subordinate on the back with a rousing "Good work, Hiro!" will not create the desired impression in Hiro's mind that the expatriate intended. In fact, the behavior will likely create the opposite impression.[82]

Making a Poor Impression

At first glance, the idea of consciously trying to make a bad impression in the workplace seems absurd. But an interesting new line of impression management research has uncovered both motives and tactics for making oneself look *bad*. In a survey of the work experiences of business students at a large northwestern US university, more than half "reported witnessing a case of someone intentionally looking bad at work."[83] Why? Four motives came out of the study:

> (1) *Avoidance:* Employee seeks to avoid additional work, stress, burnout, or an unwanted transfer or promotion. (2) *Obtain concrete rewards:* Employee seeks to obtain a pay raise or a desired transfer, promotion, or demotion. (3) *Exit:* Employee seeks to get laid off, fired, or suspended, and perhaps also to collect unemployment or workers' compensation. (4) *Power:* Employee seeks to control, manipulate, or intimidate others, get revenge, or make someone else look bad.[84]

Within the context of these motives, *unfavorable* upward impression management makes sense.

Five unfavorable upward impression management tactics identified by the researchers are as follows:

OB Exercise — How Much Do You Rely on Upward Impression Management Tactics?

Instructions

Rate yourself on each item according to how you behave on your current (or most recent) job. Add your circled responses to calculate a total score. Compare your score with our arbitrary norms.

	Rarely				Very Often

Job-Focused Tactics

1. I play up the value of my positive work results and make my supervisor aware of them. 1 — 2 — 3 — 4 — 5
2. I try to make my work appear better than it is. 1 — 2 — 3 — 4 — 5
3. I try to take responsibility for positive results, even when I'm not solely responsible for achieving them. 1 — 2 — 3 — 4 — 5
4. I try to make my negative results not as severe as they initially appear to my supervisor. 1 — 2 — 3 — 4 — 5
5. I arrive at work early and/or work late to show my supervisor I am a hard worker. 1 — 2 — 3 — 4 — 5

Supervisor-Focused Tactics

6. I show an interest in my supervisor's personal life. 1 — 2 — 3 — 4 — 5
7. I praise my supervisor on his/her accomplishments. 1 — 2 — 3 — 4 — 5
8. I do personal favors for my supervisor that I'm not required to do. 1 — 2 — 3 — 4 — 5
9. I compliment my supervisor on her/his dress or appearance. 1 — 2 — 3 — 4 — 5
10. I agree with my supervisor's major suggestions and ideas. 1 — 2 — 3 — 4 — 5

Self-Focused Tactics

11. I am very friendly and polite around my supervisor. 1 — 2 — 3 — 4 — 5
12. I try to act as a model employee around my supervisor. 1 — 2 — 3 — 4 — 5
13. I work harder when I know my supervisor will see the results. 1 — 2 — 3 — 4 — 5

Total score = _____

Arbitrary Norms

13–26 = Free agent
27–51 = Better safe than sorry
52–65 = Hello, Hollywood

SOURCE: Adapted from S J Wayne and G R Ferris, "Influence Tactics, Affect, and Exchange Quality in Supervisor-Subordinate Interactions: A Laboratory Experiment and Field Study," *Journal of Applied Psychology*, October 1990, pp. 487–99.

- *Decreasing performance*—restricting productivity, making more mistakes than usual, lowering quality, neglecting tasks.
- *Not working to potential*—pretending ignorance, having unused capabilities.
- *Withdrawing*—being tardy, taking excessive breaks, faking illness.
- *Displaying a bad attitude*—complaining, getting upset and angry, acting strangely, not getting along with co-workers.
- *Broadcasting limitations*—letting co-workers know about one's physical problems and mistakes, both verbally and nonverbally.[85]

Recommended ways to manage employees who try to make a bad impression can be found throughout this book. They include more challenging work, greater autonomy, better feedback, supportive leadership, clear and reasonable goals, and a less stressful work setting.

Research Evidence on Organizational Politics and Impression Management

Field research involving employees in real organizations rather than students in contrived laboratory settings has yielded these useful insights:

- In a study of 514 nonacademic university employees in the southwestern United States, white men had a greater understanding of organizational politics than did racial and ethnic minorities and white women. The researchers endorsed the practice of using mentors to help women and minorities develop their political skills.[86]

- Another study of 68 women and 84 men employed by five different service and industrial companies in the United States uncovered significant gender-based insights about organizational politics. In what might be termed the battle of the sexes,

  it was found that political behavior was perceived more favorably when it was performed against a target of the opposite gender. . . . Thus subjects of both sexes tend to relate to gender as a meaningful affiliation group. This finding presents a different picture from the one suggesting that women tend to accept male superiority at work and generally agree with sex stereotypes which are commonly discriminatory in nature.[87]

- In a recent survey of 172 team members in a large company's research and development unit, perceived higher levels of team politics were associated with lower organizational commitment, lower job satisfaction, poorer job performance, and lower unit effectiveness.[88]

The results of a recent cross-cultural laboratory study are noteworthy. A unique study of 38 Japanese Americans and 39 European Americans at the University of Utah showed how impression management can cause problems across cultures. Consistent with Japanese tradition, the Japanese Americans tended to publicly report their job performance in a self-effacing (or modest) way, *despite confiding in private that they had performed as well as the European Americans.* This Japanese cultural tendency toward understatement created a false impression for third-party European American evaluators (who were kept unaware of any cultural distinctions). According to the researchers, "Japanese American participants were seen as less competent and less likeable than their European American counterparts because of their tendency to downplay their performance."[89] The old American expression "It pays to toot your own horn" appears to be as true as ever. Too much tooting, however, can brand one as arrogant, self-centered, and overbearing. This sort of delicate cultural balancing act makes cross-cultural dealings very challenging.

Managing Organizational Politics

Organizational politics cannot be eliminated. A manager would be naive to expect such an outcome. But political maneuvering can and should be managed to keep it constructive and within reasonable bounds. Harvard's Abraham Zaleznik put the issue this way: "People can focus their attention on only so many things. The more it lands on politics, the less energy—emotional and intellectual—is available to attend to the problems that fall under the heading of real work."[90]

Table 16-4   *How to Keep Organizational Politics within Reasonable Bounds*

- Screen out overly political individuals at hiring time.
- Create an open-book management system.
- Make sure every employee knows how the business works and has a personal line of sight to key results with corresponding measureable objectives for individual accountability.
- Have nonfinancial people interpret periodic financial and accounting statements for all employees.
- Establish formal conflict resolution and grievance processes.
- As an ethics filter, do only what you would feel comfortable doing on national television.
- Publicly recognize and reward people who get real results without political games.

SOURCE: Adapted in part from discussion in LB MacGregor Server, "The End of Office Politics as Usual" (New York: American Management Association, 2002), pp. 184–99.

An individual's degree of politicalness is a matter of personal values, ethics, and temperament. People who are either strictly nonpolitical or highly political generally pay a price for their behavior. The former may experience slow promotions and feel left out, while the latter may run the risk of being called self-serving and lose their credibility. People at both ends of the political spectrum may be considered poor team players. A moderate amount of prudent political behavior generally is considered a survival tool in complex organizations. Experts remind us that

political behavior has earned a bad name only because of its association with politicians. On its own, the use of power and other resources to obtain your objectives is not inherently unethical. It all depends on what the preferred objectives are.[91]

With this perspective in mind, the practical steps in Table 16–4 are recommended. How many of the Enron- and World Com-type scandals could have been prevented with this approach? Remember: measurable objectives are management's first line of defense against negative expressions of organizational politics.[92]

Summary of Key Concepts

1. *Explain the concept of mutuality of interest.* Managers are constantly challenged to foster mutuality of interest (a win–win situation) between individual and organizational interests. Organization members need to actively cooperate with actual and potential adversaries for the common good.

2. *Name at least three "soft" and two "hard" influence tactics, and summarize the practical lessons from influence research.* Five soft influence tactics are rational persuasion, inspirational appeals, consultation, ingratiation, and personal appeals. They are more friendly and less coercive than the four hard influence tactics: exchange, coalition tactics, pressure, and legitimating tactics. According to research, soft tactics are better for

generating commitment and are perceived as more fair than hard tactics. Ingratiation—making the boss feel good through compliments and being helpful—can slightly improve performance appraisal results and make the boss like you a lot more. Influence through domination is a poor strategy for both men and women. Influence is a complicated and situational process that needs to be undertaken with care, especially across cultures.

3. *Identify and briefly explain Cialdini's six principles of influence and persuasion.* They are liking (people tend to like those who like them), reciprocity (belief that good and bad deeds should be repaid in kind), social proof (people tend to follow those most like themselves), consistency (people tend to do what they are publicly committed to

doing), authority (people tend to defer to and respect credible experts), and scarcity (people tend to want more of what has limited availability).

4. *Identify and briefly describe French and Raven's five bases of power, and discuss the responsible use of power.* French and Raven's five bases of power are reward power (rewarding compliance), coercive power (punishing noncompliance), legitimate power (relying on formal authority), expert power (providing needed information), and referent power (relying on personal attraction). Responsible and ethical managers strive to use socialized power (primary concern is for others) rather than personalized power (primary concern for self). Research found higher organizational commitment among employees with bosses who used uplifting power than among those with power-hungry bosses who relied on dominating power.

5. *Define the term* empowerment, *and discuss the realities of open-book management.* Empowerment involves sharing varying degrees of power and decision-making authority with lower-level employees to tap their full potential. Surveys indicate widespread use of open-book management, whereby managers share more information than usual about innovations, company finances, and strategy. This act of trust carries with it the risk of betrayal. But advocates of empowerment and open-book management say the promises of more teamwork and greater competitiveness outweigh the risks.

6. *Explain why delegation is the highest form of empowerment, and discuss the connections among delegation, trust, and personal initiative.* Delegation gives employees more than a participatory role in decision making. It allows them to make their *own* work-related decisions. Managers tend to

delegate to employees they trust. Employees can get managers to trust them by demonstrating personal initiative (going beyond formal job requirements and being self-starters).

7. *Define* organizational politics, *and explain what triggers it.* Organizational politics is defined as intentional acts of influence to enhance or protect the self-interests of individuals or groups. Uncertainty triggers most politicking in organizations. Political action occurs at individual, coalition, and network levels. Coalitions are informal, temporary, and single-issue alliances.

8. *Distinguish between favorable and unfavorable impression management tactics.* Favorable upward impression management can be job-focused (manipulating information about one's job performance), supervisor-focused (praising or doing favors for the boss), or self-focused (being polite and nice). Unfavorable upward impression management tactics include decreasing performance, not working to potential, withdrawing, displaying a bad attitude, and broadcasting one's limitations.

9. *Explain how to manage organizational politics.* Since organizational politics cannot be eliminated, managers need to keep it within reasonable bounds. Measurable objectives for personal accountability are key. Participative management also helps, especially in the form of open-book management. Formal conflict resolution and grievance programs are helpful. Overly political people should not be hired, and employees who get results without playing political games should be publicly recognized and rewarded. The "how-would-it-look-on-TV" ethics test can limit political maneuvering.

Discussion Questions

1. Of the nine generic influence tactics, which do you use the most when dealing with friends, parents, your boss, or your professors? Would other tactics be more effective?

2. Which of Cialdini's six principles of influence and persuasion have you observed lately? What were the circumstances and was the influence attempt successful?

3. Before reading this chapter, did the term *power* have a negative connotation for you? Do you view it differently now? Explain.

4. What base(s) of power do you rely on in your daily affairs? (Use the OB Exercise on page 566 to assess your power bases at work.) Do you handle power effectively and responsibly?

5. In your opinion, how much empowerment is too much in today's workplaces?

6. What are the main advantages and drawbacks of the trend toward increased delegation?

7. Why do you think organizational politics is triggered primarily by uncertainty?

8. What personal experiences have you had with coalitions? Explain any positive or negative outcomes.

9. According to the OB Exercise on page 581, how heavily do you rely on upward impression management tactics? What are the career implications of your approach to impression management?

10. How much impression management do you see in your classroom or workplace today? Citing specific examples, are those tactics effective?

Internet Exercise

www.influenceatwork.com
www.fastcompany.com

Influence and political tactics are an inescapable part of modern organizational life, as discussed in this chapter. The purpose of this exercise is to broaden your understanding of organizational influence and politics and help you deal with them effectively.

A Free Quiz on Social Influence

Do you get the feeling advertisers, the media, politicians, salespeople, parents and teachers, and friends sometimes are trying to trick you by manipulating words and images in self-serving ways? According to Professor Robert B Cialdini and his colleagues, you are right to feel a bit put upon. After all, as their research has documented, each of us is the recipient (or victim) of countless social influence attempts during every waking hour. The Internet site **www.influenceatwork.com** provides a brief inside look at social influence so we will not be unfairly or unwittingly manipulated. At the home page, click on the "What's Your Influence Quotient?" icon. The short 10-item quiz (and answers) will get you thinking about the power and pervasiveness of social influence. Back at the home page, you might want to select the heading "About Us" from the main menu, for relevant background.

Interesting and Practical Advice on Organizational Politics

A pair of articles in the April–May 1998 issue of *Fast Company* magazine are must reading. Here's how to get to them online. Go to *Fast Company's* Internet home page, (**www.fastcompany.com**) and click on "Dynamic Archives" under the main menu heading "Magazine." Scroll down to issue number 14 and select "Table of Contents—April/May 1998." Finally, scroll down the table of contents for issue number 14 and select these two articles: "The Bad Guy's (and Gal's) Guide to Office Politics" (1½ pages) and "The Good Guy's (and Gal's) Guide to Office Politics" (6½ pages). You may want to print copies. We recommend you read the Good Guy's article first.

Questions

1. Having taken the influence quiz, are you more aware of day-to-day influence processes and tactics? Explain.

2. Generally, do you see social influence as a constructive or sinister force in society? Explain.

3. Is it possible that employees are becoming more difficult to influence because they have become hardened or numbed as a result of excessive exposure to influence attempts?

4. How can managers use social influence *ethically?*

5. On balance, now that you have read the office politics articles, do you regard workplace politics positively or negatively? Explain.

6. What was the most *useful* advice you obtained from the politics articles?

OB in Action Case *Study*

Organizational Politics, Enron-Style[93]

The Enron scandal has been told as a kind of Greek tragedy, a cautionary tale of hubris, even a battle of the sexes. But it can perhaps be best understood as a brutal competition. The miracle of the marketplace is supposed to be that competition is healthy—that the struggle to create something better, faster and cheaper benefits nearly everyone. That's the theory, at least, that some people use to explain why greed is good. But throw in pride (and lust), and sometimes the game goes out of control. This is the story of how Jeff Skilling and Rebecca Mark took their rivalry and drove it—and a multibillion-dollar company, its employees and its stockholders—right off the edge of a cliff.

While the drama played out, Enron founder Ken Lay seemed more interested in schmoozing Washington and going to charity events in Houston than running the company day to day. The two young dynamos vying for his favor offered competing models of the future. To Mark, the road to riches lay in building ever-grander castles, massive energy infrastructures. But to Skilling, tangible assets like power plants were just toys. The real money, he argued, was in the action—the trading, buying and selling. They each had an enormous interest in justifying their respective visions.

Inside Enron, Mark was sometimes known as "Mark the Shark." Blond and tall and toned, she was sleek and fast and knew how to bite. When she entered the utility business in the early 80s, it was populated with frumpy males in baggy suits and short-sleeved shirts with pocket protectors. Mark wore stiletto heels and tightly tailored size-6 Escada suits. She was a builder. Her job was to create and develop power plants and sell the electricity they made. In the sleepy, once tightly regulated world of power companies she was regarded as both a curiosity and a whirlwind, able to use her femininity and no-nonsense manner to disarm, then buffalo the men sitting across the table. By the mid-90s, she had constructed or acquired five plants in the United States and was on her way to buying or building well in excess of 15 in Europe, Asia, South America, and the Middle East.

But inside her own company, she had competition. Like her, Jeff Skilling had been born middle class and Middle Western, gone to college in Texas and to Harvard Business School. They both turned 40 in 1993; both were clearly on track for the top jobs at Enron. But Skilling saw himself as the true visionary. Buying power plants and selling their product—that was Old Think, argued Skilling. In the new, wired, free-for-all economy, the greatest rewards would go to those who made markets, who bought and sold—but didn't actually own much of anything. Constructing and running power plants was for chumps: it required huge capital investments and never produced the return on investment he was after. Anyone could build a factory, Skilling said. But it took a special genius—a whiz kid who had not just been a Harvard Business School grad but a high-ranking Baker scholar—to manipulate all the pieces, to make them add up to more than the sum of their parts. (As it turned out, it also took creative and possibly fraudulent accounting that masked losses and debts and recorded projected and far-from-certain future profits as present earnings.) And why stop at gas and electricity? Why not trade water or broadband capacity? By the time Skilling was done, Enron would be trading securities based on weather data.

Skilling was aggressive and brash, not so much articulate and smooth as cunning and willful. He thrived on one-upmanship and didn't mind trying to embarrass the less-quick-witted or anyone who challenged him. In one conference call with Wall Street analysts he dismissed one nagging questioner as an "a—hole." Skilling wanted to stomp not just Enron's competitors in the corporate world but any potential rival within Enron. In 1993 he persuaded his boss—Ken Lay—to cut him a piece of Mark's business. Skilling was given control of Enron's power plants in the United States; he promptly sold these assets in order to have more cash for his plans. (Skilling's spokeswoman says he never considered Mark a direct rival.) At first, Mark was baffled by Skilling's raid on her turf—especially since it was a sneak attack. She had never been given a chance to make her case. She regarded Skilling as a flashy consultant type who had never done the hard work of building anything.

Rather than pout, Mark just pushed herself harder. She became a world traveler, ranging round the globe buying and building plants. She lived high and, in retrospect, paid too much, especially for a $3 billion plant in India that immediately became enmeshed in local political intrigue. But she wanted to prove that her way was the golden road. As she flew around in her corporate jet and smart suits, she

began to get noticed. She worked with Henry Kissinger to lobby the Chinese prime minister on the need for Western-built pipelines and plants. She spoke on the phone to the Israeli prime minister and raised the gender awareness of a high-ranking official in Qatar. At first, the Qatari official refused to address her directly, but by the end of three hours, he was gushing, "It's a shame you haven't been here before. We would have resolved the issues a long time ago."

In foreign capitals, Enron was no longer being confused with Exxon. Mark had every reason to believe her bosses would be pleased with her efforts to extend and enshrine the Enron brand. She was, like other Enron executives, showered in stock options. But she didn't get quite the glory she anticipated. Perhaps because Lay saw himself as Enron's pitchman, he didn't seem to welcome Mark's high profile.

Lay's boy, it soon became clear, was Skilling. While Mark globe-trotted, Skilling was filling headquarters with his own troops. He was not looking for "fuzzy skills," a former employee recalls. His recruits talked about a socialization process called "Enronizing." Family time? Quality of life? Forget it. Anybody who did not embrace the elbows-out culture "didn't get it." They were "damaged goods" and "shipwrecks," likely to be fired by their bosses at blistering annual job reviews known as rank-and-yank sessions. The culture turned paranoid: former CIA and FBI agents were hired to enforce security. Using "sniffer" programs, they would pounce on anyone E-mailing a potential competitor. The "spooks," as the former agents were called, were known to barge into offices and confiscate computers.

Some employees found the cultural revolution troubling. The Reverend James Nutter of Palmer Memorial Episcopal Church heard from so many unhappy Enron souls that he penned a letter to Skilling: "These people don't belong to you," Nutter recalls writing. "They belong to God." But many Enronites worshiped Mammon instead. The real status symbol at Enron was not a new Ferrari but one of the company's half-dozen parking spaces monitored by security cameras. Skilling would take his favorites, "The Mighty Man Force," as one employee called them, on macho adventure trips. They raced across Mexico on a 1,000-mile bike tour. While tearing through the rugged Australian Outback, the overexuberant Mighty Men trashed several expensive SUVs they'd rented.

Enron parties were suitably imperial, with Tiffany glassware as door prizes and waiters standing by at all times with flutes of champagne. Some of the informal partying was less classy. . . .

Sex suffused the Enron atmosphere. Skilling divorced his wife and became engaged to an Enron secretary, whom he promoted to a $600,000 job and whom insiders immediately dubbed "Va Voom!" One top executive, Lou Pai, divorced his wife and married a former stripper. Several women who were believed to be sleeping with their bosses were called "The French Lieutenants' Women." Staffers fearful of the next rank-and-yank session worried that these women were acting as spies. The most celebrated affair was between two top executives, Ken Rice and Amanda Martin. Their affection, described by Enron staffers to *Newsweek* as "touchy feely" and "obscene," was visible through the windows of Martin's office.

Mark apparently had her own intramural affair. In the late 80s, after she was divorced, she had a relationship with an Enron consultant, John Wing. Some of Mark's colleagues believed their relationship continued after Wing joined Enron. Some employees found the office romances and salacious gossip so disturbing that they proposed the company adopt a formal policy against fraternization, according to a former personnel executive. The company let the suggestion drop.

Mark was not above ostentatious revelry. At a party to celebrate the development of the Enron power plant in India, she brought a small elephant into a resort outside Houston (at the same party, dressed in leather, she rode in on the back of a Harley-Davidson). But for the most part, she remained outside the Lay-Skilling in-crowd, working in a separate building downtown. She failed to fully realize how hard Skilling was working to undermine her.

In 1997, Skilling was given another chunk of Mark's territory—energy development in parts of Europe. Too late, Mark realized that Skilling was playing for keeps. The two had a "short and extremely acrimonious" discussion, she says. But by 1998, Skilling was Enron's chief operating officer. Mark was made vice chairman, a fancy title for a position described by Enron insiders as "the ejection seat."

Mark had one last play. That same year she took over a small water company called Azurix spun off by Enron. Mark had grand plans for Azurix: essentially to control as much of the world's drinking water as possible and sell it for a profit. Yet lacking adequate financing from Enron, she took the company public before it was ready. But the stock quickly crashed. Azurix invested heavily in an English company—but again was ensnared in local politics, and the project turned out to be a loser. To help her make deals, she brought in the hard-charging Amanda Martin, who, like Mark, was

stylish and well educated. But she had misgivings about Martin. Some of her colleagues suspected that Martin was a spy for Skilling. Martin dismisses the notion, but says she understands why some people believed it. "I was one of the few people coming out of Jeff's camp," she says.

Mark left herself open to attack. When she tried to buy a company that provided services to water utilities, there were grumbles that she was overpaying. As it turned out, the services company was run by her fiance. An employee urged Enron's general counsel to look into Mark's potential conflict of interest. The whistle-blower? Martin. The deal was scuttled. According to a person close to Mark, it was Mark herself who decided to kill it.

By August 2000 it was time to go, and Mark was forced out. In terms of her own finances, the timing was fortunate. Mark sold her stock at a big profit [$56 million, total]. Outsiders, including Enron shareholders, were kept in the dark, but Skilling's empire was already starting to rot from within. Desperate to keep the price of the stock climbing, Enron's management was creating hundreds of off-the-books "entities," some of which served to hide or disguise heavy debts and losses. By 2001, the stock price was beginning to slide. Skilling won the ultimate prize—he succeeded Ken Lay as CEO in January 2001. But by August he was gone, claiming "personal reasons" for his early retirement.

Questions for Discussion

1. Which of the nine generic influence tactics are evident in this case? What were the consequences?
2. What role did personalized power play in this case? What were the consequences?
3. Which of the five bases of power can you find in this case? Explain.
4. How important were political coalitions at Enron? Explain.
5. Why was a highly charged political climate unavoidable at Enron?
6. What could/should have been done to tone down the politics at Enron?

Personal Awareness and Growth Exercise

How Political Are You?

Objectives

1. To get to know yourself a little bit better.
2. Within an organizational context, to assess your political tendencies.
3. To consider the career implications of your political tendencies.

Introduction

Organizational politics is an unavoidable feature of modern organizational life. Your career success, job performance, and job satisfaction can hinge on your political skills. But it is important to realize that some political tactics can cause ethical problems.

Instructions

For each of the 10 statements below, select the response that best characterizes your behavior. You do not have to engage in the behavior at all times to answer true.[94]

1. You should make others feel important through an open appreciation of their ideas and work.   _____ True   _____ False
2. Because people tend to judge you when they first meet you, always try to make a good first impression.   _____ True   _____ False
3. Try to let others do most of the talking, be sympathetic to their problems, and resist telling people that they are totally wrong.   _____ True   _____ False
4. Praise the good traits of the people you meet and always give people an opportunity to save face if they are wrong or make a mistake.   _____ True   _____ False
5. Spreading false rumors, planting misleading information, and backstabbing are necessary, if somewhat unpleasant, methods to deal with your enemies.   _____ True   _____ False
6. Sometimes it is necessary to make promises that you know you will not or cannot keep.   _____ True   _____ False
7. It is important to get along with everybody, even with those who are generally recognized as windbags, abrasive, or constant complainers.   _____ True   _____ False
8. It is vital to do favors for others so that you can call in these IOUs at times when they will do you the most good.   _____ True   _____ False
9. Be willing to compromise, particularly on issues that are minor to you, but important to others.   _____ True   _____ False
10. On controversial issues, it is important to delay or avoid your involvement if possible.   _____ True   _____ False

Scoring and Interpretation

The author of this quiz recommends the following scoring system:

A confirmed organizational politician will answer "true" to all 10 questions. Organizational politicians with fundamental ethical standards will answer "false" to Questions 5 and 6, which deal with deliberate lies and uncharitable behavior. Individuals who regard manipulation, incomplete disclosure, and self-serving behavior as unacceptable will answer "false" to all or almost all of the questions.[95]

Questions for Discussion

1. Did this instrument accurately assess your tendencies toward organizational politics? Explain.
2. Do you think a confirmed organizational politician would answer this quiz honestly? Explain.
3. Will your political tendencies help or hinder your career? Explain.
4. Are there any potential ethical problems with any of your answers? Which ones?
5. How important is political behavior for career success today? Explain, relative to the industry or organization you have in mind.

Group Exercise

You Make Me Feel So Good!

Objectives

1. To introduce a different type of impression management and sharpen your awareness of impression management.
2. To promote self-awareness and diversity awareness by comparing your perceptions and ethics with others.

Introduction

This is a group discussion exercise designed to enhance your understanding of impression management. Personal interpretations are involved, so there are no strictly right or wrong answers.

Researchers recently have explored *beneficial* impression management, the practice of helping friends and significant others look good. This new line of inquiry combines the established OB topics of social support (discussed relative to stress in Chapter 19) and impression management (discussed in this chapter.) In this exercise, we explore the practical and ethical implications of "strategically managing information to make your friends look good." We also consider impression management in general.

Instructions

This is a two-stage exercise: a private note-taking part, followed by a group discussion.

Stage 1 (5 to 7 minutes): Read the two scenarios in the box below and then rate each one according to the following three scales:

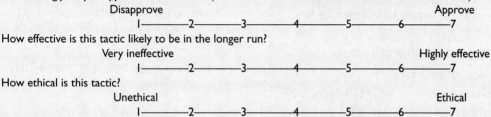

How strongly do you approve of this tactic? (Mark an "X" for scenario I and an "O" for scenario 2.)

Disapprove   Approve
I————————2————————3————————4————————5————————6————————7

How effective is this tactic likely to be in the longer run?

Very ineffective   Highly effective
I————————2————————3————————4————————5————————6————————7

How ethical is this tactic?

Unethical   Ethical
I————————2————————3————————4————————5————————6————————7

SCENARIOS[96]

1. A high school ballplayer buoys the spirits of a teammate who struck out at a key moment by emphasizing the latter's game-winning hit last week and noting that even the greatest big-league hitters fail about 7 times out of 10. He may privately suspect his teammate has only mediocre baseball talent, but by putting the best side to his comments and not sharing his doubts, he makes the teammate feel better, builds his confidence so he can face tomorrow's game in a more optimistic frame of mind, and boosts the teammate's image in front of the other players who can hear his reassuring words.

2. At a party, a college student describes her roommate to a potential date she knows her friend finds extremely attractive. She stresses her friend's intelligence, attractiveness, and common interests but fails to mention that her friend can also be quite arrogant.

Stage 2 (10 to 15 minutes): Join two or three others in a discussion group and compare scores for both scenarios. Are there big differences of opinion, or is there a general consensus? Next, briefly discuss these questions: How do *you* create a good first impression in *specific* situations? What goes through your mind when you see someone trying to make a good impression for themselves or for someone else? *Note:* Your instructor may ask you to pick a spokesperson to briefly report the results of your discussion to the class. If so, be sure to keep notes during the discussion.

Questions for Discussion

1. Is the whole practice of impression management a dishonest waste of time, or does it have a proper place in society? Why?

2. In what situations can impression management attempts backfire?

3. How do you know when someone has taken impression management too far?

4. How would you respond to a person who made this statement? "I never engage in impression management."

Ethical Dilemma

Your Job: Up in Smoke?[97]

Smokers have been banned from lighting up on airplanes, at work, and in restaurants. Now, a nicotine habit could cost a smoker a job. As of March 25, [2002,] St. Cloud, Florida (population 19,000), requires applicants for city jobs to swear they've been tobacco-free for a year. New hires can't smoke or dip and can be tested to make sure they're not cheating. (Current employees are exempt.)

Other Florida cities have similar laws, but none go as far: North Miami bans smokers from applying for city jobs, too, but relents after they're hired; Coral Gables won't let smokers be cops.

Boosters say the restrictions mean fewer lost workdays, higher productivity, and lower health-insurance costs. Eric Nieves, St. Cloud's human-resources director, says 6% to

12% of the $1.3 million the city spends on health insurance is tobacco-related.

But civil-rights advocates say saving money is not worth the loss of privacy. Smoking is a health risk, "but so is high blood pressure and cholesterol," says Angie Brooks of the American Civil Liberties Union, which is considering whether to file suit. "It's a very slippery slope."

And some say the law will make hiring harder. Says public works director Bob MacKichan: "I could have the most qualified person there is, but now I don't even get to see the application."

What is your position on this ethically charged workplace power play?

1. Smoking is hazardous to all involved and should be discouraged in every possible way. Explain.

2. This is an outrageous abuse of power. Smokers have rights, too. Explain.

3. Current no-smoking policies in most workplaces are strict enough already. Explain.

4. Exempting current employees from a tobacco-free policy for new hires is an unacceptable double standard that could hurt morale and productivity. Explain.

5. Employees in each particular organization should be allowed to vote on tobacco-free hiring. Explain.

6. Invent other options. Discuss.

For an interpretation of this situation, visit our Web site, **www.mhhe.com/kreitner.**

Chapter Seventeen

Leadership

Learning Objectives

When you finish studying the material in this chapter, you should be able to:

1 Define the term leadership, and explain the difference between leading versus managing.

2 Review trait theory research, and discuss the idea of one best style of leadership, using the Ohio State studies and the Leadership Grid as points of reference.

3 Explain, according to Fiedler's contingency model, how leadership style interacts with situational control.

4 Discuss House's revised path–goal theory and Hersey and Blanchard's situational leadership theory.

5 Define and differentiate transactional and charismatic leadership.

6 Explain how charismatic leadership transforms followers and work groups.

7 Summarize the managerial implications of charismatic leadership.

8 Explain the leader–member exchange model of leadership.

9 Describe the substitutes for leadership, and explain how they substitute for, neutralize, or enhance the effects of leadership.

10 Describe servant-leadership.

The attributes and skills required of leaders expanded dramatically [after September 11, 2001].

As people everywhere reacted to the terrorist attacks that left thousands dead in New York and Washington, they looked to government, business, religious, and other leaders for guidance and wisdom. In addition to directions on how to cope with the immediate crisis—everything from locating victims to repairing communication and transportation links—they sought leaders who could provide perspective, calm their fears, and inspire confidence in their ability to combat further attacks. As Napoleon said, "a leader is a dealer in hope."

The challenge fell more heavily than usual on business executives because the victims at the World Trade Center . . . were mostly employees at work. Suddenly, heads of brokerage firms, law firms, insurance companies, and other concerns found themselves searching for missing staff members, informing employees' relatives that their loved ones were likely dead and offering grief counseling to survivors.

Cantor Fitzgerald, the bond-trading firm that lost 600 employees, followed the crisis-management maxim of putting people first but also getting back to business quickly. Chairman Howard Lutnick wept with employees' relatives at a hastily convened family-services

Marty Evans, President of the American Red Cross, demonstrated effective leadership during the 1989 San Francisco earthquake.
(c) American Red Cross

center at the Pierre Hotel in Manhattan. He shared his grief at losing his brother and won kudos for his emotional honesty, though some victims' families worry about what benefits they will receive. At the same time, his surviving lieutenants worked around the clock at backup offices in New Jersey and London to save Cantor's computer systems. By Thursday morning, despite gaping holes in the staff, they had reopened Cantor's electronic bond-trading network. . . .

Beyond crisis management, however, the most important task for leaders is to help employees feel confident and capable of carrying on. While acknowledging our common vulnerability, "leaders must emphasize the importance of each person's actions and appeal to the better aims of their natures—to be the best managers, soldiers, students, best whoever they can be," says Nancy Koehn, a business historian at Harvard Business School.

Great historical figures like Lincoln and Churchill did this by talking frankly about the gravity of crises they faced yet mobilizing action. "When Lincoln told Americans in his second inaugural address to act with malice toward none, with charity toward all, with firmness in the right . . . to finish the work we are in, he was trying to make sense of the carnage of the Civil War while stirring hope," Ms Koehn says. Similarly, business leaders today, faced with rebuilding, must challenge employees to move forward.

Marty Evans, [former] national executive director of the Girl Scouts of the USA and a former Navy rear admiral, agrees that even though employees may show more of their personality quirks during times of duress, they often become more able and willing to work together. [Ms Evans is now president of the American Red Cross.] "It's been a . . . [time] of incredible tragedy, but we've also seen the best of people," she says. "It's a leader's job to nudge people into that better space."

[Following the terrorist attack,] Ms Evans drew on lessons she learned in 1989, when she was in charge of the Navy's emergency efforts during the San Francisco earthquake. Then, she recalls; "I didn't have a choice but to make important decisions when all I had was incomplete information." City officials asked her to send a ship so they could try to restore some electrical power. Some of her staff warned that the idea would never work. "But there was a voice in the back of my head telling me that the Navy had to try to render help," she says, "so we sent the ship and . . . the lights went on."

Another key to maneuvering through crises is having strong deputies. When the earthquake hit, Ms Evans's admiral was away from the base, but she was prepared to step in. "Leaders don't choose where they are when things happen, so you always have to make sure your No. 2 and No. 3 person is ready to be in charge," she says.

At Girl Scout headquarters in New York . . . [the week of the attack], Ms Evans and her staff set aside a room for meditation and prayer. They also created a Web page to suggest ways Girl Scouts could respond. "People need space and time to grieve, but they also need structure to help them go on," she says.[1]

For Discussion

How can leaders instill hope in others during a crisis like September 11? Discuss.

Someone once observed that a leader is a person who finds out which way the parade is going, jumps in front of it, and yells "Follow me!" The plain fact is that this approach to leadership has little chance of working in today's rapidly changing world. As illustrated in the chapter opening case, leadership involves much more than simply taking charge. Howard Lutnick not only had to deal with the emotions of losing family members and valued employees, he also needed to focus on the operational issues at hand. In short, successful leaders are those individuals who can step into a difficult situation and make a noticeable difference. But how much of a difference can leaders make in modern organizations?

OB researchers have discovered that leaders can make a difference. One study, for instance, revealed that leadership was positively associated with net profits from 167 companies over a time span of 20 years.[2] Research also showed that a coach's leadership skills affected the success of his or her team. Specifically, teams in both Major League Baseball and college basketball won more games when players perceived the coach to be an effective leader.[3] Rest assured, leadership makes a difference.

After formally defining the term *leadership,* this chapter focuses on the following areas: (1) trait and behavioral approaches to leadership, (2) alternative situational theories of leadership, (3) charismatic leadership, and (4) additional perspectives on leadership. Because there are many different leadership theories within each of these areas, it is impossible to discuss them all. This chapter reviews those theories with the most research support.

What Does Leadership Involve?

Because the topic of leadership has fascinated people for centuries, definitions abound. This section presents a definition of leadership and highlights the similarities and differences between leading versus managing.

What Is Leadership?

Disagreement about the definition of leadership stems from the fact that it involves a complex interaction among the leader, the followers, and the situation. For example, some researchers define leadership in terms of personality and physical traits, while others believe leadership is represented by a set of prescribed behaviors. In contrast, other researchers believe that leadership is a temporary role that can be filled by anyone. There is a common thread, however, among the different definitions of leadership. The common thread is social influence.

Within an organizational context, **leadership** is defined as "a social influence process in which the leader seeks the voluntary participation of subordinates in an effort to reach organizational goals."[4] Tom Peters and Nancy Austin, authors of the best-seller, *A Passion for Excellence,* describe leadership in broader terms:

> Leadership means vision, cheerleading, enthusiasm, love, trust, verve, passion, obsession, consistency, the use of symbols, paying attention as illustrated by the content of one's calendar, out-and-out drama (and the management thereof), creating heroes at all levels, coaching, effectively wandering around, and numerous other things. Leadership must be present at all levels of the organization. It depends on a million little things done with obsession, consistency, and care, but all of those million little things add up to nothing if the trust, vision, and basic belief are not there.[5]

As you can see from this definition, leadership clearly entails more than wielding power and exercising authority and is exhibited on different levels. At the individual level, for example, leadership involves mentoring, coaching, inspiring, and motivating. Leaders build teams, generate cohesion, and resolve conflicts at the group level. Finally, leaders build culture and generate change at the organizational level.[6]

There is one component of leadership missing from the above definition: the follower's perspective. Research from this point of view reveals that people seek, admire, and respect leaders who foster three emotional responses in others. Followers want organizational leaders to create feelings of *significance* (what one does at work is important and meaningful), *community* (a sense of unity encourages people to treat others with respect and dignity and to work together in pursuit of organizational goals), and *excitement* (people are engaged and feel energy at work).[7]

Leadership

Influencing employees to voluntarily pursue organizational goals.

Leading versus Managing

It is important to appreciate the difference between leadership and management to fully understand what leadership is all about. Bernard Bass, a leadership expert, concluded that "leaders manage and managers lead, but the two activities are not synonymous."[8] Bass tells us that although leadership and management overlap, each entails a unique set of activities or functions. Broadly speaking, managers typically perform functions associated with planning, investigating, organizing, and control, and leaders deal with the interpersonal aspects of a manager's job. Leaders inspire others, provide emotional support, and try to get employees to rally around a common goal. Leaders also play a key role in creating a vision and strategic plan for an organization. Managers, in turn, are charged with implementing the vision and strategic plan. Table 17–1 summarizes the key differences found between leaders and managers.[9]

The distinction between leaders and managers is more than a semantic issue for four reasons:

1. It is important from a hiring standpoint. Because leaders and managers perform a subset of unique functions, it is important to recruit and select people who have the required intellectual abilities, experience, and job-relevant knowledge to perform their jobs.

2. Differences may affect group effectiveness. Work group performance can be increased by staffing a productive mix of leaders and managers.

3. Successful organizational change is highly dependent upon effective leadership throughout an organization. Senior executives cannot create change on their own. According to organizational change expert John Kotter, successful organizational transformation is 70% to 90% leadership and 10% to 30% management.[10]

4. Distinctions between leading and managing highlight the point that leadership is not restricted to people in particular positions or roles. Anyone from the bottom to the top of an organization can be a leader. Many informal leaders have contributed to organizational effectiveness. This conclusion supports Warren Bennis's point about leaders and managers. Bennis characterized managers as people who do things right and leaders as individuals who do the right things.

Table 17–1   *Differences between Leaders and Managers*

Leaders	Managers
Innovate	Administer
Develop	Maintain
Inspire	Control
Long-term view	Short-term view
Ask what and why	Ask how and when
Originate	Initiate
Challenge the status quo	Accept the status quo
Do the right things	Do things right

SOURCE: Distinctions were taken from W G Bennis, *On Becoming a Leader* (Reading, MA: Addison-Wesley, 1989).

Trait and Behavioral Theories of Leadership

This section examines the two earliest approaches used to explain leadership. Trait theories focused on identifying the personal traits that differentiated leaders from followers. Behavioral theorists examined leadership from a different perspective. They tried to uncover the different kinds of leader behaviors that resulted in higher work group performance. Both approaches to leadership can teach current and future managers valuable lessons about leading.

Trait Theory

At the turn of the 20th century, the prevailing belief was that leaders were born, not made. Selected people were thought to possess inborn traits that made them successful leaders. A **leader trait** is a physical or personality characteristic that can be used to differentiate leaders from followers.

> **Leader trait**
> Personal characteristics that differentiate leaders from followers.

Before World War II, hundreds of studies were conducted to pinpoint the traits of successful leaders. Dozens of leadership traits were identified. During the postwar period, however, enthusiasm was replaced by widespread criticism. Studies conducted by Ralph Stogdill in 1948 and by Richard Mann in 1959, which sought to summarize the impact of traits on leadership, caused the trait approach to fall into disfavor.

Stogdill's and Mann's Findings
Based on his review, Stogdill concluded that five traits tended to differentiate leaders from average followers: (1) intelligence, (2) dominance, (3) self-confidence, (4) level of energy and activity, and (5) task-relevant knowledge.[11] Among the seven categories of personality traits examined by Mann, intelligence was the best predictor of leadership.[12] Unfortunately, the overall pattern of research findings revealed that both Stogdill's and Mann's key traits did not accurately predict which individuals became leaders in organizations. People with these traits often remained followers.

Contemporary Trait Research
Two OB researchers concluded in 1983 that past trait data may have been incorrectly analyzed. By applying modern statistical techniques to an old database, they demonstrated that the majority of a leader's behavior could be attributed to stable underlying traits.[13] Unfortunately, their methodology did not single out specific traits.

A 1986 meta-analysis by Robert Lord and his associates remedied this shortcoming. Based on a reanalysis of past studies, Lord concluded that people have leadership *prototypes* that affect their perceptions of who is and who is not an effective leader. Your **leadership prototype** is a mental representation of the traits and behaviors that you believe are possessed by leaders. We thus tend to perceive that someone is a leader when he or she exhibits traits or behaviors that are consistent with our prototypes.[14] Lord's research demonstrated that people are perceived as being leaders when they exhibit the traits associated with intelligence, masculinity, and dominance. More recently, a study of 6,052 middle-level managers from 22 European countries revealed that leadership prototypes are culturally based. In other words, leadership prototypes

> **Leadership prototype**
> Mental representation of the traits and behaviors possessed by leaders.

Perceptions of Russian President Vladimir Putin, U.S. President George W. Bush, Nigerian President Olusegun Obasanjo, and Canadian Prime Minister Jean Chretien are likely to vary across countries because leadership prototypes are influenced by national cultural values. What are your perceptions of these leaders?

AP/Wide World Photos

are influenced by national cultural values.[15] Researchers have not yet identified a set of global leadership prototypes.

Another pair of leadership researchers attempted to identify key leadership traits by asking the following open-ended question to more than 20,000 people around the world: "What values (personal traits or characteristics) do you look for and admire in your superiors?" The top four traits included honesty, forward-looking, inspiring, and competent.[16] The researchers concluded that these four traits constitute a leader's credibility. This research suggests that people want their leaders to be credible and to have a sense of direction. This conclusion is consistent with recent concerns regarding ethical and legal lapses at companies such as Enron, Tyco, and Global Crossing.

A deep cynicism has settled over corporate America as many employees in a variety of businesses wonder how much, if at all, they can trust their top bosses.

The trigger event was the Enron scandal. But while more becomes known about the energy trader's rotten numbers, and the cheating and lying that apparently prevailed in its senior ranks, accounting problems and ethical breaches are surfacing at a growing list of other companies.

The trust quotient is especially low among employees at troubled firms such as Tyco and Global Crossing, who have lost jobs and retirement savings, and feel they are bearing the brunt of their bosses' mistakes.

"Whatever company I work for in the future, I'll never again trust at face value what top executives say," says a former vice president of marketing at Global Crossing.[17]

Gender and Leadership

The increase of women in the workforce has generated much interest in understanding the similarities and differences in female and male leaders. Three separate meta-analyses and a series of studies conducted by consultants across the country uncovered the following differences: (1) Men and women were seen as displaying more task and social leadership, respectively;[18] (2) women used a more democratic or participative style than men, and men used a more autocratic and direc-

Table 17–2   *A Scorecard of Male-Female Leadership Ratings Derived from 360-Degree Evaluations*

Skill*	Men	Women
Motivating others		√ √ √ √ √
Fostering communication		√ √ √ √**
Producing high-quality work		√ √ √ √ √
Strategic planning	√ √	√ √**
Listening to others		√ √ √ √ √
Analyzing issues	√ √	√ √**

*Each check mark denotes which group scored higher in the respective studies.
**In one study, women's and men's scores in these categories were statistically even.

SOURCE: R Sharpe, "As Leaders, Women Rule," *Business Week*, November 20, 2000, p. 75. The data came from Hagberg Consulting Group, Management Research Group, Lawrence A Pfaff Personnel Decisions International Inc., and Advanced Teamware Inc.

tive style than women;[19] (3) men and women were equally assertive,[20] and (4) women executives, when rated by their peers, managers, and direct reports, scored higher than their male counterparts on a variety of effectiveness criteria (see Table 17–2).[21]

In spite of these positive results, the same behavior by a male and female can be interpreted differently and lead to opposite consequences. Consider the case of Deborah Hopkins, former chief financial officer at Lucent Technologies:

Ms Hopkins, 46 years old and widely viewed as one of America's hottest female executives, had been at the maker of phone-industry equipment just over a year. . . . Ms Hopkins's management technique, which earned her the nickname "Hurricane Debby," fell flat at Lucent. There, she was known for unforgiving candor, in which she typically cut off colleagues in midsentence. . . . Being a woman didn't help, say people close to Ms Hopkins. Indeed, she was the fourth high-ranking female executive to leave Lucent, starting with Ms Fiorina [Carly Fiorina is CEO of Hewlett-Packard] in 1999. And while traits such as candor and abrasiveness can be considered good qualities in male chief executives in a tough turn-around situation, Ms Hopkins was criticized for her personality.[22]

Trait Theory in Perspective   We can no longer afford to ignore the implications of leadership traits. Traits play a central role in how we perceive leaders. Recalling the Chapter 7 discussion of social perception, it is important to determine the traits embodied in people's schemata (or mental pictures) for leaders. If those traits are inappropriate (i.e., foster discriminatory selection and invalid performance appraisals), they need to be corrected through training and development. Consider the stereotypes associated with who gets selected for corporate assignments overseas.

While women represent about half of the global workforce, surveys indicate they count for less than 12% of the expatriate population. Why? Because many male managers still believe women aren't interested in overseas jobs or won't be effective at them. The managers cite dual-career complications, gender prejudice in many countries, and the risk of sexual harassment. That's hogwash, according to researchers at Loyola University (Chicago). Their recent survey of 261 female expats and their supervisors concluded that

Table 17–3 *Leadership Traits Identified by Famous Organizational Leaders*

Colin Powell (former Chairman of the Joint Chiefs of Staff and Current Secretary of State)	Larry Bossidy (former CEO of Allied Signal)	Carly Fiorina (CEO of Hewlett-Packard Co.)	Jack Welch (former CEO of General Electric)
1. Ability to execute	1. Ability to execute	1. Self-confidence	1. Ability to execute
2. Visionary	2. Ability to grow professionally	2. Visionary	2. Ability to energize others
3. Proactive communicator	3. Multiple work experiences in various functional areas	3. Proactive communicator	3. The edge to make tough decisions
4. Flexible	4. A team orientation	4. Flexible	4. High energy
5. Challenges the status quo		5. A team orientation	
6. Ability to execute			

SOURCES: Derived from O Harai, *The Leadership Secrets of Colin Powell* (New York: McGraw-Hill, 2002); L Bossidy, "The Job No CEO Should Delegate," *Harvard Business Review,* March 2001, pp. 47–49; P-W Tam, "The Chief Does Double Duty: How H-P's Fiorina Manages to Run Global Corporation while Waging Proxy Fight," *The Wall Street Journal,* February 7, 2002, pp. B1, B4; and T A Stewart, "The Contest for Welch's Throne Begins: Who Will Run GE?" *Fortune,* January 11, 1999, p. 27.

women are just as interested as men in foreign assignments and just as effective once there. In fact, contends Linda Stroh, one of the researchers, the traits considered crucial for success overseas—knowing when to be passive, being a team player, soliciting a variety of perspectives—are more often associated with women's management styles than men's.[23]

Managers should be careful to avoid using gender-based stereotypes when making overseas assignments. Moreover, organizations may find it beneficial to consider selected leadership traits when choosing among candidates for leadership positions. Gender should not be used as one of these traits. Consider, for example, the leadership traits that Colin Powell, Larry Bossidy, Carly Fiorina, and Jack Welch believe effective leaders need to have in the 21st century (see Table 17–3). The table reveals both agreement and disagreement in preferred traits across these leaders.

Behavioral Styles Theory

This phase of leadership research began during World War II as part of an effort to develop better military leaders. It was an outgrowth of two events: the seeming inability of trait theory to explain leadership effectiveness and the human relations movement, an outgrowth of the Hawthorne Studies. The thrust of early behavioral leadership theory was to focus on leader behavior, instead of on personality traits. It was believed that leader behavior directly affected work group effectiveness. This led researchers to identify patterns of behavior (called leadership styles) that enabled leaders to effectively influence others.

The Ohio State Studies
Researchers at Ohio State University began by generating a list of behaviors exhibited by leaders. At one point, the list contained 1,800 statements that described nine categories of leader behavior. Ultimately, the Ohio State

Figure 17–1   *Four Leadership Styles Derived from the Ohio State Studies*

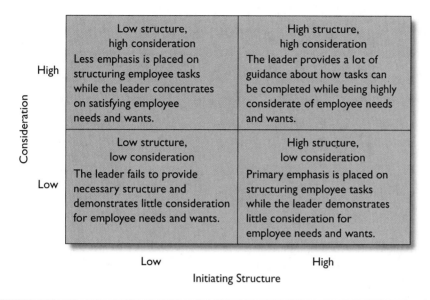

researchers concluded there were only two independent dimensions of leader behavior: consideration and initiating structure. **Consideration** involves leader behavior associated with creating mutual respect or trust and focuses on a concern for group members' needs and desires. **Initiating structure** is leader behavior that organizes and defines what group members should be doing to maximize output. These two dimensions of leader behavior were oriented at right angles to yield four behavioral styles of leadership (see Figure 17–1).

It initially was hypothesized that a high-structure, high-consideration style would be the one best style of leadership. Through the years, the effectiveness of the high-high style has been tested many times. Overall, results have been mixed. Researchers thus concluded that there is not one best style of leadership.[24] Rather, it is argued that effectiveness of a given leadership style depends on situational factors.

University of Michigan *Studies*

As in the Ohio State studies, this research sought to identify behavioral differences between effective and ineffective leaders. Researchers identified two different styles of leadership: one was employee centered, the other was job centered. These behavioral styles parallel the consideration and initiating-structure styles identified by the Ohio State group. In summarizing the results from these studies, one management expert concluded that effective leaders (1) tend to have supportive or employee-centered relationships with employees, (2) use group rather than individual methods of supervision, and (3) set high performance goals.[25]

Blake and Mouton's Managerial/Leadership Grid

Perhaps the most widely known behavioral styles model of leadership is the Managerial Grid. Behavioral scientists Robert Blake and Jane Srygley Mouton developed and trademarked the grid. They use it to demonstrate that there *is* one best style of leadership. Blake and Mouton's Managerial Grid (renamed the **Leadership Grid** in 1991) is a matrix formed by the

Consideration
Creating mutual respect and trust with followers.

Initiating structure
Organizing and defining what group members should be doing.

Leadership Grid
Represents four leadership styles found by crossing concern for production and concern for people.

Figure 17–2 *The Leadership Grid*

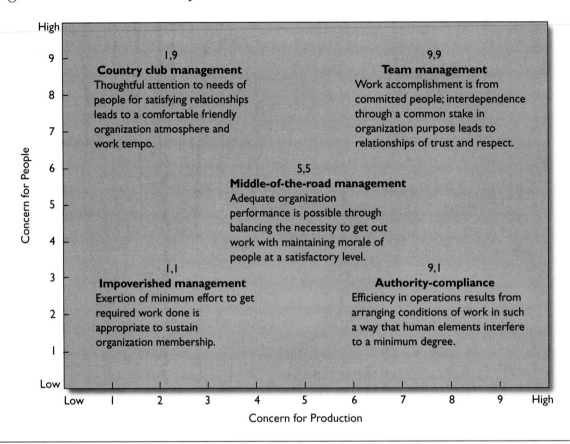

intersection of two dimensions of leader behavior (see Figure 17–2). On the horizontal axis is "concern for production." "Concern for people" is on the vertical axis.

Blake and Mouton point out that "the variables of the Managerial Grid are *attitudinal and conceptual,* with *behavior* descriptions derived from and connected with the thinking that lies behind action."[26] In other words, concern for production and concern for people involve attitudes and patterns of thinking, as well as specific behaviors. By scaling each axis of the grid from 1 to 9, Blake and Mouton were able to plot five leadership styles. Because it emphasizes teamwork and interdependence, the 9,9 style is considered by Blake and Mouton to be the best, regardless of the situation.

In support of the 9,9 style, Blake and Mouton cite the results of a study in which 100 experienced managers were asked to select the best way of handling 12 managerial situations. Between 72% and 90% of the managers selected the 9,9 style for each of the 12 situations.[27] Moreover, Blake and Mouton report, "The 9,9, orientation . . . leads to productivity, satisfaction, creativity, and health."[28] Critics point out that Blake and Mouton's research may be self-serving. At issue is the grid's extensive use as a training and consulting tool for diagnosing and correcting organizational problems.

Behavioral /tyles Theory in Perspective

By emphasizing leader *behavior*, something that is learned, the behavioral style approach makes it clear that leaders are made, not born. This is the opposite of the trait theorists' traditional assumption. Given what we know about behavior shaping and model-based training, leader *behaviors* can be systematically improved and developed. Consider, for example, how the U.S. Postal Service is striving to grow and develop leadership talent within the organization.

> The United States Postal Service's Advanced Leadership Program was conceived and introduced in 1998. Its aim: "to develop a cadre of leaders who are prepared to take over leadership positions within the Postal Service because of the significant number of leaders that will leave over the next few years," explains Olaf Jaehnigen, ALP program manager.
>
> The concept for ALP came out of a competency model. The model, based on information gathered by Postal Service executives and officers, was built by the service's employee development staff in conjunction with an external firm specializing in competency modeling. The competencies, 31 in all, are part cognitive and part behavioral. "The Postal Service has said that these competencies are the things that we really want our leaders to have," says Jaehnigen. "And if we see candidates that are strong in all of these competencies we can rest, relatively assured, that they will perform well."
>
> The model became the building blocks for the ALP curriculum, delivered via four weeks of residential study over a nine-month period and a 15-semester academic component. Weeks two, three, and four comprise business foundation, business decisions, and business leadership, respectively. "We ground them in the principles of finance, strategy, and decision-making using generic models and simulations," says Dot Fisher, one of the program's three moderators. "Then we use what they learn to compare the Postal Service with its major competitors."[29]

Behavioral styles research also revealed that there is no one best style of leadership. The effectiveness of a particular leadership style depends on the situation at hand. For instance, employees prefer structure over consideration when faced with role ambiguity.[30] Finally, research also reveals that it is important to consider the difference between how frequently and how effectively managers exhibit various leader behaviors. For example, a manager might ineffectively display a lot of considerate leader behaviors. Such a style is likely to frustrate employees and possibly result in lowered job satisfaction and performance. Because the frequency of exhibiting leadership behaviors is secondary in importance to effectiveness, managers are encouraged to concentrate on improving the effective execution of their leader behaviors.[31] At this time we would like you to complete the OB Exercise on page 604.

The exercise gives you the opportunity to test the behavioral styles theory by assessing your teacher's leadership style and your associated class satisfaction and role clarity. Are you satisfied with this class? If yes, the behavioral styles approach is supported if your teacher displayed both high consideration and initiating structure. In contrast, the behavioral style approach is not supported if you are satisfied with this class and your teacher exhibits something other than the standard high-high style. Do your results support the proposition that there is one best style of leadership? Are your results consistent with past research that showed leadership behavior depends on the situation at hand? The answer is yes if you prefer initiating structure over consideration when faced with high role ambiguity. The answer also is yes if you prefer consideration over structure when role ambiguity is low. We now turn our attention to discussing alternative situational theories of leadership.

OB Exercise Assessing Teacher Leadership Style, Class Satisfaction, and Student Role Clarity

Instructions

A team of researchers converted a set of leadership measures for application in the classroom. For each of the items shown here, use the following rating scale to circle the answer that best represents your feelings. Next, use the scoring key to compute scores for your teacher's leadership style and your class satisfaction and role clarity.

1 = Strongly disagree
2 = Disagree
3 = Neither agree nor disagree
4 = Agree
5 = Strongly agree

1. My instructor behaves in a manner which is thoughtful of my personal needs.   1 — 2 — 3 — 4 — 5

2. My instructor maintains a friendly working relationship with me.   1 — 2 — 3 — 4 — 5

3. My instructor looks out for my personal welfare.   1 — 2 — 3 — 4 — 5

4. My instructor gives clear explanations of what is expected of me.   1 — 2 — 3 — 4 — 5

5. My instructor tells me the performance goals for the class.   1 — 2 — 3 — 4 — 5

6. My instructor explains the level of performance that is expected of me.   1 — 2 — 3 — 4 — 5

7. I am satisfied with the variety of class assignments.   1 — 2 — 3 — 4 — 5

8. I am satisfied with the way my instructor handles the students.   1 — 2 — 3 — 4 — 5

9. I am satisfied with the spirit of cooperation among my fellow students.   1 — 2 — 3 — 4 — 5

10. I know exactly what my responsibilities are.   1 — 2 — 3 — 4 — 5

11. I am given clear explanations of what has to be done.   1 — 2 — 3 — 4 — 5

Scoring Key

Teacher consideration (1, 2, 3)   _____

Teacher initiating structure (4, 5, 6) _____

Class satisfaction (7, 8, 9) _____

Role clarity (10, 11)   _____

Arbitrary Norms

Low consideration = 3–8

High consideration = 9–15

Low structure = 3–8

High structure = 9–15

Low satisfaction = 3–8

High satisfaction = 9–15

Low role clarity = 2–5

High role clarity = 6–10

SOURCE: The survey was adapted from A J Kinicki and C A Schriesheim, "Teachers as Leaders: A Moderator Variable Approach," *Journal of Educational Psychology*, 1978, pp. 928–35.

*S*ituational Theories

Situational leadership theories grew out of an attempt to explain the inconsistent findings about traits and styles. **Situational theories** propose that the effectiveness of a particular style of leader behavior depends on the situation. As situations change, different styles become appropriate. This directly challenges the idea of one best style of leadership. Let us closely examine three alternative situational theories of leadership that reject the notion of one best leadership style.

*S*ituational
theories

Propose that leader
styles should match
the situation at hand.

Fiedler's Contingency Model

Fred Fiedler, an OB scholar, developed a situational model of leadership. It is the oldest and one of the most widely known models of situational leadership. Fiedler's model is based on the following assumption:

> The performance of a leader depends on two interrelated factors: (1) the degree to which the situation gives the leader control and influence—that is, the likelihood that [the leader] can successfully accomplish the job; and (2) the leader's basic motivation—that is, whether [the leader's] self-esteem depends primarily on accomplishing the task or on having close supportive relations with others.[32]

With respect to a leader's basic motivation, Fiedler believes that leaders are either task motivated or relationship motivated. These basic motivations are similar to initiating structure/concern for production and consideration/concern for people. Consider the basic leadership motivation possessed by Oracle Corp. CEO Lawrence Ellison.

Oracle Corp. CEO Lawrence J Ellison isn't afraid to go it alone, on land or at sea. Last month, because of what he considered "prima donna" behavior, Ellison demoted one of four veteran skippers of his elite yachts, which will compete for the America's Cup this fall in New Zealand. It was the second such move in less than a year. Ellison, a respected skipper himself, says he'll pick up the slack at the helm. . . .

Three years ago, rather than playing his normal big-think role, Ellison gradually took

Oracle Corp.'s CEO Lawrence J. Ellison is a task-motivated leader. His desire to improve Oracle's financial performance has led to the departure of several key executives of the company. Because Ellison is task and not relationship-motivated, what, if any, future problems might arise at Oracle?

over daily management and transformed the company's internal operations using Internet technology. That ranged from centralizing data-processing operations to automating sales. Some results were positive: Oracle's operating margins doubled in two years.

In other areas, Ellison has been his own enemy. His insistence on running operations led to the departure of a handful of key executives, starting with former President Raymond J Lane some 21 months ago. Lane had helped lead the company to nine straight years of healthy growth. Next to go was Gary L Bloom, who was being groomed for a top slot but left to become CEO of Veritas Software Corp. after Ellison made it clear that he would continue his tight control of Oracle.[33]

Ellison clearly has used a task motivation style in attempting to help Oracle improve its financial performance.

Fiedler's theory also is based on the premise that leaders have one dominant leadership style that is resistant to change. He suggests that leaders must learn to manipulate or influence the leadership situation in order to create a match between their leadership style and the amount of control within the situation at hand. After discussing the components of situational control and the leadership matching process, we review relevant research and managerial implications.[34]

Situational Control

Situational control refers to the amount of control and influence the leader has in her or his immediate work environment. Situational control ranges from high to low. High control implies that the leader's decisions will produce predictable results because the leader has the ability to influence work outcomes. Low control implies that the leader's decisions may not influence work outcomes because the leader has very little influence. There are three dimensions of situational control: leader–member relations, task structure, and position power. These dimensions vary independently, forming eight combinations of situational control (see Figure 17–3).

The three dimensions of situational control are defined as follows:

- **Leader–member relations** reflect the extent to which the leader has the support, loyalty, and trust of the work group. This dimension is the most important component of situational control. Good leader–member relations suggest that the leader can depend on the group, thus ensuring that the work group will try to meet the leader's goals and objectives.

- **Task structure** is concerned with the amount of structure contained within tasks performed by the work group. For example, a managerial job contains less structure than that of a bank teller. Because structured tasks have guidelines for how the job should be completed, the leader has more control and influence over employees performing such tasks. This dimension is the second most important component of situational control.

- **Position power** refers to the degree to which the leader has formal power to reward, punish, or otherwise obtain compliance from employees.[35]

Linking Leadership Motivation and Situational Control

Fiedler's complete contingency model is presented in Figure 17–3. The last row under the Situational Control column shows that there are eight different leadership situations. Each situation represents a unique combination of leader–member relations, task structure, and position power. Situations I, II, and III represent high control situations.

Figure 17–3   *Representation of Fiedler's Contingency Model*

Situational Control	High Control Situations			Moderate Control Situations			Low Control Situations	
Leader-member relations	Good	Good	Good	Good	Poor	Poor	Poor	Poor
Task structure	High	High	Low	Low	High	High	Low	Low
Position power	Strong	Weak	Strong	Weak	Strong	Weak	Strong	Weak
Situation	I	II	III	IV	V	VI	VII	VIII
Optimal Leadership Style		Task-Motivated Leadership			Relationship-Motivated Leadership			Task-Motivated Leadership

SOURCE: Adapted from F E Fiedler, "Situational Control and a Dynamic Theory of Leadership," in *Managerial Control and Organizational Democracy,* eds B King, S Streufert, and F E Fiedler (New York: John Wiley & Sons, 1978), p. 114.

Figure 17–3 shows that task-motivated leaders are hypothesized to be most effective in situations of high control. Under conditions of moderate control (situations IV, V, and VI), relationship-motivated leaders are expected to be more effective. Finally, the results orientation of task-motivated leaders is predicted to be more effective under conditions of low control (situations VII and VIII).

Research and Managerial Implications   The overall accuracy of Fiedler's contingency model was tested through a meta-analysis of 35 studies containing 137 leader style–performance relations. According to the researchers' findings, (1) the contingency theory was correctly induced from studies on which it was based; (2) for laboratory studies testing the model, the theory was supported for all leadership situations except situation II; and (3) for field studies testing the model, three of the eight situations (IV, V, and VII) produced completely supportive results, and partial support was obtained for situations I, II, III, VI, and VIII. A more recent meta-analysis of data obtained from 1,282 groups also provided mixed support for the contingency model.[36] These findings suggest that Fiedler's model needs theoretical refinement.[37]

The major contribution of Fiedler's model is that it prompted others to examine the contingency nature of leadership. This research, in turn, reinforced the notion that there is no one best style of leadership. Leaders are advised to alter their task and relationship orientation to fit the demands of the situation at hand.

Path–Goal Theory

Path–goal theory was originally proposed by Robert House in the 1970s.[38] It was based on the expectancy theory of motivation discussed in Chapter 9. Recall that expectancy theory is based on the idea that motivation to exert effort increases as one's effort→performance→outcome expectations improve. Leader behaviors thus are expected to be acceptable when employees view them as a source of satisfaction or as paving the way to future satisfaction. In addition, leader behavior is predicted to be motivational to the extent it (1) reduces roadblocks that interfere with goal accomplishment, (2) provides the guidance and support needed by employees, and (3) ties meaningful rewards to goal accomplishment.

House proposed a model that describes how leadership effectiveness is influenced by the interaction between four leadership styles (directive, supportive, participative, and achievement-oriented) and a variety of contingency factors. **Contingency factors** are situational variables that cause one style of leadership to be more effective than another. Path–goal theory has two groups of contingency variables. They are employee characteristics and environmental factors. Five important employee characteristics are locus of control, task ability, need for achievement, experience, and need for clarity. Two relevant environmental factors are task structure (independent versus interdependent tasks) and work group dynamics. In order to gain a better understanding of how these contingency factors influence leadership effectiveness, we illustratively consider locus of control (see Chapter 5), task ability and experience, and task structure.

Employees with an internal locus control are more likely to prefer participative or achievement-oriented leadership because they believe they have control over the work environment. Such individuals are unlikely to be satisfied with directive leader behaviors that exert additional control over their activities. In contrast, employees with an external locus tend to view the environment as uncontrollable, thereby preferring the structure provided by supportive or directive leadership. An employee with high task ability and experience is less apt to need additional direction and thus would respond negatively to directive leadership. This person is more likely to be motivated and satisfied by participative and achievement-oriented leadership. Oppositely, an inexperienced employee would find achievement-oriented leadership overwhelming as he or she confronts challenges associated with learning a new job. Supportive and directive leadership would be helpful in this situation. Finally, directive and supportive leadership should help employees experiencing role ambiguity. However, directive leadership is likely to frustrate employees working on routine and simple tasks. Supportive leadership is most useful in this context.

There have been about 50 studies testing various predictions derived from House's original model. Results have been mixed, with some studies supporting the theory and others not.[39] House thus proposed a new version of path–goal theory in 1996 based on these results and the accumulation of new knowledge about OB.

A Reformulated Theory   The revised theory is presented in Figure 17–4.[40] There are three key changes in the new theory. First, House now believes that leadership is more complex and involves a greater variety of leader behavior. He thus identified eight categories of leadership styles or behavior (see Table 17–4). The need for an expanded list of leader behaviors is supported by current research and descriptions of business leaders.[41] Consider the different leader behaviors exhibited by Dieter Zetsche. Zetsche, a German executive, was appointed CEO of the Chrysler Group shortly after Daimler and Chrysler merged into DaimlerChrysler.

Contingency factors
Variables that influence the appropriateness of a leadership style.

Figure 17–4   *A General Representation of House's Revised Path–Goal Theory*

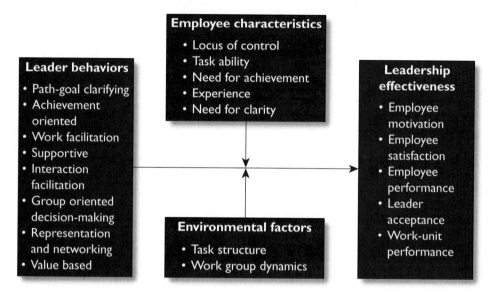

Employee characteristics

- Locus of control
- Task ability
- Need for achievement
- Experience
- Need for clarity

Leader behaviors

- Path-goal clarifying
- Achievement oriented
- Work facilitation
- Supportive
- Interaction facilitation
- Group oriented decision-making
- Representation and networking
- Value based

Environmental factors

- Task structure
- Work group dynamics

Leadership effectiveness

- Employee motivation
- Employee satisfaction
- Employee performance
- Leader acceptance
- Work-unit performance

Now, Zetsche, 48, has to turn Chrysler into something it hasn't been for a while: a low-cost producer. "I'm pretty confident we'll get our act together," says Zetsche. "But it's taking longer than I thought when I first came in." . . .

Along the way, the German engineer has confounded his critics in Detroit, who included almost everybody he works with, by turning out to be a decent, even likable fellow. He has spread a lot of misery, but he has done it with such sensitivity—and often in person—that potential antagonists usually decide to cooperate instead. After so many layoffs, no one expected Zetsche to address a United Auto Workers convention in Las Vegas. . . . Indeed, few CEOs have ever ventured to speak at the union's gatherings. Zetsche not only gave a speech but also mingled with the delegates for five hours. "The union and the company are working very well together," says UAW Vice President Nate Gooden, who handles relations with Chrysler. . . .

As it turned out, Zetsche had just the combination of humility and warmth to ease tensions among Chrysler's demoralized staff. He eats in the cafeteria, interrupts plant tours to talk with workers, and even promised to shave his head (he's already half-bald) if the new Dodge Ram again topped the J D Power & Associates quality survey. His town hall meetings are so popular that plant officials resort to a lottery to choose participants.

Zetsche's decisive leadership is welcome relief for an outfit that drifted aimlessly after the merger. "There's not an employee around here who didn't know this company was in trouble," says James D Donlon III, senior vice president and controller. "They just needed somebody to get up and tell it like it is." That's true for those outside Chrysler as well. Three weeks into the job, Zetsche demanded that suppliers swallow an immediate 5% price cut. That alone should save Chrysler $2 billion this year. . . .

In terms of product development, Zetsche wants Chrysler to balance style with thrift—an approach he calls "disciplined pizzazz." He is overhauling the vehicle-development process to put more focus on the earliest stages. By pulling together teams from all areas

Table 17–4   *Categories of Leader Behavior within the Revised Path–Goal Theory*

Category of Leader Behavior	Description of Leader Behaviors
Path–goal clarifying behaviors	Clarifying employees' performance goals; providing guidance on how employees can complete tasks; clarifying performance standards and expectations; use of positive and negative rewards contingent on performance
Achievement-oriented behaviors	Setting challenging goals; emphasizing excellence; demonstrating confidence in employees' abilities
Work facilitation behaviors	Planning, scheduling, organizing, and coordinating work; providing mentoring, coaching, counseling, and feedback to assist employees in developing their skills; eliminating roadblocks; providing resources; empowering employees to take actions and make decisions
Supportive behaviors	Showing concern for the well-being and needs of employees; being friendly and approachable; treating employees as equals
Interaction facilitation behaviors	Resolving disputes; facilitating communication; encouraging the sharing of minority opinions; emphasizing collaboration and teamwork; encouraging close relationships among employees
Group-oriented decision-making behaviors	Posing problems rather than solutions to the work group; encouraging group members to participate in decision making; providing necessary information to the group for analysis; involving knowledgeable employees in decision making
Representation and networking behaviors	Presenting the work group in a positive light to others; maintaining positive relationships with influential others; participating in organizationwide social functions and ceremonies; doing unconditional favors for others
Value-based behaviors	Establishing a vision, displaying passion for it, and supporting its accomplishment; demonstrating self-confidence; communicating high performance expectations and confidence in others' abilities to meet their goals; giving frequent positive feedback

SOURCE: Descriptions were adapted from R J House, "Path–Goal Theory of Leadership: Lessons, Legacy, and a Reformulated Theory," *Leadership Quarterly,* 1996, pp. 323–52.

of the company—design, engineering, marketing, manufacturing, and purchasing—Zetsche hopes to reduce waste and resolve nagging quality problems without diminishing Chrysler's creative instincts.[42]

Dieter Zetsche exhibited path–goal clarifying behaviors, achievement-oriented behaviors, supportive behaviors, interaction facilitation behaviors, group-oriented decision-making behaviors, and representation and networking behaviors.

The second key change involves the role of intrinsic motivation (discussed in Chapter 8) and empowerment (discussed in Chapter 16) in influencing leadership effectiveness. House places much more emphasis on the need for leaders to foster intrinsic motivation through empowerment. The current list of leader behaviors shown in Table 17–4, for example, contains many of the recommendations derived from the building blocks for intrinsic motivation presented in Figure 8–7. Shared leadership represents the final change in the revised theory. That is, path–goal theory is based on the premise that an employee does not have to be a supervisor or manager to engage in leader behavior. Rather, House believes that leadership is shared among all employees within an organization.

Research and Managerial Implications   There are not enough direct tests of House's revised path–goal theory using appropriate research methods and statistical procedures to draw overall conclusions. Research on charismatic leadership, however, which is discussed in the next section, is supportive of the revised model.[43] Future research is clearly needed to assess the accuracy of this model. That said, there still are two important managerial implications. First, effective leaders possess and use more than one style of leadership. Managers are encouraged to familiarize themselves with the different categories of leader behavior outlined in path–goal theory and to try new behaviors when the situation calls for them. Second, a small set of employee characteristics (i.e., ability, experience, and need for independence) and environmental factors (task characteristics of autonomy, variety, and significance) are relevant contingency factors.[44] Managers are advised to modify their leadership style to fit these various employee and task characteristics.

Hersey and Blanchard's Situational Leadership Theory

Situational leadership theory (SLT) was developed by management writers Paul Hersey and Kenneth Blanchard.[45] According to the theory, effective leader behavior depends on the readiness level of a leader's followers. **Readiness** is defined as the extent to which a follower possesses the ability and willingness to complete a task. Willingness is a combination of confidence, commitment, and motivation.

Readiness

Follower's ability and willingness to complete a task.

The SLT model is summarized in Figure 17–5. The appropriate leadership style is found by cross referencing follower readiness, which varies from low to high, with one of four leadership styles. The four leadership styles represent combinations of task- and relationship-oriented leader behaviors (S_1 to S_4). Leaders are encouraged to use a "telling style" for followers with low readiness. This style combines high task-oriented leader behaviors, such as providing instructions, with low relationship-oriented behaviors, such as close supervision (see Figure 17–5). As follower readiness increases, leaders are advised to gradually move from a telling, to a selling, to a participating, and, ultimately, to a delegating style. In the most recent description of this model, the four leadership styles depicted in Figure 17–5 are referred to as telling or directing (S_1), persuading or coaching (S_2), participating or supporting (S_3), and delegating (S_4).[46]

Although SLT is widely used as a training tool, it is not strongly supported by scientific research. For instance, leadership effectiveness was not attributable to the predicted interaction between follower readiness and leadership style in a study of 459 salespeople.[47] Moreover, a study of 303 teachers indicated that SLT was accurate only for employees with low readiness. This finding is consistent with a survey of 57 chief nurse executives in California. These executives did not delegate in accordance with SLT.[48] Finally, researchers have concluded that the self-assessment instrument used to measure leadership style and follower readiness is inaccurate and should be used with caution.[49] In summary, managers should exercise discretion when using prescriptions from SLT.

Figure 17–5 *Situational Leadership Model*

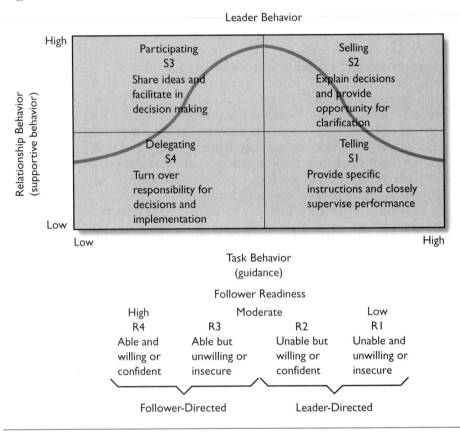

From Transactional to Charismatic Leadership

New perspectives of leadership theory have emerged in the past 15 years, variously referred to as "charismatic," "heroic," "transformational," or "visionary" leadership.[50] These competing but related perspectives have created confusion among researchers and practicing managers. Fortunately, Robert House and Boas Shamir have given us a practical, integrated theory. It is referred to as *charismatic leadership.*

This section begins by highlighting the differences between transactional and charismatic leadership. We then discuss a model of the charismatic leadership process and its research and management implications.

International OB

The CEO of Shire Pharmaceuticals Effectively Uses Transactional Leadership

"It takes an enormous amount of energy and time to filter out what isn't critical and focus on essentials," says Rolf Stahel, CEO of Shire Pharmaceuticals, the UK company that developed the most widely prescribed drugs for Attention Deficit Disorder and HIV/AIDS.

He and his top executives pore over sales, inventory, marketing and other data on a daily, weekly and monthly basis to determine whether Shire is meeting its 18-month and longer-range growth forecasts. "If you have a good planning system, you can find out quickly when things start to go wrong," he says.

Mr Stahel uses a traffic-light system to differentiate between issues that require his immediate attention from those that need little oversight. "Areas that aren't going well get a red light—and action now," he says.

An advocate of managing by walking around, Mr Stahel travels frequently to Shire's operations in other countries, and every six months joins his sales managers to make customer calls on doctors. He welcomes suggestions from customers as well as his professional advisers, including Shire's outside auditors. "I'm disappointed if at the end of an audit they don't tell me things that can be improved," he says.

SOURCE: Excerpted from C Hymowitz, "In the Lead: How CEOs Can Keep Informed Even as Work Stretches across the Globe," *The Wall Street Journal*, February 12, 2002, p. B1.

What Is the Difference between Transactional and Charismatic Leadership?

Most of the models and theories previously discussed in this chapter represent transactional leadership. **Transactional leadership** focuses on the interpersonal transactions between managers and employees. Leaders are seen as engaging in behaviors that maintain a quality interaction between themselves and followers. The two underlying characteristics of transactional leadership are that (1) leaders use contingent rewards to motivate employees and (2) leaders exert corrective action only when subordinates fail to obtain performance goals. Rolf Stahel, CEO of Shire Pharmaceuticals, effectively uses transactional leadership to help organize and run the company (see the International OB above).

In contrast, **charismatic leadership** emphasizes "symbolic leader behavior, visionary and inspirational messages, nonverbal communication, appeal to ideological values, intellectual stimulation of followers by the leader, display of confidence in self and followers, and leader expectations for follower self-sacrifice and for performance beyond the call of duty."[51] Charismatic leadership can produce significant organizational change and results because it "transforms" employees to pursue organizational goals in lieu of self-interests. Charismatic leadership was instrumental for Mathew Szulik, CEO of Red Hat, a Linux operating system provider with 750 employees, as he pursued global expansion of the company's products and services.

> For CEO Mathew Szulik, employees of Red Hat feed off the company's rebel reputation by believing in a unified cause. "Our people believe they are changing the world of computing and reshaping its culture," he says. "And our challenge was and always will be to find people who are willing to work 24 hours a day, seven days a week, not so they can drive a Porsche or BMW, but because they feel they are fundamentally redefining their industry."[52]

Let us now examine how charismatic leadership transforms followers.

Transactional leadership
Focuses on interpersonal interactions between managers and employees.

Charismatic leadership
Transforms employees to pursue organizational goals over self-interests.

How Does Charismatic Leadership Transform Followers?

Charismatic leaders transform followers by creating changes in their goals, values, needs, beliefs, and aspirations. They accomplish this transformation by appealing to followers' self-concepts—namely, their values and personal identity. Figure 17–6 presents a model of how charismatic leadership accomplishes this transformation process.

Figure 17–6 shows that organizational culture is a key precursor of charismatic leadership. You may recall from our discussion of organizational culture in Chapter 3 that long-term financial performance was highest for organizations with an adaptive culture. Organizations with adaptive cultures anticipate and adapt to environmental changes and focus on leadership that emphasizes the importance of service to customers, stockholders, and employees. This type of management orientation involves the use of charismatic leadership.

Charismatic leaders first engage in three key sets of leader behavior. If done effectively, these behaviors positively affect individual followers and their work groups. These positive effects, in turn, influence a variety of outcomes. Before discussing the model of charismatic leadership in more detail, it is important to note two general conclusions about charismatic leadership.[53] First, the two-headed arrow between organizational culture and leader behavior in Figure 17–6 reveals that individuals with

Figure 17–6   *A Charismatic Model of Leadership*

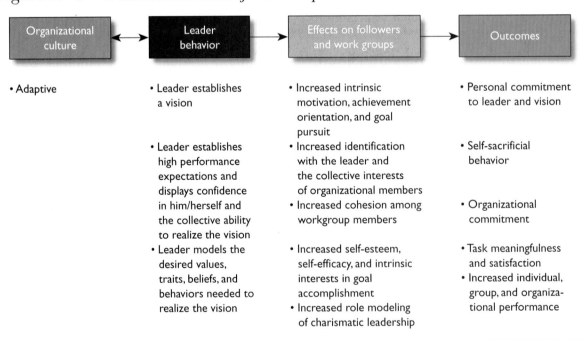

SOURCES: Based in part on D A Waldman and F J Yammarino, "CEO Charismatic Leadership: Levels-of-Management and Levels-of-Analysis Effects," *Academy of Management Review,* April 1999, pp. 266–85; and B Shamir, R J House, and M B Arthur, "The Motivational Effects of Charismatic Leadership: A Self-Concept Based Theory," *Organization Science,* November 1993, pp. 577–94.

charismatic behavioral tendencies are able to influence culture. This implies that charismatic leadership reinforces the core values of an adaptive culture and helps to change dysfunctional aspects of an organization's culture that develop over time. Second, charismatic leadership has effects on multiple levels within an organization. For example, Figure 17–6 shows that charismatic leadership can positively influence individual outcomes (e.g., motivation), group outcomes (e.g., group cohesion), and organizational outcomes (e.g., financial performance). You can see that the potential for positive benefits from charismatic leadership is quite widespread.

Charismatic Leader Behavior   The first set of charismatic leader behaviors involves establishing a common vision of the future. A vision is "a realistic, credible, attractive future for your organization."[54] According to Burt Nanus, a leadership expert, the "right" vision unleashes human potential because it serves as a beacon of hope and common purpose. It does this by attracting commitment, energizing workers, creating meaning in employees' lives, establishing a standard of excellence, promoting high ideals, and bridging the gap between an organization's present problems and its future goals and aspirations.[55] In contrast, the "wrong" vision can be very damaging to an organization.

Consider what happened to Coastal Physician Group Inc. as it pursued the vision of its founder Dr Steven Scott. Dr Scott's vision was to create networks of physician practices and then sell the network services to health care providers:

> Today, his dream of a physician-led revolution has turned into a nightmare. Major clients and top executives have fled. Coastal is abandoning many of its businesses, selling clinics, and trying to resuscitate its original activity, staffing hospitals. . . .
>
> Dr Scott himself, a 48-year-old workaholic obstetrician turned entrepreneur, sits in his fenced-in two-story brick home here, cooling his heels and sipping iced tea. In May, his handpicked board ousted him as chief executive officer and put him on "sabbatical." The CEO who made a practice of calling subordinates at home at night is now barred, by motion of the board, from speaking to Coastal's employees. He also can't enter its offices, even though he owns the building. . . .
>
> Current management describes him as an arrogant boss who ruined Coastal through a series of missteps and can't bear to let go.[56]

As you can see, Coastal Physician Group's vision produced disastrous results. This highlights the fact that charismatic leaders do more than simply establish a vision. They also must gain input from others in developing an effective implementation plan.[57]

The second set of leader behaviors involves two key components:

1. Charismatic leaders set high performance expectations and standards because they know challenging, attainable goals lead to greater productivity.

2. Charismatic leaders need to publicly express confidence in the followers' ability to meet high performance expectations. This is essential because employees are more likely to pursue difficult goals when they believe they can accomplish what is being asked of them.

The third and final set of leader behaviors involves being a role model. Through their actions, charismatic leaders model the desired values, traits, beliefs, and behaviors needed to realize the vision.

Motivational Mechanisms Underlying the Positive Effects of Charismatic Leadership

Charismatic leadership positively affects employee motivation (see Figure 17–6). One way in which this occurs is by increasing the intrinsic value of an employee's effort and goals. Leaders do this by emphasizing the symbolic value of effort; that is, charismatic leaders convey the message that effort reflects important organizational values and collective interests. Followers come to learn that their level of effort represents a moral statement. For example, high effort represents commitment to the organization's vision and values, whereas low effort reflects a lack of commitment.

Charismatic leadership increases employees' effort → performance expectancies by positively contributing to followers' self-esteem and self-efficacy. Leaders also increase the intrinsic value of goal accomplishment by explaining the organization's vision and goals in terms of the personal values they represent. This helps employees to personally connect with the organization's vision. Charismatic leaders further increase the meaningfulness of actions aimed toward goal accomplishment by showing how goals move the organization toward its positive vision, which then gives followers a sense of growth and development, both of which are important contributors to a positive self-concept.

Research and Managerial Implications

The charismatic model of leadership presented in Figure 17–6 has been supported by research. Studies have shown that charismatic leadership was positively related to followers' self-concept, identification with and trust in the leader, positive self-sacrifice, identification with the work group, and with the work group's motivation.[58] A meta-analysis of 54 studies further indicated that charismatic leaders were viewed as more effective leaders by both supervisors and followers and had followers who exerted more effort and reported higher levels of job satisfaction than noncharismatic leaders.[59] Other studies revealed that charismatic leadership was positively associated with employees' safety consciousness, individual performance, and satisfaction with the leader.[60] At the organizational level, a meta-analysis demonstrated that charismatic leadership was positively correlated with organizational measures of effectiveness.[61] Finally, a study of 31 presidents of the United States indicated that charisma significantly predicted presidential performance.[62]

These results underscore five important managerial implications. First, the best leaders are not just charismatic, they are both transactional and charismatic. Leaders should attempt these two types of leadership while avoiding a laissez-faire or wait-and-see style. Laissez-faire leadership is the most ineffective leadership style.

Second, charismatic leadership is not applicable in all organizational situations. According to a team of experts, charismatic leadership is most likely to be effective when

1. The situation offers opportunities for "moral" involvement.

2. Performance goals cannot be easily established and measured.

3. Extrinsic rewards cannot be clearly linked to individual performance.

4. There are few situational cues or constraints to guide behavior.

5. Exceptional effort, behavior, sacrifices, and performance are required of both leaders and followers.[63]

Third, although it is difficult to enhance an individual's charisma, evidence suggests that employees at any level in an organization can be trained to be more transactional and charismatic.[64] Ford Motor Company, for example, is using its Leadership Development Center to roll out a large-scale leadership development program aimed at creating transformational leaders.[65] Fourth, charismatic leaders can be ethical or unethical. Whereas ethical charismatic leaders enable employees to enhance their self-concepts, unethical ones select or produce obedient, dependent, compliant, and dissatisfied followers. Top management can create and maintain ethical charismatic leadership by

1. Creating and enforcing a clearly stated code of ethics.
2. Recruiting, selecting, and promoting people with high morals and standards.
3. Developing performance expectations around the treatment of employees—these expectations can then be assessed in the performance appraisal process.
4. Training employees to value diversity.
5. Identifying, rewarding, and publicly praising employees who exemplify high moral conduct.[66]

Finally, a charismatic leader's enthusiasm can lead to employment promises that cannot be met. Consider the experience of Mary Shea.

> Mary Shea, an Oakland, California, lawyer specializing in employment litigation, including options litigation, says that charismatic leaders are not uncommon in the Internet world. She says that in the Internet economy there is a faction of "overzealous companies" and "true believers who made employment offers they couldn't back up." The result was that many employees "trusted these often very charismatic leaders" whose zeal outstripped—and even supplanted—their business acumen. Shea speculates that in the three California counties that form the heart of Silicon Valley and the Internet economy—Santa Clara, San Francisco, and San Mateo—there are at least 100 options-related lawsuits pending, and that more are on the way.[67]

Organizations need to create a check-and-balance system that precludes charismatic leaders from making unrealistic or unethical employment contracts.

Additional Perspectives on Leadership

This section examines three additional approaches to leadership: leader–member exchange theory, substitutes for leadership, and servant-leadership. We spend more time discussing leader–member exchange theory and substitutes for leadership because they have been more thoroughly investigated.

The Leader–Member Exchange (LMX) Model of Leadership

The leader–member exchange model of leadership revolves around the development of dyadic relationships between managers and their direct reports. This model is quite different from those previously discussed in that it focuses on the quality of relationships between managers and subordinates as opposed to the behaviors or traits of either

Figure 17–7   *A Role-Making Model of Leadership*

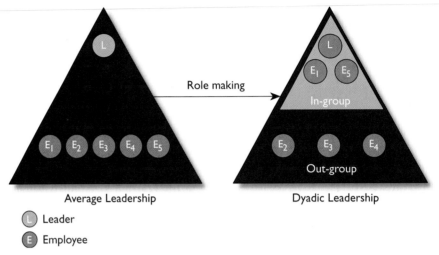

SOURCE: Adapted from F Dansereau Jr, G Graen, and W J Haga, "A Vertical Dyad Linkage Approach to Leadership within Formal Organizations," *Organizational Behavior and Human Performance*, February 1975, p. 72.

leaders or followers. It also is different in that it does not assume that leader behavior is characterized by a stable or average leadership style as does the Leadership Grid and Fiedler's contingency theory. In other words, these models assume a leader treats all subordinates in about the same way. This traditional approach to leadership is shown in the left side of Figure 17–7. In this case, the leader (designated by the circled L) is thought to exhibit a similar pattern of behavior toward all employees (E_1 to E_5). In contrast, the LMX model is based on the assumption that leaders develop unique one-to-one relationships with each of the people reporting to them. Behavioral scientists call this sort of relationship a *vertical dyad*. The forming of vertical dyads is said to be a naturally occurring process, resulting from the leader's attempt to delegate and assign work roles. As a result of this process, two distinct types of leader–member exchange relationships are expected to evolve.[68]

In-group exchange

A partnership characterized by mutual trust, respect, and liking.

One type of leader–member exchange is called the **in-group exchange.** In this relationship, leaders and followers develop a partnership characterized by reciprocal influence, mutual trust, respect and liking, and a sense of common fates. Figure 17–7 shows that E_1 and E_5 are members of the leader's in-group. In the second type of exchange, referred to as an **out-group exchange,** leaders are characterized as overseers who fail to create a sense of mutual trust, respect, or common fate.[69] E_2, E_3, and E_4 are members of the out-group on the right side of Figure 17–7.

Out-group exchange

A partnership characterized by a lack of mutual trust, respect, and liking.

Research Findings   If the leader–member exchange model is correct, there should be a significant relationship between the type of leader–member exchange and job-related outcomes. Research supports this prediction. For example, a positive leader–member exchange was positively associated with job satisfaction, job performance, goal commitment, organizational citizenship behavior, and satisfaction with leadership.[70] The type of leader–member exchange also was found to predict not only turnover among nurses and computer analysts but also career outcomes, such as promotability, salary level, and receipt of bonuses over a seven-year period.[71] Finally, studies also have identified a variety of variables that influence the quality of an LMX. For example, LMX was related to personality similarity and demographic similarity.[72] Further, the quality of an LMX was positively related to the level of trust between a manager and his or her direct reports, the manager's use of positive contingent rewards, and the amount of effort the dyad partners put into the relationship.[73]

Managerial Implications   There are four managerial implications associated with the LMX model of leadership. First, relationship building plays a key role in leadership and OB. This implies that it is important for organizations to design human resource systems and activities that proactively promote relationship building.[74] It also suggests that managers should make it a point to focus on relationship building within their work units. Second, leaders are encouraged to establish high performance expectations for all of their direct reports because setting high performance standards fosters high-quality LMXs. Third, because personality and demographic similarity between leaders and followers is associated with higher LMXs, managers need to be careful that they don't create a homogeneous work environment in the spirit of having positive relationships with their direct reports. Our discussion of diversity in Chapter 2 clearly documented that there are many positive benefits of having a diverse workforce. The fourth implication pertains to those of us who find ourselves in a poor LMX. Before providing advice about what to do in this situation, we would like you to assess the quality of your current leader–member exchange. The OB Exercise on page 620, contains a measure of leader–member exchange that segments an LMX into four subdimensions: mutual affection, loyalty, contribution to work activities, and professional respect.[75]

What is the overall quality of your LMX? Do you agree with this assessment? Which subdimensions are high and low? If your overall LMX and associated subdimensions are all high, you should be in a very good situation with respect to the relationship between you and your manager. Having a low LMX overall score or a low dimensional score, however, reveals that part of the relationship with your manager may need improvement. OB researcher Robert Vecchio offers the following tips to both followers and leaders for improving the quality of leader–member exchanges:

1. New employees should offer their loyalty, support, and cooperativeness to their manager.

2. If you are an out-group member, either accept the situation, try to become an in-group member by being cooperative and loyal, or quit.

3. Managers should consciously try to expand their in-groups.

4. Managers need to give employees ample opportunity to prove themselves.[76]

Finally, you may want to try using some of the impression management techniques discussed in Chapter 16 in order to improve your LMX.

Substitutes for Leadership

Virtually all leadership theories assume that some sort of formal leadership is necessary, whatever the circumstances. But that basic assumption is questioned by this model of leadership. Specifically, some OB scholars propose that there are a variety of situational

OB Exercise   Assessing Your Leader–Member Exchange

Instructions

For each of the items shown below, use the following scale and circle the answer that best represents how you feel about the relationship between you and your current manager/supervisor. If you are not currently working, complete the survey by thinking about a previous manager. Remember, there are no right or wrong answers. After circling a response for each of the 12 items, use the scoring key to compute scores for the subdimensions within your leader–member exchange.

1 = Strongly disagree
2 = Disagree
3 = Neither agree nor disagree
4 = Agree
5 = Strongly agree

1. I like my supervisor very much as a person.	1——2——3——4——5
2. My supervisor is the kind of person one would like to have as a friend.	1——2——3——4——5
3. My supervisor is a lot of fun to work with.	1——2——3——4——5
4. My supervisor defends my work actions to a superior, even without complete knowledge of the issue in question.	1——2——3——4——5
5. My supervisor would come to my defense if I were "attacked" by others.	1——2——3——4——5
6. My supervisor would defend me to others in the organization if I made an honest mistake.	1——2——3——4——5
7. I do work for my supervisor that goes beyond what is specified in my job description.	1——2——3——4——5
8. I am willing to apply extra efforts, beyond those normally required, to meet my supervisor's work goals.	1——2——3——4——5
9. I do not mind working my hardest for my supervisor.	1——2——3——4——5
10. I am impressed with my supervisor's knowledge of his/her job.	1——2——3——4——5
11. I respect my supervisor's knowledge of and competence on the job.	1——2——3——4——5
12. I admire my supervisor's professional skills.	1——2——3——4——5

Scoring Key

Mutual affection (add items 1–3) _____
Loyalty (add items 4–6) _____
Contribution to work activities (add items 7–9) _____
Professional respect (add items 10–12) _____
Overall score (add all 12 items) _____

Arbitrary Norms

Low mutual affection = 3–9
High mutual affection = 10–15
Low loyalty = 3–9
High loyalty = 10–15
Low contribution to work activities = 3–9
High contribution to work activities = 10–15
Low professional respect = 3–9
High professional respect = 10–15
Low overall leader–member exchange = 12–38
High overall leader–member exchange = 39–60

SOURCE: Survey items were taken from R C Liden and J M Maslyn, "Multidimensionality of Leader–Member Exchange: An Empirical Assessment through Scale Development," *Journal of Management*, 1998, p. 56.

variables that can substitute for, neutralize, or enhance the effects of leadership. These situational variables are referred to as **substitutes for leadership.**[77] Substitutes for leadership can thus increase or diminish a leader's ability to influence the work group. For example, leader behavior that initiates structure would tend to be resisted by independent-minded employees with high ability and vast experience. Consequently, such employees would be guided more by their own initiative than by managerial directives.

Substitutes for leadership
Situational variables that can substitute for, neutralize, or enhance the effects of leadership.

Kerr and Jermier's Substitutes for Leadership Model

According to Steven Kerr and John Jermier, the OB researchers who developed this model, the key to improving leadership effectiveness is to identify the situational characteristics that can either substitute for, neutralize, or improve the impact of a leader's behavior. Table 17–5 lists the various substitutes for leadership. Characteristics of the subordinate, the task, and the organization can act as substitutes for traditional hierarchical leadership. Further, different characteristics are predicted to negate different types of leader behavior. For example, tasks that provide feedback concerning accomplishment, such as taking a test, tend to negate task-oriented but not relationship-oriented leader behavior (see Table 17–5). Although the list in Table 17–5 is not all-inclusive, it shows that there are more substitutes for task-oriented leadership than for relationship-oriented leadership.

Table 17–5   *Substitutes for Leadership*

Characteristic	Relationship-Oriented or Considerate Leader Behavior Is Unnecessary	Task-Oriented or Initiating Structure Leader Behavior Is Unnecessary
Of the Subordinate		
1. Ability, experience, training, knowledge		X
2. Need for independence	X	X
3. "Professional" orientation	X	X
4. Indifference toward organizational rewards	X	X
Of the Task		
5. Unambiguous and routine		X
6. Methodologically invariant		X
7. Provides its own feedback concerning accomplishment		X
8. Intrinsically satisfying	X	
Of the Organization		
9. Formalization (explicit plans, goals, and areas of responsibility)		X
10. Inflexibility (rigid, unbending rules and procedures)		X
11. Highly specified and active advisory and staff functions		X
12. Closely knit, cohesive work groups	X	X
13. Organizational rewards not within the leader's control	X	X
14. Spatial distance between superior and subordinates	X	X

SOURCE: Adapted from S Kerr and J M Jermier, "Substitutes for Leadership: Their Meaning and Measurement," *Organizational Behavior and Human Performance*, December 1978, pp. 375–403.

Research and Managerial Implications   Two different approaches have been used to test this model. The first is based on the idea that substitutes for leadership are contingency variables that moderate the relationship between leader behavior and employee attitudes and behavior. Recent studies have revealed that contingency relationships did not support the model.[78] This demonstrates that substitutes for leadership do not moderate the effect of a leader's behavior as suggested by Kerr and Jermier. The second approach to test the substitutes model examined whether substitutes for leadership have a direct effect on employee attitudes and behaviors. A meta-analysis of 36 different samples revealed that the combination of substitute variables and leader behaviors significantly explained a variety of employee attitudes and behaviors. Interestingly, the substitutes for leadership were more important than leader behaviors in accounting for employee attitudes and behaviors.[79]

The key implication is that managers should be attentive to the substitutes listed in Table 17–5 because they directly influence employee attitudes and performance. Managers can positively influence the substitutes through employee selection, job design, work group assignments, and the design of organizational processes and systems.[80]

Servant-Leadership

Servant-leadership is more a philosophy of managing than a testable theory. The term *servant-leadership* was coined by Robert Greenleaf in 1970. Greenleaf believes that great leaders act as servants, putting the needs of others, including employees, customers, and community, as their first priority. **Servant-leadership** focuses on increased service to others rather than to oneself.[81]

It would seem that organizations could use a dose of servant-leadership in this day and age of corporate misdoings and scandals. Consider the following examples.

> CEO L Dennis Kozlowski of Tyco International Ltd. was indicted and Samuel D Waksal, CEO of IMClone Systems Inc., was accused of egregious breaches of trust and abuse of power within eight days of each other. Meanwhile, in Houston, a jury deliberated on the fate of Andersen Worldwide, once one of the nation's most respected auditing firms, accused of destroying evidence in the investigation of Enron Corp. [it was later found guilty]. These scandals follow a parade of outgoing CEOs that included Kenneth L Lay of Enron, Bernard J Ebbers of WorldCom, and John J Rigas of Adelphia, all forced to step down amid questions of abuse, incompetence, or both. Over the same period, other CEOs supplemented their mammoth paychecks by cashing in giant option grants just before steep stock declines.[82]

Because the focus of servant-leadership is serving others over self-interest, servant-leaders are less likely to engage in self-serving behaviors that hurt others (e.g., stockholders and employees).

More and more companies are trying to instill a philosophy of servant-leadership into their organizational cultures. Consider how TDI Industries is attempting to embed servant-leadership into its culture.

> A major player in the high-turnover construction industry, TDI's workforce is a loyal lot: 368 of the company's 1,413 employees have been with the Dallas-based company for more than five years, and more than 85 have been there for at least 20 years.
>
> Why? Because of TDI's commitment to the personal and professional development of each employee, which is best illustrated in the company's "People Objective." This objective promises to ensure that employees will succeed as a "total person," grow with the

*∫*ervant-
leadership

Focuses on increased
service to others
rather than to oneself.

company, and feel important. Through extensive personal and professional training programs, TDI cultivates well-rounded employees, while simultaneously enhancing its bottom line.

For TDI, creating an environment that promotes longevity begins with the concept of servant leadership. Based on Robert Greenleaf's Servant as Leader theory, the philosophy—in which managers (servants) cultivate employees (leaders) by serving and meeting the needs of others—lies at the heart of nearly all business functions.

To keep servant-leadership central to TDI's corporate culture, new employees are assigned to servant-leadership discussion groups, which meet weekly for six weeks to discuss particular elements of servant-leadership and how to apply the concept to all areas of their particular job. Additionally, TDI's employees who supervise at least one person must go through more extensive servant-leadership training at TDI's Leadership Institute.[83]

This example illustrates that it takes more than words to embed servant-leadership into an organization's culture. Servant-leadership must be reinforced through organizational structure, systems, and rewards for it take hold. At the individual level, however, managers also need to commit to a set of behaviors underlying servant-leadership.

According to Jim Stuart, co-founder of the leadership circle in Tampa, Florida, "Leadership derives naturally from a commitment to service. You know that you're practicing servant-leadership if your followers become wiser, healthier, more autonomous—and more likely to become servant-leaders themselves."[84] Servant-leadership is not a quick-fix approach to leadership. Rather, it is a long-term, transformational approach to life and work. Table 17–6 presents 10 characteristics possessed by servant-leaders. One can hardly go wrong by trying to adopt these characteristics.

Table 17–6   *Characteristics of the Servant-Leader*

Servant-Leadership Characteristics	Description
1. Listening	Servant-leaders focus on listening to identify and clarify the needs and desires of a group.
2. Empathy	Servant-leaders try to empathize with others' feelings and emotions. An individual's good intentions are assumed even when he or she performs poorly.
3. Healing	Servant-leaders strive to make themselves and others whole in the face of failure or suffering.
4. Awareness	Servant-leaders are very self-aware of their strengths and limitations.
5. Persuasion	Servant-leaders rely more on persuasion than positional authority when making decisions and trying to influence others.
6. Conceptualization	Servant leaders take the time and effort to develop broader based conceptual thinking. Servant-leaders seek an appropriate balance between a short-term, day-to-day focus and a long-term, conceptual orientation.
7. Foresight	Servant-leaders have the ability to foresee future outcomes associated with a current course of action or situation.
8. Stewardship	Servant-leaders assume that they are stewards of the people and resources they manage.
9. Commitment to the growth of people	Servant-leaders are committed to people beyond their immediate work role. They commit to fostering an environment that encourages personal, professional, and spiritual growth.
10. Building community	Servant-leaders strive to create a sense of community both within and outside the work organization.

SOURCE: These characteristics and descriptions were derived from L C Spears, "Introduction: Servant-Leadership and the Greenleaf Legacy," In *Reflections on Leadership: How Robert K Greenleaf's Theory of Servant-Leadership Influenced Today's Top Management Thinkers,* ed L C Spears (New York: John Wiley & Sons, 1995), pp. 1–14.

Summary of Key Concepts

1. *Define the term* leadership, *and explain the difference between leading versus managing.* Leadership is defined as a social influence process in which the leader tries to obtain the voluntary participation of employees in an effort to reach organizational objectives. Leadership entails more than having authority and power. Although leadership and management overlap, each entails a unique set of activities or functions. Managers typically perform functions associated with planning, investigating, organizing, and control, and leaders deal with the interpersonal aspects of a manager's job. Table 17–1 summarizes the differences between leading and managing.

2. *Review trait theory research, and discuss the idea of one best style of leadership, using the Ohio State studies and the Leadership Grid as points of reference.* Historical leadership research did not support the notion that effective leaders possessed unique traits from followers. However, teams of researchers reanalyzed this historical data with modern-day statistical procedures. Results revealed that individuals tend to be perceived as leaders when they possess one or more of the following traits: intelligence, dominance, and masculinity. Another study further demonstrated that employees value credible leaders. Credible leaders are honest, forward-looking, inspiring, and competent. Research also examined the relationship between gender and leadership. Results demonstrated that (a) men and women were seen as displaying more task and social leadership, respectively, (b) leadership styles varied by gender, (c) men and women were equally assertive, and (d) women were rated as more effective than men on a variety of criteria.

The Ohio State studies revealed that there were two key independent dimensions of leadership behavior: consideration and initiating structure. Authors of the Leadership Grid proposed that leaders should adopt a style that demonstrates high concern for production and people. Research did not support the premise that there is one best style of leadership.

3. *Explain, according to Fiedler's contingency model, how leadership style interacts with situational control.* Fiedler believes leader effectiveness depends on an appropriate match between leadership style and situational control. Leaders are either task motivated or relationship motivated. Situation control is composed of leader–member relations, task structure, and position power. Task-motivated leaders are effective under situations of both high and low control. Relationship-motivated leaders are more effective when they have moderate situational control.

4. *Discuss House's revised path–goal theory and Hersey and Blanchard's situational leadership theory.* There are three key changes in the revised path–goal theory. Leaders now are viewed as exhibiting eight categories of leader behavior (see Table 17–4) instead of four. In turn, the effectiveness of these styles depends on various employee characteristics and environmental factors. Second, leaders are expected to spend more effort fostering intrinsic motivation through empowerment. Third, leadership is not limited to people in managerial roles. Rather, leadership is shared among all employees within an organization. According to situational leadership theory (SLT), effective leader behavior depends on the readiness level of a leader's followers. As follower readiness increases, leaders are advised to gradually move from a telling to a selling to a participating and, finally, to a delegating style. Research does not support SLT.

5. *Define and differentiate transactional and charismatic leadership.* There is an important difference between transactional and charismatic leadership. Transactional leaders focus on the interpersonal transactions between managers and employees. Charismatic leaders motivate employees to pursue organizational goals above their own self-interests. Both forms of leadership are important for organizational success.

6. *Explain how charismatic leadership transforms followers and work groups.* Organizational culture is a key precursor of charismatic leadership, which is composed of three sets of leader behavior. These leader behaviors, in turn, positively affect followers' and work groups' goals, values, beliefs, aspirations, and motivation. These positive effects are then associated with a host of preferred outcomes.

7. *Summarize the managerial implications of charismatic leadership.* There are five managerial implications: (1) The best leaders are both transactional and charismatic. (2) Charismatic leadership is not applicable in all organizational situations. (3) Employees at any level in an organization can be trained to be more transactional and charismatic. (4) Top management needs to promote and reinforce ethical charismatic leadership because charismatic leaders can be ethical or unethical. (5) A charismatic leader's enthusiasm can lead to employment promises that cannot be met. This can lead to costly lawsuits.

8. *Explain the leader–member exchange model of leadership.* This model revolves around the development of dyadic relationships between managers and their direct reports. These leader–member exchanges qualify as either in-group or out-group relationships. Research supports this model of leadership.

9. *Describe the substitutes for leadership, and explain how they substitute for, neutralize, or enhance the effects of leadership.* There are 14 substitutes for leadership (see Table 17–5) that can substitute for, neutralize, or enhance the effects of leadership. These substitutes contain characteristics of the subordinates, the task, and the organization. Research shows that substitutes directly influence employee attitudes and performance.

10. *Describe servant-leadership.* Servant-leadership is more a philosophy than a testable theory. It is based on the premise that great leaders act as servants, putting the needs of others, including employees, customers and community, as their first priority.

Discussion Questions

1. Is everyone cut out to be a leader? Explain.

2. Has your college education helped you develop any of the traits that characterize leaders? Explain.

3. Should organizations change anything in response to research pertaining to gender and leadership? If yes, describe your recommendations.

4. What leadership traits and behavioral styles are possessed by the president of the United States?

5. Does it make more sense to change a person's leadership style or the situation? How would Fred Fiedler and Robert House answer this question?

6. Describe how a college professor might use House's revised path–goal theory to clarify student's path–goal perceptions.

7. Identify three charismatic leaders, and describe their leadership traits and behavioral styles.

8. Have you ever worked for a charismatic leader? Describe how he or she transformed followers.

9. Have you ever been a member of an in-group or out-group? For either situation, describe the pattern of interaction between you and your manager.

10. In your view, which leadership theory has the greatest practical application? Why?

Internet Exercise

www.leader-values.com

The topic of leadership has been important since the dawn of time. History is filled with examples of great leaders such as Mohandas Gandhi, Martin Luther King, and Bill Gates. These leaders likely possessed some of the leadership traits discussed in this chapter, and they probably used a situational approach to lead their followers. The purpose of this exercise is for you to evaluate the leadership styles of an historical figure.

Go to the Internet home page for Leadership Values (**www.leader-values.com**), and select the subheading "4 E's" on the left side of the screen. This section provides an overview of leadership and suggests four essential traits/behaviors that are exhibited by leaders: to envision, enable, empower, and energize. After reading this material, go back to the home page, and select the subheading "Historical Leaders" from the list on the left-hand side of the page. Next, choose one of the leaders from the list of his-

torical figures, and read the description about his or her leadership style. You may want to print all of the material you read thus far from this Web page to help you answer the following questions.

Questions

1. Describe the 4 E's of leadership.

2. To what extent do the 4 E's overlap with the theories and models of leadership discussed in this chapter?

3. Using any of the theories or models discussed in this chapter, how would you describe the leadership style of the historical figure you investigated?

4. Was this leader successful in using the 4 E's of leadership? Describe how he or she used the 4 E's.

OB in Action Case Study

Successful CEOs from Genuity Inc. and Factiva Rely on Similar but Different Leadership Styles

In June 2000, Genuity CEO Paul Gudonis made Internet IPO history when the company raised nearly $2 billion in the largest US public offering. While Amazon's Jeff Bezos, Oracle's Larry Ellison, and Cisco's John Chambers grabbed magazine covers and headlines during the past three years, Gudonis—an electrical engineer equipped with a Harvard MBA and 20 years of telecommunications and technology management experience—concentrated on guiding Genuity through an extraordinary growth spurt. Since 1994 with 50 employees and $5 million in revenues, it has reached 5,000 employees and revenues of $1 billion.

Gudonis' main concentration is to set corporate strategy and tightly focus the company on chief objectives. That strategy contains a handful of bold objectives: to be no. 1 in Internet traffic on Genuity's network backbone; to rank tops in network infrastructure and broadband; to be no. 1 in quality and customer satisfaction; and to be considered the company with the highest quality work/life environment.

Genuity's objectives are etched onto a plastic badge that Gudonis distributes to every new employee at the company's weekly orientation programs. "I spend a lot of my time communicating to our people, which probably contrasts with the role of Old Economy CEOs," he says. "Last year, we hired nine people a day, so I want everybody to walk around with our objectives hanging off their employee ID badge. I had one young man who stood up during orientation and said, 'Let me get this straight, if I'm working on something that's not on the card, I should stop what I'm doing?' I said, 'Exactly. That's exactly why I'm handing this out.'"

Besides establishing corporate strategy and communicating to employees, Gudonis identifies management development as a critical, and perhaps the most challenging, component of his leadership role. "When you have a company that is growing exponentially," he notes, "the pace of your employees' personal growth must remain ahead of the business growth. We cannot let their jobs outgrow their capabilities." To this end, Gudonis instituted a formal management development program and he holds senior leadership meetings twice a year for the company's top 75 managers. . . .

He also stresses the importance of training and development to his workforce, informing each orientation audience that Genuity promoted 600 employees in 2000. He also spells out specific success stories such as the temp who in four years became director of project management for Genuity's European Internet backbone, or the sales rep who in five years became a regional vice president with a 100-person team.

Gudonis cites the employee review process as another difference between New and Old Economy approaches to leadership. "Given our dynamic industry, I don't know what your objectives as an employee should be for this coming December," Gudonis explains. "While we do have an annual plan, every 90 days I lay out my objectives to my direct reports. They write down their quarterly objectives and review them with me and then with their teams throughout the organization." Also, every 90 days each employee is eligible for a bonus, depending on overall company performance and how each individual performed against his or her quarterly objectives.[85]

Last December, Clare Hart set some boundaries that would surprise many CEOs—not that she set them, but that it took her a year to do it. Hart's management style is decidedly open. So open, in fact, that she doesn't have an office.

But with the first year of serving as Factiva's CEO under her belt, she knew it was time to set some limits. "My lead-

ership style is about being very approachable, and it was especially important during our first year that I spent time enabling that openness," Hart explains. Ownership also is a big piece of Hart's leadership style. Responsibilities among her leadership team are clear-cut, with no dual-ownership or dual-reporting structures. Each month, all leadership team members compile a report on their area. The reports are then combined and shared among the respective teams and condensed into Hart's report to the board of directors.

Open communication among the leadership team is further facilitated throughout the year with 10 two-day meetings in which business strategy and key issues are worked out. Team members are asked to share appropriate information from the minutes of these meetings with the managers in their areas, with the intent that all 850 employees understand what is accomplished in these meetings. "Each Factiva executive is in his or her respective role because of the intellect, skills, experience and attitude he or she brings to the job," Hart says: "I do not want to do anything that gets in the way of an individual guiding his or her team towards the achievement of our corporate goals."

Through this process, Hart believes, the company is cultivating independent, proactive leaders who aren't afraid to take charge. "I recently watched a senior manager give a presentation to the leadership team, and it was obvious just by how she presented the material that she feels as if everything she does matters to the business. That's the way I want everybody to feel."[86]

Questions for Discussion

1. Based on the discussion of leading versus managing, did Paul Gudonis and Clare Hart exhibit more leadership or managerial behaviors? Use Table 17–1 to answer this question.

2. Citing examples, which different leadership traits and styles were displayed by Gudonis and Hart?

3. Did Gudonis and Hart display more transactional or charismatic leadership? Explain.

4. To what extent are the different styles of Gudonis and Hart consistent with research regarding gender and leadership? Discuss your rationale.

5. What did you learn about leadership from this case? Use examples to reinforce your conclusions.

Personal Awareness and Growth Exercise

How Ready Are You to Assume the Leadership Role?

Objectives

1. To assess your readiness for the leadership role.

2. To consider the implications of the gap between your career goals and your readiness to lead.

Introduction

Leaders assume multiple roles. Roles represent the expectations that others have of occupants of a position. It is important for potential leaders to consider whether they are ready for the leadership role because mismatches in expectations or skills can derail a leader's effectiveness. This exercise assesses your readiness to assume the leadership role.[87]

Instructions

For each statement, indicate the extent to which you agree or disagree with it by selecting one number from the scale provided. Circle your response for each statement. Remember, there are no right or wrong answers. After completing the survey, add your total score for the 20 items, and record it in the space provided.

1 = Strongly disagree
2 = Disagree
3 = Neither agree nor disagree
4 = Agree
5 = Strongly agree

1. It is enjoyable having people count on me for ideas and suggestions.		1—2—3—4—5
2. It would be accurate to say that I have inspired other people.		1—2—3—4—5
3. It's a good practice to ask people provocative questions about their work.		1—2—3—4—5
4. It's easy for me to compliment others.		1—2—3—4—5
5. I like to cheer people up even when my own spirits are down.		1—2—3—4—5
6. What my team accomplishes is more important than my personal glory.		1—2—3—4—5
7. Many people imitate my ideas.		1—2—3—4—5
8. Building team spirit is important to me.		1—2—3—4—5
9. I would enjoy coaching other members of the team.		1—2—3—4—5
10. It is important to me to recognize others for their accomplishments.		1—2—3—4—5
11. I would enjoy entertaining visitors to my firm even if it interfered with my completing a report.		1—2—3—4—5
12. It would be fun for me to represent my team at gatherings outside our department.		1—2—3—4—5
13. The problems of my teammates are my problems too.		1—2—3—4—5
14. Resolving conflict is an activity I enjoy.		1—2—3—4—5
15. I would cooperate with another unit in the organization even if I disagreed with the position taken by its members.		1—2—3—4—5
16. I am an idea generator on the job.		1—2—3—4—5
17. It's fun for me to bargain whenever I have the opportunity.		1—2—3—4—5
18. Team members listen to me when I speak.		1—2—3—4—5
19. People have asked me to assume the leadership of an activity several times in my life.		1—2—3—4—5
20. I've always been a convincing person.		1—2—3—4—5

Total score:_____

Norms for Interpreting the Total Score[88]

90–100 = High readiness for the leadership role
60–89 = Moderate readiness for the leadership role
40–59 = Some uneasiness with the leadership role
39 or less = Low readiness for the leadership role

Questions for Discussion

1. Do you agree with the interpretation of your readiness to assume the leadership role? Explain why or why not.

2. If you scored below 60 and desire to become a leader, what might you do to increase your readiness to lead? To answer this question, we suggest that you study the statements carefully—particularly those with low responses—to determine how you might change either an attitude or a behavior so that you can realistically answer more

questions with a response of "agree" or "strongly agree."

3. How might this evaluation instrument help you to become a more effective leader?

Group Exercise

Exhibiting Leadership within the Context of Running a Meeting[89]

Objectives

1. To consider the types of problems that can occur when running a meeting.

2. To identify the leadership behaviors that can be used to handle problems that occur in meetings.

Introduction

Managers often find themselves playing the role of formal or informal leader when participating in a planned meeting (e.g., committees, work groups, task forces, etc.). As a leader, individuals often must handle a number of interpersonal situations that have the potential of reducing the group's productivity. For example, if an individual has important information that is not shared with the group, the meeting will be less productive. Similarly, two or more individuals who engage in conversational asides could disrupt the normal functioning of the group. Finally, the group's productivity will also be threatened by two or more individuals who argue or engage in personal attacks on one another during a meeting. This exercise is designed to help you practice some of the behaviors necessary to overcome these problems and at the same time share in the responsibility of leading a productive group.[90]

Instructions

Your instructor will divide the class into groups of four to six. Once the group is assembled, briefly summarize the types of problems that can occur when running a meeting—start with the material presented in the preceding introduction. Write your final list on a piece of paper. Next, for each problem on the group's list, the group should brainstorm a list of appropriate leader behaviors that can be used to handle the problem. Use the guidelines for brainstorming discussed in Chapter 11. Try to arrive at a consensus list of leadership behaviors that can be used to handle the various problems encountered in meetings.

Questions for Discussion

1. What type of problems that occur during meetings are most difficult to handle? Explain.

2. Are there any particular leader behaviors that can be used to solve multiple problems during meetings? Discuss your rationale.

3. Was there a lot of agreement about which leader behaviors were useful for dealing with specific problems encountered in meetings? Explain.

Ethical Dilemma

Doug Durand's Staff Engages in Questionable Sales Activities[91]

In his 20 years as a pharmaceutical salesman, Douglas Durand thought he had seen it all. Then, in 1995, he signed on as vice president for sales at TAP Pharmaceutical Products Inc. in Lake Forest, Illinois. Several months later, in disbelief, he listened to a conference call among his sales staff: They were openly discussing how to bribe urologists. Worried about a competing drug coming to market, they

wanted to give a 2% "administration fee" up front to any doctor who agreed to prescribe TAP's new prostate cancer drug, Lupron. When one of Durand's regional managers fretted about getting caught, another quipped: "How do you think Doug would look in stripes?" Durand didn't say a word. "That conversation scared the heck out of me," he recalls. "I felt very vulnerable." . . .

For years, TAP sales reps had encouraged doctors to charge government medical programs full price for Lupron they received at a discount or gratis. Doing so helped TAP establish Lupron as the prostrate treatment of choice, bringing in annual sales of $800 million, about a quarter of the company's revenues. . . .

Durand grew increasingly concerned. Colleagues told him he didn't understand TAP's culture. He was excluded from top marketing and sales meetings. Then came the crack about how he would look in stripes. Durand's stomach knotted in fear that he would become the company scapegoat. Yet he left trapped: If he left within a year, he wouldn't be able to collect his bonus. He also doubted that anyone would hire him if he bolted so hastily.

What would you do if you were Doug Durand?

1. It's a tough market, and giving kickbacks is nothing more than a form of building product loyalty. I wouldn't make a big issue about this practice.

2. I wouldn't do anything because I would not receive my bonus and it wouldn't look good on my résumé to leave the job within one year.

3. I would gather information about TAP and send it to a federal prosecutor. After all, TAP is giving kickbacks and it is encouraging doctors to charge full price for a drug they receive on a discount.

4. I would go to TAP's president and get his or her blessing for our sales activities.

5. Invent other options. Discuss.

For an interpretation of this situation, visit our Web site, **www.mhhe.com/kreitner.**

Chapter Eighteen

Creating Effective Organizations

Learning Objectives

When you finish studying the material in this chapter, you should be able to:

1 Describe the four characteristics common to all organizations, and explain the difference between closed and open systems.

2 Define the term *learning organization*.

3 Describe horizontal, hourglass, and virtual organizations.

4 Describe the four generic organizational effectiveness criteria, and discuss how managers can prevent organizational decline.

5 Explain what the contingency approach to organization design involves.

6 Describe the relationship between differentiation and integration in effective organizations.

7 Discuss Burns and Stalker's findings regarding mechanistic and organic organizations.

8 Define and briefly explain the practical significance of centralization and decentralization.

9 Discuss the effective management of organizational size.

Figure 18–2   *Sample Organization Chart for a Hospital (executive and director levels only)*

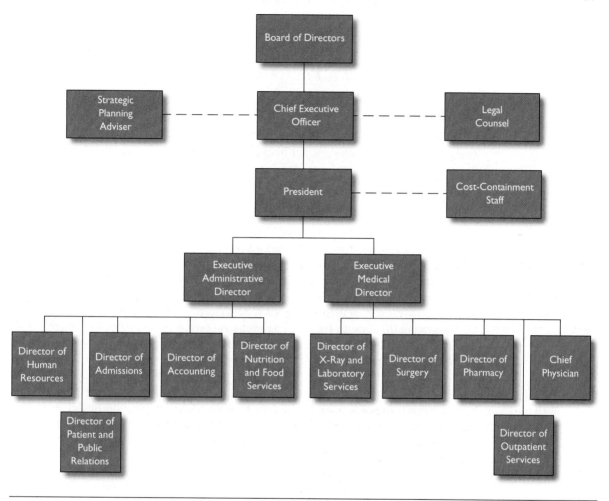

sis on leanness and administrative efficiency dictates spans of control as wide as possible but guarding against inadequate supervision and lack of coordination. Wider spans also complement the trend toward greater worker autonomy and empowerment.

Line and ∫taff Positions

The organization chart in Figure 18–2 also distinguishes between line and staff positions. Line managers such as the president, the two executive directors, and the various directors occupy formal decision-making positions within the chain of command. Line positions generally are connected by solid lines on organization charts. Dotted lines indicate staff relationships. **Staff personnel** do background research and provide technical advice and recommendations to their **line managers,** who have the authority to make decisions. For example, the cost-containment specialists in the sample organization chart merely advise the president on relevant matters. Apart from supervising the work of their own staff assistants, they have no line authority over other organizational members. Modern trends such as cross-functional teams and reengineering are blurring the distinction between line and staff.

∫taff personnel
Provide research, advice, and recommendations to line managers.

Line managers
Have authority to make organizational decisions.

According to a study of 207 police officers in Israel, line personnel exhibited greater job commitment than did their staff counterparts.[9] This result was anticipated because the line managers' decision-making authority empowered them and gave them comparatively more control over their work situations.

An Open-System Perspective of Organizations

Closed system

A relatively self-sufficient entity.

Open system

Organism that must constantly interact with its environment to survive.

To better understand how organizational models have evolved over the years, we need to know the difference between closed and open systems. A **closed system** is said to be a self-sufficient entity. It is "closed" to the surrounding environment. In contrast, an **open system** depends on constant interaction with the environment for survival. The distinction between closed and open systems is a matter of degree. Because every worldly system is partly closed and partly open, the key question is: How great a role does the environment play in the functioning of the system? For instance, a battery-powered clock is a relatively closed system. Once the battery is inserted, the clock performs its time-keeping function hour after hour until the battery goes dead. The human body, on the other hand, is a highly open system because it requires a constant supply of life-sustaining oxygen from the environment. Nutrients also are imported from the environment. Open systems are capable of self-correction, adaptation, and growth, thanks to characteristics such as homeostasis and feedback control.

Historically, management theorists downplayed the environment as they used closed-system thinking to characterize organizations as either well-oiled machines or highly disciplined military units. They believed rigorous planning and control would eliminate environmental uncertainty. But that proved unrealistic. Drawing upon the field of general systems theory that emerged during the 1950s, organization theorists suggested a more dynamic model for organizations.[10] The resulting open-system model likened organizations to the human body. Accordingly, the model in Figure 18–3, reveals the organization to be a living organism that transforms inputs into various outputs. The outer boundary of the organization is permeable. People, information, capital, and goods and services move back and forth across this boundary. Moreover, each of the five organizational subsystems—goals and values, technical, psychosocial, structural, and managerial—is dependent on the others. Feedback about such things as sales and customer satisfaction or dissatisfaction enables the organization to self-adjust and survive despite uncertainty and change.[11] In effect, the organization is alive.

Learning Organizations

Learning organization

Proactively creates, acquires, and transfers knowledge throughout the organization.

In recent years, organization theorists have extended the open-system model by adding a "brain" to the "living body." Organizations are said to have human-like cognitive functions, such as the abilities to perceive and interpret, solve problems, and learn from experience. Today, managers read and hear a good deal about learning organizations and knowledge management (as discussed in Chapter 11).[12] Peter Senge, a professor at the Massachusetts Institute of Technology, popularized the term *learning organization* in his best-selling book entitled *The Fifth Discipline*. He described a learning organization as "a group of people working together to collectively enhance their capacities to create results that they truly care about."[13] A practical interpretation of these ideas results in the following definition. A **learning organization** is one that proactively creates, acquires, and transfers knowledge and that changes its behavior on the basis of new knowledge and insights.[14]

Figure 18–3   *The Organization as an Open System*

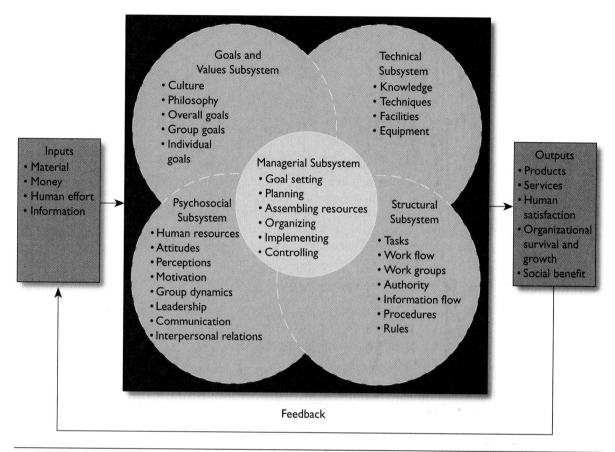

SOURCE: This model is a combination of Figures 5–2 and 5–3 in F E Kast and J E Rosenzweig, *Organization and Management: A Systems and Contingency Approach,* 4th ed (New York: McGraw-Hill, 1986), pp. 112, 114. Copyright © 1986. Reproduced with permission of the McGraw-Hill Companies.

Learning organizations actively try to infuse their organizations with new ideas and information. They do this by constantly scanning their external environments, hiring new talent and expertise when needed, and by devoting significant resources to train and develop their employees. Next, new knowledge must be transferred throughout the organization. Learning organizations strive to reduce structural, process, and interpersonal barriers to the sharing of information, ideas, and knowledge among organizational members. Finally, behavior must change as a result of new knowledge. Learning organizations are results oriented. They foster an environment in which employees are encouraged to use new behaviors and operational processes to achieve corporate goals. Consider Ernst & Young's approach, for example:

Ernst & Young figures that its knowledge falls into three categories of "content." The first is benchmark data—studies, surveys, industry facts, and figures. "Each year we buy about $30 million of this stuff in the United States alone, so that's valuable right there," says [chief knowledge officer John] Peetz. "The second content is point-to-point knowledge, which is people sharing what they know. And finally, we've got expert knowledge, or the best people in a given area who know how to solve specific problems." To tie this together, Ernest & Young created "power packs," or databases on specific business areas that employees load into laptops. Those packs also contain contact information for the firm's network of subject matter experts. If a consultant runs into a glitch in a supply-chain management proposal, for example, he or she can instantly find and get help from Ernst & Young's most experienced supply-chain master.[15]

Now let us see how this evolution of ideas is reshaping organizations.

The Changing Shape of Organizations

Organizations are basically tools invented to get things done through collective action. As any carpenter or plumber knows, different jobs require different tools. So it is with organizations. When the situation changes significantly, according to contingency thinking, a different type of organization may be appropriate. The need for new organizations is greater than ever today because managers face revolutionary changes. *Fortune* magazine offered this perspective:

> We all sense that the changes surrounding us are not mere trends but the workings of large, unruly forces; the globalization of markets; the spread of information technology and computer networks; the dismantling of hierarchy, the structure that has essentially organized work since the mid-19th century. Growing up around these is a new, information-age economy, whose fundamental sources of wealth are knowledge and communication rather than natural resources and physical labor.[16]

What sorts of organizations will prosper in the age of the Internet and E-Business? Will they be adaptations of the traditional pyramid-shaped organization? Or will they be radically different? Let us put our imaginations to work by envisioning the shape of tomorrow's organizations, the rough outlines of which are visible today.

New-Style versus Old-Style Organizations

Organization theorists Jay R Galbraith and Edward E Lawler III have called for a "new logic of organizing."[17] They recommend a whole new set of adjectives to describe organizations (see Table 18–1). Traditional pyramid-shaped organizations, conforming to the old-style pattern, tend to be too slow and inflexible today. Leaner, more flexible organizations are needed to accommodate today's strategic balancing act between cost, quality, and speed. These new-style organizations embrace the total quality management (TQM) principles discussed in Chapter 1. This means they are customer focused, dedicated to continuous improvement and learning, and structured around teams. These qualities, along with computerized information technology, hopefully enable big organizations to mimic the speed and flexibility of small organizations (see the International OB on page 641).

Three New Organizational Patterns

Figure 18–4 illustrates three radical departures from the traditional pyramid-shaped organization. Each is the logical result of various trends that are evident today. In other words, we have exaggerated these new organizations for instructional purposes. You will

Flexibility, Not Lower Wages, Gives Foreign Automakers the Edge over Detroit

BusinessWeek By forcing foreign-based manufacturers to hike their nonunion wages, the UAW [United Auto Workers Union] helps to level the playing field for GM, Ford, and Chrysler. Not completely, though: Detroit auto makers still have an estimated $1,600-per-vehicle cost disadvantage versus the Japanese, according to a Deutsche Banc Alex. Brown Inc. analysis. But it's flexibility, not wages, that gives nonunion transplants a productivity edge, most experts agree. "Even if they paid union scale and even if their benefits came up, I think they would still be more efficient," says Van Bussmann, Chrysler's former chief economist and now senior vice president of global forecasting for J D Power & Associates Inc.

For one thing, Japanese-owned factories typically build two or more models on a single assembly line. That's especially helpful as auto makers turn out more low-volume niche models. If sales of one model start to wane, they can quickly crank up production of another. But Big Three factories were designed to build large volumes of a single model. All the Detroit companies are racing to make their plants more flexible.

SOURCE: Excerpted from J Muller, "Autos: A New Industry," *Business Week*, July 15, 2002, p. 104.

likely encounter various combinations of these pure types in the years ahead. Let us imagine life in the organizations of tomorrow. (Importantly, these characterizations are not intended to be final answers. We simply seek to stimulate thoughtful discussion.)

Horizontal Organizations Despite the fact that *reengineering* became synonymous with huge layoffs and has been called a passing fad, it will likely have a lasting effect on organization design. Namely, it helped refine the concept of a horizontally oriented organization. Unlike traditional vertically oriented organizations with functional units such as production, marketing, and finance, horizontal organizations are

Table 18–1 *Profiles of the New-Style and Old-Style Organizations*

New	Old
Dynamic, learning	Stable
Information rich	Information is scarce
Global	Local
Small and large	Large
Product/customer oriented	Functional
Skills oriented	Job oriented
Team oriented	Individual oriented
Involvement oriented	Command/control oriented
Lateral/networked	Hierarchical
Customer oriented	Job requirements oriented

SOURCE: J R Galbraith and E E Lawler III, "Effective Organizations: Using the New Logic of Organizing," p. 298 in *Organizing for the Future: The New Logic for Managing Complex Organizations*, eds J R Galbraith, E E Lawler III, and Associates. Copyright 1993 Jossey-Bass Inc. Publishers. Reprinted by permission of Jossey-Bass Inc., a subsidiary of John Wiley & Sons Inc.

Figure 18–4   *The Shape of Tomorrow's Organizations*

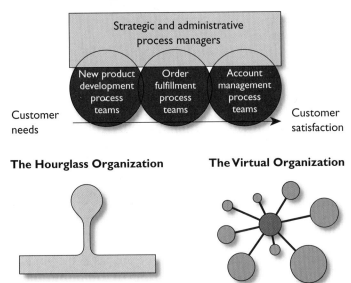

flat and built around core processes aimed at satisfying customers. *Fortune* magazine characterized horizontal organizations this way:

> The horizontal corporation includes these potent elements: Teams will provide the foundation of organizational design. They will not be set up inside departments, like marketing, but around core processes, such as new-product development. Process owners, not department heads, will be the top managers, and they may sport wonderfully weird titles; GE Medical Systems has a "vice president of global sourcing and order to remittance."
>
> Rather than focusing single-mindedly on financial objectives or functional goals, the horizontal organization emphasizes customer satisfaction. Work is simplified and hierarchy flattened by combining related tasks—for example, an account-management process that subsumes the sales, billing, and service functions—and eliminating work that does not add value. Information zips along an internal superhighway: The knowledge worker analyzes it, and technology moves it quickly across the corporation instead of up and down, speeding up and improving decision making.
>
> Okay, so some of this is derivative; the obsession with process, for example, dates back to total quality management. Part of the beauty of the horizontal corporation is that it distills much of what we know about what works in managing today. Its advocates call it an "actionable model"—jargon for a plan you can work with—that allows companies to use ideas like teams, supplier-customer integration, and empowerment in ways that reinforce each other. A key virtue, says Pat Hoye, dealer-service support manager at Ford Motor, is that the horizontal corporation is the kind of company a customer would design. The customer, after all, doesn't care about the service department's goals or the dealer's sales targets; he just wants his car fixed right and on time—so the organization makes those objectives paramount. In most cases, a horizontal organization requires some employees to be organized functionally where their expertise is considered critical, as in human

resources or finance. But those departments are often pared down and judiciously melded into a design where the real authority runs along process lines.[18]

What will it be like to work in a horizontal organization?[19] It will be a lot more interesting than traditional bureaucracies with their functional ghettos. Most employees will be *close to the customer* (both internal and external)—asking questions, getting feedback, and jointly solving problems. Constant challenge also will come from being on cross-functional teams where co-workers with different technical specialties work side-by-side on projects. Sometimes people will find themselves dividing their time among several projects. Blurred and conflicting lines of authority will break the traditional unity-of-command principle. Project goals and deadlines will tend to replace the traditional supervisor role. Training in both technical and teamwork skills will be a top priority. Multiskilled employees at all levels will find themselves working on different teams and various projects during the year. Paradoxically, self-starters and team players will thrive. Because of the flatness of the organization, lateral transfers will be more common than traditional vertical promotions. This will be a source of discontent for many of those who want to move upward. Constant change will take its toll in terms of interpersonal conflict, personal stress, and burnout. Skill-based pay will supplement pay-for-performance.

Hourglass Organizations
This pattern gets its name from the organization's pinched middle. Thanks to modern information technology, a relatively small executive group will be able to coordinate the efforts of numerous operating personnel who make goods or render services. Multiple and broad layers of middle managers who served as conduits for information in old-style organizations will be unnecessary in hourglass organizations. Competition for promotions among operating personnel will be intense because of the restricted hierarchy. Lateral transfers will be more common. Management will compensate for the lack of promotion opportunities with job rotation, skill training, and pay-for-performance. What few middle managers there are will be cross-functional problem solvers who also possess a number of technical skills. The potential for alienation between the executive elite and those at the base of the hourglass will be great, thus giving labor unions an excellent growth opportunity.

Virtual Organizations
Like virtual teams, discussed in Chapter 13, modern information technology allows people in virtual organizations to get something accomplished despite being geographically dispersed.[20] Instead of relying heavily on face-to-face meetings, as before, members of virtual organizations send E-mail and voicemail messages, exchange project information over the Internet, and convene videoconferences among far-flung participants. In addition, cellular phones have made the dream of doing business from the beach a reality! This disconnection between work and location is causing managers to question traditional assumptions about centralized offices and factories. Why have offices for people who are never there because they are out finding and helping customers? Why have a factory when it is less expensive to contract out the work? Indeed, many so-called virtual organizations are really a *network* of several independent contractors or organizations hooked together contractually and electronically. A prime example is Indigo Partners, a five-woman, one-man management consulting firm:

> The partners tackle projects on their own or in small teams. There is no hierarchy; there are no regularly scheduled meetings. [Jennifer] Overholt and her cohorts—an intense and experienced bunch, many of whom have young children—labor in their homes, setting their own hours and workload. Anyone can leave the partnership for any length of time and for any reason. . . .

Michelle Lee has a virtual lock on a balanced life as a founding member of Indigo Partners, a loosely-structured virtual organization of management consultants. They all work at home and link up electronically. Lee and her busy colleagues team up as projects dictate and don't need permission to take some time off for family and other outside commitments. They have no hard assets such as an office building. Instead, they rely on their connections, brains, and hard work.

(c) Kate Powers

Indigo Partners has no overhead, no assets to manage. There is no central office or secretarial pool. There are no accounting services. Most projects are bid on a fixed-price basis, so there's no need to track hours. The partners' equity is in themselves, and they are constantly boosting their own value through education and experience. For projects that require heavy lifting, they temporarily bulk up by using people from a large pool of specialized freelancers that they have personally recruited.[21]

The Internet provides the glue for this loose confederation.

Here is how we envision life in the emerging virtual organizations and organizational networks. Things will be very interesting and profitable for the elite core of entrepreneurs and engineers who hit on the right business formula. Turnover among the financial and information have nots—data entry, customer service, and production employees—will be high because of glaring inequities and limited opportunities for personal fulfillment and growth. Telecommuters who work from home will feel liberated and empowered (and sometimes lonely). Commitment, trust, and loyalty could erode badly if managers do not heed this caution by Charles Handy, a British management expert. According to Handy: "A shared commitment still requires personal contact to make the commitment feel real. *Paradoxically, the more virtual an organization becomes the more its people need to meet in person.*"[22] Independent contractors, both individuals and organizations, will participate in many different organizational networks and thus have diluted loyalty to any single one. Substandard working conditions and low pay at some smaller contractors will make them little more than Internet-age sweatshops. Companies living from one contract to another will offer little in the way of job security and benefits. Opportunities to start new businesses will be numerous, but prolonged success could prove elusive at Internet speed.

Be Prepared for Some Surprises

The only certainty about tomorrow's organizations is they are not a cure-all and will produce their fair share of surprises.[23] For instance, consider what happened at Cisco Systems during the 2000–2002 recession.

It turned out that Cisco's networked-manufacturing model was not nearly as accurate as [CEO John] Chambers had boasted. Only 40% of what Cisco sells is actually made by the company. Instead, a network of suppliers and contract manufacturers delivers an unusually large chunk of Cisco-branded merchandise direct to customers. This business model was supposed to keep fixed costs to a minimum, eliminate the need for inventory, and give management an instantaneous, real-time fix on orders, shipments, and demand.

The highly hyped systems, however, failed to account for the double and triple ordering by customers tired of long waits for shipments. So Cisco began to stockpile parts and finished products. . . .

When a weakening economy brought capital spending to a near halt, Chambers found himself stuck with billions of dollars of inventory he didn't expect to have. In April [2001] he wrote off $2.2 billion of excess inventory and cut 18% of Cisco's staff, or 8,500 employees.[24]

If you are a flexible and adaptable person who sees problems as opportunities, are a self-starter capable of teamwork, and are committed to life-long learning, don't worry. You will likely thrive in tomorrow's organizations.

Organizational Effectiveness (and the Threat of Decline)

How effective are you? If someone asked you this apparently simple question, you would likely ask for clarification before answering. For instance, you might want to know if they were referring to your grade point average, annual income, actual accomplishments, ability to get along with others, public service, or perhaps something else entirely. So it is with modern organizations. Effectiveness criteria abound. For example, Scott McNealy, CEO of computer maker Sun Microsystems, walks in his customers' shoes when judging the effectiveness of his company. McNealy explained:

There are few metrics to which I pay closer attention than "system uptime"—how often Sun systems are up and running at customer sites. The most important commitment that we can make as a company is to share our customers' risk. Most of our customers face the same risk: computer systems that go down when people need them.

I wish I could say that the concept of focusing on system uptime came to me in a flash of brilliance. But it didn't; it came straight from a customer. One of the most eye-opening customer comments that I've heard was "You have to understand that we guarantee the availability of our solutions to *our* customers at much higher levels than you ever guarantee your systems to us."

That's why we assemble real-time data on system availability at customer sites. We use that data to determine the causes of downtime.[25]

Assessing organizational effectiveness is an important topic for an array of people, including managers, stockholders, government agencies, and OB specialists. The purpose of this section is to introduce a widely applicable and useful model of organizational effectiveness; we will also deal with the related problem of organizational decline.

Generic Organizational-Effectiveness Criteria

A good way to better understand this complex subject is to consider four generic approaches to assessing an organization's effectiveness (see Figure 18–5). These effectiveness criteria apply equally well to large or small and profit or not-for-profit

Figure 18–5 *Four Ways to Assess Organizational Effectiveness*

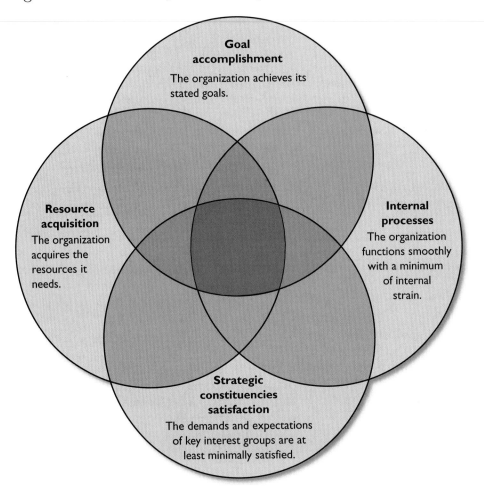

SOURCES: Adapted from discussion in K Cameron, "Critical Questions in Assessing Organizational Effectiveness." *Organizational Dynamics,* Autumn 1980, pp. 66–80; and K S Cameron, "Effectiveness as Paradox: Consensus and Conflict in Conceptions of Organizational Effectiveness," *Management Science,* May 1986, pp. 539–53.

organizations. Moreover, as denoted by the overlapping circles in Figure 18–5, the four effectiveness criteria can be used in various combinations. The key thing to remember is "no single approach to the evaluation of effectiveness is appropriate in all circumstances or for all organization types."[26] What do Coca-Cola and France Télécom, for example, have in common, other than being large profit-seeking corporations? Because a multidimensional approach is required, we need to look more closely at each of the four generic effectiveness criteria.

Goal Accomplishment Goal accomplishment is the most widely used effectiveness criterion for organizations. Key organizational results or outputs are compared with previously stated goals or objectives. Deviations, either plus or minus, require corrective action. This is simply an organizational variation of the personal goal-setting process discussed in Chapter 9. Effectiveness, relative to the criterion of goal accomplishment, is gauged by how well the organization meets or exceeds its goals.[27]

Productivity improvement, involving the relationship between inputs and outputs, is a common organization-level goal.[28] Goals also may be set for organizational efforts such as minority recruiting, pollution prevention, and quality improvement. Given today's competitive pressures and E-Business revolution, *innovation* and *speed* are very important organizational goals worthy of measurement and monitoring.[29] Toyota recently gave us a powerful indicator of where things are going in this regard. The Japanese automaker announced it could custom-build a car in just five days! A customer's new Toyota would roll off the Ontario, Canada, assembly line just five days after the order was placed. A 30-day lag was the industry standard at the time.[30]

Resource Acquisition   This second criterion relates to inputs rather than outputs. An organization is deemed effective in this regard if it acquires necessary factors of production such as raw materials, labor, capital, and managerial and technical expertise. Charitable organizations such as the Salvation Army judge their effectiveness in terms of how much money they raise from private and corporate donations.

Internal Processes   Some refer to this third effectiveness criterion as the "healthy systems" approach. An organization is said to be a healthy system if information flows smoothly and if employee loyalty, commitment, job satisfaction, and trust prevail. Goals may be set for any of these internal processes. Healthy systems, from a behavioral standpoint, tend to have a minimum of dysfunctional conflict and destructive political maneuvering. M Scott Peck, the physician who wrote the highly regarded book, *The Road Less Traveled,* characterizes healthy organizations in ethical terms:

> A healthy organization, Peck says, is one that has a genuine sense of community: It's a place where people are emotionally present with one another, and aren't afraid to talk about fears and disappointments—because that's what allows us to care for one another. It's a place where there is authentic communication, a willingness to be vulnerable, a commitment to speaking frankly and respectfully—and a commitment not to walk away when the going gets tough.[31]

Strategic Constituencies Satisfaction   Organizations both depend on people and affect the lives of people. Consequently, many consider the satisfaction of key interested parties to be an important criterion of organizational effectiveness.

A **strategic constituency** is any group of individuals who have some stake in the organization—for example, resource providers, users of the organization's products or services, producers of the organization's output, groups whose cooperation is essential for the organization's survival, or those whose lives are significantly affected by the organization.[32]

Strategic constituencies (or *stakeholders*) generally have competing or conflicting interests.[33] For instance, when pilots and other unionized employees were winning generous wage increases at major US airlines in mid-2001, profit-conscious investors and cost-conscious ticket buyers weren't cheering.[34] Strategic constituents or stakeholders can be identified systematically through a stakeholder audit.[35] A **stakeholder audit** enables management to identify all parties significantly impacted by the organization's performance (see Figure 18–6). Conflicting interests and relative satisfaction among the listed stakeholders can then be dealt with.

A never-ending challenge for management is to strike a workable balance among strategic constituencies so as to achieve at least minimal satisfaction on all fronts.

Strategic constituency
Any group of people with a stake in the organization's operation or success.

Stakeholder audit
Systematic identification of all parties likely to be affected by the organization.

Figure 18–6   *A Sample Stakeholder Audit Identifying Strategic Constituencies*

SOURCE: Reprinted from "The Stakeholder Audit Goes Public" by N C Roberts et al. *Organizational Dynamics,* Winter 1989 © 1989. With permission from Elsevier Science.

Multiple Effectiveness Criteria: Some Practical Guidelines

Experts on the subject recommend a multidimensional approach to assessing the effectiveness of modern organizations. This means no single criterion is appropriate for all stages of the organization's life cycle. Nor will a single criterion satisfy competing stakeholders. Well-managed organizations mix and match effectiveness criteria to fit the unique requirements of the situation.[36] Managers need to identify and seek input from strategic constituencies. This information, when merged with the organization's stated mission and philosophy, enables management to derive an appropriate *combination* of effectiveness criteria. The following guidelines are helpful in this regard:

- *The goal accomplishment approach* is appropriate when "goals are clear, consensual, time-bounded, measurable."[37]
- *The resource acquisition approach* is appropriate when inputs have a traceable effect on results or output. For example, the amount of money the American Red Cross receives through donations dictates the level of services provided.
- *The internal processes approach* is appropriate when organizational performance is strongly influenced by specific processes (e.g., cross-functional teamwork).
- *The strategic constituencies approach* is appropriate when powerful stakeholders can significantly benefit or harm the organization.[38]

Keeping these basic concepts of organizational effectiveness in mind, we turn our attention to preventing organizational decline.

The Ever-Present Threat of Organizational Decline

Sadly, there are many examples of organizational decline and failure in the wake of the recent corporate scandals and recession. Some failed because of illegal acts. Enron, for one, had the dubious honor of going from number seven on the 2001 *Fortune* 500 list to bankruptcy within a single year! During that time, Enron shareholders saw their shares plummet from $83 a share to 67 cents, when the stock was finally delisted. Thousands of Enron jobs evaporated and employee retirement plans and dreams were wiped out.[39] Other companies tripped over strategic blunders and bad luck. As Enron was self-destructing and taking auditor Arthur Andersen with it, losses mounted at Ford Motor Company as it faced Explorer rollover lawsuits and saw its J D Power and Associates quality ratings go from first to last in just three years.[40] Kmart, the once-giant retailer, also slipped into bankruptcy and lost a stunning $1 billion in the month of April 2002 alone.[41] Although the problems at these particular companies varied, all of them turned the corner from success to decline suddenly and dramatically. Donald N Sull, a strategy professor at the London Business School, added this perspective:

> One of the most common business phenomena is also one of the most perplexing: when successful companies face big changes in their environment, they often fail to respond effectively. Unable to defend themselves against competitors armed with new products, technologies, or strategies, they watch their sales and profits erode, their best people leave, and their stock valuations tumble. Some ultimately manage to recover—usually after painful rounds of downsizing and restructuring—but many don't.[42]

Researchers call this downward spiral **organizational decline** and define it as "a decrease in an organization's resource base."[43] The term *resource* is used very broadly in this context, encompassing money, talent, customers, and innovative ideas and products. Managers seeking to maintain organizational effectiveness need to be alert to the problem because experts tell us "decline is almost unavoidable unless deliberate steps are taken to prevent it."[44] The first key step is to recognize the early warning signs of organizational decline.

Organizational decline

Decrease in organization's resource base (money, customers, talent, innovations).

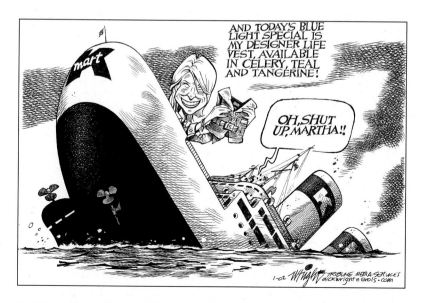

Early Warning Signs of Decline

Short of illegal conduct, there are 14 early warning signs of organizational decline:

1. Excess personnel.
2. Tolerance of incompetence.
3. Cumbersome administrative procedures.
4. Disproportionate staff power (e.g., technical staff specialists politically overpower line managers, whom they view as unsophisticated and too conventional).
5. Replacement of substance with form (e.g., the planning process becomes more important than the results achieved).
6. Scarcity of clear goals and decision benchmarks.
7. Fear of embarrassment and conflict (e.g., formerly successful executives may resist new ideas for fear of revealing past mistakes).
8. Loss of effective communication.
9. Outdated organizational structure.[45]
10. Increased scapegoating by leaders.
11. Resistance to change.
12. Low morale.
13. Special interest groups are more vocal.
14. Decreased innovation.[46]

Managers who monitor these early warning signs of organizational decline are better able to reorganize in a timely and effective manner.[47] However, research has uncovered a troublesome perception tendency among entrenched top management teams. In companies where there had been little if any turnover among top executives, there was a tendency to attribute organizational problems to *external* causes (e.g., competition, the government, technology shifts). Oppositely, *internal* attributions tended to be made by top management teams with *many* new members. Thus, proverbial "new blood" at the top appears to be a good insurance policy against misperceiving the early-warning signs of organizational decline.[48]

Preventing Organizational Decline

The time to start doing something about organizational decline is when everything is going *right.* For it is during periods of high success that the seeds of decline are sown.[49] *Complacency* is the number one threat because it breeds overconfidence and inattentiveness. As one management writer recently explained:

> In organizations, complacency is a side effect of success. Growth brings bloat, and bloat slows the organization's response to competitive threats. It is after sustained periods of success that organizations run the highest risk of getting hurt. At the moment of a company's greatest triumph, senior management's most important duty is to make sure that the butterflies are still fluttering in everybody's belly.[50]

Judging from what has been written about Enron, complacency also can breed arrogance and unethical or illegal conduct.[51]

Total quality management advocates remind us that *continuous improvement* is the first line of defense against organizational decline. Japan's Toyota is a world leader in this regard.

Of all the slogans kicked around Toyota City, the key one is *kaizen,* which means "continuous improvement" in Japanese. While many other companies strive for dramatic breakthroughs, Toyota keeps doing lots of little things better and better. . . .

One consultant calls Toyota's strategy "rapid inch-up": Take enough tiny steps and pretty soon you outdistance the competition. . . .

In short, Toyota is the best carmaker in the world. And it keeps getting better. Says Iwao Isomura, chief of personnel: "Our current success is the best reason to change things." Extensive interviews with Toyota executives in the United States and Japan demonstrate the company's total dedication to continuous improvement. What is often mistaken for excessive modesty is, in fact, an expression of permanent dissatisfaction—even with exemplary performance.[52]

General Motors, whose US market share dropped from 51% to 28% over the last 40 years, has worked hard to catch up with Toyota. But it is chasing a moving target. According to *Business Week:* "In 1987, GM . . . had 180 problems per 100 cars in a JD Power quality study, versus 127 for Toyota. By 2002, in a redesigned survey, GM's quality had improved to 130 defects per 100 cars and trucks versus 107 for Toyota."[53] *Kaizen* works!

The Contingency Approach to Organization Design

According to the **contingency approach to organization design,** organizations tend to be more effective when they are structured to fit the demands of the situation.[54] A contingency approach can be put into practice by first assessing the degree of environmental uncertainty. (see Figure 18–7).[55] For example, Nokia, the Finnish mobile phone

Contingency approach to organization design
Creating an effective organization–environment fit.

Figure 18–7   *Assessing Environmental Uncertainty*

	Low	Moderate	High
1. How strong are social, political, and economic pressures on the organization?	Minimal	Moderate	Intense
2. How frequent are technological breakthroughs in the industry?	Infrequent	Occasional	Frequent
3. How reliable are resources and supplies?	Reliable	Occasional, predictable shortages	Unreliable
4. How stable is the demand for the organization's product or service?	Highly stable	Moderately stable	Unstable

SOURCE: Kreitner, Robert, *Management,* eighth edition. Copyright © 2001 by Houghton Mifflin Company. Used with permission.

powerhouse, faces a high degree of environmental uncertainty. This was the situation for Nokia in 2002, in the face of a sharp decline in sales growth:

> Figuring out what increasingly confused customers want is another challenge. Mobile phones used to be about talking—anytime, anywhere. Now they're becoming devices for sending and receiving data, as well. More than half of new phones come with built-in Web browsers, and a growing number include digital cameras or music players. Leaders in the PC business, including Microsoft and Intel Corp., have concluded that this is their moment to barge in....
>
> In the past, only Nokia and a few others had the technical chops to design the special-purpose electronics that go into cell phones. Now, once-esoteric components are available off the shelf from multiple suppliers, and companies like Motorola, Texas Instruments, and France's Wavecom are hawking ready-to-assemble phone kits.
>
> The upshot? It's easier than ever for low-cost producers to cobble together me-too phones and undercut Nokia. Retail prices for handsets have fallen from an average of $275 five years ago to $155.[56]

Next, the contingency model calls for using various organization design configurations to achieve an effective organization–environment fit. This section presents two classic contingency design studies.

Differentiation and Integration: The Lawrence and Lorsch Study

In their classic text, *Organization and Environment,* Harvard researchers Paul Lawrence and Jay Lorsch explained how two structural forces simultaneously fragment the organization and bind it together. They cautioned that an imbalance between these two forces—labeled *differentiation* and *integration*—could hinder organizational effectiveness.

Differentiation

Division of labor and specialization that cause people to think and act differently.

Differentiation Splits the Organization Apart   **Differentiation** occurs through division of labor and technical specialization. A behavioral outcome of differentiation is that technical specialists such as computer programmers tend to think and act differently than specialists in, say, accounting or marketing. Excessive differentiation can cause the organization to bog down in inefficiency, miscommunication, conflict, and politics. Thus, differentiation needs to be offset by an opposing structural force to ensure needed *coordination*. This is where integration enters the picture (see Figure 18–8).

Integration

Cooperation among specialists to achieve a common goal.

Integration Binds the Organization Together   **Integration** occurs when specialists cooperate to achieve a common goal. According to the Lawrence and Lorsch model, integration can be achieved through various combinations of the following six mechanisms: (1) a formal hierarchy; (2) standardized policies, rules, and procedures; (3) departmentalization; (4) committees and cross-functional teams; (5) human relations training, and (6) individuals and groups acting as liaisons between specialists.

Achieving the Proper Balance   When Lawrence and Lorsch studied successful and unsuccessful companies in three industries, they concluded the following: *As environmental complexity increased, successful organizations exhibited higher de-*

Figure 18–8   *Differentiation and Integration Are Opposing Structural Forces*

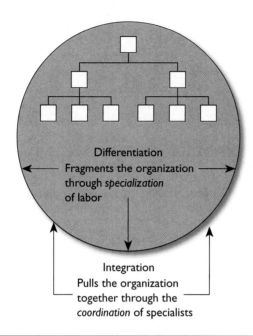

grees of both differentiation and integration. In other words, an effective balance was achieved. Unsuccessful organizations, in contrast, tended to suffer from an imbalance of too much differentiation and not enough offsetting integration. Managers need to fight this tendency if their growing and increasingly differentiated organizations are to be coordinated.

Lawrence and Lorsch also discovered that "the more differentiated an organization, the more difficult it is to achieve integration."[57] Managers of today's complex organizations need to strive constantly and creatively to achieve greater integration.[58] For example, how does 3M Company, with its dozens of autonomous divisions and more than 60,000 products, successfully maintain its competitive edge in technology? Among other things, 3M makes sure its technical specialists frequently interact with one another so cross-fertilization of ideas takes place. Art Fry, credited with inventing the now ubiquitous Post-it Notes, actually owes much of his success to colleague Spencer Silver, an engineer down the hall who created an apparently useless semi-adhesive. If Fry and Silver had worked in a company without a strong commitment to integration, we probably would not have Post-it Notes. 3M does not leave this sort of cross-fertilization of ideas to chance. It organizes for integration with such things as a Technology Council that regularly convenes researchers from various divisions and an annual science fair at which 3M scientists enthusiastically hawk their new ideas, not to customers, but to each other![59]

Mechanistic versus Organic Organizations

A second landmark contingency design study was reported by a pair of British behavioral scientists, Tom Burns and G M Stalker. In the course of their research, they drew

Mechanistic organizations

Rigid, command-and-control bureaucracies.

a very instructive distinction between what they called mechanistic and organic organizations. **Mechanistic organizations** are rigid bureaucracies with strict rules, narrowly defined tasks, and top-down communication. For example, when *Business Week* correspondent Kathleen Deveny spent a day working in a McDonald's restaurant, she found a very mechanistic organization:

> Here every job is broken down into the smallest of steps, and the whole process is automated....
>
> Anyone could do this, I think. But McDonald's restaurants operate like Swiss watches, and the minute I step behind the counter I am a loose part in the works....
>
> I bag French fries for a few minutes, but I'm much too slow. Worse, I can't seem to keep my station clean enough. Failing at French fries is a fluke, I tell myself....
>
> I try to move faster, but my co-workers are [leaving me behind].[60]

This sort of mechanistic structure is necessary at McDonald's because of the competitive need for uniform product quality, speedy service, and cleanliness. Oppositely, **organic organizations** are flexible networks of multitalented individuals who perform a variety of tasks.[61] The Institute for Genomic Research in Rockville, Maryland, headed by PhD pharmacologist Claire M Fraser, is a prime example of a highly organic organization.

Organic organizations

Fluid and flexible networks of multitalented people.

> Fraser has little patience for formality or for hierarchy. The institute's organizational lines mostly run horizontally, not vertically. "There are no walls, no departmental barriers," she says. "We're what you might find in industry, where groups are formed to tackle a particular problem. And when the task is completed, the groups go away and new groups are

Claire M Fraser, a PhD pharmacologist, is president of The Institute for Genomic Research in Rockville, Maryland. Fraser created a highly organic organization where high-powered researchers enjoy flexibility and project-based teamwork.

(c) Katherine Lambert

Table 18–2   *Characteristics of Mechanistic and Organic Organizations*

Characteristic	Mechanistic Organization		Organic Organization
1. Task definition and knowledge required	Narrow; technical	→	Broad; general
2. Linkage between individual's contribution and organization's purpose	Vague or indirect	→	Clear or direct
3. Task flexibility	Rigid; routine	→	Flexible; varied
4. Specification of techniques, obligations, and rights	Specific	→	General
5. Degree of hierarchical control	High	→	Low (self-control emphasized)
6. Primary communication pattern	Top-down	→	Lateral (between peers)
7. Primary decision-making style	Authoritarian	→	Democratic; participative
8. Emphasis on obedience and loyalty	High	→	Low

SOURCE: Adapted from discussion in T Burns and G M Stalker, *The Management of Innovation* (London: Tavistock, 1961), pp. 119–25.

formed." Teamwork is crucial to the institute's success. "We're not a good place for loners, people who are more comfortable doing traditional biology," she says. "This is large-scale biology, and that means people have to come together to solve problems."[62]

A Matter of Degree   Importantly, as illustrated in Table 18–2, each of the mechanistic-organic characteristics is a matter of degree. Organizations tend to be *relatively* mechanistic or *relatively* organic. Pure types are rare because divisions, departments, or units in the same organization may be more or less mechanistic or organic. From an employee's standpoint, which organization structure would you prefer?

Different Approaches to Decision Making   Decision making tends to be centralized in mechanistic organizations and decentralized in organic organizations. **Centralized decision making** occurs when key decisions are made by top management. **Decentralized decision making** occurs when important decisions are made by middle- and lower-level managers. Generally, centralized organizations are more tightly controlled while decentralized organizations are more adaptive to changing situations.[63] Each has its appropriate use. For example, both Delta Air Lines and General Electric are very respected and successful companies, yet the former prefers centralization while the latter pushes decentralization.

Experts on the subject warn against extremes of centralization or decentralization. The challenge is to achieve a workable balance between the two extremes. A management consultant put it this way:

> The modern organization in transition will recognize the pull of two polarities: a need for greater centralization to create low-cost shared resources; and, a need to improve market responsiveness with greater decentralization. Today's winning organizations are the ones that can handle the paradox and tensions of both pulls. These are the firms that analyze the optimum organizational solution in each particular circumstance, without prejudice for one type of organization over another. The result is, almost invariably, a messy mixture of decentralized units sharing cost-effective centralized resources.[64]

Centralization and decentralization are not an either-or proposition; they are an *and-also* balancing act.

Centralized decision making
Top managers make all key decisions.

Decentralized decision making
Lower-level managers are empowered to make important decisions.

Relevant Research Findings
When they classified a sample of actual companies as either mechanistic or organic, Burns and Stalker discovered one type was not superior to the other. Each type had its appropriate place, depending on the environment. When the environment was relatively *stable and certain,* the successful organizations tended to be *mechanistic. Organic* organizations tended to be the successful ones when the environment was *unstable and uncertain.*[65]

In a more recent study of 103 department managers from eight manufacturing firms and two aerospace organizations, managerial skill was found to have a greater impact on a global measure of department effectiveness in organic departments than in mechanistic departments. This led the researchers to recommend the following contingencies for management staffing and training:

> If we have two units, one organic and one mechanistic, and two potential applicants differing in overall managerial ability, we might want to assign the more competent to the organic unit since in that situation there are few structural aids available to the manager in performing required responsibilities. It is also possible that managerial training is especially needed by managers being groomed to take over units that are more organic in structure.[66]

Another interesting finding comes from a study of 42 voluntary church organizations. As the organizations became more mechanistic (more bureaucratic) the intrinsic motivation of their members decreased. Mechanistic organizations apparently undermined the volunteers' sense of freedom and self-determination. Additionally, the researchers believe their findings help explain why bureaucracy tends to feed on itself: "A mechanistic organizational structure may breed the need for a more extremely mechanistic system because of the reduction in intrinsically motivated behavior."[67] Thus, bureaucracy begets greater bureaucracy.

Most recently, field research in two factories, one mechanistic and the other organic, found expected communication patterns. Command-and-control (downward) communication characterized the mechanistic factory. Consultative or participative (two-way) communication prevailed in the organic factory.[68]

Both Mechanistic and Organic Structures Are Needed
Although achievement-oriented students of OB typically express a distaste for mechanistic organizations, not all organizations or subunits can or should be organic. For example, as mentioned earlier, McDonald's could not achieve its admired quality and service standards without extremely mechanistic restaurant operations. Imagine the food and service you would get if McDonald's employees used their own favorite ways of doing things and worked at their own pace! On the other hand, mechanistic structure alienates some employees because it erodes their sense of self-control.

Three Important Contingency Variables: Technology, Size, and Strategic Choice

Both contingency theories just discussed have one important thing in common. Each is based on an *environmental imperative,* meaning the environment is said to be the primary determinant of effective organizational structure. Other organization theorists disagree. They contend that factors such as the organization's core technology, size, and corporate strategy hold the key to organizational structure. This section examines the significance of these three additional contingency variables.

The Effect of Technology on Structure— Woodward and Beyond

Joan Woodward proposed a *technological imperative* in 1965 after studying 100 small manufacturing firms in southern England. She found distinctly different structural patterns for effective and ineffective companies based on technologies of low, medium, or high *complexity.* Effective organizations with either low- or high-complexity technology tended to have an organic structure. Effective organizations based on a technology of medium complexity tended to have a mechanistic structure. Woodward concluded that technology was the overriding determinant of organizational structure.[69]

Since Woodward's landmark work, many studies of the relationship between technology and structure have been conducted. Unfortunately, disagreement and confusion have prevailed. For example, a comprehensive review of 50 studies conducted between 1965 and 1980 found six technology concepts and 140 technology-structure relationships.[70] A statistical analysis of those studies prompted the following conclusions:

- The more the technology requires *interdependence* between individuals or groups, the greater the need for integration (coordination).

- "As technology moves from routine to nonroutine, subunits adopt less formalized and [less] centralized structures."[71]

Additional insights can be expected in this area as researchers coordinate their definitions of technology and refine their methodologies.[72]

Organizational Size and Performance

Size is an important structural variable subject to two schools of thought. According to the first school, economists have long extolled the virtues of economies of scale. This approach, often called the "bigger is better" model, assumes the per-unit cost of production decreases as the organization grows. In effect, bigger is said to be more efficient. For example, on an annual basis, DaimlerChrysler supposedly can produce its 100,000th car less expensively than its 10th car.

The second school of thought pivots on the law of diminishing returns. Called the "small is beautiful" model,[73] this approach contends that oversized organizations and subunits tend to be plagued by costly behavioral problems. Large and impersonal organizations are said to breed apathy and alienation, with resulting problems such as turnover and absenteeism. Two strong advocates of this second approach are the authors of the popular book *In Search of Excellence:*

> In the excellent companies, small in *almost every case* is beautiful. The small facility turns out to be the most efficient; its turned-on, motivated, highly productive worker, in communication (and competition) with his peers, outproduces the worker in the big facilities time and again. It holds for plants, for project teams, for divisions—for the entire company.[74]

Is Complexity the Issue? (A Case against Mergers?)   Recent research suggests that when designing their organizations, managers should follow a middle ground between "bigger is better" and "small is beautiful" because both models have been oversold. Indeed, a newer perspective says *complexity,* not size, is the central issue.[75] British management teacher and writer Charles Handy, cited earlier, offered this instructive perspective:

> Growth does not have to mean more of the same. It can mean better rather than bigger. It can mean leaner or deeper, both of which might improve rather than expand the current position. Businesses can grow more profitable by becoming better, or leaner, or deeper, more concentrated, without growing bigger. Bigness, in both business and life, can lead to a lack of focus, too much complexity and, in the end, too wide a spread to control. We have to know when big is big enough.[76]

We do not have a definite answer to the question of how big is too big, but the excessive complexity argument is compelling. This argument may also help explain why many mergers have been disappointing in recent years. According to *Business Week,* the "historic surge of consolidations and combinations is occurring in the face of strong evidence that mergers and acquisitions, at least over the past 35 years or so, have hurt more than helped companies and shareholders."[77] A prime case in point today is Lockheed Martin Corp.:

> The $27 billion Bethesda [Maryland] based company became the world's No. I defense contractor by leading the post-cold-war consolidation, becoming a favorite among analysts and at the Pentagon. Recent setbacks have those cheerleaders asking some tough questions. "Has this company just gotten too big and too complex?" asks Merrill Lynch & Co. aerospace analyst Byron K Callan. Says a top Defense Dept. official: "You can't have 50 priorities—the product suffers."[78]

Research Insights Researchers measure the size of organizations and organizational subunits in different ways. Some focus on financial indicators such as total sales or total asset value. Others look at the number of employees, transactions (such as the number of students in a school district), or capacity (such as the number of beds in a hospital). A meta-analysis[79] of 31 studies conducted between 1931 and 1985 that related organizational size to performance found:

- Larger organizations (in terms of assets) tended to be more productive (in terms of sales and profits).
- There were "no positive relationships between organizational size and efficiency, suggesting the absence of net economy of scale effects."[80]
- There were zero to slightly negative relationships between *subunit* size and productivity and efficiency.
- A more recent study examined the relationship between organizational size and employee turnover over a period of 65 months. Turnover was unrelated to organizational size.[81]

Striving for Small Units in Big Organizations In summary, bigger is not necessarily better and small is not necessarily beautiful.[82] Hard-and-fast numbers regarding exactly how big is too big or how small is too small are difficult to come by. Management consultants offer some rough estimates (see Table 18–3). Until better evidence is available, the best that managers can do is monitor the productivity, quality, and efficiency of divisions, departments, and profit centers. Unwieldy and overly complex units need to be promptly broken into ones of more manageable size. The trick is to *create smallness within bigness.*[83] Cisco Systems' CEO John Chambers explained

Table 18–3   *Organizational Size: Management Consultants Address the Question of How Big Is Too Big?*

> Peter F Drucker, well-known management consultant:
>
> The real growth and innovation in this country has been in medium-size companies that employ between 200 and 4,000 workers. If you are in a small company, you are running all out. You have neither the time nor the energy to devote to anything but yesterday's crisis.
>
> A medium-sized company has the resources to devote to new products and markets, and it's still small enough to be flexible and move fast. And these companies now have what they once lacked—they've learned how to manage.
>
> Thomas J Peters and Robert H Waterman, Jr, best-selling authors and management consultants:
>
> A rule of thumb starts to emerge. We find that the lion's share of the top performers keep their division size between $50 and $100 million, with a maximum of 1,000 or so employees each. Moreover, they grant their divisions extraordinary independence—and give them the functions and resources to exploit.
>
> ---
>
> SOURCES: Excerpted from J A Byrne, "Advice from the Dr. Spock of Business," *Business Week*, September 28, 1987, p. 61; and T J Peters and R H Waterman Jr, *In Search of Excellence* (New York: Harper & Row, 1982), pp. 272–73.

the logic of this approach in a recent question-and-answer exchange with *Fast Company* magazine:

Q. As Cisco has grown, you've redefined people's jobs in a very unusual way. Instead of letting managers build up ever-larger empires, you've constantly split up their duties, in what Cisco calls "divide and grow." Why do you do that?

A. It's one of the hardest things to grasp, but the more successful a group is, the more you ought to split it up. In sales, that allows a more focused approach to the customer. It forces you to cover each of the bases in order to achieve your overall goals. If you have multiple accounts, you can let opportunities slip away and still have what looks like a good year. But then you're leaving room to make your competitors strong. The same thing is true with R&D or other groups.

Now, this sort of approach only works if you can empower the people who work for you.[84]

Strategic Choice and Organizational Structure

In 1972, British sociologist John Child rejected the environmental imperative approach to organizational structure. He proposed a *strategic choice* model based on behavioral rather than rational economic principles.[85] Child believed structure resulted from a political process involving organizational power holders. According to the strategic choice model that has evolved from Child's work,[86] an organization's structure is determined largely by a dominant coalition of top-management strategists.[87]

A Strategic Choice Model   As Figure 18–9 illustrates, specific strategic choices or decisions reflect how the dominant coalition perceives environmental constraints and the organization's objectives. These strategic choices are tempered by the

Figure 18–9   *The Relationship between Strategic Choice and Organizational Structure*

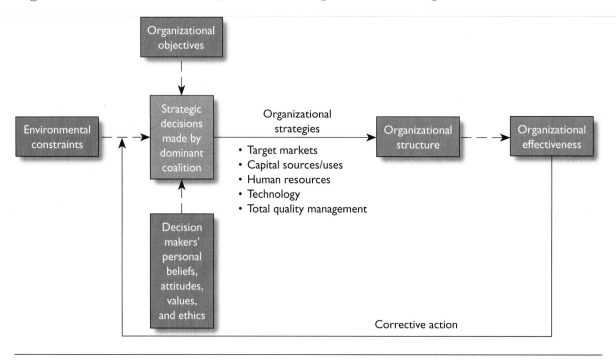

decision makers' personal beliefs, attitudes, values, and ethics. For example, consider this unusual relationship between top management's ethics and corporate strategy, as reported by *Business Ethics* magazine:

> As a manufacturer and retailer of outdoor clothing and equipment, it's natural for Patagonia to be concerned about the environment. But as a for-profit business, it's also natural for the company to feel a need to look at its bottom line.
>
> Patagonia has found a way to do both, and to turn upside down traditional concepts of how companies grow in the bargain.
>
> The company first warned its customers of the impending change in its [1992] fall/winter catalog. . . . "We are limiting Patagonia's growth in the United States with the eventual goal of halting growth altogether. We dropped 30% of our clothing line. . . .
>
> "What does this mean to you? Well, last fall you had a choice of five ski pants; now you may choose between two. This is, of course, unAmerican, but two styles of ski pants are all anyone needs."
>
> And . . . [the 1993] catalog featured the following message: "At Patagonia, as a company, and as individuals, we sometimes find the array of choices dizzying. But the choices must be faced, resolved soberly, and judicious action taken. To fully include environmental concerns in our ordinary work is to give something back to the planet that sustains us, and that we have taxed so heavily. It's a complex process, but the simplest of gifts."
>
> To that end, say Patagonia spokespeople Lu Setnicksa and Mike Harrelson, the company has embarked on an aggressive effort to examine everything from the materials it uses to produce its products, to which products it actually makes, to what kind of paper it uses in its copying machines.[88]

A more efficient Patagonia enjoyed increased profits, despite an initial decrease in sales revenue. According to a recent search of Patagonia's Web site, the company still prefers "the human scale to the corporate."[89] Directing our attention once again to Figure 18–9, the organization is structured to accommodate its mix of strategies. Ultimately, corrective action is taken if organizational effectiveness criteria are not met.

Research and Practical Lessons   In a study of 97 small and mid-size companies in Quebec, Canada, strategy and organizational structure were found to be highly interdependent. Strategy influenced structure and structure influenced strategy. This was particularly true for larger, more innovative, and more successful firms.[90]

Strategic choice theory and research teaches managers at least two practical lessons. First, the environment is just one of many codeterminants of structure. Second, like any other administrative process, organization design is subject to the byplays of interpersonal power and politics.

Summary of Key Concepts

1. *Describe the four characteristics common to all organizations, and explain the difference between closed and open systems.* They are coordination of effort (achieved through policies and rules), a common goal (a collective purpose), division of labor (people performing separate but related tasks), and a hierarchy of authority (the chain of command). Closed systems, such as a battery-powered clock, are relatively self-sufficient. Open systems, such as the human body, are highly dependent on the environment for survival. Organizations are said to be open systems.

2. *Define the term* learning organization. A learning organization is one that proactively creates, acquires, and transfers knowledge and changes its behavior on the basis of new knowledge and insights.

3. *Describe horizontal, hourglass, and virtual organizations.* Horizontal organizations are flat structures built around core processes aimed at identifying and satisfying customer needs. Cross-functional teams and empowerment are central to horizontal organizations. Hourglass organizations have a small executive level; a short and narrow middle-management level (because information technology links the top and bottom levels), and a broad base of operating personnel. Virtual organizations typically are families of interdependent companies. They are contractual and fluid in nature.

4. *Describe the four generic organizational effectiveness criteria, and discuss how managers can prevent organizational decline.* They are goal accomplishment (satisfying stated objectives), resource acquisition (gathering the necessary productive inputs), internal processes (building and

maintaining healthy organizational systems), and strategic constituencies satisfaction (achieving at least minimal satisfaction for all key stakeholders). Because complacency is the leading cause of organizational decline, managers need to create a culture of continuous improvement. Decline automatically follows periods of great success if preventive steps are not taken to avoid the erosion of organizational resources (money, customers, talent, and innovative ideas).

5. *Explain what the contingency approach to organization design involves.* The contingency approach to organization design calls for fitting the organization to the demands of the situation. Environmental uncertainty can be assessed in terms of social, political, economic, technological, resource, and demand factors.

6. *Describe the relationship between differentiation and integration in effective organizations.* Harvard researchers Lawrence and Lorsch found that successful organizations achieved a proper balance between the two opposing structural forces of differentiation and integration. Differentiation forces the organization apart. Through a variety of mechanisms—including hierarchy, rules, teams, and liaisons—integration draws the organization together.

7. *Discuss Burns and Stalker's findings regarding mechanistic and organic organizations.* British researchers Burns and Stalker found that mechanistic (bureaucratic, centralized) organizations tended to be effective in stable situations. In unstable situations, organic (flexible, decentralized) organizations were more effective. These findings underscored the need for a contingency approach to organization design.

8. *Define and briefly explain the practical significance of centralization and decentralization.* Because key decisions are made at the top of centralized organizations, they tend to be tightly controlled. In decentralized organizations, employees at lower levels are empowered to make important decisions. Contingency design calls for a proper balance.

9. *Discuss the effective management of organizational size.* Regarding the optimum size for organizations, the challenge for today's managers is to achieve smallness within bigness by keeping subunits at a manageable size.

Discussion Questions

1. How many organizations directly affect your life today? List as many as you can.

2. What would an organization chart of your current (or last) place of employment look like? Does the chart you have drawn reveal the hierarchy (chain of command), division of labor, span of control, and line–staff distinctions? Does it reveal anything else? Explain.

3. Why is it appropriate to view modern organizations as open systems?

4. Which of the three new organizational configurations probably will be most prevalent 10 to 15 years from now? Why?

5. How would you respond to a manager who claimed the only way to measure a business's effectiveness is in terms of how much profit it makes?

6. Why is it important to focus on the role of complacency in organizational decline?

7. In a nutshell, what does contingency organization design entail?

8. What is wrong with an organization having too much differentiation and too little integration?

9. If organic organizations are popular with most employees, why can't all organizations be structured in an organic fashion?

10. How can you tell if an organization (or subunit) is too big?

Internet Exercise

www.fortune.com

There is no single way to measure organizational effectiveness, as discussed in this chapter. Different stakeholders want organizations to do different and often conflicting things. The purpose of this exercise is to introduce alternative effectiveness criteria and to assess real companies with them.

Each year, *Fortune* magazine publishes a ranking of America's Most Admired Companies. Some might pass this off as simply a corporate image popularity contest. But we view it as much more. *Fortune* applies a set of eight attributes that arguably could be called effectiveness criteria. You can judge for yourself by going to *Fortune*'s Internet site (**www.fortune.com**) and selecting "America's Most Admired" under the heading "Companies." (For a broader global perspective, select "Global Most Admired.") Briefly check out the "Methodology and FAQ" section before clicking on "Key Attributes." Survey the top 10 and bottom 10 companies for each of the eight attributes (nine attributes for the global list). You may want to print copies of your lists for possible class discussion.

Questions

1. Do you agree that the eight (or nine) key attributes are really organizational effectiveness criteria? Explain. What other attributes would you add to the list? Which would you remove from the list?

2. In terms of relative importance, how would you rank the eight (or nine) key attributes? Explain your reasoning.

3. Were you surprised by how any of the companies were ranked? Explain.

4. All things considered, which particular company do you admire most? Why? Which one do you admire the least? Why?

OB in Action Case Study

Steve Ballmer Attempts to Remake Microsoft in Bill Gates' Shadow[91]

BusinessWeek There isn't another company in the world as closely identified with its leader as Microsoft Corp. has been with William H Gates III. When the PC revolution erupted in the mid-1980s, it was Gates who emerged as chief pitchman for the clunky machines that suddenly appeared on many desktops. When tech stocks soared to unimaginable heights, Gates's multi-billions landed him atop the lists of the world's wealthiest. And when Microsoft found itself in the crosshairs of federal antitrust regulators, Gates personified the abuse of market power. He was lord over a software behemoth that in 27 years has racked up nearly $50 billion in profits and that calls the tune for one of the world's most crucial industries. Gates is to our era what Rockefeller and Carnegie were to theirs.

But Gates no longer runs Microsoft. He gave up the chief executive role 2½ years ago to his best friend and longtime management sidekick, Steven A Ballmer. The burly, eats-nails-for-breakfast Detroit native thrives on the discipline of organizational management the way Gates thrills to the intricacies of technology. In 2000, Gates gave his pal free rein to restructure the way Microsoft manages finance, sales, product development, marketing, even strategic planning. And Ballmer took him up on it, big time.

Today, after a transition that had its rocky moments, it's clear that a new era has dawned at Microsoft: The powerhouse that Gates built is being reconstructed by Ballmer. And Gates doesn't seem to mind. Ask Gates about Ballmer's thumbprint on the company, and he laughs at the understatement. "Thumbprint? He's got big thumbs," Gates says. "Steve's the no. 1 guy, and I'm the no. 2 guy.... I have a strong voice, a strong recommendation, but Steve has to decide."

Indeed, if Gates is Rockefeller, then Ballmer is shaping up to be Microsoft's Jack Welch—not a visionary founder but a leader, like the legendary General Electric Co. CEO, with the force of personality and management chops to reinvent a company in his own image. The 46-year-old Ballmer is not content to tend the machine Gates designed. His goal: to create a "great, long-lasting company" that will be even more successful in its second quarter-century than it was in its first. "We've done well," he says. Now, "there's an opportunity to really be amazing—to be amazing as a business, to be amazing in the positive impact that we have on society. But we have to do some things a little bit differently to be as amazing as we hope we can be."

After more than two years of trial and error as a new CEO, Ballmer has come up with his prescription for achieving amazingness. He spelled it out publicly for the first time in a June 6 [2002] memo to 50,000 employees under the heading "Realizing Potential." Typically, crossing-the-Rubicon moments in Microsoft's history have been heralded by a call-to-arms memo. The "Internet Tidal Wave" E-mail that Gates sent out in 1995, for instance, spurred a sleepy Microsoft to become a force to be reckoned with on the Net. Ballmer's memo, too, is a clarion call. He lays out a new mission statement—agreed on by the company's top executives during a March [2002] meeting—and describes the path to get there.

The new mission sounds simple enough, but it's audacious in scope: "To enable people and businesses throughout the world to realize their full potential." That's far broader than the company's basic goal of building software for any device, anywhere. For the first time, Microsoft's mission is not just about technology. It's also about improving the way the company handles relationships with customers and others in the technology industry. "This is not just a fluffy statement of principles, but really a call to action," Ballmer writes.

Indeed, the CEO is calling on his colleagues to do nothing less than rethink every aspect of the way they do their jobs. He has put in place a set of management processes aimed at bridging the gap between the sales and product-development sides of the company. He has empowered a second tier of executives to run their businesses with less supervision, breaking from Microsoft's heritage of placing every important decision in the hands of Gates and Ballmer. And, in response to the frustration of corporate customers, he has ordered his engineers, salesforce, and managers to improve the quality of their products and services.

To make it all stick, Ballmer has concocted a dizzying array of meetings, reviews, and examinations that force people to do their jobs differently. It includes everything from rank-and-file employees grading their supervisors to an accounting system for managers that helps them weigh spending trade-offs to quarterly off-site brainstorming meetings for top execs. Each new process is designed to hook into the next so decisions can be made quickly—and can later be measured. This is light-years from the ad hoc way Microsoft took action before. The final touch: Ballmer is making adoption of the new corporate values part of every employee's annual performance review.

Ballmer's hope is that his code of conduct also will make Microsoft a better corporate citizen. He says the company's core values of honesty, integrity, and respect must shine through with customers, partners, and the tech industry. Microsoft's five-year antitrust case has put a severe strain on its relationships with the rest of the industry, but Ballmer believes that by being open with others about its plans, Microsoft can regain the industry's trust. "We're going to work even harder on these positive relationships, whether that means an investment of time, an investment of energy, or being honest and open and respectful," he says. . . .

Ballmer also has to battle himself. Simply put, he's a grade-A control freak. He's obsessive about understanding every detail of a business—sales, costs, marketing—to the point where he might know how well the Office suite sold in Sweden last quarter. When he became president in 1998, he moved his office to RedWest, the nearby campus that's home to Microsoft's online businesses, and spent a year running the operation. When Paul Gross stepped down as the leader of Microsoft's wireless-computing group last year, Ballmer took control of the division for nine months before handing off the job to Pieter Knook in February. "He'll have to learn to delegate. He wants to, but he's not wired that way," says a former Microsoft executive.

It's not clear that the company's other managers are capable of changing their ways, either. In his memo, Ballmer says he wants his people to be "respectful" and "accountable" toward outsiders and each other. That's an about-face from the culture he and Gates created, where hard-charging and hypercompetitive executives advanced by out-thinking each other and pummeling competitors. Moreover, Microsoft has torn through a string of chief operating officers, brought in from the outside, whose job it was to institute management processes. Most failed. "Many employees see these things as manifestations of old-line companies," says David B Yoffie, a management professor at Harvard Business School. "It just isn't Microsoft." Ballmer has one advantage, though—he's not some outsider trying to impose a foreign structure on the company. . . .

Even though Gates and Ballmer have long been best buddies, the transfer of power was anything but smooth. Gates resisted handing off authority at first, struggling to give up high-level decisions that he had made for decades. "So, the first six months were definitely harder than we expected. And even the second six months were just so-so," Gates admits. Some staff meetings devolved into shouting matches. At one meeting, Gates approved a budget hike to add more people for a project. Ballmer vetoed him, barking, "You put me in charge of the company. Let me run it," say execs familiar with the meeting. Neither Gates nor Ballmer recall the incident, though Ballmer says it could have happened since the pair often spar in meetings. "Bill had to acclimate to the idea that he could defer decisions to

Steve," says Senior Vice President Craig Mundie. It took some time, but the duo eventually grew into their new roles. "It's a cautionary note to anybody who wants to try something like that," Gates says.

Ballmer's first stabs at retooling weren't any easier. He realized he couldn't manage Microsoft the way Gates had. There were just too many moving parts, and it was too unwieldy. "Despite the fact that I think I'm a pretty bright guy, I knew I wasn't bright enough to run the whole company the way I ran sales, where I had a pretty complete model of what we were up to all in my head," Ballmer says, smacking himself in the forehead with the heel of his hand, as if driving home how hard it was to get his mind around Microsoft.

There was—and is—plenty to boggle a mind. The company is not only large, it's no longer the racehorse it once was. Growth roared along at an average 36% a year through the 1990s but slowed in the past two fiscal years. . . .

The problem has been that the two biggest growth engines—the Windows operating system and Office suite of applications—are slowing as PC sales wane. Even though Microsoft has had success in some new markets, such as databases and software for handhelds, it has struggled in the fledgling markets for interactive TV and cell phones. That left Ballmer looking for alternatives—a key reason why Microsoft last year jumped into the game-console business with Xbox and into the accounting-software business with the acquisition of Great Plains Software Inc.

Ballmer realized that Microsoft needed new methods to manage an ever-more-complex company. He first tried to organize around different kinds of customers. The idea was to get product-development groups more connected to users. But the reorganization didn't work. Decisions about such widely used products as Windows, for example, spread across too many of the new divisions. Not even a year into his new job, Ballmer was stressed out and looked it.

Now, Ballmer feels like he's on the right track. He has lost 52 pounds in the past year. He is tanned and clearly comfortable in his CEO role. A series of epiphanies brought him to this place—the result of reorganizational experiments, face-to-face meetings with execs at other companies, and thirsty reading of management books. *Good to Great* by management guru James C Collins and Welch's *Jack: Straight from the Gut* got him to think about solving a wide variety of problems systematically, rather than trying to fix them on an ad hoc basis.

From this patchwork, Ballmer stitched together a quilt of management processes that, he says, especially suits Microsoft. Ballmer elevated the importance of something he calls the "organizational health index," a key factor in measuring executive performance. Taken from Procter & Gamble, the OHI is a survey of employees who are asked to rate their bosses on their leadership skills. By studying

GE, Ballmer crafted a new system to identify and promote promising managers.

Perhaps Ballmer's biggest innovation is something called the Executive P&L, launched in April [2000]. It's a balance sheet that divides the company into seven distinct businesses and gives each unit's leader the financial tools to measure its performance. Ballmer hopes the device will empower execs who have long worked in an environment where everything was run by the CEO. In the past, managers would know the costs of developing a product but not the cost of selling it. Now, they can see their costs end-to-end, giving them the information necessary to make decisions about allocating resources without having to run it by Ballmer.

To some managers, it's liberating. On June 3 [2002], Senior Vice President Doug Burgum walked Ballmer through his financial plan for his corporate-applications group for the coming fiscal year. Ballmer seized on an unusually large bump in R&D spending. In the end, he made it clear it was up to Burgum to decide how much to spend. "In some ways, the review felt like a really good board meeting," says Burgum, who ran Great Plains Software. . . .

Gates had his "think weeks," where he secluded himself at his family's retreat in Hood Canal in northwest Washington to ruminate on the Next Big Thing in technology. Ballmer has created "management sync weeks," weeklong events every quarter with day-after-day of meetings involving the executive staff and board members. The idea is to coordinate themes and strategies among the company's important decision-making groups. The first sync week begins June 17 [2002].

It's not enough to have new business processes, though. Ballmer wants to change the way people behave, too. He needs managers who are willing to work collaboratively. "People have to be very open, self-critical, almost relentlessly honest, and, at the same time, respectful," he says. Ballmer also wants people who are driven to finish projects on time. Under Ballmer's regime, powerful executives at the company are so-called finishers, such as Office applications boss Raikes, Chief Financial Officer John Connors, and sales chief Orlando Ayala. . . .

Ballmer has always been a tough boss. He's known for eviscerating business plans at annual reviews, sometimes humiliating execs in the process. One former top exec says he'd rather put his arm in a food processor than work for

Ballmer again. "Steve is a pain in the ass to work for," the exec says. Ballmer says he's trying to improve. "A lot of people would like to see me balance a little bit more the fun side with the tough side," he says. "I think I've hit a better balance than I had in the past." . . .

At a March [2002] management retreat attended by 84 people in Sun River, Oregon, sales chief Ayala made a plea to other Microsoft execs to put the customer first. Ayala said customers often think Microsoft doesn't care about producing great products, and they believe Microsoft feels it can get away with shoddy work because it has a monopoly. "Some of us should lose our jobs," Ayala says. "All of us are accountable." He got a standing ovation. At the end of the retreat, Ballmer decided to make customer trust the focus of September's management sync week. He got a standing ovation, too.

A taller order will be to remake Microsoft into a company that can grow rapidly and profit handsomely, while also being seen as trustworthy by customers and its industry brethren. If Ballmer can pull that off, Microsoft executives won't be the only ones applauding.

Questions for Discussion

1. What evidence of new-style and old-style organizations (see Table 18–1) do you find in this case?
2. What criteria should Ballmer use to measure the effectiveness of Microsoft? Explain.
3. Using Figure 18–7 as a guide, how much environmental uncertainty does Microsoft face? Explain.
4. Relative to the Lawrence and Lorsch model, what attempts at integration (coordination) can you detect in this case? How important is organizational integration at Microsoft? Explain.
5. Is Ballmer trying to create a more mechanistic or more organic organization? Explain.
6. What examples of decentralization can you find in this case?
7. What should Ballmer do about the sheer size and complexity of Microsoft? Does he have the right management style to implement your recommendation? Explain.

Personal Awareness and Growth Exercise

Organization Design Field Study

Objectives

1. To get out into the field and talk to a practicing manager about organizational structure.
2. To increase your understanding of the important distinction between mechanistic and organic organizations.
3. To broaden your knowledge of contingency design, in terms of organization-environment fit.

Introduction

A good way to test the validity of what you have just read about organizational design is to interview a practicing manager. (*Note:* If you are a manager, simply complete the questionnaire yourself.)

Instructions

Your objective is to interview a manager about aspects of organizational structure, environmental uncertainty, and organizational effectiveness. A *manager* is defined as anyone who supervises other people in an organizational set-ting. The organization may be small or large and for-profit or not-for-profit. Higher-level managers are preferred, but middle managers and first-line supervisors are acceptable. If you interview a lower-level manager, be sure to remind him or her that you want a description of the overall organization, not just an isolated subunit. Your interview will center on the adaptation of Table 18–2, as discussed below.

When conducting your interview, be sure to explain to the manager what you are trying to accomplish. But assure the manager that his or her name will not be mentioned in class discussion or any written projects. Try to keep side notes during the interview for later reference.

Questionnaire

The following questionnaire, adapted from Table 18–2, will help you determine if the manager's organization is relatively mechanistic or relatively organic in structure. *Note:* For items 1 and 2 on the following questionnaire, have the manager respond in terms of the average nonmanagerial employee. (Circle one number for each item.)

Characteristics

1. Task definition and knowledge required	Narrow; technical	1—2—3—4—5—6—7	Broad; general
2. Linkage between individual's contribution and organization's purpose	Vague or indirect	1—2—3—4—5—6—7	Clear or direct
3. Task flexibility	Rigid; routine	1—2—3—4—5—6—7	Flexible; varied
4. Specification of techniques, obligations, and rights	Specific	1—2—3—4—5—6—7	General
5. Degree of hierarchical control	High	1—2—3—4—5—6—7	Low (self-control emphasized)
6. Primary communication pattern	Top-down	1—2—3—4—5—6—7	Lateral (between peers)
7. Primary decision-making style	Authoritarian	1—2—3—4—5—6—7	Democratic; participative
8. Emphasis on obedience and loyalty	High	1—2—3—4—5—6—7	Low

Total score = _____

Additional Question about the Organization's Environment

This organization faces an environment that is (circle one number):
Stable and certain   1—2—3—4—5—6—7—8—9—10   Unstable and uncertain

Additional Questions about the Organization's Effectiveness

1. Profitability (if a profit-seeking business):
   Low   1—2—3—4—5—6—7—8—9—10   High
2. Degree of organizational goal accomplishment:
   Low   1—2—3—4—5—6—7—8—9—10   High
3. Customer or client satisfaction:
   Low   1—2—3—4—5—6—7—8—9—10   High
4. Employee satisfaction:
   Low   1—2—3—4—5—6—7—8—9—10   High

Total effectiveness score = _____
(Add responses from above)

Questions for Discussion

1. Using the following norms, was the manager's organization relatively mechanistic or organic?

    8–24 = Relatively mechanistic

    25–39 = Mixed

    40–56 = Relatively organic

2. In terms of Burns and Stalker's contingency theory, does the manager's organization seem to fit its environment? Explain.

3. Does the organization's degree of effectiveness reflect how well it fits its environment? Explain.

Group Exercise

Stakeholder Audit Team

Objectives

1. To continue developing your group interaction and teamwork skills.

2. To engage in open-system thinking.

3. To conduct a stakeholder audit and thus more fully appreciate the competing demands placed on today's managers.

4. To establish priorities and consider trade-offs for modern managers.

Introduction

According to open-system models of organizations, environmental factors—social, political, legal, technological, and economic—greatly affect what managers can and cannot do. This exercise gives you an opportunity to engage in open-system thinking within a team setting. It requires a team meeting of about 20 to 25 minutes followed by a 10- to 15-minute general class discussion. Total time required for this exercise is about 30 to 40 minutes.

Instructions

Your instructor will randomly assign you to teams with five to eight members each. Choose one team member to act as recorder/spokesperson. Either at your instructor's prompting or as a team, choose one of these two options:

1. Identify an organization that is familiar to everyone on your team (it can be a local business, your college or university, or a well-known organization such as McDonald's, Wal-Mart, or Southwest Airlines).

2. Select an organization from any of the OB in Action Case Studies following each chapter in this book.

Next, using Figure 18–6 as a model, do a *stakeholder audit* for the organization in question. This will require a team brainstorming session followed by brief discussion. Your team will need to make reasonable assumptions about the circumstances surrounding your target organization.

Finally, your team should select the three (or more) *high-priority* stakeholders on your team's list. Rank them number one, number two, and so on. (*Tip:* A top-priority stakeholder is one with the greatest short-term impact on the success or failure of your target organization.) Be prepared to explain to the entire class your rationale for selecting each high-priority stakeholder.

Questions for Discussion

1. How does this exercise foster open-system thinking? Give examples.

2. Did this exercise broaden your awareness of the complexity of modern organizational environments? Explain.

3. Why do managers need clear priorities when it comes to dealing with organizational stakeholders?

4. How many *trade-offs* (meaning one party gains at another's expense) can you detect in your team's list of stakeholders? Specify them.

5. Does your experience with doing a stakeholder audit strengthen or weaken the validity of the ecosystem model of organizations? Explain.

6. How difficult was it for your team to complete this assignment? Explain.

Ethical Dilemma

A Smokin' Deal for the Ex-CEO of Philip Morris[92]

BusinessWeek When Geoffrey Bible retires from cigarette-and-food giant Philip Morris on August 31 [2002], he will end a 15-year run at the top of one of the largest companies in the world. Although Bible will no longer be calling the shots, he'll still be free to call up the corporate jet. According to his exit agreement, filed with the Securities & Exchange Commission, Philip Morris will provide its onetime leader with the following benefits, in exchange for occasionally being available as a consultant, for as long as he lives:

- An office near his home, including a secretary.

- An unlimited phone-calling card.

- Two cell phones and two fax machines, plus the cost of maintenance.

- Security at his home and at his vacation home.

- Access to the corporate plane, dining room, and gym.

- A company car and driver or a car allowance of up to $100,000 a year.

- Up to $15,000 a year for financial-advisory services.

While it seems amazing that a man who earned $50 million in salary, bonus, and other compensation in 2001 could need all this, executive-pay experts say this isn't unheard of.

As the term is used in Figure 18–9, did the "dominant coalition" at Philip Morris exceed ethical limits in this case?

1. Bible is being justly rewarded for his long and successful tenure at a top company. Explain.

2. People who criticize situations such as this are just jealous. They would gladly accept such a package. Explain.

3. This is just another greedy CEO take-the-money-and-run story. It is clearly unethical. Explain.

4. This is unfair for other Philip Morris stakeholders, including employees and stockholders. Explain.

5. The government should pass legislation to limit exit packages for corporate executives. What should be the limits?

6. Invent other options. Discuss.

For an interpretation of this situation, visit our Web site, **www.mhhe.com/kreitner.**

Chapter Nineteen

Managing Change and Stress

Learning Objectives

When you finish studying the material in this chapter, you should be able to:

1 Discuss the external and internal forces that create the need for organizational change.

2 Describe Lewins change model and the systems model of change.

3 Discuss Kotter's eight steps for leading organizational change.

4 Demonstrate your familiarity with the four identifying characteristics of organization development (OD).

5 Summarize the 10 reasons employees resist change.

6 Discuss the five personal characteristics related to resistance to change.

7 Identify alternative strategies for overcoming resistance to change, and discuss the managerial recommendations for leading change.

8 Define the term *stress*, and describe the model of occupational stress.

9 Discuss the stress moderators of social support, hardiness, and Type A behavior.

10 Contrast the five dominant stress-reduction techniques.

The latest crisis for Jeffrey R. Immelt came as they all have in his short tenure as chairman and CEO of General Electric Co.: without warning. This time, it was a quarterly earnings announcement. Despite an economy that Immelt describes as the toughest he has seen in 20 years, he was delivering a solid, 17% earnings increase before an accounting change. And just as investors had demanded, he was offering more detail. In a first for GE, Chief Financial Officer Keith S. Sherin would field questions from analysts. But the moment of triumph, as it has so many times in the past seven months, slipped away. Instead of responding with cheers and a runup in the stock on April 11, investors bailed because of flat revenues and GE's cautious outlook. By the end of the day, shares had plunged 9.3%, and Chairman Immelt was peeved, to say the least. "The bottom line is that we met our numbers. We absolutely, positively met our numbers," he says. To buck up morale, Immelt phoned top managers and later dashed off a companywide e-mail reminding employees of GE's strong position in its markets. Imagine former chief Jack Welch having to do that. . . .

For years, GE sat at the top of the marketplace as the world's most valuable, and for some, the most admirable company. But an economic downturn and corporate scandals forced General Electric's new CEO Jeffrey Immelt to face unprecedented scrutiny and cautious investors.
AP/Wide World Photos

In quiet moments, while sipping the Diet Coke that always seems at hand, Immelt admits that the criticism has been more intense than he had imagined—and his ability to counter it less effective than he had hoped. Indeed, he has spent twice as much time communicating with Wall Street as he had expected. "I hate the criticism, but it's not a personal thing," he says. "I get up the next day and say, 'These guys don't get it.' " Still, he adds: "I'd be lying if I didn't say I felt stress. But it's never about this company. It's about wanting the world to see and to touch and to feel how different we are."

The pressure isn't likely to slacken anytime soon. GE stock has been slashed by almost half since October 2000, and in just the past six weeks the company has lost almost $100 billion in market value. . . .

Immelt is determined to reshape GE for the next generation. Between battling crises, he has already launched several initiatives. His immediate push is to slash the company's administrative and support staff, now a full 40% of employees, while making the front-line workers obsessed with helping customers. That's right—obsessed. He will measure managers by how much they improve their customers' bottom lines—something Welch never did—and by how much time they spend in front of their customers. He wants GE to take the Six Sigma quality program and other innovations deep into a client's operations. Add to that more globalization, more business via the Web, and a more diverse senior staff. In short, a more modern GE.

Indeed, GE already looks different in at least one respect: Since Immelt was named chairman-elect in late 1999, 50% of all senior executive hires and 54% of new corporate officers are women, minorities, or foreign employees. He has put teeth into mentoring programs and made [an executive] directly responsible for a diversity forum. He has also funneled a lot more money into research and development.

Immelt hasn't spent a day more than necessary at company headquarters in Fairfield, Connecticut. He has made it a priority to keep up the global travel, visiting customers and employees; he even devoted 21 full days for the annual "Session C" assessment of top talent, which ends in mid-May. He's out of the office almost 70% of the time, calling his wife, Andy, and 15-year-old daughter, Sarah, each night from different parts of the world.[1]

> **For Discussion**
>
> What are the forces of change at General Electric? Describe what Immelt is doing in response to these forces of change.

Jeff Immelt's experiences at GE are not the exception. Increased global competition, startling breakthroughs in information technology, and calls for greater corporate ethics are forcing companies to change the way they do business. Employees want satisfactory work environments, customers are demanding greater value, and investors want more integrity in financial disclosures. The rate of organizational and societal change is clearly accelerating.

Companies no longer have a choice—they must change to survive. Unfortunately, it is not easy to successfully implement organizational change. The GE case, for example, illustrates that successful organizational change requires managerial commitment, an implementation plan, and buy-in from all employees. Peter Senge, a well-known expert on the topic of organizational change, made the following comment about organizational change during an interview with *Fast Company* magazine:

> When I look at efforts to create change in big companies over the past 10 years, I have to say that there's enough evidence of success to say that change is possible—and enough evidence of failure to say that it isn't likely.[2]

If Senge is correct, then it is all the more important for current and future managers to learn how they can successfully implement organizational change. This final chapter was written to help managers navigate the journey of change.

Specifically, we discuss the forces that create the need for organization change, models of planned change, resistance to change, and how managers can better manage the stress associated with organizational change.

Forces of Change

How do organizations know when they should change? What cues should an organization look for? Although there are no clear-cut answers to these questions, cues signaling the need for change are found by monitoring the forces for change.

Organizations encounter many different forces for change. These forces come from external sources outside the organization and from internal sources. This section examines the forces that create the need for change. Awareness of these forces can help managers determine when they should consider implementing an organizational change. The external and internal forces for change are presented in Figure 19–1.

Figure 19–1   *The External and Internal Forces for Change*

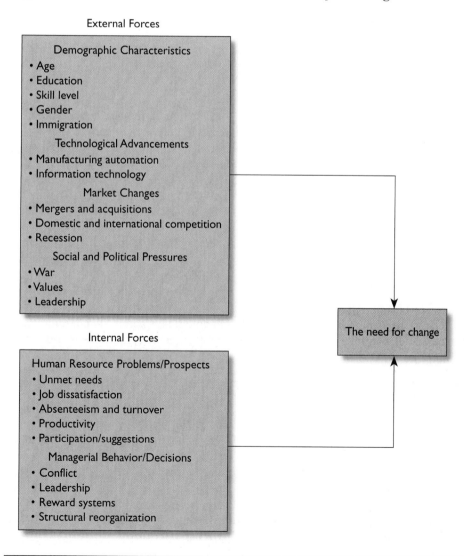

External Forces

External forces for change originate outside the organization. Because these forces have global effects, they may cause an organization to question the essence of what business it is in and the process by which products and services are produced. There are four key external forces for change: demographic characteristics, technological advancements, market changes, and social and political pressures. Each is now explored.

Demographic Characteristics

Chapter 2 provided a detailed discussion of demographic changes occurring in the US workforce. We concluded that organizations need to effectively manage diversity if they are to receive maximum contribution and commitment from employees. Consider the implications associated with hiring the 80 million people dubbed the Net or Echo-Boom Generation—people born between 1977 and 1997.

> Employers will have to face the new realities of the Net Generation's culture and values, and what it wants from work if they expect to attract and retain those talents and align them with corporate goals. . . . The new wave of 80 million young people entering the workforce during the next 20 years are technologically equipped and, therefore, armed with the most powerful tools for business. That makes their place in history unique: No previous generation has grown up understanding, using, and expanding on such a pervasive instrument as the PC.[3]

Technological Advancements

Both manufacturing and service organizations are increasingly using technology as a means to improve productivity and market competitiveness. Manufacturing companies, for instance, have automated their operations with robotics, computerized numerical control (CNC), which is used for metal cutting operations, and computer-aided design (CAD). CAD is a computerized process of drafting and designing engineering drawings of products. Companies also are using computer-integrated manufacturing (CIM). This highly technical process attempts to integrate product design with product planning, control, and operations. In contrast to these manufacturing technologies, the service sector of the US economy is using a host of computerized technologies to obtain, store, analyze, retrieve, and communicate information.

Development and use of information technologies is probably one of the biggest forces for change. Organizations, large and small, for profit and not for profit, all must adapt to using a host of information technologies. Experts also predict that E-business will continue to create evolutionary change in organizations around the world.

Market Changes

The emergence of a global economy is forcing companies to change the way they do business. For example, many Japanese companies are having to discontinue their jobs-for-life philosophy because of increased international competition, and Chinese companies increasingly are adopting an international mind-set. Ping An Insurance Company is a good example of a Chinese company that has experienced tremendous growth by internationalizing its operations (see the International OB on page 675). US companies are also forging new partnerships and alliances with their suppliers and potential competitors. For example, AOL has created alliances with drkoop.com, GTE, US West, Sun, and Nintendo, while Oracle has between 15,000 and 16,000 business alliances.[4]

International OB   China's Ping An Insurance Company Grows and Learns from International Markets

Ping An is a company devoted to learning from around the world. Its CEO, Peter Ma, understands that the employee of the future must see, think, act, and mobilize not only with a Chinese mind-set, but also with a global one. Ma's company continues to break new ground, as it has since it was founded in 1988, as China's first partially employee-owned company. From US$30 million in assets and 10 employees in 1988, it has grown to a US$30 billion company with more than 130,000 employees. Ping An's secret to success is its ability to keep one foot in traditional Chinese culture and one foot in the world, constantly learning and modernizing Chinese culture. For Ping An, to be a global company no longer means just doing business internationally or being world class at home and abroad. It now also means learning aggressively from around the world.

SOURCE: Excerpted from R Rosen and P Digh, "Developing Globally Literate Leaders," *Training & Development*, May 2001, p. 72.

∫ocial and Political Pressures   These forces are created by social and political events. For example, the collapse of Enron has created increased focus on the process by which organizations conduct financial reporting. The tobacco companies also are experiencing a lot of pressure to alter the way they market their products within the United States.

This pressure is being exerted through legislative bodies that represent the American populace. Political events can create substantial change. For instance, Russian President Vladimir Putin is instituting changes aimed at increasing US investment in business opportunities within Russia.

> Jokes aside, Putin is serious about cleaning up Russia. He realizes the entrepreneurial sector can never achieve its potential without a full-scale battle against corruption. What's more, Putin wants closer ties to the West—an initiative that has prompted Putin's cooperation with the United States in the fight against terrorism and his resistance to OPEC's call for big cuts in oil exports. But Putin knows that Western investment will not pour in without a major improvement in corporate governance.
>
> So Putin is leading the Kremlin's biggest crackdown on corruption since the Soviet Union's collapse. A high-profile probe of suspect bureaucrats—as seen in the charges pending against Railways Minister Nikolai Aksyonenko for illegally spending Ministry funds—is making headlines. But a second, less-sensational effort is the heart of this campaign: the drive to limit the myriad opportunities for bribery and pilferage that plague business and government.[5]

Although it is difficult for organizations to predict changes in political forces, many organizations hire lobbyists and consultants to help them detect and respond to social and political changes.

Internal Forces

Internal forces for change come from inside the organization. These forces may be subtle, such as low job satisfaction, or can manifest in outward signs, such as low productivity and conflict. Internal forces for change come from both human resource problems and managerial behavior/decisions.

Internal forces for change
Originate inside the organization.

Human Resource Problems/Prospects   These problems stem from employee perceptions about how they are treated at work and the match between individual and organization needs and desires. Chapter 6 highlighted the relationship between an employee's unmet needs and job dissatisfaction. Dissatisfaction is a symptom of an underlying employee problem that should be addressed. Unusual or high levels of absenteeism and turnover also represent forces for change. Organizations might respond to these problems by using the various approaches to job design discussed in Chapter 8, by reducing employees' role conflict, overload, and ambiguity (recall our discussion in Chapter 12), and by removing the different stressors discussed in the final section of this chapter. Prospects for positive change stem from employee participation and suggestions.

Managerial Behavior/Decisions   Excessive interpersonal conflict between managers and their subordinates is a sign that change is needed. Both the manager and the employee may need interpersonal skills training, or the two individuals may simply need to be separated. For example, one of the parties might be transferred to a new department. Inappropriate leader behaviors such as inadequate direction or support may result in human resource problems requiring change. As discussed in Chapter 17, leadership training is one potential solution for this problem. Inequitable reward systems—recall our discussion in Chapters 9 and 10—and the type of structural reorganizations discussed in Chapter 18 are additional forces for change. Finally, managerial decisions are a powerful force for change. For example, Jacques Nasser, former CEO of Ford Motor Company, instituted a host of internal changes aimed at improving Ford's financial position, productivity, quality, organizational culture, and customer satisfaction.

> Almost as soon as he ascended to the corner office, Nasser began overhauling Ford, unveiling one initiative after another. He signed agreements to partner with Microsoft Corp. and Yahoo! Inc. on the Web. He pushed out Ford's Old Guard and brought in talented young stars from the auto industry and beyond. He flattened Ford's bureaucracy, giving more autonomy to regional executives, and shook up senior managers by tying their bonuses to gains in customer service. Gone were the days of automatic promotions and seniority. "You've got to earn a promotion" he thundered at young execs shortly after becoming CEO. "The days of entitlement at Ford Motor Co. are gone forever."[6]

Unfortunately, these changes did not help the company overcome its financial and quality problems: Nasser ultimately was let go by Ford.[7]

Models and Dynamics of Planned Change

American managers are criticized for emphasizing short-term, quick-fix solutions to organizational problems. When applied to organizational change, this approach is doomed from the start. Quick-fix solutions do not really solve underlying problems, and they have little staying power. Researchers and managers alike have thus tried to identify effective ways to manage the change process. This section sheds light on their insights. After discussing different types of organizational changes, we review Lewin's change model, a systems model of change, Kotter's eight steps for leading organizational change, and organizational development.

Figure 19–2   *A Generic Typology of Organizational Change*

Types of Change

A useful three-way typology of change is displayed in Figure 19–2.[8] This typology is generic because it relates to all sorts of change, including both administrative and technological changes. Adaptive change is lowest in complexity, cost, and uncertainty. It involves reimplementation of a change in the same organizational unit at a later time or imitation of a similar change by a different unit. For example, an adaptive change for a department store would be to rely on 12-hour days during the annual inventory week. The store's accounting department could imitate the same change in work hours during tax preparation time. Adaptive changes are not particularly threatening to employees because they are familiar.

Innovative changes fall midway on the continuum of complexity, cost, and uncertainty. An experiment with flexible work schedules by a farm supply warehouse company qualifies as an innovative change if it entails modifying the way other firms in the industry already use it. Unfamiliarity, and hence greater uncertainty, make fear of change a problem with innovative changes.

At the high end of the continuum of complexity, cost, and uncertainty are radically innovative changes. Changes of this sort are the most difficult to implement and tend to be the most threatening to managerial confidence and employee job security.[9] They can tear the fabric of an organization's culture. Resistance to change tends to increase as changes go from adaptive to innovative to radically innovative.

Lewin's Change Model

Most theories of organizational change originated from the landmark work of social psychologist Kurt Lewin. Lewin developed a three-stage model of planned change which explained how to initiate, manage, and stabilize the change process.[10] The three stages are unfreezing, changing, and refreezing. Before reviewing each stage, it is important to highlight the assumptions underlying this model:[11]

1. The change process involves learning something new, as well as discontinuing current attitudes, behaviors, or organizational practices.

2. Change will not occur unless there is motivation to change. This is often the most difficult part of the change process.

3. People are the hub of all organizational changes. Any change, whether in terms of structure, group process, reward systems, or job design, requires individuals to change.

4. Resistance to change is found even when the goals of change are highly desirable.

5. Effective change requires reinforcing new behaviors, attitudes, and organizational practices.

Let us now consider the three stages of change.

Unfreezing
The focus of this stage is to create the motivation to change. In so doing, individuals are encouraged to replace old behaviors and attitudes with those desired by management. Managers can begin the unfreezing process by disconfirming the usefulness or appropriateness of employees' present behaviors or attitudes. In other words, employees need to become dissatisfied with the old way of doing things. Benchmarking is a technique that can be used to help unfreeze an organization. **Benchmarking** "describes the overall process by which a company compares its performance with that of other companies, then learns how the strongest-performing companies achieve their results."[12] For example, one company for which we consulted discovered through benchmarking that their costs to develop a computer system were twice as high as the best companies in the industry, and the time it took to get a new product to market was four times longer than the benchmarked organizations. These data were ultimately used to unfreeze employees' attitudes and motivate people to change the organization's internal processes in order to remain competitive.

Moreover, providing employees with relevant financial information is another common method to create the motivation to change. Consider how Tush Nikollaj used this approach to unfreeze his organization.

> Last January he gathered his upper managers in a conference room and confessed that in the space of six months, the company had gone from turning a profit to losing $130,000 a month. He drew one stark, startling graph on a whiteboard. The graph, which depicted sales, recurring revenues, and expenses, showed that Logical Net Corp., an $8-million Internet service provider based in Albany, NY, was likely to go bankrupt by April. . . .
>
> He realized that the only way he could avoid bankruptcy would be if all his employees moved to cut costs and raise revenues—drastically. To motivate swift action, Nikollaj knew he'd need buy-in.[13]

After unfreezing his employees with this dire financial information, Nikollaj began the change stage by brainstorming different options for improving the company's financial position.

Changing
Because change involves learning, this stage entails providing employees with new information, new behavioral models, or new ways of looking at things.[14] The purpose is to help employees learn new concepts or points of view. Consider, for example, the organizational changes implemented by KPMG Consulting as it transforms itself from an organization run by a partnership to one that is publicly held and focuses on meeting financial goals:

> The massive mahogany desks and expansive offices once occupied by KPMG's venerated partners have given way to cookie-cutter work spaces, pint-size offices, and managing directors. . . . KPMG Consulting has already laid off 800 of its 10,000 employees in the past

Benchmarking

Process by which a company compares its performance with that of high-performing organizations.

16 months, for which it will take a $15 million to $20 million charge....Those who are left have had to adapt to an environment in which the focus is firmly on the numbers. Instead of measuring profitability once a year—standard operating procedure in the partnership—the company now monitors financials constantly. Every Friday, Senior Vice President Kenneth C Taormina grills his sales force on every would-be client: "I go through every single deal [asking] 'What do we need to get it done?' " Even the office kitty that partners dipped into freely for moral-building activities such as staff dinners is now under scrutiny.[15]

Directors at KPMG are clearly trying to get employees to become more customer focused and cost conscious. During a change process like that at KPMG, organizations use role models, mentors, consultants, benchmarking results, and training to facilitate change. Experts recommend that it is best to convey the idea that change is a continuous learning process rather than a one-time event.

Refreezing   Change is stabilized during refreezing by helping employees integrate the changed behavior or attitude into their normal way of doing things. This is accomplished by first giving employees the chance to exhibit the new behaviors or attitudes. Once exhibited, positive reinforcement is used to reinforce the desired change. Additional coaching and modeling also are used at this point to reinforce the stability of the change.

A Systems Model of Change

A systems approach takes a "big picture" perspective of organizational change. It is based on the notion that any change, no matter how large or small, has a cascading effect throughout an organization.[16] For example, promoting an individual to a new work group affects the group dynamics in both the old and new groups. Similarly, creating project or work teams may necessitate the need to revamp compensation practices. These examples illustrate that change creates additional change. Today's solutions are tomorrow's problems. A systems model of change offers managers a framework to understand the broad complexities of organizational change. The three main components of a systems model are inputs, target elements of change, and outputs (see Figure 19–3).[17]

Inputs   All organizational changes should be consistent with an organization's mission, vision, and resulting strategic plan. A **mission statement** represents the "reason" an organization exists, and an organization's *vision* is a long-term goal that describes "what" an organization wants to become. Consider how the difference between mission and vision affects organizational change. Your university probably has a mission to educate people. This mission does not necessarily imply anything about change. It simply defines the university's overall purpose. In contrast, the university may have a vision to be recognized as the "best" university in the country. This vision requires the organization to benchmark itself against other world-class universities and to create plans for achieving the vision. While vision statements point the way, strategic plans contain the detail needed to create organizational change.

A **strategic plan** outlines an organization's long-term direction and actions necessary to achieve planned results. Strategic plans are based on considering an organization's strengths and weaknesses relative to its environmental opportunities and threats. This comparison results in developing an organizational strategy to attain desired outputs such as profits, customer satisfaction, quality, adequate return on investment, and

Mission statement
Summarizes "why" an organization exists.

Strategic plan
A long-term plan outlining actions needed to achieve desired results.

Figure 19–3   *A Systems Model of Change*

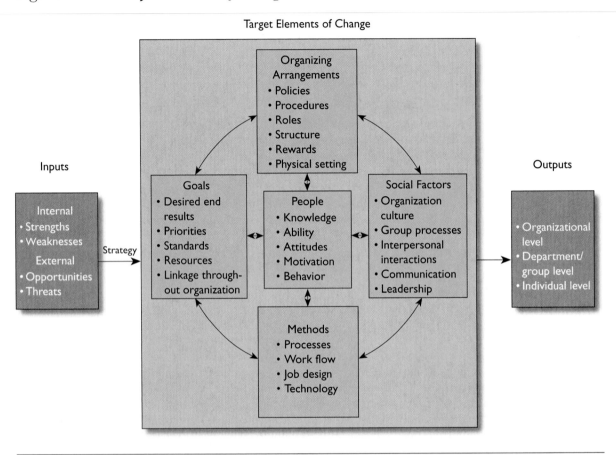

Target Elements of Change

Inputs

Internal
• Strengths
• Weaknesses

External
• Opportunities
• Threats

Strategy

Organizing Arrangements
• Policies
• Procedures
• Roles
• Structure
• Rewards
• Physical setting

Goals
• Desired end results
• Priorities
• Standards
• Resources
• Linkage throughout organization

People
• Knowledge
• Ability
• Attitudes
• Motivation
• Behavior

Social Factors
• Organization culture
• Group processes
• Interpersonal interactions
• Communication
• Leadership

Methods
• Processes
• Work flow
• Job design
• Technology

Outputs

• Organizational level
• Department/ group level
• Individual level

SOURCES: Adapted from D R Fuqua and D J Kurpius, "Conceptual Models in Organizational Consultation," *Journal of Counseling & Development,* July–August 1993, pp. 602–18; and D A Nadler and M L Tushman, "Organizational Frame Bending: Principles for Managing Reorientation," *Academy of Management Executive,* August 1989, pp. 194–203.

acceptable levels of turnover and employee commitment (see Figure 19–3). In summary, organizations tend to commit resources to counterproductive or conflicting activities when organizational changes are not consistent with its strategic plan.

Target elements of change

Components of an organization that may be changed.

Target Elements of Change

Target elements of change represent the components of an organization that may be changed. As shown in Figure 19–3, change can be directed at realigning organizing arrangements, social factors, methods, goals, and people.[18] The choice is based on the strategy being pursued or the organizational problem at hand. For example, Ford Motor Company is targeting organizing arrangements, methods, and goals in order to compete for the increasing demand of "crossover vehicles." These vehicles combine the looks and four-wheel-drive capability of sport-utility vehicles with the seating capacity of minivans and comfortable ride of a larger sedan.

Indeed, the proliferation of models will reward the nimble. Companies that can most quickly develop innovative new autos on a shoestring will be able to sell profitably at lower

Finished vans sit at the end of a production line in the Avon Lake, Ohio, Ford assembly plant. The plant assembles the Ford Mercury Villager, Nisson Quest, and the Ford Econoline Vans. How will Ford's inflexible plant design affect its ability to respond to changes in consumer preferences?

AP/Wide World Photos

volumes. Toyota Motor Corp. and Volkswagen, for example, could be big winners, since both are skilled at incorporating shared components among different models to save money. Toyota, Honda, and, increasingly, GM have flexible factories that can build several different vehicles on the same assembly line at one time, enabling them to switch output as demand shifts. "The key is flexibility, low costs, and being fast to market," says GM Chief Executive G Richard Wagoner Jr. . . .

Such flexibility eludes old-style mass manufacturers like Ford. The no.2 automaker is geared to cranking out hundreds of thousands of Tauruses, Explorers, and F-150 pickups, with as many as three factories dedicated to each vehicle. . . .

That's why converting the body shops at as many as one-third of its 21 North American assembly plants is a top priority of Ford's . . . [new] restructuring plan. Unlike Ford's European operations, which recently retooled three body shops to allow those plants to make two or three completely different models simultaneously, none of Ford's North American body shops is flexible. They are severely limited in their ability to build more than one model on an assembly line. So, for instance, as demand for Taurus drops, the auto maker can't put those facilities or employees to work making something more popular, without spending millions and shutting a plant for months.[19]

Outputs   Outputs represent the desired end results of a change. Once again, these end results should be consistent with an organization's strategic plan. Returning to the above example regarding Ford, the organizational changes are geared toward increasing flexibility, decreasing costs, and decreasing the time it takes to bring a new car to market. Figure 19–3 indicates that change may be directed at the organizational level, department/group level, or individual level. Change efforts are more complicated and difficult to manage when they are targeted at the organizational level. This occurs because organizational-level changes are more likely to affect multiple target elements of change shown in the model.

Kotter's Eight Steps for Leading Organizational Change

John Kotter, an expert in leadership and change management, believes that organizational change typically fails because senior management commits one or more of the following errors:[20]

1. Failure to establish a sense of urgency about the need for change.
2. Failure to create a powerful-enough guiding coalition that is responsible for leading and managing the change process.
3. Failure to establish a vision that guides the change process.
4. Failure to effectively communicate the new vision.
5. Failure to remove obstacles that impede the accomplishment of the new vision.
6. Failure to systematically plan for and create short-term wins. Short-term wins represent the achievement of important results or goals.
7. Declaration of victory too soon. This derails the long-term changes in infrastructure that are frequently needed to achieve a vision.
8. Failure to anchor the changes into the organization's culture. It takes years for long-term changes to be embedded within an organization's culture.

Kotter recommends that organizations should follow eight sequential steps to overcome these problems (see Table 19–1).

Each of the steps shown in Table 19–1 is associated with the eight fundamental errors just discussed. These steps also subsume Lewin's model of change. The first four steps represent Lewin's "unfreezing" stage. Steps 5, 6, and 7 represent "changing," and step 8 corresponds to "refreezing." The value of Kotter's steps is that it provides specific recommendations about behaviors that managers need to exhibit to successfully lead organizational change. It is important to remember that Kotter's research reveals that it is ineffective to skip steps and that successful organizational change is 70% to 90% leadership and only 10% to 30% management. Senior managers are thus advised to focus on leading rather than managing change.[21]

Organization Development

Organization development (OD) is an applied field of study and practice. A pair of OD experts defined **organization development** as follows:

Organization development

A set of techniques or tools used to implement organizational change.

> Organization development is concerned with helping managers plan change in organizing and managing people that will develop requisite commitment, coordination, and competence. Its purpose is to enhance both the effectiveness of organizations and the well-being of their members through planned interventions in the organization's human processes, structures, and systems, using knowledge of behavioral science and its intervention methods.[22]

As you can see from this definition, OD constitutes a set of techniques or interventions that are used to implement organizational change. These techniques or interventions apply to each of the change models discussed in this section. For example, OD is used

Table 19–1   *Steps to Leading Organizational Change*

Step	Description
1. Establish a sense of urgency	Unfreeze the organization by creating a compelling reason for why change is needed.
2. Create the guiding coalition	Create a cross-functional, cross-level group of people with enough power to lead the change.
3. Develop a vision and strategy	Create a vision and strategic plan to guide the change process.
4. Communicate the change vision	Create and implement a communication strategy that consistently communicates the new vision and strategic plan.
5. Empower broad-based action	Eliminate barriers to change, and use target elements of change to transform the organization. Encourage risk taking and creative problem solving.
6. Generate short-term wins	Plan for and create short-term "wins" or improvements. Recognize and reward people who contribute to the wins.
7. Consolidate gains and produce more change	The guiding coalition uses credibility from short-term wins to create more change. Additional people are brought into the change process as change cascades throughout the organization. Attempts are made to reinvigorate the change process.
8. Anchor new approaches in the culture	Reinforce the changes by highlighting connections between new behaviors and processes and organizational success. Develop methods to ensure leadership development and succession.

SOURCE: The steps were developed by J P Kotter, *Leading Change* (Boston: Harvard Business School Press, 1996).

during Lewin's "changing" stage. It also is used to identify and implement targeted elements of change within the systems model of change. Finally, OD might be used during Kotter's steps 1, 3, 5, 6, and 7. In this section, we briefly review the four identifying characteristics of OD and its research and practical implications.[23]

OD Involves Profound Change   Change agents using OD generally desire deep and long-lasting improvement. OD consultant Warner Burke, for example, who strives for fundamental *cultural* change, wrote: "By fundamental change, as opposed to fixing a problem or improving a procedure, I mean that some significant aspect of an organization's culture will never be the same."[24]

OD Is Value-Loaded   Owing to the fact that OD is rooted partially in humanistic psychology, many OD consultants carry certain values or biases into the client organization. They prefer cooperation over conflict, self-control over institutional control, and democratic and participative management over autocratic management. In addition to OD being driven by a consultant's values, some OD practitioners now believe that there is a broader "value perspective" that should underlie any organizational change. Specifically, OD should always be customer focused. This approach implies that organizational interventions should be aimed at helping to satisfy customers' needs and thereby provide enhanced value of an organization's products and services.[25]

OD Is a Diagnosis/Prescription Cycle   OD theorists and practitioners have long adhered to a medical model of organization. Like medical doctors, internal and external OD consultants approach the "sick" organization, "diagnose" its ills, "prescribe" and implement an intervention, and "monitor" progress.

OD Is Process-Oriented

Ideally, OD consultants focus on the form and not the content of behavioral and administrative dealings. For example, product design engineers and market researchers might be coached on how to communicate more effectively with one another without the consultant knowing the technical details of their conversations. In addition to communication, OD specialists focus on other processes, including problem solving, decision making, conflict handling, trust, power sharing, and career development.

OD Research and Practical Implications

Before discussing OD research, it is important to note that many of the topics contained in this book are used during OD interventions. For example, role analysis, which was discussed in Chapter 12, is used to enhance cooperation among work group members by getting them to discuss their mutual expectations. Team building also is commonly used as an OD technique. It is used to improve the functioning of work groups and was reviewed in Chapter 13. The point is that OD research has practical implications for a variety of OB applications previously discussed. OD-related interventions produced the following insights:

- A meta-analysis of 18 studies indicated that employee satisfaction with change was higher when top management was highly committed to the change effort.[26]

- A meta-analysis of 52 studies provided support for the systems model of organizational change. Specifically, varying one target element of change created changes in other target elements. Also, there was a positive relationship between individual behavior change and organizational-level change.[27]

- A meta-analysis of 126 studies demonstrated that multifaceted interventions using more than one OD technique were more effective in changing job attitudes and work attitudes than interventions that relied on only one human-process or technostructural approach.[28]

- A survey of 1,700 firms from China, Japan, the United States, and Europe revealed that (1) US and European firms used OD interventions more frequently than firms from China and Japan and (2) some OD interventions are culture free and some are not.[29]

There are four practical implications derived from this research. First, planned organizational change works. However, management and change agents are advised to rely on multifaceted interventions. As indicated elsewhere in this book, goal setting, feedback, recognition and rewards, training, participation, and challenging job design have good track records relative to improving performance and satisfaction. Second, change programs are more successful when they are geared toward meeting both short-term and long-term results. Managers should not engage in organizational change for the sake of change. Change efforts should produce positive results. Third, organizational change is more likely to succeed when top management is truly committed to the change process and the desired goals of the change program. This is particularly true when organizations pursue large-scale transformation. Finally, the effectiveness of OD interventions is affected by cross-cultural considerations. Managers and OD consultants should not blindly apply an OD intervention that worked in one country to a similar situation in another country.

Understanding and Managing Resistance to Change

We are all creatures of habit. It generally is difficult for people to try new ways of doing things. It is precisely because of this basic human characteristic that most employees do not have enthusiasm for change in the workplace. Rare is the manager who does not have several stories about carefully cultivated changes that died on the vine because of resistance to change. It is important for managers to learn to manage resistance because failed change efforts are costly. Costs include decreased employee loyalty, lowered probability of achieving corporate goals, a waste of money and resources, and difficulty in fixing the failed change effort. This section examines employee resistance to change, relevant research, and practical ways of dealing with the problem.

Why People Resist Change in the Workplace

No matter how technically or administratively perfect a proposed change may be, people make or break it. Individual and group behavior following an organizational change can take many forms (see Figure 19–4). The extremes range from acceptance to active resistance. **Resistance to change** is an emotional/behavioral response to real or imagined threats to an established work routine.

Resistance to change
Emotional/behavioral response to real or imagined work changes.

Figure 19–4   *The Continuum of Responses to Change*

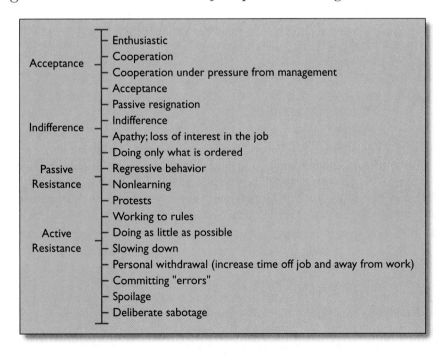

SOURCE: A S Judson, *Changing Behavior in Organizations: Minimizing Resistance to Change* (Cambridge, MA: Basil Blackwell Inc., 1991), p. 48. Used with permission.

Figure 19–4 shows that resistance can be as subtle as passive resignation and as overt as deliberate sabotage. Managers need to learn to recognize the manifestations of resistance both in themselves and in others if they want to be more effective in creating and supporting change. For example, managers can use the list in Figure 19–4 to prepare answers and tactics to combat the various forms of resistance.

Now that we have examined the manifestations of resistance to change, let us consider the reasons employees resist change in the first place. Ten of the leading reasons are listed here:[30]

1. *An individual's predisposition toward change.* This predisposition is highly personal and deeply ingrained. It is an outgrowth of how one learns to handle change and ambiguity as a child. Consider the hypothetical examples of Mary and Jim. Mary's parents were patient, flexible, and understanding. From the time Mary was weaned from a bottle, she was taught that there were positive compensations for the loss of immediate gratification. She learned that love and approval were associated with making changes. In contrast, Jim's parents were unreasonable, unyielding, and forced him to comply with their wishes. They forced him to take piano lessons even though he hated them. Changes were demands for compliance. This taught Jim to be distrustful and suspicious of change. These learned predispositions ultimately affect how Mary and Jim handle change as adults.[31] Dell Computer Corporation recognizes how important an individual's predisposition toward change can be and tries to hire people with positive predispositions:

   > Dell actively seeks and cultivates a certain type of employee mind-set. For example, potential employees are told early on that their former titles may not correlate exactly with positions at Dell because the company structure is relatively flat. "We have to strip the paradigm that titles and levels mean anything," says ... [Steve Price, vice president of human resources for Dell's Public and Americas International Group]. "People have to park their egos at the door." Furthermore, Dell's employees have to move away from the paradigm that more means better. "It's just the reverse," says Price. "When we take half of what you have away from you and tell you to go rebuild it, that's a sign of success." ... "We typically attract people for whom change is not a problem," says ... [Jim Koster, director of human resources for customer service].[32]

2. *Surprise and fear of the unknown.* When innovative or radically different changes are introduced without warning, affected employees become fearful of the implications. Grapevine rumors fill the void created by a lack of official announcements. Harvard's Rosabeth Moss Kanter recommends appointing a transition manager charged with keeping all relevant parties adequately informed.[33]

3. *Climate of mistrust.* Trust, as discussed in Chapter 13, involves reciprocal faith in others' intentions and behavior. Mutual mistrust can doom to failure an otherwise well-conceived change. Mistrust encourages secrecy, which begets deeper mistrust. Managers who trust their employees make the change process an open, honest, and participative affair. Employees who, in turn, trust management are more willing to expend extra effort and take chances with something different.

4. *Fear of failure.* Intimidating changes on the job can cause employees to doubt their capabilities. Self-doubt erodes self-confidence and cripples personal growth and development.

5. *Loss of status or job security.* Administrative and technological changes that threaten to alter power bases or eliminate jobs generally trigger strong resistance.

For example, most corporate restructuring involves the elimination of managerial jobs. One should not be surprised when middle managers resist restructuring and participative management programs that reduce their authority and status.

6. *Peer pressure.* Someone who is not directly affected by a change may actively resist it to protect the interests of his or her friends and co-workers.

7. *Disruption of cultural traditions or group relationships.* Whenever individuals are transferred, promoted, or reassigned, cultural and group dynamics are thrown into disequilibrium.

8. *Personality conflicts.* Just as a friend can get away with telling us something we would resent hearing from an adversary, the personalities of change agents can breed resistance.

9. *Lack of tact or poor timing.* Undue resistance can occur because changes are introduced in an insensitive manner or at an awkward time. Proposed organizational changes are more likely to be accepted by others when managers effectively explain or "sell" the value of their proposed changes. This can be done by explaining how a proposed change is strategically important to an organization's success.[34]

10. *Nonreinforcing reward systems.* Individuals resist when they do not foresee positive rewards for changing. For example, an employee is unlikely to support a change effort that is perceived as requiring him or her to work longer with more pressure.

Research on Resistance to Change

The classic study of resistance to change was reported in 1948 by Lester Coch and John R P French. They observed the introduction of a new work procedure in a garment factory. The change was introduced in three different ways to separate groups of workers. In the "no participation" group, the garment makers were simply told about the new procedure. Members of a second group, called the "representative" group, were introduced to the change by a trained co-worker. Employees in the "total participation" group learned of the new work procedure through a graphic presentation of its cost-saving potential. Mixed results were recorded for the representative group. The no participation and total participation groups, meanwhile, went in opposite directions. Output dropped sharply for the no participation group, while grievances and turnover climbed. After a small dip in performance, the total participation group achieved record-high output levels while experiencing no turnover.[35] Since the Coch and French study, participation has been the recommended approach for overcoming resistance to change.[36]

Empirical research uncovered five additional personal characteristics related to resistance to change. The first involves an employee's commitment to change. **Commitment to change** is defined as a mind-set "that binds an individual to a course of action deemed necessary for the successful implementation of a change initiative."[37] A recent series of studies showed that an employee's commitment to change was a significant and positive predictor of behavioral support for a change initiative.[38] In order to bring this concept to life, we would like you to complete a shortened version of a commitment to change instrument presented in the OB Exercise on page 688. Were you committed to the change? Did this level of commitment affect your behavioral support for what management was trying to accomplish?

The second personal characteristic is resilience to change. **Resilience to change** is a composite characteristic reflecting high self-esteem, optimism, and an internal locus of control: Self-esteem and locus of control were discussed in Chapter 5. People with high resilience are expected to be more open and adaptable toward change. In support

Commitment to change
A mind-set of doing whatever it takes to effectively implement change.

Resilience to change
Composite personal characteristic reflecting high self-esteem, optimism, and an internal locus of control.

OB Exercise — Does Your Commitment to a Change Initiative Predict Your Behavioral Support for the Change?

Instructions

First, think of a time in which a previous or current employer was undergoing a change initiative that required you to learn something new or to discontinue an attitude, behavior, or organizational practice. Next, evaluate your commitment to this change effort by indicating the extent to which you agree with the following survey items: Use the rating scale shown below. Finally, assess your behavioral support for the change.

1 = Strongly disagree
2 = Disagree
3 = Neither agree nor disagree
4 = Agree
5 = Strongly agree

1. I believe in the value of this change	1——2——3——4——5
2. This change serves an important purpose	1——2——3——4——5
3. This change is a good strategy for the organization	1——2——3——4——5
4. I have no choice but to go along with this change	1——2——3——4——5
5. It would be risky to speak out against this change	1——2——3——4——5
6. It would be too costly for me to resist this change	1——2——3——4——5
7. I feel a sense of duty to work toward this change	1——2——3——4——5
8. It would be irresponsible of me to resist this change	1——2——3——4——5
9. I feel obligated to support this change	1——2——3——4——5

Total score = _____

Arbitrary Norms

9–18 = Low commitment
19–35 = Moderate commitment
36–45 = High commitment

Behavioral Support for the Change

Overall, I modified my attitudes and behavior in line with what management was trying to accomplish	1——2——3——4——5

SOURCE: Survey items were obtained from L Herscovitch and J P Meyer, "Commitment to Organizational Change: Extension of a Three-Component Model," *Journal of Applied Psychology*, June 2002, p. 477.

---

of this prediction, a study of 130 individuals working in the areas of public housing and community development revealed that resilience to change was associated with respondents' willingness to accommodate or accept a specific organizational change. In turn, willingness to accept change was positively related to job satisfaction and negatively associated with work irritations and intentions to quit.[39]

The third and fourth characteristics were identified in a study of 514 employees from six organizations headquartered in four different continents (North America, Europe, Asia, and Australia). Results revealed that personal dispositions pertaining to having a "positive self-concept" and "tolerance for risk" were positively related to coping with change. That is, people with a positive self-concept and a tolerance for risk handled organizational change better than those without these dispositions.[40]

Finally, high levels of self-efficacy (recall our discussion in Chapter 5) were negatively associated with resistance to change.[41]

The preceding research is based on the assumption that individuals directly or consciously resist change. Some experts contend that this is not the case. Rather, there is a growing belief that resistance to change really represents employees' responses to obstacles in the organization that prevent them from changing.[42] For example, John Kotter, the researcher who developed the eight steps for leading organizational change that were discussed earlier in this chapter, studied more than 100 companies and concluded that employees generally wanted to change but were unable to do so because of obstacles that prevented execution. He noted that obstacles in the organization's structure or in a "performance appraisal system [that] makes people choose between the new vision and their own self-interests" impeded change more than an individual's direct resistance.[43] This new perspective implies that a systems model such as that shown in Figure 19–3 should be used to determine the causes of failed change. Such an approach would likely reveal that ineffective organizational change is due to faulty organizational processes and systems as opposed to employees' direct resistance. In conclusion, a systems perspective suggests that people do not resist change, per se, but rather that individuals' antichange attitudes and behaviors are caused by obstacles within the work environment.

Alternative Strategies for Overcoming Resistance to Change

We previously noted that participation historically has been the recommended approach for overcoming resistance to change. More recently, however, organizational change experts criticized the tendency to treat participation as a cure-all for resistance to change. They prefer a contingency approach because resistance can take many forms and, furthermore, because situational factors vary (see Table 19–2). As seen in Table 19–2, participation + involvement does have its place, but it takes time that is not always available. Also as indicated in Table 19–2, each of the other five methods has its situational niche, advantages, and drawbacks. In short, there is no universal strategy for overcoming resistance to change. Managers need a complete repertoire of change strategies.

Moreover, there are four additional recommendations managers should consider when leading organizational change. First, an organization must be ready for change. Just as a table must be set before you can eat, so must an organization be ready for change before it can be effective.[44] The OB Exercise on page 691 contains a survey that assesses an organization's readiness for change. Use the survey to evaluate a company that you worked for or are familiar with that undertook a change effort. What was the company's readiness for change, and how did this evaluation relate to the success of the change effort?

Second, do not assume that people are consciously resisting change. Managers are encouraged to use a systems model of change to identify the obstacles that are affecting the implementation process. Third, radical innovative change is more likely to succeed when middle-level managers are highly involved in the change process.[45] Hewlett-Packard successfully implemented change by following this recommendation.

[W]hen new executives were charged with turning around Hewlett-Packard's Santa Rosa Systems division, which produces test and measurement equipment for electronic systems,

Table 19–2   *Six Strategies for Overcoming Resistance to Change*

Approach	Commonly Used in Situations	Advantages	Drawbacks
Education + communication	Where there is a lack of information or inaccurate information and analysis.	Once persuaded, people will often help with the implementation of the change.	Can be very time consuming if lots of people are involved.
Participation + involvement	Where the initiators do not have all the information they need to design the change and where others have considerable power to resist.	People who participate will be committed to implementing change, and any relevant information they have will be integrated into the change plan.	Can be very time consuming if participators design an inappropriate change.
Facilitation + support	Where people are resisting because of adjustment problems.	No other approach works as well with adjustment problems.	Can be time consuming, expensive, and still fail.
Negotiation + agreement	Where someone or some group will clearly lose out in a change and where that group has considerable power to resist.	Sometimes it is a relatively easy way to avoid major resistance.	Can be too expensive in many cases if it alerts others to negotiate for compliance.
Manipulation + co-optation	Where other tactics will not work or are too expensive.	It can be a relatively quick and inexpensive solution to resistance problems.	Can lead to future problems if people feel manipulated.
Explicit + implicit coercion	Where speed is essential and where the change initiators possess considerable power.	It is speedy and can overcome any kind of resistance.	Can be risky if it leaves people mad at the initiators.

SOURCE: Reprinted by permission of *Harvard Business Review*. Exhibit from "Choosing Strategies for Change" by J P Kotter and L A Schlesinger, March/April 1979. Copyright © 1979 by the Harvard Business School of Publishing Corporation; all rights reserved.

they enlisted a task force of eight middle managers to collect employees' views about the current leadership (negative) and customers' views about the division's performance (also negative). The result was candid, detailed feedback that sometimes felt like "an icy bucket of water over the head," as one executive described it, but that also allowed executives to adjust their change proposals on the fly. Middle managers were consulted early and often about strategic and operational questions. As a result, they understood better what the senior team was trying to accomplish and felt more comfortable supporting executives' intentions. The end result was one of the speediest turnarounds ever of an HP division.[46]

Fourth, employees' perceptions or interpretations of a change significantly affect resistance. Employees are less likely to resist when they perceive that the benefits of a change overshadow the personal costs. At a minimum then, managers are advised to (1) provide as much information as possible to employees about the change, (2) inform employees about the reasons/rationale for the change, (3) conduct meetings to address employees' questions regarding the change, and (4) provide employees the opportunity to discuss how the proposed change might affect them.[47] These recommendations underscore the importance of communicating with employees throughout the process of change.

OB Exercise   Assessing an Organization's Readiness for Change

Instructions
Circle the number that best represents your opinions about the company being evaluated.

3 = Yes
2 = Somewhat
1 = No

1. Is the change effort being sponsored by a senior-level executive (CEO, COO)?	3——2——1
2. Are all levels of management committed to the change?	3——2——1
3. Does the organization culture encourage risk taking?	3——2——1
4. Does the organization culture encourage and reward continuous improvement?	3——2——1
5. Has senior management clearly articulated the need for change?	3——2——1
6. Has senior management presented a clear vision of a positive future?	3——2——1
7. Does the organization use specific measures to assess business performance?	3——2——1
8. Does the change effort support other major activities going on in the organization?	3——2——1
9. Has the organization benchmarked itself against world-class companies?	3——2——1
10. Do all employees understand the customers' needs?	3——2——1
11. Does the organization reward individuals and/or teams for being innovative and for looking for root causes of organizational problems?	3——2——1
12. Is the organization flexible and cooperative?	3——2——1
13. Does management effectively communicate with all levels of the organization?	3——2——1
14. Has the organization successfully implemented other change programs?	3——2——1
15. Do employees take personal responsibility for their behavior?	3——2——1
16. Does the organization make decisions quickly?	3——2——1

Total score: _____

Arbitrary Norms
40–48 = High readiness for change
24–39 = Moderate readiness for change
16–23 = Low readiness for change

SOURCE: Based on the discussion contained in T A Stewart, "Rate Your Readiness to Change," *Fortune*, February 7, 1994, pp. 106–10.

Dynamics of Stress

We all experience stress on a daily basis. Although stress is caused by many factors, researchers conclude that stress triggers one of two basic reactions: active fighting or passive flight (running away or acceptance), the so-called **fight-or-flight response.**[48] Physiologically, this stress response is a biochemical "passing gear" involving hormonal changes that mobilize the body for extraordinary demands. Imagine how our prehistoric ancestors responded to the stress associated with a charging saber-toothed tiger. To avoid being eaten, they could stand their ground and fight the beast or run away. In either case, their bodies would have been energized by an identical hormonal change, involving the release of adrenaline into the bloodstream.

Fight-or-flight response
To either confront stressors or try to avoid them.

In today's hectic urbanized and industrialized society, charging beasts have been replaced by problems such as deadlines, role conflict and ambiguity, financial responsibilities, information overload, technology, traffic congestion, noise and air pollution, family problems, and work overload. As with our ancestors, our response to stress may or may not trigger negative side effects, including headaches, ulcers, insomnia, heart attacks, high blood pressure, and strokes. The same stress response that helped our prehistoric ancestors survive has too often become a factor that seriously impairs our daily lives.

Because stress and its consequences are manageable, it is important for managers to learn as much as they can about occupational stress. After defining stress, this section provides an overview of the dynamics associated with stress by presenting a model of occupational stress, discussing moderators of occupational stress, and reviewing the effectiveness of several stress-reduction techniques.

Defining Stress

To an orchestra violinist, stress may stem from giving a solo performance before a big audience. While heat, smoke, and flames may represent stress to a firefighter, delivering a speech or presenting a lecture may be stressful for those who are shy. In short, stress means different things to different people. Managers need a working definition.

Stress

Behavioral, physical, or psychological response to stressors.

Formally defined, **stress** is "an adaptive response, mediated by individual characteristics and/or psychological processes, that is a consequence of any external action, situation, or event that places special physical and/or psychological demands upon a person."[49] This definition is not as difficult as it seems when we reduce it to three interrelated dimensions of stress: (1) environmental demands, referred to as stressors, that produce (2) an adaptive response that is influenced by (3) individual differences.

Hans Selye, considered the father of the modern concept of stress, pioneered the distinction between stressors and the stress response. Moreover, Selye emphasized that both positive and negative events can trigger an identical stress response that can be beneficial or harmful. He referred to stress that is positive or produces a positive outcome as **eustress.** Receiving an award in front of a large crowd or successfully completing a difficult work assignment both are examples of stressors that produce eustress. He also noted that

Eustress

Stress that is good or produces a positive outcome.

- Stress is not merely nervous tension.
- Stress can have positive consequences.
- Stress is not something to be avoided.
- The complete absence of stress is death.[50]

These points make it clear that stress is inevitable. Efforts need to be directed at managing stress, not at somehow escaping it altogether.

A Model of Occupational Stress

Figure 19–5 presents an instructive model of occupational stress. The model shows that an individual initially appraises four types of stressors. This appraisal then motivates an individual to choose a coping strategy aimed at managing stressors, which, in turn, produces a variety of outcomes. The model also specifies several individual differences that moderate the stress process. A moderator is a variable that causes the relationship between two variables—such as stressors and cognitive appraisal—to be stronger for some people and weaker for others. Three key moderators are discussed in the next section. Let us now consider the remaining components of this model in detail.

Figure 19–5   *A Model of Occupational Stress*

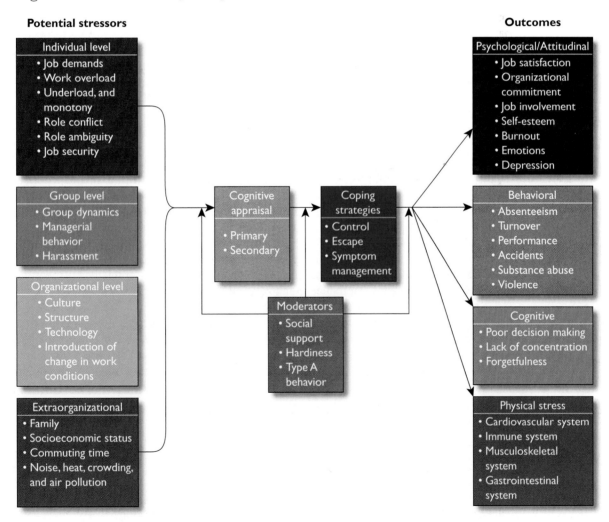

*ſ*tressors

Environmental factors
that produce stress.

*ſ*tressors   **Stressors** are environmental factors that produce stress. Stated differently, stressors are a prerequisite to experiencing the stress response. Figure 19–5 shows the four major types of stressors: individual, group, organizational, and extraorganizational. Individual-level stressors are those directly associated with a person's job duties. For example, the National Institute for Occupational Safety and Health found that 75% of computer videoscreen users reported occasional aching or burning eyes at work. Experts also estimated that computer-related problems resulted in more than 12 million annual eye exams.[51] The most common examples of individual stressors are job demands, work overload, role conflict, role ambiguity, everyday hassles, perceived control over events occurring in the work environment, and job characteristics. Consider, for example, the stressors contained in Bill Northrop's job.

> Bill Northrop's job is so stressful that "some days, when you get home, the muscles in your neck are like banjo strings," he says. A Sioux Falls, South Dakota, snow-plow operator, Mr Northrop, 53 years old, gets up at 3:30 AM to face subzero temperatures and snowy wind. Impatient drivers sometimes pass him as he clears the county's 330 miles of blacktop, putting both in danger. The good part: He still has a boy-like love of the equipment. "We've got the king-size Tonka toys," he says.[52]

Job security is another important individual-level stressor to manage because it is associated with increased job satisfaction, organization commitment, and performance, and it is decreasing. A recent survey of 150 executives, for instance, revealed that job loss due to a merger was cited as their number one concern at work. This fear is being fueled by the large number of mergers that have occurred over the last few years.[53]

Group-level stressors are caused by group dynamics (recall our discussion in Chapter 12) and managerial behavior. Managers create stress for employees by (1) exhibiting inconsistent behaviors, (2) failing to provide support, (3) showing lack of concern, (4) providing inadequate direction, (5) creating a high-productivity environment, and (6) focusing on negatives while ignoring good performance. Sexual harassment experiences represent another group-level stressor. Studies show that harassing experiences are negatively associated with work, supervision, and promotion satisfaction and are positively related to ambiguity, conflict, and stress.[54]

Organizational stressors affect large numbers of employees. Organizational culture, which was discussed in Chapter 3, is a prime example. For instance, a high-pressure environment that places chronic work demands on employees fuels the stress response.[55] In contrast, research provides preliminary support for the idea that participative management can reduce organizational stress.[56] The increased use of information technology is another source of organizational stress.

Extraorganizational stressors are those caused by factors outside the organization. For instance, in Chapter 6 we discussed how conflicts associated with balancing one's career and family life are stressful. Socioeconomic status is another extraorganizational stressor. Stress is higher for people with lower socioeconomic status, which represents a combination of (1) economic status, as measured by income, (2) social status, assessed by education level, and (3) work status, as indexed by occupation. These stressors are likely to become more important in the future.

Cognitive Appraisal of *ſ*tressors   Cognitive appraisal reflects an individual's overall perception or evaluation of a situation or stressor. It is an important component within the stress process because people interpret the same stressors differently. For example, some individuals perceive unemployment as a positive liberating experience, whereas others perceive it as a negative debilitating one.[57]

Figure 19–5 shows that people make two types of appraisals when evaluating the potential impact of stressors on their lives: primary and secondary appraisals.[58] A **primary appraisal** results in categorizing a situation or stressor as irrelevant, positive, or stressful. Stress appraisals are obviously the most important in terms of our current discussion because they imply that a situation or stressor is perceived as harmful, threatening, or challenging.

A **secondary appraisal** only occurs in response to a stressful primary appraisal and entails an assessment of what might and can be done to reduce the level of perceived stress. During this evaluation a person considers which coping strategies are available and which ones are most likely to help resolve the situation at hand. Ultimately, the combination of an individual's primary and secondary appraisal influences the choice of coping strategies used to reduce stress.

Coping Strategies

Coping strategies are characterized by the specific behaviors and cognitions used to cope with a situation. People use a combination of three approaches to cope with stressors and stress (see Figure 19–5). The first, called a **control strategy,** consists of using behaviors and cognitions to directly anticipate or solve problems. A control strategy has a take-charge tone. Consider the behavior of quitting a job in order to gain flexibility in your life. Kathy Dawson, for example, resigned from a six-figure job at Pinnacle Brands Inc., a trading-card company in Grand Prairie, Texas, because she wanted to spend more time with her two young daughters. She coped by starting a personnel consulting company.[59]

In contrast to tackling the problem head-on, an **escape strategy** amounts to avoiding the problem. Behaviors and cognitions are used to avoid or escape situations. Individuals use this strategy when they passively accept stressful situations or avoid them by failing to confront the cause of stress (an obnoxious co-worker, for instance). Finally, a **symptom management strategy** consists of using methods such as relaxation, meditation, medication, or exercise to manage the symptoms of occupational stress.

Stress Outcomes

Theorists contend stress has psychological/attitudinal, behavioral, cognitive, and physical health consequences or outcomes. Imagine the stress outcomes experienced by New Yorkers after the Sept. 11 tragedy.

> The strain of months of living with searing memories, frequent terrorist alerts and fears about what the future will bring is taking a toll. "People have said to me, 'we are shouting at each other and we are not even angry,' " says Henry Spitz, who heads the couples therapy program at Columbia University medical school. "There is a background tension that is there all the time," he says. The level of irritability is so high, it's "like chalk on a blackboard." . . .
>
> Already more employees say they are feeling depressed or anxious or having trouble sleeping, says Irene Lovitz, who heads the employee-assistance program at Merrill Lynch & Co., whose corporate headquarters are next to ground zero.[60]

Many others outside of New York similarly felt anxious and depressed following the terrorists attacks. Do you recall your feelings?

A large body of research supports the negative effects of perceived stress on many aspects of our lives.[61] Workplace stress is negatively related to job satisfaction, organizational commitment, positive emotions, and performance.[62] Research also shows that stress is associated with negative behaviors such as yelling and verbal abuse, and violence toward others. These stress outcomes are very costly. Experts estimate the

Primary appraisal
Determining whether a stressor is irrelevant, positive, or stressful.

Secondary appraisal
Assessing what might and can be done to reduce stress.

Control strategy
Coping strategy that directly confronts or solves problems.

Escape strategy
Coping strategy that avoids or ignores stressors and problems.

Symptom management strategy
Coping strategy that focuses on reducing the symptoms of stress.

Do you recall how you felt days after the September 11 attacks? These New Yorkers are reminded of this tragedy eight months later because they must walk past spray painted directions for triage, first aid and other important information needed in the first days after the World Trade Center collapse. The strain of living with painful memories, terrorist alerts, and fear of the future were just some of the stress outcomes experienced by New Yorkers after the tragedy.

AP/Wide World Photos

cost of workplace violence in the United States to be between $6.4 billion and $36 billion in lost productivity, insurance payments, and increased security.[63] Finally, ample evidence supports the conclusion that stress negatively affects our physical health. Stress contributes to the following health problems: lessened ability to ward off illness and infection, high blood pressure, coronary artery disease, tension headaches, back pain, diarrhea, and constipation.[64] In fact, it's stressful to even think about all these problems!

Moderators of Occupational Stress

Moderators, once again, are variables that cause the relationships between stressors, perceived stress, and outcomes to be weaker for some people and stronger for others. Managers with a working knowledge of important stress moderators can confront employee stress in the following ways:

1. Awareness of moderators helps identify those most likely to experience stress and its negative outcomes. Stress-reduction programs then can be formulated for high-risk employees.

2. Moderators, in and of themselves, suggest possible solutions for reducing negative outcomes of occupational stress.

Keeping these objectives in mind, we will examine three important moderators: social support, hardiness, and Type A behavior.

Social Support   Talking with a friend or taking part in a bull session can be comforting during times of fear, stress, or loneliness. For a variety of reasons, meaningful social relationships help people do a better job of handling stress. **Social support** is the amount of perceived helpfulness derived from social relationships. Importantly, social support is determined by both the quantity and quality of an individual's social relationships. We receive four types of social support from others:

- *Esteem support.* Providing information that a person is accepted and respected despite any problems or inadequacies.
- *Informational support.* Providing help in defining, understanding, and coping with problems.
- *Social companionship.* Spending time with others in leisure and recreational activities.
- *Instrumental support.* Providing financial aid, material resources, or needed services.[65]

Social support
Amount of helpfulness derived from social relationships.

Research shows that social support is negatively related to physiological processes and mortality. In other words, people with low social support tend to have poorer cardiovascular and immune system functioning and tend to die earlier than those with strong social support networks.[66] Further, social support protects against the perception of stress, depression, psychological problems, pregnancy complications, anxiety, loneliness, high blood pressure, and a variety of other ailments. In contrast, negative social support, which amounts to someone undermining another person, negatively affects one's mental health.[67] We are well advised to avoid people who try to undermine us.

Social support research highlights two practical recommendations. First, managers are advised to keep employees informed about external and internal social support systems. Internally, managers can use esteem and informational support while administering daily feedback and coaching. Second, participative management programs and company-sponsored activities that make employees feel they are an important part of an extended family can be rich sources of social support. Employees need time and energy to adequately maintain their social relationships. If organizational demands are excessive, employees' social relationships and support networks will suffer, resulting in stress-related illness and decreased performance.

Hardiness   Suzanne Kobasa, a behavioral scientist, identified a collection of personality characteristics that neutralize occupational stress. This collection of characteristics, referred to as **hardiness,** involves the ability to perceptually or behaviorally transform negative stressors into positive challenges. Hardiness embraces the personality dimensions of commitment, locus of control, and challenge.[68]

Hardiness
Personality characteristic that neutralizes stress.

Commitment reflects the extent to which an individual is involved in whatever he or she is doing. Committed people have a sense of purpose and do not give up under pressure because they tend to invest themselves in the situation. As discussed in Chapter 5, individuals with an *internal locus of control* believe they can influence the events that affect their lives. People possessing this trait are more likely to foresee stressful events, thereby reducing their exposure to anxiety-producing situations. Moreover, their perception of being in control leads "internals" to use proactive coping strategies. *Challenge* is represented by the belief that change is a normal part of life. Hence, change is seen as an opportunity for growth and development rather than a threat to security.

Research supports the moderating influence of hardiness on the stress process. For example, a five-year study of 259 managers from a public utility revealed that hardiness—commitment, locus of control, and challenge—reduced the probability of illness following exposure to stress.[69] The three components of hardiness also were found to directly influence how 276 members of the Israeli Defense Forces appraised stressors and ultimately coped with them. Hardy individuals interpreted stressors less negatively and were more likely to use control coping strategies than unhardy people.[70] Furthermore, additional research demonstrated that hardy individuals displayed lower stress, burnout, and psychological distress and higher job satisfaction than their less hardy counterparts.[71] Finally, a study of 73 pregnant women revealed that hardy women had fewer problems during labor and more positive perceptions about their infants than unhardy women.[72]

One practical offshoot of this research is organizational training and development programs that strengthen the characteristics of commitment, personal control, and challenge. Because of cost limitations, it is necessary to target key employees or those most susceptible to stress (e.g., air traffic controllers). The hardiness concept also meshes nicely with job design. Enriched jobs are likely to fuel the hardiness components of commitment and challenge. A final application of the hardiness concept is as a diagnostic tool. Employees scoring low on hardiness would be good candidates for stress-reduction programs.

Type A Behavior Pattern   According to Meyer Friedman and Ray Rosenman (the cardiologists who isolated the Type A syndrome in the 1950s):

Type A behavior pattern

Aggressively involved in a chronic, determined struggle to accomplish more in less time.

> **Type A behavior pattern** is an action-emotion complex that can be observed in any person who is aggressively involved in a chronic, incessant struggle to achieve more and more in less and less time, and if required to do so, against the opposing efforts of other things or persons. It is not psychosis or a complex of worries or fears or phobias or obsessions, but a socially acceptable—indeed often praised—form of conflict. Persons possessing this pattern also are quite prone to exhibit a free-floating but extraordinarily well-rationalized hostility. As might be expected, there are degrees in the intensity of this behavior pattern.[73]

While labeling Type A behavior as "hurry sickness," Friedman and Rosenman noted that Type A individuals frequently tend to exhibit most of the behaviors listed in Table 19–3.

Because Type A behavior is a matter of degree, it is measured on a continuum. This continuum has the hurried, competitive Type A behavior pattern at one end and the more relaxed Type B behavior pattern at the other. Take a moment to complete the Type A survey contained in the OB Exercise on page 700. This exercise will help you better understand the characteristics of the Type A behavior pattern. Where did you fall on the Type A continuum?

Table 19–3   *Type A Characteristics*

1. Hurried speech; explosive accentuation of key words.
2. Tendency to walk, move, and eat rapidly.
3. Constant impatience with the rate at which most events take place (e.g., irritation with slow-moving traffic and slow-talking and slow-to-act people).
4. Strong preference for thinking of or doing two or more things at once (e.g., reading this text and doing something else at the same time).
5. Tendency to turn conversations around to personally meaningful subjects or themes.
6. Tendency to interrupt while others are speaking to make your point or to complete their train of thought in your own words.
7. Guilt feelings during periods of relaxation or leisure time.
8. Tendency to be oblivious to surroundings during daily activities.
9. Greater concern for things worth *having* than with things worth being.
10. Tendency to schedule more and more in less and less time; a chronic sense of time urgency.
11. Feelings of competition rather than compassion when faced with another Type A person.
12. Development of nervous tics or characteristic gestures.
13. A firm belief that success is due to the ability to get things done faster than the other guy.
14. A tendency to view and evaluate personal activities and the activities of other people in terms of "numbers" (e.g., number of meetings attended, telephone calls made, visitors received).

SOURCE: Adapted from M Friedman and R H Rosenman, *Type A Behavior and Your Heart* (Greenwich, CT: Fawcett Publications, 1974), pp. 100–2.

Let us now consider the pros and cons of being Type A. OB research has demonstrated that Type A employees tend to be more productive than their Type B co-workers. For instance, Type A behavior yielded a significant and positive correlation with 766 students' grade point averages, the quantity and quality of 278 university professors' performance, and sales performance of 222 life insurance brokers.[74] On the other hand, Type A behavior is associated with some negative consequences.

A meta-analysis of 99 studies revealed that Type A individuals had higher heart rates, diastolic blood pressure, and systolic blood pressure than Type B people. Type A people also showed greater cardiovascular activity when they encountered the following situations:

1. Receipt of positive or negative feedback.

2. Receipt of verbal harassment or criticism.

3. Tasks requiring mental as opposed to physical work.[75]

Unfortunately for Type A individuals, these situations are frequently experienced at work. A second meta-analysis of 83 studies further demonstrated that the hard-driving and competitive aspects of Type A are related to coronary heart disease, but the speed and impatience and job involvement aspects are not. This meta-analysis also showed that feelings of anger, hostility, and aggression were more strongly related to heart disease than was Type A behavior.[76]

Do these results signal the need for Type A individuals to quit working so hard? Not necessarily. First off, the research indicated that feelings of anger, hostility, and aggression were more detrimental to our health than being Type A. We should all attempt to reduce these negative emotions. Second, researchers have developed stress-reduction techniques to help Type A people pace themselves more realistically and

OB Exercise   Where Are You on the Type A–B Behavior Continuum?

Instructions

Indicate the extent to which each statement is true of you.

	Not at All True of Me	Neither Very True Nor Very Untrue of Me	Very True of Me
1. I hate giving up before I'm absolutely sure that I'm licked.	1 —— 2 —— 3 —— 4 —— 5		
2. Sometimes I feel that I shouldn't be working so hard, but something drives me on.	1 —— 2 —— 3 —— 4 —— 5		
3. I thrive on challenging situations. The more challenges I have, the better.	1 —— 2 —— 3 —— 4 —— 5		
4. In comparison to most people I know, I'm very involved in my work.	1 —— 2 —— 3 —— 4 —— 5		
5. It seems as if I need 30 hours a day to finish all the things I'm faced with.	1 —— 2 —— 3 —— 4 —— 5		
6. In general, I approach my work more seriously than most people I know.	1 —— 2 —— 3 —— 4 —— 5		
7. I guess there are some people who can be nonchalant about their work, but I'm not one of them.	1 —— 2 —— 3 —— 4 —— 5		
8. My achievements are considered to be significantly higher than those of most people I know.	1 —— 2 —— 3 —— 4 —— 5		
9. I've often been asked to be an officer of some group or groups.	1 —— 2 —— 3 —— 4 —— 5		

Total score = _____

Arbitrary Norms

9–22 = Type B
23–35 = Balanced Type A and Type B
36–45 = Type A

SOURCE: Taken from R D Caplan, S Cobb, J R P French Jr, R Van Harrison, and S R Pinneau Jr, *Job Demands and Worker Health* (HEW Publication No. [NIOSH] 75–160). (Washington, DC: US Department of Health, Education, and Welfare, 1975), pp. 253–54.

achieve better balance in their lives; they are discussed in the next section. Management can help Type A people, however, by not overloading them with work despite their apparent eagerness to take an ever-increasing work load. Managers need to actively help rather than unthinkingly exploit Type A individuals.

Stress-Reduction Techniques

International data reveal that Americans are fatter, do less strenuous exercise, and eat less healthful foods than people from Australia, Britain, France, and Japan. Still, the number of obese people increased over the last decade in all of these countries.[77] All told, the National Council on Compensation Insurance estimates that stress-related medical and disability payments cost US companies $26 billion a year plus an additional $95 billion a year in lost productivity.[78] It is, therefore, not surprising that organizations are increasingly implementing a variety of stress-reduction programs to help employees cope with modern-day stress. One study, for instance, revealed that 91% of US employers offer some form of health promotion program.[79]

When you're stressed do you reach for the junk food? Surgeon General David Satcher reports that Americans' increasing obesity will result in 300,000 deaths per year from illnesses directly caused by being overweight. He believes that obesity may soon kill more Americans than cigarettes. So go easy on the junk food!

AP/Wide World Photos

There are many different stress-reduction techniques available. The four most frequently used approaches are muscle relaxation, biofeedback, meditation, and cognitive restructuring. Each method involves somewhat different ways of coping with stress (see Table 19–4).

Two teams of OB researchers reviewed the research on stress management interventions. Although much of the published research is methodologically weak, results offer preliminary support for the conclusion that muscle relaxation, biofeedback, meditation, and cognitive restructuring all help employees cope with occupational stress.[80]

Some researchers advise organizations not to implement these stress-reduction programs despite their positive outcomes. They rationalize that these techniques relieve *symptoms* of stress rather than eliminate stressors themselves.[81] Thus, they conclude that organizations are using a Band-Aid approach to stress reduction. A holistic approach has subsequently been offered as a more proactive and enduring solution.

A **holistic wellness approach** encompasses and goes beyond stress reduction by advocating that individuals strive for "a harmonious and productive balance of physical, mental, and social well-being brought about by the acceptance of one's personal responsibility for developing and adhering to a health promotion program."[82] Five dimensions of a holistic wellness approach are as follows:

Holistic wellness approach
Advocates personal responsibility for healthy living.

1. *Self-responsibility.* Take personal responsibility for your wellness (e.g., quit smoking, moderate your intake of alcohol, wear your seat belt). A study of 4,400 people revealed that continuous smoking throughout one's life reduces life expectancy by 18 years.[83]

Table 19–4   *Stress-Reduction Techniques*

Technique	Descriptions	Assessment
Muscle relaxation	Uses slow deep breathing and systematic muscle tension reduction.	Inexpensive and easy to use; may require a trained professional to implement.
Biofeedback	A machine is used to train people to detect muscular tension; muscle relaxation is then used to alleviate this symptom of stress.	Expensive due to costs of equipment; however, equipment can be used to evaluate effectiveness of other stress-reduction programs.
Meditation	The relaxation response is activated by redirecting one's thoughts away from oneself; a four-step procedure is used to attain passive stress-free state of mind.	Least expensive, simple to implement, and can be practiced almost anywhere.
Cognitive restructuring	Irrational or maladaptive thoughts are identified and replaced with those that are rational or logical.	Expensive because it requires a trained psychologist or counselor.
Holistic wellness	A broad, interdisciplinary approach that goes beyond stress reduction by advocating that people strive for personal wellness in all aspects of their lives.	Involves inexpensive but often behaviorally difficult lifestyle changes.

2. *Nutritional awareness.* Because we are what we eat, try to increase your consumption of foods high in fiber, vitamins, and nutrients—such as fresh fruits and vegetables, poultry, and fish—while decreasing those high in sugar and fat.

3. *Stress reduction and relaxation.* Use techniques to relax and reduce the symptoms of stress.

4. *Physical fitness.* Exercise regularly to maintain strength, flexibility, endurance, and a healthy body weight. A recent review of employee fitness programs indicated that they were a cost-effective way to reduce medical costs, absenteeism, turnover, and occupational injuries. Fitness programs also were positively linked with job performance and job satisfaction.[84]

5. *Environmental sensitivity.* Be aware of your environment and try to identify the stressors that are causing your stress. A control coping strategy might be useful to eliminate stressors.

Summary of Key Concepts

1. *Discuss the external and internal forces that create the need for organizational change.* Organizations encounter both external and internal forces for change. There are four key external forces for change: demographic characteristics, technological advancements, market changes, and social and political pressures. Internal forces for change come from both human resource problems and managerial behavior/decisions.

2. *Describe Lewin's change model and the systems model of change.* Lewin developed a three-stage model of planned change that explained how to initiate, manage, and stabilize the change process. The three stages were *unfreezing*, which entails creating the motivation to change, *changing*, and stabilizing change through *refreezing*. A systems model of change takes a big picture perspective of change. It focuses on the

interaction among the key components of change. The three main components of change are inputs, target elements of change, and outputs. The target elements of change represent the components of an organization that may be changed. They include organizing arrangements, social factors, methods, goals, and people.

3. *Discuss Kotter's eight steps for leading organizational change.* John Kotter believes that organizational change fails for one or more of eight common errors. He proposed eight steps that organizations should follow to overcome these errors. The eight steps are: (1) establish a sense of urgency, (2) create the guiding coalition, (3) develop a vision and strategy, (4) communicate the change vision, (5) empower broad-based action, (6) generate short-term wins, (7) consolidate gains and produce more change, and (8) anchor new approaches in the culture.

4. *Demonstrate your familiarity with the four identifying characteristics of organization development (OD).* The identifying characteristics of OD are that it (*a*) involves profound change, (*b*) is value loaded, (*c*) is a diagnosis/prescription cycle, and (*d*) is process oriented.

5. *Summarize the 10 reasons employees resist change.* Resistance to change is an emotional/behavioral response to real or imagined threats to an established work routine. Ten reasons employees resist change are (1) an individual's predisposition toward change, (2) surprise and fear of the unknown, (3) climate of mistrust, (4) fear of failure, (5) loss of status or job security, (6) peer pressure, (7) disruption of cultural traditions or group relationships, (8) personality conflicts, (9) lack of tact or poor timing, and (10) nonreinforcing reward systems.

6. *Discuss the five personal characteristics related to resistance to change.* The first entails an employee's commitment to change, which reflects a mind-set of doing whatever it takes to effectively implement change. Resilience to change, a composite characteristic reflecting high self-esteem, optimism, and an internal locus of control, is the second personal characteristic. People with a positive self-concept and a tolerance for risk also handle change better than those without these two dispositions. High levels of self-efficacy also are negatively associated with resistance to change.

7. *Identify alternative strategies for overcoming resistance to change, and discuss the managerial recommendations for leading change.* Organizations must be ready for change. Assuming an organization is ready for change, the alternative strategies for overcoming resistance to change are education + communication, participation + involvement, facilitation + support, negotiation + agreement, manipulation + co-optation, and explicit + implicit coercion. Each has its situational appropriateness and advantages and drawbacks.

8. *Define the term* stress *and describe the model of occupational stress.* Stress is an adaptive reaction to environmental demands or stressors that triggers a fight-or-flight response. This response creates hormonal changes that mobilize the body for extraordinary demands. According to the occupational model of stress, the stress process begins when an individual cognitively appraises stressors. This appraisal then motivates an individual to choose a coping strategy aimed at reducing stressors, which, in turn, results in a variety of stress outcomes.

9. *Discuss the stress moderators of social support, hardiness, and Type A behavior.* People use each of these moderators to help reduce the impact of stressors that are appraised as harmful, threatening, or challenging. Social support represents the amount of perceived helpfulness derived from social relationships. People use four types of support (esteem, informational, social, and instrumental) to reduce the impact of stress. Hardiness is a collection of personality characteristics that neutralize stress. It includes the characteristics of commitment, locus of control, and challenge. The Type A behavior pattern is characterized by someone who is aggressively involved in a chronic, determined struggle to accomplish more and more in less and less time. Management can help Type A individuals by not overloading them with work despite their apparent eagerness to take on an ever-increasing workload.

10. *Contrast the five dominant stress-reduction techniques.* Muscle relaxation, biofeedback, meditation, cognitive restructuring, and a holistic wellness approach are predominant stress-reduction techniques. Slow and deep breathing and a conscious effort to relieve muscle tension are common denominators of muscle relaxation. Biofeedback relies on a machine to train people to detect bodily signs of stress. This awareness facilitates proactive coping with stressors. Meditation activates the relaxation response by redirecting one's thoughts away from oneself. Cognitive restructuring entails identifying irrational or maladaptive thoughts and replacing them with rational or logical thoughts.

   Holistic wellness is a broad, interdisciplinary approach advocating that people strive for personal wellness in all aspects of their lives. The five key components underlying this approach are self-responsibility, nutritional awareness, stress reduction and relaxation, physical fitness, and environmental sensitivity.

Discussion Questions

1. Which of the external forces for change do you believe will prompt the greatest change between now and the year 2010?

2. Have you worked in an organization where internal forces created change? Describe the situation and the resulting change.

3. How would you respond to a manager who made the following statement? "Unfreezing is not important, employees will follow my directives."

4. What are some useful methods that can be used to refreeze an organizational change?

5. Have you ever observed the systems model of change in action? Explain what occurred.

6. Have you ever resisted a change at work? Explain the circumstances and your thinking at the time.

7. Which source of resistance to change do you think is the most common? Which is the most difficult for management to deal with?

8. Describe the behavioral and physiological symptoms you have observed in others when they are under stress.

9. How can someone increase their hardiness and reduce their Type A behavior?

10. Have you used any of the stress-reduction techniques? Evaluate their effectiveness.

Internet Exercise   **www.queendom.com**

We highlighted in this chapter how people cope with stress by using a variety of control, escape, and symptom management strategies. Your ability to effectively cope with your Type A tendencies is very important because ineffective coping can make a stressful situation even worse.

A Free Type A Personality Test

The purpose of this exercise is to provide you with feedback on your Type A behavior. Go to the Internet home page for Body-Mind Queendom (www.queendom.com), and select the main menu heading "Tests and Profiles." At the "Tests, Tests, Tests . . . " page, scroll down to the heading "Top Tests" and click on "Type A Personality Test."

Complete it, and submit your score for automatic scoring. (*Note:* Our use of this questionnaire is for instructional purposes only and does not constitute an endorsement of any products that may or may not suit your needs. There is no obligation to buy anything.) You will receive a score and interpretation.

Questions

1. How did you score? Are you surprised by the results?

2. Based on the interpretation of your results, what can you do to improve your Type A tendencies? How might you also reduce your level of perceived stress?

OB in Action Case Study

Gateway Is Implementing a Measurement Management System in Order to Turn Around the Company[85]

Can a pony-tailed computer guru change his management spots?

Ted Waitt is trying.

The co-founder and chief executive of Gateway Inc. has long been centrally involved in most of the personal-computer maker's decisions, from its advertising selection to corporate partnerships. But Gateway's losses are piling up and its market share is falling, indicating that the old ways aren't working.

Now, Mr Waitt is making a battlefield conversion. Borrowing from methods long used by arch-rival Dell Computer Corp., Gateway is moving to rigorous measurement and discipline. At the company's new Poway, California, headquarters, a 9-foot-by-12-foot screen visible to all employees projects a running, daily tally comparing sales and costs with forecasts.

In the past, underperformers might have faced a hallway chat with Ted. But since January, executives' goals are meticulously spelled out and their performances are graded by the company's top human resources executive, not Mr Waitt. Regular reviews have already led to the departure of four sales managers.

"Accountability is objectively different than at any point in the past. It's focus, discipline and metrics. That's what Dell has done better than we did." a chastened Mr Waitt says.

The new routine includes measuring customers' abandoned calls at telephone sales centers, where managers are automatically clued in whenever the number of hang-ups exceeds a certain level. If sales fail to meet forecasts, executives up the ladder are notified even if the company is behind by as little as an hour, says David G Turner, the company's senior vice president of sales and marketing. The response may be as simple as a call to staff the phone centers or a Web price change to lure more buyers.

The first week Gateway began tracking so-called adherence rates—or its ability to hit goals on everything from the number of phone calls resulting from each ad to the number of callers converted to customers—managers hit their numbers a miserable 60% of the time. "The next week was 80%; it quickly got to 98%," Mr Turner says. Indeed, managers now attend training classes to learn what the company is measuring and why.

Gateway executives also are learning to make decisions on the numbers and not defer to Mr Waitt. John D Heubusch, Gateway's vice president of strategy, says that in the past, managers either held off making choices until they talked to Mr Waitt or invoked his name to gather others' support. . . .

Skeptics say changing Gateway won't be easy. "They were a very undisciplined organization," a former Gateway executive says. "They did a lot of shooting from the hip."

This time, there isn't much choice. The company had a loss of $1 billion last year as sales fell 37% to $6.1 billion. For the year, it projects a pretax loss of as much as $250 million on revenue of between $4.5 billion and $5 billion. The California Public Employees' Retirement System has put Gateway on its focus list of poor performers. Twice this year Moody's Investors Service cut the company's credit rating.

Questions for Discussion

1. What were the internal and external forces for change at Gateway?

2. Using Figure 19–2, how would you classify the changes occurring at Gateway? Explain.

3. Use the systems model of change shown in Figure 19–3 to discuss how Gateway has attempted to implement organizational change. Based on this assessment, what would you have done differently if you were Ted Waitt? Discuss.

4. Based on Gateway's past organizational culture and business practices, do you expect employees to resist this new organizational change? Discuss your rationale. If you predict resistance, discuss what could be done to reduce it.

5. Based on everything that you have learned about organizational behavior, what is your opinion about Gateway's approach to organizational change? Explain.

Personal Awareness and Growth Exercise

Applying the Systems Model of Change

Objectives

1. To help you understand the diagnosis step of planned organizational change.

2. To give you a practical diagnostic tool to assess which target elements of change in Figure 19–3 should be changed during a change process.

Introduction

Diagnosis is the first step in planned organizational change. It is used to identify past or current organizational problems that inhibit organizational effectiveness. As indicated in Figure 19–3, there are five organizational areas in which to look for problems: organizing arrangements, social factors, methods, goals, and people. In this exercise, you will be asked to complete a brief survey assessing these five areas of an organization.

Instructions

If you currently have a full- or part-time job, think of your organization and describe it by circling an appropriate response for each of the following 18 statements. Calculate a total score for each diagnostic area. Then connect the set of points for your organization in a vertical profile. If you are not currently employed, describe the last organization you worked for. If you have never worked, use your current university or school as your frame of reference.

After completing the survey, think of an ideal organization: an organization that you believe would be most effective. How do you believe this organization would stand in terms of the five diagnostic areas? We would like you to assess this organization with the same diagnostic survey. Circle your responses with a different color or marking. Then vertically connect the set of points for your ideal organization. Calculate a total score for each diagnostic area.

Organizational Diagnostic Survey

1 = Strongly disagree
2 = Disagree
3 = Neutral
4 = Agree
5 = Strongly agree

Organizing Arrangements

1. The company has the right recognition and rewards in place to support its vision and strategies.   1—2—3—4—5
2. The organizational structure facilitates goal accomplishment.   1—2—3—4—5
3. Organizational policies and procedures are administered fairly.   1—2—3—4—5

Total Organizing Arrangements score = _____ _____

Social Factors

4. The culture promotes adaptability and flexibility.   1—2—3—4—5
5. Interpersonal and group conflict are handled in a positive manner.   1—2—3—4—5
6. Horizontal and vertical communication is effective.   1—2—3—4—5
7. Leaders are good role models and decision makers.   1—2—3—4—5

Total Social Factors score = _____ _____

Methods

8. The work flow promotes higher quality and quantity of performance.   1—2—3—4—5
9. Technology is effectively utilized.   1—2—3—4—5
10. People focus on solving root cause problems rather than symptoms.   1—2—3—4—5

Total Methods score = _____ _____

Goals

11. I am aware of the organization's vision and strategic goals.   1—2—3—4—5
12. I have all the tools and resources I need to do my job.   1—2—3—4—5
13. Corporate goals are cascaded down the organization.   1—2—3—4—5
14. I am evaluated against specific standards of performance.   1—2—3—4—5

Total Goals score = _____ _____

People

15. This organization inspires the very best in me in the way of job performance.   1—2—3—4—5
16. I understand my job duties and responsibilities.   1—2—3—4—5
17. I like working in this company.   1—2—3—4—5
18. People are motivated to do the best job they can.   1—2—3—4—5

Total People score = _____ _____

Questions for Discussion

1. Based on your evaluation of your current organization, which diagnostic area(s) is most in need of change?

2. Based on a comparison of your current and ideal organizations, which diagnostic area(s) is most in need of change? If your answer is different from the first question, explain the difference.

3. What sort of intervention would be appropriate for your work group or organization? Give details.

Group Exercise

Creating Personal Change through Force-Field Analysis[86]

Objectives

1. To apply force-field analysis to a behavior or situation you would like to change.
2. To receive feedback on your strategies for bringing about change.

Introduction

The theory of force-field analysis is based on the premise that people resist change because of counteracting positive and negative forces. Positive forces for change are called *thrusters*. They propel people to accept change and modify their behavior. In contrast, *counterthrusters* or *resistors* are negative forces that motivate an individual to maintain the status quo. People frequently fail to change because they experience equal amounts of positive and negative forces to change.

Force-field analysis is a technique used to facilitate change by first identifying the thrusters and resistors that exist in a specific situation. To minimize resistance to change, it is generally recommended to first reduce or remove the negative forces to change. Removing counterthrusters should create increased pressure for an individual to change in the desired direction. Managers can also further increase motivation to change by following up the reduction of resistors with an increase in the number of positive thrusters of change.

Instructions

Your instructor will pair you up with another student. The two of you will serve as a team that evaluates the completeness of each other's force-field analysis and recommendations. Once the team is assembled, each individual should independently complete the Force-Field Analysis Form presented after these instructions. Once both of you complete this activity, one team member should present results from steps 2 through 5 from the five-step Force-Field Analysis Form. The partner should then evaluate the results by considering the following questions with his or her team member:

1. Are there any additional thrusters and counterthrusters that should be listed? Add them to the list.
2. Do you agree with the strength evaluations of thrusters and counterthrusters in step 4? Ask your partner to share his or her rationale for the ratings. Modify the ratings as needed.
3. Examine the specific recommendations for change listed in step 5, and evaluate whether you think they will produce the desired changes. Be sure to

consider whether the focal person has the ability to eliminate, reduce, or increase each thruster and counterthruster that is the basis for a specific recommendation. Are there any alternative strategies you can think of?

4. What is your overall evaluation of your partner's intervention strategy?

FORCE-FIELD ANALYSIS FORM[87]

Step 1

In the space provided, please identify a number of personal problems you would like to solve or aspects of your life you would like to change. Be as imaginative as possible. You are not limited to school situations. For example, you may want to consider your work environment if you are currently employed, family situation, interpersonal relationships, club situations, and so forth. It is important that you select some aspects of your life that you would like to change but which up to now have made no effort to do.

_____

_____

_____

_____

_____

_____

Step 2

Review in your mind the problems or aspects listed in step 1. Now select one that you would really like to change and which you believe lends itself easily to force-field analysis. Select one that you will feel comfortable talking about to other people.

Step 3

On the form following step 4, indicate existing forces that are pushing you in the direction of change. Thrusters may be forces internal to the self (pride, regret, and fear) or they may be external to the self (friends, the boss, a professor). Also list existing forces that are preventing you from changing. Again, the counterthruster may be internal to the self (uncertainty, fear) or external to the self (poor instruction, limited resources, lack of support mechanisms).

Step 4

In the space to the right of your list of thrusters and counterthrusters indicate the relative strength. For consistency, use a scale of 1 to 10, with 1 indicating a weak force and 10 indicating a high force.

Thrusters   **Strength**

_____   _____
_____   _____
_____   _____
_____   _____
_____   _____
_____   _____

Counterthrusters   **Strength**

_____   _____
_____   _____
_____   _____
_____   _____
_____   _____
_____   _____

Step 5

Analyze your thrusters and counterthrusters, and develop a strategy for bringing about the desired change. Remember that it is possible to produce the desired

results by strengthening existing thrusters, introducing new thrusters, weakening or removing counterthrusters, or some combination of these. Consider the impact of your change strategy on the system's internal stress (i.e., on yourself and others), the likelihood of success, the availability of resources, and the long-term consequences of planned changes. Be prepared to discuss your recommendations with the partner in your group.

_____
_____
_____
_____
_____
_____
_____
_____

Questions for Discussion

1. What was your reaction to doing a force-field analysis? Was it insightful and helpful?

2. Was it valuable to receive feedback about your force-field analysis from a partner? Explain.

3. How would you assess the probability of effectively implementing your recommendations?

Ethical Dilemma

What Would You Do if Your Boss Had a Serious Mental Illness?[88]

Paul Gottlieb was a 40-something rising star in the publishing world, sought after for top positions at major book publishers in New York City. In meetings with authors, business associates, and employees, he was a take-charge executive. No one realized that sometimes at the end of the day, Mr Gottlieb would sit at his desk, exhausted, and think about jumping out the window. . . .

Coping with employee depression is increasingly on the minds of workplace managers. But what happens when the boss is the one with a mental illness? The repercussions on a business, its employees and stockholders can be enormous if the illness interferes with a leader's performance. . . .

Securities laws require public companies to disclose anything that materially affects the company, and that can theoretically include serious health problems of key executives.

Assume that your boss suffers from a serious mental condition and he or she is trying to withhold this information from others? What would you do?

1. Nothing. The boss's mental condition is none of my business.

2. I would not say a word because I could be ignored or punished for saying anything. Identify the pros and cons of this option.

3. Discuss the issue only with my boss and encourage him or her to get help. Explain your rationale.

4. Discuss the issue with someone from the human resources department. Explain your rationale.

5. Invent other options. Discuss.

For an interpretation of this situation, visit our Web site, **www.mhhe.com/kreitner.**

OB in Action Video Case

Virtual Disagreement at Saber Union

Total run time for both parts: 15 minutes, 52 seconds.

About the Manager's Hot Seat video series: To achieve a high degree of realism, McGraw-Hill/Irwin created these videos around the concept of having real-life managers deal with challenging hypothetical situations without the aid of a script. Each Manager's Hot Seat video has two parts. Both parts are followed by the guest manager's view of what went right and wrong in the "hot seat." What would *you* do in the manager's hot seat?

Characters: Guest manager A Ralph Ramos, in real life, is director of network services at New York University's School of Medicine. His "hot seat" position in this video is senior manager in the claims department of Saber Union, a giant insurance company. Angela Zanoni is a claims investigator for the company and has been telecommuting as part of a small-scale experiment for six months.

Situation: The two have had a positive working relationship, deepened by family ties to a small Colombian village outside Bogotá. They often chatted during breaks and at lunchtime before Angela started telecommuting. The meeting in Part 1 has been called because Zanoni is unhappy and Ramos isn't sure why. Ramos is a smart, fast-paced manager who is concerned about two deadlines Zanoni has missed.

Links to textual material: Chapter 15: communicating and listening. Chapter 16: influence tactics and power. Chapter 17: leadership. Chapter 18: virtual organizations. Chapter 19: managing change.

For Class Discussion (following Part 1)

1. As a test of your communication and listening skills, what is Zanoni's real problem? Explain.
2. What influence tactics were evident in the first meeting? Explain.
3. What are Ramos's and Zanoni's respective power bases? Are they using them effectively? Explain.
4. How would you characterize Ramos's leadership style? Explain.
5. What did Ramos do right (and wrong) in the first meeting?
6. What should he do to prepare for the follow-up meeting?

For Class Discussion (following Part 2)

1. What did Zanoni's nonverbal communication (body language) say to Ramos in both meetings? Explain.
2. What did Ramos do right (and wrong) in the second meeting?
3. Does Ramos's admitted bias against people working outside the office constitute resistance to change? Explain what he should do.
4. What practical lessons about "managing from a distance" come from this snapshot of a virtual organization?

Learning Module C
Research Methods in Organizational Behavior

As a future manager, you probably will be involved in developing and/or implementing programs for solving managerial problems. You may also be asked to assess recommendations derived from in-house research reports or judge the usefulness of management consulting proposals. These tasks might entail reading and evaluating research findings presented both in scientific and professional journal articles. Thus, it is important for managers to have a basic working knowledge of the research process. Moreover, such knowledge can help you critically evaluate research information encountered daily in newspaper, magazine, and television reports. These conclusions are all the more important when you consider them in light of results obtained from two recent studies. The first was a national survey about the extent to which Americans believe or accept poll results reported on TV or in a newspaper. Results revealed that 33% of adults generally believed in what they heard or read: 44% did not.[1] The second study, which was conducted by the National Science Foundation, indicated that most people could not tell good scientific studies from bad ones.[2] If people cannot judge the difference between good and bad research, then how do they know what to believe about research results pertaining to organizational or societal problems? As a specific case in point, let us consider the issue of whether to wear rear-seat lap belts while riding in an automobile.

A study conducted by the National Transportation Safety Board (NTSB) concluded, "Instead of protecting people, rear-seat lap belts can cause serious or fatal internal injuries in the event of a head-on crash."[3] Despite previous recommendations to wear seat belts, do you now believe rear-seat lap belts are dangerous? To answer this question adequately, one needs to know more about how the NTSB's study was conducted and what has been found in related studies. Before providing you with this information, however, this advanced learning module presents a foundation for understanding the research process. Our purpose is not to make you a research scientist. The purpose is to make you a better consumer of research information, such as that provided by the NTSB.

The Research Process

Research on organizational behavior is based on the scientific method. The *scientific method* is a formal process of using systematically gathered data to test hypotheses or to explain natural phenomena. To gain a better understanding of how to evaluate this process, we discuss a model of how research is conducted, explore how researchers measure organizationally relevant variables, highlight three ways to evaluate research methods, and provide a framework for evaluating research conclusions. We also discuss how to read a research article. Finally, we return to the NTSB study and evaluate its conclusions on the basis of lessons from this learning module.

Figure C–1   *Model of the Research Process*

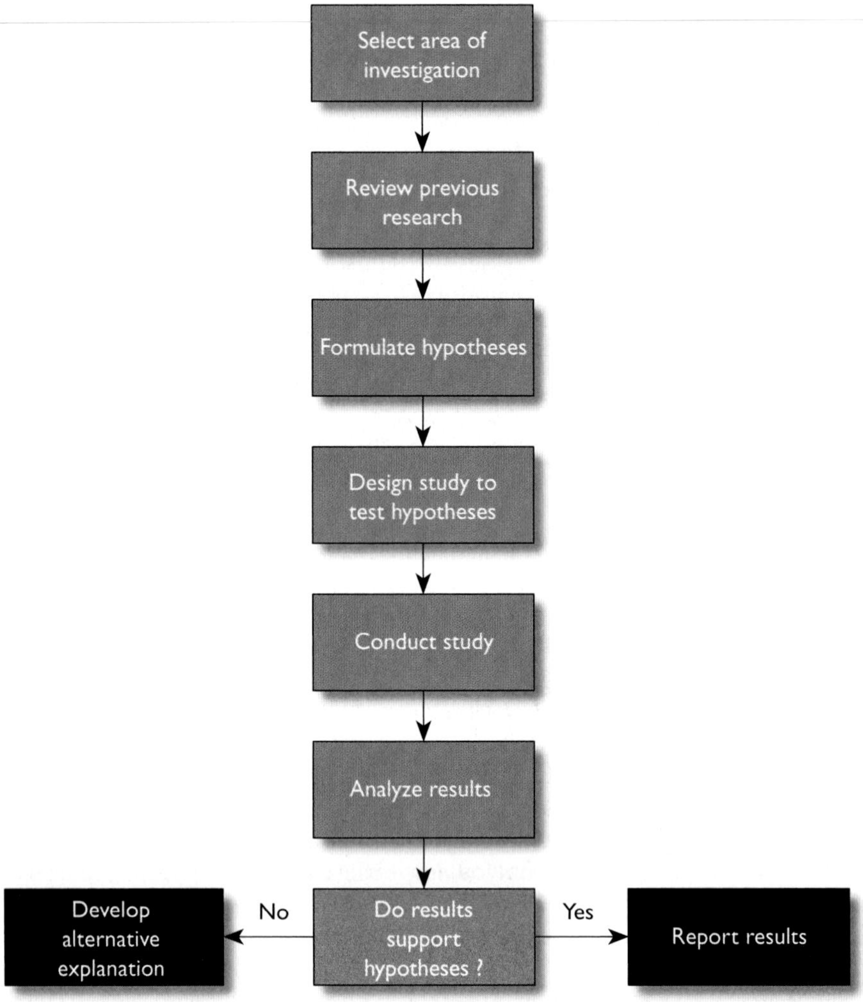

SOURCE: V R Boehm, "Research in the 'Real World': A Conceptual Model," *Personnel Psychology,* Autumn 1980, p. 496. Used with permission.

A Model of the Research Process

A flowchart of the research process is presented in Figure C–1. Organizational research is conducted to solve problems. The problem may be one of current interest to an organization, such as absenteeism or low motivation, or may be derived from published research studies. In either case, properly identifying and attempting to solve the problem necessitates a familiarity with previous research on the topic. This familiarity contributes background knowledge and insights for formulating a hypothesis to solve the problem. Students who have written formal library-research papers are well-acquainted with this type of *secondary* research.

According to a respected researcher: "A *hypothesis* is a conjectural statement of the relation between two or more variables. Hypotheses are always in declarative form, and they relate, either generally or specifically, variables to variables."[4] Regarding the problem of absenteeism, for instance, a manager might want to test the following hypothesis: "Hourly employees who are dissatisfied with their pay are absent more often than those who are satisfied." Hypothesis in hand, a researcher is prepared to design a study to test it.

There are two important, interrelated components to designing a study. The first consists of deciding how to measure independent and dependent variables. An *independent variable* is a variable that is hypothesized to affect or cause a certain state of events. For example, a study demonstrated that losing one's job led to lower self-esteem and greater depression.[5] In this case, losing one's job, the independent variable, produced lower levels of self-esteem and higher levels of depression. A *dependent variable* is the variable being explained or predicted. Returning to the example, self-esteem and depression were the dependent variables (the variables being explained). In an everyday example, those who eat less (independent variable) are likely to lose weight (dependent variable). The second component of designing a study is to determine which research method to use (recall the discussion in Chapter 1). Criteria for evaluating the appropriateness of different research methods are discussed in a later section.

After a study is designed and completed, data are analyzed to determine whether the hypothesis is supported. Researchers look for alternative explanations of results when a hypothesis is not supported.[6]

Measurement and Data Collection

"In its broadest sense, measurement is the assignment of numerals to objects or events according to rules."[7] Organizational researchers measure variables. Job satisfaction, turnover, performance, and perceived stress are variables typically measured in OB research. Valid measurement is one of the most critical components of any research study because research findings are open to conflicting interpretations when variables are poorly measured.[8] Poor measurement reduces the confidence one has in applying research findings. Four techniques are frequently used to collect data: (1) direct observation, (2) questionnaires, (3) interviews, and (4) indirect methods.

Observation
This technique consists of recording the number of times a prespecified behavior is exhibited. For example, psychologist Judith Komaki developed and validated an observational categorization of supervisory behavior. She then used the instrument to identify behavior differences between effective and ineffective managers from a large medical insurance firm. Managerial effectiveness was based on superior ratings. Results indicated that effective managers spent more time monitoring their employees' performance than did ineffective managers. Komaki more recently applied the same instrument to examine the performance of sailboat captains competing in a race. Similar to the managerial study, skippers finished higher in the overall race standings when they monitored and rewarded their crews.[9] There are few "valid" observational schemes for use in OB research outside of Komaki's taxonomy.

Questionnaires
Questionnaires ask respondents for their opinions or feelings about work-related issues. They generally contain previously developed and validated instruments and are self-administered. Given their impersonal nature, poorly designed questionnaires are susceptible to rater bias. Nevertheless, a well-developed survey can be an accurate and economical way to collect large quantities of data.[10]

Interviews   Interviews rely on either face-to-face or telephone interactions to ask respondents questions of interest. In a *structured* interview, interviewees are asked the same questions in the same order. *Unstructured* interviews do not require interviewers to use the same questions or format. Unstructured interviews are more spontaneous. Structured interviews are the better of the two because they permit consistent comparisons among people. Accordingly, human resource management experts strongly recommend structured interviews during the hiring process to permit candidate-to-candidate comparisons.[11]

Indirect Methods   These techniques obtain data without any direct contact with respondents. This approach may entail observing someone without his or her knowledge. Other examples include searching existing records, such as personnel files, for data on variables such as absenteeism, turnover, and output. This method reduces rater error and generally is used in combination with one of the previously discussed techniques.

Evaluating Research Methods

All research methods can be evaluated from three perspectives: (1) generalizability, (2) precision in control and measurement, and (3) realism of the context.[12] *Generalizability,* which also is referred to as external validity, reflects the extent to which results from one study are generalizable to other individuals, groups, or situations. *Precision in control and measurement* pertains to the level of accuracy in manipulating or measuring variables. A *realistic context* is one that naturally exists for the individuals participating in the research study. In other words, realism implies that the context is not an artificial situation contrived for purposes of conducting the study. Table C–1 presents an evaluation of the five most frequently used research methods in terms of these three perspectives.

In summary, there is no one best research method. Choosing a method depends on the purpose of the specific study.[13] For example, if high control is necessary, as in testing for potential radiation leaks in pipes that will be used at a nuclear power plant, a laboratory experiment is appropriate (see Table C–1). In contrast, sample surveys would be useful if a company wanted to know the generalizable impact of a television commercial for light beer.

Table C–1   *Assessment of Frequently Used Research Methods*

Method	Generalizability	Precision in Control and Measurement	Realistic Context
Case study	Low	Low	High
Sample survey	High	Low	Low
Field study	Moderate	Moderate	High
Laboratory experiment	Low	High	Low
Field experiment	Moderate	Moderate	Moderate

SOURCE: Adapted in part from J E McGrath, J Martin, and R A Kulka, *Judgment Calls in Research* (Beverly Hills, CA: Sage Publications, 1982).

Evaluating Research Conclusions

There are several issues to consider when evaluating the quality of a research study.[14] The first is whether results from the specific study are consistent with those from past research. If not, it is helpful to determine why discrepancies exist. For instance, it is insightful to compare the samples, research methods, measurement of variables, statistical analyses, and general research procedures across the discrepant studies. Extreme differences suggest that future research may be needed to reconcile the inconsistent results. In the meantime, however, we need to be cautious in applying research findings from one study that are inconsistent with those from a larger number of studies.

The type of research method used is the second consideration. Does the method have generalizability (see Table C–1)? If not, check the characteristics of the sample. If the sample's characteristics are different from the characteristics of your work group, conclusions may not be relevant for your organization. Sample characteristics are very important in evaluating results from both field studies and experiments.

The level of precision in control and measurement is the third factor to consider. It is important to determine whether valid measures were used in the study. This can be done by reading the original study and examining descriptions of how variables were measured. Variables have questionable validity when they are measured with one-item scales or "ad-hoc" instruments developed by the authors. In contrast, standardized scales tend to be more valid because they are typically developed and validated in previous research studies. We have more confidence in results when they are based on analyses using standardized scales. As a general rule, validity in measurement begets confidence in applying research findings.

Finally, it is helpful to brainstorm alternative explanations for the research results. This helps to identify potential problems within research procedures.

Reading a Scientific Journal Article

Research is published in scientific journals and professional magazines. *Journal of Applied Psychology* and *Academy of Management Journal* are examples of scientific journals reporting OB research. *Harvard Business Review* and *HRMagazine* are professional magazines that sometimes report research findings in general terms. Table C–2 contains a list of 50 highly regarded management journals and magazines. You may find this list to be a useful source of information when writing term papers.

Scientific journal articles report results from empirical research studies, overall reviews of research on a specific topic, and theoretical articles. To help you obtain relevant information from scientific articles, let us consider the content and structure of these three types of articles.[15]

Empirical Research Studies

Reports of these studies contain summaries of original research. They typically comprise four distinct sections consistent with the logical steps of the research process model shown in Figure C–1. These sections are as follows:

- *Introduction.* This section identifies the problem being investigated and the purpose of the study. Previous research pertaining to the problem is reviewed and sometimes critiqued.

Table C–2   *A List of Highly Regarded Management Journals and Magazines*

1. *Administrative Science Quarterly*	26. *Journal of Occupational Behavior*
2. *Journal of Applied Psychology*	27. *Public Administration Quarterly*
3. *Organizational Behavior and Human Decision Processes*	28. *Journal of Organizational Behavior Management*
4. *Academy of Management Journal*	29. *Organizational Dynamics*
5. *Psychological Bulletin*	30. *Monthly Labor Review*
6. *Industrial and Labor Relations Review*	31. *Journal of World Business*
7. *Journal of Personality and Social Psychology*	32. *Journal of Business Research*
8. *Academy of Management Review*	33. *Group and Organization Management*
9. *Industrial Relations*	34. *Human Resource Planning*
10. *Journal of Labor Economics*	35. *Journal of Management Studies*
11. *Personnel Psychology*	36. *Administration and Society*
12. *American Psychologist*	37. *Negotiation Journal*
13. *Journal of Labor Research*	38. *Arbitration Journal*
14. *Journal of Vocational Labor*	39. *Compensation and Benefits Review*
15. *Journal of Applied Behavioral Science*	40. *Journal of Collective Negotiations in the Public Sector*
16. *Occupational Psychology*	41. *Public Personnel Management*
17. *Sloan Management Review*	42. *Journal of Management Education**
18. *Journal of Conflict Resolution*	43. *Review of Business and Economic Research*
19. *Human Relations*	44. *Personnel Journal*
20. *Journal of Human Resources*	45. *Journal of Small Business Management*
21. *Labor Law Journal*	46. *SAM Advanced Management Journal*
22. *Harvard Business Review*	47. *Business Horizons*
23. *Social Forces*	48. *Business and Public Affairs*
24. *Journal of Management*	49. *HRMagazine***
25. *California Management Review*	50. *Training and Development****

*Formerly *Organizational Behavior Teaching Review*
**Formerly *Personnel Administrator*
***Formerly *Training and Development Journal*
SOURCE: Adapted by permission from M M Extejt and J E Smith, "The Behavior Sciences and Management: An Evaluation of Relevant Journals," *Journal of Management*, September 1990, p. 545.

- *Method.* This section discusses the method used to conduct the study. Characteristics of the sample or subjects, procedures followed, materials used, measurement of variables, and analytic procedures typically are discussed.

- *Results.* A detailed description of the documented results is presented.

- *Discussion.* This section provides an interpretation, discussion, and implications of results.

Review Articles

These articles, including meta-analyses, are critical evaluations of material that has already been published. By organizing, integrating, and evaluating previously published material, the author of a review article considers the progress of current research toward clarifying a problem."[16] Although the structure of these articles is not as clear-cut as reports of empirical studies, the general format is as follows:

- A statement of the problem.
- A summary or review of previous research that attempts to provide the reader with the state of current knowledge about the problem (meta-analysis frequently is used to summarize past research).
- Identification of shortcomings, limitations, and inconsistencies in past research.
- Recommendations for future research to solve the problem.

Theoretical Articles

These articles draw on past research to propose revisions to existing theoretical models or to develop new theories and models. The structure is similar to that of review articles.

Back to the NTSB Study

This module was introduced with a National Transportation Safety Board study that suggested it is not safe to wear rear-seat lap belts while riding in an automobile. Given what we have just discussed, take a few minutes now to jot down any potential explanations for why the NTSB findings conflict with past research supporting the positive benefits of rear-seat lap belts. Now compare your thoughts with an evaluation presented in the *University of California, Berkeley Wellness Letter*:

> Critics claim that the NTSB study paints a misleadingly scary picture by focusing on 26 unrepresentative accidents, all unusually serious and all but one frontal. The National Highway Traffic Safety Administration has strongly disputed the board's findings, citing five earlier studies of thousands of crashes showing that safety belts—including lap belts—are instrumental in preventing death and injury. And a new study of 37,000 crashes in North Carolina shows that rear-seat lap belts reduce the incidence of serious injury and death by about 40%...
>
> In the meantime, most evidence indicates that you should continue to use rear-seat lap belts. You can minimize the risk of injury by wearing them as low across the hips as possible and keeping them tight.[17]

The NTSB findings were based on a set of unrepresentative serious frontal accidents. In other words, the NTSB's sample was not reflective of the typical automobile accident. Thus, the generalizability of the NTSB results is very limited. Buckle up!

Glossary

ability Stable characteristic responsible for a person's maximum physical or mental performance.

accountability practices Focus on treating diverse employees fairly.

adaptive perspective Assumes that adaptive cultures enhance a firm's financial performance.

affective component The feelings or emotions one has about an object or situation.

affirmative action Focuses on achieving equality of opportunity in an organization.

aggressive style Expressive and self-enhancing, but takes unfair advantage of others.

alternative dispute resolution Avoiding costly lawsuits by resolving conflicts informally or through mediation or arbitration.

Americans with Disabilities Act Prohibits discrimination against the disabled.

anticipatory socialization Occurs before an individual joins an organization, and involves the information people learn about different careers, occupations, professions, and organizations.

Asch effect Giving in to a unanimous but wrong opposition.

assertive style Expressive and self-enhancing, but does not take advantage of others.

attention Being consciously aware of something or someone.

attitude Learned predisposition toward a given object.

availability heuristic Tendency to base decisions on information readily available in memory.

behavioral component How one intends to act or behave toward someone or something.

benchmarking Process by which a company compares its performance with that of high-performing organizations.

bounded rationality Constraints that restrict rational decision making.

brainstorming Process to generate a quantity of ideas.

building blocks of intrinsic motivation Essential work environment characteristics needed for intrinsic motivation.

care perspective Involves compassion and an ideal of attention and response to need.

career plateauing The end result when the probability of being promoted is very small.

case study In-depth study of a single person, group, or organization.

causal attributions Suspected or inferred causes of behavior.

centralized decision making Top managers make all key decisions.

change and acquisition Requires employees to master tasks and roles and to adjust to work group values and norms.

charismatic leadership Transforms employees to pursue organizational goals over self-interests.

closed system A relatively self-sufficient entity.

coalition Temporary groupings of people who actively pursue a single issue.

coercive power Obtaining compliance through threatened or actual punishment.

cognitions A person's knowledge, opinions, or beliefs.

cognitive categories Mental depositories for storing information.

cognitive component The beliefs or ideas one has about an object or situation.

cognitive style A perceptual and judgmental tendency, according to Jung's typology.

cohesiveness A sense of "we-ness" helps group stick together.

collaborative computing Using computer software and hardware to help people work better together.

collectivist culture Personal goals less important than community goals and interests.

commitment to change A mind-set of doing whatever it takes to effectively implement change.

communication Interpersonal exchange of information and understanding.

communication competence Ability to effectively use communication behaviors in a given context.

communication distortion Purposely modifying the content of a message.

conflict One party perceives its interests are being opposed or set back by another party.

conflict triangle Conflicting parties involve a third person rather than dealing directly with each other.

consensus Presenting opinions and gaining agreement to support a decision.

consideration Creating mutual respect and trust with followers.

contingency approach Using management tools and techniques in a situationally appropriate manner; avoiding the one-best-way mentality.

contingency approach to organization design   Creating an effective organization–environment fit.

contingency factors   Variables that influence the appropriateness of a leadership style.

continuous reinforcement   Reinforcing every instance of a behavior.

control strategy   Coping strategy that directly confronts or solves problems.

core job dimensions   Job characteristics found to various degrees in all jobs.

creativity   Process of developing something new or unique.

cross-cultural management   Understanding and teaching behavioral patterns in different cultures.

cross-cultural training   Structured experiences to help people adjust to a new culture/country.

cross-functionalism   Team made up of technical specialists from different areas.

culture   Beliefs and values about how a community of people should and do act.

culture shock   Anxiety and doubt caused by an overload of new expectations and cues.

decentralized decision making   Lower-level managers are empowered to make important decisions.

decision making   Identifying and choosing solutions that lead to a desired end result.

decision-making style   A combination of how individuals perceive and respond to information.

delegation   Granting decision-making authority to people at lower levels.

Delphi technique   Process to generate ideas from physically dispersed experts.

development practices   Focus on preparing diverse employees for greater responsibility and advancement.

developmental relationship strength   The quality of relationships among people in a network.

devil's advocacy   Assigning someone the role of critic.

dialectic method   Fostering a debate of opposing viewpoints to better understand an issue.

differentiation   Division of labor and specialization that causes people to think and act differently.

distributive justice   The perceived fairness of how resources and rewards are distributed.

diversity   The host of individual differences that make people different from and similar to each other.

diversity of developmental relationships   The variety of people in a network used for developmental assistance.

dysfunctional conflict   Threatens organization's interests.

E-business   Running the *entire* business via the Internet.

electronic mail   Uses the Internet/intranet to send computer-generated text and documents.

emotional intelligence   Ability to manage oneself and interact with others in mature and constructive ways.

emotions   Complex human reactions to personal achievements and setbacks that may be felt and displayed.

empowerment   Sharing varying degrees of power with lower-level employees to tap their full potential.

enacted values   The values and norms that are exhibited by employees.

encounter phase   Employees learn what the organization is really like and reconcile unmet expectations.

equity sensitivity   An individual's tolerance for negative and positive equity.

equity theory   Holds that motivation is a function of fairness in social exchanges.

ERG theory   Three basic needs—existence, relatedness, and growth—influence behavior.

escalation of commitment   Sticking to an ineffective course of action too long.

escape strategy   Coping strategy that avoids or ignores stressors and problems.

espoused values   The stated values and norms that are preferred by an organization.

ethics   Study of moral issues and choices.

ethnocentrism   Belief that one's native country, culture, language, and behavior are superior.

eustress   Stress that is good or produces a positive outcome.

expatriate   Anyone living or working in a foreign country.

expectancy   Belief that effort leads to a specific level of performance.

expectancy theory   Holds that people are motivated to behave in ways that produce valued outcomes.

expert power   Obtaining compliance through one's knowledge or information.

explicit knowledge   Information that can be easily put into words and shared with others.

external factors   Environmental characteristics that cause behavior.

external forces for change   Originate outside the organization.

external locus of control   Attributing outcomes to circumstances beyond one's control.

extinction   Making behavior occur less often by ignoring or not reinforcing it.

extranet   Connects internal employees with selected customers, suppliers, and strategic partners.

extrinsic motivation   Motivation caused by the desire to attain specific outcomes.

extrinsic rewards   Financial, material, or social rewards from the environment.

feedback   Objective information about performance.

field study   Examination of variables in real-life settings.

fight-or-flight response   To either confront stressors or try to avoid them.

fit perspective Assumes that culture must align with its business or strategic context.

formal group Formed by the organization.

functional conflict Serves organization's interests.

fundamental attribution bias Ignoring environmental factors that affect behavior.

genderflex Temporarily using communication behaviors typical of the other gender.

glass ceiling Invisible barrier blocking women and minorities from top management positions.

goal What an individual is trying to accomplish.

goal commitment Amount of commitment to achieving a goal.

goal difficulty The amount of effort required to meet a goal.

goal specificity Quantifiability of a goal.

Golem effect Loss in performance due to low leader expectations.

grapevine Unofficial communication system of the informal organization.

group Two or more freely interacting people with shared norms and goals and a common identity.

group cohesiveness A "we feeling" binding group members together.

groupthink Janis's term for a cohesive in-group's unwillingness to realistically view alternatives.

hardiness Personality characteristic that neutralizes stress.

hierarchical communication Exchange of information between managers and employees.

high-context cultures Primary meaning derived from nonverbal situational cues.

holistic wellness approach Advocates personal responsibility for healthy living.

human capital The productive potential of one's knowledge and actions.

hygiene factors Job characteristics associated with job dissatisfaction.

impression management Getting others to see us in a certain manner.

individualistic culture Primary emphasis on personal freedom and choice.

informal group Formed by friends or those with common interests.

information richness Information-carrying capacity of data.

in-group exchange A partnership characterized by mutual trust, respect, and liking.

initiating structure Organizing and defining what group members should be doing.

instrumental cohesiveness Sense of togetherness based on mutual dependency needed to get the job done.

instrumental values Personally preferred ways of behaving.

instrumentality A performance→outcome perception.

integration Cooperation among specialists to achieve a common goal.

intelligence Capacity for constructive thinking, reasoning, problem solving.

interactional justice Extent to which people feel fairly treated when procedures are implemented.

intermittent reinforcement Reinforcing some but not all instances of behavior.

internal factors Personal characteristics that cause behavior.

internal forces for change Originate inside the organization.

internal locus of control Attributing outcomes to one's own actions.

Internet A global system of computer networks.

intranet An organization's private Internet.

intrinsic motivation Motivation caused by positive internal feelings.

intrinsic rewards Self-granted, psychic rewards.

job design Changing the content or process of a specific job to increase job satisfaction and performance.

job enlargement Putting more variety into a job.

job enrichment Building achievement, recognition, stimulating work, responsibility, and advancement into a job.

job involvement Extent to which an individual is immersed in his or her present job.

job rotation Moving employees from one specialized job to another.

job satisfaction An affective or emotional response to one's job.

judgmental heuristics Rules of thumb or shortcuts that people use to reduce information-processing demands.

justice perspective Based on the ideal of reciprocal rights and driven by rules and regulations.

knowledge management Implementing systems and practices that increase the sharing of knowledge and information throughout an organization.

laboratory study Manipulation and measurement of variables in contrived situations.

law of effect Behavior with favorable consequences is repeated; behavior with unfavorable consequences disappears.

leader–member relations Extent that leader has the support, loyalty, and trust of work group.

leader trait Personal characteristics that differentiate leaders from followers.

leadership Influencing employees to voluntarily pursue organizational goals.

Leadership Grid Represents four leadership styles found by crossing concern for production and concern for people.

leadership prototype Mental representation of the traits and behaviors possessed by leaders.

learned helplessness Debilitating lack in one's ability to control the situation.

learning organization Proactively creates, acquires, and transfers knowledge throughout the organization.

legitimate power Obtaining compliance through formal authority.

liaison individuals Those who consistently pass along grapevine information to others.

line managers Have authority to make organizational decisions.

linguistic style A person's typical speaking pattern.

listening Actively decoding and interpreting verbal messages.

low-context cultures Primary meaning derived from written and spoken words.

maintenance roles Relationship-building group behavior.

management Process of working with and through others to achieve organizational objectives efficiently and ethically.

management by objectives Management system incorporating participation in decision making, goal setting, and feedback.

managing diversity Creating organizational changes that enable all people to perform up to their maximum potential.

mechanistic organizations Rigid, command-and-control bureaucracies.

mentoring Process of forming and maintaining developmental relationships between a mentor and a junior person.

met expectations The extent to which one receives what he or she expects from a job.

meta-analysis Pools the results of many studies through statistical procedure.

mission statement Summarizes "why" an organization exists.

monochronic time Preference for doing one thing at a time because time is limited, precisely segmented, and schedule driven.

motivation Psychological processes that arouse and direct goal-directed behavior.

motivators Job characteristics associated with job satisfaction.

mutuality of interest Balancing individual and organizational interests through win–win cooperation.

need for achievement Desire to accomplish something difficult.

need for affiliation Desire to spend time in social relationships and activities.

need for power Desire to influence, coach, teach, or encourage others to achieve.

need hierarchy theory Five basic needs—physiological, safety, love, esteem, and self-actualization—influence behavior.

needs Physiological or psychological deficiencies that arouse behavior.

negative inequity Comparison in which another person receives greater outcomes for similar inputs.

negative reinforcement Making behavior occur more often by contingently withdrawing something negative.

negotiation Give-and-take process between conflicting interdependent parties.

noise Interference with the transmission and understanding of a message.

nominal group technique Process to generate ideas and evaluate solutions.

nonassertive style Timid and self-denying behavior.

nonverbal communication Messages sent outside of the written or spoken word.

norm Shared attitudes, opinions, feelings, or actions that guide social behavior.

normative beliefs Thoughts and beliefs about expected behavior and modes of conduct.

open system Organism that must constantly interact with its environment to survive.

operant behavior Skinner's term for learned, consequence-shaped behavior.

optimizing Choosing the best possible solution.

organic organizations Fluid and flexible networks of multitalented people.

organization System of consciously coordinated activities of two or more people.

organization chart Boxes-and-lines illustration showing chain of formal authority and division of labor.

organization development A set of techniques or tools used to implement organizational change.

organizational behavior Interdisciplinary field dedicated to better understanding and managing people at work.

organizational citizenship behaviors (OCBs) Employee behaviors that exceed work-role requirements.

organizational commitment Extent to which an individual identifies with an organization and its goals.

organizational culture Shared values and beliefs that underlie a company's identity.

organizational decline Decrease in organization's resource base (money, customers, talent, innovations).

organizational identification Organizational values or beliefs become part of one's self-identity.

organizational moles Those who use the grapevine to enhance their power and status.

organizational politics Intentional enhancement of self-interest.

organizational socialization Process by which employees learn an organization's values, norms, and required behaviors.

ostracism Rejection by other group members.

out-group exchange A partnership characterized by a lack of mutual trust, respect, and liking.

participative management Involving employees in various aspects of decision making.

pay for performance Monetary incentives tied to one's results or accomplishments.

perception Process of interpreting one's environment.

perceptual model of communication Process in which receivers create their own meaning.

performance appraisal Judgmental evaluation of one's traits, behavior, or accomplishments as basis for personnel decisions and development plans.

persistence Extent to which effort is expended on a task over time.

personal initiative Going beyond formal job requirements and being an active self-starter.

personality Stable physical and mental characteristics responsible for a person's identity.

personality conflict Interpersonal opposition driven by personal dislike or disagreement.

personalized power Directed at helping oneself.

polychronic time Preference for doing more than one thing at a time because time is flexible and multidimensional.

position power Degree to which leader has formal power.

positive inequity Comparison in which another person receives lesser outcomes for similar inputs.

positive reinforcement Making behavior occur more often by contingently presenting something positive.

primary appraisal Determining whether a stressor is irrelevant, positive, or stressful.

proactive personality Action-oriented person who shows initiative and perseveres to change things.

problem Gap between an actual and desired situation.

procedural justice The perceived fairness of the process and procedures used to make allocation decisions.

programmed conflict Encourages different opinions without protecting management's personal feelings.

propensity to trust A personality trait involving one's general willingness to trust others.

proxemics Hall's term for the study of cultural expectations about interpersonal space.

punishment Making behavior occur less often by contingently presenting something negative or withdrawing something positive.

quality circles Small groups of volunteers who strive to solve quality-related problems.

rational model Logical four-step approach to decision making.

readiness Follower's ability and willingness to complete a task.

realistic job preview Presents both positive and negative aspects of a job.

reality shock A newcomer's feeling of surprise after experiencing unexpected situations or events.

recruitment practices Attempts to attract qualified, diverse employees at all levels.

referent power Obtaining compliance through charisma or personal attraction.

representativeness heuristic Tendency to assess the likelihood of an event occurring based on impressions about similar occurrences.

resilience to change Composite personal characteristic reflecting high self-esteem, optimism, and an internal locus of control.

resistance to change Emotional/behavioral response to real or imagined work changes.

respondent behavior Skinner's term for unlearned stimulus–response reflexes.

reward equality norm Everyone should get the same rewards.

reward equity norm Rewards should be tied to contributions.

reward power Obtaining compliance with promised or actual rewards.

role ambiguity Others' expectations are unknown.

role conflict Others have conflicting or inconsistent expectations.

role overload Others' expectations exceed one's ability.

roles Expected behaviors for a given position.

sample survey Questionnaire responses from a sample of people.

satisficing Choosing a solution that meets a minimum standard of acceptance.

scenario technique Speculative forecasting method.

schema Mental picture of an event or object.

scientific management Using research and experimentation to find the most efficient way to perform a job.

secondary appraisal Assessing what might and can be done to reduce stress.

self-concept Person's self-perception as a physical, social, spiritual being.

self-efficacy Belief in one's ability to do a task.

self-esteem One's overall self-evaluation.

self-fulfilling prophecy People's expectations determine behavior and performance.

self-managed teams Groups of employees granted administrative oversight for their work.

self-management leadership Process of leading others to lead themselves.

self-monitoring Observing one's own behavior and adapting it to the situation.

self-serving bias Taking more personal responsibility for success than failure.

self-talk Evaluating thoughts about oneself and one's circumstances.

sense of choice The ability to use judgment and freedom when completing tasks.

sense of competence Feelings of accomplishment associated with doing high-quality work.

sense of meaningfulness The task purpose is important and meaningful.

sense of progress Feeling that one is accomplishing something important.

servant-leadership Focuses on increased service to others rather than to oneself.

sex-role stereotype Beliefs about appropriate roles for men and women.

shaping Reinforcing closer and closer approximations to a target behavior.

situational theories Propose that leader styles should match the situation at hand.

skill Specific capacity to manipulate objects.

social capital The productive potential of strong, trusting, and cooperative relationships.

social loafing Decrease in individual effort as group size increases.

social power Ability to get things done with human, informational, and material resources.

social support Amount of helpfulness derived from social relationships.

socialized power Directed at helping others.

socio-emotional cohesiveness Sense of togetherness based on emotional satisfaction.

span of control The number of people reporting directly to a given manager.

staff personnel Provide research, advice, and recommendations to line managers.

stakeholder audit Systematic identification of all parties likely to be affected by the organization.

stereotype Beliefs about the characteristics of a group.

strategic constituency Any group of people with a stake in the organization's operation or success.

strategic plan A long-term plan outlining actions needed to achieve desired results.

strength perspective Assumes that the strength of corporate culture is related to a firm's financial performance.

stress Behavioral, physical, or psychological response to stressors.

stressors Environmental factors that produce stress.

substitutes for leadership Situational variables that can substitute for, neutralize, or enhance the effects of leadership.

symptom management strategy Coping strategy that focuses on reducing the symptoms of stress.

tacit knowledge Information gained through experience that is difficult to express and formalize.

target elements of change Components of an organization that may be changed.

task roles Task-oriented group behavior.

task structure Amount of structure contained within work tasks.

team Small group with complementary skills who hold themselves mutually accountable for common purpose, goals, and approach.

team-based pay Linking pay to teamwork behavior and/or team results.

team building Experiential learning aimed at better internal functioning of groups.

team viability Team members satisfied and willing to contribute.

telecommuting Doing work that is generally performed in the office away from the office using different information technologies.

terminal values Personally preferred end-states of existence.

theory A story defining key terms, providing a conceptual framework, and explaining why something occurs.

Theory Y McGregor's modern and positive assumptions about employees being responsible and creative.

360-degree feedback Comparison of anonymous feedback from one's

superior, subordinates, and peers with self-perceptions.

total quality management An organizational culture dedicated to training, continuous improvement, and customer satisfaction.

transactional leadership Focuses on interpersonal interactions between managers and employees.

trust Reciprocal faith in others' intentions and behavior.

Type A behavior pattern Aggressively involved in a chronic, determined struggle to accomplish more in less time.

underemployment The result of taking a job that requires less education, training, or skills than possessed by a worker.

unity of command principle Each employee should report to a single manager.

upward feedback Subordinates evaluate their boss.

valence The value of a reward or outcome.

value attainment The extent to which a job allows fulfillment of one's work values.

value system The organization of one's beliefs about preferred ways of behaving and desired end-states.

values Enduring belief in a mode of conduct or end-state.

valuing diversity Emphasizes the awareness, recognition, understanding, and appreciation of human differences.

virtual team Information technology allows group members in different locations to conduct business.

vision Long-term goal describing "what" an organization wants to become.

withdrawal cognitions Overall thoughts and feelings about quitting a job.

workforce demographics Statistical profiles of adult workers.

Endnotes

CHAPTER I

[1] Reprinted by permission of *Harvard Business Review.* From "Investing in Relationships" by J Hoffer Gittell, June 2001. Copyright © 2001 by the Harvard Business School Publishing Corporation; all rights reserved.

[2] "James F Parker," *Fast Company,* May 2002, p 62.

[3] Adams, *The Dilbert Principle* (New York: HarperBusiness, 1996), p 51. Also see D Kersten, "Dilbert Moves into Dot-Com Purgatory," *USA Today,* April 8, 2002, p 7B.

[4] J Pfeffer and J F Veiga, "Putting People First for Organizational Success," *Academy of Management Executive,* May 1999, p 37.

[5] Adapted from ibid.

[6] See J A Byrne, "How to Fix Corporate Governance," *Business Week,* May 6, 2002, pp 68–78.

[7] For the case against layoffs, see J R Morris, W F Cascio, and C E Young, "Downsizing after All These Years: Questions and Answers about Who Did It, How Many Did It, and Who Benefited from It," *Organizational Dynamics,* Winter 1999, pp 78–87; and D Rigby, "Look Before You Lay Off," *Harvard Business Review,* April 2002, pp 20–21.

[8] Data from Pfeffer and Veiga, "Putting People First for Organizational Success," p 47. Also see C A O'Reilly and Pfeffer, *Hidden Value: How Great Companies Achieve Extraordinary Results with Ordinary People* (Boston: Harvard Business School Press, 2000); and J P Guthrie, "High-Involvement Work Practices, Turnover, and Productivity: Evidence from New Zealand," *Academy of Management Journal,* February 2001, pp 180–90.

[9] For inspiring examples, see R Levering and M Moskowitz, "The 100 Best Companies to Work for: The Best in the Worst of Times," *Fortune,* February 4, 2002, pp 60–90.

[10] See J Collins, *Good to Great: Why Some Companies Make the Leap . . . and Others Don't* (New York: Harper Business, 2001); and J Collins, "How Great Companies Tame Technology," *Newsweek,* April 29, 2002, p 51.

[11] H Mintzberg, "The Manager's Job: Folklore and Fact," *Harvard Business Review,* July–August 1975, p 61. For an alternative perspective, see R J Samuelson, "Why I Am Not a Manager," *Newsweek,* March 22, 1999, p 47. Also see C A Walker, "Saving Your Rookie Managers from Themselves," *Harvard Business Review,* April 2002, pp 97–102.

[12] See, for example, H Mintzberg, "Managerial Work: Analysis from Observation," *Management Science,* October 1971, pp B97–B110; and F Luthans, "Successful vs. Effective Real Managers," *Academy of Management Executive,* May 1988, pp 127–32. For an instructive critique of the structured observation

method, see M J Martinko and W L Gardner, "Beyond Structured Observation: Methodological Issues and New Directions," *Academy of Management Review,* October 1985, pp 676–95. Also see N Fondas, "A Behavioral Job Description for Managers," *Organizational Dynamics,* Summer 1992, pp 47–58.

[13] See L B Kurke and H E Aldrich, "Mintzberg Was Right!: A Replication and Extension of *The Nature of Managerial Work,*" *Management Science,* August 1983, pp 975–84.

[14] For example, see H Bruch and S Ghoshal, "Beware the Busy Manager," *Harvard Business Review,* February 2002, pp 62–69.

[15] Validation studies can be found in E Van Velsor and J B Leslie, *Feedback to Managers, Volume II: A Review and Comparison of Sixteen Multi-Rater Feedback Instruments* (Greensboro, NC: Center for Creative Leadership, 1991); and F Shipper, "A Study of the Psychometric Properties of the Managerial Skill Scales of the Survey of Management Practices," *Educational and Psychological Measurement,* June 1995, pp 468–79. Also see F Shipper and C S White, "Mastery, Frequency, and Interaction of Managerial Behaviors Relative to Subunit Effectiveness," *Human Relations,* January 1999, pp 49–66; and F Shipper and J Davy, "A Model and Investigation of Managerial Skills, Employees' Attitudes and Managerial Performance," *Leadership Quarterly,* in press.

[16] For example, see S B Parry, "Just What Is a Competency? (And Why Should You Care?)" *Training,* June 1998, pp 58–64.

[17] See F Shipper, "Mastery and Frequency of Managerial Behaviors Relative to Sub-Unit Effectiveness," *Human Relations,* April 1991, pp 371–88.

[18] Ibid.

[19] Data from F Shipper, "A Study of Managerial Skills of Women and Men and Their Impact on Employees' Attitudes and Career Success in a Nontraditional Organization," paper presented at the Academy of Management Meeting, August 1994, Dallas, Texas. The same outcome for on-the-job studies is reported in A H Eagly and B T Johnson, "Gender and Leadership Style: A Meta-Analysis," *Psychological Bulletin,* September 1990, pp 233–56.

[20] For instance, see J B Rosener, "Ways Women Lead," *Harvard Business Review,* November–December 1990, pp 119–25; and C Lee, "The Feminization of Management," *Training,* November 1994, pp 25–31.

[21] Based on F Shipper and J E Dillard Jr, "A Study of Impending Derailment and Recovery of Middle Managers across Career Stages," *Human Resource Management,* Winter 2000, pp 331–45.

[22] B E Becker, M A Huselid, and D Ulrich, *The HR Scorecard: Linking People, Strategy, and Performance* (Boston: Harvard Business School Press, 2001), p 4.

[23] See D Stamps, "Measuring Minds," *Training,* May 2000, pp 76–85; and C A Bartlett and S Ghoshal, "Building Competitive Advantage through People," *MIT Sloan Management Review,* Winter 2002, pp 34–41.

[24] For details, see **www.intel.com**; select "Intel Innovation in Education" under the heading "About Intel."

[25] Data from "The 100 Best Companies to Work For," *Fortune,* February 4, 2002, p 84. Also see G Anders, "The Reeducation of Silicon Valley," *Fast Company,* April 2002, pp 100–8.

[26] Inspired by P S Adler and S Kwon, "Social Capital: Prospects for a New Concept," *Academy of Management Review,* January 2002, pp 17–40. Also see R A Baaron and G D Markman, "Beyond Social Capital: How Social Skills Can Enhance Entrepreneurs' Success," *Academy of Management Executive,* February 2000, pp 106–16.

[27] L Prusak and D Cohen, "How to Invest in Social Capital," *Harvard Business Review,* June 2001, p 93.

[28] Data from "What Makes a Job OK," *USA Today,* May 15, 2000, p 1B.

[29] See M Hammer, *The Agenda: What Every Business Must Do to Dominate the Decade* (New York: Crown Business, 2001).

[30] Essential sources on reengineering are M Hammer and J Champy, *Reengineering the Corporation: A Manifesto for Business Revolution* (New York: HarperCollins, 1993); and J Champy, *Reengineering Management: The Mandate for New Leadership* (New York: HarperCollins, 1995). Also see "Anything Worth Doing Is Worth Doing from Scratch," *Inc.,* May 18, 1999 (20th Anniversary Issue), pp 51–52.

[31] For thoughtful discussion, see G G Dess, A M A Rasheed, K J McLaughlin, and R L Priem, "The New Corporate Architecture," *Academy of Management Executive,* August 1995, pp 7–20.

[32] See, for example, W A Randolph, "Re-thinking Empowerment: Why Is It So Hard to Achieve?" *Organizational Dynamics,* Fall 2000, pp 94–107; and W A Randolph and M Sashkin, "Can Organizational Empowerment Work in Multinational Settings?" *Academy of Management Executive,* February 2002, pp 102–15.

[33] P C Judge, "Provocation 101," *Fast Company,* January 2002, p 110.

[34] See J B Miner, "The Validity and Usefulness of Theories in an Emerging Organizational Science," *Academy of Management Review,* April 1984, pp 296–306.

[35] B S Lawrence, "Historical Perspective: Using the Past to Study the Present," *Academy of Management Review,* April 1984, p 307.

[36] Evidence indicating that the original conclusions of the famous Hawthorne studies were unjustified may be found in R G Greenwood, A A Bolton, and R A Greenwood, "Hawthorne a Half Century Later: Relay Assembly Participants Remember," *Journal of Management,* Fall–Winter 1983, pp 217–31; and R H Franke and J D Kaul, "The Hawthorne Experiments: First Statistical Interpretation," *American Sociological Review,* October 1978, pp 623–43. For a positive interpretation of the Hawthorne studies, see J A Sonnenfeld, "Shedding Light on the Hawthorne Studies," *Journal of Occupational Behaviour,* April 1985, pp 111–30.

[37] See M Parker Follett, *Freedom and Coordination* (London: Management Publications Trust, 1949).

[38] See D McGregor, *The Human Side of Enterprise* (New York: McGraw-Hill, 1960).

[39] For a recent story of a manager's switch from Theory X to Theory Y, see D Dorsey, "Andy Pearson Finds Love," *Fast Company,* August 2001, pp 78–86.

[40] J Hall, "Americans Know How to Be Productive if Managers Will Let Them," *Organizational Dynamics,* Winter 1994, p 38.

[41] See D W Organ, "Elusive Phenomena," *Business Horizons,* March–April 2002, pp 1–2.

[42] See, for example, R Zemke, "TQM: Fatally Flawed or Simply Unfocused?" *Training,* October 1992, p 8.

[43] For example, see L Silverman, "Critical Shift: The Future of Quality in Organizational Performance," *Nonprofit World,* November–December 2000, pp 27–28; E Naumann, D W Jackson, Jr, and M S Rosenbaum, "How to Implement a Customer Satisfaction Program," *Business Horizons,* January–February 2001, pp 37–46; and J J Kline, "How Quality Award-Winning Governments Handle Customer Service," *Journal of Organizational Excellence,* Summer 2001, pp 41–47.

[44] L Wah, "The Almighty Customer," *Management Review,* February 1999, p 17.

[45] "Thomas M Siebel: Siebel Systems," *Business Week,* January 8, 2001, p 63. Also see R S Allen and R H Kilmann, "Aligning Reward Practices in Support of Total Quality Management," *Business Horizons,* June 2001, pp 77–84.

[46] Instructive background articles on TQM are R Zemke, "A Bluffer's Guide to TQM," *Training,* April 1993, pp 48–55; R R Gehani, "Quality Value-Chain: A Meta-Synthesis of Frontiers of Quality Movement," *Academy of Management Executive,* May 1993, pp 29–42; P Mears, "How to Stop Talking about, and Begin Progress toward, Total Quality Management," *Business Horizons,* May–June 1993, pp 11–14; and the Total Quality Special Issue of *Academy of Management Review,* July 1994.

[47] M Sashkin and K J Kiser, *Putting Total Quality Management to Work* (San Francisco: Berrett-Koehler, 1993), p 39.

[48] R J Schonberger, "Total Quality Management Cuts a Broad Swath—Through Manufacturing and Beyond," *Organizational Dynamics,* Spring 1992, p 18. Also see K Y Kim, J G Miller, and J Heineke, "Mastering the Quality Staircase, Step by Step," *Business Horizons,* January–February 1997, pp 17–21; R Bell and B Keys, "A Conversation with Curt W Reimann on the Background and Future of the Baldrige Award," *Organizational Dynamics,* Spring 1998, pp 51–61; and B Kasanoff, "Are You Ready for Mass Customization?" *Training,* May 1998, pp 70–78.

[49] Based on C Hui, S S K Lam, and J Schaubroeck, "Can Good Citizens Lead the Way in Providing Quality Service? A Field Quasi Experiment," *Academy of Management Journal,* October 2001, pp 988–95.

[50] Deming's landmark work is W E Deming, *Out of the Crisis* (Cambridge, MA: MIT, 1986).

[51] See M Trumbull, "What Is Total Quality Management?" *The Christian Science Monitor,* May 3, 1993, p 12; and J Hillkirk, "World-Famous Quality Expert Dead at 93," *USA Today,* December 21, 1993, pp 1B–2B.

[52] Based on discussion in M Walton, *Deming Management at Work* (New York: Putnam/Perigee, 1990).

[53] Ibid., p 20.

[54] Adapted from D E Bowen and E E Lawler III "Total Quality-Oriented Human Resources Management," *Organizational Dynamics,* Spring 1992, pp 29–41.

[55] See T F Rienzo, "Planning Deming Management for Service Organizations," *Business Horizons,* May–June 1993, pp 19–29. Also see M R Yilmaz and S Chatterjee, "Deming and the Quality of Software Development," *Business Horizons,* November–December 1997, pp 51–58.

[56] For details, see T J Douglas and W Q Judge, Jr, "Total Quality Management Implementation and Competitive Advantage: The Role of Structural Control and Exploration," *Academy of Management Journal,* February 2001, pp 158–69; and K B Hendricks and V R Singhal, "The Long-Run Stock Price Performance of Firms with Effective TQM Programs," *Management Science,* March 2001, pp 359–68.

[57] For example, see J R Dew, "Learning from Baldrige Winners at the University of Alabama," *Journal of Organizational Excellence,* Spring 2001, pp 49–56; R B Chase and S Dasu, "Want to Perfect Your Company's Service? Use Behavioral Science," *Harvard Business Review,* June 2001, pp 79–84; A W Ulwick, "Turn Customer Input into Innovation," *Harvard Business Review,* January 2002, pp 91–97; and S Thomke and E von Hippel, "Customers as Innovators: A New Way to Create Value," *Harvard Business Review,* April 2002, pp 74–81.

[58] For more on Berners-Lee and the future of the Web, see O Port, "The Next Web," *Business Week,* March 4, 2002, pp 97–102.

[59] See J O'C Hamilton, "The Harder They Fall," *Business Week* **E.BIZ,** May 14, 2002, pp EB14, EB16.

[60] B DeLollis, "Revenue Takes Wing on Airlines' Web Sites," *USA Today,* March 12, 2002, p 8B.

[61] See S E Ante, "In Search of the Net's Next Big Thing," *Business Week,* March 26, 2001, pp 140–41; T J Mullaney, "Break Out the Black Ink," *Business Week,* May 13, 2002, pp 74, 76; J Useem, "Our 10 Principles of the New Economy, Slightly Revised," *Business 2.0,* August–September 2001, p 85; and H Green, "Lessons of the Cyber Survivors," *Business Week,* April 22, 2002, p 42.

[62] R D Hof, "How E-Biz Rose, Fell, and Will Rise Anew," *Business Week,* May 13, 2002, p 67.

[63] Ibid.

[64] See G Hamel, "Is This All You Can Build with the Net? Think Bigger," *Fortune,* April 30, 2001, 134–38; and B Rosenbloom, "The Ten Deadly Myths of E-Commerce," *Business Horizons,* March–April 2002, pp 61–66.

[65] M J Mandel and R D Hof, "Rethinking the Internet," *Business Week,* March 26, 2001, p 118. Also see B Powell, "The New World Order," *Fortune,* May 14, 2001, pp 134, 136.

[66] A Bernasek, "Buried in Tech." *Fortune,* April 16, 2001, p 52.

[67] W Echikson, "Nestlé: An Elephant Dances," *Business Week* **E.BIZ,** December 11, 2000, pp EB47–EB48. Also see B Sosnin. "Digital Newsletters 'E-volutionize' Employee Communications," *HR Magazine,* May 2001, pp 99–107.

[68] For more, see G Meyer, "eWorkbench: Real-Time Tracking of Synchronized Goals," *HR Magazine,* April 2001, pp 115–18.

[69] R Moss Kanter. *Evolve! Succeeding in the Digital Culture of Tomorrow* (Boston: Harvard Business School Press, 2001), p 206. Also see R Moss Kanter, "You Are Here," *Inc.,* February 2001, pp 84–90.

[70] Data from "Hurry Up and Decide!" *Business Week,* May 14, 2001.

[71] W C Symonds, "Giving It the Old Online Try," *Business Week,* December 3, 2001, p 80. Also see K Tyler, "Take E-Learning to the Next Step," *HR Magazine,* February 2002, pp 56–61.

[72] F Vogelstein, "Flying on the Web in a Turbulent Economy," *Fortune,* April 30, 2001, p 143.

[73] Boeing's problems are discussed in S Holmes and M France, "Boeing's Secret," *Business Week,* May 20, 2002, pp 110–20.

[74] See B Lessard and S Baldwin, *Net Slaves: True Tales of Working the Web* (New York: McGraw-Hill, 2000); and C Wilder and J Soat, "A Question of Ethics," *Information Week.com,* February 19, 2001, pp 38–50.

[75] H L Tosi, Jr, and J W Slocum, Jr, "Contingency Theory: Some Suggested Directions," *Journal of Management,* Spring 1984, p 9.

[76] For empirical evidence in a cross-cultural study, see D I Jung and B J Avolio, "Effects of Leadership Style and Followers' Cultural Orientation on Performance in Groups and Individual Task Conditions," *Academy of Management Journal,* April 1999, pp 208–18.

[77] See S L Rynes, J M Bartunek, and R L Daft, "Across the Great Divide: Knowledge Creation and Transfer between Practitioners and Academics," *Academy of Management Journal,* April 2001, pp 340–55.

[78] See R L Daft, "Learning the Craft of Organizational Research," *Academy of Management Review,* October 1983, pp 539–46.

[79] See K E Weick, "Theory Construction as Disciplined Imagination," *Academy of Management Review,* October 1989, pp 516–31. Also see D A Whetten's article in the same issue, pp 490–95.

[80] Theory-focused versus problem-focused research is discussed in K E Weick, "Agenda Setting in Organizational Behavior: A Theory-Focused Approach," *Journal of Management Inquiry,* September 1992, pp 171–82. Also see the collection of articles about theory in the October 1999 issue of *Academy of Management Review.*

[81] For instance, see M R Buckley, G R Ferris, H J Bernardin, and M G Harvey, "The Disconnect between the Science and Practice of Management," *Business Horizons,* March–April 1998, pp 31–38. Also see D Cohen, "Research: Food for Future Thought," *HR Magazine,* May 2001, p 184.

[82] Complete discussion of this technique can be found in J E Hunter, F L Schmidt, and G B Jackson, *Meta-Analysis. Cumulating Research Findings across Studies* (Beverly Hills, CA: Sage Publications, 1982); and J E Hunter and F L Schmidt, *Methods of Meta-Analysis: Correcting Error and Bias in Research Findings* (Newbury Park, CA: Sage Publications, 1990). Also see R Hutter Epstein, "The Number-Crunchers Drugmakers Fear and Love," *Business Week,* August 22, 1994, pp 70–71.

[83] Limitations of meta-analysis technique are discussed in P Bobko and E F Stone-Romero, "Meta-Analysis May Be Another Useful Tool, but It Is Not a Panacea," in *Research in Personnel and Human Resources Management,* vol. 16, ed G R Ferris (Stamford, CT: JAI Press, 1998), pp 359–97.

[84] For an interesting debate about the use of students as subjects, see J Greenberg, "The College Sophomore as Guinea Pig: Setting the Record Straight," *Academy of Management Review,* January 1987, pp 157–59; and M E Gordon, L A Slade, and N Schmitt, "Student Guinea Pigs: Porcine Predictors and Particularistic Phenomena," *Academy of Management Review,* January 1987, pp 160–63.

[85] Good discussions of case studies can be found in A S Lee, "Case Studies as Natural Experiments," *Human Relations,* February 1989, pp 117–37; and K M Eisenhardt, "Building Theories from Case Study Research," *Academy of Management Review,* October 1989, pp 532–50. The case survey technique is discussed in R Larsson, "Case Survey Methodology: Analysis of Patterns across Case Studies," *Academy of Management Journal,* December 1993, pp 1515–46.

[86] Based on discussion found in J M Beyer and H M Trice, "The Utilization Process: A Conceptual Framework and Synthesis of Empirical Findings," *Administrative Science Quarterly,* December 1982, pp 591–622. Also see S Albers Mohrman, C B Gibson, and A M Mohrman, Jr, "Doing Research That Is Useful to Practice: A Model and Empirical Exploration," *Academy of Management Journal,* April 2001, pp 357–75.

[87] See J J Martocchio, "Age-Related Differences in Employee Absenteeism: A Meta-Analysis," *Psychology & Aging,* December 1989, pp 409–14.

[88] J Schettler, "Marcus Buckingham," *Training,* November 2001, p 51. Also see D Jones, "Rule-Breaking Turns into Boss-Training," *USA Today,* February 20, 2002, pp 1B–2B.

[89] These research results are discussed in detail in J B Miner and N R Smith, "Decline and Stabilization of Managerial Motivation over a 20-Year Period," *Journal of Applied Psychology,* June 1982, pp 297–305.

[90] See J B Miner, J M Wachtel, and B Ebrahimi, "The Managerial Motivation of Potential Managers in the United States and Other Countries of the World: Implications for National Competitiveness and the Productivity Problem," in *Advances in International Comparative Management,* vol. 4, ed B Prasad (Greenwich, CT: JAI Press, 1989), pp 147–70; and J B Miner, C C Chen, and K C Yu, "Theory Testing under Adverse Conditions: Motivation to Manage in the People's Republic of China," *Journal of Applied Psychology,* June 1991, pp 343–49.

[91] See J B Miner, B Ebrahimi, and J M Wachtel, "How Deficiencies in Motivation to Manage Contribute to the United States' Competitiveness Problem (and What Can Be Done about It)," *Human Resource Management,* Fall 1995, pp 363–87.

[92] Based on K M Bartol and D C Martin, "Managerial Motivation among MBA Students: A Longitudinal Assessment," *Journal of Occupational Psychology,* March 1987, pp 1–12.

[93] G Gendron, "My Son, the Downsizer," *Inc.,* May 2002, pp 22, 24.

LEARNING MODULE A

[1] R Blumenstein, D Solomon, and K Chen, "As Global Crossing Crashed, Executives Got Loan Relief, Pension Payouts," *The Wall Street Journal,* February 21, 2002, p B1.

[2] Details of these examples can be found in L Wah, "Lip-Service Ethics Programs Prove Ineffective," *Management Review,* June 1999, p 9; and "Workplace Ethics Dilemma," *USA Today,* February 15, 1999, p 1B.

[3] L Wah, "Lies in the Executive Wing," *Management Review,* May 1999, p 9.

[4] R Lieber, "New Hidden Fees Hit Overseas Travel," *The Wall Street Journal,* April 23, 2001, p D1.

[5] See C Gilligan, "In a Different Voice: Women's Conceptions of Self and Morality," *Harvard Educational Review,* November 1977, pp 481–517.

[6] The following discussion is based on A J Daboub, A M A Rasheed, R L Priem, and D A Gray, "Top Management Team Characteristics and Corporate Illegal Activity," *Academy of Management Review,* January 1995, pp 138–70.

[7] L Simpson, "Taking the High Road," *Training,* January 2002, p 38.

[8] S Branch, "The 100 Best Companies to Work for in America," *Fortune,* January 11, 1999, p 128.

[9] The role of incentives and ethical behavior was investigated by A E Tenbrunsel, "Misrepresentation and Expectations of Misrepresentation in an Ethical Dilemma: The Role of Incentives and Temptation," *Academy of Management Journal,* June 1998, pp 330–39.

[10] The following discussion is based on Daboub et al., "Top Management Team Characteristics and Corporate Illegal Activity."

[11] R Miller, "O'Neill Has the White House Running Scared," *Business Week,* March 11, 2002, p 32.

[12] See "SEC Charges Fraud by Xerox: $10 Million Fine a Record," *Arizona Republic,* April 12, 2002, p D1.

[13] Results can be found in T Jackson, "Cultural Values and Management Ethics: A 10-Nation Study," *Human Relations,* October 2001, pp 1267–1302.

[14] The following discussion is based on Daboub et al., "Top Management Team Characteristics and Corporate Illegal Activity."

[15] T Gutner, "Blowing Whistles—and Being Ignored," *Business Week,* March 18, 2002, p 107.

[16] Results are discussed in ibid.

[17] C Gilligan and J Attanucci, "Two Moral Orientations: Gender Differences and Similarities," *Merril-Palmer Quarterly,* July 1988, pp 224–25.

[18] Results can be found in S Jaffee and J Hyde, "Gender Differences in Moral Orientation: A Meta-Analysis," *Psychological Bulletin,* September 2000, pp 703–26.

[19] Ibid, p 719.

[20] See Ch. 6 in K Hodgson, *A Rock and a Hard Place: How to Make Ethical Business Decisions When the Choices Are Tough* (New York: AMACOM, 1992), pp 66–77.

[21] Adapted from W E Stead, D L Worrell, and J Garner Stead, "An Integrative Model for Understanding and Managing Ethical Behavior in Business Organizations," *Journal of Business Ethics,* March 1990, pp 233–42.

[22] For an excellent review of integrity testing, see D S Ones and C Viswesvaran, "Integrity Testing in Organizations," in *Dysfunctional Behavior in Organizations: Violent and Deviant Behavior,* eds R W Griffin et al. (Stamford, CT: JAI Press, 1998), pp 243–76.

[23] The ethics test is discussed in D Fandray, "The Ethical Company," *Workforce,* December 2000, pp 75–77.

[24] These scenarios were excerpted from L M Dawson, "Women and Men, Morality, and Ethics," *Business Horizons,* July–August 1995, pp 62, 65.

[25] Comparative norms were obtained from Dawson, "Women and Men, Morality and Ethics." Scenario 1: would sell (28% males, 57% females); would not sell (66% males, 28% females); unsure (6% males, 15% females). Scenario 2: would consult (84% males, 32% females); would not consult (12% males, 62% females); unsure (4% males, 6% females).

[26] The following trends were taken from Dawson, "Women and Men, Morality and Ethics." Women were likely to primarily respect feelings, ask "who will be hurt?", avoid being judgmental, search for compromise, seek solutions that minimize hurt, rely on communication, believe in contextual relativism, be guided by emotion, and challenge authority. Men were likely to primarily respect rights, ask "who is right?", value decisiveness, make unambiguous decisions, seek solutions that are objectively fair, rely on rules, believe in blind impartiality, be guided by logic, and accept authority.

CHAPTER 2

[1] Excerpted from J Cohen, "I/Os in the Know Offer Insights on Generation X Workers," *Monitor on Psychology,* February 2002, pp 66–67.

[2] J K Laabs, "Thinking Outside the Box at the Container Store," *Workforce,* March 2001, p 35.

[3] "Ford Settles Racial Harassment Suit," *Arizona Republic,* December 22, 2001, p D1.

[4] W Zellner, "Slugfests: A Texas-Size Case of Discrimination?" *Business Week,* March 18, 2002, p 14.

[5] The following discussion is based on material in R R Thomas, Jr, *Redefining Diversity* (New York: AMACON, 1996), pp 4–9.

[6] This distinction is made by M Loden, *Implementing Diversity* (Chicago: Irwin, 1996).

[7] H Collingwood, "Who Handles a Diverse Work Force Best?" *Working Women,* February 1996, p 25.

[8] See A Karr, "Work Week: A Special News Report about Life on the Job—and Trends Taking Shape There," *The Wall Street Journal,* June 1, 1999, p A1.

[9] A description of Ford's program can be found in E Garsten, "Ford Muslim Workers Organize 'Islam,' " *Arizona Republic,* December 13, 2001, p D2.

[10] R Thomas, Jr, "From Affirmative Action to Affirming Diversity," *Harvard Business Review,* March–April 1990, pp 107–17.

[11] Opposition to affirmative action was investigated by E H James, A P Brief, J Dietz, and R R Cohen, "Prejudice Matters: Understanding the Reactions of Whites to Affirmative Action Programs Targeted to Benefit Blacks," *Journal of Applied Psychology,* December 2001, pp 1120–28.

[12] For a thorough review of relevant research, see M E Heilman, "Affirmative Action: Some Unintended Consequences for Working Women," in *Research in Organizational Behavior,* vol 16, eds B M Staw and L L Cummings (Greenwich, CT: JAI Press, 1994), pp 125–69.

[13] Results from this study can be found in M E Heilman, W S Battle, C E Keller, and R A Lee, "Type of Affirmative Action Policy: A Determinant of Reactions to Sex-Based Preferential Selection?" *Journal of Applied Psychology,* April 1998, pp 190–205.

[14] See J Kaufman, "How Workplaces May Look without Affirmative Action," *The Wall Street Journal,* March 20, 1995, pp B1, B7.

[15] Valuing diversity is discussed by R R Thomas, Jr, *Beyond Race and Gender* (New York: American Management Association, 1991).

[16] Results are summarized in R S Allen and K A Montgomery, "Applying an Organizational Development Approach to Creating Diversity," *Organizational Dynamics,* Fall 2001, pp 149–61.

[17] V J Weaver, "What These CEOs and Their Companies Know about Diversity," *Business Week,* September 10, 2001, special advertising section.

[18] See S Rynes and B Rosen, "A Field Survey of Factors Affecting the Adoption and Perceived Success of Diversity Training," *Personnel Psychology,* Summer 1995, pp 247–70.

[19] A M Morrison, *The New Leaders: Guidelines on Leadership Diversity in America* (San Francisco: Jossey-Bass, 1992), p 78.

[20] Results can be found in N London-Vargas, *Faces of Diversity* (New York: Vantage Press, 1999).

[21] Weaver, "What These CEOs and Their Companies Know about Diversity."

[22] Labor force statistics can be found in H N Fullerton, Jr, and M Toossi, "Employment Outlook: 2000–10," *Monthly Labor Review,* November 2001, pp 21–38.

[23] Ibid.

[24] Results from this study are summarized in "The Big Picture: This Is Progress?" *Business Week,* March 11, 2002, p 10.

[25] Results can be found in K S Lyness and D E Thompson, "Above the Glass Ceiling: A Comparison of Matched Samples of Female and Male Executives," *Journal of Applied Psychology,* June 1997, pp 359–75.

[26] This study was conducted by K S Lyness and M K Judiesch, "Are Women More Likely to Be Hired or Promoted into Management Positions?" *Journal of Vocational Behavior,* February 1999, pp 158–73.

[27] These statistics were obtained from Women in Politics, April 2, 2002 (www.onlinewomeninpolitics.org/statistics.html); and Learning Partnership, January 1, 2002 (www.learningpartnership.org/facts/human.html).

[28] See T Wilen, "Women Working Overseas," *Training & Development,* May 2001, pp 120–22.

[29] Details of this study can be found in B R Ragins, B Townsend, and M Mattis, "Gender Gap in the Executive Suite: CEOs and Female Executives Report on Breaking the Glass Ceiling," *Academy of Management Executive,* February 1998, pp 28–42.

[30] Here are the ranks for each career strategy: Strategy 1 = 12; Strategy 2 = 6; Strategy 3 = 5; Strategy 4 = 11; Strategy 5 = 9; Strategy 6 = 3; Strategy 7 = 10; Strategy 8 = 1; Strategy 9 = 7; Strategy 10 = 8; Strategy 11 = 4; Strategy 12 = 2; and Strategy 13 = 13.

[31] See "Race-Based Charges FY 1992–FY 2001," February 22, 2002 (www.eeoc.gov/stats/race.html).

[32] See "Median Household Income by Race and Hispanic Origin: 1967 to 2000," U.S. Census Bureau, September 26, 2001 (www.census.gov/hhes/income/income00/incxrace.html).

[33] Results can be found in R J Contrada, R D Ashmore, M L Gary, E Coups, J D Egeth, A Sewell, K Ewell, T M Goyal, and V Chasse, "Measures of Ethnicity-Related Stress: Psychometric Properties, Ethnic Group Differences, and Associations with Well-Being," *Journal of Applied Social Psychology,* 2001, pp 1775–1820.

[34] See S Kravetz, "Work Week: A Special News Report about Life on the Job—And Trends Taking Shape There," *The Wall Street Journal,* April 13, 1999, p A1.

[35] For a review of this research, see L Roberson and C J Block, "Racioethnicity and Job Performance: A Review and Critique of Theoretical Perspectives on the Causes of Group Differences," in *Research in Organizational Behavior,* vol 23, eds B M Staw and R I Sutton (New York: JAI Press, 2001), pp 247–326.

[36] See J Hopkins, "Hispanics Stump for Success," *USA Today,* May 21, 2001, pp B1, B2.

[37] Minority-owned businesses are discussed by J Hopkins, "Shift in Power Creates Tension in Minorities," *USA Today,* April 4, 2002, pp D1, D4.

[38] See "No. 249. Educational Attainment, by Race, and Hispanic Origin," US Census Bureau, March 28, 2001 (www.census.gov/statab/freq/00s0249.txt).

[39] See D Dooley and J Prause, "Underemployment and Alcohol Misuse in the National Longitudinal Survey of Youth," *Journal of Studies on Alcohol,* November 1998, pp 669–80; and D C Feldman, "The Nature, Antecedents and Consequences of Underemployment," *Journal of Management,* 1966, pp 385–407.

[40] See "Unemployment Rate, 2000 Annual Average," Bureau of Labor Statistics, March 2000 (www.bls.gov/emp/emptab7.htm).

[41] Literacy statistics can be found in D Baynton, "America's $60 Billion Problem," *Training,* May 2001, pp 51–56.

[42] "Facts on Literacy," *National Literacy Facts,* August 27, 1998 (www.svs.net/wpci/Litfacts.htm).

[43] See Baynton, "America's $60 Billion Problem."

[44] See A R Karr, "Work Week: A Special News Report about Life on the Job—And Trends Taking Shape There," *The Wall Street Journal,* May 18, 1999, p A1.

[45] See H London, "The Workforce, Education, and the Nation's Future," Summer 1998 (www.hudson.org/american_outlook/articles_sm 98/london.htm).

[46] The supply and demand for labor are discussed in K Ellis, "Mind the Gap," *Training,* January 2002, pp 30–35.

[47] S Armour, "Welcome Mat Rolls Out for Hispanic Workers: Corporate America Cultivates Talent as Ethnic Population Booms," *USA Today,* April 12, 2001, pp 1B, 2B.

[48] D A Thomas, "The Truth about Mentoring Minorities: Race Matters," *Harvard Business Review,* April 2001, p 107.

[49] See Ellis, "Mind the Gap."

[50] P M Elsass and D A Ralston, "Individual Responses to the Stress of Career Plateauing," *Journal of Management,* Spring 1989, p 35.

[51] Supportive findings can be found in D R Ettington, "Successful Career Plateauing," *Journal of Vocational Behavior,* February 1998, pp 72–88.

[52] These recommendations were taken from G M McEvoy and M J Blahna, "Engagement or Disengagement? Older Workers and the Looming Labor Shortage," *Business Horizons,* September–October 2001, p 50.

[53] These statistics were obtained from "Sex-Based Charges FY 1992–FY 2001; Age Discrimination in Employment Act (ADEA) Charges FY 1992–FY 2001; Americans with Disabilities Act of 1990 (ADA) Charges FY 1992–FY 2001; and Sexual Harassment Charges EEOC & FEPAs Combined: FY 1992–FY 2001," February 22, 2002 (www.eeoc.gov/stats/harass.html).

[54] See D Brady, "Give Nursing Moms a Break at the Office," *Business Week,* August 6, 2001, p 70.

[55] A A Johnson, "The Business Case for Work-Family Programs," *Journal of Accountancy,* August 1995, pp 55–56.

[56] See R J Ely and D A Thomas, "Cultural Diversity at Work: The Effects of Diversity Perspectives on Work Group Processes and Outcomes," *Administrative Science Quarterly,* June 2001, pp 229–73; and Roberson and Block, "Racioethnicity and Job Performance."

[57] Research on gay and lesbian employees can be found in B R Ragins and J M Cornwell, "Pink Triangles: Antecedents and Consequences of Perceived Workplace Discrimination against Gay and Lesbian Employees," *Journal of Applied Psychology,* December 2001, pp 1244–61.

[58] See "The State of the Workforce for Lesbian, Gay, Bisexual and Transgender Americans 2001," *Human Rights Campaign Foundation* (www.hrc.org/worknet/publications/state_workplace/2001/SOW2001.pdf).

[59] Statistics on disabilities can be found in "Table 2. Labor Force Status—Work Disability Status of Civilians 16 to 74 Years Old, by Educational Attainment and Sex: 2001," March 2001 (www.census.gov/hhes/www/disable/cps/cps201.html); and "Chartbook on Work and Disability in the United States," 1998 (www.infouse.com/disabilitydata/workdisability_1_.html).

[60] See P Digh, "People with Disabilities Show What They Can Do," *HR Magazine,* June 1998, pp 141–45.

[61] Ibid.

[62] R Koonce, "Redefining Diversity," *Training & Development,* December 2001, p 24.

[63] R S Allen and K A Montgomery, "Applying an Organizational Development Approach to Creating Diversity," *Organizational Dynamics,* Fall 2001, p 149.

[64] See R W Thompson, "Diversity among Managers Translates into Profitability," *HR Magazine,* April 1999, p 10.

[65] For research on TMT demographics, see K Y Williams, "Demography and Diversity in Organizations: A Review of 100 Years of Research," in *Research in Organizational Behavior,* vol 20, eds B M Staw and L L Cummings (Greenwich, CT: JAI Press, 1998), pp 77–140.

[66] See R Moss-Kanter, *The Change Masters* (New York: Simon and Schuster, 1983); and L K Larkey, "Toward a Theory of Communicative Interactions in Culturally Diverse Workgroups," *Academy of Management Review,* April 1996, pp 463–91.

[67] See Williams, "Demography and Diversity in Organizations."

[68] Ibid.

[69] See W E Watson, K Kumar, and L K Michaelson, "Cultural Diversity's Impact on Interaction Process and Performance: Comparing Homogeneous and Diverse Task Groups," *Academy of Management Journal,* June 1993, pp 590–602.

[70] Results can be found in J A Chatman and F J Flynn, "The Influence of Demographic Heterogeneity on the Emergence and Consequences of Cooperative Norms in Work Teams," *Academy of Management Journal,* October 2001, pp 956–74; and F J Flynn, J A Chatman, and S E Spataro, "Getting to Know You: The Influence of Personality on Impressions and Performance of Demographically Different People in Organizations," *Administrative Science Quarterly,* September 2001, pp 414–42.

[71] The relationship between conflict and stages of group development is discussed by D C Lau and J K Murnighan, "Demographic Diversity and Faultlines: The Compositional Dynamics of Organizational Groups," *Academy of Management Review,* April 1998, pp 325–40.

[72] See J A Chatman, J T Polzer, S G Barsade, and M A Neale, "Being Different Yet Feeling Similar: The Influence of Demographic Composition and Organizational Culture on Work Processes and Outcomes," *Administrative Science Quarterly,* December 1998, pp 749–80.

[73] These barriers were taken from discussions in Loden, *Implementing Diversity;* E E Spragins, "Benchmark: The Diverse Work Force," *Inc.,* January 1993, p 33; and Morrison, *The New Leaders.*

[74] See the related discussion in R J Ely and D A Thomas, "Cultural Diversity at Work: The Effects of Diversity Perspectives on Work Group Processes and Outcomes," *Administrative Science Quarterly,* June 2001, pp 229–73.

[75] This discussion is based on R R Thomas, Jr, *Redefining Diversity* (New York, AMACOM, 1996).

[76] D J Gaiter, "Eating Crow: How Shoney's, Belted by a Lawsuit, Found the Path to Diversity," *The Wall Street Journal,* April 16, 1996, pp A1, A11.

[77] P Dass and B Parker, "Strategies for Managing Human Resource Diversity: From Resistance to Learning," *Academy of Management Executive,* May 1999, p 69.

[78] Gaiter, "Eating Crow."

[79] Dass and Parker, "Strategies for Managing Human Resource Diversity," p 73.

[80] M Littman, "Best Bosses Tell All," *Working Woman,* October 2000, p 52.

[81] M Bolch, "The Coming Crunch," *Training,* April 2001, pp 56–57.

[82] For complete details and results from this study, see Morrison, *The New Leader.*

[83] Koonce, "Redefining Diversity," pp 24, 26.

[84] Empirical support is provided by H Ibarra, "Race, Opportunity, and Diversity of Social Circles in Managerial Networks," *Academy of Management Journal,* June 1995, pp 673–703.

[85] Koonce, "Redefining Diversity," p 26.

[86] R Kazel, "Hotel Speaks Employees' Languages," *Business Insurance,* November 24, 1997, p 14.

[87] "Winning with Diversity: In Pursuit of Excellence McGraw-Hill's Diversity Program Is a Source of Power," *Business Week,* September 10, 2001, special advertising section.

[88] "Winning with Diversity: Diversity in an Affiliated Company Aligned, Yet Autonomous," *Business Week,* September 10, 2001, special advertising section.

[89] This exercise was modified from Gardenswartz and Rowe, *Diverse Teams at Work* (New York: McGraw-Hill, 1994), pp 60–61 © 1994. Reproduced with permission of The McGraw-Hill Companies.

[90] D A Blackmon and N Harris, "Racial Bind: Black Utility Workers in Georgia See Nooses as Sign of Harassment," *The Wall Street Journal,* April 2, 2001, pp A1, A8.

CHAPTER 3

[1] Excerpted from M Mangalindan and S L Hwang, "Gang of Six: Coterie of Early Hires Made Yahoo! a Hit but an Insular Place," *The Wall Street Journal,* March 9, 2001, pp A1, A6.

[2] C L Bernick, "When Your Culture Needs a Makeover," *Harvard Business Review,* June 2001, p 54.

[3] K Freiberg and J Freiberg, *Nuts! Southwest Airlines' Crazy Recipe for Business and Personal Success* (Austin, TX: Bard Press, 1996), p 144.

[4] E H Schein, "Culture: The Missing Concept in Organization Studies," *Administrative Science Quarterly,* June 1996, p 236.

[5] This figure and related discussion are based on C Ostroff, A Kinicki, and M Tamkins, "Organizational Culture and Climate," in *Comprehensive Handbook of Psychology,* vol. 12, eds W C Borman, D R Ilgen, and R J Klimoski (New York: Wiley & Sons, in press).

[6] S H Schwartz, "Universals in the Content and Structure of Values: Theoretical Advances and Empirical Tests in 20 Countries," in *Advances in Experimental Social Psychology,* ed M P Zanna (New York: Academic Press, 1992), p 4.

[7] "How to Build an Employee Brand," *HRFocus,* September 2001, p 3.

[8] C Terhune, "Home Depot's Home Improvement," *The Wall Street Journal,* March 8, 2001, pp B1, B4.

[9] Results can be found in S Clarke, "Perceptions of Organizational Safety: Implications for the Development of Safety Culture," *Journal of Organizational Behavior,* March 1999, pp 185–98.

[10] See Terhune, "Home Depot's Home Improvement."

[11] For an example of profiling organizational values see T J Kalliath, A C Bluedorn, and D F Gillespie, "A Confirmatory Factor Analyses of the Competing Values Instrument," *Educational and Psychological Measurement,* February 1999, pp 143–58.

[12] See the discussion in J R Detert, R G Schroeder, and J J Mauriel, "A Framework for Linking Culture and Improvement Initiatives in Organizations," *Academy of Management Review,* October 2000, pp 850–63.

[13] Details of this model can be found in V Sathe, "Implications of Corporate Culture: A Manager's Guide to Action," *Organizational Dynamics,* Autumn 1983, pp 4–23.

[14] The Southwest Airlines example was based on material contained in the "Southwest Airlines Fact Sheet," March 4, 2002 (www.southwest.com).

[15] K D Godsey, "Slow Climb to New Heights," *Success,* October 1996, p 21.

[16] Southwest's mission statement can be found in "Customer Service Commitment," October 9, 2001 (www.southwest.com).

[17] These statistics come from "History: We Weren't Just Airborne Yesterday," March 11, 2002 (www.southwest.com).

[18] See Ostroff, Kinicki, and Tamkins, "Organizational Culture and Climate."

[19] The validity of these cultural types was summarized and supported by R A Cooke and J L Szumal, "Using the Organizational Culture Inventory to Understand the Operating Cultures of Organizations," in *Handbook of Organizational Culture and Climate,* eds N M Ashkanasy, C P M Wilderom, and M F Peterson (Thousand Oaks, CA: Sage Publications, 2000), pp 147–62.

[20] Subcultures were examined by G Hofstede, "Identifying Organizational Subcultures: An Empirical Approach," *Journal of Management Studies,* January 1998, pp 1–2.

[21] An historical overview of research on organizational culture is provided by H M Trice and J M Beyer, *The Cultures of Work Organizations* (Englewood Cliffs, NJ: Prentice Hall, 1993).

[22] See W G Ouchi, *Theory Z: How American Business Can Meet the Japanese Challenge* (Reading, MA: Addison-Wesley Publishing, 1981).

[23] See T E Deal and A A Kennedy, *Corporate Cultures: The Rites and Rituals of Corporate Life* (Reading, MA: Addison-Wesley Publishing, 1982).

[24] See T J Peters and R H Waterman, Jr. *In Search of Excellence* (New York: Harper & Row, 1982).

[25] Ibid., pp 75–76.

[26] Measures of organizational culture are reviewed and discussed by N M Ashkanasy, L E Broadfoot, and S Falkus, "Questionnaire Measures of Organizational Culture," in *Handbook of Organizational Culture and Climate,* eds N M Ashkanasy, C P M Wilderom, and M F Peterson (Thousand Oaks, CA: Sage Publications, 2000), pp 131–46.

[27] See Cooke and Szumal, "Using the Organizational Culture Inventory to Understand the Operating Cultures of Organizations."

[28] Supportive results are found in A Van Vianen, "Person-Organization Fit: The Match between Newcomers' and Recruiters' Preferences for Organizational Cultures," *Personnel Psychology,* Spring 2000, pp 113–50.

[29] See C Wilderom, U Glunk, and R Maslowski, "Organizational Culture as a Predictor of Organizational Performance," in *Handbook of Organizational Culture and Climate,* eds N Ashkanasy, C Wilderom, and M Peterson (Thousand Oaks, CA: Sage Publications, 2000), pp 193–210.

[30] Results can be found in J P Kotter and J L Heskett, *Corporate Culture and Performance* (New York: Free Press, 1992).

[31] The process of merging cultures during an organizational merger is discussed by E Krell, "Merging Corporate Cultures," *Training,* May 2001, pp 68–78.

[32] Results can be found in S Zamanou and S R Glaser, "Moving toward Participation and Involvement," *Group and Organization Management,* December 1994, pp 475–502.

[33] The relationship between organizational change and culture is discussed by M J Hatch, "The Cultural Dynamics of Organizing and Change," in *Handbook of Organizational Culture and Climate,* eds N M Ashkanasy, C P M Wilderom, and M F Peterson (Thousand Oaks, CA: Sage Publications, 2000), pp 245–60.

[34] This perspective was promoted by Deal and Kennedy, *Corporate Cultures.*

[35] H Lancaster, "Managing Your Career: Traditional Managers Have to Jump Hurdles to Join Internet Firms," *The Wall Street Journal,* March 30, 1999, p B1.

[36] R H Kilman, M J Saxton, and R Serpa, *Gaining Control of the Corporate Culture* (San Francisco: Jossey-Bass, 1986), p 356.

[37] These results can be found in Kotter and Heskett, *Corporate Culture and Performance.*

[38] W W George, "Medtronic's Chairman William George on How Mission-Driven Companies Create Long-Term Shareholder Value," *Academy of Management Executive,* November 2001, p 46.

[39] S McCartney, "Airline Industry's Top-Ranked Woman Keeps Southwest's Small-Fry Spirit Alive," *The Wall Street Journal,* November 30, 1996, pp B1, B11.

[40] The mechanisms were based on material contained in E H Schein, "The Role of the Founder in Creating Organizational Culture," *Organizational Dynamics,* Summer 1983, pp 13–28.

[41] See the description in T Begley and D Boyd, "Articulating Corporate Values through Human Resource Policies," *Business Horizons,* July–August 2000, pp 8–12.

[42] Excerpted from D F Kuratko, R D Ireland, and J S Hornsby, "Improving Firm Performance through Entrepreneurial Actions: Acordia's Corporate Entrepreneurship Strategy," *Academy of Management Executive,* November 2001, p 67.

[43] The program is described in C Cole, "Eight Values Bring Unity to a Worldwide Company," *Workforce,* March 2001, pp 44–45.

[44] D Jones, "Welch: Nurture Best Workers, Lose Bottom 10%," *USA Today,* February 27, 2001, p 2B.

[45] C Hymowitz, "Does Rank Have Too Much Privilege?" *The Wall Street Journal,* February 26, 2002, p B1.

[46] R Charan, "Conquering a Culture of Indecision," *Harvard Business Review,* April 2001, p 79.

[47] M France and W Zellner, "Enron's Fish Story," *Business Week,* February 25, 2002, p 40.

[48] Excerpted from T Galvin, "Birds of a Feather," *Training,* March 2001, p 60.

[49] See N M Tichy and C DeRose, "The Pepsi Challenge: Building a Leader-Driven Organization," *Training & Development,* May 1996, pp 58–66.

[50] J Van Maanen, "Breaking In: Socialization to Work," in *Handbook of Work, Organization, and Society,* ed R Dubin (Chicago: Rand-McNally, 1976), p 67.

[51] For an instructive capsule summary of the five different organizational socialization models, see J P Wanous, A E Reichers, and S D Malik, "Organizational Socialization and Group Development: Toward an Integrative Perspective," *Academy of Management Review,* October 1984, pp 670–83, Table 1.

[52] Supportive evidence is provided by R W Griffeth and P W Hom, *Retaining Valued Employees* (Thousand Oaks, CA: Sage Publications, 2001), pp 46–65.

[53] See J M Phillips, "Effects of Realistic Job Previews on Multiple Organizational Outcomes: A Meta-Analysis," *Academy of Management Journal,* December 1998, pp 673–90.

[54] S Wisbauer, "In His Own Words, Welch Tells How to Jolt a Business Back to Life: Jack and the People Factory," *Fortune,* September 17, 2001, p 76.

[55] Galvin, "Birds of a Feather," p 66.

[56] Reprinted by permission of *Harvard Business Review.* From "No Ordinary Boot Camp" by N M Tichy, April 2001. Copyright © 2001 by the Harvard Business School Publishing Corporation; all rights reserved.

[57] For a thorough review of socialization research, see B E Ashforth, *Role Transitions in Organizational Life: An Identity-Based Perspective* (Mahwah, NJ: Lawrence Erlbaum Associates, 2001), pp 87–108.

[58] Results can be found in H Klein and N Weaver, "The Effectiveness of an Organizational-Level Orientation Training Program in the Socialization of New Hires," *Personnel Psychology,* Spring 2000, pp 47–66.

[59] See D Cable and C Parsons, "Socialization Tactics and Person-Organization Fit," *Personnel Psychology,* Spring 2001, pp 1–23.

[60] A review of stage model research can be found in Ashforth, *Role Transitions in Organizational Life.*

[61] See A M Saks and B E Ashforth, "Proactive Socialization and Behavioral Self-Management," *Journal of Vocational Behavior,* June 1996, pp 301–23.

[62] For a thorough review of research on the socialization of diverse employees with disabilities see A Colella, "Organizational Socialization of Newcomers with Disabilities: A Framework for Future Research," in *Research in Personnel and Human Resources Management,* ed G R Ferris (Greenwich, CT: JAI Press, 1996), pp 351–417.

[63] This definition is based on the network perspective of mentoring proposed by M Higgins and K Kram, "Reconceptualizing Mentoring at Work: A Developmental Network Perspective," *Academy of Management Review,* April 2001, pp 264–88.

[64] Supportive results can be found in J E Wallace, "The Benefits of Mentoring for Female Lawyers," *Journal of Vocational Behavior,* June 2001, pp 366–91.

[65] Career functions are discussed in detail in K Kram, *Mentoring of Work: Developmental Relationships in Organizational Life* (Glenview, IL: Scott, Foresman, 1985).

[66] This discussion is based on Higgins and Kram, "Reconceptualizing Mentoring at Work."

[67] K McLaughlin, "A Strong Foundation," *Training,* March 2001, p 84.

[68] This discussion is based on Higgins and Kram, "Reconceptualizing Mentoring at Work."

[69] Supportive results can be found in T Allen, M Poteet, and J Russell, "Protégé Selection by Mentors: What Makes the Difference?" *Journal of Organizational Behavior,* May 2000, pp 271–82.

[70] I Mochari, "Roll Out the Welcome Mat," *Inc.,* May 1999, p 101.

[71] J A Byrne, M France, and W Zellner, "Corporate Culture: The Environment Was Ripe for Abuse," *Business Week,* February 25, 2002, pp 118–20.

[72] The survey items were adapted from D Cable and C Parsons, "Socialization Tactics and Person-Organization Fit," *Personnel Psychology,* Spring 2001, pp 1–23.

[73] See E H Schein, *The Corporate Culture Survival Guide* (San Francisco: Jossey-Bass, 1999).

[74] K Brown and J Weil, "How Andersen's Embrace of Consulting Altered the Culture of the Auditing Firm," *The Wall Street Journal,* March 12, 2002, pp C1, C16.

ANSWERS TO OB EXERCISE

[1] The whiteboard is a shared object at Setpoint. There are two shared sayings. Employees talk about monitoring GP—gross profit—during their "weekly huddles." Employees at Setpoint like to ride dirt bikes together, and they put photos of their experiences on the bulletin board. This is a shared doing. Controlling cash and conducting the weekly huddles to review the budget are two additional shared behaviors among employees at Setpoint. Finally, the management system at Setpoint seems to fuel employee motivation, a component of shared feelings.

[2] While the management system at Setpoint is a mechanism for controlling employee behavior, the implementation of the system allows employees much freedom to determine how they can control costs and increase gross profit.

CHAPTER 4

[1] Excerpted from K Capell, "MTV's World," *Business Week,* February 18, 2002, pp 81–82.

[2] Ibid., pp 81–82.

[3] Data from Ibid.

[4] Based on J S Lublin, "An Overseas Stint Can Be a Ticket to the Top," *The Wall Street Journal,* January 29, 1996, pp B1, B5.

[5] Data from M A Carpenter, W G Sanders, and H B Gregersen, "Bundling Human Capital with Organizational Context: The Impact of International Assignment Experience on Multinational Firm Performance and CEO Pay," *Academy of Management Journal,* June 2001, pp 493–511. Also see "International Experience Aids Career," *USA Today,* January 28, 2002, p 1B.

[6] G Dutton, "Building a Global Brain," *Management Review,* May 1999, p 35.

[7] See L Eden and S Lenway, "Introduction to the Symposium—Multinationals: The Janus Face of Globalization," *Journal of International Business Studies,* Third Quarter 2001, pp 383–400.

[8] M Mabry, "Pin a Label on a Manager—And Watch What Happens," *Newsweek,* May 14, 1990, p 43.

[9] Ibid.

[10] M Javidan and R J House, "Cultural Acumen for the Global Manager: Lessons from Project GLOBE," *Organizational Dynamics,* Spring 2001, p 292. (Emphasis added.)

[11] For instructive discussion, see J S Black, H B Gregersen, and M E Mendenhall, *Global Assignments: Successfully Expatriating and Repatriating International Managers* (San Francisco: Jossey-Bass, 1992), Ch 2.

[12] F Trompenaars and C Hampden-Turner, *Riding the Waves of Culture: Understanding Cultural Diversity in Global Business,* 2nd ed (New York: McGraw-Hill, 1998), pp 6–7.

[13] See G Strauss, "Catastrophe Suspends Business as Usual in USA," *USA Today,* September 12, 2001, pp 1B–2B; and B Powell, "Battered but Unbroken," *Fortune,* October 1, 2001, pp 68–80.

[14] "How Cultures Collide," *Psychology Today,* July 1976, p 69.

[15] See C L Sharma, "Ethnicity, National Integration, and Education in the Union of Soviet Socialist Republics," *The Journal of East and West Studies,* October 1989, pp 75–93; and R Brady and P Galuszka, "Shattered Dreams," *Business Week,* February 11, 1991, pp 38–42.

[16] See R Inglehart and W E Baker, "Modernization's Challenge to Traditional Values: Who's Afraid of Ronald McDonald," *The Futurist,* March–April 2001, pp 16–21.

[17] G Farrell, "Capitalism Comes to German Town," *USA Today,* December 11, 2001, p 6B.

[18] J Main, "How to Go Global—And Why," *Fortune,* August 28, 1989, p 73.

[19] An excellent contrast between French and American values can be found in C Gouttefarde, "American Values in the French Workplace," *Business Horizons,* March–April 1996, pp 60–69.

[20] W D Marbach, "Quality: What Motivates American Workers?" *Business Week,* April 12, 1993, p 93.

[21] See G A Sumner, *Folkways* (New York: Ginn, 1906). Also see J G Weber, "The Nature of Ethnocentric Attribution Bias: Ingroup Protection or Enhancement?" *Journal of Experimental Social Psychology,* September 1994, pp 482–504.

22 "House English-only Bill Aims at Federal Agencies," *USA Today,* July 25, 1996, p 3A. For another example of ethnocentric behavior, see J Cox, "Summers Has Slightly Tense Relationship with Japanese," *USA Today,* May 13, 1999, p 2B.

23 D A Heenan and H V Perlmutter, *Multinational Organization Development* (Reading, MA: Addison-Wesley, 1979), p 17.

24 Data from R Kopp, "International Human Resource Policies and Practices in Japanese, European, and United States Multinationals," *Human Resource Management,* Winter 1994, pp 581–99. Also see G Balabanis, A Diamantopoulos, R D Mueller, and T C Melewar, "The Impact of Nationalism, Patriotism and Internationalism on Consumer Ethnocentric Tendencies," *Journal of International Business Studies,* First Quarter 2001, pp 157–75.

25 J S Osland and A Bird, "Beyond Sophisticated Stereotyping: Cultural Sensemaking in Context," *Academy of Management Executive,* February 2000, p 67.

26 "Fujio Mitarai: Canon," *Business Week,* January 14, 2002, p 55.

27 See L G Conway III, A G Ryder, R G Tweed, and B W Sokol, "Intranational Cultural Variation: Exploring Further Implications of Collectivism within the United States," *Journal of Cross-Cultural Psychology,* November 2001, pp 681–97. Also see T Lenartowicz and K Roth, "Does Subculture within a Country Matter? A Cross-Cultural Study of Motivational Domains and Business Performance in Brazil," *Journal of International Business Studies,* Second Quarter 2001, pp 305–25; and C Dawson, "Ghosn's Way: Why Japan Inc. Is Following a *Gaijin,*" *Business Week,* May 20, 2002, p 58.

28 See "How Cultures Collide," pp 66–74, 97; and M Munter, "Cross-Cultural Communication for Managers," *Business Horizons,* May–June 1993, pp 69–78.

29 Relationship building in China is discussed in L M Yi and P Ellis, "Insider-Outsider Perspectives of *Guanxi,*" *Business Horizons,* January–February 2000, pp 25–30; and S H Ang, "The Power of Money: A Cross-Cultural Analysis of Business-Related Beliefs," *Journal of World Business,* Spring 2000, pp 43–60.

30 The German management style is discussed in R Stewart, "German Management: A Challenge to Anglo-American Managerial Assumptions," *Business Horizons,* May–June 1996, pp 52–54.

31 I Adler, "Between the Lines," *Business Mexico,* October 2000, p 24.

32 The tips were excerpted from R Drew, "Working with Foreigners," *Management Review,* September 1999, p 6.

33 For background, see Javidan and House, "Cultural Acumen for the Global Manager," pp 289–305; and the entire Spring 2002 issue of *Journal of World Business.*

34 R House, M Javidan, P Hanges, and P Dorfman, "Understanding Cultures and Implicit Leadership Theories across the Globe: An Introduction to Project GLOBE," *Journal of World Business,* Spring 2002, p 4.

35 Visit the GLOBE project's Internet site for updates (http://mgmt3.ucalgary.ca/web/globe.nsf/index).

36 Adapted from the list in House, Javidan, Hanges, and Dorfman, "Understanding Cultures and Implicit Leadership Theories across the Globe," pp 5–6.

37 See D Oyserman, H M Coon, and M Kemmelmeier, "Rethinking Individualism and Collectivism: Evaluation of Theoretical Assumptions and Meta-Analyses," *Psychological Bulletin,* January 2002, pp 3–72; S Soh and F T L Leong, "Validity of Vertical and Horizontal Individualism and Collectivism in Singapore: Relationships with Values and Interests," *Journal of Cross-Cultural Psychology,* January 2002, pp 3–15; and J Kurman and N Sriram, "Interrelationships among Vertical and Horizontal Collectivism, Modesty, and Self-Enhancement," *Journal of Cross-Cultural Psychology,* January 2002, pp 71–86.

38 Data from Trompenaars and Hampden-Turner, *Riding the Waves of Culture,* Ch 5. For relevant research evidence, see Y A Fijneman, M E Willemsen, and Y H Poortinga, "Individualism–Collectivism: An Empirical Study of a Conceptual Issue," *Journal of Cross-Cultural Psychology,* July 1996, pp 381–402; D I Jung and B J Avolio, "Effects of Leadership Style and Followers' Cultural Orientation on Performance in Groups and Individual Task Conditions," *Academy of Management Journal,* April 1999, pp 208–18; T M Singelis, M H Bond, W F Sharkey, and C S Y Lai, "Unpacking Culture's Influence on Self-Esteem and Embarrassability: The Role of Self-Construals," *Journal of Cross-Cultural Psychology,* May 1999, pp 315–41; and M J Bresnahan, R Ohashi, W Y Liu, R Nebashi, and C Liao, "A Comparison of Response Styles in Singapore and Taiwan," *Journal of Cross-Cultural Psychology,* May 1999, pp 342–58.

39 As quoted in E E Schultz, "Scudder Brings Lessons to Navajo, Gets Some of Its Own," *The Wall Street Journal,* April 29, 1999, p C12.

40 Trompenaars and Hampden-Turner, *Riding the Waves of Culture,* p 56.

41 For related readings, see E Mosakowski and P C Earley, "A Selective Review of Time Assumptions in Strategy Research," *Academy of Management Review,* October 2000, pp 796–812; and M J Waller, J M Conte, C B Gibson, and M A Carpenter, "The Effect of Individual Perceptions of Deadlines on Team Performance," *Academy of Management Review,* October 2001, pp 586–600.

42 For a comprehensive treatment of time, see J E McGrath and J R Kelly, *Time and Human Interaction: Toward a Social Psychology of Time* (New York: Guilford Press, 1986). Also see L A Manrai and A K Manrai, "Effects of Cultural-Context, Gender, and Acculturation on Perceptions of Work versus Social/Leisure Time Usage," *Journal of Business Research,* February 1995, pp 115–28.

43 A good discussion of doing business in Mexico is G K Stephens and C R Greer, "Doing Business in Mexico: Understanding Cultural Differences," *Organizational Dynamics,* Summer 1995, pp 39–55. Also see P Seldon, *The Business*

Traveler's World Guide (New York: McGraw-Hill, 1998), pp 311–17.

[44] R W Moore, "Time, Culture, and Comparative Management: A Review and Future Direction," in *Advances in International Comparative Management,* vol. 5, ed S B Prasad (Greenwich, CT: JAI Press, 1990), pp 7–8.

[45] See A C Bluedorn, C F Kaufman, and P M Lane, "How Many Things Do You Like to Do at Once? An Introduction to Monochronic and Polychronic Time," *Academy of Management Executive,* November 1992, pp 17–26.

[46] "Multitasking" term drawn from S McCartney, "The Breaking Point: Multitasking Technology Can Raise Stress and Cripple Productivity," *Arizona Republic,* May 21, 1995, p D10.

[47] O Port, "You May Have to Reset This Watch—In a Million Years," *Business Week,* August 30, 1993, p 65.

[48] See E T Hall, *The Hidden Dimension* (Garden City, NY: Doubleday, 1966).

[49] "How Cultures Collide," p 72.

[50] For relevant reading, see C T Burris, N R Branscombe, and L M Jackson, "For God and Country: Religion and the Endorsement of National Self-Stereotypes," *Journal of Cross-Cultural Psychology,* July 2000, pp 517–27; L Grensing-Pophal, "Workplace Chaplains," *HR Magazine,* August 2000, pp 54–62; and E Cose, "Even a Tragic Quake Fails to Level India's Caste System," *USA Today,* February 13, 2001, p 13A.

[51] Results adapted from and value definitions quoted from S R Safranski and I-W Kwon, "Religious Groups and Management Value Systems," in *Advances in International Comparative Management,* vol. 3, eds R N Farner and E G McGoun (Greenwich, CT: JAI Press, 1988), pp 171–83.

[52] Ibid., p 180.

[53] N J Adler, *International Dimensions of Organizational Behavior,* 4th ed (Cincinnati: South-Western, 2002), p 11. (Emphasis added.)

[54] See D Matsumoto, R J Grissom, and D L Dinnel, "Do Between-Culture Differences Really Mean That People Are Different? A Look at Some Measures of Cultural Effect Size," *Journal of Cross-Cultural Psychology,* July 2001, pp 478–90.

[55] M Javidan and R J House, "Leadership and Cultures around the World: Findings from GLOBE—An Introduction to the Special Issue," *Journal of World Business,* Spring 2002, p 1.

[56] For complete details, see G Hofstede, *Culture's Consequences: International Differences in Work-Related Values,* abridged ed (Newbury Park, CA: Sage Publications, 1984); G Hofstede, "The Interaction between National and Organizational Value Systems," *Journal of Management Studies,* July 1985, pp 347–57; and G Hofstede, "Management Scientists Are Human," *Management Science,* January 1994, pp 4–13. For replications and extensions of Hofstede's work, see A Merritt, "Culture in the Cockpit: Do Hofstede's Dimensions Replicate?" *Journal of Cross-Cultural Psychology,* May 2000, pp 283–301; K Sivakumar and C Nakata, "The Stampede toward Hofstede's Framework: Avoiding the Sample Design Pit in Cross-Cultural Research," *Journal of*

International Business Studies, Third Quarter 2001, pp 555–74; and J K Sebenius, "The Hidden Challenge of Cross-Border Negotiations," *Harvard Business Review,* March 2002, pp 76–85.

[57] See G Hofstede and M H Bond, "Hofstede's Culture Dimensions: An Independent Validation Using Rokeach's Value Survey," *Journal of Cross-Cultural Psychology,* December 1984, pp 417–33. A more recent study using the Chinese Value Survey is reported in D A Ralston, D J Gustafson, P M Elsass, F Cheung, and R H Terpstra, "Eastern Values: A Comparison of Managers in the United States, Hong Kong, and the People's Republic of China," *Journal of Applied Psychology,* October 1992, pp 664–71.

[58] G Hofstede, "Cultural Constraints in Management Theories," *Academy of Management Executive,* February 1993, p 90.

[59] Confucian values are discussed in P Ghauri and T Fang, "Negotiating with the Chinese: A Socio-Cultural Analysis," *Journal of World Business,* Fall 2001, pp 303–25.

[60] For complete details, see G Hofstede and M H Bond, "The Confucius Connection: From Cultural Roots to Economic Growth," *Organizational Dynamics,* Spring 1988, pp 4–21.

[61] See P M Rosenzweig, "When Can Management Science Research Be Generalized Internationally?" *Management Science,* January 1994, pp 28–39.

[62] A follow-up study is J P Johnson and T Lenartowicz, "Culture, Freedom and Economic Growth: Do Cultural Values Explain Economic Growth?" *Journal of World Business,* Winter 1998, pp 332–56.

[63] For details, see D Hartog, et al., "Emics and Etics of Culturally-Endorsed Implicit Leadership Theories: Are Attributes of Charismatic/Transformational Leadership Universally Endorsed?" *Leadership Quarterly,* in press.

[64] For example, see M F R Kets de Vries, "A Journey into the 'Wild East': Leadership Style and Organizational Practices in Russia," *Organizational Dynamics,* Spring 2000, pp 67–81; and F C Brodbeck, M Frese, and M Javidan, "Leadership Made in Germany: Low on Compassion, High on Performance," *Academy of Management Executive,* February 2002, pp 16–29.

[65] M Vande Berg, "Siemens: Betting That Big Is Once Again Beautiful," *Milken Institute Review,* Second Quarter 2002, p 47.

[66] Data from D Beck, "What Negotiating Tactics Reveal about Executives," February 11–17, 2002, (www.careerjournal.com).

[67] J S Black and H B Gregersen, "The Right Way to Manage Expats," *Harvard Business Review,* March–April 1999, p 53. A more optimistic picture is presented in R L Tung, "American Expatriates Abroad: From Neophytes to Cosmopolitans," *Journal of World Business,* Summer 1998, pp 125–44. For interesting expatriate metaphors, see A Harzing, "Of Bears, Bumble-Bees, and Spiders: The Role of Expatriates in Controlling Foreign Subsidiaries," *Journal of World Business,* Winter 2001, pp 366–79.

[68] Adapted from R L Tung, "Expatriate Assignments: Enhancing Success and Minimizing Failure," *Academy of Management Executive,* May 1987, pp 117–26.

69 S Dallas, "Rule No. 1: Don't Diss the Locals," *Business Week,* May 15, 1995, p 8.

70 These insights come from Tung, "American Expatriates Abroad"; P M Caligiuri and W F Cascio,"*Can We Send Her There?* Maximizing the Success of Western Women on Global Assignments," *Journal of World Business,* Winter 1998, pp 394–416; L K Stroh, A Varma, and S J Valy-Durbin, "Why Are Women Left Home: Are They Unwilling to Go on International Assignments?" *Journal of World Business,* Fall 2000, pp 241–55; A Varma, L K Stroh, and L B Schmitt, "Women and International Assignments: The Impact of Supervisor-Subordinate Relationships," *Journal of World Business,* Winter 2001, pp 380–88; and H Scullion and C Brewster, "The Management of Expatriates: Messages from Europe?" *Journal of World Business,* Winter 2001, pp 346–65.

71 A good resource book is M W McCall, Jr, and G P Hollenbeck, *Developing Global Executives: The Lessons of International Experience* (Boston: Harvard Business School Press, 2002). Also see Y Baruch, "No Such Thing as a Global Manager," *Business Horizons,* January–February 2002, pp 36–42; and A K Gupta and V Govindarajan, "Cultivating a Global Mindset," *Academy of Management Executive,* February 2002, pp 116–26.

72 See J I Sanchez, P E Spector, and C L Cooper, "Adapting to a Boundaryless World: A Developmental Expatriate Model," *Academy of Management Executive,* May 2000, pp 96–106; M Janssens, "Developing a Culturally Synergistic Approach to International Human Resource Management," *Journal of World Business,* Winter 2001, pp 429–50; and A C Poe, "Selection Savvy," *HR Magazine,* April 2002, pp 77–83.

73 Data from "E-Pulse," *Training,* January 2002, p 60.

74 J S Lublin, "Younger Managers Learn Global Skills," *The Wall Street Journal,* March 31, 1992, p B1.

75 See P C Earley, "Intercultural Training for Managers: A Comparison of Documentary and Interpersonal Methods," *Academy of Management Journal,* December 1987, pp 685–98; and J S Black and M Mendenhall, "Cross-Cultural Training Effectiveness: A Review and a Theoretical Framework for Future Research," *Academy of Management Review,* January 1990, pp 113–36.

76 See E Marx, *Breaking through Culture Shock: What You Need to Succeed in International Business* (London: Nicholas Brealey Publishing, 2001).

77 See H H Nguyen, L A Messe, and G E Stollak, "Toward a More Complex Understanding of Acculturation and Adjustment," *Journal of Cross-Cultural Psychology,* January 1999, pp 5–31; S Jun, J W Gentry, and Y J Hyun, "Cultural Adaptation of Business Expatriates in the Host Marketplace," *Journal of International Business Studies,* Second Quarter 2001, pp 369–77; and M Lazarova and P Caligiuri, "Retaining Repatriates: The Role of Organizational Support Practices," *Journal of World Business,* Winter 2001, pp 389–401.

78 K L Miller, "How a Team of Buckeyes Helped Honda Save a Bundle," *Business Week,* September 13, 1993, p 68.

79 B Newman, "For Ira Caplan, Re-Entry Has Been Strange," *The Wall Street Journal,* December 12, 1995, p A12.

80 See Black, Gregersen, and Mendenhall, *Global Assignments,* p 227.

81 Ibid., pp 226–27.

82 See A C Poe, "Welcome Back," *HR Magazine,* March 2000, pp 94–105; and J Barbian, "Return to Sender," *Training,* January 2002, pp 40–43.

83 Excerpted from J Useem, "Exxon's African Adventure," *Fortune,* April 15, 2002, 102–14. © 2001 Time, Inc. All rights reserved.

84 This list of work goals is quoted from I Harpaz, "The Importance of Work Goals: An International Perspective," *Journal of International Business Studies,* First Quarter 1990, p 79.

85 Adapted from a seven-country summary in ibid., Table 2, p 81.

86 See A Nimgade, "American Management as Viewed by International Professionals," *Business Horizons,* November–December 1989, pp 98–105; W A Hubiak and S J O'Donnell, "Do Americans Have Their Minds Set against TQM?" *National Productivity Review,* Summer 1996, pp 19–32; and Adler, *International Dimensions of Organizational Behavior,* pp 84–91.

87 Excerpted from M V Gratchev, "Making the Most of Cultural Differences," *Harvard Business Review,* October 2001, pp 28, 30.

CHAPTER 5

1 Excerpted from C Fishman, "What if You'd Worked at Enron?" *Fast Company,* May 2002, pp 104, 106.

2 D Seligman, "The Trouble with Buyouts," *Fortune,* November 30, 1992, p 125.

3 S I Cheldelin and L A Foritano, "Psychometrics: Their Use in Organisation Development," *Journal of Managerial Psychology,* no. 4, 1989, p 21.

4 See L Yu, "Does Diversity Drive Productivity?" *MIT Sloan Management Review,* Winter 2002, p 17; and L Grensing-Pophal, "Reaching for Diversity," *HR Magazine,* May 2002, pp 52–56.

5 Data from "If We Could Do It Over Again," *USA Today,* February 19, 2001, p 4D.

6 V Gecas, "The Self-Concept," in *Annual Review of Sociology,* eds R H Turner and J F Short, Jr (Palo Alto, CA: Annual Reviews Inc., 1982), vol. 8, p 3. Also see T A Judge and J E Bono, "Relationship of Core Self-Evaluations Traits—Self-Esteem, Generalized Self-Efficacy, Locus of Control, and Emotional Stability—with Job Satisfaction and Job Performance: A Meta-Analysis," *Journal of Applied Psychology,* February 2001, pp 80–92; and A Erez and T A Judge, "Relationship of Core Self-Evaluations to Goal Setting, Motivation, and Performance," *Journal of Applied Psychology,* December 2001, pp 1270–79.

[7] L Festinger, *A Theory of Cognitive Dissonance* (Stanford, CA: Stanford University Press, 1957), p 3.

[8] See D C Barnlund, "Public and Private Self in Communicating with Japan," *Business Horizons,* March–April 1989, pp 32–40; and the section on "Doing Business with Japan" in P R Harris and R T Moran, *Managing Cultural Differences,* 4th ed (Houston: Gulf Publishing, 1996), pp 267–76.

[9] See F Luthans, "Positive Organizational Behavior: Developing and Managing Psychological Strengths," *Academy of Management Executive,* February 2002, pp 57–72.

[10] Based in part on a definition found in Gecas, "The Self-Concept." Also see N Branden, *Self-Esteem at Work: How Confident People Make Powerful Companies* (San Francisco: Jossey-Bass, 1998).

[11] H W Marsh, "Positive and Negative Global Self-Esteem: A Substantively Meaningful Distinction or Artifacts?" *Journal of Personality and Social Psychology,* April 1996, p 819.

[12] Ibid.

[13] For related research, see B Gray-Little and A R Hafdahl, "Factors Influencing Racial Comparisons of Self-Esteem: A Quantitative Review," *Psychological Bulletin,* no. 1, 2000, pp 26–54.

[14] See S J Rowley, R M Sellers, T M Chavous, and M A Smith, "The Relationship between Racial Identity and Self-Esteem in African American College and High School Students," *Journal of Personality and Social Psychology,* March 1998, pp 715–24.

[15] N Hellmich, "Emphasizing Achievement, Not Faint Praise," *USA Today,* October 24, 1995, p 1D. Also see "All Shall Have Prizes," *The Economist,* April 14, 2001, p 56.; and M Elias, "Church Boosts Kids' Self-Esteem," *USA Today,* August 27, 2001, p 7D.

[16] See J A Stein, M D Newcomb, and P M Bentler, "The Relative Influence on Vocational Behavior and Family Involvement on Self-Esteem: Longitudinal Analyses of Young Adult Women and Men," *Journal of Vocational Behavior,* June 1990, pp 320–38.

[17] Based on P G Dodgson and J V Wood, "Self-Esteem and the Cognitive Accessibility of Strengths and Weaknesses after Failure," *Journal of Personality and Social Psychology,* July 1998, pp 178–97.

[18] Details may be found in B R Schlenker, M F Weigold, and J R Hallam, "Self-Serving Attributions in Social Context: Effects of Self-Esteem and Social Pressure," *Journal of Personality and Social Psychology,* May 1990, pp 855–63. Also see P Sellers, "Get Over Yourself," *Fortune,* April 30, 2001, pp 76–88.

[19] See R F Baumeister, L Smart, and J M Boden, "Relation of Threatened Egotism to Violence and Aggression: The Dark Side of High Self-Esteem," *Psychological Review,* January 1996, pp 5–33; and R Vermunt, D van Knippenberg, B van Knippenberg, and E Blaauw, "Self-Esteem and Outcome Fairness: Differential Importance of Procedural and Outcome Considerations," *Journal of Applied Psychology,* August 2001, pp 621–28.

[20] E Diener and M Diener, "Cross-Cultural Correlates of Life Satisfaction and Self-Esteem," *Journal of Personality and Social Psychology,* April 1995, p 662. For cross-cultural evidence of a similar psychological process for self-esteem, see T M Singelis, M H Bond, W F Sharkey, and C S Y Lai, "Unpackaging Culture's Influence on Self-Esteem and Embarrassability," *Journal of Cross-Cultural Psychology,* May 1999, pp 315–41.

[21] Based on data in F L Smoll, R E Smith, N P Barnett, and J J Everett, "Enhancement of Children's Self-Esteem through Social Support Training for Youth Sports Coaches," *Journal of Applied Psychology,* August 1993, pp 602–10.

[22] W J McGuire and C V McGuire, "Enhancing Self-Esteem by Directed-Thinking Tasks: Cognitive and Affective Positivity Asymmetries," *Journal of Personality and Social Psychology,* June 1996, p 1124.

[23] M E Gist, "Self-Efficacy: Implications for Organizational Behavior and Human Resource Management," *Academy of Management Review,* July 1987, p 472. Also see A Bandura, "Self-Efficacy: Toward a Unifying Theory of Behavioral Change," *Psychological Review,* March 1977, pp 191–215; T J Maurer and K D Andrews, "Traditional, Likert, and Simplified Measures of Self-Efficacy," *Educational and Psychological Measurement,* December 2000, pp 965–73; and S L Anderson and N E Betz, "Sources of Social Self-Efficacy Expectations: Their Measurement and Relation to Career Development," *Journal of Vocational Behavior,* February 2001, pp 98–117.

[24] D Rader, " 'I Knew What I Wanted to Be,' " *Parade Magazine,* November 1, 1992, p 4.

[25] Based on D H Lindsley, D A Brass, and J B Thomas, "Efficacy-Performance Spirals: A Multilevel Perspective," *Academy of Management Review,* July 1995, pp 645–78.

[26] See, for example, V Gecas, "The Social Psychology of Self-Efficacy," in *Annual Review of Sociology,* eds W R Scott and J Blake (Palo Alto, CA: Annual Reviews, Inc., 1989), vol. 15, pp 291–316; C K Stevens, A G Bavetta, and M E Gist, "Gender Differences in the Acquisition of Salary Negotiation Skills: The Role of Goals, Self-Efficacy, and Perceived Control," *Journal of Applied Psychology,* October 1993, pp 723–35; D Eden and Y Zuk, "Seasickness as a Self-Fulfilling Prophecy: Raising Self-Efficacy to Boost Performance at Sea," *Journal of Applied Psychology,* October 1995, pp 628–35; and S M Jex, P D Bliese, S Buzzell, and J Primeau, "The Impact of Self-Efficacy on Stressor-Strain Relations: Coping Style as an Explanatory Mechanism," *Journal of Applied Psychology,* June 2001, pp 401–9.

[27] For more on learned helplessness, see Gecas, "The Social Psychology of Self-Efficacy"; M J Martinko and W L Gardner, "Learned Helplessness: An Alternative Explanation for Performance Deficits," *Academy of Management Review,* April 1982, pp 195–204; C R Campbell and M J Martinko, "An Integrative Attributional Perspective of Empowerment and Learned Helplessness: A Multimethod Field Study," *Journal of Management,* no. 2, 1998, pp 173–200; and A Dickerson and M A Taylor, "Self-Limiting Behavior in Women: Self-Esteem and Self-Efficacy as Predictors," *Group and Organization Management,* June 2000, pp 191–210.

28 Research on this connection is reported in R B Rubin, M M Martin, S S Bruning, and D E Powers, "Test of a Self-Efficacy Model of Interpersonal Communication Competence," *Communication Quarterly,* Spring 1993, pp 210–20.

29 T Petzinger Jr, "Bob Schmonsees Has a Tool for Better Sales, and It Ignores Excuses," *The Wall Street Journal,* March 26, 1999, p B1.

30 Data from A D Stajkovic and F Luthans, "Self-Efficacy and Work-Related Performance: A Meta-Analysis," *Psychological Bulletin,* September 1998, pp 240–61.

31 Based in part on discussion in Gecas, "The Social Psychology of Self-Efficacy."

32 See S K Parker, "Enhancing Role Breadth Self-Efficacy: The Roles of Job Enrichment and Other Organizational Interventions," *Journal of Applied Psychology,* December 1998, pp 835–52.

33 The positive relationship between self-efficacy and readiness for retraining is documented in L A Hill and J Elias, "Retraining Midcareer Managers: Career History and Self-Efficacy Beliefs," *Human Resource Management,* Summer 1990, pp 197–217. Also see A M Saks, "Longitudinal Field Investigation of the Moderating and Mediating Effects of Self-Efficacy on the Relationship between Training and Newcomer Adjustment," *Journal of Applied Psychology,* April 1995, pp 211–25; and S P Brown, S Ganesan, and G Challagalla, "Self-Efficacy as a Moderator of Information-Seeking Effectiveness," *Journal of Applied Psychology,* October 2001, pp 1043–51.

34 See A D Stajkovic and Fred Luthans, "Social Cognitive Theory and Self-Efficacy: Going Beyond Traditional Motivational and Behavioral Approaches," *Organizational Dynamics,* Spring 1998, pp 62–74.

35 See P C Earley and T R Lituchy, "Delineating Goal and Efficacy Effects: A Test of Three Models," *Journal of Applied Psychology,* February 1991, pp 81–98; and J B Vancouver, C M Thompson, and A A Williams, "The Changing Signs in the Relationships among Self-Efficacy, Personal Goals, and Performance," *Journal of Applied Psychology,* August 2001, pp 605–20.

36 See W S Silver, T R Mitchell, and M E Gist, "Response to Successful and Unsuccessful Performance: The Moderating Effect of Self-Efficacy on the Relationship between Performance and Attributions," *Organizational Behavior and Human Decision Processes,* June 1995, pp 286–99; and S Berglas, "The Very Real Dangers of Executive Coaching," *Harvard Business Review,* June 2002, pp 89–92.

37 For a model of "leadership self-efficacy," see L L Paglis and S G Green, "Leadership Self-Efficacy and Managers' Motivation for Leading Change," *Journal of Organizational Behavior,* March 2002, pp 215–35.

38 M Snyder and S Gangestad, "On the Nature of Self-Monitoring: Matters of Assessment, Matters of Validity," *Journal of Personality and Social Psychology,* July 1986, p 125.

39 T Morganthau, "Throwing Long," *Newsweek,* August 19, 1996, p 29.

40 Data from D V Day, D J Schleicher, A L Unckless, and N J Hiller, "Self-Monitoring Personality at Work: A Meta-Analytic Investigation of Construct Validity," *Journal of Applied Psychology,* April 2002, pp 390–401. Also see S W Gangestad and M Snyder, "Self-Monitoring: Appraisal and Reappraisal," *Psychological Bulletin,* July 2000, pp 530–55; and I M Jawahar, "Attitudes, Self-Monitoring, and Appraisal Behaviors," *Journal of Applied Psychology,* October 2001, pp 875–83.

41 Data from M Kilduff and D V Day, "Do Chameleons Get Ahead? The Effects of Self-Monitoring on Managerial Careers," *Academy of Management Journal,* August 1994, pp 1047–60.

42 Data from D B Turban and T W Dougherty, "Role of Protege Personality in Receipt of Mentoring and Career Success," *Academy of Management Journal,* June 1994, pp 688–702.

43 See F Luthans, "Successful vs. Effective Managers," *Academy of Management Executive,* May 1988, pp 127–32. Also see W H Turnley and M C Bolino, "Achieving Desired Images while Avoiding Undesired Images: Exploring the Role of Self-Monitoring in Impression Management," *Journal of Applied Psychology,* April 2001, pp 351–60.

44 M G Pratt, "To Be or Not to Be? Central Questions in Organizational Identification," in *Identity in Organizations,* eds D A Whetten and P C Godfrey (Thousand Oaks, CA: Sage Publications, 1998), p 172. Also see S Albert, B E Ashforth, and J E Dutton, "Organizational Identity and Identification: Charting New Waters and Building New Bridges," *Academy of Management Review,* January 2000, pp 13–17; J L Pierce, T Kostova, and K T Dirks, "Toward a Theory of Psychological Ownership in Organizations," *Academy of Management Review,* April 2001, pp 298–310; and A Smidts, A T H Pruyn, and C B M van Riel, "The Impact of Employee Communication and Perceived External Prestige on Organizational Identification," *Academy of Management Journal,* October 2001, 1051–62.

45 See G Dessler, "How to Earn Your Employees' Commitment," *Academy of Management Executive,* May 1999, pp 58–67.

46 Based on C Sertoglu and A Berkowitch, "Cultivating Ex-Employees," *Harvard Business Review,* June 2002, pp 20–21.

47 For more, see B Filipczak, "The Soul of the Hog," *Training,* February 1996, pp 38–42.

48 See A Bandura, *Social Learning Theory* (Englewood Cliffs, NJ: Prentice Hall, 1977). A further refinement is reported in A D Stajkovic and F Luthans, "Social Cognitive Theory and Self-Efficacy: Going beyond Traditional Motivational and Behavioral Approaches," *Organizational Dynamics,* Spring 1998, pp 62–74. Also see M Uhl-Bien and G B Graen, "Individual Self-Management: Analysis of Professionals' Self-Managing Activities in Functional and Cross-Functional Work Teams," *Academy of Management Journal,* June 1998, pp 340–50.

49 Bandura, *Social Learning Theory,* p 13.

50 For related research, see M Castaneda, T A Kolenko, and R J Aldag, "Self-Management Perceptions and Practices: A Structural Equations Analysis," *Journal of Organizational Behavior,* January 1999, pp 101–20.

51 "Career Self-Management," *Industry Week,* September 5, 1994, p 36.

52 For more, see C Joinson, "Employee, Sculpt Thyself. . . with a Little Help," *HR Magazine,* May 2001, pp 61–64; and R A Heifetz and M Linsky, "A Survival Guide for Leaders," *Harvard Business Review,* June 2002, pp 65–74.

53 S R Covey, *The 7 Habits of Highly Effective People* (New York: Simon & Schuster, 1989), p 42. Also see J Waldroop and T Butler, "Managing away Bad Habits," *Harvard Business Review,* September–October 2000, pp 89–98; and A Manning, "Fix Your Inner World before Tackling the Universe," *USA Today,* January 15, 2001, p 6D.

54 "Labor Letter: A Special News Report on People and their Jobs in Offices, Fields, and Factories," *The Wall Street Journal,* October 15, 1985, p 1.

55 R McGarvey, "Rehearsing for Success," *Executive Female,* January–February 1990, p 36.

56 D S Looney, "Mental Toughness Wins Out," *Christian Science Monitor,* July 31, 1998, p B4.

57 See M Boyle, "Picture a Perfect Job Hunt," *Fortune,* February 4, 2002, p 162.

58 C Zastrow, *Talk to Yourself: Using the Power of Self-Talk* (Englewood Cliffs, NJ: Prentice Hall, 1979), p 60. Also see C P Neck and R F Ashcraft, "Inner Leadership: Mental Strategies for Nonprofit Staff Members," *Nonprofit World,* May–June 2000, pp 27–30.

59 E Franz, "Private Pep Talk," *Selling Power,* May 1996, p 81.

60 Drawn from discussion in A Bandura, "Self-Reinforcement: Theoretical and Methodological Considerations," *Behaviorism,* Fall 1976, pp 135–55.

61 R Kreitner and F Luthans. "A Social Learning Approach to Behavioral Management: Radical Behaviorists 'Mellowing Out,' " *Organizational Dynamics,* Autumn 1984, p 63.

62 See R F Rakos and M V Grodek, "An Empirical Evaluation of a Behavioral Self-Management Course in a College Setting." *Teaching of Psychology,* October 1984, pp 157–62.

63 Data from L M Godat and T A Brigham, "The Effect of a Self-Management Training Program on Employees of a Mid-Sized Organization," *Journal of Organizational Behavior Management,* no. 1, 1999, pp 65–83.

64 See F Luthans and T R V Davis, "Behavioral Self-Management—The Missing Link in Managerial Effectiveness," *Organizational Dynamics,* Summer 1979, pp 54–59; and C A Frayne and G P Latham, "Application of Social Learning Theory to Employee Self-Management of Attendance," *Journal of Applied Psychology,* August 1987, pp 387–92. Also see G P Latham and C A Frayne, "Self-Management Training for Increasing Job Attendance: A Follow-up and a Replication," *Journal of Applied Psychology,* June 1989, pp 411–16.

65 For a good overview, see L R James and M D Mazerolle, *Personality in Work Organizations* (Thousand Oaks, CA: Sage Publications, 2002).

66 The landmark report is J M Digman, "Personality Structure: Emergence of the Five-Factor Model," *Annual Review of Psychology,* vol. 41, 1990, pp 417–40. Also see M R Barrick and M K Mount, "Autonomy as a Moderator of the Relationships between the Big Five Personality Dimensions and Job Performance," *Journal of Applied Psychology,* February 1993, pp 111–18; and C Viswesvaran and D S Ones, "Measurement Error in 'Big Five Factors' Personality Assessment: Reliability Generalization across Studies and Measures," *Educational and Psychological Measurement,* April 2000, pp 224–35.

67 Data from S V Paunonen et al., "The Structure of Personality in Six Cultures," *Journal of Cross-Cultural Psychology,* May 1996, pp 339–53; and K Yoon, F Schmidt, and R Ilies, "Cross-Cultural Construct Validity of the Five-Factor Model of Personality among Korean Employees," *Journal of Cross-Cultural Psychology,* May 2002, pp 217–35.

68 See M R Barrick and M K Mount, "The Big Five Personality Dimensions and Job Performance: A Meta-Analysis," *Personnel Psychology,* Spring 1991, pp 1–26. Also see R P Tett, D N Jackson, and M Rothstein, "Personality Measures as Predictors of Job Performance: A Meta-Analytic Review," *Personnel Psychology,* Winter 1991, pp 703–42.

69 Barrick and Mount, "The Big Five Personality Dimensions and Job Performance," p 18. Also see H Moon, "The Two Faces of Conscientiousness: Duty and Achievement Striving in Escalation of Commitment Dilemmas," *Journal of Applied Psychology,* June 2001, pp 533–40; M R Barrick, G L Stewart, and M Piotrowski, "Personality and Job Performance: Test of the Mediating Effects of Motivation among Sales Representatives," *Journal of Applied Psychology,* February 2002, pp 43–51; and L A Witt, L A Burke, M R Barrick, and M K Mount, "The Interactive Effects of Conscientiousness and Agreeableness on Job Performance," *Journal of Applied Psychology,* February 2002, pp 164–69.

70 Based on S E Seibert and M L Kraimer, "The Five-Factor Model of Personality and Career Success," *Journal of Vocational Behavior,* February 2001, pp 1–21.

71 J M Crant, "Proactive Behavior in Organizations," *Journal of Management,* no. 3, 2000, p 439.

72 Ibid., pp 439–41.

73 B Hagenbaugh, "Economics Majors Build Brand Name with Unmentionables," *USA Today,* May 20, 2002, p 3B.

74 See discussion in Barrick and Mount, "The Big Five Personality Dimensions and Job Performance: A Meta-Analysis," pp 21–22. Also see J M Cortina, M L Doherty, N Schmitt, G Kaufman, and R G Smith, "The 'Big Five' Personality Factors in the IPI and MMPI: Predictors of Police Performance," *Personnel Psychology,* Spring 1992, pp 119–40; M J Schmit and A M Ryan, "The Big Five in Personnel Selection: Factor Structure in Applicant and Nonapplicant Populations," *Journal of Applied Psychology,* December 1993, pp 966–74; and C Caggiano, "Psychopath," *Inc.,* July 1998, pp 77–85.

75 M K Mount and M R Barrick, "The Big Five Personality Dimensions: Implications for Research and Practice in Human

Resources Management," in *Research in Personnel and Human Resources Management,* ed G R Ferris (Greenwich, CT: JAI Press, 1995), vol. 13, p 189. See J M Collins and D H Gleaves, "Race, Job Applicants, and the Five-Factor Model of Personality: Implications for Black Psychology, Industrial/Organizational Psychology, and the Five-Factor Theory," *Journal of Applied Psychology,* August 1998, pp 531–44.

76 See M Hofman, "Doesn't Work Well with Others," *Inc.,* January 2000, p 95; S Bates, "Personality Counts," *HR Magazine,* February 2002, pp 28–34; and D Patel, "Testing, Testing, Testing," *HR Magazine,* February 2002, p 112.

77 W Lambert, "Psychological Tests Designed to Weed Out Rogue Cops Get a 'D,'" *The Wall Street Journal,* September 1995, p A1. Also see A M Ryan, R E Ployhart, and L A Friedel, "Using Personality Testing to Reduce Adverse Impact: A Cautionary Note," *Journal of Applied Psychology,* April 1998, pp 298–307.

78 For more, see S Stark, O S Chernyshenko, K Chan, W C Lee, and F Drasgow, "Effects of the Testing Situation on Item Responding: Cause for Concern," *Journal of Applied Psychology,* October 2001, pp 943–53. Also see G M Alliger and S A Dwight, "A Meta-Analytic Investigation of the Susceptibility of Integrity Tests to Faking and Coaching," *Educational and Psychological Measurement,* February 2000, pp 59–72.

79 R Lieber, "Wired for Hiring: Microsoft's Slick Recruiting Machine," *Fortune,* February 5, 1996, p 124.

80 For an instructive update, see J B Rotter, "Internal versus External Control of Reinforcement: A Case History of a Variable," *American Psychologist,* April 1990, pp 489–93. A critical review of locus of control and a call for a meta-analysis can be found in R W Renn and R J Vandenberg, "Differences in Employee Attitudes and Behaviors Based on Rotter's (1966) Internal-External Locus of Control: Are They All Valid?" *Human Relations,* November 1991, p 1161–77.

81 J Fierman, "What's Luck Got to Do with It?" *Fortune,* October 16, 1995, p 149.

82 For an overall review of research on locus of control, see P E Spector, "Behavior in Organizations as a Function of Employee's Locus of Control," *Psychological Bulletin,* May 1982, pp 482–97; the relationship between locus of control and performance and satisfaction is examined in D R Norris and R E Niebuhr, "Attributional Influences on the Job Performance–Job Satisfaction Relationship," *Academy of Management Journal,* June 1984, pp 424–31; salary differences between internals and externals were examined by P C Nystrom, "Managers' Salaries and Their Beliefs about Reinforcement Control," *Journal of Social Psychology,* August 1983, pp 291–92.

83 See S R Hawk, "Locus of Control and Computer Attitude: The Effect of User Involvement," *Computers in Human Behavior,* no. 3, 1989, pp 199–206. Also see S S K Lam and J Schaubroeck, "The Role of Locus of Control in Reactions to Being Promoted and to Being Passed Over: A Quasi Experiment," *Academy of Management Journal,* February 2000, pp 66–78.

84 These recommendations are from Spector, "Behavior in Organizations as a Function of Employee's Locus of Control."

85 See C D Fisher and N M Ashkanasy, "The Emerging Role of Emotions in Work Life: an Introduction," *Journal of Organizational Behavior,* March 2000, pp 123–29; P M Muchinsky, "Emotions in the Workplace: The Neglect of Organizational Behavior," *Journal of Organizational Behavior,* November 2000, pp 801–5; and N M Ashkanasy and C S Daus, "Emotion in the Workplace: The New Challenge for Managers," *Academy of Management Executive,* February 2002, pp 76–86.

86 S Hamm, "Bill's Co-Pilot," *Business Week,* September 14, 1998, pp 85, 87.

87 G Anders, "John Chambers after the Deluge," *Fast Company,* July 2001, p 108.

88 R S Lazarus, *Emotion and Adaptation* (New York: Oxford University Press, 1991), p 6. Also see, Goleman, *Emotional Intelligence,* pp 289–90; and J A Russell and L F Barrett, "Core Affect, Prototypical Emotional Episodes, and Other Things Called *Emotion:* Dissecting the Elephant," *Journal of Personality and Social Psychology,* May 1999, pp 805–19.

89 Based on discussion in R D Arvey, G L Renz, and T W Watson, "Emotionality and Job Performance: Implications for Personnel Selection," in *Research in Personnel and Human Resources Management,* vol. 16, ed G R Ferris (Stamford, CT: JAI Press, 1998), pp 103–47. Also see K Dogan and R P Vecchio, "Managing Envy and Jealousy in the Workplace," *Compensation & Benefits Review,* March–April 2001, pp 57–64.

90 See D L Coutu, "Managing Emotional Fallout: Parting Remarks from America's Top Psychiatrist," *Harvard Business Review,* February 2002, pp 55–59.

91 J A Byrne and H Timmons, "Tough Times," *Business Week,* October 29, 2001, p 66. Also see J E Dutton, P J Frost, M C Worline, J M Lilius, and J M Kanov, "Leading in Times of Trauma," *Harvard Business Review,* January 2002, pp 54–61.

92 See R Hampson, "A Last-Minute Change in FDR Speech Still Inspires," *USA Today,* November 1, 2001, p 2A; and A D Marcus, "Living with Fear," *Money,* December 2001, pp 124–29.

93 Data from J Hilton and U Shankar, "2001 Motor Vehicle Traffic Crashes Injury and Fatality Estimates Early Assessment," National Center for Statistics and Analysis, May 30, 2002 (www.nhtsa.dot.gov); and R Hampson, "WTC Recovery Effort Concludes without a Word," *USA Today,* May 31, 2002, p 2A.

94 Based on 2000 data from Mothers Against Drunk Driving, May 30, 2002 (www.madd.org/stats).

95 D Goleman, *Emotional Intelligence* (New York: Bantam Books, 1995), p 34. For more, see Q N Huy, "Emotional Capability, Emotional Intelligence, and Radical Change," *Academy of Management Review,* April 1999, pp 325–45.

96 See "What's Your EQ at Work," *Fortune,* October 26, 1998, p 298; M Davies, L Stankov, and R D Roberts, "Emotional Intelligence: In Search of an Elusive Construct," *Journal of Personality and Social Psychology,* October 1998, pp 989–1015; S Fox and P E Spector, "Relations of Emotional Intelligence, Practical Intelligence, General Intelligence, and Trait Affectivity with Interview Outcomes: It's Not all Just 'G,' " *Journal of Organizational Behavior,* April 2000, pp 203–20; J M George, "Emotions and Leadership: The Role of Emotional Intelligence," *Human Relations,* August 2000, pp 1027–55; V U Druskat and S B Wolff, "Building the Emotional Intelligence of Groups," *Harvard Business Review,* March 2001, pp 80–90; and D Goleman, R Boyatzis, and A McKee, "Primal Leadership: The Hidden Driver of Great Performance," *Harvard Business Review,* Special Issue: Breakthrough Leadership, December 2001, pp 43–51.

[97] Data from S D Pugh, "Service with a Smile: Emotional Contagion in the Service Encounter," *Academy of Management Journal,* October 2001, pp 1018–27.

[98] Drawn from P Totterdell, S Kellett, K Teuchmann, and R B Briner, "Evidence of Mood Linkage in Work Groups," *Journal of Personality and Social Psychology,* June 1998, pp 1504–15. Also see C D Fisher, "Mood and Emotions while Working: Missing Pieces of Job Satisfaction," *Journal of Organizational Behavior,* March 2000, pp 185–202; K M Lewis, "When Leaders Display Emotion: How Followers Respond to Negative Emotional Expression of Male and Female Leaders," *Journal of Organizational Behavior,* March 2000, pp 221–34; and A Singh-Manoux and C Finkenauer, "Cultural Variations in Social Sharing of Emotions: An Intercultural Perspective," *Journal of Cross-Cultural Psychology,* November 2001, pp 647–61.

[99] "Ulrich Schumacher," *Business Week,* June 11, 2001, p 82.

[100] N M Ashkanasy and C S Daus, "Emotion in the Workplace: The New Challenge for Managers," *Academy of Management Executive,* February 2002, p 79. Also see J Schaubroeck and J R Jones, "Antecedents of Workplace Emotional Labor Dimensions and Moderators of Their Effects on Physical Symptoms," *Journal of Organizational Behavior,* March 2000, pp 163–83; and "The Killer Smile: The Cost of Service at Any Cost," *Training,* May 2000, p 22.

[101] Data from A M Kring and A H Gordon, "Sex Differences in Emotions: Expression, Experience, and Physiology," *Journal of Personality and Social Psychology,* March 1998, pp 686–703.

[102] Excerpted from B Morris, "Overcoming Dyslexia," *Fortune,* May 13, 2002, pp 54–70. © 2001 Time Inc. All rights reserved.

[103] Adapted in part from James and Mazerolle, *Personality in Work Organizations,* p 89.

[104] Excerpted from J Macht, "To Get Ahead, Get Mad," *Business 2.0,* May 2002, p 94. © Time, Inc. All rights reserved.

CHAPTER 6

[1] Excerpted from E Krell, "Greener Pastures," *Training,* November 2001, pp 54–59.

[2] Data from "The 100 Best Companies to Work For," *Fortune,* February 4, 2002, p 72.

[3] M Rokeach, *The Nature of Values* (New York: Free Press, 1973), p 5.

[4] See S H Schwartz and W Bilsky, "Toward a Theory of the Universal Content and Structure of Values: Extensions and Cross-Cultural Replications," *Journal of Personality and Social Psychology,* May 1990, pp 878–91. For other values-related research, see G R Maio and J M Olson, "Values as Truisms: Evidence and Implications," *Journal of Personality and Social Psychology,* February 1998, pp 294–311; B M Meglino and E C Ravlin, "Individual Values in Organizations: Concepts, Controversies, and Research," *Journal of Management,* no. 3, 1998, pp 351–89; L A King and C K Napa, "What Makes a Life Good?" *Journal of Personality and Social Psychology,* July 1998, pp 156–65; R A Rodriguez, "Challenging Demographic Reductionism: A Pilot Study Investigating Diversity in Group Composition," *Small Group Research,* December 1998, pp 744–59; and M W Allen, S H Ng and M Wilson, "A Functional Approach to Instrumental and Terminal Values and the Value-Attitude-Behaviour System of Consumer Choice," *European Journal of Marketing,* January 2002, pp 111–35.

[5] S H Schwartz and A Bardi, "Value Hierarchies across Cultures: Taking a Similarities Perspective," *Journal of Cross-Cultural Psychology,* May 2001, p 287. Also see D Akiba and W Klug, "The Different and the Same: Reexamining East and West in a Cross-Cultural Analysis of Values," *Social Behavior and Personality,* Fall 1999, pp 467–74; S H Schwartz and G Sagie, "Value Consensus and Importance: A Cross-National Study," *Journal of Cross-Cultural Psychology,* July 2000, pp 465–97; and J G Bruhn, "Managing Tough and Easy Organizational Cultures," *Health Care Manager,* December 2001, pp 1–10.

[6] See M Rokeach, *Beliefs, Attitudes, and Values* (San Francisco: Jossey-Bass, 1968). For related research, see S W Smith, J B Ellis, and H Yoo, "Memorable Messages as Guides to Self-Assessment of Behavior: The Role of Instrumental Values," *Communication Monographs,* December 2001, pp 325–39.

[7] Data from M Rokeach and S J Ball-Rokeach, "Stability and Change in American Value Priorities, 1968–1981," *American Psychologist,* May 1989, pp 775–84. For an alternative model of personal values, see S H Schwartz, G Melech, A Lehmann, S Burgess, M Harris, and V Owens, "Extending the Cross-Cultural Validity of the Theory of Basic Human Values with a Different Method of Measurement," *Journal of Cross-Cultural Psychology,* September 2001, pp 519–42; and P B Smith, M F Peterson, and S H Schwartz, "Cultural Values, Sources of Guidance, and Their Relevance to Managerial Behavior: A 47-Nation Study," *Journal of Cross-Cultural Psychology,* March 2002, pp 188–208.

[8] "Kirby Dyess," *Fast Company,* March 1999, p 90.

[9] W Shapiro, "Peace Corp Inexpensive, Yet Priceless," *USA Today,* May 5, 1999, p 15A.

[10] E Shapiro, "Time Warner Defines, Defends System of Values," *The Wall Street Journal,* April 9, 1999, p B1. Also see R Grover, "AOL: John Malone Wants to Be Heard," *Business Week,* May 13, 2002, pp 86–88.

[11] Ibid., p B4.

[12] B Moses, "The Busyness Trap," *Training,* November 1998, p 42.

[13] See E T Behr, "Acting from the Center," *Management Review,* March 1998, pp 51–55; and J D Beckett. "NOBLE Ideas for Businesses," *Management Review,* March 1999, p 62.

[14] See K Fackelmann, "New Moms with Jobs Hit Record High," *USA Today,* October 24, 2000, p 1A; M J Cetron and O Davies, "Trends Now Changing the World: Economics and Society, Values and Concerns, Energy and Environment," *The Futurist,* January–February 2001, pp 30–43; S Armour, "More Gen Xers Juggle Jobs, Parents' Care," *USA Today,* April 26, 2002, p 1B; and D Patel, "Different Choices," *HR Magazine,* May 2002, p 144.

[15] K W Smola and C D Sutton, "Generational Differences: Revisiting Generational Work Values for the New Millennium," *Journal of Organizational Behavior,* June 2002, p 379.

[16] S Shellenbarger, "Wed., 1:30 P.M., Lunch: Emotional Discussion with Family Member," *The Wall Street Journal,* March 27, 2002, p B1.

[17] P L Perrewé and W A Hochwarter, "Can We Really Have It All? The Attainment of Work and Family Values," *Current Directions in Psychological Science,* February 2001, p 31.

[18] Data from S A Hewlett, "Executive Women and the Myth of Having It All," *Harvard Business Review,* April 2002, pp 66–73. Also see K S Peterson, "We're Working More, but Less around the House," *Arizona Republic,* March 18, 2002, p E1; and G Koretz, "Marriage's 'Unique Effect,' " *Business Week,* May 13, 2002, p 32.

[19] Based on T D Allen, "Family-Supportive Work Environments: The Role of Organizational Perceptions," *Journal of Vocational Behavior,* June 2001, pp 414–35.

[20] "The 100 Best Companies to Work For," p 84.

[21] Based on S C Clark, "Work Cultures and Work/Family Balance," *Journal of Vocational Behavior,* June 2001, pp 348–65.

[22] T R Nielson, D S Carlson, and M J Lankau, "The Supportive Mentor as a Means of Reducing Work-Family Conflict," *Journal of Vocational Behavior,* December 2001, pp 374–75.

[23] Based on S Parasuraman and C A Simmers, "Type of Employment, Work-Family Conflict and Well-Being: A Comparative Study," *Journal of Organizational Behavior,* August 2001, pp 551–68.

[24] R Rapoport, L Bailyn, J K Fletcher, and B H Pruitt, *Beyond Work-Family Balance: Advancing Gender Equity and Workplace Performance* (San Francisco: Jossey-Bass, 2002), p 36. Also see L Bailyn, "The Myth of Having It All," *Harvard Business Review,* June 2002, pp 146–47.

[25] M Fishbein and I Ajzen, *Belief, Attitude, Intention and Behavior: An Introduction to Theory and Research* (Reading, MA: Addison-Wesley Publishing, 1975), p 6.

[26] For a discussion of the difference between values and attitudes, see B W Becker and P E Connor, "Changing American Values—Debunking the Myth," *Business,* January–March 1985, pp 56–59.

[27] The components or structure of attitudes is thoroughly discussed by A P Brief, *Attitudes in and around Organizations* (Thousand Oaks, CA: Sage, 1998), pp 49–84.

[28] See B M Staw and J Ross, "Stability in the Midst of Change: A Dispositional Approach to Job Attitudes," *Journal of Applied Psychology,* August 1985, pp 469–80. Also see J Schaubroeck, D C Ganster, and B Kemmerer, "Does Trait Affect Promote Job Attitude Stability?" *Journal of Organizational Behavior,* March 1996, pp 191–96.

[29] Data from P S Visser and J A Krosnick, "Development of Attitude Strength Over the Life Cycle: Surge and Decline," *Journal of Personality and Social Psychology,* December 1998, pp 1389–410.

[30] I Ajzen, "The Theory of Planned Behavior," *Organizational Behavior and Human Decision Processes,* vol. 50 (1991), p 188.

[31] See R P Steel and N K Ovalle II. "A Review and Meta-Analysis of Research on the Relationship between Behavioral Intentions and Employee Turnover," *Journal of Applied Psychology,* November 1984, pp 673–86. Also see A Kirschenbaum and J Weisberg, "Employee's Turnover Intentions and Job Destination Choices," *Journal of Organizational Behavior,* February 2002, pp 109–125.

[32] Drawn from I Ajzen and M Fishbein, *Understanding Attitudes and Predicting Social Behavior* (Englewood Cliffs, NJ: Prentice Hall, 1980); and K I van der Zee, A B Bakker, and P Bakker, "Why Are Structured Interviews so Rarely Used in Personnel Selection?" *Journal of Applied Psychology,* February 2002, pp 176–84. Also see D Albarracín, B T Johnson, M Fishbein, and P A Muellerleile, "Theories of Reasoned Action and Planned Behavior as Models of Condom Use: A Meta-Analysis," *Psychological Bulletin,* January 2001, pp 142–61; K A Finlay, D Trafimow, and A Villarreal, "Predicting Exercise and Health Behavioral Intentions: Attitudes, Subjective Norms, and Other Behavioral Determinants," *Journal of Applied Social Psychology,* February 2002, pp 342–58; and M Riketta, "Attitudinal Organizational Commitment and Job Performance: A Meta-Analysis," *Journal of Organizational Behavior,* May 2002, pp 257–66.

[33] See P W Hom and C L Hulin, "A Competitive Test of the Prediction of Reenlistment by Several Models," *Journal of Applied Psychology,* February 1981, pp 23–39. Also see P R Warshaw, R Calantone, and M Joyce, "A Field Study Application of the Fishbein and Ajzen Intention Model," *Journal of Social Psychology,* February 1986, pp 135–365.

[34] Data from D A Kravitz and J Platania, "Attitudes and Beliefs about Affirmative Action: Effects of Target and of Respondent Sex and Ethnicity," *Journal of Applied Psychology,* December 1993, pp 928–38.

[35] Based on evidence in C J Thomsen, A M Basu, and M Tippens Reinitz, "Effects of Women's Studies Courses on Gender-Related Attitudes of Women and Men," *Psychology of Women Quarterly,* September 1995, pp 419–26.

[36] See B Fishel, "A New Perspective: How to Get the Real Story from Attitude Surveys," *Training,* February 1998, pp 91–94.

[37] L Yerkes, *Fun Works: Creating Places Where People Love to Work* (San Francisco: Berrett-Koehler, 2001), p 73. Also see R Boyatzis, A McKee, and D Goleman, "Reawakening Your Passion for Work," *Harvard Business Review,* April 2002, pp 87–94.

[38] For a review of the development of the JDI, see P C Smith, L M Kendall, and C L Hulin, *The Measurement of Satisfaction in Work and Retirement* (Skokie, IL: Rand McNally, 1969).

[39] For norms on the MSQ, see D J Weiss, R V Dawis, G W England, and L H Lofquist, *Manual for the Minnesota Satisfaction Questionnaire* (Minneapolis: Industrial Relations Center, University of Minnesota, 1967).

[40] See A J Kinicki, R M McKee-Ryan, C A Schriesheim, and K P Carson, "Assessing the Construct Validity of the Job Descriptive Index: A Review and Meta-Analysis," *Journal of Applied Psychology,* February 2002, pp 14–32.

[41] W Zeller, C Palmeri, M France, J Weber, and D Carney, "Jeff Skilling: Enron's Missing Man," *Business Week,* February 11, 2002, p 39.

[42] D Wessel, "How Loyalty Comes by Degrees," *The Wall Street Journal,* May 17, 2001, p A1.

[43] Ibid.

[44] See R P Tett and J P Meyer, "Job Satisfaction, Organizational Commitment, Turnover Intention, and Turnover: Path Analysis Based on Meta-Analytic Findings," *Personnel Psychology,* Summer 1993, pp 259–93.

[45] Results can be found in M Riketta, "Attitudinal Organizational Commitment and Job Performance: A Meta-Analysis," *Journal of Organizational Behavior,* March 2002, pp 257–66.

[46] Supportive results are presented in R D Hackett, L M Lapierre, and P A Hausdorf, "Understanding the Links between Work Commitment Constructs," *Journal of Vocational Behavior,* June 2001, pp 392–413.

[47] This recommendation was supported by T Heffner and J R Rentsch, "Organizational Commitment and Social Interaction: A Multiple Constituencies Approach," *Journal of Vocational Behavior,* December 2001, pp 471–90.

[48] I M Paullay, G M Alliger, and E F Stone-Romero, "Construct Validation of Two Instruments Designed to Measure Job Involvement and Work Centrality," *Journal of Applied Psychology,* April 1994, p 224.

[49] Yerkes, *Fun Works,* p 126.

[50] Ibid.

[51] Results can be found in S P Brown, "A Meta-Analysis and Review of Organizational Research on Job Involvement," *Psychological Bulletin,* September 1996, pp 235–55.

[52] This recommendation is supported by K W Thomas, *Intrinsic Motivation at Work* (San Francisco: Berrett-Koehler, 2000).

[53] Results can be found in J M Diefendorff, D J Brown, A M Kamin, and R G Lord, "Examining the Roles of Job Involvement and Work Centrality in Predicting Organizational Citizenship Behaviors and Job Performance," *Journal of Organizational Behavior,* February 2002, pp 93–108.

[54] S B Parry, "The Quest for Competencies," *Training,* July 1996, p 48. Also see K Tyler, "Put Applicants' Skills to the Test," *HR Magazine,* January 2000, pp 74–80; J Sandberg, "Understanding Human Competence at Work: An Interpretative

Approach," *Academy of Management Journal,* February 2000, pp 9–25; and E A Day, W Arthur Jr, and D Gettman, "Knowledge Structures and the Acquisition of a Complex Skill," *Journal of Applied Psychology,* October 2001, pp 1022–33.

[55] See D L Coutu, "How Resilience Works," *Harvard Business Review,* May 2002, pp 46–55.

[56] See "Nappers of the World, Lie Down and Be Counted!" *Training,* May 2000, p 24; K Fackelmann, "Deep Sleep Beats All-Nighter for Retaining What You Learn," *USA Today,* November 27, 2000, p 10D; D M Osborne, "Sleep: The Final Frontier," *Inc.,* September 2001, p 68; and A Pomeroy, "The Doctor Is Still In," *HR Magazine,* February 2002, pp 36–42.

[57] A Pomeroy, "Sleep Deprivation and Medical Errors," *HR Magazine,* February 2002, p 42.

[58] For interesting reading on intelligence, see M Elias, "Mom's IQ, Not Family Size, Key to Kids' Smarts," *USA Today,* June 12, 2000, p 1D; R Sapolsky, "Score One for Nature—or Is It Nurture?" *USA Today,* June 21, 2000, p 17A; and D Lubinski, R M Webb, M J Morelock, and C P Benbow, "Top 1 in 10,000: A 10-Year Follow-Up of the Profoundly Gifted," *Journal of Applied Psychology,* August 2001, pp 718–29.

[59] For an excellent update on intelligence, including definitional distinctions and a historical perspective of the IQ controversy, see R A Weinberg, "Intelligence and IQ," *American Psychologist,* February 1989, pp 98–104.

[60] Ibid.

[61] S L Wilk, L Burris Desmarais, and P R Sackett, "Gravitation to Jobs Commensurate with Ability: Longitudinal and Cross-Sectional Tests," *Journal of Applied Psychology,* February 1995, p 79.

[62] B Azar, "People Are Becoming Smarter—Why?" *APA Monitor,* June 1996, p 20. Also see " 'Average' Intelligence Higher than It Used to Be," *USA Today,* February 18, 1997, p 6D.

[63] For related research, see M J Ree and J A Earles, "Predicting Training Success: Not Much More than g," *Personnel Psychology,* Summer 1991, pp 321–32.

[64] See F L Schmidt and J E Hunter, "Employment Testing: Old Theories and New Research Findings," *American Psychologist,* October 1981, p 1128. Also see Y Ganzach, "Intelligence and Job Satisfaction," *Academy of Management Journal,* October 1998, pp 526–39.

[65] See I Briggs Myers (with P B Myers), *Gifts Differing* (Palo Alto, CA: Consulting Psychologists Press, 1980). Mentions of the MBTI can be found in B O'Reilly, "Does Your Fund Manager Play the Piano?" *Fortune,* December 29, 1997, pp 139–44; T A Stewart, "Escape from the Cult of Personality Tests," *Fortune,* March 16, 1998, p 80; J T Adams III, "What's Your Type?" *HR Magazine,* June 1999, p 8; and T Petzinger Jr, "With the Stakes High, a Lucent Duo Conquers Distance and Culture," *The Wall Street Journal,* April 23, 1999, p B1.

[66] For a complete discussion of each cognitive style, see J W Slocum, Jr, and D Hellriegel, "A Look at How Managers' Minds Work," *Business Horizons,* July–August 1983, pp 58–68; and W

Taggart and D Robey, "Minds and Managers: On the Dual Nature of Human Information Processing and Management," *Academy of Management Review,* April 1981, pp 187–95. Also see M Wood Daudelin, "Learning from Experience through Reflection," *Organizational Dynamics,* Winter 1996, pp 36–48.

[67] See B K Blaylock and L P Rees, "Cognitive Style and the Usefulness of Information," *Decision Sciences,* Winter 1984, pp 74–91.

[68] Additional material on cognitive styles may be found in F A Gul, "The Joint and Moderating Role of Personality and Cognitive Style on Decision Making," *The Accounting Review,* April 1984, pp 264–77; B H Kleiner, "The Interrelationship of Jungian Modes of Mental Functioning with Organizational Factors: Implications for Management Development," *Human Relations,* November 1983, pp 997–1012; and J L McKenney and P G W Keen, "How Managers' Minds Work," *Harvard Business Review,* May–June 1974, pp 79–90.

[69] See G H Rice, Jr, and D P Lindecamp, "Personality Types and Business Success of Small Retailers," *Journal of Occupational Psychology,* June 1989, pp 177–82. Also see S Goldman and W M Kahnweiler, "A Collaborator Profile for Executives of Nonprofit Organizations," *Nonprofit Management and Leadership,* Summer 2000, pp 435–50.

[70] W L Gardner and M J Martinko, "Using the Myers-Briggs Type Indicator to Study Managers: A Literature Review and Research Agenda," *Journal of Management,* no. 1, 1996, p 77.

[71] For example, see F Ramsoomair, "Relating Theoretical Concepts to Life in the Classroom: Applying the Myers-Briggs Type Indicator," *Journal of Management Education,* February 1994, pp 111–16. For related material, see S Shapiro and M T Spence, "Managerial Intuition: A Conceptual and Operational Framework," *Business Horizons,* January–February 1997, pp 63–68.

[72] See A J Kinicki, F M McKee, and K J Wade, "Annual Review, 1991–1995: Occupational Health," *Journal of Vocational Behavior,* October 1996, pp 190–220.

[73] For a review of these models, see Brief, *Attitudes in and around Organizations.*

[74] See A R Karr, "Work Week: A Special News Report about Life on the Job—and Trends Taking Shape There," *The Wall Street Journal,* June 29, 1999, p A1.

[75] For a review of need satisfaction models, see E F Stone, "A Critical Analysis of Social Information Processing Models of Job Perceptions and Job Attitudes," in *Job Satisfaction: How People Feel about Their Jobs and How It Affects Their Performance,* eds C J Cranny, P Cain Smith, and E F Stone (New York: Lexington Books, 1992), pp 21–52.

[76] See J P Wanous, T D Poland, S L Premack, and K S Davis, "The Effects of Met Expectations on Newcomer Attitudes and Behaviors: A Review and Meta-Analysis," *Journal of Applied Psychology,* June 1992, pp 288–97.

[77] K Dobbs, "Plagued by Turnover? Train Your Managers," *Training,* August 2000, p 64.

[78] A complete description of this model is provided by E A Locke, "Job Satisfaction," in *Social Psychology and*

Organizational Behavior, eds M Gruneberg and T Wall (New York: John Wiley & Sons, 1984).

[79] See the related discussion in Perrewé and Hochwarter, "Can We Really Have It All?" pp 29–33.

[80] Results can be found in J Cohen-Charash and P E Spector, "The Role of Justice in Organizations: A Meta-Analysis," *Organizational Behavior and Human Decision Processes,* November 2001, pp 278–321.

[81] A thorough discussion of this model is provided by T A Judge and R J Larsen, "Dispositional Affect and Job Satisfaction: A Review and Theoretical Extension," *Organizational Behavior and Human Decision Processes,* September 2001, pp 67–98.

[82] Supportive results can be found in H M Weiss, J P Nicholas, and C S Daus, "An Examination of the Joint Effects of Affective Experiences and Job Beliefs on Job Satisfaction and Variances in Affective Experiences Over Time," *Organizational Behavior and Human Decision Processes,* April 1999, pp 1–24; and B M Staw and J Ross, "Stability in the Midst of Change: A Dispositional Approach to Job Attitudes," *Journal of Applied Psychology,* August 1985, pp 469–80.

[83] See R D Arvey, T J Bouchard, Jr, N L Segal, and L M Abraham, "Job Satisfaction: Environmental and Genetic Components," *Journal of Applied Psychology,* April 1989, pp 187–92.

[84] See C Dormann and D Zapf, "Job Satisfaction: A Meta-Analysis of Stabilities," *Journal of Organizational Behavior,* August 2001, pp 483–504.

[85] P Wakeman, "The Good Life and How to Get It," *Inc.,* February 2001, p 50.

[86] See Kinicki, McKee-Ryan, Schriesheim, and Carson, "Assessing the Construct Validity of the Job Descriptive Index."

[87] D W Organ, "The Motivational Basis of Organizational Citizenship Behavior," in *Research in Organizational Behavior,* eds B M Staw and L L Cummings (Greenwich, CT: JAI Press, 1990), p 46.

[88] Results can be found in J A LePine, A Erez, and D E Johnson, "The Nature and Dimensionality of Organizational Citizenship Behavior: A Critical Review and Meta-Analysis," *Journal of Applied Psychology,* February 2002, pp 52–65.

[89] Supportive results can be found in P M Podsakoff, S B MacKenzie, J B Paine, and D G Bachrach, "Organizational Citizenship Behaviors: A Critical Review of the Theoretical and Empirical Literature and Suggestions for Future Research," *Journal of Management,* 2000, pp 513–63.

[90] Supportive findings are presented in ibid; and LePine, Erez, and Johnson, "The Nature and Dimensionality of Organizational Citizenship Behavior."

[91] Results can be found in D J Koys, "The Effects of Employee Satisfaction, Organizational Citizenship Behavior, and Turnover on Organizational Effectiveness: A Unit-Level, Longitudinal Study," *Personnel Psychology,* Spring 2001, pp 101–14.

[92] See R D Hackett, "Work Attitudes and Employee Absenteeism: A Synthesis of the Literature," *Journal of Occupational Psychology,* 1989, pp 235–48.

[93] A thorough review of the various causes of employee turnover is provided by T R Mitchell and T W Lee, "The Unfolding Model of Voluntary Turnover and Job Embeddedness: Foundations for a Comprehensive Theory of Attachment," in *Research in Organizational Behavior,* eds B M Staw and R I Sutton (New York: JAI Press, 2001), pp 189–246.

[94] Results can be found in P W Hom and A J Kinicki, "Toward a Greater Understanding of How Dissatisfaction Drives Employee Turnover," *Academy of Management Journal,* October 2001, pp 975–87.

[95] Costs of turnover are discussed by R W Griffeth and P W Hom, *Retaining Valued Employees* (Thousand Oaks, CA: Sage Publications, 2001).

[96] Techniques for reducing employee turnover are thoroughly discussed in ibid.

[97] Results can be found in R W Griffeth, P W Hom, and S Gaertner, "A Meta-Analysis of Antecedents and Correlates of Employee Turnover: Update, Moderator Tests, and Research Implications for the Next Milennium," *Journal of Management,* 2000, pp 463–488.

[98] See P W Hom and R W Griffeth, *Employee Turnover* (Cincinnati: South Western, 1995), pp 35–50; and C Kalb and A Rogers, "Stress," *Newsweek,* June 14, 1999, pp 56–63.

[99] Results can be found in M A Blegen, "Nurses' Job Satisfaction: A Meta-Analysis of Related Variables," *Nursing Research,* January–February 1993, pp 36–41.

[100] The various models are discussed in T A Judge, C J Thoresen, J E Bono, and G K Patton, "The Job Satisfaction–Job Performance Relationship: A Qualitative and Quantitative Review," *Psychological Bulletin,* May 2001. pp 376–407.

[101] Results can be found in ibid.

[102] Ibid.

[103] These issues are discussed by C Ostroff, "The Relationship between Satisfaction, Attitudes, and Performance: An Organizational Level Analysis," *Journal of Applied Psychology,* December 1992, pp 963–74.

[104] Results can be found in J K Harter, F L Schmidt, and T L Hayes, "Business-Unit-Level Relationship between Employee Satisfaction, Employee Engagement, and Business Outcomes: A Meta-Analysis," *Journal of Applied Psychology,* April 2002, pp 268–79.

[105] Reprinted by permission of *Harvard Business Review.* From "Retention through Redemption" by D M Abrashoff, February 2001. Copyright © 2001 by the Harvard Business School Publishing Corporation; all rights reserved.

[106] The questionnaire and scoring key are from J W Slocum, Jr, and D Hellriegel, "A Look at How Managers' Minds Work," *Business Horizons,* July–August 1983, pp 58–68.

[107] This exercise was based on S M Dunphy and K E Aupperle, "Flight Plan: Motivation," *Training & Development,* October 2001, pp 18–19.

[108] Excerpted from M Schneider, "How an MBA Can Bend Your Mind," *Business Week,* April 1, 2002, p 12.

CHAPTER 7

[1] Excerpted from M Conlin, "Taking Precautions—or Harassing Workers?" *Business Week,* December 3, 2001, p 84.

[2] Details may be found in R Eisenberger, P Fasolo, and V Davis–LaMastro, "Perceived Organizational Support and Employee Diligence, Commitment, and Innovation," *Journal of Applied Psychology,* February 1990, pp 51–59.

[3] Supportive results are found in R Eisenberger, S Armeli, B Rexwinkel, P D Lynch, and L Rhoades, "Reciprocation of Perceived Organizational Support," *Journal of Applied Psychology,* February 2001, pp 42–51.

[4] S T Fiske and S E Taylor, *Social Cognition,* 2nd ed (Reading, MA: Addison-Wesley Publishing, 1991), pp 1–2.

[5] Adapted from discussion in Fiske and Taylor, *Social Cognition,* pp 247–50.

[6] The negativity bias was examined and supported by O Ybarra and W G Stephan, "Misanthropic Person Memory," *Journal of Personality and Social Psychology,* April 1996, pp 691–700.

[7] E Rosch, C B Mervis, W D Gray, D M Johnson, and P Boyes-Braem, "Basic Objects in Natural Categories," *Cognitive Psychology,* July 1976, p 383.

[8] Washing clothes.

[9] Results can be found in M Rotundo, D-H Nguyen, and P R Sackett, "A Meta-Analytic Review of Gender Differences in Perceptions of Sexual Harassment," *Journal of Applied Psychology,* October 2001, pp 914–22.

[10] Mood and information processing is discussed by J P Forgas and J M George, "Affective Influences on Judgments and Behavior in Organizations: An Information Processing Perspective," *Organizational Behavior and Human Decision Processes,* September 2001, pp 3–34.

[11] See A J Kinicki, P W Hom, M R Trost, and K J Wade, "Effects of Category Prototypes on Performance-Rating Accuracy," *Journal of Applied Psychology,* June 1995, pp 354–70.

[12] The relationship between depression and information processing is discussed by A Zelli and K A Dodge, "Personality Development from the Bottom Up," in *The Coherence of Personality,* eds D Cervone and Y Shoda (New York: Guilford Press, 1999), pp 94–126.

[13] For a thorough discussion about the structure and organization of memory, see L R Squire, B Knowlton, and G Musen, "The Structure and Organization of Memory," in *Annual Review of Psychology,* eds L W Porter and M R Rosenzweig (Palo Alto, CA: Annual Reviews Inc., 1993), vol. 44, pp 453–95.

[14] Results can be found in C M Marlowe, S L Schneider, and C E Nelson, "Gender and Attractiveness Biases in Hiring Decisions: Are More Experienced Managers Less Biased?" *Journal of Applied Psychology,* February 1996, pp 11–21.

[15] Details of this study can be found in C K Stevens, "Antecedents of Interview Interactions, Interviewers' Ratings,

and Applicants' Reactions," *Personnel Psychology,* Spring 1998, pp 55–85.

[16] See R C Mayer and J H Davis, "The Effect of the Performance Appraisal System on Trust for Management: A Field Quasi-Experiment," *Journal of Applied Psychology,* February 1999, pp 123–36.

[17] Results can be found in W H Bommer, J L Johnson, G A Rich, P M Podsakoff, and S B Mackenzie, "On the Interchangeability of Objective and Subjective Measures of Employee Performance: A Meta-Analysis," *Personnel Psychology,* Autumn 1995, pp 587–605.

[18] See J I Sanchez and P D L Torre, "A Second Look at the Relationship between Rating and Behavioral Accuracy in Performance Appraisal," *Journal of Applied Psychology,* February 1996, pp 3–10.

[19] The effectiveness of rater training was supported by D V Day and L M Sulsky, "Effects of Frame-of-Reference Training and Information Configuration on Memory Organization and Rating Accuracy," *Journal of Applied Psychology,* February 1995, pp 158–67.

[20] Results can be found in J S Phillips and R G Lord, "Schematic Information Processing and Perceptions of Leadership in Problem-Solving Groups," *Journal of Applied Psychology,* August 1982, pp 486–92.

[21] C Hymowitz, "Just How Much Should a Boss Reveal to Others about a Staffer's Firing?" *The Wall Street Journal,* March 19, 2002, p B1.

[22] S Power, "Mickey Mouse, Nike Give Advice on Air Security," *The Wall Street Journal,* January 24, 2002, p B4.

[23] C M Judd and B Park, "Definition and Assessment of Accuracy in Social Stereotypes," *Psychological Review,* January 1993, p 110.

[24] For a thorough discussion of stereotype accuracy, see M C Ashton and V M Esses, "Stereotype Accuracy: Estimating the Academic Performance of Ethnic Groups," *Personality and Social Psychology Bulletin,* February 1999, pp 225–36.

[25] Results can be found in E H James, "Race-Related Differences in Promotions and Support: Underlying Effects of Human and Social Capital," *Organization Science,* September–October 2000, pp 493–508.

[26] The study was conducted by K S Lyness and D E Thompson, "Climbing the Corporate Ladder: Do Female and Male Executives Follow the Same Route?" *Journal of Applied Psychology,* February 2000, pp 86–101.

[27] The process of stereotype formation and maintenance is discussed by S T Fiske, M Lin, and S L Neuberg, "The Continuum Model: Ten Years Later," in *Dual-Process Theories in Social Psychology,* eds S Chaiken and Y Trope (New York: Guilford Press, 1999) pp 231–54.

[28] This discussion is based on material presented in G V Bodenhausen, C N Macrae, and J W Sherman, "On the Dialectics of Discrimination," in *Dual-Process Theories in Social Psychology,* eds S Chaiken and Y Trope (New York: Guilford Press, 1999) pp 271–90.

[29] Results are reported in "USA Today Snapshots®," *USA Today,* March 15, 2001, p 8D.

[30] Results are reported in "USA Today Snapshots®," *USA Today,* March 14, 2001, p 5D.

[31] See B P Allen, "Gender Stereotypes Are Not Accurate: A Replication of Martin (1987) Using Diagnostic vs. Self-Report and Behavioral Criteria," *Sex Roles,* May 1995, pp 583–600.

[32] Results can be found in V E Schein, R Mueller, T Lituchy, and J Liu, "Think Manager—Think Male: A Global Phenomenon?" *Journal of Organizational Behavior,* January 1996, pp 33–41.

[33] See J D Olian, D P Schwab, and Y Haberfeld, "The Impact of Applicant Gender Compared to Qualifications on Hiring Recommendations: A Meta-Analysis of Experimental Studies," *Organizational Behavior and Human Decision Processes,* April 1988, pp 180–95.

[34] Results from the meta-analyses are discussed in K P Carson, C L Sutton, and P D Corner, "Gender Bias in Performance Appraisals: A Meta-Analysis," paper presented at the 49th Annual Academy of Management Meeting, Washington, DC: 1989. Results from the field study can be found in T J Maurer and M A Taylor, "Is Sex by Itself Enough? An Exploration of Gender Bias Issues in Performance Appraisal," *Organizational Behavior and Human Decision Processes,* November 1994, pp 231–51.

[35] See J Landau, "The Relationship of Race and Gender to Managers' Ratings of Promotion Potential," *Journal of Organizational Behavior,* July 1995, pp 391–400.

[36] Results from this study can be found in M Biernat, C S Crandall, L V Young, D Kobrynowicz, and S M Halpin, "All That You Can Be: Stereotyping of Self and Others in a Military Context," *Journal of Personality and Social Psychology,* August 1998, pp 301–17.

[37] For a complete review, see S R Rhodes, "Age-Related Differences in Work Attitudes and Behavior: A Review and Conceptual Analysis," *Psychological Bulletin,* March 1983, pp 328–67.

[38] Results were reported in E Kaplan-Leiserson, "Aged to Perfection," *Training & Development,* October 2001, pp 16–17.

[39] See G M McEvoy, "Cumulative Evidence of the Relationship between Employee Age and Job Performance," *Journal of Applied Psychology,* February 1989, pp 11–17.

[40] A thorough discussion of the relationship between age and performance is contained in D A Waldman and B J Avolio, "Aging and Work Performance in Perspective: Contextual and Developmental Considerations," in *Research in Personnel and Human Resources Management,* ed G R Ferris (Greenwich, CT: JAI Press, 1993), vol. 11, pp 133–62.

[41] For details, see B J Avolio, D A Waldman, and M A McDaniel, "Age and Work Performance in Nonmanagerial Jobs: The Effects of Experience and Occupational Type," *Academy of Management Journal,* June 1990, pp 407–22.

[42] D H Powell, "Aging Baby Boomers: Stretching Your Workforce Options," *HR Magazine,* July 1998, p 83.

[43] D G Albrecht, "Getting Ready for Older Workers," *Workforce,* February 2001, p 58.

[44] Results can be found in R W Griffeth, P W Hom, and S Gaertner, "A Meta-Analysis of Antecedents and Correlates of Employee Turnover: Update, Moderator Tests, and Research Implications for the Next Millennium," *Journal of Management,* 2000, pp 463–88.

[45] See J J Martocchio, "Age-Related Differences in Employee Absenteeism: A Meta-Analysis," *Psychology and Aging,* December 1989, pp 409–14.

[46] Various racial stereotypes are discussed by N London-Vargas, *Faces of Diversity* (New York: Vantage Press, 1999).

[47] See "Household Data Annual Averages: Employed Persons by Detailed Occupation, Sex, Race, and Hispanic Origin," Bureau of Labor Statistics, 2001 (www.bls.gov/cps/cpsaat11.pdf).

[48] Details of the study on race and attitudes may be found in J H Greenhaus, S Parasuraman, and W M Wormley, "Effects of Race on Organizational Experiences, Job Performance Evaluations, and Career Outcomes," *Academy of Management Journal,* March 1990, pp 64–86.

[49] Results from these studies can be found in A I Huffcutt and P L Roth, "Racial Group Differences in Employment Interview Evaluations," *Journal of Applied Psychology,* April 1998, pp 179–89; and T-R Lin, G H Dobbins, and J-L Farh, "A Field Study of Race and Age Similarity Effects on Interview Ratings in Conventional and Situational Interviews," *Journal of Applied Psychology,* June 1992, pp 363–71.

[50] See D A Waldman and B J Avolio, "Race Effects in Performance Evaluations: Controlling for Ability, Education, and Experience," *Journal of Applied Psychology,* December 1991, pp 897–901; and E D Pulakos, L A White, S H Oppler, and W C Borman, "Examination of Race and Sex Effects on Performance Ratings," *Journal of Applied Psychology,* October 1989, pp 770–80.

[51] Results can be found in Landau, "The Relationship of Race and Gender to Managers' Ratings of Promotion Potential."

[52] C M Schall, "The Americans with Disabilities Act—Are We Keeping Our Promise? An Analysis of the Effect of the ADA on the Employment of Persons with Disabilities," *Journal of Vocational Rehabilitation,* June 1998, p 191.

[53] Statistics on disabilities can be found in "Table 2. Labor Force Status—Work Disability Status of Civilians 16 to 74 Years Old, by Educational Attainment and Sex: 2001," March 2001 (www.census.gov/hhes/www/disable/cps/cps201.html).

[54] See "Employment Rates of People with Disabilities," National Organization of Disability, July 2001 (www.nod.org).

[55] Disability stereotypes are discussed by A Colella, "Organizational Socialization of Newcomers with Disabilities: A Framework for Future Research," in *Research in Personnel and Human Resources Management,* ed G R Ferris (Greenwich, CT: JAI Press, 1996), vol. 14, pp 351–417.

[56] The discussion about the performance of disabled employees and the costs of their employment was based on P Digh,

"People with Disabilities Show What They Can Do," *HR Magazine,* June 1998, pp 141–45.

[57] See Day and Sulsky, "Effects of Frame-of-Reference Training and Information Configuration on Memory Organization and Rating Accuracy."

[58] The background and results for this study are presented in R Rosenthal and L Jacobson, *Pygmalion in the Classroom: Teacher Expectation and Pupils' Intellectual Development* (New York: Holt, Rinehart & Winston, 1968).

[59] D B McNatt, "Ancient Pygmalion Joins Contemporary Management: A Meta-Analysis of the Result," *Journal of Applied Psychology,* April 2000, pp 314–22.

[60] Ibid.

[61] A summary of the samples used in past research is contained in N M Kierein and M A Gold, "Pygmalion in Work Organizations: A Meta-Analysis," *Journal of Organizational Behavior,* December 2000, pp 913–28.

[62] The Golem effect is defined and investigated by O B Davidson and D Eden, "Remedial Self-Fulfilling Prophecy: Two Field Experiments to Prevent Golem Effects among Disadvantaged Women," *Journal of Applied Psychology,* June 2000, pp 386–98.

[63] The role of positive expectations at Microsoft is discussed by S Hamm and O Port, "The Mother of All Software Projects," *Business Week,* February 22, 1999, pp 69, 72.

[64] Pygmalion leadership training is discussed by D Eden, D Geller, A Gewirtz, R Gordon-Terner, I Inbar, M Liberman, Y Pass, I Salomon-Segev, and M Shalit, "Implanting Pygmalion Leadership Style through Workshop Training: Seven Field Experiments," *Leadership Quarterly,* Summer 2000, pp 171–210.

[65] Kelley's model is discussed in detail in H H Kelley, "The Processes of Causal Attribution," *American Psychologist,* February 1973, pp 107–28.

[66] This research is discussed by J A Lepine and L Van Dyne, "Peer Responses to Low Performers: An Attributional Model of Helping in the Context of Groups," *Academy of Management Review,* January 2001, pp 67–84.

[67] See P D Sweeney, K Anderson, and S Bailey, "Attributional Style in Depression: A Meta-Analytic Review," *Journal of Personality and Social Psychology,* May 1986, pp 974–91.

[68] Results can be found in P J Corr and J A Gray, "Attributional Style as a Personality Factor in Insurance Sales Performance in the UK," *Journal of Occupational Psychology,* March 1996, pp 83–87.

[69] See G E Prussia, A J Kinicki, and J S Bracker, "Psychological and Behavioral Consequences of Job Loss: A Covariance Structure Analysis Using Weiner's (1985) Attribution Model," *Journal of Applied Psychology,* June 1993, pp 382–94.

[70] See B Weiner, *An Attributional Theory of Motivation and Emotion* (New York: Springer-Verlag, 1985).

[71] Results from these studies can be found in D A Hofmann and A Stetzer, "The Role of Safety Climate and Communication in Accident Interpretation: Implications for Learning from Negative Events," *Academy of Management Journal,* December 1998, pp 644–57; and I Choi, R E Nisbett, and A Norenzayan, "Causal Attribution Across Cultures: Variation and Universality," *Psychological Bulletin,* January 1999, pp 47–63.

[72] D Bickley, "Russians Won't Stop Whining," *Arizona Republic,* February 23, 2002, p C1.

[73] Results can be found in E W K Tsang, "Self-Serving Attributions in Corporate Annual Reports: A Replicated Study," *Journal of Management Studies,* January 2002, pp 51–65.

[74] This research is summarized by T S Duval and P J Silvia, "Self-Awareness, Probability of Improvement, and the Self-Serving Bias," *Journal of Personality and Social Psychology,* January 2002, pp 49–61.

[75] Ibid., p 58.

[76] Details may be found in S E Moss and M J Martinko, "The Effects of Performance Attributions and Outcome Dependence on Leader Feedback Behavior Following Poor Subordinate Performance," *Journal of Organizational Behavior,* May 1998, pp 259–74; and E C Pence, W C Pendleton, G H Dobbins, and J A Sgro, "Effects of Causal Explanations and Sex Variables on Recommendations for Corrective Actions Following Employee Failure," *Organizational Behavior and Human Performance,* April 1982, pp 227–40.

[77] See D Konst, R Vonk, and R V D Vlist, "Inferences about Causes and Consequences of Behavior of Leaders and Subordinates," *Journal of Organizational Behavior,* March 1999, pp 261–71.

[78] See M Miserandino, "Attributional Retraining as a Method of Improving Athletic Performance," *Journal of Sport Behavior,* August 1998, pp 286–97.

[79] Excerpted from A Fisher, "Finished at Forty," *Fortune,* February 1, 1999, pp 50–54, 60.

[80] This exercise was modified from one contained in L Gardenwartz and A Rowe, *Diverse Teams at Work* (New York: McGraw-Hill, 1994), p 169. © 1994. Reproduced with permission of The McGraw-Hill Companies.

[81] The worksheet was adapted from ibid, p 169.

[82] Excerpted from Jason Leopold, "En-Ruse? Workers at Enron Say They Posed as Busy Traders to Impress Visiting Analysts," *The Wall Street Journal,* February 17, 2002, p C1.

CHAPTER 8

[1] Excerpted from J L Lunsford, "Lean Times: With Airbus on Its Tail, Boeing Is Rethinking How It Builds Planes," *The Wall Street Journal,* October 5, 2001, pp A1, A16.

[2] T R Mitchell, "Motivation: New Direction for Theory, Research, and Practice," *Academy of Management Review,* January 1982, p 81.

[3] This discussion is based on T R Mitchell, "Matching Motivational Strategies with Organizational Contexts," in *Research in Organizational Behavior,* vol. 19, eds L L Cummings and B M Staw (Greenwich, CT: JAI Press, 1997), pp 57–149.

[4] S Boehle, "From Humble Roots," *Training,* October 2000, p 108.

[5] Ibid., pp 106–13.

[6] See D Foust, "Whipping a Behemoth into Shape," *Business Week,* January 21, 2002, p 64.

[7] Mitchell, "Motivation," p 83.

[8] The role of emotions at work is thoroughly discussed by N M Ashkanasy and C S Daus, "Emotion in the Workplace: The New Challenge for Managers," *Academy of Management Executive,* February 2002, pp 76–86.

[9] For a complete description of Maslow's theory, see A H Maslow, "A Theory of Human Motivation," *Psychological Review,* July 1943, pp 370–96.

[10] M Murray, "An Added Benefit for Workers: Flexibility," *The Wall Street Journal,* April 29, 2001, p D7.

[11] K Tyler, "A Roof over Their Heads," *HR Magazine,* February 2001, p 41.

[12] For a complete review of ERG theory, see CP Alderfer, *Existence, Relatedness, and Growth: Human Needs in Organizational Settings* (New York: Free Press, 1972).

[13] See ibid; and J P Wanous and A Zwany, "A Cross-Sectional Test of Need Hierarchy Theory," *Organizational Behavior and Human Performance,* February 1977, pp 78–97.

[14] See S Glazer, "Past, Present and Future of Cross-Cultural Studies in Industrial and Organizational Psychology," in *International Review of Industrial and Organizational Psychology,* vol. 17, eds C L Cooper and I T Robertson (West Sussex, England: John Wiley, 2002), pp 145–86.

[15] Results can be found in "Women's Work Hours on Rise, Survey Says," *Arizona Republic,* May 8, 2002, p A11.

[16] L Buchanan, "Managing One-to-One," *Inc.,* October 2001, p 87.

[17] Results can be found in S D Bluen, J Barling, and W Burns, "Predicting Sales Performance, Job Satisfaction, and Depression by Using the Achievement Strivings and Impatience–Irritability Dimensions of Type A Behavior," *Journal of Applied Psychology,* April 1990, pp 212–16; and D C McClelland, *The Achieving Society* (New York: Free Press, 1961).

[18] H A Murray, *Explorations in Personality* (New York: John Wiley & Sons, 1938), p 164.

[19] Recent studies of achievement motivation can be found in H Grant and C S Dweck, "A Goal Analysis of Personality and Personality Coherence," in *The Coherence of Personality,* eds D Cervone and Y Shoda (New York: Guilford Press, 1999), pp 345–71.

[20] See K G Shaver, "The Entrepreneurial Personality Myth," *Business and Economic Review,* April–June 1995, pp 20–23.

[21] Research on the affiliative motive can be found in R F Baumeister and M R Leary, "The Need to Belong: Desire for Interpersonal Attachments as a Fundamental Human Motivation," *Psychological Bulletin,* May 1995, pp 497–529.

[22] Results from these studies are discussed in S Shellenbarger, "Along with Benefits and Pay, Employees Seek Friends on the Job," *The Wall Street Journal,* February 20, 2002, p B1; and D Jones, "Rule-Breaking Turns into Boss-Training," *USA Today,* February 20, 2002, pp 1B, 2B.

[23] See the following studies: D K McNeese-Smith, "The Relationship between Managerial Motivation, Leadership, Nurse Outcomes and Patient Satisfaction," *Journal of Organizational Behavior,* March 1999, pp 243–59; and A M Harrell and M J Stahl, "A Behavioral Decision Theory Approach for Measuring McClelland's Trichotomy of Needs," *Journal of Applied Psychology,* April 1981, pp 242–47.

[24] For a review of the foundation of achievement motivation training, see D C McClelland, "Toward a Theory of Motive Acquisition," *American Psychologist,* May 1965, pp 321–33. Evidence for the validity of motivation training can be found in H Heckhausen and S Krug, "Motive Modification," in *Motivation and Society,* ed A J Stewart (San Francisco: Jossey-Bass, 1982).

[25] Results can be found in D B Turban and T L Keon, "Organizational Attractiveness: An Interactionist Perspective," *Journal of Applied Psychology,* April 1993, pp 184–93.

[26] See D Steele Johnson and R Perlow, "The Impact of Need for Achievement Components on Goal Commitment and Performance," *Journal of Applied Social Psychology,* November 1992, pp 1711–20.

[27] J L Bowditch and A F Buono, *A Primer on Organizational Behavior* (New York: John Wiley & Sons, 1985), p 210.

[28] This framework was proposed by M A Campion and P W Thayer, "Development and Field Evaluation of an Interdisciplinary Measure of Job Design," *Journal of Applied Psychology,* February 1985, pp 29–43.

[29] These outcomes are discussed by J R Edwards, J A Scully, and M D Brtek, "The Nature and Outcomes of Work: A Replication and Extension of Interdisciplinary Work-Design Research," *Journal of Applied Psychology,* December 2000, pp 860–68.

[30] G D Babcock, *The Taylor System in Franklin Management,* 2nd ed (New York: Engineering Magazine Company, 1917), p 31.

[31] For a thorough discussion, see F B Copley, *Frederick W Taylor: The Principles of Scientific Management* (New York: Harper & Brothers, 1911).

[32] Supporting results can be found in B Melin, U Lundberg, J Söderlund, and M Granqvist, "Psychological and Physiological Stress Reactions of Male and Female Assembly Workers: A Comparison between Two Different Forms of Work Organization," *Journal of Organizational Behavior,* January 1999, pp 47–61; and S Melamed, I Ben-Avi, J Luz, and M S Green, "Objective and Subjective Work Monotony: Effects on Job Satisfaction, Psychological Distress, and Absenteeism in Blue-Collar Workers," *Journal of Applied Psychology,* February 1995, pp 29–42.

[33] See Edwards, Scully, and Brtek, "The Nature and Outcomes of Work."

[34] T Aeppel, "More, More, More: Rust-Belt Factor Lifts Productivity, and Staff Finds It's No Picnic," *The Wall Street Journal,* May 18, 1999, p A1.

[35] See ibid, pp A1, A10.

[36] This type of program was developed and tested by M A Campion and C L McClelland, "Follow-Up and Extension of the Interdisciplinary Costs and Benefits of Enlarged Jobs," *Journal of Applied Psychology,* June 1993, pp 339–51.

[37] S F Gale, "Bringing Good Leaders to Light," *Training,* June 2001, p 41.

[38] See F Herzberg, B Mausner, and B B Snyderman, *The Motivation to Work* (New York: John Wiley & Sons, 1959).

[39] F Herzberg, "One More Time: How Do You Motivate Employees?" *Harvard Business Review,* January–February 1968, p 56.

[40] For a thorough review of research on Herzberg's theory, see C C Pinder, *Work Motivation: Theory, Issues, and Applications* (Glenview, IL: Scott, Foresman, 1984).

[41] J R Hackman, G R Oldham, R Janson, and K Purdy, "A New Strategy for Job Enrichment," *California Management Review,* Summer 1975, p 58.

[42] Definitions of the job characteristics were adapted from J R Hackman and G R Oldham, "Motivation through the Design of Work: Test of a Theory," *Organizational Behavior and Human Performance,* August 1976, pp 250–79.

[43] A review of this research can be found in M L Ambrose and C T Kulik, "Old Friends, New Faces: Motivation Research in the 1990s," *Journal of Management,* 1999, pp 231–92.

[44] C L Cole, "Sun Microsystems' Solution to Traffic That Doesn't Move? Satellite Work Centers," *Workforce,* January 2001, pp 108, 110.

[45] Results can be found in M R Kelley, "New Process Technology, Job Design, and Work Organization: A Contingency Model," *American Sociological Review,* April 1990, pp 191–208.

[46] Productivity studies are reviewed in R E Kopelman, *Managing Productivity in Organizations* (New York: McGraw-Hill, 1986).

[47] The turnover meta-analysis was conducted by R W Griffeth, P W Hom, and S Gaertner, "A Meta-Analysis of Antecedents and Correlates of Employee Turnover: Update, Moderator Tests, and Research Implications for the Next Millennium," *Journal of Management,* 2000, pp 463–88. Absenteeism results are discussed in Y Fried and G R Ferris, "The Validity of the Job Characteristics Model: A Review and Meta-Analysis," *Personnel Psychology,* Summer 1987, pp 287–322.

48 See K Dobbs, "Knowing How to Keep Your Best and Brightest," *Workforce,* April 2001, pp 557–60.

49 A thorough discussion of reengineering and associated outcomes can be found in J Champy, *Reengineering Management: The Mandate for New Leadership* (New York: Harper Business, 1995).

50 See J D Jonge, C Dormann, P P M Hanssen, M F Dollard, J A Landeweerd, and F J N Nihuis, "Testing Reciprocal Relationships between Job Characteristics and Psychological Well-Being: A Cross-Lagged Structural Equation Model," *Journal of Occupational and Organizational Psychology,* March 2001, pp 29–46.

51 This description was taken from Edwards, Scully, and Brtek, "The Nature and Outcomes of Work."

52 S Armour, "Young Tech Workers Face Crippling Injuries," *USA Today,* February 9, 2001, p 2B.

53 This description was taken from Edwards, Scully, and Brtek, "The Nature and Outcomes of Work."

54 These descriptions were excerpted from J Prichard, "Reinventing the Office," *Arizona Republic,* January 16, 2002, p D1.

55 Armour, "Young Tech Workers Face Crippling Injuries," p 2B.

56 The guidelines are summarized in "How to Cope with the New Standard," *HR Focus,* January 2001, pp 1, 13, 14.

57 The relationship between self-management and intrinsic motivation is discussed by K W Thomas, *Intrinsic Motivation at Work: Building Energy and Commitment* (San Francisco: Berrett-Koehler Publishers, 2000).

58 The definition and discussion of intrinsic motivation were drawn from R M Ryan and E L Deci, "Intrinsic and Extrinsic Motivations: Classic Definitions and New Directions," *Comtemporary Educational Psychology,* January 2000, pp 54–67.

59 The definition and discussion of extrinsic motivation were drawn from ibid.

60 See E L Deci, R Koestner, and R M Ryan, "A Meta-Analytic Review of Experiments Examining the Effects of Extrinsic Rewards on Intrinsic Motivation," *Psychological Bulletin,* November 1999, pp 627–68; and R Eisenberger, W D Pierce, and J Cameron, "Effects of Reward on Intrinsic Motivation— Negative, Neutral, and Positive: Comment on Deci, Koestner, and Ryan (1999)," *Psychological Bulletin,* November 1999, pp 677–91.

61 See K W Thomas, E Jansen, and W G Tymon, Jr, "Navigating in the Realm of Theory: An Empowering View of Construct Development," in *Research in Organizational Change and Development,* vol. 10, eds W A Pasmore and R W Woodman (Greenwich, CT: JAI Press, 1997), pp 1–30.

62 See E L Deci and R M Ryan, "The 'What' and 'Why' of Goal Pursuits: Human Needs and Self-Determination of Behavior," *Psychological Inquiry,* December 2000, pp 227–68.

63 Thomas, *Intrinsic Motivation at Work,* p 44.

64 Results are presented in J Barbian, "In the Battle to Attract Talent, Companies Are Finding New Ways to Keep Employees Smiling," *Training,* January 2001, pp 93–96.

65 Thomas, *Intrinsic Motivation at Work,* p 44.

66 Details are provided in K Dobbs, "Knowing How to Keep Your Best and Brightest," *Workforce,* April 2001, pp 57–60.

67 Thomas, *Intrinsic Motivation at Work,* p 44.

68 Results were presented in M Littman, "Best Bosses Tell All," *Working Woman,* October 2000, p 51.

69 Thomas, *Intrinsic Motivation at Work,* p 44.

70 This study is summarized by S Ellingwood, "On a Mission," *Gallup Management Journal,* Winter 2001, pp 6–7.

71 Littman, "Best Bosses Tell All," p 55.

72 Ibid., p 54.

73 Excerpted from Buchanan, "Managing One-to-One," pp 84, 87.

74 The complete JDS can be found in J R Hackman and G R Oldham, *Work Redesign* (Reading, MA: Addison-Wesley, 1980).

75 The JDS and its norms were adapted from Hackman and Oldham, *Work Redesign,* pp 280, 281, 317.

76 Excerpted from S Shellenbarger, "Employees Are Seeking Fewer Hours; Maybe Bosses Should Listen," *The Wall Street Journal,* February 21, 2001, p B1.

CHAPTER 9

1 Excerpted from E O Welles, "Great Expectations," *Inc.,* March 2001, pp 70, 72.

2 See L Festinger, *A Theory of Cognitive Dissonance* (Stanford, CA: Stanford University Press, 1957).

3 Retaliation in response to perceived injustice was investigated by D P Skarlicki and R Folger, "Retaliation in the Workplace: The Roles of Distributive, Procedural, and Interactional Justice," *Journal of Applied Psychology,* June 1997, pp 434–43.

4 A Geller, "Theft by US Employees Rises," *Arizona Republic,* March 25, 2002, p D1.

5 The generalizability of the equity norm was examined by J K Giacobbe-Miller, D J Miller, and V I Victorov, "A Comparison of Russian and US Pay Allocation Decisions, Distributive Justice Judgments, and Productivity Under Different Payment Conditions," *Personnel Psychology,* Spring 1998, pp 137–63.

6 The choice of a comparison person is discussed by P P Shah, "Who Are Employees' Social Referents? Using a Network Perspective to Determine Referent Others," *Academy of Management Journal,* June 1998, pp 249–68.

7 M N Bing and S M Burroughs, "The Predictive and Interactive Effects of Equity Sensitivity in Teamwork-Oriented Organizations," *Journal of Organizational Behavior,* May 2001, p 271.

[8] Types of equity sensitivity are discussed in ibid., pp 271–90; and K S Sauley and A G Bedeian, "Equity Sensitivity: Construction of a Measure and Examination of Its Psychometric Properties," *Journal of Management,* 2000, pp 885–910.

[9] Results can be found in Y Cohen-Charash and P E Spector, "The Role of Justice in Organizations: A Meta-Analysis," *Organizational Behavior and Human Decision Processes,* November 2001, pp 278–321.

[10] For a thorough review of organizational justice theory and research, see R Cropanzano, D E Rupp, C J Mohler, and M Schminke, "Three Roads to Organizational Justice," in *Research in Personnel and Human Resources Management,* vol. 20, eds G R Ferris (New York: JAI Press, 2001), pp 269–329.

[11] J A Colquitt, D E Conlon, M J Wesson, C O L H Porter, and K Y Ng, "Justice at the Millennium: A Meta-Analytic Review of 25 Years of Organizational Justice Research," *Journal of Applied Psychology,* June 2001, p 426.

[12] E Tahmincioglu, "Electronic Workplace Vulnerable to Revenge," *Arizona Republic,* August 6, 2001, p D1.

[13] Results can be found in R W Griffeth, R P Vecchio, and J W Logan, Jr, "Equity Theory and Interpersonal Attraction," *Journal of Applied Psychology,* June 1989, pp 394–401; and R P Vecchio, "Predicting Worker Performance in Inequitable Settings," *Academy of Management Review,* January 1982, pp 103–10.

[14] See J Greenberg, "Stealing in the Name of Justice: Informational and Interpersonal Moderators of Theft Reactions to Underpayment Inequity," *Organizational Behavior and Human Decision Process,* February 1993, pp 81–103.

[15] Results from these two studies can be found in Cohen-Charash and Spector, "The Role of Justice in Organizations"; and Colquitt, Conlon, Wesson, Porter, and Ng, "Justice at the Millennium."

[16] R C Ford, "Darden Restaurants CEO Joe Lee on the Impact of Core Values: Integrity and Fairness," *Academy of Management Executive,* February 2002, p 35.

[17] The role of voice in justice perceptions was investigated by D R Avery and M A Quiñones, "Disentangling the Effects of Voice: The Incremental Roles of Opportunity, Behavior, and Instrumentality in Predicting Procedural Fairness," *Journal of Applied Psychology,* February 2002, pp 81–86.

[18] Supporting studies were conducted by D P Skarlicki, R Folger, and P Tesluk, "Personality as a Moderator in the Relationship between Fairness and Retaliation," *Academy of Management Journal,* February 1999, pp 100–8.

[19] Supportive results can be found in B J Tepper, "Health Consequences of Organizational Injustice: Tests of Main and Interactive Effects," *Organizational Behavior and Human Decision Processes,* November 2001, pp 197–215; and S Fox, P E Spector, and D Miles, "Counterproductive Work Behavior (CWB) in Response to Job Stressors and Organizational Justice: Some Mediator and Moderator Tests for Autonomy and Emotions," *Journal of Vocational Behavior,* December 2001, pp 291–309.

[20] The role of equity in organizational change is thoroughly discussed by A T Cobb, R Folger, and K Wooten, "The Role Justice Plays in Organizational Change," *Public Administration Quarterly,* Summer 1995, pp 135–51.

[21] A comparison of individual and group perceptions of justice was conducted by E A Lind, L Kray, and L Thompson, "The Social Comparison of Injustice: Fairness Judgments in Response to Own and Others' Unfair Treatment by Authorities," *Organizational Behavior and Human Decision Processes,* July 1998, pp 1–22.

[22] See B M Goldman, "Toward an Understanding of Employment Discrimination Claiming: An Integration of Organizational Justice and Social Information Processing Theories," *Personnel Psychology,* Summer 2001, pp 361–86.

[23] Results can be found in K W Mossholder, N Bennett, and C L Martin, "A Multilevel Analysis of Procedural Justice Context," *Journal of Organizational Behavior,* March 1998, pp 131–41.

[24] The relationship between organizational justice and customer service is discussed by D E Bowen, S W Gilliland, and R Folger, "HRM Service Fairness: How Being Fair with Employees Spills Over to Customers," *Organizational Dynamics,* Winter 1999, pp 7–23.

[25] For a complete discussion of Vroom's theory, see V H Vroom, *Work and Motivation* (New York: John Wiley & Sons, 1964).

[26] E E Lawler III, *Motivation in Work Organizations* (Belmont, CA: Wadsworth, 1973), p 45.

[27] M Conlin and R Berner, "A Little Less in the Envelope This Week," *Business Week,* February 18, 2002, p 65.

[28] See J Chowdhury, "The Motivational Impact of Sales Quotas on Effort," *Journal of Marketing Research,* February 1993, pp 28–41; and C C Pinder, *Work Motivation* (Glenview, IL: Scott, Foresman, 1984), ch 7.

[29] M Frase-Blunt, "Driving Home Your Awards Program," *HR Magazine,* February 2001, p 109.

[30] The measurement and importance of valence was investigated by N T Feather, "Values, Valences, and Choice: The Influence of Values on the Perceived Attractiveness and Choice of Alternatives," *Journal of Personality and Social Psychology,* June 1995, pp 1135–51; and A Pecotich and G A Churchill, Jr, "An Examination of the Anticipated-Satisfaction Importance Valence Controversy," *Organizational Behavior and Human Performance,* April 1981, pp 213–26.

[31] "Federal Express's Fred Smith," *Inc.,* October 1986, p 38.

[32] For a thorough discussion of the model, see L W Porter and E E Lawler III, *Managerial Attitudes and Performance* (Homewood, IL: Richard D Irwin, 1968).

[33] Results can be found in W van Eerde and H Thierry, "Vroom's Expectancy Models and Work-Related Criteria: A Meta-Analysis," *Journal of Applied Psychology,* October 1996, pp 575–86.

[34] See J P Wanous, T L Keon, and J C Latack, "Expectancy Theory and Occupational/Organizational Choices: A Review

and Test," *Organizational Behavior and Human Performance,* August 1983, pp 66–86.

[35] These results are based on G P Latham, "The Importance of Understanding and Changing Employee Outcome Expectancies for Gaining Commitment to an Organizational Goal," *Personnel Psychology,* Autumn 2001, pp 707–16; C L Haworth and P E Levy, "The Importance of Instrumentality Beliefs in the Prediction of Organizational Citizenship Behaviors," *Journal of Vocational Behavior,* August 2001, pp 64–75; R M Lynd-Stevenson, "Expectancy-Value Theory and Predicting Future Employment Status in the Young Unemployed," *Journal of Occupational and Organizational Psychology,* March 1999, pp 101–6; E D Pulakos and N Schmitt, "A Longitudinal Study of a Valence Model Approach for the Prediction of Job Satisfaction of New Employees," *Journal of Applied Psychology,* May 1983, pp 307–12; A J Kinicki, "Predicting Occupational Role Choices for Involuntary Job Loss," *Journal of Vocational Behavior,* October 1989, pp 204–18; T A DeCotiis and J-Y LeLouarn, "A Predictive Study of Voting Behavior in a Representation Election Using Union Instrumentality and Work Perceptions," *Organizational Behavior and Human Performance,* February 1981, pp 103–18; P W Hom, "Expectancy Prediction of Reenlistment in the National Guard," *Journal of Vocational Behavior,* April 1980, pp 235–48; D F Parker and L Dyer, "Expectancy Theory as a Within-Person Behavioral Choice Model: An Empirical Test of Some Conceptual and Methodological Refinements," *Organizational Behavior and Human Performance,* October 1976, pp 97–117; and A W Stacy, K F Widaman, and G A Marlatt, "Expectancy Models of Alcohol Use," *Journal of Personality and Social Psychology,* May 1990, pp 918–28.

[36] For a review of the criticisms of expectancy theory, see F J Landy and W S Becker, "Motivation Theory Reconsidered," in *Research in Organizational Behavior,* vol. 9, eds L L Cummings and B M Staw (Greenwich, CT: JAI Press, 1987), pp 1–38.

[37] Components of coaching are discussed by M Fleschner, "The Winning Season: How Legendary Wrestling Coach Dan Gable Built Championships to Last," *Selling Power,* April 1998, pp 14, 16.

[38] Supportive results are presented in L Morris, "Employees Not Encouraged to Go Extra Mile," *Training & Development,* April 1996, pp 59–60.

[39] See D R Spitzer, "Power Rewards: Rewards That Really Motivate," *Management Review,* May 1996, pp 45–50; and A Kohn, *Punished by Rewards: The Trouble with Gold Stars, Incentive Plans, A's, Praise, and Other Bribes* (Boston: Houghton Mifflin, 1993).

[40] Results from these studies can be found in G D Jenkins, Jr, A Mitra, N Gupta, and J D Shaw, "Are Financial Incentives Related to Performance? A Meta-Analytic Review of Empirical Research," *Journal of Applied Psychology,* October 1998, pp 777–87.

[41] See S Kerr, "Organizational Rewards: Practical, Cost-Neutral Alternatives That You May Know, But Don't Practice," *Organizational Dynamics,* Summer 1999, pp 61–70.

[42] E Zehnder, "A Simpler Way to Pay," *Harvard Business Review,* April 2001, pp 54, 56.

[43] R Charan, "Conquering a Culture of Indecision," *Harvard Business Review,* April 2001, pp 75–82.

[44] E A Locke, K N Shaw, L M Saari, and G P Latham, "Goal Setting and Task Performance: 1969–1980," *Psychological Bulletin,* July 1981, p 126.

[45] Ibid.

[46] A thorough discussion of MBO is provided by P F Drucker, *The Practice of Management* (New York: Harper, 1954); and P F Drucker, "What Results Should You Expect? A User's Guide to MBO," *Public Administration Review,* January–February 1976, pp 12–19.

[47] Results from both studies can be found in R Rodgers and J E Hunter, "Impact of Management by Objectives on Organizational Productivity," *Journal of Applied Psychology,* April 1991, pp 322–36; and R Rodgers, J E Hunter, and D L Rogers, "Influence of Top Management Commitment on Management Program Success," *Journal of Applied Psychology,* February 1993, pp 151–55.

[48] M Campbell, "Dream Work: How Steven Spielberg, the Most Successful Film Director of All Time, Turned His Dreams into Reality," *Selling Power,* April 1999, pp 92–93.

[49] Supportive results can be found in G Oettingen, H-J Pak, and K Schnetter, "Self-Regulation of Goal Setting: Turning Free Fantasies about the Future into Binding Goals," *Journal of Personality and Social Psychology,* May 2001, pp 736–53.

[50] "Empire Builders," *Business Week e.biz,* May 14, 2001, p EB-28.

[51] Results can be found in P M Wright, "Operationalization of Goal Difficulty as a Moderator of the Goal Difficulty-Performance Relationship," *Journal of Applied Psychology,* June 1990, pp 227–34.

[52] This linear relationship was not supported by P M Wright, J R Hollenbeck, S Wolf, and G C McMahan, "The Effects of Varying Goal Difficulty Operationalizations on Goal Setting Outcomes and Processes," *Organizational Behavior and Human Decision Processes,* January 1995, pp 28–43.

[53] See Locke, Shaw, Saari, and Latham, "Goal Setting and Task Performance: 1969–1980"; and A J Mento, R P Steel, and R J Karren, "A Meta-Analytic Study of the Effects of Goal Setting on Task Performance: 1966–1984," *Organizational Behavior and Human Decision Processes,* February 1987, pp 52–83.

[54] Results from the meta-analysis can be found in R E Wood, A J Mento, and E A Locke, "Task Complexity as a Moderator of Goal Effects: A Meta-Analysis," *Journal of Applied Psychology,* August 1987, pp 416–25.

[55] See the related discussion in L A King, "Personal Goals and Personal Agency: Linking Everyday Goals to Future Images of the Self," in *Personal Control in Action: Cognitive and Motivational Mechanisms,* eds M Kofta, G Weary, and G Sedek (New York: Plenum Press, 1998), pp 109–28.

[56] See R P DeShon and R A Alexander, "Goal Setting Effects on Implicit and Explicit Learning of Complex Tasks," *Organizational Behavior and Human Decision Processes,* January 1996, pp 18–36.

[57] Results can be found in K H Doerr, T R Mitchell, T D Klastorin, and K A Brown, "Impact of Material Flow Policies and Goals on Job Outcomes," *Journal of Applied Psychology,* April 1996, pp 142–52.

[58] Supportive results can be found in K L Langeland, C M Johnson, and T C Mawhinney, "Improving Staff Performance in a Community Mental Health Setting: Job Analysis, Training, Goal Setting, Feedback, and Years of Data," *Journal of Organizational Behavior Management,* 1998, pp 21–43.

[59] See E A Locke and G P Latham, *A Theory of Goal Setting and Task Performance* (Englewood Cliffs, NJ: Prentice Hall, 1990).

[60] See J J Donovan and D J Radosevich, "The Moderating Role of Goal Commitment on the Goal Difficulty-Performance Relationship: A Meta-Analytic Review and Critical Reanalysis," *Journal of Applied Psychology,* April 1998, pp 308–15.

[61] Results can be found in G H Seijts and G P Latham, "The Effect of Distal Learning, Outcome, and Proximal Goals on a Moderately Complex Task," *Journal of Organizational Behavior,* May 2001, pp 291–307.

[62] For information on how to best measure goal commitment, see H J Klein, M J Wesson, J R Hollenbeck, P M Wright, and R P DeShon, "The Assessment of Goal Commitment: A Measurement Model Meta-Analysis," *Organizational Behavior and Human Decision Processes,* May 2001, pp 32–55.

[63] See the related discussion in T P Flannery, D A Hofrichter, and P E Platten, *People, Performance, & Pay* (New York: Free Press, 1996).

[64] See P M Wright, J M George, S R Farnsworth, and G C McMahan, "Productivity and Extra-Role Behavior: The Effects of Goals and Incentives on Spontaneous Helping," *Journal of Applied Psychology,* June 1993, pp 374–81.

[65] Supporting results can be found in S W Gilliland and R S Landis, "Quality and Quantity Goals in a Complex Decision Task: Strategies and Outcomes," *Journal of Applied Psychology,* October 1992, pp 672–81.

[66] See J A Colquitt and M J Simmering, "Conscientiousness, Goal Orientation, and Motivation to Learn During the Learning Process: A Longitudinal Study," *Journal of Applied Psychology,* August 1998, pp 654–65.

[67] D VandeWalle, S P Brown, W L Cron, and J W Slocum, Jr, "The Influence of Goal Orientation and Self-Regulated Tactics on Sales Performance: A Longitudinal Field Test," *Journal of Applied Psychology,* April 1999, p 250.

[68] See D VandeWalle, "Goal Orientation: Why Wanting to Look Successful Doesn't Always Lead to Success," *Organizational Dynamics,* 2001, pp 162–71; and D VandeWalle, W L Cron, and J W Slocum Jr, "The Role of Goal Orientation Following Performance Feedback," *Journal of Applied Psychology,* August 2001, pp 629–40.

[69] E A Locke and G P Latham, *Goal Setting: A Motivational Technique That Works!* (Englewood Cliffs, NJ: Prentice-Hall, 1984), p 79.

[70] T R Mitchell, "Motivation: New Directions for Theory, Research, and Practice," *Academy of Management Review,* January 1982, p 81.

[71] Elements of an effective appraisal system are discussed by C Joinson, "Making Sure Employees Measure Up," *HR Magazine,* March 2001, pp 36–41.

[72] C Hymowitz, "Ranking Systems Gain Popularity but Have Many Staffers Riled," *The Wall Street Journal,* May 15, 2001, p B1.

[73] See D J Burrough, "More Firms Rank Employees," *Arizona Republic,* May 20, 2001, p E1.

[74] "HMO Clerks Who Pare Doctor Visits Rewarded," *Arizona Republic,* May 18, 2002, p A10.

[75] See J Appleby, "HMO to Pay Bonuses for Good Care," *USA Today,* July 11, 2001, p 3B.

[76] P L Moore, "The Most Aggressive CEO," *Business Week,* May 28, 2001, p 77.

[77] Excerpted from M Conlin, "The Big Squeeze on Workers," *Business Week,* May 13, 2002, pp 96–97.

[78] Actual survey rankings are as follows: (1) interesting work, (2) full appreciation of work done, (3) feeling of being in on things, (4) job security, (5) good wages, (6) promotion and growth in the organization, (7) good working conditions, (8) personal loyalty to employees, (9) tactful discipline, and (10) sympathetic help with personal problems.

[79] Reprinted by permission of Kinicki and Associates, Inc. "The Case of the Missing Form," by A Kinicki, *Performance Management Systems,* pp 3–34, 3–35. Copyright © 1992 by Kinicki and Associates, Inc.; all rights reserved.

[80] Excerpted from C Bellamy, "Teacher Resigns as School Backs Plagiarizing Kids," *Arizona Republic,* February 10, 2002, p A21.

CHAPTER 10

[1] Excerpted from A C Poe, "Online Recognition," *HR Magazine,* June 2002, pp 95–103.

[2] "Workplace Changes Employees Want to See," *Management Review,* January 1999, p 6.

[3] R Aubrey and P M Cohen, *Working Wisdom: Timeless Skills and Vanguard Strategies for Learning Organizations* (San Francisco: Jossey-Bass, 1995), p 4.

[4] For instance, see "Worker Retention Presents Challenge to US Employers," *HR Magazine,* September 1998, p 22; L Wah, "An Ounce of Prevention," *Management Review,* October 1998, p 9; S Armour, "Cash or Critiques: Which Is Best?" *USA Today,* December 16, 1998, p 6B; R R Callister, M W Kramer, and D B Turban, "Feedback Seeking Following Career Transitions," *Academy of Management Journal,* August 1999, pp 429–38;

and T D Ludwig and F S Geller, "Intervening to Improve the Safety of Occupational Driving: A Behavior-Change Model and Review of Empirical Evidence," *Journal of Organizational Behavior Management,* no. 4, 2000, pp 1–124.

5 Data from "Fortune 500 Largest US Corporations," *Fortune,* April 15, 2002, p F57.

6 As quoted in C Fishman, "Fred Smith," *Fast Company,* June 2001, p 66.

7 C Bell and R Zemke, "On-Target Feedback," *Training,* June 1992, p 36. Also see R Zemke, "The Feather Factor: You Gotta Believe," *Training,* May 2002, p 10.

8 Both the definition of feedback and the functions of feedback are based on discussion in D R Ilgen, C D Fisher, and M S Taylor, "Consequences of Individual Feedback on Behavior in Organizations," *Journal of Applied Psychology,* August 1979, pp 349–71; and R E Kopelman, *Managing Productivity in Organizations: A Practical People-Oriented Perspective* (New York: McGraw-Hill, 1986), p 175.

9 See P C Earley, G B Northcraft, C Lee, and T R Lituchy, "Impact of Process and Outcome Feedback on the Relation of Goal Setting to Task Performance," *Academy of Management Journal,* March 1990, pp 87–105. Also see D VandeWalle, W L Cron, and J W Slocum Jr, "The Role of Goal Orientation following Performance Feedback," *Journal of Applied Psychology,* August 2001, pp 629–40.

10 Data from A N Kluger and A DeNisi, "The Effects of Feedback Interventions on Performance: A Historical Review, a Meta-Analysis, and a Preliminary Feedback Intervention Theory," *Psychological Bulletin,* March 1996, pp 254–84.

11 Data from K D Harber, "Feedback to Minorities: Evidence of a Positive Bias," *Journal of Personality and Social Psychology,* March 1998, pp 622–28.

12 See D M Herold and D B Fedor, "Individuals' Interaction with Their Feedback Environment: The Role of Domain-Specific Individual Differences," in *Research in Personnel and Human Resources Management,* vol. 16, ed G R Ferris (Stamford, CT: JAI Press, 1998), pp 215–54.

13 H Lancaster, "Scott Adams Offers Valuable Lessons from Life with Dilbert," *The Wall Street Journal,* August 8, 1995, p B1.

14 For relevant research, see J S Goodman, "The Interactive Effects of Task and External Feedback on Practice Performance and Learning," *Organizational Behavior and Human Decision Processes,* December 1998, pp 223–52.

15 See P E Levy, M D Albright, B D Cawley, and J R Williams, "Situational and Individual Determinants of Feedback Seeking: A Closer Look at the Process," *Organizational Behavior and Human Decision Processes,* April 1995, pp 23–37; M R Leary, E S Tambor, S K Terdal, and D L Downs, "Self-Esteem as an Interpersonal Monitor: The Sociometer Hypothesis," *Journal of Personality and Social Psychology,* June 1995, pp 518–30; and M A Quinones, "Pretraining Context Effects: Training Assignment as Feedback," *Journal of Applied Psychology,* April 1995, pp 226–38.

16 See T Matsui, A Okkada, and T Kakuyama, "Influence of Achievement Need on Goal Setting, Performance, and Feedback Effectiveness," *Journal of Applied Psychology,* October 1982, pp 645–48.

17 S J Ashford, "Feedback-Seeking in Individual Adaptation: A Resource Perspective," *Academy of Management Journal,* September 1986, pp 465–87. Also see D B Fedor, R B Rensvold, and S M Adams, "An Investigation of Factors Expected to Affect Feedback Seeking: A Longitudinal Field Study," *Personnel Psychology,* Winter 1992, pp 779–805; and M F Sully De Luque and S M Sommer, "The Impact of Culture on Feedback-Seeking Behavior: An Integrated Model and Propositions," *Academy of Management Review,* October 2000, pp 829–49.

18 See D B Turban and T W Dougherty, "Role of Protege Personality in Receipt of Mentoring and Career Success," *Academy of Management Journal,* June 1994, pp 688–702. Also see M E Burkhardt, "Social Interaction Effects Following a Technological Change: A Longitudinal Investigation," *Academy of Management Journal,* August 1994, pp 869–98.

19 See D M Herold, C K Parsons, and R B Rensvold, "Individual Differences in the Generation and Processing of Performance Feedback," *Educational and Psychological Measurement,* February 1996, pp 5–25.

20 See B D Bannister, "Performance Outcome Feedback and Attributional Feedback: Interactive Effects on Recipient Responses," *Journal of Applied Psychology,* May 1986, pp 203–10.

21 For complete details, see P M Podsakoff and J-L Farh, "Effects of Feedback Sign and Credibility on Goal Setting and Task Performance," *Organizational Behavior and Human Decision Processes,* August 1989, pp 45–67. Also see S J Ashford and A S Tsui, "Self-Regulation for Managerial Effectiveness: The Role of Active Feedback Seeking," *Academy of Management Journal,* June 1991, pp 251–80.

22 W S Silver, T R Mitchell, and M E Gist, "Responses to Successful and Unsuccessful Performance: The Moderating Effect of Self-Efficacy on the Relationship between Performance and Attributions," *Organizational Behavior and Human Decision Processes,* June 1995, p 297. Also see T A Louie, "Decision Makers' Hindsight Bias after Receiving Favorable and Unfavorable Feedback," *Journal of Applied Psychology,* February 1999, pp 29–41.

23 J M Kouzes and B Z Posner, *Credibility: How Leaders Gain and Lose It, Why People Demand It* (San Francisco: Jossey-Bass, 1993), p 25.

24 See R B Jelley and R D Goffin, "Can Performance-Feedback Accuracy Be Improved? Effects of Rater Priming and Rating-Scale Format on Rating Accuracy," *Journal of Applied Psychology,* February 2001, pp 134–44; G L Graham, "If You Want Honesty, Break Some Rules," *Harvard Business Review,* April 2002, pp 42–47; S Aryee, P S Budhwar, and Z X Chen, "Trust as a Mediator of the Relationship between Organizational Justice and Work Outcomes: Test of a Social Exchange Model," *Journal of Organizational Behavior,* May 2002, pp 267–85.

25 See S E Moss and M J Martinko, "The Effects of Performance Attributions and Outcome Dependence on Leader Feedback Behavior Following Poor Subordinate Performance," *Journal of Organizational Behavior,* May 1998, pp 259–74; and K Leung, S Su, and M W Morris, "When Is Criticism *Not* Constructive? The Roles of Fairness Perceptions and Dispositional Attributions in Employee Acceptance of Critical Supervisory Feedback," *Human Relations,* September 2001, pp 1123–54.

26 B Uttal, "Behind the Fall of Steve Jobs," *Fortune,* August 5, 1985, p 22.

27 Based on discussion in Ilgen, Fisher, and Taylor, "Consequences of Individual Feedback on Behavior in Organizations," pp 367–68. Also see A M O'Leary-Kelly, "The Influence of Group Feedback on Individual Group Member Response," in *Research in Personnel and Human Resources Management,* vol. 16, ed G R Ferris (Stamford, CT: JAI Press, 1998), pp 255–94.

28 See P C Earley, "Computer-Generated Performance Feedback in the Magazine-Subscription Industry," *Organizational Behavior and Human Decision Processes,* February 1988, pp 50–64.

29 See M De Gregorio and C D Fisher, "Providing Performance Feedback: Reactions to Alternate Methods," *Journal of Management,* December 1988, pp 605–16.

30 For details, see R A Baron, "Countering the Effects of Destructive Criticism: The Relative Efficacy of Four Interventions," *Journal of Applied Psychology,* June 1990, pp 235–45. Also see M L Smith, "Give Feedback, Not Criticism," *Supervisory Management,* February 1993, p 4.

31 C O Longenecker and D A Gioia, "The Executive Appraisal Paradox," *Academy of Management Executive,* May 1992, p 18. Also see "It's Still Lonely at the Top," *Training,* April 1993, p 8.

32 See M R Edwards, A J Ewen, and W A Verdini, "Fair Performance Management and Pay Practices for Diverse Work Forces: The Promise of Multisource Assessment," *ACA Journal,* Spring 1995, pp 50–63.

33 See G D Huet-Cox, T M Nielsen, and E Sundstrom, "Get the Most from 360-Degree Feedback: Put It on the Internet," *HR Magazine,* May 1999, pp 92–103; and J Day, "Simple, Strong Team Ratings," *HR Magazine,* September 2000, pp 159–61.

34 This list is based in part on discussion in H J Bernardin, "Subordinate Appraisal: A Valuable Source of Information about Managers," *Human Resource Management,* Fall 1986, pp 421–39.

35 For a complete list, see "Companies Where Employees Rate Executives," *Fortune,* December 27, 1993, p 128. Also see S Gruner, "Turning the Tables," *Inc.,* May 1996, pp 87–89.

36 Data from D Antonioni, "The Effects of Feedback Accountability on Upward Appraisal Ratings," *Personnel Psychology,* Summer 1994, pp 349–56.

37 H J Bernardin, S A Dahmus, and G Redmon, "Attitudes of First-Line Supervisors toward Subordinate Appraisals," *Human Resource Management,* Summer–Fall 1993, p 315.

38 See L Atwater, P Roush, and A Fischthal, "The Influence of Upward Feedback on Self- and Follower Ratings of Leadership," *Personnel Psychology,* Spring 1995, pp 35–59.

39 Data from J W Smither, M London, N L Vasilopoulos, R R Reilly, R E Millsap, and N Salvemini, "An Examination of the Effects of an Upward Feedback Program Over Time," *Personnel Psychology,* Spring 1995, pp 1–34.

40 Data from K E Morical, "A Product Review: 360 Assessments," *Training & Development,* April 1999, pp 43–47. Also see N E Fried, "360° Software Shootout: Comparing Features with Needs," *HR Magazine* (Focus), December 1998, pp 8–13.

41 Data from J L Seglin, "Reviewing Your Boss," *Fortune,* June 11, 2001, p 248.

42 See A S DeNisi and A N Kluger, "Feedback Effectiveness: Can 360-Degree Appraisals Be Improved?" *Academy of Management Executive,* February 2000, pp 129–39; and J Ghorpade, "Managing Five Paradoxes of 360-Degree Feedback," *Academy of Management Executive,* February 2000, pp 140–50.

43 B O'Reilly, "360 Feedback Can Change Your Life," *Fortune,* October 17, 1994, p 93.

44 For a comprehensive overview of 360-degree feedback, see W W Tornow and M London, *Maximizing the Value of 360-Degree Feedback* (San Francisco: Jossey-Bass, 1998).

45 See M M Harris and J Schaubroeck, "A Meta-Analysis of Self-Supervisor, Self-Peer, and Peer-Supervisor Ratings," *Personnel Psychology,* Spring 1988, pp 43–62, and J Lane and P Herriot, "Self-Ratings, Supervisor Ratings, Positions and Performance," *Journal of Occupational Psychology,* March 1990, pp 77–88. Also see J R Williams and P E Levy, "The Effects of Perceived System Knowledge on the Agreement between Self-Ratings and Supervisor Ratings," *Personnel Psychology,* Winter 1992, pp 835–47; R F Martell and M R Borg, "A Comparison of the Behavioral Rating Accuracy of Groups and Individuals," *Journal of Applied Psychology,* February 1993, pp 43–50; J D Makiney and P E Levy, "The Influence of Self-Ratings versus Peer Ratings on Supervisors' Performance Judgments," *Organizational Behavior and Human Decision Processes,* June 1998, pp 212–28; G W Cheung, "Multifaceted Conceptions of Self-Other Ratings Disagreement," *Personnel Psychology,* Spring 1999, pp 1–36; and T A Beehr, L Ivanitskaya, C P Hansen, D Erofeev, and D M Gudanowski, "Evaluation of 360-Degree Feedback Ratings: Relationships with Each Other and with Performance and Selection Predictors," *Journal of Organizational Behavior,* November 2001, pp 775–88.

46 Fisher Hazucha, S A Hezlett, and R J Schneider, "The Impact of 360-Degree Feedback on Managerial Skills Development," *Human Resource Management,* Summer–Fall 1993, p 42. Also see M K Mount, T A Judge, S E Scullen, M R Sytsma, and S A Hezlett, "Trait, Rater and Level Effects in 360-Degree Performance Ratings," *Personnel Psychology,* Autumn 1998, pp 557–76.

47 J F Brett and L E Atwater, " "360° Feedback: Accuracy, Reactions, and Perceptions of Usefulness," *Journal of Applied Psychology,* October 2001, p 930.

48 D E Coates, "Don't Tie 360 Feedback to Pay," *Training,* September 1998, pp 68–78.

49 List excerpted from D W Bracken, "Straight Talk about Multirater Feedback," *Training & Development,* September 1994, p 46. Also see D Antonioni, "Designing an Effective 360-Degree Appraisal Feedback Process," *Organizational Dynamics,* Autumn 1996, pp 24–38.

50 Jack Welch, "Jack and the People Factory," *Fortune,* September 17, 2001, p 82.

51 For supporting evidence of employees' desire for prompt feedback, see D H Reid and M B Parsons, "A Comparison of Staff Acceptability of Immediate versus Delayed Verbal Feedback in Staff Training," *Journal of Organizational Behavior Management,* no. 2, 1996, pp 35–47.

52 See R S Allen and R H Kilmann, "Aligning Reward Practices in Support of Total Quality Management," *Business Horizons,* May–June 2001, pp 77–84; and T R Mitchell, B C Holtom, and T W Lee, "How to Keep Your Best Employees: Developing an Effective Retention Policy," *Academy of Management Executive,* November 2001, pp 96–108.

53 Strategic models of pay and rewards are discussed in C Joinson, "Pay Attention to Pay Cycles," *HR Magazine,* November 1998, pp 71–78; M Bloom and G T Milkovich, "A SHRM Perspective on International Compensation and Reward Systems," in *Research in Personnel and Human Resources Management,* supplement 4, ed G R Ferris (Stamford, CT: JAI Press, 1999), pp 283–303; and J Dolmat-Connell, "Developing a Reward Strategy That Delivers Shareholder and Employee Value," *Compensation & Benefits Review,* March–April 1999, pp 46–53. Also see A Etzioni, "The Good Society: Goals beyond Money," *The Futurist,* July–August 2001, pp 68+66.

54 For example, see B Nelson, *1001 Ways to Reward Employees* (New York: Workman Publishing, 1994); and "Emerging Optional Benefits," *Management Review,* December 1998, p 8. For more on stock options, see J Staiman and K Tompson, "Designing and Implementing a Broad-Based Stock Option Plan," *Compensation & Benefits Review,* July–August 1998, pp 23–40; "Stock Options as Bait," *Management Review,* February 1999, p 6; and A Tergesen, "Making the Most of Your Stock Options," *Business Week,* May 31, 1999, pp 178–80.

55 W J Wiatrowski, "Family-Related Benefits in the Workplace," *Monthly Labor Review,* March 1990, p 28. For recent data, see L H Geary and M J Powe, "Corporate America's Best Benefits," *Money,* December 2001, pp 140–47.

56 K I Kim, H-J Park, and N Suzuki, "Reward Allocations in the United States, Japan, and Korea: A Comparison of Individualistic and Collectivistic Cultures," *Academy of Management Journal,* March 1990, pp 188–98. Also see C C Chen, J R Meindl, and H Hui, "Deciding on Equity or Parity: A Test of Situational, Cultural, and Individual Factors," *Journal of Organizational Behavior,* March 1998, pp 115–29; and M Buchanan, "Wealth Happens," *Harvard Business Review,* April 2002, pp 49–54.

57 See T Gutner, "Progress? Not as Much as You Thought," *Business Week,* February 18, 2002, p 108.

58 Based on M Bloom, "The Performance Effects of Pay Dispersion on Individuals and Organizations," *Academy of Management Journal,* February 1999, pp 25–40.

59 See G Colvin, "The Great CEO Pay Heist," *Fortune,* June 25, 2001, pp 64–70; G Strauss, "Coke CEO's 2001 Pay Package: $200M," *USA Today,* February 5, 2002, p 2B; and A Backover, "Qwest CEO Compensation Hits $217.3M," *USA Today,* April 10, 2002, p 2B.

60 List adapted from J L Pearce and R H Peters, "A Contradictory Norms View of Employer–Employee Exchange," *Journal of Management,* Spring 1985, pp 19–30.

61 Ibid., p 25.

62 M Von Glinow, "Reward Strategies for Attracting, Evaluating, and Retaining Professionals," *Human Resource Management,* Summer 1985, p 193.

63 T Cunneff, "Insider," *People,* April 22, 2002, p 47.

64 "The 100 Best Companies to Work For," *Fortune,* February 4, 2002, p 90.

65 D R Spitzer, "Power Rewards: Rewards That Really Motivate," *Management Review,* May 1996, p 47. Also see S Kerr, "An Academy Classic: On the Folly of Rewarding A, while Hoping for B," *Academy of Management Executive,* February 1995, pp 7–14.

66 List adapted from discussion in Spitzer, "Power Rewards: Rewards that Really Motivate," pp 45–50. Also see L Lavelle, "Thinking beyond the One-Size-Fits-All Pay Cut,' *Business Week,* December 3, 2001, p 45; and A Fox, "The Right Rewards?" *HR Magazine,* May 2002, p 8.

67 See, for example, T P Flannery, D A Hofrichter, and P E Platten, *People, Performance, and Pay: Dynamic Compensation for Changing Organizations* (New York: Free Press, 1996).

68 See R Ganzel, "What's Wrong with Pay for Performance?" *Training,* December 1998, pp 34–40; R Plachy and S Plachy, "Rewarding Employees Who Truly Make a Difference," *Compensation & Benefits Review,* May–June 1999, pp 34–39; M A Stiffler, "Incentive Compensation and the Web," *Compensation & Benefits Review,* January–February 2001, pp 15–19; E Zehnder, "A Simpler Way to Pay," *Harvard Business Review,* April 2001, pp 53–61; R Berner, "The Economy's Bonus Setback," *Business Week,* January 14, 2002, p 24; and D Fiedler, "Should You Adjust Your Sales Compensation?" *HR Magazine,* February 2002, pp 79–82.

69 For both sides of the "Does money motivate?" debate, see N Gupta and J D Shaw, "Let the Evidence Speak: Financial Incentives *Are* Effective!!" *Compensation & Benefits Review,* March–April 1998, pp 26, 28–32; A Kohn, "Challenging Behaviorist Dogma: Myths about Money and Motivation," *Compensation & Benefits Review,* March–April 1998, pp 27, 33–37; and B Ettorre, "Is Salary a Motivator?" *Management Review,* January 1999, p 8. Also see W J Duncan, "Stock Ownership and Work Motivation," *Organizational Dynamics,* Summer 2001, pp 1–11.

70 Data from D Kiley, "Crafty Basket Makers Cut Downtime, Waste," *USA Today,* May 10, 2001, p 3B.

[71] Data from N J Perry, "Here Come Richer, Riskier Pay Plans," *Fortune,* December 19, 1988, p 51. Also see W Zellner, "Trickle-Down Is Trickling Down at Work," *Business Week,* March 18, 1996, p 34.

[72] Data from M Bloom and G T Milkovich, "Relationships among Risk, Incentive Pay, and Organizational Performance," *Academy of Management Journal,* June 1998, pp 283–97.

[73] For details, see G D Jenkins, Jr, N Gupta, A Mitra, and J D Shaw, "Are Financial Incentives Related to Performance? A Meta-Analytic Review of Empirical Research," *Journal of Applied Psychology,* October 1998, pp 777–87.

[74] See M J Mandel, "Those Fat Bonuses Don't Seem to Boost Performance," *Business Week,* January 8, 1990, p 26.

[75] Based on discussion in R Ricklefs, "Whither the Payoff on Sales Commissions?" *The Wall Street Journal,* June 6, 1990, p B1.

[76] G Koretz, "Bad Marks for Pay-by-Results," *Business Week,* September 4, 1995, p 28. Also see S Bates, "Now, the Downside of Pay for Performance," *HR Magazine,* March 2002, p 10.

[77] B Geber, "The Bugaboo of Team Pay," *Training,* August 1995, pp 25–26. Also see E Neuborne, "Companies Save, but Workers Pay," *USA Today,* February 25, 1997, pp 1B–2B.

[78] Ranking based on research evidence in F Trompenaars, *Riding the Waves of Culture: Understanding Diversity in Global Business* (Chicago: Irwin Professional Publishing, 1994), p 52.

[79] P V LeBlanc and P W Mulvey, "Research Study: How American Workers See the Rewards of Work," *Compensation & Benefits Review,* January–February 1998, pp 24–28.

[80] R Mitchell, "Managing by Values," *Business Week,* August 1, 1994, p 50. Also see J D Shaw, M K Duffy, and E M Stark, "Team Reward Attitude: Construct Development and Initial Validation," *Journal of Organizational Behavior,* December 2001, pp 903–17.

[81] J S Dematteo, L T Eby, and E Sundstrom, "Team-Based Rewards: Current Empirical Evidence and Directions for Future Research," in *Research in Organizational Behavior,* vol. 20, eds B M Staw and L L Cummings (Greenwich, CT: JAI Press, 1998), p 152. Also see T R Zenger and C R Marshall, "Determinants of Incentive Intensity in Group-Based Rewards," *Academy of Management Journal,* April 2000, pp 149–63; and M Natter, A Mild, M Feurstein, G Dorffner, and A Taudes, "The Effect of Incentive Schemes and Organizational Arrangements on the New Product Development Process," *Management Science,* August 2001, pp 1029–45.

[82] For example, see R L Heneman and C von Hippel, "Balancing Group and Individual Rewards: Rewarding Individual Contributions to the Team," *Compensation & Benefits Review,* July–August 1995, pp 63–68; A Muoio, "At SEI, Teamwork Pays," *Fast Company,* April 1999, p 186; L N McClurg, "Team Rewards: How Far Have We Come?" *Human Resource Management,* Spring 2001, pp 73–86; and C Garvey, "Steer Teams with the Right Pay," *HR Magazine,* May 2002, pp 71–78.

[83] See C Ginther, "Incentive Programs That Really Work," *HR Magazine,* August 2000, pp 117–20.

[84] For a recent unconventional perspective, see R J DeGrandpre, "A Science of Meaning? Can Behaviorism Bring Meaning to Psychological Science?" *American Psychologist,* July 2000, pp 721–38.

[85] See E L Thorndike, *Educational Psychology: The Psychology of Learning, Vol. II* (New York: Columbia University Teachers College, 1913).

[86] Discussion of an early behaviorist who influenced Skinner's work can be found in P J Kreshel, "John B Watson at J Walter Thompson: The Legitimation of 'Science' in Advertising," *Journal of Advertising,* no. 2, 1990, pp 49–59. Recent discussions involving behaviorism include M R Ruiz, "B F Skinner's Radical Behaviorism: Historical Misconstructions and Grounds for Feminist Reconstructions," *Psychology of Women Quarterly,* June 1995, pp 161–79; J A Nevin, "Behavioral Economics and Behavioral Momentum," *Journal of the Experimental Analysis of Behavior,* November 1995, pp 385–95; and H Rachlin, "Can We Leave Cognition to Cognitive Psychologists? Comments on an Article by George Loewenstein," *Organizational Behavior and Human Decision Processes,* March 1996, pp 296–99.

[87] For recent discussion, see J W Donahoe, "The Unconventional Wisdom of B F Skinner: The Analysis-Interpretation Distinction," *Journal of the Experimental Analysis of Behavior,* September 1993, pp 453–56.

[88] See B F Skinner, *The Behavior of Organisms* (New York: Appleton-Century-Crofts, 1938).

[89] For modern approaches to respondent behavior, see B Azar, "Classical Conditioning Could Link Disorders and Brain Dysfunction, Researchers Suggest," *APA Monitor,* March 1999, p 17.

[90] For interesting discussions of Skinner and one of his students, see M B Gilbert and T F Gilbert, "What Skinner Gave Us," *Training,* September 1991, pp 42–48; and "HRD Pioneer Gilbert Leaves a Pervasive Legacy," *Training,* January 1996, p 14. Also see F Luthans and R Kreitner, *Organizational Behavior Modification and Beyond: An Operant and Social Learning Approach* (Glenview, IL: Scott, Foresman, 1985).

[91] The effect of praise is explored in C M Mueller and C S Dweck, "Praise for Intelligence Can Undermine Children's Motivation and Performance," *Journal of Personality and Social Psychology,* July 1998, pp 33–52.

[92] C Salter, "Customer Service," *Fast Company,* May 2002, p 86. Also see R Kegan and L L Lahey, "More Powerful Communication: From the Language of Prizes and Praising to the Language of Ongoing Regard," *Journal of Organizational Excellence,* Summer 2001, pp 11–17.

[93] Research on punishment is reported in B P Niehoff, R J Paul, and J F S Bunch, "The Social Effects of Punishment Events: The Influence of Violator Past Performance Record and Severity of the Punishment on Observers' Justice Perceptions and Attitudes," *Journal of Organizational Behavior,* November 1998, pp 589–602; and L E Atwater, D A Waldman, J A Carey, and P Cartier, "Recipient and Observer Reactions to Discipline: Are Managers Experiencing Wishful Thinking?" *Journal of Organizational Behavior,* May 2001, pp 249–70.

94 See C B Ferster and B F Skinner, *Schedules of Reinforcement* (New York: Appleton-Century-Crofts, 1957).

95 Our choice is "b," variable ratio, because it is the "slot machine" effect. But instead of possibly being reinforced after a variable number of lever pulls on a slot machine, the AccuData employees have a chance of being reinforced (monthly and annually) after attending a variable number of after-work training sessions. For another example, see C Caggiano, "Hot Tips," *Inc.,* April 1999, p 104.

96 See L M Saari and G P Latham, "Employee Reactions to Continuous and Variable Ratio Reinforcement Schedules Involving a Monetary Incentive," *Journal of Applied Psychology,* August 1982, pp 506–8.

97 P Brinkley-Rogers and R Collier, "Along the Colorado, the Money's Flowing," *Arizona Republic,* March 4, 1990, p A12.

98 M Schrage, "Actually, I'd Rather Have That Favor than a Raise," *Fortune,* April 16, 2001, p 412.

99 Data from K L Alexander, "Continental Airlines Soars to New Heights," *USA Today,* January 23, 1996, p 4B; and M Knez and D Simester, "Making Across-the-Board Incentives Work," *Harvard Business Review,* February 2002, pp 16–17.

100 Excerpted from C Garvey, "Not Always a Good Fit," *HR Magazine,* May 2002, p 73.

101 This exercise is adapted from material in D M Herold and C K Parsons, "Assessing the Feedback Environment in Work Organizations: Development of the Job Feedback Survey," *Journal of Applied Psychology,* May 1985, pp 290–305.

102 Excerpted from J A Byrne, "How to Fix Corporate Governance," *Business Week,* May 6, 2002, p 72.

LEARNING MODULE B

1 T Galvin, "The Weakest Link," *Training,* December 2001, p 8. Also see M Boyle, "Performance Reviews: Perilous Curves Ahead," *Fortune,* May 28, 2001, pp 187–88; and D Kiley and D Jones, "Ford Alters Worker Evaluation Process," *USA Today,* July 11, 2001, p 1B.

2 Data from D Stamps, "Performance Appraisals: Out of Sync and as Unpopular as Ever," *Training,* August 1995, p 16.

3 For example, see K McKirchy, *Powerful Performance Appraisals: How to Set Expectations and Work Together to Improve Performance* (Franklin Lakes, NJ: Career Press, 1998); and T Coens and M Jenkins, *Abolishing Performance Appraisals: Why They Backfire and What to Do Instead* (San Francisco: Berrett-Koehler, 2000).

4 See J N Cleveland, K R Murphy, and R E Williams, "Multiple Uses of Performance Appraisal: Prevalence and Correlates," *Journal of Applied Psychology,* February 1989, pp 130–35.

5 B Rice, "Performance Review: The Job Nobody Likes," *Psychology Today,* September 1986, p 32.

6 See G E Calvasina, R V Calvasina, and E J Calvasina, "Management and the EEOC," *Business Horizons,* July–August 2000, pp 3–7; and N H Woodward, "Help from the EEOC?" *HR Magazine,* September 2001, pp 123–28.

7 L Grensing-Pophal, "Motivate Managers to Review Performance," *HR Magazine,* March 2001, p 46.

8 See "Performance Appraisals—Reappraised," *Management Review,* November 1983, p 5. Eight common performance appraisal errors are discussed in T R Lowe, "Eight Ways to Ruin a Performance Review," *Personnel Journal,* January 1986, pp 60–62. Also see G L Blakely, "The Effects of Performance Rating Discrepancies on Supervisors and Subordinates," *Organizational Behavior and Human Decision Processes,* February 1993, pp 57–80; and J H Dulebohn and G R Ferris, "The Role of Influence Tactics in Perceptions of Performance Evaluations' Fairness," *Academy of Management Journal,* June 1999, pp 288–303.

9 For details, see G H Dobbins, R L Cardy, and D M Truxillo, "The Effects of Purpose of Appraisal and Individual Differences in Stereotypes of Women on Sex Differences in Performance Ratings: A Laboratory and Field Study," *Journal of Applied Psychology,* August 1988, pp 551–58. A similar finding is reported in P R Sackett, C L Z DuBois, and A Wiggins Noe, "Tokenism in Performance Evaluation: The Effects of Work Group Representation on Male-Female and White-Black Differences in Performance Ratings," *Journal of Applied Psychology,* April 1991, pp 263–67.

10 Data from B Klaas and A S DeNisi, "Managerial Reactions to Employee Dissent: The Impact of Grievance Activity on Performance Ratings," *Academy of Management Journal,* December 1989, pp 705–17.

11 W S Swan and P Margulies, *How to Do a Superior Performance Appraisal* (New York: John Wiley, 1991), p 8.

12 K N Wexley and R Klimoski, "Performance Appraisal: An Update," in *Research in Personnel and Human Resources Management,* vol. 2, eds K M Rowland and G R Ferris (Greenwich, CT: JAI Press, 1984), pp 55–56.

13 B Jacobson and B L Kaye, "Career Development and Performance Appraisal: It Takes Two to Tango," *Personnel,* January 1986, p 27.

14 Supporting discussion is provided by K N Wexley, "Appraisal Interview," in *Performance Assessment,* ed R A Berk (Baltimore, MD: Johns Hopkins Press Ltd., 1986).

15 See D Grote, "Painless Performance Appraisals Focus on Results, Behaviors," *HR Magazine,* October 1998, pp 52–58.

16 See, for example, R Rodgers and J E Hunter, "Impact of Management by Objectives on Organizational Productivity," *Journal of Applied Psychology,* April 1991, pp 322–36; and R Rodgers, J E Hunter, and D L Rogers, "Influence of Top Management Commitment on Management Program Success," *Journal of Applied Psychology,* February 1993, pp 151–55.

17 Indeed, research found rater differences to be more important than format differences. See C E J Härtel, "Rating Format Research Revisited: Format Effectiveness and Acceptability Depend on Rater Characteristics," *Journal of Applied Psychology,* April 1993, pp 212–17. Also see T J Maurer, J K

Palmer, and D K Ashe, "Diaries, Checklists, Evaluations, and Contrast Effects in Measurement of Behavior," *Journal of Applied Psychology,* April 1993, pp 226–31.

[18] See A M Morrison, "Performance Appraisal: Getting from Here to There," *Human Resource Planning,* no. 2, 1984, pp 73–77. Also see C Lee, "Smoothing Out Appraisal Systems," *HR Magazine,* March 1990, pp 72–76; and J Conger, D Finegold, and E E Lawler III, "CEO Appraisals: Holding Corporate Leadership Accountable," *Organizational Dynamics,* Summer 1998, pp 7–20.

[19] Results are presented in K Kraiger and J K Ford, "A Meta-Analysis of Ratee Race Effects in Performance Ratings," *Journal of Applied Psychology,* February 1985, pp 56–65.

[20] Based on R C Mayer and J H Davis, "The Effect of the Performance Appraisal System on Trust for Management: A Field Quasi-Experiment," *Journal of Applied Psychology,* February 1999, pp 123–36.

[21] Data from B D Cawley, L M Keeping, and P E Levy, "Participation in the Performance Appraisal Process and Employee Reactions: A Meta-Analytic Review of Field Experiments," *Journal of Applied Psychology,* August 1998, pp 615–33.

[22] M S Taylor, S S Masterson, M K Renard, and K B Tracy, "Managers' Reactions to Procedurally Just Performance Management Systems," *Academy of Management Journal,* October 1998, pp 568–79. Also see S S K Lam, M S M Yik, and J Schaubroeck, "Responses to Formal Performance Appraisal Feedback: The Role of Negative Affectivity," *Journal of Applied Psychology,* February 2002, pp 192–201.

[23] Research results extracted from F J Landy and J L Farr, "Performance Rating," *Psychological Bulletin,* January 1980, pp 72–107; Wexley and Klimoski, "Performance Appraisal: An Update"; Rice, "Performance Review: The Job Nobody Likes"; J W Hedge and M J Kavangh, "Improving the Accuracy of Performance Evaluations; Comparisons of Three Methods of Performance Appraiser Training," *Journal of Applied Psychology,* February 1988, pp 68–73; and R Klimoski and L Inks, "Accountability Forces in Performance Appraisal," *Organizational Behavior and Human Decision Processes,* April 1990, pp 194–208. Also see H M Findley, W F Giles, and K W Mossholder, "Performance Appraisal Process and System Facets: Relationships with Contextual Performance," *Journal of Applied Psychology,* August 2000, pp 634–40.

CHAPTER 11

[1] Excerpted from J A Byrne, L Lavelle, N Byrnes, M Vickers, and A Borrus, "How to Fix Corporate Governance," *Business Week,* May 6, 2002, p 78.

[2] For a review of research on rational decision making, see K E Stanovich, *Who Is Rational?* (Mahwah, NJ: Lawrence Erlbaum, 1999), pp 1–31.

[3] G L White, "GM Takes Advice from Disease Sleuths to Debug Cars," *The Wall Street Journal,* April 8, 1999, p B1.

[4] See W F Pounds, "The Process of Problem Finding," *Industrial Management Review,* Fall 1969, pp 1–19.

[5] Scenario planning is discussed by S Schnaars and P Ziamou, "The Essentials of Scenario Writing," *Business Horizons,* July–August 2001, pp 25–31.

[6] Risk and decision making is discussed by S W Williams, *Making Better Business Decisions* (Thousand Oaks, CA: Sage Publications, 2002), pp 77–88.

[7] Results can be found in J P Byrnes, D C Miller, and W D Schafer, "Gender Differences in Risk Taking: A Meta-Analysis," *Psychological Bulletin,* May 1999, pp 367–83.

[8] The implementation process and its relationship to decision outcomes is discussed by S J Miller, D J Hickson, and D C Wilson, "Decision-Making in Organizations," in *Handbook of Organization Studies,* eds S R Clegg, C Hardy, and W R Nord (London: Sage Publications, 1996), pp 293–312.

[9] H A Simon, "Rational Decision Making in Business Organizations," *American Economic Review,* September 1979, p 510.

[10] For a complete discussion of bounded rationality, see H A Simon, *Administrative Behavior,* 2nd ed (New York: Free Press, 1957); J G March and H A Simon, *Organizations* (New York: John Wiley, 1958); H A Simon, "Altruism and Economics," *American Economic Review,* May 1993, pp 156–61; and R Nagel, "A Survey on Experimental Beauty Contest Games: Bounded Rationality and Learning," in *Games and Human Behavior,* eds D V Budescu, I Erev, and R Zwick (Mahwah, NJ: 1999), pp 105–42.

[11] Biases associated with using shortcuts in decision making are discussed by A Tversky and D Kahneman, "Judgment under Uncertainty: Heuristics and Biases," *Science,* September 1974, pp 1124–31; and D Stahlberg, F Eller, A Maass, and D Frey, "We Knew It All Along: Hindsight Bias in Groups," *Organizational Behavior and Human Decision Processes,* July 1995, pp 46–58.

[12] M D Hovanesian, "Don't Just Analyze the Market, Analyze the Investor," *Business Week,* May 21, 2001, pp 124–25.

[13] Results can be found in "The Big Picture: 'Hurry Up and Decide!'" *Business Week,* May 14, 2001, p 16.

[14] D W De Long and P Seemann, "Confronting Conceptual Confusion and Conflict in Knowledge Management," *Organizational Dynamics,* Summer 2000, p 33.

[15] See L Hollman, "The Power of Knowledge Management Software," *Call-Center Magazine,* January 2002, pp 30–38.

[16] Reprinted from *Organizational Dynamics* by from R Cross, A Parker, L Prusak, and S P Borgatti, "Knowing What We Know: Supporting Knowledge Creation and Sharing In Social Networks," Fall 2001, p. 109 © 2001 with permission from Elsevier Science.

[17] R Lubit, "Tacit Knowledge and Knowledge Management: The Keys to Sustainable Competitive Advantage," *Organizational Dynamics,* 2001, p 166.

[18] A M Hayashi, "When to Trust Your Gut," *Harvard Business Review,* February 2001, p 61.

[19] See Lubit, "Tacit Knowledge and Knowledge Management."

[20] Reprinted from *Organizational Dynamics* by from Cross, Parker, Prusak, and Borgatti, "Knowing What We Know: Supporting Knowledge Creation and Sharing In Social Networks," Fall 2001, p. 109 © 2001 with permission from Elsevier Science.

[21] Ibid.

[22] Results can be found in W H Stewart Jr and P L Roth, "Risk Propensity Differences between Entrepreneurs and Managers: A Meta-Analytic Review," *Journal of Applied Psychology,* February 2001, pp 145–53.

[23] This definition was derived from A J Rowe and R O Mason, *Managing with Style: A Guide to Understanding, Assessing and Improving Decision Making* (San Francisco: Jossey-Bass, 1987).

[24] The discussion of styles was based on material contained in ibid.

[25] P Shishkin, "Tough Tactics: European Regulators Spark Controversy with 'Dawn Raids,' " *The Wall Street Journal,* March 1, 2002, p A1.

[26] See Rowe and Mason, *Managing with Style* and M J Dollinger and W Danis, "Preferred Decision-Making Styles: A Cross-Cultural Comparison," *Psychological Reports,* 1998, pp 755–61.

[27] The details of this case are discussed in J Ross and B M Staw, "Organizational Escalation and Exit: Lessons from the Shoreham Nuclear Power Plant," *Academy of Management Journal,* August 1993, pp 701–32.

[28] See ibid.

[29] Psychological determinants of escalation are discussed by J H Hammond, R L Keeney, and H Raiffa, "The Hidden Traps in Decision Making," *Harvard Business Review,* September–October 1998, pp 47–58.

[30] Results can be found in S L Kirby and M A Davis, "A Study of Escalating Commitment in Principal-Agent Relationships: Effects of Monitoring and Personal Responsibility," *Journal of Applied Psychology,* April 1998, pp 206–17.

[31] Supportive results can be found in H Moon, "Looking Forward and Looking Back: Integrating Completion and Sunk-Cost Effects within an Escalation-of-Commitment Progress Decision," *Journal of Applied Psychology,* February 2001, pp 104–13.

[32] See D A Hantula and J L D Bragger, "The Effects of Feedback Equivocality on Escalation of Commitment: An Empirical Investigation of Decision Dilemma Theory," *Journal of Applied Social Psychology,* February 1999, pp 424–44.

[33] Results can be found in C R Greer and G K Stephens, "Escalation of Commitment: A Comparison of Differences between Mexican and US Decision Makers," *Journal of Management,* 2001, pp 51–78.

[34] See Ross and Staw, "Organizational Escalation and Exit."

[35] Supportive results are provided by G McNamara, H Moon, and P Bromiley, "Banking on Commitment: Intended and Unintended Consequences of an Organization's Attempt to Attenuate Escalation of Commitment," *Academy of Management Journal,* April 2002, pp 443–52; and J C Edwards,

"Self-Fulfilling Prophecy and Escalating Commitment," *Journal of Applied Behavioral Science,* September 2001, pp 343–60.

[36] See B M Staw and J Ross, "Behavior in Escalation Situations: Antecedents, Prototypes, and Solutions," in *Research in Organizational Behavior,* vol. 9, eds L L Cummings and B M Staw (Greenwich, CT: JAI Press, 1987), pp 39–78; and W S Silver and T R Mitchell, "The Status Quo Tendency in Decision Making," *Organizational Dynamics,* Spring 1990, pp 34–36.

[37] Results can be found in C K W De Dreu and M A West, "Minority Dissent and Team Innovation: The Importance of Participation in Decision Making," *Journal of Applied Psychology,* December 2001, pp 1191–201.

[38] These recommendations were derived from R Y Hirokawa, "Group Communication and Decision-Making Performance: A Continued Test of the Functional Perspective," *Human Communication Research,* October 1988, pp 487–515.

[39] See the related discussion in B B Baltes, M W Dickson, M P Sherman, C C Bauer, and J S LaGanke, "Computer-Mediated Communication and Group Decision Making: A Meta-Analysis," *Organizational Behavior and Human Decision Processes,* January 2002, pp 156–79.

[40] These guidelines were derived from G P Huber, *Managerial Decision Making* (Glenview, IL: Scott, Foresman, 1980), p 149.

[41] G W Hill, "Group versus Individual Performance: Are N + 1 Heads Better than One?" *Psychological Bulletin,* May 1982, p 535.

[42] D Pringle, "Finnish Line: Facing Big Threat from Microsoft, Nokia Places a Bet," *The Wall Street Journal,* May 22, 2002, p A16.

[43] J H Davis, "Some Compelling Intuitions about Group Consensus Decisions, Theoretical and Empirical Research, and Interpersonal Aggregation Phenomena: Selected Examples, 1950–1990," *Organizational Behavior and Human Decision Processes,* June 1992, pp 3–38.

[44] Supporting results can be found in J Hedlund, D R Ilgen, and J R Hollenbeck, "Decision Accuracy in Computer-Mediated versus Face-to-Face Decision-Making Teams," *Organizational Behavior and Human Decision Processes,* October 1998, pp 30–47.

[45] See J R Winquist and J R Larson, Jr, "Information Pooling: When It Impacts Group Decision Making," *Journal of Personality and Social Psychology,* February 1998, pp 371–77.

[46] Results are presented in J T Delaney, "Workplace Cooperation: Current Problems, New Approaches," *Journal of Labor Research,* Winter 1996, pp 45–61.

[47] For an extended discussion of this model, see M Sashkin, "Participative Management Is an Ethical Imperative," *Organizational Dynamics,* Spring 1984, pp 4–22.

[48] See G Yukl and P P Fu, "Determinants of Delegation and Consultation by Managers," *Journal of Organizational Behavior,* March 1999, pp 219–32.

[49] Supporting results can be found in J Hunton, T W Hall, and K H Price, "The Value of Voice in Participative Decision

Making," *Journal of Applied Psychology,* October 1998, pp 788–97; and C R Leana, R S Ahlbrandt, and A J Murrell, "The Effects of Employee Involvement Programs on Unionized Workers' Attitudes, Perceptions, and Preferences in Decision Making," *Academy of Management Journal,* October 1992, pp 861–73.

[50] Results can be found in B D Cawley, L M Keeping, and P E Levy, "Participation in the Performance Appraisal Process and Employee Reactions: A Meta-Analytic Review of Field Investigations," *Journal of Applied Psychology,* August 1998, pp 615–33.

[51] Results are contained in J A Wagner III, C R Leana, E A Locke, and D M Schweiger, "Cognitive and Motivational Frameworks in US Research on Participation: A Meta-Analysis of Primary Effects," *Journal of Organizational Behavior,* 1997, pp 49–65.

[52] See E A Locke, D M Schweiger, and G R Latham, "Participation in Decision Making: When Should It Be Used?" *Organizational Dynamics,* Winter 1986, pp 65–79.

[53] A thorough discussion of this issue is provided by W A Randolph, "Navigating the Journey to Empowerment," *Organizational Dynamics,* Spring 1995, pp 19–32.

[54] Results are presented in J Barbian, "Decision Making: The Tyranny of Managers," *Training,* January 2002, p 19.

[55] Results can be found in S A Mohrman, E E Lawler III, and G E Ledford, Jr, "Organizational Effectiveness and the Impact of Employee Involvement and TQM Programs: Do Employee Involvement and TQM Programs Work?" *Journal for Quality and Participation,* January–February 1996, pp 6–10.

[56] See R Rodgers, J E Hunter, and D L Rogers, "Influence of Top Management Commitment on Management Program Success," *Journal of Applied Psychology,* February 1993, pp 151–55.

[57] G M Parker, *Team Players and Teamwork: The New Competitive Business Strategy* (San Francisco, CA: Jossey-Bass, 1990).

[58] These recommendations were obtained from Parker, *Team Players and Teamwork.*

[59] Supportive results can be found in S Mohammed and E Ringseis, "Cognitive Diversity and Consensus in Group Decision Making: The Role of Inputs, Processes, and Outcomes," *Organizational Behavior and Human Decision Processes,* July 2001, pp 310–35.

[60] See A F Osborn, *Applied Imagination: Principles and Procedures of Creative Thinking,* 3rd ed (New York: Scribners, 1979).

[61] See W H Cooper, R Brent Gallupe, S Pollard, and J Cadsby, "Some Liberating Effects of Anonymous Electronic Brainstorming," *Small Group Research,* April 1998, pp 147–78; and P B Paulus, T S Larey, and A H Ortega, "Performance and Perceptions of Brainstormers in an Organizational Setting," *Basic and Applied Social Psychology,* August 1995, pp 249–65.

[62] These recommendations were derived from C Caggiano, "The Right Way to Brainstorm," *Inc.,* July 1999, p 94; and G

McGartland, "How to Generate More Ideas in Brainstorming Sessions," *Selling Power,* July–August 1999, p 46.

[63] See J G Lloyd, S Fowell, and J G Bligh, "The Use of the Nominal Group Technique as an Evaluative Tool in Medical Undergraduate Education," *Medical Education,* January 1999, pp 8–13; and A L Delbecq, A H Van de Ven, and D H Gustafson, *Group Techniques for Program Planning: A Guide to Nominal Group and Delphi Processes* (Glenview, IL: Scott, Foresman, 1975).

[64] See N C Dalkey, D L Rourke, R Lewis, and D Snyder, *Studies in the Quality of Life: Delphi and Decision Making* (Lexington, MA: Lexington Books: D C Heath and Co., 1972).

[65] Benefits of the Delphi technique are discussed by N I Whitman, "The Committee Meeting Alternative: Using the Delphi Technique," *Journal of Nursing Administration,* July–August 1990, pp 30–36.

[66] A thorough description of computer-aided decision-making systems is provided by M C Er and A C Ng, "The Anonymity and Proximity Factors in Group Decision Support Systems," *Decision Support Systems,* May 1995, pp 75–83.

[67] Excerpted from T E Weber, "How Bringing Doctors Together Online Helps Brothers Build Business," *The Wall Street Journal,* April 2, 2001, p B1.

[68] Supportive results can be found in S S Lam and J Schaubroeck, "Improving Group Decisions by Better Polling Information: A Comparative Advantage of Group Decision Support Systems," *Journal of Applied Psychology,* August 2000, pp 565–73; and I Benbasat and J Lim, "Information Technology Support for Debiasing Group Judgments: An Empirical Evaluation," *Organizational Behavior and Human Decision Processes.* September 2000, pp 167–83.

[69] Results can be found in Baltes, Dickson, Sherman, Bauer, and LaGanke, "Computer-Mediated Communication and Group Decision Making."

[70] M Arndt, "3M: A Lab for Growth?" *Business Week,* January 21, 2002, p 50.

[71] This definition was adapted from one provided by R K Scott, "Creative Employees: A Challenge to Managers," *Journal of Creative Behavior,* First Quarter, 1995, pp 64–71.

[72] E T Smith, "Are You Creative?" *Business Week,* September 30, 1985, pp 81–82. For a review of research about the left and right hemispheres of the brain, see T Hines, "Left Brain/Right Brain Mythology and Implications for Management and Training," *Academy of Management Review,* October 1987, pp 600–6.

[73] Excerpted from S Stern, "How Companies Can Be More Creative," *HR Magazine,* April 1998, p 59.

[74] These stages are thoroughly discussed by S W. Williams, *Making Better Business Decisions* (Thousand Oaks, CA: Sage Publications, 2002).

[75] Details of this study can be found in M Basadur, "Managing Creativity: A Japanese Model," *Academy of Management Executive,* May 1992, pp 29–42.

[76] Ibid.

[77] "Caring Enough," *Selling Power,* June 1999, p 18.

[78] See R J Sternberg, "What Is the Common Thread of Creativity?" *American Psychologist,* April 2001, pp 360–62.

[79] P Magnusson, "Small Biz vs. the Terrorists," *Business Week,* March 4, 2002, p 68.

[80] T A Matherly and R E Goldsmith, "The Two Faces of Creativity," *Business Horizons,* September–October 1985, p 9.

[81] This discussion is based on research reviewed in M A Collins and T M Amabile, "Motivation and Creativity," in *Handbook of Creativity,* eds R J Sternberg (Cambridge, UK: Cambridge University Press, 1999), pp 297–311; and G J Feist, "A Meta-Analysis of Personality in Scientific and Artistic Creativity," *Personality and Social Psychology Review,* 1998, pp 290–309.

[82] Personality and creativity were investigated by S Taggar, "Individual Creativity and Group Ability to Utilize Individual Creative Resources: A Multilevel Model," *Academy of Management Journal,* April 2002, pp 315–30; and J M George and J Zhou, "When Openness to Experience and Conscientiousness Are Related to Creative Behavior: An Interactional Approach," *Journal of Applied Psychology,* June 2001, pp 513–24.

[83] J M Higgins, "Innovate or Evaporate: Seven Secrets of Innovative Corporations," *The Futurist,* September–October 1995, p 46.

[84] See the related discussion in T M Amabile, "How to Kill Creativity," *Harvard Business Review,* September–October 1998, pp 77–87.

[85] R P Weiss, "How to Foster Creativity at Work," *Training & Development,* February 2001, pp 64–65.

[86] L Simpson, "Fostering Creativity," *Training,* December 2001, p 86.

[87] Reprinted by permission of *Harvard Business Review.* An excerpt from "How Smithkline Beecham Makes Better Resource—Allocation Decisions," March–April 1998. Copyright © 1998 by the president and fellows of Harvard College; all rights reserved.

[88] The survey and detailed norms can be found in A J Rowe and R O Mason, *Managing with Style: A Guide to Understanding, Assessing, and Improving Decision Making* (San Francisco: Jossey-Bass, 1987).

[89] Excerpted from E J Pollock, "Limited Partners: Lawyers for Enron Faulted Its Deals, Didn't Force Issue," *The Wall Street Journal,* May 22, 2002, pp A1, A18.

CHAPTER 12

[1] Excerpted from A C Logue, "Girl Gangs," *Training & Development,* January 2001, pp 24–28.

[2] E Van Velsor and J Brittain Leslie, "Why Executives Derail: Perspectives across Time and Cultures," *Academy of Management Executive,* November 1995, p 62.

[3] Ibid., p 63.

[4] See R A Baron and G D Markman, "Beyond Social Capital: How Social Skills Can Enhance Entrepreneurs' Success," *Academy of Management Executive,* February 2000, pp 106–16; L Prusak and D Cohen, "How to Invest in Social Capital," *Harvard Business Review,* June 2001, pp 86–93; and P S Adler and S Kwon, "Social Capital: Prospects for a New Concept," *Academy of Management Review,* January 2002, pp 17–40.

[5] This definition is based in part on one found in D Horton Smith, "A Parsimonious Definition of 'Group': Toward Conceptual Clarity and Scientific Utility," *Sociological Inquiry,* Spring 1967, pp 141–67.

[6] E H Schein, *Organizational Psychology,* 3rd ed (Englewood Cliffs, NJ: Prentice Hall, 1980), p 145. For more, see L R Weingart, "How Did They Do That? The Ways and Means of Studying Group Process," in *Research in Organizational Behavior,* vol. 19, eds L L Cummings and B M Staw (Greenwich, CT: JAI Press, 1997), pp 189–239.

[7] See E Bonabeau, "Predicting the Unpredictable," *Harvard Business Review,* March 2002, pp 109–16; and R Cross and L Prusak, "The People Who Make Organizations Go—or Stop," *Harvard Business Review,* June 2002, pp 105–12.

[8] J Castro, "Mazda U.," *Time,* October 20, 1986, p 65.

[9] For more, see M S Cole, W S Schaninger Jr, and S G Harris, "The Workplace Social Exchange Network: A Multilevel, Conceptual Examination," *Group & Organization Management,* March 2002, pp 142–67.

[10] For an instructive overview of five different theories of group development, see J P Wanous, A E Reichers, and S D Malik, "Organizational Socialization and Group Development: Toward an Integrative Perspective," *Academy of Management Review,* October 1984, pp 670–83.

[11] See B W Tuckman, "Developmental Sequence in Small Groups," *Psychological Bulletin,* June 1965, pp 384–99; and B W Tuckman and M A C Jensen, "Stages of Small-Group Development Revisited," *Group & Organization Studies,* December 1977, pp 419–27. An instructive adaptation of the Tuckman model can be found in L Holpp, "If Empowerment Is So Good, Why Does It Hurt?" *Training,* March 1995, p 56.

[12] Alternative group development models are discussed in L N Jewell and H J Reitz, *Group Effectiveness in Organizations* (Glenview, IL: Scott, Foresman, 1981), pp 15–20; and R S Wellins, W C Byham, and J M Wilson, *Empowered Teams: Creating Self-Directed Work Groups That Improve Quality, Productivity, and Participation* (San Francisco: Jossey-Bass, 1991).

[13] For related research, see C Kampmeier and B Simon, "Individuality and Group Formation: The Role of Independence and Differentiation," *Journal of Personality and Social Psychology,* September 2001, pp 448–62.

[14] For related research, see K Aquino and A Reed II, "A Social Dilemma Perspective on Cooperative Behavior in Organizations: The Effects of Scarcity, Communication, and Unequal Access on the Use of a Shared Resource," *Group & Organization Management,* December 1998, pp 390–413; B Fehr, "Laypeople's Conceptions of Commitment," *Journal of*

Personality and Social Psychology, January 1999, pp 90–103; G L Stewart, C C Manz, and H P Sims, Jr, *Team Work and Group Dynamics* (New York: Wiley, 1999); and B L Riddle, C M Anderson, and M M Martin, "Small Group Socialization Scale: Development and Validity," *Small Group Research,* October 2000, pp 554–72.

[15] Jewell and Reitz, *Group Effectiveness in Organizations,* p 19. Also see C B Gibson, A E Randel, and P C Earley, "Understanding Group Efficacy: An Empirical Test of Multiple Assessment Methods," *Group & Organization Management,* March 2000, pp 67–97; V U Druskat and S B Wolff, "Building the Emotional Intelligence of Groups," *Harvard Business Review,* March 2001, pp 80–90; S W Lester, B M Meglino, and M A Korsgaard, "The Antecedents and Consequences of Group Potency: A Longitudinal Investigation of Newly Formed Work Groups," *Academy of Management Journal,* April 2002, pp 352–68; and A Edmondson, R Bohmer, and G Pisano, "Speeding Up Team Learning," *Harvard Business Review,* October 2001, pp 125–32.

[16] Based on J F McGrew, J G Bilotta, and J M Deeney, "Software Team Formation and Decay: Extending the Standard Model for Small Groups," *Small Group Research,* April 1999, pp 209–34.

[17] Ibid., p 232.

[18] Ibid., p 231.

[19] D Davies and B C Kuypers, "Group Development and Interpersonal Feedback," *Group & Organizational Studies,* June 1985, p 194.

[20] Ibid., pp 184–208.

[21] C J G Gersick, "Marking Time: Predictable Transitions in Task Groups," *Academy of Management Journal,* June 1989, pp 274–309.

[22] D K Carew, E Parisi-Carew, and K H Blanchard, "Group Development and Situational Leadership: A Model for Managing Groups," *Training and Development Journal,* June 1986, pp 48–49. For evidence linking leadership and group effectiveness, see G R Bushe and A L Johnson, "Contextual and Internal Variables Affecting Task Group Outcomes in Organizations," *Group & Organization Studies,* December 1989, pp 462–82.

[23] See C Huxham and S Vangen, "Leadership in the Shaping and Implementation of Collaboration Agendas: How Things Happen in a (Not Quite) Joined-Up World," *Academy of Management Journal,* December 2000, pp 1159–75; and N Sivasubramaniam, W D Murry, B J Avolio, and D I Jung, "A Longitudinal Model of the Effects of Team Leadership and Group Potency on Group Performance," *Group & Organization Management,* March 2002, pp 66–96.

[24] Negative social impact on individuals is documented in G Blau, "Influence of Group Lateness on Individual Lateness: A Cross-Level Examination," *Academy of Management Journal,* October 1995, pp 1483–96.

[25] G Graen, "Role-Making Processes within Complex Organizations," in *Handbook of Industrial and Organizational Psychology,* ed M D Dunnette (Chicago: Rand McNally, 1976), p 1201. Also see L Van Dyne and J A LePine, "Helping and Voice Extra-Role Behaviors: Evidence of Construct and Predictive Validity," *Academy of Management Journal,* February 1998, pp 108–19.

[26] Other role determinants are explored in H Ibarra "Network Centrality, Power, and Innovation Involvement: Determinants of Technical and Administrative Roles," *Academy of Management Journal,* June 1993, pp 471–501. Role modeling applications are covered in J Barbian, "A Little Help from Your Friends," *Training,* March 2002, pp 38–41.

[27] G L Miles, "Doug Danforth's Plan to Put Westinghouse in the 'Winner's Circle,' " *Business Week,* July 28, 1986, p 75.

[28] For a review of research on the role episode model, see L A King and D W King, "Role Conflict and Role Ambiguity: A Critical Assessment of Construct Validity," *Psychological Bulletin,* January 1990, pp 48–64. Consequences of role perceptions are discussed in R C Netemeyer, S Burton, and M W Johnston, "A Nested Comparison of Four Models of the Consequences of Role Perception Variables," *Organizational Behavior and Human Decision Processes,* January 1995, pp 77–93.

[29] Schein, *Organizational Psychology,* p 198.

[30] Ibid. The relationship between interrole conflict and turnover is explored in P W Hom and A J Kinicki, "Toward a Greater Understanding of How Dissatisfaction Drives Employee Turnover," *Academy of Management Journal,* October 2001, pp 975–87.

[31] See D Moore, "Role Conflict: Not Only for Women? A Comparative Analysis of 5 Nations," *International Journal of Comparative Sociology,* June 1995, pp 17–35; S Shellenbarger, "More Men Move Past Incompetence Defense to Share Housework," *The Wall Street Journal,* February 21, 1996, p B1; and K S Peterson, "Pleasant Division of Labor = Less Than Half," *USA Today,* March 15, 1999, p 1D.

[32] "Liz Dolan," *Fast Company,* February–March 1999, p 89. Also see N Yang, C C Chen, J Choi, and Y Zou, "Sources of Work-Family Conflict: A Sino-U.S. Comparison of the Effects of Work and Family Demands," *Academy of Management Journal,* February 2000, pp 113–23.

[33] See D J Brass, K D Butterfield, and B C Skaggs, "Relationships and Unethical Behavior: A Social Network Perspective," *Academy of Management Review,* January 1998, pp 14–31.

[34] Schein, *Organizational Psychology,* p 198. Four types of role ambiguity are discussed in M A Eys and A V Carron, "Role Ambiguity, Task Cohesion, and Task Self-Efficacy," *Small Group Research,* June 2001, pp 356–73.

[35] Drawn from M Peterson et al., "Role Conflict, Ambiguity, and Overload: A 21-Nation Study," *Academy of Management Journal,* April 1995, pp 429–52.

[36] Based on Y Fried, H A Ben-David, R B Tiegs, N Avital, and U Yeverechyahu, "The Interactive Effect of Role Conflict and Role Ambiguity on Job Performance," *Journal of Occupational*

and Organizational Psychology, March 1998, pp 19–27. Also see A Risberg, "Employee Experiences of Acquisition Processes," *Journal of World Business,* Spring 2001, pp 58–84; M R Beauchamp and S R Bray, "Role Ambiguity and Role Conflict within Interdependent Teams," *Small Group Research,* April 2001, pp 133–57; and S R Bray and L R Brawley, "Role Efficacy, Role Clarity, and Role Performance Effectiveness," *Small Group Research,* April 2002, pp 233–53.

[37] 1 = A; 2 = C; 3 = A; 4 = A; 5 = C; 6 = A; 7 = C; 8 = A; 9 = C; 10 = C.

[38] R R Blake and J Srygley Mouton, "Don't Let Group Norms Stifle Creativity," *Personnel,* August 1985, p 28.

[39] See K L Gammage, A V Carron, and P A Estabrooks, "Team Cohesion and Individual Productivity: The Influence of the Norm for Productivity and the Identifiability of Individual Effort," *Small Group Research,* February 2001, pp 3–18; M M Colman and A V Carron, "The Nature of Norms in Individual Sport Teams," *Small Group Research,* April 2001, pp 206–22; and M C Higgins, "Follow the Leader? The Effects of Social Influence on Employer Choice," *Group & Organization Management,* September 2001, pp 255–82.

[40] A Dunkin, "Pepsi's Marketing Magic: Why Nobody Does It Better," *Business Week,* February 10, 1986, p 52.

[41] D C Feldman, "The Development and Enforcement of Group Norms," *Academy of Management Review,* January 1984, pp 50–52.

[42] See D M Casperson, "Mastering the Business Meal," *Training & Development,* March 2001, pp 68–69; J M Marques, D Abrams, and R G Serodio, "Being Better by Being Right: Subjective Group Dynamics and Derogation of In-Group Deviants When Generic Norms Are Undermined," *Journal of Personality and Social Psychology,* September 2001, pp 436–47; and T Wildschut, C A Insko, and L Gaertner, "Intragroup Social Influence and Intergroup Competition," *Journal of Personality and Social Psychology,* June 2002, pp 975–92.

[43] Feldman, "The Development and Enforcement of Group Norms."

[44] See R G Netemeyer, M W Johnston, and S Burton, "Analysis of Role Conflict and Role Ambiguity in a Structural Equations Framework," *Journal of Applied Psychology,* April 1990, pp 148–57; and G W McGee, C E Ferguson, Jr, and A Seers, "Role Conflict and Role Ambiguity: Do the Scales Measure These Two Constructs?," *Journal of Applied Psychology,* October 1989, pp 815–18.

[45] See S E Jackson and R S Schuler, "A Meta-Analysis and Conceptual Critique of Research on Role Ambiguity and Role Conflict in Work Settings," *Organizational Behavior and Human Decision Processes,* August 1985, pp 16–78.

[46] Based on C S Crandall, A Eshleman, and L O'Brien, "Social Norms and the Expression and Suppression of Prejudice: The Struggle for Internalization," *Journal of Personality and Social Psychology,* March 2002, pp 359–78. Also see J A Chatman and F J Flynn, "The Influence of Demographic Heterogeneity on the Emergence and Consequences of Cooperative Norms in Work Teams," *Academy of Management Journal,* October 2001, pp 956–74.

[47] See K D Benne and P Sheats, "Functional Roles of Group Members," *Journal of Social Issues,* Spring 1948, pp 41–49.

[48] See H J Klein and P W Mulvey, "Two Investigations of the Relationships among Group Goals, Goal Commitment, Cohesion, and Performance," *Organizational Behavior and Human Decision Processes,* January 1995, pp 44–53; and D F Crown and J G Rosse, "Yours, Mine, and Ours: Facilitating Group Productivity through the Integration of Individual and Group Goals," *Organizational Behavior and Human Decision Processes,* November 1995, pp 138–50.

[49] A Zander, "The Value of Belonging to a Group in Japan," *Small Group Behavior,* February 1983, pp 7–8. Also see P R Harris and R T Moran, *Managing Cultural Differences,* 4th ed (Houston: Gulf Publishing, 1996), pp 267–76.

[50] For example, see B Grofman, S L Feld, and G Owen, "Group Size and the Performance of a Composite Group Majority: Statistical Truths and Empirical Results," *Organizational Behavior and Human Performance,* June 1984, pp 350–59.

[51] See P Yetton and P Bottger, "The Relationships among Group Size, Member Ability, Social Decision Schemes, and Performance," *Organizational Behavior and Human Performance,* October 1983, pp 145–59.

[52] This copyrighted exercise may be found in J Hall, "Decisions, Decisions, Decisions," *Psychology Today,* November 1971, pp 51–54, 86, 88.

[53] Yetton and Bottger, "The Relationships among Group Size, Member Ability, Social Decision Schemes, and Performance," p 158.

[54] Based on R B Gallupe, A R Dennis, W H Cooper, J S Valacich, L M Bastianutti, and J F Nunamaker, Jr, "Electronic Brainstorming and Group Size," *Academy of Management Journal,* June 1992, pp 350–69. Also see H Barki and A Pinsonneault, "Small Group Brainstorming and Idea Quality: Is Electronic Brainstorming the Most Effective Approach?" *Small Group Research,* April 2001, pp 158–205; and T J Kramer, G P Fleming, and S M Mannis, "Improving Face-to-Face Brainstorming through Modeling and Facilitation," *Small Group Research,* October 2001, pp 533–57.

[55] Data from E Salas, D Rozell, B Mullen, and J E Driskell, "The Effect of Team Building on Performance: An Integration," *Small Group Research,* June 1999, pp 309–29.

[56] Drawn from B Mullen, C Symons, L-T Hu, and E Salas, "Group Size, Leadership Behavior, and Subordinate Satisfaction," *Journal of General Psychology,* April 1989, pp 155–69. Also see P Oliver and G Marwell, "The Paradox of Group Size in Collective Action: A Theory of the Critical Mass. II.," *American Sociological Review,* February 1988, pp 1–8.

[57] T Howard, "FTC Impasse Allows Pepsi, Quaker Deal," *USA Today,* August 2, 2001, p 1B.

[58] See, for example, K Hawkins and C B Power, "Gender Differences in Questions Asked During Small Decision-Making Group Discussions," *Small Group Research,* April 1999,

pp 235–56; R K Shelly and P T Munroe, "Do Women Engage in Less Task Behavior Than Men?" *Sociological Perspectives,* Spring 1999, pp 49–67; and L E Sandelands, "Male and Female in Organizational Behavior," *Journal of Organizational Behavior,* March 2002, pp 149–65.

[59] See L Smith-Lovin and C Brody, "Interruptions in Group Discussions: The Effects of Gender and Group Composition," *American Sociological Review,* June 1989, pp 424–35.

[60] E M Ott, "Effects of the Male-Female Ratio at Work," *Psychology of Women Quarterly,* March 1989, p 53.

[61] Data from B A Gutek, A Groff Cohen, and A M Konrad, "Predicting Social-Sexual Behavior at Work: A Contact Hypothesis," *Academy of Management Journal,* September 1990, pp 560–77. Also see C A Pierce and H Aguinis, "A Framework for Investigating the Link between Workplace Romance and Sexual Harassment," *Group & Organization Management,* June 2001, pp 206–29.

[62] Data from M Rotundo, D Nguyen, and P R Sackett, "A Meta-Analytic Review of Gender Differences in Perceptions of Sexual Harassment," *Journal of Applied Psychology,* October 2001, pp 914–22. Also see J H Wayne, C M Riordan, and K M Thomas, "Is All Sexual Harassment Viewed the Same? Mock Juror Decisions in Same- and Cross-Gender Cases," *Journal of Applied Psychology,* April 2001, pp 179–87; L J Munson, A G Miner, and C Hulin, "Labeling Sexual Harassment in the Military: An Extension and Replication," *Journal of Applied Psychology,* April 2001, pp 293–303; A B Malamut and L R Offermann, "Coping with Sexual Harassment: Personal, Environmental, and Cognitive Determinants," *Journal of Applied Psychology,* December 2001, pp 1152–66; and M E Bergman, R D Langhout, L M Cortina, P A Palmieri, and L F Fitzgerald, "The (Un)reasonableness of Reporting: Antecedents and Consequences of Reporting Sexual Harassment," *Journal of Applied Psychology,* April 2002, pp 230–42.

[63] See S A Lobel, R E Quinn, L St. Clair, and A Warfield, "Love without Sex: The Impact of Psychological Intimacy between Men and Women at Work," *Organizational Dynamics,* Summer 1994, pp 5–16.

[64] S J South, C M Bonjean, W T Markham, and J Corder, "Female Labor Force Participation and the Organizational Experiences of Male Workers," *Sociological Quarterly,* Summer 1983, p 378.

[65] B T Thornton, "Sexual Harassment, 1: Discouraging It in the Work Place," *Personnel,* April 1986, p 18. Good updates include G L Maatman Jr, "A Global View of Sexual Harassment," *HR Magazine,* July 2000, pp 151–58; J A Segal, "HR as Judge, Jury, Prosecutor, and Defender," *HR Magazine,* October 2001, pp 141–54; and J W Janove, "Sexual Harassment and the Three Big Surprises," *HR Magazine,* November 2001, pp 123–30.

[66] Data from T Galvin, "2001 Industry Report," *Training,* October 2001, pp 41, 54.

[67] I Pave, "A Woman's Place Is at GE, Federal Express P&G . . .," *Business Week,* June 23, 1986, p 78. Also see L Yu, "Does Diversity Drive Productivity?" *MIT Sloan Management Review,* Winter 2002, p 17; and L Grensing-Pophal, "Reaching for Diversity," *HR Magazine,* May 2002, pp 52–56.

[68] Diversity and group effectiveness are examined in D C Lau and J K Murnighan, "Demographic Diversity and Faultlines: The Compositional Dynamics of Organizational Groups," *Academy of Management Review,* April 1998, pp 325–40; B L Kelsey, "The Dynamics of Multicultural Groups: Ethnicity as a Determinant of Leadership," *Small Group Research,* October 1998, pp 602–23; D C Thomas, "Cultural Diversity and Work Group Effectiveness: An Experimental Study," *Journal of Cross-Cultural Psychology,* March 1999, pp 242–63; and L M Millhous, "The Experience of Culture in Multicultural Groups: Case Studies of Russian-American Collaboration in Business," *Small Group Research,* June 1999, pp 280–308.

[69] For details, see R A Rodriguez, "Challenging Demographic Reductionism: A Pilot Study Investigating Diversity in Group Composition," *Small Group Research,* December 1998, pp 744–59.

[70] Blake and Mouton, "Don't Let Group Norms Stifle Creativity," p 29.

[71] For additional information, see S E Asch, *Social Psychology* (Englewood Cliffs, NJ: Prentice Hall, 1952), ch 16.

[72] See T P Williams and S Sogon, "Group Composition and Conforming Behavior in Japanese Students," *Japanese Psychological Research,* no. 4, 1984, pp 231–34; and T Amir, "The Asch Conformity Effect: A Study in Kuwait," *Social Behavior and Personality,* no. 2, 1984, pp 187–90.

[73] Data from R Bond and P B Smith, "Culture and Conformity: A Meta-Analysis of Studies Using Asch's (1952b, 1956) Line Judgment Task," *Psychological Bulletin,* January 1996, pp 111–37.

[74] J L Roberts and E Thomas, "Enron's Dirty Laundry," *Newsweek,* March 11, 2002, p 26. Also see G Farrell and J O'Donnell, "Watkins Testifies Skilling, Fastow Duped Lay, Board," *USA Today,* February 15, 2002, pp 1B–2B; and M Schminke, D Wells, J Peyrefitte, and T C Sebora, "Leadership and Ethics in Work Groups: A Longitudinal Assessment," *Group & Organization Management,* June 2002, pp 272–93.

[75] For a comprehensive update on groupthink, see the entire February–March 1998 issue of *Organizational Behavior and Human Decision Processes* (12 articles).

[76] I L Janis, *Groupthink,* 2nd ed (Boston: Houghton Mifflin, 1982), p 9. Alternative models are discussed in K Granstrom and D Stiwne, "A Bipolar Model of Groupthink: An Expansion of Janis's Concept," *Small Group Research,* February 1998, pp 32–56; and A R Flippen, "Understanding Groupthink From a Self-Regulatory Perspective," *Small Group Research,* April 1999, pp 139–65.

[77] Ibid. For an alternative model, see R J Aldag and S Riggs Fuller, "Beyond Fiasco: A Reappraisal of the Groupthink Phenomenon and a New Model of Group Decision Processes," *Psychological Bulletin,* May 1993, pp 533–52. Also see A A Mohamed and F A Wiebe, "Toward a Process Theory of Groupthink," *Small Group Research,* August 1996, pp 416–30.

[78] L Baum, "The Job Nobody Wants," *Business Week,* September 8, 1986, p 60. Also see J G Koretz, "Friendly Boards Are Not All Bad," *Business Week,* June 14, 1999, p 34; W

Shapiro, "Groupthink a Danger for White House War Planners," *USA Today,* October 3, 2001, p 7A; and K Brooker, "Trouble in the Boardroom," *Fortune,* May 13, 2002, pp 113–16.

[79] Details of this study may be found in M R Callaway and J K Esser, "Groupthink: Effects of Cohesiveness and Problem-Solving Procedures on Group Decision Making," *Social Behavior and Personality,* no. 2, 1984, pp 157–64. Also see C R Leana, "A Partial Test of Janis's Groupthink Model: Effects of Group Cohesiveness and Leader-Behavior on Defective Decision Making," *Journal of Management,* Spring 1985, pp 5–17; and G Moorhead and J R Montanari, "An Empirical Investigation of the Groupthink Phenomenon," *Human Relations,* May 1986, pp 399–410. A more modest indirect effect is reported in J N Choi and M U Kim, "The Organizational Application of Groupthink and Its Limitations in Organizations," *Journal of Applied Psychology,* April 1999, pp 297–306.

[80] Adapted from discussion in Janis, *Groupthink,* ch 11.

[81] J A Byrne, "How to Fix Corporate Governance," *Business Week,* May 6, 2002, p 78. Also see J A Byrne, "Restoring Trust in Corporate America," *Business Week,* June 24, 2002, pp 30–35.

[82] Based on discussion in B Latane, K Williams, and S Harkins, "Many Hands Make Light the Work: The Causes and Consequences of Social Loafing," *Journal of Personality and Social Psychology,* June 1979, pp 822–32; and D A Kravitz and B Martin, "Ringelmann Rediscovered: The Original Article," *Journal of Personality and Social Psychology,* May 1986, pp 936–41.

[83] See J A Shepperd, "Productivity Loss in Performance Groups: A Motivation Analysis," *Psychological Bulletin,* no. 1, 1993, pp 67–81; R E Kidwell, Jr, and N Bennett, "Employee Propensity to Withhold Effort: A Conceptual Model to Intersect Three Avenues of Research," *Academy of Management Review,* July 1993, pp 429–56; S J Karau and K D Williams, "Social Loafing: Meta-Analytic Review and Theoretical Integration," *Journal of Personality and Social Psychology,* October 1993, pp 681–706; and S G Scott and W O Einstein, "Strategic Performance Appraisal in Team-Based Organizations: One Size Does Not Fit All," *Academy of Management Executive,* May 2001, pp 107–16.

[84] See S J Zaccaro, "Social Loafing: The Role of Task Attractiveness," *Personality and Social Psychology Bulletin,* March 1984, pp 99–106; J M Jackson and K D Williams, "Social Loafing on Difficult Tasks: Working Collectively Can Improve Performance," *Journal of Personality and Social Psychology,* October 1985, pp 937–42; and J M George, "Extrinsic and Intrinsic Origins of Perceived Social Loafing in Organizations," *Academy of Management Journal,* March 1992, pp 191–202.

[85] For complete details, see K Williams, S Harkins, and B Latane, "Identifiability as a Deterrent to Social Loafing: Two Cheering Experiments," *Journal of Personality and Social Psychology,* February 1981, pp 303–11.

[86] See J M Jackson and S G Harkins, "Equity in Effort: An Explanation of the Social Loafing Effect," *Journal of*

Personality and Social Psychology, November 1985, pp 1199–1206.

[87] Both studies are reported in S G Harkins and K Szymanski, "Social Loafing and Group Evaluation," *Journal of Personality and Social Psychology,* June 1989, pp 934–41.

[88] Data from J A Wagner III, "Studies of Individualism-Collectivism: Effects on Cooperation in Groups," *Academy of Management Journal,* February 1995, pp 152–72. Also see P W Mulvey and H J Klein, "The Impact of Perceived Loafing and Collective Efficacy on Group Goal Processes and Group Performance," *Organizational Behavior and Human Decision Processes,* April 1998, pp 62–87; P W Mulvey, L Bowes-Sperry, and H J Klein, "The Effects of Perceived Loafing and Defensive Impression Management on Group Effectiveness," *Small Group Research,* June 1998, pp 394–415; and L Karakowsky and K McBey, "Do My Contributions Matter? The Influence of Imputed Expertise on Member Involvement and Self-Evaluations in the Work Group," *Group & Organization Management,* March 2001, pp 70–92.

[89] S G Rogelberg, J L Barnes-Farrell, and C A Lowe, "The Stepladder Technique: An Alternative Group Structure Facilitating Effective Group Decision Making," *Journal of Applied Psychology,* October 1992, p 730.

[90] P Hoversten, "Thiokol Wavers, Then Decides to Launch," *USA Today,* January 22, 1996, p 2A. Copyright 1996, USA Today. Reprinted with permission.

[91] This paragraph and the balance of the case are excerpted from P Hoversten, P Edmonds, and H El Nasser, "Debate Raged before Doomed Launch," *USA Today,* January 22, 1996, pp 1A–2A. Copyright 1996, *USA Today.* Reprinted with permission.

[92] Twenty items excerpted from S A Wheelan and J M Hochberger, "Validation Studies of the Group Development Questionnaire," *Small Group Research,* February 1996, pp 143–70.

[93] From *Developing Management Skills* by D A Whetten and K S Cameron. Copyright © 1984 by Scott, Foresman and Company. Reprinted by permission of Addison Wesley Educational Publishers, Inc.

[94] Excerpted from K Thomas, "The Kids Are All Right," *USA Today,* May 28, 2002, pp 1D–2D.

CHAPTER 13

[1] Excerpted from A Overholt, "Virtually There?" *Fast Company,* March 2002, pp 111–12.

[2] For a good overview, see the entire March 2001 issue of *Journal of Organizational Behavior.*

[3] See P F Drucker, "The Coming of the New Organization," *Harvard Business Review,* January–February 1988, pp 45–53.

[4] J Pfeffer and J F Veiga, "Putting People First for Organizational Success," *Academy of Management Executive,* May 1999, p 41.

[5] See N Enbar, "What Do Women Want? Ask 'Em," *Business Week,* March 29, 1999, p 8; and M Hickins, "Duh! Gen Xers Are Cool with Teamwork," *Management Review,* March 1999, p 7.

[6] J R Katzenbach, and D K Smith, *The Wisdom of Teams: Creating the High-Performance Organization* (New York: HarperBusiness, 1999), p 45. Sports teams are discussed in N Katz, "Sports Teams as a Model for Workplace Teams: Lessons and Liabilities," *Academy of Management Executive,* August 2001, pp 56–67; R Fusaro, "The Big Comeback," *Harvard Business Review,* January 2002, p 20; and G Colvin, "Think You Can Bobsled? Ha!" *Fortune,* March 18, 2002, p 50.

[7] For an interesting case study, see P F Levy, "The Nut Island Effect: When Good Teams Go Wrong," *Harvard Business Review,* March 2001, pp 51–59.

[8] J R Katzenbach and D K Smith, "The Discipline of Teams," *Harvard Business Review,* March–April 1993, p 112.

[9] "A Team's-Eye View of Teams," *Training,* November 1995, p 16.

[10] See E Sundstrom, K P DeMeuse, and D Futrell, "Work Teams," *American Psychologist,* February 1990, pp 120–33.

[11] For an alternative typology of teams, see S G Scott and Walter O Einstien, "Strategic Performance Appraisal in Team-Based Organizations: One Size Does Not Fit All," *Academy of Management Executive,* May 2001, pp 107–16.

[12] See G Van der Vegt, B Emans, and E Van de Vliert, "Effects of Interdependencies in Project Teams," *Journal of Social Psychology,* April 1999, pp 202–14; and A L Kristof-Brown and C K Stevens, "Goal Congruence in Project Teams: Does the Fit between Members' Personal Mastery and Performance Goals Matter?" *Journal of Applied Psychology,* December 2001, pp 1083–95.

[13] For a description of medical teams in action, see J Appleby and R Davis, "Teamwork Used to Be a Money Saver; Now It's a Lifesaver," *USA Today,* March 1, 2001, pp 1B–2B.

[14] P King, "What Makes Teamwork Work?" *Psychology Today,* December 1989, p 16.

[15] See R S Landis, "A Note on the Stability of Team Performance," *Journal of Applied Psychology,* June 2001, pp 446–50; M A Marks, J E Mathieu, and S J Zaccaro, "A Temporally Based Framework and Taxonomy of Team Processes," *Academy of Management Review,* July 2001, pp 356–76; M A Marks, M J Sabella, C S Burke, and S J Zacccaro, "The Impact of Cross-Training on Team Effectiveness," *Journal of Applied Psychology,* February 2002, pp 3–13; and J N Choi, "External Activities and Team Effectiveness: Review and Theoretical Development," *Small Group Research,* April 2002, pp 181–208.

[16] Sundstrom, DeMeuse, and Futrell, "Work Teams," p 122.

[17] For more on team-member satisfaction, see M A Griffin, M G Patterson, and M A West, "Job Satisfaction and Teamwork: The Role of Supervisor Support," *Journal of Organizational Behavior,* August 2001, pp 537–50; and C M Mason and M A Griffin, "Group Task Satisfaction: Applying the Construct of Job Satisfaction to Groups," *Small Group Research,* June 2002, pp 271–312.

[18] Other team criteria are discussed in N R Anderson and M A West, "Measuring Climate for Work Group Innovation: Development and Validation of the Team Climate Inventory," *Journal of Organizational Behavior,* May 1998, pp 235–58; and M J Stevens and M A Campion, "Staffing Work Teams: Development and Validation of a Selection Test for Teamwork Settings," *Journal of Management,* no. 2 (1999), pp 207–28.

[19] For example, see C O Longenecker and M Neubert, "Barriers and Gateways to Management Cooperation and Teamwork," *Business Horizons,* September–October 2000, pp 37–44; and M D Cannon and A C Edmondson, "Confronting Failure: Antecedents and Consequences of Shared Beliefs about Failure in Organizational Work Groups," *Journal of Organizational Behavior,* March 2001, pp 161–77.

[20] H Lancaster, "Those Rotten Things You Say about Work May Be True After All," *The Wall Street Journal,* February 20, 1996, p B1.

[21] Ibid.

[22] Team problems are revealed in L Holpp, "The Betrayal of the American Work Team," *Training,* May 1996, pp 38–42; S Wetlaufer, "The Team That Wasn't," *Harvard Business Review,* November–December 1994, pp 22–38; "More Trouble with Teams," *Training,* October 1996, p 21; and E Neuborne, "Companies Save, but Workers Pay," *USA Today,* February 25, 1997, pp 1B–2B.

[23] See M J Stevens and M A Campion, "The Knowledge, Skill, and Ability Requirements for Teamwork: Implications for Human Resource Management," *Journal of Management,* Summer 1994, pp 503–30; and D L Miller, "Reexamining Teamwork KSAs and Team Performance," *Small Group Research,* December 2001, pp 745–66. Also see L L Thompson, *Making the Team: A Guide for Managers* (Upper Saddle River, NJ: Prentice Hall, 2000).

[24] P Raeburn, "Whoops! Wrong Patient," *Business Week,* June 17, 2002, p 85.

[25] See M E Haskins, J Liedtka, and J Rosenblum, "Beyond Teams: Toward an Ethic of Collaboration," *Organizational Dynamics,* Spring 1998, pp 34–50; C C Chen, X P Chen, and J R Meindl, "How Can Cooperation Be Fostered? The Cultural Effects of Individualism-Collectivism," *Academy of Management Review,* April 1998, pp 285–304; and "Roche's Big Discovery: Teamwork," *Fast Company,* January 2002, p 66.

[26] A Kohn, "How to Succeed without Even Vying," *Psychology Today,* September 1986, pp 27–28. Sports psychologists discuss "cooperative competition" in S Sleek, "Competition: Who's the Real Opponent?" *APA Monitor,* July 1996, p 8.

[27] D W Johnson, G Maruyama, R Johnson, D Nelson, and L Skon, "Effects of Cooperative, Competitive, and Individualistic Goal Structures on Achievement: A Meta-Analysis," *Psychological Bulletin,* January 1981, pp 56–57. An alternative interpretation of the foregoing study that emphasizes the influence of situational factors can be found in J L Cotton and M S Cook, "Meta-Analysis and the Effects of Various Reward

Systems: Some Different Conclusions from Johnson et al.," *Psychological Bulletin,* July 1982, pp 176–83. Also see A E Ortiz, D W Johnson, and R T Johnson, "The Effect of Positive Goal and Resource Interdependence on Individual Performance," *Journal of Social Psychology,* April 1996, pp 243–49; and S L Gaertner, J F Dovidio, M C Rust, J A Nier, B S Banker, C M Ward, G R Mottola, and M Houlette, "Reducing Intergroup Bias: Elements of Intergroup Cooperation," *Journal of Personality and Social Psychology,* March 1999, pp 388–402.

28 R Zemke, "Office Spaces," *Training,* May 2002, p 24.

29 R Lieber, "Timex Resets Its Watch," *Fast Company,* November 2001, p 48; and F Warner, "He Builds Company Towns," *Fast Company,* January 2002, pp 46, 48.

30 S W Cook and M Pelfrey, "Reactions to Being Helped in Cooperating Interracial Groups: A Context Effect," *Journal of Personality and Social Psychology,* November 1985, p 1243. Also see W E Watson, L Johnson, and D Merritt, "Team Orientation, Self-Orientation, and Diversity in Task Groups," *Group & Organization Management,* June 1998, pp 161–88.

31 See A J Stahelski and R A Tsukuda, "Predictors of Cooperation in Health Care Teams," *Small Group Research,* May 1990, pp 220–33. Also see K Aquino and A Reed II, "A Social Dilemma Perspective on Cooperative Behavior in Organizations," *Group & Organization Management,* December 1998, pp 390–413.

32 See G Colvin, "The Great CEO Pay Heist," *Fortune,* June 25, 2001, pp 64–70; C J Loomis, "This Stuff Is Wrong," *Fortune,* June 25, 2001, pp 72–84; and J A Byrne, "Restoring Trust in Corporate America," *Business Week,* June 24, 2002, pp 30–35.

33 S Armour, "Employees' New Motto: Trust No One," *USA Today,* February 5, 2002, p 2B.

34 J Barbian, "Short Shelf Life," *Training,* June 2002, p 52.

35 See R Zemke, "Trust Inspires Trust," *Training,* January 2002, p 10.

36 J D Lewis and A Weigert, "Trust as a Social Reality," *Social Forces,* June 1985, p 971. Trust is examined as an *indirect* factor in K T Dirks, "The Effects of Interpersonal Trust on Work Group Performance," *Journal of Applied Psychology,* June 1999, pp 445–55.

37 R C Mayer, J H Davis, and F D Schoorman, "An Integrative Model of Organizational Trust," *Academy of Management Review,* July 1995, p 715.

38 Lewis and Weigert, "Trust as a Social Reality," p 970. Also see C Gomez and B Rosen, "The Leader-Member Exchange as a Link between Managerial Trust and Employee Empowerment," *Group & Organization Management,* March 2001, pp 53–69; M Williams, "In Whom We Trust: Group Membership as an Affective Context for Trust Development," *Academy of Management Review,* July 2001, pp 377–96; and S Aryee, P S Budhwar, and Z X Chen, "Trust as a Mediator of the Relationship between Organizational Justice and Work Outcomes: Test of a Social Exchange Model," *Journal of Organizational Behavior,* May 2002, pp 267–85.

39 For an interesting trust exercise, see G Thompson and P F Pearce, "The Team-Trust Game," *Training & Development Journal,* May 1992, pp 42–43.

40 M Powell, "Betrayal," *Inc.,* April 1996, p 24. Also see L Prusak and D Cohen, "How to Invest in Social Capital," *Harvard Business Review,* June 2001, pp 86–93; and G Colvin, "Tapping the Trust Fund," *Fortune,* April 29, 2002, p 44.

41 See G L Graham, "If You Want Honesty, Break Some Rules," *Harvard Business Review,* April 2002, pp 42–47.

42 For support, see G M Spreitzer and A K Mishra, "Giving Up Control without Losing Control: Trust and Its Substitutes' Effects on Managers' Involving Employees in Decision Making," *Group & Organization Management,* June 1999, pp 155–87.

43 Adapted from F Bartolomé, "Nobody Trusts the Boss Completely—Now What?" *Harvard Business Review,* March–April 1989, pp 135–42. Also see R Zemke, "Can You Manage Trust?" *Training,* February 2000, pp 76–83.

44 W Foster Owen, "Metaphor Analysis of Cohesiveness in Small Discussion Groups," *Small Group Behavior,* August 1985, p 416. Also see S A Carless and C De Paola, "The Measurement of Cohesion in Work Teams," *Small Group Research,* February 2000, pp 71–88; and A V Carron and L R Brawley, "Cohesion: Conceptual and Measurement Issues," *Small Group Research,* February 2000, pp 89–106.

45 This distinction is based on discussion in A Tziner, "Differential Effects of Group Cohesiveness Types: A Clarifying Overview," *Social Behavior and Personality,* no. 2: (1982) pp 227–39.

46 B Mullen and C Copper, "The Relation between Group Cohesiveness and Performance: An Integration," *Psychological Bulletin,* March 1994, p 224.

47 Ibid. Additional research evidence is reported in P J Sullivan and D L Feltz, "The Relationship between Intrateam Conflict and Cohesion within Hockey Teams," *Small Group Research,* June 2001, pp 342–55; and A Chang and P Bordia, "A Multidimensional Approach to the Group Cohesion–Group Performance Relationship," *Small Group Research,* August 2001, pp 379–405.

48 Based on B Mullen, T Anthony, E Salas, and J E Driskell, "Group Cohesiveness and Quality of Decision Making: An Integration of Tests of the Groupthink Hypothesis," *Small Group Research,* May 1994, pp 189–204. Also see L D Sargent and C Sue-Chan, "Does Diversity Affect Group Efficacy? The Intervening Role of Cohesion and Task Interdependence," *Small Group Research,* August 2001, pp 426–50; and D I Jung and J J Sosik, "Transformational Leadership in Work Groups: The Role of Empowerment, Cohesiveness, and Collective-Efficacy on Perceived Group Performance," *Small Group Research,* June 2002, pp 313–36.

49 G L Miles, "The Plant of Tomorrow Is in Texas Today," *Business Week,* July 28, 1986, p 76.

50 See, for example, P Jin, "Work Motivation and Productivity in Voluntarily Formed Work Teams: A Field Study in China,"

Organizational Behavior and Human Decision Processes, 1993, pp 133–55. The related topic of commitment is discussed in B Fehr, "Laypeople's Conceptions of Commitment," *Journal of Personality and Social Psychology,* January 1999, pp 90–103.

[51] Based on discussion in E E Lawler III and S A Mohrman, "Quality Circles: After the Honeymoon," *Organizational Dynamics,* Spring 1987, pp 42–54.

[52] For a report on 8,000 quality circles in Mexico, see R Carvajal, "Its Own Reward," *Business Mexico,* special edition 1996, pp 26–28.

[53] The historical development of quality circles is discussed by C Stohl, "Bridging the Parallel Organization: A Study of Quality Circle Effectiveness," in *Organizational Communication,* ed M L McLaughlin (Beverly Hills, CA: Sage Publications, 1987), pp 416–30; T Li-Ping Tang, P Smith Tollison, and H D Whiteside, "The Effect of Quality Circle Initiation on Motivation to Attend Quality Circle Meetings and on Task Performance," *Personnel Psychology,* Winter 1987, pp 799–814; and N Kano, "A Perspective on Quality Activities in American Firms," *California Management Review,* Spring 1993, pp 12–31. Also see the discussion of quality circles in J B Keys, L T Denton, and T R Miller, "The Japanese Management Theory Jungle—Revisited," *Journal of Management,* Summer 1994, pp 373–402.

[54] Based on discussion in K Buch and R Spangler, "The Effects of Quality Circles on Performance and Promotions," *Human Relations,* June 1990, pp 573–82.

[55] See G R Ferris and J A Wagner III, "Quality Circles in the United States: A Conceptual Reevaluation," *Journal of Applied Behavioral Science,* no. 2 (1985), pp 155–67.

[56] Lawler and Mohrman, "Quality Circles: After the Honeymoon," p 43. Also see E E Lawler III, "Total Quality Management and Employee Involvement: Are They Compatible?" *Academy of Management Executive,* February 1994, pp 68–76.

[57] See M L Marks, "The Question of Quality Circles," *Psychology Today,* March 1986, pp 36–38, 42, 44, 46.

[58] See A K Naj, "Some Manufacturers Drop Effort to Adopt Japanese Techniques," *The Wall Street Journal,* May 7, 1993, p A1.

[59] See E E Adam, Jr, "Quality Circle Performance," *Journal of Management,* March 1991, pp 25–39.

[60] See R P Steel and R F Lloyd, "Cognitive, Affective, and Behavioral Outcomes of Participation in Quality Circles: Conceptual and Empirical Findings," *Journal of Applied Behavioral Science,* no. 1 (1988), pp 1–17; M L Marks, P H Mirvis, E J Hackett, and J F Grady, Jr, "Employee Participation in a Quality Circle Program: Impact on Quality of Work Life, Productivity, and Absenteeism," *Journal of Applied Psychology,* February 1986, pp 61–69; and Buch and Spangler, "The Effects of Quality Circles on Performance and Promotions." Additional research is reported in T Li-Ping Tang, P Smith Tollison, and H D Whiteside, "Differences between Active and Inactive Quality Circles in Attendance and Performance," *Public Personnel Management,* Winter 1993, pp 579–90; and C

Doucouliagos, "Worker Participation and Productivity in Labor-Managed and Participatory Capitalist Firms: A Meta-Analysis," *Industrial and Labor Relations Review,* October 1995, pp 58–77.

[61] See B S Bell and S W J Kozlowski, "A Typology of Virtual Teams: Implications for Effective Leadership," *Group & Organization Management,* March 2002, pp 14–49.

[62] See W F Cascio, "Managing a Virtual Workplace," *Academy of Management Executive,* August 2000, pp 81–90; C Joinson, "Managing Virtual Teams," *HR Magazine,* June 2002, pp 69–73; and D Robb, "Virtual Workplace," *HR Magazine,* June 2002, pp 105–13.

[63] Based on P Bordia, N DiFonzo, and A Chang, "Rumor as Group Problem Solving: Development Patterns in Informal Computer-Mediated Groups," *Small Group Research,* February 1999, pp 8–28.

[64] See K A Graetz, E S Boyle, C E Kimble, P Thompson, and J L Garloch, "Information Sharing in Face-to-Face, Teleconferencing, and Electronic Chat Groups," *Small Group Research,* December 1998, pp 714–43.

[65] Based on F Niederman and R J Volkema, "The Effects of Facilitator Characteristics on Meeting Preparation, Set Up, and Implementation," *Small Group Research,* June 1999, pp 330–60; and B Whitworth, B Gallupe, and R McQueen, "Generating Agreement in Computer-Mediated Groups," *Small Group Research,* October 2001, pp 625–65.

[66] Based on J J Sosik, B J Avolio, and S S Kahai, "Inspiring Group Creativity: Comparing Anonymous and Identified Electronic Brainstorming," *Small Group Research,* February 1998, pp 3–31. For practical advice on brainstorming, see C Caggiano, "The Right Way to Brainstorm," *Inc.,* July 1999, p 94.

[67] Based on M M Montoya-Weiss, A P Massey, and M Song, "Getting It Together: Temporal Coordination and Conflict Management in Global Virtual Teams," *Academy of Management Journal,* December 2001, pp 1251–62.

[68] Data from C Joinson, "Teams at Work," *HR Magazine,* May 1999, pp 30–36.

[69] B Dumaine, "Who Needs a Boss?" *Fortune,* May 7, 1990, p 52.

[70] A B Cheney, H P Sims, Jr, and C C Manz, "Teams and TQM," *Business Horizons,* September–October 1994, pp 22–23.

[71] See M Moravec, O J Johannessen, and T A Hjelmas, "The Well-Managed SMT," *Management Review,* June 1998, pp 56–58; and "Case Study in C-Sharp Minor," *Training,* October 1998, p 21.

[72] See R M Yandrick, "A Team Effort," *HR Magazine,* June 2001, pp 136–41.

[73] See R T Keller, "Cross-Functional Project Groups in Research and New Product Development: Diversity, Communications, Job Stress, and Outcomes," *Academy of Management Journal,* June 2001, pp 547–55; and K Lovelace, D L Shapiro, and L R Weingart, "Maximizing Cross-Functional

New Product Teams' Innovativeness and Constraint Adherence: A Conflict Communications Perspective," *Academy of Management Journal,* August 2001, pp 779–93.

[74] A Erdman, "How to Keep That Family Feeling," *Fortune,* April 6, 1992, p 95.

[75] See "1996 Industry Report: What Self-Managing Teams Manage," *Training,* October 1996, p 69.

[76] Drawn from P S Goodman, R Devadas, and T L Griffith Hughson, "Groups and Productivity: Analyzing the Effectiveness of Self-Managing Teams," in *Productivity in Organizations,* eds J P Campbell, R J Campbell and Associates (San Francisco: Jossey-Bass, 1988), pp 295–327. Also see E F Rogers, W Metlay, I T Kaplan, and T Shapiro, "Self-Managing Work Teams: Do They Really Work?" *Human Resource Planning,* no. 2 (1995), pp 53–57; and V U Druskat and S B Wolff, "Effects and Timing of Developmental Peer Appraisals in Self-Managing Work Groups," *Journal of Applied Psychology,* February 1999, pp 58–74.

[77] Based on R C Liden, S J Wayne, and M L Kraimer, "Managing Individual Performance in Work Groups," *Human Resource Management,* Spring 2001, pp 63–72.

[78] See M H Jordan, H S Feild, and A A Armenakis, "The Relationship of Group Process Variables and Team Performance: A Team-Level Analysis in a Field Setting," *Small Group Research,* February 2002, pp 121–50.

[79] B L Kirkman and D L Shapiro, "The Impact of Cultural Values on Job Satisfaction and Organizational Commitment in Self-Managing Work Teams: The Mediating Role of Employee Resistance," *Academy of Management Journal,* June 2001, p 565.

[80] See R E Walton, "Work Innovations at Topeka: After Six Years," *Journal of Applied Behavioral Science,* 1977, pp 422–33.

[81] See P Thoms, J K Pinto, D H Parente, and V U Druskat, "Adaptation to Self-Managing Work Teams," *Small Group Research,* February 2002, pp 3–31.

[82] See Dumaine, "Who Needs a Boss?" pp 55, 58; and J Hillkirk, "Self-Directed Work Teams Give TI Lift," *USA Today,* December 20, 1993, p 8B. A good contingency model for empowering teams is presented in R C Liden, S J Wayne, and L Bradway, "Connections Make the Difference," *HR Magazine,* February 1996, pp 73–79.

[83] Data from S Alper, D Tjosvold, and K S Law, "Interdependence and Controversy in Group Decision Making: Antecedents to Effective Self-Managing Teams," *Organizational Behavior and Human Decision Processes,* April 1998, pp 33–52.

[84] See M S O'Connell, D Doverspike, and A B Cober, "Leadership and Semiautonomous Work Team Performance: A Field Study," *Group & Organization Management,* March 2002, pp 50–65.

[85] Based on K Lowry Miller, "GM's German Lessons," *Business Week,* December 20, 1993, pp 67–68.

[86] See E Brown, "War Games to Make You Better at Business," *Fortune,* September 28, 1998, pp 291–96; M Hickins, "A Day at the Races," *Management Review,* May 1999, pp 56–61; J Rendon, "Corporate Bondage," *Business 2.0,* September 26, 2000, pp 204–7; and C Dahle, "Can This Off-Site Be Saved?" *Fast Company,* October 2001, pp 118–27.

[87] R Henkoff, "Companies that Train Best," *Fortune,* March 22, 1993, p 73.

[88] See M J McCarthy, "A Management Rage: Beating the Drums for the Company," *The Wall Street Journal,* August 13, 1996, pp A1, A6.

[89] An excellent resource is W G Dyer, *Team Building: Current Issues and New Alternatives,* 3rd ed (Reading, MA: Addison-Wesley, 1995). Also see G L Stewart, C C Manz, and H P Sims, Jr, *Team Work and Group Dynamics* (New York: Wiley, 1999).

[90] S Bucholz and T Roth, *Creating the High-Performance Team* (New York: John Wiley & Sons, 1987), p xi.

[91] Ibid., p 14. Also see V U Druskat and S B Wolff, "Building the Emotional Intelligence of Groups," *Harvard Business Review,* March 2001, pp 80–90; and A Edmondson, R Bohmer, and G Pisano, "Speeding Up Team Learning," *Harvard Business Review,* October 2001, pp 125–32.

[92] P King, "What Makes Teamwork Work?" *Psychology Today,* December 1989, p 17. A critical view of teams is presented in C Casey, " 'Come, Join Our Family': Discipline and Integration in Corporate Organizational Culture," *Human Relations,* February 1999, pp 155–78.

[93] Adapted from C C Manz and H P Sims, Jr, "Leading Workers to Lead Themselves: The External Leadership of Self-Managing Work Teams," *Administrative Science Quarterly,* March 1987, pp 106–29. Also see C C Manz, *Mastering Self-Leadership: Empowering Yourself for Personal Excellence* (Englewood Cliffs, NJ: Prentice Hall, 1992); M Uhl-Bien and G B Graen, "Individual Self-Management: Analysis of 'Professional' Self-Managing Activities in Functional and Cross-Functional Work Teams," *Academy of Management Journal,* June 1998, pp 340–50; G E Prussia, J S Anderson, and C C Manz, "Self-Leadership and Performance Outcomes: The Mediating Influence of Self-Efficacy," *Journal of Organizational Behavior,* September 1998, pp 523–38; and P Troiano, "Nice Guys Finish First," *Management Review,* December 1998, p 8.

[94] Excerpted from N M Tichy, "No Ordinary Boot Camp," *Harvard Business Review,* April 2001, pp 63–70. For more on Trilogy, go to **www.trilogy.com.**

[95] Questionnaire items adapted from C Johnson-George and W C Swap, "Measurement of Specific Interpersonal Trust: Construction and Validation of a Scale to Assess Trust in a Specific Other," *Journal of Personality and Social Psychology,* December 1982, pp 1306–17; and D J McAllister, "Affect- and Cognition-Based Trust as Foundations for Interpersonal Cooperation in Organizations," *Academy of Management Journal,* February 1995, pp 24–59.

[96] Ten questionnaire items excerpted from W G Dyer, *Team Building: Current Issues and New Alternatives,* 3rd ed (Reading, MA: Addison-Wesley, 1995), pp 96–99.

[97] S Williams, "All Smoke, No Fire," *Fast Company,* April 1996, p 134. (Also in *Fast Company*'s Dynamic Archives at **www.fastcompany.com.**)

CHAPTER 14

[1] Excerpted from M Boitano, "You Got a Problem with That?" *Fortune,* June 11, 2001, pp 196[B]–196[F].

[2] D Tjosvold, *Learning to Manage Conflict: Getting People to Work Together Productively* (New York: Lexington Books, 1993), p xi.

[3] Ibid., pp xi–xii.

[4] J A Wall, Jr, and R Robert Callister, "Conflict and Its Management," *Journal of Management,* no. 3 (1995), p 517.

[5] Ibid., p 544.

[6] K Cloke and J Goldsmith, *Resolving Conflicts at Work: A Complete Guide for Everyone on the Job* (San Francisco: Jossey-Bass, 2000), pp 25, 27, 29.

[7] Ibid., pp 31–32. Also see M Delahoussaye, "Don't Get Mad, Get Promoted," *Training,* June 2002, p 20; and R E Shea, "Break the Retaliation Cycle," *HR Magazine,* July 2002, pp 89–96.

[8] See K Dobbs, "The Lucrative Menace of Workplace Violence," *Training,* March 2000, pp 54–62; S C Douglas and M J Martinko, "Exploring the Role of Individual Differences in the Prediction of Workplace Aggression," *Journal of Applied Psychology,* August 2001, pp 547–59; and K Tyler, "Afraid to Fly, and It Shows," *HR Magazine,* September 2001, pp 64–74.

[9] See S Alper, D Tjosvold, and K S Law, "Interdependence and Controversy in Group Decision Making: Antecedents to Effective Self-Managing Teams," *Organizational Behavior and Human Decision Processes,* April 1998, pp 33–52.

[10] S P Robbins, " 'Conflict Management' and 'Conflict Resolution' Are Not Synonymous Terms," *California Management Review,* Winter 1978, p 70.

[11] Cooperative conflict is discussed in Tjosvold, *Learning to Manage Conflict: Getting People to Work Together Productively.* Also see A C Amason, "Distinguishing the Effects of Functional and Dysfunctional Conflict on Strategic Decision Making: Resolving a Paradox for Top Management Teams," *Academy of Management Journal,* February 1996, pp 123–48.

[12] K Brooker, "Can Anyone Replace Herb?" *Fortune,* April 17, 2000, p 190.

[13] K Brooker, "I Built This Company, I Can Save It," *Fortune,* April 30, 2001, p 102.

[14] Adapted in part from discussion in A C Filley, *Interpersonal Conflict Resolution* (Glenview, IL: Scott, Foresman, 1975), pp 9–12; and B Fortado, "The Accumulation of Grievance Conflict," *Journal of Management Inquiry,* December 1992, pp 288–303. For related research on the antecedents of marital conflict, see P R Amato and A Booth, "The Legacy of Parents' Marital Discord: Consequences for Children's Marital Quality," *Journal of Personality and Social Psychology,* October 2001, pp 627–38.

[15] Adapted from discussion in Tjosvold, *Learning to Manage Conflict,* pp 12–13.

[16] L Gardenswartz and A Rowe, *Diverse Teams at Work: Capitalizing on the Power of Diversity* (New York: McGraw-Hill, 1994), p 32.

[17] F Keenan, "EMC: Turmoil at the Top?" *Business Week,* March 11, 2002, pp 58–60.

[18] See L M Andersson and C M Pearson, "Tit for Tat? The Spiraling Effect of Incivility in the Workplace," *Academy of Management Review,* July 1999, pp 452–71. Also see A C Poe, "An Office Undivided," *HR Magazine,* February 2000, pp 58–64; C M Pearson, L M Andersson, and C L Porath, "Assessing and Attacking Workplace Incivility," *Organizational Dynamics,* Fall 2000, pp 123–37; and R Rosell, "The Respectful Workplace," *Training,* November 2001, p 80.

[19] M Elias, "Study: Rudeness Is Poisoning US Workplace," *USA Today,* June 14, 2001, p 1D.

[20] Data from D Stamps, "Yes, Your Boss Is Crazy," *Training,* July 1998, pp 35–39. Also see L Huggler, "Companies on the Couch," *HR Magazine,* November 1997, pp 80–84; and J C Connor, "The Paranoid Personality at Work," *HR Magazine,* March 1999, pp 120–26.

[21] See S H Milne and T C Blum, "Organizational Characteristics and Employer Responses to Employee Substance Abuse," *Journal of Management,* no. 6, 1998, pp 693–715; J Kline, Jr, and L Sussman, "An Executive Guide to Workplace Depression," *Academy of Management Executive,* August 2000, pp 103–14; J A Segal, "I'm Depressed— Accommodate Me!" *HR Magazine,* February 2001, pp 139–48; L Tanner, "With Less Stigma, More Drugs, Treatment for Depression Soars," *USA Today,* January 9, 2002, p 9D; K Tyler, "Happiness from a Bottle?" *HR Magazine,* May 2002, pp 30–37; and S Berfield, "A CEO and His Son," *Business Week,* May 27, 2002, pp 72–80.

[22] See J Muller, "Keeping an Investigation on the Right Track," *Business Week,* July 5, 1999, p 84.

[23] See Bencivenga, "Dealing with the Dark Side;" and C Lee, "Tips for Surviving Rude Encounters," *Training,* July 1999, p 29; and V Jockin, R D Arvey, and M McGue, "Perceived Victimization Moderates Self-Reports of Workplace Aggression and Conflict," *Journal of Applied Psychology,* December 2001, pp 1262–69.

[24] Also see H Weeks, "Taking the Stress out of Stressful Conversations," *Harvard Business Review,* July–August 2001, pp 112–19; and M Delahoussaye, "I'm Not OK, You're Not OK," *Training,* February 2002, p 70.

[25] Drawn from J C McCune, "The Change Makers," *Management Review,* May 1999, pp 16–22.

[26] Based on discussion in G Labianca, D J Brass, and B Gray, "Social Networks and Perceptions of Intergroup Conflict: The Role of Negative Relationships and Third Parties," *Academy of Management Journal,* February 1998, pp 55–67. Also see C Gómez, B L Kirkman, and D L Shapiro, "The Impact of Collectivism and In-Group/Out-Group Membership on the Evaluation Generosity of Team Members," *Academy of*

Management Journal, December 2000, pp 1097–106; J M Twenge, R F Baumeister, D M Tice, and T S Stucke, "If You Can't Join Them, Beat Them: Effects of Social Exclusion on Aggressive Behavior," *Journal of Personality and Social Psychology,* December 2001, pp 1058–69; T Kessler and A Mummendey, "Is There Any Scapegoat Around? Determinants of Intergroup Conflicts at Different Categorization Levels," *Journal of Personality and Social Psychology,* December 2001, pp 1090–102; and T Kessler and A Mummendey, "Sequential or Parallel? A Longitudinal Field Study Concerning Determinants of Identity-Management Strategies," *Journal of Personality and Social Psychology,* January 2002, pp 75–88.

[27] See M Mikulincer and P R Shaver, "Attachment Theory and Intergroup Bias: Evidence That Priming the Secure Base Schema Attenuates Negative Reactions to Out-Groups," *Journal of Personality and Social Psychology,* July 2001, pp 97–115.

[28] Labianca, Brass, and Gray, "Social Networks and Perceptions of Intergroup Conflict, p 63 (emphasis added).

[29] For example, see S C Wright, A Aron, T McLaughlin-Volpe, and S A Ropp, "The Extended Contact Effect: Knowledge of Cross-Group Friendships and Prejudice," *Journal of Personality and Social Psychology,* July 1997, pp 73–90.

[30] See C D Batson, M P Polycarpou, E Harmon-Jones, H J Imhoff, E C Mitchener, L L Bednar, T R Klein, and L Highberger, "Empathy and Attitudes: Can Feeling for a Member of a Stigmatized Group Improve Feelings toward the Group?" *Journal of Personality and Social Psychology,* January 1997, pp 105–18.

[31] Evidence that it pays to ignore interpersonal conflicts in teams is reported in C K W De Dreu, and A E M Van Vianen, "Managing Relationship Conflict and the Effectiveness of Organizational Teams," *Journal of Organizational Behavior,* May 2001, pp 309–28.

[32] For a good overview, see N J Adler, *International Dimensions of Organizational Behavior,* 4th ed (Cincinnati: South-Western, 2002).

[33] For example, see A S Hubbard, "Cultural and Status Differences in Intergroup Conflict Resolution: A Longitudinal Study of a Middle East Dialogue Group in the United States," *Human Relations,* March 1999, pp 303–26; and P F Buller, J J Kohls, and K S Anderson, "When Ethics Collide: Managing Conflicts across Cultures," *Organizational Dynamics,* Spring 2000, pp 52–66.

[34] "Negotiating South of the Border," *Harvard Management Communication Letter,* August 1999, p 12.

[35] A Rosenbaum, "Testing Cultural Waters," *Management Review,* July–August 1999, p 43 © 1999 American Management Association International. Reprinted by permission of American Management Association International, New York, NY. All rights reserved. (www.amanet. org)

[36] See R L Tung, "American Expatriates Abroad: From Neophytes to Cosmopolitans," *Journal of World Business,* Summer 1998, pp 125–44.

[37] R A Cosier and C R Schwenk, "Agreement and Thinking Alike: Ingredients for Poor Decisions," *Academy of*

Management Executive, February 1990, p 71. Also see J P Kotter, "Kill Complacency," *Fortune,* August 5, 1996, pp 168–70; and S Caudron, "Keeping Team Conflict Alive," *Training & Development,* September 1998, pp 48–52.

[38] For example, see "Facilitators as Devil's Advocates," *Training,* September 1993, p 10. Also see K L Woodward, "Sainthood for a Pope?" *Newsweek,* June 21, 1999, p 65.

[39] Good background reading on devil's advocacy can be found in C R Schwenk, "Devil's Advocacy in Managerial Decision Making," *Journal of Management Studies,* April 1984, pp 153–68.

[40] See G Katzenstein, "The Debate on Structured Debate: Toward a Unified Theory," *Organizational Behavior and Human Decision Processes,* June 1996, pp 316–32.

[41] W Kiechel III, "How to Escape the Echo Chamber," *Fortune,* June 18, 1990, p 130.

[42] See D M Schweiger, W R Sandberg, and P L Rechner, "Experiential Effects of Dialectical Inquiry, Devil's Advocacy, and Consensus Approaches to Strategic Decision Making," *Academy of Management Journal,* December 1989, pp 745–72.

[43] See J S Valacich and C Schwenk, "Devil's Advocacy and Dialectical Inquiry Effects on Face-to-Face and Computer-Mediated Group Decision Making," *Organizational Behavior and Human Decision Processes,* August 1995, pp 158–73.

[44] Other techniques are presented in Cloke and Goldsmith, *Resolving Conflicts at Work,* pp 229–35.

[45] As quoted in D Jones, "CEOs Need X-Ray Vision in Transition," *USA Today,* April 23, 2001, p 4B.

[46] Based on C K W De Dreu and M A West, "Minority Dissent and Team Innovation: The Importance of Participation in Decision Making," *Journal of Applied Psychology,* December 2001, pp 1191–201.

[47] A statistical validation for this model can be found in M A Rahim and N R Magner, "Confirmatory Factor Analysis of the Styles of Handling Interpersonal Conflict: First-Order Factor Model and Its Invariance Across Groups," *Journal of Applied Psychology,* February 1995, pp 122–32. Also see C K W De Dreu, A Evers, B Beersma, E S Kluwer, and A Nauta, "A Theory-Based Measure of Conflict Management Strategies in the Workplace," *Journal of Organizational Behavior,* September 2001, pp 645–68; and M A Rahim, *Managing Conflict in Organizations* (Westport, CT: Greenwood Publishing Group, 2001).

[48] M A Rahim, "A Strategy for Managing Conflict in Complex Organizations," *Human Relations,* January 1985, p 84.

[49] "Female Officers Draw Fewer Brutality Suits," *USA Today,* May 2, 2002, p 3A.

[50] P Ruzich, "Triangles: Tools for Untangling Interpersonal Messes," *HR Magazine,* July 1999, p 129.

[51] For background, see D L Jacobs, "First, Fire All the Lawyers," *Inc.,* January 1999, pp 84–85; and P S Nugent, "Managing Conflict: Third-Party Interventions for Managers," *Academy of Management Executive,* February 2002, pp 139–54.

52 See M Bordwin, "Do-It-Yourself Justice," *Management Review,* January 1999, pp 56–58.

53 B Morrow and L M Bernardi, "Resolving Workplace Disputes," *Canadian Manager,* Spring 1999, p 17.

54 Adapted from discussion in K O Wilburn, "Employment Disputes: Solving Them Out of Court," *Management Review,* March 1998, pp 17–21; and Morrow and Bernardi, "Resolving Workplace Disputes," pp 17–19, 27. Also see W H Ross and D E Conlon, "Hybrid Forms of Third-Party Dispute Resolution: Theoretical Implications of Combining Mediation and Arbitration," *Academy of Management Review,* April 2000, pp 416–27.

55 Wilburn, "Employment Disputes," p 19. Also see B P Sunoo, "Hot Disputes Cool Down in Online Mediation," *Workforce,* January 2001, pp 48–52.

56 For background on this contentious issue, see S Armour, "Arbitration's Rise Raises Fairness Issue," *USA Today,* June 12, 2001, pp 1B–2B; T J Heinsz, "The Revised Uniform Arbitration Act: An Overview," *Dispute Resolution Journal,* May–July 2001, pp 28–39; C Hirschman, "Order in the Hearing!" *HR Magazine,* July 2001, pp 58–64; J D Wetchler, "Agreements to Arbitrate," *HR Magazine,* August 2001, pp 127–34; and J Biskupic, "Supreme Court Ruling Defends Power of EEOC," *USA Today,* January 16, 2002, p 2B.

57 See R E Jones and B H Melcher, "Personality and the Preference for Modes of Conflict Resolution," *Human Relations,* August 1982, pp 649–58.

58 See R A Baron, "Reducing Organizational Conflict: An Incompatible Response Approach," *Journal of Applied Psychology,* May 1984, pp 272–79.

59 See G A Youngs, Jr, "Patterns of Threat and Punishment Reciprocity in a Conflict Setting," *Journal of Personality and Social Psychology,* September 1986, pp 541–46.

60 For more details, see V D Wall, Jr, and L L Nolan, "Small Group Conflict: A Look at Equity, Satisfaction, and Styles of Conflict Management," *Small Group Behavior,* May 1987, pp 188–211. Also see S M Farmer and J Roth, "Conflict-Handling Behavior in Work Groups: Effects of Group Structure, Decision Processes, and Time," *Small Group Research,* December 1998, pp 669–713.

61 Based on B Richey, H J Bernardin, C L Tyler, and N McKinney, "The Effects of Arbitration Program Characteristics on Applicants' Intentions toward Potential Employers," *Journal of Applied Psychology,* October 2001, pp 1006–13.

62 See M E Schnake and D S Cochran, "Effect of Two Goal-Setting Dimensions on Perceived Intraorganizational Conflict," *Group & Organization Studies,* June 1985, pp 168–83. Also see O Janssen, E Van De Vliert, and C Veenstra, "How Task and Person Conflict Shape the Role of Positive Interdependence in Management Teams," *Journal of Management,* no. 2 (1999), pp 117–42.

63 Drawn from L H Chusmir and J Mills, "Gender Differences in Conflict Resolution Styles of Managers: At Work and at Home," *Sex Roles,* February 1989, pp 149–63.

64 See K K Smith, "The Movement of Conflict in Organizations: The Joint Dynamics of Splitting and Triangulation," *Administrative Science Quarterly,* March 1989, pp 1–20. Also see J B Olson-Buchanan, F Drasgow, P J Moberg, A D Mead, P A Keenan, and M A Donovan, "Interactive Video Assessment of Conflict Resolution Skills," *Personnel Psychology,* Spring 1998, pp 1–24; and D E Conlon and D P Sullivan, "Examining the Actions of Organizations in Conflict: Evidence from the Delaware Court of Chancery," *Academy of Management Journal,* June 1999, pp 319–29.

65 Based on C Tinsley, "Models of Conflict Resolution in Japanese, German, and American Cultures," *Journal of Applied Psychology,* April 1998, pp 316–23; and S M Adams, "Settling Cross-Cultural Disagreements Begins with 'Where' Not 'How,'" *Academy of Management Executive,* February 1999, pp 109–10. Also see K Ohbuchi, O Fukushima, and J T Tedeschi, "Cultural Values in Conflict Management: Goal Orientation, Goal Attainment, and Tactical Decision," *Journal of Cross-Cultural Psychology,* January 1999, pp 51–71; and R Cropanzano, H Aguinis, M Schminke, and D L Denham, "Disputant Reactions to Managerial Conflict Resolution Tactics: A Comparison among Argentina, the Dominican Republic, Mexico, and the United States," *Group & Organization Management,* June 1999, pp 124–54.

66 Based on a definition in M A Neale and M H Bazerman, "Negotiating Rationally: The Power and Impact of the Negotiator's Frame," *Academy of Management Executive,* August 1992, pp 42–51.

67 See D A Whetten and K S Cameron, *Developing Management Skills,* 3rd ed (New York: HarperCollins, 1995), pp 425–30. Also see J K Sebenius, "Six Habits of Merely Effective Negotiators," *Harvard Business Review,* April 2001, pp 87–95; A Fisher, "Being Lowballed on Salary? How to Eke out More Bucks," *Fortune,* April 30, 2001, p 192; and G Koretz, "She's a Woman, Offer Her Less," *Business Week,* May 7, 2001, p 34.

68 M H Bazerman and M A Neale, *Negotiating Rationally* (New York: The Free Press, 1992), p 16. Also See J F Brett, G B Northcraft, and R L Pinkley, "Stairways to Heaven: An Interlocking Self-Regulation Model of Negotiation," *Academy of Management Review,* July 1999, pp 435–51.

69 Good win–win negotiation strategies can be found in R R Reck and B G Long, *The Win–Win Negotiator: How to Negotiate Favorable Agreements That Last* (New York: Pocket Books, 1987); R Fisher and W Ury, *Getting to YES: Negotiating Agreement without Giving In* (Boston: Houghton Mifflin, 1981); and R Fisher and D Ertel, *Getting Ready to Negotiate: The Getting to YES Workbook* (New York: Penguin Books, 1995). Also see D M Kolb and J Williams, "Breakthrough Bargaining," *Harvard Business Review,* February 2001, pp 88–97; and K A Wade-Benzoni, A J Hoffman, L L Thompson, D A Moore, J J Gillespie, and M H Bazerman, "Barriers to Resolution in Ideologically Based Negotiations: The Role of Values and Institutions," *Academy of Management Review,* January 2002, pp 41–57.

70 See L R Weingart, E B Hyder, and M J Prietula, "Knowledge Matters: The Effect of Tactical Descriptions on Negotiation

Behavior and Outcome," *Journal of Personality and Social Psychology,* June 1996, pp 1205–17.

[71] Data from J L Graham, A T Mintu, and W Rodgers, "Explorations of Negotiation Behaviors in Ten Foreign Cultures Using a Model Developed in the United States," *Management Science,* January 1994, pp 72–95.

[72] For more, see C H Tinsley, "How Negotiators Get to Yes: Predicting the Constellation of Strategies Used across Cultures to Negotiate Conflict," *Journal of Applied Psychology,* August 2001, pp 583–93; and P Ghauri and T Fang, "Negotiating with the Chinese: A Socio-Cultural Analysis," *Journal of World Business,* Fall 2001, pp 303–25.

[73] For supporting evidence, see J K Butler, Jr, "Trust Expectations, Information Sharing, Climate of Trust, and Negotiation Effectiveness and Efficiency," *Group & Organization Management,* June 1999, pp 217–38.

[74] See H J Reitz, J A Wall, Jr, and M S Love, "Ethics in Negotiation: Oil and Water or Good Lubrication?" *Business Horizons,* May–June 1998, pp 5–14; M E Schweitzer and Jeffrey L Kerr, "Bargaining under the Influence: The Role of Alcohol in Negotiations," *Academy of Management Executive,* May 2000, pp 47–57; and A M Burr, "Ethics in Negotiation: Does Getting to Yes Require Candor?" *Dispute Resolution Journal,* May–July 2001, pp 8–15.

[75] For related research, see A E Tenbrunsel, "Misrepresentation and Expectations of Misrepresentation in an Ethical Dilemma: The Role of Incentives and Temptation," *Academy of Management Journal,* June 1998, pp 330–39.

[76] Based on R L Pinkley, T L Griffith, and G B Northcraft, " 'Fixed Pie' a la Mode: Information Availability, Information Processing, and the Negotiation of Suboptimal Agreements," *Organizational Behavior and Human Decision Processes,* April 1995, pp 101–12.

[77] Based on A E Walters, A F Stuhlmacher, and L L Meyer, "Gender and Negotiator Competitiveness: A Meta-Analysis," *Organizational Behavior and Human Decision Processes,* October 1998, pp 1–29.

[78] Based on B Barry and R A Friedman, "Bargainer Characteristics in Distributive and Integrative Negotiation," *Journal of Personality and Social Psychology,* February 1998, pp 345–59. Also see C K W De Dreu, E Giebels, and E Van de Vliert, "Social Motives and Trust in Integrative Negotiation: The Disruptive Effects of Punitive Capability," *Journal of Applied Psychology,* June 1998, pp 408–22.

[79] For more, see J P Forgas, "On Feeling Good and Getting Your Way: Mood Effects on Negotiator Cognition and Bargaining Strategies," *Journal of Personality and Social Psychology,* March 1998, pp 565–77.

[80] Drawn from J M Brett and T Okumura, "Inter- and Intracultural Negotiation: US and Japanese Negotiators," *Academy of Management Journal,* October 1998, pp 495–510. Also see W L Adair, T Okumura, and J M Brett, "Negotiation Behavior when Cultures Collide: The United States and Japan," *Journal of Applied Psychology,* June 2001, pp 371–85. More negotiation research is reported in A D Galinsky and T Mussweiler, "First Offers as Anchors: The Role of Perspective-Taking and Negotiator Focus," *Journal of Personality and Social Psychology,* October 2001, pp 657–69.

[81] Excerpted from S Holmes, "Pulp Friction at Weyerhaeuser," *Business Week,* March 11, 2002, pp 66, 68.

[82] The complete instrument may be found in M A Rahim, "A Measure of Styles of Handling Interpersonal Conflict," *Academy of Management Journal,* June 1983, pp 368–76. A validation study of Rahim's instrument may be found in E Van De Vliert and B Kabanoff, "Toward Theory-Based Measures of Conflict Management," *Academy of Management Journal,* March 1990, pp 199–209.

[83] This case is quoted from David A. Whetten and Kim S Cameron, *Developing Management Skills.* Copyright © 1984 by Scott, Foresman and Company. Reprinted by permission of Addison Wesley Educational Publishers, Inc.

[84] Excerpted from S Hamm, "Less Ego, More Success," *Business Week,* July 23, 2001, p 59.

CHAPTER 15

[1] R O Crockett, "Digital Distractions: The Office Gossips' New Water Cooler," *Business Week,* June 24, 2002, p 14.

[2] Results can be found in A Smidts, A T H Pruyn, and C B M van Riel, "The Impact of Employee Communication and Perceived External Prestige on Organizational Identification," *Academy of Management Journal,* October 2001, pp 1051–62.

[3] See P G Clampitt and C W Downs, "Employee Perceptions of the Relationship between Communication and Productivity: A Field Study," *Journal of Business Communication,* 1993, pp 5–28.

[4] Results can be found in D Fenn, "Benchmark: What Drives the Skills Gap?" *Inc.,* May 1996, p 111.

[5] J L Bowditch and A F Buono, *A Primer on Organizational Behavior,* 4th ed (New York: John Wiley & Sons, 1997), p 120.

[6] For a review of these criticisms see L L Putnam, N Phillips, and P Chapman, "Metaphors of Communication and Organization," in *Handbook of Organization Studies,* eds S R Clegg, C Hardy, and W R Nord (London: Sage Publications, 1996), pp 375–408.

[7] D Ray and L Ferrari, "At One of America's Best Companies to Work for, CEO Hal Rosenbluth Raises Employee Appreciation to an Art Form," *Selling Power,* July–August 1999, p 18.

[8] Results of this study can be found in C M Fiol, "Corporate Communications: Comparing Executives' Private and Public Statements," *Academy of Management Journal,* April 1995, pp 522–36.

[9] M Orey, "Lawyer's Firing Signals Turmoil in Legal Circles," *The Wall Street Journal,* May 21, 2001, p B1.

[10] Cross-cultural issues in communication are discussed by L Gardenswartz and A Rowe, "Cross-Cultural Awareness." *HR Magazine,* March 2001, pp 139–42.

[11] J Weil, "Two Andersen Employees Believed Enron Shredding Was Firm's Policy," *The Wall Street Journal,* March 13, 2002, p C1.

[12] Ibid.

[13] S R Axley, "Managerial and Organizational Communication in Terms of the Conduit Metaphor," *Academy of Management Review,* July 1984, pp 428–37.

[14] For a thorough discussion of these barriers, see C R Rogers and F J Roethlisberger, "Barriers and Gateways to Communication," *Harvard Business Review,* July–August 1952, pp 46–52.

[15] Ibid., p 47.

[16] M Rich, "Shut Up So We Can Do Our Jobs!" *The Wall Street Journal,* August 29, 2001, p B1.

[17] The role of jargon in communication is discussed by R Spragins, "Don't Talk to Me That Way," *Fortune Small Business,* February 2002, p 26.

[18] Results can be found in J D Johnson, W A Donohue, C K Atkin, and S Johnson, "Communication, Involvement, and Perceived Innovativeness," *Group & Organization Management,* March 2001, pp 24–52; and B Davenport Sypher and T E Zorn, Jr, "Communication-Related Abilities and Upward Mobility: A Longitudinal Investigation," *Human Communication Research,* Spring 1986, pp 420–31.

[19] Communication competence is discussed by J S Hinton and M W Kramer, "The Impact of Self-Directed Videotape Feedback on Students' Self-Reported Levels of Communication Competence and Apprehension," *Communication Education,* April 1998, pp 151–61; and L J Carrell and S C Willmington, "The Relationship between Self-Report Measures of Communication Apprehension and Trained Observers' Ratings of Communication Competence," *Communication Reports,* Winter 1998, pp 87–95.

[20] 1. *False.* Clients always take precedence, and people with the greatest authority or importance should be introduced first.

2. *False.* You should introduce yourself. Say something like "My name is _____. I don't believe we've met."

3. *False.* It's OK to admit you can't remember. Say something like "My mind just went blank, your name is?" Or offer your name and wait for the other person to respond with his or hers.

4. *False.* Business etiquette has become gender neutral.

5. *a. Host.* This enables him or her to lead their guest to the meeting place.

6. *False.* Not only is it rude to invade public areas with your conversation, but you never know who might hear details of your business transaction or personal life.

7. *b. 3 feet.* Closer than this is an invasion of personal space. Farther away forces people to raise their voices. Because communication varies from country to country, you should also inform yourself about cultural differences.

8. *True.* An exception to this would be if your company holds an event at the beach or the pool.

9. *False.* Just wave your hand over it when asked, or say "No thank you."

10. *True.* The person who initiated the call should redial if the connection is broken.

11. *True.* If you must use speakerphone, you should inform all parties who's present.

12. *True.* You should record a greeting such as "I'm out of the office today, March 12. If you need help, please dial _____ at extension. . ."

[21] See E Raudsepp, "Are You Properly Assertive?" *Supervision,* June 1992, pp 17–18; and D A Infante and W I Gorden, "Superiors' Argumentativeness and Verbal Aggressiveness as Predictors of Subordinates' Satisfaction," *Human Communication Research,* Fall 1985, pp 117–25.

[22] J A Waters, "Managerial Assertiveness," *Business Horizons,* September–October 1982, p 25.

[23] M Pacelle and R B Schmitt, "Last Chapter: A Bankruptcy Lawyer Famed for Theatrics Sees His Job Go Bust," *The Wall Street Journal,* February 27, 2002, p A1.

[24] See Waters, "Managerial Assertiveness," p 27.

[25] W D St. John, "You Are What You Communicate," *Personnel Journal,* October 1985, p 40.

[26] This statistic was obtained from A Warfield, "Do You Speak Body Language?" *Training & Development Journal,* April 2001, pp 60–61.

[27] The importance of nonverbal communication is discussed by L K Guerrero and J A DeVito, *The Nonverbal Communication Reader: Classic and Contemporary Readings,* 2nd ed (Prospect Heights, IL: Waveland Press, 1999).

[28] See H Aguinis and C A Henle, "Effects of Nonverbal Behavior on Perceptions of a Female Employee's Power Bases," *Journal of Social Psychology,* August 2001, pp 537–49.

[29] Results can be found in S D Kelly, D J Barr, R B Church, and K Lynch, "Offering a Hand to Pragmatic Understanding: The Role of Speech and Gesture in Comprehension and Memory," *Journal of Memory and Language,* May 1999, pp 577–92.

[30] Related research is summarized by J A Hall, "Male and Female Nonverbal Behavior," in *Multichannel Integrations of Nonverbal Behavior,* eds A W Siegman and S Feldstein (Hillsdale, NJ: Lawrence Erlbaum, 1985), pp 195–226.

[31] Results can be found in Hall, "Male and Female Nonverbal Behavior."

[32] See J A Russell, "Facial Expressions of Emotion: What Lies Beyond Minimal Universality?" *Psychological Bulletin,* November 1995, pp 379–91.

[33] Norms for cross-cultural eye contact are discussed by C Engholm, *When Business East Meets Business West: The Guide to Practice and Protocol in the Pacific Rim* (New York: John Wiley & Sons, 1991).

[34] St. John, "You Are What You Communicate," p 43.

[35] See J Joyner, "Listening Increases Support from Co-Workers," *Computing—Canada,* October 19, 2001, p 31.

[36] Statistics were reported in M Burley-Allen, "Listen Up," *HR Magazine,* November 2001, pp 115–20.

[37] Ibid.

[38] For a summary of supporting research, see K W Watson and L L Barker, "Listening Behavior: Definition and Measurement," in *Communication Yearbook* 8, ed R N Bostrom (Beverly Hills, CA: Sage Publications, 1984); and L B Comer and T Drollinger, "Active Empathetic Listening and Selling Success: A Conceptual Framework," *Journal of Personal Selling & Sales Management,* Winter 1999, pp 15–29.

[39] See S R Covey, *The 7 Habits of Highly Effective People* (New York: Simon & Schuster, 1989).

[40] Results are presented in J C Tingley, *Genderflex: Men and Women Speaking Each Other's Language at Work* (New York: American Management Association, 1994).

[41] D Tannen, "The Power of Talk: Who Gets Heard and Why," *Harvard Business Review,* September–October 1995, p 139.

[42] For a thorough review of the evolutionary explanation of sex differences in communication, see A H Eagly and W Wood, "The Origins of Sex Differences in Human Behavior," *American Psychologist,* June 1999, pp 408–23.

[43] See D Tannen, "The Power of Talk, pp 160–73; and D Tannen, *You Just Don't Understand: Women and Men in Conversation* (New York: Ballantine Books, 1990).

[44] Research on gender differences can be found in A Mulac, J J Bradac, and P Gibbons, "Empirical Support for the Gender-as-Culture Hypothesis: An Intercultural Analysis of Male/Female Language Differences," *Human Communications Research,* January 2001, pp 121–52; and K Hawkins and C B Power, "Gender Differences in Questions Asked during Small Decision-Making Group Discussions," *Small Group Research,* April 1999, pp 235–56.

[45] This definition was taken from Tingley, *Genderflex,* p 16.

[46] Tannen, "The Power of Talk," pp 147–48.

[47] Results can be found in D Clark, "Managing the Mountain," *The Wall Street Journal,* June 21, 1999, p R4.

[48] A C Poe, "Don't Touch That 'Send' Button!" *HR Magazine,* July 2001, pp 74–75.

[49] R L Daft and R H Lengel, "Information Richness: A New Approach to Managerial Behavior and Organizational Design," in *Research in Organizational Behavior,* eds B M Staw and L L Cummings (Greenwich, CT: JAI Press, 1984), p 196.

[50] K Chen, "Work Week: A Special News Report about Life on the Job—and Trends Taking Shape There," *The Wall Street Journal,* July 10, 2001, p A1.

[51] See V Anand, C C Manz, and W H Glick, "An Organizational Memory Approach to Information Management," *Academy of Management Review,* October 1998, pp 796–809; and J Webster and L K Trevino, "Rational and Social Theories as Complementary Explanations of Communications Media Choices: Two Policy-Capturing Studies," *Academy of Management Journal,* December 1995, pp 1544–72.

[52] See R E Rice and D E Shook, "Relationships of Job Categories and Organizational Levels to Use of Communication Channels, Including Electronic Mail: A Meta-Analysis and Extension," *Journal of Management Studies,* March 1990, pp 195–229.

[53] C Redding, *Communication within the Organization: An Interpretive Review of Theory and Research* (New York: Industrial Communication Council, 1972).

[54] Results from this study are discussed by D Krackhardt and J R Hanson, "Informal Networks: The Company Behind the Chart," *Harvard Business Review,* July–August 1993, pp 104–11.

[55] C Hymowitz, "In the Lead: Need to Boost Morale? Try Good Food, Fitness and Communication," *The Wall Street Journal,* May 28, 2002, p B1.

[56] Organizational benefits of the grapevine are discussed by T Galpin, "Pruning the Grapevine," *Training & Development,* April 1995, pp 28–32; and J Smythe, "Harvesting the Office Grapevine," *People Management,* September 1995, pp 24–27.

[57] Results can be found in S J Modic, "Grapevine Rated Most Believable," *Industry Week,* May 15, 1989, pp 11, 14.

[58] H B Vickery III, "Tapping into the Employee Grapevine," *Association Management,* January 1984, pp 59–60.

[59] A thorough discussion of organizational moles is provided by J G Bruhn and A P Chesney, "Organizational Moles: Information Control and the Acquisition of Power and Status," *Health Care Supervisor,* September 1995, pp 24–31.

[60] The most recent research is discussed by S M Crampton, J W Hodge, and J M Mishra, "The Informal Communication Network: Factors Influencing Grapevine Activity," *Public Personnel Management,* Winter 1998, pp 569–584 , "Pruning the Company Grapevine," *Supervision,* September 1986, p 11; and R Half, "Managing Your Career: 'How Can I Stop the Gossip?' " *Management Accounting,* September 1987, p 27.

[61] L Grensing-Pophal, "Got the Message?" *HR Magazine,* April 2001, pp 75–76.

[62] For a thorough discussion of communication distortion, see E W Larson and J B King, "The Systematic Distortion of Information: An Ongoing Challenge to Management," *Organizational Dynamics,* Winter 1996, pp 49–61.

[63] J Fulk and S Mani, "Distortion of Communication in Hierarchical Relationships," in *Communication Yearbook* 9, ed M L McLaughlin (Beverly Hills, CA: Sage Publications, 1986), p 483.

[64] For a review of this research, see Fulk and Mani, "Distortion of Communication in Hierarchical Relationships," pp 483–510.

[65] A Stuart, "Cutting the Cord," *Inc. Tech,* March 2001, p 78.

[66] The impact of information technology on OB is thoroughly discussed by R P Gephart, Jr, "Introduction to the Brave New Workplace: Organizational Behavior in the Electronic Age," *Journal of Organizational Behavior,* June 2002, pp 327–44.

[67] Statistics were obtained from M Roman, "In Business This Week: America, Land of the Web Surfers," *Business Week,* February 18, 2002, p 46.

[68] Results can be found in D Smith, "One-Tenth of College Students Are Dependent on the Internet, Research Finds," *Monitor on Psychology,* May 2001, p 10.

[69] Results were reported in A Petersen, "A Fine Line: Companies Face a Delicate Task When It Comes to Deciding What to Put on Their Intranets: How Much Is Too Much?" *The Wall Street Journal,* June 21, 1999, p R8.

[70] See J Useem, "For Sale Online: You," *Fortune,* July 5, 1999, pp 67–78.

[71] See S J Wells, "Communicating Benefits Information Online," *HR Magazine,* February 2001, pp 69–76.

[72] "Websmart," *Business Week e.biz,* May 14, 2001, p EB56.

[73] See D Buss, "Spies Like Us," *Training,* December 2001, pp 44–48.

[74] Results from this study are summarized in G Kortez, "Economic Trends: Big Bro Is Eyeing Your E-Mail," *Business Week,* June 4, 2001, p 30.

[75] Statistics are reported in C Tejada, "Work Week: A Special News Report about Life on the Job—and Trends Taking Shape There," *The Wall Street Journal,* May 8, 2001, p A1; and J Wallace, "The (E-Mail) Postman Rings More than Twice," *HR Magazine,* March 2001, p 176.

[76] Results are summarized in S Armour, "Boss: It's in the E-mail," *USA Today,* August 10, 1999, p 3B.

[77] See B Hemphill, "File, Act, or Toss?" *Training & Development,* February 2001, pp 38–41.

[78] Results can be found in J Yaukey, "E-Mail Out of Control for Many: Take Steps to Ease Load," *The Wall Street Journal,* May 8, 2001, p F1.

[79] M Rose and M Peers, "AOL's Latest Internal Woe: 'You've Got Mail'—'Oops, No You Don't,' " *The Wall Street Journal,* March 22, 2002, p B1.

[80] See "Overwhelmed by Spam," *Business Week,* April 22, 2002, p 16.

[81] Results can be found in M S Thompson and M S Feldman, "Electronic Mail and Organizational Communication: Does Saying 'Hi' Really Matter?" *Organization Science,* November–December 1998, pp 685–98.

[82] See the discussion in S Prasso, "Workers, Surf at Your Own Risk," *Business Week,* June 11, 2001, p 14.

[83] E Krell, "Videoconferencing Gets the Call," *Training,* December 2001, p 38.

[84] F Keenan and S E Ante, "The New Teamwork," *Business Week e.biz,* February 18, 2002, p EB14.

[85] Challenges associated with virtual operations are discussed by S O'Mahony and S R Barley, "Do Digital Telecommunications Affect Work and Organization? The State of Our Knowledge," in *Research in Organizational Behavior,* vol. 21, eds R I Sutton and B M Staw (Stamford, CT: JAI Press, 1999), pp 125–61.

[86] S Shellenbarger, "Work and Family: 'Telework' Is on the Rise, But It Isn't Just Done from Home Anymore," *The Wall Street Journal,* January 23, 2002, p B1.

[87] Statistic was reported in M Mallory, "Telecommuting Concept Slowly Gaining Converts," *Arizona Republic,* June 24, 2002, p D1.

[88] Supporting evidence can be found in D E Bailey and N B Kurland, "A Review of Telework Research: Findings, New Directions, and Lessons for the Study of Modern Work," *Journal of Organizational Behavior,* June 2002, pp 383–400; and S Shellenbarger, "Work and Family: This Time, Firms See Work-Life Plans as Aid during the Downturn," *The Wall Street Journal,* March 28, 2001, p B1.

[89] Excerpted from H Green, "Winging into Wireless," *Business Week e.biz,* February 18, 2002, pp EB8–9.

[90] Excerpted from S Craig and K Scannell, "Settling Accounts: How Spat over Clients Cost a Securities Firm Record Punitive Award," *The Wall Street Journal,* September 29, 2001, pp A1, A2.

CHAPTER 16

[1] C Woodyard, "Teams of Employees Search and Destroy Work Bottlenecks," *USA Today,* May 9, 2001, p 3B.

[2] H Malcolm and C Sokoloff, "Values, Human Relations, and Organization Development," in *The Emerging Practice of Organizational Development,* eds W Sikes, A Drexler, and J Gant (San Diego: University Associates, 1989), p 64.

[3] See D Kipnis, S M Schmidt, and I Wilkinson, "Intraorganizational Influence Tactics: Explorations in Getting One's Way," *Journal of Applied Psychology,* August 1980, pp 440–52. Also see C A Schriesheim and T R Hinkin, "Influence Tactics Used by Subordinates: A Theoretical and Empirical Analysis and Refinement of the Kipnis, Schmidt, and Wilkinson Subscales," *Journal of Applied Psychology,* June 1990, pp 246–57; and G Yukl and C M Falbe, "Influence Tactics and Objectives in Upward, Downward, and Lateral Influence Attempts," *Journal of Applied Psychology,* April 1990, pp 132–40.

[4] Based on Table 1 in G Yukl, C M Falbe, and J Y Youn, "Patterns of Influence Behavior for Managers," *Group & Organization Management,* March 1993, pp 5–28. An additional influence tactic is presented in B P Davis and E S Knowles, "A Disrupt-then-Reframe Technique of Social Influence," *Journal of Personality and Social Psychology,* February 1999, pp 192–99.

[5] For related reading, see M Lippitt, "How to Influence Leaders," *Training & Development,* March 1999, pp 18–22; and L Schlesinger, "I've Got Three Words for You: Suck It Up," *Fast Company,* April 1999, p 104.

[6] Based on discussion in G Yukl, H Kim, and C M Falbe, "Antecedents of Influence Outcomes," *Journal of Applied Psychology,* June 1996, pp 309–17.

[7] Data from ibid.

[8] Data from G Yukl and J B Tracey, "Consequences of Influence Tactics Used with Subordinates, Peers, and the Boss," *Journal of Applied Psychology,* August 1992, pp 525–35. Also see C M Falbe and G Yukl, "Consequences for Managers of Using Single Influence Tactics and Combinations of Tactics," *Academy of Management Journal,* August 1992, pp 638–52.

[9] Data from R A Gordon, "Impact of Ingratiation on Judgments and Evaluations: A Meta-Analytic Investigation," *Journal of Personality and Social Psychology,* July 1996, pp 54–70. Also see S J Wayne, R C Liden, and R T Sparrowe, "Developing Leader-Member Exchanges," *American Behavioral Scientist,* March 1994, pp 697–714; A Oldenburg, "These Days, Hostile Is Fitting for Takeovers Only," *USA Today,* July 22, 1996, pp 8B, 10B; and J H Dulebohn and G R Ferris, "The Role of Influence Tactics in Perceptions of Performance Evaluations' Fairness," *Academy of Management Journal,* June 1999, pp 288–303.

[10] Data from Yukl, Kim, and Falbe, "Antecedents of Influence Outcomes."

[11] Data from B J Tepper, R J Eisenbach, S L Kirby, and P W Potter, "Test of a Justice-Based Model of Subordinates' Resistance to Downward Influence Attempts," *Group & Organization Management,* June 1998, pp 144–60. Also see A Somech and A Drach-Zahavy, "Relative Power and Influence Strategy: The Effects of Agent/Target Organizational Power on Superiors' Choices of Influence Strategies," *Journal of Organizational Behavior,* March 2002, pp 167–79.

[12] J E Driskell, B Olmstead, and E Salas, "Task Cues, Dominance Cues, and Influence in Task Groups," *Journal of Applied Psychology,* February 1993, p 51. No gender bias was found in H Aguinis and S K R Adams, "Social-Role versus Structural Models of Gender and Influence Use in Organizations: A Strong Inference Approach," *Group & Organization Management,* December 1998, pp 414–46.

[13] Yukl, Falbe, and Youn, "Patterns of Influence Behavior for Managers," p 27.

[14] B Moses, "You Can't Make Change; You Have to Sell It," *Fast Company,* April 1999, p 101. Also see B Breen, "Trickle-Up Leadership," *Fast Company,* November 2001, pp 70, 72.

[15] For more, see A Sloan and M Hosenball, "No Accounting for It," *Newsweek,* February 25, 2002, pp 34–35; K McCoy, "Kozlowski's Fall from Grace," *USA Today,* June 7, 2002, pp 1B–2B; J O'Donnell, "ImClone CEO Denies Tipping off Brother," *USA Today,* June 14, 2002, p 1B; C Haddad, D Foust, and S Rosenbush, "WorldCom's Sorry Legacy," *Business Week,* July 8, 2002, pp 38–40; and A Sloan, "Bad Boys Club," *Newsweek,* July 1, 2002, pp 44–46.

[16] S Bates, "Poll: Employees Skeptical about Management Actions," *HR Magazine,* June 2002, p 12.

[17] See M J Mandel, "A New Economy Needs a New Morality," *Business Week,* February 25, 2002, pp 114–15.

[18] Adapted from R B Cialdini, "Harnessing the Science of Persuasion," *Harvard Business Review,* October 2001, pp 72–79. Also see G A Williams and Robert B Miller, "Change the Way You Persuade," *Harvard Business Review,* May 2002, pp 64–73.

[19] Cialdini, "Harnessing the Science of Persuasion," p 77.

[20] D Tjosvold, "The Dynamics of Positive Power," *Training and Development Journal,* June 1984, p 72. Also see T A Stewart, "Get with the New Power Game," *Fortune,* January 13, 1997, pp 58–62; and "The Exercise of Power," *Harvard Business Review,* May 2002, p 136.

[21] M W McCall, Jr, *Power, Influence, and Authority: The Hazards of Carrying a Sword,* Technical Report No. 10 (Greensboro, NC: Center for Creative Leadership, 1978), p 5. For an excellent update on power, see E P Hollander and L R Offermann, "Power and Leadership in Organizations," *American Psychologist,* February 1990, pp 179–89. Also see R Greene, *The 48 Laws of Power* (New York: Viking, 1998); and N B Kurland and L H Pelled, "Passing the Word: Toward a Model of Gossip and Power in the Workplace," *Academy of Management Review,* April 2002, pp 428–38.

[22] D Weimer, "Daughter Knows Best," *Business Week,* April 19, 1999, pp 132, 134.

[23] For an update, see C L Bernick, "When Your Culture Needs a Makeover," *Harvard Business Review,* June 2001, pp 53–61.

[24] L H Chusmir, "Personalized versus Socialized Power Needs among Working Women and Men," *Human Relations,* February 1986, p 149.

[25] See B Lloyd, "The Paradox of Power," *The Futurist,* May–June 1996, p 60; and R Lubit, "The Long-Term Organizational Impact of Destructively Narcissistic Managers," *Academy of Management Executive,* February 2002, pp 127–38.

[26] D W Cantor and T Bernay, *Women in Power: The Secrets of Leadership* (Boston: Houghton Mifflin, 1992), p 40; and K Morris, "Trouble in Toyland," *Business Week,* March 15, 1999, p 40.

[27] See J R P French and B Raven, "The Bases of Social Power," in *Studies in Social Power,* ed D Cartwright (Ann Arbor: University of Michigan Press, 1959), pp 150–67. Also see J M Whitmeyer, "Interest-Network Structures in Exchange Networks," *Sociological Perspectives,* Spring 1999, pp 23–47; and C M Fiol, E J O'Connor, and H Aguinis, "All for One and One for All? The Development and Transfer of Power across Organizational Levels," *Academy of Management Review,* April 2001, pp 224–42.

[28] Data from J R Larson, Jr, C Christensen, A S Abbott, and T M Franz, "Diagnosing Groups: Charting the Flow of Information in Medical Decision-Making Teams," *Journal of Personality and Social Psychology,* August 1996, pp 315–30.

[29] Details may be found in Chusmir, "Personalized versus Socialized Power Needs among Working Women and Men," pp 149–59. For a review of research on individual differences in the need for power, see R J House, "Power and Personality in Complex Organizations," in *Research in Organizational Behavior,* ed B M Staw and L L Cummings (Greenwich, CT: JAI Press, 1988), pp 305–57.

[30] B Filipczak, "Is It Getting Chilly in Here?" *Training,* February 1994, p 27.

[31] Data from J Onyx, R Leonard, and K Vivekananda, "Social Perception of Power: A Gender Analysis," *Perceptual and Motor Skills,* February 1995, pp 291–96.

[32] P M Podsakoff and C A Schriesheim, "Field Studies of French and Raven's Bases of Power: Critique, Reanalysis, and Suggestions for Future Research," *Psychological Bulletin,* May 1985, p 388. Also see M A Rahim and G F Buntzman, "Supervisory Power Bases, Styles of Handling Conflict with Subordinates, and Subordinate Compliance and Satisfaction," *Journal of Psychology,* March 1989, pp 195–210; D Tjosvold, "Power and Social Context in Superior-Subordinate Interaction," *Organizational Behavior and Human Decision Processes,* June 1985, pp 281–93; and C A Schriesheim, T R Hinkin, and P M Podsakoff, "Can Ipsative and Single-Item Measures Produce Erroneous Results in Field Studies of French and Raven's (1950) Five Bases of Power? An Empirical Investigation," *Journal of Applied Psychology,* February 1991, pp 106–14.

[33] See T R Hinkin and C A Schriesheim, "Relationships between Subordinate Perceptions and Supervisor Influence Tactics and Attributed Bases of Supervisory Power," *Human Relations,* March 1990, pp 221–37. Also see D J Brass and M E Burkhardt, "Potential Power and Power Use: An Investigation of Structure and Behavior," *Academy of Management Journal,* June 1993, pp 441–70; and K W Mossholder, N Bennett, E R Kemery, and M A Wesolowski, "Relationships between Bases of Power and Work Reactions: The Mediational Role of Procedural Justice," *Journal of Management,* no. 4, 1998, pp 533–52.

[34] See H E Baker III, " 'Wax On—Wax Off:' French and Raven at the Movies," *Journal of Management Education,* November 1993, pp 517–19.

[35] Based on P A Wilson, "The Effects of Politics and Power on the Organizational Commitment of Federal Executives," *Journal of Management,* Spring 1995, pp 101–18. For related research, see J B Arthur, "Effects of Human Resource Systems on Manufacturing Performance and Turnover," *Academy of Management Journal,* June 1994, pp 670–87.

[36] For related research, see L G Pelletier and R J Vallerand, "Supervisors' Beliefs and Subordinates' Intrinsic Motivation: A Behavioral Confirmation Analysis," *Journal of Personality and Social Psychology,* August 1996, pp 331–40.

[37] As quoted in G Smith, "Here Comes Abby," *Business Week,* July 8, 2002, p 62.

[38] As quoted in W A Randolph and M Sashkin, "Can Organizational Empowerment Work in Multinational Settings?" *Academy of Management Executive,* February 2002, p 104. (Emphasis added.)

[39] As quoted in J Angwin and M Peers, "Executive Shares Secrets to Management Success," Career Journal from *The Wall Street Journal,* February 11, 2002 (www.careerjournal.com).

[40] R M Hodgetts, "A Conversation with Steve Kerr," *Organizational Dynamics,* Spring 1996, p 71. Also see R

Forrester, "Empowerment: Rejuvenating a Potent Idea," *Academy of Management Executive,* August 2000, pp 67–80; M Kaminski, J S Kaufman, R Graubarth, and T G Robins, "How Do People Become Empowered? A Case Study of Union Activists," *Human Relations,* October 2000, pp 1357–83; and P Haspeslagh, T Noda, and F Boulos, "It's Not Just about the Numbers," *Harvard Business Review,* July–August 2001, pp 65–73.

[41] Data from "HR Pulse," *HR Magazine,* September 1998, p 18. Also see R Aggarwal and B J Simkins, "Open Book Management—Optimizing Human Capital," *Business Horizons,* September–October 2001, pp 5–13.

[42] L Shaper Walters, "A Leader Redefines Management," *Christian Science Monitor,* September 22, 1992, p 14.

[43] For related discussion, see M M Broadwell, "Why Command and Control Won't Go Away," *Training,* September 1995, pp 62–68; R E Quinn and G M Spreitzer, "The Road to Empowerment: Seven Questions Every Leader Should Consider," *Organizational Dynamics,* Autumn 1997, pp 37–49; and I Cunningham and L Honold, "Everyone Can Be a Coach," *HR Magazine,* June 1998, pp 63–66.

[44] For a 15-item empowerment scale, see Table 1 on p 103 of B P Niehoff, R H Moorman, G Blakely, and J Fuller, "The Influence of Empowerment and Job Enrichment on Employee Loyalty in a Downsizing Environment," *Group & Organization Management,* March 2001, pp 93–113.

[45] S Chandler, "United We Own," *Business Week,* March 18, 1996, p 96.

[46] For more on delegation, see L Bossidy, "The Job No CEO Should Delegate," *Harvard Business Review,* March 2001, pp 46–49.

[47] See S Gazda, "The Art of Delegating," *HR Magazine,* January 2002, pp 75–78.

[48] M Memmott, "Managing Government Inc.," *USA Today,* June 28, 1993, p 2B. Also see R C Ford and C P Heaton, "Lessons from Hospitality That Can Serve Anyone," *Organizational Dynamics,* Summer 2001, pp 30–47.

[49] R Kreitner, *Management,* 8th ed (Boston: Houghton Mifflin, 2001), p 315. Also see C A Walker, "Saving Your Rookie Managers from Themselves," *Harvard Business Review,* April 2002, pp 97–102.

[50] Drawn from G Yukl and P P Fu, "Determinants of Delegation and Consultation by Managers," *Journal of Organizational Behavior,* March 1999, pp 219–32. Also see C A Schriesheim, L L Neider, and T A Scandura, "Delegation and Leader-Member Exchange: Main Effects, Moderators, and Measurement Issues," *Academy of Management Journal,* June 1998, pp 298–318.

[51] For practical tips on building trust, see C Joinson, "Managing Virtual Teams," *HR Magazine,* June 2002, pp 69–73.

[52] M Frese, W Kring, A Soose, and J Zempel, "Personal Initiative at Work: Differences between East and West Germany," *Academy of Management Journal,* February 1996, p 38. (Emphasis added.) For comprehensive updates, see D J

Campbell, "The Proactive Employee: Managing Workplace Initiative," *Academy of Management Executive,* August 2000, pp 52–66; and M Frese and D Fay, "Personal Initiative: An Active Performance Concept for Work in the 21st Century," in *Research in Organizational Behavior,* vol. 23, eds B M Staw and R I Sutton (New York: JAI, 2001), pp 133–87.

[53] See J A Belasco and R C Stayer, "Why Empowerment Doesn't Empower: The Bankruptcy of Current Paradigms," *Business Horizons,* March–April 1994, pp 29–41; and W A Randolph, "Re-thinking Empowerment: Why Is It So Hard to Achieve?" *Organizational Dynamics,* Fall 2000, pp 94–107.

[54] For complete details, see C R Leana, "Power Relinquishment versus Power Sharing: Theoretical Clarification and Empirical Comparison of Delegation and Participation," *Journal of Applied Psychology,* May 1987, pp 228–33.

[55] M D Fulford and C A Enz, "The Impact of Empowerment on Service Employees," *Journal of Managerial Issues,* Summer 1995, p 172.

[56] Data from A J H Thorlakson and R P Murray, "An Empirical Study of Empowerment in the Workplace," *Group & Organization Management,* March 1996, pp 67–83.

[57] Data from C S Koberg, R W Boss, J C Senjem, and E A Goodman, "Antecedents and Outcomes of Empowerment: Empirical Evidence from the Health Care Industry," *Group & Organization Management,* March 1999, pp 71–91. Also see K Aquino, S L Grover, M Bradfield, and D G Allen, "The Effects of Negative Affectivity, Hierarchical Status, and Self-Determination on Workplace Victimization," *Academy of Management Journal,* June 1999, pp 260–72.

[58] Based on B L Kirkman and B Rosen, "Beyond Self-Management: Antecedents and Consequences of Team Empowerment," *Academy of Management Journal,* February 1999, pp 58–74. Also see W J Burpitt and W J Bigoness, "Leadership and Innovation among Teams: The Impact of Empowerment," *Small Group Research,* August 1997, pp 414–23.

[59] Based on J P Guthrie, "High-Involvement Work Practices, Turnover, and Productivity: Evidence from New Zealand," *Academy of Management Journal,* February 2001, pp 180–90.

[60] W A Randolph, "Navigating the Journey to Empowerment," *Organizational Dynamics,* Spring 1995, p 31.

[61] D J Burrough, "Office Politics Mirror Popular TV Program," *Arizona Republic,* February 4, 2001, p EC1.

[62] L B MacGregor Serven, *The End of Office Politics as Usual* (New York: American Management Association, 2002), p 5.

[63] R Bhasin, "On Playing Corporate Politics," *Pulp & Paper,* October 1985, p 175. Also see G R Ferris, P L Perrewé, W P Anthony, and D C Gilmore, "Political Skill at Work," *Organizational Dynamics,* Spring 2000, pp 25–37; R M Kramer, "When Paranoia Makes Sense," *Harvard Business Review,* July 2002, pp 62–69; and J Barbian, "Office Politics: Swinging with the Sharks," *Training,* July 2002, p 16.

[64] R W Allen, D L Madison, L W Porter, P A Renwick, and B T Mayes, "Organizational Politics: Tactics and Characteristics of

Its Actors," *California Management Review,* Fall 1979, p 77. A comprehensive update can be found in K M Kacmar and R A Baron, "Organizational Politics: The State of the Field, Links to Related Processes, and an Agenda for Future Research," in *Research in Personnel and Human Resources Management,* vol. 17, ed G R Ferris (Stamford, CT: JAI Press, 1999), pp 1–39. Also see M C Andrews and K M Kacmar, "Discriminating among Organizational Politics, Justice, and Support," *Journal of Organizational Behavior,* June 2001, pp 347–66.

[65] See P M Fandt and G R Ferris, "The Management of Information and Impressions: When Employees Behave Opportunistically," *Organizational Behavior and Human Decision Processes,* February 1990, pp 140–58.

[66] First four based on discussion in D R Beeman and T W Sharkey, "The Use and Abuse of Corporate Politics," *Business Horizons,* March–April 1987, pp 26–30.

[67] A Raia, "Power, Politics, and the Human Resource Professional," *Human Resource Planning,* no. 4 (1985), p 203.

[68] A J DuBrin, "Career Maturity, Organizational Rank, and Political Behavioral Tendencies: A Correlational Analysis of Organizational Politics and Career Experience," *Psychological Reports,* October 1988, p 535.

[69] This three-level distinction comes from A T Cobb, "Political Diagnosis: Applications in Organizational Development," *Academy of Management Review,* July 1986, pp 482–96.

[70] An excellent historical and theoretical perspective of coalitions can be found in W B Stevenson, J L Pearce, and L W Porter, "The Concept of 'Coalition' in Organization Theory and Research," *Academy of Management Review,* April 1985, pp 256–68.

[71] L Baum, "The Day Charlie Bradshaw Kissed off Transworld," *Business Week,* September 29, 1986, p 68.

[72] See A Nierenberg, "Masterful Networking," *Training & Development,* February 1999, pp 51–53.

[73] Allen, Madison, Porter, Renwick, and Mayes, "Organizational Politics," p 77.

[74] See J Barbian, "It's Who You Know," *Training,* December 2001, p 22; and S Bing, "Throwing the Elephant: Zen and the Art of Managing Up," *Fortune,* March 18, 2002, pp 115–16.

[75] A Rao, S M Schmidt, and L H Murray, "Upward Impression Management: Goals, Influence Strategies, and Consequences," *Human Relations,* February 1995, p 147.

[76] See W L Gardner and B J Avolio, "The Charismatic Relationship: A Dramaturgical Perspective," *Academy of Management Review,* January 1998, pp 32–58; L Wah, "Managing—Manipulating?—Your Reputation," *Management Review,* October 1998, pp 46–50; M C Bolino, "Citizenship and Impression Management: Good Soldiers or Good Actors?" *Academy of Management Review,* January 1999, pp 82–98; and W H Turnley and M C Bolino, "Achieving Desired Images while Avoiding Undesired Images: Exploring the Role of Self-Monitoring in Impression Management," *Journal of Applied Psychology,* April 2001, pp 351–60.

77 See A Wheat, "Work That Room," *Fortune,* May 27, 2002, 187–90; and A Heller, "How to Give Your Career a Lift," *Business Week,* July 8, 2002, p 10.

78 S Friedman, "What Do You Really Care About? What Are You Most Interested In?" *Fast Company,* March 1999, p 90. Also see B M DePaulo and D A Kashy, "Everyday Lies in Close and Casual Relationships," *Journal of Personality and Social Psychology,* January 1998, pp 63–79.

79 See S J Wayne and G R Ferris, "Influence Tactics, Affect, and Exchange Quality in Supervisor-Subordinate Interactions: A Laboratory Experiment and Field Study," *Journal of Applied Psychology,* October 1990, pp 487–99. For another version, see Table 1 (p 246) in S J Wayne and R C Liden, "Effects of Impression Management on Performance Ratings: A Longitudinal Study," *Academy of Management Journal,* February 1995, pp 232–60.

80 See R Vonk, "The Slime Effect: Suspicion and Dislike of Likeable Behavior toward Superiors," *Journal of Personality and Social Psychology,* April 1998, pp 849–64; and M Wells, "How to Schmooze Like the Best of Them," *USA Today,* May 18, 1999, p 14E.

81 See A Montagliani and R A Giacalone, "Impression Management and Cross-Cultural Adaptation," *Journal of Social Psychology,* October 1998, pp 598–608.

82 M E Mendenhall and C Wiley, "Strangers in a Strange Land: The Relationship between Expatriate Adjustment and Impression Management," *American Behavioral Scientist,* March 1994, pp 605–20.

83 T E Becker and S L Martin, "Trying to Look Bad at Work: Methods and Motives for Managing Poor Impressions in Organizations," *Academy of Management Journal,* February 1995, p 191.

84 Ibid., p 181. Also see M K Duffy, D C Ganster, and M Pagon, "Social Undermining in the Workplace," *Academy of Management Journal,* April 2002, pp 331–51.

85 Adapted from ibid., pp 180–81.

86 Data from G R Ferris, D D Frink, D P S Bhawuk, J Zhou, and D C Gilmore, "Reactions of Diverse Groups to Politics in the Workplace," *Journal of Management,* no. 1, 1996, pp 23–44. For other findings from the same database, see G R Ferris, D D Frink, M C Galang, J Zhou, K M Kacmar, and J L Howard, "Perceptions of Organizational Politics: Prediction, Stress-Related Implications, and Outcomes," *Human Relations,* February 1996, pp 233–66. Also see M L Randall, R Cropanzano, C A Bormann, and A Birjulin, "Organizational Politics and Organizational Support as Predictors of Work Attitudes, Job Performance, and Organizational Citizenship Behavior," *Journal of Organizational Behavior,* March 1999, pp 159–74.

87 A Drory and D Beaty, "Gender Differences in the Perception of Organizational Influence Tactics," *Journal of Organizational Behavior,* May 1991, pp 256–57. Also see L A Rudman, "Self-Promotion as a Risk Factor for Women: The Costs and Benefits of Counterstereotypical Impression Management," *Journal of Personality and Social Psychology,* March 1998, pp 629–45; and J Tata, "The Influence of Gender on the Use and Effectiveness of Managerial Accounts," *Group & Organization Management,* September 1998, pp 267–88.

88 Based on L A Witt, T F Hilton, and W A Hochwarter, "Addressing Politics in Matrix Teams," *Group & Organization Management,* June 2001, pp 230–47.

89 S A Akimoto and D M Sanbonmatsu, "Differences in Self-Effacing Behavior between European and Japanese Americans," *Journal of Cross-Cultural Psychology,* March 1999, pp 172–73.

90 A Zaleznik, "Real Work," *Harvard Business Review,* January–February 1989, p 60.

91 C M Koen, Jr, and S M Crow, "Human Relations and Political Skills," *HR Focus,* December 1995, p 11.

92 See L A Witt, "Enhancing Organizational Goal Congruence: A Solution to Organizational Politics," *Journal of Applied Psychology,* August 1998, pp 666–74.

93 Excerpted from J L Roberts and E Thomas, "Enron's Dirty Laundry," *Newsweek,* March 11, 2002, pp 22–28.

94 Ten quiz items quoted from J F Byrnes, "Connecting Organizational Politics and Conflict Resolution," *Personnel Administrator,* June 1986, p 49.

95 Scoring system quoted from ibid.

96 B R Schlenker and T W Britt, "Beneficial Impression Management: Strategically Controlling Information to Help Friends," *Journal of Personality and Social Psychology,* April 1999, p 559.

97 Excerpted from K Tse and D Foust, "At Risk from Smoking: Your Job," *Business Week,* April 15, 2002, p 12.

CHAPTER 17

1 Excerpted from C Hymowitz, "In the Lead: In a Crisis, Leaders Put People First, but Also Get Back to Business," *The Wall Street Journal,* August 18, 2001, p B1.

2 See S Lieberson and J F O'Connor, "Leadership and Organizational Performance: A Study of Large Corporations," *American Sociological Review,* April 1972, pp 117–30.

3 Results can be found in K T Dirks, "Trust in Leadership and Team Performance: Evidence from NCAA Basketball," *Journal of Applied Psychology,* December 2000, pp 1004–12; and D Jacobs and L Singell, "Leadership and Organizational Performance: Isolating Links between Managers and Collective Success," *Social Science Research,* June 1993, pp 165–89.

4 C A Schriesheim, J M Tolliver, and O C Behling, "Leadership Theory: Some Implications for Managers," *MSU Business Topics,* Summer 1978, p 35.

5 T Peters and N Austin, *A Passion for Excellence* (New York: Random House, 1985), pp 5–6.

6 The multiple levels of leadership are discussed by F J Yammarino, F Dansereau, and C J Kennedy, "A Multiple-Level Multidimensional Approach to Leadership: Viewing Leadership through an Elephant's Eye," *Organizational Dynamics,* 2001, pp 149–63.

[7] See R Goffee and G Jones, "Followership: It's Personal, Too," *Harvard Business Review,* December 2001, p 148.

[8] B M Bass, *Bass & Stogdill's Handbook of Leadership: Theory, Research, and Managerial Applications,* 3rd ed, (New York: Free Press, 1990), p 383.

[9] For a thorough discussion about the differences between leading and managing, see G Weathersby, "Leading vs. Management," *Management Review,* March 1999, p 5; and A Zalesnik, "Managers and Leaders: Are They Different?" *Harvard Business Review,* May–June 1977, pp 67–78.

[10] The role of leadership within organizational change is discussed by J P Lotter, *Leading Change* (Boston: Harvard Business School Press, 1996).

[11] For complete details, see R M Stogdill, "Personal Factors Associated with Leadership: A Survey of the Literature," *Journal of Psychology,* 1948, pp 35–71; and R M Stogdill, *Handbook of Leadership* (New York: Free Press, 1974).

[12] See R D Mann, "A Review of the Relationships between Personality and Performance in Small Groups," *Psychological Bulletin,* July 1959, pp 241–70.

[13] See D A Kenny and S J Zaccaro, "An Estimate of Variance Due to Traits in Leadership," *Journal of Applied Psychology,* November 1983, pp 678–85.

[14] Perceptions of leadership were examined by R F Martell and A L DeSmet, "A Diagnostic-Ratio Approach to Measuring Beliefs about the Leadership Abilities of Male and Female Managers," *Journal of Applied Psychology,* December 2001, pp 1223–31; and R A Baron, G D Markman, and A Hirsa, "Perceptions of Women and Men as Entrepreneurs: Evidence for Differential Effects of Attributional Augmenting," *Journal of Applied Psychology,* October 2001, pp 923–29.

[15] Results from this study can be found in F C Brodbeck et al., "Cultural Variation of Leadership Prototypes across 22 European Countries," *Journal of Occupational and Organizational Psychology,* March 2000, pp 1–29.

[16] Results can be found in J M Kouzes and B Z Posner, *The Leadership Challenge* (San Francisco: Jossey-Bass, 1995).

[17] C Hyowitz, "In the Lead: Managers Must Respond to Employee Concerns about Honest Business," *The Wall Street Journal,* February 19, 2002, p B1.

[18] Gender and the emergence of leaders was examined by A H Eagly and S J Karau, "Gender and the Emergence of Leaders: A Meta-Analysis," *Journal of Personality and Social Psychology,* May 1991, pp 685–710; and R K Shelly and P T Munroe, "Do Women Engage in Less Task Behavior than Men?" *Sociological Perspectives,* Spring 1999, pp 49–67.

[19] See A H Eagly, S J Karau, and B T Johnson, "Gender and Leadership Style among School Principals: A Meta-Analysis," *Educational Administration Quarterly,* February 1992, pp 76–102.

[20] Supportive findings are contained in J M Twenge, "Changes in Women's Assertiveness in Response to Status and Roles: A

Cross-Temporal Meta-Analysis, 1931–1993," *Journal of Personality and Social Psychology,* July 2001, pp 133–45.

[21] For a summary of this research, see R Sharpe, "As Leaders, Women Rule," *Business Week,* November 20, 2000, pp 74–84.

[22] D K Berman and J S Lublin, "Restructuring, Personality Clashes Led to Lucent Executive's Exit," *The Wall Street Journal,* May 16, 2001, p B1.

[23] H Lancaster, "Managing Your Career: To Get Shipped Abroad, Women Must Overcome Prejudice at Home," *The Wall Street Journal,* June 29, 1999, p B1.

[24] This research is summarized and critiqued by E A Fleishman, "Consideration and Structure: Another Look at Their Role in Leadership Research," in *Leadership: The Multiple-Level Approaches,* eds F Dansereau and F J Yammarino (Stamford, CT: JAI Press, 1998), pp 51–60.

[25] See V H Vroom, "Leadership," in *Handbook of Industrial and Organizational Psychology,* ed M D Dunnette (Chicago: Rand McNally, 1976).

[26] R R Blake and J S Mouton, "A Comparative Analysis of Situationalism and 9,9 Management by Principle," *Organizational Dynamics,* Spring 1982, p 23.

[27] Ibid., pp 28–29. Also see R R Blake and J S Mouton, "Management by Grid Principles or Situationalism: Which?" *Group & Organization Studies,* December 1981, pp 439–55.

[28] Ibid., p 21.

[29] M Delahoussaye, "Licking the Leadership Crisis," *Training,* January 2002, p 26.

[30] See Bass, *Bass & Stogdill's Handbook of Leadership,* chs 20–25.

[31] The relationships between the frequency and mastery of leader behavior and various outcomes were investigated by F Shipper and C S White, "Mastery, Frequency, and Interaction of Managerial Behaviors Relative to Subunit Effectiveness," *Human Relations,* January 1999, pp 49–66.

[32] F E Fiedler, "Job Engineering for Effective Leadership: A New Approach," *Management Review,* September 1977, p 29.

[33] J Kerstetter, S Hamm, and A Park, "Larry's One-Man Show," *Business Week,* March 25, 2002, pp 64–65.

[34] For more on this theory, see F E Fiedler, "A Contingency Model of Leadership Effectiveness," in *Advances in Experimental Social Psychology,* vol. 1, ed L Berkowitz (New York: Academic Press, 1964): and F E Fiedler, *A Theory of Leadership Effectiveness* (New York: McGraw-Hill, 1967).

[35] Additional information on situational control is contained in F E Fiedler, "The Leadership Situation and the Black Box in Contingency Theories," in *Leadership Theory and Research: Perspectives and Directions,* eds M M Chemers and R Ayman (New York: Academic Press, 1993), pp 2–28.

[36] See L H Peters, D D Hartke, and J T Pohlmann, "Fiedler's Contingency Theory of Leadership: An Application of the Meta-Analyses Procedures of Schmidt and Hunter," *Psychological Bulletin,* March 1985, pp 274–85. The meta-analysis was

conducted by C A Schriesheim, B J Tepper, and L A Tetrault, "Least Preferred Co-Worker Score, Situational Control, and Leadership Effectiveness: A Meta-Analysis of Contingency Model Performance Predictions," *Journal of Applied Psychology,* August 1994, pp 561–73.

[37] A recent review of the contingency theory and suggestions for future theoretical development is provided by R Ayman, M M Chemers, and F Fiedler, "The Contingency Model of Leadership Effectiveness: Its Levels of Analysis," in *Leadership: The Multiple-Level Approaches,* eds Dansereau and Yammarino, pp 73–94.

[38] For more detail on this theory, see R J House, "A Path–Goal Theory of Leader Effectiveness," *Administrative Science Quarterly,* September 1971, pp 321–38.

[39] This research is summarized by R J House, "Path–Goal Theory of Leadership: Lessons, Legacy, and a Reformulated Theory," *Leadership Quarterly,* Autumn 1996, pp 323–52.

[40] See ibid.

[41] Supportive results can be found in B Alimo-Metcalfe and R J Alban-Metcalfe, "The Development of a New Transformational Leadership Questionnaire," *Journal of Occupational and Organizational Psychology,* March 2001, pp 1–27.

[42] J Muller and C Tierney, "Can This Man Save Chrysler?" *Business Week,* September 17, 2001, pp 86, 88–89.

[43] Supportive results can be found in D Charbonneau, J Barling, and E K Kelloway, "Transformational Leadership and Sports Performance: The Mediating Role of Intrinsic Motivation," *Journal of Applied Social Psychology,* July 2001, pp 1521–34.

[44] Results can be found in P M Podsakoff, S B MacKenzie, M Ahearne, and W H Bommer, "Searching for a Needle in a Haystack: Trying to Identify the Illusive Moderators of Leadership Behaviors," *Journal of Management,* 1995, pp 422–70.

[45] A thorough discussion of this theory is provided by P Hersey and K H Blanchard, *Management of Organizational Behavior: Utilizing Human Resources,* 5th ed (Englewood Cliffs, NJ: Prentice Hall, 1988).

[46] A comparison of the original theory and its latent version is provided by P Hersey and K Blanchard, "Great Ideas Revisited," *Training & Development,* January 1996, pp 42–47.

[47] Results can be found in J R Goodson, G W McGee, and J F Cashman, "Situational Leadership Theory," *Group & Organization Studies,* December 1989, pp 446–61.

[48] The first study was conducted by R P Vecchio, "Situational Leadership Theory: An Examination of a Prescriptive Theory," *Journal of Applied Psychology,* August 1987, pp 444–51. Results from the study of nurse executives can be found in C Adams, "Leadership Behavior of Chief Nurse Executives," *Nursing Management,* August 1990, pp 36–39.

[49] See D C Lueder, "Don't Be Misled by LEAD," *Journal of Applied Behavioral Science,* May 1985, pp 143–54; and C L Graeff, "The Situational Leadership Theory: A Critical View," *Academy of Management Review,* April 1983, pp 285–91.

[50] For details on these theories, see H B Jones, "Magic, Meaning and Leadership: Weber's Model and the Empirical Literature," *Human Relations,* 2001, pp 753–771; J McGregor Burns, *Leadership* (New York: Harper & Row, 1978); N M Tichy and M A Devanna, *The Transformational Leader* (New York: John Wiley & Sons, 1986); J M Kouzes and B Z Posner, *The Leadership Challenge: How to Get Extraordinary Things Done in Organizations* (San Francisco: Jossey-Bass, 1990); B Bass and B J Avolio, "Transformational Leadership: A Response to Critiques," in *Leadership Theory and Research: Perspectives and Directions,* eds M M Chemers and R Ayman (New York: Academic Press, 1993), pp 49–80; B Nanus, *Visionary Leadership* (San Francisco: Jossey-Bass, 1992); and B Shamir, R J House, and M B Arthur, "The Motivational Effects of Charismatic Leadership: A Self-Concept Based Theory," *Organization Science,* November 1993, pp 577–94.

[51] Shamir, House, and Arthur, "The Motivational Effects of Charismatic Leadership," p 578.

[52] R Zemke and J Barbian, "The New Leaders," *Training,* August 2001, p 34.

[53] This discussion is based on D A Waldman and F J Yammarino, "CEO Charismatic Leadership: Levels-of-Management and Levels-of-Analysis Effects," *Academy of Management Review,* April 1999, pp 266–85.

[54] Nanus, *Visionary Leadership,* p 8.

[55] See ibid.

[56] N Deogun, "Bitter Medicine: Network of Doctors, Touted as a Panacea, Develops Big Problems," *The Wall Street Journal,* August 26, 1996, p A1.

[57] A process for creating an organization vision is outlined by S Yearout, G Miles, and R H Koonce, "Multi-Level Visioning," *Training & Development,* March 2001, pp 31–39.

[58] Supportive results can be found in N Sivasubramaniam, W D Murry, B J Avolio, and D I Jung, "A Longitudinal Model of the Effects of Team Leadership and Group Potency on Group Performance," *Group & Organization Management,* March 2002, pp 66–96; and J Paul, D L Costley, J P Howell, P W Dorfman, and D Trafimow, "The Effects of Charismatic Leadership on Followers' Self-Concept Accessibility," *Journal of Applied Social Psychology,* September 2001, pp 1821–44.

[59] Results can be obtained from T G DeGroot, D S Kiker, and T C Cross, "A Meta-Analysis to Review the Consequences of Charismatic Leadership," paper presented at the annual meeting of the Academy of Management, Cincinnati, Ohio, 1996.

[60] See J Barling, C Loughlin, and E K Kelloway, "Development and Test of a Model Linking Safety-Specific Transformation Leadership and Occupational Safety," *Journal of Applied Psychology,* June 2002, pp 488–96; and J A Conger, R N Kanungo, and S T Menon, "Charismatic Leadership and Follower Effects," *Journal of Organizational Behavior,* November 2000, pp 747–68.

[61] See K B Lowe, K G Kroeck, and N Sivasubramaniam, "Effectiveness Correlates of Transformational and Transactional Leadership: A Meta-Analytic Review of the MLQ Literature," *Leadership Quarterly,* 1996, pp 385–425.

[62] Results can be found in R J House, W D Spangler, and J Woycke, "Personality and Charisma in the US Presidency: A Psychological Theory of Leader Effectiveness," *Administrative Science Quarterly,* September 1991, pp 364–96.

[63] See B Shankar Pawar and K K Eastman, "The Nature and Implications of Contextual Influences on Transformational Leadership: A Conceptual Examination," *Academy of Management Review,* January 1997, pp 80–109.

[64] Supporting research is summarized by Bass and Avolio, "Transformation Leadership," pp 49–80.

[65] Ford's program is thoroughly discussed by S D Friedman, "Leadership DNA: The Ford Motor Story," *Training & Development,* March 2001, pp 23–29.

[66] These recommendations were derived from J M Howell and B J Avolio, "The Ethics of Charismatic Leadership: Submission or Liberation," *Academy of Management Executive,* May 1992, pp 43–54.

[67] E O Welles, "Options, Equity, and Rancor," *Inc.,* July 2001, p 52.

[68] See F Dansereau, Jr, G Graen, and W Haga, "A Vertical Dyad Linkage Approach to Leadership within Formal Organizations," *Organizational Behavior and Human Performance,* February 1975, pp 46–78; and R M Dienesch and R C Liden, "Leader–Member Exchange Model of Leadership: A Critique and Further Development," *Academy of Management Review,* July 1986, pp 618–34.

[69] These descriptions were taken from D Duchon, S G Green, and T D Taber, "Vertical Dyad Linkage: A Longitudinal Assessment of Antecedents, Measures, and Consequences," *Journal of Applied Psychology,* February 1986, pp 56–60.

[70] Supportive results can be found in S J Wayne, L M Shore, W H Bommer, and L E Tetrick, "The Role of Fair Treatment and Rewards in Perceptions of Organizational Support and Leader–Member Exchange," *Journal of Applied Psychology,* June 2002, pp 590–98; C A Schriesheim, S L Castro, and F J Yammarino, "Investigating Contingencies: An Examination of the Impact of Span of Supervision and Upward Controllingness on Leader–Member Exchange Using Traditional and Multivariate Within- and Between-Entities Analysis," *Journal of Applied Psychology,* October 2000, pp 659–77; and C Cogliser and C A Schriesheim, "Exploring Work Unit Context and Leader–Member Exchange: A Multi-Level Perspective," *Journal of Organizational Behavior,* August 2000, pp 487–511.

[71] A turnover study was conducted by G B Graen, R C Liden, and W Hoel, "Role of Leadership in the Employee Withdrawal Process," *Journal of Applied Psychology,* December 1982, pp 868–72. The career progress study was conducted by M Wakabayashi and G B Graen, "The Japanese Career Progress Study: A 7-Year Follow-Up," *Journal of Applied Psychology,* November 1984, pp 603–14.

[72] A review of this research can be found in R T Sparrowe and R C Liden, "Process and Structure in Leader–Member Exchange," *Academy of Management Review,* April 1997, pp 522–52.

[73] Supportive results can be found in C Gomez and B Rosen, "The Leader–Member Exchange as a Link between Managerial Trust and Employee Empowerment," *Group & Organization Management,* March 2001, pp 53–69; and J M Maslyn and M Uhl-Bien, "Leader–Member Exchange and Its Dimensions: Effects of Self-Effort and Other's Effort on Relationship Quality," *Journal of Applied Psychology,* August 2001, pp 697–708.

[74] Suggestions for relationship building are provided by M Uhl-Bien, G B Graen, and T A Scandura, "Implications of Leader–Member Exchange (LMX) for Strategic Human Resource Management Systems: Relationships as Social Capital for Competitive Advantage," in *Research in Human Resources Management,* vol. 18, ed G R Ferris (Stamford, CT: JAI Press, 2000), pp 137–85.

[75] The reliability and validity of this measure is provided by R C Liden and J M Maslyn, "Multidimensionality of Leader–Member Exchange: An Empirical Assessment through Scale Development," *Journal of Management,* 1998, pp 43–72.

[76] These recommendations are from R P Vecchio, "Are You In or Out with Your Boss?" *Business Horizons,* November–December 1986, pp 76–78.

[77] For an expanded discussion of this model, see S Kerr and J Jermier, "Substitutes for Leadership: Their Meaning and Measurement," *Organizational Behavior and Human Performance,* December 1978, pp 375–403.

[78] Results can be found in S D Dionne, F J Yammarino, L E Atwater, and L R James, "Neutralizing Substitutes for Leadership Theory: Leadership Effects and Common-Source Bias," *Journal of Applied Psychology,* June 2002, pp 454–64; and P M Podsakoff, S B MacKenzie, M Ahearne, and W H Bommer, "Searching for a Needle in a Haystack: Trying to Identify the Illusive Moderators of Leadership Behaviors," *Journal of Management,* 1995, pp 422–70.

[79] For details of this study, see P M Podsakoff, S B MacKenzie, and W H Bommer, "Meta-Analysis of the Relationship between Kerr and Jermier's Substitutes for Leadership and Employee Job Attitudes, Role Perceptions, and Performance," *Journal of Applied Psychology,* August 1996, pp 380–99.

[80] See the related discussion in J P Howell, D E Bowen, P W Dorfman, S Kerr, and P M Podsakoff, "Substitutes for Leadership: Effective Alternatives to Ineffective Leadership," in *Leadership: Understanding the Dynamics of Power and Influence in Organizations,* ed R P Vecchio (Notre Dame, IN: University of Notre Dame Press, 1997), pp 381–95.

[81] An overall summary of servant-leadership is provided by L C Spears, *Reflections on Leadership: How Robert K Greenleaf's Theory of Servant-Leadership Influenced Today's Top Management Thinkers* (New York: John Wiley & Sons, 1995).

[82] J A Byrne, "Restoring Trust in Corporate America: Business Must Lead the Way to Real Reform," *Business Week,* June 24, 2002, pp 31–32.

[83] T Galvin, "Birds of a Feather," *Training,* March 2001, p 84.

[84] J Stuart, *Fast Company,* September 1999, p 114.

[85] Excerpted from E Krell, "The New Leaders," *Training,* August 2001, p 35.

86 Excerpted from K Ellis, "The New Leaders," *Training,* August 2001, p 36.

87 The scale used to assess readiness to assume the leadership role was taken from A J DuBrin, *Leadership: Research Findings, Practice, and Skills* (Boston: Houghton Mifflin Company, 1995), pp 10–11.

88 The norms were taken from ibid.

89 This exercise was based on one contained in L W Mealiea, *Skills for Managers in Organizations* (Burr Ridge, IL: Irwin, 1994), pp 96–97.

90 The introduction was excerpted from ibid., p 96.

91 Excerpted from C Haddad and A Barrett, "A Whistle-Blower Rocks an Industry," *Business Week,* June 24, 2002, pp 126, 128.

CHAPTER 18

1 Excerpted from F Keenan and S E Ante, "The New Teamwork," *Business Week e.biz,* February 18, 2002, pp EB12–EB15.

2 C I Barnard, *The Functions of the Executive* (Cambridge, MA: Harvard University Press, 1938), p 73. Also see M C Suchman, "Managing Legitimacy: Strategic and Institutional Approaches," *Academy of Management Review,* July 1995, pp 571–610.

3 Drawn from E H Schein, *Organizational Psychology,* 3rd ed (Englewood Cliffs, NJ: Prentice Hall, 1980), pp 12–15.

4 For interesting and instructive insights about organization structure and theory, see J G March, "Continuity and Change in Theories of Organizational Action," *Administrative Science Quarterly,* June 1996, pp 278–87; and J Ofori-Dankwa and S D Julian, "Complexifying Organizational Theory: Illustrations Using Time Research," *Academy of Management Review,* July 2001, pp 415–30.

5 For related research, see S Finkelstein and R A D'Aveni, "CEO Duality as a Double-Edged Sword: How Boards of Directors Balance Entrenchment Avoidance and Unity of Command," *Academy of Management Journal,* October 1994, pp 1079–108.

6 See M Cecere, "Drawing the Lines," *Harvard Business Review,* November 2001, p 24.

7 For an interesting historical perspective of hierarchy, see P Miller and T O'Leary, "Hierarchies and American Ideals, 1900–1940," *Academy of Management Review,* April 1989, pp 250–65.

8 For an excellent overview of the span of control concept, see D D Van Fleet and A G Bedeian, "A History of the Span of Management," *Academy of Management Review,* July 1977, pp 356–72. Also see E E Lawler III and J R Galbraith, "New Roles for the Staff: Strategic Support and Service," in *Organizing for the Future: The New Logic for Managing Complex Organizations,* eds J R Galbraith, E E Lawler III, and Associates (San Francisco: Jossey-Bass, 1993), pp 65–83.

9 M Koslowsky, "Staff/Line Distinctions in Job and Organizational Commitment," *Journal of Occupational Psychology,* June 1990, pp 167–73.

10 A management-oriented discussion of general systems theory—an interdisciplinary attempt to integrate the various fragmented sciences—may be found in K E Boulding, "General Systems Theory—The Skeleton of Science," *Management Science,* April 1956, pp 197–208. For recent systems-related ideas, see A M Webber, "How Business Is a Lot Like Life," *Fast Company,* April 2001, pp 130–36; E Bonabeau and C Meyer, "Swarm Intelligence: A Whole New Way to Think about Business," *Harvard Business Review,* May 2001, pp 106–14; S Godin, "Survival Is Not Enough," *Fast Company,* January 2002, pp 90–94; E K Clemons and J A Santamaria, "Maneuver Warfare: Can Modern Military Strategy Lead You to Victory?" *Harvard Business Review,* April 2002, pp 56–65; and C Oswick, T Keenoy, and D Grant, "Metaphor and Analogical Reasoning in Organization Theory: Beyond Orthodoxy," *Academy of Management Review,* April 2002, pp 294–303.

11 For more on this subject, see V-W Mitchell, "Organizational Homoeostasis: A Role for Internal Marketing," *Management Decision,* no. 2, 1992, pp 3–7. Biological metaphors are explored in T Petzinger Jr, "A New Model for the Nature of Business: It's Alive!" *The Wall Street Journal,* February 26, 1999, pp B1, B4; and T Petzinger Jr, "Two Doctors Give New Meaning to Taking Your Business to Heart," *The Wall Street Journal,* April 30, 1999, p B1.

12 For updates, see V Anand, W H Glick, and C C Manz, "Thriving on the Knowledge of Outsiders: Tapping Organizational Social Capital," *Academy of Management Executive,* February 2002, pp 87–101; S L Berman, J Down, and C W L Hill, "Tacit Knowledge as a Source of Competitive Advantage in the National Basketball Association," *Academy of Management Journal,* February 2002, pp 13–31; D Coutu, "The Anxiety of Learning," *Harvard Business Review,* March 2002, pp 100–6; and R S Bhagat, B L Kedia, P D Harveston, and H C Triandis, "Cultural Variations in the Cross-Border Transfer of Organizational Knowledge: An Integrative Framework," *Academy of Management Review,* April 2002, pp 204–21.

13 R M Fulmer and J B Keys, "A Conversation with Peter Senge: New Development in Organizational Learning," *Organizational Dynamics,* Autumn 1998, p 35.

14 This definition was based on D A Garvin, "Building a Learning Organization," *Harvard Business Review,* July–August 1993, pp 78–91.

15 J Stuller, "Chief of Corporate Smarts," *Training,* April 1998, p 32. For more on learning organizations, see R S Snell, "Moral Foundations of the Learning Organization," *Human Relations,* March 2001, pp 319–42; A Edmondson, R Bohmer, and G Pisano, "Speeding Up Team Learning," *Harvard Business Review,* October 2001, pp 125–32; and B Breen, "Lilly's R&D Prescription," *Fast Company,* April 2002, pp 44, 46.

16 T A Stewart, "Welcome to the Revolution," *Fortune,* December 13, 1993, p 66. Also see J A Byrne, "Management by Web," *Business Week,* August 28, 2000, pp 84–96; and J Child and R G McGrath, "Organizations Unfettered: Organizational Form in an Information-Intensive Economy," *Academy of Management Journal,* December 2001, pp 1135–48.

17 See J R Galbraith and E E Lawler III, "Effective Organizations: Using the New Logic of Organizing," in

Organizing for the Future: The New Logic for Managing Complex Organizations, eds J R Galbraith, E E Lawler III, and Associates (San Francisco: Jossey-Bass, 1993).

[18] R Jacob, "The Struggle to Create an Organization for the 21st Century," *Fortune,* April 3, 1995, pp 91–92. © Time Inc. All rights reserved.

[19] See S Sonnesyn Brooks, "Managing a Horizontal Revolution," *HR Magazine,* June 1995, pp 52–58; and M Hequet, "Flat and Happy," *Training,* April 1995, pp 29–34.

[20] See C M Christensen, "Limits of the New Corporation," *Business Week,* August 28, 2000, pp 180–81; R Häcki and J Lighton, "The Future of the Networked Company," *McKinsey Quarterly,* no. 3 (2000), pp 26–39; and M A Schilling and H K Steensma, "The Use of Modular Organizational Forms: An Industry-Level Analysis," *Academy of Management Journal,* December 2001, pp 1149–68.

[21] J Bick, "Solo: The New Face of Self-Employment," *Inc.,* November 2001, p 88.

[22] C Handy, *The Hungry Spirit* (New York: Broadway Books, 1998), p 186. (Emphasis added.)

[23] For a discussion of Amazon.com, see K Maney, "Better Watch Out, Better Not Cry: Bezos Is Coming to Town," *USA Today,* December 12, 2001, p 3B.

[24] J A Byrne and B Elgin, "Cisco: Behind the Hype," *Business Week,* January 21, 2002, p 58.

[25] As quoted in L McCauley, "Measure What Matters," *Fast Company,* May 1999, pp 97–98.

[26] K Cameron, "Critical Questions in Assessing Organizational Effectiveness," *Organizational Dynamics,* Autumn 1980, p 70. Also see K Gawande and T Wheeler, "Measures of Effectiveness for Governmental Organizations," *Management Science,* January 1999, pp 42–58; E J Walton and S Dawson, "Managers' Perceptions of Criteria of Organizational Effectiveness," *Journal of Management Studies,* March 2001, pp 173–200; M Beer, "How to Develop an Organization Capable of Sustained High Performance: Embrace the Drive for Results-Capability Development Paradox," *Organizational Dynamics,* Spring 2001, pp 233–47; and K H Roberts and R Bea, "Must Accidents Happen? Lessons from High-Reliability Organizations," *Academy of Management Executive,* August 2001, pp 70–78.

[27] See J Collins, "Turning Goals into Results: The Power of Catalytic Mechanisms," *Harvard Business Review,* July–August 1999, pp 71–82.

[28] See, for example, R O Brinkerhoff and D E Dressler, *Productivity Measurement: A Guide for Managers and Evaluators* (Newbury Park, CA: Sage Publications, 1990); and J McCune, "The Productivity Paradox," *Management Review,* March 1998, pp 38–40.

[29] See M Ozer, "The Role of Flexibility in Online Business," *Business Horizons,* January–February 2002, pp 61–69; and O Port, "The Next Web," *Business Week,* March 4, 2002, pp 96–102.

[30] Data from M Maynard, "Toyota Promises Custom Order in 5 Days," *USA Today,* August 6, 1999, p 1B.

[31] "Interview: M Scott Peck," *Business Ethics,* March–April 1994, p 17.

[32] Cameron, "Critical Questions in Assessing Organizational Effectiveness," p 67. Also see W Buxton, "Growth from Top to Bottom," *Management Review,* July–August 1999, p 11.

[33] See R K Mitchell, B R Agle, and D J Wood, "Toward a Theory of Stakeholder Identification and Salience: Defining the Principle of Who and What Really Counts," *Academy of Management Review,* October 1997, pp 853–96; W Beaver, "Is the Stakeholder Model Dead?" *Business Horizons,* March–April 1999, pp 8–12; J Frooman, "Stakeholder Influence Strategies," *Academy of Management Review,* April 1999, pp 191–205; T M Jones and A C Wicks, "Convergent Stakeholder Theory," *Academy of Management Review,* April 1999, pp 206–21; and I M Jawahar and G L McLaughlin, "Toward a Descriptive Stakeholder Theory: An Organizational Life Cycle Approach," *Academy of Management Review,* July 2001, pp 397–414.

[34] See M Adams, "Big Raises Pound Airlines at a Bad Time," *USA Today,* July 5, 2001, p 1B.

[35] See N C Roberts and P J King, "The Stakeholder Audit Goes Public," *Organizational Dynamics,* Winter 1989, pp 63–79; and I Henriques and P Sadorsky, "The Relationship between Environmental Commitment and Managerial Perceptions of Stakeholder Importance," *Academy of Management Journal,* February 1999, pp 87–99.

[36] See C Ostroff and N Schmitt, "Configurations of Organizational Effectiveness and Efficiency," *Academy of Management Journal,* December 1993, pp 1345–61; and M Boyle, "The Right Stuff," *Fortune,* March 4, 2002, pp 85–86.

[37] K S Cameron, "Effectiveness as Paradox: Consensus and Conflict in Conceptions of Organizational Effectiveness," *Management Science,* May 1986, p 542.

[38] Alternative effectiveness criteria are discussed in Ibid.; A G Bedeian, "Organization Theory: Current Controversies, Issues, and Directions," in *International Review of Industrial and Organizational Psychology,* eds C L Cooper and I T Robertson (New York: John Wiley & Sons, 1987), pp 1–33; and M Keeley, "Impartiality and Participant-Interest Theories of Organizational Effectiveness," *Administrative Science Quarterly,* March 1984, pp 1–25.

[39] For details, see A Sloan, "Lights Out for Enron," *Newsweek,* December 10, 2001, pp 50–51; W Zellner and S A Forest, "The Fall of Enron," *Business Week,* December 17, 2001, pp 30–36; B McLean, "Why Enron Went Bust," *Fortune,* December 24, 2001, pp 58–68; and G Farrell and D Jones, "How Did Enron Come Unplugged?" *USA Today,* January 14, 2002, pp 1B–2B.

[40] Data from K Naughton, "Ford's 'Perfect Storm,'" *Newsweek,* September 17, 2001, pp 48–50.

[41] Data from "Kmart Posts $1 Billion Loss in April," *USA Today,* May 24, 2002, p 1B.

[42] D N Sull, "Why Good Companies Go Bad," *Harvard Business Review,* July–August 1999, pp 42–52. Also see H B

Cohen, "The Performance Paradox," *Academy of Management Executive,* August 1998, pp 30–40.

[43] M A Mone, W McKinley, and V L Barker III, "Organizational Decline and Innovation: A Contingency Framework," *Academy of Management Review,* January 1998, p 117.

[44] P Lorange and R T Nelson, "How to Recognize—and Avoid—Organizational Decline," *Sloan Management Review,* Spring 1987, p 47.

[45] Excerpted from ibid., pp 43–45. Also see E E Lawler III and J R Galbraith, "Avoiding the Corporate Dinosaur Syndrome," *Organizational Dynamics,* Autumn 1994, pp 5–17; and K Labich, "Why Companies Fail," *Fortune,* November 14, 1994, pp 52–68.

[46] For details, see K S Cameron, M U Kim, and D A Whetten, "Organizational Effects of Decline and Turbulence," *Administrative Science Quarterly,* June 1987, pp 222–40. Also see A G Bedeian and A A Armenakis, "The Cesspool Syndrome: How Dreck Floats to the Top of Declining Organizations," *Academy of Management Executive,* February 1998, pp 58–63. For a relevant list of strategic issues, see A J Slywotzky and D J Morrison, *How Digital Is Your Business?* (New York: Crown Business, 2000), pp 23–24.

[47] Twelve dysfunctional consequences of decline are discussed and empirically tested in K S Cameron, D A Whetten, and M U Kim, "Organizational Dysfunctions of Decline," *Academy of Management Journal,* March 1987, pp 126–38. Also see D K Hurst, *Crisis and Renewal: Meeting the Challenge of Organizational Change* (Boston: Harvard Business School Press, 1995); Z Rosenblatt and Z Sheaffer, "Brain Drain in Declining Organizations: Toward a Research Agenda," *Journal of Organizational Behavior,* June 2001, pp 409–24; G C Mueller, W McKinley, M A Mone, and V L Barker III, "Organizational Decline—A Stimulus for Innovation?" *Business Horizons,* November–December 2001, pp 25–34; D N James, "The Trouble I've Seen," *Harvard Business Review,* March 2002, pp 42–49; and K H Hammonds, "Five Habits of Highly Reliable Organizations," *Fast Company,* May 2002, pp 124–28.

[48] Data from V L Barker III and P W Patterson, Jr, "Top Management Team Tenure and Top Manager Causal Attributions at Declining Firms Attempting Turnarounds," *Group & Organization Management,* September 1996, pp 304–36. Related research is reported in V L Barker III, P W Patterson Jr, and G C Mueller, "Organizational Causes and Strategic Consequences of the Extent of Top Management Team Replacement during Turnaround Attempts," *Journal of Management Studies,* March 2001, pp 235–70.

[49] For related reading, see C R Eitel, "The Ten Disciplines of Business Turnaround," *Management Review,* December 1998, p 13; J R Morris, W F Cascio, and C E Young, "Downsizing After All These Years: Questions and Answers about Who Did It, How Many Did It, and Who Benefited from It," *Organizational Dynamics,* Winter 1999, pp 78–87; and S Kuczynski, "Help! I Shrunk the Company!" *HR Magazine,* June 1999, pp 40–45.

[50] B Treasurer, "How Risk-Taking Really Works," *Training,* January 2000, p 43.

[51] See J L Roberts and E Thomas, "Enron's Dirty Laundry," *Newsweek,* March 11, 2002, pp 22–28.

[52] A Taylor III, "Why Toyota Keeps Getting Better and Better and Better," *Fortune,* November 19, 1990, pp 66–67.

[53] J Muller, "Autos: A New Industry," *Business Week,* July 15, 2002, p 106.

[54] For updates, see J M Pennings, "Structural Contingency Theory: A Reappraisal," *Research in Organizational Behavior* vol 14 (Greenwich, CT: JAI Press, 1992), pp 267–309; and M Goold and A Campbell, "Do You Have a Well-Designed Organization?" *Harvard Business Review,* March 2002, pp 117–24.

[55] See G J Lewis and B Harvey, "Perceived Environmental Uncertainty: The Extension of Miller's Scale to the Natural Environment," *Journal of Management Studies,* March 2001, pp 201–34.

[56] A Reinhardt, "Nokia's Next Act," *Business Week,* July 1, 2002, p 57.

[57] P R Lawrence and J W Lorsch, *Organization and Environment* (Homewood, IL: Richard D Irwin, 1967), p 157.

[58] Pooled, sequential, and reciprocal integration are discussed in J W Lorsch, "Organization Design: A Situational Perspective," *Organizational Dynamics,* Autumn 1977, pp 2–14. Also see J E Ettlie and E M Reza, "Organizational Integration and Process Innovation," *Academy of Management Journal,* October 1992, pp 795–827; and A L Patti and J P Gilbert, "Collocating New Product Development Teams: Why, When, Where, and How?" *Business Horizons,* November–December 1997, pp 59–64.

[59] See B Dumaine, "Ability to Innovate," *Fortune,* January 29, 1990, pp 43, 46. For good reading on innovation and technology, see O Port, "Getting to 'Eureka!' " *Business Week,* November 10, 1997, pp 72–75; J W Gurley, "Got a Good Idea? Better Think Twice," *Fortune,* December 7, 1998, pp 215–16; J C McCune, "The Technology Treadmill," *Management Review,* December 1998, pp 10–12; and L Yates and P Skarzynski, "How Do Companies Get to the Future First?" *Management Review,* January 1999, pp 16–22.

[60] K Deveny, "Bag Those Fries, Squirt That Ketchup, Fry That Fish," *Business Week,* October 13, 1986, p 86.

[61] See D A Morand, "The Role of Behavioral Formality and Informality in the Enactment of Bureaucratic versus Organic Organizations," *Academy of Management Review,* October 1995, pp 831–72.

[62] P Raeburn, "A Genome Project against Disease," *Business Week,* July 1, 2002, p 85.

[63] See G P Huber, C C Miller, and W H Glick, "Developing More Encompassing Theories about Organizations: The Centralization-Effectiveness Relationship as an Example," *Organization Science,* no. 1 (1990), pp 11–40; and C Handy, "Balancing Corporate Power: A New Federalist Paper," *Harvard Business Review,* November–December 1992,

pp 59–72. Also see W R Pape, "Divide and Conquer," *Inc. Technology,* no. 2, 1996, pp 25–27; and J Schmidt, "Breaking Down Fiefdoms," *Management Review,* January 1997, pp 45–49.

64 P Kaestle, "A New Rationale for Organizational Structure," *Planning Review,* July–August 1990, p 22. Also see M E Raynor and J L Bower, "Lead from the Center: How to Manage Divisions Dynamically," *Harvard Business Review,* May 2001, pp 92–100; and R F Freeland, "When Organizational Messiness Works," *Harvard Business Review,* May 2002, pp 24–25.

65 Details of this study can be found in T Burns and G M Stalker, *The Management of Innovation* (London: Tavistock, 1961).

66 D J Gillen and S J Carroll, "Relationship of Managerial Ability to Unit Effectiveness in More Organic versus More Mechanistic Departments," *Journal of Management Studies,* November 1985, pp 674–75.

67 J D Sherman and H L Smith, "The Influence of Organizational Structure on Intrinsic versus Extrinsic Motivation," *Academy of Management Journal,* December 1984, p 883.

68 See J A Courtright, G T Fairhurst, and L E Rogers, "Interaction Patterns in Organic and Mechanistic Systems," *Academy of Management Journal,* December 1989, pp 773–802.

69 See J Woodward, *Industrial Organization: Theory and Practice* (London: Oxford University Press, 1965); and P D Collins and F Hull, "Technology and Span of Control: Woodward Revisited," *Journal of Management Studies,* March 1986, pp 143–64.

70 See L W Fry, "Technology-Structure Research: Three Critical Issues," *Academy of Management Journal,* September 1982, pp 532–52.

71 Ibid., p 548. Also see R Reese, "Redesigning for Dial Tone: A Socio-Technical Systems Case Study," *Organizational Dynamics,* Autumn 1995, pp 80–90.

72 For example, see C C Miller, W H Glick, Y-D Wang, and G P Huber, "Understanding Technology-Structure Relationships: Theory Development and Meta-Analytic Theory Testing," *Academy of Management Journal,* June 1991, pp 370–99; and K H Roberts and M Grabowski, "Organizations, Technology and Structuring," in *Handbook of Organization Studies,* eds S R Clegg, C Hardy, and W R Nord (Thousand Oaks, CA: Sage Publications, 1996), pp 409–23.

73 The phrase "small is beautiful" was coined by the late British economist E F Schumacher. See E F Schumacher, *Small Is Beautiful: Economics as if People Mattered* (New York: Harper & Row, 1973).

74 T J Peters and R H Waterman, Jr, *In Search of Excellence* (New York: Harper & Row, 1982), p 321. Also see T Peters, "Rethinking Scale," *California Management Review,* Fall 1992, pp 7–29.

75 See, for example, W McKinley, "Decreasing Organizational Size: To Untangle or Not to Untangle?" *Academy of*

Management Review, January 1992, pp 112–23; W Zellner, "Go-Go Goliaths," *Business Week,* February 13, 1995, pp 64–70; T Brown, "Manage 'BIG!'" *Management Review,* May 1996, pp 12–17; and E Shapiro, "Power, Not Size, Counts," *Management Review,* September 1996, p 61.

76 Handy, *The Hungry Spirit,* pp 107–8. Also see C Handy, "The Doctrine of Enough," *Management Review,* June 1998, pp 52–54.

77 P L Zweig, "The Case against Mergers," *Business Week,* October 30, 1995, p 122. Also see M Arndt, "Let's Talk Turkeys," *Business Week,* December 11, 2000, pp 44–46; J L Bower, "Not All M&As Are Alike—and That Matters," *Harvard Business Review,* March 2001, pp 92–101; M L Marks and P H Mirvis, "Making Mergers and Acquistions Work: Strategic and Psychological Preparation," *Academy of Management Executive,* May 2001, pp 80–92; E Barker, "Size Counts," *Inc.,* July 2001, pp 42–49; M Arndt, "How Companies Can Marry Well," *Business Week,* March 4, 2002, p 28; and A Sloan, "Memo to CEOs: Bigger Isn't Better," *Newsweek,* May 13, 2002, p 60.

78 S Crock, "A Lean, Mean Fighting Machine It Ain't," *Business Week,* January 11, 1999, p 41.

79 R Z Gooding and J A Wagner III, "A Meta-Analytic Review of the Relationship between Size and Performance: The Productivity and Efficiency of Organizations and Their Subunits," *Administrative Science Quarterly,* December 1985, pp 462–81.

80 Ibid., p 477.

81 Results are presented in P G Benson, T L Dickinson, and C O Neidt, "The Relationship between Organizational Size and Turnover: A Longitudinal Investigation," *Human Relations,* January 1987, pp 15–30. Also see M Yasai-Ardekani, "Effects of Environmental Scarcity and Munificence on the Relationship of Context to Organizational Structure," *Academy of Management Journal,* March 1989, pp 131–56.

82 See E E Lawler III, "Rethinking Organization Size," *Organizational Dynamics,* Autumn 1997, pp 24–35; O Harari, "Honey, I Shrunk the Company!" *Management Review,* December 1998, pp 39–41; and J C McCune, "Stuck in the Middle?" *Management Review,* February 1999, pp 44–49.

83 See D McGinn, "Honey, I Shrunk the Store," *Newsweek,* June 3, 2002, pp 36–37.

84 G Anders, "John Chambers after the Deluge," *Fast Company,* July 2001, p 108.

85 See J Child, "Organizational Structure, Environment and Performance: The Role of Strategic Choice," *Sociology,* January 1972, pp 1–22.

86 See J Galbraith, *Organization Design* (Reading, MA: Addison-Wesley Publishing, 1977); J R Montanari, "Managerial Discretion: An Expanded Model of Organization Choice," *Academy of Management Review,* April 1978, pp 231–41; and H R Bobbitt, Jr, and J D Ford, "Decision-Maker Choice as a Determinant of Organizational Structure," *Academy of Management Review,* January 1980, pp 13–23.

[87] For an alternative model of strategy making, see S L Hart, "An Integrative Framework for Strategy-Making Processes," *Academy of Management Review,* April 1992, pp 327–51. Also see C McDermott and K K Boyer, "Strategic Consensus: Marching to the Beat of a Different Drummer?" *Business Horizons,* July–August 1999, pp 21–28; R S Dooley and G E Fryxell, "Attaining Decision Quality and Commitment from Dissent: The Moderating Effects of Loyalty and Competence in Strategic Decision-Making Teams," *Academy of Management Journal,* August 1999, pp 389–402; M A Carpenter and J D Westphal, "The Strategic Context of External Network Ties: Examining the Impact of Director Appointments on Board Involvement in Strategic Decision Making," *Academy of Management Journal,* August 2001, pp 639–60; and J Denis, L Lamothe, and A Langley, "The Dynamics of Collective Leadership and Strategic Change in Pluralistic Organizations," *Academy of Management Journal,* August 2001, pp 809–37.

[88] S Perlstein, "Less Is More," *Business Ethics,* September–October 1993, p 15.

Business Ethics

P.O. Box 8439

Minneapolis, MN 55408

Reprinted with permission from *Business Ethics,* P.O. Box 8439, Minneapolis, MN 55408. www.business-ethics.com/612/879-0695.

[89] "Our Culture: about Patagonia," July 17, 2002, (www.patagonia.com/culture).

[90] Details may be found in D Miller, "Strategy Making and Structure: Analysis and Implications for Performance," *Academy of Management Journal,* March 1987, pp 7–32. For more, see T L Amburgey and T Dacin, "As the Left Foot Follows the Right? The Dynamics of Strategic and Structural Change," *Academy of Management Journal,* December 1994, pp 1427–52; and M W Peng and P S Heath, "The Growth of the Firm in Planned Economies in Transition: Institutions, Organizations, and Strategic Choice," *Academy of Management Review,* April 1996, pp 492–528.

[91] Excerpted from J Greene, "Ballmer's Microsoft," *Business Week,* June 17, 2002, pp 66–74.

[92] Excerpted from N Byrnes, "At Philip Morris, Perks for Life," *Business Week,* July 15, 2002, p 12.

CHAPTER 19

[1] Excerpted from D Brady, "The Education of Jeff Immelt," *Business Week,* April 29, 2002, pp 80, 82–83, 86.

[2] A M Webber, "Learning for a Change," *Fast Company,* May 1999, p 180.

[3] M L Alch, "Get Ready for the Net Generation," *Training & Development,* February 2000, pp 32, 34.

[4] A discussion of strategic alliances and partnerships is contained in D Sparks, "Special Report: Partners," *Business Week,* October 25, 1999, pp 106–12.

[5] P Starobin and C Belton, "Cleanup Time," *Business Week,* January 14, 2002, p 46.

[6] J Muller, "Ford: Why It's Worse than You Think," *Business Week,* June 25, 2001, p 81.

[7] See Special Report, "The Fallen," *Business Week,* January 14, 2002, p 78.

[8] This three-way typology of change was adapted from discussion in P C Nutt, "Tactics of Implementation," *Academy of Management Journal,* June 1986, pp 230–61.

[9] Types of organizational change are discussed by K E Weick and R E Quinn, "Organizational Change and Development," in *Annual Review of Psychology,* vol. 50, eds J T Spence, J M Darley, and D J Foss (Palo Alto, CA: Annual Reviews, 1999), pp 361–86.

[10] For a thorough discussion of the model, see K Lewin, *Field Theory in Social Science* (New York: Harper & Row, 1951).

[11] These assumptions are discussed in E H Schein, *Organizational Psychology,* 3rd ed (Englewood Cliffs, NJ: Prentice Hall, 1980).

[12] C Goldwasser, "Benchmarking: People Make the Process," *Management Review,* June 1995, p 40.

[13] I Mochari, "The Talking Cure," *Inc.,* November 2001, p 122.

[14] An individual model of change is discussed by J M George and G R Jones, "Towards a Process Model of Individual Change in Organizations," *Human Relations,* April 2001, pp 419–44.

[15] L Lavelle, "KPMG's Brave Leap into the Cold," *Business Week,* May 21, 2001, pp 72, 73.

[16] A cascading model of organizational change is presented in R M Miles, "Accelerating Corporate Transformations by Rapidly Engaging All Employees," *Organizational Dynamics,* 2001, pp 313–21.

[17] A case study application of a systems model of change can be found in A Cabrera, E F Cabrera, and S Barajas, "The Key Role of Organizational Culture in a Multi-System View of Technology-Driven Change," *International Journal of Information Management,* June 2001, pp 245–61.

[18] A thorough discussion of the target elements of change can be found in M Beer and B Spector, "Organizational Diagnosis: Its Role in Organizational Learning," *Journal of Counseling & Development,* July–August 1993, pp 642–50.

[19] K Kerwin and D Welch, "Attack of the Killer Crossovers," *Business Week,* January 28, 2002, pp 98, 100.

[20] These errors are discussed by J P Kotter, "Leading Change: The Eight Steps to Transformation," in *The Leader's Change Handbook,* eds J A Conger, G M Spreitzer, and E E Lawler III (San Francisco: Jossey-Bass, 1999) pp 87–99.

[21] The type of leadership needed during organizational change is discussed by J P Kotter, *Leading Change* (Boston: Harvard Business School Press, 1996); and B Ettorre, "Making Change," *Management Review,* January 1996, pp 13–18.

22 M Beer and E Walton, "Developing the Competitive Organization: Interventions and Strategies," *American Psychologist,* February 1990, p 154.

23 An historical overview of the field of OD can be found in N A M Worren, K Ruddle, and K Moore, "From Organizational Development to Change Management," *Journal of Applied Behavioral Science,* September 1999, pp 273–86.

24 W W Burke, *Organization Development: A Normative View* (Reading, MA: Addison-Wesley Publishing, 1987), p 9.

25 See the related discussion in H Hornstein, "Organizational Development and Change Management: Don't Throw the Baby out with the Batch Water," *Journal of Applied Behavioral Science,* June 2001, pp 223–26.

26 See R Rodgers, J E Hunter, and D L Rogers, "Influence of Top Management Commitment on Management Program Success," *Journal of Applied Psychology,* February 1993, pp 151–55.

27 Results can be found in P J Robertson, D R Roberts, and J I Porras, "Dynamics of Planned Organizational Change: Assessing Empirical Support for a Theoretical Model," *Academy of Management Journal,* June 1993, pp 619–34.

28 Results from the meta-analysis can be found in G A Neuman, J E Edwards, and N S Raju, "Organizational Development Interventions: A Meta-Analysis of Their Effects on Satisfaction and Other Attitudes," *Personnel Psychology,* Autumn 1989, pp 461–90.

29 Results can be found in C-M Lau and H-Y Ngo, "Organization Development and Firm Performance: A Comparison of Multinational and Local Firms," *Journal of International Business Studies,* First Quarter 2001, pp 95–114.

30 Adapted in part from B W Armentrout, "Have Your Plans for Change Had a Change of Plan?" *HR Focus,* January 1996, p 19; and A S Judson, *Changing Behavior in Organizations: Minimizing Resistance to Change* (Cambridge, MA: Blackwell, Inc., 1991).

31 See "Vulnerability and Resilience," *American Psychologist,* January 1996, pp 22–28.

32 C Joinson, "Moving at the Speed of Dell," *HR Magazine,* April 1999, p 52.

33 See R Moss Kanter, "Managing Traumatic Change: Avoiding the 'Unlucky 13,' " *Management Review,* May 1987, pp 23–24.

34 Supportive results can be found in J E Dutton, S J Ashford, R M O'Neill, and K A Lawrence, "Moves That Matter: Issue Selling and Organizational Change," *Academy of Management Journal,* August 2001, pp 716–36.

35 See L Coch and J R P French Jr, "Overcoming Resistance to Change," *Human Relations,* 1948, pp 512–32.

36 For a thorough review of the role of participation in organizational change, see W A Pasmore and M R Fagans, "Participation, Individual Development, and Organizational Change: A Review and Synthesis," *Journal of Management,* June 1992, pp 375–97.

37 L Herscovitch and J P Meyer, "Commitment to Organizational Change: Extension of a Three-Component Model," *Journal of Applied Psychology,* June 2002, p 475.

38 Ibid., pp 474–87.

39 Results can be found in C R Wanberg and J T Banas, "Predictors and Outcomes of Openness to Changes in a Reorganizing Workplace," *Journal of Applied Psychology,* February 2000, pp 132–42.

40 Results from this study can be found in T A Judge, C J Thoresen, V Pucik, and T W Welbourne, "Managerial Coping with Organizational Change: A Dispositional Perspective," *Journal of Applied Psychology,* February 1999, pp 107–22.

41 See Wanberg and Banas, "Predictors and Outcomes of Openness to Changes in a Reorganizing Workplace," pp 132–42.

42 See the related discussion in E B Dent and S G Goldberg, "Challenging 'Resistance to Change,' " *Journal of Applied Behavioral Science,* March 1999, pp 25–41.

43 J P Kotter, "Leading Change: Why Transformation Efforts Fail," *Harvard Business Review,* 1995, p 64.

44 Readiness for change is examined by L T Eby, D M Adams, J E A Russell, and S H Gaby, "Perceptions of Organizational Readiness for Change: Factors Related to Employees' Reactions to the Implementation of Team-Based Selling," *Human Relations,* March 2000, pp 419–42.

45 See Q N Huy, "In Praise of Middle Managers," *Harvard Business Review,* September 2001, pp 72–79.

46 Ibid., p 76.

47 For a discussion of how managers can reduce resistance to change by providing different explanations for an organizational change, see D M Rousseau and S A Tijoriwala, "What's a Good Reason to Change? Motivated Reasoning and Social Accounts in Promoting Organizational Change," *Journal of Applied Psychology,* August 1999, pp 514–28.

48 The stress response is thoroughly discussed by H Selye, *Stress without Distress* (New York: J B Lippincott, 1974).

49 J M Ivancevich and M T Matteson, *Stress and Work: A Managerial Perspective* (Glenview, IL: Scott, Foresman, 1980), pp 8–9.

50 See Selye, *Stress without Distress.*

51 See S Armour, "Experts Give PC-Related Eyestrain a Close Look," *USA Today,* February 10, 1999, p 1B.

52 C Tejada, "Work Week: A Special New Report about Life on the Job-and-Trends Taking Shape There," *The Wall Street Journal,* February 26, 2002, p A1.

53 See L A Wah, "An Executive's No. 1 Fear," *American Management Association International,* January 1998, p 87.

54 Supportive results can be found in V J Magley, C L Hulin, L F Fitzgerald, and M DeNardo, "Outcomes of Self-Labeling Sexual Harassment," *Journal of Applied Psychology,* June 1999, pp 390–402.

55 The relationship between work demands and stress was investigated by E Demerouti, A B Bakker, F Nachreiner, and W B Schaufeli, "The Job Demands-Resources Model of Burnout," *Journal of Applied Psychology,* June 2001, pp 499–512.

56 See J M Plas, *Person-Centered Leadership: An American Approach to Participatory Management* (Thousand Oaks, CA: Sage, 1996).

57 See the related discussion in F M McKee-Ryan and A J Kinicki, "Coping with Job Loss: A Life-Facet Perspective," in *International Review of Industrial and Organizational Psychology,* eds C L Cooper and I T Robertson (West Sussex, England: John Wiley & Sons, 2002), pp 1–30.

58 The discussion of appraisal is based on R S Lazarus and S Folkman, *Stress, Appraisal, and Coping* (New York: Springer Publishing, 1984).

59 This example was taken from S N Mehta, "Hear Them Roar: More Women Quit Lucrative Jobs to Start Their Own Businesses," *The Wall Street Journal,* November 11, 1996, pp A1, A4.

60 L Lagnado, "Bracing for Trauma's Second Wave: Depression, Irritability, Angst Return to New York City Six Months after Sept. 11," *The Wall Street Journal,* March 5, 2002, p B1.

61 For reviews of this research see K Sparks, B Faragher, C L Cooper, "Well-Being and Occupational Health in the 21st Century Workplace," *Journal of Occupational and Organizational Psychology,* November 2001, pp 489–509; and R M Ryan and E L Deci, "On Happiness and Human Potentials: A Review of Research on Hedonic and Eudaimonic Well-Being," in *Annual Review of Psychology,* eds S T Fiske, D L Schacter, and C-Z Waxler (Palo Alto, CA: Annual Reviews, 2001), pp 141–66.

62 Supportive results can be found in A J Kinicki, F M McKee-Ryan, C A Schriesheim, and K P Carson, "Assessing the Construct Validity of the Job Descriptive Index: A Review and Meta-Analysis," *Journal of Applied Psychology,* February 2002, pp 14–32; M A Cavanaugh, W R Boswell, M V Roehling, and J W Boudreau, "An Empirical Examination of Self-Reported Work Stress among US Managers," *Journal of Applied Psychology,* February 2000, pp 65–74; and J R Edwards and N P Rothbard, "Work and Family Stress and Well-Being: An Examination of Person-Environment Fit in the Work and Family Domains," *Organizational Behavior and Human Decision Processes,* February 1999, pp 85–129.

63 These statistics were reported in J Daw, "Road Rage, Air Rage and Now Desk Rage," *Monitor on Psychology,* July–August 2001, pp 52–54.

64 Supportive results can be found in D C Ganster, M L Fox, and D J Dwyer, "Explaining Employees' Health Care Costs: A Prospective Examination of Stressful Job Demands, Personal Control, and Physiological Reactivity," *Journal of Applied Psychology,* October 2001, pp 954–64; and R S DeFrank and J M Ivancevich, "Stress on the Job: An Executive Update," *Academy of Management Executive,* August 1998, pp 55–66.

65 Types of support are discussed by S Cohen and T A Wills, "Stress, Social Support, and the Buffering Hypothesis," *Psychological Bulletin,* September 1985, pp 310–57.

66 See the discussion in R A Clay, "Research to the Heart of the Matter," *Monitor on Psychology,* January 2001, pp 42–45.

67 Supportive results can be found in L L Schirmer and F G Lopez, "Probing the Social Support and Work Strain Relationship among Adult Workers: Contributions of Adult Attachment Orientations," *Journal of Vocational Behavior,* August 2001, pp 17–33.

68 This pioneering research is presented in S C Kobasa, "Stressful Life Events, Personality, and Health: An Inquiry into Hardiness," *Journal of Personality and Social Psychology,* January 1979, pp 1–11.

69 See S C Kobasa, S R Maddi, and S Kahn, "Hardiness and Health: A Prospective Study," *Journal of Personality and Social Psychology,* January 1982, pp 168–77.

70 Results can be found in V Florian, M Mikulincer, and O Taubman, "Does Hardiness Contribute to Mental Health during a Stressful Real Life Situation? The Roles of Appraisal and Coping," *Journal of Personality and Social Psychology,* April 1995, pp 687–95; and K L Horner, "Individuality in Vulnerability: Influences on Physical Health," *Journal of Health Psychology,* January 1998, pp 71–85.

71 See C Robitschek and S Kashubeck, "A Structural Model of Parental Alcoholism, Family Functioning, and Psychological Health: The Mediating Effects of Hardiness and Personal Growth Orientation," *Journal of Counseling Psychology,* April 1999, pp 159–72.

72 B Priel, N Gonik, and B Rabinowitz, "Appraisals of Childbirth Experience and Newborn Characteristics: The Role of Hardiness and Affect," *Journal of Personality,* September, 1993, pp 299–315.

73 M Friedman and R H Rosenman, *Type A Behavior and Your Heart* (Greenwich, CT: Fawcett Publications, 1974), p 84. (Boldface added.)

74 See C Lee, L F Jamieson, and P C Earley, "Beliefs and Fears and Type A Behavior: Implications for Academic Performance and Psychiatric Health Disorder Symptoms," *Journal of Organizational Behavior,* March 1996, pp 151–77; S D Bluen, J Barling, and W Burns, "Predicting Sales Performance, Job Satisfaction, and Depression by Using the Achievement Strivings and Impatience-Irritability Dimensions of Type A Behavior," *Journal of Applied Psychology,* April 1990, pp 212–16; and M S Taylor, E A Locke, C Lee and M E Gist, "Type A Behavior and Faculty Research Productivity: What Are the Mechanisms?" *Organizational Behavior and Human Performance,* December 1984, pp 402–18.

75 Results from the meta-analysis are contained in S A Lyness, "Predictors of Differences between Type A and B Individuals in Heart Rate and Blood Pressure Reactivity," *Psychological Bulletin,* September 1993, pp 266–95.

76 See S Booth-Kewley and H S Friedman, "Psychological Predictors of Heart Disease: A Quantitative Review"

Psychological Bulletin, May 1987, pp 343–62. More recent results can be found in T Q Miller, T W Smith, C W Turner, M L Guijarro, A J Hallet, "A Meta-Analytic Review of Research on Hostility and Physical Health," *Psychological Bulletin,* March 1996, pp 322–48.

[77] Results from this study were reported in R Winslow and P Landers, "Obesity: A World-Wide Woe," *The Wall Street Journal,* July 1, 2002, pp B1, B4.

[78] These statistics were derived from J Norman, "Stress Relief Is Good Business," *Arizona Republic,* March 25, 2002, pp D1, D5.

[79] Results are presented in "Employers Promote Healthy Habits," *HR Magazine,* February 1999, pp 32, 34.

[80] See S Reynolds, E Taylor, and D A Shapiro, "Session Impact in Stress Management Training," *Journal of Occupational Psychology,* June 1993, pp 99–113; and J M Ivancevich, M T Matteson, S M Freedman, and J S Phillips, "Worksite Stress Management Interventions," *American Psychologist,* February 1990, pp 252–61.

[81] An evaluation of stress-reduction programs is conducted by P A Landsbergis and E Vivona-Vaughan, "Evaluation of an Occupational Stress Intervention in a Public Agency," *Journal of Organizational Behavior,* January 1996, pp 29–48; and D C Ganster, B T Mayes, W E Sime, and G D Tharp, "Managing Organizational Stress: A Field Experiment," *Journal of Applied Psychology,* October 1982, pp 533–42.

[82] R Kreitner, "Personal Wellness: It's Just Good Business," *Business Horizons,* May–June 1982, p 28.

[83] Results are presented in "The 18-Year Gap," *University of California, Berkeley Wellness Letter,* January 1991, p 2.

[84] A thorough review of this research is provided by D L Gebhardt and C E Crump, "Employee Fitness and Wellness Programs in the Workplace," *American Psychologist,* February 1990, pp 262–72.

[85] Excerpted from G McWilliams, "Gateway Adopts Tough New Style as Sales Tumble," *The Wall Street Journal,* May 28, 2002, pp B1, B4.

[86] Based on a group exercise in L W Mealiea, *Skills for Managers in Organizations* (Burr Ridge, IL: Irwin, 1994), pp 198–201. © 1994. Reproduced with permission of the McGraw-Hill Companies.

[87] The force-field analysis form was quoted directly from ibid., pp 199, 201.

[88] Excerpted from E Tanouye, "What Happens When It's the Boss Who's Suffering?" *The Wall Street Journal,* June 13, 2001, pp B1, B6.

LEARNING MODULE C

[1] See "Do Americans Trust Media Polls?" *USA Today,* May 18, 1999, p 1A.

[2] This study is discussed in A Finkbeiner, "Some Science Is Baloney; Learn to Tell the Difference," *USA Today,* September 11, 1997, p 15A.

[3] "Buckle Up in the Rear Seat?" *University of California, Berkeley Wellness Letter,* August 1987, p 1.

[4] F N Kerlinger, *Foundations of Behavioral Research* (New York: Holt, Rinehart & Winston, 1973), p 18. (Emphasis added.)

[5] See A H Winefield and M Tiggemann, "Employment Status and Psychological Well-Being: A Longitudinal Study," *Journal of Applied Psychology,* August 1990, pp 455–59.

[6] See P J Frost and R E Stablein, eds, *Doing Exemplary Research* (Newbury Park, CA: Sage, 1992); and S Begley, "The Meaning of Junk," *Newsweek,* March 22, 1993, pp 62–64.

[7] S S Stevens, "Mathematics, Measurement, and Psychophysics," in *Handbook of Experimental Psychology,* ed S S Stevens (New York: John Wiley & Sons, 1951), p 1.

[8] A thorough discussion of the importance of measurement is provided by D P Schwab, "Construct Validity in Organizational Behavior," in *Research in Organizational Behavior,* eds B M Staw and L L Cummings (Greenwich, CT: JAI Press, 1980), pp 3–43.

[9] See J L Komaki, "Toward Effective Supervision: An Operant Analysis and Comparison of Managers at Work," *Journal of Applied Psychology,* May 1986, pp 270–79. Results from the sailing study can be found in J L Komaki, M L Desselles, and E D Bowman, "Definitely Not a Breeze: Extending an Operant Model of Effective Supervision to Teams," *Journal of Applied Psychology,* June 1989, pp 522–29.

[10] A thorough discussion of the pros and cons of using surveys or questionnaires is provided by J A Krosnick, "Survey Research," in *Annual Review of Psychology,* eds J T Spence, J M Darley, and D J Foss (Palo Alto, CA: 1999), pp 537–67.

[11] See F L Schmidt and M Rader, "Exploring the Boundary Conditions for Interview Validity: Meta-Analytic Validity Findings for a New Interview Type," *Personnel Psychology,* Summer 1999, pp 445–64; and M A McDaniel, D Whetzel, F L Schmidt, and S Maurer, "The Validity of Employment Interviews: A Comprehensive Review and Meta-Analysis," *Journal of Applied Psychology,* August 1994, pp 599–616.

[12] A complete discussion of research methods is provided by T D Cook and D T Campbell, *Quasi-Experimentation: Design & Analysis Issues for Field Settings* (Chicago: Rand McNally, 1979).

[13] Ibid.

[14] For a thorough discussion of the guidelines for conducting good research, see L Wilkinson, "Statistical Methods in Psychology Journals," *American Psychologist,* August 1999, pp 594–604.

[15] This discussion is based on material presented in the *Publication Manual of the American Psychological Association,* 4th ed (Washington, DC: American Psychological Association, 1994).

[16] Ibid., p 5.

[17] "Buckle Up in the Rear Seat?"

Name and Company Index

Subject Index